T̶ _____ OF LORDS

The Judicial
House of Lords
1876–2009

Edited by
LOUIS BLOM-COOPER
BRICE DICKSON
and
GAVIN DREWRY

OXFORD
UNIVERSITY PRESS

OXFORD
UNIVERSITY PRESS

Great Clarendon Street, Oxford OX2 6DP

Oxford University Press is a department of the University of Oxford.
It furthers the University's objective of excellence in research, scholarship,
and education by publishing worldwide in

Oxford New York

Auckland Cape Town Dar es Salaam Hong Kong Karachi
Kuala Lumpur Madrid Melbourne Mexico City Nairobi
New Delhi Shanghai Taipei Toronto

With offices in

Argentina Austria Brazil Chile Czech Republic France Greece
Guatemala Hungary Italy Japan Poland Portugal Singapore
South Korea Switzerland Thailand Turkey Ukraine Vietnam

Oxford is a registered trade mark of Oxford University Press
in the UK and in certain other countries

Published in the United States
by Oxford University Press Inc., New York

British Library Cataloguing in Publication Data

Data available

Library of Congress Cataloging in Publication Data

The Judicial House of Lords, 1876–2009 / edited by Louis Blom-Cooper,
Brice Dickson, and Gavin Drewry.

p. cm.

Includes bibliographical references and index.

ISBN 978–0–19–953271–1 (alk. paper)

1. Courts of last resort—Great Britain—History. 2. Courts of last resort—England—History.
3. Great Britain. Parliament. House of Lords—History. 4. England and Wales. Parliament. House
of Lords—History. I. Blom-Cooper, Louis Jacques. II. Dickson, Brice. III. Drewry, Gavin.

KD7632.J83   2009
347.42'039–dc22   2009019866

Typeset by Newgen Imaging Systems (P) Ltd., Chennai, India
Printed in Great Britain
on acid-free paper by
Antony Rowe Ltd, Chippenham, Wiltshire

ISBN 978–0–19–953271–1 (Hbk.)
ISBN 978–0–19–969333–7 (Pbk.)

1 3 5 7 9 10 8 6 4 2

Acknowledgements

Looking back three years, to the early months of 2006 when this project was first conceived, we have ruefully to confess that our initial feelings of excitement and enthusiasm may then have been clouded by the merest modicum of anxiety. While we ourselves were wholly convinced that this valedictory tribute to the judicial work of the House of Lords was a wholly fitting and worthwhile enterprise, would others—on whom the success of such an undertaking would ultimately depend—share our conviction? We knew that if the job was worth doing it had to be done well; in fact, very well indeed. This would have to be a top-quality product, covering every (or almost every) aspect of the appellate function, and this would require us to recruit a high-class team of distinguished contributors—judges, practitioners, academics, and other top professionals—all of them busy and important people, able, between them, to cover all the angles. Was this really possible?

As we began, cautiously, to make our initial soundings, our anxieties on this score were quickly laid to rest. Well aware that our plans would make no headway at all without judicial backing, we decided at the outset to consult Lord Bingham of Cornhill, the Senior Law Lord—scheduled to retire from judicial office just before the appellate functions of the House of Lords were to pass to the new Supreme Court but still, throughout the period of this book's gestation, a very active and most distinguished presence at the top of the judicial tree. To our great pleasure and gratitude, he took no persuading of the merits of the project and has been an enormous source of wise and friendly advice and behind-the-scenes support throughout—and subsequently agreed to contribute a chapter to this volume. His name merits a very high place in the long list of those to whom the editors are deeply indebted.

Then there are our contributors—41 of them in total. When we began to approach people to write chapters for this collection, we were greatly heartened by the fact that almost everyone we asked not only said yes, but did so with little or no visible hesitation and indeed, invariably, with warm expressions of support and goodwill. In total, quite remarkably, we had only three or four refusals, in all cases with manifest regret. What is more, everyone who did accept our invitation delivered their contributions as requested and (almost) everyone did so on time without, we hope, undue nagging on our part. Editorial requests and suggestions were duly taken on board. This book is the sum of their contributions and we thank them both for the substance of those contributions and for their friendly cooperation—without which our editorial burden would have been so very much heavier.

We also thank, very warmly, Sharon Witherspoon and the Trustees of the Nuffield Foundation, who supported the project with a Small Grant; also Royal

Holloway, University of London, which administered that grant. Our publisher, Oxford University Press—in particular Rebecca Smith and her successor Chris Champion—supported us from the outset and turned our manuscript into a most attractive volume. Public Administration International very kindly allowed us to use their Central London premises for several of our editorial meetings. We also gratefully acknowledge the contribution of Ronagh McQuigg, of Queen's University Belfast, who painstakingly researched and drafted the 'pen portraits' of all the Lords of Appeal since 1876 and Terence McCleave, also of Queen's, who gave valuable assistance with the Table of Cases.

We end with a very special thank you to Ruth Massey. Ruth was a key member of the editorial team from the outset, recruited as our editorial manager, to keep the project moving, to liaise with contributors, and to keep the editors on their toes. She did all these things with delightful charm and impressive efficiency. Ian Aitkenhead ably supported her in her role, as well as acting as a valued research assistant to one of the editors. We are very grateful to them both.

We end with the customary (but no less valid for that) absolution, that those we have acknowledged share the responsibility for the content of their own contributions, but it is the editors who must take full responsibility for the book as a whole, and the blame for any errors or omissions.

Louis Blom-Cooper
Brice Dickson
Gavin Drewry

April 2009

Summary Contents

PART C: DEVELOPMENT OF THE COURT

PART D: REGIONAL AND EXTERNAL PERSPECTIVES

PART E: SPECIFIC AREAS

Appendices

Detailed Contents

PART B: THE JUDGES

Appendices

Editors' Introduction

The reinstatement in 1876 of the House of Lords as the final court of appeal for the United Kingdom (after the aborted abolition of 1873) was the product of political gymnastics that had little, if anything, to do with the needs of the legal system. It had everything to do with the prestige of the upper House of Parliament. On 12 June 2003 the announcement of a supreme court to succeed the Appellate Committee of the House of Lords (established in 1948) was likewise the result of political manoeuvrings—abrupt and unheralded within the legal profession. The editors of the present volume are of the opinion that the demise of the Lords of Appeal in Ordinary in October 2009, 133 years after their creation, calls for a commemorative volume describing their contribution to the legal life of British society.

When two of us (Louis Blom-Cooper and Gavin Drewry) were engaged in the late 1960s in our study of the House of Lords, which led to the publication of *Final Appeal* in 1972, we were acutely aware that the hierarchy of appeals was 'once again a source of dispute'.[1] The legal reformers of the post-war period were actively propagating the idea that one appeal sufficed in a modern system of justice. Professor Robert Stevens had concluded in an article published in 1964 that: 'It will be interesting to see whether the judicial reformers of the 1960s will be any more successful than the judicial reformers of a hundred years ago in abolishing the double appeal in general, and in particular the semblance of the House of Lords as the final court of appeal.'[2] Reviewing *Final Appeal* in 1973, not uncritically, the late Mr Justice Windeyer (then a judge of the High Court of Australia) supported our advocacy for retention of the judicial House of Lords:

As a judicial tribunal it can stand between the Crown and the subjects of the realm; and it exercises a supervisory jurisdiction over all courts within the realm and all agencies of Government. It may be hoped that nothing will be allowed to imperil, or even to seem to diminish, that. On it hangs the power of the law to regulate social welfare to new ways important today, and to protect ancient liberties.[3]

Over the past four decades the editors have not been conscious of there having been any revival of the desire to abolish the House of Lords in its judicial capacity, even in the midst of incessant attempts to reform the legislative institution in a bicameral parliamentary system. Indeed, the assumption of commentators, both expressed and implied, has appeared unequivocally to favour retention. Given this politico-legal background, it is perhaps not so surprising that during the passage of

---

[1] R Stevens, 'The Appellate Committee of the House of Lords and the Judicial Committee of the Privy Council 1876–1964' (1964) 80 LQR 343.
[2] ibid, 369.   [3] (1973) 89 LQR 282, 289.

the Constitutional Reform Bill in 2004–5 there was not a whisper—let alone a whimper—of discontent about the existence of a three-tier court structure, despite much contemporary public concern about the twin problems of cost and delay in both trial and appellate litigation. The succession of the judicial House of Lords by a UK supreme court, exercising a virtually identical jurisdiction, has involved merely a change of venue, and then only a short walk across Parliament Square. Neither the judicial reformers of 1873 nor those of the 1960s have found their counterparts today. A second tier of appellate court is firmly entrenched in our legal system.

Undoubtedly, the quality of judicial output over recent years has countered any arguable ground for public dissatisfaction. Notwithstanding the recent outbursts from politicians about some House of Lords decisions, there has been no expressed desire to be rid of this judicial obstacle to the ever-increasing resort to legislative and governmental action that impinges more and more on citizens' lives. But while there is no major quarrel with the quality of the jurisprudence of the judicial House of Lords, we think there is a discrete major factor that has bolstered the need for a final court of appeal for the whole of the United Kingdom. The process of devolution for Scotland, Wales, and Northern Ireland has necessitated the cementing of the Union. Hilaire Belloc's cautionary advice to 'keep a-hold of Nurse for fear of finding something worse' is apt in this context. The distribution of legislative power to the separate parts of the United Kingdom demands a strengthening of judicial cultures. The rule of law itself requires a correspondingly bright line to be drawn between the three independent judiciaries and the actions of government.

There is a further reason for retaining the final court of appeal for England and Wales, Scotland, and Northern Ireland. Whereas in the 1960s the judicial House of Lords was essentially a final port of call for aspiring litigants in private law litigation, the court's role today has become that of final arbiter of public law issues, the very matters referred to by Mr Justice Windeyer—protection of the fundamental rights of citizens, coupled with its supervisory jurisdiction over public authorities. Litigation in the private law field frequently now goes no further than the Court of Appeal, and the importance of the Human Rights Act 1998 has accentuated the role of the House of Lords in the judicial control of public authorities.

The idea for this book thus stemmed from a wish to revisit familiar territory and from a strong desire to commemorate the achievements of a prominent legal institution in British society. To that end we invited experts in various aspects of the judicial House of Lords to write about it in both an engaging and a scholarly fashion. Collectively the contributions are intended to provide a broad picture, painted on the canvas of legal policy and the practice of law in a modern democratic country. Apart from the chapter on the Judicial Committee of the Privy Council by Sir Kenneth Keith (Chapter 18), and reference to that court in the contributions from the Commonwealth, we did not ask our various contributors to take account of the output from the Privy Council, even though the judgments are largely the product of Law Lords, many of them reflecting in extra-territorial contexts the development of law in the United Kingdom. (It is worth noting that today the Law Lords spend about 40 per cent of their time sitting in the Privy Council.)

Inevitably, in a book which seeks to commemorate the achievements of a final court of appeal over 133 years there will be gaps in the coverage of the subject matter, if only because the size of the volume would otherwise become editorially unmanageable and unwieldy for the reader. Hence we acknowledge that there are topics which have received either partial attention or none at all. They include: bankruptcy and insolvency law, company law, consumer law, criminal procedure and evidence (other than the burden and standard of proof), education law, employment law, equity and trusts, landlord and tenant law, local government law, mental health law, prison law, private international law, and welfare law.

Nor have we been able to include an account of the work of the Lords of Appeal outside the courtroom. We are conscious, for example, that many Lords of Appeal have presided over important public inquiries. Indeed, for the past 11 years one Lord of Appeal, Lord Saville, has spent nearly all his time on one such inquiry into the deaths caused by British soldiers in Derry on 'Bloody Sunday', 30 January 1972. While the reports emanating from these inquiries have often had profound consequences for society, we felt we had to eliminate them from our study because they do not relate specifically to the adjudication role that is the central focus of this work. For the same reason we have eschewed any examination of the extra-judicial writings of the Law Lords, even though in recent years, especially since the relaxation of the Kilmuir Rules by Lord Chancellor Mackay in 1987, there has been an increasing number of these writings appearing in the pages of the country's leading law journals. That particular bank of material must, we feel, be left to other scholars to analyse.

At an early stage of our project, the Government announced that the new Supreme Court of the United Kingdom would be housed in a refurbished Middlesex Guildhall, on the west side of Parliament Square, to be occupied by the Justices of the Supreme Court and the administration of the Court at the beginning of the law year in October 2009. Once judicial review proceedings seeking to prevent the dismantling of the works of art in the building had been concluded,[4] the date of October 2009 became a firm target. As we write (February 2009) nothing looks like disturbing the timetable. Throughout the days of compiling the table of contents, selecting the various contributors, and performing our editorial role we have kept in our sights the aim of having the publication of this commemorative volume coincide with the change-over of the venue of the court from the Palace of Westminster to Middlesex Guildhall.

---

[4] *R (SAVE Britain's Heritage) v Westminster CC* [2007] EWHC 807 (Admin).

To meet that timetable, we needed to deliver the complete manuscript to Oxford University Press early in 2009. This meant that we would be covering 133 years of judicial output, but alas not the final year's output (indeed, it may be that the last judgments—or should we still call them speeches?—will not be delivered until the autumn of 2009, by which time the new Supreme Court will already be operational). Our cut-off point for the inclusion of material therefore had to be 31 October 2008. We considered delaying publication until the summer of 2010, by which time the last decisions of the Appellate Committee could safely be accommodated. But we came to the conclusion that we should publish the book at the moment of the final court of appeal's demise. As Evelyn Waugh once wrote: 'Do realise that a letter need not be a bald chronicle of events.' The purpose of this book is to provide some overall appraisal of the work of this hugely important legal institution of modern Britain. It is not intended to be an exhaustive account of everything the judicial House of Lords has—or has not—done since 1876.

We trust that this collection of essays will provide the reader with a rich and diverse range of perspectives on the history, work, and contribution of the House of Lords in its judicial capacity. While it would be impertinent for us, and in any event a nigh-impossible task, to evaluate the quality of judicial output over the 133 years, we are confident at least in concluding, with a suitable dose of diffidence, that within the English-speaking world the reputation of the United Kingdom's final court of appeal has been of a consistently high order. There have—perhaps inevitably in any human institution—been some occasional troughs among the peaks, but overall individual judgments have reflected sound legal analysis of an ever-burgeoning host of social and human problems. The country has been well served by all 112 lawyers who have been appointed to occupy the highest judicial office and their output bears very favourable comparison with that of apex courts in other common law jurisdictions.

In Part A of the book the contributors address basic features of the House of Lords as a judicial institution: the origins of its judicial function, the troubled history during the 1870s, the way it has been serviced by officialdom, the relationship between the House and the Court of Appeal, and the very recent process by which the House has been replaced by the Supreme Court. Part B moves on to consider the judges who have served in the House: the role of the Lord Chancellor, the criteria for appointment as a Lord of Appeal in Ordinary, the profile of those who have been appointed so far, the way they have handled the doctrine of precedent, the style in which they have written their judgments, and the contribution they have made as legislators when the House is sitting as a Chamber of Parliament. We are particularly grateful to Lord Bingham, the Senior Law Lord from 2000 to 2008, for contributing a chapter to this Part, and also to Lord Hope, the current Second Senior Law Lord, for his valuable chapter on Law Lords as legislators.

Part C contains five chapters which consider the development of the House's jurisprudence during five distinct periods in the court's history between 1876 and 2008. It is obviously difficult to choose where to draw the dividing lines when breaking up such a long period, but we feel confident that the lines chosen do represent important turning points in the House's development. Because of the increased number of decisions issued by the Law Lords in the past 30 years or so, proportionately more attention has been paid to the 1982–2000 and 2000–8 periods than to the earlier ones. Needless to say, not every significant decision reached by the Law Lords has been referred to, in whatever period is under scrutiny. Contributors were asked to highlight what they considered to be the most significant and representative decisions.

The book then proceeds, in Part D, to reflect a number of regional and external perspectives on the House of Lords. There are chapters on the experience of Scotland and Ireland (pre- and post-partition), on the relationship between the House and the Privy Council, on the impact of the House in both 'old' and 'new' Commonwealth jurisdictions, on how the House compares with the US Supreme Court, and on whether the role played by the House is now so very different from that played by constitutional courts in Europe. Again, we are particularly grateful to retired senior judges from many of these jurisdictions for their insights and analyses. Part D concludes with three chapters allowing non-judicial perspectives to be brought to bear: those of two legal practitioners (a solicitor and barrister), a commercial lawyer with wide experience of working within the financial hub of the United Kingdom—the City of London, and a political scientist (one of the editors). These external views have been included to help drive home the point that the House's *modus operandi* and output deeply affect the day-to-day work of lawyers, financiers, and politicians, even if that is not always clearly understood by the people concerned.

Part E is the longest in the book, containing 15 chapters that examine specific areas of the law about which the House has had a lot to say in the course of the past 133 years. This is where the selectivity of the editors is most apparent, but we believe that the inevitable lack of space for some topics has not diminished the quality of analysis encountered in the chapters which remain. Once more, the contributors of these chapters have not been able to comment on every relevant House of Lords decision, having been asked to focus instead on highlights and trends. There should be something for everyone in this Part, whatever their interests may be.

The book's appendices are intended to be an *aide mémoire* for anyone wanting to be reminded of the sequence of appointments to the office of Lord of Appeal (or Lord Chancellor) and of the background of the individuals in question. Regrettably, there was no room to include a list of all the decisions issued by the House during its illustrious history: that would require a book almost as sizeable as this one.

Preface to the Paperback Edition

The Final Year of the Judicial House of Lords

In our Introduction to the hardback version of this book in July 2009, we emphasised that the book was not intended to be an exhaustive account of everything the House of Lords had done during its 133 year history. In particular, we explained that in order to meet the publication schedule contributors were unable to consider decisions taken by the Law Lords during their last year in office (October 2008 to September 2009). One or two reviewers expressed their regret at that omission, so we are taking advantage of the appearance of this paperback edition to add a few comments about that last batch of cases. In doing so we cannot be any more comprehensive in our approach than the hardback edition was regarding previous years' cases; we can merely seek to identify what we think are significant landmarks in the court's jurisprudence.

It was a year typical of recent times, for while it contained a mix of some criminal and civil cases it was dominated by public law cases, and especially by cases raising human rights issues. Many of the decisions were unremarkable and did not develop the law in any appreciable way, but a few indicated quite clearly the prevailing mindset of the outgoing court. This was perhaps most clearly evident in both the first and the last of the year's decisions. In *R (Bancoult) v Secretary of State for Foreign and Commonwealth Affairs*[1] the Lords decided by 3 v 2 that the UK government did not break any law when it issued a prerogative order preventing the inhabitants of the Chagos Islands in the Indian Ocean from exercising their right to live there. While their Lordships ostensibly split on the interpretation of the government's right to make laws "for the peace, order and good government" of the territory, and on the applicability of the Colonial Laws Validity Act 1865, a deeper division is discernible in their approach to human rights and the rule of law. The majority, led by Lord Hoffmann,[2] did not see any legal objection to the government doing what it deemed best in all the circumstances, while the minority (Lords Mance and Bingham) felt that the government's action was contrary to the rule of law and fundamental rights. At a conference shortly after the decision was announced, when Lord Bingham had retired, he admitted to one of this book's editors that he found the majority's decision "remarkable", and in his book published in 2009, *The Rule of Law*,[3] he

---

[1] [2008] UKHL 61, [2009] 1 AC 453.

[2] The other two judges in the majority were Lords Rodger and Carswell.

[3] Allen Lane, London. Sadly, Lord Bingham passed away on 11 September 2010. The obituaries acknowledged that in many people's eyes he was the greatest British judge of his generation, as Chapter 16 of this book helps to demonstrate.

strongly reasserted his allegiance to that basic democratic value. While the decision in *Bancoult* may not have much purchase as a precedent, because of the unlikelihood of comparable facts arising in relation to any other UK overseas territory in the future, it nevertheless leaves an unpleasant taste in the mouth.

In the year's last case, *R (Purdy) v DPP*,[4] deliberately chosen by the Law Lords to be their swan song (and pronounced in a crowded Upper Chamber), a completely different bench from that which sat in *Bancoult* held that English law on the crime of assisted suicide was in need of clarification and that the Director of Public Prosecutions should develop a new policy identifying the facts and circumstances which he would consider when deciding whether to exercise his statutory discretion to prosecute someone for aiding and abetting an assisted suicide abroad. The House's ruling was reached on the basis of Article 8 of the European Convention on Human Rights and in particular on that aspect of the right to a private life which touches upon a person's desire to end his or her life at the moment of their own choosing. It built upon the decision of the European Court of Human Rights in *Pretty v UK*,[5] where that Court had disagreed with the House's view that access to assisted suicide did not even engage Article 8. *Purdy* was, we submit, an intensely humane decision, one that stands in stark contrast to the rather authoritarian approach to human rights adopted in *Bancoult*. It was an unusual example of the House of Lords trespassing on the discretion of the DPP.

These were important cases, but it is worth noting that neither of them, nor indeed any other case decided during the House of Lords' last year, was decided by more than the normal quota of five Law Lords. In his role as Senior Law Lord, it seems that Lord Phillips of Worth Matravers was not keen to maintain the trend that had developed in recent years towards using seven or even nine judges in cases of especial importance. This reluctance was, however, soon overcome when the Supreme Court got up and running, for in the 89 decisions issued during the first 18 months of that Court's existence, it has sat as a court of more than five judges on no fewer than 24 occasions (27%).[6] In 2008-09, by way of contrast, the House had been content to use just five judges when ruling that the Royal Ulster Constabulary had not violated any human rights in the manner in which it policed disturbances at Holy Cross Primary School in North Belfast in 2001,[7] that the "kettling" of protestors by the Metropolitan Police during a demonstration in London in the same year was not a deprivation of anyone's right to liberty under Article 5 of the European Convention,[8] and that it was not a breach of the right under Article 3 of the Convention to be free from torture and inhuman or degrading ill-treatment or punishment to deport people to

---

[4] [2009] UKHL 45, [2010] 1 AC 345.
[5] (2002) 35 EHRR 1.
[6] 16 cases involved seven judges; eight cases involved nine judges.
[7] *E v Chief Constable of the RUC* [2008] UKHL 66, [2009] 1 AC 536.
[8] *Austin v Metropolitan Police Commissioner* [2009] UKHL 5, [2009] 1 AC 564.

Algeria or Jordan, so long as there were either official assurances from the foreign government or an appropriate Memorandum of Understanding between that government and the UK government promising that ill-treatment would not occur.[9]

Two broad fields of law dominated the decisions of the House of Lords in its final year, fields that hardly featured at all in the court's first half century of decisions. No fewer than nine of the 59 decisions concerned the law on asylum, deportation or extradition, while a further nine dealt with the law on housing, whether privately owned housing or housing rented out by social landlords such as local authorities. In each of these two fields human rights considerations again predominated. The right to a family life under Article 8 of the European Convention was held to play a crucial role in deciding whether to extradite the mother of a seven-year-old child,[10] but a person who was a fugitive from justice was not permitted to rely on the passage of time since his flight to argue that there had been a fatal delay in bringing criminal proceedings against him.[11] In the housing field the House of Lords held in favour of the state or local authorities when ruling that taking away a person's disability premium if that person becomes homeless was not a denial of his or her right to property under Article 1 of the First Protocol to the European Convention,[12] that a homeless man could not be prioritised in his application for accommodation just because a court had issued a shared residence order requiring his children to live alternative weeks with each of their parents,[13] and that a council's policy to give preference to some existing tenants over others who were in priority groups was not unlawful.[14] But a local council was held not to be entitled to treat as a homeless person, rather than as a child with accommodation needs, a 17-year-old who had been thrown out of the family home and presented himself to a local children's services authority.[15] Nor could a council refuse to treat as homeless a woman who was in a women's refuge as a result of domestic violence.[16]

Apart from the decision in *Purdy*, there were two other notable decisions on the right to life during the House's last year. In *R (L) (A Patient) v Secretary of State for Justice* their Lordships found that there had not been an Article 2-compliant investigation into the attempted suicide of a 20-year-old prisoner at Feltham Young Offenders Centre in 2002.[17] In *Savage v South Essex Partnership*

---

[9] *RB (Algeria) v Secretary of State for the Home Department* [2009] UKHL 10, [2010] 2 AC 110.
[10] *EM (Lebanon) v Secretary of State for the Home Department* [2008] UKHL 64, [2009] 1 AC 1198.
[11] *Gomes v Government of the Republic of Trinidad and Tobago* [2009] UKHL 21, [2009] 1 WLR 1038.
[12] *R (RJM) v Secretary of State for Work and Pensions* [2008] UKHL 63, [2009] 1 AC 311.
[13] *Holmes-Moorhouse v Richmond upon Thames London Borough Council* [2009] UKHL 7, [2009] 1 WLR 413.
[14] *R (Ahmad) v Newham London Borough Council* [2009] UKHL 14, [2009] 3 All ER 755.
[15] *R (G) v Southwark London Borough Council* [2009] UKHL 26, [2009] 1 WLR 34.
[16] *Birmingham City Council v Ali* [2009] UKHL 36, [2009] 1 WLR 1506.
[17] [2008] UKHL 68, [2009] 1 AC 588.

NHS Foundation they held that, in the circumstances, a health trust had a positive obligation to prevent the suicide of a person compulsorily detained under the Mental Health Act 1983.[18] These were two significant steps along the road to a more comprehensive formulation of the duty to protect life which the Strasbourg court has said is implicit in the European Convention.[19]

As regards the right not to be ill-treated (protected by Article 3 of the Convention) an unfortunate split emerged between their Lordships in *R (Wellington) v Secretary of State for the Home Department.*[20] The three in the majority – Lord Hoffmann, Lady Hale and Lord Carswell – appeared to suggest that a less demanding standard could be applied when considering whether someone could be extradited to a country where he or she might suffer ill-treatment (in this case the USA, where the applicant faced life imprisonment without the possibility of parole); Lord Brown and Lord Scott disagreed, saying that the same standard should apply whether the treatment was to occur abroad or in the United Kingdom. Especially when read alongside the House's decision regarding deportation to countries where torture is rife,[21] the majority's position will appear troubling to many, the more so since it seems to endorse the concept of a 'whole life' sentence for murder.

The House issued one declaration of incompatibility during the year, in a case about the way in which lists are compiled under the Care Standards Act 2000 of people considered unsuitable to work with vulnerable adults.[22] It refused to issue declarations in a case concerning the Home Secretary's power to reject a Parole Board recommendation[23] and in a further case concerning the compatibility with Convention rights of indeterminate sentences for public protection passed under the Criminal Justice Act 2003.[24] No declaration was issued in a case where the procedure for issuing control orders against suspected terrorists was challenged, but the House did say that the relevant provisions of the Prevention of Terrorism Act 2005 should be 'read down' under section 3 of the Human Rights Act 1998 so as to ensure that the prospective controlee is made aware of the essence of the case against him or her.[25] This endorses what the House had already said in an earlier application by the same controlee concerning the acceptability of the special advocate system in control order cases.[26]

In the field of private law the three most noteworthy decisions of the year are probably *Thorner v Major,*[27] where the House distinguished one of its decisions

---

[18] [2008] UKHL 74, [2009] 1 AC 681.
[19] *Osman v UK* (2000) 29 EHRR 245
[20] [2008] UKHL 72, [2009] 1 AC 335.
[21] See the text at n. 9 above.
[22] *R (Wright) v Secretary of State for Health* [2009] UKHL 3, [2009] 1 AC 739.
[23] *R (Black) v Secretary of State for Justice* [2009] UKHL 1, [2009] 1 AC 949.
[24] *R (Walker) v Secretary of State for Justice* [2009] UKHL 22, [2010] 1 AC 553.
[25] *Secretary of State for the Home Department v AF (No 3)* [2009] UKHL 28, [2010] 2 AC 269.
[26] *Secretary of State for the Home Dept v MB and AF* [2007] UKHL 46, [2008] 1 AC 440.
[27] [2008] UKHL 18, [2009] 1 WLR 776.

of the previous year[28] and held that a person claiming land owned by a farmer who had died intestate could indeed rely on the doctrine of proprietary estoppel to substantiate his claim; *Gray v Thames Trains Ltd*,[29] where the principle of *ex turpi causa non oritur actio* was applied in order to deny damages to a claimant who, having pleaded guilty to manslaughter on the grounds of diminished responsibility, tried to sue the train company responsible for the railway accident which had caused his mental instability; and *Fisher v Brooker*,[30] where the House ruled that in the law of intellectual property there is no doctrine of adverse possession, so a claim for a share of copyright in Procul Harem's 'Whiter Shade of Pale' could be defeated only if the defendant had suffered some detriment as a result of the claimant's delay in asserting his rights.

To summarise, in its last year the Appellate Committee of the House of Lords does not appear to have behaved any differently from how it has behaved in immediately preceding years and it does not seem to have been positioning itself in such a way as to provide a contrast between its own *modus operandi* and that which the Supreme Court might be expected to adopt. It continued to allow organisations to intervene in appeals and in the great majority of cases it delivered multiple judgments rather than a single judgment of the court. The House does seem to have deliberately opted to go out with a flourish by choosing to make the *Purdy* case its last decision: the case would have received significant publicity anyway, but extra attention was paid to it precisely because it marked the end of an era. The decision showed that the judges in the United Kingdom's top court were very conscious of the value of consultative and nuanced law-making. There was in fact no fanfare at the end of the case. Lord Phillips simply closed the proceedings by saying that this was the last decision of the House's Appellate Committee. As it happened, the Committee had to reconvene the very next day, 31 July 2009, in order to hear a procedural petition connected with the ongoing appeal in *R (E) v Governing Body of JFS*. That was the case which was to become the highlight, even in the eyes of several of the Justices, of the first year of the new UK Supreme Court.[31]

Louis Blom-Cooper
Brice Dickson
Gavin Drewry

May 2011.

---

[28] *Cobbe v Yeoman's Row Management Ltd* [2008] UKHL 55, [2008] 1 WLR 1752.
[29] [2009] UKHL 33, [2010] 1 AC 497.
[30] [2009] UKHL 41, [2009] 1 WLR 1764.
[31] [2009] UKSC 15, [2010] 2 AC 728. See, e.g., the interview with Lady Hale on ukscblog.com (16 September 2010).

Notes on Contributors

Justice **Adarsh Sein Anand** was called to the Bar in 1964 (Inner Temple). He was Chief Justice of the Supreme Court of India 1998–2001, and Chairperson of the National Human Rights Commission (India) 2003–6. He is an Honorary Bencher of The Inner Temple, a Fellow of University College London, an Honorary Fellow of the Society for Advanced Legal Studies, London, an Honorary Professor of Law at the Nalsar University, Hyderabad, and a Visiting Professor at the National Law School India University, Bangalore. He was awarded the second highest Civilian Award—*Padma Vibhushan*— by the President of India in 2008 for providing fair and efficient administration of justice and protection and promotion of Human Rights. Publications include *Development of the Constitution of Jammu and Kashmir* (1994) and *Justice for Women—Concerns and Expressions* (2004).

David Anderson QC practises from London with particular emphasis on EU law, public law, and human rights. He is Visiting Professor at King's College London, a Trustee of BIICL, a member of the Advisory Board of SSEES, a Recorder, and a Bencher of the Middle Temple. He is the author of *References to the European Court* (2nd edn with Marie Demetriou, 2002).

Eric Barendt is Goodman Professor of Media Law, University College London (appointed 1990). Formerly he was Fellow and Tutor in Law at St Catherine's College Oxford. He is the author of many books, including *Freedom of Speech* (2nd edn 2005) and *Libel and the Media* (1997), and is an editor of *The Journal of Media Law*.

Michael J Beloff QC is a practising Barrister and Senior Ordinary Appeal Judge in Jersey and Guernsey. He was President of Trinity College, Oxford 1996–2006. He was the first Chairman of the Administrative Law Bar Association and is now a Vice-President and Emeritus Chairman. He was called to the Bar by Gray's Inn in 1967, became a Queen's Counsel in 1981, was a Recorder of the Crown Court 1984–95, a Master of the Bench of Gray's Inn in 1988 (Treasurer 2008), and a Deputy High Court Judge 1989–96. He has been a Member of the Court of Arbitration for Sport since 1996 and has served as an arbitrator at the last four summer Olympics. He has written and contributed to many publications, including *The Sex Discrimination Act* (1976); *European Community Law in English Courts* (1999); and *Law and the Spirit of Inquiry: Essays in Honour of Sir Louis Blom-Cooper QC* (1999).

Lord Bingham of Cornhill was called to the Bar (Gray's Inn) in 1959. He was appointed a Queen's Counsel in 1972, Recorder in 1975, and Judge of the High Court (QBD) in 1980. He sat on the Court of Appeal from 1986, was Master of the Rolls 1992–6, and was Lord Chief Justice of England and Wales 1996–2000. He was the Senior Law Lord 2000–8, and was appointed a Knight of the Garter in 2005, the only professional judge to be so appointed. Publications include *The Business of Judging* (2000).

Michael Blair QC is in independent practice at the Bar, specialising in financial services and financial regulation. Until 2000 he was the General Counsel to the Board of the

Financial Services Authority. He was Treasurer of the Middle Temple in 2008, and holds or has held a number of public appointments, including Chairmanship of the Review Body on Doctors' and Dentists' Remuneration and membership of the Competition Appeal Tribunal.

Sir **Louis Blom-Cooper** QC was called to the Bar by the Middle Temple in July 1952, and was made a Bencher of the Inn in 1978. He took silk in 1970, and was a Deputy High Court Judge from 1992 to 1996, as well as a Judge of Appeal in the Court of Appeal of Jersey and of Guernsey from 1989 to 1996. Publications include *Final Appeal: A Study of the House of Lords in its Judicial Capacity* (1972), co-authored with Gavin Drewry, and *The Court of Appeal* (2007), with Gavin Drewry and Charles Blake.

Lord Brodie is a Senator of the College of Justice. A graduate of the Universities of Edinburgh (LLB 1972) and Virginia (LLM 1973), he was admitted to the Faculty of Advocates (Scottish Bar) in 1976, appointed Queen's Counsel (Scotland) in 1987, and was called to the English Bar (Lincoln's Inn) in 1991. Previous posts include part-time member of the Mental Welfare Commission for Scotland 1985–96, and Advocate Depute 1997–9. He was appointed a judge in 2002. Lord Brodie is currently Chairman of the Judicial Studies Committee for Scotland (2006–).

Laurence Burgorgue-Larsen is Professor in Law at the University Paris I-Panthéon Sorbonne and at the Institute Ortega y Gasset in Madrid (Masters in Law and International Relations), at the University Autonomar (Masters in European Law). She researches in the areas of human rights law, comparative law, and European and international law. She has edited several publications, including *La France face à la Charte des droits fondamentaux de l'Union européenne* (2005), and is the author of *L'Espagne et la Communauté européenne* (1995); *Libertés fondamentales* (2003); and, more recently, with A Úbeda de Torres, *Les grandes décisions de la Cour interaméricaine des droits de l'homme* (2008).

Justice **Arthur Chaskalson** QC was admitted to the Johannesburg Bar in 1956 and took silk in July 1971. A former member of the Johannesburg Bar Council (1967–71, 1973–84), Chairman of the Johannesburg Bar (1976, 1982), member and later Convenor of the National Bar Examination Board (1979–91), and Vice Chairman of the General Council of the Bar of South Africa (1982–7), in June 1994 he was appointed the first President of South Africa's new Constitutional Court, which is the highest court in the land in all constitutional matters. He is the President of the International Commission of Jurists (elected in 2001, having been a Commissioner since 1995). He became Chief Justice of South Africa in 2001 and retired from that position in 2005.

Paul Craig has been Professor of English Law at St John's College Oxford since 1998, and previous to that was Professor of Law at Worcester College, Oxford. He researches and teaches in the areas of constitutional law, administrative law, and EU law. His most recent books are *EU Administrative Law* (2006); *EU Law: Text, Cases and Materials* (4th edn 2007, jointly with Gráinne de Búrca); and *Administrative Law* (6th edn 2008).

Stephen Cretney practised for some time as a solicitor but has spent most of his career in academia (latterly as a Senior Research Fellow at All Souls College, Oxford). He served as a Law Commissioner (with responsibility for the Commission's family law work) from 1978 to 1983. He is a Fellow of the British Academy, a Queen's Counsel (*honoris causa*), and an Honorary Bencher of the Inner Temple. He is the author of many books and other publications, including *Same Sex Relationships: From 'Odious Crime' to 'Gay Marriage'* (2006); *Family Law in the Twentieth Century: A History* (paperback edn 2005); *Law, Law Reform and the Family* (1998); and *Principles of Family Law* (7th edn, jointly, 2002).

Brice Dickson has been Professor of International and Comparative Law at Queen's University Belfast since 2005. Prior to that he served for six years as Northern Ireland's first Chief Commissioner of Human Rights, in the wake of the Belfast (Good Friday) Agreement of 1998, and before that he was the foundation Professor of Law at the University of Ulster from 1991. His latest book is an edited collection entitled *Judicial Activism in Common Law Supreme Courts* (2007).

Gavin Drewry has been Professor of Public Administration at Royal Holloway, University of London, since 1989. He began his academic career in 1966, at Bedford College, employed as a research assistant to Louis Blom-Cooper in the Legal Research Unit at the College and served subsequently as Lecturer, then Reader, in Government. He has written extensively on parliament and the legislative process, on public sector reform, on legal and parliamentary mechanisms of public accountability, and on the history and reform of legal institutions. He is an elected member of the Executive Committee of the International Institute of Administrative Sciences and is an Honorary Professor in the Faculty of Law at UCL.

David Feldman is Rouse Ball Professor of English Law at the University of Cambridge (since 2004; Chairman of the Faculty of Law 2006–9) and Fellow of Downing College, Cambridge, and a Judge of the Constitutional Court of Bosnia and Herzegovina (since 2002; Vice-President 2006–9). He is a Queen's Counsel (*honoris causa*), a Fellow of the British Academy, an Honorary Bencher of Lincoln's Inn, and an Academic Associate of Chambers at 39 Essex Street, London. He was the first Legal Adviser to the Parliamentary Joint Select Committee on Human Rights (2000–4), and has taught at the Universities of Bristol and Birmingham (where he was Dean of the Law Faculty 1997–2000) and the Australian National University. Publications include *The Law Relating to Entry, Search and Seizure* (1986); *Civil Liberties and Human Rights in England and Wales* (2nd edn 2002); and, as editor and contributor, *English Public Law* (2nd edn 2009), and he has written many articles on human rights, constitutional and administrative law, and criminal procedure.

Brigid Hadfield is Professor of Constitutional Law in the School of Law, University of Essex.

Baroness Hale of Richmond became the first woman Lord of Appeal in Ordinary after a varied career, first as an academic lawyer at Manchester University, then as a member of the Law Commission for England and Wales, and finally as a Judge, first in the Family Division of the High Court, then in the Court of Appeal, and now in the House of Lords. Throughout her career she has specialised in issues relating to the family, women and children, and mental health.

Dame **Rosalyn Higgins** QC was a member of the International Court of Justice from 1995 to 2009 and its President from 2006 to 2009. Previously, she was Professor of

International Law at the University of London (London School of Economics). She practised in public international law and petroleum law before English courts and international tribunals, taking silk in 1986 and becoming a Bencher of the Inner Temple in 1989. She was a member of the UN Committee on Human Rights (1985–95). Publications include *UN Peacekeeping: Documents and Commentary* (four volumes, 1969–81), *Problems and Process: International Law and How We Use It* (1994), and *Themes and Theories: Selected Essays, Speeches and Writings in International Law* (2009).

Sir **Anthony Hooper** was appointed a Lord Justice of Appeal in 2004, having been a judge of the High Court of Justice, QBD, from 1995 to 2004 and Presiding Judge, NE Circuit, 1997–2000. At the Bar he practised largely in the field of criminal law. Before then he taught law for 11 years at various universities in both England and Canada.

Lord Hope of Craighead practised at the Scottish Bar between 1965 and 1989. He was Dean of the Faculty of Advocates from 1986 to 1989 and was Lord Justice General for Scotland and Lord President of the Court of Session from 1989 to 1996. He has been a Lord of Appeal in Ordinary since 1996, is the Second Senior Law Lord, and was Chairman of Sub-Committee E of the House of Lords Select Committee on the EU from 1998 to 2002.

Sir **Robin Jacob** read Natural Sciences at Cambridge, and also took an LLB from the LSE whilst reading for the Bar. He practised at the Patent Bar from 1967. From 1976 to 1981 he was the Junior Counsel for the Comptroller of Patents and for Government departments in intellectual property. He was made a Queen's Counsel in 1981 and was appointed to the Bench in 1993. From 1997 to 2001 he was Supervising Chancery Judge for Birmingham, Bristol, and Cardiff, and was appointed a Lord Justice of Appeal in 2003. He is President of the Intellectual Property Institute, Honorary President of the UK branch of the Licensing Executive Society, and Honorary President of the Association of Law Teachers. He was a Founding Governor of the Expert Witness Institute and Treasurer of Grays Inn for 2007. He is a member of the Court of Appeal and sits in most appeals in IP cases, particularly patent cases, and has written and lectured extensively on all forms of intellectual property.

Sir **Francis Jacobs** QC is Professor of Law and Jean Monnet Professor at King's College London. He was an Advocate General at the Court of Justice of the European Communities from 1988 to 2006. His most recent book is *The Sovereignty of Law: The European Way* (2007).

David Lewis Jones was Librarian to the House of Lords 1991–2006; prior to that, he served as Deputy Librarian, House of Lords, 1977–91; Law Librarian, University of Wales, Aberystwyth, 1972–7; and Assistant Librarian, Institute of Historical Research, University of London, 1970–2. He is Chairman of the Parliamentary History Yearbook Trust and the author of studies on parliamentary history.

Mr Justice **Ronan Keane** was appointed barrister-at-law, King's Inns, Dublin, 1954; Senior Counsel, 1970; Judge of the High Court, 1979; President of the Irish Law Reform Commission, 1987–92; Judge of the Supreme Court, 1996; and Chief Justice, 2000–4. His publications include *Law of Local Government in the Republic of Ireland* (1982), *Equity and the Law of Trusts in the Republic of Ireland* (1988), and *Irish Company Law* (2007).

Judge Sir **Kenneth Keith** is a Judge of the International Court of Justice. Former positions include Judge of the Supreme Court and Court of Appeal of New Zealand, and member of the Judicial Committee of the Privy Council; appeal judge in Samoa, Cook Islands, Niue, and Fiji; member and president of the New Zealand Law Commission; member of the law faculty of the Victoria University of Wellington; and member of the Office of Legal Affairs of the United Nations and of the legal division of the New Zealand Department of External Affairs.

The Hon Justice **Michael Kirby** AC CMG retired from the High Court of Australia, the nation's highest court, in 2009. Born and educated in Sydney, he was called to the New South Wales Bar. In 1975 he was appointed a Deputy President of the Australian Conciliation and Arbitration Commission. In the same year he began a decade of service as the inaugural Chairman of the Australian Law Reform Commission. In 1983 he was appointed a judge of the Federal Court of Australia and in 1984 President of the New South Wales Court of Appeal. In 1995 he was appointed to the additional post of President of the Court of Appeal of Solomon Islands. His appointment to the High Court of Australia followed in 1996. Justice Kirby has taken an active part in international bodies, including the World Health Organization, UNAIDS, UNDP, ILO, UNODC, UNESCO, OECD, and the Commonwealth Secretariat. Between 1993 and 1996 he was Special Representative of the Secretary-General for Human Rights in Cambodia. Between 1995 and 1998 he was President of the International Commission of Jurists. In 2006 he was elected an Honorary Bencher of Inner Temple.

Andrew Le Sueur is Professor of Public Law at Queen Mary, University of London. He is editor of *Public Law*, the leading journal on law and government. He acted as specialist adviser to the House of Lords Select Committee on the Constitutional Reform Bill in 2004, and edited and contributed to *Building the UK's New Supreme Court: National and Comparative Perspectives* (2004).

Mark Littman QC was called to the Bar in the Middle Temple in 1947. Following service in the Royal Navy 1941–6, he served a pupillage with John Galway Foster QC. He then joined the Chambers of the Hon Hubert Parker, the future Lord Chief Justice. He took silk in 1961. Mr Littman now carries on practice from 12, Gray's Inn Square. He was Treasurer of the Middle Temple in 1987.

Kate Malleson is Professor of Law at Queen Mary, University of London. She is the author of a wide range of publications on the judiciary and the legal system, including *Appointing Judges in an Age of Judicial Power: Critical Perspectives from Around the World* (co-edited with Peter Russell, 2006). She acted as a specialist adviser to the House of Commons Constitutional Affairs Select Committee, assisting it in its review of the provisions of the Constitutional Reform Bill.

Arthur Marriott QC has been a Solicitor of the Supreme Court of England and Wales since 1966; Solicitor of the Supreme Court of Hong Kong since 1976; Recorder since 1995; he took silk in 1997, and was appointed a Deputy High Court Judge (Commercial Court) in 1997. He has been President of the Mental Health Review Tribunals since

2000, and is a Fellow of the Chartered Institute of Arbitrators and Member of the CPR International Panel of Distinguished Neutrals. He specialises in international commercial arbitration, mediation, oil and gas law and practice, joint venture agreements, and civil engineering construction law and practice. He has written numerous articles, and co-authored the *Handbook of Arbitration Law and Practice* (2003) and (with Henry Brown) *ADR Principles and Practice* (2nd edn 1999).

Dawn Oliver FBA is Emeritus Professor of Constitutional Law, University College London, Bencher of the Middle Temple, Chair of the UK Constitutional Law Group, and a member of the executive committee of the International Association of Constitutional Law. Previous positions include editor of *Public Law* (1993–2001), and member of the Royal Commission on Reform of the House of Lords (1999) and the Fabian Society Commission on the Future of the Monarchy (2002–3). Publications include *Constitutional Reform in the United Kingdom* (2003); *Common Values and the Public-Private Divide* (1999); and (with G Drewry) *Public Service Reform: Issues of Accountability and Public Law* (1996). She has edited (with J Fedtke) *Human Rights and the Private Sphere: A Comparative Study* (2007); (with J Jowell) *The Changing Constitution* (6th edn 2007); and (with G Drewry) *The Law and Parliament* (1998).

Sir **Stephen Oliver** QC is the Presiding Special Commissioner; President of the VAT and Duties Tribunals; President of the Financial Services and Markets Tribunal; President of the Pensions Regulator Tribunal; President of the Claims Management Services Tribunal; and Chairman of the Tribunal constituted by Section 703 of the Income and Corporation Taxes Act 1998. He became a QC in 1980, a Recorder in 1985, and Deputy High Court Judge in 1990.

Sir **Fred Phillips** QC was Assistant Administrator, Grenada 1957–8; Senior Assistant Secretary, West Indies Federation, 1958–60; Cabinet Secretary, 1960–2; Senior Lecturer, West Indies University, 1962–3; Acting Administrator, St Vincent, 1965; Administrator, St Kitts/Nevis/Anguilla, 1966–7; Governor, St Kitts/Nevis/Anguilla, 1967–9; Chief Legal Adviser to Cable & Wireless, 1969–97; Chairman, Constitution Commission for St Kitts/Nevis, 1997–2000; Chairman, similar Commission for Antigua and Barbuda, 2000–2. He is the author of six books on Constitutional Law and Ethics of the Legal Profession.

Patrick Polden is a Professor of Law in the Brunel Law School. He has written on various aspects of English legal history from the eighteenth to the twentieth centuries, including property law and inheritance, the legal profession, the judiciary, and the courts. His publications include *A History of the County Court* (1999) and *Peter Thellusson's Will of 1797 and its Consequences in Chancery Law* (2002). He is currently engaged, with others, on the nineteenth-century volumes of *The Oxford History of the Laws of England*, with publication due in 2009.

Francis Reynolds QC (Hon), DCL, FBA is Professor of Law Emeritus at the University of Oxford and Emeritus Fellow of Worcester College, Oxford. He has been the Editor of *The Law Quarterly Review* since 1987, and is the writer of *Bowstead and Reynolds on Agency* (now in its 18th edition). He has written sections of several other books on commercial law, and served as Visiting Professor at universities in Singapore, Hong Kong,

Malta, Australia, and New Zealand. He is a titulary member of the Comité Maritime International.

Justice **Robert J Sharpe**, Court of Appeal for Ontario, was formerly Professor and Dean of the Faculty of Law, University of Toronto. He has written several books, including *The Law of Habeas Corpus* (3rd edn forthcoming 2010); *Injunctions and Specific Performance* (3rd edn 2000); *Brian Dickson: A Judge's Journey* (2003); and *The Charter of Rights and Freedoms* (2nd edn 2002).

JR Spencer QC LLD is a Professor of Law at the University of Cambridge, and a Fellow of Selwyn College. He has taught law at the University of Cambridge since 1970. His interests include criminal law, criminal evidence, and criminal procedure. He has written or edited books on the English legal system, comparative criminal procedure, and various aspects of the law of evidence. He lectures regularly for the Judicial Studies Board and was a consultant to Sir Robin Auld's Review of the Criminal Courts. He is an Academic Bencher of the Inner Temple and holds an Honorary Degree from the University of Poitiers.

David Steele, formerly Reader in History, University of Leeds, is the author of *Irish Land and British Politics* (1974); *Palmerston and Liberalism* (1991); *Lord Salisbury: A Political Biography* (1999); and author of the *Oxford Dictionary of National Biography* entries on Lord Chancellors Selborne and Cairns.

Robert Stevens has been Professor of Commercial Law at University College London since 2007. Previously he was a lecturer in law at the University of Oxford and a Fellow and Tutor in Law at Lady Margaret Hall, where he taught from 1994. He was called to the Bar in 1992. He has taught and lectured widely both within the Commonwealth (Australia and Canada) and Continental Europe (Germany, the Netherlands, Spain). He has lectured for the Judicial Studies Board, and holds a consultancy with Clifford Chance. He has written on subjects across private law issues, focusing most recently on the law of torts in his book *Torts and Rights* (2007).

John Tiley QC (Hon) CBE, until his retirement in 2008, FBA LLD was Professor of Tax Law and Fellow of Queens' College in the University of Cambridge, having begun teaching law there in 1967. He was made a CBE for services to tax law in 2003. He is the author of *Revenue Law* (6th edn 2008) and is a regular contributor to the British Tax Review and other UK journals. He is a founder member of the European Association of Tax Law Professors and in 1995–6 he was President of the Society of Legal Scholars (previously the Society of Public Teachers of Law). He served as an Assistant Recorder and then Recorder from 1983 to 1997. He is an Honorary Bencher of the Inner Temple.

James Vallance White CB was Fourth Clerk at the Table and Clerk of the Judicial Office in the House of Lords from 1983 to 2002. He previously served as Chief Clerk of the Public Bill Office from 1978 to 1983 and as Clerk of Committees from 1971 to 1978.

Sir **David GT Williams** MA, LLB (Cantab), LLM (California) taught at the Universities of Nottingham, Oxford, and Cambridge. At Cambridge he was Rouse Ball Professor of English Law 1983–92, President of Wolfson College 1980–92, and Vice-Chancellor of the University 1989–96. He has written many publications in the area of public law.

Derek **Wood** CBE QC has practised at the Bar since 1965 in all fields of property litigation and took silk in 1978. He has served as chairman or member of many government committees on housing, planning, property investment, and rating. Between 1991 and 2002 he was Principal of St Hugh's College Oxford. He is a Bencher and ex-Treasurer (2006) of the Middle Temple.

Tom **Zwart** is a Professor of Law at the School of Law, Utrecht University. He joined Leiden Law Faculty in 1982, became Head of the European and Legal Affairs Department of the Dutch Home Office in 1993, and moved to Utrecht in 1997. In 2007 he was appointed Director of the School of Human Rights Research, a consortium set up by five universities and the TMC Asser Institute, in which some 200 researchers are cooperating. Zwart has written extensively on topics relating to comparative law, human rights, and public law, including on 'deference' in *Judges, Transitions and Human Rights*, published by OUP. He has been an academic visitor at several law schools in Australia, China, France, the UK, and the US. In 2000 he was elected a Visiting Fellow of Wolfson College, Cambridge.

Table of Cases

Table of Legislation

NATIONAL LEGISLATION

PART A
THE INSTITUTION

1

The Judicial Role of the House of Lords before 1870

David Lewis Jones

Thomas, Duke of Gloucester, and Thomas Arundel, bishop of Ely, remonstrated with Richard II over the King's refusal to attend the parliament called in 1386:

> we have a laudable and approved custom, which none can deny, that our king has the power to call together once every year, to his parliament, the lords and great men of the realm, with the commons, as to the highest court in all the land, in which without doubt or quibble all equity ought to shine like the morning sun in his ascent, and to which both rich and poor can resort, for the refreshment and tranquillity of peace, and the redress of injuries, as to an unfailing refuge...[1]

A significant part of Parliament's role, from the reign of Edward I, lay in providing remedies for petitioners either reluctant to pursue their causes in other courts or, to a lesser extent, wishing to appeal from a lower court. With the development of the two Houses of Parliament in the fourteenth century, petitions could be and were sent to either House. The Lords claimed, by the early fifteenth century, that judgment belonged to them alone: petitions considered by the Commons were sent to the Lords for confirmation, but petitions dealt with by the Lords were not referred to the Commons.[2] There was a sharp decline in the judicial work of Parliament in the sixteenth century; only five cases are recorded in the Lords Journals between 1514 and 1589. This decline has been attributed to greater activity by the common law courts and to the development of new prerogative courts; another reason, acknowledged in the preamble to the Error from Queen's Bench Act 1584, was the infrequent meeting of Parliament: 'Forasmuch as erronious Judgementes given in the Courte called the King's

---

[1] *Knighton's Chronicle 1337–1396*, GH Martin (ed and trans) (Oxford: OUP, 1995) 357.
[2] G Dodd, *Justice and Grace: Private Petitioning and the English Parliament in the Late Middle Ages* (Oxford: OUP, 2007); see 165–6 for the 'prominence of the Lords in the petitionary process'.

Bench are only to be reformed by the High Courte of Parliament, which Court of Parliament is not in these Dayes so often holden as in aunciant Time.'[3]

When Henry Elsyng codified the rules of procedure in the House of Lords during the 1620s, he commented that 'The execucion of all our Lawes hath ben longe since distributed by the Parlement unto the inferiour Courtes, in such sorte as the Subiecte is directed where to complayne, and the Justices howe to redresse wronges and punish offences ... Yett complaynts have ever ben receaved in Parlement, asswell of pryvatt wronges, as of publique offences. And, according to the quallitye of the person, and nature of the offence, they have been reteyned, or referred to the Common Lawe.'[4] Elsyng noted that judicature still belonged to Parliament in the following instances: (1) judgments against delinquents, as well for capital crimes, as misdemeanours; (2) in reversing erroneous judgments in Parliament, or the Court of King's Bench; (3) in deciding of suits long depending in other courts, either for difficulty or delay; (4) in hearing and determining the complaints of particular persons on petition; (5) in setting at liberty any of their own Members or servants imprisoned; and in staying the proceedings at the common law against them during the privilege of Parliament; and (6) in certifying the elections and returns of Knights and Citizens for Parliament. Elsyng completed his chapter on the judicature of the House of Lords in August 1627.[5]

The previous six years had seen a remarkable revival of the judicial work of the House of Lords, which began in March 1621 when James I referred the petition of Edward Ewer, a hardened litigant, who asked that his cause in the King's Bench be sent to the House of Lords for review. A few days later, the House of Commons pressed the Lords to proceed against Sir Giles Mompesson for his misdeeds as a patentee; Edward Coke referred in warm terms to the judicial role of the Lords: 'there is a necessity in this else justice will fall to the ground and the subject in some cases cannot be relieved'. In agreeing to act against Mompesson, the House of Lords revived impeachment.[6]

Greater prosperity, more complex economic organisations and an increased population brought a considerable growth in litigation in the later sixteenth and early seventeenth centuries. Suitors were also more likely to bring their complaints to London rather than apply to a local court. There were serious delays in the administration of justice by the law courts. Other litigants were ready to follow Ewer's example; in the five parliaments held between 1621 and 1629, the House accepted 207 cases which included cases of first instance, cases which had been considered by other courts but were not appeals, and appeals. The House was

---

[3] CH McIlwain, *The High Court of Parliament and its Supremacy* (New Haven: Yale University Press, 1910) 121–37.

[4] ER Foster (ed), *Judicature in Parlement by Henry Elsyng* (London: Hambledon Press, 1991) 7.

[5] ibid, xii, 10–11.

[6] W Notestein et al (eds), *Commons Debates 1621* (New Haven: Yale University Press, 1935) vol 2, 195; parliament retains the power of impeachment, but it was last exercised when Lord Melville was impeached in 1804.

prompt to develop new procedures for handling the growing number of petitions. A standing Committee for Petitions, established in 1621, grew in size and importance throughout the 1620s. Legal assistants, summoned by writs of assistance, supported the work of the Committee. Initially, a petition was read before the whole House before it was referred to a Committee. In the Parliament of 1624 it was ordered that petitions should be sent directly to the Committee, which would present its conclusions to the House. Eventually, the Committee was allowed to decide on petitions, but with a weekly report to the House. A new and necessary precedent was created and generally accepted in 1624 when the House considered appeals from the Court of Chancery.[7]

During the long interlude of Charles I's personal rule in the 1630s, the actions of royal officials weakened popular confidence in the rule of law. When Parliament met again in 1640, the House of Lords faced a torrent of litigation, which increased following the abolition of the prerogative courts and the collapse of the Privy Council in 1641 when their unfinished litigation came to the Lords. In the first half of the 1640s, the House laboured to restore the legal order. Later, the radical passions of the time overwhelmed a House devoted to a conservative interpretation of the law. On 6 February 1648/9, the House of Lords, being 'useless and dangerous', was abolished.[8] During the debates on the case of James Nayler in December 1656, the House of Commons claimed to hold the authority of the House of Lords to sentence Nayler. The severe punishment imposed on Nayler highlighted the lack of a check on the power of the Commons and led to a debate on the concept of the 'Other House' and its judicial powers. The resolution passed by the Commons on 17 March 1657 limited these powers in civil causes to writs of error from the lower courts; to cases sent to Parliament because of difficulty; to petitions against proceedings in the courts of equity; and, to the privileges of their own House. Criminal cases could only be considered after an impeachment by the Commons. The inconclusive debates in the Protectorate Parliaments on the judicial power of the Other House did show the need for a second chamber.[9]

The restored House of Lords met in April 1660 and embarked, within five days, on its judicial work. Inevitably, the House had to deal with complaints arising from the turbulent years of the Civil War and the Interregnum; with caution and compromise, realistic solutions to these difficult problems were

---

[7] The standard work on the judicial work of the House of Lords in the seventeenth century is JS Hart, *Justice upon Petition: The House of Lords and the Reformation of Justice 1621–1675* (London: HarperCollins Academic, 1991); see ch 1 for the revival of the House as a court. For the role of legal assistants, see ER Foster, *The House of Lords 1603–1649: Structure, Procedure, and the Nature of its Business* (Chapel Hill: University of North Carolina Press, 1983) 74–6; see also A Horstman, 'A New Curia Regis: The Judicature of the House of Lords in the 1620s' (1982) 25 Historical Journal 411–22.

[8] Hart, ibid, chs 2–5 contain a detailed survey of the House's use of its judicial powers in the 1640s.

[9] P Little and DL Smith, *Parliament and Politics during the Cromwellian Protectorate* (Cambridge: CUP, 2007) 178–95; JT Rutt, *Diary of Thomas Burton Esq* (London: H Colburn, 1828) vol 1, 387–8 for the Commons' resolution.

pursued. The Act for Confirmation of Judicial Proceedings 1660 forestalled appeals based on the status of the Interregnum judges. The usual private grievances were also received but, for lack of time, many were re-scheduled for the next parliament.

The House proceeded with its judicial work, as usual, for the first six years of the parliament called on 8 May 1661. A major dispute with the House of Commons arose over the case of *Thomas Skinner v East India Company*. Skinner established a trading station in the East Indies before Cromwell granted a monopoly of the East Indies trade to the East Indies Company in 1657. After the Company confiscated his property, Skinner returned to England in 1661 and sought compensation for his considerable losses. A number of attempts by the Privy Council to mediate between Skinner and the Company failed before Charles II agreed to send the matter to the House of Lords on 19 January 1667. In the Company's answer of 28 January to Skinner's claims, a strong objection was made to the fact that 'the petition is in the nature of an original complaint' and not a petition to consider a decision by a lower court. The House held that they could proceed on the matter and found, a year later, for Skinner; in answer, the Company petitioned the Commons for relief from the 'unusual' and 'extra-ordinary' proceedings of the Lords. The House of Commons, which included men who were members of the Company, resolved that the Lords had acted arbitrarily and initiated a dispute between the two Houses that lasted throughout 1668 and 1669. At the opening of a new session in February 1670, the King asked both Houses to bring the dispute to an end. When the Commons revived the quarrel, the King ordered that all references to the dispute in the journals of both Houses be deleted and the dispute brought to an end. Both the Commons and the Company argued that the Lords did not have the right to hear first instance cases where other avenues of redress had not been pursued. This argument deterred future litigants and the House of Lords, in practice, limited its jurisdiction to appeal cases, except for impeachments and peerage claims.

Within five years another crisis had arisen between the two Houses, this time over the case of *Shirley v Fagg*, where the defendant, Sir John Fagg, was a member of the Commons, and this led that House to claim that Fagg had parliamentary privilege. Opposition peers seeking a dissolution encouraged this dispute and the Commons enlarged the quarrel when it emerged that two other Members of their House, Thomas Dalmahoy and Arthur Onslow, were also defendants in appeals before the Lords. Two of the cases were appeals from the Court of Chancery and the third was an appeal from the equity side of the Court of Exchequer. The House of Commons now added to their dispute by challenging the power of the Lords to accept appeals from the courts of equity. The King was forced to prorogue Parliament twice; the dispute was not revived when Parliament met again in 1677 and the House of Lords retained its right to an appellate jurisdiction in equity. The altercations over the judicial powers of the House of Lords were fomented by members of both Houses with other priorities: the argument over *Skinner's Case* was used as a means of preventing a new Bill limiting toleration to dissenters reaching the House of Lords; the dispute over privileges which arose from *Shirley v Fagg* and the other cases was used to scupper the Test Bill and to attack the Lord Treasurer, Lord Danby. The House of Lords defended its judicial powers fiercely; when the House of Commons imprisoned persons involved in the case against Dalmahoy, the Lords rebuked the other House sharply:

Their Lordships do judge this Order for Imprisonment to be illegal and arbitrary, and the Execution thereof a great Indignity to the King's Majesty in this His highest Court of Judicature in the Kingdom, the Lords in Parliament; where His Majesty is Highest in His Royal Estate, and where the last Resort of judging upon Writs of Error and Appeals in Equity, in all Causes, and over all Persons, is undoubtedly fixed and permanently lodged.

The House of Commons was reminded that it held no judicial authority: 'the Lower House of Parliament, who are no Court, nor have Authority to administer an oath, or give any Judgment'.[10]

By the end of the reign of Charles II, the judicial role of the House of Lords had been established for some 60 years. Around 40 per cent of the peers who attended the restored House of Lords had attended the House before the Civil Wars and their familiarity with the House's practice in receiving and considering appeals enabled the restored House to resume judicial work with relative ease. On the whole, the peers dealt fairly and expertly with the cases presented to them. The main disadvantage lay in the intermittent nature of Parliament and the fact that cases lapsed at a prorogation; the House sought to solve the latter problem by allowing, on 29 March 1673, writs of error and appeals to continue into the next session. The difficulties arising from the intermittent nature of Parliament were solved after the Glorious Revolution when Parliament met annually and, as a result, the Lords could decide a greater proportion of the cases before them.[11]

When the British Parliament met for the first time on 23 October 1707, the question of appeals from Scotland to the House of Lords was unclear. Article 19 of the Articles of Union stated that:

No causes in Scotland be cognoscible by the Courts of Chancery, Queen's Bench, Common Pleas or any other court in Westminster Hall, and that the said courts or any other of the like nature after the Union shall have no power to cognosce, review or alter the acts or sentences of the judicatures within Scotland or stop execution of the same.

The subject of an appellate jurisdiction had been raised during the discussions over the Union and it is probable that the omission of the role of the House of Lords from the Articles was deliberate. On the English side, the recent dispute in 1704–5 between the Lords and the Commons over *Ashby v White* had raised questions again in the Commons over the extent of the jurisdiction of the Lords,

---

[10] Lords Journals vol 12, 718.

[11] Hart (n 7) ch 6 has the best account of *Skinner's Case* and of *Shirley v Fagg*. See A Swatland, *The House of Lords in the Reign of Charles II* (Cambridge: CUP, 1996) ch 5 for the regular judicial work of the House.

and this was probably a factor in omitting a reference to appeals in the Articles. Scottish opinion was divided: some thought that distance would deter appeals to the Lords while others believed that such appeals would assist in reducing ministerial influence over the Court of Session. The commissioners negotiating the Union probably held that a direct reference to appeals in the Articles of Union would be controversial in Scotland. However, soon after the Union, Parliament passed the Exchequer Court (Scotland) Act 1707, which allowed appeals from that court to the House of Lords in common law and equity cases. The House of Lords received the first appeal from a decision of the Court of Session, *Rosebery v Inglis*, on 16 February 1708. Parliament was dissolved before Inglis could return his answer to the House and there were no further proceedings on this appeal. Lord Rosebery had been a Scottish Union Commissioner while five of the Scottish Union Commissioners and five of the English Union Commissioners sat on the petition committee, which reported on the appeal. The House claimed jurisdiction over Scottish criminal cases when it reversed the decision of the High Court of Justiciary in the case of *Magistrates of Elgin v Ministers of Elgin* (1713). The right of the House to accept such appeals was contentious and it was effectively ended in 1781 by the decision of Lord Mansfield who argued, in the case of *Bywater v Lord Advocate*, that there had been no appeal from the High Court to the Scottish Parliament and there could, therefore, be no appeal from the High Court to the House of Lords.

In its first order relating to Scottish appeals on 19 April 1709, the House ordered that, once notice had been served on a respondent in an appeal from a court in Scotland, the sentence or decree appealed against ought not to be carried into effect. This was an incentive for Scottish litigants to postpone judgment by appealing to the Lords; the number of Scottish appeals easily outnumbered English appeals throughout the eighteenth century. Action to reduce the number of such appeals was taken in 1808 when 139 Scottish cases were waiting for a hearing in the House. With the agreement of the Scottish judges, the Court of Session Act 1808 prohibited appeals in interlocutory matters without the leave of the Court of Session or if there was disagreement among the judges. Scottish judges were also allowed, under the Administration of Justice (Scotland) Act 1808, the power to decide whether a case being appealed merited a stay of execution. These measures had little effect in reducing the number of Scottish appeals.[12]

When Maurice Annesley appealed on 7 May 1717 to the House of Lords against the decision of the Irish House of Lords in the case of *Annesley v Sherlock*, he prompted the House of Lords to resume a long-standing dispute over jurisdiction with the House in Dublin. Following the judgment of the Irish House of Lords in *The Bishop of Derry v The Irish Society* in 1698, the Society had appealed

---

[12] DM Walker, *A Legal History of Scotland, vol 5, The Eighteenth Century* (Edinburgh: T & T Clark, 1998) 445–55; AJ MacLean, 'The 1707 Union: Scots Law and the House of Lords' (1983) 4(3) Journal of Legal History 50; AJ MacLean, 'The House of Lords and Appeals from the Court of Justiciary, 1707–1887' (1985) 30 Juridical Review ns 192.

to the English House of Lords which ruled that an appeal from the Irish Court of Chancery to the Irish House of Lords was *coram non judice,* and that such appeals had to be sent to the English House of Lords. In the following year, the English House overruled the decision of the Irish House in another Irish Chancery appeal, *Ward and ors v The Earl of Meath.* On this occasion, the Irish House voted to defend its jurisdiction and a difficult conflict was only avoided through the mediation of the Lord-Lieutenant in Dublin. *Annesley v Sherlock* reopened a dispute that had not been resolved. Despite the success of the Lord-Lieutenant in reaching an amicable settlement between the two parties in the case, the two Houses were not prepared to put their disagreement to one side and the matter now turned on the question of which House held the final jurisdiction over appeals in Ireland. In the course of the quarrel, the Irish House of Lords placed three of the judges of the Irish Court of Exchequer under arrest for heeding the decisions of the British House of Lords. In answer, the British House of Lords passed resolutions on 28 January 1719 in support of the Exchequer judges for their action 'in Obedience to the Orders of this House' and instructed the judges to prepare a Bill to secure 'the Dependency of Ireland'. The Declaratory Act of 1719 reaffirmed the appellate jurisdiction of the British House of Lords in appeals from the Irish courts. Forty years later, when the British government was weakened by the war in America and the Irish Parliament became aware of its increased power relative to London, the Declaratory Act was repealed by the Repeal of the Act for Securing Dependence of Ireland Act 1782. The position was restored to that in effect before the Declaratory Act and the British Parliament, prompted by Irish pressure, passed the Irish Appeals Act 1783 which, with great care, declared that all actions and suits in Ireland should be 'decided in His Majesty's Courts therein finally, and without appeal from thence'. Further offence was avoided by the omission of a reference to either House of Lords. Almost twenty years later, appeals from Irish courts returned to Westminster following the Act of Union in 1801.[13]

Lay peers continued to sit on appeals during the eighteenth century. In notable cases, for example the *Douglas Cause* of 1769, a large number of lay peers attended and voted on the appeal. There were occasional attempts to interfere with the course of justice, as in the case of *Bishop of London v Ffytche* (1783) when the judges advising the House recommended judgment for Ffytche by seven to one, but the spiritual peers carried the day for the Bishop of London when the House, after a long debate, voted on the appeal. Frequently, the Lord Chancellor was the only lawyer sitting on appeal, but with a number of lay peers. Gradually, it was recognised that the House needed a number of Members qualified to act as

[13] I Victory, 'The Making of the Declaratory Act 1720' in G O'Brien (ed), *Parliament, Politics and People: Essays in Eighteenth Century Irish History* (Dublin: Irish Academic Press, 1989) 9–29; DW Hayton, 'The Stanhope/Sunderland Ministry and the Repudiation of Irish Parliamentary Independence' (1998) 113 English Historical Review 610; A Lyall, 'The Irish House of Lords as a Judicial Body, 1783–1800' (1993–5) 28–30 Irish Jurist 314.

judges; rumours of a new peerage in January 1785 led *The Times* to comment: 'the business of appeals in the House of Lords [is] making an encrease of Law Lords a matter of necessity'.[14]

Except for one year, Lord Eldon held the post of Lord Chancellor from 1801 to 1827; he was a man of great legal learning but his procrastination over judgments was the despair of his fellow lawyers. At a time when the political world was divided over the question of political reform, it was inevitable that the reformers would press for changes in the administration of justice by the House of Lords. Eldon succumbed to pressure from the House of Commons for reform when he moved, on 5 March 1811, for the appointment of a select committee to consider the best mode of expediting the hearing of cases in appeal and writs of error. At that time the arrears of appeals and writs of error amounted to 270 cases. The report of the select committee, published on 20 May, recommended that the House should sit three days a week at 10am in order to reduce the arrears and that an extra judge should be appointed in Chancery to reduce the burden on the Lord Chancellor. The House agreed to meet three days a week between 10am and 3.45pm to hear appeals and an extra judge was appointed to Chancery. The House also appointed an Appeals Committee, which met, and still meets, to consider preliminary procedural matters and petitions for leave to appeal.

These reforms proved inadequate and another select committee reported that 225 appeals and 24 writs of error, which included 155 Scottish cases, were awaiting a hearing on 14 March 1823.[15] Judges in the Court of Session did not elaborate on their judgments and this prompted dissatisfied litigants to appeal to the House of Lords. The Court of Session (Scotland) Act 1825 restricted appeals in cases beginning before magistrates or sheriffs in Scotland to questions of law. The House of Lords also agreed to meet five days a week, between 10am and 4pm, to hear appeals, and measures were introduced to compel lay peers to make up a quorum, with the unfortunate result that the lay peers sitting on an appeal often changed from day to day. These arrangements reduced the arrears of appeals by 1827. Under the reforming government of Lord Grey, the new Lord Chancellor was Brougham, a man of great energy and a strong will, who abolished, between 1830 and 1834, the arrears of appeals. Anxious to extend his legal reforms to the work of the House of Lords, Brougham introduced in 1834 a Bill to separate the judicial and parliamentary duties of the Lord Chancellor, but he was persuaded to abandon his Bill on the grounds that his successful dispatch of the arrears made it unnecessary. Shortly afterwards, he was replaced as Lord Chancellor.

---

[14] *The Times*, 6 January 1785, col 3b. AS Turberville, *The House of Lords in the Age of Reform 1784–1837* (London: Faber and Faber, 1958) 185–219 contains some relevant material on this period; the judicial work of the House between 1690 and 1870 requires more detailed study.
[15] *Accounts relating to the number of appeals and writs of error heard or decided, 1813–23.* HC paper 447, sess 1823.

By the late 1830s the membership of the House included seven peers with judicial experience, and they were sufficient for a quorum to hear appeals. In the appeal of Daniel O'Connell from a decision of the Irish Queen's Bench in 1844, five of these Law Lords sat, with the assistance of 12 judges from the common law courts. This appeal was controversial on political grounds and lay peers wished to support the minority of lords who had found against O'Connell. Peel, the Prime Minister, sent his colleague, Lord Wharncliffe, to persuade the House that lay peers should not attempt to override the judgment of the Law Lords. The lay peers accepted Wharncliffe's plea and followed the Earl of Verulam's example in leaving the chamber.[16]

During the committee stage of a Chancery Reform Bill in 1855, Sir Richard Bethell, the Solicitor General, repeated current complaints about the appellate jurisdiction: the House of Lords was not performing its judicial work satisfactorily; peers hearing an appeal felt free to attend or not as they pleased, or to remain for the whole of the argument; with the exception of the Lord Chancellor, the rest of the court were 'mere volunteers'; and the House should include a judge experienced in the law of Scotland; the House was 'inferior to the lowest tribunal in what ought to be the accompaniments of a Court of Justice'.[17] In answer to the vocal criticism of reformers, the Government announced that Sir James Parke, lately a judge in the Court of Exchequer, was to be made a life peer as Baron Wensleydale. Members of the Lords opposed, successfully, the creation of a life peer, which they feared would foreshadow a reform of their House with the creation of more life peers. At the same time, the House of Lords accepted that the exercise of the judicial functions was inadequate and that a more reliable core of professional judges was required to consider appeals. Chance largely dictated the presence of sufficient members qualified to sit judicially. Following the rejection of life peerages, the House appointed a select committee to consider the appellate jurisdiction. The outcome of its reflections was the Appellate Jurisdiction (House of Lords) Bill 1856 which allowed the appointment of two salaried judicial officers in the House and four life peers and for the House to sit judicially during prorogation. After a swift passage through the Lords, the Bill failed in the Commons because the measure was insufficient for the reformers and excessive for the conservative.

After 1856, rapid changes of government ensured that there were sufficient Law Lords to cope with appeals. The House's ability to deal with Scottish appeals, which had been a grievance of long standing, was improved in 1867 when Duncan McNeill, a Scottish judge, became Lord Colonsay. Reformers had not

---

[16] There was an emphasis in the speeches of the Lord Chancellor and others on the importance of the legal opinions presented to the House: see the detailed account of *O'Connell v R* in *The Times*, 5 September 1844, 5–7. Lay members had last voted on an appeal, without a 'law lord' present, on 17 June 1834; Lord Denman expressed his concurrence with the dissenting judgment in the controversial *Bradlaugh v Clarke* (1883), but he was ignored: *The Times*, 10 April 1883, col 4e.

[17] Parl Debs (series 3) vol 139, cols 2119–20.

abandoned their campaign for a thorough review of the entire court system; in 1867, the year of the Second Reform Act, pressure in the House of Commons led to a Royal Commission on the Judicature. The Appellate Jurisdiction Bill 1870 included the Commission's proposal that the House of Lords should appoint a Judicial Committee, consisting of members and others, to hear appeals; the Bill failed and reform was again postponed.[18]

---

[18] The standard account of developments from 1800–70 is R Stevens, *Law and Politics: The House of Lords as a Judicial Body 1800–1976* (London: Weidenfeld and Nicholson, 1979) 3–47; O Anderson, 'The Wensleydale Peerage Case and the Position of the House of Lords in the Mid-nineteenth Century' (1967) 82 English Historical Review 486; for Scotland, see DM Walker, *A Legal History of Scotland, vol 6, The Nineteenth Century* (Edinburgh: LexisNexis Butterworths, 2001) 306–10.

2

The Judicial House of Lords: Abolition and Restoration 1873–6

David Steele

The setting

'The story is one of intrigue, legislation and counter-legislation that virtually defies unravelling',[1] wrote Robert Stevens in his standard account of this topic published 30 years ago. Sources not available then have made it easier to get at the motives behind the sequence of events. It is difficult to understand the comparative absence of opposition to Lord Chancellor Selborne's Supreme Court of Judicature Act in 1873 and the intensifying hostility thereafter in the law and both Houses of Parliament, unless one remembers that this is as much political as legal history. Ending the Lords' jurisdiction in final appeals, with effect from November 1875, was the concluding instalment of the first Gladstone government's reforms in church and state, unequalled since the legislative activity of the 1830s that followed the Great Reform Act. Both of the historic parties were committed to continuous, though cautious, modernisation, but Gladstone and the Gladstonians went faster and further than many of his own party thought was safe, or desirable. As the political weather changed with the development of a natural reaction, determined defenders of the Lords' political as well as judicial role attracted the support that had been wanting. They forced Selborne's Tory collaborator and successor, Lord Chancellor Cairns, to proceed by stages to the confirmation in his Appellate Jurisdiction Act of 1876 of what had been on the verge of extinction. More often than not, significant law reform reflects a political mood favourable to change that can be deemed radical by the standards of the time. But rearguard actions are sometimes successful, and the manoeuvres of 1873–6 provide a notable instance. The leading modernisers met with an unexpected check at the hand of traditionalists able to make the case for their version of a pragmatic and flexible conservatism.

---

[1] R Stevens, *Law and Politics: The House of Lords as a Judicial Body 1800–1976* (London: Weidenfeld and Nicholson, 1979) 57. I am grateful to the owners and custodians of the MSS on which I have drawn for this chapter.

The Disraeli administration, which replaced Gladstone's reforming ministry in February 1874, sought to explain Tory acquiescence in the Act of 1873 by reference to 'very great and manifest apathy' among its adherents in both Houses.[2] On the other hand, the author of the measure, Selborne, claimed that its smooth passage had been the result of a compact between the parties to effect a change arising from prolonged discussion.[3] The apathy was more apparent than real, and the compact reflected the Tories' loss of confidence in their historic role as the brake on reform after they had failed to prevent, or modify significantly, strong doses of change. The atmosphere in which the Lords' appellate function was set to end resembled that of the Blair decade in which the Constitutional Reform Act of 2005 was passed. Like New Labour's triumphs from 1997, the Liberal victory of 1868 in the first election fought on household suffrage in the boroughs seemed to knock the stuffing out of a Tory opposition without much faith in its leadership. Gladstone's popularity outside Parliament and his domination of the Commons were such that fearful conservatives—with a small 'c', that is, on both sides of the party divide— believed it might be in his power to radicalise English politics in depth.[4]

The ambiguity of Gladstone's political stance, combined with the authority he enjoyed, never greater than at this stage of his career, explains why an instalment of law reform that was not inherently divisive elicited a powerful delayed reaction. The House of Lords was perceived, by itself and by informed opinion, to be under threat. It was a time when Gladstone's colleague, Robert Lowe, was genuinely afraid of what his chief might do: if thwarted and forced out of office, he was likely to reveal himself as ' "the reddest of the red"... the tendency of his mind is all in that direction...'.[5] Misreading a complex, though essentially conservative, mind Lowe, like many others, did not appreciate the paradox that continues to intrigue historians: the contrast between Gladstone's commitment to moderating inevitable change in the spirit of the Burke he idolised, and his readiness to deploy an unnerving populism when it suited him. He had no doubt in 1873 that he would get the Judicature Bill through on his terms. 'There will be no compromising with the Lords,' he noted after a cabinet in July. '... Need not be in a hurry to display our strength.'[6] Although the public displayed little

---

[2] Hughenden Papers (B/XX/Ca) Cambridge University Library microfilm, unsigned memorandum in Cairns' hand, not dated but March 1875; for a character and assessment of this chancellor see *Oxford Dictionary of National Biography (ODNB)* (2004).

[3] Parl Debs (series 3) vol 219, cols 1387–98 (11 June 1874); in his memorandum cited in n 2 above, Cairns agreed there was 'nothing short of a compact'. For the prehistory of attempts to reform the appellate jurisdiction, see Stevens (n 1) ch 2.

[4] The national political scene in the first half of the 1870s may be approached through HCG Matthew, *Gladstone 1809–74* (Oxford: Clarendon Press, 1986) chs vii and viii, reprinted prefaces from HCG Matthew (ed), *The Gladstone Diaries, with Cabinet Minutes and Prime Ministerial Correspondence*, 14 vols (Oxford: OUP, 1968–94).

[5] JR Vincent (ed), *A Selection from the Diaries of Edward Henry Stanley, 15th Earl of Derby 1849–1878*, Camden Fifth series (London: Royal Historical Society, 1994) 98, 8 February 1872. Hereafter cited as *DD*. For Derby, see *DNB*.

[6] Gladstone Papers (BL Add MS 44663) cabinet minutes, 14 July 1873.

interest, then or later, in the question of the Lords' jurisdiction, it could always be called upon to resent the alleged obscurantism of the Upper House.

Some advocates of law reform were spoiling for a fight with a view to weakening the hereditary peerage and diluting its near-monopoly of the second chamber. In a combative address to the Social Science Association in 1872, the Attorney General, Sir John Coleridge, who professed to loathe the aristocracy before he took a peerage, fastened on the connection between an unreformed House of Lords and a legal system overdue for comprehensive reconstruction along Benthamite lines. He was scathing when he reviewed the constitution of a court of final appeal and the Lords' obdurate resistance over the years to admitting judicial life peers as a means of strengthening their jurisdiction. Comparing their pretensions with his estimate of their performance in the appellate role, Coleridge poured scorn on the existing Law Lords as being unfit for the function long since relegated to them by the peers as a whole. Quoting some lines from Milton, he likened them to the 'smallest dwarfs' of the poet's imagery. His language was not, said the *Saturday Review*, calculated to win friends for his ambitious programme.[7]

Coleridge's strictures introduce another strand in the re-telling of this episode in English political and legal history. Contemporary reverence for the law did not exclude incessant complaints about the cost and the delays of litigation within the antiquated framework of the courts and their procedures. Lawyers were pilloried as the beneficiaries of absurdity and injustice; *Bleak House* is only the best known of the Victorian novels that depict the helpless litigant in the toils of the law. Gladstone, for one, had a surprisingly low opinion of barristers and judges. They were, he told Selborne, when the Government started to think seriously of extending reform to a promising field, '*generally* second rate men'. As such, they were decidedly overpaid on promotion to the Bench.[8] Selborne of course stood up for his brethren, but the prime minister's determination to achieve some small economies for the taxpayer made judicial salaries an enjoyable topic for (unsalaried) peers and MPs in the debates of 1873 and succeeding sessions on the Judicature Bills. Selborne's Act made provision for restraining the expense of proceedings, as did Cairns in his turn.[9]

There was much more to the 1873 Judicature Act than the ending of appeals to the Lords. The re-ordering of the structure and procedures of English courts exhibited the contemporary flair for modernising without conflict. The first of the three contentious issues raised, and the one that particularly concerns us, was

---

[7] EH Coleridge, *Life and Correspondence of John Duke, Lord Coleridge, Lord Chief Justice of England*, 2 vols (London, 1904) I, 259–60, Coleridge to Sir W Heathcote, MP, 19 August 1860; II, 91–3.

[8] Gladstone Papers (44296) Gladstone to Selborne, 27 January 1872.

[9] Selborne in Parl Debs (series 3) vol 223, cols 1806–7 (29 April 1875); he regretted the absence of any such 'distinct provisions' from the Appellate Jurisdiction Bill, ibid, vol 227, col 913 (25 February 1876). In debating the bill Disraeli was to argue that 'after all the best security for cheap justice is prompt justice': Parl Debs vol 229, col 1688 (12 June 1876).

the replacement of the Lords by an altogether novel court. Secondly, Selborne committed himself, largely on the grounds of expense, and against the weight of professional opinion, to doing away with a double appeal. The Law Lords would therefore be superfluous. Lastly, Selborne and his supporters wanted to modify the existing rigid separation between common law and equity in the interests, again, of the public. Unwisely, they spoke of fusing the two before substituting convergence as the stated aim.[10] The equity Bar took fright; its practitioners made common cause with the champions of the Lords. There was plenty of material for a concerted movement, when the political climate changed, to overturn the most obvious and controversial of the innovations in Selborne's Act: the removal of the Lords from their ancient position in the hierarchy of English and British tribunals. While Selborne himself was no radical, his political sensibility as, then, a loyal Gladstonian made him responsive to the prevailing assumptions that his leader put to good use.[11] The Lords were an anachronism; there was widespread agreement that sooner or later rational reform would dispense with them entirely. Stripping their House of the appellate jurisdiction was an important move in that direction, without which the reconstruction of the legal system could not satisfy expert and enlightened thinking, assumed to be more or less the same.

The reception of Lord Selborne's Bill

In the *Fortnightly Review* articles reprinted as his classic exposition of *The English Constitution*, Walter Bagehot had dismissed the judicial House of Lords as outdated and unworthy of its responsibilities. Lord Falconer was to quote the passage as in itself a sufficient justification for the Constitutional Reform Act. The House had allowed this function to pass into the hands of a very small number of peers qualified by holding, or having held, high judicial office; its jurisdiction was otherwise a fiction. Instead of this ad hoc arrangement, confirmed as recently as 1843, Bagehot envisaged 'the supreme court of the English people [which] ought to be a great conspicuous tribunal, ought to rule all other courts, ought to have no competitor . . . ought not to be hidden beneath . . . a legislative assembly'. Writing only months after Palmerston's death, he struck a note unfamiliar to the evolutionary conservatism of Whigs and Tories; a note evocative of the rhetoric of American democracy.[12] Introducing the Judicature Bill nearly ten years later, Selborne hinted that the peers should defer to their intellectual superiors, who

[10] *The Economist*, 15 March 1873, for the equity Bar's fears, and Lord Westbury's remarks in a private letter to Cairns, 30 April 1873, Cairns Papers (PRO 30/51/9).

[11] Selborne devoted a chapter of autobiography to his Judicature Act and the reversal of its provision for final appeals, *Memorials, Pt II Personal and Political 1865–1895*, 2 vols (London, 1898) I, ch XIV.

[12] *Hansard* (series 5) vol 667, col 1566 (20 December 2004); N St John Stevas (ed), *The Collected Works of Walter Bagehot*, 15 vols (London: *The Economist*, 1965–86) V, 285.

also had the whip hand in the politics of their period. Opinion had ripened 'among the most educated and enlightened classes of society', and the fruits were there to see in his measure. A double appeal was unnecessary with a well constructed and well manned supreme court. The fears of the equity Bar were not allayed by his reminder that the distinction between common law and equitable jurisdictions had no existence outside England and countries whose legal systems were modelled on hers.[13]

Gladstone had been clear that there should be '*one court*'.[14] Accordingly, the Bill created a supreme court consisting of the Court of Appeal and the High Court with original jurisdiction. The latter's divisions corresponded initially with the old courts they replaced, but in all of them judges were invested with equal jurisdiction in equity and law, and were available, at need, to sit in other divisions. The new unity and interchangeability were to be underpinned by rules of procedure drawn with those overriding considerations in mind. All this was generally well received, enjoying as it did the prior approval, with some reservations, of Cairns and other legal luminaries: although the equity Bar was unconvinced for some time by the assurances that their livelihoods and chances of promotion to the Bench would not be adversely affected. Nevertheless, the appellate structure in a 'colossal plan' assumed a consensus that did not exist.[15] The new court was substituted for the Lords and the intermediate jurisdictions of Exchequer Chamber and the Court of Appeal in Chancery. Its composition gave every appearance of judicial strength, with nine permanent judges sitting in three divisions and, in reserve, the Lord Chancellor, the other most senior English judges, and reinforcements from their counterparts in the rest of the United Kingdom. But Cairns felt it would have been wiser to let the Lords continue to hear a progressively more restricted range of second appeals until there was 'a cessation rather than a transfer of jurisdiction'.[16] The extrusion of the Lords from the reformed machinery of justice went further than a royal commission and select committees of both Houses had recommended. The unease about this advance, which surfaced during the committee stage of the Bill in the Commons, was increased by Coleridge's language on the second reading.

The Attorney General indulged in an unsparing condemnation of the Lords and of the eminent lawyers who represented it in deciding on final appeals. 'If the Bill did nothing else,' he declared, 'but get rid of the House of Lords as a judicial tribunal, it would be worthwhile to pass it.' Had litigants organised themselves to complain of the expense and delays inflicted on them he did not believe the tribunal would have lasted so long. 'The utter irresponsibility of the judges who composed it made it a profoundly indefensible institution.'[17] Backbenchers who

---

[13] Parl Debs (series 3) vol 214, cols 331–60 (13 February 1873); quotation from col 332.
[14] Gladstone Papers (44663) cabinet minute, 14 July 1873.
[15] Selborne, *Memorials, 1865–1895*, I, 302–3, Westbury to Selborne, 16 February 1873.
[16] ibid, 309, Cairns to Selborne, 11 October 1872.
[17] Parl Debs vol 216, col 649 (9 June 1873).

shared his triumphalist mood sought the immediate inclusion of Scotland and Ireland within the scope of the new court. Selborne had left their final appeals with the Lords until it could be ascertained whether the two countries were favourable to the change. Gladstone now chose to anticipate such a reaction. His announcement in committee was the signal for the Tories to move away from supporting, in principle, the last of the major reforms undertaken by his government. The tactic they adopted in late July 1873, with the end of the session in sight, was to assert that ministers had breached the Lords' privileges by introducing a further reduction of its powers in the Lower House. To save the Bill, Gladstone gave up his amendment. It had become evident, especially in the Lords, that there was a growing disposition to question the case for abolishing that House's judicial function, without denying that the 'cheapness, simplicity and uniformity of procedure'[18] at which Selborne was aiming ought to be built into the operation of justice at the highest, as at other, levels.

One of the most honourable of men, Selborne could not suppose that Cairns' action in raising the issue of privilege was intended to derail the Bill, to which the former chancellor had committed himself and, it appeared, his party. Gladstone's antennae alerted him to double-dealing: he detected a plot between Disraeli and Cairns.[19] The main source for Disraeli's covert manoeuvres is the diary of Lord Carnarvon, a key figure in the stealthy moves to assemble a majority in the Lords that would vote down the measure; notwithstanding Gladstone's concession on Scotland and Ireland, which preserved a remnant of the Lords' jurisdiction for the time being.[20]

Carnarvon was glad to learn from Disraeli that Cairns was 'really at heart sick' of supporting Selborne. With the prudence of someone with painful experience of the other's ways, he intimated his readiness to act in the Upper House if he could be satisfied that Cairns 'was not actually a consenting but an "assenting party"' to the Bill.[21] The caution was not misplaced; speaking in the Commons next day Disraeli denied reports that he was preparing to come out against ministers: the 'mature opinion' of the country was in favour of their proposals which, with few exceptions, both Houses felt it was their duty to support.[22]

However, when Disraeli saw Cairns on the day after his declaration of continued backing for the Judicature Bill he was, in confidence, 'all in favour of extinguishing it' on its return to the peers with the Commons' amendments. Checking on Cairns' supposed eagerness to take this course, Carnarvon found him unwilling: a majority in the Lords had repeatedly yielded to the Gladstone

---

[18] Parl Debs vol 214, col 337 (13 February 1873).

[19] Selborne, *Memorials, 1865–1895*, I, 311–12; Gladstone on Disraeli's moves in Parl Debs vol 216, cols 1713 and 1723 (3 July 1873).

[20] Carnarvon Papers (BL Add MS 60905) diary, 13 July 1873, and see Sir A Hardinge, *Life of Henry Howard Molyneux Herbert, 4th Earl of Carnarvon, 1831–1890*, 3 vols (London, 1925) II, 52–3, 89–90.

[21] Carnarvon Papers (60905) diary, 13 July 1873.

[22] Parl Debs vol 217, col 365 (14 July 1873).

ministry. More importantly, Cairns considered himself 'so bound in honour' to Selborne and his measure that he could not join in killing it off.[23] Disraeli did briefly succeed in overcoming these scruples, only for Cairns to change his mind within a couple of hours.[24] Lord Derby held the ex-chancellor to the conclusion they had previously reached in discussion with the Duke of Richmond, the Tories' leader in the Lords, and Lord Salisbury, whose standing with the peers of his party made him a host in himself. Derby, seen as a potential successor to Disraeli, was and remained opposed to perpetuating the Lords' jurisdiction, arguing that Gladstone had been conciliatory in his parliamentary handling of the question, and that throwing out a Bill sure to be resurrected would be 'a foolish waste of public time'.[25] Disraeli's initial response was to reflect that Cairns and Derby had left him 'all at sea . . . again', but then to appear in the Lords on 24 July openly encouraging peers to vote for a procedural motion certain to be fatal to the Bill.[26] Cairns, Derby, and Richmond went with the Government, which prevailed, and Salisbury abstained. Most Tories, with Carnarvon prominent among them, refused to listen to the duke's pleas. As they voted, a Liberal cabinet minister thought he was witnessing the peers commit suicide. In the event, with the help of abstentions, the Lords did not court the prime minister's unbridled wrath.[27]

All this brings out what was believed to be at stake in an almost forgotten struggle. Lord Westbury, who had given Selborne's plans a qualified approval and voted with him in the division of 24 July, was not the only supporter to entertain grave doubts. Chancellor under Palmerston, Westbury looked on the reorganisation of an historic structure as levelling, while he welcomed the dismantling of the artificial and costly barrier between common law and equity. 'Why destroy?' he asked Selborne, to which the Chancellor replied that they had to distinguish between 'union and consolidation', with flexibility as the essential requirement, and the radical approach of 'destruction and re-edification'.[28] If he did not convince Westbury, he could rely on Cairns, and he later carried Richmond with him: the duke, who was not a cerebral politician, leant heavily on his plebeian colleague.[29] Among Tories, some of those who accepted that this Gladstonian injection of law reform had to be swallowed, for mainly political reasons, were not persuaded that it was necessary.[30] If there were sound arguments for retaining a

[23] Carnarvon Papers (60905) diary, 15 July 1873.

[24] ibid, (60763) Disraeli to Carnarvon, 'Monday night', July 1873.

[25] *DD*, 141, 11 July 1873; for Salisbury at this period, D Steele, *Lord Salisbury. A Political Biography* (London: UCL Press, 1999) ch 4 'The conscience of the party'.

[26] Carnarvon Papers (60767) Disraeli to Carnarvon, 'Monday night' and 28 July 1873.

[27] *DD*, 24 July 1873; A Hawkins and J Powell, *The Journal of John Wodehouse, 1st Earl of Kimberley from 1862–1902*, Camden Fifth series (Cambridge: CUP, 1997) 279–80, 24 July 1873. Hereafter cited as *Kimberley Journal*.

[28] Cairns Papers (PRO 30/51/9) Selborne to Cairns, 16 April 1873.

[29] Carnarvon Papers (60905) diary, 15 July 1873.

[30] NE Johnson (ed), *The Diary of Gathorne Hardy, later Lord Cranbrook, 1866–1892: Political Selections* (Oxford: OUP, 1981) 187, 26 July 1873; Cairns' uneasiness about a single appeal in Parl Debs vol 214, col 364 (13 February 1873).

double appeal, they pointed to the continued existence of the Lords' appellate tribunal, strengthened where it was most vulnerable, in respect of the number of judges available to serve on it. Getting rid of the established jurisdiction looked too much like radical politics. To have attacked the peers, law reformers began to realise, was a mistake: but Selborne and Cairns viewed the substitution of a court for the Lords as integral to the modernisation of the law to which they were committed. In this they were sustained by Derby, the most progressive of Tories.

Lord Cairns' honour

It was in Cairns' power to put an end to the Judicature Bill in the late summer of 1873, probably for the duration of that Parliament. By-elections registered the decline in the ministry's fortunes since the great days of 1869–70. Disraeli's tactics at this juncture were dictated by the unashamed opportunism that made him a dangerous foe. 'It is of great importance,' he told Cairns, 'that the impotence of the government should be demonstrated to the country. This is the high political course which ought to [be] above all petty considerations of the merit or demerits of their measures.'[31] Linked to Selborne by 'professional brotherhood', friendship, and 'that deeper... more abiding... regard... due to the belief that... there is a common purpose of life',[32] Cairns did not relish Disraeli's attitude to political warfare, used though they were to working together. The Bill received the Royal Assent in August 1873, with an effective date of November 1874, but the unfinished business of Scottish and Irish appeals remained. As the victors in the general election of February 1874, the Tories, with Cairns again chancellor, brought in legislation to end those appeals and at the same time to provide for the continuation of a double appeal in the guise of a re-hearing on broader grounds than those in Selborne's Act. It was only the start of a two-year battle to expand those grounds and rescue the Lords' jurisdiction, with improvements to it. The outcome reflected Lord Salisbury's influential views in private correspondence and in debate on the second chamber's value as a place where legislators and judges influenced each other to their mutual benefit.[33]

Cairns' first Bill of 1874 was withdrawn at the close of the session and the Government legislated to postpone the effective date for the operation of the 1873 Act for a year.[34] Taking the title from the recommendations of a Lords select committee in 1872, Cairns restyled Selborne's tribunal 'an Imperial Court of Appeal' to which colonial and ecclesiastical as well as Scottish and Irish appeals

---

[31] Cairns Papers (PRO 30/51/1) Disraeli to Cairns, 1873/4; the first part of this letter is missing.
[32] ibid, (PRO 30/51/9) Sir R Palmer (Selborne) to Cairns, 18 October 1872.
[33] Selborne Papers, Lambeth Palace Library, MS 1865, Salisbury to Selborne, 24 February 1873; Parl Debs vol 215, cols 1283–9 (1 May 1873), a withdrawn amendment.
[34] Supreme Court of Judicature Act (1873) Amendment Bill; Supreme Court of Judicature Act (1873) Suspension Act.

were to go. He made it clear that the second principal feature of his court—the enlarged provision for a re-hearing by the first of the three divisions where the judges in the other two were not unanimous—was 'virtually a second appeal'. Opposition to his recension of Selborne's arrangements for final appeals, he warned the peers, would be tantamount to a breach of faith with the Commons and sure to provoke a clash between the Houses.[35] Selborne repaid Cairns' loyalty with interest: they now had 'a truly Imperial Court', the end result of so much argument; a preference for the Lords' jurisdiction as it stood discounted legal in favour of political reasoning.[36] The House bowed to the combination of Cairns and Selborne, but the latter's remarks implicitly acknowledged the feeling that the wave of aggressive modernisation under Gladstone was spent. Conservatives, on either side, nevertheless had difficulty in believing that they could turn the clock back. When Cairns outlined his new legislation to the cabinet in March 1874, Carnarvon entered a plea for the Lords that made little impression on his colleagues, but ministers in the Commons were perceptibly more sympathetic to his representations.[37] After the general election, MPs, without distinction of party, were less frightened of questioning the obligation to change at the pace of the last six years. When Cairns' Bill reached the Commons, the lawyers there hardly concealed their resentment of the eminent modernisers. Watkin Williams, a Liberal barrister who was about to emerge as one of the rescuers of the Lords' jurisdiction, alluded to the natural reluctance of his profession to speak out against its political heads and the dispensers of legal patronage.[38]

Another Liberal, Sir George Bowyer, now sitting as an Irish home ruler, was one of Disraeli's contacts outside his own party.[39] As such, Bowyer had unsuccessfully tried to persuade him to oppose single appeals and the new court to hear them. He held Cairns mainly responsible for the Tories' compliant attitude in 1873, but he commented acidly on their desire to be seen supporting 'a great judicial reform', conceived in a progressive spirit. In 1874 the return of a thinly disguised double appeal encouraged him to urge that it should go to the Lords. The obstacle was Cairns and his intellectual subjection to Selborne.[40] Inside the Tory cabinet, Derby insisted that they must not lose the chancellor's Bill. To deprive the Lords of their function one year, and hand it back the next, would be ridiculous. After taking soundings, Derby assured the prime minister that the peers could be relied on; nor was there any evidence among them of a wider

[35] Parl Debs vol 218, cols 1808–23 (7 May 1874); quotation from cols 1817 and 1823.
[36] ibid, vol 219, cols 1387–98 (11 June 1874); quotation from col 1387. In the final outcome of this struggle over the Lords' jurisdiction colonial and ecclesiastical appeals remained with the Judicial Committee of the Privy Council.
[37] Carnarvon Papers (60906) diary, 4 March 1874.
[38] Parl Debs vol 221, cols 142–3.
[39] The 7th baronet, reader in law at the Middle Temple; an Englishman who sat for Irish constituencies, *ODNB*.
[40] Hughenden Papers (B/XXI/B) Bowyer to Disraeli, 4 July, 16 March, and 8 June 1873.

dissatisfaction with the Government.[41] Yet some weeks later Cairns concluded that they would have to withdraw the bill in the face of gathering opposition on their side.[42] Announcing his decision, Disraeli said an interval was needed for 'calm and at the same time energetic and vigorous, discussion', seeming to invite fundamental reconsideration.[43] To allow for that interval of reflection and further debate, the operation of the Selborne Act was deferred, until November 1875.

In the Lords an extremely disappointed Selborne feared that the House would recover its jurisdiction, for reasons he found quite unconvincing. Cairns laid the blame on resistance, 'however limited', in the Commons.[44] Their exchange struck Bowyer as a '*pezzo concertato*'. He implored Disraeli to take the opportunity of arresting the erosion of the Lords' place in the British constitution: if their appellate jurisdiction went, the House itself would not long survive.[45] Disraeli was a ready listener, telling Carnarvon that he had always disliked this part of Selborne's reforms, and that he expected no real objection from his Lord Chancellor to dropping it.[46] In fact, Cairns' retreat was tactical: he had no intention of going back, if he could help it, on the principle of excluding the Lords from an agreed reform. His quiet determination led to a dramatic scene in an autumn cabinet on the legislative programme for 1875. 'Suddenly like thunder in a clear sky a storm broke', wrote Carnarvon. It is evident from his account that Cairns, seconded by the Duke of Richmond, tried to pre-empt the opposition that was to be expected from Carnarvon, and possibly from others. The Lord Chancellor and the duke wanted to bring their colleague into line, although he had consistently declined to give them his vote. With the help of Salisbury, who insisted that his closest associate in the Government should not be coerced, Carnarvon held his own. Cairns declared that his personal honour was at stake in the reintroduction of the Bill he had been obliged to withdraw. On that note the cabinet decided to go ahead.[47]

Like the press, ministers paid little attention to the cross-party lobby of peers, MPs, and Queen's Counsel organised that autumn, the Committee for Preserving the Jurisdiction of the House of Lords as a Court of Final Appeal for the United Kingdom, which ought to be ranked with the best known movements of the kind in modern parliamentary history. Its moving spirit was a Tory barrister and MP, WT Charley, who had stood up for the Lords in 1873 when their cause appeared hopeless. He enlisted over 50 MPs, including Watkin Williams and Bowyer. Among the peers he recruited, there were three dukes and a judge, Lord Penzance,

[41] ibid, (B/XX/S) Derby to Disraeli, 8 and 17 June 1874.

[42] ibid, (B/XX/Ca) Cairns to Disraeli, 25 July 1874.

[43] Parl Debs vol 221, col 763 (27 July 1874).

[44] Parl Debs vol 221, cols 1387–9 (6 August 1874).

[45] Hughenden Papers (B/XXI/B) Bowyer to Disraeli, 7 August 1874.

[46] Carnarvon Papers (60906) diary, 26 September 1874.

[47] ibid, 20 November 1874; Carnarvon asked Salisbury in December if there was any hope of saving the Lords' jurisdiction 'in some sense', Salisbury Papers, Hatfield House, HHM/3M/E.

who had come out against Cairns earlier in the year.[48] Bowyer ensured that Disraeli was kept informed of the lobby's growth as the Scottish and Irish Bars joined their English brethren, with expressions of support from the solicitors.[49] The committee exploited the efficiency with which the Law Lords were now functioning under a stay of execution. This disposed of one of the strongest arguments against them; the waiting list for a hearing and the duration of cases had been sharply reduced since the beginning of the decade. By June 1875 the committee's Commons membership had climbed to 138.[50] Against this background, Cairns' second attempt to legislate, little changed from the first, ran into trouble at once when introduced in February 1875.[51] Selborne greeted it 'with great satisfaction', but Penzance thought that the provision for final appeals could not be an acceptable substitute for the Lords. It lacked the dignity and independence of the House, being no more than a division of the Court of Appeal, with its judges returning to other divisions on completion of a three-year term. 'It had nothing about it Imperial except the name.'[52] Even before the second reading the Bill's likely fate was plain, although the possibility of Cairns' resignation was a factor holding the Government back, until the eve of the session and beyond, from a commitment to maintain the Lords at the apex of the structure in the 1873 Act.[53]

Peers allowed the Bill to go into committee, at which point the Duke of Buccleuch, a member of Charley's committee, put down an amendment to uphold their jurisdiction. It triggered a counter-move which ministers had been considering: a meeting of the Tory peers, attended by Disraeli, held on 3 March at Richmond's house.[54] The duke described the occasion as 'the most disagreeable... I ever assisted at'; the irritation of years with the Tory leadership's unwillingness to stand and fight burst forth.[55] Disraeli's ingenuity and diplomacy were taxed to the limit in arranging what one of the cabinet called 'the most extraordinary solution', and another said, 'This looks unpleasantly like surrender...'[56] Cairns' Bill was to be withdrawn, while a respected party figure on the Commons back benches, Spencer Walpole, would propose the retention of the judicial House of Lords.[57] Designed to spare Cairns' feelings, to some extent,

[48] Hughenden Papers (B/XX/Ca) printed list of the committee's membership, February 1875; for Charley see *ODNB*.

[49] ibid, (B/XXI/B) Bowyer to Disraeli, 30 November and 16 December 1874; 26 February 1875.

[50] Parl Debs vol 224, col 1666, WT Charley (10 June 1875).

[51] Again entitled the Supreme Court of Judicature Act (1873) Amendment Bill.

[52] Parl Debs vol 222, cols 739–41 (9 February 1875).

[53] Goodwood Papers, West Sussex Record Office, MS 867, Lord Malmesbury, Lord Privy Seal, to the Duke of Richmond, Lord President and leader of the Lords, 14 February 1875.

[54] ibid, and 3 March 1875, the list of 73 peers present.

[55] Hughenden Papers (B/XX/Le) Richmond to Disraeli, 4 March 1875.

[56] WF Monypenny and GE Buckle, *The Life of Benjamin Disraeli, Earl of Beaconsfield*, 2 vols (London: John Murray, new edn 1929) II, 715, Disraeli to the Queen, 5 March 1875; Carnarvon Papers (60907) diary, 3 March 1875; *DD*, 197–8, 4 March 1875.

[57] Goodwood Papers, MS 867, Cairns to Richmond, 3 March 1875; the chancellor supplied Walpole with a form of words for his motion.

the understanding with the Tory peers may have stopped him from resigning. But when he withdrew his Bill on 9 March, a Liberal opponent recorded that he was 'white with rage. Every tone in his voice quivered with suppressed fury.'[58] Responding to the conflicting pressures on him,[59] Disraeli had extricated his government from immediate embarrassment or worse. Buccleuch's amendment was not debated, and neither was Walpole's motion. The question hung in the air: exactly what was to replace the Bill? Aided by Derby, who told the Lords that he deeply regretted the decision forced on ministers by 'imperative necessity',[60] Cairns managed to avoid capitulating to his Tory assailants and their Liberal sympathisers whom Derby estimated at around half the other side's strength in the Upper House alone.[61] A rift had opened between the cabinet as a whole and the rank and file Tories sitting behind them at Westminster. The party's display of a 'violent and reactionary' temper made Derby think that he might not be able to stay in it 'either as leader or follower'.[62]

Disraeli did not want, and could not afford, to lose Derby, an old friend and his foreign secretary, who opposed either compromise or surrender on abolishing the Lords' jurisdiction; while after the humiliating withdrawal of his Bill Cairns was, according to Carnarvon, 'entirely converted to the necessity of a change of front', and said later, in private, that he could envisage routing *all* final appeals from the United Kingdom to their House.[63] Conscious of being divided themselves on the question, the Liberal leaders were nonetheless speculating that the Disraeli ministry might be on the verge of breaking up.[64] In its Judicature Bills the Government had been obliged to grapple with a problem created by Gladstone. Retaining Scottish and Irish appeals to the Lords once the English business was removed seemed 'absurd' to Disraeli, but the situation was an awkward one.[65] After meeting the Tory peers he had explained to the Queen that they had gone from 'greatest apathy' when Selborne passed the Act to the state of indignation he had striven to calm. The peers and, undeniably, the party, 'were, and still are ... in a great mess'. Disraeli was sure of Cairns, whatever happened;[66] Derby was the man who had to be won over: the prime minister approached him with 'many professions of his confidence in my judgement, his wish to do all that I approved

[58] *Kimberley Journal*, 293, 9 March 1875.

[59] eg from opponents of the bill: Lord Beauchamp to the Prime Minister, 2 and 3 March 1875, Hughenden Papers (B/XX/Ln); and WT Charley to Montagu Corry, Disraeli's secretary, 3 March 1875, ibid, (B/XXI/C).

[60] Parl Debs vol 222, cols 1377–8 (8 February 1875).

[61] *DD*, 197–8, 4 March 1875.

[62] *DD*, 198, 6 March 1875.

[63] Carnarvon Papers (60907) diary, 10 and 30 March 1875.

[64] *Kimberley Journal*, 293, 11 March 1875; Lord Zetland (ed), *The Letters of Disraeli to Lady Bradford and Lady Chesterfield*, 2 vols (London: John Murray, 1929) I, 222–3, to Lady Chesterfield, 21 March 1875.

[65] ibid, 212, to Lady Chesterfield, 11 March 1875.

[66] Monypenny and Buckle (n 56) II, 715, Disraeli to the Queen, 5 March 1875; Zetland, *Letters of Disraeli*, I, 213–16, to Lady Chesterfield, 4 March 1875 and 8 March 1875.

and nothing else, and so forth . . . partly sincere . . . very evidently dictated by an apprehension that I should disapprove'.[67] This friendly conversation paved the way for yet another Bill from Cairns. The Lords would continue to hear the Scottish and Irish appeals. On the other hand, Selborne's, and Cairns' court of appeal would take final appeals from England from November 1876; no mention was made of any other destination. As a sop to the public desire, real or imagined, for a financial saving, a smaller number of judges would be appointed to the court. When Disraeli asked for his support at the cabinet of 8 April, Derby gave it reluctantly, 'compelled to say that though not much liking it, there was no alternative'.[68]

Arriving at a 'compromise'[69]

Giving his altered proposals to the peers next day, Cairns addressed their disappointment at the failure to leave English appeals with the House. He repeated what he was saying privately, that the Law Lords had never disposed of cases so briskly.[70] Yet he did not agree that the Lords' exercise of their power should be left more or less intact, with some change to enhance such admitted strength. He distinguished between 'substance and what is comparatively insubstantial'. The question of single or double appeal belonged to the first category. Whether the hearing of final appeals was to be located in the Lords, or, for the sake of argument, in the Judicial Committee of the Privy Council, or in a new court, appeared 'if I do not say unimportant but . . . of minor importance, . . . a matter, perhaps, of sentiment . . . privilege . . . traditionary honour and dignity . . .'.[71] Unsurprisingly, the implications of this for the hearing of English appeals after November 1876, and the suggestion that the efforts on behalf of the Lords had confused form and substance, sent the committee fighting in its defence into action where it was most effective, inside the governing party, with publicity as a threat held in reserve. There was a muffled explosion. The veteran chairman of committees in the House, Lord Redesdale, who resisted the 1873 Act when few others were inclined to do so, had become a leading figure in Charley's organisation. As such, he had an interview with Disraeli, at the prime minister's request, after Cairns' speech. The Duke of Buccleuch's amendment and the ministerially inspired motion in the Commons, both calling for confirmation of the ancient jurisdiction in its entirety, had not been pressed, on the understanding that government would act in their spirit. Cairns' latest Bill and his language on its

---

[67] *DD*, 201, 18 March 1875; Salisbury Papers, HHM/3M/E, Disraeli to Salisbury, 30 March and 2 April 1875.

[68] *DD*, 206, 8 April 1875; the rest of Selborne's Act came into force from November 1875, under the legislation of 1874.

[69] The term Derby used; ibid, 282, 3 March 1876.

[70] Carnarvon Papers (60907) diary, 30 March 1875.

[71] Parl Debs vol 223, cols 574–89 (9 April 1875); quotation from col 587.

introduction were hard to square with that assumption. 'Some peers,' Redesdale later reminded Disraeli, 'openly declared that they considered themselves sold, with other strong expressions.' Similar protests had been reaching the prime minister, and could not be disregarded: 'the crisis is rather critical', he had written to the Queen. Charley was almost certainly right in reporting that a majority in both Houses wished to roll back the encroachment upon the Lords.[72]

At the interview with Redesdale, Disraeli pleaded 'complications in the cabinet', gave an assurance that he personally approved of the committee's aims, and asked for the 'quiet passage' of a new Bill in return for a promise of legislating to meet the wishes of his loyal critics next year. Redesdale agreed to this and delivered his side of the bargain.[73] Without its completion, he stressed, Toryism as an idea and a policy would undoubtedly suffer, unnecessarily because they had the 'peculiar advantage' of much Liberal support for the course he was urging.[74] The watching Liberal leaders, whose deliberations were known to Disraeli in some detail, hoped that their rivals would be discomfited, or even brought down, by their own followers without the Liberals whose involvement would expose the disagreements among them.[75] 'Still we are an united cabinet', Disraeli asserted to Salisbury, another key figure, when its unity was problematical.[76] It was a union that left Cairns free to make his unwise remarks, which implied that after his legislation's effective date the Lords might have to be content with the literally marginal business from Scotland and Ireland. Now, after the interview with Redesdale on 11 April, the impression spread that, although government spokesmen still professed to be dealing with an open question, the committee of both Houses and parties had won its battle. The strongest Tory administration since Peel's had run away, said a Liberal in the Commons, expressing the general view.[77]

What had the ministry run away from? There had been a reaction against the Gladstonian 'mania for change', as a conservative Liberal designated it.[78] There was renewed confidence in the validity of sentiment as a constituent of the accumulated wisdom that makes institutions work. The Lords' appellate jurisdiction, Bowyer told the Commons in June 1875, when the current Bill relating to it came before them, was sentiment. Reiterating a point he made in letters addressed to *The Times* in 1873, and little noticed then, and in his correspondence with Disraeli, he dwelt on feeling—prejudice in Burke's sense of the word—as the

---

[72] Hughenden Papers (B/XXI/R) Redesdale to Disraeli, 31 October 1875, recalling what passed at the interview on 11 April; Monypenny and Buckle (n 56) II, 715, Disraeli to the Queen, 5 March 1875; Hughenden Papers (B/XXI/C) Charley to Corry, 7 April 1875.

[73] The Supreme Court of Judicature Act (1873) Amendment Act 1875.

[74] Hughenden Papers (B/XXI/R) Redesdale to Disraeli, 31 October 1875.

[75] Zetland, *Letters of Disraeli*, I, 221, 223, to Lady Chesterfield, 19 and 21 March 1875; *Kimberley Journal*, 293, 11 and 19 March 1875.

[76] Salisbury Papers, HHM/3M/E, 2 April 1875.

[77] Parl Debs vol 224, cols 1653–4, Osborne Morgan (10 June 1875).

[78] Parl Debs vol 224, cols 1841–2, Lord Elcho (14 June 1875).

animating force of otherwise desiccated traditions: 'What was patriotism? Sentiment. What was loyalty? Sentiment.'[79] Tradition, in this instance, had been
vindicated by the abandonment of a single appeal, and by Cairns' acknowledgement that the Law Lords had mended their ways and lately achieved
impressive results in their handling of appeals. There was good reason to think
that the two Lord Chancellors concerned did not have a plausible answer to the
question Westbury had asked: 'Why destroy?' The much less distinguished
lawyers—led by Charley and Bowyer—who criticised Selborne and Cairns saw
more clearly than they did that the concept of 'the High Court of Parliament'
was still meaningful: Parliament was where law and politics met, as they must
meet somewhere, and the review and interpretation of the laws by judges in the
House of Lords should be seen, Bowyer insisted, as *res integra* to that interaction.[80]

   This last was a point that Bowyer put to Salisbury, who thought that his
House's jurisdiction, vested in the tiny handful of peers qualified by judicial
office, was the fiction that its critics maintained. Salisbury had a radical streak and
hesitated to commit himself to anything more than a strong court of final appeal,
whatever its form.[81] However, the pressure from his party and allied Liberals was
irresistible, particularly in their confidential remonstrances. Some of them had
voted against their convictions in 1873–4; to be invited to do so again was too
much to ask when the original indictment of the Lords had been so largely
retracted. Parliament passed Cairns' second Bill of the 1875 session in the
expectation that the partisans of the Lords would get what they wanted next year.
The suspicion lingered that Cairns would contrive to frustrate them, and Selborne continued to cite the judges' unanimous endorsement in 1873 of abolishing the Lords' function.[82] There are glimpses of the personal animus feeding
the conflict between the two Lord Chancellors and some of their enemies. The
pair were deeply religious lawyer-politicians, among the ablest men produced by
the Bar in their century, and they had the defects of their virtues. Bowyer said
Selborne thought himself infallible. It was a pity, observed Lord Elcho, another
member of the committee, with reference to Selborne's attack on it at a City
dinner, that he had 'infused all his Christianity into his Psalmody, and had not
reserved a little for his prose . . .'.[83]

   Towards the end of 1875, Redesdale felt he should remind Disraeli of what he
had said at their April meeting. Even so, Cairns apparently needed prompting in

---

[79] Parl Debs vol 224, cols 1657–61 (10 June 1875); Bowyer, *Four Letters reprinted from The Times on the Appellate Jurisdiction of the House of Lords and the New Court of Appeal* (London, 1873); Hughenden Papers (B/XXI/B) Bowyer to Disraeli, 26 February [1875].

[80] ibid, 8 June and 30 November 1874; and (B/XXI/C) Charley to Corry, 7 April 1875.

[81] ibid, (B/XXI/B) Bowyer to Disraeli, 16 August 1873; Parl Debs vol 223, cols 1087–90 (16 April 1875).

[82] ibid, vol 219, cols 1395–6 (11 June 1874); vol 222, cols 1372–6 (9 March 1875).

[83] Hughenden Papers (B/XXI/B) Bowyer to Disraeli, 16 August 1873; Parl Debs vol 224, col 1843 (14 June 1875).

cabinet. His Appellate Jurisdiction Bill[84] repealed the prospective abolition of the Lords' tribunal, which was reinforced by the creation of two Lords of Appeal in Ordinary, and provision for two more in due course. They were to be peers during office, in deference to the aversion with which the Lords viewed life peerages, but from 1887 sat for life. To Gladstone's mortification, these appointments carried a salary—of £6,000 a year—undeserved and unnecessary, to his thinking, for '*generally* second rate men'. Cairns' notes for his speech introducing the Bill showed how he tried to justify the sacrifice of his professional opinions to political expediency. Though he had always had doubts about a single appeal, he did not pretend, to himself anyway, that he cared for his own legislation. It must have cost an effort to write: 'I don't sacrifice utility but superfluity to be avoided, 1. for itself. 2. for example.'[85] A strengthened, and more expensive, judicial House offended against the criteria that guided Selborne with Cairns' approval when the structure of the courts was pared down in 1873. For all his Ulster Toryism, Cairns resembled Selborne and many of the most powerful minds of his generation of lawyers. Utility was their guide, but not their god, as it had been for Bentham. They considered they had won the argument over the Lords, although defeated in a political battle such as neither they, nor anyone else, had foreseen.[86]

Derby made the best of, for him, an unsatisfactory outcome, typically of his side of the controversy. It was a 'compromise', which Cairns had been 'adroit and lucky' in getting accepted by a reluctant party. The Lords had been made to admit the judicial peers they had kept out since Palmerston's day. Moreover, Derby reflected that the strengthened jurisdiction was, as before, a constitutional fiction: the reformed Law Lords would still function, as such, separately from the rest of the peerage. He found it strange that the peers should be well content with their achievement. They had rejected, on second thoughts, the excision of an anomaly, the removal of which promised to prolong their existence as an anachronism, 'with whatever remnants of prestige may still belong to the institution...'.[87] Yet he knew quite well that the progressive opinion with which he aligned himself on this question and some others had suffered a political reverse. Without the provisions affecting the Lords, the 1873 Act's extensive changes—'this revolution... it amounts to no less', said Sir Alexander Cockburn[88]—were a bold and imaginative reform which lawyers could assimilate. *With* those provisions, the reformers on the Woolsack, enjoying, it should be emphasised, an unusually supportive press headed by *The Times*, entered the political arena, carried forward by the seemingly remorseless Gladstonian tide. Once that tide had turned,

---

[84] Hughenden Papers (B/XXI/R) Redesdale to Disraeli, 31 October 1875; Carnarvon Papers (60907) diary, 6 November 1875; (60856) Redesdale to Carnarvon, 3 November 1875.

[85] Goodwood Papers, MS 868, Cairns' notes for his speech of 11 February 1876.

[86] On Selborne and Cairns as modernisers, see *ODNB*.

[87] *DD*, 282, 3 March 1876; Goodwood Papers, MS 866, Derby's minute, April 1874.

[88] Cairns Papers (PRO 30/29/51/6) Lord Chief Justice Cockburn to Cairns, 30 July 1876.

successful but scarcely distinguished barristers and MPs, largely inspired by Charley and Bowyer, organised the rescue of the doomed jurisdiction, forcing Disraeli to change course. They demonstrated the resilience and the adaptability of English tradition. The Act of 1876 not only preserved and improved the Law Lords, it breathed some new life into their House with the introduction of judicial peerages. That element made a distinctive contribution, as Salisbury, among others, had argued that it would, until quite recently when it began to question the legitimacy of its presence in the light of the Continental rather than the English doctrine of the separation of powers. Bagehot was wrong, as he quite often was, when he deplored the settlement in the Act, and the way in which it was reached, as making for 'abundant . . . mischief and reaction'.[89]

---

[89] *Hansard* (series 5) vol 667, col 1208, Lord Goodhart (14 December 2004); St John Stevas (n 12) VII, 285, 'The Appellate Jurisdiction Bill' (*The Economist*, 17 June 1976).

3

The Judicial Office

James Vallance White

A distinguished co-editor of this volume once referred to the Judicial Office of the House of Lords as a 'cave of mystery',[1] after the name of the head of the office[2] of the day. In fact there was nothing very strange about it—the office simply provided for the House of Lords what the court service of England and Wales provided for the other courts. What might have seemed mysterious was the fact that, because the court in this case was also a House of Parliament, its judicial activities had to be filtered through the prism of parliamentary procedure. The Judicial Office acted as the parliamentary conduit by which lawyers, litigants, and the public approached the Law Lords, and it was by that same channel that the judgments and orders of the Law Lords were delivered. It is therefore fitting that a few paragraphs should be devoted to an office so long connected with the judicial work of the House, at a time when, in the prophetic words of another scholar,[3] 'all memories of the parliamentary status and trappings of the final appeal will fade into the footnotes of constitutional history'.

The House of Lords is administered by a body of officials known collectively as the Parliament Office. This consists of a number of departments, each responsible for a particular area of activity of the House, and the Judicial Office was one such department. In the 1990s, in obedience to the vogue for identifying 'aims and objectives', it described its task as 'enabling the House to fulfil its judicial functions, and to assist and support the Lords of Appeal in carrying out their responsibilities'. Unlike other departments in the Parliament Office, the Judicial Office retained its name and functions, and (until 1995) its geographical location within the Palace of Westminster largely unchanged throughout its existence. Its relationship with its parent body, however, did change in ways which reflected the changing role of the Law Lords within the House of Lords.

---

[1] L Blom-Cooper and G Drewry, *Final Appeal: A Study of the House of Lords in its Judicial Capacity* (Oxford: Clarendon Press, 1972).

[2] Sir Richard Cave, KCBO, CB, Principal Clerk of the Judicial Office 1959–77 and Fourth Clerk at the Table (Judicial) 1970–7.

[3] David Steele (personal comment); see ch 2 in this volume.

At the head of all the departments of the Parliament Office is the Clerk of the Parliaments, and as Registrar of the House all judgments and judicial orders went out over his signature. The day-to-day affairs of the office were delegated to the Principal Clerk of the Judicial Office who directed both the work of the general office, which dealt with those members of the legal profession and the public who had judicial business in the House, and that of the Law Lords' office, which provided administrative support for the Lords of Appeal. Of the two parts of the office the latter was of comparatively recent origin: until the early 1970s it can scarcely be said to have existed at all since the Law Lords' personal staff consisted of a single individual. The head of the Judicial Office was also the Taxing Officer for all legal costs allowed by the House. Until 1975 taxation work took place in the office of the House of Lords' Accountant, but in that year a member of the Accountant's staff was transferred to the Judicial Office as Taxing Clerk and thereafter worked directly under the head of the office in preparing papers for taxation.

The first recorded mention of a Clerk of the Judicial Office is in 1854[4] (at a time when the Government was making its first and unsuccessful attempt[5] to strengthen the House by the addition of judicial life peers), but it is difficult to be precise about his duties, and about the nature or number of staff in the office at that time. After 1876 things become a little clearer. We have an unbroken list of the heads of the office, a list which includes Edward Fairfax Taylor,[6] whose acclaimed (but sadly posthumous) translation of the *Aeneid* into Spenserian stanzas was published in 1903. It is also possible to catch glimpses of what life may have been like for those who worked in the office.

One such glimpse appears from the Clerk of the Parliaments' plea to the House of Lords Offices' Committee[7] in 1879, asking for additional remuneration for the 'Second, Third and Fourth Clerks' because of 'additional attendance required in the Judicial Office in consequence of the judicial sittings of the House in November and December during the prorogation'. One of the most serious criticisms of the period before the passing of the Appellate Jurisdiction Act in 1876 had been the length of time taken to hear appeals; and the reason for this delay was that the Lord Chancellor (with whatever judicial help he was able to muster) could only sit when Parliament was in session; and since Parliament tended to be prorogued in July or August and not to sit again until February, this period of inactivity was a serious impediment to judicial efficiency. The problem was addressed by the 1876 Act, which enabled judicial sittings to continue uninterrupted throughout prorogation and even to take place during a dissolution of Parliament. Thus members of the Parliament Office assigned to the Judicial Office were deprived of several months of what their colleagues (and until 1876 they themselves) had considered to be a well-earned period of rest.

---

[4] Edward Meredith Parratt. Entered Parliament Office 1830, promoted to Chief Clerk in 1874 and retired in 1886.
[5] See the Wensleydale case, HL Journals 1856.   [6] Judicial Clerk 1896–1902.
[7] Forerunner of the present day Administration Committee.

The reference to 'Second, Third and Fourth Clerks' is puzzling, since it is not clear what they did. The archives are not revealing, but since, before 1876, the judicial work of the House was largely the province of the Lord Chancellor, it is reasonable to assume that he and his staff would have taken many of the decisions which in more recent times would have been taken by the Senior Law Lord and the head of the Judicial Office. The three Clerks, whose leisure had been so cruelly curtailed, would have undertaken the tasks later done by those working in the general office: they would have received petitions and appeals, checked the accompanying documents, arranged for payment of the appropriate fees and, most importantly, would have negotiated the dates on which hearings would take place. All of this would have been done in the large, airy Judicial Business Room (as it was then called—a room now divided into two) on the first floor above the Chancellor's Gate, overlooking Old Palace Yard and Westminster Abbey's King Henry VII Chapel. For a picture of their lives (in the absence of archival material) it is perhaps best to turn to Anthony Trollope. In *Framley Parsonage* the hero, the Revd Mark Robarts, has a brother, John, who is a Clerk in the office of the Lord Petty Bag. A friend of Mark has just been appointed to that office, and Mark visits his brother to arrange a meeting with his friend. He is impressed to see the effects of responsibility on John who, having been 'occasionally careless, not to say slovenly, in his dress', is now much improved: 'his jaunty frock-coat fitted him to perfection, not a hair on his head was out of place, his waistcoat and trousers now glossy and new'. Appointment to the Lord Petty Bag's office (as doubtless to a Clerkship in the House of Lords) made John and his colleagues 'quite respectable in their walk in life'. John did however complain of 'the enormous deal of fagging' he had to endure. When asked to explain, he said that much of his time was engaged in fending off peeresses who believed (mistakenly) that there was a vacancy for a 'lobby messenger' in the office, a job each of these ladies coveted for a favourite footman; and in case this seems too far-fetched an analogy for modern times, it is a fact that all staff in the House of Lords below the rank of Clerk were referred to indiscriminately as 'messengers' until well into the second half of the twentieth century. To anyone whose memory goes back that far, John Robarts' mode of recruitment will not be wholly unfamiliar; such was the Human Resources Office of the day.

When the Appellate Jurisdiction Act was passed in 1876 it preserved the judicial House of Lords not because its judicial reputation was high—indeed Mr Gladstone was disobliging enough to refer to those who then exercised the jurisdiction as 'generally second rate men'[8]—but because to many, especially in the Conservative party, it seemed of paramount importance, for historic and constitutional reasons, to maintain the connection between the upper House and the final court of appeal. By the middle of the twentieth century there were few who would have sought to defend the settlement on those grounds, but by that time

---

[8] Gladstone Papers (44138) Gladstone to Selborne, 27 January 1872; see Steele, above, p 28.

the reputation of the House as a court was high enough for it to resist challenges to its continuation for another half century.

In the opening years of the twentieth century attention was directed more to the political activities of the House of Lords rather than to its judicial work, but by the inter-war years the situation had changed. For one thing, the Law Lords were beginning to win a high reputation as a judicial forum, thus reducing the number of those who doubted the value of a second appellate tier; and this was happening at a time when the reputation of the House as a legislative body was in decline. Compared with what it had been in the Victorian era, and even in the years before 1914 when it struggled to stem the reforms of the Liberal govern-ment, the post-war House was something of a political backwater. Notwith-standing the introductory words of the Parliament Act of 1911,[9] the House was still (apart from the bishops and the Law Lords) a wholly hereditary body; and after Lord Curzon's failure to succeed to the premiership in 1923 it was generally accepted that thereafter no member of the Upper House would serve as Prime Minister.[10] In this less active House the Law Lords loomed large. For one thing, there was their sheer physical presence: before the appointment of the Appellate Committee in 1948, the Law Lords occupied the Chamber from 10.30 in the morning until 4 o'clock in the afternoon and public business only began after that. It was rare in those days for the House to sit much beyond 6.30 in the evening, so that in crude terms of sitting hours, the Law Lords accounted for the larger part of the Lords' time. Thus the Judicial Office found itself at the heart of the day-to-day work of the House. It must be remembered that Lords' Select Committees (which since the 1970s have played such an important role in the modern House) hardly existed at that time, so that apart from the Judicial Office the most significant departments in the Parliament Office were the Private Bill and Public Bill Offices. This had distinct advantages for the Judicial Office, and particularly for the head of the office.

Until well into the twentieth century, the senior posts in the Parliament Office (Clerk of the Parliaments, Clerk Assistant, and Reading Clerk) were gifts of government patronage; and before 1930 no member of the office had ever been promoted to the Table of the House. In that year, however, the head of the Judicial Office, Henry Badeley, was appointed Clerk Assistant. He retained his responsibilities for the Judicial Office for a further 11 years until, in 1941, he was appointed Clerk of the Parliaments; and when he retired in 1949[11] the vacant place at the Table was once again filled by the head of the Judicial Office, Victor Goodman,[12] who also continued to be in charge of the Judicial Office until he

---

[9] The Preamble to the Act stated the Government's intention to replace the hereditary House with an assembly made up on a popular basis.

[10] Whether the objection to Curzon was personal or constitutional is immaterial: the result was the same.

[11] Raised to the peerage as Baron Badeley in the same year.

[12] Clerk of the Parliaments 1959–63.

was promoted to the post of Clerk Assistant. In later years it would have been difficult for the responsibilities of the head of the Judicial Office and those of a Table Clerk to be combined; but in those days it clearly worked well enough, largely because (since a Table Clerk had to attend throughout the sitting whether for judicial or public business) it seemed reasonable that the man who worked most closely with the Law Lords should be one of the Clerks manning the Table.

After 1945 three developments were significantly to affect the House, the Law Lords and, consequently, the Judicial Office: first, the gradual withdrawal of the Lord Chancellor from the judicial business of the House, and the evolution of the post of 'Senior Law Lord'; secondly, the establishment of the Appellate Committee in 1948; and thirdly, the arrival of life peers in 1958.

Lord Chancellor and Senior Law Lord

In the inter-war years the Lord Chancellor presided progressively less over appeals to the House. This diminution was not sudden, nor was it even, and it is possible to identify years in the 1920s and the 1930s when the Lord Chancellor presided over a majority of appeals, and also years when he presided in single figures or not at all. After the second world war that trend continued and accelerated. In reality, however, it was not so much the diminution of the number of times that the Lord Chancellor presided which was as significant as the fact that he increasingly withdrew from playing the coordinating role over the House as a judicial body which heads of division are expected to play in relation to the judges who sit in their courts. For the most part this vacuum did not greatly matter—the Law Lords were well able, with the help of the Judicial Office, to mind their own house, and probably the only practical effect was the disengagement of the Lord Chancellor from the process of choosing which Law Lords were to sit on future cases. Again no exact date can be assigned; all that can be said with certainty is that until the 1960s the meetings that decided these matters took place in the Lord Chancellor's room between him and his Permanent Secretary and (occasionally) the Clerk of the Judicial Office and the Registrar of the Privy Council. By the early 1980s the meetings were held in the Law Lords' conference room and took place between the two Senior Law Lords together with the head of the Judicial Office and the Registrar of the Privy Council. At that time the Lord Chancellor's Permanent Secretary still attended from time to time, or at least was invited to attend; but by the middle of the decade even this vestige of the Lord Chancellor's involvement had disappeared.

One of the consequences of the Lord Chancellor's withdrawal was that from around the time of Lord Reid,[13] the term 'Senior Law Lord' was increasingly used

---

[13] Lord of Appeal in Ordinary 1948–75.

to describe the Law Lord who had, to all intents and purposes, taken over the position previously occupied by the Lord Chancellor. Again dates can only be assigned to the formal steps by which the post can be said to have been developed, and these are set out by Michael Beloff QC in his chapter in this volume.[14] It should be emphasised, however, that those steps—the appointment by Letters Patent of which Law Lords were to preside in the absence of the Lord Chancellor—did nothing to identify the other duties which attached to the post. Indeed, Lord Hailsham of St Marylebone[15] disliked the expression 'Senior Law Lord' so much that he was liable to greet it with the expostulation 'Kindly remember that *I* am the senior Law Lord'; and as late as 1993 the Judicial Office was being asked to provide the Lord Chancellor with papers dealing with such matters as a new edition of the Practice Directions and progress on the new arrangements by which counsel were required to provide estimates of the time, in hours, which they would need before the Appellate Committee. Thus officials, in both the Lord Chancellor's office and the Judicial Office, were not encouraged to rely too heavily on the ultimate authority of the 'Senior Law Lord'. During the last three decades of the twentieth century, the Senior Law Lord, whilst acknowledged as *primus inter pares*, was inclined to put more emphasis on the last word of that phrase than on the first. By and large this did not greatly matter—the House of Lords was not usually in need of organisation as were the lower courts. However, there were occasions when the lack of an acknowledged central authority was felt, and when it led to disruptions in judicial procedures which were thought by some to have damaged the Law Lords' reputation. Such failings in the way in which the House operated as a judicial body might have been avoided if either the Lord Chancellor had retained the role he had played in the past or (more realistically) if a substitute with clearly defined authority and responsibilities had been established.

Lord Chancellors were aware of this possible weakness and tentative steps were taken to address it, such as the appointment in 1996 and again in 1998 of a single presiding Law Lord instead of following the custom dating from 1984, of appointing two presiding Law Lords. But nothing really changed until 2000, when Lord Bingham of Cornhill[16] was appointed direct from the post of Lord Chief Justice of England and Wales to that of Senior Law Lord. Although his formal position was the same as that of his predecessors, Lord Bingham was the first Law Lord (who was not Lord Chancellor) who was acknowledged as having a leadership role significantly different from what had gone before. Nevertheless, the post of Senior Law Lord would still have to wait another five years before it received official recognition in legislation—and the occasion for such recognition was the Constitutional Reform Act 2005, which provided for its abolition.

---

[14] ch 15 below.   [15] Lord Chancellor 1970–4, 1979–87.
[16] Senior Law Lord 2000–8. See ch 16 in this volume.

The establishment of the Appellate Committee

Until 1948, appeals to the House of Lords were heard in the Chamber. Although referred to as 'judicial sittings', the proceedings were essentially the same as those for public business, with the mace on the Woolsack and a bishop reading prayers. At about 4 o'clock in the afternoon, the hearing would be suspended and the House adjourned. Then at 4.30 the sitting would be resumed for the House to transact its public business.

The destruction of the Commons' Chamber by an enemy bomb in 1941 led to a fundamental change in the way the Lords carried out their judicial role. Until the Commons could be rebuilt, that House sat in the Lords' Chamber, and the Lords moved into the King's Robing Room at the southern end of the palace. After the war the noise of rebuilding work made conditions in the Robing Room so intolerable that it was suggested that, as a purely temporary measure, an Appellate Committee should be appointed so that the Law Lords could hear appeals in one of the upstairs committee rooms where they would not be disturbed by the noise. In the light of later developments it is perhaps surprising to read in Hansard that the Lord Chancellor did not have an altogether easy task in persuading the House to agree to this suggestion. He was at pains to stress its temporary nature, which, he promised, would come to an end as soon as the building works were completed, and that meanwhile the committee should be authorised only to *hear* appeals: judgment, or any order arising from an appeal, would be made in the House following a report from the committee. But, like other aspects of the British constitution, the temporary expedient soon became a permanent fixture because it was so obviously more convenient than the arrangements that had preceded it. However, the conveniences did not come without a price: because the House now advanced the time of sitting to 2.30 in the afternoon, the services of the Law Lords for parliamentary purposes were denied to the House until after 4pm; and since the Lord Chancellor was expected to take his place on the Woolsack at the beginning of each day's sitting, it was more difficult for him to sit judicially. Viscount Simon[17] foresaw even more momentous implications:

If the Lord Chancellor was seriously prevented from sitting [judicially] the question may arise whether some rearrangement of duties is not required which might lead to a demand for the appointment of a Ministry of Justice—a constitutional change which, I believe, would be very much against the public interest of this country. For a Minister of Justice would never be one of the great offices in a Cabinet. It would mean the creation of yet another ministry and of a department staffed by officials who would be likely more and more to concern themselves with the judicial work of this country from the lowest to the highest courts.[18]

---

[17] Lord Chancellor 1940–5.   [18] *The Listener*, December 1949.

In spite of these reservations, by the early 1950s it was clear that the Appellate Committee had become a fixture, and indeed the term was increasingly used to refer to the judicial House of Lords itself.

For the Judicial Office the establishment of the Appellate Committee had the effect of maintaining the number of Clerks at what was probably an unnecessarily high level, since it was considered essential that the Committee should be attended throughout its sitting by a senior member of the office. There is no point in pretending that this was anything but an unwelcome chore which was of no help to anyone, least of all to the Law Lords. In the early years of the Committee's existence the arrangement was accepted with resignation, but later, when the House began to change with the arrival of life peers, and especially when the House began regularly to appoint Select Committees (where the Clerk played an essential role), the hours spent in the Appellate Committee were resented. Whenever the Clerk of the Parliaments assigned a Clerk to the Judicial Office (usually for a term of two to three years) the news was received with gloom; it was felt that the Parliament Office had better things to offer, and that time spent in the Judicial Office was, at the least, unhelpful to a career. This unsatisfactory state of affairs came to an end in 1972 when the Law Lords agreed to dispense with the constant attendance of a Clerk in the Appellate Committee. The Judicial Office was then reduced to two Clerks, the head of the office and his deputy, an arrangement which lasted until 2009.

Life Peers

In 1958 Life Peers (other than the spiritual peers and the Law Lords) were admitted to the House of Lords for the first time, and with their arrival the institution began to change rapidly. For the Law Lords the change had two consequences: first it was soon recognised that they, and the other holders of high judicial office who had been raised to the peerage, no longer had a monopoly of legal expertise. Although their status undoubtedly gave them great authority in the House, nevertheless theirs were no longer the only voices listened to with respect on legal matters. The other consequence was the increasing pressure on space within the Palace of Westminster. When he designed the Palace in the middle of the nineteenth century, Sir Charles Barry had made ample provision for the Great Officers of State (such as the Earl Marshall and the Lord Great Chamberlain) and for the officers of the House and the staff, much of it in the form of spacious residential accommodation. What Barry had not considered was the need to provide rooms for peers, not even for members of the Government. In this he reflected the times: it was no more considered that a peer might need a room in the House of Lords than he would in his club—the Library and refreshment rooms sufficed for all his needs when he was not actually sitting in the Chamber. In 1876 it was readily acknowledged that rooms would have to be provided for the newly appointed judges, and these were found in what became known as the Law Lords' Corridor, leading from the Peers' Lobby to the river front, conveniently close to the Chamber and to the Library. The arrangement worked satisfactorily until, in 1948, the establishment of the Appellate Committee removed the need for the Law Lords to be close to the Chamber; and when in the same year, the number of Lords of Appeal in Ordinary was increased to nine, the corridor became inconveniently crowded. By the 1960s it was generally agreed that the situation had become intolerable and alternatives were urgently sought. Until a solution was found, however, some of the Law Lords had to endure an uncomfortable few years occupying rooms which Barry had never intended for human habitation for the good reason that they had no windows.

It was around this time, in the mid-60s, that the possibility was first mooted of moving the Law Lords (together with what was referred to as 'the entire judicial apparatus') to Middlesex Guildhall in Parliament Square—indeed into the very building now chosen as the site for the Supreme Court. Memoranda passed between ministers and officials stressing the advantages of extra space for the Law Lords and for the members of the House who would inherit the abandoned accommodation. The proposal foundered because, as Sir David Stephens,[19] the Clerk of the Parliaments, pointed out in December 1965, the move might 'raise the danger that [the Appellate Committee] may become an adjunct or outstation, an "outdoor" committee, rather than an integral part of the House, and could indeed easily become a Supreme Court of Appeal on its own'. Since the Government was not at that time prepared to introduce the legislation necessary for such a step, the Law Lords, and the Judicial Office, remained in the Palace of Westminster.

The solution eventually decided upon was that the Law Lords should move to the second floor on the West Front. By 1972 this area had been greatly improved by the building works in State Officers Court, and for the first time the Law Lords had their own self-contained area which provided space for staff and a conference room. It is curious that criticism of the alleged inadequacy of the Law Lords' facilities began to be voiced just at the very time that those facilities were better than they had ever been. Before then, when the accusation could have been made with justice, there is no record of dissatisfaction with facilities, only with accommodation. All this time the Judicial Office remained in its original location on the first floor, West Front, where it was now at least closer to the Law Lords than it had been. Nevertheless, the pressure on space continued to increase, and from that time onwards the Law Lords were regarded (as Stephens had predicted) as a discrete group who, having been moved once, might well be moved again. Further attempts to persuade them to move were indeed made, driven by the desire of the political parties to provide rooms for those who took their whip, and each failed primarily because the suggested options were too far away from the

---

[19] Clerk of the Parliaments 1963–74.

House to be reconcilable with the constitutional position that it was the jurisdiction of the House which the Law Lords exercised.

One proposal should be recorded because it did at least partly succeed. In 1994 it was suggested that the Law Lords should move into the suite of rooms on the South Front of the palace recently vacated by the Lord Chancellor's civil servants. The proposal appeared to offer the advantage of proximity to the Appellate Committee rooms, but it foundered when permission was denied to drill the necessary passage to the Committee corridor through a corner of the Lord Chancellor's residence. This meant that the Law Lords would have had to walk three times as far in order to reach a point only a few yards away from where they had started. Not surprisingly, they preferred to stay where they were. What survived of the proposal was that the Judicial Office left the area it had occupied since records began, and moved to what had been the Staff Superintendent's flat at the south end of the (new) Law Lords' Corridor. Thus, finally, and little more than a decade before the office was disbanded, the Law Lords, their staff, and the Judicial Office were all gathered together in one adjacent area.

The final decades

I became Principal Clerk of the Judicial Office in October 1983. The occasion was not a happy one, since it was brought about by the sad and untimely death of John Webb,[20] who had succeeded Dick Cave in 1977.

Following Cave was always going to be hard. Some institutions have among them individuals who seem so quintessentially to represent that institution that it is difficult to imagine it surviving once they have left the scene. Cave was such a one. With his somewhat Dickensian exterior and the inimitable stateliness of his gait, he seemed to embody a Judicial Office, and indeed a House of Lords, which had long disappeared. He was well aware of this, and it was the mixture of conscious self-mockery and strict adherence to every nuance of precedent and procedure—especially those to do with dress codes—that made him the unusual character he was. However, none of this prevented him from being a courteous and reliable guide through all the intricacies of judicial practice in the House during the 1960s and most of the 1970s; and he will be remembered with affection by the members of the legal profession who knew him at that time.

After Cave's retirement, John Webb made a start in reforming the office, in an attempt to meet the demands of growing judicial activity. In particular, he tackled the controversial matter of petitions for leave to appeal, the numbers of which had increased alarmingly. He began the process of simplifying the procedure for considering petitions (which was not completed at the time of his death) without which there was a danger that the system would have seized up. This was the

---

[20] Principal Clerk of the Judicial Office and Fourth Clerk at the Table (Judicial) 1977–83.

situation when I arrived in 1983, as much of a *tabula rasa* as can well be conceived. My only knowledge came from what little I could remember from my time as a junior Clerk in the office nearly 20 years before; and those memories were mostly to do with sitting in the Appellate Committee, wrestling with the annual judicial statistics—Cave insisted that these should be drawn up using a complex system of coloured crayons and I could never grasp the difference between purple and mauve, thus doubling the number of criminal appeals apparently allowed by the House—and interviewing the 'petitioners in person' who used to haunt the office in those days, and who were often more in need of the services of a psychiatrist than someone with an often less than perfect grasp of the Judicial Standing Orders and Practice Directions of the House, in which in any case they showed little interest.

In fact the Judicial Office was a very different place from what it had been, even as recently as 20 years before. It had become more detached from the rest of the Parliament Office, and for understandable reasons. For one thing, it was the only department which did not have a counterpart in the Commons. Almost all its contacts, oral, written, and telephonic, were with the legal profession and it had little to do with other parts of the parliamentary organisation. This comparative remoteness made it more difficult to apply to the Judicial Office the general policy of moving post-holders between the different departments of the Parliament Office, which by then had become management policy, and this was particularly true of those who held the higher posts (the two higher executive officers in charge of the judicial general office and of the Law Lords' private office). It also meant that for day-to-day purposes the Judicial Office was left more to its own devices than it had been.

Since 1948 no head of the Judicial Office had been promoted to the Table of the House; and this is not surprising since one of the criteria for a Table appointment is that the candidate should be well known to members; this was difficult to achieve for someone whose working life was so far removed from the rest of the House. Perhaps because this handicap was recognised, a curious consolation prize was adopted in 1970 when a new post of 'Fourth Clerk at the Table (Judicial)' was created. The reasons for this apparent generosity were perhaps not entirely selfless. Although the Appellate Committee had by then become a permanent feature of judicial proceedings, the Law Lords still reverted to the old custom of hearing appeals in the Chamber (as Lord Chancellor Jowitt had promised in 1948) whenever the House was not sitting for public business. In practice this meant two to three weeks in October and sometimes a week or so at the end of the short recesses, but whenever it happened it was necessary for one of the three Table Clerks to sit in the Chamber, a duty which was doubtless as irksome to them as it had been to the junior Clerks in the Judicial Office when they had to attend throughout the sittings of the Appellate Committee. The creation of the Fourth Clerkship relieved the Table Clerks of their immediate problem, although it was soon overtaken by a further development. The House was by then regularly sitting late into the night—or indeed the morning—and it was decided to extend the duty of sitting at the Table to all Clerks above a certain grade, thus removing the original purpose of the Fourth Clerkship. Nevertheless the appointment to the Fourth Clerkship was made for the head of the Office in 1977 and 1983. It was not repeated in 2002.

In the final decades of its existence, the main preoccupation of the Judicial Office was to improve the facilities available to the Law Lords, and thus to address the criticism frequently heard from the Law Lords and others which made unflattering contrasts between conditions in the House of Lords and other supreme courts. The Judicial Office made two assumptions: first, that the House valued the presence of the Law Lords, and secondly, that the Law Lords themselves were satisfied with the 1876 settlement, if only they were given facilities adequate to cope with an increasing judicial workload. I believed (wrongly as it turned out) that if there were ever to be an unpicking of the 1876 arrangements, the change would come as a result of the Law Lords' dissatisfaction with their conditions rather than as a result of a unilateral government decision. These assumptions were based on the views of the majority of the Law Lords in the 1980s and early 1990s; they did not take account of the views of those appointed from the mid-1990s, some of whom had misgivings about the propriety of combining the judicial and legislative roles—the very basis of the 1876 settlement.

Progress in the improvement of the facilities was certainly made, but it has to be admitted that the base line was in some respects embarrassingly low. There is among the Judicial Office papers a file entitled 'Dictionary for the Law Lords'. It is a set of memoranda passing between the Principal Clerk, Librarian, Clerk of the Parliaments, and Lord Simonds[21] (at that time Chairman of the Library Committee) asking that 'the lady who types for the Law Lords' be provided with a Shorter Oxford Dictionary. She made this request because, as she put it, 'Law Lords often use words in their obsolete or old fashioned sense' and the only volume with which she had been provided was the Concise Oxford. There were many dictionaries available in the Library, but at that time female members of staff were denied access to those facilities. The Clerk of the Parliaments, demurring at the expense of a Shorter Oxford Dictionary, asked the Librarian whether 'without breaching some important principal [he might feel able] to allow [the typist] to use the Library. I put this to you not merely on grounds of economy but also because it seems a reasonable use of the facilities available to the Law Lords.' After anxious discussions between the Librarian and Lord Simonds it was finally agreed that the secretary might consult the dictionaries in the Library at any time before 1 pm on sitting days, with no restriction on non-sitting days. Reporting this happy arrangement to the Clerk of the Parliaments, the Librarian admitted 'times have changed, and so has the feeling in the House generally about women'. This was in

---

[21] Lord Chancellor 1951–4.

May 1965, and shows perhaps that the Judicial Office had some way to go before they could persuade the Law Lords to be satisfied with their lot.

By the end of the century it could at least be claimed that the most obvious deficiencies had been removed. By that time the Law Lords had adequate secretarial assistance and their office was managed by an officer of Higher Executive rank with a deputy. In the face of fierce competition from other departments in the Parliament Office, a large conference room and law library was created out of a room that had previously belonged to the Private Bill Office, making the smaller conference room available for additional staff. Use of the government car service was extended to the Law Lords and the two Committee rooms used by the Appellate Committees were air-conditioned and refurbished with full Pugin treatment and in accordance with the Law Lords' own specifications. Finally, an ambition long cherished by the Law Lords was realised in 1999 when four judicial assistants were appointed on one-year contracts. In order to achieve this last improvement it was necessary, with some historic irony, yet again to ask the Yeoman Usher of the Black Rod to vacate his accommodation, just as had happened in 1876 when his predecessor had had to give up his sitting room in the (original) Law Lords' Corridor for Lord Gordon, one of the first Lords of Appeal in Ordinary to be appointed.

In achieving these improvements the Judicial Office had one great advantage. Unlike a government department, the House of Lords is not subject to budgetary constraints. So long as the Clerk of the Parliaments (as Accounting Officer) was persuaded that something was needed and that it was desired by the Law Lords, money was forthcoming. The benefits of this comparative financial independence were vividly illustrated in 1994 when the Lord Chancellor decided to increase the number of Lords of Appeal in Ordinary to 12. For this, parliamentary approval was required under the provisions of the Appellate Jurisdiction Act 1947, and before agreeing to set this in motion the Prime Minister asked that the Treasury should satisfy itself that the increase was justified. Accordingly the Treasury asked for 'an analysis of the average sitting days of the existing Lords of Appeal in Ordinary and an assessment of whether more could be done to manage the workload effectively'. Their request was made in the first instance to the Lord Chancellor's Department (under the mistaken but perhaps understandable impression that they were responsible for the work of the Law Lords) but it soon found its way to the Judicial Office. Enquiries about what information the Treasury would find helpful revealed a degree of ignorance about the judicial House of Lords which threatened a wearying period of explanation. Nevertheless a paper was produced which concluded with the words: 'in reviewing the workload of the Lords of Appeal certain general assumptions have been made; i) appeals to the House of Lords . . . are heard by panels of five; ii) the duties of those who hold high judicial office may involve them spending some of their time away from Westminster; iii) the current sitting times in hours per day, days per week and weeks per year are the maximum which can be reconciled with the nature of the work and the institution in which much of that work takes place'. The Lord Chancellor's Department accepted and supported both the premises and the conclusion of the paper and accordingly the Judicial Office was spared what the department chillingly referred to as 'a more detailed and extensive examination of the work of the Law Lords with, no doubt, appropriate cost-analysis'. Their recommendation to the Treasury concluded: 'there were unlikely to be any radical or more effective ways of organising the workload, nor were there any obvious economies of scale to be realised. It was important not to see...the House of Lords...as capable of responding to the intensive managerial approach which we have applied to the Court Service in recent years. We concluded that there was little or no scope for a structural or management analysis.' With that welcome endorsement the Judicial Office could turn to what really mattered: finding rooms for the two new Lords of Appeal.

In spite of these improvements, the popular perception that the Law Lords were poorly provided for persisted, so that in his evidence to the Select Committee on the Constitutional Reform Bill 2004 Lord Falconer [22] cited it as one of the reasons for the move to the Supreme Court; 'as we all know, the accommodation for the Law Lords [in the Palace of Westminster] leaves a lot to be desired. Their offices are cramped and inconveniently located. Constraints of space available limit the number of support staff.'[23] The views of the Lord Chancellor were not shared by all the Law Lords, and were described as 'exaggerated' by Lord Hope of Craighead, a serving Lord of Appeal in Ordinary, in his evidence to the same Committee.[24]

The twenty-first century

By the middle of the 1990s it was generally assumed that the Labour Party would be returned at the next election; and the party was committed to a radical reform of the House of Lords. In planning for the future the Judicial Office could not be certain that the position of the Law Lords would be unaffected by whatever changes were coming. It would, for example, be difficult for the court to remain part of a wholly elected House—though not entirely unthinkable, since that was precisely the arrangement adopted by the United States in the years immediately following independence.

In the aftermath of the Labour victory in May 1997, however, fears of any immediate change to the existing judicial arrangements seemed premature. The new Lord Chancellor, Lord Irvine of Lairg,[25] was a strong supporter of the judicial House of Lords, and made it clear that he intended to exercise his right to preside

---

[22] Lord Chancellor 2003–7.
[23] Select Committee on the Constitutional Reform Bill, vol 2, p 10.
[24] ibid, 190.   [25] Lord Chancellor 1997–2003.

over judicial sittings from time to time as his predecessors had done. Furthermore the Royal Commission on the House of Lords, appointed by the Government soon after taking office, reported that, in their view, the current system worked well and, with a few minor modifications, should be left as it was. Since by then the Law Lords' working conditions were no longer as open to criticism as they had been, and since the Government appeared to be concentrating on the position of the hereditary peers rather than the judiciary, there seemed reasonable grounds to expect that the settlement of 1876 would last at least for the foreseeable future. At the same time the Judicial Office was encountering a wholly new order of problems which would have been incomprehensible to earlier generations.

I refer to the gradual but perceptible increase in the belligerence displayed by some members of the legal profession to the judicial rules of the House, set out in the Standing Orders and Practice Directions. Because these differed in a number of important ways from the rules in the lower courts, it was the task of the Judicial Office to explain to litigants exactly what the House required. Increasingly the Office found that the rules were being challenged. Some attributed this to the Human Rights Act, some to the arrival of a Labour government with the attendant speculation about the future of the House of Lords, and some put it down to the so-called 'end of deference'. Probably it was a mixture of all three, but whatever the reason, it certainly presented the office with a new set of problems. One firm of solicitors even tried to bring a case against me for having written to inform them that their client's petition for leave to appeal had been refused; and I understand that my successor fared even worse when, in 2005, Parliament Office funds had to be used in order to resist a motion for judicial review in the High Court following his refusal to receive a petition for leave to appeal, which was inadmissible under the *Lane v Esdaile* [26] rule. Others objected to the requirement to lodge security for costs when presenting an appeal; and there were frequent failures to conform to the manner in which the Practice Directions (which reflected the wishes of the Law Lords) required documents to be presented. The Law Lords themselves were cajoled into giving reasons for refusing leave to appeal. (The 'reason' was distinctly formulaic, stating that 'in the opinion of the Committee the petition did not disclose a point of law which merited an appeal to the House'—which is rather like answering the question 'why don't you like eating bananas?' with the reply: 'because I don't like the taste of bananas'. Nevertheless it appeared to satisfy the requirements.) All this led to an awareness that the time might be coming when the judicial business of the House could no longer be left entirely in the hands of those who were essentially general administrators, knowledgeable in parliamentary procedure, but not lawyers. This had never been a problem in the past but we recognised that it might be necessary in the future to include at least one person in the office who was legally qualified.

---

[26] *Lane v Esdaile* [1891] AC 210 decided that no appeal might be brought to the House of Lords against an order of the Court of Appeal refusing leave to appeal to that court.

One area where this change of atmosphere was particularly keenly felt was the taxation of costs. The head of the Judicial Office had always acted as Taxing Officer, and this arrangement seems to have been satisfactory so long as it was essentially a matter of playing umpire between two sides, one to pay costs and the other to be paid. Arguments were made on the one side, then on the other, and the Taxing Officer was there to oversee what usually ended up as a mutually agreed compromise. With the taxation of bills payable out of legal aid (that is, public) funds, the situation was very different since there was no one to represent the 'paying party', in effect the taxpayer. In these cases the Taxing Officer found himself arguing with lawyers who were deploying ingenious reasons why it would be grossly unfair not to allow a fee or a charging rate greatly in excess of the guideline figures and the amounts allowed in recent comparable cases. I was acutely aware that I was an amateur operating in a world of professionals, and my only comfort was that if someone (usually a barrister) really felt that my judgment was wrong, he or she had the right of appeal, ultimately to the Law Lords themselves. In my time as Taxing Officer there were three such appeals, the first quite soon after I took over. The Appeal Committee which heard the petition was chaired by Lord Templeman,[27] who certainly lived up to his nickname of 'Sid Vicious' on that occasion. In the years that followed I found that sight of the transcript of that hearing often had a sobering effect on those who were contemplating an appeal, although it is true that one of my decisions was overturned following the third appeal. That happened not long before my retirement, and was one of the factors which led me to suggest that my successor should be given some professional help with taxation. Accordingly, from October 2002 a costs judge of the High Court was appointed an Officer of the House, and sat with the Principal Clerk on taxation hearings until the establishment of the Supreme Court. I understand that these hearings now take up far more time than they used to, and that the level of fees allowed has risen substantially. At the time of writing (December 2008), there has been no appeal against any decision of this duumvirate.

Whether the Human Rights Act was indeed partly responsible for the complaints against Judicial Office procedures it was certainly the cause of the virtual end of the Lord Chancellor's participation in the hearing of appeals. Holders of that office had always been scrupulous in avoiding any case where there might be any question of government interest, but after the passage of the Act the criteria for judging where the line should be drawn became so much stricter that it proved impossible to be confident that a challenge to the presence of the Lord Chancellor would not be made, sometimes at a time inconveniently close to the scheduled start of the hearing. Even tax cases, on which Lord Irvine's predecessor, Lord Mackay of Clashfern,[28] had frequently sat, were held to be out of bounds since it was argued that the Treasury had an interest in the taxpayer losing the appeal. Until the appointment of Lord Bingham as Senior Law Lord in 2000, it had been

---

[27] Lord of Appeal in Ordinary 1982–94.   [28] Lord Chancellor 1987–97.

the practice, at the end of each term, to send the list of those who were to sit in the following term to the Lord Chancellor, both for his approval (although by the 1990s this was largely a formality) and with a request that he would indicate on which cases he wished to sit. After June 2000, the Lord Chancellor left it to Lord Bingham to suggest cases where, in his opinion, there was little danger of a challenge on Human Rights Act grounds.

The same approach to the human rights legislation led to a disinclination among some of the serving Law Lords to speak in the House. Some, indeed, felt that it was wrong in any circumstances to give an opinion in a legislative forum, while others took the more traditional view that their status as peers gave them a right, and indeed a duty, to speak so long as they were careful not to say anything which might disqualify them from a judicial hearing in the future—the same criteria, that is, which applied to any holder of high judicial office who gave a public lecture.

In 1995 the Principal Clerk of the Judicial Office was appointed to the newly created post of Registrar of Lords' Interests, as recommended by Lord Griffiths[29] in his report to the House on the declaration of interests.[30] A sub-committee of the Privileges Committee was also appointed to oversee the Register, with Lord Griffiths as its first chairman, and after his resignation, all subsequent chairmen (until the end of 2008) were former Lords of Appeal. After the change of government in 1997, it became mandatory for all members of the House to register all their interests, including those which had not needed to be declared under the original, less stringent, rules. Although this made the Registrar's task more demanding, it was generally agreed that the Judicial Office was the appropriate place for the post, and its establishment went a long way towards bringing the Judicial Office into closer contact with the wider parliamentary organisation.

Thus as the twentieth century gave way to the twenty-first, it was clear that not only was the House, both 'lay' and judicial, very different from what it had been a quarter of a century before, but that further changes were likely in the not too distant future; but in the first few years of the century there was no expectation that these changes would not take place within the general context of the 1876 Appellate Jurisdiction Act. However, on 12 June 2003, in a statement expected to be concerned with ministerial changes, the Government announced that the jurisdiction of the House of Lords would be ended and that its functions would in the future be carried out by a supreme court. This is not the place to discuss the merits of that decision, but it is worth reflecting on the difference between the way it was announced, and the years—indeed decades—of public debate which had preceded the settlement of 1876. Although it is true that a number of eminent lawyers and academics over the years had expressed their support for the

---

[29] Lord of Appeal in Ordinary 1985–93.
[30] Third Report of the Procedure Committee on the Declaration and Registration of Interests, 1995.

establishment of a supreme court, there had not been the succession of government green and white papers which might have been expected to precede an announcement of such constitutional importance, nor was it made in fulfilment of a manifesto commitment. Nevertheless, having taken the decision, the Government proceeded to implement it by legislation in the next parliamentary session, culminating with Royal Assent to the Constitutional Reform Act 2005.

For the Judicial Office the decision meant that it would become redundant after the transfer to the new court, and each individual member had to decide whether he or she should, if it were possible, transfer with the court or be absorbed into other parts of the Parliament Office. One of the difficulties in providing for the future was that it seems not to have been generally appreciated that, as parliamentary officials, members of the Judicial Office were not civil servants, so that there could be no question of a straight transfer, as often happens when ministries are amalgamated or reorganised. It would therefore be surprising if morale among the members of the office had not suffered to some extent.

However, the Judicial Office did have a new 'aim and objective': to ensure that the transfer to the new court was carried through as smoothly as possible, and, whilst the transfer was being planned, that the judicial work of the House continued to function with as little interruption as possible. In spite of some natural misgivings about their personal futures once the familiar structure was dismantled, it must have been an exhilarating experience to have had a part in planning the most far-reaching reform of the highest tier of the judiciary in modern times. And perhaps those Lords of Appeal in Ordinary who on 1 October 2009 will become Justices of the Supreme Court will carry with them to their new home—geographically so close but so distant in other ways—some kind memories of that group of parliamentary officials who for a century and a half helped a court to operate within a House of Parliament.

4

The House of Lords and the English Court of Appeal

Gavin Drewry and Louis Blom-Cooper

The relationship between the House of Lords and the courts below is complex and multi-faceted. Its most obvious aspects are defined by the formal rules that underpin the appellate function: for instance, the rules of precedent that render House of Lords' decisions binding on lower courts, and the procedures and criteria relating to the granting of leave to appeal. Knowledge of such matters is important, not just to litigants and their legal representatives who have to navigate their way through such procedural complexities, but also to those of a more conceptual disposition, seeking to explain the operation and the rationale of a two-tier appellate system. These aspects of the relationship between the intermediate appeal courts—in particular the Court of Appeal—and the House of Lords are particularly germane to the distinction between 'review' and 'supervision', discussed later in this chapter.

The 'relationship' between courts is not, however, just to do with things like rights of appeal and the doctrine of precedent. Although this chapter is concerned largely with such formal matters, it is important to remember that the relationship between the House of Lords and lower courts also manifests itself in other, less formal and more 'sociological', ways. For one thing, the English higher judiciary is a tightly knit fraternity (and, increasingly in recent years, a sorority) with its epicentre in the Inns of Court. In its very early days, the Court of Appeal used to do some of its business in Westminster Hall;[1] those days are long past, but the Palace of Westminster is within easy walking distance of Fleet Street and the Inns. Judges—including Law Lords and Lords and Lady Justices of Appeal—regularly mingle together, there and elsewhere, in all kinds of social as well as professional contexts.[2] Their conversation doubtless touches from time to time upon legal issues. (In any case, one hopes and assumes that judges do read one another's judgments.)

---

[1] G Drewry, L Blom-Cooper, and C Blake, *Court of Appeal* (Oxford: Hart Publishing, 2007) 34.

[2] Scottish and Northern Irish judges have their own professional networks and it is perhaps worth reflecting whether Law Lords from those parts of the UK feel in any way marginalised (however unintentionally) by their English colleagues.

Another relationship derives from the career structure of the judiciary: even though there may be no formal judicial promotion structure, ambitious Lord and Lady Justices of Appeal will inevitably see advancement to the House of Lords as a desirable career goal. The Court of Appeal (and the other intermediate appeal courts) is a reservoir of talent—and a forum in which to demonstrate appellate capability[3] for appointments to the House of Lords. Moreover, looking at relationships in managerial terms, the top court serves, in effect, as an instrument of professional accountability—peer review, in a literal sense—for the judges below. Those who may sometimes complain that judges are not sufficiently accountable for their performance would do well to remember the important quality-control function that is provided by the appellate system—though a final appeal court, by virtue of its finality, is where the accountability buck stops (thus prompting the classical question, *quis custodiet...*?). We will return later to this aspect of the relationship.

The remainder of this chapter looks in more detail at the relationship between the Court of Appeal in England and Wales and the House of Lords. In adopting this focus we are of course omitting consideration of, but not forgetting, the several other courts *a quo*; but the Court of Appeal is the one that provides the House of Lords with four-fifths of its caseload. According to the annual *Judicial Statistics*, in the period 2002 to 2007, 68.8 per cent of appeals presented to the Lords came from the Civil Division of the Court of Appeal, and 10 per cent from the Criminal Division.

We begin our account by looking at the civil jurisdictions of the two courts. Some of the material in the following sections is adapted from our own, recently published, study (co-authored with Charles Blake) of the Civil Division of the Court of Appeal,[4] a study that drew in turn upon our much earlier research into the appellate functions of the House of Lords, published in 1972 in *Final Appeal*.

The Court of Appeal—Civil Jurisdiction

The Court of Appeal, normally constituted of ten benches of three Lords Justices hearing full appeals,[5] disposes annually of about a dozen times as many appeals as the House of Lords, whose appellate committees normally consist of five Lords of Appeal, usually sitting in just one division at any one time.[6] Thus the annually

---

[3] See ch 7 in this volume.   [4] See note 1 above.

[5] In 2008, the maximum number of judges in the Court of Appeal was increased from 37 to 38, to enable a Lord or Lady Justice to serve as Chair of the Law Commission without reducing the capacity of the Court: see *Hansard*, HL, vol 702, cols 746 ff (12 June 2008).

[6] With a current establishment, since 1994, of 12 Lords of Appeal (plus the possibility of calling upon the services of retired Law Lords under the age of 75) it is sometimes possible to have two five-judge Appellate Committees sitting at the same time. In practice, however, Law Lords are often busy elsewhere—sitting in the Judicial Committee of the Privy Council, presiding over official enquiries, or undertaking judicial engagements overseas (eg in Hong Kong)—so parallel sittings, though by no means unknown, are not common. The appointment of Lord

published *Judicial Statistics*[7] indicate that in 2004 the Court of Appeal (Civil Division) disposed of 1,059 appeals,[8] while the House of Lords disposed of 77 (52 of them from the Court of Appeal).[9] In the same year, the Court of Appeal disposed of 2,402 applications for permission to appeal;[10] the House of Lords disposed of 271 petitions for leave to appeal (202 of them from the Court of Appeal (Civil Division)).[11] On the face of it, there might appear to be some pertinent questions to be asked in this context about the relative cost-effectiveness of the two institutions in terms of their respective deployment of expensive judicial manpower.

However, we must not of course proceed from the *a priori* assumption that both courts are performing exactly the same role: if they were, then even more troubling questions about apparent duplication of effort would arise. The House of Lords (with its strict requirement of leave to appeal) nowadays reverses the Court of Appeal in more than half of the appeals it hears[12]—a very significant increase on the corresponding figure 40 or 50 years ago, when the reversal rate was just over one-third.[13] So the House of Lords, composed mainly of former members of the Court of Appeal, is looking again at a small, and hand-picked proportion of the latter's case-load and coming, in most cases, to different conclusions. This may, of course be a consequence of the criteria for granting leave to appeal: the Appeal Committee will surely be much more likely to grant leave in cases where it looks as though the Court of Appeal might have got it wrong (and/or was divided) than in cases where it has manifestly got it right. But it may also be the case—as we argue later—that the House of Lords has decided, when considering petitions for leave to appeal, to pay special attention to certain *kinds* of high-profile case, leaving the more routine, and perhaps less headline-grabbing, ones to the Court of Appeal.

In any event, the bottom line must surely be, particularly given that the number of opportunities to appeal has been severely restricted since the civil justice reforms of the late 1990s, that the continued existence of the House of Lords—and of its

---

Saville of Newdigate to chair the Bloody Sunday inquiry has meant that, from May 2000 when he last sat on an appeal (*Dimond v Lovell* [2002] 1 AC 384), the House has in practice had only 11 full-time Law Lords to call upon.

[7] Renamed *Judicial and Court Statistics* in 2006: for simplicity's sake, we have retained the former title throughout this chapter.

[8] *Judicial Statistics 2004*, Cm 6565, Table 1.9.

[9] ibid, Table 1.4. The House of Lords also has a criminal jurisdiction (discussed later in this chapter), and hears cases from Scotland (civil appeals only) and Northern Ireland.

[10] ibid, Table 1.11.　　　[11] ibid, Table 1.3.

[12] According to the *Judicial Statistics*, in the period 2002–7, the House of Lords reversed the Court of Appeal (wholly or in part) in 169 out of the 310 appeals heard—a reversal rate of 54.5 per cent.

[13] In the period covered by *Final Appeal* (Oxford: Clarendon Press, 1972), namely 1952–70 (Table 48), 144 out of 405 appeals from the Court of Appeal (Civil Division) were allowed wholly or in part by the House of Lords—a reversal rate of 35.6 per cent. The apparent increase should be interpreted with caution, not least because of some idiosyncrasies in the *Judicial Statistics* (particularly in their treatment of consolidated and conjoined appeals, which are counted multiple times). However, other factors may be relevant: for instance, the fact that the House of Lords now takes almost exclusive responsibility for the granting of leave to appeal—see below.

prospective successor, the Supreme Court—can be justified only if it can be shown to be performing an appellate function that is both *important* in its own right, and *different* from that of the Court of Appeal. And, given that appeals reaching the House of Lords will already (other than in a tiny number of 'leapfrog' cases—see below) have been subject to at least one dose of appellate scrutiny, then the work of the House of Lords must also derive some benefit from the spadework done in the court below. In the brave 'new public management' world of efficiency, effectiveness, and value for money that has come, since the Thatcher years, to characterise official policy towards the delivery and funding of public services, including the administration of justice, duplication of functions is not an affordable luxury.

Review and supervision

In October 1996, faced with a mounting backlog of appeals in the Court of Appeal, the Lord Chancellor commissioned Sir Jeffery Bowman, a former senior partner of the top accountancy firm, PricewaterhouseCoopers, to undertake a review of the Civil Division of the Court. The Bowman Report[14] came up with a number of important recommendations—including a new requirement of obtaining permission to appeal in almost all cases that seek to progress to the Court of Appeal, and a tough regime of judicial case management—the details of which need not concern us here. More germane to the present discussion is the fact that the Report looked at the rationale of an appeals system, and concluded that appeals serve a much broader function than merely correcting wrong decisions as far as they concern the parties to a dispute. It noted that there is also a wider public purpose in ensuring confidence in the administration of justice and, where appropriate, in clarifying the law, and rules of practice and procedure, and helping to maintain the standards of performance of first instance courts and tribunals.

This corresponds closely to the argument that we put forward in *Final Appeal* to explain the rationale of a two-level appellate process. There we argued that appeals serve two separate but related purposes. The first is best termed *review*. This is the means of correcting mistakes at first instance and of creating some kind of continuity, consistency, and certainty in the administration of justice. To borrow the kind of managerial vocabulary that has become familiar in the discussion of public services, review is about both *quality-control* in the administration of justice and providing a mechanism of *accountability* in respect of those exercising judicial functions in the lower courts. The second function is termed *supervision*. This is the process of laying down fresh precedents and statutory interpretations and updating old ones for the guidance of lower courts in the hierarchy—including the intermediate appeal courts. It also consists in resolving

---

[14] <http://www.dca.gov.uk/civil/bowman/bowfr.htm>. See Drewry, Blom-Cooper, and Blake (n 1) ch 2.

legal problems of a particularly high order, both of difficulty and of public importance, that arise in that important minority of 'hard' cases that require judicial attention of the highest order. In managerial vocabulary, this has to do with top-down leadership and the formulation and refining of policy.

We would add, in passing, that the exercise of effective leadership requires that the messages from on high are framed in clear and unambiguous language—a factor to be borne in mind when considering the relative merits of retaining multiple House of Lords judgments rather than single composite ones.

It is important also to note that, although the two functions are closely interconnected, there is an important difference of emphasis between them. Review is principally to do with achieving justice for individual litigants in the instant case while supervision has primarily to do with addressing legal problems in the wider public interest. This highlights the most important distinction—or, at least, a major difference of emphasis—between the respective functions of the Court of Appeal and of the House of Lords. As Lord Bingham observed in *R v Secretary of State for Trade and Industry, ex p Eastaway* (a decision of the House of Lords that reaffirmed the rule in *Lane v Esdaile*, discussed below):

In its role as a supreme court the House must necessarily concentrate its attention on a relatively small number of cases recognised as raising legal questions of general public importance. It cannot seek to correct errors in the application of settled law, even where such are shown to exist.[15]

At the time of our work on *Final Appeal*, most appeals ending up in the House of Lords had obtained leave from the Court of Appeal. Of the 366 civil appeals heard by the House of Lords in the period 1952–68 that required leave,[16] 286 (78.1 per cent) had obtained leave from the court below.[17] But nowadays—as we shall see—the position is strikingly different. Since the Court of Appeal nowadays very rarely grants leave to take a case further, it falls to the House of Lords, in effect, to cherry-pick the cases it wishes to hear—to control its own docket, as Americans might say. 'Justice *à la carte*' is a term that is sometimes used. The role of the Court of Appeal is mainly one of review, although if an appeal stops there, as most do, the Court inevitably acts also *de facto* as a supervisory body in many instances. This is particularly so in relation to important points of practice and procedure, an area where the House of Lords very seldom seeks to intrude.

One other major change since the days of *Final Appeal* is the sharp diminution in the proportion of Revenue appeals in the caseload of the House of Lords. In the period 1952–68, such appeals constituted more than 30 per cent of all Lords appeals.[18] The torrent of Revenue business (even including post-1972 VAT cases)

---

[15] [2000] 1 WLR 2222, 2228B.

[16] The main exception was, and still is, appeals from the Inner House of the Scottish Court of Session. These lie, in general, as of right, subject to the petition being signed by two counsel, certifying that the appeal is reasonable.

[17] See *Final Appeal* (n 13) Table 5.   [18] ibid, Table 11.

has since dwindled to little more than a mere trickle: the annual *Judicial Statistics* for the six years 2001–7 suggest that the current proportion is about 7 per cent.

However, the shrinkage of the House's engagement in tax-related matters has been offset by a substantial growth in the number of judicial review and (since 2000) human rights appeals. *Final Appeal* identified just 14 appeals in the subject categories of administrative and constitutional law, out of 349 appeals heard by the House in the period 1952–68—just 4 per cent. The *Judicial Statistics* for the five years 2003–7 (by which time the first human rights appeals under the 1998 Act were beginning to reach the House) show that, of the 279 appeals determined, 35 were in the field of administrative law and 63 involved human rights—a figure, adding the two categories together, of 35.1 per cent.[19]

And the growing volume of such business tells only part of the story. Many of the cases in these subject categories have been very high profile events that have brought the House of Lords into an unaccustomed media spotlight, and have sometimes given rise to interesting tensions between the judiciary and the executive. The landmark decision of a nine-judge Appellate Committee in December 2004, in a human rights case involving the detention of suspected Al-Qa'ida terrorists on the orders of the Home Secretary, exercising powers conferred by the Anti-terrorism, Crime and Security Act 2001, is one of many instances that could be cited in this context.[20] And the judgments delivered by the members of another nine-judge Appellate Committee in October 2005, concerning the constitutionality of the Parliament Act 1949, which had been used to enact the Hunting Act 2004, are major landmarks in contemporary constitutional law.[21]

If it was only a slight exaggeration to suggest that the House of Lords in the 1950s and 1960s functioned substantially as a specialist tax tribunal, it is surely no more of an exaggeration to suggest that it has now become a court specialising substantially in public law. And this has interesting implications for the role and public perception of the final appellate court when it moves from the House of Lords and is re-badged with the evocative title of Supreme Court. Meanwhile, we would reiterate our concluding remark in *Court of Appeal*: 'the Court of Appeal will remain firmly in place, occupying its crucial position as, to all intents and purposes, the court of last resort—indeed, a supreme court—for most civil appellants'.[22]

Leave to appeal

The Administration of Justice (Appeals) Act 1934, implementing a recommendation of the Business of the Courts Committee, chaired by Lord Hanworth MR,[23]

---

[19] Some caution must be exercised in comparing statistics in *Final Appeal* with those in the *Judicial Statistics*, because they are compiled and presented somewhat differently.

[20] *A v Secretary of State for the Home Department* [2005] 2 AC 68.

[21] *R (Jackson) v Attorney General* [2006] 1 AC 262.   [22] n 1, 185.

[23] Second Interim Report, Cmd 4471, 1934.

imposed a requirement of leave to appeal to the House of Lords in place of the absolute right of appeal that had existed hitherto. Leave was to be granted either by the Court of Appeal, to which application had first to be made, or by the House of Lords itself. So, if both bodies refused leave, the Court of Appeal would become the final court for the parties in that case. This procedure remains in place. The origin of the leave requirement seems to have lain more in concerns about the workload of the Judicial Committee of the Privy Council, most of whose members are Lords of Appeal, than in concerns about that of the House of Lords itself.[24]

Those who supported the 1934 Act apparently did so more out of concern to protect poor litigants who had won their cases in the lower courts from any further challenge than being actuated by arguments about the desired nature and form of the appellate process. A multiplicity of appeals was seen as a source of delay and as a device that enabled one party, usually the stronger one, to force a settlement on the other. In particular, it was felt that an unlimited right of appeal placed great power in the hands of large corporations and government departments. Concerns about the powerful litigious leverage of the latter were becoming evident even though public law still remained undeveloped and the Crown Proceedings Act 1947 (removing many anomalous and outdated procedural and substantive privileges and immunities of the state) had yet to be enacted. The modernisation of judicial review, culminating in the establishment of an Administrative Court, lay even further in the future.

The requirement of leave to appeal has remained firmly in place since its first introduction. Our own research on the Court of Appeal has confirmed that losing parties in the Court of Appeal do, fairly routinely, ask for leave to go to the Lords—on the principle, perhaps, that making such an application takes little time or trouble, and that there is surely no harm in asking, even if, in the overwhelming majority of cases, the answer is bound to be no. Moreover, any party who intends to petition the House of Lords for leave (or wishes to keep open the possibility of doing so) must first have applied for and been refused leave in the Court of Appeal. Our examination of 398 Court of Appeal transcripts in the first six months of 2001 found that applications for leave to petition the Lords were made in 147 cases (36.3 per cent of the total). But only two of these applications were granted. The policy is clear. The Appeal Committee of the House of Lords now decides which cases are to reach the House, rather than the court below.

The strict requirement of leave to appeal, now applied almost exclusively by the House of Lords itself,[25] goes to the heart of the 'review' function. If the job of a final appeal court is to pay in-depth attention to the small proportion of difficult

---

[24] See R Stevens, *Law and Politics* (London: Weidenfeld and Nicolson, 1979) 189.
[25] See B Dickson, 'The Processing of Appeals in the House of Lords' [2007] LQR 571–2.

cases that raise important issues of principle, then it must have control of both the quantity and quality of its caseload. As our colleague, Brice Dickson has observed,

The main reason for having a second tier appeal court is to ensure that first tier appeal courts do not make wrong, or inconsistent, decisions. To perform this role efficiently the House itself needs to be able to choose the cases it wants to deal with. If judges in the first tier appeal courts would *prefer* the House to hear a further appeal, they can intimate as much when issuing their judgments.[26]

Lord Bingham of Cornhill, delivering a lecture to the Constitution Unit at University College London, in May 2002, on the prospective establishment of the new Supreme Court, was in no doubt on the matter:

I am very clearly of the opinion that since the House can, under existing arrangements, hear only some 60–80 full appeals a year, there must be a power to decide which those cases should be. If, as in many countries in Europe and elsewhere there existed an unfettered right of appeal, the inevitable consequence would be the summary dismissal of the overwhelming majority of those appeals, probably on paper without a hearing. I doubt whether such a process would be very satisfying to litigants brought up on our tradition.[27]

In *Final Appeal*, the present authors quoted Mr Justice Frankfurter's words concerning the right of appeal to the US Supreme Court, that bear upon this point (always remembering, of course, that there are important procedural differences between that court and the House of Lords):

...the judgments of this court are collective judgments. Such judgments presuppose ample time and freshness of mind for private study and reflection in preparation for discussion at conference. Without adequate study there cannot be adequate reflection; without adequate reflection there cannot be adequate discussion; without adequate discussion there cannot be that fruitful interchange of minds which is indispensable to thoughtful unhurried decision and its formulation in learned and impressive decisions. It is therefore imperative that the docket [ie list of cases for hearing] be kept down so that its volume does not preclude wide adjudication. This can be avoided only if the Court rigorously excludes any case from coming here that does not rise to the significance of inevitability in meeting the responsibilities vested in this Court.[28]

In this respect, the Court of Appeal's growing reluctance to grant leave to appeal to the House of Lords may be seen as inevitable, and perhaps overdue. Lord

---

[26] ibid. However, Dickson also observes (at 587) that, in practice, the present procedures operate 'rather idiosyncratically', and he concludes that 'the House is not in as much control of its caseload as it needs to be'.

[27] <http://www.ucl.ac.uk/constitution-unit/files/90.pdf>.

[28] *Dick v New York Life Insurance Co*, 359 US 437, 458–9 (1959), quoted in *Final Appeal* (note 13 above) 119. As was pointed out in a footnote, the 'collective' character of Supreme Court judgments is not exactly replicated in the House of Lords, or indeed in the Court of Appeal, where separate assenting (and dissenting) judgments are common.

Bingham of Cornhill was certainly of that mind, in his lecture to the Constitution Unit, cited above:

I would not, for my part, echo the criticism, sometimes heard, that the Court of Appeal is nowadays too reluctant to grant leave: no division of that court can know what cases are competing for the attention of the House, and the decision is usually best left to the House unless considerations of time weigh in favour of immediate leave. If the Court of Appeal considers the case to be one which probably does merit consideration by the House, it can helpfully give its reasons for holding that opinion when refusing leave and the House will then have the benefit of its view.

By the same token, it can be argued that the introduction of a post-Bowman permission to appeal requirement in the Court of Appeal has been conducive to the exercise of a more effective review function by that court, particularly in those cases that are not destined to proceed to the Lords.

The demise of oral hearings

So far as petitioning the House of Lords is concerned, a major change in the operation of the means of turning an intermediate appeal into a final one, dating back to the 1970s, has been effectively to remove an oral hearing from the process. If the Court of Appeal refuses leave to appeal to the Lords (which it almost invariably does today even if the broad, unstated, but generally recognised criterion of general public importance is met), a renewed application to the House of Lords will normally be dealt with on the papers without a hearing before a three-judge Appeals Committee. Only if the committee is divided will there be an oral hearing of such an application.

In *Final Appeal*[29] we noted the significance in this context of a decision of the House of Lords in 1891, in *Lane v Esdaile*.[30] Here it was held that no appeal can lie to the House of Lords from the Court of Appeal's refusal of leave to appeal *to itself*,[31] since such a refusal does not constitute a 'judgment or order' within the meaning of the Appellate Jurisdiction Act 1876.

The rule was subsequently restated in section 54 of the Access to Justice Act 1999, which provides, in line with *Lane v Esdaile*, that 'no appeal may be made against a decision of a court under this section to give or refuse permission...'. Direction 1.14 of the House of Lords' *Practice Directions and Standing Orders Applicable to Civil Appeals* provides that the categories of petition that are not admissible include 'petitions for leave to appeal to the House of Lords from a refusal by the Court of Appeal to grant leave to appeal to that court from a judgment or order of a lower

---

[29] n 13, 128–9.   [30] [1891] AC 210.

[31] At the time of *Lane v Esdaile* there was of course no general requirement to obtain permission to appeal. However, leave was required, for instance, in order to appeal from the interlocutory ruling of a judge in chambers or, as in *Lane v Esdaile* itself, where an appeal was out of time.

court, or from any other preliminary decision of the Court of Appeal in respect of a case in which leave to appeal to the Court of Appeal was not granted'.

We noted in *Final Appeal* that the rediscovery of this useful precedent in the 1950s enabled the Appeal Committee of the House of Lords to dispose summarily of a high proportion of unmeritorious petitions for leave (which in those days were considered in oral hearings before the Appeal Committee). Our own research has found, however, that a significant number of petitions covered by the *Lane v Esdaile* rule are still lodged by aspiring appellants, often in the face of well-intended informal advice from the staff of the Judicial Office that they stand no chance of success because they are clearly inadmissible. The potential deterrent effect of having to pay a substantial fee (currently £570) is much blunted by the availability of fairly liberal provisions for the waiver of fees for petitioners in receipt of state benefits—a modern version of what used to be called the *in forma pauperis* procedure. And, although Article 6 of the European Convention on Human Rights certainly does not confer an unlimited right of appeal, the House of Lords has tended in recent years to err on the side of caution in its approach to even the most unmeritorious and incompetent petitions.

The major change, more than 70 years ago, abolishing the unrestricted right of appeal to the Lords, more recently replicated by the introduction of a permission requirement for the Court of Appeal, did not give rise to any serious discussion about abolishing either the Court of Appeal or the House of Lords. Indeed, the judicial role of the Lords hardly featured at all in recent discussions of the future of the second chamber, though the issue was on the table, at least by implication, in the debates about the establishment of the Supreme Court and the enactment of the Constitutional Reform Act 2005. Still less has there been any examination of the relationship between the two courts.

'Leapfrog' appeals

A development that was first recommended by the Evershed Committee in 1953,[32] the leapfrog appeal, enjoyed some popularity when it was first introduced in 1970.[33] However, perhaps for reasons given by Megarry J in *IRC v Church Commissioners for England*,[34] which gave a restricted interpretation of the requirement that a leapfrog case must relate 'wholly or mainly to the construction of an enactment',[35] the procedure fell out of favour and is seldom used today. Our co-editorial colleague, Brice Dickson, has noted that, in the 30-year period 1967–96, there were only 54 such appeals. He concluded from this that, 'clearly

---

[32] *Final Report of the Committee on Supreme Court Practice and Procedure*, Cmnd 8878, 1953, paras 483–530.

[33] Administration of Justice Act 1969, Part II. See G Drewry, 'Leapfrogging—and a Lords Justices' Eye View of the Final Appeal' (1973) 89 LQR 260.

[34] [1975] 1 WLR 251.   [35] Administration of Justice Act 1969, s 12(3)(a).

this fast-track facility for appeals has not done much to alleviate the burden on the Court of Appeal, since [in the period under review] leapfrog appeals represent[ed] less than five percent of the combined total of these civil appeals'.[36]

The low take-up rate of the procedure may be explained in part by its being little known (or its having been forgotten) by advocates and those who instruct them. The first-instance court must certify that such an appeal is appropriate and that the criteria specified in the legislation are met (a point of law of general importance arising from the construction of legislation, a binding precedent in the Court of Appeal or the House of Lords, and the House agrees to take the case). It seems unlikely that such an issue would be actively canvassed before the court of first instance has given judgment.

It is probable, moreover, that the Law Lords themselves are reluctant to be deprived of the benefit of the preliminary spade-work done by the Court of Appeal on a difficult case—even in those instances where, in the event, their Lordships prove all too willing to trample over that spade-work by allowing the appeal. In this respect, the leapfrog procedure, while serving the cause of expedition, conflates the review and supervision functions, and risks starving the former of some of the raw material that is needed to do the job properly. And this is probably why, in the very rare instances (on average, no more than one a year) where a certified leapfrog application comes before the Appeal Committee, leave is usually refused.

However, there still are occasional reminders that the leapfrog procedure is not quite defunct. Thus in July 2005, in *Jones v Ceredigion County Council (No 2)*,[37] the Court of Appeal was called upon to consider a rather curious jurisdictional point relating to the procedure. The substance of the case had to do with the interpretation of a statutory provision requiring local education authorities to provide free school transport. The judge at first instance, having decided against the county council, granted it a leapfrog certificate, allowing it to apply to the House of Lords for leave to appeal in respect of two points at issue in his decision. He also gave permission to appeal to the Court of Appeal in the event of the House of Lords refusing leave. The House of Lords then granted leave in respect of one of the issues, but refused it in respect of the other. The 1969 Act says that if, in a leapfrog case, the House of Lords grants leave, 'no appeal from the decision of the judge to which the [leapfrog] certificate relates shall lie to the Court of Appeal'. So did the Court of Appeal now have jurisdiction to hear the appeal in respect of the issue in which the Lords had refused leave? By a majority, the Court decided that it did have jurisdiction in these circumstances. The House of Lords held that it would undermine the purpose of the leapfrog procedure if different appeals against the same order could proceed at the same time in different courts but their Lordships nevertheless found that they could not deprive an applicant of

---

[36] B Dickson, 'The Lords of Appeal and their Work 1967–96' in B Dickson and P Carmichael (eds), *The House of Lords: Its Parliamentary and Judicial Roles* (Oxford: Hart, 1999) 127–54, at 146.
[37] [2007] 1 WLR 1400.

the option of appealing to the Court of Appeal instead of the House of Lords, even where a certificate under section 12 of the 1969 Act had been granted, if the House had granted leave to appeal only on conditions which were unacceptable to the applicant.[38]

Leapfrogging is thus a mixed blessing, which is why the courts are so cautious about deploying it. It reflects an admirable desire for expedition and economy, but at the risk of cutting corners in the rigorous exercise of the review functions of the House of Lords. Exceptionally difficult cases of high public importance may be better decided by the iterative attention of two appellate courts rather than by just one. But if leapfrogging is to be used then we would argue, in line with our contention later in this chapter, that there should be parity between civil and criminal appellate justice, that the procedure should be extended—in exceptional cases, of course—to criminal as well as to civil appeals.

The Criminal Division of the Court of Appeal

Criminal appeals have always been the poor relation in the hierarchy of the appellate system of courts. Before 1960 access to the House of Lords in criminal cases was almost unheard of. When criminal appeals were first established in 1907, the Court of Criminal Appeal was effectively the last port of call. Only with the fiat of the Attorney General could a case reach the final court of appeal. The Attorney General might give his certificate that the case raised 'a point of law of exceptional public importance' and that it was 'in the public interest that a further appeal should be brought'. But the fiat was, predictably, rarely granted.

The fiat procedure was deeply unpopular. It contrasted starkly with the civil procedure which had no certification provision, only a requirement of leave from the Court of Appeal or the House of Lords. There was concern that the fiat was politically oriented, since the Crown was always a party, either as an applicant for the fiat or as respondent to the convicted person aspiring to take his or her case to the final court of appeal. The fiat procedure survived until 1960, by which time the House of Lords began to hear appeals, the notable one being *DPP v Smith*,[39] the Attorney General granting his fiat to the Director of Public Prosecutions seeking to upgrade to murder a manslaughter decision of the Court of Appeal.

The Administration of Justice Act 1960 replicated the certification procedure, to be effected by the Court of Criminal Appeal, amending the formula that the appeal must raise a point of law of *exceptional* public importance, to the lesser requirement that it raised a point of *general* public importance. Armed with the certificate, the aspiring appellant could seek leave either from the Court of Criminal Appeal (after 1966, it became, and has remained as the Court of Appeal (Criminal Division)) or the House of Lords. The result of these new arrangements

[38] [2007] 1 WLR 1400.   [39] [1961] AC 290.

was, predictably, that the number of appeals which the House of Lords had to deal with rose sharply.

The development was not always to the liking of the House of Lords. In *Lawrence v Metropolitan Police Commissioner*[40] Viscount Dilhorne (a former Attorney General) castigated the Court of Appeal for granting leave too readily. He wrote: 'I must confess to some surprise that a certificate for leave to appeal should have been granted in this case. I can say with some confidence that, prior to the Administration of Justice Act 1960, it is most unlikely that the Attorney General's fiat would have been granted for an appeal in such a case as this', the case involving a basic point about the law of theft, both in theory and practice. The retort was for the Court of Appeal readily to certify points of law of general public importance, but routinely to refuse leave to appeal, thus leaving the House of Lords to select the cases it wished to hear (a trend that has also been noted in respect of civil appeals). The policy of restraint, however, did not lead to a reduction in the number of appeals; over the rest of the twentieth century the numbers continued to rise. The relationship between the civil and criminal appellate jurisdiction remained the same. The portfolio of criminal appeals in the House of Lords was left for their Lordships to dine upon *à la carte*, save for the fact that the menu was prescribed by the certification procedure which the Court was disposed to grant where there was a genuine point of law of general public importance.

If the civil appellate system never needed an additional sifting process of prior certification, what was the reason for imposing it in the criminal justice system? It is not easy to discern any plausible reason for maintaining the distinction, save for the historical fact that appellate machinery in the criminal law had developed its separate judicial culture and the judiciary exhibited a disinclination to advocate any change. There was a hint of discrimination against offenders of the criminal law. But the case law emanating from the Lords, up until the 1980s, was displaying distinct disquiet lower down the judicial ladder. A political scientist writing about the jurisprudence of the Law Lords stated: 'By common consent, including at least some of the Law Lords themselves and many of their juniors on the Court of Appeal, the Lords have not shone in their task of controlling and developing the criminal law.'[41] If that reflected too harsh a view, it would be tempered if the writer were reconsidering the state of play in 2008. The more recent output has shown a distinct improvement, although the view from the Lords Justices of Appeal was still silently critical of the Law Lords in certain aspects of the criminal process, particularly where it involved directions to juries.

Outside professional circles, there have been rumblings about the requirement of a certificate, which stands in the way of an unsuccessful appellant in the Court of Appeal (Criminal Division) being allowed even to petition the Law Lords for

---

[40] [1972] AC 626.
[41] D Robertson, *Judicial Discretion in the House of Lords* (Oxford: Clarendon Press, 1998) 109.

leave. The Runciman Commission on Criminal Justice in its 1993 report[42] described the certification procedure as 'unduly restrictive', and recommended its abolition: 'The need to obtain the leave of either the Court of Appeal or the House of Lords before proceeding further is by itself a sufficient filter.' No legislative response was forthcoming, and in his Review of the Criminal Courts in 2001[43] Sir Robin Auld did not allude to this issue in the part of the report dealing with some issues relating to appeals to the House of Lords, although he did recommend the introduction of a form of the leapfrog procedure 'from the Crown Court' to the House of Lords similar to that applicable to civil appeals (see above). But the climate among legal practitioners began to revive the issue, in the light of the Human Rights Act 1998. Although the European Convention on Human Rights does not anywhere specifically establish the right of appeal in either civil or criminal proceedings, appellate rights, civil and criminal, are envisaged as part of the municipal systems of the Member States of the Council of Europe. Article 6 (a fair trial before an independent and impartial tribunal in public) makes no distinction in this respect in relation 'to the determination of his civil rights and obligations or of any criminal charge against him'. Protocol 7 to the Convention, which the UK has not so far ratified, does import appellate rights in criminal matters.

It has also been a disfigurement of the criminal appellate system that the unsuccessful appellant in the intermediate court of appeal should not seek any comfort from a dissentient voice, however important that voice is in the result. Section 1(5) of the Criminal Appeal Act 1907 prevented separate judgments in the Court of Criminal Appeal without the leave of the presiding judge. This rule was perpetuated (though with different wording) in section 2(4) of the Criminal Appeal Act 1966 which excludes separate judgments unless the presiding judge considers that it is convenient that separate judgments should be pronounced. The last instance of separate judgments (which included a notable dissent from the self-granting permission of the presiding judge) was *Commissioners of Customs and Excise v Harz and Power*.[44] The Divisional Court of the Queen's Bench Division (which hears appeals by way of case stated from the magistrates' court) has never excluded separate judgments, even though it may consist usually of only two [or more] judges. The introduction in the Administration of Justice Act 1960 of appeals from the Divisional Court meant that, for the first time, the supervisory jurisdiction of the House of Lords could permeate directly downwards to the work of the magistrates' court, which statistically includes the vast bulk of criminal trials (well over 90 per cent). Yet the disparate modes of appeal upwards have remained stubbornly unchanged. (Certification in criminal cases before the Divisional Court, however, is similarly required as a *sine qua non* to the granting

---

[42] Cm 2263, para 10.79.
[43] <http://www.criminal-courts-review.org.uk>, ch 12, paras 112–17, pp 655–8.
[44] [1967] 1 AC 760. The majority in the Court of Appeal (Thesiger J dissenting) was unanimously upheld in the House of Lords.

of leave to the House of Lords.) Many of the leading House of Lords cases in the criminal jurisdiction have originated in the magistrates' courts, including all extradition cases, of which the House of Lords has heard not a few.[45] *Sweet v Parsley*,[46] for example, started out its forensic life in the magistrates' court. It is not just a plea for judicial tidiness that demands reform of the criminal appellate system, but also an adherence to the principle of equal access to justice.

There is a whiff of change in the procedures and practices to be adopted by the Supreme Court in the shape of a serious proposal to reform the leave process in the criminal appellate system. The senior judges who serve in the Court of Appeal (Criminal Division)—that is, the Lords Justices of Appeal who sit regularly to preside over its sittings, together with the High Court Judges of the Queen's Bench Division and some senior Circuit Judges—are suggesting privately a modification of the existing procedure. On the footing that some important points of law are receiving insufficient attention under the pressure of the present heavy work-load, the Court, in appropriate circumstances, will resolve to adjourn the hearing of an important appeal and reconvene with a court of five judges, the original three members, plus two additional judges.

In one sense, there is nothing abnormal about such a proposal. The Court has no upper limit on the number of judges who comprise the Court. It was the same with the original Court of Criminal Appeal, which once sat with 13 judges, all members of the King's Bench Division who happened to be in London on the relevant day in 1924! They heard argument in *R v Norman*,[47] re-argued after it had initially been argued before five judges.[48] The appeal was decided by 9 to 4, a rare instance of a declared dissent. At that time a small percentage (around 5 per cent) of reported cases was heard by five-judge courts; they were regarded as having a greater authority, but there was no legal foundation for that. A three-judge court had precisely the same powers as a larger-composed court. The most frequent reason for convening a five-judge court was to deal with some tricky precedent which the judges wished to unravel by distinguishing the earlier authorities.[49]

In 2007 the Lord Chief Justice convened a five-judge court to decide whether the Court of Appeal (Criminal Division) was bound by the House of Lords' decision in *R v Smith (Morgan)* which was not followed by the majority decision (6 to 3) of the Judicial Committee of the Privy Council in *Attorney General for Jersey v Holley*. Exceptionally, the five judges said that *Holley* was now the law relating to the interpretation of section 3 of the Homicide Act 1957 on provocation as a partial defence to murder. The Court certified a point of law of general importance but refused leave to appeal to the House of Lords. On a petition by

---

[45] See the latest, *Norris v USA* [2008] 1 AC 920.   [46] [1970] AC 132.
[47] (1924) 18 Cr App R 81.
[48] *The Times*, 15 April 1924 and 29 April 1924, p 9.
[49] The Court of Appeal itself has ruled that it makes no difference (in terms of precedential value) whether its decisions are taken by two-judge, three-judge, or five-judge courts. See *Limb v Union Jack Removals Ltd* [1998] 1 WLR 1354.

the appellant, the Appeal Committee of the House of Lords refused to give leave, thereby, by implication, overruling its previous decision in *Smith (Morgan)*. No reference was made to the power under the Practice Statement of 1966 to overrule a previous decision![50]

The only novelty in the new proposal is the recognition of an important point of law demanding more mature consideration by an enlarged composition. Thus, at a stroke, it is expected, or at least hoped, that there will be fewer cases (particularly those touching on issues that will potentially impact on the procedures of trial courts and their task of simplifying issues for untutored jurors) of which the Law Lords are perceived as having only remote ideas of what goes on in a criminal trial. The theory is that the judiciary in the Court of Appeal (Criminal Division) is more in touch with the system of trial by judge and jury, and will thereby hand down rulings in tune with the dual task of judge and jury. The proposal has a superficial attraction, although there is a suspicion that it is designed to cut off criminal appeals from going to the final court of appeal; moreover, it does not require legislation, only a change of practice dictated by the Lord Chief Justice. But it seems contrary to any liberal concept of criminal justice. It should be discussed in the seminar rooms of our schools of law—and go no further.

The proposal would set the seal on the devalued appellate function in criminal justice. In so doing, it would perpetuate an anomaly. If there is a need for some mechanism for limiting the caseload of the final court of appeal, then a certification procedure might be justified. But it can be justified only if the convicted criminal (and/or indeed the Crown) is equiparated with their counterpart in the civil justice system. To maintain the present distinction is to treat the criminal process as an inferior brand of justice. Whatever the past has inflicted on our legal system, access to justice must be indiscriminate in the full sense of the word.

[50] See ch 9 in this volume.

5

From Appellate Committee to
Supreme Court: A Narrative

*Andrew Le Sueur**

Introduction

This chapter attempts to chart the principal events leading up to the Government's decision on 12 June 2003 to announce that the judicial business of the House of Lords would be transferred to a supreme court, on to the enactment of the Constitutional Reform Act 2005, and the first steps towards practical realisation of the new court. The policy to have a supreme court was, from the outset, inextricably linked—at least in the minds of officials and ministers—with a decision to abolish the office of Lord Chancellor (later revised, following parliamentary pressure in the House of Lords, to retaining a much-reformed post of Lord Chancellor). This chapter is a case study on the British constitution's 'flexible' character and the absence of strong normative controls of the constitutional reform *process*.

An idea whose time had yet not come

The creation of a supreme court did not feature on New Labour's constitutional reform agenda until the second year of the second term of the Blair administration. Indeed, between May 1997 and 12 June 2003—at least in public—the Government was opposed to the idea that the Law Lords might move from the Palace of Westminster.

The years of saying 'no'

There was no mention of the Law Lords or other judiciary-related institutional reforms in the Cook-Maclennan Agreement (a statement of cross-party consensus

* I am grateful to a number of people who took the time to comment on a draft of this chapter. I had two small supporting roles in the events described: as one of the specialist advisers to the House of Commons Constitutional Affairs Committee; and as the specialist adviser to the ad hoc House of Lords Select Committee on the Constitutional Reform Bill.

on constitutional change negotiated between Labour and the Liberal Democrats before the 1997 general election).[1] In January 2000, the report of the Royal Commission on the future of the House of Lords, chaired by Lord Wakeham, concluded that '[t]here is no reason why the second chamber should not continue to exercise the judicial functions of the present House of Lords'[2] and recommended that '[t]he Lords of Appeal in Ordinary should continue to be *ex officio* members of the reformed second chamber and carry out its judicial functions'.[3] Against this background it was unsurprising that the Government's November 2001 White Paper on House of Lords reform was 'committed to maintaining judicial membership of the House of Lords'.[4] Not only was it envisaged at the time that the Law Lords would carry on conducting judicial business as part of a reformed upper chamber, but in a new partly elected/partly appointed House, all the Law Lords 'should continue to be members of the Lords until age 75, whether or not they sit judicially'.[5] Only ten weeks before the announcement from 10 Downing Street on 12 June 2003 of the package of reforms—a supreme court, abolition of the office of Lord Chancellor, a judicial appointments commission for England and Wales—the then Lord Chancellor, Lord Irvine of Lairg, told a House of Commons select committee, '[t]here is a future for everything, but there are no present plans for a new supreme court building.'[6] He assured the MPs that '[w]e have a very, very high quality system which rests on customs, conventions and traditions that are special to us. You should only interfere with them if you are absolutely sure that you can produce a better product as a result.'[7]

Reform ideas simmer on the back burner

While reform of the Law Lords did not make it onto the Government's public policy agenda until mid-2003, proposals for change nonetheless simmered gently on the back burner. In 1999, JUSTICE (the all-party law reform organisation) published a paper by a distinguished working party arguing that the senior judiciary should be separated from the legislature.[8] In 2001, an ESRC-funded research project at UCL's Constitution Unit made a modest contribution to the debate by seeking to

---

[1] *Report of the Joint Consultative Committee on Constitutional Reform* (1997).

[2] *A House for the Future* (Cm 4534) para 9.5.

[3] ibid, recommendation 57.

[4] *The House of Lords—Completing the Reform* (Cm 5291) para 81. The White Paper envisaged a mainly appointed House, with 20 per cent elected members.

[5] ibid.

[6] Evidence to the House of Commons Select Committee on the Lord Chancellor's Department, 2 April 2003 (HC 611-I of 2002–03) Q59. Lord Irvine seemed to assume that, if there were to be a new building, the Lord Chancellor would nonetheless continue to be president of the court, even if ministerial business meant that he could only rarely sit as a judge (Q48).

[7] ibid, Q51.

[8] Referred to in *A House for the Future* (Cm 4534) para 9.1. The working party was chaired by Lord Alexander of Weedon QC, the chairman of JUSTICE who was a former chairman of the Bar Council and a Conservative peer.

identify and evaluate a range of options for change, drawing on the experiences of several other jurisdictions.[9] The most important catalyst, however, was the appointment of Lord Bingham of Cornhill as the Senior Law Lord in 2000. The Law Lords were led for the first time by an advocate for reform[10] (though the Law Lords as a whole remained divided on the supreme court question). In a report made in February 2002, the House of Commons Public Administration Select Committee, persuaded by Lord Bingham's views, recommended that 'the law lords should leave the second chamber at the next general election but one'.[11]

Behind the scenes in government, there were also some people sympathetic to change. Pat McFadden, a policy adviser to Labour leader John Smith and then Tony Blair, has been credited with articulating 'a view widely shared across government' that the three-in-one role of the Lord Chancellor was unsustainable,[12] though it may be more accurate to say that this was a minority view, albeit of some influence.

Accommodation practicalities during the 1990s

As well as principled arguments for reform, there continued to be practical consideration of the adequacy or otherwise of the Law Lords' accommodation and facilities within the Palace of Westminster. At official level, moves were suggested from time to time well before the Labour constitutional reforms. As early as the 1960s, officials considered the possibility of acquiring Middlesex Guildhall for use by the Law Lords, but the idea made no headway.[13] Rosemary Pattenden reports that 'a project in the early 1990s to move the court out of Westminster to Milbank was dropped in the face of fierce resistance from the Law Lords'.[14] The possibility of a move to the old Lord Advocate's Department in Fielden House, Great College Street, was also considered at official level during the 1990s.[15] Speaking in December 2004, Lord Woolf CJ said:[16]

---

[9] A Le Sueur and R Cornes, *The Future of the UK's Highest Courts* (London: UCL Constitution Unit, 2001).

[10] In 'The Evolving Constitution' (JUSTICE Annual Law Lecture, 4 October 2001 published in [2002] EHRLR 1), acknowledging that his views were not shared in Government, Lord Bingham argued that 'institutional structure should reflect practical reality' and that there was an acute shortage of space in the Palace of Westminster: 'Not for the first time, constitutional reform may be the child of administrative necessity.' In 'A New Supreme Court for the United Kingdom' (UCL Constitution Unit Spring Lecture 2002), he pointed to the changing character of the upper chamber, incorporation of Convention rights, and jurisdiction over devolution issues as three reasons why change was now desirable. See also Lord Steyn's Neill Lecture at All Souls College, Oxford, 1 March 2002 (published as 'The Case for a Supreme Court' (2002) 118 LQR 382).

[11] 5th Report of 2001–02: *The Second Chamber: Continuing the Reform* (HC 494) para 153.

[12] A Seldon, *Blair Unbound* (London: Simon & Schuster, 2007) 215.

[13] Private information. See p 38 above.

[14] *English Criminal Appeals 1844–1994: Appeals Against Conviction and Sentence in England and Wales* (Oxford: Clarendon Press, 1996) 311, note 8.

[15] Private information. Fielden House was acquired by the House of Lords in 2001 for office space for peers.

[16] *Hansard*, HL, vol 667 col 1557 (20 December 2004). Lord Woolf was a Lord of Appeal in Ordinary 1992–6.

I can remember a time, I think about nine years ago [that would have been around 1995], when the Law Lords considered moving from this House to occupy what was undoubtedly a prestigious building in Chancery Lane, the then empty Public Records Office. Some of the most senior Law Lords and myself went to inspect the building, and we thought that there would be very real advantages in making the move—for only one reason, that of the improved accommodation. But at the time, because the Law Lords were split, that proposition was taken no further.

The U-turn

As Robert Stevens concedes, 'Piecing together [the] rather bizarre story is not easy.'[17] By mid-2003, an inner circle of senior advisers in Number 10 were converted to the pressing need for reform of the office of Lord Chancellor and (though it did not *have* to follow) the creation of a supreme court. The political context for the plans had little to do with constitutional reform aspirations per se and everything to do with continuing concerns about the future shape and management of two government departments—the Home Office (led at the time by David Blunkett MP) and the Lord Chancellor's Department (LCD) (led by Lord Irvine). The view of the problems from inside Number 10 and the Cabinet Office was that there were 'machinery of government' issues that needed to be addressed. In the preceding years, a culmination of developments had resulted in the LCD 'coming of age' as a major government department, with a large budget and oversight from a Commons select committee.[18] A plan in 2001 to move ministerial responsibility for HM Court Service from the LCD to a department led by Blunkett had been vehemently opposed by Irvine—and those in the senior judiciary who knew about it.[19] Blunkett and Irvine had also clashed on issues of policy and presentation several times. There was also a great deal of inter-departmental rivalry on criminal justice and immigration and asylum.[20]

Over a series of meetings Blair encouraged Lord Irvine—one of his great mentors—to sign up to the whole package of reforms that had by 2003 been developed by the inner circle of advisers, including the replacement of the Lord Chancellorship with a Secretary of State for Justice, and a supreme court. Irvine would not. 'Sacking,' Seldon says, 'was inevitable'.[21] Perhaps so; but after six years

---

[17] *The English Judges: Their Role in the Changing Constitution* (Oxford: Hart, 2005) 155. For early attempts, see A Le Sueur, 'New Labour's (Surprisingly) Quick Steps on the Road to Constitutional Reform' [2003] PL 368; 'Judicial Power in the Changing Constitution', ch 13 in J Jowell and D Oliver (eds), *The Changing Constitution* (Oxford: OUP, 5th edn 2004).

[18] See Select Committee on the Lord Chancellor's Department, Minutes of Evidence 15 July 2003, Q1 (Sir Heyden Phillips).

[19] F Gibbs, 'Is this an unseemly rush to change?' *The Times*, 1 May 2007.

[20] S Pollard, *David Blunkett* (London: Hodder & Stoughton, 2005) 268–71.

[21] Seldon (n 12) 217. There had been press speculation for some months that either Lord Williams of Mostyn or Lord Falconer would replace Lord Irvine after the general election; see eg N Watt and C Dyer, 'A law unto himself' *The Guardian*, 12 February 2003, 2.

as Lord Chancellor it must be open to question whether Irvine's time in office was in any event running out, whatever his views on the package of reforms presented to him.

Whether because there was insufficient time as a result of a Cabinet reshuffle forced on the Prime Minister—who had planned one for July rather than mid-June 2003—or because the reforms were 'so sensitive' because of Lord Irvine's opposition to them,[22] the scheme is said not to have been scrutinised, as would be usual, by a Cabinet sub-committee. Nor, in what must rank among the low points of collective Cabinet government, was there any discussion of the plans in full Cabinet.

D-Day: constitutional reform by press release and briefing journalists

When Alan Milburn MP made his sudden decision in mid-June 2003 to leave front-line politics to spend more time with his young family—he was Secretary of State for Health and a close confidant of Tony Blair—it is unlikely that he foresaw the immediate chain of events that would be unleashed. This was not just a Cabinet reshuffle; this was constitutional reform (though not according to any formal process of the type found in other states which respect constitutional principles). A Cabinet meeting was held on the morning of 12 June 2003, described by Alastair Campbell as 'pretty surreal because everyone knew there was going to be a reshuffle'.[23] The judiciary-related reforms about to be announced by Number 10 were not on the agenda. Lord Irvine stayed after Cabinet and spoke to Blair in private. Campbell recounts:[24]

Previously, TB had argued that he needed to shake things up and put an elected MP in charge of the new department, so when he told Derry it would be Charlie F, he was particularly pissed off. 'You are getting rid of me and putting in another peer, that's not exactly what I expected.' As he left, he looked pretty miserable.

At a press briefing at 5.45pm on 12 June 2003, the Prime Minister's Official Spokesman is recorded as telling journalists: 'Derry Irvine was retiring from government and he would be replaced by Charles Falconer in what will be a new Department for Constitutional Affairs.'[25] (It is a testament to how quickly the new

---

[22] K Ahmed, 'Cabinet ignored over history legal reforms' *The Observer*, 15 June 2003 ('The issue of the departure of Derry Irvine, one of Tony Blair's oldest friends and mentor, was so sensitive that the Prime Minister would allow it to be discussed only by a small circle of his closest advisers. He never even set up a Cabinet sub-committee to scrutinise and improve policies before they were made public, as is customary').

[23] A Campbell and R Stott, *The Blair Years: Extracts from the Alastair Campbell Diaries* (London: Arrow Books, 2008) 704. Campbell was the PM's Director of Communications and Strategy 1997–2003.

[24] ibid.

[25] <http://www.number-10.gov.uk/output/Page3895.asp> (last visited 12 July 2008). The Prime Minister made a Statement to the House of Commons six days later but added nothing of substance on the Supreme Court proposals: *Hansard*, HC, vol 407, col 357 (18 June 2003).

constitutional arrangements have bedded down that it now looks constitutionally surprising, to say the least, that a prime minister had power, for entirely political reasons, to remove the head of the judiciary from office with no more formality than sacking any other government minister.) The spokesman explained that as part of the 'process of modernisation' of the legal system, a supreme court would be established along with a new judicial appointments system in England and Wales. Journalists were told that Lord Falconer of Thoroton would not fulfil the judicial functions of the Lord Chancellor or (as it soon became apparent, erroneously) the role of speaker of the House of Lords, even in a transitional period. Senior officials were said to be 'infuriated' by the inept press briefing.[26] There was a deep irony, apparently unnoticed within government, that reforms justified as aiming to enhance public perceptions of judicial independence were announced as an executive fiat.

The proposal for the supreme court was consequential on the Government's wish to abolish the office of Lord Chancellor. Disentangling the various roles of the Lord Chancellor[27] and creating a judicial appointments commission for England and Wales involved redistribution of power, some of it away from the executive; creating a new supreme court of the type envisaged by the Government did not.[28]

An early judicial shot across the bow of government—reminding officials and ministers who needed to be reminded that the Appellate Committee and the planned supreme court were not merely English institutions—came from Lord Hope of Craighead, one of the two Scottish Law Lords. In a televised interview for BBC Scotland on 27 June 2003, he warned of the need to protect the integrity of the Scottish legal system and said that there were many as yet unanswered questions.[29]

The Government states its (new) case

The House of Commons select committee on the Lord Chancellor's Department, chaired by Alan Beith MP, was quick off the mark. On 30 June 2003 they held an evidence session with the new Secretary of State for Constitutional Affairs/Lord Chancellor, Lord Falconer. Asked about the supreme court proposals, Lord Falconer told the committee that the Government now thought,[30]

...as Lord Bingham and Steyn have argued very persuasively, that you should clearly separate the two [final court of appeal and second chamber]. The difficulties of

---

[26] Seldon (n 12) 217.

[27] Head of the judiciary in England and Wales, an occasional judge, the Speaker of the House of Lords, the ministerial head of a medium-sized department with political responsibility for important and sometimes controversial areas of policy, a lawyer of stature at the heart of government responsible for defending the rule of law and independence of the judiciary.

[28] See K Malleson, ch 6 in A McDonald (ed), *Reinventing Britain: Constitutional Change under New Labour* (London: Politico's, 2007) 145–6.

[29] The video is available at <http://news.bbc.co.uk/1/hi/scotland/3026934.stm> (last visited 12 July 2008).

[30] Minutes of Evidence, 30 June 2003, Q21.

the final Court of Appeal being in the legislature are to some extent revealed by the statement that Lord Bingham made on behalf of the Law Lords in the year 2000 indicating those things they would speak on in the Lords normally, and those things they would not normally speak on in relation to the Lords. The two things they said they would not normally speak on were things involving strong party political dispute or things that they might come to have to decide themselves in court sitting as a judge. Now, since June 2000 one can see a large number of areas where they have spoken where it is very difficult to know precisely where the line should be drawn, far better, we think, that there is clarity between what is the final court and what is the legislature.

The Prime Minister explains

On 8 July 2003, the Prime Minister appeared before the House of Commons Liaison Committee. Alan Beith MP asked about the reforms announced a month earlier. Mr Blair was exasperated at the focus on process rather than substance: 'It has always been a matter of fascination to me that some people who have campaigned for changes over a long period of time then find a reason for being against them when you actually introduce them', he said.[31] He went on: 'I felt it was important that the changes all came together. It is in the very nature of changes to do with the re-shuffle that obviously there is a more restricted discussion. I think it is also fair to say that discussions about these types of changes had been around for a considerable period of time.'[32]

Bad relations between ministers and judiciary

The Government's decision to launch the largest scale judiciary-related reforms since the nineteenth century coincided—and it did seem to be a matter of coincidence rather than causation—with fragile relations between ministers and judges. The tensions related both to issues of substance and to the governance of the courts and would continue for much of the reform period. David Blunkett, the Home Secretary, told one interviewer: 'Frankly I am fed up with having to deal with a situation where Parliament debates issues and the judges overturn them.'[33] Judges criticised the Home Office in particular on sentencing guidelines,[34] on immigration and asylum judgments,[35] and in early

---

[31] Minutes of Evidence, 8 July 2003, Q276. The committee consists of the chairmen of the main Commons select committees. This is the only committee in front of which the Prime Minister routinely appears.

[32] ibid, Q277.   [33] Quoted in *The Independent,* 20 February 2003.

[34] Pollard (n 20) 273.

[35] A Bradley, 'Judicial Independence Under Attack' [2003] PL 397.

2004, on a proposal in the Asylum and Immigration (Treatment of Claimants, etc) Bill which would have ousted the jurisdiction of the courts to supervise the legality of certain asylum decisions.[36] Pollard argues that the combative tone of ministerial denouncements of certain judgments and the judiciary in general was sanctioned at the highest level:[37]

Blair was increasingly annoyed with a judiciary that he felt was one of the most culpable 'forces of conservatism'... Blair himself was considering an all-out attack on the judiciary, and was happy to let his Home Secretary [Blunkett] wade in first. Blair had explicitly asked Blunkett to take on the judiciary, and Blunkett was keen to oblige.

Lord Rawlinson of Ewell, a former Attorney General, told the House of Lords: '... in my 48 consecutive years in one or other of the Houses of Parliament I have never known such antagonism as there is at the moment between the judiciary and the executive'.[38] Lord Goodhart echoed this in a letter to *The Times* that same day: 'There has clearly been a serious breakdown of confidence between the Lord Chancellor and the senior judiciary.' Some commentators suggested that Blunkett's 'determination to go on picking fights with the judiciary has justifiably alarmed many potential supporters of the legislation'.[39]

Consultations on a momentous but modest proposal

From the perspective of Number 10, prior public consultation on the judiciary and departmental reforms before 12 June 2003 was nigh on impossible with Lord Irvine so strongly opposed to them. Senior members of the judiciary, and then only some of them, were given only a few hours' or minutes' notice of the announcement—'it came as an immense shock', Lord Woolf CJ said later.[40] Nor had there been discussion with the Scottish Executive.[41] Lord Hope, one of the Scottish Law Lords, later remarked: 'When the whole issue of the Supreme Court arose last summer it did seem to me that the way it was being presented had overlooked the existence of a separate jurisdiction in Scotland.'[42] Some suggested that a Royal Commission should have been set up to investigate whether there

---

[36] A Le Sueur, 'Three Strikes and it's Out? The UK Government's Strategy to Oust Judicial Review from Immigration and Asylum Decision-making' [2004] PL 224.

[37] Pollard (n 20) 273.

[38] *Hansard*, HL, vol 658, col 1041 (8 March 2004).Tensions had also been high during John Major's administration: A Le Sueur, 'The Judicial Review Debate: From Partnership to Friction' (1996) 31 Government and Opposition 8.

[39] Editorial, 'Day of judgment' *The Guardian,* 8 March 2004.

[40] 'A new constitutional consensus', speech at the University of Hertfordshire, 10 February 2005.

[41] Annabell Ewing MP, *Hansard*, HC, vol 408, col 174 (1 July 2003).

[42] House of Lords Select Committee on the Constitutional Reform Bill, Evidence (HL Paper 121-II 2003–04) Q644.

was a need for change to the Appellate Committee and, if so, the merits of the various options for change.[43]

A series of consultation papers was published by the new Department for Constitutional Affairs (DCA) during July 2003, including a 50-page paper on the Supreme Court which posed 23 questions.[44] It did not seek views on *whether* there should be a supreme court; that had already been decided. It sought views instead on a range of issues most of which would prove to be relatively uncontroversial. The DCA made it plain from the outset that the new court would have no new remedial powers or any greater jurisdiction than the Appellate Committee of the House of Lords. It was envisaged that the new court would be made up of the same judges, and the same type of judges, as the Appellate Committee. The only significant change proposed to the court's jurisdiction, compared to the Appellate Committee, was that it should take over devolution cases from the Judicial Committee of the Privy Council (JCPC)—hardly a radical step as the small number of 'devolution issue' cases were already determined by the Law Lords sitting in the JCPC. This did not however stop some commentators conjuring up the spectre that the new court would seek to enlarge its powers to strike down Acts of Parliament as unconstitutional.[45] On most issues, however, what was proposed was 'intensely conservative'.[46]

The consultation exercise prompted 173 responses, 39 of which were from judges or judicial organisations and 59 from the legal professions.[47] The Law Lords were split on the question (not asked in the consultation paper) of whether there should be a supreme court of the kind envisaged by the DCA: four supported the proposal (Lords Bingham, Steyn, Saville, and Walker) and six opposed it (Lords Nicholls, Hoffmann, Hope, Hutton, Millett, and Rodger).[48] In a separate response, Lord Hobhouse said he was 'in principle in favour of setting up a United Kingdom Supreme Court and therefore would support a properly structured and implemented proposal. However the Consultation Paper does not contain such a proposal'.[49]

Support from the Scottish Executive for the supreme court proposal was essential. The Scottish judiciary and the two Scottish Law Lords (Hope and

---

[43] eg Lord Cullen of Whitekirk and the Senators of the College of Justice (ie the senior judiciary in Scotland) in their response to the DCA consultation.

[44] *Constitutional Reform: A Supreme Court for the United Kingdom* (CP 11/03).

[45] Lord Rees-Mogg (a former editor of *The Times*): House of Lords Select Committee on the Constitutional Reform Bill, Evidence (HL Paper 121-II 2003–04), Q231.

[46] R Stevens, 'Reform in Haste and Repent at Leisure: Iolanthe, the Lord High Executioner and *Brave New World*' ch 1 in D Morgan (ed), *Constitutional Innovation: The Creation of a Supreme Court for the United Kingdom* (London: LexisNexis Butterworths, 2004) 33.

[47] <http://www.dca.gov.uk/consult/supremecourt/scresp.htm> (last visited 12 July 2008).

[48] <http://www.dca.gov.uk/consult/supremecourt/responses/sc164.pdf> (last visited 12 July 2008). The view of Lord Scott of Foscote is not recorded. Baroness Hale of Richmond, a supporter of the principle of a supreme court, replaced Lord Millett on his retirement in January 2004.

[49] <http://www.dca.gov.uk/consult/supremecourt/responses/sc070.pdf> (last visited 12 July 2008).

Rodger) were not supporters of change. Questions of the compatibility of the proposal with Article XIX of the Act of Union and the Claim of Right were raised. The Scottish Nationalist Party—then still some years away from power—questioned the need for Scottish appeals to be dealt with by a court in London. The Scottish Executive, then a Labour-Liberal Democrat coalition, welcomed the proposals:[50] '... the right of appeal to the House of Lords on civil matters has served the Scottish justice system well,' they said, and 'the UK Supreme Court is the appropriate forum for final determination of all [devolution] matters'.

The phoney war

There was a great deal of interest and concern in Parliament about all aspects of the DCA's judiciary-related reforms. In both Houses the Liberal Democrats supported the thrust of the Government's proposals. The Conservatives broadly supported the plans to reform the judicial appointments system in England and Wales but were strongly opposed to the abolition of the Lord Chancellor (which was portrayed as undermining practical arrangements for the protection of the rule of law) and (for largely pragmatic reasons related to the cost of the project) the creation of a supreme court.

The 2003–5 parliamentary session: the Loyal Address in the Lords

The start of each parliamentary session involves several days of wide-ranging debate on the Government's legislative programme that has just been announced in the Queen's Speech at the State Opening of Parliament. The motion debated is a formal one moved by the Government: 'Most Gracious Sovereign—We, Your Majesty's most dutiful and loyal subjects, the Lords Spiritual and Temporal in Parliament assembled, beg leave to thank Your Majesty for the most gracious Speech which Your Majesty has addressed to both Houses of Parliament.' The Queen's Speech included the Constitutional Reform Bill—and also a bill to remove the remaining 92 hereditary peers from the Lords. It is unusual for the Opposition to move an amendment to the motion, but this year they did. Lord Strathclyde, for the Conservatives, moved:[51]

...at the end of the Address to insert 'but regrets the decision of Your Majesty's Government to abandon the search for cross-party consensus on constitutional reform and to launch unilateral proposals for changes to this House that could gravely weaken

---

[50] <http://www.dca.gov.uk/consult/supremecourt/responses/sc138.pdf> (last visited 12 July 2008).
[51] *Hansard*, HL, vol 667, col 193 (2 December 2004).

the House; and calls on Your Majesty's Government to respect the formal undertakings given to this House, to withdraw their current proposals and to undertake meaningful consultation with Parliament and the senior judiciary before proceeding with legislation'.

In a symbolic shot across the Government's bows, the Conservative amendment was carried 188 votes to 108—the first time a government had been defeated on such a procedure since 1914.

Commons Constitutional Affairs Committee report

In November 2003, Alan Beith's Constitutional Affairs Committee (as it was now called) launched a major inquiry into the reforms, with seven evidence sessions. In one of them Lord Lloyd of Berwick, a Lord of Appeal in Ordinary 1993–9, argued, 'we have a Supreme Court in all but name at the moment. Everybody accepts that the Law Lords are completely independent of politics' and that 'the cost of setting up a brand new Supreme Court is out of all proportion to the non-existent benefit which is purely a theoretical one' to do with the separation of powers, which he did not accept was a principle of the British constitution.[52] Lord Lloyd was to become a key player in the opposition to the reforms. The committee's report, published on 3 February 2004, recorded that 'Both those in favour of the change and those against were united in emphasising that the present system was one which worked. The arguments for change were about principle and perception.'[53] The committee recommended that '[t]he Constitutional Reform Bill is a clear candidate for examination in draft'[54]—meaning that there should be a period of pre-legislative scrutiny to enable a parliamentary committee to take expert evidence on the proposals outlined in a draft bill before the Government formally introduced a bill to start the legislative process.

The Concordat

Six months on from the announcement by Number 10, Lord Falconer announced on 26 January 2004 that agreement[55] had been reached with Lord Woolf CJ on the principles and practices relating to the transfer of functions from the Lord Chancellor.[56] But while that agreement was a significant milestone, its focus was on England and Wales and it said nothing about the supreme court proposal.

---

[52] Minutes of evidence, 27 November 2003, QQ 204, 227, 228 (HC 48-II of 2003–04).
[53] *Judicial Appointments and a Supreme Court (Court of Final Appeal)* (HC 48-I of 2003–04) para 23.
[54] ibid, para 188.
[55] <http://www.dca.gov.uk/consult/lcoffice/judiciary.htm> (last visited 12 July 2008).
[56] *Hansard*, HL, vol 657, col 1211 (12 February 2004).

Mistakes admitted, detailed proposals announced

On 3 February 2004, the Prime Minister appeared before the House of Commons Liaison Committee again. He conceded that combining constitutional reforms with a Cabinet reshuffle some eight months previously had not been a good idea: 'I think we could have in retrospect—this is entirely my responsibility —done it better.'[57] The pace was quickening. On 9 February 2004, Lord Falconer made an oral statement to the House of Lords on the proposed supreme court. He reminded the House that 'the key objective is to achieve a full and transparent separation between the judiciary and the legislature'.[58] He went on to outline the main features of the court that would be contained in the forthcoming Constitutional Reform Bill. Lord Kingsland, from the Conservative front bench, argued that the scheme 'undermines the strength of the judiciary as an arm of the constitution in this country'[59] and called for the impending bill to be published in draft to allow detailed scrutiny.

'Take note' debate in the Lords

The first full debate on the detailed proposals—the bill was still not published— was in the House of Lords on 12 February 2004. Only the most optimistic minister could read it as an encouraging start to the next phase. Lord Kingsland again pressed for a draft bill, though Lord Lester of Herne Hill for the Liberal Democrats expressed support for the supreme court plans. The tone of the rest of the debate was remarkable for being overwhelmingly critical of the proposals and for the contributions from the senior judiciary (whose right to speak in the Lords would be removed by the bill).

Lord Nicholls of Birkenhead—a serving Law Lord—described the plan to abolish the Appellate Committee as 'put forward with the best of intentions' but 'misguided' and 'harmful'.[60] Lord Cullen of Whitekirk—the head of the Scottish judiciary—followed, making his maiden speech in the House; he said that his fellow judges in Scotland had misgivings about the proposal for a supreme court and sought assurance that the bill would contain safeguards about the independence of Scots law.[61] Lord Hoffmann—a serving Law Lord—also spoke, lamenting that '[i]t is sad that a great constitutional change should be adopted as a quick fix for personal squabbles in the Cabinet' (referring to the departure of Lord Irvine).[62] Lord Hobhouse—another Law Lord—urged that the priority of Government should be to ensure adequate resources for existing courts.[63] Lord Woolf CJ said, 'the question of whether we have a Supreme Court is quite independent of any other reforms' and confessed that he did 'not regard the

---

[57] Tony Blair, Minutes of Evidence, Liaison Committee, 3 February 2004 (HC 310-I, 2003–04).
[58] *Hansard*, HL, vol 657, col 927 (9 February 2004).
[59] ibid, col 933.   [60] *Hansard*, HL, vol 657, col 1228 (12 February 2004).
[61] ibid, col 1231.   [62] ibid, col 1259.   [63] ibid, col 1266.

question of a new building for the Supreme Court as a burning issue'.[64] Lord Millett—who had retired as a Law Lord a month earlier—explained that he had 'long advocated the creation of a Supreme Court' but was dismayed by the Government's proposals. There were, he said, 'compelling grounds for a physical move' but there was a risk that much of value in the current arrangements might be lost. His support for a supreme court was 'heavily conditional' on suitable accommodation being found, which he said should be near the Royal Courts of Justice and Inns of Court.[65] Lord Hope—a Law Lord—took a different view of facilities: lack of space or assistance did not 'in the least' inhibit his work. He described his practice 'quite often of sitting and listening to debates to enable myself to keep in touch with ideas and events' and expressed concern about the cost of a new court.[66] Lord Lloyd, Lord Donaldson of Lymington, and Lord Mackay of Clashfern also spoke.

Lord Bingham, true to his self-denying ordinance, did not take part; nor did Lord Steyn. Also missing from the list of speakers (though he was in the chamber) was Lord Irvine.

The Constitutional Reform Bill introduced in the Lords

As we have noted, calls for the Bill to be published in draft followed by a period of pre-legislative scrutiny had been made by the all-party Commons Constitutional Affairs Committee and by the Conservatives in the Lords. The Government decided not to heed these calls and introduced the Bill into the House of Lords on 24 February 2004. By this stage, nobody could imagine that this was going to be constitutional reform by consensus. There was never any doubt the Bill would secure approval in the Commons: the Government had a majority of 165 over all other parties, and the central features of the proposals were supported by the Liberal Democrats. But in the Lords, the terrain was altogether more difficult. The Government had no overall majority and many of the non-party affiliated cross-benchers—including Lord Lloyd of Berwick and other retired judges—had already made clear their scepticism or hostility to the package of reforms. Although by introducing the bill to the Lords rather than the Commons the Government precluded the use of the Parliament Acts to present the Bill for Royal Assent in the face of sustained Lords' opposition,[67] the tactical decision was taken to start in the Lords; a head of steam opposed to the bill had already built up there that would only be exacerbated if the Bill were placed in the Commons first.

---

[64] ibid, col 1291.
[65] ibid, col 1294. In the Law Lords' response to the DCA consultation paper, Lord Millett had been identified as against the proposals.
[66] ibid, cols 1299–1300.
[67] The Government was contemplating using the Parliament Acts to force through the Hunting Bill and for a bill (which never materialised) to remove the remaining 92 hereditary peers.

A few days before the Constitutional Reform Bill was due to start its passage through the House of Lords, Lord Woolf CJ in a lecture at Cambridge University made clear his views of the issues at stake. 'We cannot,' he told his audience, 'take the continued individual and collective independence of the judiciary for granted.'[68] Much of the speech focused on the role of the Lord Chancellor, and Lord Woolf CJ said, '. . . since the 12 June, I have personally, with reluctance, joined those who say the Lord Chancellor can no longer play his traditional role as Head of the Judiciary unless his responsibilities are significantly reduced'. On the plans for a new court, he said, referring to its role as 'subordinate to the will of Parliament as expressed in legislation' that '[a]mong the Supreme Courts of the world, our Supreme Court will, because of its more limited role, be a poor relation. We will be exchanging a first class Final Court of Appeal for a second class Supreme Court.' He explained that he was not 'wholly hostile to the idea of a new Supreme Court' but he favoured deferring a decision until a building had been found and decisions had been taken as to whether or not the House of Lords (in its legislative capacity) was to be wholly or substantially elected. For ministers and officials, this was an inauspicious start. Also hovering in the ether were continuing concerns about clause 11 of the Asylum and Immigration (Treatment of Claimants etc) Bill, due to be debated in the Lords the following week.[69]

Second reading in the Lords

A second reading debate offers the House an opportunity to consider the general policy of a Bill. At the Bill's second reading debate on 8 March 2004, the Government was faced with an almost unprecedented procedural motion in the name of Lord Lloyd of Berwick, supported by the Conservatives,[70] which sought to commit the Bill to an ad hoc select committee with powers to take evidence (rather than, as normal in the Lords, proceed to the next stage of scrutiny in the form of a Committee of the Whole House).[71] Attempts by the Government Chief Whip to dissuade him from doing so had failed.[72] The Government was opposed to this as it would involve delay and require the Bill to 'carry over' into the next parliamentary session. In interviews to the press, Peter Hain MP, Leader of the

---

[68] 'The Rule of Law and a Change in the Constitution', Squire Centenary Lecture, 3 March 2004 (published in *The Times* that day and later in [2004] CLJ 317).

[69] See above. The Government backed down on the ouster clause.

[70] Lord Strathclyde, Opposition Leader in the Lords, had some weeks earlier called for a joint committee of peers and MPs to review the judiciary-related proposals and the plan to remove the remaining 92 hereditary peers: B Russell, 'Lords threaten to reduce Labour programme to a "shambles"' *The Independent*, 12 January 2004.

[71] R Walters, 'A Procedural Throwback: The Select Committee on the Constitutional Reform Bill (HL)' (2005) 73 The Table 11.

[72] *Hansard*, HL, vol 658, cols 998–9 (8 March 2004). Lord Grocott explained to Lord Lloyd that 'it would make it extremely difficult for business managers such as myself to argue with other colleagues in government that major legislation should start in this House if the effect [of the Lloyd proposal] were to delay it or even prevent it proceeding to the other Chamber'.

House of Commons, made the Government's position plain: 'What peers are proposing is completely undemocratic. We cannot allow it to happen.'[73] Commentators were divided on the merits of the Bill and the tactics to delay it. A leader in *The Times* opined that 'the principles at the core of this Bill are commendable' and suggested that '[m]uch of the opposition to the Bill is based on sentimental traditionalism or short-term opportunism'.[74]

Opening the debate, Lord Falconer argued 'that the time has come to reflect the reality of our constitutional arrangements. The Law Lords are appointed to the final Court of Appeal, not the legislature. They are judges.'[75] The Bill, he said, 'seeks to make our constitution more transparent and logical by creating at the apex of the judicial systems a Supreme Court which is visibly independent of the legislature'.[76] For the Conservatives, Lord Kingsland expressed concern that the Bill proposed to give a Secretary of State 'quite extensive veto powers over the selection of judges in the Supreme Court'[77] and dismissed the new supreme court as 'pointless and extravagant'.[78] For the Liberal Democrats, Lord Lester opposed committing the Bill to a select committee; he welcomed the thrust of the reforms contained in the Bill but expressed concerns about the scope for political interference in the supreme court appointments process; he argued that the selection commission should provide only one name rather than a short list and that he was against a further round of consultation with 'politicians in Scotland, Northern Ireland and Wales, and with secret soundings by Ministers with senior judges'.[79]

Lord Lloyd—a self-avowed 'constitutional realist' rather than a 'purist'[80]—followed, reminding the House of the Government's commitment, as part of the modernisation of Parliament, to publish major Bills in draft and to permit pre-legislative scrutiny.[81] He gave two examples of how a select committee would assist: it would enable evidence to be gathered about the costs of creating a supreme court; and it would enable a cost/benefit analysis. He sought to reassure peers on the Liberal Democrat benches that the proposal to commit the Bill to a select committee was not intended to wreck the Bill. Simon Hoggart in *The Guardian* wrote: 'In his quiet, not quite bumbling way, he was coruscating about the government, and the way it was proceeding not on the basis of fact, but on what he called "a double perception"; a perception of what the public perception might be'—a phrase borrowed from Lord Norton of Louth (a Conservative peer and professor of government) to emphasise the absence of any hard evidence that the public were confused by having the highest court in the land situated in Parliament.[82]

[73] P Webster, 'Labour vows to defeat Lords in power struggle' *The Times*, 8 March 2004.

[74] 'Law and diplomacy: a split decision on the details of legal reform' *The Times*, 26 February 2004. The editorial added, anticipating by some months a Conservative proposal: 'A separation of powers does not have to involve a physical separation of powers and a plush new residence.'

[75] *Hansard*, HL, vol 658, col 981 (8 March 2004).

[76] ibid, col 982.   [77] ibid, col 985.   [78] ibid, col 986.   [79] ibid, col 992.

[80] ibid, col 996.   [81] ibid, col 994.

[82] 'When a crisis is just a few silly jokes' *The Guardian*, 9 March 2004.

Lord Carter (a former Labour chief whip in the Commons) argued that the Lloyd proposal was 'completely unprecedented and the procedure of such a committee is singularly inappropriate for the consideration of a major Bill'.[83] He warned that as the question of the select committee procedure has become a matter of party political controversy 'the Law Lords should not participate or vote on this amendment or indeed take part in proceedings on the Bill'[84] in line with Lord Bingham's June 2000 statement.[85] Nor, he added, should retired Law Lords who were still eligible to sit. He stated that if the Lloyd proposal was carried 'the Government would be acting entirely properly and well within their rights if they withdrew the Bill and immediately introduced a No. 2 Bill in the Commons. In that event, this House would lose the advantage of being the first House to consider the Bill, which would then, of course, become subject to the Parliament Acts.'[86] The House of Lords, he cautioned, 'should not allow itself to become party to a confrontation between some elements of the judiciary and the Government'.[87]

Lord Woolf CJ spoke in favour of the Bill proceeding in the normal way, if only to ensure that provisions on judicial appointments in England and Wales, which were 'urgently necessary', could be brought into force without delay. With the ink barely dry on the concordat, he was concerned that the Bill might not pass.[88] Returning to a theme introduced in his Cambridge lecture a week earlier, he said '. . . the position as to the Supreme Court is different'. The judiciary of England and Wales 'has no agreed position that I can report to the House' and he was himself 'ambivalent on the subject'. The idea of hiving off supreme court reform to a different and later Bill was not, however, one that would ever be attractive to the Government.

The second reading debate was, as Lord Goodhart remarked in his winding-up speech, 'a long and, frankly, repetitive debate',[89] with 46 speeches, ending at 11.30pm. Lord Irvine did not speak, but he did vote with the Government against the Lloyd proposal. Lord Hoffmann, then a serving Law Lord, voted for the proposal—the only full-time judge to vote.[90] At the end of the nine-hour debate, the Lloyd amendment was carried by 216 votes to 183. Ministers were said to be 'taken aback by the defeat, believing that support from the Liberal Democrat peers would see them through'.[91]

---

[83] *Hansard*, HL, vol 658, col 999 (8 March 2004). Lord Carter went on to become a member of the select committee.
[84] ibid col 1000.   [85] See further ch 9 in this volume.   [86] ibid, col 1002.
[87] ibid, col 1003.   [88] ibid, col 1005.   [89] ibid, col 1098.
[90] This did not go unnoticed. Peter Riddell described his vote as 'a wholly indefensible political action' and suggested, 'Not for the first time he should take lessons on conflict of interest' *The Times*, 10 March 2004.
[91] P Webster, 'Ministers in deal with Tories after Lords sabotage' *The Times*, 10 March 2004. The Conservatives 'mounted a formidable whipping operation'.

Lords Select Committee on the Bill: an unusual step

Although there had been talk of the Government withdrawing the Bill, this was probably never seriously on the cards. Agreement through 'the usual channels' was reached with the Conservatives: the Bill would go to a select committee, but subject to understandings: the Bill would not be 'killed off'; the select committee would work to a strict timetable of three months; and the Bill would be 'carried over' into the following parliamentary session.[92]

During the second reading debate Lord Carter had warned: 'You cannot give pre-legislative scrutiny to a substantive Bill'.[93] Yet this is what the unusual procedural development attempted, in a way, to do.[94] Given the procedural novelty of referring the Bill to a select committee, it is plausible to suggest that few members of the House of Lords realised that the committee would have powers to amend the Bill.

The 16 members of the committee, broadly reflecting the party composition of the House of Lords as a whole, consisted of five Labour,[95] five Conservative,[96] three Liberal Democrat,[97] and three crossbenchers.[98] They had considerable experience of government (six were former cabinet ministers; one a former chief whip) and law (seven had some background in practice). In stark contrast to the arrangements in other select committees, the committee included a member of the Executive in the form of Lord Falconer—a necessity as a minister was needed to be in charge of what was a 'real' not merely a draft Bill.

The committee met twice a week between 24 March and 24 June 2004, for meetings of two to three hours. The first phase of its work was evidence-taking, hearing from 32 witnesses in public sessions and receiving written evidence from more than 80 others. In a second phase, the committee held deliberative meetings in private and agreed a report.[99] In the final phase of the committee's work, the Bill was (behind closed doors) considered clause by clause. Over 400 amendments

---

[92] ibid.   [93] *Hansard*, HL, vol 658, col 1103 (8 March 2004).

[94] From the perspective of 2008, the committee does not seem so unusual. Since 2006, bills in the House of Commons have been committed to Public Bill Committees for their clause-by-clause scrutiny; these committees have power to take evidence and amend the bill.

[95] The chairman, Lord Richard (a barrister, former minister, and EU Commissioner); Lord Falconer; Lord Carter; Lord Elder (a former Labour Party adviser); Baroness Gibson of Market Rasen (with a background in trades unions).

[96] Lord Carlisle of Bucklow (formerly Mark Carlisle MP and Secretary of State for Education and Science); Lord Howe of Aberavon (formerly Geoffrey Howe QC, MP, successively Chancellor of the Exchequer, Foreign Secretary, Leader of the House of Commons); Lord Kingsland (a QC and the shadow Lord Chancellor); Lord Crickhowell (formerly Nicholas Edwards MP); and Lord Windlesham (a former minister and Leader of the House of Lords).

[97] Lord Holme of Cheltenham (chairman of the House of Lords Constitution Committee); Lord Goodhart (a QC); and Lord Maclennan of Rogart (formerly Robert Maclennan MP).

[98] Viscount Bledisloe (in professional life Christopher Bathurst QC, a commercial silk); Lord Craig of Radley (a former Chief of Defence Staff); and Lord Lloyd of Berwick.

[99] HL Paper No 125-I (2003–04).

were made, all of them with government support. Some were drafting points; others the result of the policy work that continued within the DCA.

What did the select committee achieve? On the two large issues—abolition of the office of Lord Chancellor and creation of the supreme court—the committee was more or less evenly divided. In any event, the committee recognised that these were matters for the House as a whole to determine. Lord Lloyd had assured the House that the point of the committee would not be to 'wreck' the Bill and any attempt to press those issues in committee would on that basis have been inappropriate. Lord Lloyd had hoped that the committee would gather evidence of the costs of a supreme court, but on this front, the committee managed to make little progress as a suitable site had not yet been agreed. One of the most significant aspects debated was how the new court might be given greater budgetary and administrative independence from central government; the Government agreed to bring forward amendments when the Bill returned to the chamber.

Views on the success of the committee were mixed. Michael Zander, writing in the *New Law Journal,* was unimpressed:[100]

Unsurprisingly, the Select Committee failed to agree on the main controversial topics. The arguments for and against are set out, but with no analysis or discussion of their merits. Where the Select Committee failed to agree, that fact is baldly stated without any indication as to which individual members took what position, nor even of the numbers holding different views.

For the Government, Lord Falconer made a more charitable assessment, conceding that '[t]he committee made real progress in improving the Bill'.[101] Shortly before the select committee reported, he told *The Times*: 'It has been difficult, challenging—but incredibly worthwhile.'[102] There was clearly relief within government that, after the initial focus on the inept way the plans had been announced and the procedural wrangles when the Bill was introduced, attention was now firmly on the substance of the proposals. Lord Woolf CJ also praised the work of the select committee.[103]

All-clear from the Scottish Parliament

At the same time as the Lords select committee, the Scottish Parliament Justice 2 Committee was carrying out scrutiny of the supreme court proposals in the Bill. In their report, Justice 2 agreed with the Government's case for establishing a supreme court; agreed that no leave requirement should be introduced for Scottish civil cases; supported a proposed amendment designed to safeguard the

---

[100] 'Constitutional Reform Debate Rumbles On' (2004) 154 NLJ 1074.
[101] *Hansard*, HL, vol 663, col 1184 (13 July 2004).
[102] F Gibb, 'The cheerful chappie who rolls on undeflated' *The Times,* 22 June 2004.
[103] 'A New Constitutional Consensus', speech at the University of Hertfordshire, 10 February 2005. The House of Lords had been a 'remarkably effective revising chamber' and the select committee 'undoubtedly resulted in improvements'.

separate identity of Scots law; and recommended that in Scottish devolution cases there 'should be an absolute majority' of Scottish judges and that it was desirable for 'a majority of Scottish judges in all Scottish cases'.[104]

Bill recommitted to Committee of the Whole House

On 13 July 2004, the bill returned to the floor of the House of Lords from the select committee. Lord Richard explained what had been achieved by the select committee on the supreme court and other issues.[105] Lord Kingsland for the Conservatives explained that his party now accepted 'the new architecture of the Bill' in relation to the Lord Chancellor: they accepted he should be a minister and not a judge, but in an occasionally ill-tempered debate they continued to press for 'the Lord Chancellor' rather than 'the Secretary of State' as the minister in the Bill.

The summer recess intervened with no further debate on the supreme court. The Bill reached the final day of its committee stage in the Lords on 11 October 2004. Lord Lloyd moved a group of amendments, supported by cross-bencher Viscount Bledisloe, and Conservatives Lord Kingsland and Lord Norton, that represented a further attempt to block the creation of the supreme court (though it would have kept the appointments process outlined in the Bill for the Law Lords).[106] Lord Goodhart for the Liberal Democrats dismissed them as 'wrecking amendments'.[107] In his last speech to the House, Lord Cooke of Thorndon, the great New Zealand judge who sat from time to time as a Law Lord, supported the amendments. He argued that '[t]he separation of powers is said to lie behind the Bill—a doctrine that is foreign to the British constitution and is in any case undermined by the Bill itself. The genesis of the Bill and such drive as has impelled it has come from the executive.'[108] Lord Hope's unplanned contribution to the debate focused on accommodation; he doubted that the two prime contenders—Somerset House and Middlesex Guildhall—were appropriate.[109] Lord Lloyd withdrew the amendments, saying '. . . before we can consider sensibly the question of the supreme court on Report [the next stage of the legislative process], we must have a firm decision on where it is going to be accommodated and what it is going to cost'.[110]

Joint Committee on Human Rights reports

On 17 November 2004 the Joint Committee on Human Rights reported on the bill, stating:[111]

We therefore conclude that, although Article 6 does not per se require the abolition of the Appellate Committee of the House of Lords and the creation of a new and separate

---

[104] Justice 2 Committee, 4th Report, 2004 (Session 2), Constitutional Reform Bill, SP Paper 163.
[105] *Hansard*, HL, vol 663, col 1140 (13 July 2004).
[106] *Hansard*, HL, vol 665, col 55 (11 October 2004).   [107] ibid, col 64.
[108] ibid, col 67.   [109] ibid, cols 67–8.   [110] ibid, col 76.
[111] 21st Report of 2003–04 (HL 210/HC 1282), para 1.70.

Supreme Court, such a step would make it much less likely that violations of Article 6(1) will occur in practice, or that individual members of the highest court will have to recuse themselves from hearing particular appeals because of their involvement in some relevant way in their legislative capacity.

The new 2004–5 parliamentary session starts: report stage in the Lords

As negotiated by the parties, the Constitutional Reform Bill was 'carried over' to the new session so that it could continue where it had left off.[112] The Bill had its report stage debate on 7 December 2004. There was consensus that the Bill should have an opening clause on the Lord Chancellor's role in relation to the rule of law, though the precise scope of that clause was not yet agreed.[113] Lord Lloyd pressed an amendment that '[n]o person is qualified to be Lord Chancellor unless he is a member of the House of Lords'.[114] In a wide-ranging speech, Lord Woolf CJ continued to express concern that the Bill might not reach the statute book.[115] He praised the Bill as 'a piece of great reforming legislation. If it is given life, it will rank in importance with the great constitutional instruments of the past.' On the question of the supreme court, he acknowledged that he had not personally 'been vocal in support' but he now recognised that 'it would have very real advantages over the Appellate Committee. It would make our final court of appeal more accessible to the public; it would be more in accord with the separation of powers; and its role would be more understandable to the public.'[116] He explained that his previous reservations were 'primarily financial', concerning the stature of the building for the new court and whether it would take money away from the existing courts. He announced that 'subject to there being a suitable sunrise clause,' the supreme court proposal 'will have my support and that of the Judges' Council'.[117] Lord Lloyd's amendment, requiring the Lord Chancellor to be a member of the Lords not the Commons, was carried by 229 to 206. A Conservative amendment requiring him to be a lawyer was carried 215 to 175.

The report stage debate continued on 14 December 2004. At 9.30pm the previous evening, the Lord Chancellor had made a formal written statement on the choice of Middlesex Guildhall and the anticipated capital costs.[118] Lord Lloyd moved an amendment that once more sought to retain the Law Lords ('The House of Lords, when exercising its appellate jurisdiction, is the Supreme Court of the United Kingdom') and that the Lords of Appeal in Ordinary shall be

---

[112] *Hansard*, HL, vol 667, col 23 (24 November 2004).

[113] *Hansard*, HL, vol 667, col 738 (7 December 2004). The Government's amendment sought to stress that the Lord Chancellor's duty was 'not cognisable in law'.

[114] ibid, col 749.   [115] ibid, col 759.   [116] ibid, col 759.

[117] ibid, col 758. A 'sunrise clause' prevents specified sections of an Act of Parliament from being brought into force until certain circumstances are satisfied.

[118] *Hansard*, HL, vol 667, col WS71 (14 December 2004).

appointed in accordance with the provisions set out in the Bill.[119] He was clearly disappointed that Lord Woolf CJ and the Judges' Council now supported a supreme court. He argued that the Judges' Council should not be directly concerned with whether a supreme court was established and suggested that, with the exception of Lord Woolf CJ and Lord Phillips, members of the Judges' Council 'can have little idea of what the work of the Law Lords actually involves'.[120] Lord Lloyd reminded the House of the Law Lords' doubts about the suitability of Middlesex Guildhall and the considerable capital costs of £32.5 million. Lord Howe of Aberavon spoke to a similar amendment, which provided that the supreme court shall be 'situated within the House of Lords, but not entitled to use the chamber of the House of Lords for the hearing of appeals or the giving of judgments'.[121] After two hours of debate, Lord Lloyd withdrew his amendment, once again avoiding a vote—saying that the Government had so far failed to provide the House with sufficient information about the costs of refurbishing Middlesex Guildhall.

The Government brought forward amendments, fulfilling commitments made to the select committee, to give greater detail to the governance arrangements for the supreme court and to increase the independence of the court in this respect.[122] These were agreed without a division, as were government amendments on fees, the appointments process, and an annual report. Finally, the House agreed a 'sunrise clause', under which the supreme court provisions would not be brought into force 'unless the Minister is satisfied that the supreme court will at that time be provided with accommodation in accordance with written plans that he has approved' and that the Law Lords are satisfied with those plans.[123]

Third reading in the Lords

On 20 December 2004, with the Christmas recess imminent, the Bill had its third reading debate. The Government tabled 14 pages of amendments. A new clause 1 on the Lord Chancellor's role in relation to rule of law was agreed (and is s 1 of the Constitutional Reform Act 2005).

Lord Lloyd returned to his amendment, withdrawn after lengthy debate at report stage, seeking to allow the Law Lords, sitting as the supreme court, to remain in the House of Lords.[124] Lord Nicholls of Birkenhead, the Second Senior Law Lord, rose to speak. He argued that the current accommodation and secretarial assistance provided to the Law Lords was satisfactory. He said that while the site of the Middlesex Guildhall is superb 'unhappily the same cannot be said of the building itself'.[125] He rejected the notion that any principle of separation of powers or Article 6 of the European Convention on Human Rights required the creation of a supreme court. Lord Woolf CJ followed, explaining why he had

---

[119] ibid, col 1180.   [120] ibid, col 1182.   [121] ibid, col 1194.
[122] ibid, col 1236.   [123] ibid, col 1322.
[124] *Hansard*, HL, vol 667, col 1548 (20 December 2004).   [125] ibid, col 1553.

come to change his view on the matter.[126] He reminded the House that the Law Lords were split and that those who supported a supreme court 'would not think it right to get involved in any way in the debate taking place, and so we have not heard from them'. Referring to the impending hearing in *R (Jackson) Attorney General* (on the Hunting Act and the scope of the Parliament Acts),[127] Lord Woolf CJ said: 'A few years back, litigation of that kind would simply never have been anticipated.' Half the Law Lords, he said, felt uneasy about being members of the House of Lords. He urged the House to vote in favour of the supreme court. Lord Lloyd's last ditch attempt to retain the Law Lords failed. His amendment was lost by 199 votes to 133, as was a Conservative 'half-way house' amendment that would have located the supreme court in the Palace of Westminster.

An approach from the Home Secretary

A week before the third reading debate in December 2004, the Law Lords—sitting as a panel of nine—handed down their judgment in *A v Secretary of State for the Home Department*.[128] In one of the most significant decisions under the Human Rights Act 1998, they held that provisions of the Anti-terrorism, Crime and Security Act 2001, giving the Home Secretary power to detain foreign nationals suspected of terrorism without charge or trial, were incompatible with Convention rights. It was a blow to the Government. Charles Clarke MP, who had just taken over as Home Secretary following David Blunkett's resignation, sought, through an intermediary, to have a confidential meeting with the Law Lords as the Government considered how to respond to the declaration of incompatibility.[129] Lord Bingham declined to meet, taking the view that it would be constitutionally inappropriate to do so.[130] Mr Clarke was perplexed and aggrieved by the rebuff.[131] Despite the change of Home Secretary, the gulf of understanding between Government and the judiciary was as wide as ever.

The Bill goes to the Commons

The Bill had its second reading debate in the House of Commons on 17 January 2005. By then speculation was mounting that a general election would be called

---

[126] ibid, col 1556.   [127] [2006] 1 AC 262.   [128] [2005] 2 AC 68.

[129] A regime of 'control orders' was introduced by the Terrorism Act 2005.

[130] J Rozenberg, 'Not the usual channels' *The Daily Telegraph*, 10 November 2005, reporting on an interview with Lord Bingham.

[131] Eighteen months later, then out of office, Mr Clarke wrote, 'One of my depressing experiences as Home Secretary was the outright refusal of any of the Law Lords to discuss the principles behind these matters in any forum, private or public, formal or informal. That attitude has to change', *Evening Standard*, 3 July 2006. Mr Clarke subsequently explained his frustrations to the House of Lords Constitution Committee: see 6th Report of 2006–07, *Relations between the Executive, the Judiciary and Parliament* (HL Paper 151) para 93.

by the Prime Minister in May, so pressure was on for the Bill to complete all its stages in time.[132] The mood of the debate was different to what had been seen in the Lords; in part this was because there simply was not the same vehement opposition to the Bill; and in part because there were, of course, no retired or serving judges in the Commons able to speak with the particular kind of authority that comes from professional engagement with an issue.

Opening the second reading debate, Christopher Leslie MP, the minister in charge of the Bill, was able to say: 'The Lord Chief Justice and members of the senior judiciary support the Government, and a select committee of the House of Lords has meticulously scrutinised the Bill.'[133] All sides of the debate made reference to Lord Woolf CJ's views, especially his conversion to the cause of a supreme court. Dominic Grieve MP, for the Conservatives, dismissed the supreme court as 'a costly white elephant'.[134] He argued that the position of the Law Lords[135]

> ... has unique characteristics that are beneficial to the way in which we do governmental business in this country. It allows the Law Lords to participate in debate in the other place and they have shown themselves—as I said to the Minister and he acknowledged at the outset—perfectly capable of choosing their words with sufficient care and choosing the debates in which they intervene sufficiently carefully to ensure that no criticism attaches to them. That is what the Minister wants to get rid of, but it has real value as a constant reminder in the legislature of the view of the judiciary.

In a debate dominated by speeches from MPs with professional backgrounds in the law, much of the focus was on the office of Lord Chancellor and judicial appointments in England and Wales rather than on the supreme court.

The question of how the Bill should to be scrutinised in detail also came to the boil: after failed negotiations between 'the usual channels', the Government business managers proposed a 'programme motion' that the House, without debate, should agree to deal with only 21 clauses and Schedule 8 on the floor of the House over two days, and other clauses and schedules in standing committee. In exasperation, front bench Conservative spokesman Mr Grieve resorted to quoting the words of Labour minister Herbert Morrison: 'You cannot play about with the British Constitution in a Committee Upstairs, to put it colloquially.'[136] By convention, Bills of 'first class constitutional importance' have in the past had all or at least some parts of their committee stage scrutiny on the floor of the House, enabling all MPs to take part.[137] During the course of the second reading debate, the Government thought again and offered an additional day on the floor

---

[132] The Prime Minister was to request a dissolution of Parliament on 11 April and the general election was held on 5 May 2005.

[133] *Hansard*, HC, vol 429, col 555 (17 January 2005); Mr Leslie lost his seat in the general election.

[134] ibid, col 587.   [135] ibid, col 587.   [136] ibid, col 578.

[137] R Hazell, 'Time for a New Constitutional Convention: Parliamentary Scrutiny of Constitutional Bills 1997–2005' [2006] PL 247.

of the House. On a division as to whether the Bill should be given a second reading, the Government, supported by the Liberal Democrats, inevitably won (329 votes to 126). After further talks, the Government agreed to allow the whole of the committee stage to be taken on the floor of the House over three days.

Committee stage in the Commons

The first day of committee on 31 January 2005 included a two-hour debate—largely among Conservative Members and (not on the only occasion) with a Eurosceptic undercurrent—on clause 1 on the Lord Chancellor's duties in relation to the rule of law and whether that principle should be further defined in the Bill; the proposed amendment was not carried.

By this point, the Government had accepted the decision of the House of Lords 'to retain the title and formal office of Lord Chancellor'[138] and amendments were therefore agreed without a division that replaced references to 'Minister' with 'Lord Chancellor' throughout the Bill. Mr Leslie explained to the House that the Government was content with the compromise because it included substantial reform: the Lord Chancellor would no longer be head of the judiciary in England and Wales, sit as a judge, or be speaker of the House of Lords. On a division, the clause requiring the Lord Chancellor to be a member of the House of Lords—an amendment made by the Lords—was removed.[139] So, too, was the clause requiring the Lord Chancellor to have a legal qualification.[140]

On the second day, the Commons turned to consider the supreme court.[141] The Conservatives moved amendments that would have enabled the supreme court to be situated in the Palace of Westminster.[142] There was an extended debate on the merits and demerits of Middlesex Guildhall and of the costs of the proposed new court. There was a further rehearsal of arguments about public perceptions of independence. The Conservative amendments were rejected.

Government amendments, accepted without a division, introduced a new clause modifying the Northern Ireland Act 1998 to clarify that under the devolution settlement the supreme court would be an 'excepted matter' (in other words, exclusively a matter for the UK Parliament) and rights of appeal to the court, and legal aid for such appeals, would be 'reserved matters' (retained by the UK Parliament but able to be transferred to the Northern Ireland Assembly at some point in the future).[143]

Annabelle Ewing, the Scottish Nationalist Party MP for Perth, moved an amendment to the effect that no final appeal in civil cases in Scotland would lie to the supreme court (following her advocacy of the point at second reading).[144] She was soon interrupted by Labour MP Keith Vaz, who pointed out that there were no Conservative backbenchers present in the chamber: 'After the fuss they made

---

[138] *Hansard*, HC, vol 430, col 621 (31 January 2005).   [139] ibid, col 663.
[140] ibid, col 681.   [141] *Hansard*, HC, vol 430, col 717 (1 February 2005).
[142] ibid, col 719.   [143] ibid, col 749.   [144] ibid, col 750.

yesterday about the constitutional importance of the Bill, they cannot be bothered to turn up to listen to this important debate.'[145] In the division, the committee voted 411: 4 against the amendment.

The committee of the whole House went on to consider a Conservative amendment that sought to provide: 'Nothing in this Act shall prevent the conferment of a life peerage on a judge of the Supreme Court.'[146] The minister responded that '[t]he amendments are clearly contrary to one of the key principles behind the proposals for a separate supreme court and for the functional separation of the judiciary from the legislature'.[147] The amendment failed. And that was effectively the end of debate on the supreme court. The committee went on to consider judicial discipline.

The third and final allotted day for the committee stage was on 1 March 2005—the day after the House had considered the Prevention of Terrorism Bill which introduced a regime of control orders to replace the detention without charge of foreign national terrorist suspects.[148] The committee of the whole House (to the evident irritation of some Members) spent time debating whether the 'Senior Courts' was the appropriate term for the Court of Appeal, High Court, and Crown Court in England and Wales—which the Bill proposed should cease being called the 'Supreme Court of Judicature' after the UK Supreme Court started work. There followed debate on a group of government amendments dealing with the allocation of Lord Chancellor functions. There was debate also on the Lord Chancellor's oath, his duty to provide resources, and the Speakership of the House of Lords. The Conservatives pressed to the vote an amendment that sought to disqualify the Lord Chancellor from holding further ministerial office, but lost despite support from Liberal Democrats.

In a final division, dozens of government amendments—including new clauses and schedules—were approved without debate due to lack of time. It took the Deputy Speaker half an hour to read them out. Liberal Democrat Simon Hughes MP lamented: 'This is the second day in a row—I understand that today's context is not as controversial as yesterday's—when a major constitutional Bill, on the Floor of the House, has not been debated.'[149] Third reading followed immediately afterwards. The Bill was passed.

Ping-pong

Parliamentary procedure dictated that the Bill was then returned to the House of Lords as (unless the exceptional powers under the Parliament Acts are being used)

---

[145] ibid, col 751.   [146] ibid, col 759.   [147] ibid, col 760.
[148] *Hansard*, HC, vol 431, col 644 (28 February 2005). There were angry exchanges in the House over the way the Government had programmed debate on that Bill; many Members were concerned that important clauses affecting liberty would not be properly scrutinised.
[149] ibid, col 913.

both Houses must agree on the final text before a Bill can be presented for Royal Assent. Most of this final stage in the legislative process was concerned with the office of Lord Chancellor rather than the supreme court. On 15 March 2005, the Lords considered the Commons amendments to the Bill. There was debate on the 'Lord' and 'lawyer' requirements for the office of Lord Chancellor, inserted by the Lords but subsequently removed by the Commons. By 215 votes to 199, the House voted in favour of reintroducing the 'Lord' and 'lawyer' requirements. A series of amendments made by the Commons were agreed without substantial debate or divisions. At 7.14pm on 16 March 2005, the Bill returned to the Commons. The Government put forward a compromise in a clause that listed the various factors any of which prime ministers may take into account in appointing Lord Chancellors in the future—including experience as 'a qualifying practitioner' and 'a teacher of law in a university' (see now s 2 of the Constitutional Reform Act 2005). The Commons agreed.

The Commons amendments were considered by the Lords on 21 March 2005. Many Conservatives and Cross Benchers remained unhappy with the proposals that had emerged from the Commons, but the Conservative whips did not impose a three line whip for the vote. The bill received Royal Assent on 24 March 2005, five sitting days before Parliament was prorogued for the general election.

What did scrutiny of the Bill achieve?

Looking at the Constitutional Reform Bill as a whole, there can be no doubt that parliamentary scrutiny secured a significant substantive change to the Government's proposals in relation to the office of Lord Chancellor. In relation to the Supreme Court proposals, however, the amendments made to the Bill were more modest. Those significant amendments that were made in relation to the Supreme Court were instigated in response to the select committee's work (see Table 1).

A building fit for a Supreme Court

The Government's plan for a supreme court required a twin-track approach: it was necessary to put in place legislation to provide a legal basis for the new court; a building also had to be found. The latter was never going to be straightforward. For many of those opposed to or unconvinced by the Government's proposals for a new court, the suitability and cost of a new building was a key consideration. Without this information, they argued, it was impossible to carry out even the most rudimentary cost/benefit analysis of the reforms. After some hesitation, the Government agreed that the provisions of the Constitutional Reform Act creating

Table 1

Bill as introduced to the Lords	Constitutional Reform Act 2005
No provision for lay representation on selection commissions for Justices of the Supreme Court	At least one member of the five-person commission must be a lay person (Sch 8)
Selection commission must submit a list of two to five candidates, with comments, to the Minister	Selection commission must select one person only, with the Lord Chancellor having power to notify the selection to the Prime Minister, reject it, or require the commission to reconsider the selection (s 28)
No express provision about different jurisdictions of the UK	'Nothing in this Part is to affect the distinctions between the separate legal systems of the parts of the United Kingdom' (s 41)
Court constituted if panel has uneven number of at least three judges, one of whom is a permanent judge	More than half those judges must be permanent judges (s 42)
Minister has power to disallow Supreme Court Rules submitted to him by the President	Lord Chancellor has no discretion to disallow Rules (s 46)
'The Minister may appoint such officers and staff as he thinks appropriate for the purpose of discharging his general duty in relation to the Supreme Court.'	Lord Chancellor must consult President about the appointment of the chief executive; chief executive must carry out functions in accordance with directions given by President (s 48)
	President appoints officers and staff of the court (s 49)
	Express provision for Scottish Minister to make payments by way of contribution to the costs incurred by the Lord Chancellor in providing the Court with resources (s 50(4))
	Express requirement for Lord Chancellor to consult legal professional bodies over court fees (s 52)
	Chief executive required to make an annual report, which the Lord Chancellor will lay before Parliament (s 54)
	Northern Ireland Act 1998 amended to make the Supreme Court an 'excepted matter' and rights of appeal 'reserved matters' (s 58)
	Renaming the Supreme Court of Judicature—the Court of Appeal, High Court, and Crown Court in England and Wales—the Senior Courts (s 59) Sunrise clause (s 148)

the Supreme Court should not be brought into force until such time as a building was ready.[150]

---

[150] Constitutional Reform Act 2005, s 148. In policy terms, it was recognised that for the Supreme Court to start life in the Palace of Westminster would undermine the aim of improving public understanding that the judiciary and legislature were separate; Black Rod also indicated that it would be unacceptable in practical terms for the Supreme Court to be located in the Palace of Westminster, even on an interim basis.

Previous attempts in the 1990s to relocate the Appellate Committee away from the Palace of Westminster—to Milbank and Chancery Lane—had foundered almost immediately because of the Law Lords' rejection of those premises.[151] Against that background, the DCA, in close consultation with the Law Lords, drew up a 'statement of requirements' for the accommodation and facilities of the Supreme Court in August 2003.[152] It was soon decided that the Judicial Committee of the Privy Council, currently located in Downing Street, should also move to the new building.

Initially, the search was confined to suitable buildings within one mile of Charing Cross, but this was later extended to two miles.[153] A long-list of 48 properties was identified, whittled down to a short list of eight discussed with the Law Lords,[154] based on advice from property agents Knight Frank. Two possible sites suitable for a new-build were also considered following an approach from Land Securities plc: in Fetter Lane near the Royal Courts of Justice and a site at Buckingham Gate; the former was regarded as too large and the latter insufficiently prestigious.[155] The choice eventually came down to two buildings: the New Wing of Somerset House (a mid-nineteenth century part of the Grade I listed complex facing Waterloo Bridge, occupied by Revenue officials) and Middlesex Guildhall in Parliament Square (a Grade II* listed building completed in 1913, most recently used as a Crown Court centre but previously also a local authority chamber). Somerset House 'was in the end rejected because of the difficulty in persuading the Revenue to relocate and because of other problems in adapting it to the needs of the new court'.[156] Its cause was not helped by its location on the busy approach to Waterloo Bridge and noise from passing buses.

The Law Lords were unimpressed by the other contender, Middlesex Guildhall. Giving evidence to the House of Commons Constitutional Affairs Committee on 11 December 2003, Lord Bingham said bluntly: 'I do not fancy the Middlesex

---

[151] See text at n 13 above.

[152] 'The space requirement was calculated on the basis of providing at least three hearing rooms requiring 500 m², 14 judicial chambers and ancillary accommodation totalling 1300 m², staff accommodation and facilities totalling 800 m², 400 m² of public area and facilities and 550 m² for library and records storage': *Hansard*, HC, vol 658, col 534W (26 February 2004). Lord Nicholls of Birkenhead chaired the Law Lords' working party: *Hansard*, HL, vol 667, col 1553 (20 December 2004).

[153] *R (SAVE Britain's Heritage) v Westminster CC* [2007] EWHC 807 (Admin) para 5 (Collins J).

[154] Central and Staple Court, WC2; 4 Mathew Parker Street, SW1; New Wing, Somerset House, WC2; Field House, Breams Buildings, EC4; Victoria House, Bloomsbury Square, WC1; Middlesex Guildhall, Parliament Square, SW1; Stewart House, 24 Kingsway, WC2; and St Dunstan's House EC4: *Hansard*, HC, vol 460, col 134W (8 May 2007); *Hansard*, HL, vol 657, col WA28 (27 January 2004). English Heritage suggested 10 Whitehall Place, SW1, a building formerly occupied by Department for the Environment, Food and Rural Affairs.

[155] *Hansard*, HC, vol 460, col 1248W (22 May 2007), Vera Baird MP. Lord Falconer told the House of Commons Constitutional Affairs Committee these new build sites were too small to 'produce the revenue that would make it worthwhile for the developer to build': Constitutional Affairs, Minutes of Evidence, 17 April 2007, Q71.

[156] *SAVE Britain's Heritage* (n 153) para 6 (Collins J).

Guildhall at all.'[157] He repeated his concerns in April 2004 to the House of Lords select committee on the Bill. Given what were then understood to be the constraints involved in converting the listed building, the 'impression will always remain that the Supreme Court has been crudely thrust into a building designed and built for quite another purpose', he told the committee.[158]

On 13 December 2004—as the Bill neared the end of its passage through the Lords—the Lord Chancellor finally announced that Middlesex Guildhall had been selected, acknowledging the reservations of the Law Lords.[159] At the time, Middlesex Guildhall was used as a Crown Court and seven courtrooms were closed at the end of March 2007. The Government's estimate of the 'set-up cost' of the Supreme Court was £56.9 million.[160] Capital construction costs are to be met by rent over a 30-year period as part of a leases-and-lease-back arrangement.[161] Conservation architects Feilden + Mawson, supported by Foster and Partners during the design and planning stages, were engaged following a competitive tender,[162] and the Kier Group plc won the contract for the works. The Supreme Court was originally expected to open for business in October 2008,[163] but soon moved to October 2009 to reflect the time needed to prepare the new court facilities.

In November 2006, planning permission and listed building consent were granted by Westminster City Council—to the dismay of SAVE Britain's Heritage, a campaign group for threatened historic buildings. The group said, 'the wonderful gothic revival interiors would, under the proposals, be stripped of their remarkable fittings'.[164] They launched a judicial review challenge, arguing that Westminster City Council had acted unlawfully; in March 2007 Collins J rejected their claim.[165] In April the House of Commons Constitutional Affairs Committee took evidence on the controversy, hearing from representatives of SAVE, the Victorian Society, Lord Falconer, and the permanent secretary to the DCA.[166]

---

[157] Minutes of Evidence, Q454.
[158] Memorandum by Lord Bingham of Cornhill, 30 April 2004 (published at 114–15 of HL Paper 125-II (2003–04)).
[159] *Hansard*, HL, vol 679, col WS29 (1 March 2006): Lord Falconer acknowledged that 'there are some members who remain unconvinced that the building can, even re-designed as proposed, provide a suitable modern setting for the Supreme Court of the UK'.
[160] *Hansard*, HL, vol 700, col WA102 (26 March 2008). This is £36.7m for building work and £20.2m for professional fees, furniture, IT, and library facilities. It was announced in July 2008 that unexpected structural repairs would cost a further £2m.
[161] *Hansard*, HC, vol 457, col 1170W (8 February 2007). The rent payable to Kier is £2.1m per annum, increasing at a rate of 2.5% per annum for 30 years: *Hansard*, HL, vol 692, col 119WS (14 June 2007).
[162] *Hansard*, HC, vol 435, col 546W (7 June 2005).
[163] *Hansard*, HC, vol 441, col 2385W (26 January 2006); *Hansard*, HC, vol 441, col 1447W (19 January 2006).
[164] *The Guildhall Testimonial: Stop this folly* (London: SAVE Britain's Heritage, 2006).
[165] *SAVE Britain's Heritage* (n 153).
[166] Constitutional Affairs, Minutes of Evidence, 17 April 2007.

Implementation

With the legislation on the statute book and the building work under way, the next phase was to prepare for the transfer of judicial functions to the new court. This required close working between officials in the Ministry of Justice Supreme Court Implementation Programme and the Law Lords.[167] Planning for a wide range of matters in addition to the building was required including: information technology; the rules of court;[168] and the court's website. The Law Lords formed a sub-committee (chaired by Lord Hope, with Baroness Hale and Lord Mance) to work with officials on the Supreme Court Implementation Programme within the Department of Constitutional Affairs (later the Ministry of Justice).[169] Monthly meetings were held with officials; from time to time there were meetings with Lord Falconer (and, after Gordon Brown's reshuffle as the in-coming Prime Minister in June 2007, his successor Jack Straw MP).

In January 2007, Lord Bingham published the draft UK Supreme Court Rules for consultation. That month Jenny Rowe was appointed as the court's first chief executive by the Lord Chancellor in consultation with Lord Bingham.[170] At the suggestion of Lord Justice Carnwath, a series of six seminars for members of the judiciary, practitioners, and academics was held at Queen Mary University of London between January and June 2007 to encourage an exchange of views about a range of issues relating to the working practices of the new court.[171] These seminars were followed by a larger conference in November 2008, organised by the Ministry of Justice.[172]

In an irony of timing, the great judicial advocate of a UK Supreme Court—Lord Bingham—was required to retire at the end of September 2008. His successor as Senior Law Lord was destined to become, under the terms of the

---

[167] The Ministry of Justice (MoJ) replaced the DCA in May 2007. The MoJ took on responsibilities for criminal law and sentencing, prisons, probation, and re-offending reduction that previously fell within the ambit of the Home Office. The creation of the MoJ caused concern among the judiciary of England and Wales but seems not to have had any significant impact on the Supreme Court project.

[168] Work on the rules and practice directions was led by Lord Walker, supported by Louise di Mambro (Judicial Office Registrar) and a team of lawyers from the MoJ: Supreme Court Implementation Programme, *Newsletter*, issue 5 (July 2008), 1.

[169] *Hansard*, HL, vol 693, col 1095 (4 July 2007).

[170] M Berlins, 'Who will be the first president of the new supreme court?' *The Guardian*, 21 January 2008, 10 (describing her as 'a much respected and influential éminence grise in the corridors of legal power').

[171] See A Le Sueur, *A Report on Six Seminars About the UK Supreme Court* (Queen Mary School of Law Legal Studies Research Paper No 1/2008) <http://papers.ssrn.com/sol3/papers.cfm?abstract_id=1324749> (last visited 9 March 2009).

[172] See J Rozenberg, 'Senior judge wants top court to avoid crime' *Daily Telegraph* (online), 17 November 2008; F Gibb, 'The £60 million makeover: new building, new law lords, new postcode' *The Times* (online), 20 November 2008; M Berlins, 'Let's end the lottery in the lords' *The Guardian* (online), 24 November 2008.

Constitutional Reform Act 2005, the first President of the Supreme Court when jurisdiction transferred in October 2009. With this in mind, in October 2007, with the agreement of Lord Bingham, Jack Straw announced that the new appointments process contained in Part 3 of the 2005 Act would be adopted on a voluntary basis (pending its coming into force in 2009) for future Law Lords appointments, including that of the next Senior Law Lord. This required a five-person selection panel to be formed, initiated by but independent from the Ministry of Justice, consisting of the Senior Law Lord (Lord Bingham), the Second Senior Law Lord (Lord Hoffmann), and a representative from each of three judicial appointments commissions (for England and Wales, for Northern Ireland, and for Scotland), one of whom must be a non-lawyer.[173] In April 2008 it was announced—as widely anticipated—that Lord Phillips of Worth Matravers, the Lord Chief Justice of England and Wales, had been appointed with effect from October 2008.

---

[173] These were Baroness Prashar (Judicial Appointments Commission of England and Wales), Sir Neil McIntosh (Judicial Appointments Board for Scotland)—both non-legally qualified—and Lord Justice Anthony Campbell (Northern Ireland Judicial Appointments Commission). The panel did not interview the successful candidate: House of Lords Constitution Committee, Minutes of Evidence, 9 July 2008, Q52 (Lord Phillips).

PART B

THE JUDGES

6

The Lord Chancellor as Head of the Judiciary[1]

Dawn Oliver

Introduction

Among the many roles of the old-style, pre-Constitutional Reform Act Lord Chancellor, that of head of the judiciary was the oddest, and the most inconsistent with any idea of the separation of powers. And yet it more or less worked. Although it is impossible to identify specific statutory or formal provisions as to the old-style Lord Chancellor's role as head of the judiciary, that role was of central importance, especially to many members of the judiciary,[2] and when the CRA reforms were announced it was the end of this role that caused the most anguish among judges. This was partly due to the way in which the changes were announced—by press release, and without any prior consultation with the judiciary. This generated an atmosphere of suspicion and mistrust of the Government's motives. But it was also because it was only when the changes were announced that many of those affected focused on the implications and came to appreciate some of the benefits of the old system and to articulate their fears. These included that the change would result in greater exposure of conflicts between the executive and the judiciary, and a change in the culture of government resulting from the absence of an old-style Lord Chancellor, in that the importance of the rule of law and judicial independence might be downgraded.[3]

The scope of this subject—the role of the Lord Chancellor as head of the judiciary—is not however clear-cut. Before the Constitutional Reform Act 2005 the phrase 'head of the judiciary' was not much used in the literature on the office

---

[1] I am most grateful to Sir Derek Oulton and Sir Thomas Legg for providing information about the role of the Lord Chancellor as head of the judiciary.

[2] But note that Lord Coleridge as Lord Chief Justice resented 'the enthroning of the Chancellor upon the neck of all of us': EH Coleridge, *Life and Correspondence of John Duke, Lord Coleridge, Lord Chief Justice of England, 1904*, vol ii, 359, quoted in R Stevens, *The English Judges* (Oxford: Hart, 2002) 91–2.

[3] See D Oliver, 'Constitutionalism and the Abolition of the Office of Lord Chancellor' (2004) 57 *Parliamentary Affairs* 754.

of Lord Chancellor or the judiciary.[4] Woodhouse, in her seminal book on *The Office of Lord Chancellor*, makes only passing reference to the head of the judiciary role in her treatment of 'The Lord Chancellor's Constitutional Role':

If the Lord Chancellor were to lose his judicial and appointing roles, logic and constitutional propriety dictate that he should also give up his position as head of the judiciary, a position he came to occupy because of these roles. The head of the judiciary can hardly be someone who is not a judge, nor should he be a government minister.[5]

It was not always easy to determine whether the old-style Lord Chancellor was exercising his role as head of the judiciary, or his role as a member of the Cabinet—or both, at any given time. (His role as Speaker of the House of Lords did not raise difficulties of that kind.) There were grey areas between the head of the judiciary and member of the Cabinet roles and the lines were fuzzy. In the run-up to the changes in the Constitutional Reform Act 2005 there had been no expressions of concern about past conscious abuse by Lord Chancellors of their position as head of the judiciary. The concerns expressed by commentators such as Lord Steyn and Woodhouse were about the potential for abuse in the future. (As we shall see, however, there were a very few occasions on which the exercise of the Lord Chancellor's various roles raised eyebrows, though not on the ground that deliberate abuse was suspected.)

The grey areas and fuzziness may be illustrated in a number of ways. The Lord Chancellor was regarded as being 'at the apex of the judicial pyramid'.[6] He was President of the Supreme Court,[7] *ex officio* member of the Court of Appeal,[8] and President of the Chancery Division of the High Court.[9] All this was clearly part of the Lord Chancellor's role in relation to the judiciary, rather than as a member of the Cabinet. But these presidential and *ex officio* membership roles may have been separate from the head of the judiciary role: now, under the Constitutional Reform Act 2005, the Lord Chief Justice of England and Wales 'holds the office of President of the Courts of England and Wales *and* is Head of the Judiciary of England and Wales'.[10] Thus the Lord Chief Justice now has two separate roles or titles, one in relation to 'courts' and the other in relation to 'the judiciary'. The same was true of the old-style Lord Chancellor.

The 2005 Act says quite a lot about the role of the Lord Chief Justice as President of the Courts of England and Wales. By section 7(3) the President is

---

[4] The head of the judiciary role is not discussed in Robert Stevens, *The Independence of the Judiciary: The View from the Lord Chancellor's Office* (Oxford: Clarendon Press, 1993) or *The English Judges* (n 2). *Halsbury's Laws of England* on *Constitutional Law and Human Rights*, vol 8(2) makes no reference to the role of head of the judiciary in its discussions either of the Lord Chancellor or of the judiciary. Discussion of these matters tends to focus on the judiciary of England and Wales and to ignore the fact that there are separate judiciaries in Scotland and Northern Ireland.

[5] D Woodhouse, *The Office of Lord Chancellor* (Oxford: Hart, 2001) 206.

[6] A Bradney, 'The Judicial Activity of the Lord Chancellor 1946–87: A Pellet' (1989) 16 JLS 360.

[7] Supreme Court Act 1981, s 1.   [8] ibid, s 2.   [9] s 5(1)(a).   [10] s 7(1), my italics.

President of and entitled to sit in any of the courts listed in section 7(4)—the Court of Appeal, the High Court, the Crown Court, the county courts, and the magistrates' courts. He is not however Senior President of Tribunals[11]—that office falls to a specially designated judge, as from 12 November 2007 Sir Robert Carnwath.

By section 7(2), as President of the Courts of England and Wales, the Lord Chief Justice has responsibility for (i) representing the views of the judiciary of England and Wales to Parliament, to the Lord Chancellor, and to Ministers of the Crown generally; (ii) the maintenance of appropriate arrangements for the welfare, training, and guidance of the judiciary of England and Wales within the resources made available by the Lord Chancellor; and (iii) the maintenance of appropriate arrangements for the deployment of the judiciary of England and Wales and the allocation of work within courts.

The 2005 Act says nothing further, however, about the Lord Chief Justice's role as 'head of the judiciary'. So it is by no means clear that the presidential roles of the Lord Chief Justice—and therefore of the pre-Constitutional Reform Act Lord Chancellor—form part of the 'head of the judiciary' function.

Woodhouse states that the responsibility for upholding judicial independence derived from the Lord Chancellor's position as head of the judiciary.[12] But it must also have had executive aspects. And it is now clear that the responsibilities for upholding judicial independence can be placed on others than the head of the judiciary: they are so placed under the Constitutional Reform Act 2005. The new-style Lord Chancellor—no longer head of the judiciary—now has the role of upholding the independence of the judiciary under section 3(1) of the Constitutional Reform Act 2005, along with other Ministers of the Crown and all those with responsibility for matters relating to the judiciary or otherwise to the administration of justice.

The Constitutional Reform Act does not in terms place the statutory duty to uphold the independence and integrity of the judiciary upon the Lord Chief Justice of England and Wales or counterparts in Scotland and Northern Ireland. That is not of course to deny that it is part of the role of the Lord Chief Justice to do just that. The point highlights the degree to which the system always has relied, and still does rely, though to a lesser extent, on often unarticulated understandings.

The Lord Chief Justice's responsibilities as head of the judiciary are now set out in the Concordat,[13] the soft law document agreed between Lord Chancellor

[11] See provisions in relation to the Senior President of Tribunals in the Tribunals, Courts and Enforcement Act 2007, Part I and Schedule 1. Some tribunals have UK-wide jurisdiction.

[12] Woodhouse (n 5) 15.

[13] <http://www.dca.gov.uk/consult/lcoffice/judiciary>. And see the Lord Chancellor's judiciary related functions in the *Report of the Select Committee on the Constitutional Reform Bill*, HL Paper 125, 2003–4, 202–24 (Appendix). See also provisions as to the roles of the Lord Chief Justices of England and Wales, and of Northern Ireland, and the Lord President, in the Tribunals, Courts and Enforcement Act 2007.

Falconer and Lord Chief Justice Woolf to settle the relationships between the Lord Chancellor/Secretary of State, the Lord Chief Justice, the Government, and the judiciary when the reforms took effect. This document does not employ the phrase 'head of the judiciary'. And yet, of course, the Lord Chief Justice has a central role in maintaining judicial independence and integrity, and in communications between the judiciary, the executive, and Parliament.

An important aspect of the role of the Lord Chancellor was to act as a buffer or link between the judiciary and the Government. This is discussed below. Here, too, it is not clear what head-dress a Lord Chancellor was wearing. Lord Mishcon, in a House of Lords debate on the relationship between the Lord Chancellor and a judge, commented that the Lord Chancellor was required to wear too many hats.[14] Perhaps, when acting as a buffer, he was wearing a bowler hat (or a safety helmet, depending on the sense in which 'buffer' is used) over a full bottomed wig. The metaphors have changed over the years, mutating from engineering (Albert Napier described the role of Lord Chancellor as being 'a kind of universal joint between cabinet, judiciary and parliament'[15]) to railways to hatting and wigmaking.

Thus the extent of the role of the old-style Lord Chancellor as head of the judiciary was not clear-cut. Let us not be too pedantic about these matters, however. We shall consider the overall broadly judiciary-related roles of the old-style Lord Chancellor in what follows.

The Lord Chancellor in the Appellate Committee and the Privy Council

The rights of the Lord Chancellor to sit on the Appellate Committee of the House of Lords and the Judicial Committee of the Privy Council formed part of the head of the judiciary role, but in a peculiar way. The jurisdiction of the Appellate Committee—and aspects of the Judicial Committee's jurisdiction—extended to the whole of the United Kingdom. The Lord Chancellor was the Lord High Chancellor of Great Britain, with jurisdiction therefore over Scotland as well as England and Wales—though it is not clear what the jurisdiction over Scotland amounted to. The 'Head of the Judiciary of England and Wales' role of the old-style Lord Chancellor (and of the new-style Lord Chief Justice) does not of course extend to Scotland—or Northern Ireland. However, the Lord Chancellor had power to advise on the appointment of Northern Ireland judges. His position in the Appellate and Judicial Committees therefore implied an additional special status as 'head' or 'president' of those courts; but this did not imply any further

---

[14] *Hansard*, HL, vol 553, col 768 (27 April 1994).
[15] See his *Dictionary of National Biography* entry on Sir Claude Schuster; see also the *DNB* entry by Sir Derek Oulton on Sir George Coldstream.

special status in relation to the judiciaries of Scotland and Northern Ireland—or countries from which appeal lay to the Privy Council.

It was as Speaker of the House of Lords rather than as head of the judiciary that the Lord Chancellor presided over the House of Lords when it was sitting as the highest court of appeal.[16] Here two of the Lord Chancellor's roles—Speaker of the House of Lords and head of the judiciary—ran in parallel. The role had particularly strong credibility until the Second World War, since the Lord Chancellor sat regularly in the Appellate Committee of the House of Lords. He would sit until 4pm, when he would move into his Speaker and executive roles.

The House of Commons chamber was bombed in 1941 and the Commons then took over the chamber of the House of Lords. The Lords were moved to the Royal Gallery in the Palace of Westminster and the Law Lords took to sitting in a Committee Room. When the House was prorogued and the Chamber therefore empty, the Law Lords would sit in the Chamber, emphasising their membership of the House. The Upper Chamber would sit in the mornings with the Lord Chancellor in position as Speaker; thus it was no longer possible for him to sit judicially.[17] Thus does the British Constitution change.

After the end after the Second World War and the rebuilding of the Commons Chamber the Lord Chancellor resumed sitting, but only occasionally, in the Appellate Committee of the House of Lords—and in the Judicial Committee of the Privy Council. From the 1960s he sat only exceptionally because of the timetable of government business and the expansion of the work of the Lord Chancellor's Office, which included in due course the reforms to the court system under the Courts Act 1971 and the establishment of the Court Service. It became accepted that the Lord Chancellor should not sit on public law cases: the Appellate Committee's case-load in public law was substantial from the 1970s, so his role as judge became proportionately diminished. There were however exceptions, which will be noted below, particularly the cases of *Pepper v Hart*[18] and *DPP v Jones*.[19] Lord Chancellors continued to sit on private law cases.

The justification for the Lord Chancellor continuing to sit as a judge was to maintain the credibility of the role as head of the judiciary rather than that he should have the opportunity to observe candidates for judicial appointment who appeared before the Committee and thus form a view about their suitability for appointment—a justification sometimes put forward in the past for the Lord Chancellor sitting as a judge.

The old-style Lord Chancellors were entitled not only to preside when sitting in the Appellate Committee and to sit on such cases as they chose, but also to select the judicial panels in the House of Lords.[20] They were also entitled to preside when sitting on the Judicial Committee of the Privy Council and to select

---

[16] House of Lords Standing Order 83(1) and (4). That status did not of course extend to the Judicial Committee of the Privy Council.
[17] See the discussion by James Vallance White, ch 3 in this volume.   [18] [1993] AC 593.
[19] [1999] 2 AC 240.   [20] See ch 3 in this volume.

panels there. In practice the selection depended upon such matters as the availability of Law Lords, problems caused when someone went sick, the fact that
newly-appointed Law Lords could not sit on appeals from their own decisions in
lower courts, the desirability of having a Scot to hear a Scottish appeal, special
expertise, and so on. By the late 1970s, when Lord Hailsham became Lord
Chancellor, the guidelines or criteria included: judicial expertise; the need not to
have judges with political experience sitting on politically sensitive cases; and that
one or two judges from Scotland or one from Northern Ireland should sit in
appeals from those jurisdictions.

In the 1970s, under Lord Hailsham, the Permanent Secretary and the Clerk in
charge of the Judicial Office in the House of Lords[21] would take the main
decisions on the selection of panels and put them to the Lord Chancellor for
approval. The Private Secretary to the Lord Chancellor's Permanent Secretary
would then get out the invitation letters.[22] From early in the 1980s the selection
of panels was delegated by the Lord Chancellor to the Senior Law Lord, and in
practice it was dealt with by the Clerk of the Judicial Office of the House of Lords
and the Judicial Clerk of the Privy Council, who then reported direct to the two
Senior Law Lords. However, the Lord Chancellor retained the right to select
panels if he wished, and to sit on what cases he chose, even political ones, and if so
to preside. There was a scuffle over this in 1998 when Lord Lester QC asked a
number of questions in the House of Lords about the powers of the Lord
Chancellor in such matters and the constraints under which Lord Irvine, the then
Lord Chancellor operated—if any. Lord Irvine maintained his right to decide who
should sit, to sit himself, and to preside when he did so, though it was implicit
that these powers would not be abused, for instance for party political or government advantage.[23] Lord Steyn was strongly critical of this position in a public
lecture in 2002.[24]

When sitting as a judge the Lord Chancellor acted on his personal responsibility and under judicial oath.[25] This indicates that a strong concept of the
separation of the judicial from the political role formed part of the conventions,
culture and tradition of the old arrangements.

However, there were some surprising exercises by Lord Chancellors of their
right to sit as a judge. For instance, in *Pepper v Hart*[26] Lord Chancellor Mackay

---

[21] See ch 3 in this volume.

[22] I am grateful to Sir Derek Oulton, Permanent Secretary at the time, for this account. See also
Woodhouse (n 5) 121 and AA Paterson, *The Law Lords* (London: Palgrave Macmillan, 1982) 87,
referred to in Woodhouse.

[23] See D Oliver, 'The Lord Chancellor, the Judicial Committee of the Privy Council and
Devolution' [1999] PL 1; *Hansard*, HL, vol 592 (30 July 1998) WA 220; *Hansard*, HL, vol 593 (20
October 1998) WE 137 and 138; *Hansard*, HL, vol 593, cols 1971–85 (28 October 1998).

[24] Lord Steyn, 'The Case for a Supreme Court' (2002) 118 LQR 382.

[25] Home Affairs Committee, *Third Report Judicial Appointments Procedures* (1995–6) HC 52-
II, Appendix 1, Memorandum from the LCD.

[26] [1993] AC 593; D Oliver, '*Pepper v Hart*. A Suitable Case for Reference to Hansard?' [1993]
PL 5.

(Lord Chancellor from 1987 to 1997) sat on a case the decision in which would affect his own Department's expenditure. He based his reasoning in part on the fact that if the courts looked in *Hansard* for evidence of the intentions of Parliament when interpreting ambiguous Acts this would increase the costs of legal aid, for which his Department was responsible. It was on this ground that he dissented from the majority and decided the case in favour of the Inland Revenue and against the taxpayer.

Lord Chancellor Irvine (Lord Chancellor from 1997 to 2004) sat and presided on the case of *DPP v Jones*,[27] where anti-government demonstrations were in issue. In that case the Lord Chancellor found that the defendants had not committed the offence of trespassory assembly on the highway, and thus upheld their right in the circumstances to demonstrate (for instance, against the Government) on the highway. There was no implication of bias in his decision. But if he had found the other way there would inevitably have been concerns about the propriety of his sitting in the case.

Judicial appointments, and the deployment and discipline of judges

The old-style Lord Chancellor also had responsibility for judicial appointments. Woodhouse notes that this responsibility 'has its origins in his position as the Sovereign's first minister. In modern times it is more easily reconciled with his role as head of the judiciary'.[28] In reality the function had both head of the judiciary and executive aspects. This is reflected in the arrangements under Chapter 2 of the Constitutional Reform Act and the Concordat: appointments are not part of the role of the Lord Chief Justice as head of the judiciary, except that he is consulted by the Lord Chancellor and he or his nominee is to be a member of Judicial Appointments Commission selection panels.

Early in the 1980s new systems for judicial appointments were introduced under Lord Hailsham. These were worked out by the Permanent Secretary, Sir Derek Oulton and his Deputy, Thomas Legg.[29] The system was more formalised than hitherto. The Master of the Rolls, the Lord Chief Justice, the Vice Chancellor, and the President of the Family Division had important advisory roles in relation to appointments of High Court Judges. Appointments to lower courts were made by the Lord Chancellor, who obtained advice from civil servants. The revamped system still relied on the 'soundings' which attracted widespread criticism for their secrecy, for the fact that it was possible for a good candidate to be blackballed by a member of the higher judiciary and yet not to know why, and that aspirants to the Bench with high profiles—large practices in the High Court,

---

[27] [1999] 2 AC 240.   [28] Woodhouse (n 5) 133.
[29] Legg also overhauled the Silk Round at that time.

Court of Appeal, and House of Lords—had a better chance of appointment than possibly equally able aspirants with lower profiles. The numbers of women and members of ethnic minorities continued to be low. And this was the case despite efforts by Lord Chancellors Mackay and Irvine in particular to widen the pool and attract applicants from a broad range of practitioners.

We have already noted that a convention developed that the Lord Chancellor would not make appointments to the High Court and the Court of Appeal without discussion with the Heads of Division. In effect a collegiate appointment system grew up. A system for the oversight of the processes of appointment was grafted onto this under Lord Chancellor Irvine, in accordance with the recommendations of Sir Leonard Peach:[30] Commissioners for Judicial Appointments, led by Professor Sir Colin Campbell, oversaw the appointments process from 2001 until the new system came into effect in 2007.[31]

Under the old as under the new system arrangements have to be made for the deployment of judges—to divisions of the High Court, to circuits, to roles on circuit such as presiding judge, to the Employment Appeal Tribunal and so on. These decisions were made by the Lord Chancellor, in practice in consultation with the Lord Chief Justice or his deputy. Under the Concordat these deployment responsibilities are shared in various ways, involving consultation between the Lord Chief Justice and the Lord Chancellor. Thus, by analogy, this aspect of the role of the old-style Lord Chancellor appears to have involved a mixture of head of the judiciary and executive aspects, though these were not labelled as clearly as they are now.

The Lord Chancellor also had some *de facto* roles in what were then the informal disciplinary processes governing judges' conduct.[32] By way of example, Lord Chancellor Mackay asked Wood J to 'consider his position' when he refused to change his practice in relation to cases in the Employment Appeal Tribunal, where the Lord Chancellor took the view that the practice was incurring unnecessary delay and expense. Wood J replied: 'You have demanded that I exercise my judicial function in a way which you regard as best suited to your Executive purposes, but I have to say that in all the circumstances . . . I cannot regard compliance with your demand as conducive to justice.' This exchange gave rise to concerns that the Lord Chancellor was seeking to interfere inappropriately with the judge's function and to undermine his independence.[33] In fact of course the Lord Chancellor had no power to dismiss the judge, but he could have redeployed him. Presumably no concerns would have been aroused had the Lord

---

[30] Report to the Lord Chancellor, *An Independent Scrutiny of the Appointment Process for Judges and Queen's Counsel in England and Wales*, 1999.

[31] See also Sir Thomas Legg, 'Judges for a New Century' [2001] PL 62.

[32] See Stevens, *Independence of the Judiciary* (n 4) 88–92.

[33] For a full account see D Oliver, 'The Lord Chancellor's Department and the Judges' [1994] PL 157; Sir Francis Purchas, 'Lord Mackay and the Judiciary' (1994) 144 NLJ 527; see also *Hansard*, HL, vol 553, cols 751–804 (27 April 1994).

Chief Justice of the day remonstrated with a judge in his informal role as 'professional head of the judiciary'. (In fact the Lord Chief Justice had been privy to the matter and did not consider the pressure on the judge had been that he should resign.) It was the fact that the Lord Chancellor was a member of the executive which lay behind the concerns both of the judge and of commentators.

Development of the law

Leadership can take many forms. Other chapters in this collection may consider examples of cases where the Lord Chancellor played a leadership role in the development of the law. We shall not engage in that issue here, save to note that Woodhouse suggests that successive Lord Chancellors had built up a patchy record on this—not surprisingly perhaps, since for the most part they had not had judicial experience before being appointed and had been active politicians with less than full-time practice at the Bar and thus little practical experience of the workings of the law when they were appointed.[34]

One matter in which the Lord Chancellor of the day, Lord Gardiner, did play an important role was the issuing of the Practice Statement of 1966. The Lord Chancellor and the Lords of Appeal in Ordinary announced that they proposed to modify their then practice and, 'while treating former decisions of this House as normally binding, to depart from a previous decision when it appears right to do so'.[35]

The Lord Chancellor as protector of the judiciary

One of the most constitutionally important roles of the old-style Lord Chancellor was to act as advocate, protector, and champion of the judiciary in relation to politicians and the media and to uphold judicial independence and integrity. The Kilmuir Rules, 1955[36] provide an example of the Lord Chancellor acting to protect judges from controversy. Lord Kilmuir LC set out in a letter to the Director General of the BBC his view, in his capacity as head of the judiciary, that the judiciary should be isolated from the controversies of the day; by keeping silent a judge's reputation for wisdom and impartiality remains unassailable. 'As a general rule it is undesirable for members of the judiciary to broadcast on the wireless or to appear on television.' But he acknowledged that he had no disciplinary jurisdiction over the judges and each would decide for himself whether he considered it compatible with his office to accept an invitation to broadcast.

---

[34] Woodhouse (n 5) 105–10.

[35] *Practice Statement* [1966], pp 128ff 3 All ER 77. The Practice Statement is discussed in ch 9 of this volume 1 WCR 1234; [1966].

[36] These are set out in R Brazier, *Constitutional Texts* (Oxford: OUP, 1990) 595. See also AW Bradley [1986] PL 383.

On becoming Lord Chancellor in 1987 Lord Mackay stated that while judges should obey the spirit of the Rules, they would be trusted to decide for themselves whether to talk to the media and advised that they should in any case be careful not to say anything which might damage their authority or prejudice the performance of their work.[37] Thus the protective role of the Lord Chancellor diminished. And judges have been far readier than before to write articles and give public lectures about law-related matters: in fact it might now be said to be expected of senior judges that they will do so.

The Lord Chancellor as link and buffer between the executive and the judiciary and as champion of the judiciary

To the end it remained important to most of the judges that the Lord Chancellor should be, and be seen to be, what was to many of them a vital link and buffer between them and the Government.[38] (The Lord Chancellor is now, under the new arrangements, regarded by the Ministry of Justice as a 'bridge between the judiciary and the government'.[39]) The judges would defer to the Lord Chancellor despite the fact that he was a member of Her Majesty's Government, because of his position as head of the judiciary. This aspect of the Lord Chancellor's role was credible for so long as he still sat as a judge, even if only from time to time. Latterly however, in the years leading up to the changes of 2005, the Lord Chancellor sat only very rarely. His role as member of the Cabinet and chair of important Cabinet Committees concerned with constitutional reform came to dominate. Thus the 'head of the judiciary' role, though important in its influence on relations between the judiciary and the executive became in reality increasingly less credible in the run up to the 2005 Act.

The role as *link*[40] took the form of regular contacts and exchanges between the Lord Chancellor and the Lord Chief Justice.[41] The pattern of such contact dates back to Coldstream's period as Permanent Secretary in the LCO from 1954. He, the Lord Chancellor, and the Lord Chief Justice would meet weekly, briefing one another on matters of concern. Their discussions would cover judicial

---

[37] Brazier, ibid, 597.

[38] See for instance Lord Hailsham LC, 'The Office of Lord Chancellor and the Separation of Powers' (1989) 8 Civil Justice Quarterly 308: 'The Lord Chancellor is the judges' friend at court, whether he is acting as their public defender in Parliament or as their private representative in Whitehall. For this purpose he is to be regarded as the representative of the judicial body and not simply as a member of the executive.' See also D Oliver [1998] PL 157, 160–1; Woodhouse (n 5).

[39] See *The Governance of Britain. Judicial Appointments*, Cm 7210, October 2007, para 4.15. Here the metaphor has moved from mechanical (universal joint/link/buffer) to civil engineering. So far no reference to cricket—level playing fields and the like—or sailing (close to the wind, tight ships, etc). But cricket is unlikely to be played by Scots such as Lord Chancellors Mackay and Irvine, and sailing is less of a national sport in Scotland than in England.

[40] Note the shift to a chainmaking metaphor here.

[41] I am grateful to Sir Thomas Legg for this information.

appointments, judicial manpower, any concerns of the judges about the running of the courts, how to deal with complaints about judges, and so on. The relationship developed into one of mutual respect and partnership between the Lord Chancellor and the Lord Chief Justice. Thus for instance, Sir Thomas Legg, when Deputy Permanent Secretary, met the Deputy Chief Justice (an unofficial position dating back to 1983 when Lord Justice Tasker Watkins became Deputy) regularly, almost daily—often on the way to the Office. They discussed the judicial workload, any needs for more judges, who should be appointed resident judges and presiding judges on the circuits, and so on. In the 1980s monthly meetings between the Lord Chancellor, the Lord Chief Justice, and the Heads of Division came to be held as a matter of course. The agenda for these meetings included judicial appointments, and thus a convention developed that appointments to the High Court and the Court of Appeal would not be made without discussion with the Heads of Division.

The provisions in the Constitutional Reform Act 2005 and the Concordat transferring the role of head of the judiciary to the Lord Chief Justice are then in many ways the formalisation of a position that had been evolving in that direction over several decades.

The role of the Lord Chancellor as a *buffer* between the judges and the Government rested on the ability of a strong Lord Chancellor to communicate to Cabinet colleagues both the concerns of the judges and the importance of judicial independence and the rule of law. He would also convey to the judges concerns of the executive.[42]

It is in fact difficult to determine how Lord Chancellors performed this role, and to what extent their performance of it rested on their role as head of the judiciary as opposed to the First Minister of the Prime Minister or respect for their historic and cultural role as a voice for the judges and the rule of law in government. Cabinet minutes are not published and what takes place in Cabinet is confidential and protected by collective ministerial responsibility, so information is not available about specific instances of Lord Chancellors exercising a role as protectors of the judiciary and the rule of law. A number of Lord Chancellors claimed that this was part of their role (for instance, Lord Hailsham,[43] Lord Mackay,[44] and Lord Irvine[45]) and it, or the belief in it, was important to the judges.

For the most part the buffer function operated well and limited or prevented damaging open collisions between the judiciary and ministers. But in the 15 years or so prior to the Constitutional Reform Act there had been an increased

---

[42] See for instance *Hansard*, HC, vol 475, col 155 (4 December 2001), discussed in Stevens (n 2) 126.

[43] See n 39 above.

[44] 'The Lord Chancellor in the 1990s', Mishcon lecture, March 1991; 'The Chancellor in the 1990s' [1991] CLP 241.

[45] See *Human Rights, Constitutional Law and the Development of the English Legal System* (Oxford: Hart, 2003) 204–8.

willingness, on the part of Home Secretaries in particular—Howard under the Conservative government and Blunkett under Labour—to criticise individual judges for their decisions.[46] What we can infer from this about the role of the Lord Chancellor is doubtful. It may be that Lord Chancellors in this period were less respected in Cabinet than their predecessors; or that judges were more activist and provocative in their decisions; or that the political culture, at least among Home Secretaries, changed and respect for the rule of law and the independence of the judiciary gave way to politics and partisanship.[47] It cannot have been ignorance of the rule of law on the part of Howard, a barrister. Whatever the causes, a divergence of culture between the legal and political establishments—in effect the emergence of two cultures in place of the one that was epitomised by the Lord Chancellor—raises serious issues as to the channels of communication between the two and whether the link and buffer roles that are now formalised will be as effective as they used to be in defusing conflict and preserving a culture of respect for the rule of law in government.

Lastly, the role of the Lord Chancellor as champion of the judiciary in the Cabinet. The Lord Chancellor became increasingly political from the 1980s as his department and its budget (covering the Court Service and legal aid) grew and he was in competition with other departments for Treasury funds. These factors generated conflicts between the roles of the Lord Chancellor as Cabinet member, and as head of the judiciary. By way of example, Lord Chancellor Mackay was responsible for the reforms in the Government's Courts and Legal Services Act 1990. These were strongly and openly objected to by the Lord Chief Justice, Lord Lane on behalf of the judges, on independence grounds. The Lord Chancellor's role as champion of the judiciary had become incompatible with his role as Cabinet member.

Mixed or separate roles?

It is not clear when the Lord Chancellor was acting in the role of head of the judiciary in these 'link and buffer' matters and when he was acting as a member of the Cabinet. Here the lines of separation were particularly fuzzy. It may well be that the Lord Chancellor was exercising both roles simultaneously in doing so, and obeying a particular and exceptional convention that he should not act in a partisan way and he should act on his own responsibility rather than being bound by government policy and collective responsibility in performing the executive role.

This link and buffer aspect of the role of the Lord Chancellor involved there being appropriate channels of communication, through him, between the

---

[46] See Stevens (n 2) 129–36 for an account of confrontations between Lord Chancellor Irvine and Home Secretary David Blunkett.

[47] For discussion see A Le Sueur, 'The Judicial Review Debate. From Partnership to Friction' (1996) 31 Government and Opposition 8–26.

judiciary and the executive, through which the concerns of each could be voiced and responded to—this is where Napier's 'universal joint' metaphor was so apt.[48] Whether the Lord Chancellor was regarded as head of the judiciary or a member of the Cabinet in so doing is not clear. Perhaps to the judiciary he was their Head and ambassador and to the Cabinet a member of their team. But the answer to the question whether the Lord Chancellor was acting as head of the judiciary or member of the executive or advocate for the rule of law is less important than the fact that the changes to the office of Lord Chancellor caused considerable concern among the judiciary when the reforms were first mooted. The loss of this link or buffer or universal joint between the judiciary and the executive was regretted by the judiciary, but not apparently by the executive.

So what has happened to this link and buffer role? The largely unwritten understandings about it are not referred to with much specificity in the Concordat. Instead section 1 of the Constitutional Reform Act purports not to affect 'the existing principle of the rule of law' (about the meaning of which there is a good deal of debate,[49] among academics at least[50]); and by section 3(1) the Lord Chancellor and other Ministers of the Crown are required to uphold 'the continued independence of the judiciary'. The Lord Chief Justice of England and Wales and the heads of the judiciaries of Scotland and Northern Ireland[51] may make representations to Parliament. And of course they enjoy a general freedom to communicate with the Lord Chancellor. These are pretty bland substitutes for what was a rich and complex unwritten culture.

Whether these arrangements will substitute for the old ones remains to be seen. And whether new-style Lord Chancellors, especially those who are not lawyers or who are members of the House of Commons hoping for promotion, will interpret their role as a link, buffer, or bridge between the judiciary and the executive in the same ways as the old-style ones did will also be interesting to see.

The Lord Chancellor's Office and Department and the Permanent Secretary

As we have seen, it is not easy to separate out the role of the old-style Lord Chancellor as head of the judiciary from the other roles that attached to the office—Member of the Cabinet and Speaker of the House of Lords. The lines were fuzzy. The mixing of roles extended also to the Lord Chancellor's Office staff, the upper echelons of which consisted entirely of lawyers—some 12 in the

---

[48] See n 15 above.

[49] See Lord Bingham, 'The Rule of Law' (2007) 66 CLJ 67–85 for an authoritative judicial view.

[50] See for instance P Craig, 'Formal and Substantive Conceptions of the Rule of Law: An Analytical Framework' [1997] PL 467; J Jowell, 'The Rule of Law and its Underlying Values' in J Jowell and D Oliver (eds), *The Changing Constitution* (Oxford: OUP, 6th edn 2007).

[51] Constitutional Reform Act 2005, s 5(1).

1960s and 1970s.[52] Over a period the dominance of lawyers in the Department declined and the Department came to resemble more closely other government Departments, staffed by non-lawyer civil servants. (As from 1989 the Lord Chancellor's Department included a small separate legal department.)

The position of the Permanent Secretary in the Lord Chancellor's Office and Department was statutory. The holder had a range of roles. He was an Officer of the Supreme Court under the Administration of Justice Act 1922 and the Judicature Act 1925 and held office during good behaviour, subject to the judicial retiring age. This requirement was removed in 1990, after which it was no longer necessary for the Permanent Secretary to be an officer of the Supreme Court. Sir Hayden Phillips was the first non-lawyer Permanent Secretary of the Lord Chancellor's Department and, from 2003 to 2004, of the Department for Constitutional Affairs.

Under the earlier system the Permanent Secretary was also the Clerk of the Crown in Chancery—ie not a civil servant—and an officer of both Houses of Parliament. Hence the order of priority of the Office's functions and those of the Permanent Secretary were to serve the Lord Chancellor as head of the judiciary first (but not when he was deciding an appeal in the Lords), then to serve him in his role as Speaker of the House of Lords—which was not demanding—and lastly to serve him in his role as member of the Cabinet. The work of the Permanent Secretary reflected the mix of the Lord Chancellor's roles.

Reflections

The Lord Chancellor's status as head of the judiciary was a matter of convention and culture as much as of law. It rested only in part on his being entitled to sit in the highest courts in England and Wales and his right to preside in the Appellate Committee of the House of Lords and the Judicial Committee of the Privy Council. Perhaps most significantly, his position also rested on the high regard in which he was held by judges, politicians, and parliamentarians: the Lord Chancellor enjoyed the highest status in the official order of precedence, after the Archbishop of Canterbury and above, and with a higher salary than, the Prime Minister.[53] He was listened to with respect in Cabinet. This may be taken as acknowledgement of the importance of the law, the courts, and the rule of law in England and Wales, and in the UK as a whole.

However, it was inevitable that the head of the judiciary would in due course be a person who was a judge and not also a member of the executive and legislature. The pressures for change came from a number of quarters: the lack of clarity

---

[52] The Lord Chancellor's Office became a Department in the 1970s, after the Courts Act 1971. The arrangements in relation to the judiciary did not change at that time.

[53] See *Burke's Peerage*, Table of Precedence, and *Halsbury's Laws*, vol 8(2) para 481 n 1.

about when it was or was not appropriate for a Lord Chancellor to sit as a judge in cases involving governmental interests, coupled with the case law of the European Court of Human Rights on Article 6 of the ECHR, indicating that the UK arrangements were unlikely to stand up if challenged before that court; the steady rise over a long period in the importance of the Lord Chief Justice as the recognised professional head of the judiciary—the Chief; in recent years the combination of aggressive criticism of the judges by Home Secretaries and other ministers which Lord Chancellors had not been able to restrain; rather stubborn insistence by Lord Chancellor Irvine on his own authority to determine how the powers of the office should be exercised and increasingly unconvincing assertions that he could be both a party politician and head of the judiciary; and finally the increased workload attaching to the Cabinet and executive roles of the Lord Chancellor.

The new-style Lord Chancellor continues to enjoy a high status under the new arrangements. Whether this lasts will depend greatly on the ways in which each new-style Lord Chancellor approaches the task. Whether the culture of respect for the rule of law, which the Constitutional Reform Act purports to protect, remains unchanged in future will depend in part on the personalities of Lord Chancellors and Lord Chief Justices and their relationships with one another and the institutions they represent; and in part on the way in which the culture within government develops—whether it diverges from the rule of law culture of the judiciary and the legal establishment and moves towards a more political approach. These are matters on which the holder of the office of Lord Chancellor has an important constitutional and democratic responsibility to show leadership.

7

Appointments to the House of Lords: Who Goes Upstairs

Kate Malleson

Very little is known outside legal circles about the 110 men and one woman who have been appointed to the judicial House of Lords since 1876. When compared with the judges of the highest courts in other common law systems, most notably the US Supreme Court, the Law Lords have carried out their work in relative obscurity. Their appointments have rarely received much media coverage and the public has generally seen the judges as an amorphous group of learned old men with little to distinguish one from the other. With the exception of a few important scholarly works, academics have tended to share this disinterest.[1] One reasonable explanation for this neglect is that it is an appropriate response to the far more limited role that the Judicial Home of Lords has played, at least until relatively recently, in the political and constitutional system of the UK compared to many of its Supreme Court and Constitutional Courts counterparts. This argument is persuasive up to a point. One would certainly not expect new appointments to the judicial House of Lords to attract the same interest as the election of MPs or the appointment of ministers. Nevertheless, the increasing importance of many recent House of Lords judgments could reasonably have been expected to have resulted in a stronger spotlight being turned on the membership of the Court. One reason why this has not happened is that the judges themselves have generally been at pains to avoid publicity and to nurture a culture of anonymity around the Court. Despite the wider significance of their decisions in recent years, the Law Lords have generally succeeded in perpetuating their image as a body of legal decision-makers who operate outside the political system.

The advent of the new Supreme Court may bring about a shift in the balance between the role of the Court, the attitude of the individual judges, and the

---

[1] See, eg, L Blom-Cooper and G Drewry, *Final Appeal: A Study of the House of Lords in its Judicial Capacity* (Oxford: Clarendon Press, 1972); AA Paterson, *The Law Lords* (London: Palgrave Macmillan, 1982); D Robertson, *Judicial Discretion in the House of Lords* (Oxford: Clarendon Press, 1998); R Stevens, *Law and Politics: The House of Lords as a Judicial Body 1800–1976* (London: Weidenfeld and Nicholson, 1979).

interest in their judgments outside the Court resulting in more attention being paid to the membership of the new body. If so, this needs to be informed by an understanding of who has sat in the Lords to date and how they got there. This is not just of historical interest in shedding light on the reasoning behind past decisions of the Appellate Committee, but also tells us a great deal about the nature of the judicial system and the legal profession during the twentieth and early twenty-first centuries. In quantitative terms the Law Lords may constitute a very thin upper crust of the judiciary but as the apex of the court structure they reflect many of the priorities and values that have underpinned the legal system, and will continue to do so as the first Supreme Court Justices take their places in Middlesex Guildhall.

The make-up of the Law Lords

As many of the chapters in this volume illustrate, the development of the law in a range of different fields has often been influenced by the particular attitudes of individual Law Lords. The form of judgments delivered by the Appellate Committee, allowing each judge to express their different reasoning, is both a cause and a consequence of the high degree of intellectual individualism in the House of Lords compared to many other top courts around the world. Contrary to the popular image of bland uniformity, the personal assumptions, ideologies, and values of the Law Lords have played a vital role in the court's decision-making over the years. It is for good reason that lawyers appearing before the Appellate Committee have rejoiced or despaired on learning which judges have been allocated to hear a particular case.[2] Evidence of the underlying values underpinning the judges' decisions can usually only be glimpsed in their judgments. Occasionally it is much more explicit; an example being Lord Templeman's famous comment in the *Gillick* case that '[t]here are many things which a girl under 16 needs to practise but sex is not one of them'.[3] More recently, the disclosure of Lord Hoffmann's association with Amnesty International after he had sat on the *Pinochet* case not only led to the case being reheard, but raised a wider debate about the influence of the judges' political views in human rights cases.[4] Although such decisions have from time to time attracted considerable public attention, for the most part the work of the Appellate Committee has been very low profile. Paradoxically, therefore, the Law Lords have achieved their anonymity in the public eye despite the fact that it has long been recognised that the views of individual Law Lords can have a

---

[2] The process by which judges in general and the Law Lords in particular are allocated to sit on a case is one which merits a separate analysis, given the importance of the make-up of each panel in the outcome of cases (see Robertson, ibid).

[3] *Gillick v West Norfolk and Wisbech AA* [1986] 1 AC 112.

[4] See K Malleson, 'Judicial Bias and Disqualification after *Pinochet (No 2)*' (2000) 63 MLR 119.

profound effect on the development of the law in areas of great political and social importance.

One reason why the strong individualistic culture in the decision-making of the Court has generally passed unnoticed outside legal circles is that it arose within the context of a remarkable degree of homogeneity amongst the judges in terms of social background and career pattern. An overview of the appointments made to the Court from the late nineteenth century onwards shows that Law Lords have tended to be strikingly similar in their origins and experiences. Most obviously, until the appointment of Baroness Hale in 2003, all the Law Lords were male. Likewise, they were all white and generally appointed relatively late in life, in their 50s or early 60s. In terms of social background they were almost all been raised in comfortable middle or upper middle class backgrounds and been educated privately. The background of Lord Denning was very much an exception, as he was often keen to point out. The historical review of the Lords undertaken by Blom-Cooper and Drewry in 1969 found that '[t]he picture is one of unexciting but worthy professionalism'. This summary remained broadly accurate 20 years later.[5]

The lack of diversity in the composition of the Law Lords in terms of gender, ethnicity, and class was for most of its history quite predictable, given the general lack of diversity in these respects in all institutions of power during the twentieth century. Likewise, the fact that, politically, the judges' outlook was generally conservative with a small c is to be expected, since courts rarely contain radicals of either political hue. Few judges are by background or inclination revolutionaries. More noteworthy, however, was the degree of homogeneity amongst the Law Lords in terms of geographical representation and career patterns. With the exception of the presence of two Law Lords who by convention were appointed from Scotland, the great majority of the judges spent their working lives as members of the Bar in London before joining the Bench. None were former solicitors and very few spent any part of their career in academia.[6] Moreover, a very high proportion had traditionally been drawn from a limited number of elite commercial chambers.[7]

This thumbnail sketch of the membership of the Court might not have been surprising in the 1950s but by the 1990s it had become the subject of growing concern as the lack of diversity in the make-up of the Court increasingly stood in contrast to the changing composition of many other public institutions.[8] The

---

[5] Blom-Cooper and Drewry (n 1) 167. One surprising aspect of their findings was the relatively high number of Law Lords whose parents' occupations were professions such as teachers, indicating solid middle class backgrounds rather than more aristocratic or wealthy origins.

[6] Baroness Hale being a path-breaker in this respect as well, having been a professor of law before her appointment to the High Court.

[7] R Stevens, *The English Judge: Their Role in the Changing Constitution* (Oxford: Hart, 2nd edn 2005) 39.

[8] As early as 1972 JUSTICE recommended that academic lawyers should be promoted both to the Court of Appeal and the Lords. JUSTICE, *The Judiciary: The Report of a Sub-Committee* (1972), paras 21–8. See also S Shetreet, *Judges on Trial: A Study of the Appointment and Accountability of the English Judiciary* (Amsterdam: North-Holland 1976) 59.

standard response to criticisms of the relative homogeneity of the Court was that it would take time for a more diverse range of qualified candidates to 'trickle up' onto the Bench, given the fact that Law Lords were appointed after a long career in practice and therefore reflect the make-up of those who entered the legal profession 30 years earlier. This argument was somewhat weakened, however, by the fact that many other top courts in common law countries around the world had succeeded in diversifying their membership despite being similarly drawn from those who have first had a career of some kind in legal practice. Indeed, the make-up of the Appellate Committee in 2009 stood in stark contrast with many of its Supreme Court and Constitutional Court counterparts.

This diversity gap was most notable in terms of gender and ethnicity. The Canadian Supreme Court, for example, by 2007 had four women amongst its nine members, including the Chief Justice. Six of the 12 Israeli Supreme Court Justices are women and it has always included judges from a range of different religious and ethnic backgrounds. Likewise the South African Constitutional Court is known as the 'rainbow court' because of its broad ethnic and gender. In addition to these visible forms of diversity, most other top courts draw their members from a far wider range of career backgrounds. Most have judges who have been promoted up from the lower courts, or have been appointed from academia, private practice, the Attorney General's office, the prosecution service, or the government service.[9] An underlying explanation for the slow pace of change in the make-up of the Law Lords compared to these courts is the relative lack of political pressure for change that was brought to bear on the court. A more immediate explanation is found in the nature of the career paths of the Law Lords and the process of appointment to the Appellate Committee.

The career path to the Lords

It is common to claim that there is not and has never been a career judiciary in the UK.[10] What is usually meant by this is that judges do not progress through the judicial ranks in a way which is common in many civil law systems and that appointment to the Bench is regarded as an end in itself which follows a successful career in practice. While it is clearly accurate to say that there is no formal judicial career structure of the kind found in France or Germany, it is also the case that there is a distinct and relatively rigid career path through the upper judicial ranks in England and Wales. Since the middle of the twentieth century all judges in the Court of Appeal have been promoted from the High Court.[11] With the exception of seven Law Lords, promoted directly from the Bar and five promoted

---

[9] See Baroness Hale, 'A Supreme Court for the UK?' [2004] LS 14.

[10] See L Blom-Cooper, G Drewry, and C Blake, *The Court of Appeal* (Oxford: Hart, 2007) 112 and Shetreet (n 8) 79. Both works argued that this the traditional view 'defies reality'.

[11] Blom-Cooper et al, ibid, 111.

directly from the High Court, all Law Lords since 1876 have been promoted from the Court of Appeal.[12] For at least a proportion of those judges appointed to the High Court, therefore, the prospect of promotion to the Court of Appeal and the Law Lords has been a real one. Lord Denning's claim in 1955 that '[o]nce a man becomes a judge, he has nothing to gain from further promotion and does not seek it' was not, even at the time, plausible.[13] A more candid perspective is found in the admission by Lord Justice Kerr in 1985 that promotion to the House of Lords was something he thought about '... nearly every day, and not only I'.[14] An accurate description of the nature of the judicial career would therefore be that there is not one judicial career path but two. The lower judiciary, drawn predominantly from the solicitors' branch of the profession, and the upper judiciary drawn from certain sections of the Bar. The Bar currently constitutes approximately 10 per cent of the legal profession and yet it is from this group that the senior judges are almost wholly drawn. Until very recently, there was almost no promotion from the lower judicial ranks to the High Court and above.

The consequence of this closed promotions system through the higher courts is that the recruitment pool of the Law Lords has been a very narrow one and the composition of the Law Lords is inevitably a direct reflection of the composition of the High Court bench.[15] This funnel at the top of the system would not, of itself, limit the make-up of the Court if the appointments process to the High Court drew in a wide range of candidates. Nor is there any structural reason why it should not do so. The formal eligibility requirements for higher judicial office, have, for some years, been flexible enough to allow almost all qualified lawyers, in theory, to find a path to the High Court. Moreover, one of the defining features of the UK legal professions from the latter half of the twentieth century has been their increasingly flexible and varied career patterns, particularly compared to many other jurisdictions where highly restrictive practices in the legal profession are still common. Over 100,000 practitioners are today occupied in England and Wales in a great range of different legal positions in the public and private sectors. Yet most of these, however talented they might be, have no real prospect of ever being appointed to sit as a judge in the High Court bench.

Since the Bar established itself as the senior branch of the profession in the nineteenth century, and the commercial Bar in London emerged as the inner core of that senior branch, the career path from those chambers to the Law Lords has been 'a golden road'.[16] By definition, only a small proportion of even those elite

---

[12] Lord Atkinson (1905), Lord Shaw (1909), Lord Robson (1910), Lord Thankerton (1929), Lord Macmillan (1930), Lord Reid (1948), Lord Radcliffe (1949). See Shetreet (n 8) 79.

[13] Lord Denning, *The Road to Justice* (London: Stevens & Sons, 1955) 17.

[14] Sir Michael Kerr, *As Far as I Remember* (Oxford: Hart, 2006) 320. Quoted in Blom-Cooper et al (n 10) 113.

[15] Two Law Lords were recruited directly from the High Court: Lord Wilberforce and Lord Simon of Glaisdale.

[16] This term was used by one respondent judge in the author's earlier empirical review of the judicial appointments process to describe his career path from commercial chambers in London to the bench.

members of the Bar would achieve that goal but for the most talented and well-connected young lawyers amongst that group, the career path that could lead to that ultimate goal was always a clear one. A similar hierarchy of authority explains the absence of appointment of academics to the appellate courts, in contrast with many other top courts around the world. The fact that academic lawyers in England and Wales have never enjoyed the status of their European and North American counterparts explains why, until the appointment of Baroness Hale, no former Professor of Law had become a Law Lord.

Most official accounts of the deficiencies of the judicial selection process have shied away from acknowledging that the hierarchical ranking of the legal profession is directly responsible for the composition of the senior judiciary. Nevertheless, few members of the Bar or the judiciary now seek to argue, as they once did, that advocacy skills acquired by barristers in the upper courts are a prerequisite for higher judicial office. Yet equally few are willing openly to acknowledge that the prioritising of the commercial Bar was driven by factors other than the objective search for the very best candidates, in particular the high proportion of members of the senior judiciary based in those chambers and so with a strong continuing connection with barristers in that field of work. Although it is now generally accepted that those in the traditional recruitment pool do not hold a monopoly on the skills or experiences required for judicial office, there is a strong consensus that those appointed to the higher judiciary have consistently been of the highest calibre. In order to square this circle, many lawyers and judges now take the position put forward recently by Lord Phillips that 'the system demonstrably ensured that those who were appointed were good; it did not, however, demonstrably ensure that the good were appointed'.[17]

The consultation process

Establishing the connection between the career path to the Law Lords and the hierarchy of status and authority within the legal profession provides an underlying explanation as to why certain lawyers have been appointed to the higher courts and others have not, but it does not explain the mechanisms by which that filter process has operated in practice. Given the combination of the broad eligibility requirements and the varied nature of the legal profession, some mechanism was needed to keep certain candidates on the 'golden road' to the Lords and others off it. This mechanism was the consultation process whereby senior judges were asked their views on the suitability of the candidates. Regarded as the heart of the judicial appointments process, the consultations process shaped the composition of all ranks of the judiciary, but had a particular significance for

[17] Lord Phillips, 'Constitutional Reform: One Year On', Judicial Studies Board Annual Lecture, March 2007.

the higher judiciary where the views of the judges were, for many years, the determining factor in the decision-making process. The central role of the consultations process meant that, as one former permanent secretary to the Lord Chancellor noted, the judges 'select themselves'.[18] The fact that appointment to the upper judicial ranks was, until very recently by invitation only, inevitably perpetuated this. Only those judges who had the strong support of their peers in the Court of Appeal and their future colleagues in the Lords could hope to be tapped on the shoulder. As the requirements of open and competitive selection processes became the norm in public life, the retention of the system of appointment by invitation only to the senior judiciary became increasingly unsustainable and was removed for all ranks below the Lords under the new system of judicial appointment commission established by the Constitutional Reform Act 2005. The new Supreme Court joins all other posts in being advertised and open to all qualified applicants.

The creation of a system of open selection is not, however, inherently incompatible with the consultations process which still has strong defenders. In common with all peer-based appointments, promotions, or performance review systems, it allows decisions to be based on the knowledge and views of those who best know the work and characteristics of the candidates. The argument for the value of this input is particularly persuasive in relation to positions such as the senior judiciary where it is difficult for those without high levels of expertise to make well-informed objective assessments of the quality of candidates' work and their suitability for the office. However, the price paid by all peer-based systems, as reflected in the composition of the Law Lords, has always been that of self-replication. Given our natural tendency to favour, consciously or unconsciously, those who have similar approaches, backgrounds and experiences as ourselves, the consultation process has effectively reinforced the tendency to exclude those who are outside the inner circle and so to reinforce the background homogeneity of the judges.

The role of politics in the appointments process to the Lords

One possible counter to this tendency towards self-replication amongst appointments to the Lords might have come from the political input to the decision-making process. In common with most top courts, the appointments process to the Law Lords was formally controlled by the executive.[19] The choice of appointment was that of the Prime Minister who by convention acted on the advice of her or his political appointee, the Lord Chancellor. Neither the Prime Minister nor the Lord Chancellor was obliged by any constitutional or statutory

---

[18] Quoted in R Stevens, 'A Loss of Independence? Judicial Independence and the Separation of Powers' (1999) 19 OJLS 390.

[19] Constitutionally, the appointments were made by the Queen on the advice of her Prime Minister after consultation with the Lord Chancellor.

requirement to consult with the judiciary, so that they could have made their selection quite legitimately from a wide pool of senior lawyers and judges on the basis of the likely ideological outlook in much the same way as the US President selects the appointees to the Supreme Court. In practice, the two appointments systems have developed along very different lines as regards the part played by political influence in the decision-making process. The central role played by the judiciary in the selection process through the consultations process has been matched by a general rejection of the role of party politics in the selection of the senior judges in the UK. Lord Bingham when Lord Chief Justice, for example, claimed in 1996 that no account was taken of a candidate's political views.[20] Similarly, Lord Irvine in evidence to the Home Affairs Select Committee in 1997 stated, 'Politics has never been a factor in appointment to the professional judiciary and as far as I am concerned it never will be, nor should be.'[21] The appointments made by both Lord Irvine and Lord Mackay during their time on the Woolsack provide support for these claims. The former Conservative Lord Chancellor, Lord Mackay, appointed a number of notably liberal-minded judges while the Labour Lord Chancellor, Lord Irvine, was responsible for the selection in 1998 of two strongly conservative judges: Lord Hobhouse and Lord Millett. Research carried out by Salzberger in the 1990s on the effect of the decisions of Court of Appeal judges on their prospects of promotion to the House of Lords also confirmed that there did not seem to be any correlation between 'loyalty' to the Government and promotion.[22]

This recognition that party politics played little or no role in the Appellate Committee appointments decisions should not, however, lead to the bald assertion that the appointments process was free of all political influence. While Lord Irvine may have been right to claim that during his tenure party politics was not a factor in the appointments decision, his suggestion that politics had never played a part is inaccurate. Before the Second World War the connection between political career and a legal career was a close one. Writing about the judicial appointments process in 1926, Harold Laski pointed out that all the senior judicial offices of the day, including the Lord Chief Justice and Master of the Rolls, had come to the Bench after careers in politics with many senior judges being appointed after serving as Attorney General or Solicitor General. His research found that there was a clear correlation between the political persuasion of the judges and the Lord Chancellor who appointed them and he concluded that judicial office was often a reward for political service.[23] Thirty years later, the

---

[20] Lord Bingham, *Judicial Independence* (London: Judicial Studies Board, 1996) 5.

[21] Home Affairs Select Committee, *The Work of the Lord Chancellor's Department, Minutes of evidence,* 13 October 1997, vol II para 82.

[22] E Salzberger, 'The Judges of the English Court of Appeal: Public Decision-Making Characteristics and the Chances of Promotion to the House of Lords' in S Nagel (ed), *Handbook of Global Legal Policy: Among and Within Nations* (New York: Marcel Dekker, 2000) 223.

[23] H Laski, 'The Technique of Judicial Appointment' (1926) 26 Mich L Rev 533–4.

picture was very different and political patronage had largely disappeared with very few senior judges being appointed after a political career.[24] The history of this depoliticisation process has yet to be written. One particularly odd feature of this change is that it came about over a period when the senior judiciary moved from relative passivity to the first awakenings of a more engaged and active decision-making. The time, in fact, when one might have expected the executive to wish to keep a stronger hold on the selection decisions of those appointed to the Lords and Court of Appeal rather than effectively handing it over to the judges themselves.

In addition to this historical qualification to the claim of non-political appointments, a second distinction has to be made between the influence of appointees' party political support and their broad ideological values. The claim that the appointments process to the Lords was, by convention, free of politics implicitly refers to party politics. The term 'non-politicisation' is shorthand for saying that if a candidate for high judicial office was an active supporter of a mainstream political party this had little relevance one way or the other for his or her chances of appointment. Any suggestion that no account was taken of candidates' general political views in the broadest sense is more problematic. Just as judges did not take their place on the Appellate Committee as ideological virgins, so the Lord Chancellors who appointed them were not unaware of their appointees' views. What influence this knowledge has had on specific appointments decisions will never be fully known, given the confidential and closed nature of the decision-making process. But it would be naïve to imagine that it has not sometimes been significant in deciding between candidates who have broadly similar levels of support amongst the senior judges. Although we do not know the basis on which Prime Ministers and Lord Chancellors went about the process of selecting from the possible candidates in each case, we do know that some Prime Ministers did more than rubber-stamp their Lord Chancellor's decision and played an active part in the process of determining the final selection. Lord Mackay, when Lord Chancellor, was asked about the decision-making process and the role of the then Prime Minister, Margaret Thatcher. His characteristically diplomatic response was also very revealing:

Chairman: I think you answered, just to confirm to Peter Butler, that all your recommendations [to the Prime Minister] had been accepted?

Lord Mackay: I was careful not to say that. What I did say was that I make these recommendations in confidence to the Prime Minister. I have never been disappointed by any recommendation that the Prime Minister has made to Her Majesty during my time—neither surprised nor disappointed.[25]

On the basis of such evidence the Committee reported that it was left with 'some qualms' about the role of the Prime Minister in the appointments process and

---

[24] Stevens (n 18); Shetreet (n 8) 71.
[25] Home Affairs Select Committee, *The Work of the Lord Chancellor's Department, Minutes of evidence*, 13 October 1997, vol II para 459.

questioned whether he or she should continue to play a part in the system.[26]
These concerns were taken on board when the proposals for the new judicial
appointments process were drawn up in 2003 and the provisions of the Constitutional Reform Act 2005 removed the Prime Minister from the process,
leaving the Lord Chancellor alone to recommend the final decision to the Queen
in relation to all judicial appointments, including that of the new Supreme Court.

Lessons for the Supreme Court

A broad-brush overview of the Law Lords reveals a body of judges who were
generally highly regarded, both in the UK and abroad, in terms of their integrity
and their intellectual ability. Socially and politically conservative, drawn from a
narrow background and a tightly defined legal career, they generally commanded
the confidence of the legal community and enjoyed high public regard combined
with a low public profile.

How different will the picture be of the new Supreme Court, should a similar
review be carried out in the future? Given the general trend towards greater
openness and public knowledge in both our legal and political institutions, it is
unlikely that the Court will be able or willing to function with such a high degree
of anonymity. If the trend in the Appellate Committee's decision-making continues on its current trajectory and the Supreme Court takes its place as a leading
member of the global community of top courts, then the sort of intense public
attention attracted by the *Pinochet* case will become a more common phenomenon. One consequence of this shift will be that the lack of diversity in the
composition of the Court will attract more attention and the political pressure for
change will build. The ability of the Law Lords to side-step the connection
between institutional legitimacy and diversity is likely to become much harder for
the Supreme Court. Experience from other supreme courts shows that it is quite
possible to identify very high quality candidates from outside the traditional
recruitment pool. For the Supreme Court that will mean a rethink of the traditional assumption that candidates should inevitably be drawn from the Court of
Appeal.[27] In the future, the selection process may not, in all instances at least, be a
case of simply moving upstairs.

---

[26] ibid, vol I para 128.
[27] Stevens is not alone in the view that it would be a 'disaster' if the new Supreme Court were
staffed entirely by Court of Appeal judges. See Stevens (n 7) 152.

8

The Law Lords: Who Has Served

Tom Bingham

The judicial function of the House of Lords was saved from the axe in 1876 not out of respect for its quality or value but from a belief that removing it would diminish the standing of the House. As late as the 1960s authoritative voices were challenging the need for an appeal from (in England and Wales) the Court of Appeal,[1] or were agnostic on the question.[2] But while, in the debates that preceded enactment of the Constitutional Reform Act 2005, there was much argument over whether a separate supreme court was desirable or whether the Appellate Committee of the House should continue more or less as it was, there was no pressure to do away with the further right of appeal altogether. So it seems that the 109 men and one woman who have held office as Lords of Appeal in Ordinary since the first appointment under the 1876 Act in October of that year up to the time of writing (October 2008) must have got some things right (unless the courts of appeal in the three UK jurisdictions have increasingly got things wrong). So it is perhaps worth taking a closer look at these 110 individuals.

The professional background of 83 of those appointed was wholly or mainly[3] in England and Wales, 19 in Scotland, and eight in Ireland or Northern Ireland, the Irish total being reduced by the absence of any appointment between that of Lord MacDermott in April 1947 and Lord Lowry in August 1988. All had been barristers, although one (the first Lord Russell of Killowen) had first practised as a solicitor. All were men, until the welcome appointment of Baroness Hale in 2004.

The schools most favoured by future Law Lords (or most skilful at educating them) were Eton (eight), Winchester (seven), and the Edinburgh Royal Academy

---

[1] G Gardiner and A Martin, *Law Reform Now* (London: Victor Gollancz, 1963).

[2] Louis Blom-Cooper and Gavin Drewry, starting from an agnostic position, concluded in their book *Final Appeal: A Study of the House of Lords in its Judicial Capacity* (Oxford: Clarendon Press, 1972) that a second appeal to a final court of appeal should be retained, and in 1999 ('The Appellate Function' in B Dickson and P Carmichael (eds), *The House of Lords: Its Parliamentary and Judicial Roles* (Oxford: Hart, 1999)) they endorsed the enduring value of the House of Lords in its judicial capacity.

[3] There were those, like Lord Carson, who practised with success in more than one jurisdiction. Lord Macnaghten, although brought up in County Antrim, which he later represented in Parliament, practised exclusively in England.

(six), but more were educated at grammar schools in England and Wales and their equivalents elsewhere than went to Eton. All attended a university, save three (Lords Fitzgerald, Donovan, and Bridge, the last of whom obtained a degree in mathematics at the Open University after retirement). The range of universities attended was broad (Belfast, Cambridge, Cape Town, Dublin, Edinburgh, Galway, Glasgow, Heidelberg, Liverpool, London, Melbourne, Oxford, Paris, and Stellenbosch), and a number of Law Lords attended more than one (in recent years, Lords Slynn, Nicholls, Steyn, Hoffmann, Hope, Scott, and Rodger). The subjects most frequently studied were classics, law (often as a second degree), and mathematics, but some studied other subjects including modern history (Lords Keith of Avonholm, Cohen, Devlin, Roskill, and Bingham), chemistry (Lords Somervell, Diplock, and Neuberger), PPE (Lords Kilbrandon and Fraser), and mechanical sciences (Lord Upjohn). Oxford (52) and Cambridge (40) were the most popular choices of university, among colleges Trinity (12) and St John's (seven) at Cambridge; Balliol (12, or 13 if Lord Rodger, a junior research fellow, be included), New College (nine), and Magdalen (six) at Oxford. Not all graduated with the highest honours, although most of them did: but Lord Thankerton was placed in the third class in both parts of the Cambridge law tripos in 1894 and 1895, and Viscount Dilhorne, as the *DNB* delicately puts it, 'secured a third in law [at Oxford] in 1926'. Several held fellowships at an Oxford or Cambridge college for a time before embarking on legal practice, most recently Lords Goff, Lloyd, Hoffmann, and Rodger, but only Baroness Hale had held a professorial chair. All save six were married, but only one was married more than twice. Two fathers and sons held office as Lords of Appeal in Ordinary (Lords Watson and Thankerton; Lords Keith of Avonholm and Keith of Kinkel), and there was one father-son-grandson succession, all Lords Russell of Killowen.

In contrast with later appointees, a majority of those appointed up to 1930 had previously served as members of the House of Commons, which no Law Lord has done since Lords Donovan (appointed January 1964), Dilhorne (June 1969), and Simon of Glaisdale (April 1971). This no doubt reflects the increasingly apolitical nature of the appointments process. Up to 1930 also a significant minority of appointees (Scots and Irishmen prominent among them) had held no previous judicial office and were appointed straight from the Bar: Lords Gordon (October 1876), Watson (April 1880), Macnaghten (January 1887), Russell of Killowen (May 1894), Atkinson (December 1905), Shaw of Dunfermline (February 1909), Robson (October 1910), Cave (November 1918), Carson (June 1921), Thankerton (May 1929), and Macmillan (February 1930). Since then, only Lords Reid (October 1948) and Radcliffe (June 1949) have been so appointed.

The mean age of appointees over the period was fractionally under 63. The oldest appointees were Lords Lindley and Romer (71½) and Brightman (70), although Viscounts Maugham and Simonds were respectively 73 and 72 on reappointment after serving as Lord Chancellor. The youngest appointees were Lords Radcliffe (50), MacDermott (51), Watson (52), Robertson (54) and

Sumner (54). The average term of service, excluding those currently (October 2008) serving, was just under nine years. But this figure conceals wide variations. Lords Reid (October 1948 to January 1975) and Macnaghten (January 1887 to February 1913) served for over 26 years, Lord Atkinson (December 1905 to February 1928) over 22, Lord Shaw of Dunfermline (February 1909 to April 1929) over 20, and Lord Keith of Kinkel (January 1977 to September 1996) just under 20. By contrast, the first Lord Russell of Killowen served for only 57 days (7 May to 2 July 1894), Lord Lane for just over six months (28 September 1979 to 15 April 1980), and Lord Goddard for 18 months (19 July 1944 to 21 January 1946) before, in each case, becoming Lord Chief Justice of England. Lord Bowen served for just over six months (September 1893 to April 1894) before he died, and Lord Greene for under a year (June 1949 to May 1950) before ill health compelled him to retire. Terms of under three years were also served by Lords Gordon (October 1876 to August 1879), Hannen (January 1891 to August 1893), Robson (October 1910 to August 1912), Roche (October 1935 to January 1938), Devlin (October 1961 to January 1964), and Evershed (April 1962 to January 1965). Lord Mackay served for just over two years before becoming Lord Chancellor (October 1985 to October 1987) and Lord Phillips for nearly one and a half years (January 1999 to June 2000) before appointment as Master of the Rolls and then Lord Chief Justice of England and Wales and reappointment as a Lord of Appeal in Ordinary as Senior Law Lord.

The average age of Law Lords on giving up office, for whatever reason, was 71½. This average also conceals wide variations. Lord Reid was 84½, Lords Atkinson and Macnaghten 83, Viscount Dunedin 82, Lord Thankerton 80. The youngest elective retirees were Lord Devlin (58) and Lord Robson (59). But Lord MacDermott gave up office aged 55 to become Lord Chief Justice of Northern Ireland and Lord Mackay at 60 to become Lord Chancellor. Lord Bowen was only 59 when he died, one of 18 Law Lords to die in office: it was a relatively common occurrence in earlier days, but no one has died in office since Lords Upjohn and Donovan (1971) and Diplock (1985). Of the last 18 Law Lords to retire (otherwise than to take up another judicial office) only two had effectively reached the statutory retirement age of 75: Lords Lowry (1994) and Bingham (2008).

Lord Phillips was selected to succeed as Senior Law Lord (and prospective first President of the Supreme Court) in October 2008 by the procedure laid down in the Constitutional Reform Act 2005, adopted informally because the relevant sections of the Act had not come into force. All other appointments since 1876 have been made by the traditional process: the Sovereign, on the advice of the Prime Minister, who is him- or herself advised by the Lord Chancellor and who has all but invariably accepted the Lord Chancellor's advice. In recent years, the Lord Chancellor has, when filling a vacancy made by the retirement or impending retirement of a Law Lord with an English or Welsh background, consulted the other Law Lords and some of the most senior judges. The ensuing discussion has focused exclusively on the perceived judicial quality of those seen as candidates. There has been no consideration at all of candidates' political allegiance, almost all candidates neither having nor ever having had any such allegiance. There has similarly been no discussion of candidates' supposed leanings or ideologies.

Are there, as the Lords of Appeal in Ordinary evolve into Justices of the Supreme Court, any lessons to be learned from the foregoing history? Perhaps:

(1) The seeming impossibility nowadays of combining a serious career in representative politics with legal practice at the highest level makes it unlikely that the political experience of the earlier Law Lords will be repeated in the future. The apolitical nature of the appointments process now, as in recent years, makes such appointments less likely. While the independence of the judges is rightly regarded in this country as fundamental, the absence of experience in public administration among the members of the highest tribunal must be regretted: its deliberations would be enriched if some of its members had direct personal experience of the democratic and bureaucratic process as of the civil and criminal trial.

(2) While there is no exact correlation between a Law Lord's tenure as such and the enduring value of his or her contribution to the law, it is probably true that most of those who have made the greatest contribution have served for significant periods of time. One might instance, looking back (but eschewing reference to those still living), the 26-year tenure of Lords Macnaghten and Reid, the 18 years of Lord Dunedin, the 17 years of Lords Wilberforce and Diplock, the 16 years of Lords Sumner and Atkin and the second Lord Russell of Killowen, and the 15 years of Lord Macmillan. While there are obvious exceptions (such as Lord Devlin and Lord Mustill), few of those who served for very short periods had the opportunity to make a comparable mark.

(3) Thus, it is suggested, the task of those selecting future Justices of the Supreme Court is not to choose seasoned judges nearing the end of distinguished careers to spend two or three years in the Supreme Court before retirement but to choose outstandingly able younger candidates who would have time to mature and develop in office. There would be obvious risks in this more adventurous approach, and it might well lead to more appointments direct from professional practice and from academe. But it may be an approach worth considering in order to achieve a blend of youthful energy with seasoned experience in a court fully attuned to the contemporary world.

(4) The problem of giving recruits to the Supreme Court time to develop and mature is exacerbated by the current retirement age of 70. The reduction of the retirement age from 75 to 70 may in retrospect be recognised as an error. As already noted, relatively few of those entitled to serve until 75 chose to do so. There has not in practice been a problem of senile judges who should have retired and declined to do so. And Law Lords, like the rest of the population, live (and, it is hoped, retain their faculties) for longer. The first

ten Law Lords appointed after 1876 died at an average age of 72; the comparable figures for the last ten Law Lords to die is 86. The earlier retirement age is not compensated by earlier appointment to less senior judicial office: the trend is, if anything, upwards.

(5) The 2005 Act lays down two significant criteria for the selection of Justices of the Supreme Court: appointment must be on merit,[4] and the court must include judges with knowledge of and experience of practice of the law of each part of the United Kingdom.[5] The first of these, merit, re-states the test that Lord Chancellors have sought to apply for many years. But the term is not self-defining. It directs attention to proven professional achievement as a necessary condition, but also enables account to be taken of wider considerations, including the virtue of gender and ethnic diversity, values which the mandatory lay element in the selection panel is no doubt intended to promote. The second criterion, representation across the UK jurisdictions, has been consistently met since 1876 in relation to Scotland and, for roughly half the period, in relation to Ireland or Northern Ireland. Despite producing some notable Law Lords (such as Lords Atkin, Morris of Borth-y-Gest, and Edmund-Davies) Wales enjoyed no separate jurisdictional voice, being part of a unitary system embracing England and Wales. But Welsh devolution is in its infancy and if the pace of devolution quickens to develop a distinctively Welsh legal identity, the language of the Act is wide enough to enable its claim to representation to be heard.

As the Law Lords progress across Parliament Square to their new home on the western side and their metamorphosis into Justices of the Supreme Court, two questions are likely to follow them. The first is whether the President of the Supreme Court will simply be the Senior Law Lord under a grander name or whether the new office will lead to an enhancement of the role as well as the title, recognising that the holder is no longer just the senior professional playing under the captaincy of the gentleman Lord Chancellor. Judicially, it seems likely that the President's role will depend on his (or in due course her) judicial standing, personality, and ability to persuade uncertain colleagues. Administratively, it seems certain that the burden will be heavier. It also seems certain that the public profile of the office will be higher (it could scarcely be otherwise), which will give the holder the opportunity, whether accepted or not, to play a more prominent part on the public stage.

The second, and more important, question is whether its transformation into a supreme court will change, substantively, the way in which the Appellate Committee has done its work. There are those who predict that re-constitution as a supreme court, in a building of its own, will lead the new court to be more assertive, more interventionist, less respectful of governmental authority, than its

---

[4] s 27(5).   [5] s 27(8).

noble predecessor. But the new court will enjoy no powers not exercised by the Appellate Committee, save that of ruling on devolution issues, previously exercised by almost exactly the same people sitting as the Judicial Committee of the Privy Council. The accommodation of the new court falls well short of the grandiose. The Committee in recent years has not been notably quiescent and passive. The new Justices will not need reminding of the elementary constitutional fact that they will continue to lack the power most characteristic of supreme courts around the world, that of nullifying legislation as unconstitutional. For reasons which are difficult to identify, courts tend to operate in cycles, with a phase of legal growth and development being followed by a period of retrenchment and relative passivity. It may be, but time alone will tell, that the earlier years of the Supreme Court will be a period of consolidation rather than heightened activity.

As the sun finally sets on the House of Lords as a judicial body, even those who regarded the establishment of a supreme court as a reform long overdue must experience a twinge of nostalgic regret. A chapter in our legal history comes to an end. But a new one opens, and, as TS Eliot wrote,

> Time present and time past
> Are both perhaps present in time future,
> And time future contained in time past.[6]

The new Justices will be the beneficiaries of what the Law Lords, labouring mightily and on the whole fruitfully, over 133 years, bequeath to them.

---

[6] *Burnt Norton*, from *Four Quartets*.

9

1966 and All That: The Story of the Practice Statement[1]

Louis Blom-Cooper

Their lordships regard the use of precedent as an indispensable foundation upon which to decide what is the law and its application to individual cases. It provides at least some degree of certainty upon which individuals can rely in the conduct of their affairs, as well as a basis for orderly development of legal rules.

Their lordships nevertheless recognise that too rigid adherence to precedent may lead to injustice in a particular case and also unduly restrict the proper development of the law. They propose therefore to modify their present practice and, while treating former decisions of this House as normally binding, to depart from a previous decision when it appears right to do so.

In this connection they will bear in mind the danger of disturbing retrospectively the basis on which contracts, settlements of property, and fiscal arrangements have been entered into and also the especial need for certainty as to the criminal law.

This announcement is not intended to affect the use of precedent elsewhere than in this House.

By no stretch of the imagination can 26 July 1966 be regarded as an earth-shattering day in the life of the country, or even its legal system. But the Practice Statement[2] by the Lord Chancellor (Lord Gardiner) and the Lords of Appeal in Ordinary that day, before judgments were given in the House of Lords, dropped a pebble into the judicial pool that produced not merely a few ripples but also a seismic wave in English juridical thinking. And the doom-laden opponents, such as Lord Halsbury, of modifying the absolute rule of *stare decisis* could hardly today fault the loosening of the bonds of the doctrine of precedent in the final court of appeal. The Practice Statement has utterly disproved Professor John Langbein's gloomy prognostication in the Cornell Law Review for 1968[3] that it 'will not rescue English law from its century of petrification or the House of Lords from what had become burgeoning disrepute'. Rather, the story of that legally

---

[1] For the title of this chapter I have purloined the phrase from Professor Julius Stone's article '1966 and All That: Loosing the Chains of Precedent' (1969) Columbia L Rev 1162.
[2] *Practice Statement (HL: Judicial Precedent)* [1966] 1 WLR 1234, [1966] 3 All ER 77.
[3] 53 Cornell L Rev 807.

historic event displays the carapace of traditional English lawyers' disinclination readily to accept radical change and to the cautious application of such change, once it is ultimately conceded.

The doctrine of self-binding precedent is usually attributed to Lord Halsbury, the Lord Chancellor, sitting in 1898 with Lords Macnaghten, Morris, and James of Hereford in *London Street Tramways Co Ltd v London CC*.[4] But the true provenance of the rule can be traced to a decision of the House in 1861, a decade or so before the statutory rationalisation during the 1870s of the judicial House of Lords. In *Beamish v Beamish*[5] their Lordships were being invited to reconsider a doctrine laid down in *R v Millis*[6] by a House equally divided—thus the appeal had been dismissed—in its opinion on what constituted a common law marriage. Lord Campbell, who had dissented in *Millis*, nevertheless spoke firmly against reversing the decision. He said that 'the law laid down as your *ratio decidendi*, being clearly binding on all inferior tribunals,... if it were not considered as equally binding upon Your Lordships, this House would be *arrogating to itself the right of altering the law, and legislating by its own separate authority*' (italics supplied)—a judicial affirmation of the sovereignty of Parliament. Lord Halsbury adopted a different tack to support the rule:

Of course I do not deny that cases of individual hardship may arise, and there may be a current of opinion in the profession that such and such an opinion is erroneous; but what is that occasional interference with what is perhaps abstract injustice, as compared with the inconvenience—the disastrous inconvenience—of having each question subject to being reargued and the dealings of mankind rendered doubtful by reason of different decisions, so that in truth and in fact there would be no real final court of appeal?[7]

As an Irish judge caustically observed in 1965 (perspicaciously anticipating the Practice Statement): '[T]his argument from inconvenience would come more suitably from the mouth of an executive officer than from that of a judge.'[8]

Before 1861, the situation had been somewhat different, with the House of Lords more than willing to overrule previous decisions, where those decisions seemed erroneous. In 1840, in the case of *Birtwhistle v Vardill*,[9] Lord Brougham said that judges, 'in deciding important questions, should adopt the course, where they have gone wrong, of at once, in an open and manly way, retracing their steps, rather than persist in their error'. And in 1852, in *Bright v Hutton*,[10] Lord St Leonards addressed the House with these words: 'You are not bound by any rule of law which you may lay down, if upon a subsequent occasion you should

---

[4] [1898] AC 375. A single judgment—the other three merely agreed—was delivered *ex tempore* on 25 April 1898, the respondent not having been called on to reply.
[5] (1861) 9 HL Cases 274, 338–9; 11 Eng Rep 735, 761.   [6] (1844) 10 Cl & F 534, 8 ER 844.
[7] *London Street Tramways Co Ltd v London CC* [1898] AC 375, 380.
[8] Kingsmill Moore J in *AG v Ryan's Car Hire Ltd* [1965] 642, 654; see also *O'Brien v Mirror Group Newspapers* [2001] IR 1, where Keane CJ speaks of the importance of 'certainty, stability and practicability' of the law on which the doctrine is grounded.
[9] 7 Cl & F 895, 922.   [10] (1852) 3 HLC 341, 389, 10 ER 133.

find reason to differ from that rule; that is, that this House, like every court of justice, possesses an inherent power to correct an error into which it may have fallen.'

The doctrine of binding precedent has been the subject of academic attack ever since Lord Halsbury's famous ruling. Professor W Barton Leach pointed out in 1967 that *stare decisis* is a habit of mind in all walks of life—the professions, business, family life. One does what one has done before in similar circumstances. But when it is obvious that one's previous actions have turned out badly, or that circumstances are essentially different, the intelligent human being reviews the problem anew; if, with due consideration to desiderata of stability and continuity, he concludes that something different should be done in the future, a different course is generally charted.[11]

The genesis of the movement towards reform, usually attributed to Lord Gardiner and his co-authors in *Law Reform Now* in 1963, can be more properly traced in the legal literature to that radical Law Lord, Lord Wright, in a tailpiece to an outstanding article in the Cambridge Law Journal in 1943, entitled, with delicious simplicity, *Precedents*.[12] Lord Wright ended his plea for change with his own residue of caution: '[T]he instinct of inertia is as potent in judges as in other people . . . Precedents would still be precedents, though not coercive but merely persuasive.' After 1943, apart from the distinct advocacy for change by Lord Wright, other judicial figures were similarly outspoken. Lord Cohen adumbrated the change in 1951. He said: 'This House, being a part of Parliament, is not in theory so strictly bound by precedent as is the Court of Appeal, though it naturally treats with great respect and rarely disturbs earlier decisions of its own.'[13] Lord Denning, in a dissenting judgment in 1959, was typically outspoken:[14]

It seems to me that when a particular precedent—even of your Lordships' House—comes into conflict with a fundamental principle—also of your Lordships' House, then the fundamental principle must prevail. This must at least be true when, on the one hand, the particular precedent leads to absurdity or injustice and, on the other hand, the fundamental principle leads to consistency and fairness. It would, I think, be a great mistake to cling too closely to particular precedent at the expense of fundamental principle.

Other voices joined a chorus that maintained that the rigid rule of *stare decisis* must in a court of ultimate resort give place to a more elastic formula. Among the critics of the rigid rule was Lord Reid, who, in *Midland Silicones Ltd v Scruttons*

---

[11] 'Revisionism in the House of Lords: The Bastion of Rigid *Stare Decisis* Falls' (1967) 80 Harvard L Rev 797.

[12] (1944) 8 CLJ 118. Twelve years earlier, in the case of *Birch v Brown* [1931] AC 605, Lord Macmillan had pre-empted the discussion when he suggested that precedents 'must often be stepping stones rather than halting places'.

[13] 'Jurisdiction, Practice and Procedure of the Court of Appeal' (1951) 11 CLJ 3. Lord Cohen sat as a Lord of Appeal in Ordinary from 1951–60 and was, significantly, a member of the Appellate Committee in *Public Trustee v Inland Revenue Comrs* [1960] AC 398, which 'reconsidered' Lord Macnaghten's previous dictum. See below.

[14] *London Transport Executive v Betts* [1959] AC 213, 217.

Ltd,[15] said: 'I have on more than one occasion stated my view that this rule is too rigid and that it does not in fact create certainty... But I am bound by the rule until it is altered.' The Practice Statement of July 1966 was hence inevitable, the only question being when and how the change could be effected, and consequentially how it would be applied.[16]

In *Final Appeal* (1972) Professor Drewry and I wrote that no one could have contemplated the Practice Statement of 1966 coming into being so long as Viscount Simonds was still in harness—nor, we might have added, so long as he was alive.[17] That outstanding judge had an unusual career history. Appointed a Chancery judge in 1937, he was appointed a Lord of Appeal in Ordinary direct from the High Court bench in 1944. In 1951 he was appointed Lord Chancellor in the Churchill government, but gave way to Lord Kilmuir in 1954, whereupon, instead of retreating into the limbo which his age might have indicated—he was then 73, at a time before there was any retiring age for the higher judiciary; that only came in 1959—he returned as the Senior Law Lord. During the seven years of his final stint as a Law Lord, Viscount Simonds left an indelible imprint on the work of the Appellate Committee. Endowed with a powerful intellect, he ranks as a legal giant. He epitomised the classical legalistic conservative lawyer, whose total commitment to *stare decisis* and the rigid rule that ensnared even the final court of appeal was manifest in some of his judgments. Not infrequently he had cause to chastise Lord Denning for the latter's irreverent attitude to binding precedent.

After Viscount Simonds' retirement in 1962 it was the conventional wisdom in legal circles that any inclination by an incoming Labour Lord Chancellor to promote the change would not be forthcoming. And opposition from the immediately preceding Senior Law Lord would have persisted. Not so, it would now appear. Whatever views Viscount Simonds had held, there is at least a hint that he had abandoned any implacable hostility, even to the point of not actively opposing the change. Viscount Simonds died in 1971, aged 90, not having publicly aired his views in July 1966, or thereafter. The questioning here of the conventional wisdom derives judicially from Lord Reid, an impeccable source.

In a trademark appeal which lasted 13 days in the Appellate Committee, the report of the case, appearing only in the specialist Reports of Patent Cases,[18] unusually contains extensive extracts from the oral argument of counsel (16 pages of the printed report). During the course of the hearing mention was made of a case construing provisions of the Finance Act 1894 which had first introduced estate duty into tax law.[19] Counsel cited the case, which evoked the following

[15] [1962] AC 446.

[16] For a fuller account of the background to the Practice Statement, see Alan Paterson's *The Law Lords* (London: Macmillan, 1982) 143–53.

[17] Viscount Simonds was against the change, even as late as 1962; according to Lord Denning, in earlier discussions of the question, 'Lord Simonds wouldn't have it at all.' See footnote in Paterson, ibid, at 151.

[18] *Re GE Trade Mark* [1973] RPC 297.

[19] *Cowley v Inland Revenue Comrs* [1899] AC 198.

response from Lord Reid: 'I think some people take the view that Lord Simonds was the progenitor of our present practice that we can reconsider decisions of this House because what in fact was done was that they reconsidered *Cowley's* case.'[20]

Cowley's case had indeed been 'reconsidered' in *Public Trustee v Inland Revenue Commissioners*[21] at the end of 1959 before Viscount Simonds and Lords Radcliffe, Cohen, and Keith of Avonholm. For over 60 years Lord Macnaghten's judgment in *Cowley's* case had been accepted as laying down a principle for the determination of estate duty cases. Lord Macnaghten had made a remark, drawing a distinction between property passing for estate duty purposes under section 1 of the Finance Act 1894 and property deemed to pass under section 2(1) of the Act. The two sections, Lord Macnaghten had held, 'were mutually exclusive'. That judicial pronouncement had been repeatedly followed and made the *ratio* of subsequent decisions, and must, in very many cases which never reached the courts, have been accepted as determining the liability to duty. In 1950 the Master of the Rolls, Sir Raymond Evershed (later Lord Evershed) referred to the 'celebrated pronouncement of Lord Macnaghten which has constituted one of the most significant decisions in the interpretation of the Finance Act 1894'.[22] Viscount Simonds' judgment reveals the dilemma of a Law Lord faced with a judicial pronouncement that dictated the decisions of the courts (including the House of Lords). He wrote:

What, then, my Lords, is the proper course to be taken? I believe that I yield to no one in the importance I attach to the rule of precedent. But this case stands alone in my experience. Observations so patently wrong (may I be forgiven for saying so) that they leave only a sense of wonderment . . . all these factors [previous judicial comments on the Macnaghten blunder] lead me to the conclusion that I can properly invite your Lordships to say that section 1 and section 2 [of the Finance Act 1894] are not mutually exclusive.[23]

True enough, the Law Lords in 1959 were compelled only to disapprove the reasoning—or, if you like, a dictum[24]—of Lord Macnaghten, and were not, at least not directly, calling into question Lord Halsbury's judgment in the *London Street Tramways* case. As a commentator in the British Tax Review cryptically observed, 'the extraordinary thing is that the statement of the law long accepted as one of the most significant pronouncements on the interpretation of the Finance Act 1894 is torn to pieces, and it makes little difference to the law in practice. This in itself is a minor mystery of the law.'[25]

Viscount Simonds confessed to his sole experience of doubting the efficacy of *stare decisis* in all its forms. His dictum did not bite directly on the rule of binding precedent of their Lordships' previous decisions. But may the experience not have

---

[20] The report is notable for a pithy judgment from Lord Reid: see 316, lines 18–25.
[21] [1960] AC 398.   [22] *Re Duke of Norfolk* [1950] Ch 467, 473.
[23] [1960] AC 398, 415–16.
[24] ibid, 405–6. Viscount Simonds said that what Lord Macnaghten had said in *Cowley's* case in relation to sections 1 and 2 'was a mere dictum'.
[25] 1960 BTR 65.

materially weakened Viscount Simonds' stance on the issue? After all, he was not averse to getting rid of antiquated law, so long as it was the product of the lower courts. In *Plato Films Ltd v Speidel*[26] he wrote: ' . . . long though the decision has stood unchallenged, I should not hesitate to reverse it if it was one of those cases in which serious inconvenience would follow from perpetuating an erroneous construction of a ruling of law'. Lord Reid's allusion to his predecessor being, 'in some people's view at least, the progenitor of the Practice Statement' may have been a polite nod in the direction of acquiescence by Lord Simonds, if only reluctantly, to the pronounced shift in judicial outlook that preceded the Practice Statement.

Even if Viscount Simonds should no longer be affixed with outright hostility to the Practice Statement, the prime credit must go to Lord Gardiner and Lord Reid for writing the epitaph to an ill-conceived rule of law, and for introducing the reform. Since there was no pending case before the Appellate Committee, the Practice Statement could not operate as a judicial decision: it was not strictly law. Yet its acceptance by all the serving Lords of Appeal in Ordinary indicates that they and the Lord Chancellor had simply got together to effect a change that all of them, except in legal theory, accepted was not part of any curial proceeding; nor was it a legislative act, but was treated as a rule of practice to be (and which has been) observed with a regularity of subsequent judicial behaviour. *London Street Tramways* has never been 'reconsidered'—neither in *Public Trustee v IRC*, nor in any subsequent decision of their Lordships.

Whatever stirrings there might have been at the Palace of Westminster after the advent of the Labour administration in 1964, the impetus for the abandonment of the pure doctrine of *stare decisis* came from Edinburgh in the shape of the Scottish Law Commission, which led to its counterpart in England joining in the proposal for reform. But even that fact obscures the true beginning, which derived from the promptings of that distinctive academic lawyer, Professor TB Smith (later Sir Tom Smith). Professor Smith was no black-letter lawyer; he saw the law as a series of grand themes, so that as the academic on the Commission he was in pole position to propose in the Law Commission's First Programme an item on 'Judicial Precedent'. Professor Smith had previously written a monograph on judicial precedent in Scots law, arguing for a loose and flexible approach. Characteristically for a very Scots lawyer, he found that all he saw to be wrong with the law north of the border was traceable to the rigidity of the English doctrine. Tracing the Scottish history of the matter, Smith included a view expressed by Lord Cooper of Culross (his judicial hero and distinguished President of the Court of Session) that the doctrine had had a stifling effect upon the law of Scotland. Professor Smith added his own historical perspective of previous Scottish judges who had exhibited an activist approach to the moulding of Scots law, as well as noting the recent writings in England of Lord Gardiner and

---

[26] [1961] AC 1090, 1124.

Professor Andrew Martin (one of the first commissioners on the English Law Commission) in their edition of *Law Reform Now*.

The appearance at the end of 1965 of the Scottish Law Commission's First Programme, with the recommendation that for Scottish appeals to the House of Lords the doctrine established in *London Street Tramways v London CC*[27] (following a case considered by the House of Lords four years earlier in a Scottish appeal which involved the interpretation of a statute, the principle having been considered by the House in subsequent English appeals) should not apply, led to a joint meeting of the two Commissions in January 1966. The outcome of that meeting was an agreement that the Scottish Law Commission should make recommendations for a short Bill to allow the House of Lords to reverse its decisions in Scottish cases; the English Law Commission indicated that it might include a similar provision for England and Wales. Interestingly, although no such recommendation appeared in its First Programme, there appeared to be an inclination to extend the reform to the lower courts in England and Wales which could be dealt with gradually, to be achieved by the process of codification, which both chairmen (Lord (then Mr Justice) Scarman and Lord Kilbrandon) strongly favoured. We still await that development.

The Scottish Law Commission set to work, by way of preparing a paper setting out the argument for the necessary change in Scotland; it annexed a draft statutory provision. Sensing constitutional difficulties presented by the legislative proposal, the Commission consulted officials at the House of Lords. At that point, the focus shifted from the parliamentary process to a simpler and non-legislative action by the Law Lords. The Principal Clerk to the Appellate Committee of the House of Lords, Richard Cave,[28] wrote to the Secretary of the Scottish Commission, saying that the correspondence between the Scottish Commission and the officials in Parliament (including parliamentary draftsmen) had been submitted to the Lord Chancellor (Lord Gardiner). The English Commission was, by March 1966, well versed in what was afoot and displayed enthusiastic support, which was coupled with a commitment to consider without delay the English point of view. In April 1966, the two Commissions were alerted to the Lord Chancellor's interest in the topic, and sensed that the reform was coming without parliamentary action, and speedily. Clearly, Lord Gardiner had alighted on the Scottish initiative to promote the cause he had espoused so volubly before he became Lord Chancellor.

The Lord Chancellor instantly sought to canvass the opinion of Lord Reid and the other Lords of Appeal in Ordinary, and a meeting took place between them.

---

[27] [1898] AC 375.

[28] Richard Cave had been a member of the Judicial Office since 1945. A legal journal once paid tribute to the office and to the Principal Clerk by remarking, 'To those whose work is on the outer circumference of its approaches, the oracular pronouncements which spasmodically emerge from that cave of mystery, the Judicial Department [*sic*] of the House of Lords, always provide material for interesting meditations'—hence the reference to the 'cave of mystery' in James Vallance White's engaging chapter on the Judicial Office, ch 3 of this volume.

On 22 June 1966 the Lord Chancellor's Department told Lord Kilbrandon that the Law Lords intended to change their position as regards *stare decisis*. Lord Reid drafted the proposed statement, which was considered by all his judicial brethren, and an 'outer circle' of former Lords of Appeal (including, one surmises, Viscount Simonds), the Lord Chief Justice (Lord Parker), and the Master of the Rolls (Lord Denning) were consulted. The draft was urgently attended to, since Lord Gardiner and Lord Reid were keen to make the statement before the summer recess. And so the Practice Statement was duly made on 26 July 1966. The rest is history. A Scottish initiative had produced, with remarkable ease, a reform that served further to cement within the two jurisdictions the work of the United Kingdom's final court of appeal.

In essence, the Practice Statement meant that the legislature and judiciary could in future share the burden of law reform, the former possessing primacy in lawmaking. Since 1966 the judicial contribution, though modest, has been significant; the Practice Statement has been applied only where the judiciary has sensed the disinclination of politicians to act promptly and in areas appropriate for judicial determination.

The severe, self-imposed limitation on the power to reverse its early decisions 'only sparingly' has been best exemplified by the House of Lords' attitude to the law of murder. When in 1998 Lord Mustill referred to the rule of English law, that a person can be guilty of murder if he or she merely intended to cause grievous bodily harm, as a 'conspicuous anomaly', and said that the law of homicide was 'permeated by anomaly, fiction, misnomer and obsolete reasoning',[29] he was adamant in asserting that the House of Lords at the end of the twentieth century was in no position to abolish the four-century-old rule of common law. He said:

My Lords, in a system based on binding precedent there could be no ground for doubting a long course of existing law, and certainly none which could now permit this House even to contemplate such a fundamental change as to abolish the grievous harm rule; and counsel rightly hinted at no such idea.[30]

Lord Mustill added later in his judgment:

I am willing to follow old laws until they are overturned, but not to make a new law on a basis for which there is no principle.[31]

A year later, in *R v Powell*,[32] two defendants appealed against their convictions for murder on the basis that they were secondary parties to events where deaths had occurred in the course of joint enterprises which were in themselves criminal. The House of Lords ruled that a secondary party might kill with intent so to do or with intent to cause grievous bodily harm, except that if the primary party's lethal act was fundamentally different from that foreseen by the secondary party, the

---

[29] *Attorney General's Reference (No 3 of 1994)* [1998] AC 245, 250.   [30] ibid, 258.
[31] ibid, 262.   [32] [1999] 1 AC 1.

latter would not be guilty of murder (nor of manslaughter). Lord Hutton gave the single, reasoned judgment.[33] Both Lord Mustill and Lord Steyn[34] made heartfelt pleas for parliamentary intervention; they were entirely persuaded that the House of Lords in its judicial capacity could not effect change in this area of the criminal law. Lord Mustill reaffirmed his earlier statement:

Once again, an appeal to this House has shown how badly our country needs a law of homicide, or a new law of punishment of homicide, or preferably both. The judges can do nothing about this, being held fast by binding authorities on the one hand and a mandatory statute [the mandatory penalty of life imprisonment for murder, after the passing of the Murder (Abolition of the Death Penalty) Act 1965] on the other. Only Parliament has the powers, if it will choose to exercise them. It may not be a popular choice, but surely it is justice that counts.[35]

Professor Brice Dickson summed up the record of the Law Lords in the area of homicide law since 1995 as 'disunited and unambitious'.[36] Although the Government in 2004 initiated a review of the law of murder by the Law Commission, which reported in November 2006,[37] parliamentary action is in prospect only to revise the partial defences to the present law of murder. (The Government in December 2007 had restricted the immediate review by officials to only four aspects of the law of homicide.) If Parliament is unable, unwilling, or incapable of tackling the subject, either at all or only peripherally, can and should the UK Supreme Court exceptionally step in and clear up the 'mess' which its predecessors created 400 years ago and which has since perpetuated on numerous occasions?

Given the limitations on lawmaking, what then have been the criteria for the House of Lords departing from precedent?[38] The Practice Statement expressly stated that the House of Lords would treat its former decisions as 'normally binding' and would depart from a previous decision only when it appeared right to do so. Throughout the last 40 years the power to overrule has been exercised in 21 cases (see the Appendix to this chapter). Lord Reid observed in *R v National Insurance Commissioners, ex p Hudson* that the power would ordinarily be exercised where the previous wrong decision was 'thought to be impeding the proper development of the law or to have led to results which were unjust or contrary to public policy'.[39] Likewise, Lord Scarman, in *Khawaja*,[40] clarified the

---

[33] Ten years later, in *R v Rahman* [2009] 1 AC 129, Lord Bingham elaborated on the reasoning established in *Powell*.

[34] [1991] 1 AC 1, 15.   [35] ibid, 12.

[36] 'Judicial Activism in the House of Lords 1995–2007', ch 9 in B Dickson (ed), *Judicial Activism in Common Law Supreme Courts* (Oxford: OUP, 2007).

[37] *Murder, Manslaughter and Infanticide*, Law Commission Report No 204, HC30 (London: The Stationery Office).

[38] For an analysis of the cases in the civil jurisdiction where the Practice Statement was relied on, see Matthew Sheridan, 'Appeals to the House of Lords', ch 5 in Sir Michael Burton (ed), *Civil Appeals* (EMS Professional Publishing, first published looseleaf, 2002).

[39] [1972] AC 944, 966.   [40] [1984] AC 74.

understanding about the necessity to use the power sparingly. He observed that before departing from a precedent of its own making, the House of Lords must be satisfied on two counts: first, that continued adherence to the precedent would involve the risk of injustice and would obstruct the proper development of the law; and, second, that a departure from the precedent was the safe and appropriate way of remedying the injustice and developing the law. Lord Carswell, in *A v Hoare*,[41] amplified the two factors by noting that the elimination of anomalies in the existing law, together with the various artificial types of claim which they have spawned, provided an ample reason for invoking the Practice Statement so that justice may in future be done as Parliament intended. And Lord Hope, in *Re Spectrum Plus*, reaffirmed the essential feature of precedent under the Practice Statement as the degree of certainty for the guidance of those seeking to regulate their affairs according to the law.[42]

The Practice Statement has been considered on a number of occasions with the precautionary note that it should not be lightly invoked, even when the earlier decision being reconsidered was itself not unanimous. As Lord Wilberforce said in *Fitzleet v Cherry*:

Nothing could be more undesirable... than to permit litigants, after a decision has been given by this House with all appearance of finality, to return to this House in the hope that a differently constituted committee might be persuaded to take the view which its predecessors rejected. True that the earlier decision was by a majority: I say nothing as to its correctness or as to the validity of the reasoning by which it was supported. That there were two eminently possible views is shown by the support for each by at any rate two members of the House. But doubtful issues have to be resolved and the law knows no better way of resolving them than by the considered majority opinion of the ultimate tribunal.[43]

Nothing untoward has occurred as regards application of the Practice Statement. Of course, many cases have arisen where it was unnecessary for any reliance on the Practice Statement: the House of Lords has felt able, without departure from the indispensable foundation of the doctrine of precedent, to distinguish the instant appeal from earlier decisions.

The list of cases in the Appendix to this chapter reflects a not inconsiderable number of cases—21 in 40 years—where a previous decision has been overtly declared to have been wrongly decided, or no longer in conformity with public policy, and has thus been overruled. But there are other cases where overruling has probably taken place without explicit reliance on the Practice Statement. Such an instance occurred in *Moodie v Inland Revenue Commissioners*.[44] There it was fully recognised that the decision in *Inland Revenue Commissioners v Plummer*[45] was

---

[41] [2008] 1 AC 844.   [42] [2005] 2 AC 680, para 63.
[43] [1977] 3 All ER 996. Lord Wilberforce's cautionary approach did not deter the majority of the Privy Council in *Boyce and Joseph v R* [2005] 1 AC 400, overruling *Roodal v The State* [2005] 1 AC 328.
[44] [1993] 1 WLR 266.   [45] [1980] AC 896.

inconsistent with a later decision of the House of Lords in *Ramsey (WT) Ltd v Inland Revenue Commissioners.*[46] Lord Templeman, delivering the main judgment of the House, said:

If it were necessary to invoke the 1966 Practice Statement I have no doubt that this would be an appropriate course to take, but in my opinion it is sufficient to state that the decision in *Plummer's* case would have been different if the appeal had been heard after the enunciation by the House of the *Ramsay* principle.

Clearly, *Plummer's* case was wrongly decided and might, therefore, qualify for the application of the Practice Statement, in spite of the vigorous plea by counsel for the taxpayer (the ultimate loser in the appeal) that on a proper reading of the Practice Statement the case did not qualify as one that was impeding the development of the law and that no injustice would be caused if it were left unreversed. Counsel's reasoning went uncontroverted. There may be similar instances of implicit overruling, but my limited researches have not uncovered any. Hence the Practice Statement may have in some instances not been relied on, but it may yet have facilitated the circumnavigation of earlier rocky decisions.

    Time and opportunity are relevant factors in determining the application of the Practice Statement. *Rondel v Worsley,*[47] for example, stood uneasily unreversed for 30 years. The immunity for advocates from professional negligence claims had until then been firmly based on the traditional attitude towards the honorarial hiring of barristers (solicitors had not until then enjoyed the same protection for their activities as courtroom advocates). Lord Reid, in his judgment, based his decision for protecting all advocates on the public policy of that time, while also recognising that in the future the ending of the immunity would be likely. In fact, the death-knell of the immunity was rung in 1995 by Lord Lowry in *Spring v Guardian Assurance plc,*[48] when he stated that he could not understand how the submissions made by counsel for Mr Rondel had failed in 1968 to persuade their Lordships. And, also in 1995, an assenting judgment by a justice of appeal in the Court of Appeal of Jersey in *Picot v Crills*[49] declared that *Rondel v Worsley* did not bind the law of Jersey and was probably no longer good law even in England. The overruling of *Rondel v Worsley* came not before time.[50]

    Although the Practice Statement notes that attention should be paid to the 'especial need for clarity as to the criminal law', it has been in that field that some of the best-known cases invoking the Practice Statement have been decided—*DPP v Camplin*[51] (reasonable man in homicide); *R v Shivpuri*[52] (liability for impossible attempts to commit a crime); *R v Howe*[53] (duress no defence to

---

[46] [1982] AC 300.   [47] [1969] 1 AC 191.   [48] [1995] 2 AC 296.

[49] [1995] Jersey L Rev 33.

[50] The author must confess to having been the losing counsel in *Rondel v Worsley* and, fortuitously, to have seized the opportunity to repeat his failed submissions as the assenting member of the Court of Appeal of Jersey.

[51] [1978] AC 705.   [52] [1987] AC 1.   [53] [1987] AC 411.

murder); and *R v G*[54] (recklessness redefined). That says no more than that their Lordships seem to be less sure-footed when considering the criminal law. The potential applicability of the Practice Statement in the criminal law context was considered by the Court of Criminal Appeal in *R v Taylor*,[55] where Lord Goddard said:[56]

The Court of Appeal in civil matters usually considers itself bound by its own decisions or by decisions of a court of co-ordinate jurisdiction. For instance, it considers itself bound by its own decisions and by those of the Exchequer Chamber; and, as is well known, the House of Lords also always considers itself bound by its own decisions. In civil matters this is essential in order to preserve the rule of *stare decisis*.

This court, however, has to deal with questions involving the liberty of the subject, and if it finds, on reconsideration, that, in the opinion of a full court assembled for that purpose, the law has been either misapplied or misunderstood in a decision which it has previously given, and that, on the strength of that decision, an accused person has been sentenced and imprisoned it is the bounden duty of the court to reconsider the earlier decision with a view to seeing whether that person had been properly convicted. The exceptions which apply in civil cases ought not to be the only ones applied in such a case as the present, and in this particular instance the full court of seven judges[57] is unanimously of the opinion that the decision in *Rex v Treanor*[58] was wrong.

It is noteworthy that, where their Lordships are inclined at the outset of an appeal to call into question an earlier decision suspected of error, the practice has been to empanel a court of seven or even nine judges. However, this has not been an invariable practice: as the Appendix below shows, a normal court of five Law Lords has not been inhibited from reversing one of its earlier decisions.

But recent events in the Judicial Committee of the Privy Council have indicated some scope for a difference in approach among the Law Lords. Three times since the beginning of the twenty-first century the Board has exercised its undoubted power to reverse its earlier decisions—the Board, incidentally, has never considered itself to be bound by its own previous decisions.[59] In two of the cases[60] there was disagreement about whether earlier decisions had been wrongly decided. The third case was altogether more worrying, in that the seven members of the Board were unanimous that the earlier decision of the Board was erroneous, but disagreed (by four to three) whether there should be a reversal of the earlier decision.[61] The division focused on the need to do justice, while at the same time reflecting the values inherent in the principle of *stare decisis*.[62] The dissenting

---

[54] [2004] 1 AC 1034.   [55] [1950] KB 368.   [56] At 371.

[57] Lord Goddard CJ, with Humphreys, Stable, Cassels, Hallett, Morris, and Parker JJ.

[58] (1939) 27 Cr App R 35.

[59] *Cushing v Dupry* (1880) 5 App Cas 409; *Read v Bishop of Lincoln* [1892] AC 644; *Will v Bank of Montreal* [1931] 3 DLR 526; *Gideon Nkambule v R* [1950] AC 379.

[60] *Lewis v AG of Jamaica* [2001] 2 AC 50; *Boyce and Joseph v R* [2005] 1 AC 400.

[61] *Gibson v Government of the USA* [2007] 1 WLR 2367.

[62] See the illuminating article by Derek O'Brien, 'The Privy Council Overrules Itself—Again!' [2008] PL 28.

judgment of Lords Hoffmann, Carswell, and Mance, expressing the conservative approach to *stare decisis*, ruled that the earlier, erroneous decision did not impede the proper development of the law, for the simple reason—there were other reasons—that the decision had been specifically adopted by the [Bahamian] legislature. If the underlying purpose of the Practice Statement was to recognise that the final court of appeal should supplement (where appropriate) the primary power of Parliament to change the law, then the view of the minority in the Privy Council should have prevailed over the liberal approach of the majority (Lord Woolf, Lord Scott of Foscote, Lord Brown of Eaton-under-Heywood—who delivered the majority judgment—and Sir Christopher Rose, a recently retired Lord Justice of Appeal).

In *Attorney General for Jersey v Holley* [63] nine serving Law Lords sitting in the Privy Council determined an appeal which involved consideration of a House of Lords decision in *R v Smith (Morgan)* [64] on the thorny issue of the law of provocation as a partial defence to murder. The Board was split six to three, the minority view (Lord Bingham of Cornhill, Lord Hoffmann, and Lord Carswell) being that the law had been correctly stated in *Smith (Morgan)* and that the Court of Appeal of Jersey had correctly applied the House of Lords decision in that case. The judgment of the majority (Lords Nicholls of Birkenhead, Hope of Craighead, Scott of Foscote, Walker of Gestingthorpe, and Rodger of Earlsferry and Lady Hale of Richmond) thought that an earlier decision of the Privy Council in 1997 [65] was right and the House of Lords in *Smith (Morgan)* wrong.

The decision in *Holley* presented a peculiar problem for courts in England and Wales. Should they adhere to strict rules of precedent and follow loyally the decision in *Smith (Morgan)*? Or should they accept the ruling of the Privy Council in *Holley* (assuming that the law of murder, with the partial defence of provocation, was the same in Jersey and England)? The answer was provided in *R v James* [66] by a five-judge Court of Appeal (Criminal Division) presided over by the Lord Chief Justice. The Court said that there were exceptional reasons that justified the Court in following the Privy Council and not being bound by the House of Lords. The Court certified that the case raised a point of law of genuine public importance, but refused leave to appeal to the House of Lords, which in its turn refused leave to appeal. Thus, in effect, their Lordships in the Appeal Committee were applying the Practice Statement in deciding not to endorse the decision in *Smith (Morgan)* without explicitly saying that *Smith (Morgan)* was wrongly decided. The episode could be added to the list of 21 cases where the Practice Statement has been explicitly applied. But what a tortuous judicial path to tread in order to produce finality on a legal issue of some importance. The Law Commission's endorsement of the decision in

---

[63] [2005] 2 AC 580.   [64] [2001] 1 AC 146.   [65] *Luc Thiet Thuan v R* [1997] AC 131.
[66] [2006] QB 588.

Holley has not stifled debate over the proper direction to juries in murder trials.[67]

This case and the trilogy of recent Privy Council cases argue for some elucidation of the power to reverse earlier decisions. The policy that prompted and brought about the Practice Statement perhaps itself needs reconsidering, not in order to change the now-established practice but to elucidate its proper scope. A decision to overrule should rest upon some special reason(s) over and above a belief that the prior case was wrongly decided, or even if not wrongly decided, that it should be reversed on grounds of public policy.

Alongside the issue of the binding precedent of the House of Lords' decisions, there has been discussion about the House overruling its previous erroneous decisions only for the future, leaving such earlier erroneous decisions to apply to all transactions entered into before the decisions were reconsidered by the House of Lords. The opportunity for adopting this not uncontroversial procedure was considered but not taken in *National Westminster Bank v Spectrum Plus Ltd*.[68]

The classical approach—that prospective overruling has no place in our legal system—was crisply stated by Lord Reid in *Midland Baptist (Trust) Association v Birmingham Corporation* (a case concerning compulsory acquisition and compensation):

We cannot say that the law was one thing yesterday but is to be something different tomorrow. If we decide that [the existing rule] is wrong we must decide that it always has been wrong and that would mean that in many completed transactions owners have received too little compensation. But that often happens where an existing decision is reversed.[69]

After an exhaustive examination by Lord Nicholls in the *Spectrum Plus* case of the complex issues involved, the principle of prospective overruling[70] was accepted, but in the instant case not applied, because the dispute about the interpretation of a statute was thought not to be susceptible to prospective overruling. If the Law Lords were to interpret a statute only prospectively, it would be sanctioning the continued misapplication of the statute in relation to extant transactions or past events. The introduction of prospective overruling cannot long be postponed, and ought to receive full review as part of the debate over the future scope of the Practice Statement.

The experience of the Practice Statement in 1966 has finally dispelled whatever was left of the myth that judges do not make law. At the same time it has had a profound effect on the psyche of appellate judges, such that the Court of Appeal might now be enticed to follow suit, at least in the Civil Division, where it has become effectively the final court of appeal in private law litigation. The

---

[67] See Law Commission Report No 304, *Murder, Manslaughter and Infanticide* (2006) para 5.45, p 87.

[68] [2005] 2 AC 680.   [69] [1970] AC 874, 898–9.

[70] See M Arden, 'Prospective Overruling' (2004) 120 LQR 7.

sharpening of awareness of the creativity of the appellate task, and consequentially a more overt concern with the search for a more just rule, as well as the discarding of some forensic deadwood, cannot sensibly be confined to the judges in the final court of appeal. The phenomenon should extend to the intermediate appellate court. Following the Court of Appeal's own decision in *Actavis v Merck*[71] exposing and removing some of the unnecessary limitations imposed on itself by the decision in *Young v Bristol Aeroplane Co*,[72] a practice statement along the lines of the 1966 precedent might be a welcome development in the freedom of appellate judges generally to create law.

[71] *The Times*, 5 June 2008.
[72] [1944] KB 718. The rule in *Young v Bristol Aeroplane Co* had been earlier adumbrated in *Velasquez v DRC* [1914] 3 KB 458, 461 and was endorsed on appeal by the House of Lords, [1946] AC 163, 169 *per* Viscount Simon. This application was affirmed by the Northern Ireland Court of Appeal in *Parkinson v Watson* [1956] NI 1, 7, 11 and recently in *R (Johnson) v Havering LBC* [2008] QB 1, 35 (para 62) and 42 (para 86).

APPLICATION OF THE PRACTICE STATEMENT 1966

Case	Case(s) reconsidered	Subject	Action taken in relation to earlier case
Conway v Rimmer [1968] AC 910	*Duncan v Cammell, Laird & Co* [1942] AC 624	The doctrine of Crown privilege	Overruled
British Rlys Board, ex p Herrington [1972] AC 877	*Addie and Sons v Dumbreck* [1929] AC 358	The liability of occupiers to a trespasser	Overruled
EL Oldendorff & Co GmbH v Tradax Export SA; The Johanna Oldendorff [1974] AC 479	*Sociedad Financeria de Bienes Raices SA v Agrimpex Hungarian Trading Co; The Aello* [1961] AC 135	Whether ship can be judged to have 'arrived' on anchoring at usual waiting place	Declined to follow
Miliangos v George Frank (Textiles) Ltd [1976] AC 443	*Re United Rlys of the Havana and Regla Warehouses Ltd* [1961] AC 1007	Whether damages can be awarded in a currency other than sterling	Overruled
Dick v Burgh of Falkirk [1976] SC (HL) 1	*Darling v Gray & Sons* [1892] AC 576	Whether a defendant owes a common law duty of care to a victim's relatives	Overruled
DPP v Camplin [1978] AC 705	*Bedder v DPP* [1954] 1 WLR 1119	The 'reasonable man' test for provocation	Explained (in relation to Homicide Act 1957 s 3)
Vestey v Inland Revenue Comrs [1980] AC 1148	*Congreve v Inland Revenue Comrs* [1948] 1 All ER 948	The extent of tax liability for assets transferred abroad	Overruled
Jobling v Associated Dairies Ltd [1982] AC 794	*Baker v Willoughby* [1970] AC 467	How to measure damages for loss of earnings	Declined to follow
MV Yorke Motors v Edwards [1982] 1 WLR 444	*Jacobs v Booth's Distillery Co* [1901] 85 LT 262	The extent of a court's discretion to order payment into court as condition of leave for summary judgment	Did not follow (but did not expressly over-rule)
R v Secretary of State for the Home Department, ex p Khawaja and Khera [1984] AC 74	*R v Secretary of State, ex p Zamir* [1980] AC 930	Jurisdiction over illegal immigrants	Overruled

(cont.)

(cont.)

Case	Case(s) reconsidered	Subject	Action taken in relation to earlier case
R v Shivpuri [1987] AC 1	*Anderton v Ryan* [1985] AC 560	Whether a person can be held criminally liable for an 'impossible' attempt	Overruled
R v Howe [1987] AC 417	*DPP v Lynch* [1975] AC 653	Whether duress can be a defence to murder	Overruled
Patel v Immigration Appeal Tribunal [1988] 1 AC 911	*R v Secretary of State for the Home Department, ex p Khawaja and Khera* [1984] AC 74	The rights of illegal entrants	Reconsidered part
Murphy v Brentwood DC [1991] 1 AC 398 (7 Law Lords)	*Anns v Merton LBC* [1978] AC 728	The extent of a local authority's duty of care	Overruled
Pepper v Hart [1993] AC 593	*Beswick v Beswick* [1968] AC 58; *Black-Clawson International Ltd v Papierwerke Waldhof-Aschaffenburg AG* [1975] AC 591; *Davis v Johnson* [1979] AC 264	The admissibility of information in Hansard	Declined to follow
Westdeutsche Landesbank Girozentrale v Islington BC [1996] AC 669	*Sinclair v Brougham* [1914] AC 398	The extent of liability for monies had and received	Declined to follow
Arthur JS Hall v Simons [2002] 1 AC 615 (7 Law Lords)	*Rondel v Worsley* [1969] 1 AC 191	Whether advocates should be immune from suit	Overruled
R v G [2004] 1 AC 1034	*R v Caldwell* [1982] AC 341	The definition of 'recklessness' in criminal law	Departed from
Lagden v O'Connor [2004] 1 AC 1067	*Dredger Liesbosch (owners) v SS Edison (owners)* [1933] AC 449	The assessment of damages in a car-hire contract	Overruled
Horton v Sadler [2007] 1 AC 307	*Walkley v Precision Forgings Ltd* [1979] 1 WLR 606	When proceedings can be issued after the limitation period has expired	Overruled
A v Hoare [2008] 1 AC 844	*Stubbings v Webb* [1993] AC 498	The limitation period for personal injuries	Overruled

10

Style of Judgments

Louis Blom-Cooper

A literary overview

The distinctive individualism of the English judge lends itself to, even invites, good writing in the composition of any judgment. Even more so is this true for the appellate judge. Relieved of the trial judge's task of fact-finding (often a tedious, if essential task) the appellate judge has the opportunity and time for reflection to craft his or her judgment in a literary style. The facts as found by the trial judge may need to be revisited and analysed alongside the applicable law, but they can be reworked in a way that does not intrude upon the flow of the judgment.

Given the constraints of the judicial process, how have the Law Lords over 133 years performed in framing and shaping their judgments? And what has been their literary quality? Writing in 1925,[1] Justice Cardozo of the US Supreme Court said in his *Law and Literature*:

I am told at times by friends that a judicial opinion has no business to be literature. The idol must be ugly, or he may be taken for a common man. The deliverance that has to be accepted without demur or hesitation must have a certain high austerity which frowns at winning graces. I fancy that not a little of this criticism is founded in misconception of the true significance of literature, or more accurately perhaps, of literary style. There are those who have perceived that the highest measure of condensation, of short and sharp and imperative directness, a directness that speaks the voice of some external and supreme authority, is consistent, none the less, with supreme literary excellence...

He went on to single out the English judiciary for special praise:

For quotable good things, for pregnant aphorisms, for touchstones of ready application, the opinions of the English judges are a mine of instruction and a treasury of joy.

Justice Cardozo might have had in mind one of many examples that flowed from the pellucid pen of Lord Macnaghten, although he singled out for special

---

[1] This appeared originally in the Yale Law Review of 1925 and was subsequently reproduced in the Harvard Law Review for 1939. Not all his admirers approved of Cardozo's literary style: see the biography, *Cardozo*, by AL Kaufman (Cambridge, MA: Harvard University Press, 2000) 447–9.

mention Lords Blackburn, Esher, Bramwell, and Bowen. Contemporaneous with Cardozo's praise, 'Q' (Sir Arthur Quiller-Couch), when compiling his *Oxford Book of English Prose*, included only three extracts from the law courts (in fact, short snippets from well-known pieces of elegance). That was a meagre trawl from the ocean that is so much bigger 80 years on. But Q, relevantly for our purpose, asked what was the cardinal virtue for judicial prose. His answer was, 'persuasion'. That hardly seems adequate as the criterion for judicial literary quality.[2] But included in the *Oxford Book*,[3] Q gives us an essay from Arthur Clutton-Brock on the 'Cardinal Virtue of Prose', where he uses the word 'justice', which Q rejected. That essay expresses precisely what I have in mind as the appropriate test.

Prose of its very nature is longer than verse, and the virtues peculiar to it manifest themselves gradually. If the cardinal virtue of poetry is love, the cardinal virtue of prose is justice; and, whereas love makes you act and speak on the spur of the moment, justice needs inquiry, patience, and a control even of the noblest passions . . . By justice here I do not mean justice only to particular people or ideas, but a habit of justice in all the processes of thought, a style tranquilized and a form moulded by that habit. The master of prose is not cold, but he will not let any word or image inflame him with a heat irrelevant to his purpose. Unhasting, unresting, he pursues it, subduing all the riches of his mind to it, rejecting all beauties that are not germane to it; making his own beauty out of the very accomplishment of it, out of the whole work and its proportions, so that you must read to the end before you know that it is beautiful. But he has his reward, for he is trusted and convinces, as those who are at the mercy of their own eloquence do not; and he gives a pleasure all the greater for being hardly noticed. In the best prose, whether narrative or argument, we are so led on as we read, that we do not stop to applaud the writer, nor do we stop to question him.[4]

I here select five examples from across the whole period of the judicial House of Lords, judgments from 1888, 1943, 1980, 2002, and 2008.

The five examples

The judgment of Lord Macnaghten in *Great Western Railway Co v Bunch*[5] is a gem. Mrs Bunch had arrived early to catch a train at Paddington station, where she handed over her Gladstone bag and other luggage to a waiting porter. They were lost; so too was the porter. She (actually, her husband) sued the railway

---

[2] Sir James Fitzjames Stephen, the famous Victorian judge, once wrote:

The way in which the man of genius rules is by *persuading* an efficient minority to coerce an indifferent and self-indulgent majority [italics supplied].
(*Liberty, Equality and Fraternity* (1873) Ch II.)

[3] 1925 edn, p 1028.   [4] From his essay, 'The Defects of English Prose'.
[5] (1888) 13 App Cas 31. See also his judgments in *Gluckstein v Barnes (Official Receiver)* [1900] AC 240 and *Lloyd v Grace, Smith & Co* [1912] AC 716.

company for her loss. The wit of Lord Macnaghten was primarily directed at the weighty formulae of law, when wheeled into place to measure the minor incidents of ordinary life. But there was a touch of gentle humour at Mrs Bunch's expense and not a little criticism both of her 'ephemeral and evanescent porter' and of the railway company. Lord Macnaghten wrote:[6]

It was said that Mrs Bunch came to the station too soon—that she came before the train was drawn up—that she broke the journey, if the journey is to be taken as having begun—and left her bag in the charge of a porter who was then not acting as the servant of the company within the scope of his authority as such, but acting as her agent in his individual capacity, and if this is not what she meant, it was an attempt on her part to saddle the company with a liability which they were not bound to undertake...Mrs Bunch, no doubt, came to the station somewhat early. But one thing railway companies try to impress on the public is to come in good time...it does not seem to me that Mrs Bunch came so unreasonably early as to relieve the company who received the baggage from the ordinary obligations flowing from that receipt...

Then I think there is nothing in the conversation which took place between Mrs Bunch and the porter. Mrs Bunch's question was a very natural one. The answer she received was just what might have been expected.[7] Nine women out of ten parting with a travelling bag on which they set any store would ask the same question. In ninety-nine times out of a hundred the same answer would be returned. I do not think that this conversation altered the relation between the parties in the least degree. It seems to me almost absurd to treat it as a solemn negotiation by which the lady abdicated such rights as she possessed against the Great Western Railway Company, and constituted this ephemeral and evanescent porter in his individual capacity the sole custodian of her Gladstone bag...

It was said that if everybody acted as Mrs Bunch acted in this case, the railway companies would require an army of porters, and that it would be almost impossible for them to carry on their business. I quite agree; but I am not much impressed by that observation. I apprehend that if all travellers acted precisely alike, if everybody arrived at a station for a particular journey at precisely the same moment, there would be no little confusion, and perhaps some consternation, among the railway officials. Whatever may be the result of your Lordships' judgment, there is no fear that it will have the effect of making everybody act alike. Some passengers will still give more trouble at the stations than others, but no one will give any more trouble for it. Things will go on just as usual. The fidgety and the nervous will still come too soon; the unready and the unpunctual will still put off their chance of arrival till the last moment, and the prudent may have their calculations upset by the many accidents and hindrances that may be met with on the way to the station. And it is just because of the irregularity of individuals that the stream of traffic is regular and easily managed.

---

[6] (1888) 13 App Cas 31, 57–8.

[7] The porter who came forward to put the luggage on a trolley was asked by Mrs Bunch to put the travelling bag into the carriage with her; and she asked him if it was safe to leave it with him. The porter replied that it would be quite safe and that he would take care of the luggage and put it onto the train. (This was footnoted, marked with an asterisk, in the judgment.)

And what is more delightful than Lord Atkin's exposition on the meaning of money? In *Perrin v Morgan*[8] he wrote:

The result of your Lordships' decision will be to relieve judges in the future from the thraldom, often I think self-imposed, of judgments in other cases believed to constrain them to give a meaning to wills which they know to be contrary to the testator's intention. In the competition for bad pre-eminence in departure from the true meaning I think I should place first the decision of Lords Justices Turner and Knight-Bruce in *Lowe v Thomas* where the testator being possessed of stocks and some cash had left his 'money' to his brother for life and on his death to the brother's two daughters with ultimate remainder to the survivor. The testator left £50 cash, and it was held that, despite the series of life interests, the bequest only passed the cash. The poorest mind would know that this was absurd, and so, plainly, did the lords justices, but they were held in thrall. A high place, however, in the competition could be given to *Re Hodgson* where a nurse asked to make her will within two days of her death and having in her case by the side of her bed some £800 in cash and £600 in savings certificates left all her 'money' to a named beneficiary. She left no next of kin and the Crown claimed and was awarded the savings certificates as *bona vacantia*. In the future the resources of the Crown will receive no such flagitious increment. I anticipate with satisfaction that henceforth the group of ghosts of dissatisfied testators who, according to a late Chancery judge, wait on the other bank of the Styx to receive the judicial personages who have misconstrued their wills, may be considerably diminished. It will be a relief to the whole legal profession that at last what the Master of the Rolls rightly called a blot on our jurisprudence has been removed...

As a classic example of judicial appreciation of the socio-political content of post-war legislation, a passage in Lord Salmon's judgment in *Johnson v Moreton*,[9] determining the degree of security of tenure accorded to tenant-farmers under the Agricultural Holdings Act 1948, could scarcely be improved upon in positioning its historical context and in its clarity of expression:

During the last war, the submarine menace was such that it would have been virtually impossible to import into this country any more goods vital for our survival than we, in fact, did. Accordingly, it is extremely doubtful whether we could have survived had it not been for the food produced by our own farms. Even in 1947 when the Agriculture Act of that year was passed, food rationing was still in existence. It must have been clear to all that it was then and always would be of vital importance, both to the national economy and security, that the level of production and the efficiency of our farms should be maintained and improved. This could be achieved only by the skill and hard work of our farmers and the amount of their earnings which they were prepared to plough back into the land from which those earnings had been derived. A very large proportion of those farmers were tenant farmers. They were tenants because they did not have the necessary capital to buy land or they could not find any land which they wanted that was for sale—or for sale at a price which they could afford. In spite of sections 23 and 25 of the Agricultural Holdings Act of 1923 which had put them in a somewhat better position than did the common law, the sword of Damocles was always hanging over their heads. If

[8] [1943] AC 399, 414.   [9] [1980] AC 37.

they were tenants for a term of years, they might receive an effective notice to quit on the date when the term expired—and this term was rarely for more and usually for less than 10 years. If they were tenants from year to year, and very many of them were, they might in any year receive an effective notice to quit at the end of the next ensuing year. Accordingly there was no great inducement for these farmers to work as hard as they could, still less to plough money back into land which they knew they might well lose sooner or later.

The security of tenure which tenant farmers were accorded by the Act of 1947 was not only for their own protection as an important section of the public, nor only for the protection of the weak against the strong; it was for the protection of the nation itself. This is why section 31(1) of the Act of 1947, reproduced by section 24(1) of the Act of 1948, gave tenant farmers the option to which I have referred and made any agreement to the contrary void.

What could be more majestically expressed than the opening paragraphs of Lord Nicholls of Birkenhead's speech in *Royal Bank of Scotland plc v Etridge (No 2)*[10] as a modern view of equitable law?

My Lords, before your Lordships' House are appeals in eight cases. Each case arises out of a transaction in which a wife charged her interest in her home in favour of a bank as security for her husband's indebtedness or the indebtedness of a company through which he carried on business. The wife later asserted she signed the charge under the undue influence of her husband. In *Barclays Bank plc v O'Brien* [1994] 1 AC 180 your Lordships enunciated the principles applicable in this type of case. Since then, many cases have come before the courts, testing the implications of the *O'Brien* decision in a variety of different factual situations. Seven of the present appeals are of this character. In each case the bank sought to enforce the charge signed by the wife. The bank claimed an order for possession of the matrimonial home. The wife raised a defence that the bank was on notice that her concurrence in the transaction had been procured by her husband's undue influence. The eighth appeal concerns a claim by a wife for damages from a solicitor who advised her before she entered into a guarantee obligation of this character.

Undue influence

The issues raised by these appeals make it necessary to go back to first principles. Undue influence is one of the grounds of relief developed by the courts of equity as a court of conscience. The objective is to ensure that the influence of one person over another is not abused. In everyday life people constantly seek to influence the decisions of others. They seek to persuade those with whom they are dealing to enter into transactions, whether great or small. The law has set limits to the means properly employable for this purpose. To this end the common law developed a principle of duress. Originally this was narrow in its scope, restricted to the more blatant forms of physical coercion, such as personal violence.

Here, as elsewhere in the law, equity supplemented the common law. Equity extended the reach of the law to other unacceptable forms of persuasion. The law will investigate the manner in which the intention to enter into the transaction was secured: 'how the intention was produced', in the oft repeated words of Lord Eldon LC, from as long

---

[10] [2002] 2 AC 773.

ago as 1807 (*Huguenin v Baseley* 14 Ves 273, 300). If the intention was produced by an unacceptable means, the law will not permit the transaction to stand. The means used is regarded as an exercise of improper or 'undue' influence, and hence unacceptable, whenever the consent thus procured ought not fairly to be treated as the expression of a person's free will. It is impossible to be more precise or definitive. The circumstances in which one person acquires influence over another, and the manner in which influence may be exercised, vary too widely to permit of any more specific criterion.

Equity identified broadly two forms of unacceptable conduct. The first comprises overt acts of improper pressure or coercion such as unlawful threats. Today there is much overlap with the principle of duress as this principle has subsequently developed. The second form arises out of a relationship between two persons where one has acquired over another a measure of influence, or ascendancy, of which the ascendant person then takes unfair advantage. An example from the 19th century, when much of this law developed, is a case where an impoverished father prevailed upon his inexperienced children to charge their reversionary interests under their parents' marriage settlement with payment of his mortgage debts: see *Bainbrigge v Browne* (1881) 18 Ch D 188.

In cases of this latter nature the influence one person has over another provides scope for misuse without any specific overt acts of persuasion. The relationship between two individuals may be such that, without more, one of them is disposed to agree a course of action proposed by the other. Typically this occurs when one person places trust in another to look after his affairs and interests, and the latter betrays this trust by preferring his own interests. He abuses the influence he has acquired . . . .

The law has long recognised the need to prevent abuse of influence in these 'relationship' cases despite the absence of evidence of overt acts of persuasive conduct. The types of relationship, such as parent and child, in which this principle falls to be applied cannot be listed exhaustively. Relationships are infinitely various. Sir Guenter Treitel QC has rightly noted that the question is whether one party has reposed sufficient trust and confidence in the other, rather than whether the relationship between the parties belongs to a particular type: see *Treitel, The Law of Contract*, 10th ed (1999), pp 380–381 . . .

Even this test is not comprehensive. The principle is not confined to cases of abuse of trust and confidence. It also includes, for instance, cases where a vulnerable person has been exploited. Indeed, there is no single touchstone for determining whether the principle is applicable . . . .

Finally, for its breadth of learning, can this judgment of Lord Bingham, in the modern era, be rivalled?

It is a long-established principle of the English common law that, subject to certain exceptions and statutory qualifications, the defendant in a criminal trial should be confronted by his accusers in order that he may cross-examine them and challenge their evidence. This principle originated in ancient Rome.[11] But in continental Europe the principle was greatly attenuated in early mediaeval times and the procedure of the

---

[11] See generally *Coy v Iowa* 487 US 1012, 1015 (1988); *Crawford v Washington* 124 S Ct 1354, 1359 (2004); D Lusty, 'Anonymous Accusers: An Historical & Comparative Analysis of Secret Witnesses in Criminal Trials' (2002) 24 Sydney L Rev 361, 363–4.

Inquisition, directed to the extirpation of heresy and the preservation of society, depended heavily on evidence given secretly by anonymous witnesses whom the suspect was denied the opportunity to confront. In England, where proof of crime depended on calling live evidence before a jury to convince it of a defendant's guilt, there was no room for such procedures. But concern as to national security and intimidation of witnesses did lead to reliance on secret, anonymous evidence and evidence not adduced in court, and thus to departures from the rule of confrontation, notably in the Court of Star Chamber and in common law trials for treason, as notoriously at the trial of Sir Walter Raleigh. The Court of Star Chamber, popular at first, came over time to attract the same popular loathing as the Inquisition, its procedures regarded as foreign, cruel, oppressive and unfair. It was promptly abolished by the Long Parliament in 1641, and steps were taken (as, for example, by the Sedition Act 1661) to bring the procedure of treason trials into line with that required at common law. Thus, in 1720, in a civil case, the court declared in *Duke of Dorset v Girdler*[12] that 'the other side ought not to be deprived of the opportunity of confronting the witnesses, and examining them publicly, which has always been found the most effectual method of discovering of the truth'.[13]

Reviewing the judgments over a century and more of judicial output, one is struck as much by the change in language as the subject matter of litigation. Those linguistic critics who struggle against the 'abuse' of language must realise that to complain is a sentimental archaism. As George Orwell wrote,[14] it is 'like preferring candles to electric light or hansom cabs to aeroplanes' or, in modern ages, to prefer the fountain pen to email. Language is not just a natural growth, but also an instrument that we shape for our own purpose. A judgment from the highest court of the land is not just a means of telling the litigating parties who has won and lost, but why the winner won and the loser lost. It is also a communication with the wider public that has an interest in the development of the law and its consequences on their lives. But perhaps we should be allowed our moans for lost linguistic habits. Do we have, for example, to endure the over-throw of Fowler's sensible split infinitive rule?

Not infrequently, but happily not too often, Law Lords have been tempted by the instant subject matter to go beyond the strict discipline of determining the legal issues posed by the litigation. It is one thing to acknowledge that judges do make law. It is altogether impermissible to indulge in sweeping statements about what ought to be the law, or commentaries on the political scene. Lord Atkin's rhetorical question[15] 'Who is my neighbour?' is well within bounds, and has indeed shaped the evolving law of torts. But Lord Diplock's penchant for exegesis on particular areas of law often proved disastrous. His judgments in *O'Reilly v Mackman*,[16] *R v Lawrence*,[17] and *R v Caldwell*[18] subsequently required judicial

---

[12] (1720) Prec Ch 531–2, 24 ER 238.   [13] *R v Davis* [2008] 1 AC 1128.
[14] In his book of essays on *Why I Write* (Harmondsworth: Penguin, 1946).
[15] In *Donoghue v Stevenson* [1932] AC 562.   [16] [1983] 2 AC 237.
[17] [1982] AC 510.   [18] [1982] AC 341.

surgery, although it must be admitted that his judgment in *GCHQ*[19] spelling out the fundamental ingredients of judicial review has proved of lasting value in the burgeoning industry of administrative law. There is a tendency in a court of last resort to convert the judicial opinion into a legal treatise which makes the judges professorial. As Judge Learned Hand once wrote to his friend, the Chief Justice of Nebraska, 'after all we are not speaking to eternity, but deciding disputes'.[20]

In the same vein Lord Macmillan spoke 60 years ago in *Read v J Lyons & Co*:[21]

Your Lordships' task in this House is to decide particular cases between litigants and Your Lordships are not called on to rationalise the law of England. That attractive, if perilous field may well be left to other hands to cultivate ... Arguments based on legal consistency are apt to mislead, for the common law is a practical code adapted to deal with the manifold diversities of human life ...

This contrasts with the civilian systems of Europe, which Lord Cooper of Culross, a distinguished Lord President of the Court of Session, described as the 'instinct to systematise'; on the other hand, 'the working rule of the common lawyer is *solvitur ambulando*'.[22]

Doubt and dissent

Lord Atkin's resounding dissent in *Liversidge v Anderson*,[23] while achieving near-universal acclaim for its forthright declaration that the majority Law Lords appeared 'more executive-minded than the executive',[24] caused offence among his judicial colleagues. The Lord Chancellor, Lord Simon, saw a copy of Lord Atkin's judgment a few days before it was delivered on 3 November 1941. He wrote about the 'very amusing citation' from Lewis Carroll's *Through the Looking-Glass*, but wondered if it was 'necessary'. It might be 'wounding' and, Lord Simon added, 'neither the dignity of the House, nor the collaboration of colleagues, nor the forces of your reasoning would suffer from the omission of the question'. Lord Atkin was unmoved. The criticism emerged publicly when Lord Maugham (who had presided over the case before the Appellate Committee) wrote a letter to the editor of *The Times*. He was particularly incensed by the reference to counsel's argument being likened to those that might have been addressed acceptably to the King's Bench at the time of Charles I: 'Counsel could not reply even to so grave an animadversion as this, but nothing in their arguments could justify such a

---

[19] *Council of Civil Service Unions v Minister for the Civil Service* [1985] AC 374.
[20] G Gunther, *Learned Hand* (New York: Knopf, 1994) 528.   [21] [1947] AC 156, 175.
[22] 'The Common Law and the Civil Law—A Scot's View' (1950) 63 Harvard L Rev 468, 470, cited in M Zander, *The Law-Making Process* (Cambridge: CUP, 6th edn 2004) 293. See also the illuminating article by Lord Rodger of Earlsferry, 'The Form and Language of Judicial Opinions' (2002) 118 LQR 226.
[23] [1942] AC 206.
[24] See the essay by Professor Heuston supporting the majority decision in (1970) 86 LQR 33.

remark.' Lord Atkin was for a time ostracized; he remained silent. The episode reflected a rare departure from the convention that disapproval among judicial colleagues should be couched in decorous language. Decorousness can often be achieved by the use of the polite *dubitante*, a useful device which both assuages the judicial conscience and avoids judicial disunity by the pronounced disagreement of the dissent. Nowadays the *dubitante* seems less often in evidence. Anyone reading the opinions of the judges of the US Supreme Court in the last two years will observe the stark difference. Justices do not spare outright hostility to rival reasoning of colleagues—most notably in the recent case involving the constitutional right of the citizen to bear arms: *District of Columbia v Heller*.[25]

Lord Hoffmann's opinion in *A v Secretary of State for Home Affairs*,[26] that a greater threat to British liberty comes not from terrorism (or indeed from individual or isolated acts of terrorism) but from the reaction of politicians and a gullible populace, and from panic legislation that follows, aroused discombobulation in government circles. If the statement was somewhat intemperate, Lord Hoffmann's sole opinion, that derogatory power in the European Convention on Human Rights encompassed armed conflict by an invading army or an internal insurrection, and not from a handful of terrorist suspects, however organised and orchestrated in their activities, hardly bearing the description of an 'emergency threatening the life of the nation',[27] may prove to win the day.

There have been other notable dissents or disagreements over the years which have exhibited the qualities of judicial prose. Lord Reid in *DPP v Shaw*,[28] Lords Diplock and Pearce in *Forde v McEldowney*,[29] Lord Dilhorne in *Dorset Yacht Co v Home Office*,[30] Lord Kilbrandon in *DPP v Hyam*,[31] and Lord Mance in *R (Bancoult) v Secretary of State for Foreign and Commonwealth Affairs*[32] are outstanding examples. Assenting judgments do not instinctively attract attention, but often they make compulsive reading. Lord Macnaghten's judgment in *Great Western Railway Co v Bunch* was the fourth of five judgments in favour of Mrs Bunch.

Since judgments are 'speeches', the convention has remained that each Law Lord has the right to give a separate assenting or dissenting opinion, even if the assents are often no more than a formulaic 'For the reasons given by Your Lordships, I agree that this appeal should be allowed [or dismissed] and that the House should make the order proposed [by the senior Law Lord]'. But the collective approach to adjudication, first employed in the 1960s, but abandoned after the poorly-received alliterative trilogy of cases in *Smith v DPP*,[33] *Sykes v DPP*,[34] and *Shaw v DPP*[35] (thereafter revived by Lord Diplock as Senior Law Lord in the 1970s) is now becoming fashionable. The collective approach has had

---

[25] No 07-290, 26 June 2008.   [26] [2006] 2 AC 221.
[27] Lord Bingham noted that interpretation, but felt unable to ally himself with it. The other Law Lords based their judgments on the applicability of the power of derogation.
[28] [1962] AC 220.   [29] [1971] AC 632   [30] [1970] AC 1004.
[31] [1975] AC 55, 90.   [32] [2008] 3 WLR 955.   [33] [1961] AC 290.
[34] [1962] AC 528.   [35] [1962] AC 220.

a renewed vigour in the years of the Bingham court.[36] More significantly, in a decision in 2008 on extradition law, *Norris v Government of the United States of America*,[37] the Appellate Committee uniquely produced a *composite* judgment. Conventionally, if not constitutionally, it is not possible for Law Lords to merge their separate opinions in a single judgment to which all of them have contributed, unless they were to speak their separate parts, like actors in a play. But who cares, if the result is clarity of expression, certainty in the legal ruling, and leads to brevity?

The shift in the style of contemporary judgments would certainly meet with the approval of Professor AWB Simpson who wrote in 1984 that 'the undisciplined individualism of English appellate judges, and their complete lack of collegiate spirit, reduces much of their work to mere confusion . . . It no longer seems possible for a single judge . . . to dominate the system as once Lord Mansfield did. Law reform seems all much better done through the more disciplined and systematic institution of the committee.'[38] This trend towards single or composite judgments chimes with the modern judicial approach which sees the final court of appeal, more distinctly since the dialogue of incompatibility in the Human Rights Act 1998, as an auxiliary to the primary legislative power of Parliament. So long as that approach pertains, there is room for both the traditional style of judgments as well as for a collegiate product. Much depends on the subject matter of the appeal. There is no better model for the appellate function, however, than in the judgment of Lord Reid in *Broome v Cassell & Co Ltd*, dealing with the issue of exemplary damages:

The very full argument which we have had in this case has not caused me to change the views which I held when *Rookes v Barnard* was decided or to disagree with any of Lord Devlin's main conclusions, but it has convinced me that I and my colleagues made a mistake in simply concurring with Lord Devlin's speech. With the passage of time I have come more and more firmly to the conclusion that it is never wise to have only one speech in this House dealing with an important question of law. My main reason is that experience has shown that those who have to apply the decision to other cases and still more those who wish to criticise it come to find it difficult to avoid treating sentences and phrases in a single speech as if they were provisions in an Act of Parliament. They do not seem to realise that it is not the function of noble and learned Lords or indeed of any judges to frame definitions or to lay down hard and fast rules. It is their function to enunciate principles and much that they say is intended to be illustrative or explanatory and not to be definitive. Where there are two or more speeches they must be read together and often it is generally much easier to see what are the principles involved and what are merely illustrations of it.

A rare, but commendable judicial approach to multiple judgments is Lord Reid's assent to a lengthy judgment of Lord Diplock in a trade mark case that was heard

---

[36] See ch 16 in this volume.   [37] [2008] 1 AC 920.

[38] AWB Simpson, 'Lord Denning as Jurist' in JL Jowell and JPWB McAuslan, *Lord Denning: The Judge and the Law* (London: Sweet & Maxwell, 1984) 51.

over 13 days in the Appellate Committee. In *GE Trade Mark* [39] Lord Reid wrote succinctly:

I have read the speech of my noble and learned friend, Lord Diplock. I am in general agreement with it apart from one matter. I agree with the view of Eve J in *Woodward v Boulton Macro Ltd* [40] that section 11 of the Act has only a limited application. If that is right then I would reach the same conclusion that this appeal should be allowed but by a shorter and simpler route. As I believe that I am alone in taking this view I do not think that it would serve any useful purpose either to set out my reasons for agreeing with Eve J or to set out the subsequent steps by which I reach my conclusion.

Even more commendable was Lord Mustill's concurrence to the single judgment of Lord Hutton in *R v Powell*, [41] adding that he had prepared a judgment coming to a different conclusion and withdrew it only because he did not want future trial judges, who had to direct juries as simply as possible, being confused by conflicting theories propounded by different Law Lords.

The problem is that if Law Lords do not share their judgments with their colleagues in advance of delivering them—if there is no collective discussion prior to judgment day—there is a substantial risk that readers of the judgments may not know precisely why the case has been decided the way that it has, with all that that means for lawyers who need to advise future potential litigants. One of the most infamous illustrations of this danger is *Boys v Chaplin*, [42] a leading decision in private international law. All five Law Lords agreed that David Boys, a member of the Royal Air Force who had been injured in a road accident in Malta caused by Mr Chaplin, a member of the Royal Navy, could recover damages in England assessed in accordance with English laws not merely regarding quantum but also the allowable heads of damage. Each Law Lord—Hodson, Guest, Donovan, Wilberforce, and Pearson—gave a different justification for coming to the same conclusion, much to the consternation of textbook writers. Dicey and Morris describe the *ratio* of the case as 'speculative', [43] while another writer says, 'though there was no dissent there were many conflicting opinions'. [44] Accidents such as occurred in *Boys v Chaplin* are to be avoided at all costs, both on the roads and in the courts.

Deliberations and delivery of judgments

Historically, the judicial arm of the House of Lords is the High Court of Parliament: the ultimate repository of royal justice. But the decline of monarchical

---

[39] [1973] RPC 297, 316.   [40] (1915) 32 RPC 173.

[41] [1999] 1 AC 1. See ch 9 in this volume.   [42] [1971] AC 356.

[43] L Collins et al (eds), *Dicey and Morris: The Conflict of Laws* (London: Sweet & Maxwell, 13th edn 2000) 1511.

[44] D McClean, *Morris: The Conflict of Laws* (London: Sweet & Maxwell, 5th edn 2000) 362.

authority and the growing separation of judicial and legislative functions brought about a metamorphosis of the court of last resort. The Appellate Jurisdiction Act 1876 was the culmination of that process.

Tradition was not, however, to be so lightly tossed aside. Anger among the traditionalists was aroused with the setting up of the Appellate Committee in 1948.[45] Thereafter their Lordships abandoned the chamber of the House for their oral hearings (except for an annual assertion of their right to sit there) in favour of a committee room upstairs at the Palace of Westminster. The convenience of conducting judicial business according to a continuous timetable and undisturbed by the legislative sittings of the House, was overwhelming. The constitutionalists contented themselves, however, with the knowledge that decisions were formally voted upon in the chamber (see below). Another quirk of the parliamentary situation has been that the Appellate Committee has to be formally appointed annually by the House; even when in the middle of 1951 the Lords returned to their former chamber, the Committee continued to function, and in November 1960 a further motion was agreed upon to enable two Appellate Committees to sit simultaneously. Thereafter their Lordships quite frequently have occupied Committee Rooms No 1 and No 2 at the same time.

Committee Room No 1 is large, half-panelled, oblong, with large windows overlooking the Thames and St Thomas' Hospital across the river. The Law Lords sit unrobed and without wigs, wearing ordinary everyday dress. They sit at a D-shaped table with the Senior Law Lord (or alternative presiding judge) in the centre. Counsel, incongruously, are kitted out in wigs and gowns, addressing the judges from a lectern. The public are seated, not too uncomfortably, at the back of the room, which adequately accommodates an audience that rarely exceeds two figures but without beckoning a wider public audience.

Hanging in Committee Room No 1 are (or were until recently) three eighteenth century tapestries, designed by Boucher for Madame de Pompadour (1755) and depicting light-hearted pastoral scenes—a background which some spectators might feel was well-suited to august proceedings—infecting a relaxed and informal atmosphere. But Committee Room No 1 also has the ghastly picture above the Senior Law Lord of the *Death of Harold*—hardly a suitable decoration. In Committee Room No 2 their Lordships have quite recently acquired a colourful picture of a youthful Richard II haranguing an expiring John of Gaunt. Did the person who arranged the hanging of the picture have recent experience of counsel addressing the Law Lords? In any event, whatever the interpretation, the picture is in striking contrast to the pastoral scenes on view in Committee Room No 1. Perhaps it reflects the changed nature of the forensic process at the highest level of appellate jurisdiction.

---

[45] The story is shortly described in L Blom-Cooper and G Drewry, *Final Appeal: A Study of the House of Lords in its Judicial Capacity* (Oxford: Clarendon Press, 1972) 111–13.

Dead judgments and reporting

There are (or were) other quiddities associated with the parliamentary forum of the final court of appeal. The judicial process had to be filtered through the prism of parliamentary procedure. Judgments of the Law Lords were delivered orally as if part of the deliberative process of a democratic legislature, however much the Law Lords acted as a final court of appeal. The attitudes of parliamentarians towards the media were to maintain an open forum, restricted in the report of its proceedings only by an insistence on the procedures and privileges of Parliament. For the Law Lords as judges the proceedings were always in public and subject to scrutiny, where only the contempt of court rules would apply.

Lord Merriman was still the President of the Probate, Divorce & Admiralty Division in October 1961 when he was invited by the Lord Chancellor to sit in the Appellate Committee in the House of Lords to hear, exceptionally, an appeal before a seven-judge court. The case was brought to determine whether the English courts had jurisdiction to deal with the petition of a wife against her husband for the annulment of their marriage on the ground of non-consummation owing to the impotence of the husband who was domiciled in Scotland and resident in the Middle East, his only connection with England having been that he resided in Newcastle-upon-Tyne for a time while working there. During the short stay in England the parties were married. The case[46] raised the question whether the fact that the marriage was celebrated in England was in itself sufficient to confer jurisdiction on the English courts to annul the marriage.

The reason for an enhanced number of Law Lords sitting on the appeal was the reconsideration of an authority from 1860[47] which had decided that the English courts did have jurisdiction in nullity petitions involving similar facts. Their Lordships sat for six days at the end of October 1961. They were clearly divided between, on the one hand, five common law and chancery judges, and on the other, two divorce judges, Lords Merriman and Hodson. In the result, on 18 January 1962, the majority overruled the 1860 decision. Lord Reid, who presided, delivered a 13-page speech, unusually lengthy for him. He announced at the end of his speech that Lord Morton of Henryton agreed. The two others —Lord Cohen (the chancery judge) delivered a five-page speech, as did Lord Morris of Borth-y-Gest—also agreed. There were the two dissenters, both of whom had prepared lengthy speeches. But on that very morning Lord Merriman had died; his prepared speech, which was in print at the House of Lords, literally died with him, but was presented by Lord Hodson, who tacked it on to his own judgment—all of it, save one short passage—which would have been delivered, since the two had agreed with their respective drafts. In the omitted

---

[46] *Ross-Smith v Ross-Smith* [1963] AC 280.
[47] *Simonin v Mallac* (1860) 2 Sw & Tr 67, 164 ER 917.

passage Lord Merriman had expressed his astonishment that Mr Justice Bateson in *Inverclyde v Inverclyde*[48] could have conceivably come to the decision he arrived at.

In the case of *Inland Revenue Commissioners v Wilsons (Dunblane) Ltd*[49] in 1954, Viscount Simon died before judgment was delivered, and his opinion was adopted by Lord Normand as his own. This procedure was followed when judgment was delivered in *Kennedy v Spratt*[50] (on appeal from the Court of Appeal in Northern Ireland), where Lord Reid stated in the House that he would adopt Lord Upjohn's opinion as his own, Lord Upjohn having died between the hearing of the appeal and the delivery of judgment. Soon after that time, however, the practice changed. The practice of one Law Lord adopting a deceased Law Lord's prepared opinion was dropped in 1972, when Lord Donovan's posthumous opinion in *Ealing London Borough Council v Race Relations Board*[51] was published, as it had been prepared while he was alive. Likewise, Lord Diplock's posthumous judgment in *Allen and Hanbury v Generics*[52] was delivered for him by Lord Fraser.

At the time of *Ross-Smith* the facilities to the Press for reporting the judgments of the House of Lords were treated as 'speeches' of the Law Lords in the Chamber of the Upper House. Judgments were invariably delivered in a quaint ceremony on the floor of the House at 10.30 in the morning before it was used for legislative and deliberative business, whereby the (usually) five Law Lords, *qua* Appellate Committee, reported back to themselves as the House of Lords proper, and took a 'vote' on the outcome of the appeal. It was in every sense a sitting of the House. The Mace was on the Woolsack, and prayers had been read, usually by a Bishop, who in all probability was seated on the spiritual side of the House. Prior to 1963 each Law Lord would read his printed opinion—often ponderously and in full. On 18 January 1962 it took three and a half hours to complete the performance.

Counsel were allowed to have copies of the printed opinions about an hour before formal judgment at 10.30, so that they might address their Lordships on the issue of costs. Nowadays, each Law Lord stands up (in order of seniority) and states merely that he would allow or dismiss the appeal 'for the reasons given in my printed speech'. They are formally described as 'Opinions of the Lords of Appeal for Judgments in the Cause [followed by the parties' names]'. (This piece of judicial gymnastics now takes place at 9.45am, usually on Wednesdays, with counsel receiving the judgments on the preceding Friday, for the sole purpose of pointing out any minor mistakes in the text, but not for re-arguing the appeal!)

In 1962, the media were allocated to the press gallery and were given the drafted opinions so that they could follow the dreary process of the reading of the speeches. When the process was complete, the journalists were taken to a room in

---

48 [1931] P 29.   49 [1954] 1 WLR 282.   50 [1972] 2 AC 83.
51 [1972] AC 342.   52 [1988] 3 All ER 1057.

the House where any corrections or amendments to the printed opinions were noted by the officers of the shorthand writers to the House of Lords. No journalist could leave until that corrective process was complete. It was well beyond the luncheon break on 18 January 1962 that journalists repaired to their newspaper offices with the Law Lords' judgments in their hot sticky hands.

The Guardian's London diary column, the following day, recited the omitted passage in Lord Merriman's judgment. The newspaper's legal correspondent was subsequently held to have breached parliamentary privilege, and was ordered by the permanent secretary to the Lord Chancellor's Department to write apologising to the Lord Chancellor. No journalist or editor could, even in 1962, have imagined that the publication of a document in legal proceedings (especially a judgment of the final court of appeal) could constitute a contempt of court—at least that was the law after the case in *Home Office v Harman*[53] and its Strasbourg aftermath. But this was Parliament, not the High Court of Justice.

Since 1990 the proceedings of Parliament have, unlike those of the courts, been televised. Thus it was that Lord Browne-Wilkinson, a distinguished member of the 1990s court, and the Senior Law Lord at the time, read out in front of the cameras in 1999 a summary of their Lordships' decision to set aside their first ruling in the *Pinochet* case,[54] on the ground that Lord Hoffmann's non-disclosure of his association with Amnesty International (a party intervening in the oral proceedings before the Appellate Committee) constituted an absolute disqualification from sitting.[55] (It is rumoured that Lord Hoffmann did mention his connection with Amnesty to Lord Slynn, the presiding Law Lord in the first appeal, but that Lord Slynn thought it not worth mentioning to the litigants.) This was undoubtedly a low point in the history of the Lords, but it was very soon afterwards eclipsed by what was clearly one of the most iconic images of the 1990s—the film of the five Law Lords issuing judgments in the second Pinochet appeal and coming to a similar conclusion to that in the first.[56] As noted elsewhere in this volume, the reputation of the House of Lords for its commitment to international human rights standards rose immensely at a stroke. The fact that the Home Secretary later opted not to exercise his discretion to extradite ex-President Pinochet because of his ill health did little to dent this well-won reputation for the House as a court.

Prolixity of judgments

The most striking difference between the judgments of the earlier years and today's output is that the former were short and to the point at issue. Brevity

---

[53] [1980] 1 AC 280.
[54] *R v Bow Street Stipendiary Magistrate, ex p Pinochet Ugarte* [2000] 1 AC 61.
[55] *R v Bow Street Metropolitan Stipendiary Magistrate, ex p Pinochet Ugarte (No 2)* [2000] 1 AC 119.
[56] *R v Bow Street Metropolitan Stipendiary Magistrate, ex p Pinochet Ugarte (No 3)* [2000] 1 AC 147.

could hardly be a term applied to the opinions handed down nowadays by the Law Lords. The length of today's judgments is not exclusively a feature of the final court of appeal in the United Kingdom. In the High Court of Australia and the Supreme Court of Canada—not to mention the inordinate verbosity of the Justices of the US Supreme Court—judgments often seem endless. The lack of brevity at home, however, is recognised judicially by the appellate judges themselves. Shortly before he left to become the UK judge in the European Court of Justice at Luxembourg, Lord Justice Schiemann (a Lord Justice of Appeal from 1995) expressed judicially his concern—he described himself as being 'perturbed'—about judgments becoming 'longer and longer'. His comments, in which he was joined specifically by Lord Justice Judge (later Lord Judge, Lord Chief Justice of England and Wales) in *HM Customs and Excise v MCA*,[57] came as a result of the Court of Appeal's consideration of a judgment given by Munby J of 223 paragraphs containing a comprehensive analysis—truly an exegesis on the subject—of the court's jurisdiction to assess and protect the interests of wives and former wives in matrimonial property. While commending the judge for his industry and erudition, Lord Justice Schiemann said that the judgment was too long 'because it dealt at length with a number of matters which the judge held were not central to the decision' (the three judgments in the Court of Appeal themselves ran to 112 paragraphs). The self-criticism reflects a general unease about the contemporary deliverance of judicial decisions at all levels of the court hierarchy.

That criticism was heartily endorsed, extra-judicially, by Lord Bingham at a discussion session on Judgment-Writing for the Senior Judiciary, held at the Royal Courts of Justice on 18 April 2007, organised by the Judicial Studies Board. He said that his heart sank whenever he had to embark on reading a judgment that sets out the table of contents or chapters as if one was being asked to read a book.

What then are the reasons for this seeming addiction to prolixity? First, and perhaps foremost, is the judicial desire in an age that demands ever more transparency and the fullest reasoning of the decision-maker, which tend towards crossing all 't's and dotting all 'i's. But that instinctive predilection to provide litigant-satisfaction, and to be seen to be doing a professional job of work, is fed nowadays by the arrival of Rank Xerox and information technology. As Lord Bingham observed: '[They] may reflect the seductive embrace of the word processor because that which is written out by hand tends to be more sparingly composed' (he himself is believed to compose all his judgments initially in manuscript, the computer taking over thereafter). The advice offered by that great American judge, Mr Justice Oliver Wendell Holmes Jr (himself an inveterate writer of pithy and succinct opinions in both the Supreme Judicial Court of Massachusetts and the US Supreme Court around the turn of the twentieth century) was to go for the essentials and express them in stinging brevity. He

[57] [2003] Fam 55.

admonished judges to observe that there was 'no need to be heavy to be weighty'.[58] Holmes was reputed to have written his draft opinions while standing up at a raised desk; when he got tired of standing he knew how his readers would feel when they read or listened to what he had written.

There is probably another reason, which is related to the content of the judicial menu served up to the Law Lords over the last two decades. Private law litigation calls primarily for the adjudication of a dispute between rival parties in dispute; the wider public might have an interest in the outcome as a development of the law as it affects them. But the predominant judicial fare put before the Law Lords today is distinctly in the areas of public law, where definitively the subject matter affects not just the litigating parties (often one of them a public authority of central or local government, alongside the growing number of interveners, usually pressure groups exhibiting specific public interests). Public law evokes decisions that involve both legal and social policy issues. They often touch sensitively on government (with both a big and small 'g'). Comprehensiveness of the subject matter in areas of administrative law leads inexorably to lengthy treatment. Yet the effort to keep a judgment short should prevail. A shorter judgment is likely to be more effective than a longer one.

Some of the problem of judicial prolixity no doubt stems from the inordinate amount of documentary material that is nowadays placed before appellate courts (both the House of Lords and the Court of Appeal) by the parties appearing. Take the following pungent opening to the judgment of Lord Justice Buxton in *R (C) v Secretary of State for Justice* of 28 July 2008,[59] a case involving the permissible physical restraints imposable on young offenders held in Secure Training Centres:

> The preparation of the appeal took an unsatisfactory form. The appellant filed a 61 page skeleton, to which was appended a 24 page 'summary of evidence', together with 89 authorities. The Secretary of State filed a further 10 authorities, and the Equality and Human Rights Commission, although only an intervener, another 23.

No wonder that Lord Justice Buxton expostulated that 'it accordingly proved difficult to reduce the proceedings to a coherent form, and that difficulty will no doubt be reflected in the judgment [of 87 paragraphs in 24 pages] that follows'. Simplicity should be the watchword of verbose advocates and judges alike.

The recipe for change lies in a striving for simplicity. Einstein is recorded as having stated as a golden rule that 'everything should be made as simple as possible, but not simpler'. Simplicity is best achieved by pruning the content of the judgment. Reciting the arguments of counsel is unnecessary. They tend to complicate the subject matter in hand, almost always by drawing fine lines and distinctions; by arguing in favour of distinctions, by suggesting analogies with

---

[58] See F Frankfurter, *Of Law and Men. Papers and Addresses of Felix Frankfurter*, P Eltman (ed) (Hamden, CN: Archon Books, 1952) 177.
[59] [2009] 2 WLR 1039.

reference to other branches of the law, by references to parliamentary debates à la *Pepper v Hart* [60] (a controversial product of the Law Lords in 1995), and by inviting the court to give a decision that will not open up the floodgates of unnecessary future litigation. Other devices are employed by counsel in their commendable, but sometimes unhelpful, effort to fulfil their mission of winning the case for the client. The court's mission is decidedly otherwise, single-mindedly to decide the issues. Arguments of counsel, which often make good reading to the academic lawyer and admiring practitioners, must be left to the law reporters. Counsel will have to derive their pleasure from that source, however gratifying it may be for an argument to be seized upon gratefully by the judge. As with other items of the forensic process, they can be consigned elsewhere. Recitation of the facts at length is rarely necessary and can be covered elsewhere. Lord Diplock once concluded a judgment by telling those curious enough to know more of the detail to go to the judgment of the judge at first instance.

Even the exposition of case law can be annexed to the judgment, with only the conclusions of chunks of cited passages from past authorities in the body of the reasoned decision. To the satisfaction of his specialist audience (the intellectual property world) Lord Justice Jacob recently did just that in *Aerotel Ltd v Telco Holdings Ltd*. [61] If the daily routine of the intermediate appellate court does not perhaps allow too often for the luxury of reserved judgments, the House of Lords rarely nowadays delivers a judgment extempore (before 1934, when aspiring litigants did not require leave to appeal, an extempore judgment was given not infrequently [62]). Citation of the case law is often overdone. It is all too easy to quote large chunks of earlier judgments, easier than to summarise them. Lord Hoffmann is an exponent of the summarising of cases, with sparing use of citations. If necessary, the parade of case law can be put into an annex, where it does not clutter up the judgment or deflect the reader from the thrust of the judicial reasoning. Statutes and statutory instruments do not need to find their way into the text. The statutory provisions immediately up for interpretation can be extracted from a lengthy recitation of a section in an Act of Parliament, not infrequently drafted incomprehensively (sometimes incomprehensibly) by parliamentary draftsmen. There are no doubt other means for shortening the text. And, whatever the length of the judgment, there is a prime virtue in helping the reader grasp the essence of the appeal. Begin the judgment with a sentence or two explaining what the point of law is. Lord Brown of Eaton-under-Heywood is an exponent of that. He once wrote:

My Lords, this appeal is all about the pre-trial detention of unconvicted defendants, and in particular the right to bail of a certain category of defendants. The category in question

---

[60] [1995] AC 593. See K Mullan, 'The Impact of *Pepper v Hart*' in B Dickson and P Carmichael (eds), *The House of Lords: Its Parliamentary and Judicial Roles* (Oxford: Hart, 1999), ch 11.

[61] [2007] 1 All ER 225.

[62] *London Street Tramways v London CC* [1898] AC 375 is one such instance: see ch 9 in this volume.

is that provided for by section 25, Criminal Justice and Public Order Act 1994, as amended, namely those charged with one of a specified number of grave offences.[63]

His injunction to judicial colleagues would be to rivet the reader's eyeball to the first words, and he or she is likely to stay with you, even if the following paragraphs (numbered, or preferably unnumbered so as to preserve the flow of judicial prose, worthy of being anthologised!) are longer than might be expected—this itself, a sentence of too great length!

[63] *R (O) v Crown Court of Harrow* [2007] 1 AC 249, 257.

11

Law Lords in Parliament

David Hope

The phenomenon of Law Lords sitting in Parliament is a comparatively recent one. Performance of the appellate function had been part of the work of the Upper House for centuries. For reasons that are explored more fully elsewhere in this volume, it had come to be regarded as part of the ordinary business of the House. This is demonstrated by the fact that for almost a hundred years after the formal opening of the new building by Queen Victoria in 1847 appeals were always heard in the Chamber as the first item of business on the day's list.

The system was not without its critics, even then. But in 1876, after much discussion and several unsuccessful attempts at reform,[1] Parliament decided not only that the appellate jurisdiction should continue but that it should be put onto a more professional footing. Judges were to sit in the House of Lords as Lords of Appeal in Ordinary. Previously it had been the practice for lay peers to participate in the hearing and determination of appeals together with peers who were learned in the law, presided over by the Lord Chancellor. An appeal from the Court of Queen's Bench in Dublin, where the appellants had been convicted, among other things, of conspiracy to excite the lieges to hatred and contempt of the Government, illustrates the disadvantages of this practice.[2] This highly charged case came on before the Lord Chancellor and four other peers who had judicial experience, referred to in the report as 'law Lords'.[3] The judges were also summoned, and nine of them attended. But other Lords too were present.[4] When the question was put, three of the four Law Lords were for allowing the appeal. The fourth was not. Some of the lay peers joined with the fourth Law Lord in voting against the decision of the majority. The Lord Chancellor reacted to this protest by refusing to declare what he considered to be the opinion of the House. The

---

[1] The history was described by the Lord Chancellor, Lord Selborne, in the debate at second reading in the House of Lords on 25 February 1876 and by the Prime Minister, Benjamin Disraeli, in the debate at second reading in the House of Commons on 12 June 1876: Parl Debs, vol 227, cols 909–17; vol 229, cols 1680–93. For a more complete account see R Stevens, *Law and Politics: The House of Lords as a Judicial Body 1800–1976* (London: Weidenfeld and Nicholson, 1979) 37–67.

[2] *O'Connell's Case* (1844) 11 Cl & F 155; Stevens, ibid, 32–3.

[3] Lords Brougham, Denman, Cottenham and Campbell.

[4] *O'Connell v R* (1844) 11 Cl & F 155; 8 ER 1061.

Leader of the House[5] then intervened, suggesting that the House should not divide on a question of that kind when the Law Lords had already given their opinion on it and the majority were in favour of reversing the judgment. He pointed out that, as the lay peers were not learned in the law and had not heard the whole case, they were not qualified to pass judgment. He proposed that they should abstain from voting. There was a short debate on the issue, following which the lay peers withdrew. The intervention of lay peers in judicial business effectively came to an end at this point. The Appellate Jurisdiction Act 1876 relieved the House from any further such embarrassment.[6]

The 1876 Act provided that appeals to the House of Lords were to be heard and determined by not less than three professionally qualified judges, designated as Lords of Appeal,[7] who were to be persons appointed by Letters Patent to be Lords of Appeal in Ordinary,[8] and such Peers of Parliament as held, or had held, any of the offices described in the Act as high judicial offices.[9] Despite these changes, it was envisaged that the traditional jurisdiction of the House would continue. It was not to have the appearance of a statutory court. At first only two judges were appointed to sit as Lords of Appeal in Ordinary.[10] Their number was increased by stages over time to twelve in keeping with the demand for their services.[11] The statute used the expression 'Lords of Appeal' to include every member of the House who was entitled to sit in a judicial capacity. The words 'the Law Lords', used colloquially, had the same wide meaning, but they came to be used to refer specifically to the Lords of Appeal in Ordinary. The Lords of Appeal in Ordinary were provided with rooms of their own in the Palace. Initially they were allocated rooms along either side of the corridor, which was then known as the Law Lords' Corridor, which leads from the Peers' Lobby to the Library Corridor. This was a satisfactory arrangement while the number of Law Lords was six or less, as these were elegant Pugin rooms with ample daylight because they all had windows. But it proved to be unsatisfactory when the numbers rose to nine. Three of the Law Lords had to occupy rooms at the east end of the Law Lords' Corridor which were without windows and amounted to little more than cubicles. By the mid-1970s the rooms on the south side of the corridor had been incorporated into an extension of the Peers' Dining Room, and the Law Lords had moved upstairs to rooms on the

---

[5] Lord Wharncliffe, ibid, 421–2. His intervention, which prevented the Tory peers from swamping the decision of the Law Lords, has been described as perhaps the moment of his life: L Strachey and R Fulford (eds), *The Greville Memoirs, 1814–1860*, vol 5 (London, 1938) 268–9.

[6] Lay peers sat together with Law Lords on the Committee for Privileges but did not vote on issues of law: see *Lord Mayhew of Twysden's Motion* [2002] 1 AC 109; *Lord Gray's Motion* [2002] 1 AC 124.

[7] Appellate Jurisdiction Act 1876, s 5.

[8] ibid, ss 5(2) and 6. The words 'in Ordinary' indicated that holders of this office, unlike other Peers, were to be paid a salary.

[9] ibid, s 5 and s 25 as amended by the Appellate Jurisdiction Act 1887, s 5.

[10] s 6 of the 1876 Act, as originally enacted, restricted their number to two. Lord Blackburn and Lord Gordon were the first to be appointed. The restriction, which was soon overlooked as their number was increased, was removed by the Administration of Justice Act 1968, s 1(5).

[11] See the Maximum Number of Judges Order 1994, art 2.

southern half of the corridor on the second floor of the west front[12] and in an adjacent corridor on the top floor of a new building in the State Officers' Court.[13] This was the part of the Palace that was known latterly as the Law Lords' Corridor, and it was where the Law Lords remained until the move to Middlesex Guildhall.

It was the convention that the Law Lords, whether in office or in retirement, should refrain from joining any political party. They were free to sit anywhere on the benches set aside for the Cross-Benchers. Frequent attendees were usually to be seen seated on the Cross-Benches proper that lie between the Bar of the House and the Clerks' table. In recent years the presence of serving Law Lords in Parliament has come to be seen as incompatible with the principle of the independence of the judiciary. But the root cause of this perceived anomaly lay in the fact that the receipt and determination of appeals was one of the functions of the House of Lords itself.

It would, of course, have been open to Parliament to confine the powers and privileges of Lords of Appeal in Ordinary to the performance of the appellate function only. If that had been done it would not have been possible for them to participate in any of the other functions of the House. It does not seem to have occurred to anyone in 1876 that this was either necessary or desirable. The reason for this is not hard to find. As it was the House itself by which appeals were to be determined, they had to be disposed of by means of speeches made and votes cast in the Chamber of the House. The Lords of Appeal had to be able to speak and to vote there to perform that function. Provision could, no doubt, have been made that the rights and privileges that they were to enjoy when speaking and voting were to be more limited than those enjoyed by other peers. But this was not done.

The only difference in the appointment of the Lords of Appeal in Ordinary from that of other peers lay in the wording of the Letters Patent, which set out their title and the grant of the rights that went with it. In the case of other peers, including other holders of high judicial office who were made life peers and were thus entitled to sit with the Lords of Appeal in Ordinary as Law Lords, the Letters Patent state that the peer may possess a seat in Parliament and may enjoy and use:

all the rights, privileges, pre-eminences, immunities, and advantages to the degree of a Baron duly and of right belonging, which Barons of Our United Kingdom have heretofore used and enjoyed, or as they do at present use and enjoy.

In the case of the Lords of Appeal in Ordinary appointed in pursuance of the Appellate Jurisdiction Act 1876 the Letters Patent stated that he[14] was:

---

[12] This floor is situated at the third level above the ground floor, as the first floor which is the level at which the Chamber is situated is known as the Principal Floor.

[13] See 'A Phoenix from the Ashes?' (2005) 121 LQR 253, 262–3.

[14] Or 'she', in the case of Baroness Hale of Richmond, who is the only woman to have been appointed a Lord of Appeal in Ordinary.

to hold the said Office so long as he shall well behave himself therein subject to the provisions of the said Act mentioned with all wages profits privileges rank and precedence whatsoever to the said Office belonging or in anywise apperraining.

The wording of the Letters Patent issued to the Lords of Appeal in Ordinary reflected the provisions of the statute. They were to hold office during good behaviour but might be removed from office on the address of both Houses of Parliament.[15]

Like every other peer, the Lords of Appeal in Ordinary received a Writ of Summons on their appointment and at the commencement of each succeeding Parliament. This is the authority for the taking of the oath of allegiance, which every peer must take before being permitted to sit, speak, and vote in the House. It was in the same terms as the Writ of Summons received by every other peer. This was unsurprising. It had never been the practice to qualify the right of any member of the House to take a full part in all its activities. It was understood from the beginning that Lords of Appeal in Ordinary were to be entitled, after taking the oath, to participate in all the work of the House irrespective of its subject matter. It was left to each individual, as in the case of every other member, to decide how little or how much use to make of that opportunity.

The rule that no distinction is made between the rights and privileges of any member of the House worked both ways. Just as it was open to a Lord of Appeal in Ordinary to engage in legislation, it was still technically possible for any member of the House to vote on the disposal of an appeal. It was not unknown for lay peers to sit in the Chamber while the Law Lords were reporting their opinions to the House. The notorious *Pinochet* case,[16] in which the first judgment was set aside because one of the Law Lords who sat on the first panel was disqualified and the appeal had to be re-heard, attracted particular attention. Many peers were present when the third judgment was delivered, amidst a blaze of publicity,[17] by a different and enlarged panel of Law Lords. But no lay peer had attempted to vote on the disposal of an appeal since Lord Denman attempted to do so in 1883.[18]

It was sometimes suggested that lay peers attempted to influence the Law Lords in their decisions, or at least that they had some part to play in them. The fact that the Law Lords' judgments were issued as judgments of the House may have contributed to this misunderstanding. So too may snatches of conversation overheard as Law Lords and lay peers met each other in the corridors on their way to or from the committee rooms. But there is no evidence that any Law Lord was ever influenced by exchanges of that kind, nor was there ever any good reason for

---

[15] Appellate Jurisdiction Act 1876, s 6.

[16] *R v Bow Street Metropolitan Stipendiary Magistrate, ex p Pinochet Ugarte* [2000] 1 AC 61; *(No 2)* [2000] 1 AC 119; *(No 3)* [2000] 1 AC 147.

[17] As the House permits its proceedings to be broadcast, the delivery in the Chamber of the first and the third judgments was broadcast on radio and television.

[18] *Bradlaugh v Clarke* (1883) 8 App Cas 354; Stevens (n 1) 34.

expecting that this might happen. It was appreciated on all sides of the House that the seniority and experience of the judges who were appointed as Law Lords made them impervious to improper influence.

Judges as legislators

Prior to the last 10 years of their membership of the House of Lords, it was the accepted practice for the Lords of Appeal in Ordinary to participate in the public business of the House as freely as they wished and as frequently as their other duties permitted. This was true also of other serving judges who, as holders of high judicial office, were eligible to sit as Law Lords. During the last ten years, however, a combination of factors led to a significant decline in their participation. By the end of this period, participation by the Lords of Appeal in Ordinary in the public business of the House had for all practical purposes ceased to exist. In practice only those Law Lords who had retired from judicial office felt able to participate. Even then, only a few of those who were in that position did so.

It is not possible in a short chapter such as this to analyse the Law Lords' contribution to the legislative process in great detail.[19] But some important stages in the history since 1876 can be identified, and some explanation can be offered for the differing approaches that were taken to their participation in the legislative process during this period.

In the early days the House devoted much more time to appellate work in proportion to its public business than it did during the last 50 years of the Law Lords' membership. Appeals were always heard in the Chamber at the outset of the day's list. It was only after these hearings had been concluded that the House settled down to legislating and engaged in debate on bills and other matters of general interest. The order of events ensured that the Law Lords were already present in the building before this started. The legal training and professional experience that had brought them into the House gave them a significant advantage over other members, apart of course from the Lord Chancellor, when the House was examining issues of law and legal practice. It was not unknown for some of the hereditary peers to have had the benefit of legal training. But detailed knowledge of how the law worked in practice lay with the Law Lords. They were expected to give the House the benefit of that knowledge and experience. Many of them felt that it was their constitutional duty to make their knowledge and experience available.

There were, from the outset, no formal restrictions on what the Law Lords could speak about or as to the circumstances in which it would be proper for them to exercise their right to vote. Indeed, given that the Writ of Summons of a

---

[19] For a more complete account, see the writer, 'Voices from the Past—The Law Lords' Contribution to the Legislative Process' (2007) 123 LQR 547.

Lord of Appeal was in exactly the same terms as the writs of all the other peers, it is difficult to see how, within the framework of the existing constitutional arrangements, a Law Lord could in practice be restrained from addressing himself to any matter before the House other than appealing to a convention. Those who did contribute to the legislative process confined their attention to issues of law on which they were equipped to speak. But, with two notable exceptions, they avoided comment on party political policy.

Lord Sumner and Lord Carson were under no such inhibitions. Lord Sumner was appointed a Lord of Appeal in Ordinary in 1913 and did not retire until 1930. He contributed frequently to debates throughout this period. The records show that he was willing to speak his mind on anything, even if the issue was the subject of political controversy. Lord Carson went even further.[20] He was appointed in May 1921 and had never been a judge. But he had been a member of the War Cabinet and was an outspoken controversialist in Irish politics. Soon after his appointment, Articles of Agreement were negotiated for a Treaty between England and Ireland. When he made his maiden speech on 14 December 1921 it was on the subject of Home Rule. It was, contrary to convention, both lengthy and controversial.[21] He followed up his maiden speech by speaking many times on the Irish Question, and he intervened repeatedly in the debates on the Irish Free State (Agreement) Bill.[22] A short time later he was criticised by the Lord Chancellor for making a political speech outside the House. He answered those criticisms two days later in a personal statement. A debate on 29 March 1922 on Law Lords and Party Politics was precipitated by this incident. It was the most comprehensive discussion on the floor of the House of the role of the Law Lords in party politics.[23]

Viscount Dunedin, who was then still serving as a Lord of Appeal in Ordinary, made a brief contribution to this debate.[24] He made it clear that, in his opinion, whatever their Lordships might think, the man in the street would not have confidence in the judges' impartiality if they were to mix themselves up in political questions. By 'political questions' he was not confining his expression of concern to issues which were party political. It can be assumed that he regarded anything that was of sufficient importance to command the attention of the House as 'political'. But he was alone in the position that he adopted. Lord Sumner, who also attended the debate but did not speak, would certainly not have agreed with him.

The Marquess of Salisbury, closing the debate on behalf of the Government,[25] said that he agreed that there was dignity to the Law Lords' office which he hoped that they would bear in mind. He hoped that the legal members of the House would continue to contribute, with all the other peers, to its counsels and

---

[20] ibid, 553–6.   [21] *Hansard*, HL, vol 48, cols 36–53.
[22] *Hansard*, HL, vol 49, cols 94–9 to 687–8.   [23] ibid, cols 931–73.
[24] ibid, cols 949–50.   [25] As Lord President of the Council.

decisions. Commenting on Lord Dunedin's remarks, he said that he was exceedingly sorry that Lord Dunedin did not take a greater part in the debates in the House. It was a good and salutory rule that the legal talent in the House should place itself at the House's service. As a lay peer, he would regret it if the Law Lords did not take what he described as their proper share in these debates.[26] The effect of the debate was to reinforce the general understanding that, while the Law Lords were being encouraged to continue to participate, they should avoid engaging in anything that was the subject of party political controversy.

As already noted, it was already the practice in 1876 for appeals to be heard in the Chamber as the first item in the day's business. This system continued until after the end of the Second World War. When the Chamber of the House of Commons was destroyed during the war by bombing, the House of Commons moved to the House of Lords Chamber. The House of Lords sat at the south end of the building in the King's Robing Room. In 1948 noise outside caused by workmen constructing a new boiler house forced the Lords of Appeal in Ordinary, as a temporary measure,[27] to seek peace and quiet upstairs on the committee corridor overlooking the River Thames.[28] This proved to be much more practical and, it was soon recognised, much more congenial. By 1951 the habit was firmly established and it became a permanent arrangement. It enabled the Law Lords to sit for most of the time in a committee room. They had to go into the Chamber of the House only when they were delivering their judgments. But, despite the move, they continued to participate in public business of the House when the day's appellate business was over. Their right to hear appeals in the Chamber was exercised when the House was in recess, usually during the first week in October of each year.

The composition of the House began to change following the enactment of the Life Peerages Act 1958. Until then the House had been made up almost exclusively of hereditary peers. Gradually, as the appointment of life peers gathered pace, it became a more broadly based institution. The Law Lords were no longer almost alone in having had the benefit of legal training and experience. Nevertheless their participation from the Cross-Benches continued to command respect. They continued to participate in the legislative process on issues on which they felt that they had something to contribute. However, there had by now been a significant change in the timing of these debates. The House now met each day for public business at 2.30pm while the Law Lords were still sitting on the Appellate Committee. In June 1954 it became the practice for the first 30 minutes of each sitting day except Friday to be made available for the putting of questions to Ministers. Nevertheless, there was a period of about an hour each

---

[26] *Hansard*, HL, vol 49, cols 970–3.

[27] Motion by Lord Jowitt, the Lord Chancellor, 11 May 1948: *Hansard*, HL, vol 155, cols 737–41. Lord Simon too emphasised that this was to be a temporary measure: cols 742–4.

[28] Note by Sir David Stephens, the Clerk of the Parliaments, to the Leader of the House, 9 December 1965, para 10.

afternoon when legislation was being debated in the House during which the Law Lords might still be hearing appeals.

At first this was not a serious obstacle to those Law Lords who wished to participate in its debates. There was no limit on the time that the House might sit late into the night, and debates on legislation not infrequently ended well after midnight. In any event, business in the House always takes priority over Committee business. From time to time this rule was invoked by the Law Lords so that they could speak in a debate in the Chamber before 4.15pm, when they would normally have concluded their appellate business. Lord Reid was a firm adherent to this rule.[29] He is recorded as having risen to his feet to speak in the second reading of the Occupiers' Liability (Scotland) Bill in 1960 at 3.15pm.[30] The importance that the Law Lords attached to maintaining their ability to take part in legislation during this period can also be seen from the fact that they declined an offer of a move to the Middlesex Guildhall in 1965 when it became available for other uses on the creation of the Greater London Council. The offer was declined on the ground that sitting in that building would make it less easy for them to participate in debates in the Chamber, and that they would be less likely to do so.[31]

The Government raised the issue of reform of the House of Lords when Labour was returned to office in 1964 under Harold Wilson. But its White Paper did not contemplate any change in the position or functions of the Law Lords.[32] It recognised that as members of the House of Lords they exercised two functions: a judicial function, as the House was the supreme appellate court of the United Kingdom; and a more general function, as ordinary but specialist members of the second chamber of Parliament. Commenting on the more general function, the White Paper noted that their responsibilities were no different from those of other peers. The convention that they did not generally participate in party political controversy was noted. But it was also acknowledged that as skilled and experienced lawyers they had a valuable part to play in the consideration of public bills and the jurisprudential aspects of legislation generally. It recommended that active Law Lords should be exempted from the attendance and age qualifications that it prescribed for other categories of voting peers. Their knowledge and experience should continue to be fully available to the reformed House for its non-judicial business. The Labour Government went out of office before the reforms that were contemplated could be implemented. But the views expressed in the White Paper seemed to reinforce the case for the participation of the Law Lords in the ordinary business of the House.

In April 1971 the problem that the timing of public business caused for the Law Lords was discussed on the floor of the House. Lord Shepherd asked the

---

[29] Lord Wilberforce recalled, in his written submission to the Royal Commission on the Reform of the House of Lords (the Wakeham Commission), that it was Lord Reid's view that priority ought to be given to legislative work, when participation in it was called for, over judicial business.
[30] *Hansard*, HL, vol 216, col 1163.   [31] See 'A Phoenix from the Ashes?' (n 13) 262.
[32] Cmnd 3799, November 1968, 24.

Leader of the House, Earl Jellicoe, whether he would make arrangements to enable the Lords of Appeal to attend and give their counsel during the committee and the report stages of the Industrial Relations Bill.[33] Earl Jellicoe acknowledged that this bill was one on which the Lords of Appeal would wish to speak and on which the House would wish to have their advice. As for their availability, he reminded the House that, as the Appeal and Appellate Committees usually adjourned by 4pm, the Law Lords could be present in the Chamber for all but a very short period in the afternoon. But he was sure that it would normally be possible for arrangements to be made to allow other business to be taken in the House until they were available, should this be thought to be necessary.

In 1978 a note was prepared in the Parliament Office on the extra-judicial activities in the House of the Lords of Appeal in Ordinary. It included a summary of the business on which they spoke between 1964 and 1977. In absolute terms they did not emerge as outstandingly active legislators, although on occasion their intervention was significant. In 1965 Lord Parker of Waddington, as Lord Chief Justice, led an unsuccessful attack on the War Damage Bill which reversed the decision of the Appellate Committee in the *Burmah Oil* case.[34] In the same year he moved two amendments to the Murder (Abolition of the Death Penalty) Bill.[35] The first would have left the penalty of life imprisonment to the discretion of the trial judge. The second retained the Government's proposal for a mandatory life sentence but gave a discretion to the trial judge to recommend a minimum term of imprisonment. His first amendment was carried by a small majority, with the support of all the Law Lords present other than the Lord Chancellor. He was prevailed upon at the Report stage to withdraw it and move, successfully, his second alternative.[36] Significant too was Lord Wilberforce's contribution to the State Immunity Act 1978, without which there would have been no exception for commercial transactions,[37] and Lord Templeman's vigorous intervention in support of an amendment to the Companies Bill of 1989[38] which was designed to circumvent a previous decision of the House[39] in which he had been a dissenting participant.[40]

Viscount Dilhorne and Lords Morris of Borth-y-gest, Wilberforce, Diplock, and Simon of Glaisdale emerged from this note as the most frequent contributors. They did not confine themselves to the legal implications of law reform. From time to time they spoke on issues of more general interest. It was predicted that, as an increasing number of law reform bills were starting in the Lords, their

---

[33] *Hansard*, HL, vol 317, cols 199–200.

[34] *Hansard*, HL, vol 264, cols 776–9. *Burmah Oil Co Ltd v Lord Advocate* [1965] AC 75; see L Blom-Cooper and G Drewry, *Final Appeal: A Study of the House of Lords in its Judicial Capacity* (Oxford: Clarendon Press, 1972) 368–73.

[35] *Hansard*, HL, vol 268, cols 1211–43.

[36] *Hansard*, HL, vol 269, col 405. It was enacted as s 1(2) of the 1965 Act.

[37] See 'Voices from the Past' (n 19) 566–8.   [38] See Companies Act 1989, s 141(4).

[39] *Bradley v Eagle Star Insurance Co Ltd* [1989] AC 957.

[40] *Hansard*, HL, vol 512, cols 1014–15, 1017.

participation could be expected to increase. This prediction was borne out by events. For example, on 18 January 1996 Lord Mustill took a leading part in the debate at second reading of the Arbitration Bill,[41] on 14 November 1996 Lord Goff of Chieveley introduced the Theft (Amendment) Bill,[42] and on 5 December 1996 Lord Browne-Wilkinson introduced the second reading of the Land Registration Bill.[43] In later years, after they retired, Lords Wilberforce, Brightman, and Simon of Glaisdale continued to attend the House regularly and contribute to debates.[44] Their example was followed a decade later by Lords Ackner, Slynn of Hadley, and Lloyd of Berwick.

The understanding that the Law Lords should avoid engaging in anything that was the subject of party political controversy extended to voting as well as to speaking. There was difference of view, however, as to whether it would ever be proper for them, while still serving, to insist on a division. During a debate on the committee stage of the Criminal Justice (Scotland) Bill in February 1980 Lord Fraser of Tullybelton said that it would be wrong for him as a judge to press for a division against the Government.[45] Others were not so inhibited. In 1977 Viscount Dilhorne pressed for a division on two amendments to the Criminal Law Bill, and in 1978 Viscount Dilhorne and Lord Diplock each pressed to divisions amendments to the Scotland Bill. Lord Scarman, while still serving, moved amendments to the Police and Criminal Evidence Bill in 1984 and on two occasions defeated the Government. Lord Ackner, also while still serving, acted as a teller in the division which resulted in the House of Lords rejecting the War Crimes Bill for a second time in 1991. Lord Diplock, while still serving as the Senior Law Lord, gave evidence to a Select Committee in 1976 on the legal demerits of a bill which would have made it a criminal offence to participate in hare coursing.[46]

On 8 June 1994 the Clerk of the Parliaments[47] issued a note on the Law Lords' participation in public business. Advice was offered as to the proprieties of their taking part in debate or in voting on bills which were the subject of controversy, especially if that controversy was of a party political nature. He pointed out that in view of the terms of the Writ of Summons and the Report of the Select Committee on the House's powers in relation to the attendance of its Members,[48] it seemed that there were no bars, other than their own discretion, in their exercise of their rights to a 'seat, place and voice' and duty to 'treat and give their counsel' as legislators. He said that the only reservation to this complete freedom was that it was incumbent on all members of the judiciary to refrain from becoming involved in party political controversy. This convention was well understood and

---

[41] *Hansard*, HL, vol 568, col 781.   [42] *Hansard*, HL, vol 575, col 1066.
[43] ibid, col 1162.
[44] See, for example, s 5 of the Trustee Delegation Act 1999 which was inserted in response to an amendment proposed by Lord Brightman: *Hansard*, HL, vol 598, cols 126–8.
[45] *Hansard*, HL, vol 404, col 1260.
[46] Report from the Select Committee on the Hare Coursing Bill, 6 May 1976, paras 864–79.
[47] MAJ (later Sir Michael) Wheeler-Booth.   [48] HL 1955–56(7), (66-1) para 67.

manifested by the fact that the Law Lords invariably sat as Cross-Benchers, although it was not based on any public written rule or statute. It rested on the recognition that the judicial reputation for the impartial administration of justice would suffer in the eyes of the public if it were transgressed. He acknowledged that it was difficult to draw the line in specific cases. Where to draw it was essentially a matter for the Law Lords themselves, not for the House or any exterior authority save that of public acceptance. He added that the Lord Chancellor's Permanent Secretary was in complete agreement with the views expressed in his note.[49] It is unlikely that the note would have been issued without the approval of the then Senior Law Lord.

Up to this point there was no sign that the position of the Law Lords as members of the House was under serious challenge. Significant changes were to come, however, when the Labour Government under Tony Blair started to reform the House of Lords. Its manifesto contained a proposal to end the right of hereditary peers to sit and vote in the House. This was proposed as the first stage in a process of reform to make the House of Lords more democratic and representative. The issue was considered by a Royal Commission on the Reform of the House of Lords, chaired by Lord Wakeham. A paper was submitted by JUSTICE which sought to take the debate one stage further. In its view there was a pressing need to create a supreme court of appeal of the United Kingdom to replace the appellate function of the House of Lords, of which the justices of the new court would not be members. The Lords of Appeal in Ordinary submitted a memorandum. It was amplified by Lord Slynn of Hadley and Lord Nicholls of Birkenhead when they appeared in person before the Commission. It acknowledged that the Law Lords might have different views on the issue, but said that the proposal by JUSTICE ought to be examined separately by a committee specially appointed for that purpose. Pending any such review, the Law Lords should continue to serve as members of the House. It was hoped that the contribution which they made to its work in the Chamber and in committees was of value. For their part, the Law Lords benefited from the wider perspective that they derived from close contact with it and their awareness of debates in the House on matters of current interest.

The first legislative step came on 11 November 1999. All but 92 of the hereditary peers were excluded from its membership.[50] The result was not just a change in the balance of power from a permanent Conservative majority. In October 2000 it was noted that many more Life Peers had been created since the Labour Government came to power than had been the case in any equivalent period since 1958 when the relevant legislation came into effect.[51] The

---

[49] The Lord Chancellor was Lord Mackay of Clashfern; his Permanent Secretary was Sir Thomas Legg QC.

[50] House of Lords Act 1999, s 1. The Act received the Royal Assent on the last day of the session, whereupon 654 hereditary Peers were removed from membership.

[51] Seventh Report of the Committee on Standards in Public Life, *Standards of Conduct in the House of Lords* (November 2000, Cm 4904-I) vol 1, para 3.18.

introduction of more and more working life peers led to an increase in the number of members of peers who were equipped to subject legislation to detailed legal scrutiny. It also led to a change in the way the House wished to conduct business. In October 2000 the advice which had previously been given to members in the Companion to the Standing Orders to attend sittings of the House 'as often as they reasonably can'[52] was changed. They were enjoined 'to attend the sittings of the House' and told that, if they could not attend, they should obtain leave of absence.[53] Although by no means all peers follow this instruction, the change reflected a general feeling on all sides of the House that those who contributed to its debates should attend regularly.

Regular attendance by those Law Lords who were interested in public business was by now becoming more and more difficult. In 2003 the times of sitting in the Chamber for public business were altered. The starting time of 2.30pm was altered to 11am on Thursdays. A rule was introduced that the House would not normally sit after 10pm each evening. The result was that a greater proportion of legislative business was now being conducted during times when the Appellate Committee was still sitting and the Law Lords were unavailable.

In the meantime the question whether the Law Lords should participate in the legislative business of the House at all had come under further scrutiny. As the Clerk of Parliaments had noted in June 1994,[54] it had for a long time been accepted that a serving Law Lord ought never to speak on a matter which was the subject of party political controversy. But it had begun to be recognised that there was a more fundamental objection to their participating in the legislative process to any extent at all. Lord Dunedin had appreciated this point many years before.[55] It had become more obvious as greater attention was paid to the principle of judicial impartiality enshrined in Article 6 of the European Convention on Human Rights and prominent human rights lawyers, including some senior judges, began to make their views felt on this issue. Greater weight was added to the argument when the Human Rights Act 1998 was enacted. It gathered pace even more when the decision of the Appellate Committee which heard the first appeal in the *Pinochet* case was set aside because one of the Law Lords was disqualified from sitting on the appeal.[56] Although Lord Wilberforce said in his submission to the Wakeham Commission in 1999 that no instance could be cited where a Law Lord's participation in a piece of legislation could be said to have affected his judgment, the risk of a serious challenge on the ground of apparent bias could no longer be ruled out.

The Wakeham Commission did not accept the proposal by JUSTICE that a supreme court of appeal should be created and its judges should no longer sit in the House. But it recommended that the principles which the Lords of Appeal

---

[52] *Companion to the Standing Orders and Guide to the Proceedings of the House of Lords* (London: The Stationery Office, 1994).
[53] *Companion* (18th edn 2000) para 1.26.   [54] See n 47.   [55] See n 24.
[56] *R v Bow Street Metropolitan Magistrate, ex p Pinochet Ugarte (No 2)* [2000] 1 AC 119.

intended to observe when participating in debates and votes in the House and considering their eligibility to sit on related cases should be set out in writing and published.[57] The Lord Chancellor, Lord Irvine of Lairg, made it clear to the then Senior Law Lord, Lord Browne-Wilkinson, that he expected such a statement to be issued as a matter of urgency. On 22 June 2000 Lord Bingham of Cornhill, who was by then Senior Law Lord,[58] made a statement to the House agreed to by all the Lords of Appeal in Ordinary in which the following general principles were set out:[59]

As full members of the House of Lords the Lords of Appeal in Ordinary have a right to participate in the business of the House. However, mindful of their judicial role they consider themselves bound by two general principles when deciding whether to participate in a particular matter, or to vote: first, the Lords of Appeal in Ordinary do not think it appropriate to engage in matters where there is a strong element of party political controversy; and secondly the Lords of Appeal in Ordinary bear in mind that they may render themselves ineligible to sit judicially if they were to express an opinion on a matter which might later be relevant to an appeal to the House.

The Lords of Appeal in Ordinary will continue to be guided by these broad principles. They stress that it is impossible to frame rules which cover every eventuality. In the end it must be for the judgment of each individual Lord of Appeal to decide how to conduct himself in any particular situation.

The wording was carefully framed to preserve the status quo. It was not designed to promote change. This would not have secured the agreement of all the then Lords of Appeal in Ordinary. But it was out of date almost as soon as it was published. Unlike his predecessors, Lord Bingham had no desire either to speak or to vote in the House whatever the circumstances. He made it clear informally that he regarded this as incompatible with the judicial function which the Lords of Appeal in Ordinary were required to perform. Lord Steyn had already taken this view.[60] Their example was followed by other recently appointed Law Lords.

It still did not have universal support, however. It was not possible for the Law Lords to detach themselves completely from the work of the House. It was the practice for Sub-Committee E of the Select Committee on the European Union to be chaired by a Lord of Appeal in Ordinary. Among the functions of the Chairman was presentation in the Chamber of reports by the Sub-Committee selected for debate in the House. On 18 June 1999 Lord Borrie spoke appreciatively of this practice and said that it would be a great loss if it were to be discontinued.[61] Lord Hoffmann and Lord Scott of Foscote felt sufficiently

---

[57] Recommendation 59.

[58] His appointment was the first occasion on which the office of Senior Law Lord was officially recognised.

[59] *Hansard*, HL, vol 614, col 419.

[60] He explained the view that he had taken on this issue during the second reading of the Counter-Terrorism Bill, 8 July 2008: *Hansard*, HL, vol 703, col 686.

[61] *Hansard*, HL, vol 602, col 624.

strongly about the Hunting Bills when they were being debated in the House to record their dissent by voting against the proposals, despite the strong element of party political controversy.[62] But the climate of opinion among the Law Lords generally had changed. Several of the Lords of Appeal in Ordinary spoke during the second reading of the Constitutional Reform Bill in 2004. But that was a special case. By then it had come to be generally recognised that it was inappropriate for a serving Law Lord to participate to any extent at all in the legislative process.

Participation in it to any meaningful extent had, in any event, by then become virtually impossible. Rules of the House require that any peer who speaks at Second Reading must be present in the House to hear the opening speeches at the start of the debate and the speeches by the closing speakers from the front benches at the end of it. Participation in debates during the committee stage used to attract the attention of many serving Law Lords. But this is only possible if the peer who wishes to do so is in touch with the issues that are being debated and has followed the progress of the argument. Changes in sitting times, coupled with the increasing demands of judicial business, put most of the legislative business out of the reach of the Law Lords even if they had wished to participate in it.

Although no restrictions are contemplated on contributions that the Law Lords may make to the work of the House after their retirement, it seems unlikely that they will make much of an impact in the future. The House is, after all, much the same as any other debating Chamber.[63] There is no substitute for actually sitting in the House and observing debates if one wants to know how best to contribute. In the past serving Law Lords became familiar with how things were done. They were able to put this knowledge to good use after their retirement. Lord Wilberforce made this point in his submission to the Wakeham Commission. He said that there would be a loss if they could not do this. But, one by one, the various reasons why serving Law Lords might wish to visit and be seen in the Chamber had disappeared. With them went any interest in the public business of the House and familiarity with its practices. It is striking how few recently retired Law Lords attend debates as compared with previous years when it was normal for them to continue to do this after retirement. The House as a whole too has already begun to lose touch with the Law Lords. If it is true that their contribution in the past was valuable even to a modest degree, this development must be seen as regrettable.

---

[62] *Hansard*, HL, vol 624, cols 77–90, Lord Hoffmann, and vol 623, col 707 and vol 624, cols 77–90, Lord Scott on the first Bill which fell with the General Election of June 2001; *Hansard*, vol 632, cols 1336–42, Lord Hoffmann and Lord Scott on the second Bill which became the Hunting Act 2004.

[63] See 'Voices from the Past' (n 19) 550.

PART C

DEVELOPMENT OF THE COURT

12

The Early Years of the House of Lords, 1876–1914

Patrick Polden

Composition[1]

The Appellate Jurisdiction Act was shorn even of the relatively minor modifications that Cairns had envisaged, for it neither created a distinct 'judicial committee' nor excluded lay peers from participation in judicial business. The latter was achieved with characteristic indirectness only when the egregious Lord Denman, unabashed by previous rebuffs, sought to add his vote to Blackburn's dissent in *Bradlaugh v Clarke* and was once more unsupported and ignored.[2] Since legally qualified peers had sometimes been very scarce, it was fortunate for defenders of the Lords' judicial role that it was unusually strong, with Lord Chancellor Cairns assisted by former chancellors in Hatherley, Chelmsford, and Selborne, and by the recently appointed Scottish judge Lord Colonsay.

This group remained intellectually dominant for a few years,[3] but as they died or, in Selborne's case, ceased to sit regularly, and with the number of Lords of Appeal in Ordinary (LAOs) raised from two to four, the common lawyers took over. Indeed, after Herschell's death in 1899, for the first time since Eldon's day there was no ex-Lord Chancellor at all. Moreover three successive chancellors were common lawyers and Halsbury's ignorance of equitable doctrines was sometimes embarrassing.[4] Only in 1912 did an equity lawyer (in the form of Haldane) again ascend the woolsack, and even then the equity element was weak.

The LAOs might be drawn directly from men of 15 years' standing at the English or Irish bar, or the Faculty of Advocates, or from among holders of 'high judicial

---

[1] All the judges mentioned below are in the *Oxford Dictionary of National Biography* (*DNB*); the most prominent are appraised by R Stevens, *Law and Politics: The House of Lords as a Judicial Body 1800–1976* (London: Weidenfeld and Nicholson, 1979).

[2] (1883) 8 App Cas 354; Stevens (n 1) 54 n 91. Eccentric son of the former Lord Chief Justice; called from Lincoln's Inn but never practised: *DNB* vol 15, 804. See also his speeches in Parl Debs (series 3) vol 310 (1887).

[3] (1895–6) 40 SJ 190. In the Law Reports volume for 1877–8 they accounted for 76 appearances out of 187; the two LAOs appeared 82 times.

[4] See eg his remarks on resulting trusts in *Smith v Coke* [1891] AC 297.

offices' for at least two years.[5] They would be barons, but would sit in the House only while they remained LAOs, and their titles would not be hereditary. With a £6,000 salary and a pension of up to £3,750, they might be made Privy Councillors and become obliged to serve on the Judicial Committee when their primary duties allowed.[6] As with other judges, there was no compulsory retirement age.

Only two LAOs were to be appointed initially, supplemented by one on the demise or retirement of each pair of salaried judges of the Privy Council.[7] The Act did not reserve places for Scottish or Irish lawyers, but the Scottish legal establishment had been among the staunchest opponents of Selborne's scheme,[8] and with Colonsay dead and the Lords still as much a Scottish as an English forum, it was evidently felt politic to choose a Scot. Unfortunately the man chosen, William Gordon, was already sick and died in 1880.[9] At 53 his successor, William Watson, was one of the youngest Law Lords, but rapidly established himself as one of the most forceful and able. His pronouncements in constitutional cases in the Privy Council were sometimes controversial but his reputation stood so high that after almost 20 years of distinguished service he was hard to replace.[10] His immediate successors fell well short. James Robertson was 'embittered by the absence of political advancement'[11] and the exigent manner in which Thomas Shaw claimed his prize got his tenure off to an unfavourable start.[12]

Though Ireland generated far fewer appeals than Scotland, the third LAO was an Irish Liberal, Sir John Fitzgerald, a clear-headed and respected judge.[13] He was followed by Sir Michael Morris, a Roman Catholic unionist who was nevertheless popular in Ireland.[14] When Morris retired in 1900, Salisbury temporarily broke the Irish succession to resolve competing claims among his English lawyers,

---

[5] Administration of Justice Act 1876 ss 5, 6. The offices were: Lord Chancellor of Great Britain or Ireland, paid judge of the Judicial Committee of the Privy Council, judge of a superior court in England, judge of one of the courts of law or equity in Dublin, judges of the Court of Session. The two-year provision was presumably intended as a safeguard against another 'Colliery explosion' like the furore surrounding the appointment of Sir Robert Collier (Lord Monkswell) in 1871, but given the power to appoint a man direct from the Bar it seems unnecessary.

[6] s 6.   [7] s 14.

[8] See eg the evidence of Scottish witnesses to the select committee of 1872 (PP 1872 (325) VII).

[9] He was third choice: A Paterson, 'Scottish Lords of Appeal, 1876–1988' [1988] Juridical Review 235, 237.

[10] R Stevens, *The Independence of the Judiciary* (Oxford: Clarendon Press, 1993) 72–6; VV Veeder, 'A Century of Judicature', in Committee of American Law Schools (eds), *Select Essays in Anglo-American Legal History* (London: Wildy, rep 1968) vol iii, 730–836, 828–31.

[11] *DNB*. Lord President of the Court of Session from 1891; CN Johnston, 'The Late Lord Robertson' (1909) 21 Juridical Review 63.

[12] Some of the 'vicious' elements of Lord Macmillan's entry in the original *DNB* entry have been toned down in the *DNB*; Stevens (n 1) 246–53.

[13] Former Attorney General and a judge of the Queen's Bench. Irish Law Lords are appraised in Lord Lowry, 'The Irish Lord of Appeal in Ordinary' in DS Greer and NM Dawson (eds), *Mysteries and Solutions in Irish Legal History* (Dublin: Four Courts Press, 2001) 193–216.

[14] Successively Attorney General, judge and Chief Justice of Common Pleas, and Lord Chief Justice. His very readable judgments scorned precedent and lacked any pretence to legal erudition (*DNB*); RJ Kelly, 'The Late Lord Morris' (1901–2) 5th ser 27 Law Magazine & Review 63.

switching Sir Nathaniel Lindley from the Rolls to accommodate Sir Richard Webster.[15] A non-political judge of wide experience, Lindley, if not quite in Macnaghten's class, provided solid judicial ballast and reassurance that the house had its quota of 'lawyers' lawyers'.[16] The outgoing Conservatives restored the Irish representation by promoting its Irish Attorney-General, Sir John Atkinson, a loyal party man, but only a moderately capable lawyer.[17]

Barring political imperatives, Sir Colin Blackburn was the obvious choice for the English LAO, for however personally ungracious, and even uncouth,[18] he was the most highly regarded common law judge of the day. The choice of his successor in 1886 was less obvious once Sir Henry James, whose political claims were indisputable, had refused. Halsbury and Salisbury bypassed the chancery bench in their search for an equity lawyer and took the Ulsterman Edward Macnaghten direct from the Bar.[19] They never regretted their decision, though others did not always appreciate the elegance and occasional humour of Macnaghten's speeches.[20] Macnaghten became the backbone of the judicial house, bringing equitable jurisprudence, albeit somewhat less expansive than Cairns' and Selborne's, and fine intellectual discrimination to bear for more than 20 years.[21]

The fourth LAO became appointable in 1891, and the first three holders were evanescent. Sir James Hannen, President of the Probate, Divorce and Admiralty Division (PDA), was already 70 and survived for only two years; Sir Charles Bowen, only 56 and almost universally loved and esteemed, was expected to lend academic distinction and urbanity to the house,[22] but died within 18 months without delivering a single judgment. The Liberal Attorney General, Sir Charles Russell, achieved his real desire—to become Lord Chief Justice—after a few months in the Lords,[23] and it was only with his successor, Sir Horace Davey, promoted from the Court of Appeal, that a period of stability ensued. Davey's political ambitions foundered on his inability to adapt a somewhat sour personality to please either the electorate or the party leadership, but he served as a

[15] Webster and Sir Edward Clarke had refused the Rolls in 1897: RFV Heuston, *Lives of the Lord Chancellors, 1885–1964* (Oxford: Clarendon Press, 1964) 52–4.

[16] He refused a hereditary peerage. Selborne appointed him to the Common Pleas in his endeavour to effect a better 'fusion' of law and equity.

[17] His appointment was criticised. '[A] cautious man who chose, if possible, narrow solutions' (*DNB*). Lowry (n 13) 198–202, is more favourable than Stevens (n 1) 259–62.

[18] See eg Sir J Hollams, *Jottings of an Old Solicitor* (London: John Murray, 1906) 105.

[19] He had refused a judgeship in 1886.

[20] Herschell once prevailed upon Macnaghten to substitute a simple concurrence for a characteristic speech: it is reproduced in (1938) 54 LQR, 522–8.

[21] According to Sir Rufus Isaacs 'one of the greatest judicial figures that the legal history of this country has ever seen': *Hansard*, HC (series 5) vol 53, cols 109–14 (1913), and see WR Kennedy (1911–12) 5th ser 37 Law Magazine & Review 455.

[22] Coleridge LCJ felt that Bowen would lend badly needed strength to the Lords: EH Coleridge, *The Life and Correspondence of John Duke, Lord Coleridge, Lord Chief Justice of England* (London: William Heinemann, 1904) ii, 380.

[23] RB O'Brien, *The Life of Lord Russell of Killowen* (London: Smith, Elder, 1901) 268–70. He probably never participated in the Lords' judicial hearings while Lord Chief Justice.

Law Lord for a dozen years, rivalling Macnaghten for the quality, if not the elegance, of his judgments.[24] His next two successors came and went quickly. Sir Richard Henn Collins was a Master of the Rolls, and like Lindley was non-political,[25] but he was not truly an equity lawyer and would hardly have filled the gap left by Davey even if he had not been chronically sick.[26] Sir William Robson was a pure common lawyer and active Liberal politician, who had been greatly overworked in piloting their contentious social reforms through the Commons. He had earned his comparative ease, but enjoyed it for less than two years before his health gave way.[27]

The third judicial element in the Lords were the holders, past and present, of the 'high judicial offices'. After 1880 only the Lord Chief Justice automatically received a peerage, and his official duties precluded regular attendance[28] but in the 1870s and 1880s the house had the occasional assistance of Lord Penzance.[29] Lord Coleridge, son of the former Lord Chief Justice, became a high court judge but perhaps felt that it would be presumptuous to offer his services.[30]

Peerages were also bestowed upon a few retired or retiring judges of varying quality. The first recipient, Sir George Bramwell (1880), was perhaps the best-known judge of his day. Vastly experienced, he would clearly strengthen the Lords' common law side, though his outspoken and unrepentant devotion to the principles of laissez faire and hostility towards equity sometimes led him into robust dissents.[31] Successive presidents of the PDA, Sir Gorell Barnes (Lord Gorell) and Sir John Bigham (Lord Mersey), were made peers. Gorell was 'a safe pair of hands' who was entrusted with several important inquiries into aspects of the law, and sat regularly in the Lords between 1909 and 1912.[32] Mersey was younger and healthier, and had been president for less than a year when he retired, ostensibly on health grounds. He was fit enough to play a major role in

---

[24] *DNB* ('as a judge, almost peerless in his time') and JB Atlay, *The Victorian Chancellors* vol 2 (London: Smith, Elder, 1908) 419 are more generous than Stevens (n 1) 118.

[25] *DNB* says that he never stood for Parliament, but Stevens (n 1) 113 calls him a failed Conservative candidate.

[26] Collins was preferred to the Attorney General Sir John Walton. Though appearing regularly in the Chancery Division as counsel, Collins was a judge of the KBD.

[27] GW Keeton, *A Liberal Attorney-General* (London: James Nesbit, 1949) 145–62. According to Stevens (n 1) 129–30, 'of all the law lords . . . [he] held the most radical opinions'.

[28] Coleridge had sat in *Dublin etc Rly v Slattery* (1877–8) 3 AC as CJCP when it was re-argued before an enlarged bench. According to Heuston (n 15) 148, Alverstone LCJ did not enjoy appellate work; he certainly appeared out of his depth in the '*Wee Frees*' case (Bannatyne v Overtoun [1904] AC 515): RFV Heuston, 'Judicial Prosopography' (1986) 102 LQR 90, 111–12.

[29] After a curious judicial career, Penzance's last—and controversial—position was as judge under the Public Worship Regulation Act 1874. He died in 1899.

[30] Despite doubts about whether a peer might practise at the Bar ('Junior Devil', *A Chance Medley* (Boston: Little, Brown & Co, 1912) 202), it was resolved in *Re Kinross* [1905] AC 468 that peers might appear as counsel in the Lords.

[31] C Fairfield, *Some Account of George Willshere, Baron Bramwell of Hever, and his Opinions* (London: Macmillan, 1898) and several articles in (1994) 38 Am J Legal History. He retired in 1892.

[32] JED de Montmorency, *John Gorell Barnes, First Lord Gorell, 1848–1913, A Memoir* (London: John Murray, 1920) 100–15.

the Judicial Committee's handling of prize cases during the war.[33] None of the others made much of an impression. Sir Ventris Field was deaf and irascible;[34] Sir Henry Lopes (Lord Ludlow) was genial and popular but one of the least capable judges in the Court of Appeal,[35] and Sir Henry Hawkins (Lord Brampton) had even fewer claims to sit on the highest court and lived down to his reputation.

Among the Scots, the Presidents of the Court Session, such as Moncrieff, were seen only occasionally, but Sir Alexander Shand, a former judge in that court, received a peerage in 1892 and for 10 years gave conscientious and capable, if undistinguished, service.[36] A sitting Lord of Session, Sir Alexander Kinnear, was similarly honoured, but seldom sat even after he finally left the bench in 1913.[37] Of the Irish Lord Chancellors Lord O'Hagan was a considerable asset,[38] but Lord Ashbourne was a more doubtful asset; Loreburn tried to keep him away, but he was still sitting occasionally under Haldane.[39]

The eligible categories were enlarged by the Appellate Jurisdiction Act 1887. Originally designed to retain Blackburn's services,[40] the bill was expanded during its passage to qualify unpaid judges of the Judicial Committee if they were made peers.[41] Lord Hobhouse devoted himself almost exclusively to the Privy Council[42] but Lord James of Hereford, harshly described by Selborne as 'almost a statesman, almost a lawyer, almost a gentleman',[43] made a useful addition to the Liberal element.[44]

The number of judicial peers therefore varied considerably from session to session until 1912 and 1913, when things changed appreciably. This came about partly through an unusually large number of comings and goings. There was a new Chancellor in Haldane, a much more sophisticated lawyer than his

[33] *DNB*; Stevens (n 1) 114. He lived until 1929 and is best known nowadays for having chaired the inquiry into the sinking of *The Titanic*.

[34] Persuaded to retire in 1890 (age 77), he sat in the Lords only during the following two years, though he lived until 1907.

[35] Made a peer in the Diamond Jubilee Honours List on the understanding that he would remain in the Court of Appeal until asked to retire, he nevertheless retired on his own initiative soon afterwards: Heuston (n 15) 54.

[36] He died during the hearing of *Free Church of Scotland v Overton* [1904] AC 515, where 'his judgment might have been crucial to the outcome.

[37] A non-political judge whose 'judicial legacy was full of solid achievement rather than of sparkling insight' (*DNB*).

[38] Lord Chancellor 1868–74, 1880–1, but active in the Lords while out of office. As a common lawyer he had more in common with Blackburn than with the English equity lawyers.

[39] Financial need largely impelled him to become Lord Chancellor in 1885 and he served Conservative administrations in that capacity until 1905, despite modest legal attainments.

[40] The debates (Parl Debs (series 3) vol 310, cols 745–52 (1887)) include fulsome tributes to Blackburn. The 'Blackburn clause' proved of little immediate value; Blackburn did not continue, probably because of advancing senility, and no other retired LAO made much use of it.

[41] s 5. It was Selborne's amendment (cols 1063–4).

[42] LT Hobhouse and JL Hammond, *Lord Hobhouse, A Memoir* (London: Edward Arnold, 1905) Lord Davey, 203.

[43] E Marjoribanks and I Colvin, *Life of Lord Carson* (vol 2, London: Victor Gollancz Ltd, 1934) 188.

[44] James rejected several high judicial posts. He was a peer and a member of the Judicial Committee from 1895.

immediate predecessors, perhaps more like Selborne in his occasional divagations into sophistry. Macnaghten died mid-hearing[45] and was replaced by a rising star of the chancery division, Robert Parker,[46] and Robson was succeeded by the elderly but awesomely intelligent Fletcher Moulton.[47]

The number of LAOs was also raised, as a side effect of a long debate over the future of the Judicial Committee, precipitated by persistent discontent among the dominions. Grandiose schemes for an 'Imperial Court of Appeal' combining both fora were never likely to command the necessary degree of political and professional support at home and abroad, and the only direct effect on the Lords was the implementation of a promise made by Loreburn in advance of the Imperial Conference of 1911 to strengthen the Judicial Committee with two top class lawyers.[48] Dissenting voices grumbled that two bodies which in 1910 had sat on only 163 days ought to be able to manage without more judges,[49] but the undertaking had been given and Andrew Graham Murray, Lord Dunedin (the Lord President of the Court of Session)[50] and Sir John Hamilton (Lord Sumner), a recent promotion to the Court of Appeal, were appointed.[51] With the bestowal of a peerage upon the Unionist MP and eminent counsel CA Cripps (Lord Parmoor),[52] these changes gave the Lords a very different look as the country went to war.

Politics

Politics intruded into the judicial activities of the Lords at several points, as was to be expected, since those who sabotaged Selborne's scheme sought to preserve the integration of the legislative body with the judicature. The 'compromise' kept judicial sittings in the chamber and made the LAOs full members of the peerage.

---

[45] *Glasgow and South-Western Rly v Boyd* [1913] AC 404.

[46] A judge only since 1906, but soon recognised as 'a great addition of legal strength' to the Lords (*DNB*). Though a firm adherent of the declaratory theory of law, Parker's ability to resort to principle was somewhat reminiscent of Cairns: Stevens (n 1) 303–6.

[47] '[A] nineteenth century liberal rather than a radical, an imperialist who believed in free trade... he thought that law ought to play a relatively small part in the life of society...' (Stevens (n 1) 254). He preferred the Privy Council and early in the war he was seconded to head a government committee organising the manufacture of explosives: HF Moulton, *Life of Lord Moulton* (London: Nisbet & Co, 1922).

[48] Stevens (n 10) 17–21.

[49] *Hansard*, HC (series 5) vol 53, cols 109–14, 141–55, 173–218, especially J Martin at 173–95 (1913).

[50] Dunedin had already been sitting occasionally, eg in *Mason v Provident Clothing and Supply Co Ltd* [1913] AC 724.

[51] Both were Conservatives, though it had been rumoured that the new judges would be chosen to placate the Labour party and Irish Nationalists: *Hansard*, HC (series 5) vol 56, col 2201, JM Hogge (1913).

[52] '... an intellectual and an iconoclast': Stevens (n 1) 255–9.

Political considerations influenced appointments at all levels of the judiciary, but were particularly prominent in the Scottish and Irish appointments as LAO. All three Irishmen[53] were active in politics and appointed by their own party, while all of the Scots had decided political affiliations. Some of the English LAOs, such as Blackburn, Bowen, and Lindley, had no party allegiance[54] but even the most out-and-out political appointments, Russell and Robson, were Attorney Generals, acknowledged to have a claim (though its strength and scope were disputed) to the highest judicial offices.[55] And whatever their politics, all the English LAOs were eminently qualified as lawyers.

In the House there was no convention that limited the legal peers' participation in debate to non-party or legal questions.[56] Fitzgerald and Morris engaged fully in the frequent debates on Irish questions and initially Macnaghten was active in debate (and sometimes outspoken too) and even took charge of government bills. Such participation remained acceptable until the early 1920s but there were early signs that openly partisan interventions in the increasingly fraught Edwardian atmosphere were less welcome; in 1905 Robertson was criticised for an openly party political speech[57] and Macnaghten ceased to speak in debates after 1903. Voting was a different matter, however, and in a momentous division on the budget (30 November 1909) Halsbury was accompanied into the 'no' lobby by Atkinson, Collins, and Macnaghten, as well as Ashbourne and Alverstone, with only Lord Coleridge entering the 'yes' lobby with the Lord Chancellor.[58] In the even more crucial division on the Parliament Bill in 1911 Shaw and Robson voted with the majority, but Atkinson was a 'ditcher'.[59]

The third direct intrusion of politics was in the selection of panels for particular cases. By the 1970s it was established that a case with strong political overtones should be heard by 'non-political' judges,[60] and by then the everyday business of selection was performed by the Judicial Office and Lord Chancellor's Department.[61] In earlier times there was no such convention, and Lord Chancellors evidently kept the management of the panels to themselves.[62] Comparatively few Lords' cases had important political implications, though those Robson listed as

---

[53] That is, men taken from the Irish bar or bench; Macnaghten and Collins made their careers in England.

[54] James, who declined to become an LAO, might have been a rather weak appointment. Salisbury ignored Sir Edward Clarke's readiness to become one, presumably because of his low view of Clarke's abilities: Heuston (n 15) 52–4.

[55] J Llewellyn Edwards, *The Law Officers of the Crown* (London: Sweet & Maxwell, 1964) 309–34.

[56] Lindley, who often voted, never spoke, but only from modesty: *Autobiography* (MS copy in King's College, London library) 128.

[57] 'Junior Devil' (n 30) 339.   [58] ibid, 143.

[59] *Hansard*, HL (series 5) vol 9, col 1073.

[60] AA Paterson, *The Law Lords* (London: Palgrave Macmillan, 1982) 88.

[61] Stevens (n 1) 85–7.

[62] See the instance of Halsbury adroitly exchanging James and Davey, quoted in Stevens (n 1) 86n.

'legal in form but political in fact'[63] were increasing. Inferences of 'packing' cannot safely be drawn simply from the identity of the panel in any case,[64] but that Halsbury resorted to such tactics is beyond doubt. Nor was he alone; Selborne may have done so in *Bradlaugh v Clarke*,[65] and there are several instances under Loreburn, notably *Board of Education v Rice*.[66]

Jurisdiction and business

The scope for appeals from the English courts was somewhat enlarged by the judicature reforms. Interlocutory appeals from common law were less severely restricted and final decisions were no longer subjected to the limitations of the writ of action.[67] Access from chancery had always been easier, but it was not possible to 'leapfrog' the new court of appeal like the court of appeals in chancery.[68] All appeals were now by way of rehearing and commenced by petition.[69] Admiralty appeals were transferred from the Privy Council and the only major restrictions were in divorce, where appeals were restricted to matters of law.[70] There was still no proper appeal in criminal cases[71] until 1907, and the first appeal from the new Court of Criminal Appeal arrived in 1910.[72] A few statutes forbade or limited an appeal to the Lords in particular subjects, but none was of great importance.

Nevertheless there was no sudden and dramatic rise in the number of appeals presented. The increase over the first 30 years, though impressive in percentage terms, was modest in actual numbers, and Sir John MacDonell estimated that only 7 per cent of Court of Appeal judgments were appealed, around one in 2,000 high court writs.[73] The Lords grew busier in the early 1900s, though with curious fluctuations; a rising trend which threatened their ability to cope, with 112 in 1908 and 108 the next year, went into reverse in 1910, the number of petitions

---

[63] '...it would be idle to deny the resolute bias of many of the Judges—there and elsewhere. That bias will probably operate more than ever in cases that touch on labour, educational, constitutional and, for the future...revenue questions': Heuston (n 15) 151.
[64] Heuston, 'Judicial Prosopography' (n 28).   [65] (1883) 8 App Cas 354.
[66] [1911] AC 179; Stevens (n 1) 85–7.
[67] *Civil Judicial Statistics 1894*: PP 1896 [C 8263] XVIV, 1.
[68] Select Committee on the House of Lords' Appellate Jurisdiction, 1872, evidence of WJ Farrer, qq 723, 772.
[69] Appellate Jurisdiction Act 1876, s 4. The re-hearing, however, was of a very restricted character and seldom permitted the reception of new evidence or the examination of witnesses.
[70] Stevens (n 1) 71.
[71] In theory a writ of error lay, but in practice this was obsolete.
[72] Criminal Appeal Act 1907, s 1(6); *R v Ball* [1911] AC 47. In *Mackintosh v Lord Advocate* (1876–77) 2 App Cas 41, the House decided that no appeal lay from the High Court of Justiciary: AJ McLean, 'The House of Lords and Appeals from the High Court of Justiciary' [1985] Juridical Review 192.
[73] *Civil Judicial Statistics 1894*. Average appeals presented: 1873–7, 49, 1893–4, 66.

falling to 71 in 1913.[74] Obviously, not every petition proceeded to a hearing, and the proportion which did, which had been very high in the 1870s, fell considerably around the turn of the century, though with sizeable variations.[75]

The most notable change was that English appeals became predominant. The long dominance of Scottish appeals was already waning before the Judicature Acts,[76] and the relative decline continued; in 1870 just 19 of 51 appeals heard were English; in 1910 they made up 59 out of 74, though for a while there were odd years in which Scottish appeals still preponderated.[77] Irish appeals had never been very numerous and seldom rose above half a dozen a year, though the Lords had still to handle occasional divorce bills from Ireland.[78]

The range of subjects under appeal was so various as to resist convenient classification.[79] The affairs of shipping firms, railway companies, waterworks, and other large undertakings featured strongly, but so did contract cases (commercial and private), marriage settlements, and wills. The Lords increasingly found themselves required to interpret statutes, but these were mostly private and local acts with no general significance. Public health and other local government functions came increasingly to the fore; in 1913 public authorities featured on one side or (occasionally) both in 14 of 39 cases in the official reports. As in the high court, corporations formed a growing proportion of litigants, with 22 of the 1913 cases involving one or more, as against 13 in 45 cases in 1877–8. Cases on company law seem comparatively small in number, but perhaps the most surprisingly underrepresented subject is negligence, at least until after 1906, when Workmen's Compensation Act cases increased. Tax cases also made a more frequent appearance, though until 1900 stamp duty was as likely to be at issue as income tax.

Organisation and procedure

The hybrid nature of the House was mirrored in its clerical services. The Judicial Office formed a part of the House's clerical establishment, and comprised a chief clerk (in effect the registrar) whose juniors were not employed exclusively on judicial work.[80] They were appointed by the Clerk of the Parliaments, a position

[74] *Civil Judicial Statistics.* The decennial figures in L Blom-Cooper and G Drewry, *Final Appeal: A Study of the House of Lords in its Judicial Capacity* (Oxford: Clarendon Press, 1972) Tables 2a and 2b are very useful, and official statistics need to be read in conjunction with their valuable 'Statistical Annex' at 39.

[75] *Civil Judicial Statistics 1900*: PP 1902 [Cd 1115] CXVII, 191.

[76] Stevens (n 1) 69; Blom-Cooper and Drewry (n 74) Tables 2a, 2b and pp 32–5.

[77] eg *Civil Judicial Statistics 1884*: PP 1885 [C 4508] LXXXVI, 1.

[78] Blom-Cooper and Drewry (n 74) Tables 2a, 2b, and see eg *Hart's Divorce Bill* [1898] AC 305.

[79] See Stevens' attempt in *Law and Politics* (n 1) 69–72. His sample years include unreported cases, whereas the comment below is based primarily upon an examination of the Law Reports Appeal Cases at five-yearly intervals from 1877–8.

[80] CM Denison and CH Scott, *The Practice and Procedure of the House of Lords in English, Scotch and Irish Cases under the Appellate Jurisdiction Act 1876* (London: Butterworths, 1879) 27; Lord Donoughmore (Lord President) to Lord Curzon, 17 Feb 1917, NA PRO LCO 2/387.

held by Sir HJL Graham for 31 years from 1885. Graham had served as the Lord Chancellor's Principal Secretary for five years, and the potential for friction inherent in a situation where the Lord Chancellor necessarily exercised a practical dominion over the judicial office while the Clerk retained formal authority was never translated into actuality.[81] Nevertheless it was one which exasperated Muir McKenzie, whose efforts to rationalise it were evidently fruitless, for the Lord President referred in a barbed note to 'a High Authority who often advises the Lord Chancellor who is most anxious to confer Home Rule on the Judicial Office. He has been consistently defeated for more years than it would be decent for me to mention.'[82]

There were some significant changes in procedure in the aftermath of the 1876 Act, when the relevant standing orders were consolidated.[83] At last hearings could be held when Parliament was prorogued or during a dissolution, and the delivery of judgments was no longer liable to be delayed by those interruptions.[84] All petitions were still scrutinised by the Appellate Committee, which rejected those solely concerned with costs or with practice questions of no general importance.[85] However, neither the committee nor the House itself would reject an appeal solely because it was trivial.[86] The Law Lords had grumbled repeatedly about such appeals, especially from Scotland,[87] but the only new barrier was indirect. The existing safeguards of counsel's signature and a £500 recognisance were acknowledged to be ineffective,[88] and so a bond or cash deposit of £200 was also required.[89] This may have deterred frivolous appeals, but it scarcely covered the average cost. Despite some economies, printing costs remained high[90] and although counsel were normally limited to two per side, the fees of fashionable leaders were becoming grossly inflated. In 1900 the averaged taxed cost of an

---

[81] Graham to Lord Chancellor, Feb 1917; Schuster's memorandum, Feb 1917, NA PRO LCO 2/387.

[82] 17 Feb 1917, ibid.

[83] Denison and Scott (n 80) 221. Curiously, the standing orders were silent on whether execution of the judgment below should be stayed. Practice fluctuated over time. Before 1876 a special application had been required and it had become usual to apply first to the court below. However, by 1924 it had become routine for the Court of Appeal to send applicants to the Lords; Haldane and the Law Lords then agreed that the Court of Appeal was the more suitable forum: NA PRO LCO 2/1007.

[84] Denison and Scott (n 80) 117–25; Appellate Jurisdiction Act 1876, ss 8, 9.

[85] Denison and Scott (n 80) 71. Proceedings of the committee are occasionally reported, eg *Caledonian Rly Co v Barrie* [1903] AC 126 and *Bowie v MSS of Ailsa* [1888] AC 371.

[86] Denison and Scott (n 80) 71.

[87] Blom-Cooper and Drewry (n 74) 33–4. Most Scottish witnesses before the Select Committee in 1872 were defensive about this, but one suggested a ban on litigants in person, no doubt recalling their Lordships' harrowing experience with the indefatigable and indomitable Mrs Shedden: D McLaurin, q 680 and see *Final Appeal* (n 74) 35.

[88] Select Committee 1872, evidence of Lord Advocate, qq 445–50.

[89] Denison and Scott (n 80) 48–52.

[90] Select Committee 1872, evidence of Sir John Shaw-Lefevre, Clerk of the Parliaments, qq 867–71; (1902) 113 LT 26.

appeal allowed to a successful party was £354, but by 1907 it had risen to £441.[91] The full cost was considerably higher.[92]

Not surprisingly, therefore, there were more attempts to invoke the *in forma pauperis* procedure. Cairns had launched a strong attack upon abuses in 1874,[93] but it was Herschell, following a collective protest in *Blair v North British Insurance Co*,[94] who pushed a short bill through referring all such applications to the House's appeal committee for preliminary scrutiny.[95] That evidently had some effect,[96] but appeals that the Lords viewed as trivial still arrived.[97]

The Lords in action

The panel

The 1876 Act adopted the select committee's recommendation for a quorum of three.[98] In the early years, with only two LAOs, a three-man court was common, but later four became more usual and five common; four was presumably considered satisfactory because disagreements were rare, and if one occurred the Lord Chancellor might either accept a 2:2 vote, which allowed the judgment below to stand, or have it re-argued before a larger panel, as Loreburn did in *Colquhoun v Faculty of Advocates*.[99] Larger panels were never frequent, and the muster of nine in *Allen v Flood* was seldom equalled.[100] Until the additional LAOs in 1913 there were signs of a struggle to keep up the numbers; it was said that the Bishop of Bristol had once to sit to keep the house quorate, and colonial lawyers were affronted by the spectacle of Law Lords apparently attempting to sit in both Lords and Privy Council simultaneously.[101]

---

[91] *Civil Judicial Statistics 1900, 1910*: PP 1902 [Cd 1115] CXVII, 1; PP 1912–13 [Cd 6047] CX 187. In 1900 brief fees were allowed at 50–70g for a leader, with two-thirds for a junior, and refreshers had become accepted. Taxation took off around a quarter to a third of the costs claimed in party and party taxation.

[92] In *Scott v Scott* [1913] AC 417 the Attorney General had the Treasury Solicitor instruct counsel for the respondent since the case was of such public importance that it ought to be fully argued. If there are other instances of this, they must have been few.

[93] *Davis v Lewis*, unreported, and see A Munns to Lord Chancellor, 15 Feb 1876, NA PRO LCO 1/3.

[94] (1890) 15 App Cas 495.

[95] Appeals (Forma Pauperis) Act 1893 (56 & 57 Vict c 22). For background see P Polden, 'Doctor in Trouble' (2001) 22 Journal of Legal History 37, 54–9.

[96] *In forma* cases were reduced to an average of two a year: *Civil Judicial Statistics 1905*: PP 1907 [Cd 3477] XCVIII, 243.

[97] Stevens (n 1) 72.   [98] Select Committee 1872, resolutions.

[99] [1908] Sess Cas 10 [HL]; Stevens (n 1) 86.

[100] [1898] AC 1. RE Megarry, *A Second Miscellany-at-Law* (London: Stevens, 1973) 61 says that the ten judges who decided (by 8:2) *Powell v Kempton Park Racecourse* [1899] AC 143 were the largest panel. Eight judges sat in *Bank of England v Vagliano Bros* [1891] AC 107.

[101] W Durran, *The Lawyer—our old-man-of-the-sea* (London: Kegan Paul, 1913) 467, quoting *Sunday Times*, 31 July 1910. Stevens (n 10) 18 n 45. It was not unusual for the two bodies to sit concurrently, though a bill of 1911 sought to restrict this: *Hansard*, HC (series 5) vol 53, col 198, HA Watt (1913).

There was always a strong likelihood that the Lord Chancellor would be presiding, for they evidently made this one of their highest priorities; thus in 1893 Herschell sat in all 33 reported cases; in 1898 Halsbury was in 25 out of 31; and in 1908 Loreburn appeared in 35 out of 41. The LAOs were also regulars, as were some 'legal peers' (eg Shand and Bramwell) and ex-Lord Chancellors (eg Hatherley). To measure diligence, however, one would need to look also at the attendance in the Judicial Committee.[102]

The hearing

As in the high court, cases were beginning to take longer; in 1908 the Lords heard 84 cases in 83 days,[103] but by 1914 the average time was creeping up from one and a half days to two.[104] Delays began to be noticed; in 1905 30 cases waited more than six months for a hearing from setting down and another 42 more than a year, though things soon improved.[105] In some respects the Lords were decidedly brisk; in particular they frequently denied the respondent's counsel his opportunity, convinced that the appellant had failed to make his case.[106] Against that, however, they developed a tendency to interrupt and sometimes harass counsel, which often did nothing to speed the cause. Herschell was the most notorious exponent, leading to Lord Morris's celebrated aside that he now understood what was meant by molesting a man in his trade.[107] Watson was another offender,[108] and there was relief when Haldane made the court once more a 'listening' one.

Reserving judgment became much commoner, the House following the Court of Appeal in adopting written judgments;[109] judgment was reserved in about half the reported cases (which perhaps exaggerate its prevalence) in 1914.[110]

The judgment

Little is known about how the Lords went about framing their judgments.[111] They had no library at their disposal[112] and after *Dalton v Angus and Co* they no

---

[102] Consolidated figures for 1910–11 are in *Hansard*, HC (series 5) vol 30, col 2046 (1913).
[103] Paterson (n 60) 68.   [104] Stevens (n 1) 187.
[105] *Civil Judicial Statistics 1905*, 1906 PP 1908 [Cd 4029] CXXIII, 419; 1909 PP 1911 [Cd 5501] CII, 199.
[106] This was not new; Sir John Shaw-Lefevre told the select committee of 1872 that it had been done in 43 of 190 cases (q 886).
[107] Atlay (n 24) ii, 461. That was, of course, the point at issue in the case.
[108] E Manson, *Builders of Our Law in the Reign of Queen Victoria* (London: H Cox, 2nd edn 1904) 440–8; Lindley (n 56) 123.
[109] According to Davey they were not the rule in Selborne's day: Roundell Palmer, Earl of Selborne, *Memorials, Personal and Political* (London: Macmillan, 1898) ii, 83. Halsbury tended to give extempore judgments: Stevens (n 1) 121.
[110] Lord Hatherley, whose sight was poor, complained that to write judgments was injurious to his health: D Pannick, *Judges* (Oxford: OUP, 1987) 6.
[111] Dissenting opinions were circulated, though Halsbury refused to do so in *Allen v Flood*: Stevens (n 1) 87 n 93.
[112] A Scottish judge tartly suggested that this explained some Lords' judgments: 'Junior Devil' (n 30) 275.

longer sent for the judges to advise them.[113] Halsbury's nakedly opportunistic (and ineffectual) resort to that in *Allen v Flood*, besides the breach it caused with Herschell, was so controversial that it was never repeated, depriving posterity of the spectacle of a collection of red-robed judges 'looking rather like an omnibus full of old ladies'.[114] Nor, seemingly, did the House ever make use of assessors, a facility presumably given them to assist in admiralty cases.[115]

It gradually became more common for a panel member simply to record his concurrence in the judgment, either of a particular colleague or generally.[116] In 1877–8 only Gordon regularly did so (probably because of ill-health), but in 1908 there were 72 instances, involving 33 out of 41 reported cases, and it had become common for just one substantive speech to be given.[117] As this suggests, the House strove for, and generally achieved, a remarkable degree of unanimity.[118] Even those who have been named as frequent dissenters—Bramwell, Morris, and Davey for instance[119]—did so relatively seldom. Cases in which their Lordships were evenly, or almost evenly, divided are strikingly few.[120] Sometimes judges indicated disagreement without actually registering a dissent, like Blackburn in *Foakes v Beer*[121] and Morris in *Comber v Leyland*,[122] while Fitzgerald even contrived, to his own satisfaction at least, to deliver a speech that was completely equivocal.[123] Experience in the Judicial Committee, where dissenting opinions could not be given, may have had some influence on the little-studied evolution of this practice.

What the Lords usually agreed upon was that the appellant's cause was wrong: indeed not infrequently they would tell him so in no uncertain terms. Between 1858 and 1894 the proportion of judgments affirmed ranged between 62 to 74 per cent, though the success rate for Scottish appellants was always higher[124] and

---

[113] (1881) 6 AC 740. The only other instances after the 1876 Act were *Mordaunt v Moncrieffe* (1875–6) 1 Scottish and Divisional Appeals 374, and *Allison v Bristol Marine Ins Co* (1875–6) App Cas 209. VV Veeder, 'Advisory Opinions of the Judges of England' (1899–1900) 13 Harvard L Rev 358–70.

[114] Heuston (n 15) 119–22.

[115] Supreme Court of Judicature Act 1891 (54 & 55 Vic c 53) s 3.

[116] Lindley sometimes read his concurring judgment 'avoiding all suspicion of laziness': *Autobiography* (n 56) 128.

[117] In *Refuge Assurance Co Ltd v Kettlewell* [1909] AC 243 there was no reasoned judgment at all, Loreburn moving to affirm and Ashbourne, James, and Macnaghten concurring: Megarry (n 100) 64.

[118] CA Hereschoff, 'Dissenting Opinions' (1906–7) 5th ser 32 Law Magazine & Review 54.

[119] Veeder (n 1) 831; Stevens (n 1) 109, 118. Hobhouse dissented in two of the only three cases in which he participated.

[120] Just three instances in a six-year sample: *General Accident v McGowan* [1908] AC 207: 4:3; *Allen v Flood* [1898] AC 1: 6:3, and *Costello v The Owners of 'The Pigeon'* [1913] AC 407: 3:2. In *Harris v Earl of Chesterfield* [1914] AC 623 the 3:3 tie was eventually broken when Loreburn announced that Kinnear, who had heard the arguments but missed the speeches, favoured the respondent.

[121] (1884) 9 App Cas 605.   [122] [1898] AC 524.

[123] *Tailby v Official Receiver* (1888) 13 App Cas 523.

[124] Blom-Cooper and Drewry (n 74) Table 2b.

after 1900 there was a modest improvement in appellants' successes to around one-third.[125] Failure was all the more serious for a party since the House had relaxed its stance against granting costs to a successful appellant. What Westbury began, with surprising casualness in one case in 1871,[126] had become well established by 1877, and by 1900 it was an almost invariable practice.[127]

Jurisprudence

Since the Lords did not sit in plenary session but with a fluctuating body of judges, it could not be expected to produce a coherent jurisprudence, especially since its caseload was a haphazard mixture of the portentous and the trivial; thus in 1898, the law reports volume that features *Allen v Flood* and *London Tramways Co v LCC*[128] also contains minor cases on party walls, sewers, and parish settlements.[129]

However, there were variations in the Lords' outlook over time which reflect changes in membership.[130] The equity-dominated court of the 1870s was inclined to eschew the detailed examination of facts (and for Cairns even reported cases) and decided where possible upon principle, fitting in the previous decisions with more (Selborne and Hatherley) or less (Cairns) meticulousness.[131] This court would have enmeshed companies and other businesses within a framework of equitable obligations,[132] but it was soon succeeded by one dominated by common lawyers, who in *Salomon and Co v Salomon* and *Derry v Peek* reasserted the primacy of the common law's particularist approach.[133] In turn this period in which laissez faire and freedom of contract held sway gave way to one in which the Edwardian judges were readier to imply terms in commercial contracts.[134]

Another trend is unmistakable: the Lords were conducting a dignified retreat from any openly acknowledged law-making role. This may seem surprising given that some defenders of the Upper House as the final court of appeal argued that for the judges to be immersed in the legislature would broaden and inform their outlook.[135] Judicial reticence probably owes something to a collective unease;

---

[125] *Civil Judicial Statistics, 1894, 1905.* Halsbury's well-known reluctance to interfere with jury verdicts was one obstacle to common law appellants. Brett's division of the Court of Appeal was 'not infrequently overturned': AR Jelf, 'In Memoriam Viscount Esher' (1898–9) 5th ser 25 Law Magazine & Review 395–404, 399.

[126] *English and Foreign Credit Co v Arduin* (unreported). In *Denny v Hancock* (1870–71) 6 Ch 1 Mellish LJ had said that the Lords never did so.

[127] Denison and Scott (n 80) 141–69.   [128] [1898] AC 1, 375.

[129] *Bethnal Green Vestry v London School Board* [1898] AC 190; *Pasmore v Oswaldthwaite UDC* [1898] AC 387; *Plymouth Poor Guardians v Axminster Poor Guardians* [1898] AC 586.

[130] This section draws heavily on Stevens (n 1) and PS Atiyah, *The Rise and Fall of Freedom of Contract* (Oxford: Clarendon Press, 1979).

[131] Atiyah, ibid, 671–4; Stevens (n 1) 114–16.

[132] eg *Erlanger v New Sombrero Phosphate Co* (1877–78) 3 App Cas 1218.

[133] [1896] AC 22; (1889) 14 App Cas 337.   [134] Stevens (n 1) 143–6.

[135] R Abel-Smith and R Stevens, *Lawyers and the Courts* (London: Heinemann, 1967) 124.

after the Third Reform Act in 1885, even the legislative role of the Lords seemed vulnerable and the legitimacy of unelected judges as law-makers was highly questionable. The controversies aroused by their decisions in the great sequence of trade union cases may well have strengthened this feeling: the constitutional crisis of 1911 almost certainly did.

One manifestation of this concern was an ostensible, and sometimes ostentatious, adherence to the strict affirmation in *London Tramways* of the self-denying ordinance that the Lords would not overturn their earlier decisions.[136] The case is actually a rather flimsy basis for such a portentous doctrine. Only Halsbury made a substantive speech, and, like his concurring colleagues (Macnaghten, Morris, and James) and the reporter, viewed it as merely endorsing a position generally taken up since 1860, albeit with exceptions, although judges from time to time bemoaned their inability to overturn inconvenient precedents, notably concerning restrictions on the equity of redemption.[137]

In reality the doctrine of *stare decisis* was never operated in so rigid a fashion as Halsbury's formulation would suggest: indeed no one was more adept and unscrupulous in escaping the chains of precedents than Halsbury himself— most outrageously in *Quinn v Leathem*.[138] Others were more subtle but equally effective, culminating in the sophistry of Haldane's reshaping of the law of collateral advantages in mortgages in *Kreglinger (G & C) v New Patagonia Meat and Cold Storage Company*.[139] The importance of *London Tramways*, however, lies in its unequivocal avowal that the Law Lords did not make law: they only ascertained it, and once discovered it could not be altered save by Parliament.[140]

The second manifestation of this reticence was in the construction of statutes. The dominant approach was increasingly to disclaim any attempt to uncover and implement the underlying policy of an enactment, and rather to apply the so-called 'golden rule', giving each word and phrase its 'normal' or 'natural' meaning. In practice, this distinction was often unworkable and probably no judge was rigidly consistent in applying it. This mattered little when local acts were construed, but was more sensitive in politically charged legislation such as the Workmen's Compensation Acts, Education Acts, and tax statutes. In workmen's

---

[136] [1898] AC 375. D Pugsley, '*London Tramways* (1898)' (1996) 17 Journal of Legal History 172–84 explains the background and the implicit rebuff to Sir FM Pollock's contrary view.

[137] *Bradley v Carritt* [1903] AC 253 (Lindley); *Samuel v Jarrah Timber and Wood Paving Corporation* [1901] AC 323 (Macnaghten). See also *Foakes v Beer* (1884) 9 App Cas 605 (Blackburn).

[138] [1901] AC 495; Stevens (n 1) 90–2. Like others, Halsbury was apt to declare that inconvenient precedents turned on a question of fact rather than law.

[139] [1914] AC 25; Stevens (n 1) 97–100. See also *Nocton v Ashburton* [1914] AC 932 in which Haldane led the Lords in deliberately undoing much of the mischief wrought by *Derry v Peek*: *The Correspondence of Mr Justice Holmes and Sir Frederick Pollock*, M de Wolfe Howe (ed) (Cambridge, Mass: Harvard UP, 2nd edn 1962) vol 1, 215.

[140] Herschell was a particularly strenuous advocate of this viewpoint: Stevens (n 1) 122; Atiyah (n 130) 831–4.

compensation differing attitudes could be distinguished[141] but in general the Lords were more prone to adopt a purposive construction than Collins MR's rigidly literalist division of the Court of Appeal.[142] In contrast there were signs that an initially even-handed approach to tax statutes was yielding to one which insisted that the revenue must bring the taxpayer within the narrowest, most literal reading of the statute in order to exact tax.[143] In general the Law Lords' public stance was that they were not junior partners in the legislative process, but disinterested, dispassionate technicians. Indeed, when the legislature positively invited judges to develop the law, as with the 'just and reasonable' charges clauses of the Railway and Canal Traffic Acts, some of the most eminent recoiled with almost comical dismay.[144]

This attitude went together with a gradual retreat from the boldness, and sometimes dogmatism, of some High Victorian judges into a substantive formalism which treated the common law as 'a self-contained objective system of rules'.[145] Equity's 'capacity for parthogenesis' withered, the potential of the adventurous decision in *Hughes v Metropolitan Railway*[146] remaining to be exploited by Denning. Inasmuch as considerations of public policy openly informed decisions at all, they usually took the form of a rather outmoded adherence to laissez faire, a stance which allowed cartels to strangle rivals[147] and gave anti-competitive arrangements in restraint of trade free rein.[148] In tort the same thinking informed a drift towards insistence that liability should be fault-based[149] and a narrow view of the scope of fraud.[150] There were of course cases which invited a broad statement of the law—Macnaghten's abiding re-ordering of 'the wilderness of legal charity' into four categories is one example[151]—but perhaps the most striking is *Scott v Scott*. This arose from the breach of an order of Bargrave Deane J that a nullity case be heard *in camera* and the evidence not reported. Only Atkinson declined to make general observations about the legitimacy of orders of this sort. The others—Haldane, Halsbury, Loreburn, and Shaw—approached it in characteristically individual styles and were prepared to countenance exceptions of varying width, but all of them trenchantly affirmed the paramount constitutional importance of open

---

[141] As later expounded by Lord Dunedin: Stevens (n 1) 169.

[142] ibid, 165–70; PWJ Bartrip, *Workmen's Compensation in Twentieth Century Britain* (London: Gower, 1987) 62–3.

[143] Stevens (n 1) 170–6.   [144] Atiyah (n 130) 558–9.

[145] Stevens (n 10) 22. On the changing content of judgments see S Hedley, 'Words, Words, Words...Making Sense of Legal Judgments' in C Stebbings (ed), *Law Reporting in England* (London: Hambledon, 1995) 169–86.

[146] (1877) 2 App Cas 439; Atiyah (n 130) 671–2; Stevens (n 1) 138.

[147] *Mogul Steamship Co v McGregor* [1892] AC 25; Atiyah (n 130) 697; Stevens (n 1) 158–9.

[148] *Nordenfelt v Maxim Nordenfelt Guns and Ammunition Co* [1894] AC 535; Atiyah (n 130) 697.

[149] Stevens (n 1) 151–4.   [150] Stevens (n 1) 156–7.

[151] *Comrs for Special Purposes of Income Tax v Pemsel* [1891] AC 531. Halsbury delayed this decision for over a year because he found himself in a minority.

justice.[152] In general, however, the House did not actively seek such ambitious tasks.[153]

In the light of the above, there was also a predictable reluctance to engage in any supervisory review of executive power. In *Metropolitan Asylum District v Hill* the Lords took a narrow view of the scope of delegated powers of a public body where they encroached upon private property rights,[154] but when it came to reviewing decisions made under delegated powers the furthest they would go was to enforce procedural due process, declining to investigate the propriety of actual decisions.[155] Haldane aspired to separate law from politics altogether[156] and with their almost complete abdication in *Local Government Board v Arlidge*,[157] the Law Lords took a long step towards doing so.

---

[152] [1913] AC 417. For the background see SM Cretney, "'Disgusted, Buckingham Palace": Divorce, Indecency and the Press, 1926' in *Law, Law Reform and the Family* (Oxford: OUP, 1998) 91–114.

[153] Despite the urging of Brett MR: (1889–90) 34 SJ 2.

[154] (1881) 6 App Cas 193; Stevens (n 1) 160–1.

[155] The position taken up in *Board of Education v Rice* [1911] AC 179; Stevens (n 1) 178–9.

[156] Stevens (n 1) 219.   [157] [1915] AC 120.

13

A Developing Jurisdiction, 1914–45

David GT Williams

Survival and consolidation

Two appeal courts

The judicial House of Lords survived and consolidated its position as the final appellate court during the period 1914–45. There were still echoes, however, of the complex manoeuvrings of the 1870s over the need for a second tier of appeal.[1] Lord Parmoor wrote in 1936 against 'constituting the House of Lords as the ultimate Court of Appeal', partly because of the expense of 'a multiplicity of appeals'.[2] A little earlier, in the wake of the Second Interim Report of the Business of Courts Committee,[3] a restriction on civil appeals to the House of Lords—requiring leave from either the Court of Appeal or the House itself—had been provided for in the Administration of Justice (Appeals) Act 1934. Even so, there were suggestions that 'we could have contemplated with equanimity the entire abolition of the final appeal';[4] and in 1940 a legal writer claimed that it 'is difficult to justify two appeal courts'.[5]

One of the factors that helped to reinforce the House of Lords as the final appeal court was that it heard appeals from Scotland (in civil cases) and Northern Ireland as well as from England and Wales. In other words, it was the final appeal court for the United Kingdom, and the presence of Scottish Law Lords in particular was important. Scottish Law Lords in the period under review were Lord Shaw of Dunfermline (1909–29), Lord Dunedin (1913–32), Lord Thankerton (1929–48), and Lord Macmillan (1930–9 and 1941–7). The last two along with Lord Atkin constituted the majority of the House of Lords in the classic case of *Donoghue v Stevenson*,[6] and RM Jackson—taking account of Lord Atkin's Welsh roots—wrote in 1940:[7]

---

[1] See R Stevens, 'The Final Appeal: Reform of the House of Lords and Privy Council' (1964) 80 LQR 343.

[2] Lord Parmoor, *A Retrospect* (London, Toronto: William Heinemann Ltd, 1936) 75–6.

[3] Cmd 4471 of 1933. The Chairman of the Committee was Lord Hanworth MR.

[4] (1934) 177 Law Times 357.

[5] RM Jackson, *The Machinery of Justice in England* (Cambridge: CUP, 1st edn 1940) 74.

[6] [1932] AC 562.   [7] Jackson (n 5) 75.

The presence of Scots' lawyers in the House of Lords is all to the good, acting as a continual reminder that other systems of law may have rules that are worth investigation. If some present racial myths gain strength in England we may see a rebellion against a state of affairs in which two Scotsmen and one Welshman may lay down the law of England, but so far we have escaped such adolescent neuroticism.

The Law Lords and the public

The number of Lords of Appeal in Ordinary was increased to six in 1913 and to seven in 1929. In manning the House of Lords they were joined by serving and retired Lord Chancellors: when Lord Birkenhead became Lord Chancellor in 1919, for instance, Lord Finlay, Lord Buckmaster, and Lord Haldane still participated actively.[8] Other peers with judicial or appropriate legal experience also participated: these included Lords Wrenbury, Parmoor, and Phillimore.

Despite the wide range of subject matter in appeals to the House of Lords, the Law Lords rarely achieved much publicity. Outside their judicial work they were cautious. The so-called Kilmuir Rules of 1955[9]—based on the principle that so long as 'a judge keeps silent his reputation for wisdom and impartiality remains unassailable'—had long been anticipated. Nevertheless many individual judges, including Law Lords, were sometimes exposed to publicity through their involvement in extra-judicial activities on behalf of the Executive. Lord Moulton was a Law Lord from 1912 to 1921 but in that period 'he was in fact only engaged in judicial duties for about three years, the remainder being devoted to War Work' and subsequently to other duties.[10] In the period after the Armistice in 1918 Lord Cave 'found himself often asked to render special service outside his judicial work'.[11] Other Law Lords sat on a variety of commissions or committees, often in areas unrelated to legal administration.[12] Lord Macmillan's extensive experience of such bodies included that of chairing the Royal Commission on Canadian Banking and Currency at the invitation of the Prime Minister of Canada;[13] and at the outset of the Second World War he stepped down from the judicial House of Lords to become Minister of Information for what he called a 'brief and

---

[8] Sir Charles Mallet, *Lord Cave. A Memoir* (London: John Murray, 1931) 225. See generally RFV Heuston, *Lives of the Lord Chancellors 1885–1940* (Oxford: Clarendon Press, 1964) and *Lives of the Lord Chancellors 1940–1970* (Oxford: Clarendon Press, 1987).

[9] See a debate in the (legislative) House of Lords initiated by Lord Irvine of Lairg on 5 June 1996: *Hansard*, HL, vol 572, cols 1256–7. The Kilmuir Rules were abandoned in the 1980s.

[10] H Fletcher Moulton, *The Life of Lord Moulton* (London: Nisbet & Co Ltd, 1922) 69–70. See esp chs 7 and 8.

[11] Mallet (n 8) 236.

[12] See KC Wheare, *Government by Committee. An Essay on the British Constitution* (Oxford: Clarendon Press, 1955) 85–6.

[13] Lord Macmillan, *A Man of Law's Tale. The Reminiscences of the Rt Hon Lord Macmillan* (London: Macmillan & Co Ltd, 1952) ch x ('In the Chair') and 334–9.

inglorious period of four months', only to be re-appointed to the House of Lords in July 1941.[14]

In assessing the public role of the Law Lords, some reference should be made to the problems of blending judicial and legislative or political functions in the House of Lords. There was vigorous participation by some Law Lords over the negotiations that led to the creation of the Irish Free State in 1922. The style and pace were set by Lord Carson who, as Sir Edward Carson, had for many years been embroiled in Irish controversies; and his attack on the Anglo-Irish Treaty of December 1921 led Lord Birkenhead, the Lord Chancellor, to suggest that 'as a constructive effort of state-craft, it would have been immature upon the lips of a hysterical school-girl'.[15] Lord Sumner intervened strongly in support of Lord Carson, expressing concerns about the speed and imprecision of the Treaty.[16] Lord Cave also expressed concerns.[17] This entire episode reflected what Lord Irvine was in 1996 to describe as 'a basic tension between judicial engagement in political controversy and public confidence in the judges' political impartiality in deciding disputes according to law'.[18]

Private and public law

Judicial quality

There were several outstanding Law Lords and Lord Chancellors in the period under review. Of the Law Lords, mention could be made of Lord Sumner (1913–30), described by Holdsworth as 'a master of English prose',[19] a quality which he demonstrated in his discussion in *Bowman v Secular Society*[20] of 'the basis and limits of religious toleration'; and of Lord Porter (1938–54), who was appointed to the House of Lords directly from the High Court and who delivered many important opinions in commercial law and on issues of statutory interpretation. Particular mention should be made, however, of Lords Wright, Macmillan, and Atkin.

Lord Wright (1932–5 and 1937–47) was also appointed directly from the High Court and the break in his service was because he was briefly Master of the Rolls. Originally a law teacher, he fought in his judicial capacity 'against subtle

---

[14] At 163. See generally ch ix ('The Ministry of Information'). As Minister of Information he was based in the Senate House of the University of London.

[15] *Hansard*, HL, vol 48, col 204 (16 December 1921). Lord Birkenhead's views are set out in his *Points of View*, vol 2 (London: Hodder and Stoughton, 1922) ch XVII ('Judges and Politics').

[16] *Hansard*, HL, vol 48, cols 160ff (15 December 1921). See David Williams, 'Bias: The Judges and the Separation of Powers' [2000] PL 45, 45–46; Heuston (1964) (n 8) 385–6; John Campbell, *FE Smith: First Earl of Birkenhead* (London: Jonathan Cape Ltd, 1983; Pimlico ed 1991) 575–85 (Pimlico ed).

[17] Mallet (n 8) 253.   [18] *Hansard*, HL, vol 572, col 1259 (5 June 1996).

[19] Sir William Holdsworth, *Essays in Law and History*, AL Goodhart and HG Hanbury (eds) (Oxford: Clarendon, 1946) 233. See A Lentin, *The Last Political Law Lord: Lord Sumner (1859–1934)* (Cambridge: Cambridge Scholars Publishing, 2008).

[20] [1917] AC 406, 466–7.

distinctions, unnecessary fictions, and historical survivals which are a hindrance to the proper development of the law';[21] and he also ranged widely in his extra-judicial writings and addresses.[22] Lord Macmillan brought to English law, it has been written, 'a width of outlook which can be attributed in part to this training in another system of law and in part to his great experience of many Royal Commissions and other Government committees'.[23] Lord Atkin (1928–44) is the most widely remembered of the Law Lords 1914–45 for many incisive opinions and especially his speeches in *Donoghue v Stevenson*[24] (when he was in the majority with Lord Macmillan) and *Liversidge v Anderson*[25] (where he was the sole dissenting voice while Lords Macmillan and Wright were in the majority). In 1944 his judicial style was described as 'chaste, composed, easy, accurate'.[26]

The judicial House of Lords delivered many important rulings in private law, especially in contract and tort, during the period under review.[27] There were several specialist areas including tax law where statutory interpretation was prominent, but it was one case in the law of tort which has captured the imagination. That was *Donoghue v Stevenson,*[28] which, on appeal from the Court of Session in Scotland, concerned the alleged decomposed snail in the ginger beer bottle. It was described in the *Annual Survey* for 1932 as 'the greatest case of the year',[29] but a writer in the *Canadian Bar Review* saw Lord Atkin's speech as 'at once stamped as perhaps the most impressive and certainly the most authoritative effort ever made to generalise the English law of negligence'.[30] The same writer went further by claiming that *Rylands v Fletcher*[31] and *Donoghue v Stevenson* 'may with justice be regarded as the two most important cases in the law of torts'.[32] Yet Geoffrey Lewis, the biographer of Lord Atkin, wrote:[33]

The revolution brought about by *Donoghue v Stevenson* was so quiet that it passed completely unnoticed by the general public who were so closely affected by it; and its true nature was perhaps not fully understood even by the profession until Lord Devlin's speech in 1963 in the *Hedley Byrne Case.*

---

[21] AL Goodhart (1947) 63 LQR 261.

[22] Lord Wright of Durley, *Legal Essays and Addresses* (Cambridge: CUP, 1939). See the Review by RST Chorley at (1940) 4 MLR 69.

[23] AL Goodhart (1947) 63 LQR 259.   [24] [1932] AC 562.   [25] [1942] AC 206.

[26] Lord Wright, 'In Memoriam: Lord Atkin of Aberdovey 1867–1944' (1944) 60 LQR 332, 333. See an early comment in the *Annual Survey of English Law 1929* (London: LSE, 1930) 151 with reference to Lord Atkin's speech in an insurance case calling for 'simple, intelligible, and unambiguous language' to be used by businessmen in their contracts. See generally Geoffrey Lewis, *Lord Atkin* (London: Butterworths, 1983).

[27] See generally L Blom-Cooper and G Drewry, *Final Appeal. A Study of the House of Lords in its Judicial Capacity* (Oxford: Clarendon Press, 1972); R Stevens, *Law and Politics. The House of Lords as a Judicial Body, 1800–1976* (London: Weidenfeld and Nicolson, 1979); A Paterson, *The Law Lords* (London and Basingstoke: Macmillan, 1982).

[28] [1932] AC 562.   [29] At 148.

[30] FC Underhay, 'Tort Liability of Manufacturers' (1932) 10 Canadian Bar Rev 615, 628–9.

[31] LR 3 HL 330 (1868).   [32] Underhay (n 30) 629.

[33] Lewis (n 26) 67. The case referred to is *Hedley Byrne & Co Ltd v Heller and Partners* [1964] AC 465, HL.

By contrast to the activity of the House of Lords in areas such as contract and tort, criminal law fared badly. Appeals from the then Court of Criminal Appeal required the fiat of the Attorney-General and this was not readily given: hence the controversy over its refusal in the *Casement* decision in 1916.[34] It has been recorded that in 'the half-century or so of the fiat procedure only twenty-three criminal cases went to the Lords', underlining the claim that criminal law was long 'the Cinderella of the English legal system'.[35] In addition, criminal appeals could not (and still cannot) come from Scotland; and it was not until the Administration of Justice Act 1960 that an appeal could be taken from rulings of the Divisional Court on appeals from magistrates' courts. The exclusion of appeal from cases which began in magistrates' courts meant, for instance, that the Lords were unable to offer authoritative guidance on the law of public order. Between the wars there were undoubtedly significant rulings in criminal law generally—as in *Woolmington v Director of Public Prosecutions*[36] on the presumption of innocence—but the overall picture is patchy.

The overall picture in constitutional law and in matters of human rights was also patchy, though it is necessary to take account of the role of the Law Lords sitting in the Judicial Committee of the Privy Council if one is seeking to present a balanced view. Lord Macmillan for instance, delivered 152 written opinions in the House of Lords and some 75 in the Privy Council.[37] A further factor of great relevance is the experience of war, post-war, and emergency problems which influenced so much of the period under review both as to emergency legislation and as to the slow emergence of administrative law.

Emergency powers and the impact of war

Bearing in mind that the two world wars of the twentieth century covered almost one-third of the period under review, it is scarcely surprising that a number of decisions of the judicial House of Lords were directly or indirectly affected by the mood and temper of the times. At the very end of the period there was the case of *Joyce v Director of Public Prosecutions*[38] where the appellant, an American citizen, had been convicted of treason by virtue of the duty of allegiance which he owed through holding a British passport. A 4:1 decision rejecting the appeal was delivered on 18 December 1945, Joyce was executed on 3 January 1946, and the

---

[34] *R v Casement* [1917] 1 KB 98. See generally JLIJ Edwards, *The Law Officers of the Crown* (London: Sweet & Maxwell, 1964) 246–56. The fiat procedure was abolished and replaced in the Administration of Justice Act 1960, on which see DGT Williams, 'The Administration of Justice Act 1960' [1961] Crim LR 87–104.

[35] Blom-Cooper and Drewry (n 27) 272 and 270 respectively.

[36] [1935] AC 462.

[37] *Oxford Dictionary of National Biography* (Oxford: OUP, 2004) vol 35, 898 (R Stevens on Lord Macmillan) 897–9.

[38] [1946] AC 347. See JW Hall (ed), *Trial of William Joyce* (London: William Hodge, 1946) (*Notable British Trials*).

reasons were given only on 1 February 1946. The majority of the House consisted of the Lord Chancellor together with Lords Macmillan, Wright, and Simonds. In his dissent Lord Porter argued that the jury should have been left to consider whether Joyce's duty of allegiance had been terminated ahead of his allegedly treasonable acts; and the Attorney General who had given his fiat for the appeal to be heard later wrote that, of the Law Lords concerned, Lord Porter was 'the most learned and responsible' and that his dissenting view 'may well have been correct'.[39]

The mood and temper of the times are reflected in several cases. When war broke out in 1914 there was wide recognition of the national emergency, and Parliament and the public 'unhesitatingly committed to the Government legislative and executive powers which would never have been contemplated in times of peace'.[40] The Defence of the Realm Act (DORA) 1914 allowed for wide executive powers, and the outbreak of war in September 1939 likewise led to wide executive powers under the Emergency Powers (Defence) Act 1939.[41]

The judicial response in the First World War is shown in *R v Halliday, ex p Zadig*.[42] This case concerned internment under Regulation 14B, made under the authority of the legislation, where it appeared to the Secretary of State that he needed to act 'for securing the public safety or the defence of the realm'. Twelve of the 13 judges who heard the case in the Divisional Court (where Mr Justice Atkin was one of the five-strong Bench), the Court of Appeal, and the House of Lords rejected Zadig's challenge to the legality of his internment. The one dissenting voice was that of Lord Shaw of Dunfermline, who contended that Parliament would not have left authority for detention without trial to be determined by inference rather than expressly. His 'blistering attack'[43] on the majority view won admirers and critics, but the dominant judicial statement was that 'it may be necessary in a time of great public danger to entrust great powers to His Majesty in Council, and that Parliament may do so feeling certain that such powers will be reasonably exercised'.[44]

In the Second World War a different challenge, based on statutory interpretation of Regulation 18B, came in *Liversidge v Anderson*.[45] In his book *In the*

---

[39] Lord Shawcross, *Life Sentence. The Memoirs of Lord Shawcross* (London: Constable, 1995) 82.

[40] CK Allen, *Law and Orders. An Inquiry into the Nature and Scope of Delegated Legislation and Executive Powers in England* (London: Stevens & Sons, 1st edn 1945) 35.

[41] See CT Carr, 'Crisis Legislation in Britain' (1940) XL Columbia L Rev 1309 where the author refers to DORA 1914, the Restoration of Order in Ireland Act 1920, the peacetime Emergency Powers Act 1920, and the Emergency Powers (Defence) Act 1939. See generally C Rossiter, *Constitutional Dictatorship. Crisis Government in Modern Democracies* (Princeton: Princeton University Press, 1948) Part 3 ('Crisis Government in Britain').

[42] [1917] AC 260. See D Foxton, '*R v Halliday, ex p Zadig* in Retrospect' (2003) 119 LQR 455.

[43] KD Ewing and CA Gearty, *The Struggle for Civil Liberties. Political Freedom and the Rule of Law in Britain 1914–1945* (Oxford: OUP, 2000) 86–7. On the use of Regulation 14B see AWB Simpson, *In the Highest Degree Odious. Detention without Trial in Wartime Britain* (Oxford: Clarendon, 1992) ch 2.

[44] [1917] AC at 268–9 (Lord Finlay, the Lord Chancellor).

[45] [1942] AC 206. See GW Keeton, '*Liversidge v Anderson*' (1941–2) 5 MLR 162; CK Allen, 'Regulation 18B and Reasonable Cause' (1942) 58 LQR 232; RFV Heuston, '*Liversidge v Anderson* in Retrospect' (1970) 86 LQR 33; E Mureinik, '*Liversidge* in Decay' (1985) 102 South African LJ 77.

Highest Degree Odious[46] Brian Simpson has given an extensive account of the emergence and operation of Regulation 18B, the successor to Regulation 14B. Regulation 18B gave powers of detention when, for instance, the Home Secretary 'has reasonable cause to believe any person to be of hostile origin or associations'. The particular background to the case was the detention of Robert William Liversidge who without success made representations to an Advisory Committee set up under 18B and then launched an action for false imprisonment through which he sought particulars of the grounds on which the Home Secretary had acted. The lower courts rejected the application for such particulars and the House of Lords by a 4:1 majority also held against Liversidge. The decision of the House—which consisted of Viscount Maugham, a former Lord Chancellor, and Lords Atkin, Macmillan, Wright, and Romer—was announced on 3 November 1941. In effect the ruling of the majority was that the words 'if the Secretary of State has reasonable cause' should mean 'if the Secretary of State thinks he has reasonable cause'. In his famous dissent Lord Atkin invoked precedent in support of an objective interpretation of the wording in 18B; he viewed with apprehension the approach of the majority who, on a matter of statutory construction, showed themselves to be more executive-minded than the executive; he stated that some of the Attorney General's arguments on behalf of the Home Secretary might have been addressed acceptably to the Court of King's Bench in the time of Charles I; and he invoked Humpty Dumpty in support. He insisted that '[i]n this country, amid the clash of arms, the laws are not silent. They may be changed, but they speak the same language in war as in peace.'[47]

Lord Atkin's dissent has been applauded by many, both at the time[48] and in subsequent cases.[49] But it has also attracted scepticism or criticism, both subsequently[50] and immediately after the decision of the House of Lords was announced. Lord Simon, the Lord Chancellor, had not sat in that case but saw a draft of the dissent and sought a modification of the remarks about Humpty Dumpty—to no avail. After the decision was announced Viscount Maugham wrote to *The Times* to protest about the attack on the Attorney General's arguments and he followed that with a statement in the legislative House of Lords.[51]

---

[46] Simpson (n 43).   [47] [1942] AC at 225–47.   [48] Allen (n 45).

[49] See Lord Radcliffe's comments in the Privy Council in *Nakkuda Ali v Jayaratne* [1951] AC 66, 76–7, and Lord Reid's reference in the House of Lords in *Ridge v Baldwin* [1964] AC 40, 73 to 'the very peculiar decision' in *Liversidge v Anderson*. In *Inland Revenue Commissioners v Rossminster Ltd* [1980] AC 952, 1011 Lord Diplock said—somewhat ambiguously—that the majority in 1941 'were expediently and, at that time, perhaps excusably wrong'. See also Lord Bingham, *The Business of Judging. Selected Essays and Speeches* (Oxford: OUP, 2000) 211–21 ('Mr Perlzweig, Mr Liversidge, and Lord Atkin').

[50] See AWB Simpson, 'Rhetoric, Reality, and Regulation 18B' (The Child & Co Oxford Lecture, 12 May 1987) esp 31–2; Simpson (n 43) 363. When Lord Atkin died in 1944 HC Gutteridge suggested that his sense of indignation 'caused him to express himself with a freedom which was perhaps unwarranted by the circumstances': 'In Memoriam: Lord Atkin of Aberdovey 1867–1944' (1944) 60 LQR 334, 340.

[51] See Stevens (n 27) 287; RFV Heuston, *Essays in Constitutional Law* (London: Stevens & Sons, 2nd edn 1964) 175; and Lewis (n 26) 132ff and esp 138–47.

The prevailing judicial philosophy, reflected in the majority opinions in both *ex p Zadig* and *Liversidge v Anderson* is perhaps explained in Lord Sumner's words in another case affected by wartime considerations:

> Experience in the present war must have taught us all that many things are done in the name of the Executive in such times purporting to be for the common good, which Englishmen have been too patriotic to contest. When the precedents of this war come to be relied on in wars to come, it must never be forgotten that much was voluntarily submitted to which might have been disputed, and that the absence of contest and even of protest is by no means always an admission of the right.

The case in question was *Attorney General v De Keyser's Royal Hotel*,[52] decided after the First World War. It concerned a claim for compensation for compulsory occupation of premises by the War Office during the war. The Crown claimed a prerogative power to take the land without compensation as of right, despite the existence of a statutory right to compensation in the same circumstances. The legislation, said the House of Lords, had not abrogated the royal prerogative but the royal prerogative had been superseded for the time being. The decision confirmed the role of the courts in defining the ambit of the prerogative, though not yet with claims to review the exercise of the prerogative. But the case illustrated the readiness of the Executive to take advantage of national emergencies.

A less happy result of the emergency climate was *Duncan v Cammell, Laird & Co*[53] in the Second World War, when a panel of seven in the judicial House of Lords ruled on Crown privilege, later to be known as public interest immunity. It arose from the loss of the submarine *Thetis* during a trial dive in Liverpool Bay a few months before the outbreak of war. In a test action for negligence against those responsible for the construction of the submarine various documents were sought in the process of discovery: these included plans and specifications of the vessel. Lord Simon, the Lord Chancellor, gave the sole opinion: he recognised the constitutional importance of the decision, he unsurprisingly rejected the disclosure of the detailed documents, but he then roamed far beyond the facts and merits of the case. A Minister's objection to disclosure on the ground that it would be injurious to the public interest cannot, he insisted, be questioned by the courts; and, as examples of the public interest being at risk, he spoke of circumstances 'where disclosure would be injurious to national defence, or to good diplomatic relations, or where the practice of keeping a class of documents secret is necessary for the proper functioning of the public service'.[54] It would be some years before the unnecessary breadth of that statement, particularly as to so-called 'class' claims, could be corrected.[55]

---

[52] [1920] AC 508. Lord Sumner's remarks (at 563) are quoted in Allen (n 40) 210.
[53] [1942] AC 624.   [54] [1942] AC 642.
[55] See *Conway v Rimmer* [1968] AC 910.

It is not surprising, given the influence of wartime considerations, that administrative law generally was largely in a state of sluggishness in the period under review.

Administrative law

The recognition of administrative law or of the need for the courts to exercise some measure of supervision over the executive was not entirely absent in the years from 1914 to 1945. Positive developments were impeded, however, both by the influence of wartime and emergency demands and by a decision of the House of Lords announced only two weeks or so before the outbreak of the First World War. This was *Local Government Board v Arlidge*[56] which Lord Wright was to describe some 30 years later as 'the charter of the administrative court'.[57] Even at the time it was regarded as significant enough to encourage Dicey to write about its establishment of the principle, as he saw it, that 'a Government department when it exercised judicial or quasi-judicial jurisdiction under a statute is bound to act with judicial fairness and equity, but is not in any way bound to follow the rules of procedure which prevail in English courts'.[58] The case arose from the refusal of a borough council in London to end an order forbidding on grounds of health the use of a particular house for human habitation. Subsequently the President of the Local Government Board rejected an appeal against that refusal, even though the owner of the property complained that 'he was not allowed to appear before the officer who made the decision or to see the report of the inspector who held the inquiry'.[59] The House of Lords, 'so far from disapproving the procedure adopted by the department, regarded it as complying with all the essentials of justice and as having done complete justice to Mr Arlidge'.[60] One legal writer has recently commented that by 'denying the courts even a limited role in protecting procedural due process, British administrative law was to sleep for the next fifty years'.[61]

What followed does not offer a tidy or consistent picture. In *Roberts v Hopwood*[62] the House of Lords was concerned with a challenge to the exercise of

---

[56] [1915] AC 120.   [57] 'Liberty and the Common Law' (1945) 9 CLJ 2, 10.
[58] 'The Development of Administrative Law in England' (1915) 31 LQR 148, 149. See note (1914) 28 Harvard L Rev 198.
[59] See HWR Wade and CF Forsyth, *Administrative Law* (Oxford: OUP, 9th edn 2004) 484. See also WI Jennings, 'Courts and Administrative Law—The Experience of English Housing Legislation' (1936) 49 Harvard L Rev 426, 439–41.
[60] CT Carr, *Concerning English Administrative Law* (New York: Columbia University Press, 1941) (quoted in Bernard Schwartz, *Law and the Executive in Britain. A Comparative Study* (New York UP and CUP, 1949) 237).
[61] R Stevens, *The English Judges. Their Role in the Changing Constitution* (Oxford: Hart, 2002) 19.
[62] [1925] AC 578. The House of Lords consisted of Lords Buckmaster, Atkinson, Sumner, Wrenbury, and Carson. See D Williams, 'Law and Administrative Discretion' (1994) 2 Indiana J of Global Legal Studies 191; N Branson, *Poplarism 1919–1925: George Lansbury and the Councillors' Revolt* (London: Lawrence and Wishart, 1979) ch 14; B Keith-Lucas, 'Poplarism' [1962] PL 52.

discretion by a local authority. In the 1920s the Council of Poplar, one of the poorest areas in London, sought to maintain a position as a model employer, under statutory authority to pay to its servants such wages as they might 'think fit', to pay its own employees, male or female, a minimum wage of £4.00 a week. The House of Lords agreed with the argument of counsel that the discretion 'conferred upon the council is not an uncontrolled discretion, but must be exercised reasonably'[63] and it was held that there had been an abuse of discretion by the council. There was also some reference to the alleged duty owed by elected councillors to local ratepayers. Lord Atkinson added his view that the Poplar councillors had 'allowed themselves to be guided . . . by some eccentric principles of socialistic philanthropy, or by a feministic ambition to secure the equality of the sexes in the matter of wages in the world of labour'.[64] Lest an impression is given that the judiciary as a whole was ill-equipped to handle such cases, it should be borne in mind that a majority of the Court of Appeal in the case[65]—Lord Justices Scrutton and Atkin—had held for the council; and the future Lord Atkin rejected the concept of a duty to ratepayers as opposed 'to the local community as a whole' and he stressed that it is 'essential to remember that we are dealing with powers given to public bodies consisting of representatives elected by the public on a wide franchise for comparatively short periods'.[66] Here one sees the seeds of administrative law as recognised in the later twentieth century and beyond.

The seeds of a new-style administrative law were also sown by legal writers in the inter-war years. Lord Hewart, the Lord Chief Justice, offered in *The New Despotism* 'a note of warning' about 'the pretensions and encroachments of bureaucracy';[67] various academic writers sought to keep pace with and interpret law and practice;[68] and the Report of the Committee on Ministers' Powers (the Donoughmore Report) appeared in 1932.[69] One of the academic writers noted that administrative law in England 'still has an air of novelty, and in many minds connotes a state of affairs which is in conflict with the principles of our Common Law'.[70]

Conclusion

By 1945 the House of Lords in its judicial capacity was well established in the hierarchy of courts of the United Kingdom. In this chapter less than justice has

---

[63] [1925] AC 580.   [64] ibid, 594.   [65] *R v Roberts, ex p Scurr* [1924] 2 KB 695.
[66] At 725–6.
[67] Lord Hewart of Bury, *The New Despotism* (London: Ernest Benn Ltd, 1929) v (Prefatory Note).
[68] CT Carr, *Delegated Legislation* (Cambridge: CUP, 1921) and *Concerning English Administrative Law* (n 60); WA Robson, *Justice and Administrative Law* (London: Stevens & Sons, 3rd edn 1951; 1st edn appeared in 1928); FJ Port, *Administrative Law* (London: Longmans, Green and Co, 1929).
[69] Cmd 4060. See DGT Williams, 'The Donoughmore Report in Retrospect' [1982] Public Administration 273–92. The Committee included Sir William Holdsworth, Professor HJ Laski, Sir Claud Schuster, Lord Justice Scott, and Gavin Simonds KC.
[70] Port (n 68) xi.

been done to the considerable contribution of the Law Lords to the common law, to commercial and tax law, and to statutory interpretation in general. The weaknesses of the House of Lords lay in criminal law and administrative law; the contribution of the Law Lords to constitutional law was slight save where the Judicial Committee of the Privy Council was involved; and the impact of war and national emergency perhaps distorted the work of the Law Lords and influenced public appreciation of the judicial House of Lords. Nevertheless there was a basis laid on which future Law Lords could develop the law in many areas in later years. The legacy of such judges as Lords Atkin, Macmillan, and Wright remains important in the law of the United Kingdom.

14

Towards a System of Administrative Law: The Reid and Wilberforce Era, 1945–82

Louis Blom-Cooper and Gavin Drewry

If, during the last years of the nineteenth century and the first half of the twentieth century, the reputation of the House of Lords for high quality appellate adjudication had been considerable, such reputation was unsullied by any temptation to get embroiled in political controversies. The daily diet of the Law Lords was litigation in the arena of private law, with the exception of revenue appeals. Even though they sat judicially in the parliamentary forum, they were not publicly encouraged, nor did they exhibit any disposition to play in their judicial capacity any role as watchdogs of constitutional propriety.

The majority decision in *Liversidge v Anderson* in 1942,[1] in the face of a stinging rebuke from their dissenting colleague, Lord Atkin—castigating his colleagues for being 'more executive-minded than the executive' and for adopting a 'Humpty Dumpty' approach to statutory interpretation—could perhaps be justified at the time. On the basis that to have questioned the Home Secretary's exercise of an unfettered discretionary power to determine, without any evidence, an alien's threat to the security of the nation in wartime, the decision might have been a step, far too far, in the exercise of their judicial role were they to try to fetter ministerial decision-making. The judges confined themselves to what Professor Ivor Jennings called their 'sphere of small diameter'.[2] If all that seems strange now, in the light of the modern development of judicial review and the burgeoning of administrative law, the genesis of a British style of public (and hence, since the Human Rights Act 1998, quasi-constitutional) law can be traced directly to the sixth decade of the last century.

---

[1] [1942] AC 206.
[2] *The Law of the Constitution* (London: University of London Press, 5th edn 1959) 254, cited by Professor Anthony King in *The British Constitution* (Oxford: OUP, 2007) 115.

Bias to the fore

The furore over a highly politicised piece of litigation was echoed in the mode of post-war Britain in its forensic guise. As if in response to Aneurin Bevan's grim warning to the judges against sabotaging the impending legislative programme of the Labour administration,[3] the House of Lords, in line with *Liversidge v Anderson*, continued to tread warily. In *Franklin v Minister of Town and Country Planning*[4] in 1947 the House went out of its way to postulate a narrow interpretation of the common law rule against bias in a ministerial decision-maker—an astonishing decision to a reader 60 years on. The Minister had spoken at a public meeting in the town hall of Stevenage, which he was planning to designate as the first new town under the impending New Towns Act 1946. The Minister (Mr Lewis Silkin) was recorded as saying that he wanted to carry out a daring exercise in town planning, to which he added, addressing the audience: 'It is no good you jeering: it is going to be done!' (applause and boos; cries of 'Dictator!') The legislation was duly passed and the objections were subject to a public inquiry before an inspector who reported to the Minister in favour of an order designating Stevenage as a new town. The Minister duly made the order. Stevenage became the first new town in post-war Britain. The objectors challenged the Minister's order.

Mr Justice Henn Collins quashed the order on the ground that the Minister had failed to act judicially. On the evidence before him he held that any issue raised by the objectors was 'forejudged'. The Court of Appeal (Lord Oaksey, Lords Justices Morton and Tucker) agreed that the Minister was under a duty to act judicially, but held that, on the basis of the evidence inaccurately evaluated by the judge, he had fulfilled his duty, and they reversed the decision to quash. The House of Lords in a single judgment from Lord Thankerton dismissed the appeal, holding that both lower courts had misstated the law, declaring that the Minister's decision was 'purely administrative' and that any reference to judicial duty or bias was 'irrelevant to the present case'.[5]

It is not without significance that at the end of the argument by the applicants' counsel over three days, Lord Thankerton told the Attorney-General (Sir Hartley Shawcross) that their Lordships did not find it necessary to hear him, 'but if there is any additional authority you wish us to consider, would you let us know?', to which Sir Hartley responded: 'It is idle to talk of natural justice in a case of this kind or of any necessity for an appearance of justice. If that were so, *Liversidge v Anderson* could not have been decided as it was.'

Two of the leading academics on Administrative Law initially supported the decision. De Smith in the second edition of *Constitutional and Administrative Law* in 1973 thought that the decision was 'sensible, though the term "purely administrative" may have been unfortunate'. The latest edition of de Smith does

---

[3] *Hansard*, HC, vol 425, col 1893 (23 July 1946).   [4] [1948] AC 87.   [5] At 102.

not repeat that verdict, but merely recites the case in an analysis of administrative law between 1935 and 1947.[6] Likewise, Professor HWR Wade in the sixth edition of his *Administrative Law* in 1988 thought that there was much to be said for 'the middle road followed by the Court of Appeal. It is a virtue for a Minister to have a policy and to advocate it ... The law must allow for the departmental bias which he is expected and required to have.'[7] When the Minister comes to make his decision, the question is, has he 'a mind which is open to persuasion?' In the ninth edition of Wade's *Administrative Law* in 2004, the case of *Franklin* is recited, with the authors' comment that 'judges later became more sensitive to natural justice'.[8]

Franklin was relied upon by counsel for the respondent in *Ridge v Baldwin* (see below) but was not referred to in the majority judgment. Could it be that *Franklin* was impliedly overruled in anticipation of the 1966 Practice Statement, then only a few years away? *Franklin* could not escape today's jurisprudence on bias.[9] And, to adopt modern case law on the control of a Minister's discretionary power, had not the Minister at that meeting in Stevenage 'fettered his discretion' when coming to his final decision? In 1956 in a rare case in planning law, *East Elloe RDC v Smith*,[10] Lord Radcliffe said that 'an order, even if not made in good faith, is still an act capable of legal consequences. It bears no brand of invalidity upon its forehead.' Could that save *Franklin* today?

Until the 1960s public law issues rarely surfaced beyond the Court of Appeal, and when occasionally such issues did emerge the constitutional response was dismissive. Thus in an appeal from Northern Ireland in *OD Cars v Belfast Corporation*[11] on the issue of compensation, Viscount Simonds expostulated that 'such a determination of rights can be affected without a cry being raised that Magna Carta is dethroned or a sacred principle of liberty infringed',[12] although it is fair to point out that in considering the principle of eminent domain, Viscount Simonds did cite the opinions of Mr Justice Holmes and Mr Justice Brandeis of the US Supreme Court.[13]

Criminal appeals

As a result of the Administration of Justice Act 1960, abolishing the procedure of the Attorney General's fiat being required for any appeal from the Court of Criminal Appeal, the Law Lords began to hear criminal appeals. Until then only a

---

[6] SA De Smith and R Brazier, *Constitutional and Administrative Law* (Harmondsworth: Penguin, 8th edn 1998) 6-039.

[7] At 491–2.

[8] At 421. See also the trenchant comment of Professor John Griffith in *Judicial Politics since 1920: A Chronicle* (Oxford: Blackwell, 1993) 50.

[9] See *Porter v Magill* [2002] 2 AC 357, 494H, *per* Lord Hope, and *Helow v Secretary of State for the Home Department (Scotland)* [2008] 1 WLR 2416.

[10] [1956] AC 736.   [11] [1960] 1 All ER 65.   [12] [1960] AC 490, 519.

[13] The citing of US authorities became more common in recent years, with the exception of Lord Diplock who demonstrated a distaste for the citation of American authorities.

dozen or so cases had filtered through.[14] Outstandingly in criminal jurisprudence, the Law Lords declared the resounding principle in *Woolmington v DPP*[15] on the burden and standard of proof.

A trilogy of cases in the first years of the sixth decade got the Law Lords off to a bad start in developing the criminal law. Before the most notorious of the three cases, *DPP v Smith*,[16] came *Shaw v DPP*[17] which revived a lurking fear in the public mind that the judges might one day strike out in favour of creating new crimes. In that case the publisher of a booklet, the *Ladies Directory*, filled his magazine with sexually suggestive advertisements together with the addresses or telephone numbers of prostitutes; he was prosecuted on an indictment containing three counts, one of which raised a howl of protest. The Law Lords, over a vigorous dissent from Lord Reid, declared that the courts constituted the residual guardians of the public morals of society, and that their Lordships could fill the gap by resort to the use of the crime of conspiring to corrupt public morals. It took a few years—until 1970—for their Lordships ultimately to reverse their stance. Courts cannot any longer create new criminal offences.

In *DPP v Sykes*[18] the dormant offence of misprision of felony (the non-disclosure of the commission of a felony) was revived in all its pristine glory, although the precise ambit of the offence was left vague; this time the legislative axe came swiftly; the decision was superseded by section 5 of the Criminal Law Act 1967. But the credibility of the Law Lords to shape and fashion a modern criminal law was disturbed, above all, by the first of the trilogy of cases, *DPP v Smith*,[19] where the accused, having been stopped by a police officer (whom he knew and liked) drove off with the constable on the bonnet of the accelerating vehicle. The officer was thrown off the bonnet and was killed by an oncoming car. Was it a case of murder or manslaughter? The trial court brought in a murder verdict. The Court of Criminal Appeal substituted manslaughter, on the ground that the trial judge had wrongly directed the jury on the application of the foreseeability of the reasonable man. The House of Lords reinstated the verdict of murder. This is not the place to discuss the legal conundrum posed by the case. Suffice it to say, it evoked immediate academic criticism, professional hostility, and judicial conflict within the Commonwealth; no less a figure than Sir Owen Dixon, the Chief Justice of Australia, declared that in future the High Court of Australia would feel free from being bound by the decisions of the House of Lords.[20] Another member of that court, Mr Justice Fullager, exclaimed extrajudicially: 'I understand that in England they are now hanging people for manslaughter.'[21]

The single judgment, delivered by the Lord Chancellor, Lord Kilmuir (reportedly drafted by Lord Parker, the Lord Chief Justice, who was sitting as a

---

[14] See ch 32 in this volume.   [15] [1935] AC 462: see ch 33 in this volume.
[16] [1961] AC 290.   [17] [1962] AC 220: for a discussion of this case see ch 32 in this volume.
[18] [1962] AC 528.   [19] [1961] AC 290.   [20] *Parker v R* (1963) 111 CLR 610, 632.
[21] Smith was granted a reprieve by the Home Secretary in advance of the appeal to the House of Lords restoring the death penalty.

supernumerary Law Lord[22]), had one juristic curiosity, which has hitherto gone unnoticed by the commentators. The judgment relied, for its proposition of foreseeability as the first test for the mental element in the crime of murder, on an extensive passage in the classic work of Oliver Wendell Holmes Jr, in his book *The Common Law*.[23] That passage was treated as if it were a binding judicial authority and not just as the persuasive opinion of a legal author, even though the author later became the distinguished US Supreme Court Justice, Mr Justice Holmes. That mistake had not been made in 1935 by Lord Sankey in the famous case of *Woolmington v DPP* where Sir Michael Foster (a distinguished eighteenth century judge) was rightly treated 'as a textbook writer' whose work, *Foster's Crown Law*,[24] had misled generations of judges and textbook writers.[25] *Smith v DPP* deserves to be revisited in the light of recent attempts to reform the 'messy' law of murder.[26]

Even after the jurisdiction of the House of Lords was extended in 1960 to entertain criminal appeals, few cases involving the sentencing powers of the criminal courts came to the final court of appeal. A notable exception was *Kennedy v Spratt*,[27] an appeal from Northern Ireland about minimum sentences (see below). Another appeal on statutory construction, *DPP v Ottewell*,[28] contains a breathtaking pronouncement by Lord Reid (in the light of recent events, notably the Criminal Justice Act 2003 with its 'starting points' in Schedule 21 to the Act) as to the appropriate distribution between government and judiciary of the power to determine the precise term of imprisonment to be passed on the individual offender. Responding to a submission by the Attorney General that 'an extended term of imprisonment' meant extended beyond the normal sentence for that type of crime, Lord Reid wrote as follows:

I reject the [submission] without hesitation. It was rather tentatively suggested by the learned Attorney-General that there is a 'tariff' for each kind of offence which is varied upwards or downwards according to the circumstances of the offence and the character of the accused. But offences of a particular kind vary so vastly in gravity that there cannot and *should not be* any 'normal' sentence and there is no workable standard by which to judge whether any particular standard is extended beyond what is 'normal'.

Civil obligations

During the early post-war period there was nothing remarkable about decisions in the field of private law, save for the distinct infrequency of cases involving the

---

[22] The other Law Lords were Lord Goddard (the former Lord Chief Justice), Lord Denning, and Lord Tucker.

[23] 1881.   [24] 1762.   [25] See further Hooper, ch 33 in this volume.

[26] See the Law Commission's report No 304 (2006) and also L Blom-Cooper and TP Morris, *Fine Lines and Distinctions: a study of murder, manslaughter and infanticide and other unlawful killings* (Oxford: Hart, forthcoming 2009).

[27] [1972] AC 83.   [28] [1970] AC 642.

rights and wrongs in civil obligation. Litigation as between private citizens had not grown, except in the pressing social areas of housing, until 1964. The volume of Appeal Cases in the official law reports series for that year occupied 1486 pages, compared with 869 for 1963. Thereafter there was no falling-off in reportable decisions of the House of Lords. In subsequent years there were often two volumes.

The output in those years was overshadowed by the decision in *Hedley Byrne and Co Ltd v Heller and Partners Ltd*[29] which opened up a new era of the tort of negligence by embracing liability for negligent misstatements contained in bank and other employment references (the beginnings of the law on professional negligence) but also extending the law of damages providing a remedy for economic loss. But this development of the law of torts and contractual liability might not have come about—at least not until some time later.

The appeal came on for hearing before Lords Radcliffe, Cohen, MacDermott, Jenkins, and Guest (a very chancery-slanted court, since three of the five Law Lords were from the chancery Bar and judiciary). At the end of the first day's hearing, when counsel for the appellant advertising agency appeared to be making little headway, Lord Radcliffe announced that the hearing would have to be abandoned, because on that day the Government had appointed him to preside over the public inquiry—under the Tribunals of Inquiry (Evidence) Act 1921— to investigate the affairs of the admiralty clerk, John Vassall. Gerald Gardiner QC (counsel for the appellant) was known to have persuaded the Lord Chancellor (Lord Dilhorne) to empanel a court of common law judges; so it turned out that judicial creativity in the law of negligence was achieved by a panel consisting of Lords Reid, Morris of Borth-y-Gest, Hodson, Devlin, and Pearce, who unanimously proclaimed the important principle of negligent misrepresentation (though they dismissed the appeal on the specific facts of the case).

If *Hedley Byrne* had removed any doubts about the ambit of liability for professional negligence, *Rondel v Worsley*[30] a few years later confirmed the breadth of the professional duty of care, even though the decision retrogressively reaffirmed the traditional immunity of barristers (and extended it to include solicitor-advocates) for anything done or said in the course of advocacy. It took three decades for the House of Lords (sitting as a seven-judge panel) to remove the anomalous immunity,[31] although Lord Reid had indicated that the public policy which sustained the immunity might very well change in time.

---

[29] [1964] AC 645.

[30] [1969] 1 AC 191. The contrary view, expressed in a separate assenting judgment in the Court of Appeal of Jersey, *Picot v Crills* 1995 JLR 33, at 46–7—that the decisions of the House of Lords are not binding in Jersey but are only of persuasive authority—was amply supported by Mr Richard Southwell QC (a member of the Jersey Court of Appeal 1994–2005): see *The Sources of Jersey Law*, an essay written by Mr Southwell in *A Celebration of Autonomy 1204–2004: 800 years of Channel Islands' Law*, ed Philip Bailhache, Bailiff of Jersey 1994–2009, [2009] Jersey L Rev 33–5.

[31] *Hall v Simmons* [2002] 1 AC 615. It has to be noted that the High Court of Australia declined to follow in the footsteps of the House of Lords, although Mr Justice Kirby delivered a powerful dissent: see *D'Orta-Ekenaike v Victoria Legal Aid* (2005) 223 CLR 1.

In the same category of importance in the law of negligence must come the decision in *Home Office v Dorset Yacht Co.*[32] In May 1970 the Law Lords decisively ended the surprising absence of any judicial consideration of the legal consequences flowing from the actions of escaped prisoners from penal institutions. Insurers of a privately-owned yacht company successfully there established the civil liability of the Home Office as vicariously responsible for Borstal officers authorised to look after Borstal boys housed temporarily in a camp as part of an extra-custodial scheme of training. Seven Borstal boys, by definition convicted of moderately serious offences, but camping lawfully on Brownsea Island in Poole Harbour, left their camp beds one night and, unhindered by sleeping custodians, boarded a motor yacht lying unattended at the water's edge. Intoxicated by the liquor found and consumed on board, the boys started up the yacht's engines and inexpertly cavorted around the harbour, crashing the yacht on shore. (Within hours they were all apprehended ashore; they were ultimately treated harshly, with lengthy custodial sentences.)

That prisoners escape or abscond from the lawful custody of penal institutions is all too common an experience to avoid general concern among the public and the victims of crime. When they do escape, prisoners sometimes steal things, and do other damage to property as well as injure people, sometimes in the vicinity of the penal institution, sometimes miles away and often days or weeks after their escape. Yet astonishingly, apart from a decision of dubious authority in 1951 in Ipswich County Court there appeared to be no precedent for a valid cause of action against the prison authorities. *Dorset Yacht Co* provided the Law Lords with the opportunity to determine in a private lawsuit the scope (if any) of the tortious liability of the prison authorities for the negligence of their prison-officer servants.

If the result in favour of the insurers of a private owner of property was a piece of creative law-making (with lasting effect), it cannot be claimed as an outstandingly fine juristic effort. It reflected the judicial mood of the time in the final court of appeal, although the dissenting judgment of Viscount Dilhorne deserves a place among the annals of valuable dissents, recognising that the desired change in the law would be better served in Parliament and not in the courts.

The reasoning (or lack of it) in the judgments of the Law Lords did not enhance the acknowledged, growing reputation for the new and welcome jurisprudence of the court. Lord Reid's leading judgment proceeded on traditional lines, taking forward the principle that in the field of the law of negligence, when a new point emerges, one should ask not whether it is covered by authority but whether the principle, enunciated by Lord Atkin as 'who is my neighbour', covers the case. Only public policy: who should bear the loss caused by the carelessness of the Borstal officers—the innocent yacht owners (or rather their insurers) or the Home Office—caused Lord Reid to pause in his judgment favouring the

---

[32] [1970] AC 1004.

property owners. He confessed to being impressed by a seven-judge decision of the Court of Appeals for the State of New York in 1955, where a prisoner, who had escaped from an open prison-farm, so threatened a local farmer that the latter died from a heart attack. The claim by the deceased's widow ultimately failed.[33] Judge Froessel in the single judgment wrote this:

But, even beyond the fact that fundamental legal principles will not permit affirmance here, public policy also requires that the State be not held liable. To hold otherwise would impose a heavy responsibility upon the State, or dissuade the wardens and principal keepers of our prison system from continued experimentation with 'minimum security' work details—which provide a means for encouraging better-risk prisoners to exercise their senses of responsibility and honor and so prepare themselves for their eventual return to society. Since 1917, the Legislature has expressly provided for out-of-prison work, Correction Law § 182, and its intention should be respected without fostering the reluctance of prison officials to assign eligible men to minimum security work, lest they thereby give rise to costly claims against the State, or indeed inducing the State itself to terminate this 'salutary procedure' looking toward rehabilitation.[34]

To which Lord Reid responded:

It may be that public servants of the State of New York are so apprehensive, easily dissuaded from doing their duty and intent on preserving public funds from costly claims that they could be influenced in this way. But my experience leads me to believe that Her Majesty's servants are made of sterner stuff.

Whatever may be the rival stoutness of heart among New York prison authorities and the English prison officer, Lord Reid omitted from Judge Froessel's statement the opening words of the paragraph—namely, 'But, beyond the fact that fundamental legal principles will not permit affirmance here [that is, upholding the decision of the Appellate Division of the Supreme Court of New York]...etc'. The plain fact is that the New York Court of Appeals did not decide the case on grounds of public policy. The State of New York was absolved from a claim made on behalf of Mr Williams' estate only because, even if negligent in permitting the prisoner's escape, the state owed no duty to Mr Williams.[35] The passage in Judge Froessel's judgment was a mere makeweight to bolster the legal principles delineating the scope of a public authority's duty to take care.

The reasoning of Judge Froessel is to be found in a passage that defined the limit of the state's duty. The escaped prisoner 'was being *punished*, and for that reason deprived of his liberty. If the state negligently permitted the prisoner's premature return to society, it breached only that *public duty* to *punish*, a duty

---

[33] *Williams v State of New York* 127 NE 2d 545 (1955). [34] ibid, 550 [15].
[35] Even Lord Edmund-Davies (as Lord Justice Edmund-Davies, as a member of the Court of Appeal in *Dorset Yacht*) incorrectly interpreted Froessel J's judgment, saying that the Court of Appeal absolved the state from a claim, 'not, it would seem, on the ground that no duty was owed,' but because, even if negligent in permitting the escape, the state could not have foreseen that it would lead to injury.

owed to the members of the community collectively but importing no "crushing burden" of liability to individuals for the breach thereof'.[36] The state's carelessness was 'negligence in the air' or 'in the abstract', and was not joined to Williams' death by the element of foreseeability: Williams' death 'may not be included within the class of consequences of the state's negligence for which it must answer in damages'.

The decision in *Williams* exemplified the sound principle of the English common law that a person's mere failure to confer a benefit upon another person—including the prevention of harm to that other person through the action of a third party—cannot, without more ado, be actionable. *Dorset Yacht* breached that principle, and is rescuable as a decision only if the facts of the case provide 'more ado'. In *Gorringe v Calderdale Metropolitan Borough Council*[37] Lord Hoffmann noted that the liability of the Home Office for the damage to the yacht by the Borstal boys was not just for having failed to prevent the damage, but for having taken them to Brownsea Island and, while there, failing to supervise them. Did that one added factor provide the 'more ado'? Both the escaped prisoner in New York state and the Borstal boys were treated alike in open conditions as part of progressive programmes in penal policy. Supervision (or rather, the lack of it) was intrinsic to a policy of putting the prisoners on trust not to abscond and to behave in a socially responsible way. Short of shackling the Borstal boys to their dormitory bedsteads (an absurd, if not impractical idea) or posting a nightwatchman or two (also not in conformity with encouraging a sense of responsibility) supervision could not reasonably be contemplated, at least not during the hours of darkness and sleep. Lord Hoffmann's explanation does not save *Dorset Yacht* from its fate as a flawed decision.

Even if the issue of liability were essentially (if not primarily) one of public policy, the Law Lords barely (if at all) addressed the ultimate policy issue, whether such damage ought to be paid for by property owners' insurers and their premium payers, on the one hand, or by the Home Office and the taxpayers, on the other hand. In practice, ever since the Ipswich case, the Home Office had made *ex gratia* payments to victims suffering from the crimes of escaped prisoners, but always declined to do so if the claimants were insured. Hence the Home Office resisted the claim of the yacht's insurers—and lost. Nothing, we suspect, has changed since in practice. Of Lord Reid's judgment, it might be said that 'reason still keeps its throne, but nods a little, that's all'.[38]

The emerging public law

In the space of five or so years a cluster of five decisions emanating from the Appellate Committee set the seal on an astonishing display of judicial creativity

---

[36] Author's italics.   [37] [2004] 1 WLR 1057, 1069.

[38] George Farquhar (1677–1707), a Restoration playwright, in his play *The Recruiting Officer* (1706).

that inaugurated a new era of public law decision-making in the succeeding four decades. The quintuplet of cases began in 1963 with *Ridge v Baldwin*,[39] through *Burmah Oil v Lord Advocate*,[40] *Conway v Rimmer*,[41] *Padfield v Ministry of Agriculture, Fisheries and Food*[42] to *Anisminic v Foreign Compensation Commission*.[43] As Professor John Griffith (a fearless critic of the English judiciary) wrote in *Judicial Politics since 1920: A Chronicle*: 'In 1962 the attitude of the senior judiciary to the exercise of the powers of public authorities began to change dramatically',[44] and later, added that 'the House of Lords, led by Lord Reid, restored the position of the highest court to the position of some eminence'. All five appeals were presided over by Lord Reid, who in that year had become the Senior Law Lord in succession to Viscount Simonds. Lord Reid was, beyond question, the pre-eminent actor in the dramatic events of that period—an actor who was to dictate the court's role for the rest of the twentieth century and beyond.

James Scott Cumberland Reid (always called Scott Reid) was, by the criteria for appointment up to that point, an unusual candidate for the final court of appeal, on which he served for 26 years. In that time he delivered well over 500 judgments, the great majority of which were on English law, in which he had never practised. He went from the Edinburgh Academy as a scholar to Jesus College, Cambridge, where he obtained first-class honours in Part One of both the natural sciences (1910) and law tripos (1911). His legal studies (which, the author of the *Dictionary of National Biography* tells us, 'he found arid and remote from the living law practised in London') were his only direct contact with English law until his appointment in 1948, direct from practice at the Scottish Bar. After wartime service he returned to the Bar. His practice was distinguished rather than extensive, mainly because he devoted a good deal of his energy to becoming an active politician. Although not a noted forensic figure, he became Dean of the Faculty of Advocates from 1946–8 when he was appointed a Lord of Appeal in Ordinary.

Reid became an MP in 1931. In 1936 he had become Solicitor-General for Scotland and in 1941 was appointed Lord Advocate, holding office until the Labour Party formed a government in 1945. Reid held onto his parliamentary seat in an election that resulted nationwide in a landslide victory for Labour, at which point he returned to practice, while continuing an active political role in opposition.

Those commentators who are keen to observe that, in the past, appointments to the higher judiciary were politically motivated often fail to note that Reid was offered (and finally accepted, after consulting political colleagues to test his future political career—Lady Reid was often heard to say that her husband should have

---

[39] [1964] AC 40.   [40] [1965] AC 75.   [41] [1968] AC 910.   [42] [1968] AC 997.
[43] [1969] 2 AC 147.
[44] Chapter 4 in *The New Look of the Sixties* (Oxford: Blackwell, 1993) 106.

become Prime Minister) and accepted a direct appointment to the House of Lords from Clement Attlee. The offer to a Conservative MP by the Labour Prime Minister of the vacancy in the final court of appeal (following the death of the Scottish Law Lord, Lord Thankerton[45]) was almost certainly prompted by an appreciation of Reid's potential contribution to the development of the law, including Attlee's awareness of Reid's experience in public administration and his ministerial post (albeit as a law officer), no doubt observed at close quarters during the wartime administration.

Given the quite exceptional politico-legal career of Reid—not least the absence of any judicial experience prior to his entering the Lords—the appointment was inspirational and showed great foresight of what was to be his transformative role in the development of the final court of appeal. In 1962 his pre-eminent position was consolidated by his appointment as Senior Law Lord—a position that might cautiously be characterised as *primus inter pares*, but one which offers pole position for leadership of the final court of appeal.

1. *Ridge v Baldwin*

Ridge v Baldwin might seem an unpromising case to alight upon as foreshadowing the emergence of an entirely novel judicial approach to the control of government and administrative authorities, since the appeal to the House of Lords arose indirectly out of nothing more than police corruption (albeit at the high level of a provincial police force) and concerned the pension rights of a Chief Constable. But Lord Reid's carefully crafted judgment (supported by three of his colleagues on the appeal[46]), while acknowledging at the outset that 'we do not have a developed system of administrative law—perhaps because until fairly recently we did not need it', proceeded thereafter to lay the foundation for what today is recognisably a highly developed system of administrative law. Academic writers such as William Robson (see Chapter 25) had debunked Dicey's ill-directed hostility towards the development of a British *droit administratif*; it now fell to the judges—led by Lord Reid—to deliver the new jurisprudence.

Mr Ridge (the Chief Constable of Brighton) had left the dock at the Old Bailey in March 1958, acquitted by the jury of corruption, but to ringing tones from the trial judge (Mr Justice, later Lord, Donovan) casting grave reflections on his conduct and expressing the view that the Brighton Police Force needed a new leader. The very next day the watch committee (then the authority for the local police force) met and instantly dismissed Mr Ridge from office. Some days later Mr Ridge's solicitor was permitted to address the committee on his behalf. With three dissentions, the committee adhered to its previous decision. He had

---

[45] Like Lord Reid, Lord Thankerton (William Watson) had served as a Conservative MP and held office as Lord Advocate (1924–9) before being appointed as a Lord of Appeal.

[46] The sole dissenter was Lord Evershed in a lengthy traditional judgment (he never wrote shortly).

obviously not been given any notice of the meeting and hence had been provided with no opportunity of being heard in his own defence. To invoke the well-established principle of natural justice was an obvious basis for the challenge to his summary dismissal. But what transpired from the judgments was something a good deal more comprehensive than just a successful claim against the watch committee.

First and foremost the judgment freed the courts from the conceptual restrictions which they had created for themselves over the years. No longer would it be necessary to demonstrate that the decision under challenge was judicial or quasi-judicial. Put simply, a public authority, in addressing the rights or interests of an individual citizen, had to proceed fairly, and that meant giving full sway to the notion of telling the individual what is alleged against him or her, and hearing his or her defence or explanation before reaching any decision. The overall duty to act fairly extended to ministerial decision-making and not just to inferior tribunals overseen by the prerogative writs of certiorari, mandamus and prohibition. That extension was immediately adopted at the lower level of the court structure.[47] Three years after *Ridge v Baldwin*, and without the case even being cited, the Divisional Court (composed of Parker LCJ, Salmon LJ, and Blain J) in *Re HK*[48] held that an immigration officer exercising on behalf of the Home Secretary powers under the Commonwealth Immigrants Act 1962 had to act fairly in refusing entry to the UK, whether he was acting administratively, creatively, or quasi-judicially. Blain J put it bluntly: '...by which I mean applying his mind dispassionately to fair analysis'. Judicial insistence on fairness has ever since been the hallmark of our administrative law.[49]

Second, Lord Reid explained that one reason why the decisions of the courts on natural justice had been found difficult to reconcile was that insufficient attention had been paid to the great difference between various kinds of cases in which it had been sought to apply the principle. What a Minister ought to do in considering objections to a planning scheme may be very different from what a public authority or Minister ought to do in considering whether to dismiss somebody from an official post. In considering a scheme other factors had to be weighed in the balance. Decisions by ministers, officials, and bodies of various kinds which adversely affected property rights or privileges of persons had to be viewed differently. Sometimes the functions of a Minister or department may also, however, be of the same character as those of a watch committee, in which case the rules of natural justice applied.

---

[47] See an interesting slant on the case as decided in the Court of Appeal by Professor SA de Smith, 'The Brighton Conspiracy Case and Administrative Law' (1962) 25 MLR 455.

[48] [1967] 2 QB 1017.

[49] As long ago as 1929 Maugham J (later Lord Maugham) observed that it was improper to refer to *natural* justice, since justice is a man-made concept; and whoever heard of unnatural justice? Presciently he preferred that judges talked about fairness: see *Maclean v Workers' Union* [1929] 1 Ch 602, 624.

Lord Reid's judgment in *Ridge v Baldwin* was characteristically peppered with wise remarks. He railed at the perennial fallacy that because something cannot be 'cut and dried', it cannot exist. He went on to observe that the idea of negligence is equally insusceptible of exact definition, an idea that resonates in judicial decisions on the law of torts to this day:

For a long time it was thought that, at least in theory, intention or mental state of some kind was a necessary ingredient in negligence. But life would be impossible in modern conditions unless on the highway and in the market place we were entitled to rely on the other man behaving like a reasonable man. So we now apply a purely objective standard. The other man may have been doing his best, and he may not realise that his best is not good enough, but if he causes damage by falling short of the ordinary standard he must pay.[50]

2. *Burmah Oil v Lord Advocate*

Conflict between the executive arm of government and the courts could not have been more direct and acute than in the decision in *Burmah Oil v Lord Advocate*.[51] In 1942, when the Japanese Army was on the doorstep of British forces in Rangoon, a policy was adopted by the British Army of destroying, in advance of the enemy troops, oil installations owned by the Burmah Oil Company, a company registered in Scotland. Action was brought in the Scottish courts for compensation. The Government warned the company that if it were to succeed in its claim, legislation would be introduced to indemnify the Crown so that no money would be paid. Undaunted, the trial judge (Lord Kilbrandon) found for the claimants, only to be reversed by the First Division of the Inner House of the Court of Session, which in turn was reversed by the House of Lords (Lords Reid, Pearce, and Upjohn, with Lords Radcliffe and Hodson dissenting). The issue was whether the destruction of the oil installations was 'battle damage', for which no compensation was payable, or 'denial damage' where it was payable. Lord Radcliffe's powerful dissent was based on the proposition that it was for those 'who fill and empty the public purse to decide where, by whom and on what conditions and within what limitations such compensation is to be made payable'.[52] Against a chorus of parliamentary opposition, including the Lord Chief Justice, Lord Parker, the Government (now the incoming Labour administration) passed the War Damage Act 1965 retrospectively reversing the House of Lords decision.

Apart from its constitutional implications, the judgment reflected the expanding doctrine of government responsibility for torts and the right of the

---

[50] For other *mots justes* from Lord Reid, see *Gollins v Gollins* [1964] AC 644 and *Southern Portland Cement v Cooper* [1974] AC 623 at 640: 'Chance probability or likelihood is always a matter of degree . . . a line of extreme probability.'
[51] [1965] AC 75.
[52] The politico-legal saga is recounted in L Blom-Cooper and G Drewry, *Final Appeal: A Study of the House of Lords in its Judicial Capacity* (Oxford: Clarendon Press, 1972) 368–73.

subject to sue the Crown.[53] But it also prompted a due respect for the proper relationship between the courts and executive government, in which the former gave notice that they would not be intimidated by Ministers of the Crown.

3. *Conway v Rimmer*

Conway v Rimmer[54] not only extended the courts' powers in areas where the prerogative powers of the Sovereign had reigned, but it also did so by the use for the first time of the power to reverse its own previous decisions. Professor Griffith quarrelled with the decision. He said:[55]

No doubt Ministers had in the past on occasion claimed [Crown] privilege more for their own protection and that of their civil servants than because they believed the public interest would be endangered by disclosure. But it is not clear why judges rather than Ministers should have the final decision in such matters. The details of the principle are not easy to see nor did the five Law Lords who each delivered separate opinions greatly clarify the circumstances in which they believed they should review the executive powers of government. Lord Reid gave one example of a class of documents where the Ministerial decision should not be reviewed. Cabinet minutes '*and the like*'[56] ought not to be disclosed. But his reason was that disclosure would create or fan ill-informed or captious public or political criticism. The business of government is difficult enough as it is, and no government could contemplate with equanimity the inner working of the government machine being exposed to the gaze of those ready to criticise without adequate knowledge of the background and perhaps with some axe to grind.

The scope of what today is called 'public interest immunity'—always a vexing subject for the judiciary—would continue to surprise Professor Griffith, but Lord Reid's 'the like' has been amply demonstrated in recent years.[57]

4. *Padfield v Ministry of Agriculture, Fisheries and Food*

Even greater scope for judicial curtailment of ministerial powers came in *Padfield v Ministry of Agriculture, Fisheries and Food*.[58] There, a statute, the Agricultural Marketing Act 1958 which established the Milk Marketing Board, appeared to give the Minister a clear choice to act in one way or in an alternative way. The Law Lords decided, however, that the Minister should have acted only in the way that their Lordships thought would have been appropriate. With the development of *Wednesbury* unreasonableness and a development of the concept of proportionality, the reasoning of their Lordships in *Padfield* does not appear discordant with legal principles. But in its day the decision did not go uncriticised professionally. How did their Lordships come to reach such a forward-looking decision?

---

[53] See *Dorset Yacht Co Ltd v Home Office* [1970] AC 1004.
[54] [1968] AC 910. See also ch 9 in this volume.   [55] *Judicial Politics since 1920* (n 8) 85–6.
[56] Emphasis added.   [57] See *Roberts v Parole Board* [2005] 2 AC 738.
[58] [1968] AC 997.

The Milk Marketing Board administered a scheme by which dairy farmers sold their milk to the Board at different prices in each of eleven regions in England and Wales, the differentials reflecting the varying costs of transporting the milk from the producers to the consumers. The South Eastern Region sought to get the differentials changed in its favour by the Board. The Board consisted largely of members elected by the individual regions and any change in favour of one region would disadvantage the rest. The South Eastern Region failed to get a majority for its proposals. It then asked the Minister of Agriculture, Fisheries and Food to refer their proposal to a committee of investigation under section 19 of the Act. Section 19 provided:

[A] committee for investigation shall be charged with the duty, *if the Minister in any case so directs*, of considering and reporting to the Minister on any complaint made to the Minister as to the operation of any scheme which, in the opinion of the Minister, could not be considered by a consumers' committee.[59]

The Minister took the view that this complaint was not suitable for investigation by the committee of investigation and that the question was one for the Board to decide. So he refused the request from the South Eastern Region which then resorted to the courts, asking for an order requiring the Minister to make the reference to the committee. The Court of Appeal, by a majority which included Lord Justice Diplock, held that the Minister was entitled not to refer the complaint and that this was made clear by the words 'if the Minister in any case so directs'. The majority's view was essentially that the Minister's decision was one of policy for which he was accountable to Parliament, not to the courts.

The House of Lords, by a majority, allowed the appeal and supported the farmers. Lord Reid said:

Parliament must have conferred the discretion [on the Minister] with the intention that it should be used to promote the policy and objects of the Act; the policy and objects of the Act must be determined by construing the Act as a whole and construction is always a matter of law for the court. In a matter of this kind it is not possible to draw a hard and fast line, but if the Minister, by reason of his having misconstrued the Act or for any other reason, so uses his discretion as to thwart or run counter to the policy and objects of the Act, then our law would be very defective if persons aggrieved were not entitled to the protection of the court.

5. *Anisminic v Foreign Compensation Commission*

For a court traditionally respectful of the legislature's supreme law-making power, *Anisminic v Foreign Compensation Commission*[60] was a blockbuster. Even the legal profession found their Lordships' audacity breathtaking. The assertion of the

[59] Emphasis added.   [60] [1969] 2 AC 147.

scope of judicial power was a foretaste of things to come. 'Ouster clauses in legislation' were not automatically judge-proof, as later events demonstrated.

Anisminic Ltd owned mining property in Egypt which they claimed was worth over £4 million. On the outbreak of hostilities in the autumn of 1956, the property was occupied by Israeli forces and damaged to the extent of £½ million. The property was sequestrated by the Egyptian government on 1 November 1956 and on 29 April 1957 that government authorised the sale of the property to an agency of the Egyptian government, TEDO, for £½ million. Subsequently the Egyptian government paid the UK Government £27½ million in full and final compensation for all property seized from UK owners.

It was the responsibility of the UK Government to decide who was entitled to participate in the distribution of this compensation and how much each claimant should receive. For this purpose, machinery was at hand, for in 1950 the Foreign Compensation Act had established the Foreign Compensation Commission (FCC). Introducing the Bill, the Minister of State had said:[61]

It is really more appropriate that what is essentially a judicial function of assessing claims and the shares of each different claimant should be performed now by a standing body, a judicial body, which should not merely advise the Secretary of State but actually take the decision and actually distribute the money.

The chairman of the FCC was appointed by the Lord Chancellor, and its members by the Secretary of State.

In 1962 an Order in Council was made under the Act of 1950, giving directions to the FCC to govern the distribution to the claimants of the Egyptian money. The Order provided that the FCC should treat a claim as established if satisfied that (a) the applicant is 'the owner of the property or is the successor in title of such a person', and (b) the applicant and any person who became successor in title were British nationals on 31 October 1956 and 28 February 1959. Anisminic made a claim to the FCC which ruled against the company on the ground that its successor in title, TEDO, was not a British national. Anisminic brought an action to have this ruling set aside and Browne J found in its favour. The Court of Appeal reversed this, but the House of Lords restored the decision of Browne J.

Lord Reid explained the problem of interpretation in these words:

The main difficulty in this case springs from the fact that the draughtsman did not state separately what conditions have to be satisfied (1) where the applicant is the original owner and (2) where the applicant claims as the successor in title of the original owner. It is clear that where the applicant is the original owner he must prove that he was a British national on the dates stated. And it is equally clear that where the applicant claims as being the original owner's successor in title he must prove that both he and the original owner were British nationals on those dates... What is left in obscurity is whether the

---

[61] *Hansard*, HC, vol 475, col 41 (8 May 1950).

provisions with regard to successors in title have any application at all in cases where the applicant is himself the original owner.

The House of Lords decided that the interpretation put on the words of the Order by the FCC was wrong and that the applicants, being the owners of the property, did not have to prove anything with regard to successors in title whose nationality was, in these circumstances, irrelevant. The difficulty about this decision was that it had previously been thought that, when a body like the FCC was invested with the apparently exclusive right to decide, the courts could intervene only on very limited grounds. These grounds would include a positive abuse of power, or a failure to provide a fair hearing, or the taking into account of some matter which was clearly not relevant to the decision.

There was an 'obscurity' in the meaning of the Order. But were the courts entitled to impose their interpretation over that of the FCC? One important reason why the Act of 1950 entrusted the FCC with the making of the decisions was that the distribution of the limited sum available depended on all claims being settled. If the decisions were challengeable in the courts, finality would be greatly postponed. To underline this, the Act provided that any determination by the FCC of an application '*shall not be called into question in any court of law*'.[62] The House of Lords' answer to this was that it could not apply to a determination which the courts decided was invalid and a nullity, and not a real determination at all.

The problem then passed back to the Government and Parliament. After further dispute, the Foreign Compensation Act 1969 provided that a person aggrieved by a determination of the FCC on any question of law (which included all questions of interpretation) could require the FCC to state a case for the Court of Appeal for a final decision. This apart, no determination or '*purported determination*' by the FCC could be called into question in any court of law except where the determination was questioned on any ground that it was contrary to natural justice, that is, that the FCC had adopted a *procedure* that was unfair. All this represented a compromise between those who wanted full access to the courts from decisions of the FCC and those who wanted to exclude the courts from the kind of supervision the Lords had adopted in the *Anisminic* case.

Thus the Law Lords seemed to envisage the transfer of decision-making from a statutory body to which decisions had been entrusted to the courts.[63] So contentious was the assertion of law-making by the judicial branch of government that Lords Morris of Borth-y-Gest (regularly a notable contributor to the

---

[62] Emphasis added.

[63] In *Re Racal Communications Ltd* [1981] AC 374, 383C Lord Diplock said: 'The break-through made by *Anisminic* was that, as respects administrative tribunals and authorities, the old distinction between errors of law that went to jurisdiction and errors of law that did not, was for practical purposes abolished. Any error of law that could be shown to have been made by them in the course of reaching their decision on matters of fact or of administrative policy would result in their having asked themselves the wrong question, with the result that the decision they reached would be a nullity.'

development of public law) and Pearson dissented. But notably, Lord Wilberforce, who had become a Law Lord in 1964, was among the majority, foreshadowing his judicial duet with Lord Reid. The two rode in tandem for the next ten years.

Lord Reid retired in 1974, aged 84, escaping the age limit imposed in the Judicial Pensions Act 1959. His period as the senior Law Lord for the last 11 years was replete with creativity, distinctively so in public law. At the annual conference in Edinburgh in 1972 of the Society of Public Teachers of Law he declared extra-judicially his adherence to principles and practicality, rather than to precedence. These lay behind his brand of judicial creativity.

There was a time when it was thought almost indecent to suggest that judges make law—they only declare it. Those with a taste for fairy tales seem to have thought that in some Aladdin's cave there is hidden the Common Law in all its splendour and that on a judge's appointment there descends on him knowledge of the magic words Open Sesame. Bad decisions are given when the judge has muddled the password and the wrong door opens. But we do not believe in fairy tales any more.

We should, I think, have regard to common sense, legal principle and public policy in that order. We are here to serve the public, the common ordinary reasonable man. He has no great faith in theories and he is quite right. What he wants and will appreciate is an explanation in simple terms which he will understand.[64]

Lord Reid's mantle

The eminence and creativity of Lord Reid cannot be gainsaid, and it takes nothing away from his reputation to remind ourselves that even the most assiduously industrious Law Lord[65] does not work alone. Special mention should be made in this context of Lord Reid's distinguished English judicial colleague, Lord Wilberforce, whose judgments—he sat on 465 appeals—often complemented those of Lord Reid (his contribution to the *Anisminic* case has already been noted). Lord Wilberforce was a Chancery silk, who was appointed to the High Court Bench in 1961, thereby being caught by the retiring age of 75. He often said that he wished he had obtained the judicial freehold; he lived to be 95, mentally alert way into his 90s. A man of high intellect (he was awarded an Oxford double first and was elected a Fellow of All Souls in 1932), his career had not been dissimilar to Lord Reid's. War service and after the German surrender he became head of the British legal section of the four-power Control Commission for the

---

[64] 'The Judge as Law-Maker' (1972) 12 JSPTL 22.

[65] In *Final Appeal* (n 52) 175–6, the present writers noted that Lord Reid sat in no fewer than 70 per cent of all the appeals (and 80 per cent of the Scottish appeals) heard by the House of Lords during the 17 years (1952–68) covered by our research. During that period he delivered 14.4 per cent of all the full judgments in English and Northern Irish civil and criminal appeals, and 22 per cent of all the full judgments in Scottish appeals.

Administration of Justice. Leaving the Commission in 1946 he became a civil servant in London with the rank of under-secretary at the Control Office for Germany and Austria (he spoke of this as the best civil service job in the world). In 1950 he stood unsuccessfully as Conservative candidate in the constituency of Kingston-upon-Hull Central, the city which his great-grandfather, William Wilberforce, had represented. He was not particularly suited to the fact-finding grind of the trial court and was clearly destined for advancement, sooner or later, to the top court. His promotion to the House of Lords in fact came unusually quickly, when Lord Dilhorne, Lord Chancellor in the out-going Conservative Government, appointed him as a Lord of Appeal in October 1964, at the age of 57, by-passing the usual stint of appellate probation in the Court of Appeal.

By this time the Reid era was well under way, and Wilberforce often showed himself to be empathetic to Lord Reid's innovative moves to develop public law. Two cases matched Reid's creativity. In *Raymond v Honey*[66] Lord Wilberforce enunciated the principle that a 'convicted person retains all civil rights which are not taken away expressly or by necessary implication', a kick-start to a series of prisoners' rights decisions, quoted regularly by every prisoners' rights advocate. And in *Tameside*,[67] discussing the exercise of the Secretary of State's power to force a local council to implement a comprehensive education policy, Wilberforce stated, in reasoning reminiscent of *Anisminic*, that:

if a judgment requires, before it can be made, the existence of some facts, then, although the evaluation of those facts is for the Secretary of State alone, the court must inquire whether those facts exist, and have been taken into account, whether the judgment has been made upon a proper self-direction as to those facts, [and] whether the judgment has not been made upon other facts which ought not to have been taken into account. If these requirements are not met, then the exercise of judgment, however bona fide it may be, becomes capable of challenge.

The two did not always ride in tandem. In *Kennedy v Spratt*[68] Lord Reid favoured applying strictly a minimum sentence of imprisonment for an offence of disorderly behaviour on a road, while Lord Wilberforce thought that the court had a discretion to impose a suspended sentence (Lord Morris of Borth-y-Gest agreed with Lord Wilberforce, while Lord Diplock readily adopted the illiberal stance, with the remarkable observation that 'the natural meaning of the words "shall be sentenced to imprisonment" is that he shall be punished for that offence by being sent to prison', ignoring the distinction between the court passing a sentence of imprisonment and ordering that the sentence shall not take effect (or

---

[66] [1983] 1 AC 1.

[67] *Secretary of State for Education and Science v Tameside MBC* [1977] AC 1014.

[68] [1972] AC 83. Since the court was equally divided 2:2 (the fifth member of the court, Lord Upjohn, having died before judgment was given; his opinion was added to that of Lord Reid) the appeal, by convention, was dismissed. Even if Lord Upjohn's view had supported Lord Morris and Lord Wilberforce, it still would not have counted and the appeal would still have been dismissed.

suspending sentence) as long recognised in English law; the distinction is not purely linguistic).

Even after the duet was over, with Lord Reid's retirement in January 1975,[69] there was still an indication of a meeting of minds between the two judicial colossi. In *Burmah Oil v Governor of the Bank of England*,[70] Lord Wilberforce wrote in a case involving public interest immunity that the Attorney General (Mr Sam Silkin) 'did not contend for any such proposition, ie, that a high level public interest can never, in any circumstances, be outweighed. In this I think he was in line with the middle of the road position taken by Lord Reid in *Conway v Rimmer*'.[71]

Procedural development

Disclosure of documents via an action for discovery had been opened up dramatically in 1974 in *Norwich Pharmacal v Customs & Excise*.[72] It set in train a whole series of cases touching on the ability of litigating parties to obtain information either to support their cause or defeat their opponent's case. Most notably, *D v NSPCC*[73] was an early example of the new-found procedure for revealing documents. A mother sought an order that the identity of the informant of child abuse should be disclosed by the voluntary organisation engaged in child protection. The application was refused only on the ground of public interest in protecting regular informants to the NSPCC. Confidentiality was in play.

Practice and procedure of the litigious process did not otherwise loom large in the work of the House of Lords, if only because the issues arose mostly in interlocutory appeals which tended to fail to get leave to appeal either from the Court of Appeal or the Lords themselves. The highlights were *Gouriet v Union of Post Office Workers*[74] (the courts cannot control the decision of the Attorney General to lend his name to the launch of relator proceedings); *Attorney General v Vernazza*[75] (a case indicating the court's power over vexatious litigants); *Pyx Granite Co v Ministry of Housing and Local Government*[76] (an early assertion of the primacy of access to justice); *R v Bracknell Justices, ex p Griffiths*[77] (restriction on right of action in mental health cases); *Hanlon v Law Society*[78] (a rare excursion into the issue of costs in legal aid); and *Granada Television v British Steel Corporation*[79] (*Norwich Pharmacal* applied). Procedural principle was most notable in

---

[69] Their last case sitting together was *Black-Clawson International Ltd v Papierwerke Waldhof-Aschaffenberg AG* [1975] AC 591, speeches being delivered on 5 March 1975, only three weeks before Lord Reid's death on 24 March 1975.
[70] [1980] AC 1014.   [71] ibid, 1113.
[72] *Norwich Pharmacal Co v Customs and Excise Comrs* [1974] AC 133, graphically described by Sir Robin Jacob in ch 39 in this volume.
[73] [1978] AC 171.   [74] [1978] AC 435.   [75] [1960] AC 965.
[76] [1960] AC 260.   [77] [1976] AC 314.   [78] [1981] AC 124.
[79] [1981] AC 1096.

the criminal jurisdiction in *Sweet v Parsley*[80] (an appeal from a conviction by a magistrates' court upheld by the Queen's Bench Divisional Court) where Lord Reid, in magisterial language, enunciated the principle that '*mens rea* is an essential ingredient of every offence unless some reason can be found for holding that it is not necessary'.

European influence

A notable failure to give full play to freedom of expression was the *Thalidomide* case, *Attorney General v Times Newspapers Ltd*,[81] in which the House of Lords, led by Lord Reid, had denied the *Sunday Times* a right to continue publishing articles accusing the Distillers company of negligence in its production and continued marketing of thalidomide, on the ground that the newspaper was interfering in the conduct of civil litigation and that such publicity was intended to bring pressure to bear on the company, thereby prejudicing a fair trial. The European Court of Human Rights declared (by 11 votes to 9) the decision incompatible with Article 10 of the ECHR; there was no 'pressing social need' to justify the interference with press freedom; the end result was a change in the law relating to journalistic output, in the Contempt of Court Act 1981. Lord Reid, while being prepared to countenance press influence by forceful comments, did not relish anyone other than the judges policing their own system of administration of justice. This echoed his reference in *Conway v Rimmer* to 'ill-informed or captious public or political criticism'.

The European influence on the legal system was only just beginning; the first reference by the House of Lords to the European Court of Justice at Luxembourg came only in 1981 in the case of *R v Henn and Darby*,[82] and the impact of the jurisprudence from Strasbourg was also slight, if only because the right of individual petition was conferred on the citizen only in 1966.

If Lord Atkin's statement in *Donoghue v Stevenson* was, according to Lord Reid in *Dorset Yacht*, 'a milestone . . . a statement of principle' in the tort of negligence, Lord Wilberforce's judgment in *Anns v Merton LBC*[83] has, in the long run, become the focus of acute debate over the liabilities of public authorities for acts and omissions that would instinctively affect the liability of the private citizen in negligence—another milestone along the thorny route of tortious liability. Lord Wilberforce approached the problem on the footing that the authority's powers and duties 'are definable in terms of public law'. The authority must give 'proper consideration to the exercise of its powers and duties, and can be held liable for damage caused only as a result of unreasonable action or acts in excess of its powers'. Only when the power or duty had become 'operational' did the ordinary duty of care, breach of which gave rise to a cause of action in negligence, apply.

---

[80] [1970] AC 132, 148.   [81] [1974] AC 273.   [82] [1981] AC 850.
[83] [1978] AC 728.

This two-step approach was reversed by the House of Lords in *Murphy v Brentwood DC*,[84] on the grounds that 'it did not proceed on any basis of principle at all, but constituted a remarkable example of judicial legislation' and 'introduced a new species of liability governed by a principle indeterminate in character'.[85] Lord Wilberforce's public law two-step test, in harmony with Lord Atkin's neighbourly metaphor, has at least been preferred in Canada[86] (notably in *Canada National Rly Co v Norsk Pacific Steamships*[87]). The perceived dangers in unlimited liability on the basis of a single test of a duty to take care are likely to revive Lord Wilberforce's legal creativity. If so, it would be as remarkable as the restoration of the rule that duress is no defence to a charge of murder.[88]

Conclusion

Twenty years before the incorporation of the European Convention on Human Rights into English law, Lord Wilberforce in a judgment in the Privy Council in *Ministry of Home Affairs v Fisher*[89] pointed the way towards a judicial approach to the interpretation of a constitutional instrument that has characterised judicial attitudes to the Human Rights Act 1998. The issue was simple enough. Did the word 'child' in the Bermudan Constitution (an inheritance from British colonial rule) include an illegitimate child? Citing Article 8 of the Convention and the Universal Declaration of Human Rights, Lord Wilberforce said that there was room for interpreting the Constitution of Bermuda with less rigidity, and greater generosity than other Acts. That generous interpretation avoided what had been called 'the austerity of tabulated legalism': it was sensible to give individuals the full measure of the fundamental freedoms referred to.[90] Up until that time only Lord Reid in *Miah v DPP*[91] had expressly referred to the Convention in House of Lords judgments. He relied on Article 7 to support the rule against retrospectivity in the criminal law.

Those two judicial pronouncements exemplify an era in which the House of Lords achieved enhanced eminence among supreme courts of the Anglo-Saxon legal system, and indeed beyond the common law. Above all, the Reid-Wilberforce era marked the beginning of a transformation of the House of Lords into a public law tribunal in embryo from a court of final appeal in private law litigation. The bottom-line definition of the rule of law is that no one—including Ministers—can be above the law. The development of administrative law jurisprudence in the 1970s and 80s (coinciding, as it happens, with the major overhaul

---

[84] [1991] 1 AC 398.   [85] ibid, 471.   [86] See ch 19(b) in this volume.
[87] [1992] 1 SCR 1021.
[88] *R v Howe* [1987] AC 417 overruling *DPP v Lynch* [1975] AC 653.
[89] The Board was composed of Lords Wilberforce, Hailsham, Salmon, and Fraser and Sir William Douglas: [1980] AC 319.
[90] At 328–9.   [91] [1974] 1 WLR 692.

of administrative law remedies and procedures that was set in train by the Law Commission) revived this most fundamental of constitutional principles from the semi-comatose state into which it had lapsed in the inter-war and post-war years. The transformation did not happen overnight: administrative law still constituted only a fraction (if an increasingly large one) of the caseload of the House of Lords. But in this context, as in so many others, quality counts for much more than quantity, and the innovative decisions, such as those discussed earlier in this chapter, set the tone, and generated the necessary momentum, for all that was to follow. On the hypothetical Law Lords' honours board in the Palace of Westminster the names of Lord Reid and Lord Wilberforce must surely merit top billing.

15

The End of the Twentieth Century: The House of Lords 1982–2000[1]

Michael J Beloff

From the close of the Wilberforce era to the start of the Bingham era the number of Law Lords at any one time fluctuated between eight and 11,[2] while the statutory maximum was gradually increased to 12.[3] Of the 34 Law Lords who sat, the majority naturally were English. The Scots continued to provide a pair at any one time: Mackay, Fraser, Keith, Jauncey, Clyde, Hope—it had become 'a firmly established convention'.[4] Lowry and Hutton had each been Chief Justice of Northern Ireland. Commercial law was represented successively by Diplock,[5] Roskill, Brandon (an admiralty specialist), Ackner, Goff, Mustill, Lloyd, Steyn, Saville, Hobhouse, and Phillips; chancery by Wilberforce, Russell, Brightman, Templeman, Oliver, Browne-Wilkinson, Nicholls, Hoffmann, and Millett; and common law by Lane, who stayed for only eight months before leaving to become Lord Chief Justice in 1980. In criminal appeals there were Edmund-Davies and Griffiths. Nolan was at the Bar a tax specialist, Scarman a planning barrister, family law first instance judge, and latterly pioneer of human rights, and Slynn returned from the European Court of Justice to lead on community law matters. Added to them were Cooke of Thorndon, a rare example of a peer of the realm who had held 'high judicial office' as President of the Court of Appeal of New Zealand, and Emslie, former Lord President[6] from Scotland. The Lord Chancellor, Hailsham, sat on 46 occasions,[7] Havers not

---

[1] For previous analyses covering this period see: S Lee, *Judging Judges* (London: Faber and Faber, 1988); D Robertson, *Judicial Discretion in the House of Lords* (Oxford: OUP, 1998); B Dickson, 'The Lords of Appeal and their Work 1967–96', ch 7 in B Dickson and P Carmichael (eds), *The House of Lords: Its Parliamentary and Judicial Roles* (Oxford: Hart, 1998), which contains useful statistical information; M Barrett, *The Law Lords* (London: Macmillan, 2001).

[2] Dickson (n 1), 129–30; Barrett (n 1).　　　[3] SI 1994/3217.

[4] S Kentridge, 'The Highest Court: Selecting the Judges', Sir David Williams Lecture, May 2002.

[5] Robertson (n 1): '*The giant of the Court in the Eighties*', p 165, albeit with a second class chemistry degree.

[6] He sat only twice (*Dictionary of National Biography*).

[7] In his spell on the Woolsack between 1979 and 1987 he 'made a particularly determined effort to sit in as many Appellate Committee cases as possible': Barrett (n 1) 10.

at all,[8] Mackay on 82, and Irvine on eight occasions only. Peter Taylor as Lord Chief Justice sat only twice.[9]

None of the Law Lords had a background in politics. Of none could it be said that he was appointed for political reasons. Jauncey, Browne-Wilkinson, Hoffmann, and Clyde served in the Courts of Appeal of Jersey and Guernsey while still at the Bar. Steyn and Hoffmann were South African émigrés.

Only a handful—Keith (who served 19 years 10 months), Mackay and Hope from north of the border, Goff and Woolf from south of it—were in their 50s at the date of appointment; Brightman alone was over 70—the choice of his former pupil, Mrs Thatcher. Most soldiered on into their 70s. A statutory retiring age was fixed in 1993 at 75:[10] Lord Bridge reflected on this phenomenon with melancholy:

[S]ince the populist image of the geriatric judge, out of touch with the real world, is now reflected in the statutory presumption of judicial incompetence at the age of 75, this is the last time I shall speak judicially in your Lordships' House. I am happy that the occasion is one when I can agree with your Lordships still in the prime of judicial life who demonstrate so convincingly that common sense and the common law here go hand in hand.[11]

By contrast, Lord Mustill (like Lord Devlin of an earlier vintage) retired at the age of 65 while in the full bloom of his judicial career, and substituted scholarship and arbitration for the more structured life of the Appellate Committee.

In his latest analysis of the contemporary corridors of power, in 2003 Anthony Sampson could write without exaggeration: 'The Law Lords could not claim to represent or know about a wide section of the population, and most of them came from similar backgrounds to forty years ago. All of them were men from Oxford or Cambridge.'[12] The same pattern prevailed through the period.[13] Only Lord Bridge was not a university graduate. In retirement he made up for any deficiency in educational qualification. He adventitiously identified his talent for advocacy in defending a young soldier at a court-martial, and was called to the Bar at the relatively late age of 30, which adds piquancy to his complaint about his compelled retirement. By the end of the period there was still no woman, or member of an ethnic minority, in the highest court in the land.[14] Initially the Lords

---

[8] He held the office for four months.

[9] Although on one of those occasions in *R v Derby Magistrates' Court, ex p B* [1996] 1 AC 487, 507, he memorably described legal professional privilege as 'the fundamental condition on which the administration of justice as a whole depends'.

[10] Judicial Pensions and Retirement Act 1993, s 26.

[11] *Ruxley Electronics v Forsyth* [1996] 1 AC 344, 354.

[12] A Sampson, *Who Runs This Place?* (London: John Murray, 2003) 183. Lord Woolf, by then Lord Chief Justice, had been to UCL. See further Barrett (n 1) 58–69 for details of background, nationality, education, and legal career of the Law Lords in 2003.

[13] JA Griffith, *The Politics of the Judiciary* (London: Fontana, 4th edn 1991) 33 for a snapshot in 1986.

[14] See, for a discussion of the why and wherefore, K Mallinson, *The New Judiciary* (Aldershot: Ashgate, 1999) ch 4.

operated on the basis of the Gardiner disposition of 1969 that, absent the Lord Chancellor, the Senior Law Lord would preside and seniority would be governed by date of appointment to that office regardless of rank in peerage.

In 1984, Lord Hailsham announced that the Royal Commission appointing the deputy speakers for the purposes of judicial sittings would be reissued in a form that identified the two Law Lords (by implication not necessarily the most senior) who were to preside in the Lord Chancellor's absence. However, on that occasion Lord Diplock and Lord Fraser were appointed; and upon successive retirements, Lord Fraser and Lord Scarman; then Lord Scarman and Lord Keith; then Lord Bridge and Lord Keith, so that a change in principle permitted continuity in practice.

Lord Diplock, in a debate on the Hailsham statement on 27 June 1984, identified two qualities—presiding and judging—as not necessarily co-existing in any one judge, and noted: 'For efficient administration of justice in the highest court in the United Kingdom seniority ought not to be the sole criterion to preside. No reflection is intended on any appellate judge that he should sit in a court presided over by one appointed later than himself.'[15] James Vallance White, Clerk of the Lords 1983–2002, suggested a third criterion:[16] the supervision of the judicial business of the House of Lords. He proposed the appointment of a single Lord of Appeal in Ordinary to be the Senior Law Lord, which would enhance his status and emphasise his waxing administrative role necessary to compensate for the Lord Chancellor's waning involvement in the judicial business of the House. He identified that role as encompassing the day-to-day organisation of the judicial timetable; the choice of which Law Lords should sit on which appeal; the selection of retired Law Lords or former Lord Chancellors when a committee could not be fully manned by Lords of Appeal in Ordinary; decisions on the expedition and postponement of appeals; advice to the House authorities on judicial matters affecting the House; and the general oversight of the Judicial Standing Orders and Practice Directions. He shared the view of John Sainty[17] in 1989 that 'there is no overall strategic supervision of the House of Lords as a Court of Law',[18] and anticipated that of Michael Wheeler-Booth[19] who wrote: 'Diarchy has never seemed a particularly effective system of government and our present arrangements seem to suffer from all the inconveniences that were made fun of in the Gondoliers.'[20] His suggestion, however, did not bear fruit until Lord Keith's retirement, when Lord Goff (1996–8) and Lord Browne-Wilkinson (1998–2000) rejoiced in a singular status recognised in the letters patent.[21]

A singular incident illuminated the potential for administrative anarchy. Before the hearing of an appeal on a judicial review brought by Lonhro[22] to compel the

---

[15] *Hansard*, HL, vol 453, 917–18.   [16] In a note dated 1 July 1991.
[17] Clerk of the Parliaments.   [18] Note of 13 July 1989.
[19] Also Clerk of the Parliaments.   [20] Note of 11 July 1991.
[21] Upon the appointment of Lord Bingham in 2000 duality was restored.
[22] *Re Lonhro plc* [1990] 1 AC 154.

Secretary of State to publish a DTI report into the acquisition by the Al Fayeds of the House of Fraser, *The Observer* (owned by Lonhro) published a special issue with extracts from and comments on the report itself. The Appellate Committee dismissed the appeal but the House then ordered that the Appeal Committee should consider whether a contempt had been committed by Lonhro and its moving spirit, 'Tiny' Rowland.

Applications were made to its members to recuse themselves on the basis that justice would not be seen to be done when the Committee both initiated the prosecution and intended to rule upon the outcome, and (more radically) to have the whole issue of contempt adjudicated upon before the High Court. The Committee declined to abdicate the House's responsibility but, as a compromise, grudgingly recused itself. A second Committee held that there was no contempt proven. The unusual procedural manoeuvres, which did not burnish the Law Lords' reputation,[23] excited the concerns of the Lord Chancellor.[24] During the 1990s Lords Keith, Templeman, Goff, and Browne-Wilkinson acted in succession as the Senior Law Lord but each had his second-in-command.[25]

Whatever may have been the problems of internal administration, the House of Lords increased control of its own agenda. The Court of Appeal came to recognise that it should render unto the Lords the choice of the things which were for the Lords. An examination of 398 Court of Appeal transcripts for the first six months of 2001 showed that applications for leave to petition the Lords were made in 147 cases, but only two were granted.[26]

Lord Bingham explained the Lords' own policy: 'In its role as a Supreme Court the House must necessarily concentrate its attention on a relatively small number of cases recognised as raising legal questions of general public importance.'[27] The Lords conventionally sat in Committees of five,[28] exceptionally, for example over

---

[23] As a member of Lonhro's legal team I watched with a mixture of awe, apprehension, and amusement as Lord Ackner and Gordon Pollock QC traded blows over the relevance of the fact that Lord Ackner's father had been Mr Rowland's dentist. (He had also been the dentist of the father of Wilfred Bourne, permanent secretary of the Lord Chancellor's Department at the time Lord Mackay was pioneering his law reform programme.) This remote relationship nonetheless enhanced Bourne's irritation at the role of Lord Ackner, as *de facto* shop steward of the Law Lords' opposition to those reforms.

[24] The issue was whether a fresh reference needed to be made before the Appellate Committee adjudicated on the contempt. James Vallance-White, Note, 29 January 1992.

[25] For general background to the constitution and organisation of hearings see *Halsbury's Laws,* 4th edn, vol 10, paras 360–9, and for its revision of practice directions for criminal and civil appeals see para 375.

[26] G Drewry, L Blom-Cooper, and C Blake, *The Court of Appeal* (Oxford: Hart, 2007) 149. See too Dickson (n 1) 143–4. In 38 cases use was made of the leapfrog provisions of the Administration of Justice Act 1969, s 12.

[27] *R v DTI, ex p Eastaway* [2000] 1 WLR 2222, *per* Lord Bingham at 2228. The limitations on the ability of a litigant to appeal to the House of Lords were explored in this case and in *Re Poh* [1983] 1 WLR 2.

[28] For a critique of this as leading to arbitrary results, and undermining the authority of the Law Lords as a body, see D Robertson, 'The House of Lords as a Political and Constitutional Court: Lessons from the Pinochet Case' in D Woodhouse (ed), *The Pinochet Case: A Legal and Constitutional Analysis* (Oxford: Hart, 2000).

the issue of the historic advocate's immunity for negligence, in a Committee of seven,[29] and even sometimes nine. This continued to mean that the outcome of a case could be dictated by composition of the Committee, as I shall repeatedly illustrate in the remainder of this chapter.

Appeals were discussed, in the Committee room, immediately after counsel had been told to 'clear the bar', in order of juniority. Drafts would be exchanged thereafter—so that Lord Y had the opportunity in his speech to claim to have had the privilege—or it might be the advantage—of reading the draft opinion of 'My noble and learned friend Lord X', but this was not viewed as any reason restricting the addition of Lord Y's own opinion. The option of a unified or unanimous joint majority opinion was rarely taken.[30] What was a bonus for the likely academic could be a burden for the legal advisers.[31] What the Law Lords had decided was clear: why they had decided it not always so.[32]

The tranquility of the orthodox process was disturbed by the General Pinochet extradition cases,[33] which set precedents in many respects: it was the first time the Law Lords had set aside one of their own decisions and ordered a rehearing. It was the first time a Law Lord had sat although disqualified: Baroness Hale told the tale.[34]

'ex p Pinochet turned on the closeness of Lord Hoffmann's links, as one of two unpaid directors of Amnesty International Charity Ltd, a charity incorporated to undertake those aspects of the work of Amnesty International which are charitable under United Kingdom law, with the unincorporated body, Amnesty International which had intervened in the case in order to support the extradition of Senator Pinochet. Lord Hoffmann was not a member of Amnesty International, had no connection with the decision to intervene in the case, nor was there any suggestion that he was unable to bring his usual judicial mind to the authorities and the arguments in the case; he was nonetheless automatically disqualified because of his involvement in protecting the same causes in the same organisation, to the suit.'

[29] *Arthur JS Hall v Simons* [2002] 1 AC 615 overruling *Rondel v Worsley* [1969] 1 AC 191 on advocates' immunity. See too *Murphy v Brentwood DC* [1991] 1 AC 420; *Pepper v Hart* [1993] AC 593; *R v Bow Street Metropolitan Stipendiary Magistrate, ex p Pinochet Ugarte, Pinochet (No 3)* [2000] 1 AC 127.

[30] In *Re Prestige Group Ltd* [1984] 1 WLR 38 Lord Diplock suggested at 338 that a single reasoned speech had 'become a frequent practice of this House when dealing with questions of statutory construction' and explained how drafts were exchanged prior to delivery. After his departure the practice dwindled. It was Diplock's dislike of dissent that was as responsible as any other factor (*DNB*).

[31] Barrett (n 1) 124–7; Robertson (n 1) 15–16. Robertson summarised the position at p 35: 'small groups of senior lawyers with enormous practical discretion coming to decisions in relation to hurried Committee meetings after exhaustive (and exhausting) oral argument'.

[32] See *Wheeler v Leicester CC* [1985] 1 AC 1054 where the Law Lords held unlawful, for a spectrum of reasons, a ban by the City Council on the use of their recreation ground by a rugby club, three of whose members had toured South Africa. Robertson (n 1) 240–4.

[33] See D Woodhouse (ed), *The Pinochet Case: A Legal and Constitutional Analysis* (Oxford: Hart, 2000) esp Robertson pp 25–31: 'Lord Hoffmann and the Question of Bias'. See too Barrett (n 1) 174–81. *Pinochet (No 1)* [2001] 1 AC 61; *Pinochet (No 2)* [2001] 1 AC 119; *Pinochet (No 3)* [2001] 1 AC 147.

[34] In *R v Abdroikov* [2007] 1 WLR 2679.

Lord Hoffmann, too, did not consider that his attitude towards the complex problem of sovereign immunity could conceivably be affected by his indirect involvement in a virtuous organisation whose general aims would not be inconsistent with those of any right thinking person.[35] It was his consequent omission to make full disclosure to (his colleagues[36] or) the parties that prompted the successful call for a rehearing.

The episode caused a certain *froideur* between Lord Slynn, who presided in *Pinochet No 1*, and Lord Hoffmann, as well as huge, if temporary, embarrassment to the House. Calls for Lord Hoffmann's resignation mercifully fell on deaf ears;[37] he was the workhorse of the Committee (of a pure thoroughbred variety) with an unrivalled range of expertise.[38]

Pinochet set another precedent too. It was the first major case in which delivery of a judgment of the House (with, unusually, oral summaries of their speeches for public consumption) was televised. Previous requests to film actual hearings made by the BBC in 1992 and 1996 had either been rejected by the Law Lords or made subject to conditions intolerable to the broadcasters.[39] If it continued to be a fundamental precept of common law that justice should not only be done, but also be seen to be done, it was not yet to be seen through the camera's lens.

The contemporary relish for case management was reflected even at the level of the Lords, in particular by the efforts to curtail excessive oral presentation. Not only were counsel increasingly asked to estimate in hours the anticipated length of submissions—an exercise complicated by their inability to predict the amount of judicial intervention—but Lord Templeman in several trenchant *dicta* trumpeted his preference for brevity.[40] In the *Tin Council* case[41] he said:

Ten counsel addressed the Appellate Committee for 26 days. This vast amount of written and oral material tended to obscure the fundamental principles . . . [I]n my opinion the length of oral argument permitted in future appeals should be subject to prior limitation by the Appellate Committee.[42]

---

[35] He told the *Daily Telegraph*, 'The fact is I am not biased, I am a lawyer, I do things as a judge.'

[36] He did discuss it with Gordon Slynn (who presided) but no action ensued.

[37] R Stevens, *The English Judges: Their Role in a Changing Constitution* (Oxford: Hart, 2005) 107–11.

[38] One legacy was a multitude of so-called Hoffmann points being taken in a variety of cases in the lower courts, until the Court of Appeal staunched the flow with a series of judicial guidelines: *Locabail v Bayfield Properties Ltd* [2000] QB 451.

[39] See J Rozenberg [1999] PL 178. The Law Lords, despite addressing the issue among themselves, never gave general permission for proceedings in Committees to be televised, thus creating an exception to the permission given by the House in 1984 for televising of their proceedings (the BBC and other authorised broadcasters had since that date been free prior to *Pinochet* to televise judgments, although they had rarely exercised that freedom.)

[40] Discussed in M Beloff QC, 'The Art of Advocacy', Margaret Howard Memorial Lecture, Oxford 2000, and 'Advocacy—A Craft Under Threat?' First Espeland Lecture 2002, Oslo.

[41] *Rayner (Mincing Lane) Ltd v DTI* [1990] 2 AC 418.

[42] At 418. See too *Banque Keyser Ullman SA v Shandia (UK) Insurance Limited* [1991] AC 249 at 280–2 ('torrent of words, written and oral'). *Ashmore v Corporation of Lloyd's* [1992] 1 WLR 446 at 453 ('every point conceivable and inconceivable without judgment or discrimination'). Between 1982 and 2000 I appeared myself before the Lords on 37 occasions. For the Bar, once Lord Diplock

Nonetheless, oral tradition of the common law survived these assaults. Even while abolishing the advocates' immunity, the Law Lords recognised the importance of the advocates. In the words of Lord Hoffmann: 'The substantial orality of the English system of trial and appellate procedure means that judges rely heavily upon the advocates appearing before them for a fair presentation of the facts and adequate alternate instruction in the law.'[43] A prominent academic briefed (unusually) in the House summed up the *mise en scène*:[44] 'Notwithstanding the informality, the atmosphere can be tense, the pressure put on counsel considerable . . .', and drew a not altogether convincing analogy with the Oxbridge tutorial.

Interventions by third parties (oral or in writing) multiplied before the Lords,[45] the *Pinochet* case providing an example—*hinc illae lacrimae*. As early as 1980[46] Anthony Lester QC was allowed a dual role, but Lord Edmund-Davies said: 'that is an indulgence which can only be allowed with the consent of the other side.'[47] Such indulgence rapidly became established practice, and the requirement for parties' consent was discarded.

Of equal note was the shift in the character of interveners: from invitees *of* the court, to applicants *to* the court; from official bodies (like the EOC), to pressure groups (like Liberty, Amnesty, or Justice). Not all commentators regarded this development with unalloyed enthusiasm,[48] but it had increased, was increasing, and seemed unlikely to diminish.

Fidelity to their own decisions still reigned at the level of the Lords, notwithstanding their freedom under the Practice Statement 1966[49] 'to depart from a precedent where it appears right to do so'. The House identified cases in which

---

(whose breathing difficulties made him almost inaudible to those at the podium) had yielded the chairmanship, the toughest characters were indeed Lord Templeman, who earned the soubriquet 'Sid Vicious' after a contemporary punk rock star, and Lord Brandon. Lords Keith and Bridge were for different reasons awkward customers: Lords Hoffmann and Hobhouse were formidable in pursuit. The others by and large muffled their intellectual acuity with courtesy. Lord Fraser's relaxed chairmanship once allowed nine days to be spent on argument over the meaning of two words: 'ordinarily resident': *Ex p Shah* [1983] 2 AC 309.

[43] *Arthur JS Hall & Co v Simons* [2002] AC 615, 692. There was, however, a marked move away from oral hearing of petitions. See Drewry, Blom-Cooper, and Blake (n 26) 159; Dickson (n 1) 153.

[44] BS Markesinis, 'Five Days in the House of Lords: Some Comparative Reflections on *White v Jones*' (1995) 3 Torts LJ 169–204.

[45] See House of Lords Practice Directions and Standing Orders Applicable to Civil Appeals, House of Lords (January 1996), Direction 34.1; *R v Secretary of State for the Home Department, ex p Venables, R v Secretary of State for the Home Department, ex p Thompson* [1998] AC 407; *Pinochet (No 1)* [2000] AC 61; *R v Immigration Appeal Tribunal, ex p Shah* [1999] 2 AC 629: see generally L Blom-Cooper QC, 'Third Party Intervention and Judicial Discretion' [2002] PL 602; S Hannett, 'Third Party Intervention in the Public Interest' [2003] PL 128.

[46] In the case of *Leyland Case v Vyas* [1980] AC 1028 raising issues of discovery in discrimination law of concern not only to the litigants but to the Commission for Racial Equality (CRE) and the Equal Opportunities Commission (EOC).

[47] At 1032–3.

[48] C Harlow, 'Public Law and Popular Justice' [2002] MLR 1; Blom-Cooper (n 45).

[49] [1966] 1 WLR 1274—a reform to which Sir Thomas Legg, later Permanent Secretary to the Lord Chancellor's Department, then the youngest member of the office, lent support, based on research, as is the practice of other supreme courts.

they could exploit it, which displayed 'no special reasons against departure' mentioned in the statement,[50] which were 'not likely to be taken into account to a significant extent by individuals ... in ordering their affairs',[51] which engaged 'a broad issue of justice and public policy and an important question of a legal principle',[52] or in which the decision challenged was in collision with 'long established principles'[53] or was 'widely regarded as an unsatisfactory decision',[54] not least when it had been the subject of 'reasoned and outspoken criticism' by leading scholars and senior judges.[55] But in fact the Lords overruled themselves on only five occasions between 1982 and 2000.[56]

Notably in *Khawaja*[57] the Lords departed from a decision which had been handed down barely three years earlier,[58] on the issue of whether a court reviewing a decision of an immigration officer that someone was an 'illegal entrant' and hence liable to summary removal was confined to a *Wednesbury* scrutiny or to an unrestricted survey of the evidence. Lord Wilberforce, who had delivered the earlier judgment, sat again but declined the 'white sheet of repentance' donned by Lord Bridge, in confessing[59] to an earlier error in interpreting the powers of a magistrates' court to enforce a maintenance order. Lord Bridge described it with modesty as 'a becoming garment'.[60] Lord Wilberforce's concurring judgment in *Khawaja* read like a dissent, whereas Lord Fraser, who had also sat in *Zamir*, readily admitted to having been on that occasion simply wrong.

The House overruled another significant Wilberforce decision, which had imposed a duty on a local authority to compensate a building owner for the cost of remedying a dangerous defect, the result of the authority's negligent failure to ensure that it was erected in conformity with the applicable standards.[61]

---

[50] *R v Secretary of State for Home Department, ex p Khawaja* [1984] AC 74, Lord Fraser of Tullybelton at 98D, Lord Bridge of Harwich at 125D.

[51] *Murphy v Brentwood DC* [1991] AC 398, *per* Lord Keith of Kinkel at 472.

[52] *R v Secretary of State for Home Department, ex p Khawaja* [1984] AC 74, *per* Lord Bridge of Harwich at 125F.

[53] *Murphy v Brentwood DC* [1991] AC 398, *per* Lord Keith of Kinkel at 471A–472A.

[54] ibid.   [55] Lord Goff in *Frost v Chief Constable of South Yorkshire* [1999] 2 AC 254, 473.

[56] *R v Shivpuri* [1987] AC 1 (it is no defence for a defendant charged with a criminal attempt for him to say that it would in fact have been impossible to commit the crime. *Anderton v Ryan* [1985] AC 560, HL overruled); *R v Howe* [1987] AC 417 (duress cannot be a defence to murder, *DPP for Northern Ireland v Lynch* [1975] AC 653 overruled); '*Murphy v Brentwood DC* [1991] 1 AC 398 (a local authority is not liable in tort for negligent application of building regulations, where the resulting defects are discovered before physical injury occurs. The loss suffered is purely economic. *Anns v Merton LBC* [1978] AC 728, HL overruled); *Khawaja* [1984] AC 74 (*Zamir v Secretary of State for the Home Department* [1980] AC 930, HL overruled); *R v Adomako* [1995] 1 AC 171 (negligent manslaughter) (*R v Seymour* [1983] 2 AC 493 not followed). See too ch 9 in this volume.

[57] n 56 The conjoined case of Khera appeared.

[58] *Zamir v secretary of State for the Home Department* [1980] AC 930, HL; 'a remarkable turn-about': Griffith (n 13) 179; for an analysis of what changed their minds: ibid, 179–81; Robertson (n 1) 309–12.

[59] *Re Wilson* [1985] AC 750.   [60] At 769.

[61] *Murphy v Brentwood DC* [1991] AC 398, another seven-member Committee overruling *Anns* [1978] AC 78 (n 56). Robertson (n 1) 211–17 describes *Murphy* as part of 'the counter-revolution'.

Prospective overruling, however, reconsidered in the next decade,[62] still remained beyond the Lords' ken.[63]

On some occasions the Lords, identifying some lacuna in the law, would recommend prompt parliamentary action. Lord Goff, commenting en route that 'hurried amendments to carefully tuned comprehensive bills are an accident prone form of proceeding',[64] noted that a provision of a mortgage advance was not a service for the purposes of section 1 of the Theft Act 1978.[65] He later seconded the bill, which became the Theft (Amendment) Act 1996 when given its second reading in the House of Lords. (Sometimes, as is the case with Private Clegg,[66] their recommendation was not succeeded by action.)[67]

On other occasions, conscious that Parliament might not be swift to act, the Law Lords themselves acted as agents for reform. They held that taxes payable by a citizen to a public authority in response to an unlawful demand were prima facie recoverable 'as of right'.[68] Lord Goff noted: 'However compelling the principle of justice may be it would never be sufficient to persuade a government to propose its legislative recognition by Parliament: caution, otherwise known as the Treasury, would never allow this to happen.'[69] He added whimsically, in response to a submission that to alter the law would be to trespass over the boundary dividing the responsibility of judges and legislators: 'although I am well aware of the existence of the boundary, I am never quite sure where to find it.'[70]

On yet other occasions the House recognised that the subject matter called for legislative intervention but knew it was a call in vain. The issue of whether feeding by tube could be withdrawn for a patient in a persistent vegetative state, according to Lord Mustill, 'cries out for exploration in depth by Parliament'.[71] Parliament preferred to leave such divisive moral decisions to the judges.

Statutory construction embraced a liberating philosophy. Lord Steyn succinctly traced the developments:[72]

Towards the end of the last century Pollock characterised the approach of judges to statutory construction as follows: 'Parliament generally changes the law for the worse, and that the business of the judges is to keep the mischief of its interference within the narrowest possible

---

[62] *Re Spectrum* [2005] 2 AC 680.

[63] *Kleinwort Benson Ltd v Lincoln CC* [1999] 2 AC 349, *per* Lord Goff at 379.

[64] At 832.   [65] *R v Preddy* [1996] AC 815.

[66] *R v Clegg* [1995] 1 AC 482 (could murder by mistake be reduced to manslaughter). Endorsed by the Law Commission in 2006.

[67] Discussed in J Rozenberg, *Trial of Strength* (London: Richard Cohen, 1997) 124–30; also *C v DPP* [1996] 1 AC 1 (presumption as to whether a child under 14 is presumed to be incapable of committing a crime was still part of English law: Rozenberg, ibid, 131–2).

[68] *Woolwich Building Society v IRC* [1993] AC 70.   [69] At 176.   [70] At 173.

[71] *Bland v Airedale NHS Trust* [1993] AC 789. See J Finnis, '*Bland*: Crossing the Rubicon' (1993) 109 LQR 329; J Rozenberg, *The Search for Justice* (London: Hodder & Stoughton, 1994) 29–30.

[72] *McGuckian v Inland Review Comrs* [1997] 1 WLR 991, 999.

bounds' . . . Whatever the merits of this observation may have been when it was made, or even earlier in this century, it is demonstrably no longer true. During the last 30 years there has been a shift away from literalist to purposive methods of construction. Where there is no obvious meaning of a statutory provision the modern emphasis is on a contextual approach designed to identify the purpose of a statute and to give effect to it.[73]

The approach to tax avoidance schemes exemplified the trend. The watershed case of *Ramsay,* dealing with artificial multi-step transactions,[74] 'seemed to herald the introduction in the United Kingdom of a judicially developed new approach to counteract tax avoidance schemes'.[75] But there was no development of a USA-type 'Business purpose' perspective. The judgment of the same academic was that the record of the UK case law in that area over the last 25 years had not been impressive.[76]

A particular milestone (or, in the view of some, millstone) was the decision in *Pepper v Hart.*[77] The Lords decided that the rule excluding reference to parliamentary material as an aid to statutory construction should be relaxed where a triple test was satisfied: that the legislation was ambiguous or obscure or, if read literally, absurd: that the material relied upon consisted of one or more statements by a Minister or other promoter of the bill; and that the statements relied upon were clear.[78] Only Lord Mackay LC, with the perspective of a Cabinet Minister, well conscious of budgetary considerations, dissented.[79] Advocates tended to honour the rule more in the breach than in the observance; and the Lords had to remind themselves of the limits as well as the reach of the principle.[80] Doubt was also cast later on the constitutional soundness of the principle itself.[81]

Construction of contracts broke further free from ancient fetters. Lord Hoffmann epitomised the changes over the previous two decades:[82]

The result has been subject to one important exception, to assimilate the way in which such documents are interpreted by judges to the common sense principles by which any

---

[73] See eg *Mandla v Dowell Lee* [1983] 2 AC 548 (Sikhs a race for the purpose of anti-discrimination law but for a criticism of judicial reasoning in this area see Robertson (n 1) ch 3). The Lords were not enthusiasts of the procedures of the CRE: *R v CRE, ex p Hillingdon BC* [1987] AC 779 and *Prestige v CRE* [1984] 1 WLR 335 when Lord Diplock said (at 347): 'No argument was advanced in that instant appeal which was not put to the House in Hillingdon, although not all such arguments were regarded as meriting specific mention in my speech.'

[74] *WT Ramsay Ltd v IRC* [1982] AC 300. See too *Furniss v Dawson* [1984] AC 474.

[75] J Freedman, 'Interpreting Tax Statutes: Tax Avoidance and the Intention of Parliament' (2007) 123 LQR 53.

[76] ibid.   [77] [1993] AC 593; see Robertson (n 1) ch 5.   [78] At 604.

[79] At 615. A purist would suggest that he should have recused himself.

[80] K Mullan, 'The Impact of Pepper and Hart' in Dickson and Carmichael (n 1) ch 11. See *Mcllimish v BMI* [1996] AC 454, *per* Lord Browne-Wilkinson at 482: 'Judges should be astute to check such misuse of the new rule by making appropriate orders as to costs wasted.'

[81] Lord Steyn, '*Pepper v Hart*: A Re-examination' (2001) 21 OJLS 59. See for further discussion of its ambit *R v Secretary of State for the Environment, Transport and the Regions, ex p Spath Holme Ltd* [2001] 2 AC 349.

[82] *West Bromwich Building Society v Investors Compensation Scheme* [1998] 1 WLR 896, 912.

serious utterance would be interpreted in ordinary life. Almost all the old intellectual baggage of 'legal' interpretation has been discarded.

Increasing use was made of academic materials.[83] As recently as 1980 Lord Wilberforce referred to 'the dangers well perceived by our predecessors but tending to be neglected in modern times, of placing reliance on textbook authority for an analysis of judicial decisions'.[84] These dangers were increasingly ignored. Wade's explanation that a public authority may only exercise powers for the public purpose for which they were conferred—a key principle of public law—was quoted with approval by Lord Bridge.[85] In *Roy*,[86] which sounded the first note of retreat from the procedural morass of *O'Reilly v Mackman*, Lord Lowry referred presciently to academic writers' (critical) analysis of the rule it purported to lay down.

In *Re M*,[87] Wade's powerful article 'Injunctive Relief Against the Crown'[88] was expressly relied upon in Lord Woolf's leading speech. Lord Goff, himself a distinguished author and a former don, made use of a variety of academic material produced by scholars on restitution in the *Woolwich* case[89] and both he and Lord Mustill considered commentary in the seminal insurance case of *Pan Atlantic*.[90] There was a growing receptiveness too to the use of foreign law.[91] In 1992 Sir Thomas Bingham MR rightly wrote,[92] 'Recent years have seen a more international outlook and growing willingness to learn from others.' Lord Steyn explained in *MacFarlane*:[93]

The discipline of comparative law does not aim at a poll of solutions adopted in different cultures. It has a different and inestimable value of sharpening focus on the weight of competing considerations.[94]

Resort was made in speeches to overseas material from the Commonwealth and the USA in the field of torts in *Murphy v Brentwood*[95] and *Arthur Hall*,[96] in the field of restitution in *Woolwich*,[97] in the field of abuse of process in

---

[83] See generally M Beloff QC, 'The Academic Influences on Judicial Review' in R Gordon (ed), *Judicial Review in the New Millennium* (London: Sweet & Maxwell, 2003).
[84] *Johnson v Agnew* [1980] AC 367, 395.
[85] *R v Tower Hamlets LBC, ex p Chetnik* [1988] AC 858, *per* Lord Bridge at 872.
[86] *Roy v Kensington & Chelsea LBC* [1992] 1 AC 624, 653.
[87] *M v Home Office* [1994] 1 AC 377.
[88] (1991) 107 LQR 41.
[89] *Woolwich Building Society v IRC* [1993] AC 70, 166–7.
[90] *Pan Atlantic Insurance Ltd v Pine Top Ltd* [1995] 1 AC 501, 517, 526, 533.
[91] C Saunders, 'Comparative Constitutional Law in the Courts: Is there a Problem?' (2006) 59 CLP 91.
[92] 'There is a World Elsewhere: The Changing Perspectives of English Law' (1992) 41 ICLQ 51.
[93] *MacFarlane v Tayside Health Board* [2000] 2 AC 59.
[94] At 81C–D. In *R v Khan* [1977] AC 558 Lord Nolan said: 'Every system of law stands to benefit by an awareness of the answers given by other courts and tribunals to similar problems' (at 583).
[95] [1991] AC 398, *per* Lord Keith at 469D–470B; Lord Bridge at 473G–474C, 476B–479.
[96] [2002] 1 AC 615 at 680–1.
[97] Lord Goff at 174: 'At this stage of the argument, I find it helpful to turn to recent developments in Canada.'

Bennett,[98] in defamation in *Derbyshire,*[99] and in the field of conflict of laws in *Patel.*[100] The globalisation of litigation itself led to significant decisions in the determination of the appropriate forum for parent company liability.[101]

International law itself continued to be treated as alien, save where expressly incorporated by statute or custom: the limited relevance of a Treaty in domestic litigation was classically explained by Lord Oliver in the *Tin Council* case.[102] Nonetheless its indirect influence was acknowledged. The principle that domestic law should, where possible, be construed as consonant with the United Kingdom's international obligations was reiterated.[103] And where international conventions fell to be construed, the House recognised that it was desirable to achieve, if possible, consistency with courts in other countries.[104]

Consistently the European Convention on Human Rights in particular remained an instrument with direct resonance only on the plane of international law. The Human Rights Act 1998, which domesticated its provisions, allowed for a gap between its enactment and implementation of two years and became directly effective in English Courts only from 2 October 2000.[105] The House of Lords resisted the invitation to smuggle in through the back door that which was barred from the front by refusing to accept that it should be a relevant influence on administrative discretion. Concomitantly they rejected as a principle of common law proportionality, whose emergence as a discrete ground for judicial review had been adumbrated as long ago as 1984 in Lord Diplock's speech in the *GCHQ* case.[106] Lord Lowry explained in *Brind*: '[T]here can be very little room for judges to operate an independent judicial review proportionality doctrine in the space which is left between the conventional judicial doctrine and the admittedly forbidden appellate approach.'[107] Nonetheless, Convention law seeped through the cracks of the national system[108] in a number of ways (although in those cases which reached the Appellate Committee the Law Lords in a self-congratulatory mode detected no gap, still less gulf, between the

---

[98] *R v Horseferry Road Magistrates' Court, ex p Bennett* [1994] AC 42, [60]–[61]; Robertson (n 1) 138–42.

[99] *Derbyshire CC v Times Newspapers Ltd* [1993] AC 534.

[100] *Airbus Industries GEI v Patel* [1999] 1 AC 119. Lord Goff said at 133: 'In this connection it is helpful to turn to other common law jurisdictions.'

[101] *Connelly v RTZ Corp plc* [1998] AC 854 where the decision turned on the availability of legal aid in England and its absence in Namibia: see generally C McClachlan, 'International Litigation and the Reworking of the Conflict of Laws' [2000] LQR 580.

[102] *Rayner (Mincing Lane) v DTI* [1990] 2 AC 418, 500–1.

[103] *Garland v British Rail Engineering Ltd* [1983] 2 AC 751 which considered the impact of Article 119 of the EU Treaty.

[104] *Fothergill v Monarch Airlines* [1981] AC 251.

[105] Although see *R v DPP, ex p Kebilene* [2000] 2 AC 236 where the applicant unsuccessfully sought to fetter the DPP's prosecutorial discretions in advance reliance on the Act.

[106] [1985] AC 374, 410.   [107] At 766–7.

[108] The Maiden Speech of Lord Bingham of Cornhill LCJ, *Hansard*, HL, vol 573, cols 1465–6 (3 July 1996); M Beloff QC and H Mountfield, 'Unconventional Convention' [1996] EHRLR 462, 490–1.

common law and the Convention).[109] Lord Browne-Wilkinson recognised extra-judicially that in those areas affected by the EC Treaties, the ECHR was indirectly incorporated into English law,[110] and the Lords fashioned independently a principle of legality by which not only ambiguous words, but also general words, should be construed as incapable of overriding basic human rights.[111]

The impact of Community law triggered by the European Communities Act 1972 resembled more a slow burning fuse than an explosion.[112] When the Spanish fishermen objected to a Fisheries Act designed to protect the interests of the native fleet, the Lords found it, almost two decades on, incompatible with the provisions of the Treaty of Rome. Lord Bridge[113] commented on the chasm between popular understanding and legal reality:

> Some public comments on the decisions of the ECJ affirming the jurisdiction of the Courts of member states to override national legislation if necessary to enable interim relief to be granted in protection of rights under community law have suggested that this was a novel and dangerous invasion by a community institution of the Sovereignty of the UK Parliament. But such comments are based on a misconception. Under the terms of the Act of 1972 it has always been clear that it was the duty of a United Kingdom Court when delivering final judgment to override any national law found to be in conflict with any directly enforceable rule of community law.

Yet in determining the extent to which UK law should be construed as compliant with EU law, the Lords oscillated between the chauvinist and the communautaire.[114]

The House of Lords considered up to 50 cases a year across a wider spectrum of subjects—and not, as is popularly believed, with an overweight of tax cases.[115] As to the quality of the Lords' judgments, David Robertson, an Oxford academic and political scientist, studied 407 cases decided between 1986 and 1995 and found them more cautious than creative: too consequentialist; too willing to leave necessary reform to Parliament; too pragmatic; too incrementalist. He described Lords as having 'the ideology of old middle-class men...but they are untypical even of that social category—they have soaked up the ethos of tough minded liberalism of those who run an administrative state'.[116] Academics may remain

---

[109] *Derbyshire CC v Times Newspapers Ltd* [1993] AC 534 (freedom of expression); *R v Governor of the Maze Prison, ex p Hone* [1988] AC 379 (prison discipline).

[110] Lord Browne-Wilkinson, 'The Infiltration of a Bill of Rights' [1992] PL 397.

[111] *R v Secretary of State for Home Department, ex p Pierson* [1998] AC 539 (the right there engaged being no aggravation of penalties), Lord Browne-Wilkinson at 523–4.

[112] See B Fitzpatrick, 'A Dualist House of Lords in a Sea of Monist Community Law?', ch 9 in Dickson and Carmichael (n 1).

[113] *R v Secretary of State for Transport, ex p Factortame Ltd* [1991] AC 603, 658–9.

[114] Fitzpatrick (n 112) 188–92. Contrast *Duke v GEC* [1988] AC 618, *per* Lord Templeman at 641: 'There is no authority for the proposition that a Court of a member state must distort the meaning of a domestic status so as to conform with community law which is not directly applicable' with *Foster v British Gas plc* [1991] 2 AC 306, *Lister v Forth Dry Dock* [1991] 1 AC 546, *Webb v EMO Cargo Ltd* [1993] 1 WLR 49.

[115] See table in (2000) 53 CLP 96–97 for the years 1997–8.   [116] Robertson (n 1) 401.

the court from whose verdict there is no appeal; but Sir Sydney Kentridge QC, closer professionally to the scene of the action, provided an alternative perspective in 2002: 'Now and at least for many years past the Appellate Committee has been intellectually impressive, impartial, fair-minded and I believe open-minded.'[117] *Tot homines, quot sententiae!* I highlight only the main developments.[118]

Judicial review[119] had its origins in the judicial interventionism of the mid-1960s. It was stimulated by, amongst other factors, the introduction of a unified application for the remedy[120] (the significant procedural divide between public and private law detected by Lord Diplock in the seminal case of *O'Reilly v Mackman*[121] injected a virus into the system which it took almost two decades to expel.[122] Fortunately that which the House had brought to birth, it also helped to bury[123]).

The 1980s and 1990s witnessed a considerable expansion of judicial activity in this sphere.[124] The Lords expanded prisoners' rights, with Lord Wilberforce expressing the principle, 'Under English law a convicted prisoner, in spite of his imprisonment, retains all civil rights which are not taken away expressly or by necessary implication.'[125] They struck down restrictions on prisoners' complaints.[126] They obliged prison governors to obey the rules of natural justice,[127] although they shrank from according to prisoners a right to damages for breach of prison rules.[128]

The libertarian lamp flickered less evenly where immigrants' rights were concerned. Immigrants' victories such as *Khawaja*[129] and *Bugdaycay*[130] (anxious scrutiny in asylum cases) were counterbalanced by executive success in *Oladehinde*[131] (Secretary of State could delegate his power to deport) and *Abdi*[132] (fast

---

[117] Kentridge (n 4).

[118] For an overview of the contribution on a wider time frame see chapters in Part D of this volume.

[119] J Jowell, 'Restraining the State: Politics, Principle and Judicial Review' (1997) 50 CLP 189, 193–4.

[120] Rules of the Supreme Court (Amendment No 3) 1977, SI 1977/1955, Supreme Court Act 1981, s 31. See also M Beloff QC, 'Proceedings in the UK' in *Judicial Review of Administrative Action* (Strasbourg: Engele Verlag, 1989).

[121] [1983] 2 AC 237.

[122] M Beloff QC, '*O'Reilly v Mackman*: A Cautionary Tale' in v Iyer (ed), *Constitutional Perspectives: Essays in Honour and in Memory of HM Seervai* (Delhi: Universal, 2001) 227.

[123] *Roy v Kensington and Chelsea and Westminster FPC* [1992] 1 AC 624, 628; *Steed v Home Department* [2000] 1 WLR 1169, 1175.

[124] Despite this, Griffiths maintains his thesis that 'The judiciary is not placed constitutionally in opposition to the government but, in the overwhelming mass of circumstances alongside it' (n 13) 317.

[125] *Raymond v Honey* [1983] AC 1, 12.   [126] Robertson (n 1) 320–8.

[127] *Leech v Governors of Parkhurst Prison* [1985] 1 AC 533; Robertson (n 1) 328–35.

[128] *R v Deputy Governor of Parkhurst Prison, ex p Hague* [1992] 1 AC 58.

[129] [1984] AC 74.   [130] [1987] AC 514; Robertson (n 1) 312.

[131] *R v Secretary of State for the Home Department, ex p Oladehinde* [1991] AC 250; Robertson (n 1) 291–300.

[132] *R v Secretary of State for Home Department, ex p Abdi* [1996] 1 WLR 298; Robertson (n 1) 319–25.

track process to remove refugees found lawful). In only one homelessness case did the applicant ever defeat the local authority in the Lords,[133] and in that case Lord Wilberforce doubted whether the Housing (Homeless Persons) Act 1977 'is as well considered as it undoubtedly is well intentioned'.[134]

In the *GCHQ* case the Lords held that in principle the prerogative power was open to review.[135] It also gave an imprimatur to the concept of a legitimate expectation giving rise to a fair hearing[136] and recognised that a mere assertion of national security could not wholly exclude judicial scrutiny. In the same appeal Lord Diplock essayed a summary of the then State of the Art, which was incomplete and soon to be rendered outdated, such was the pace of change.[137]

In 1989, the Lords issued an injunction against the Crown in reliance on paramount community law.[138] In *Re M*[139] a similar power was recognised in a purely domestic law context: a finding of contempt was made against a minister who breached an undertaking opinion on his behalf to a court, Lord Templeman observing that a contrary conclusion would 'reverse the result of the Civil War'.[140] While a general right to reasons was still no part of English public law, the Lords recognised that it existed as a sub-set of fairness, and (significantly) to assist the court in exercising its supervisory role.[141]

The Lords were astute to contain the exotic financial manoeuvres of local government.[142] They held too, by reference to EU law, that restrictions on rights of employees to bring claims for unfair dismissal and redundancy payments were indirectly discriminatory.[143] Lord Keith treated with contumely the material introduced by the Secretary of State to buttress his contention that the restriction increased the availability of part-time work, saying that it did not contain 'anything capable of being regarded as factual evidence demonstrating the correctness of these views'.[144]

The current did not flow unimpeded in a single direction. They recognised the potential for delay of valuable initiatives.[145] When the Lords held unlawful the

---

[133] Robertson (n 1) 333–67; *R v Hillingdon LBC, ex p Islam* [1983] 1 AC 688; *Din v Wandsworth LBC* [1983] 1 AC 652; *R v Hillingdon LBC, ex p Puhlhofer* [1986] 1 AC 484; *Garlick v Oldham BC* [1993] AC 509; *R v Newham DC, ex p Smith* [1994] 2 AC 402.
[134] *Islam*, ibid, 708.
[135] *Council for the Civil Service Unions v Minister for the Civil Service* [1985] AC 374.
[136] See also *R v IRC, ex p Preston* [1985] AC 835.
[137] At 408–9. It did not, for example, note the sliding scale of review—less intense in political economic matters: *Nottinghamshire CC v DoE* [1986] AC 240; Robertson (n 1) 288–300, more intense in human rights cases: *R v Home Department, ex p Bugdaycay* [1987] AC 554; Robertson (n 1) 318.
[138] *R v Secretary of State, ex p Factortame (No 2)* [1989] 1 AC 603.
[139] [1994] 1 AC 377; Robertson (n 1) 276–9. [140] At 395.
[141] *R v Secretary of State for Home Department, ex p Doody* [1994] 1 AC 531.
[142] *Hazell v Hammersmith LBC* [1992] 2 AC 1.
[143] *R v Secretary of State, ex p EOC* [1995] 1 AC 1; Robertson (n 1) 279–84.
[144] See P Maxwell, 'The House of Lords as a Constitutional Court', ch 10 in Dickson and Carmichael (n 1). *The Times* of 5 March 1994 commented that 'Britain may now have for the first time in its history a constitutional court.'
[145] *R v ITC, ex p TSW* [1996] JR 185.

decision of the Secretary of State not to introduce a statutory scheme for criminal injury compensation,[146] Lord Mustill (in the minority) said in cautionary mode:[147]

Some of the arguments addressed would have the court push to the very boundaries of the distinction between court and Parliament established in, and recognised ever since, the Bill of Rights 1689. Three hundred years have passed since then, and the political and social landscape has changed beyond recognition. But the boundaries remain; they are of crucial significance to our private and public lives; and the courts should I believe make sure that they are not overstepped.

In *Venables*[148] the Lords split again on whether the Home Secretary could set a fixed tariff for the period of detention to be served by a young offender. The majority held that the Home Secretary was not entitled to take account of the *vox populi* in the form of petitions, but Lord Lloyd said:

[I]t is to the Home Secretary that Parliament has entrusted the task of maintaining confidence in the criminal justice system and as part of that task gauging public concern in relation to a particular case when deciding on the earliest release date. I do not regard it as the function of the court to tell him how to perform that task.[149]

Truly a house divided against itself! One commentator spoke presciently of the development of the House of Lords into a true supreme court;[150] Lord Irvine in his role as putative Lord Chancellor pre-emptively counselled against judicial supremacism[151]—but in vain.

Certainty of the criminal law, a desirable component above all, was not perfectly achieved.[152] Whether or not recklessness has been replaced by gross negligence as the key element in manslaughter was not clear in the wake of the decisions in *Seymour*[153] and *Adomako*.[154] The delineation of the mental element for murder in *Moloney*[155] was qualified in *Hancock*[156] *and Woollin*. In *Gomez*,[157] when the Lords held that a person who obtains another's property by deception

---

[146] *R v Secretary of State for the Home Department, ex p Fire Brigades Union* [1995] 2 AC 513; Robertson (n 1) 267–8.

[147] At 547. Lord Mustill, however, was in the minority in seeking to subject a university visitor to judicial review. *R v University of Hull, ex p Page* [1993] AC 682.

[148] *R v Secretary of State for the Home Department, ex p Venables* [1998] AC 407. See also *R v Secretary of State for Home Department, ex p Pierson* [1998] AC 539 on the sentence of a mandatory life prisoner.

[149] At 517.

[150] M Beloff QC, 'Towards a Supreme Court: The British Experience', John Kelly Memorial Lecture, University College Dublin, 1997.

[151] Lord Irvine of Lairg, 'Judges and Decision-makers—The Theory and Practice of Wednesbury Review' [1996] PL 59.

[152] I Dennis, 'The Critical Condition of Criminal Law' [1997] CLP 213: 'Many lawyers feel that the House of Lords is at its worst in these criminal cases'. Lee (n 1) 144: 'Law Lords themselves will admit off the record that their historical performance in criminal law is woeful.' Robertson (n 1) 319.

[153] [1983] 2 AC 493.   [154] [1995] 2 AC 171.   [155] [1985] AC 905.

[156] [1986] AC 455.

[157] [1993] AC 442. *Gomez* was a split decision, with a powerful dissent by Lord Lowry.

also steals, they had to resolve two earlier inconsistent decisions of their own.[158] Recklessness is given a different meaning according to the offence involved.[159] The availability of duress as a defence to murder depended on the composition of the court determining the question[160] and exposed a 'fundamental divergence of opinion'.[161]

Sometimes the moral compass pointed unswervingly in one direction. The Lords abolished the rule that a man could not be guilty of raping his wife,[162] -considering it unnecessary to wait for legislative reform.[163] Sometimes the moral compass swivelled wildly and the Lords could plot no convincing course. By a bare majority they held that willing participants in sado-masochistic acts could nonetheless be found guilty of assault.[164] 'Society,' said Lord Templeman 'is entitled and bound to protect itself against a cult of violence. Pleasure derived from infliction of pain is a civil thing. Cruelty is uncivilised.'[165] For the minority the judges should not rush in where hitherto the legislature had feared to tread.[166]

Indeed it was sexual issues that exposed the susceptibility of the Lords to write the law according to their own personal predilections. In *Gillick*[167] (another 3:2 split) they determined that doctors were entitled to give contraceptives to minors without parental consent. Lord Templeman said epigrammatically, 'There are many things which a girl under 16 needs to practise, but sex is not one of them'.[168] Epigram was insufficient to carry the day.[169]

In family law, as elsewhere,[170] statute substantially set the framework within which the judicial exercise could be performed, notably the Children Act 1989 which provided a single body of substantive law relating to children. The Matrimonial and Family Proceedings Act 1984 developed the law on divorce 'firmly in the direction of self-sufficiency and the clear breach'.[171] In *White v*

---

[158] *Lawrence v Metropolitan Police Commissioner* [1972] AC 626 and *R v Morris* [1984] AC 320.

[159] See *DPP v Lawrence* [1982] AC 510 (reckless driving); *DPP v Morgan* [1976] AC 182 (sexual offence); see generally Dennis (n 152) 226.

[160] Compare *Howe* [1987] AC 417 (criminal damage); *Gotts* [1992] 2 AC 512.

[161] *Gotts*, per Lord Templeman at 419; see Lee (n 1) 145–7.

[162] *R v R* [1992] 1 AC 599, a decision subsequently found Convention compliant by the European Court of Human Rights [1996] 1 ELR 434 even though it overruled earlier authority with (arguably) retrospective effect; see discussion in Robertson (n 1) 119–20.

[163] Lord Keith at 623.

[164] *R v Brown* [1994] 1 AC 212—a decision also subsequently found to be Convention compliant by the European Court of Human Rights. See Robertson (n 1) 109–19.

[165] At 237.　　[166] Lord Mustill at 272–5; Lord Slynn at 282–3, 370A.

[167] *Gillick v West Norfolk and Wisbech HA* [1986] AC 112.　　[168] At 201.

[169] See *Fitzpatrick v Sterling House Association* [2001] 1 AC 27 where again by 3:2 the Lords held that a gay man would be a member of his partner's family for Rent Act purposes. By contrast, in *MacFarlane v Tayside Health Board* [2000] 2 AC 59 there was unanimity that birth after a negligent vasectomy could not give rise to a claim for damages. Lord Millett said, at 111, 'The law must take the birth of normal healthy baby to be a blessing, not a detriment.'

[170] Trusts law was another example.

[171] NA Dyer et al, *Rayden and Jackson on Divorce* (London: LexisNexis, 18th edn 2005) para 1.33. For a historical survey see S Cretney, 'Trusting the Judge: Money After Divorce' (1999) 52 CLP 286.

White[172]—30 years on—the Lords construed it by reference to the touchstone of fairness. Lord Nicholls said strikingly: 'In order to achieve a fair outcome, there is no place for discrimination between husband and wife and their respective roles,'[173] adding, 'as a general guide, equality should be departed from only if, and to the extent that, there is good reason for doing so.'[174] The full implications of the decision fell to be considered in the next decade.[175] Although the Human Fertilisation and Embryology Act 1990 regulated embryo research and prohibited certain forms of genetic engineering, the Lords had to consider indirectly when life began in the context of abortion:[176] it had too to reconsider when and in what circumstances a person would be accounted as dead[177] and to determine the circumstances in which a mentally handicapped girl should be sterilised.[178]

The Lords continued to erode the twin pillars of nineteenth century contract law, freedom of contract and sanctity of contract: mirroring again statutory reform.[179] The doctrine of duress now embraced economic duress,[180] and the doctrine of undue influence developed further[181] (although the Lords rejected the invitation earlier extended by Lord Denning to bring these diverse doctrines under the canopy of 'inequality of bargaining power').[182] The Lords recognised the existence in English law of a duty to carry on negotiations in good faith,[183] but privity of contract required legislative intervention[184] and consideration as an essential element in the formation of a contract remained inviolate.[185]

Restitution broke free of the shackles of quasi-contract and was recognised as an independent subject[186] in a case in which Lord Goff—co-author of a seminal work on restitution—gave the leading speech.

In *Anns*[187] Lord Wilberforce had laid down a test which suggested that foreseeability of damage to one person arising out of a careless act of another would give rise to liability, absent some special factor which demanded total or partial

---

[172] [2001] 1 AC 596.
[173] At 605.   [174] ibid.
[175] IM Ellman, 'Financial Settlement on Divorce: Two Steps Forward, Two To Go' (2007) 123 LQR 2, 3–9.
[176] *Royal College of Nursing v DHSS* [1981] AC 800.
[177] M Freeman, 'A Time to be Born and a Time to Die' 56 CLP 203; *Airedale NHS Trust v Bland* [1993] AC 789; S Lee, 'Uneasy Cases', ch 12 in Dickson and Carmichael (n 1); M Beloff QC, 'Life, Death and the Law', Alexander Howard Memorial Lecture, Royal College of Surgery, 2001.
[178] *Re B* [1988] AC 199.
[179] E McKendrick, 'English Contract Law—A Rich Past, An Uncertain Future' (1997) 50 CLP 25.
[180] *Universe Tankship of Monrovia v ITWF* [1983] 1 AC 366.
[181] *Barclays Bank plc v O'Brien* [1994] 2 AC 152 (the case of 'sexually transmitted debt'; Rozenberg (n 67) 128–9, Robertson (n 1) 125–30). Lord Browne-Wilkinson (at 188) balanced the policy considerations: 'It is essential that a law designed to protect the vulnerable does not render the matrimonial home unacceptable as security to financial institutions.' See also *CIBC Mortgages plc v Pitt* [1994] 1 AC 200.
[182] *National Westminster Bank plc v Morgan* [1985] AC 686; cf *Lloyds Bank v Bundy* [1971] QB 326.
[183] *Walford v Miles* [1992] 2 AC 128.   [184] Contracts (Rights of Third Parties) Act 1999.
[185] In *White v Jones* [1995] 2 AC 207, *per* Lord Goff at 262–7.
[186] *Lipkin Gorman (a firm) v Karpnale* [1991] 2 AC 548.   [187] [1978] AC 722.

immunity from suit. Between *Anns* and *Murphy*[188] the Lords considered the issues involved on more than a dozen occasions,[189] and 'over a period of 14 years from 1970 to 1984 the categories of negligence looked infinitely expandable'.[190] The boundaries of liability widened in respect of both psychiatric harm[191] and pure economic loss[192] but, fearful of the genie *Anns* had brought out of the bottle, the House sounded a retreat from *Anns,* culminating in *Caparo*[193] where a triple test of foreseeability, proximity and justice, fairness and reasonableness was said to lay the foundations for an incremental and analogical development of the law. (It had been a case of *sauter pour mieux reculer.*) But the three concepts themselves begged as many questions as they answered and Lord Lloyd suggested pessimistically that the law of negligence was 'disintegrating into a series of isolated decisions without any coherent principles at all'.[194]

The unpredictable oscillations reflected a genuine division of philosophy between conservatives such as Lord Keith and adventurers such as Lord Steyn. Lord Hoffmann was astute to avoid expanding private law remedies into public law areas, especially where a right to damages for breach of a statutory duty would have unquantifiable consequences for public funds.

He said:[195]

In my view the creation of a duty of care upon a highway authority, even on grounds of irrationality in failing to exercise a power, would inevitably expose the authority's budgetary decisions to judicial inquiry. This would distort the priorities of local authorities, which would be bound to try to play safe by increasing their spending on road improvements rather than risk enormous liabilities for personal injury accidents. They will spend less on education or social services. I think that it is important, before extending the duty of care owed by public authorities, to consider the cost to the community of the defensive measures which they are likely to take in order to avoid liability.

Indeed, substantial litigation over the existence or extent of a duty of care owed by public authorities produced inconsistent outcomes.[196] Nor did the subject of

---

[188] [1991] 1 AC 398.

[189] B Hepple, 'Negligence: The Search for Coherence' (1997) 50 CLP 68.

[190] J Murphy (ed), *Street on Torts* (Oxford: OUP, 12th edn 2007) 27.

[191] *McLoughlin v O'Brien* [1983] 1 AC 410; Robertson (n 1) 200–4 contrasts instructively the policy-laden approach of Lords Scarman and Bridge with the reliance on principle of Lords Wilberforce and Edmund-Davies, all however concurring with the result.

[192] *Junior Books v Veitchi Ltd* [1983] 1 AC 520; Robertson (n 1) 208–10.

[193] *Caparo Industries Ltd v Dickman* [1990] 2 AC 605. See also the earlier *Governors of Peabody Donation Fund v Sir Lindsay Parkinson & Co Ltd* [1985] AC 210.

[194] *Marc Rich v Bishop Rock Marine* [1996] 2 AC 211 at 230. Robertson (n 1) entitles his chapter 6 'Pure-Policy—the Law of Negligence'.

[195] *Stovin v Wise* [1996] AC 923, 958; see too his similar sentiments in *O'Rourke v Camden LBC* [1998] AC 188, 193 (duty to house the homeless).

[196] Contrast *X (Minors) v Bedfordshire CC* [1995] 2 AC 633 (on which see Robertson (n 1) 229–33), *Barnet v Enfield BC* [2001] 2 AC 550, and *W v Essex CC* [2001] 2 AC 592. See generally SH Bailey and MJ Bowman, 'Public Authority Negligence Revisited' [2000] CLJ 85 who describe it (at 132) as 'an area that has threatened to descend into chaos'.

liability for nervous shock, considered in a quartet of cases[197]—the third of which was described in the fourth by Lord Goff (dissenting) as 'a remarkable departure from . . . generally accepted principles'.[198]

But by and large the movement continued inexorably forward—if step by step, rather than by leaps and bounds. Negligence continued to colonise areas of economic loss, once part of contract's exclusive empire.[199] The concept of assumption of responsibility was injected in substitution for the narrower test based on statements relied upon:[200] next disappointed beneficiaries of a will successfully sued the testator's solicitor, although he had assumed no responsibility towards them at all.[201] This introduced, according to one commentator, 'a tendency . . . to provide a remedy where justice appeared to require it, albeit difficult to justify in terms of existing principle'.[202]

The Lords held that only *foreseeable* damage was compensable under the strict liability rule in *Rylands v Fletcher*.[203] An employer was held liable to an ex-employee for a careless reference: negligence trumped both defamation and malicious falsehood.[204]

Libel actions themselves rarely proceeded to the Lords. However, they ruled that public authorities were not entitled to sue in defamation.[205] Lord Keith said: 'It is of the highest public importance that a democratically selected governmental body should be open to uninhibited public criticism. The threat of a civil action for defamation must inevitably have an inhibiting effect on freedom of speech.' But, while other common law jurisdictions veered in the direction of giving special protection to political discussion,[206] the Lords trod a more cautious path. Qualified privilege was available in respect of political information only upon application of the established, if elasticised, common law test of whether there had been a duty to publish the material to the intended recipients and whether they had had an interest in receiving it. Judges were to take into account all the circumstances of the publication, including the nature, status, and source of the material—applying a test of responsible journalism.[207]

---

[197] *McLoughlin v O'Brien* [1983] 1 AC 410; *Alcock v Chief Constable of West Yorkshire* [1992] 1 AC 310; *Page v Smith* [1996] AC 155; *Frost v Chief Constable of West Yorkshire* [1999] 2 AC 455.

[198] *Frost*, ibid, at 473. See too his disagreement with Lord Browne-Wilkinson in an arcane discussion of the clean hands principle in equity: *Tinsley v Milligan* [1994] 1 AC 340 denying his ability to disown a century of development in the law that the latter had identified (361–2); Robertson (n 1), 130–6.

[199] *Henderson v Merrett Syndicates Ltd* [1995] 2 AC 145; Robertson (n 1) 224–5.

[200] See for a critique of the trend K Barker, 'Unreliable Assumptions in the Modern Law of Negligence' (1993) 109 LQR 461, 468–9.

[201] *White v Jones* [1995] 2 AC 207.

[202] *Charlesworth & Percy on Negligence* (London: Sweet & Maxwell, 11th edn 2006), Preface.

[203] *Cambridge Water Co v Eastern Counties Leather plc* [1994] 2 AC 264.

[204] *Spring v Guardian Assurance Co* [1995] 2 AC 296; Robertson (n 1) 145–288.

[205] *Derbyshire CC v Times Newspapers Ltd* [1993] AC 539.

[206] See M Beloff QC, 'Politicians and the Press' in *Essays in Honour of David Williams* (Oxford: OUP, 2000).

[207] *Reynolds v Times Newspapers Ltd* [2001] 2 AC 127.

And generally the Lords were not overly supportive of claims to free speech. They upheld the claim of the Secretary of State for Defence to delivery up of a document delivered anonymously to *The Guardian* about nuclear missile deployment to enable identification of the source of the leak,[208] rejecting a construction of the Contempt of Court Act 1981 which gave force to the 'constitutional right of freedom of expression'.[209] They enjoined publication of *Spycatcher* in the United Kingdom, although the information was freely available outside it,[210] despite Lord Bridge's warning that 'if the Government are determined to maintain the ban to the end, they will face inevitable condemnation and humiliation before the European Court of Human Rights at Strasbourg. Long before that they will have been condemned at the bar of public opinion in the free world.'[211] The Lords developed the law in other areas, notably linked fields of service out of the jurisdiction, stays of proceedings within it, and grant of anti-suit injunctions to restrain foreign proceedings,[212] where convenience and comity were weighed in the balance.

In employment, where in general the underpinning of statute and Community law was pervasive, the Lords' major spontaneous achievement was developing the implied term of mutual trust and compliance so as to oblige an employer not to carry on dishonest or corrupt business. In *Malik v BCC*[213] Lord Steyn said:[214]

The evolution of the term is a comparatively recent development. The obligation probably has its origin in the general duty of co-operation between contracting parties. The reason for this development is part of the history of the development of employment law in this century. The notion of a 'master and servant' relationship became obsolete. Lord Slynn of Hadley recently noted 'the changes which have taken place in the employer-employee relationship, with far greater duties imposed on the employer than in the past, whether by statute or by judicial decision, to care for the physical, financial and even psychological welfare of the employee': It was the change in legal culture which made possible the evolution of the implied term of trust and confidence.

The Lords, in defiance of the constitutional principle of separation of powers, still enjoyed both judicial and legislative powers. They continued to make occasional contributions to debate in the House, in particular in the area of lawyers' law.[215]

---

[208] *Secretary of State for Defence v Guardian Newspapers* [1985] AC 339.
[209] Lord Fraser at 359 (which Lord Diplock in the same case repudiated as 'an evocative phrase' (345)). See also *Inquiry under the Company Securities (Insider Dealing) Act 1985* [1988] AC 600; *X v Morgan Grampian Ltd* [1991] AC 1.
[210] *AG v Guardian Newspapers* [1987] 1 WLR 1248.
[211] ibid, 1280. For the sequel see *AG v Guardian Newspapers (No 2)* [1990] 1 AC 109.
[212] See *BAB v Laker Airways Ltd* [1981] AC 58; *Spiliada Maritime Corp v Cansulex Ltd* [1987] AC 460: *Airbus Industries GEI v Patel* [1999] 1 AC 119.
[213] [1998] AC 20.
[214] At 45–6.
[215] Lord Hope, 'Voices from the Past—The Law Lords' Contribution to the Legislative Process' (2007) 123 LQR 547, esp 562–5 emphasising the contributions of Lords Wilberforce, Simon, and Brightman.

There was robust criticism of Lord Mackay's Green Paper on the administration of justice from retired Law Lords,[216] but support inside and outside the House for incorporation of the Convention into domestic law.[217]

Lord Wilberforce 'played a large role in securing the enactment of the Arbitration Bill',[218] Lord Hoffmann a leading part in debates in 1996 on the Defamation Bill, and Lord Clyde and Lord Hope in 1997 on the Scotland Bill. But already the trend was towards abstinence. Lord Mustill, Lord Steyn,[219] and Lord Saville were pioneers of the vow of silence.[220] Lord Hoffmann, for example, would have been conflicted out in the case of *Al Fayed v Hamilton*,[221] which raised an issue of construction of the very bill in whose promotion he had been involved.

In 2000 no serving English Law Lord participated in a legislative debate.[222] The statement made to the House on 22 June 2000 by Lord Bingham, the Senior Law Lord, that the Law Lords had agreed that it would not be appropriate for them to engage in matters where there was a strong element of public controversy, merely validated a convention which had already grown up.[223]

The Wakeham Royal Commission on the House of Lords[224] expressed the view that '[t]here is no reason why the second chamber should not continue to exercise the judicial functions of the present House of Lords'.[225] This was mitigated only by an 'anodyne statement about when they would not participate in the legislative debates of a political nature'.[226] The Government acquiesced in this happy conclusion and 'declared itself committed to maintaining judicial membership within the House of Lords'.[227]

---

[216] They continued to be seconded to public inquiries. Lord Phillips' first sitting was delayed because of his need to conclude the BSE report; Lord Saville's judicial career was effectively terminated when he was appointed to chair the reprise of the Bloody Sunday inquiry. R Stevens, *The Independence of the Judiciary, The View from the Lord Chancellor's Office* (Oxford: Clarendon Press, 1993) 174–7.

[217] A Lester QC and D Pannick QC, *Human Rights: Law and Practice* (London: LexisNexis, 2nd edn 2004) para 1.37. Lord Scarman was the first to introduce a bill incorporating the Convention in 1985.

[218] Lord Steyn in *Lesotho Developments v Impregio SpA* [2006] 1 AC 221, [18]. 'With a strongly pragmatic approach to problems he saw no harm in a Law Lord initiating a debate on, or intervening in such topics as law reform, higher education, treaty implementation, or the protection of the weak.' Lord Neill QC on Lord Wilberforce, *DNB*.

[219] Stevens (n 37) 111.

[220] Lord Steyn, 'The Case for a Supreme Court' (2002) 118 LQR 382; Stevens (n 37) 127.

[221] [2001] AC 395.

[222] Stevens (n 37) 121.

[223] *Hansard*, HL, vol 614, col 419, 22 June 2000.

[224] *A House for the Future*, Cmnd 4534, 2000, para 9.5.

[225] See generally Stevens (n 37) 105–6. The White Paper that preceded the establishment of the Commission given no real steer in a radical direction: *Modernising More Parliament: Reforming the House of Lords*, Cmnd 4183, 1999.

[226] Stevens (n 37) 103.

[227] In *The House of Lords—Completing the Reform*, Cmnd 5291, 2001, para 81.

There was little serious questioning of the value of a second appellate tier, so as the millennium arrived, the existence of the final court of appeal was no longer much debated, as it has been by legal reformists in the post-war period.[228] The Law Lords soldiered on, enjoying the privilege of a location within the Palace of Westminster, but with facilities far less impressive than those enjoyed by members of any other supreme court.[229]

Overall, the reputation of the House of Lords for high quality appellate adjudication in private law litigation was well maintained during the last two decades of the twentieth century. And in its excursions into the developing field of public law the Law Lords built, if sometimes somewhat unevenly, on the trail-blazing of their predecessors. The *GCHQ* case in 1984[230] was certainly a landmark in English administrative law.

Publicly more exposed than ever in the past, the standing of the Law Lords at the pinnacle of the court hierarchy was, despite its occasional immersion in controversy, well established. Only those acutely sensitive to the implications of the Human Rights Act and its emphasis on the need for judges not only to be but to appear to be wholly independent, could have predicted that within another decade, it would be transformed into a supreme court wholly detached from Parliament.

---

[228] Le Sueur and R Cornes, 'What Do the Top Courts Do?' (2000) 53 CLP 53, 60–76 instancing 'the refinement of legal issues, the mode of deliberation, style of written judgments or the composition of the Court' (61). The continuing need for a second tier appeal court was affirmed in the Constitutional Reform Act 2005.

[229] Interview with James Vallance White on his retirement in *The Telegraph*, 11 July 2002. See Barrett (n 1) ch 4, 'Life on the Appellate Committee'. It is instructive to compare Lord Slynn's facilities at Luxembourg as a Judge of the ECJ (own secretary, law clerks in his cabinet) with those available to him in London as a Law Lord (typing pool, no researchers).

[230] *Council for the Civil Service Unions v Minister for the Civil Service* [1985] AC 374. Lord Diplock's speech earns the tribute of a special appendix in HWR Wade and CF Forsyth, *Administrative Law* (Oxford: OUP, 9th edn 2004).

16

A Hard Act to Follow:
The Bingham
Court, 2000–8

Brice Dickson

Introduction

It is not often that a British court can be eponymised. Naming a court after an individual judge seems antithetical to a central tenet of the British approach to administering justice—that adjudication is essentially an impersonal activity, divorced from the personality of the men and women who do the job, including those who preside in the court. Moreover the judges appointed to adjudicate in the United Kingdom's appeal courts do not ever all sit together, which reduces the likelihood of a single judge having such a degree of influence over the output of the court as to make it reasonable to link the court to his or her name. The situation is different in the United States, where commentators are accustomed to identifying the Supreme Court with whoever happens to be Chief Justice at the time, and where that court customarily sits *en banc*. Whole books have been written about the characteristics of the Warren court, the Burger court, or the Rehnquist court. Some justification is thus required for giving the present chapter the title it has. There are at least three such justifications, each of which will be given greater elaboration as the chapter proceeds.

First, in recent years the role of the Senior Law Lord has become more important, in tune with the idea that the business of the top court, as of all other courts, has to be properly managed. There is more scope than there used to be for that person to influence the way in which the House of Lords goes about its business. If the person concerned has already served as the head of another, much busier, court, it is understandable that he or she will bring to the position an awareness of a leader's potential to stamp on the court his or her ideas concerning judicial administration. When Lord Bingham of Cornhill was appointed Senior Law Lord in 2000 he had already served four years as Lord Chief Justice of England and Wales and, before that, four years as Master of the Rolls (head of the Civil Division of the Court of Appeal).

Second, Lord Bingham's tenure as Senior Law Lord coincided with a particularly important period in the constitutional history of the United Kingdom, one which saw three hugely significant events. These were the entry into force of the Human Rights Act 1998 in October 2000, the exercise of devolved powers by regional legislatures and executives in Edinburgh, Belfast, and Cardiff, all of which started to function just as the new millennium was beginning, and the decision to transfer the judicial work of the House of Lords to a new Supreme Court of the United Kingdom, now scheduled to take effect in October 2009.

The third justification for referring to 'the Bingham court' is that the quality of judgments produced by the Lords in the eight-year period during which Lord Bingham served as Senior Law Lord was noticeably high and Lord Bingham was to the forefront in contributing to that corpus of law. While there were still examples of lost opportunities and needless confusion, the House's law-making was for the most part remarkably clear and reformist. The court asserted itself in a way which gave it a particular reputation. It might be going too far to say that Lord Bingham orchestrated this state of affairs, but he certainly greatly influenced the whole court by the manner of his presiding (both when sitting and more generally), by his clear conception of the role of a judge,[1] and by the care and rigour with which he compiled his judgments. In short, he led by example. That he is very highly thought of in official circles is partly evidenced by his appointment as a Knight of the Garter in 2005, the first professional judge ever to be accorded that honour, which is in the personal gift of the Queen.

Issues of judicial administration

Lord Bingham's previous jobs as Lord Chief Justice and Master of the Rolls required him to fulfil a welter of administrative duties as well as to preside in cases raising some of the most controversial issues of the day.[2] In *Locabail (UK) Ltd v*

---

[1] Many of the speeches and articles written by Lord Bingham prior to his appointment as Senior Law Lord were published together as *The Business of Judging* (Oxford: OUP, 2000). In 'The Judge as Lawmaker: An English Perspective' (ch 3 of the book, but first published as ch 1 of P Rishworth (ed), *The Struggle for Simplicity: Essays for Lord Cooke of Thorndon* (Wellington: Butterworths, 1997)) Lord Bingham says of Lord Cooke, at 34, what others might say of him in relation to the law of the UK: 'In the law, nothing is the work of one Court or one man ... [b]ut if it be true ... that the common law in New Zealand has developed along distinctive lines peculiarly suited to the culture and customs of the people ... and if it be true, as again it plainly is, that the common law as developed in New Zealand commands high respect throughout the entire common law world, no commentator ... could fail to recognise the immense contribution, wise and scholarly as it has been, of Lord Cooke as lawmaker.' For a more recent exposition of Lord Bingham's views on judicial activism see his 2005 Maccabaean Lecture at Cardiff Law School entitled 'The Judges: Active or Passive', available at the website of the British Academy: <http://www.law.cf.ac.uk/publiclecture/transcripts/271005.pdf> (last visited 13 March 2009).

[2] eg whether it is lawful to withdraw feeding from a patient in a persistent vegetative state (*Airedale NHS Trust v Bland* [1993] AC 789); whether a health authority can deny funding for a child's leukaemia treatment (*R v Cambridge Health Authority, ex p B* [1995] 1 WLR 898); whether a

Bayfield Properties Ltd, for example, he laid down detailed guidance on what would qualify as bias, or potential bias, on the part of a judge.[3] He had also been asked to chair prominent inquiries.[4] No previous Law Lord—let alone Senior Law Lord—had been appointed with such a strong administrative background.[5] Three had been appointed as Lord Chief Justice *after* serving as a Lord of Appeal,[6] but none had travelled in the opposite direction.

When Lord Bingham succeeded Lord Browne-Wilkinson as Senior Law Lord in June 2000 he effectively displaced Lord Slynn of Hadley, who might have been expected to move from the position of Second Senior Law Lord to the top post as most of his predecessors had done before him. But Lord Bingham's talents as a presider and administrator obviously marked him out in the eyes of the then Prime Minister (Tony Blair) and Lord Chancellor (Lord Irvine) as the best man for the job, just as they had impressed John Major's Lord Chancellor, Lord Mackay, when, as Sir Thomas Bingham, he had been appointed Master of the Rolls in 1992 and Lord Chief Justice in 1996 (the latter appointment was a surprise to some, because of his lack of experience in criminal law[7]). His elevation to the post of Senior Law Lord may have been partly due to the fact that a very sound candidate was available to fill his own shoes as Lord Chief Justice (Lord Woolf—who had first been appointed to the Bench a year *before* Lord Bingham, in 1979[8]), and in turn there was another good candidate to take over Lord

---

Minister can undermine an Act of Parliament by using prerogative powers (*R v Secretary of State for the Home Department, ex p Fire Brigades Union* [1995] 2 AC 513); whether the armed forces can dismiss members who are homosexual (*R v Ministry of Defence, ex p Smith* [1996] QB 517); whether the police can be held liable for a detainee's suicide (*Reeves v Comr of the Police of the Metropolis* [1999] QB 169, reversed in the Lords); the extent of a newspaper's right to publish what turn out to be untruths (*Reynolds v Times Newspapers Ltd* [2001] 2 AC 127, affirmed by the Lords on other grounds); whether barristers are still immune from being sued (*Arthur JS Hall & Co v Simons* [2001] 1 AC 615, reversed by the Lords).

[3] [2000] QB 451.

[4] eg *Report on the supply of petroleum and petroleum products to Rhodesia* (London: HMSO, 1978, with SM Gray), written when Tom Bingham was still a practising QC, and *Inquiry into the Supervision of the Bank of Credit and Commerce International*, HC 198, 1992–3. In this latter report Sir Thomas Bingham MR, as he then was, criticised the Bank of England for not being careful enough in its oversight of the BCCI, although at the time many felt that the Bank of England had been let off rather lightly. His involvement in this inquiry meant that Lord Bingham could not sit in subsequent appeals dealing with the Bank of England's alleged public misfeasance vis-à-vis BCCI (eg *Three Rivers DC v Bank of England (No 3)* [2003] 2 AC 1 and *(No 6)* [2005] 1 AC 610), but it did not prevent him from sitting in appeals on peripheral matters (eg *BCCI v Ali* [2002] 1 AC 251, where the issue was the extent of an ex-employee's entitlement to damages for the 'stigma' of being associated with a disgraced employer).

[5] Prior to becoming Master of the Rolls, Sir Thomas Bingham had sat as a Lord Justice of Appeal for six years (1986–92) and before that as a judge of the Queen's Bench Division of the High Court for six years (1980–6).

[6] Lord Lane in 1980, Lord Goddard in 1946, and Lord Russell in 1894.

[7] In 1998 he made it clear, in the Frank Newsam Lecture delivered to senior police officers, that he favoured replacing the mandatory life sentence for murder with a discretionary life sentence: see <http://news.bbc.co.uk/1/hi/uk/65078.stm> (last visited 13 March 2009).

[8] For a collection of Lord Woolf's views on judging and other aspects of the English legal system see C Campbell-Holt (ed), *Lord Woolf: The Pursuit of Justice* (Oxford: OUP, 2008).

Woolf's mantle as Master of the Rolls (Lord Phillips of Worth-Matravers, already a Lord of Appeal at the time, although only for 17 months; when Lord Woolf retired as Lord Chief Justice in 2005, he was again succeeded by Lord Phillips). In April 2008 the Prime Minister's office announced that Lord Phillips would succeed Lord Bingham as Senior Law Lord when Lord Bingham retired on 30 September 2008, meaning that Lord Phillips would become the first President of the UK Supreme Court in October 2009. Lord Phillips has thus followed the same career path as Lord Bingham, moving from Master of the Rolls, to Lord Chief Justice, to senior judge in the top appeal court.

Lord Bingham became Senior Law Lord less than a year after the debacle of the *Pinochet* case, where the first, very liberal, decision of the Bench of five Law Lords in November 1998 had been vacated in January 1999 by a bench of five other judges because of the connections between Lord Hoffmann and the charitable arm of Amnesty International, one of the interveners in the case.[9] In the House's second decision on the appeal, in March 1999, the five Law Lords in the majority (it was a seven-judge bench) did not go as far as their brethren had gone in the first appeal, because they held that General Pinochet could be held accountable only for the actions he had taken after 29 September 1988, the date when the UN Convention Against Torture was effectively incorporated into UK law by section 134 of the Criminal Justice Act 1988.[10] The ultimate result in the appeal (notwithstanding that the Home Secretary, Jack Straw, then decided that General Pinochet should not be extradited because he was too ill to stand trial) was still a good one from a human rights point of view, but the alleged conflict of interest point had undoubtedly done some damage to the House's reputation for integrity and independence. It was important that no further unfortunate incidents should befall the House.

After Lord Bingham's appointment as Senior Law Lord Lord Slynn remained as Second Senior Law Lord for a further two years and continued to bring to bear on the House his considerable experience of EC law (he had served as a Judge of the European Court of Justice from 1988 to 1992 and as an Advocate General in Luxembourg from 1981 to 1988). The other Law Lords in post when Lord Bingham was appointed were Lords Nicholls (appointed 1994, and succeeding Lord Slynn as Second Senior Law Lord in 2002), Steyn (1995), Hoffmann (1995), Hope (1996), Clyde (1996), Hutton (1997), Saville (1997), Hobhouse (1998), and Millett (1998). A month after his appointment, the vacancy left in the House by Lord Phillips' move to become Master of the Rolls was filled by Lord Scott, a Chancery expert. Just as Lord Bingham had come to public prominence through his chairing of the inquiry into the collapse of the Bank of Credit and Commerce International in 1992,[11] so Lord Scott's name had been

---

[9] [2000] 1 AC 61 (first appeal); [2000] 1 AC 119 (decision to vacate). See too ch 26 in this volume.
[10] [2000] 1 AC 147.   [11] See n 4 above.

much in the headlines when, as Sir Richard Scott (Vice-Chancellor), he chaired the 'Arms to Iraq' inquiry, which concluded in 1996.[12] The next change of personnel was in October 2001, when Lord Rodger replaced Lord Clyde to occupy the second Scottish seat, and then Lord Walker, another Chancery lawyer, replaced Lord Slynn in October 2002.

In January 2004 there occurred the largest ever turnover in the composition of the court at any one time, when Lords Hutton, Hobhouse, and Millett—all considered to be conservative in their approach to judicial work— retired and were replaced by Lords Carswell and Brown and Lady Hale. The appointment of Lord Carswell marked the first occasion on which a retiring judge from Northern Ireland was immediately replaced by another judge from Northern Ireland, but understandably it was the appointment of Lady Hale—the first woman ever to be appointed as a 'Lord of Appeal in Ordinary'—which made the news. There were profiles of the new appointee in most of the main newspapers and on the website of the BBC. Many commentators pointed to Brenda Hale's reputation for lamenting the bias against women in many walks of life and the overwhelming maleness of the senior judiciary. She herself later queried, only half jokingly, whether her appointment was strictly speaking legal.[13] As we shall see towards the end of this chapter, in the years since her appointment Lady Hale has been to the fore in trying to change the way in which law is applied in many contexts of particular relevance to women, children, and people who have suffered mental illness (while working as an academic she had written books on family law and mental health law,[14] and while serving as the first woman to be appointed to the Law Commission, from 1984 to 1993, she specialised in considering reforms to those areas of law). By October 2008 the only other appointees to the Lords since January 2004 were Lord Mance,[15] in October 2005, who replaced Lord Steyn, and Lord Neuberger, in January 2007, who replaced Lord Nicholls. Upon Lord Nicholls' retirement Lord Hoffmann became the Second Senior Law Lord. During Lord Bingham's time in charge, however, there was the usual reliance on retired Lords of Appeal, especially Lord Mackay, and on other judicial peers, especially the serving Master of the Rolls and Lord Chief Justice.[16] Also, of course, the Lord Chancellor ceased to sit as a judge, the

---

[12] *Inquiry into the Export of Defence Equipment and Dual-Use Goods to Iraq and Related Prosecutions,* HC 115, 1995–6. Five years later Lord Scott told the BBC that it was 'regrettable and disappointing' that no changes had yet been made to legislation to prevent the sorts of abuses he had brought to light recurring. He added: 'The current legislation is appallingly outdated . . . it allows export controls to be used for any purpose whatever the government desires to use them for.' For the impact of the Scott Inquiry, see A Tomkins, *The Constitution After Scott* (Oxford: OUP, 1978).

[13] 'The House of Lords and Women's Rights, or Am I Really a Law Lord?' (2005) 25 LS 72.

[14] eg *Family, Law and Society: Cases and Materials* (London: Butterworths, 3rd edn 1991, with D Pearl), and *Mental Health Law* (London: Sweet & Maxwell, 5th edn 2005).

[15] Who happens to be married to Dame Mary Arden, a Lady Justice of Appeal since 2000 and chairperson of the Law Commission of England and Wales from 1996 to 1999.

[16] Lord Mackay sat on at least 21 occasions; Lords Phillips and Woolf, whether as MR or LCJ, sat on 22 and 17 respectively. Lord Cooke also sat 14 times and Lord Nolan eight times.

last time this occurred being in *AIB Group (UK) plc v Martin*, a case on the law of mortgages.[17]

By the time of his own retirement in September 2008 Lord Bingham had worked with 18 other Lords of Appeal, as well as with several other Lords who sat now and again (in particular Lord Woolf and Lord Phillips). Only three of his original colleagues were still in post (Lords Hoffmann, Hope, and Saville) and one of these (Lord Saville) had been effectively *hors de combat* throughout the entire period because he was serving as the full-time chairman of the second Tribunal of Inquiry into the deaths in Derry on Bloody Sunday in 1972. In accordance with the established tradition for appointing Lords of Appeal, Lord Bingham would have been centrally involved in the appointment of all eight individuals who were selected for elevation between 2000 and 2007. The Lord Chancellor would have taken soundings from many serving judges (including all the current Law Lords) but he would have paid particular attention to the views of the Senior Law Lord before recommending a name to the Prime Minister.[18] It is very likely, therefore, that Lord Bingham was a strong supporter of the appointment of the first female Lord of Appeal, Lady Hale. He had probably seen her own journal article calling for more female judges.[19] Collectively, though, the appointees were not significantly younger than previous appointees. The average age at appointment of the eight appointed between 2000 and 2007 was slightly over 62; the average age of the 30 previous Lords of Appeal (appointed between 1979 and 2000) was slightly under 63.

The Senior Law Lord, acting together with the Second Senior Law Lord, confirms which colleagues are to sit on which appeals. In practice this task is initially carried out by the Head of the Judicial Office, acting on the basis of criteria such as the judges' availability and their special expertise.[20] In the vast majority of instances the allocation made by that official will be rubber-stamped by the two senior judges. Occasionally the Senior Law Lord may decide that the case is so important that it requires a bench of more than five judges. Lord Bingham waited more than two years before convening his first seven-judge bench,[21] and did so again on four further occasions.[22] But a salient feature of

[17] [2002] 1 WLR 94. The appeal was heard on 25 October 2001 and the Lord Chancellor was Lord Irvine.

[18] Lord Irvine of Lairg was the Lord Chancellor until he was replaced by Lord Falconer of Thoroton in June 2003. Lord Falconer was in turn replaced in June 2007 by Jack Straw MP, the first member of the House of Commons to hold the office for several centuries (he was also appointed as Secretary of State for Justice).

[19] 'Equality and the Judiciary: Why Should We Want More Women Judges?' [2001] PL 489.

[20] For details see B Dickson, 'The Processing of Appeals in the House of Lords' (2007) 123 LQR 571, 589–93.

[21] In *R (Anderson) v Secretary of State for the Home Department* [2003] 1 AC 837 and *R v Lichniak* [2003] 1 AC 903. These appeals were heard together but were made the subject of separate sets of judgments.

[22] *Rees v Darlington Memorial Hospital NHS Trust* [2004] 1 AC 309; *Re Spectrum Plus Ltd* [2005] 2 AC 680; *A v Secretary of State for the Home Department (No 2)* [2006] 2 AC 221; *Kay v Lambeth LBC* [2006] 2 AC 465.

Lord Bingham's tenure of the top position was the selection of nine-judge benches, something that had not occurred since 1910.[23] He first resorted to this in 2003,[24] in a case that exposed a significant rift between the English and Scottish Lords of Appeal regarding the consequences that should follow when a defendant in a criminal case has been treated unfairly because of a delay in processing the case. The Scottish judges, reflecting the attitude struck by criminal law in their home country (from where no criminal appeals can be taken to the Lords), preferred a rule which said that the defendant's trial should in those circumstances be abandoned; the English judges, who finally won the day (by seven to two), preferred a more flexible rule which allowed for the trial to continue if some other remedy could be granted to the defendant instead of a stay of proceedings. Nine-judge benches have been convened on three subsequent occasions in the Lords[25] (and once in the Privy Council[26]). Presumably Lord Bingham's intention was to lend the decisions in these cases significantly greater weight, thereby sending a correspondingly stronger message to lower courts and, where appropriate, to the Government and Parliament.

A further method favoured by Lord Bingham for strengthening the authority of the House's judgments was the use of 'considered opinions of the Committee'. Judgments of the whole court are the norm in the Criminal Division of the Court of Appeal (unless one judge wishes to dissent[27]), but custom and practice in the Lords has always allowed for separate judicial opinions, even if some of these are very brief expressions of concurrence. No doubt drawing upon his experience of

---

[23] *R v Ball* [1911] AC 47. In *Allen v Flood* [1898] AC 1, eight judges of the High Court were summoned to give opinions alongside nine members of the House of Lords, four of whom were the then Lords of Appeal. All 17 gave written opinions.

[24] *AG's Reference (No 2 of 2001)* [2004] 2 AC 72. The decision was applied in a later case where a devolution issue had been referred to the Judicial Committee by the Lord Advocate in Scotland: *Spiers (Procurator Fiscal) v Ruddy* [2008] 1 AC 873.

[25] *A v Secretary of State for the Home Department* [2005] 2 AC 68 (whether a statutory power to detain non-British nationals indefinitely without trial was compatible with the right to liberty in Art 5 of the European Convention on Human Rights); *R (Jackson) v AG* [2006] 1 AC 262 (whether the Hunting Act 2004 had been unlawfully enacted); *R (Gentle) v The Prime Minister* [2008] 1 AC 1356 (whether Art 2 of the European Convention required an inquiry to be held into whether it was lawful to send troops to Iraq). A nine-judge bench was also convened in *Mbasogo v Logo Ltd* (whether claims by a foreign state for damages are justiciable in England if the losses sustained arose from decisions taken by the state in defence of itself and its citizens against an alleged coup) but the appeal to the Lords against the Court of Appeal's decision, [2007] QB 846, was abandoned before it could be heard. In March 2009 a nine-judge bench heard an appeal concerning the use of 'special advocates' in judicial hearings into the validity of control orders imposed under the Prevention of Terrorism Act 2005.

[26] *AG for Jersey v Holley* (see text at n 37 below). Occasionally seven judges have sat in the Privy Council, eg in *Pratt and Morgan v AG of Jamaica* [1994] 2 AC 1, where the Judicial Committee unanimously overruled its previous decision in *Riley v AG of Jamaica* [1983] 1 AC 719. Seven Law Lords also sat when the Crown (under s 4 of the Judicial Committee Act 1833) referred to the Privy Council an issue concerning the compatibility of a later Act of Parliament with the Bill of Rights 1689: *Re Parliamentary Privilege Act 1770* [1958] AC 331.

[27] For more on judgments in the Court of Appeal see G Drewry, L Blom-Cooper, and C Blake, *The Court of Appeal* (Oxford: Hart, 2007) ch 8.

dealing with criminal appeals as Lord Chief Justice, Lord Bingham first employed a collective approach to adjudication just six months after becoming Senior Law Lord, in the first criminal appeal in which he presided, *R v Forbes*.[28] He later used it on a further six criminal occasions.[29] Curiously, the same approach was adopted by Lord Nicholls when he presided in three taxation appeals in 2004,[30] and Lord Bingham himself used it in two appeals on the right to have a killing properly investigated,[31] in a Scottish appeal dealing with insolvency law,[32] and in an important case on the adjudication of immigration disputes.[33] In one 2008 decision on extradition law the Appellate Committee produced a *composite* opinion, that is, one which was compiled by a number of judges and stitched together as a whole.[34]

The great merit of collective or composite judgments is that they lead to certainty in the law, which makes it ironic that there is not yet any certainty as to when the top court will feel it appropriate to resort to the practice. Of the remaining 41 criminal appeals decided between 2000 and Lord Bingham's retirement in September 2008, 13 were decided by single judgments accompanied by four formal concurrences, but in the other 28 appeals there were multiple judgments (in eight there were five judgments), although with dissents in only three of them. In some instances the law has consequently been left somewhat unclear. This is particularly so as regards homicide law[35] where, after the three-to-two split in *R v Smith (Morgan)*,[36] decided three months before Lord Bingham's appointment, the law relating to which personal characteristics of the accused a jury is entitled to take into account when considering whether the accused's defence of provocation can succeed, was reviewed by a nine-judge Judicial Committee of the Privy Council in June 2005, with six of the nine judges preferring not to follow the earlier House of Lords' decision.[37]

---

[28] [2001] 1 AC 473; the other Law Lords who heard this appeal were Lords Steyn, Hoffmann, Cooke, and Hutton.

[29] *R v Drew* [2003] 1 WLR 1213; *R v Webber* [2004] 1 WLR 404; *R v H* [2004] 2 AC 134; *R v Montila* [2004] 1 WLR 3141; *R v Wang* [2005] 1 WLR 661; *R v Kennedy (No 2)* [2008] 1 AC 269.

[30] *Barclays Mercantile Business Finance Ltd v Mawson (Inspector of Taxes)* [2005] 1 AC 684; *IRC v Scottish Provident Institution* [2004] 1 WLR 3172; *Beynon v HM Comrs of Custom and Excise* [2005] 1 WLR 86.

[31] *R (Middleton) v West Somerset Coroner* [2004] 2 AC 182.

[32] *Henderson v 3052775 Nova Scotia Ltd* 2006 SC (HL) 85.

[33] *Huang v Secretary of State for the Home Department* [2007] 2 AC 167.

[34] *Norris v Government of the USA* [2008] 1 AC 920.

[35] See my critique of the House's decisions in this field in 'Judicial Activism in the House of Lords 1995–2007' in B Dickson (ed), *Judicial Activism in Common Law Supreme Courts* (Oxford: OUP, 2007) 404–11.

[36] [2001] 1 AC 146.

[37] *AG for Jersey v Holley* [2005] 2 AC 580; the majority comprised Lords Nicholls (who wrote for them all), Hope, Scott, Rodger, and Walker, and Lady Hale, while the dissenters were Lords Bingham, Hoffmann, and Carswell. In *R v James* [2006] QB 588 the Court of Appeal followed the Privy Council decision rather than that of the House of Lords, and the House refused leave to appeal, [2006] 1 WLR 2107.

There is evidence to show that the judicial arm of the House of Lords operated efficiently during the Bingham era. The Civil and Criminal Practice Directions were kept updated, the time taken to hear appeals was kept (usually) to just one or two days, the number of oral hearings on petitions for leave to appeal was diminished, and the average delay between the hearing of the appeal and the delivery of the judgments was reduced to just two months. Lord Bingham presided in an appeal hearing on the very first day of his appointment as a Lord of Appeal,[38] and in the first eight cases in which he presided the judgment of the House was issued within a month of the hearing.[39]

Lord Bingham's era was also noteworthy for the introduction of research assistants into their Lordships' House in 2000. While these assistants serve for only a year at a time, and do not make any direct contribution to the composition of judgments (unlike the clerks to US Supreme Court justices[40]), they do conduct research for their assigned judges and they assist them with extra-judicial work such as lectures for special occasions. They also play a key role in writing 'memos' of the petitions for appeal, which Law Lords consider when sitting in groups of three on the Appeal Committee. These memos summarise the facts of the case, the history of the litigation to date, and the issues at stake in the appeal. The employment of research assistants symbolises the modernisation of the top court over which Lord Bingham presided, even if Law Lords were still very poorly assisted in comparison with US Supreme Court justices, each of whom has four judicial clerks and two secretaries. But the greatest evidence for the House's modernisation is the development of the court's constitutional role.

The constitutional role of the Appellate Committee

A case can be made for saying that between 2000 and 2008 the House of Lords became more assertive of its own authority than in the past. On many occasions, for example, it went out of its way to chastise the Court of Appeal or Court of Session for interfering inappropriately with the discretion of a trial judge,[41] or it gave the Court of Appeal fresh guidance on what tests to apply in criminal cases,[42] or it chose to re-write the questions posed for its consideration in an appeal,[43] or it

---

[38] *Berkeley v Secretary of State for the Environment* [2001] 2 AC 603.

[39] By way of contrast, when judgments were delivered on 27 July 2000 in four appeals presided over by Lord Slynn, an average of 135 days had elapsed since the oral hearing in each case.

[40] See E Lazarus, *Closed Chambers: The Rise, Fall, and Future of the Modern Supreme Court* (New York: OUP, 1999).

[41] eg *Designers' Guild Ltd v Russell Williams (Textiles) Ltd* [2000] 1 WLR 2416; *Thomson v Kvaerner Govan Ltd* 2004 SC (HL) 1; *AH (Sudan) v Secretary of State for the Home Department* [2008] 1 AC 678, at 30 (*per* Baroness Hale). In at least two Scottish appeals their Lordships have suggested that counsel should not have certified the cases as deserving of an appeal: *Buchanan v Alba Diagnostics Ltd* 2004 SC (HL) 9 and *Wilson v Jaymarke Estates Ltd* [2007] SC(HL) 135.

[42] eg *R v Pendleton* [2002] 1 WLR 72; *R v Soneji* [2006] 1 AC 340.

[43] eg *I v DPP* [2002] 1 AC 285; *R v Hinks* [2001] 2 AC 241, at 255F (*per* Lord Hutton).

radically disagreed with the policy stance adopted by the Court of Appeal.[44] The House also confirmed that it had inherent powers to exercise any power vested in the Court of Appeal,[45] it clarified what issues could or could not be appealed to the top court,[46] and it ruled that it could continue to hear an appeal even though there might no longer be a point of law of general public importance involved in the case.[47] Moreover, by allowing more third parties to intervene in appeals than was formerly the case, the Bingham court indicated that it wished to be open to a wide range of views on contentious issues so that it could pay attention not just to the narrow concerns of the litigants but to the wider implications of the court's decision. Interveners included the National Union of Teachers,[48] the Lord Chancellor's Department,[49] the Northern Ireland Human Rights Commission,[50] Liberty,[51] Justice,[52] the Terence Higgins Trust,[53] the Redress Trust,[54] MIND,[55] CAFCASS,[56] and (on several occasions) the Office of the UN High Commissioner for Refugees.[57] In *A v Secretary of State for the Home Department (No 2)* the House permitted no fewer than 17 interventions.[58] The House was also willing to hear from *amici curiae*.[59]

In *Re Spectrum Plus Ltd*[60] the Lords unanimously accepted that they could confer upon themselves the power to overrule cases *prospectively* (ie change the law

---

[44] eg *W v Essex CC* [2001] 2 AC 592; *Tomlinson v Congleton BC* [2004] 1 AC 46; *Marcic v Thames Water Utilities Ltd* [2004] 2 AC 42; *Polanski v Condé Nast Publications Ltd* [2005] 1 WLR 637; *Brooks v Comr of Police for the Metropolis* [2005] 1 WLR 1495 (limiting examples to tort law alone).

[45] *Grobbelaar v News Group Newspapers Ltd* [2002] 1 WLR 3024.

[46] *R v Weir* [2001] 1 WLR 421 (a decision of the Appeal Committee holding that the House could not grant an extension of time to a prosecutor wishing to apply for leave to appeal); *R v H* [2007] 2 AC 270 (no appeal possible at all against a trial judge's ruling that documents in the possession of the prosecution should not be disclosed).

[47] *R (Bushell) v Newcastle Licensing Justices* [2006] 1 WLR 496 (the House proceeded with this appeal because one side to the dispute would undoubtedly lose a lot of money if it did not). Of course any court has inherent jurisdiction to determine its own practice and procedure, but some of the matters listed above go more to substance than procedure.

[48] *Eastwood v Magnox Electric plc* [2005] 1 AC 503.

[49] *Lawal v Northern Spirit Ltd* [2004] 1 All ER 856.

[50] *R (Amin) v Secretary of State for the Home Department* [2004] 1 AC 653. The Commission itself had to go to the Lords to win the right to intervene (see *Re Northern Ireland Human Rights Commission* [2002] NI 236), but it was later criticised by Lord Hoffmann for abusing this right (see *E v Chief Constable of the Royal Ulster Constabulary* [2008] 3 WLR 1208, para 3).

[51] eg *A v Secretary of State for the Home Department* [2005] 2 AC 68.

[52] eg *Secretary of State for the Home Department v MB* [2008] 1 AC 440.

[53] *N v Secretary of State for the Home Department* [2005] 2 AC 296.

[54] *R (Al-Skeini) v Secretary of State for Defence* [2008] 1 AC 153.

[55] *R (Munjaz) v Mersey Care NHS Trust* [2006] 2 AC 148.

[56] *Re B (Children) (Care Proceedings: Standard of Proof)* [2008] 3 WLR 1. CAFCASS is the Children and Family Court Advisory Support Service.

[57] eg *R (Hoxha) v Special Adjudicator* [2005] 1 WLR 1063, *R (European Roma Rights Centre) v Immigration Officer at Prague Airport* [2005] 2 AC 1, and *R v Asfaw* [2008] 1 AC 1061.

[58] [2006] 2 AC 221.

[59] eg the Attorney General in *Re Spectrum Plus Ltd* [2005] 2 AC 680 (see n 60 below), and P Jones in *Re Pantmaenog Timber Co Ltd (in liq)* [2004] 1 AC 158, the first case on the Company Directors Disqualification Act 1986 to reach the Lords.

[60] [2005] 2 AC 680. See also ch 9 in this volume.

for the future but decide the case at hand in accordance with the old law), but on the facts of the case before them they decided that it would be inappropriate to exercise this new power and Lords Steyn and Scott were against ever using the power in respect of an issue of statute law.[61] Lords Nicholls and Hope were the most explicit in saying 'never say never',[62] accepting that there may be exceptional situations where using the power would be justified, and observing that the power was already available to the Privy Council (in devolution cases) and was used by the European Court of Justice and the European Court of Human Rights.[63] The power is a significant one, giving the Lords considerable scope to develop the law for the future while not doing an injustice to the litigants before them, who must be presumed to have relied on the existing state of the law. Even more importantly, in *R (Jackson) v Attorney General* there are clear dicta from Lords Steyn and Hope that in appropriate circumstances the House might even be prepared to disapply a provision in an Act of Parliament if it were held to be in violation of a fundamental constitutional right,[64] just as United Kingdom courts are empowered to do if they find a statutory provision to be in breach of EU law.

But undoubtedly the most demanding challenge facing the House since 2000 was the coming into force of the Human Rights Act 1998 (in October 2000). I have examined elsewhere the performance of the House in this area up to February 2006, concluding that their Lordships did, on the whole, do a good job.[65] They granted leave to appeal in numerous human rights cases and they delivered many scholarly judgments which made copious references to decisions of the European Court of Human Rights. Their Lordships were careful to adhere to that Court's principles, but they were generally reluctant to develop domestic law in a way which went further in the protection of human rights unless such protection could be firmly rooted in common law precedents. While Lord Bingham sat in most of the human rights appeals, Lord Steyn was also a very prominent participant, and he wrote several articles for legal journals on the theme,[66] as well as giving interviews about the Government's approach to human rights shortly after he retired from the Bench in 2005.[67]

In the years that have elapsed since my 2006 analysis, the Lords have generally continued to limit themselves to the European Court's standards and have rejected several human rights claims which civil libertarians within the United Kingdom

---

[61] paras 45 and 125 respectively.

[62] paras 39–42 and 71–4 respectively. See too Lord Steyn at para 45.

[63] paras 17 and 23–5 (Lord Nicholls) and 68–9 (Lord Hope).

[64] [2006] 1 AC 262, para 102 (Lord Steyn) and para 107 (Lord Hope). See Lord Cooke, 'A Constitutional Retreat' (2006) 122 LQR 224.

[65] 'Safe in Their Hands? Britain's Law Lords and Human Rights' (2006) 26 LS 329.

[66] 'Democracy Through Law' [2002] EHRLR 723; 'Dynamic Interpretation Amidst an Orgy of Statutes' [2004] EHRLR 245; '2000–2005: Laying the Foundations of Human Rights Law in the United Kingdom' [2005] EHRLR 349; 'Deference: A Tangled Story' [2005] PL 346.

[67] See <http://news.bbc.co.uk/1/hi/uk_politics/4318114.stm> (last accessed 13 March 2009).

staunchly supported.[68] In several of those cases the decision was reached by a narrow majority.[69] But in one very recent case, an appeal from Northern Ireland on the right of unmarried couples to adopt, the Lords decided to go further than they felt the European Court itself might go and affirmed that the scope of Convention rights in United Kingdom domestic law is something which the top court, as well as Parliament, can determine.[70] Lord Bingham himself did not sit in this appeal, but he did give the lead judgment in *R v Davis*, where the House held that an appellant who had been convicted of murder had had an unfair trial because the conviction was based solely, or to a decisive extent, on the testimony of anonymous witnesses.[71]

The two key questions concerning the Human Rights Act which the Bingham court repeatedly had to confront were when to apply section 3 of the Act (which imposes a duty to interpret primary and secondary legislation in a way which is compatible with European Convention rights, 'so far as it is possible to do so') and when, if section 3 could not be employed, to apply instead section 4 (which empowers the House to issue a declaration that primary legislation is incompatible with Convention rights, but not a declaration that the legislation is invalid or should be 'disapplied'[72]). At first blush section 4 might seem to be the more powerful judicial tool, but in fact it simply allows a message to be sent to Parliament that unless the legislation in question is amended the United Kingdom stands in danger of losing a challenge to its law in the European Court of Human Rights. In the period under review the House resorted to section 4 on five occasions,[73] and on three further occasions it reversed the decision of the

---

[68] eg *R (Gillan) v Comr of Police for the Metropolis* [2006] 2 AC 91 (stop and search powers); *Jones v Ministry of Interior, Saudi Arabia* [2007] 1 AC 270 (civil liability for torture); *R (Al-Jedda) v Secretary of State for Defence* [2008] 1 AC 332 (relationship between UN Security Council Resolutions and the European Convention on Human Rights); *Van Colle v Chief Constable of Hertfordshire Police* [2009] 1 AC 225 (extent of positive obligation to protect life); *Re E (A Child)* [2008] 3 WLR 1208 (extent of positive obligation to prevent inhuman or degrading treatment).

[69] eg *R (Hurst) v Metropolitan Police Comr* [2007] 2 AC 189 (3:2); *Jordan v Lord Chancellor* [2007] 2 AC 226 (3:2); *Kay v Lambeth LBC* [2006] 2 AC 465 (4:3); *R v Abdroikov* [2007] 1 WLR 2679 (3:2); *YL v Birmingham CC* [2008] 1 AC 95 (3:2).

[70] *Re G (Adoption: Unmarried Couple)* [2009] 1 AC 173, where, with Lord Walker dissenting, the Lords reversed the Northern Ireland Court of Appeal and held that article 14 of the Adoption (NI) Order 1987 was in contravention of Art 8 of the ECHR because it completely prevented unmarried couples from adopting a child. See too ch 30 in this volume.

[71] [2008] 3 WLR 125. The decision led to the rapid enactment of the Criminal Evidence (Witness Anonymity) Act 2008, which is fairly certain to come under scrutiny by the European Court of Human Rights sooner or later.

[72] The term used by the House when holding that primary legislation must be overridden by EU law: see *R v Secretary of State for Transport, ex p Factortame Ltd (No 2)* [1991] 1 AC 603.

[73] *R (Anderson) v Secretary of State for the Home Department* [2003] 1 AC 837; *Bellinger v Bellinger* [2003] 2 AC 467; *A v Secretary of State for the Home Department* [2005] 2 AC 68; *R (Clift) v Secretary of State for the Home Department* [2007] 1 AC 484; *R (Baiai) v Secretary of State for the Home Department (Nos 1 and 2)* [2009] 1 AC 287. In *Doherty v Birmingham CC* [2008] 3 WLR 636 the House would have issued a s 4 declaration had the law not already been changed by the Housing and Regeneration Act 2008. See also *R (Wright) v Secretary of State for Health* [2009] 2 WLR 267.

court below to issue a declaration of incompatibility.[74] The section 3 power can have a greater impact because, once it has been exercised, it immediately changes the reach of the legislation in question and may provide the litigant with a remedy for his or her grievance. The House was particularly willing to use this power in *R v A*,[75] where it followed the approach of the Supreme Court of Canada[76] in 'reading down' (ie limiting) a rape-shield provision so as to ensure that the defendant's right to a fair trial was upheld. It also resorted to section 3 in *Ghaidan v Godin-Mendoza*, where it ruled that a gay man could be construed to be the 'spouse' of his deceased partner, whose tenancy he could then succeed to,[77] and in *Secretary of State for the Home Department v MB*,[78] where cases were referred back to the High Court with a direction that relevant statutory provisions on control orders must be read down to ensure that the controlee's right to liberty was not breached.

In a range of other cases involving the application of Convention rights the Bingham court was curiously conservative, perhaps conscious that the Human Rights Act is not viewed with universal approbation, especially by most of the tabloid press. Thus, by a majority of three to two it held that the Act does not benefit residents of a nursing home run by a private company even when most of the cost of the care provided is borne by a local authority.[79] It also held that the Act does not benefit the families of people killed by security forces in Northern Ireland prior to October 2000, while at the same time holding that inquests into deaths occurring in England and Wales before that date *could* be required to satisfy Article 2 of the European Convention.[80] It denied that the Act gives victims of torture the right to bring a civil action in the United Kingdom against the state that has carried out the torture,[81] and it allowed the right to liberty in the European Convention to be sidelined by UN Security Council Resolutions regarding the activities of British forces in Iraq.[82] In addition, their Lordships have recently confirmed that, when deciding whether a public authority has properly exercised its powers, they will look only at whether the decision ultimately emanating from the authority has violated a person's Convention rights, not at whether the authority appropriately weighed up the various human rights considerations when it was making its decision.[83] This has the potential to undermine

---

[74] *R (Alconbury Developments Ltd) v Secretary of State for the Environment, Transport and the Regions* [2003] 2 AC 295; *Wilson v First County Trust Ltd* [2004] 1 AC 816; *R (H) v Secretary of State for the Department of Health* [2006] 1 AC 441. See also *R (Black) v Secretary of State for Justice* [2009] 2 WLR 282.

[75] [2002] 1 AC 45.   [76] *R v Seaboyer* [1991] 2 SCR 577.   [77] [2004] 2 AC 557.

[78] [2008] 1 AC 440.

[79] *YL v Birmingham CC* [2008] 1 AC 95; Lord Bingham and Lady Hale dissented. The law was subsequently amended by the Health and Social Care Act 2008, s 145.

[80] Contrast *Re McKerr* [2004] 1 WLR 807 with *R (Middleton) v West Somerset Coroner* [2004] 2 AC 182.

[81] *R v Jones (Margaret)* [2007] 1 AC 136.

[82] *R (Al-Jedda) v Secretary of State for Defence* [2008] 1 AC 332.

[83] *Belfast CC v Miss Behavin' Ltd* [2007] 1 WLR 1420, confirming the approach adopted in *R (SB) v Head Teacher and Governors of Denbigh High School* [2007] 1 AC 100.

the underlying purpose of the Human Rights Act, which was surely to instill within public authorities a deep awareness of the importance of taking human rights into account at all times. In one of the last cases heard by Lord Bingham, where rights of residence were at issue outside of the context of the Human Rights Act, and, where, strangely, only five Law Lords sat, the House held by three to two that the prerogative power to make laws for the peace, order, and good government of a colony could not be made subject to any conditions—a decision which is difficult to square with a meaningful concept of the rule of law.[84] Many would argue that the House's unanimous failure to overturn the decision of the Director of the Serious Fraud Office not to continue corruption investigations relating to the alleged bribery of Saudi officials, supposedly because of dire warnings expressed by Prime Minister Tony Blair, was also most regrettable.[85]

A further seismic change in the constitutional arrangements for the United Kingdom was brought about by the devolution legislation enacted in 1998, which mostly came into effect in 1999.[86] Issues arising from Wales have not troubled their Lordships, doubtless because the Welsh Assembly has very few legislative powers. But by October 2008 20 cases on devolution issues in Scotland had reached their Lordships while sitting in the Privy Council (a jurisdiction which will be transferred to the Supreme Court of the United Kingdom in October 2009),[87] and several important cases touching upon the outworkings of the peace process in Northern Ireland had had to be resolved within the House.[88] It is very apparent that in the cases from Northern Ireland most members of the Bingham court were keen to support the political manoeuvres aimed at securing a lasting settlement there. How else can one explain the extraordinary decision, by three to two, to uphold the election of David Trimble and Mark Durkan as First and deputy First Ministers of Northern Ireland even though the election took place outside the time limit explicitly laid down in primary legislation?[89] Other indications of the Law Lords' support for the peace process can be gleaned from decisions such as *Re Northern Ireland Human Rights Commission*,[90] *R v Z*,[91] *In re McClean*,[92] and *In re Duffy*.[93]

---

[84] *R (Bancoult) v Secretary of State for Foreign and Commonwealth Affairs* [2008] 3 WLR 955; Lords Hoffmann, Rodger, and Carswell were in the majority; Lords Bingham and Mance dissented. See too ch 28 in this volume (postscript).

[85] *R (Corner House Research) v Director of Serious Fraud Office* [2008] 3 WLR 568.

[86] Scotland Act 1998; Government of Wales Act 1998; Northern Ireland Act 1998.

[87] Constitutional Reform Act 2005, s 40(4)(b) and Sch 9.

[88] See B Dickson, 'The House of Lords and the Conflict in Northern Ireland—A Sequel' (2006) 69 MLR 383. Relevant Northern Ireland appeals decided since that article include *Tweed v Parades Commission for Northern Ireland* [2007] 1 AC 650, *Jordan v Lord Chancellor* [2007] 2 AC 226, *Re Officer L* [2007] 1 WLR 2135, and *Re Duffy* [2008] NI 152.

[89] *Robinson v Secretary of State for Northern Ireland* [2002] NI 390. The dissenters were Lords Hutton and Hobhouse.

[90] [2002] NI 236 (see n 50 above).

[91] [2005] 2 AC 645 (the Real IRA was held to be a proscribed organisation).

[92] [2005] NI 490 (the process for considering the early release of prisoners was held to be fair).

[93] [2008] NI 152 (the appointment of two members of the Orange Order to the Parades Commission was held to be unlawful).

One of the first tasks Lord Bingham had to perform after taking up the post of Senior Law Lord was to notify the full House of Lords of the position adopted by the Lords of Appeal on the recommendation made in the report of the Royal Commission on Reform of the House of Lords that the Lords of Appeal 'should set out in writing and publish a statement of the principles which they intend to observe when participating in debates and votes in the second chamber and when considering their eligibility to sit on related cases'.[94] The statement read by Lord Bingham was terse and almost resentful in tone.[95] It made it clear, first, that Lords of Appeal are full members of the House of Lords who have a right to participate in the business of the House. It went on to state two rather bland principles which would bind the Lords of Appeal when deciding whether to participate or vote: '[F]irst, the Lords of Appeal in Ordinary do not think it appropriate to engage in matters where there is a strong element of party political controversy; and secondly the Lords of Appeal in Ordinary bear in mind that they might render themselves ineligible to sit judicially if they were to express an opinion on a matter which might later be relevant to an appeal to the House'. The statement added that each Lord of Appeal must decide how to conduct him- or herself in any particular situation. As regards eligibility to sit in an appeal, the statement said that the Lords of Appeal 'agree to be guided by the same principles as apply to all judges', which had recently been restated by the Court of Appeal in the *Locabail* case.[96] Lord Hope has subsequently traced the history of the involvement of Lords of Appeal in the legislative process, concluding that '[i]t is hard to point to any particular piece of legislation and say that, but for the Law Lords' participation, it would have been different from that which was enacted or that it would not have been there at all'.[97] He then gives one clear instance, and three others which were less clear, where 'it could be said that the presence of a serving Law Lord was crucial to the way a bill was dealt with in the House',[98] but none of these related to legislation enacted during the period currently under review.

Undoubtedly the greatest shock to the Appellate Committee during this period was the unexpected announcement by the Government in June 2003 that it would establish a Supreme Court of the United Kingdom and transfer the judicial functions of the House of Lords to that body. The abolition of the office of the Lord Chancellor was announced at the same time. An earlier chapter in this

---

[94] Recommendation 59 in *A House for the Future* (Cmnd 4534, 2000).

[95] *Hansard*, HL, vol 614, cols 419–20 (22 June 2000).

[96] [2000] QB 451, where Lord Bingham CJ, Lord Woolf MR and Sir Richard Scott VC gave a collective judgment.

[97] 'Voices from the Past—the Law Lords' Contribution to the Legislative Process' (2007) 123 LQR 547, 566. See too ch 11 in this volume.

[98] The clear instance was in relation to the State Immunity Act 1978. The other instances were in relation to the Scotland Bill 1978 (which was not enacted at that time, although a comparable Act was eventually enacted in 1998), the Arbitration Act 1996, the Theft (Amendment) Act 1996, and the Land Registration Act 1997.

volume explores this episode in much more detail,[99] but it is clear that the Lords of Appeal, and probably Lord Bingham as the Senior Law Lord (despite having been a strong advocate for the change in recent times), were taken completely by surprise by it.[100] When the Government later issued its consultation paper on the creation of a supreme court a month later, the Lords of Appeal responded with strong, and by no means unanimous, views.[101] Some Law Lords also referred to the matter when writing for legal journals,[102] a practice, incidentally, which has become much more common than in the past.[103] All were agreed, however, that the jurisdiction of the top court did not need to change much: it should retain the right to grant leave to appeal and should continue to decline to hear criminal cases from Scotland (even though some such cases already come to their Lordships in the Privy Council). Once it became clear that the Government was determined to go ahead with the establishment of a supreme court the Lords of Appeal rallied round to facilitate the transition. Lord Hope was appointed to chair a committee overseeing the process and little time was wasted in putting out for consultation a draft set of Rules of Procedure for the new Supreme Court. In the first half of 2008 a series of seminars on potential consequences of establishing the new Supreme Court, which involved several Lords of Appeal and were conducted under Chatham House rules, took place at Queen Mary, University of London.

The quality of the law-making

Views obviously differ as to what constitutes 'good quality' law-making on the part of judges, but most commentators would surely agree that amongst the criteria worth applying are (a) the clarity of expression in the judgments, (b) the degree to which the judgments explain how the decision relates to previous court decisions, (c) the strength of the reasoning process leading to the conclusions reached, and (d) the extent to which potential objections to the conclusions have been considered and overcome. These criteria overlap, but they are neutral as to the 'justness' of the decision reached.

Applying these criteria to the judgments of the Bingham court in the period 2000–8, it can be safely argued that the quality of the law-making was consistently high. In most areas of law the judgments issued, whether reflecting the majority or the minority view, were clear, thorough, well-reasoned, and carefully

---

[99] See ch 5.

[100] Lord Bingham himself analysed the Lord Chancellor's judicial role in 'The Old Order Changeth' (2006) 122 LQR 211.

[101] This response is available on the House of Lords' website, as is the Government's consultation paper.

[102] eg Baroness Hale, 'A New Supreme Court for the United Kingdom' (2004) 24 LS 36; Lord Cooke, 'The Law Lords: An Endangered Species' (2003) 119 LQR 49.

[103] In the years 2001–7 there were 27 lectures by former, current, or future Law Lords published in Public Law, the Law Quarterly Review, or the Cambridge Law Journal.

explained (if sometimes very long).[104] It would appear that peer pressure, if nothing else, resulted in each Law Lord striving hard to produce judgments that were comprehensive (in that they dealt with all the points raised by counsel at the hearing), categorical (in that they set out how the conclusions reached related to those reached in the judgments of their fellow judges in the appeal), and authoritative (in that they cited authorities for the principles relied upon). The practice of dividing judgments into headed sections increased and the frequency of very brief concurrences diminished.

A notable feature was the relaxed approach of the Lords to their own previous decisions—an approach which was also evident when they sat in the Privy Council.[105] There is now much less hesitation than there used to be in distinguishing or even in overruling previous decisions, even if all the principles governing this process have not yet been fully clarified.[106] Far from exhibiting a weakness in the court, this trend surely portrays a confidence and maturity which any top national court needs to have if it is to command the respect of the people. In *Kuddus v Chief Constable of Leicestershire Constabulary*[107] the Lords held that access to exemplary damages was not restricted to the categories of cases recognised before *Rookes v Barnard*;[108] in *Heaton v AXA Equity and Law Life Assurance Society plc*[109] Lord Mackay distinguished the House's very recent decision in *Jameson v CEGB*[110] regarding the impact of full and final settlements on subsequent claims against related parties; in *R (Anderson) v Secretary of State for the Home Department*[111] the House declined to follow its previous decision in *R v Secretary of State for the Home Department, ex parte Stafford*[112] because the European Court of Human Rights had in the meantime made it clear that in *Stafford* the House had adopted an interpretation of the European Convention of which the European Court itself was no longer in favour;[113] in *R v G*[114] their Lordships overruled *R v Caldwell*[115] on the meaning of 'recklessness' in criminal law; in *R (H) v Secretary of State for the Home Department*[116] they 'set aside' the ruling in *R v Oxford Regional Mental Health Review Tribunal, ex parte Secretary of State for the Home Department*,[117] where it had been held that a mental health

---

[104] For a general analysis of all the decisions taken by the House of Lords in recent years see Dickson (n 35) ch 9

[105] Since the turn of the century the Judicial Committee has already overruled its own previous decisions on three occasions: *Lewis v AG of Jamaica* [2001] 2 AC 50, *Boyce and Joseph v R* [2005] 1 AC 400, and *Gibson v Government of the USA* [2007] 1 WLR 2367. See generally D O'Brien, 'The Privy Council Overrules Itself—Again!' [2008] PL 28. On the practice in the House of Lords see ch 9 in this volume.

[106] See B Harris, 'Final Appellate Courts Overruling Their Own "Wrong" Precedents: The Ongoing Search for Principle' (2002) 118 LQR 408, which itself takes further the analysis conducted by JW Harris in 'Towards Principles of Overruling—When Should a Final Court of Appeal Second Guess?' (1990) 10 OJLS 135.

[107] [2002] 2 AC 122.   [108] [1964] AC 1129.   [109] [2002] 2 AC 329.
[110] [2000] 1 AC 455.   [111] [2003] 1 AC 837.   [112] [1999] 2 AC 38.
[113] *Stafford v UK* (2002) 35 EHRR 1121.   [114] [2004] 1 AC 1034.
[115] [1982] AC 341.   [116] [2004] 2 AC 280.   [117] [1988] AC 120.

review tribunal could not reconsider its decision to order the discharge of a patient; in *Ghaidan v Godin-Mendoza*[118] the Lords effectively refused to follow *Fitzpatrick Sterling Housing Association Ltd*[119] regarding the succession rights of gay men; in *Eastwood v Magnox Electric plc*[120] they distinguished their decision in *Johnson v Unisys Ltd*[121] regarding a claimant's entitlement to damages for unfair treatment by an employer; in *Kay v Lambeth LBC*[122] the House 'explained' its recent decision in *Harrow LBC v Qazi*[123] concerning the relationship between established property rights and the right of other persons to a home; in *Horton v Sadler*[124] it thought it right to depart from its earlier decision in *Walkley v Precision Forgings Ltd*[125] on a point to do with the law on limitation of actions; in *R v Kennedy (No 2)*[126] the Lords distinguished their decision in *R (National Grid Gas plc) v Environment Agency*[127] on the question of causation in criminal law; and in *A v Hoare*[128] they unequivocally overruled their own fairly recent decision in *Stubbings v Webb*[129] on whether a claim for damages for personal injuries caused by a sexual assault could be brought more than three years after the event. This long list of instances of re-positioning by the Law Lords is strong evidence that they are not prepared to let the law stagnate; on the contrary, they are very open to change.

The quality of the Bingham court's law-making was also enhanced by its willingness to hear counsel cite decisions reached in other jurisdictions on the points at issue. The Law Lords, in turn, frequently analysed these foreign decisions in some detail when delivering their own opinions.[130] And the references were not confined to the traditional common law jurisdictions such as the United States, Australia, and Canada. They extended to France, Germany, the Netherlands, and Israel. In this preparedness to compare its own preferred solutions with those reached elsewhere in the world the Bingham court displayed an internationalism which contrasts markedly with the disinterest in internationalism displayed by the US Supreme Court.[131] The practice also complements the growing engagement of the UK's top court with international law in general, as indicated elsewhere in this volume.[132] Probably the most remarkable examples of the House's handling of international legal sources since the turn of the century

---

[118] [2004] 2 AC 337.   [119] [2000] 1 AC 27.   [120] [2005] 1 AC 503.
[121] [2003] 1 AC 518.   [122] [2006] 2 AC 465.   [123] [2004] 1 AC 983.
[124] [2007] 1 AC 307.   [125] [1979] 1 WLR 606.   [126] [2008] 1 AC 269.
[127] [2007] 1 WLR 1780.   [128] [2008] 1 AC 844.
[129] [1993] AC 498. This decision had been held by the European Court of Human Rights not to be in breach of Art 6 of the European Convention: *Stubbings v UK* (1997) 23 EHRR 213.
[130] Most commonly in cases involving international conventions, such as *Morris v KLM Royal Dutch Airlines* [2002] 2 AC 628 and *Kirin-Amgen Inc v Hoechst Marion Roussel Ltd* [2005] 1 All ER 667, but also more generally, as in *Fairchild v Glenhaven Funeral Services Ltd* [2002] 1 AC 32.
[131] Lord Reed, 'Foreign Precedents and Judicial Reasoning: The American Debate and the British Practice' (2008) 124 LQR 253. See too Lord Cooke, 'The Road Ahead for the Common Law' (2004) 53 ICLQ 273.
[132] See ch 26 in this volume.

have been the two cases involving non-British detainees in Belmarsh Prison[133] and two further cases involving detainees in Iraq.[134]

Now and again the old saw that judges should not be 'political' raised its head during the Bingham era, leading some commentators to suggest that the Human Rights Act (for example) required judges to reveal their political leanings. The reality, of course, is that top judges have always had to decide appeals that have had political ramifications, but they have had to do so by applying the law as it stands, not in accordance with how they might want it to be. Outstanding examples of this in the current period are *Porter v Magill*, where the Lords held that Conservative councillors on Westminster City Council had adopted an unlawful policy concerning house sales;[135] *Carter v Ahsan*, on whether the Labour Party had conferred a 'qualification' for the purposes of race discrimination law;[136] *R (Countryside Alliance) v Attorney General*, on whether the ban on fox hunting was a denial of basic human rights;[137] *R (Gentle) v The Prime Minister*, on the legal implications of sending troops to Iraq in 2003;[138] and *R (Corner House Research) v Director of Serious Fraud Office*, on whether the Prime Minister had unduly influenced the Director of the Serious Fraud Office when he was investigating corruption allegations.[139]

One of the most fascinating aspects of the Bingham court was the contribution made by the first woman to be appointed to the top court. Baroness Hale is a strong proponent of the need to apply a female perspective to legal problems and in several of her judgments to date she has made it clear that she will not be cowed into falling into line with the traditional view of her male counterparts. Perhaps the most startling example of this is *R v J*,[140] where the four male judges held that it was impermissible for the Crown to prosecute a man for indecent assault in circumstances where the conduct in question was unlawful sexual intercourse with a girl under 16 and the time limit for prosecuting that latter offence had expired. Lord Bingham, underlining that it was the court's duty not to facilitate the circumvention of parliamentary intent, said any other construction of the legislation was 'impossible'.[141] Baroness Hale, just nine months into office as a

---

[133] *A v Secretary of State for the Home Department* [2005] 2 AC 68 and *A v Secretary of State for the Home Department (No 2)* [2006] 2 AC 221. Lord Bingham's approach in the former of these cases was to some extent anticipated by what he said in the 2002 Romanes Lecture at Oxford University, published as 'Personal Freedom and the Dilemma of Democracies' (2003) 52 ICLQ 841.

[134] *R (Al-Skeini) v Secretary of State for Defence* [2008] 1 AC 153 and *R (Al-Jedda) v Secretary of State for the Defence* [2008] 1 AC 322.

[135] [2002] 2 AC 357.   [136] [2008] 1 AC 696.

[137] [2008] 1 AC 719 some additional arguments against the equivalent ban in Scottish law were also dismissed in *Whaley v Lord Advocate* [2008] SC(HL) 107.

[138] [2008] 1 AC 1356. In his Grotius Lecture on 17 November 2008 (less than two months after retiring as Senior Law Lord) Lord Bingham said that the invasion of Iraq by the US, the UK, and others was a 'serious violation of international law'. See <http://www.biicl.org/news/view/-/id/109> (last visited 13 March 2009).

[139] [2008] 3 WLR 568.   [140] [2005] 1 AC 562.

[141] ibid, para 18. The legislation in question was s 14 of the Sexual Offences Act 1956.

Lord of Appeal, approached the case very much from the point of view of the young female victim of the defendant's behaviour. She said that the Sexual Offences Act 1956 'was a mess when it was enacted and became an ever greater mess with later amendments'; it was 'not possible' to discern within the Act such a coherent parliamentary intention as to require it to be interpreted in the way that her four judicial colleagues chose to interpret it, and '[a]lthough we do have to try to make sense of the words Parliament has used, we do not have to supply Parliament with the thinking it never did and the words it never used'.[142]

Baroness Hale's new perspective was made evident in several other appeals too. In *R (Hoxha) v Special Adjudicator,* a case about a claim for asylum, she focused on the gender-related violence suffered by an Albanian woman at the hands of Serbian armed forces and regretted that the issues around it had not been fully explored at an earlier stage in the proceedings;[143] in *R (R) v Durham Constabulary* she expressed considerable misgivings (while not dissenting) about the majority's ruling that the police's power to issue a warning to a young offender did not violate his or her rights under Article 6 of the European Convention;[144] in *R (Kehoe) v Secretary of State for Work and Pensions* she did dissent when her four male brethren held that the Child Support Act 1981 had not violated the right of a mother under Article 6 of the European Convention when it took away her right to go to a court to claim financial support for her children from their absent father;[145] she also dissented in *M v Secretary of State for Work and Pensions,* where a lesbian who was now living with her lover was held by the majority to be ineligible for a reduction in liability to pay child maintenance to her former husband;[146] she dissented again in *A v Head Teacher of Lord Grey School,* where her male counterparts held that the child in question had not been denied the right to education by being excluded from school;[147] and she dissented in *Down Lisburn Health and Social Service Trust v H,* on whether a child should be freed for adoption against the wishes of her mother.[148] Baroness Hale also gave the most substantive judgment in cases involving the law on mental health,[149] and on the

---

[142] ibid, para 89.   [143] [2005] 1 WLR 1063, esp para 40.

[144] [2005] 1 WLR 1184. Cf *E v Chief Constable of the Royal Ulster Constabulary* [2008] 3 WLR 1208 66, concerning police action during the Loyalist 'protest' near the Holy Cross Primary School in Belfast in 2001, where Lady Hale emphasised the rights of the children but ruled that had the police behaved as it was now being claimed they should have behaved the children's experience could have been a great deal worse (para 14).

[145] [2006] 1 AC 42.   [146] [2006] 2 AC 91.   [147] [2006] 2 AC 363.

[148] [2007] 1 FLR 121.

[149] *R (B) v Ashworth Hospital Authority* [2005] 2 AC 278; *Ward v Comr of Police for the Metropolis* [2006] 1 AC 340; *R (H) v Secretary of State for the Department of Health* [2006] 1 AC 441. In *YL v Birmingham CC* [2008] 1 AC 95 Lady Hale joined Lord Bingham in dissenting from the majority's view that a privately owned care home was not a public authority for the purposes of the Human Rights Act 1998 and in *Seal v Chief Constable of South Wales Police* she joined Lord Woolf in dissenting from the majority's view that there was an absolute statutory ban on a person suing without the leave of the High Court in respect of acts done under the Mental Health Act 1983. In *R (Munjaz) v Mersey Care NHS Trust* [2006] 2 AC 148 the House overturned the decision of the Court of Appeal on a mental health issue; the leading judgment in the Court of Appeal had been given by Hale LJ, as she then was.

care[150] or abduction[151] of children. But, needless to say, the other Law Lords have not ceded the ground completely on matters that are of great interest to their female colleague. They have continued to contribute significantly in fields such as sex discrimination law[152] and the law on ownership of the matrimonial home.[153] Lady Hale has in turn contributed valuably to the development of (amongst other areas) criminal law,[154] not an area in which she had previously specialised.

Other members of the Bingham court have acquired special reputations for their insightfulness, incisiveness, and sheer industry. Invidious though it may be to single out individuals, the brilliance of the intellect of Lord Hoffmann and the rigour and conscientiousness of Lord Hope, respectively the current and future 'deputy' leaders of the top court, bear a mention.

Conclusion

It may be hyperbole to say that the years 2000–8 represent a golden age in the history of the House of Lords, but there is little doubt that, by whatever criteria one chooses to assess it, the performance of the court in that period was very good. The challenge for judges in liberal democracies at the dawn of the twenty-first century is to play a role which reassures the public that, while not being elected officials, they have the wisdom, and above all the independence, to justify their decisions in accordance with principles and precedents, particularly in cases involving human rights and state responsibility more generally. They must be seen not as obstacles to modernisation, or as thwarters of the democratic will, but as facilitators of justice and proponents of fairness. They are called upon to adjudicate on an ever-widening array of legal issues, and the various policy considerations they have to weigh in the balance are often numerous and contradictory. Under the leadership of Lord Bingham of Cornhill the House of Lords has in recent years set a standard on all these fronts which the new Supreme Court of the United Kingdom will find difficult to emulate.

---

[150] *Re G (A Minor) (Interim Care Order: Residential Assessment)* [2006] 1 AC 576; *Re G (Children) (Residence: Same-sex Partner)* [2006] 1 WLR 2305; *R (M) v Hammersmith and Fulham LBC* [2008] 1 WLR 535.

[151] *Re J (A Child) (Return to Foreign Jurisdiction: Convention Rights)* [2006] 1 AC 80; *Re D (A Child) (Abduction: Rights of Custody)* [2007] 1 AC 619; *Re M (Children) (Abduction: Rights of Custody)* [2008] 1 AC 1288.

[152] *St Helens BC v Derbyshire* [2007] 3 All ER 81.

[153] *Stack v Dowden* [2007] 2 AC 432.

[154] eg in *R v Hasan* [2005] 2 AC 467; *R v Rimmington* [2006] 1 AC 459; *R v Abdroikov* [2007] 1 WLR 2679.

PART D

REGIONAL AND EXTERNAL PERSPECTIVES

17

From Scotland and Ireland

(a) Scotland after 1707

Philip H Brodie

The Treaty of Union

The history of the exercise by the House of Lords of an appellate jurisdiction in relation to the Scottish courts begins with the Treaty of Union[1] between Scotland and England. For England the Union meant, in large part, continuity in constitutional arrangements. For Scotland it meant quite radical change. This reflected the contemporary political reality. Despite the formalities this was not a partnership of equals.[2] By any reckoning, the balance of power was decidedly in England's favour.

The Union Agreement of 1707[3] established a new unitary state. Article I provided: '[T]he two Kingdoms of Scotland and England, shall upon the 1st May [1707]...and forever after, be united into one kingdom by the name of Great Britain...'[4] Article III provided that 'the United Kingdom of Great Britain be

<hr/>

[1] The Treaty was signed by the Commissioners for both Scotland and England in London on 22 July 1706. It was ratified, with amendments and the incorporation of the Protestant Religion and Presbyterian Church Act 1707 (c 6) APS XI, by the Scottish Estates on 16 January of the following year by the Union with England Act 1707 (c 7) APS XI and by the Parliament of England on 6 March by the Union with Scotland Act 1706 (6 Anne c 11). Why the earlier Scottish Act bears the date '1707' whereas the later English Act bears the date '1706' is explained by RK Murray (later Lord Murray) in 'The Anglo-Scottish Union' 1961 SLT (News) 161. By the beginning of the eighteenth century Scotland had adopted the Gregorian calendar. England did not dispense with the Julian calendar until 1752, hence the discrepancy.

[2] See eg MK Addo and VM Smith, 'The Relevance of Historical Fact to Certain Arguments Relating to the Legal Significance of the Acts of Union' [1998] JR 37.

[3] This is the term used by Sir Thomas Smith in *The Laws of Scotland, Stair Memorial Encyclopaedia* (hereinafter *SME*) (London: Butterworths, 1987) vol 5, para 345. As is observed by Phillips and Jackson, *Constitutional and Administrative Law* (London: Sweet & Maxwell, 8th edn 2001) para 4-006, while Englishmen refer to the English 'Act of Union', Scotsmen tend to refer to the 'Treaty'.

[4] It is usual to refer to the effect of the Treaty, as enacted, as the 'Union of the Parliaments' in contradistinction to the 'Union of the Crowns' of 1603 when King James VI of Scotland succeeded

represented by one and the same Parliament, to be styled the Parliament of Great Britain'. The composition of the new Parliament of Great Britain was provided by Article XXII of the Treaty. Of the peers of Scotland, 16 were to sit and vote in the House of Lords together with the Lords of Parliament of England. Forty-five representatives of Scotland were to be elected to sit in the House of Commons of the Parliament of Great Britain together with the Members of the House of Commons of the Parliament of England. Effectively, therefore, the Treaty provided that the new Parliament of Great Britain should inherit the two chambers of the former Parliament of England, albeit with slightly augmented memberships, together with their established powers and traditions.

The assumption of an appellate jurisdiction from the Scottish courts

By the end of the seventeenth century the House of Lords, as the English Sovereign and his council in Parliament, had established an appellate jurisdiction both in common law and equity, albeit not without controversy.[5] In Scotland, prior to 1707, matters were not quite clear-cut. The view that had prevailed in 1674, when 50 members of the Faculty of Advocates were disbarred for asserting the contrary, was that there no longer existed a right of appeal from the superior civil court, the Court of Session, to the Convention of Estates. A decision of the Court of Session, once arrived at, was therefore final. That position appeared to have been reversed by the Claim of Right of 1689[6] when the Convention of Estates enacted that there was a right to protest to the King and Parliament for 'remeid of law' against 'sentences' of the Court of Session, providing that a protestation did not stop execution of the decree or sentence, and between 1689 and 1707 the Estates exercised jurisdiction over the Court in respect of protestations.[7] However, no lesser authority than the Lord President, Viscount Stair, in the second edition of his *Institutions of the Law of Scotland*, published in 1693, argued that what had been allowed by the Claim of Right was no more than an extraordinary remedy available only in the event of excess of jurisdiction and not a more general right of appeal on an allegation of injustice.[8]

---

to the throne of England on the death of Queen Elizabeth. However, as is argued by Lord Murray, from the legal standpoint the Union of the Crowns and the Union of the Parliaments both took place in 1707, the Union being primarily a union of the crowns: Murray (n 1); RK Murray, 'Devolution in the UK—A Scottish Perspective' (1980) 96 LQR 35.

[5] L Blom-Cooper and G Drewry, *Final Appeal* (Oxford: Clarendon, 1972) 18–22; *SME* (n 3) vol 6, paras 802–3.

[6] c 28, APS ix, 39, 40, 45.   [7] *SME* (n 3) vol 6, para 809.

[8] Stair, Institutions IV, I, 56 and 61.

On 1 May 1707 the House of Lords, from being part of the English Parliament, became part of the British Parliament. It nevertheless retained its appellate jurisdiction over the English superior courts. It was also to assume an appellate jurisdiction over the Scottish superior courts and, in particular, the Court of Session. Although this was to happen apparently seamlessly there was potential for complication. The Treaty had said nothing about appeal from Scotland to the House of Lords. Article XIX provided:

[N]o causes in Scotland be cognoscible by the courts of Chancery, Queens-Bench, Common-Pleas, or any other court in Westminster-hall; and that the said courts, or any other of the like nature after the Union, shall have no power to cognosce, review or alter the acts or sentences of the judicatures within Scotland, or stop the execution of the same.[9]

However, while that seemed on the face of it quite clear, the House of Lords did not sit in Westminster-hall, nor was it of like nature to the specified courts.

If there were initial uncertainties over the availability of appeal from Scotland in civil matters,[10] they were quickly resolved. Notice was given to the House of Lords of the first 'test'[11] appeal, *Roseberie v Inglis* on 16 February 1708. It was not proceeded with but the respondent had not disputed competency and the example had been given. Unsurprisingly, English procedural forms were adopted.[12] When competency was challenged in an appeal from Scotland in the following year, the Lords held that they had jurisdiction,[13] and that has remained

---

[9] Interestingly and no doubt eloquent as to where the balance of power lay, there is no equivalent provision in the Treaty protecting English judgments against appeal to Scottish courts. As TB (later Sir Thomas) Smith put it, 'the possibility that causes in the Queen's Bench, Common-Pleas or Exchequer would be cognosced in the Parliament House [where the Court of Session sat and still sits] was too fantastic to contemplate': 'The Union of 1707 as Fundamental Law' in *Studies Critical and Comparative* (Edinburgh: W Green, 1962) 9.

[10] In *Law From Over the Border* (Edinburgh: W Green, 1950) 3, Professor Andrew Dewar Gibb expresses the view that it is a historical mystery as yet unsolved what the Commissioners for negotiating the Union really intended to do about the right of appeal. As Gibb acknowledges, Dicey and Rait in *Thoughts on the Scottish Union* at pp 192ff had proposed that the reason was to deny Scottish anti-Unionists the propaganda advantage of being able to present the prospect of an English court interfering with Scots law. AJ MacLean puts forward a different explanation in 'The 1707 Union: Scots Law and the House of Lords' 4(3) Journal of Legal History, reprinted in AKR Kiralfy and HL MacQueen, *New Perspectives in Scottish History* (London: Frank Cass, 1984) 63. He agrees with Dicey and Rait that it was well understood by the Commissioners from both countries that the result of an incorporating union meant that the House of Lords of the new British Parliament would be the sovereign judicial power in Great Britain and therefore competent to hear appeals from the Court of Session. The silence of the Treaty can therefore be taken to have been deliberate, but he argues that this had more to do with soothing English anxieties than Scottish ones. Scots law has never distinguished law and equity in the way that English law has done. In 1707 the House of Lords had only recently successfully asserted appellate jurisdiction in equity. The Court of Session was a court of both law and equity and therefore any appeal from the Court of Session might touch on what in England would be a matter for a court of equity. Such had been the intensity of the dispute on the issue of the extent of the Lords' jurisdiction that MacLean suggests that the English Commissioners considered it prudent not to re-ignite it by any express mention of appeals in the Articles of Union.

[11] Blom-Cooper and Drewry (n 5) 32.   [12] Robertson, *Reports*, preface p xv.

[13] *Greenshields v Magistrates of Edinburgh* (1709) 1 Rob 12.

the position in relation to appeals from the Inner House of the Court of Session, subject to a few statutory exceptions.[14] The approach taken with appeals from the Court of Session was not, however, adopted with the High Court of Justiciary. No appeal lies from that court.[15] Thus, while the House of Lords is the supreme civil court of appeal for Scotland it has no jurisdiction in relation to Scottish criminal cases, although the clarity of that distinction has recently been somewhat clouded by the Scotland Act 1998 and the jurisdiction that that Act confers on the Privy Council to hear an appeal against a determination of a devolution issue by two or more judges of the High Court of Justiciary.[16]

The volume of Scottish business

At the time of the negotiation of the Treaty there had been those who had assumed that the difficulty and expense associated with a journey to London would mean that appeals would be unattractive and therefore infrequent.[17] They were to be proved wrong. Disappointed litigants in the Court of Session saw advantage in undertaking the expense of a trip to London and they did so in numbers. An obvious benefit was delay. This was made the more valuable by the Order of the House of 19 April 1709[18] bringing the consequences of a Scottish appeal into conformity with the practice in English appeals by enacting that an appeal from a Scottish court prevented execution of the sentence or decree appealed against. It would seem likely that other factors were at work, including deficiencies in the Court of Session, in addition to any peculiarly Scottish pre-dilection for putting off the day of final reckoning, but whatever the precise reasons, such was the volume of appeals from north of the border that Blom-Cooper and Drewry[19] are able, remarkably, to refer to the House of Lords at the end of the eighteenth century as 'to all intents and purposes a Scottish court'. The figures bear this out: between 1794 and 1807, of 501 appeals presented to the House, 419 came from Scotland.[20]

Unsurprisingly, this gross disproportion between Scottish and English business was seen as an abuse which required to be remedied. The fault was seen to lie with

---

[14] The jurisdiction was given statutory expression in the Appellate Jurisdiction Act 1876 and now in the Court of Session Act 1988 s 40.

[15] *James Bywater* (1781) 2 Pat 563; *Mackintosh v Lord Advocate* (1876–77) 2 App Cas 41; Criminal Procedure (Scotland) Act 1995 s 124 (2); and see AJ MacLean, 'The House of Lords and Appeals from the High Court of Justiciary 1707–1887', [1985] JR 192.

[16] Scotland Act 1998, s 98 and sch 6 para 13; and see *Sinclair v HM Advocate* 2005 SCCR 446 *per* Lord Hope at [37]; and Ferguson, 'Privy Council Criminal Appeals' 2008 SLT (News) 133.

[17] MacLean (n 10) 69, citing Defoe, *History of the Union*, 161.

[18] Journal of the House of Lords, vol 18, p 713, cited in *SME* vol 6, para 818.

[19] Blom-Cooper and Drewry (n 5) 31.

[20] N Phillipson, *The Scottish Whigs and the Reform of the Court of Session 1785–1830* (Edinburgh: The Stair Society, 1990) 85.

the Court of Session. Legislation[21] was introduced in order to modify the effect of the Order of 1709 by giving the Court of Session a discretion to decide whether appeal to the House of Lords should prevent immediate execution of a sentence or decree. It also prohibited appeal from interlocutory judgments unless the Court of Session gave leave or where there was disagreement among the judges (but imposing no leave requirement for appeal against a final decree). These reforms had limited impact. The five-year period from 1811 to 1815 saw some diminution in the numbers of Scottish appeals compared with the previous five years, 193 rather than 225, but they still represented about 80 per cent of the total of all appeals.[22] There was a substantial backlog. In December 1812 the arrears of appeals and writs of error amounted to more than 276 cases, 'four-fifths of the whole arrear consisting of Scottish appeals upon questions of fact'.[23] It was in large part with a view to eradicating such appeals on fact that civil jury trial was introduced to Scotland.[24] Again, despite the hopes of the reformers, Scottish litigants' enthusiasm for the Lords was only slightly dampened. Well into the nineteenth century they continued to present appeals in disproportionately high numbers.[25] Phillipson notes that between 1835 and 1855 Scottish appeals never represented less than 39 per cent and, more usually, around 60 per cent of all the Lords' business.[26] According to statistics presented to the 1872 Select Committee on the Appellate Jurisdiction, during the period from 1865 to 1871 half of appeals and writs of error presented to the House came from the Court of Session.[27] The subsequent trend has been strongly downward. By 1880 the proportion had dropped to a third;[28] in 1903 to ten appeals from a total of 79;[29] and in 1910 to 18 from 89.[30]

More recently, while low numbers make for the possibility of significant variations year on year, the proportion of appeals coming from Scotland has been about 10 per cent of all appellate business.[31] In 2004, of 77 civil and criminal cases disposed of by the House, 10 were from Scotland.[32] In 2005 the equivalent

---

[21] Court of Session Act 1808 (c 151) s 17.   [22] Phillipson (n 20) 127.

[23] Blom-Cooper and Drewry (n 5) 31, citing Twiss, *Life of Lord Eldon*, vol 2, 238–40.

[24] This was provided by the institution of the Jury Court in terms of the Jury Trials (Scotland) Act 1815 (c 42). The new tribunal was to prove short-lived. The jurisdiction of the independent Jury Court was transferred to the Court of Session by s 1 of the Court of Session Act 1830.

[25] Echoing Blom-Cooper and Drewry's characterisation of the House of Lords in the eighteenth century, R Stevens, *Law and Politics: The House of Lords as a Judicial Body* (London: Weidenfeld & Nicolson, 1979) at 323 describes it as 'for much of the nineteenth century...predominantly a Scottish court'.

[26] Phillipson (n 20) 168.   [27] Blom-Cooper and Drewry (n 5) 35.

[28] ibid, 35, quoting Judicial Statistics (1880) C 3088, 44.

[29] ibid, 35, quoting Civil Judicial Statistics (1900) Cd 1115.

[30] ibid, 35, quoting Civil Judicial Statistics (1910) Cd 6047.

[31] In the ten years to 1997, of a total of 575 cases, 60 were Scottish appeals: Judicial Statistics, England and Wales, quoted in AA Paterson *et al*, *The Legal System of Scotland: Cases & Materials* (Edinburgh: W Green, 4th edn 1999) 89.

[32] House of Lords Judicial Business Statistics 2004.

figures were 102 and four[33] and in 2006 94 and, again, 10.[34] Even these more modest figures may be said to represent a disproportionate Scottish element in the judicial business of the House. Whereas an appeal to the House of Lords from any order or judgment of the Court of Appeal in England and Wales or in Northern Ireland may only be brought with the leave of the Court of Appeal or of the House of Lords[35] and leave will be granted only where the case raises an arguable point of general importance which ought to be considered when the appeal is brought, there is no equivalent requirement in relation to a final judgment of the Inner House of the Court of Session.[36] This is a privilege which is capable of being abused[37] and there is no question but that in recent years a number of Scottish appeals have been presented and argued which would not have got leave had such a requirement been in place.[38]

Scottish courts and Scots law

Notwithstanding that the Treaty of Union provided for a new unitary state, its two constituent parts (that 'now called England' and that 'now called Scotland'[39]) were to retain their respective courts and, at least to a certain extent and for the time being, their respective laws. There continues to be debate as to whether and to what extent the Union Agreement constitutes fundamental or higher law which has the effect, for example, of entrenching for as long as the Union remains in force, a separate Scottish legal system distinguished by its own courts and its own laws.[40] Lord President Cooper expressly reserved the question in *MacCormick v Lord Advocate*[41] and, despite arising in a number of variants in subsequent litigations,[42] it remains open. It need not be taken up here. For present purposes, it does not matter whether the relevant provisions of the Treaty are to be regarded

---

[33] House of Lords Judicial Business Statistics 2005.

[34] House of Lords Judicial Business Statistics 2006.

[35] Administration of Justice (Appeals) Act 1934, s 1(1); Judicature (Northern Ireland) Act 1978, s 42.

[36] Court of Session Act 1988, s 40(1)(a).

[37] As was pointed out by Lord Hope in *Wilson v Jaymarke* 2007 SLT 963.

[38] See J Chalmers, 'Scottish Appeals and the Proposed Supreme Court' (2004) 8 Edinburgh L Rev 4, 11.

[39] Article IX.

[40] See TB Smith, 'The Union of 1707 as Fundamental Law' [1957] PL 99, reprinted in *Studies Critical and Comparative* (n 9) 1; JDB Mitchell, *Constitutional Law* (Edinburgh: W Green, 2nd edn 1968); N MacCormick, 'Does the United Kingdom have a Constitution?' (1978) 29 NILQ 1; M Upton, 'Marriage Vows of the Elephant: The Constitution of 1707' (1989) 105 LQR 79; CR Munro, *Studies in Constitutional Law* (London: Butterworths, 2nd edn 1999) ch 5; Addo and Smith (n 2); E Wicks, 'A New Constitution for a New State? The 1707 Union of England and Scotland' (2001) 117 LQR 109; *R (Jackson) v Attorney General* [2006] 1 AC 262, *per* Lord Hope at 303Gff.

[41] 1953 SC 396 at 412.

[42] See eg *Gibson v Lord Advocate* 1975 SC 136; *Pringle, Petitioner* 1991 SLT 330; *Murray v Rogers* 1992 SLT 221; *Fraser v MacCorquadale* 1992 SLT 229; *Robbie the Pict v Hingston (No 2)* 1998 SLT 1201.

as constitutional guarantees or merely political assurances. The fact is that for all of the more than 300 years during which the House of Lords has exercised an appellate jurisdiction in respect of the Scottish courts, these courts have remained separate from and independent of their English counterparts[43] and the law which these courts have administered has remained distinct from that of England.

There appears to have been no doubt in the minds of the Commissioners who negotiated the Treaty of Union that in 1707 the laws of Scotland and England were quite different. Despite the passage of 300 years and the enactment by the 'one and the same Parliament' of an enormous amount of legislation that applies both to Scotland and England without distinction, that remains the case. It would be a foolhardy commentator who tried to explain how and why this is so in a few words or a few paragraphs. The views of scholars differ.[44] However, it may not be too controversial to say that modern Scots law is a 'mixed legal system' owing much to the civil law but also something to mediaeval feudal law and, post-nineteenth century, to the English common law. It remains different from the common law in ways that are obvious but also in ways that are more subtle.[45] A result of this difference is that the great majority of the judges who have determined Scottish appeals to the House of Lords over the history of the appellate jurisdiction have been operating a completely foreign system;[46] a state of affairs that has not escaped adverse notice.[47]

Administering a foreign system

For 160 years the tribunal to which Scots litigants appealed in such numbers functioned without the assistance of any judge appointed by reason of his knowledge of Scots law. Until 1844 lay peers sat and voted on appeals but, effectively, the judicial work of the House of Lords was done by the current Lord Chancellor; former Lord Chancellors; judges, such as Chief Justice Mansfield, who had been raised to the peerage; and, from 1827, by senior English judges

[43] '... in proper questions of jurisdiction ... the judicatories of Scotland and England are as independent of each other, within their respective territories, as if they were the judicatories of two foreign states', Lord President Inglis in *Orr Ewing v Orr Ewing's Trs* (1884) 11R 600 at 629; see also *R v Manchester Stipendiary Magistrate, ex p Granada Television* [2001] 1 AC 300, *per* Lord Hope at 304.

[44] For a measured, albeit incidental, introduction to the debate and a wealth of valuable footnotes see K Reid and R Zimmermann, 'The Development of Legal Doctrine in a Mixed System', ch 1 in *A History of Private Law in Scotland* (Oxford: OUP, 2000).

[45] Lord President Clyde was referring to the law of England when he said: 'I speak with nothing but respect of distinctions which I doubt not are useful and convenient in the administration of a system which, however much it resembles our own, is none the less animated by a genius which is subtly different from that which inspires ours': *Shillinglaw v JGR Turner* 1925 SC 807 at 817.

[46] '... as this Court is constituted without the assistance of Scotch Judges ... it is a foreign Court of Justice sitting to decide on foreign law ...': *Stewart v Porterfield* (1831) 5 W & S 515, *per* Lord Chancellor Brougham at 552.

[47] eg Gibb (n 10); TB Smith, 'English Influences on the Law of Scotland' in *Studies Critical and Comparative* (n 9) 122–4.

who were not necessarily peers but who were given a commission to act as Deputy Speaker. The English common law judges might be summoned to advise the Lords on points of English law arising in an appeal. There was no equivalent provision for summoning the Scottish judges; rather the English judges might be summoned to advise on Scots law.[48] As is frequently noticed, Lord Mansefield was Scots by birth, as were Loughborough, Erskine, and Campbell among the nineteenth-century Lord Chancellors, and one of the Deputy Speakers, Lord Chief Baron Alexander, but only Brougham (Lord Chancellor from 1832 to 1834 but active in the judicial business of the Lords long afterwards) had trained as a Scots lawyer. For all the others who voted on Scottish appeals, Scots law was a foreign system and the language of the Scottish courts a foreign language. Speaking in 1834 in support of an early and unsuccessful proposal to introduce a specialist Judicial Committee of the House of Lords, Brougham put the following question: 'Suppose a decision of the thirteen judges of Scotland appealed against. It is taken from those persons who understand the Scotch law and is to be adjudicated by a single individual who perhaps is as ignorant of the law of Scotland as of the law of Japan. Is it likely to give satisfaction?'[49] Now, of course, such a state of affairs may give complete satisfaction, at least to the successful appellant who has, one way or the other, benefited from it.[50] It has given less satisfaction to certain twentieth century academics who have seen in no small number of House of Lords decisions Scots law misunderstood and misapplied or simply ignored in favour of an English solution, often with less courtesy than might be desired.[51]

Faced with the alternative of mastering alien concepts and working through to a solution solely by reference to these concepts, with little available time and inadequate assistance from the Bar, it is not surprising to find distinguished English lawyers finding refuge in the law with which they were familiar and which by reason of familiarity will have seemed to afford the rational approach and the 'right' answer. If, as Lord Chancellor St Leonards remarked in *Duke of Atholl v Torrie*,[52]

---

[48] eg *Lord Advocate v Gordon* (1754) 1 Pat 558; *Leslie v Grant* (1763) 2 Pat 68, 161 ER 1274; *Grosset v Ogilvy* (1753) 2 Pat 12 ER 841; *Baillie v Grant* (1832) 6 W&S 40.

[49] Parl Debs (series 3) vol 25, col 1259, quoted by Gibb (n 10) 81.

[50] There is something of a tendency among Scottish commentators to regard Scottish litigants who have seen advantage in pursuing an appeal to London as obviously unscrupulous and unpatriotic to boot: '[the House of Lords] became the last refuge of the Scottish scoundrel intent on litigation': M Lynch, *Scotland: A New History* (London: Pimlico, 1991) 314–15, quoted by C McDiarmid, 'Scots Law: The Turning of the Tide' [1999] JR 156. 'Far too many Scotsmen appealed because they hoped that the Lords would misunderstand the case and reverse a judgment that had gone against them. Others appealed because they believed that English law would favour their case', Phillipson (n 20) 168. For an antidote to such an approach see Lord Rodger, 'Thinking About Scots Law' (1996) 1 Edinburgh L Rev 3 at 9: 'I have still to hear of a client who would rather lose his case than infringe some principle of Scots law ... All clients want to do is to win.'

[51] eg Gibb (n 10); Smith (n 47); DM Walker, 'Some Characteristics of Scots Law' 18 MLR 321; E Attwooll, *The Tapestry of the Law: Scotland, Legal Culture and Legal Theory* vol 26 (Deventer: Kluwer, 1997).

[52] (1851) 1 Macq 73.

the difficulty of the case arises from the difference between the law of Scotland and the law of England, there will be a temptation to reduce that difficulty by eliminating the difference. Gibb in *Law From Over the Border*[53] draws attention to cases where a number of techniques, of varying degrees of sophistication, were employed to achieve this objective. The case can be restated in English terms, using supposedly equivalent English language and English concepts and then resolved by reference to these English equivalents.[54] It may be asserted or simply assumed that the relevant Scots law is precisely the same as English law and the case then decided by reference to the English law.[55] Or it may be asserted that whatever the Scots law may be, it ought to be the same as the English law and, again, the case is decided by reference to the English law.[56] Where the rule essentially depends on what policy is adopted, it is the English policy which is applied.[57]

The Scottish Law Lords

Offensive as this may be to modern sensibilities, contemporary opinion seems to have been quite relaxed about the absence of particularly Scottish expertise among those hearing Scottish appeals. The Scottish witnesses who gave evidence to the select committee appointed to consider the appellate jurisdiction which reported in 1856 were unanimous in supporting continuation of appeal to the Lords but were divided as to the desirability of adding a Scottish judge to their numbers.[58] The second most senior judge in the Court of Session, the Lord Justice-Clerk (Hope), was firmly against it.

The first Scottish judge to sit was the former Lord President McNeill who, on his retirement in 1867, was elevated to the peerage as Lord Colonsay specifically in order to assist in the hearing of appeals. He died in 1874 when, with the passing of the Supreme Court of Judicature Act 1873, it seemed, as far as England was concerned, that the House of Lords was to lose its appellate jurisdiction. Neither this provision nor proposals first made during the passage of what became the 1873 Act and then again in a bill in 1874, that Scottish and Irish appeals would be determined by the Court of Appeal, were brought into force but shortly

---

[53] A monograph on the exercise by the House of Lords of its jurisdiction in Scottish appeals up to 1950, described by Chalmers (n 38), with justification, as 'an extended diatribe'. The index entry against 'Scots law', 'ignorance of. See House of Lords', gives an indication of the perspective of the author.

[54] eg *Annand v Scott* (1775) 2 Pat 369 at 373.

[55] *Wilson v Barnton* (1758) 2 Pat 11; *Viscount Arbuthnot v Scott* (1802) 4 Pat 337 at 343: 'Here we have no question peculiar to the law of Scotland. The law as to nuisances must be the same in both countries'; *Jaffray v Allan Stewart & Co* (1790) 3 Pat 191; *Addison v Row* (1794) 3 Pat 334.

[56] *Taylor v Fairlies Trs* (1833) 6 W & S 321.

[57] *Reid v Bartonshill Coal Co* (1858) 3 Macq 266.

[58] *Report of the Select Committee of the House of Lords on the Appellate Jurisdiction* (1856), House of Lords Sessional Papers, vol XXIV; *SME* (n 3) vol 6, para 820.

thereafter appeals to the House of Lords were placed on a new footing with the enactment of the Appellate Jurisdiction Act 1876. Among the changes provided by the 1876 Act was the creation of Lords of Appeal in Ordinary. Initially two were appointed,[59] one from England and one from Scotland, although, as it happened, Lord Blackburn, the appointment from the English bench, was Scots by birth. The Scottish candidate, Lord Gordon, had been Dean of Faculty and at the date of his elevation was Lord Advocate. He died in 1879 and, the following year, was succeeded by Lord Watson. Again, Watson was Lord Advocate at the time of his appointment. Lord Watson was succeeded in 1899 by the then Lord President Robertson who in his turn was succeeded in 1909 by Lord Shaw of Dunfermline, later Lord Craigmyle. Lord Shaw remained in office until 1929 but, following the increase in numbers of the Lords of Appeal in terms of the Appellate Jurisdiction Act 1913, the Lord President, Lord Dunedin, who had been raised to the peerage in 1905 and had sat on the Judicial Committee in that capacity, was appointed as a second Scottish Lord of Appeal in Ordinary. Dunedin retired in 1932. Since then what is now a convention of there being two Scots among the Lords of Appeal in Ordinary has been maintained. Those who have served are: Lord Thankerton 1929–48, Lord MacMillan 1930–9 and 1941–67, Lord Normand 1947–53, Lord Reid 1948–75, Lord Keith of Avonholm 1953–61, Lord Guest 1961–71, Lord Kilbrandon 1971–6, Lord Fraser of Tullybelton 1975–85, Lord Keith of Kinkel 1977–96, Lord Mackay of Clashfern 1985–7, Lord Jauncey of Tullichettle 1988–96, Lord Clyde 1996–2001, Lord Hope of Craighead 1996–, and Lord Rodger of Earlsferry 2001–.[60]

As well as the Lords of Appeal in Ordinary, a number of Scottish judges or retired judges have been elevated to the peerage. Of these judicial peers, in addition to Lord Colonsay and, before his appointment as a Lord of Appeal, Lord Dunedin, Lord Shand 1892–1904, Lord Kinnear 1897–1917, Lord Alness 1934–7, Lord Wheatley 1975–88, Lord Emslie 1980–2002, and Lord Cullen 2003– have sat on appeals. In 1987, Lord Mackay of Clashfern, then a Scottish Lord of Appeal in Ordinary, was appointed Lord Chancellor. He held office until 1997.

In *Law and Politics: The House of Lords as a Judicial Body*, Robert Stevens identifies various judicial traditions with which the Lords of Appeal in the period of his study were associated. Among these is the Scottish tradition.[61] As with the

---

[59] As explained in Stevens (n 25) 109, the 1876 Act made provision for four appointments which were made as the existing salaried judgeships in the Privy Council fell vacant.

[60] There have accordingly been 19 Scottish Lords of Appeal. Of these five were Lord Presidents, four were Lord Advocates, seven were former Lord Advocates, three were in the Inner House, and five were in the Outer House at the time of their appointment. Nine had at one time been Deans of Faculty. Eight had been Members of Parliament and a further two, unsuccessful parliamentary candidates. Watson and Thankerton were father and son, as were the two Lords Keith. For a discussion of the backgrounds, circumstances of appointment, and social characteristics of all but the three most recent holders of the office, see AA Paterson, 'Scottish Lords of Appeal 1876–1988' [1988] JR 235.

[61] Discussed by Robert Stevens in relation to different periods (n 25) 130–2, 269–82, and 507–16; and see also Paterson (n 60) 247–53.

other traditions, Stevens sees the Scottish tradition as informing the way in which those conforming to it, the Scottish Law Lords, have carried out their role as members of the final Appellate court in the United Kingdom. He singles out some of the Scots: Watson, Dunedin and, most clearly, Reid, as exercising particular influence in the Appellate Committee. He is more critical of some of the others. However, his notion of a Scottish tradition reflects the view that the Scottish Lords of Appeal have brought distinctive qualities to their office. While their social background and education may have been closely similar to those of their English colleagues,[62] a point of difference is in the nature of their professional practice when at the Bar. Successful English barristers tend to be specialists. Scottish advocates, on the other hand, even the leaders of their profession, are perforce generalists. This brings with it a broad and pragmatic or commonsensical approach to the law which Stevens has seen as a feature of the Scottish tradition. Another feature is the generally supposed Scottish preference for principle over precedent. Hackneyed as this assessment undoubtedly is, it contains at least an element of truth. In Stevens' assessment the Scottish tradition has been a source of strength: 'In short, while Scottish law lords undoubtedly take on some camouflage from their surroundings, their training and style may well be better adapted to a flexible model of the appellate process than is the English barrister's training.'[63]

The House of Lords and the Anglicisation of Scots law

The appointment of Scottish lawyers as Law Lords did not of course stop the English Law Lords thinking like English lawyers. It did mean that the more obviously irrelevant excursions into the technical arcana of English law in the course of a Scottish appeal were liable to firmly expressed correction by an irritated and better informed colleague[64] but it also exposed the Scottish members of the House to English ways of thought. It was Lord Cockburn who famously observed: 'The transplanted Scotsman must lose his Scotch law. Nothing oozes out of a man so fast as law.'[65] Scottish Lords of Appeal as well as English, have been prepared to decide Scottish cases by reference to English precedents, hence the charge, particularly associated with Sir Thomas Smith but also made by Professor David Walker, and expressed most polemically by Andrew Dewar Gibb, that the House of Lords, in the persons of its English members, has been responsible for an 'Anglicisation' of Scots law. The gravamen of the complaint is that the House of Lords has been too ready to apply an English rule in situations where there have been no more than superficial similarities between the English and Scottish systems with the result that differences of principle have been

---

[62] Paterson (n 60) 245.   [63] Stevens (n 25) 269.
[64] eg *Leitch & Co v Leydon* 1931 SC (HL) 1, *per* Lord Dunedin at 8.   [65] *Journals*, p 278.

overlooked, alien doctrines introduced, and the internal coherence and comprehensibility of Scots law undermined.

Blom-Cooper and Drewry considered the charge of Anglicisation and found it not proven in relation to the period of their study.[66] It is significant that only 14 of the 129 pages of Gibb's *Law From Over the Border* are devoted to the period following 1876 and the appointment of Lords of Appeal in Ordinary. Smith was writing at a time when there was real anxiety about the survival of Scots law as a distinct system,[67] and therefore some rhetorical exaggeration was to be expected, but he was nevertheless careful to acknowledge that the days of English Chancellors deliberately overriding Scottish principles in favour of English case law were over.[68] Moreover, while the appellate jurisdiction of the House of Lords has undoubtedly been an important conduit through which the influence of English law has made itself felt in Scotland, it is not the only one and, for all that the language of the English Law Lords has sometimes been less than tactful, it is something of a simplification to suggest that it is they and they alone who have been responsible for imposing what Smith described as 'unwelcome and retrograde English doctrines'[69] upon the Scottish system.

Given that Scotland has shared a common language and a common legislature with its economically more powerful neighbour for some hundreds of years it has been inevitable that Scots law, for all that it was originally quite distinct, has come under significant English influence. From at least the middle of the nineteenth century, as commercial and industrial development north and south of the border converged, English precedents have been freely referred to in the Scottish courts.[70] It is this history of cultural, political, and economic as well as legal interaction that has made Scots law the 'mixed' system which today's academics more often celebrate than regret. True, the emergence of the practice of citing English authority did not meet with universal approval. The same Lord Cockburn who made the observation about the transplanted Scotsman 'really' wished that Scottish counsel and judges '... could imitate the example set us by the counsel and judges of that kingdom [England], who decide their causes by their own rules and customs, without exposing themselves by referring to foreign systems, the very language of which they do not comprehend'.[71] Lord Rodger explains[72] that this shaft was aimed at, among others, John Inglis, senior counsel for the defenders in the case in which Lord Cockburn was sitting, and later successively Lord Justice-Clerk and Lord President, the leading Scots lawyer of his

---

[66] Blom-Cooper and Drewry (n 5) 375–87.

[67] Lord Cooper, 'The Scottish Legal Tradition' (1949) in *Selected Papers 1922–1954* (Edinburgh: Oliver & Boyd, 1957) 199; DM Walker, 'Some Characteristics of Scots Law' 18 MLR 321.

[68] 'The Common Law Cuckoo' in *Studies Critical and Comparative* (n 9) 96.

[69] 'English Influences on the Law of Scotland' in *Studies Critical and Comparative* (n 9) 117.

[70] Lord Rodger (n 50), citing Lord Watson, 'Recent Legal Reform' (1901) 13 JR 1 and Lord Dunedin, *Encyclopaedia of the Law of Scotland*, vol 1 (1926) preface.

[71] *Napier's Trs v Morrison* (1851) 13D 1404 at 1409.

[72] *R (Beresford) v Sunderland CC* [2004] 1 AC 889 at 909C.

generation. It was Inglis's rather than Cockburn's approach which prevailed. Accordingly, from quite an early date, cases have come to the House of Lords from the Court of Session with the arguments already developed by reference to English law. It has by no means always been a case of an unexpected ambush by alien jurisprudence on the banks of the Thames.

It is instructive to look at *Bartonshill Coal Co v Reid*,[73] if only because it is the most frequently quoted, indeed one might say notorious, example of an 'unwelcome and retrograde English doctrine' being 'imposed' on Scots law. What was in issue in *Bartonshill* was the applicability of the defence of common employment in a case of a claim by the widow and children of a miner who had been killed by the negligence of an engineman responsible for operation of the machinery for lifting a bucket containing the deceased man to the surface. The defenders had employed both the miner and the engineman. The case was tried by jury. The defenders sought a direction from the trial judge (Lord President McNeill) that if no case of direct fault was made out against the defenders then they could not be found vicariously liable for the engineman's negligence. The trial judge refused to give such a direction. He was upheld on appeal to the Inner House. The defenders appealed to the House of Lords. The appeal was allowed. The terms of the speech of Lord Chancellor Cranworth were such as to ensure that it would be repeatedly referred to over the next 150 years. In what was, after all, a Scottish appeal, he began by a full consideration of the English authority on common employment. In language that has been frequently quoted, he went on:

But if such be the law of England on what ground can it be argued not to be the law of Scotland? The law as established in England is founded on principles of universal application not on any peculiarities of English jurisprudence and unless therefore there has been a settled course of decision in Scotland to the contrary I think it would be most inexpedient to sanction a different rule to the north of the Tweed to that which prevails to the south.

Only after this pronouncement did Lord Cranworth look at the Scottish cases which, unsurprisingly, he read as not being inconsistent with his *a priori* assumption as to the universal applicability of the English rule which provided that as between servant and master there was no vicarious liability for the fault of a fellow-servant. That was to continue to be the law until abolished by section 1 of the Law Reform (Personal Injuries) Act 1948.

It is not difficult to see why Lord Cranworth's speech has provoked so much resentment. The language is arrogant and the decision does not conform to modern ideas as to where the risk of injury should lie as between worker and employer. However, to view the case simply as an example of legal imperialism on the part of an English Lord Chancellor with no Scottish involvement in the

---

[73] (1858) 3 Macq 266. Philip Simpson discusses the case and the critical commentary it has attracted in the chapter 'Vicarious Liability' in Reid and Zimmermann (n 44) 588–92.

process would be misleading. In the Court of Session the defence of common employment had been put forward from the very beginning by counsel for the employers, the by then Dean of Faculty John Inglis, as he had done in previous cases.[74] On appeal, in the Inner House, the Dean put a reference to the law of England squarely at the forefront of his argument. That he did not succeed was more on the basis of the facts of the particular case than any necessary rejection of the possibility of a defence of common employment in Scots law. Inglis did not appear in the House of Lords but had he done so it is likely that he would have continued to rely on the English case law. The view which eventually prevailed may well seem to be retrograde when viewed from the perspective of the twentieth or twenty-first centuries. It involved the unequivocal adoption of the English rule (as much a policy as anything) and to that extent can be regarded as an instance of Anglicisation, but it is less clear that it involved upsetting any principle of Scots law. The House of Lords was the medium through which the English law came to be adopted but to regard it as the sole agent is to forget the groundwork put in by Inglis and those other Scots lawyers who were of his opinion.

When giving the James Wood Lecture at the University of Glasgow in February 1998,[75] Lord Hope reflected on the role of the Scottish judge in the House of Lords, how he could be, as Lord Hope put it, 'useful to Scotland'. The answer which Lord Hope gave was maintaining contact with Scots law with a view to ensuring that appeals in Scottish cases are decided according to the principles and practice of Scots law; not always an easy task, he went on to explain, as there was nothing more difficult to resist than a desire among the others on the Appellate Committee that the law on each side of the Border should be the same. It may be, therefore, that something of the spirit of the eighteenth- and nineteenth-century Lord Chancellors lives on. If so, it is in an attenuated form. The modern practice of the Lords has been of careful respect for the distinctive character of Scots law, a shift, it has been suggested, from dismissal to deference.[76] Almost always one and usually two Scottish Lords of Appeal sit on Scottish appeals. There may be three.[77] A high proportion of the speeches, now opinions, in these cases are delivered by the Scottish members of the Judicial Committee with a consequently lower proportion being delivered by their English colleagues, a pattern accentuated when one excludes cases dealing with statutory interpretation or negligence, where it has long been accepted that there is no real difference between Scots and English law.[78] Unless the case involves United Kingdom legislation the picture is one of Scottish activity and English (and Northern Irish) restraint. The

---

[74] Simpson, ibid.

[75] Reproduced as 'Taking the Case to London—Is it All Over?' [1998] JR 135.

[76] Chalmers (n 38) 10.

[77] eg *Herd v Clyde Helicopters* 1997 SC (HL) 86; *Girvan v Inverness Farmers Dairy* 1998 SC (HL) 1; *Redrow Homes Ltd v Bett Brothers plc* 1998 SC (HL) 64.

[78] Chalmers demonstrates this by a survey of reported cases between 1993 and 2002. A similar trend emerges when the reported cases for the following five years are examined.

impression gained from reading the judgments of the House is of Scottish principles being on the one hand maintained and on the other respected. Two decisions illustrate these complementary tendencies. In *Smith v Bank of Scotland*[79] there was no issue among the members of the Committee as to the desirability, as a matter of policy, of a requirement that, if it is to be allowed to enforce a cautionary obligation a bank must have ensured that a wife acting as cautioner for her husband had been made fully aware of the consequences of the proposed transaction. Counsel for the wife had argued simply for an extension to Scotland of the English decision of *Barclays Bank plc v O'Brien*.[80] The House did not take that course. Rather, the English Law Lords (and a doubtful Lord Jauncey) followed Lord Clyde in taking the consequences of the more specifically Scottish requirement for good faith in cautionary obligations as the basis for decision. Thus, the policy objective was achieved but by what the English Law Lords were prepared to accept was the preferable Scottish route. *Burnett's Trustee v Grainger*[81] was a competition between the purchasers of a flat who had paid the price, taken delivery of a conveyance, and then taken possession of the property but not recorded title, and the trustee in sequestration of the seller acting for the general body of creditors who had recorded title. Lords Hoffmann and Hobhouse regarded the outcome to which Scots law compelled Lords Hope and Rodger as neither fair nor necessary but, in relatively short opinions, having conducted the argument in Scots terms, reluctantly accepted that their Scottish colleagues had accurately set out the law of Scotland and accordingly joined with them in refusing the appeal.

This is not to say that the generally observed discipline of the English Law Lords of refraining from delivering a substantive opinion in a case solely concerned with Scots common law does not occasionally break down when faced with the temptation of an 'interesting' case. Such was *Moncrieff v Jamieson*.[82] What was in issue was whether an express right of vehicular access to a house situated between the foot of a small cliff and the foreshore on Shetland carried with it an ancillary servitude of car parking. Full opinions from Lord Hope and Lord Rodger were supplemented by similarly extensive opinions from Lord Scott and Lord Neuberger. The authorities cited by the Scottish Law Lords were almost exclusively Scottish or Civilian. The authorities cited by the English Law Lords were almost exclusively English. Happily, the English law as to easements and the Scots law as to servitudes were found to march together on the fundamental issue as to whether a right to park existed.[83] As the Scottish observer has come to expect from the Judicial Committee, the spirit was cooperative, the approach was comparative. It is unlikely that Sir Thomas Smith would have had anything to say against it.

---

[79] 1997 SC (HL) 111.   [80] [1994] 1 AC 180.   [81] 2004 SC (HL) 19.

[82] 2007 SLT 989 *per* Lord Scott of Foscote at 998F.

[83] Lord Neuberger at 1014L, while recognising the very different concepts underlying the land laws of the respective jurisdictions.

Of course, just as English Law Lords sit in Scottish appeals, the Scottish Law Lords sit in English and Northern Irish appeals (and in appeals to the Privy Council). It is by no means uncommon for two Scottish Law Lords to sit as part of a Committee of five in an English appeal and it is in non-Scottish appeals that the Scottish Law Lords do the majority of their work. Very often they will provide an opinion in an English case. Indeed, perhaps because of their background as generalists rather than specialists, it is more common to find a Scottish Law Lord delivering a speech or opinion in an English appeal and discussing the issue in exclusively English terms than it is to find an English Law Lord making an equivalent contribution in a Scottish appeal. Blom-Cooper and Drewry raise, but do not answer, the interesting question as to whether as a result of such participation, English law may have become 'Scoticised'.[84] In closing this chapter on Scotland and the House of Lords it is worth noting the place of a speech by a Scottish Law Lord in an English appeal as a vehicle for a statement about Scots law. It may be to reinforce a point[85] or give it additional historical context[86] or to distinguish it[87] or it may be quite explicitly to address an audience north of the border[88] but in each instance it may be taken to be intended as a means whereby the House of Lords can, as Lord Hope puts it, be 'useful to Scotland'.

[84] Blom-Cooper and Drewry (n 5) 386.

[85] eg *R v Mirza* [2004] 1 AC 1118 at 1156; *Office of the King's Prosecutor, Brussels v Cando Armas* [2006] 2 AC 1 at 20G.

[86] eg *Three Rivers DC v Bank of England (No 6)* [2005] 1 AC 610 at 655E; *A v Secretary of State for the Home Department* [2005] 2 AC 68 at 132H.

[87] eg *R (Amin) v Home Secretary* [2004] 1 AC 653; *Secretary of Trade and Industry v Frid* [2004] 2 AC 508 at 515H; *Re Spectrum Plus Ltd* [2005] 2 AC 680 at 701A.

[88] eg *Miller v Miller* [2006] 2 AC 618 at 649B.

(b) Ireland

Ronan Keane

The role of the Law Lords in relation to Ireland until 1922

English law in Ireland

In considering the part played by the House of Lords as a judicial tribunal in relation to Ireland prior to 1922, it is necessary to emphasise at the outset the close similarities between Irish law and English law from the seventeenth century onwards.

The first migration of the English common law took place in the twelfth century, when a group of Norman barons invaded Ireland and, in their wake, the King's courts were established in the Pale—the region immediately surrounding Dublin—and in other coastal towns. Gaelic magnates continued to rule in the rest of the island where the indigenous Irish law, known as the brehon law, prevailed. While initially English law was administered by itinerant justices, courts of Common Pleas, King's Bench, and Exchequer, sitting in Dublin on the English model, were ultimately established.[1] There was also an Irish chancellor, but the institution of the chancery, unlike its English counterpart, was poorly staffed, and litigants seeking redress which they could not obtain in the common law courts frequently had recourse to the Irish Parliament.[2]

That body, no more than the English Parliament, was not in its original form an especially representative, let alone democratic, assembly: it was more in the nature of an emanation of the King's council. By the fifteenth century, however, the 'three estates'—the peers, commons, and lower clergy—had made their appearance. They were the germ of what later became the separate kingdom of Ireland, sharing the same crown but with its own lords and commons. However, in 1495 Poynings' Law, which required the assent of the King to the summoning of the Irish Parliament, also had the effect of decreasing the role of that

---

[1] GJ Hand, *English Law in Ireland, 1290–1324* (Cambridge: CUP, 1967) 7.
[2] HG Richardson and GO Sayles, *The Adminstration of Ireland 1172–1377* (Dublin: The Stationery Office, 1963) 15.

parliament as a court, its judicial work now being performed by the King's council and the developing court of chancery.[3]

In the sixteenth century, the Tudor monarchy embarked on its policy of bringing the entire island under its control, which culminated in the collapse of the last Gaelic redoubt in Ulster in 1603. The brehon laws were replaced by English law throughout Ireland and such evidence as exists suggests that the common law and equity as applied in Irish courts differed little from that in England: there was no parallel to the development of distinctive legal doctrines in Scotland. It should be borne in mind, however, that the destruction of the Public Records Office in the Four Courts in Dublin during the civil war which followed independence in 1922, and the absence of law reporting on any systematic basis until the nineteenth century, makes research into the early history of Irish law more difficult.

The battle between the Irish and English Houses

A form of appeal in common law cases from the Irish court of King's Bench originally lay to the English court of King's Bench or to the Irish House of Lords by the ancient procedure known as writ of error.[4] However, appeals during the seventeenth century were also heard from the Irish courts by the English House of Lords and such reports as we have of the appeals deal with cases in equity.[5] But the right of the English House to hear such appeals was vigorously challenged by the Irish House of Lords, which remained in being until the passing of the Act of Union in 1800. In the *Bishop of Derry's Case* in 1698 the English House had reversed an Irish chancery decision, but in *Annesley v Sherlock* the Irish House not merely entertained an appeal from the equity side of the Irish exchequer but went to the length of committing the Barons of the Exchequer for contempt in failing to follow their rulings.[6] However, in 1719 the Westminster Parliament intervened and passed the statute known as 'The Sixth of George the First', which made it clear that appeals from the Irish courts lay only to the English House. During the period of relative legislative independence from 1782 enjoyed by the Irish Parliament (Grattan's Parliament), the exclusive appellate jurisdiction of the Irish House was briefly reasserted. With the passing of the Act of Union in 1800, however, both Irish Houses ceased to exist and appeals from the Irish courts lay again to the House of Lords at Westminster.

---

[3] SG Ellis, *Tudor Ireland: Crown, Community and the Conflict of Cultures, 1470–1603* (London: Longman, 1985) 163.

[4] L Blom-Cooper and G Drewry, *Final Appeal: A Study of the House of Lords in its Judicial Capacity* (Oxford: Clarendon Press, 1972) 35.

[5] Such as Browne's Parliamentary Reports. See R Keane, *Equity and the Law of Trusts in Ireland* (London: Butterworths, 1988) 19.

[6] Blom-Cooper and Drewry (n 4) 35.

The Act provided that: 'all writs of error and appeals . . . which might now be finally decided by the House of Lords in either kingdom shall . . . be finally decided by the House of Lords of the United Kingdom'.

Limitations on Irish appeals to the Lords

In common law cases, appeals to the House of Lords from the court of exchequer chamber—now designated as the highest Irish court—could be brought only by a writ of error. This meant, in effect, that a common law litigant who wished to appeal to the House of Lords had to institute separate proceedings in that House. Such a proceeding, however, could only be brought where there was what was called 'an error patent on the record of a final judgment'. Accordingly, an appellant to the House of Lords in Irish common law cases had to satisfy three requirements for his appeal to be heard: there had to be a judgment (as distinct from an order), it had to be final (ie interlocutory orders could not be appealed), and there had to be an error patent on the record of the judgment.[7] The distinction between judgments and orders was a fine one but of some significance: it meant, for example, that in cases involving the prerogative writs, such as certiorari and mandamus, no appeal lay from the Irish courts to the House of Lords, unless a statute so provided. The requirement as to an 'error patent' effectively excluded appeals which did not raise any point of law.

The Irish Law Lords

The Act of Union provided for the election for life of 28 representative Irish peers to the Westminster Parliament. Until the enactment of the Appellate Jurisdiction Act in 1876, appeals from Ireland to the House of Lords followed the same course as those from England and Scotland: the appeals were heard by peers who were also lawyers, although there was in theory nothing to prevent peers who were not legally qualified from sitting on such appeals. In cases of difficulty, the judges of the lower courts were summoned to give their advice. Since the office of the Irish Lord Chancellor remained in being after the Act of Union, he frequently sat with the English Lord Chancellor and other legally qualified peers to hear the appeals from Ireland. The 1876 Act, providing for the appointment of legally qualified Lords of Appeal in Ordinary on whom life peerages were conferred, applied to Ireland as well as to the rest of the United Kingdom.

Reform of the Irish system of appeals followed the English model, with the establishment of an Irish Court of Appeal in Chancery in 1856 and of a unified Irish Court of Appeal with both a common law and chancery jurisdiction in 1876, from which appeals continued to lie to the House of Lords. The Judicature (Ireland) Act 1877 followed its English equivalent in preserving the appeals from

---

[7] *Gosford v Irish Land Commission* [1899] AC 435; *R v Barton* [1902] AC 168.

the Court of Appeal to the House of Lords, to be heard by the Lords of Appeal in Ordinary. Presumably because of the close similarity between English and Irish law and because the volume of Irish appeals was lower than those from Scotland, there was no equivalent to the convention under which at least one of the Law Lords was invariably Scottish.

There were indeed only three Law Lords from 1876 to 1922 who, on their appointment, were members of the Irish bar or bench. The first was Lord Fitzgerald, appointed in 1882, who had been Attorney General for Ireland and a judge of the Queen's Bench Division and served as a Law Lord until his death in 1889. The second was Lord Morris (on his retirement appointed to the hereditary peerage of Killanin) who came from a well-known Catholic family in the West of Ireland and had been Lord Chief Justice of Ireland before his appointment to the Lords in 1889, in which he served until his retirement in 1900. The third was Lord Atkinson, appointed in 1905, who, like his two predecessors, had been Attorney General for Ireland and served until his retirement in 1928. However, three other eminent Irishmen also became Law Lords in this period. Lord Macnaghten was the first member of the English bar to be appointed directly as a Law Lord in 1887. Lord Russell of Killowen was also appointed directly from the Bar in 1894 but served for only 57 days before being appointed Lord Chief Justice of England. Lord Carson, on his resignation as leader of the Irish unionists in the House of Commons in 1921, was also appointed directly from the Bar to the House of Lords.

The Irish appeals

Although the volume of Irish appeals to the House of Lords was never as large as those from Scotland, they were not insignificant in number. Thus, from 1833 to 1865, out of 1,076 appeals, 134 (12.3 per cent) were from Ireland. From 1866 to 1871, the corresponding figures were 230 and 21 (9.3 per cent).[8] They resulted in some judgments which made notable contributions to English and Irish law, such as the fisheries case of *Cooper v Phibbs*,[9] dealing with the operation of mistake in the law of contract. But of the Irish appeals, *Quinn v Leathem*[10] is perhaps the one that left the most enduring impression on the common law.

That case, together with the English appeal of *Allen v Flood*[11] heard three years earlier, remains a major feature of the law affecting trade disputes in England and Ireland. In *Allen v Flood*, a majority of the House of Lords had held that a trade union official who, arising out of what would now be called a demarcation dispute, induced an employer to dismiss two workers belonging to a rival trade union by threatening strike action, had not committed an actionable tort.[12] In

---

[8] Blom-Cooper and Drewry (n 4) 36.   [9] (1867) LR 2 HL 149.
[10] [1901] AC 495.   [11] [1898] AC 1.
[12] It was the last case in which the Law Lords sought the advice of the judges of the lower courts.

Quinn v Leathem the House upheld the decision of the Irish Court of Appeal that, where the trial court found that a combination of people, as distinct from an individual, using such methods had caused damage to a business, *Allen v Flood* provided no defence, since the tort of conspiracy had been committed.

The final stage

The final stage in the history of the Law Lords in relation to what became the Irish Free State arrived in 1920. The Government of Ireland Act passed in that year was the last attempt by the Westminster Parliament to provide for home rule for Ireland within the United Kingdom. It established Northern Ireland as a separate unit with its own parliament and provided for separate systems of courts in the two new jurisdictions of Northern and Southern Ireland. Courts of Appeal for both jurisdictions were established with an appeal to a High Court of Appeal for Ireland. Appeals lay from that court to the House of Lords in cases where appeals had previously lain from the Court of Appeal; in addition, there was provision for appeals in the prerogative writ cases.

With the coming into force of the Constitution of the Irish Free State in December 1922 and the consequential Westminster legislation, the 1920 Act ceased to apply in Southern Ireland. While the Constitution provided for a new court system in the Irish Free State with the Supreme Court as a court of final appeal, it also enacted that, until the establishment of the new system, the existing Southern Irish courts should remain in being and that the Court of Appeal of Southern Ireland should have the same status of a final court of appeal as the Supreme Court. There was thus no longer a right of appeal to the House of Lords, although the Constitution, implementing the relevant article of the Anglo-Irish Treaty of 1921, allowed for an appeal to the Privy Council from the Court of Appeal and, on its establishment, from the Supreme Court.

The view from Ireland 1922–2007

The constitution of the Irish Free State

The Constitution of the Irish Free State, which implemented the Anglo-Irish Treaty of 1921, applied only to the 26 counties of 'Southern Ireland', as it was described in the Government of Ireland Act 1920. The Irish Free State was to be a self-governing dominion within the British Empire, with the same constitutional practices and usages as the Dominion of Canada. The Constitution provided for the establishment of a new court system, including a supreme court, which was to be a final court of appeal, but also recognised a right of appeal from that court to the Privy Council. Thus, the House of Lords, as from December 1922, ceased to be the final court of appeal for the island of Ireland, although it retained that function in Northern Ireland.

The Constitution was unique among the founding statutes of the dominions in having been enacted by a constituent assembly elected by the people, in incorporating a bill of fundamental rights and in providing for judicial review of legislation. And while the other indicia of sovereignty—the Oireachtas or parliament, the flag, the army—may have had a more immediate, popular impact, the establishment of a new Irish judiciary with its own final court of appeal was also of great importance in an atmosphere of fervent nationalism. The majority of Irish people had little confidence in the judiciary of the old regime, which was seen by them as part of an alien system of government.

In that context, the imposition on the Irish of an appeal from the new Supreme Court to the Judicial Committee of the Privy Council, which was seen as an imperial body sitting in London, caused predictable resentment. On this matter at least, supporters and opponents of the 1921 Treaty, who had fought a bitter civil war over its signing, were united and the Free State Government used every opportunity to render the appeal procedure meaningless. In this they were helped by the manner in which the relevant part of Article 66 was worded: 'Provided that nothing in this Constitution shall impair the right of any person to petition His Majesty for special leave to appeal from the Supreme Court to His Majesty in Council or the right of His Majesty to grant such leave.' When the first applications for leave to appeal were heard, the limitations of the procedure became apparent. Lord Buckmaster remarked: '[A]s far as possible finality and supremacy are to be given to the Irish courts.'[13]

The details of the subsequent history of the procedure are outside the scope of this chapter. Its practical significance, as distinct from its symbolic importance, was small, with only two successful appeals being brought during its relatively short life. Following the accession to power in 1932 of the leader of the opposition to the Treaty, Eamon de Valera, the Oireachtas passed legislation in 1933 abolishing the right of appeal.[14] This was a patent breach of the Treaty, but when an appeal was brought on that ground, the Judicial Committee acknowledged that it was within the powers of the Oireachtas under the recently enacted Statute of Westminster to take such a step.[15]

The effect of House of Lords decisions after 1922

With the ending of the right of appeal to the House of Lords, decisions of that body were, of course, persuasive precedents only in Irish courts. However, Article 73 of the 1922 Constitution provided that the laws in force in the territory of the

---

[13] *Hull v McKenna; Freeman's Journal v Fernston* [1926] IR 402, 409.
[14] The Constitution could be amended by ordinary legislation at this stage: see below.
[15] *Moore v AG* [1935] AC 484.

Free State immediately prior to its coming into operation were to remain in force until any of them were repealed or amended by the Oireachtas. (They were not, however, to be carried over in this manner when they were inconsistent with the Constitution.) This was judicially interpreted as continuing in force not merely the pre-1922 statutes of the Westminster Parliament, but also the judge-made rules of common law and equity from that period.[16] Thus, in the early years of independence, decisions of the House of Lords prior to 1922 were considered as binding on all the courts of the Free State, including the Supreme Court, as were decisions of the former Irish Court of Appeal.

Although it was possible in theory for the Oireachtas to repeal the entire corpus of the pre-1922 law and replace it with a new civil code (possibly including elements of the ancient Irish or brehon law[17]), more pragmatic considerations prevailed. The view of both ministers and the majority of lawyers was that the existing laws should be maintained, leaving it to the Oireachtas to make such changes as might be required by conditions in the new Irish state.

While the post-1922 decisions of the House of Lords were persuasive precedents only, there were no serious indications initially of the development of a distinctive Irish jurisprudence. It was not particularly surprising that seminal English decisions, such as in the tort area *Donoghue v Stevenson*[18] and in the criminal law *DPP v Woolmington*,[19] were absorbed without difficulty into Irish law. But even where divergence might have been expected, ie in the field of constitutional law, it was slow to occur. This was despite the fact that, as we have seen, the 1922 Constitution contained a bill of fundamental rights and allowed for judicial review of legislation. However, Irish lawyers who had been brought up on Dicey and the doctrine of parliamentary sovereignty found such novel constitutional principles difficult to digest. There was the additional problem that the Constitution could be amended by ordinary legislation. This latter power could only be exercised in the first eight years of the Constitution's existence, but the Oireachtas passed an amendment extending the power for a further eight years. A majority of the Supreme Court held that this was a valid exercise of the power of amendment.[20] Thus, the power of judicial review was rendered virtually meaningless.

1937: a new Constitution

The enactment of the present Constitution in 1937 seemed to herald a new approach, since it not merely contained a new and extensive bill of rights and a

---

[16] See, eg, *Mayo-Perrott v Mayo-Perrott* [1958] IR 336. While there was some judicial support for the view that the expression 'the laws' in the relevant article of the present Constitution applied only to statute law, this has not been generally accepted. See JM Kelly, *The Irish Constitution*, Hogan and Whyte (eds) (Dublin: LexisNexis, 4th edn 2003) 2150–3.

[17] See above.   [18] [1932] AC 562 (HL).   [19] [1935] AC 462 (HL).

[20] *The State (Ryan) v Lennon* [1935] IR 170.

power of judicial review but expressly confined the power of amendment by the Oireachtas to a period of three years: thereafter amendments could only be by referendum. There were also signs of a readiness to develop the law to meet Irish conditions. This was reflected initially in a departure from the previous tendency to treat pre-1922 House of Lords and Irish Court of Appeal decisions as binding on all Irish courts in all circumstances. Thus in 1939, in *Exham v Beamish*,[21] a High Court judge, Gavan Duffy J, refused to consider himself bound to apply the pre-1922 English decisions on the rule of perpetuities which required the court to accept the possibility of a child being born to a woman long after child-bearing age, the so-called 'fertile octogenarian' principle (not, perhaps, so far-fetched a notion in our more technologically advanced age). While he acknowledged that some pre-1922 decisions reflected principles so well settled that they would have to be regarded as part of the law carried over by Article 73 of the 1922 Constitution and the 1937 Constitution (which contained an article in virtually identical terms), that did not apply to every pre-1922 decision, as where the decisions were 'repugnant to the common sense of our citizens'. But there also continued to be cases where judges felt bound to apply pre-1922 decisions, irrespective of their merits: in 1949 two members of the Supreme Court said that they considered themselves bound by the decision of the House of Lords in *Fairman v Perpetual Investment Building Society*,[22] dealing with the law on occupiers' liability, because it had been pronounced in November 1922.[23]

Such judgments must now be seen in the light of the decision of the Supreme Court in 1965 that, while it would continue to apply the general doctrine of precedent, the rule of *stare decisis* should give way in a court of final appeal to a more flexible approach, with the result that it did not have to follow its own previous decisions in every case, anticipating the Practice Statement of the English Lord Chancellor to the same effect in July 1966.[24] It seems *a fortiori* that the same principle should apply to pre-1922 decisions of the House of Lords, although the point has never been expressly decided.[25]

A new Irish constitutional jurisprudence

Hopes that the Constitution of 1937 would give birth to a new Irish jurisprudence were initially disappointed. This was due in part to the disinclination of that generation of Irish lawyers to explore the possibilities latent in a written constitution. But it also reflected the security situation during the Second World War. Although Ireland was neutral, the IRA were pursuing their violent campaign against partition and were seeking assistance from Nazi Germany. The Government introduced draconian anti-terrorist legislation and relied on provisions of the

---

[21] [1939] IR 336.   [22] [1923] AC 74.   [23] *Boylan v Dublin Corp* [1949] IR 60.
[24] *AG v Ryan's Car Hire Ltd* [1965] IR 642.
[25] See the remarks of McCarthy J in the Supreme Court in *Irish Shell Ltd v Elm Motors Ltd* [1984] IR 200, 227.

Constitution enabling such laws to be enacted in a time of emergency. Thus the development of a human rights jurisprudence was again stultified.

Ireland left the Commonwealth in 1949, but there remained a tendency to look to the English courts, and in particular the House of Lords, for guidance. However, in the 1960s, a new generation of judges, of whom Chief Justice O Dalaigh, Mr Justice Brian Walsh, and Mr Justice John Kenny were the most prominent, developed a new jurisprudence which laid particular emphasis on the role of the courts in upholding the fundamental rights guaranteed by the Constitution. In this context, decisions of the House of Lords in areas of law affecting human rights were of less significance in Ireland.

The 1960s and succeeding decades also saw an exponential growth in judicial review of decisions of public bodies in Ireland. While there was, of course, a similar development in Britain led by the House of Lords, the context was somewhat different. The expansion of judicial review was undoubtedly a response in both jurisdictions to the increasing powers of the executive, the diminishing importance of Parliament, and the vast range of functions now being entrusted to bodies other than courts. In Britain, the Law Lords, concerned no doubt by the potential for injustice inherent in unchecked parliamentary sovereignty, expanded the range of circumstances in which public bodies could be made amenable to the courts for the manner in which they exercised their functions. In Ireland, the courts could strike down the legislation governing such bodies as unconstitutional, but they also developed a principle that, since such statutes were presumed to be constitutional, it was also presumed that the Oireachtas intended the relevant bodies to act in accordance with fair procedures.[26]

The accession of Ireland and the United Kingdom to the European Communities in 1972 brought with it an abridgement of the roles of the Supreme Court and the House of Lords as final courts of appeal. More recently, the passage of legislation at Westminster to give effect to the European Convention on Human Rights and Fundamental Freedoms has given rise to a remarkable body of case law in the House of Lords in a comparatively short time. In Ireland, although legislation giving effect to the Convention has also been enacted, the results have been less dramatic, in part because of the substantial overlap between the rights guaranteed by the Convention and the Irish Constitution.

In addition to the case law from Luxembourg and Strasbourg, decisions from the United States, Canada, Australia, and other common law countries are regularly cited in Irish courts. But, as one might expect, there continues to be more citation of judgments of the House of Lords, reflecting the long, at times rather fraught, but in recent years more equable, relationship between Ireland and Britain, and we can expect this to continue as the House of Lords in its judicial capacity gives way to the new Supreme Court of the United Kingdom.

[26] *East Donegal Co-operative Ltd v AG* [1970] IR 317.

(c) Northern Ireland after 1921

Brice Dickson

When the partition of Ireland took effect in 1921, under the Government of Ireland Act 1920, appeals from what became the Irish Free State were no longer sent to the House of Lords but to the Privy Council—until 1933, when that avenue of appeal was also removed.[1] But appeals from what became the new jurisdiction of Northern Ireland continued to lie from Belfast to the House of Lords, and have done so ever since. In addition, a handful of judges based in Northern Ireland have been appointed to serve as Lords of Appeal. This account begins by examining the contribution made by those judges. During the 'troubles' in Northern Ireland (from 1968 to 1998) the British Government often called upon Law Lords to conduct inquiries into matters of public concern there, but those extra-judicial reports are beyond the remit of this work.[2]

Lords of Appeal with knowledge of Northern Ireland's law

In 1921 two of the then six Lords of Appeal in Ordinary (hereafter Lords of Appeal) were already very familiar with Northern Ireland. Lord Atkinson had practised law

---

[1] Constitution (Amendment No 22) Act 1933 (Ir).

[2] Lord Scarman investigated the disturbances of 1969 (Cmd (NI) 566; 1972); Lord Widgery, the then Lord Chief Justice of England but never a Lord of Appeal, reported on the killing of 14 civilians by SAS soldiers in Derry on 30 January 1972 (Bloody Sunday), a report that was much vilified as a whitewash (HC 220); Lord Parker, having recently retired as the Lord Chief Justice of England after serving for 12 years and also never a Lord of Appeal (although the son of one), reported on the procedures for detaining and interrogating suspected terrorists (Cmnd 4901, 1972), concluding that current interrogation techniques (including hooding and spread-eagling against a wall) were morally justified and should continue. Lord Gardiner, a Labour peer who was to become Lord Chancellor in 1974, was a member of the Parker Committee and submitted a minority report which Prime Minister Heath, to his credit, endorsed. Lord Diplock reported on legal procedures to deal with terrorist activities in Northern Ireland (Cmnd 5185, 1972) and three years later Lord Gardiner did the same (Cmnd 5847, 1975). In the 1990s Lord Lloyd of Berwick (together with Kerr J, later the Lord Chief Justice of Northern Ireland) was asked to consider terrorism in Northern Ireland when preparing a report on UK-wide legislation (Cm 3420, 1996). By then Prime Minister Blair had appointed Lord Saville to re-examine the events of Bloody Sunday (his report is due in late 2009). Lord Hutton conducted the inquiry into the death of Dr David Kelly in 2003 (HC 247, 2003–4), but that had nothing to do with the affairs of Northern Ireland. Lord Clyde, having retired as a Lord of Appeal, served as the Justice Oversight Commissioner in Northern Ireland from 2003 to 2006.

in Ireland for 25 years before being called to the Bar in England and had served as MP for Londonderry North for 10 years.[3] He sat in all six of the appeals from Northern Ireland which reached the Lords during his time there. Lord Carson, the feisty Anglo-Irish Dubliner famous for his oratorical skills in both Ireland and England, and an MP for 29 years (the last three for a constituency in Belfast), had been bitterly opposed to the island's partition. Disillusioned by the turn of events, he rejected a request to become Northern Ireland's first Prime Minister, and also the offer of a viscountcy, and instead accepted from Lloyd George the post of Lord of Appeal. But he never played an active role in that capacity and he sat in just one appeal from Northern Ireland.[4] One of the other four Lords of Appeal in 1921, Viscount Cave, a former war-time Home Secretary, was also avowedly pro-unionist, having so declared himself when debating the Home Rule Bill as a Conservative MP in 1913. He was made Lord Chancellor in 1922 and sat alongside Lord Atkinson in three appeals from Northern Ireland between then and 1928.

Lord Atkinson remained a Lord of Appeal until 1928, when he was replaced by Lord Atkin, a man with an Irish father and a predominantly Welsh upbringing. Lord Carson, despite finding the House of Lords a place 'into which the rays of the sun never penetrate',[5] stayed until 1929 and was replaced by Lord Russell of Killowen (in County Down), a unique figure in the history of the judicial work of the House of Lords in that both his father *and* his son were also Lords of Appeal in their time. His father had been a prominent Catholic lawyer who rose to become the Lord Chief Justice of England (1894–1900).[6] The second Lord Russell was, likewise, no ardent Irish nationalist. Oxford-educated, when he rejected a knighthood on being made a High Court judge, it was not on the ground that he did not want to accept a bauble from the British monarch, but rather that as the son of a peer he felt he already ranked higher than a mere knight.[7]

Although he sat in only one of the nine appeals from Northern Ireland that were heard in the Lords during his 17 years there (1929–46),[8] Lord Russell may have been perceived as the Lord of Appeal most likely to have knowledge of the legal system of Northern Ireland. In any event, only a year after he retired, Sir John MacDermott, a High Court judge from Northern Ireland who had

---

[3] Robert Stevens believes that Atkinson's appointment was 'a move designed to placate the Ulster Unionists': *Law and Politics: The House of Lords as a Judicial Body 1800–1976* (London: Weidenfeld and Nicholson, 1979) 112.

[4] *Lagan Navigation Co v Lambeg Bleaching Co* [1927] AC 226. In his biography of Lord Carson, Montgomery Hyde focuses on just two cases he dealt with in the Lords: *Russell v Russell* [1924] AC 687 (a great divorce scandal) and *Sutherland v Stopes* [1925] AC 47 (on libel law); see *Carson* (London: William Heinemann, 1953) 480–5.

[5] J Hostettler, *Sir Edward Carson: A Dream Too Far* (Chichester: Barry Rose, 2000) 282.

[6] See RB O'Brien, *The Life of Lord Russell of Killowen* (London, Edinburgh, Dublin and New York: Thomas Nelson & Sons, 1901).

[7] *Dictionary of National Biography.*   [8] This was in *Jennings v Kelly* [1940] AC 206.

served in that capacity for just three years, was appointed as a Lord of Appeal.[9] At that time Sir John was the youngest person ever to have been appointed to the office (he was 51).[10] He had been called to the Irish bar in the year of partition, and while practising in Belfast had taken up politics, serving as a Unionist MP for Queen's University from 1938–44, Minister of Public Security from 1940–1, and Attorney General for Northern Ireland from 1941–4. But any thought that his appointment to the Lords reflected a policy always to have someone with knowledge of the Northern Ireland legal system sitting there must be discarded, for just four years later he was moved back to Northern Ireland as the Lord Chief Justice of that jurisdiction, a position he held for the next 20 years. Being a peer with the requisite legal experience he was still available to sit in appeals in the Lords and he indeed did so, especially in cases involving children.[11] He even sat after retiring as the Lord Chief Justice, at the age of 77.[12] But many appeals from Northern Ireland were ones in which he was unable to sit because he had already dealt with the case in that jurisdiction's Court of Appeal or High Court. Indeed it appears that Lord MacDermott never sat as a Law Lord in an appeal from Northern Ireland. Having reviewed his judgments, Robert Stevens describes John MacDermott as bringing a 'sense of balanced creativity and policymaking to various areas of the law'.[13]

Inexplicably, after Lord MacDermott ceased to sit in the Lords (his last case was in 1973), no one from Northern Ireland was appointed as a Lord of Appeal until 1988, when Lord Lowry, who had succeeded Lord MacDermott as Lord Chief Justice of Northern Ireland, was elevated. The feeling in London may have been that, through having conducted inquiries in Northern Ireland, Lord Diplock (1968–85) and Lord Scarman (1977–86) were sufficiently *au fait* with the legal system there to be able to 'represent' that jurisdiction in the Lords during the 1970s and 1980s. But of the 11 reported cases from Northern Ireland during those decades, one or other of those Lords of Appeal sat in only six of them. The failure to promote Lord Lowry sooner may instead have been because his contribution to ensuring the stability of the judicial system in Northern Ireland at a time when it was experiencing extreme pressure was just too crucial to allow him

---

[9] Lords MacDermott and Morton were the two additional Lords of Appeal appointed when their number was raised from seven to nine by the Appellate Jurisdiction Act 1947.

[10] It might have been expected that Sir James Andrews, who had been Lord Chief Justice of Northern Ireland since 1937, was a preferable appointment, but he was already 70 by 1947. Sir James' brother, Thomas, was the designer of the *Titanic*, on which he perished in 1912. Only one subsequent Lord of Appeal has been appointed at a younger age than Lord MacDermott—Lord Radcliffe was 50 when elevated in 1949.

[11] Blom-Cooper and Drewry record him as having given 19 judgments between 1952 and 1968, and six formal concurrences; in three cases he fully dissented: *Final Appeal* (Oxford: Clarendon Press, 1972) 176. On children's issues see his judgments in, eg, *J v C* [1970] AC 668 and *Re W (An Infant)* [1971] AC 682.

[12] *R v Turner* [1974] AC 357, a case on obtaining a pecuniary advantage by deception.

[13] n 3 above, 380–4 at 383.

to be moved to the Lords before 1988. In Northern Ireland he is now viewed as a crucial player in maintaining the integrity of the legal system.[14] In any event, having been created a life peer in 1979, he was frequently invited to sit in the Lords even before being appointed as a Lord of Appeal.[15] During his five and a half years as a Lord of Appeal Lord Lowry issued several sole judgments on behalf of the House in a wide variety of legal areas, including planning, employment, tort, contempt of court, and extradition.[16] He also dissented in two important criminal appeals[17] and had strong views about the dividing line between public law and private law.[18] In *Spring v Guardian Assurance plc*, one of his last cases as a Lord of Appeal, he argued strongly that the House 'ought to think very carefully before resorting to public policy considerations which will defeat a claim that ex hypothesi is a perfectly good cause of action'.[19] When he sat as a retired Lord of Appeal in *C v DPP*,[20] a case concerning the *doli incapax* rule in criminal law for children aged 10 to 14, he delivered a very clear and convincing judgment outlining when it was appropriate for judges to engage in 'judicial legislation'. Like Lord MacDermott, incredibly, Lord Lowry never heard an appeal in the Lords that came from Northern Ireland.

After Lord Lowry retired in 1994 there was a further gap of three years before Sir Brian Hutton, who had succeeded Lord Lowry as Lord Chief Justice of Northern Ireland, was appointed a Lord of Appeal. During the following seven years Lord Hutton participated in 160 appeal hearings (38 per cent of the total) and gave judgments in 74 of them, dissenting in seven. He gave the sole judgment in six cases, all criminal appeals. In three of these he was avowedly pro-defendant, favouring wide disclosure of information by the prosecution,[21] preventing the

---

[14] See the tributes paid to him on his death in 1999 at (1999) 50 NILQ 1–11, including contributions by Sir Robert Carswell LCJ and Lord MacDermott's son, Sir John, who himself served as a judge in Northern Ireland for 25 years.

[15] A LexisNexis search reveals 18 such occasions, including *Bunge Corp v Tradax Export SA* [1981] 1 WLR 711; *Ailsa Craig Fishing Co Ltd v Malvern Shipping Co Ltd* [1983] 1 WLR 964; and *Raymond v Honey* [1983] 1 AC 1. However he appears not to have sat after July 1983.

[16] *Wyre Forest DC v Secretary of State for the Environment* [1990] 2 AC 357 (use of land as a caravan site); *R v Richmond LBC, ex p McCarthy & Stone (Developments) Ltd* [1992] 2 AC 48 (local authority's power to make charges for pre-application planning consultations); *Hughes v Greenwich LBC* [1994] 1 AC 170 (implied terms in a contract of employment); *Smith v Stages* [1989] AC 928 (acting in the course of employment); *Hampson v Department of Education and Science* [1991] 1 AC 171 (race discrimination); *Swingcastle Ltd v Gibson* [1991] 2 AC 223 (measure of damages in negligence claim); *AG v Associated Newspapers Ltd* [1994] 2 AC 238 (newspaper disclosing juror's views); *Government of Canada v Aronson* [1990] 1 AC 579 (extradition).

[17] *R v Gotts* [1992] 2 AC 412 (where his view was that duress *could* be a defence to attempted murder); *R v Gomez* [1993] AC 442 (where his view was that theft required appropriation without the consent of the owner, and he did not feel bound by the House's earlier decision in *R v Lawrence* [1972] AC 626). He voted with the 3:2 majority in *R v Brown* [1994] 1 AC 213, which held that consent was no defence to charges linked to sadomasochistic behaviour.

[18] See his judgments in *Roy v Kensington and Chelsea and Westminster Family Practitioner Committee* [1992] 1 AC 624 and *R v Secretary of State for Employment, ex p EOC* [1995] 1 AC 1.

[19] [1995] 2 AC 296, 326D.   [20] [1996] AC 1.

[21] *R v Mills and Poole* [1988] AC 382.

use of a production order power for secondary purposes,[22] and upholding the availability of the defence of diminished responsibility even to an accused who may have been drunk.[23] In the other three appeals Lord Hutton was pro-prosecution: he ruled that the police do not have to ask a driver if there are any non-medical reasons why a specimen of blood should not be taken,[24] that a person who has been declared unfit to plead cannot then rely upon the concept of diminished responsibility during the hearing into whether he or she actually did the prohibited act,[25] and that overt possession of a weapon can constitute a threat of violence even though it has not been brandished in a violent manner.[26] Among the cases where Lord Hutton dissented are *Fitzpatrick v Sterling Housing Association*,[27] *R v Kansal (No 2)*,[28] *Robinson v Secretary of State for Northern Ireland*,[29] and *Rees v Darlington Memorial Hospital NHS Trust*.[30] In these deci-sions, as in his concurring judgments, he showed that he supported the strict construction of legislation and a conservative approach to judicial law-making. Lord Hutton was also the first Lord of Appeal with previous judicial experience in Northern Ireland to hear an appeal from that jurisdiction.[31] There is not yet a convention, as is there is for Scottish appeals, that a judge from Northern Ireland must sit on appeals from Northern Ireland. In the years 2000–8 there were 18 such appeals, but in only 12 of them did a judge from Northern Ireland sit in the Lords.

As Lord Hutton was immediately succeeded by Lord Carswell in 2004, it may now be safe to assume that a convention has been created whereby once a Lord of Appeal from Northern Ireland retires he is replaced—eventually, if not imme-diately—by a senior judge from Northern Ireland, probably the Lord Chief Justice. The Constitutional Reform Act 2005 effectively requires there always to be a judge from Northern Ireland among the 12 justices on the new Supreme Court of the United Kingdom, for it says that the selection commission 'must ensure that between them the judges will have knowledge of, *and experience of practice in*, the law of each part of the United Kingdom'.[32] In his time to date as a

---

[22] *R v Southwark Crown Court, ex p Bowles* [1998] AC 641.
[23] *R v Dietschmann* [2003] 1 AC 1209.   [24] *DPP v Jackson* [1999] 1 AC 406.
[25] *R v Antoine* [2001] AC 340.   [26] *I v DPP* [2002] 1 AC 285.
[27] [2000] 1 AC 27, where he held that a gay man was not a member of his partner's family for the purpose of succeeding to a tenancy.
[28] [2002] 2 AC 69, where he repeated the view he expressed in *R v Lambert* [2002] 2 AC 545 that the Human Rights Act 1998 should not be given retrospective effect so as to apply in appeals against convictions secured before it came into force.
[29] [2002] NI 390, where he held that the election of the First and deputy First Minister in Northern Ireland was unlawful because it had not occurred within the stipulated period.
[30] [2004] 1 AC 309, where he would have given full damages to a disabled mother who became pregnant after a botched sterilisation operation.
[31] This first occurred in *McGrath v Chief Constable of the RUC* [2001] 2 AC 731.
[32] s 27(8) (emphasis added). In April 2009 it was announced that when Lord Carswell retires in June 2009 he will replaced by the current Lord Chief Justice of Northern Ireland, Sir Brian Kerr.

Lord of Appeal Lord Carswell has given the sole judgment in three appeals[33] and is considered to be one of the experts on criminal law. While he may have had a reputation for being rather conservative when he was the Lord Chief Justice, he has displayed a distinctly more liberal streak when sitting in the Lords.[34] He dissented in *R v Hayter*,[35] *Polanski v Condé Nast Publications Ltd*,[36] and *R (Carson) v Secretary of State for Work and Pensions*.[37]

The flow of appeals from Belfast[38]

Throughout the period 1921 to 2008 there was a steady flow of appeals reaching the House of Lords from Northern Ireland,[39] and in 1962 and 1978 the statutory basis for appeals from the Court of Appeal of Northern Ireland was confirmed.[40] There were 80 Northern Ireland appeals in all, an average of nearly one per year, but in the first half of the period (up to 1964) there were just 29, while in the second half there were 51. In the last few years the average has been almost three

[33] *Government of the USA v Montgomery (No 2)* [2004] 1 WLR 2241 (whether there was an unfair trial); *Akumah v London Borough of Hackney* [2005] 1 WLR 985; *R v Becouarn* [2005] 1 WLR 2589 (whether a jury can draw adverse inferences from a defendant's silence); *Re Officer L* [2007] 1 WLR 2135 (whether police officers' right to life would be violated by compelling them to give evidence without anonymity at an inquiry).

[34] See eg his judgments in *R (Ullah) v Special Adjudicator* [2004] 2 AC 323 (on the impact of the ECHR on persons liable to deportation); *R (European Roma Rights Centre) v Immigration Officer at Prague Airport* [2005] 2 AC 1 (whether a pre-entry clearance system was discriminatory); *A v Secretary of State for the Home Department (No 2)* [2006] 2 AC 221 (whether evidence that might have been obtained abroad through torture is admissible in an English criminal trial); *R (Laporte) v Chief Constable of Gloucestershire Constabulary* [2007] 2 AC 105 (on when the police can take action to prevent a breach of the peace); *R (Al-Skeini) v Secretary of State for Defence* [2008] 1 AC 153 (whether the Human Rights Act applies to acts of public authorities outside the UK); and *A v Hoare* [2008] 1 AC 844 (what limitation period applies to compensation claims for sexual assaults). He also concurred in *R (Middleton) v West Somerset Coroner* [2004] 2 AC 182 (whether inquest procedures comply with Art 2 of the ECHR); *Chief Constable of West Yorkshire Police v A (No 2)* [2005] 1 AC 51 (whether a transgender person had been discriminated against); *A v Secretary of State for the Home Department* [2005] 2 AC 68 (whether indefinite detention without trial of non-British terrorist suspects was lawful); and *R (Smith) v Parole Board* [2005] 1 AC 350 (whether the Parole Board must give a recalled prisoner an oral hearing). But for less liberal judgments see *AG's Reference (No 4 of 2002)* [2005] 1 AC 264 (whether statutory provisions created a legal or evidential burden of proof); *Secretary of State for the Home Dept v JJ* [2008] 1 AC 385 (whether a control order was in breach of Art 5 of the ECHR); and *R (Bancoult) v Secretary of State for Foreign and Commonwealth Affairs* [2008] 3 WLR 955 (whether the UK Government could lawfully prohibit Chagos Islanders from living on their islands).

[35] [2005] 1 WLR 605, on the procedure to be used when two defendants are being jointly tried.

[36] [2005] 1 WLR 637, on whether a fugitive from justice can give evidence by video link in an unrelated private law suit for defamation.

[37] [2006] 1 AC 173, where he held that a pensioner living abroad was discriminated against when denied a pension increase awarded to pensioners living in the UK.

[38] For the 'cursory glance' given by Blom-Cooper and Drewry to the appeals occurring between 1952 and 1968 see *Final Appeal* (n 11) 387–8.

[39] The first Northern Irish appeal to be decided after partition seems to have been *Ward v Laverty* in May 1924 ([1925] AC 101). The case was about whether three orphaned siblings should be raised as Presbyterians or Catholics.

[40] Northern Ireland Act 1962, s 1; Judicature (NI) Act 1978, ss 40–43.

cases per year, when it should be just two, given that the ratio of the population of
Northern Ireland to that of the UK as a whole is 1:35 and that there are about 70
cases heard in the Lords annually. In 2007 and 2008 there were actually 10
appeals heard from Northern Ireland. The success rate for these appeals is on a
par with those emanating from England and Wales, at about 50 per cent, suggesting that the Court of Appeal in Northern Ireland does not operate at an
inferior level to that in England and Wales.

Almost a third of the cases have involved criminal law, criminal procedure, or
the liability of the police, even though the first appeal on substantive criminal law
did not occur until 1961.[41] These cases laid down important rules applicable
throughout England and Wales, as well as Northern Ireland, concerning the
defences of drunkenness[42] and automatism,[43] the directions to be given to juries
when the main evidence against the accused is identificatory[44] or circumstantial,[45]
and the liability of the security forces for killing a suspected terrorist.[46] There
were almost a dozen 'constitutional' cases, where the *vires* of an Act of the
Northern Ireland Parliament[47] or of the Secretary of State for Northern Ireland,[48]
or people's human rights,[49] were at stake, though it is also interesting to note
cases in this field where leave to appeal to the Lords was refused. They did not
proceed with hearing an appeal against the decision of the Divisional Court of
Northern Ireland in *R (Hume) v Londonderry Justices*,[50] which questioned the
power of members of the British army to arrest persons in Northern Ireland,
supposedly because Parliament stepped in so quickly to reverse the effect of that
decision by passing the Northern Ireland Act 1972.[51] Nor was leave given in
appeals dealing with the legitimacy of the Safeguarding of Employment Act (NI)
1947[52] and with whether the IRA had broken its ceasefire.[53]

Another one-third of the Northern Irish appeals heard in London have
involved claims for negligence or breach of statutory duty, including a

---

[41] The Administration of Justice Act 1960 reformed the system for bringing criminal appeals to
the Lords.

[42] *AG for Northern Ireland v Gallagher* [1963] AC 349.

[43] *Bratty v AG for Northern Ireland* [1963] AC 386.

[44] *Arthurs v AG for Northern Ireland* (1970) 55 Cr App R 161.

[45] *McGreevy v DPP* [1973] 1 WLR 276.

[46] *AG for Northern Ireland's Reference (No 1 of 1975)* [1977] AC 105 and *R v Clegg* [1995] 1
AC 482.

[47] *Gallagher v Lynn* [1937] AC 863; *Belfast Corp v OD Cars* [1960] AC 490. The legitimacy of a
provision in the Betting and Lotteries Act (NI) 1957 was left open by the Lords in *McCann v
Attorney General Northern Ireland* [1961] NI 102.

[48] *Robinson v Secretary of State for Northern Ireland* [2002] NI 390.

[49] *Kelly v Northern Ireland Housing Executive* [1999] 1 AC 428; *Re Northern Ireland Human Rights
Commission* [2002] NI 236; *Cullen v Chief Constable of the RUC* [2003] 1 WLR 1763; *Re McKerr*
[2004] 1 WLR 807; *Belfast CC v Miss Behavin' Ltd* [2007] 1 WLR 1420.

[50] [1972] NI 91.

[51] For a comment on this case by Lord Carswell (who was counsel for the Crown), see
'Human Rights and the Rule of Law' [1999] J Clinical Forensic Medicine 249, 252.

[52] *Duffy v Ministry of Labour and National Insurance Fund for Northern Ireland* [1962] NI 6.

[53] *Re Williamson's Application* [2000] NI 281.

well-known decision on whether an employee was acting in the course of his employment at the time of the accident,[54] and there have been about a dozen cases focusing on contractual or employment issues.[55] Just one appeal has focused on family law,[56] and another on social security,[57] but there have been eight dealing with taxation or valuation issues. Recent years have seen an increase in judicial review applications (11 of the last 16 cases). In three of the earlier cases appeals from Northern Ireland helped to establish important general features of the House's jurisdiction: that it can hear appeals purely on cost issues,[58] that it can deal with any point arising in an appeal even though it was not one on which leave to appeal was granted,[59] and that in the event of there being an even split of opinion among the Lords of Appeal (because, say, only four were appointed to hear the appeal, or one of the five has died before being able to give judgment) the appeal must be dismissed.[60] A recurring feature in the appeals heard in the 1950s and 1960s was the deference paid by the Lords, rightly it would seem, to the views of Lord MacDermott CJ in the lower courts. In at least two cases his view as the trial judge was preferred to that of the Court of Appeal of Northern Ireland[61] and in a further three his dissent in the Court of Appeal was approved by the Lords.[62]

Legal problems relating to the 'troubles' which broke out in Northern Ireland in 1968 gave rise to no fewer than 31 appeals. The first 13 of these, decided before 1994, have been subjected to detailed legal analysis by Stephen Livingstone.[63] He concluded that the Lords' record was 'an undistinguished one' because the decisions showed 'a consistent failure to recognise, let alone fully consider, the human rights implications, and [were] frequently unsatisfactory as regards their technical aspects of reasoning and explanation'.[64] He felt that, because the House consistently upheld government action in Northern Ireland, it was not able to play a constructive role in the Northern Ireland conflict and might not be trusted with upholding human rights if and when the United Kingdom acquired

---

[54] *Century Insurance Co Ltd v Northern Ireland Road Transport Board* [1942] AC 509 (where a tanker driver struck a match to light a cigarette while transferring petrol to an underground storage tank). Other important tort cases include *Cavanagh v Ulster Weaving Co Ltd* [1960] AC 145 (where evidence of trade practice was taken not to be determinative of whether there had been negligence on the facts) and *Mallett v McMonagle* [1970] AC 166 (on how to calculate damages to a deceased's administratrix under the Fatal Accident Acts).

[55] Examples include *McEvoy v Belfast Banking Co* [1935] AC 24 and *Northern Ireland Hospitals Authority v Whyte* [1963] 1 WLR 882.

[56] *Ward v Laverty* [1925] AC 101.

[57] *Kerr v Department for Social Development* [2004] 1 WLR 1372.

[58] *Jennings v Kelly* [1940] AC 206.

[59] *AG for Northern Ireland v Gallagher* [1963] AC 349.   [60] *Kennedy v Spratt* [1972] AC 83.

[61] *AG for Northern Ireland v Gallagher* [1963] AC 349; *Northern Ireland Hospitals Authority v Whyte* [1963] 1 WLR 882.

[62] *Cavanagh v Ulster Weaving Co Ltd* [1960] AC 145; *Bill v Short Bros and Harland Ltd* [1963] NI 7; *Irwin v White, Tomkins and Courage* [1964] 1 WLR 387.

[63] 'The House of Lords and the Northern Ireland Conflict' (1994) 57 MLR 333.

[64] ibid, 334.

a Bill of Rights.[65] I myself have questioned the correctness of this analysis, arguing that the attitude of the Lords at that time was dictated not so much by the views they held on the Northern Ireland conflict as by their general conservatism and formalism. I contended that in the next 12 decisions on troubles-related cases (decided between 1994 and 2005) the Lords of Appeal were much more constructive: 'Not only are they granting leave to appeal in more such cases, they are also indulging in much fuller and more contextualised legal analyses when delivering their judgments. There is a freshness and sophistication in the judicial reasoning employed in the last ten years which were not apparent prior to then.'[66]

Having now considered the 11 cases decided since my 2006 analysis was conducted, I have no reason to think that their Lordships have become any less attuned to the sensitivities of the Northern Ireland situation. Six of those decisions can be said to relate in some way to the conflict there. In *Tweed* they allowed the Orange Order to have greater access to the information examined by the Parades Commission before it decides whether to impose conditions on marches,[67] but in *Re Duffy*, perhaps surprisingly (and contrary to the Northern Ireland Court of Appeal), they held that no reasonable Secretary of State could have appointed two members of the Orange Order to serve on the Parades Commission.[68] In *Re Officer L* the House suggested that there was no good reason to grant anonymity to police officers who were due to give evidence at an inquiry into the killing of Robert Hamill, a Catholic man attacked in Portadown by sectarian Protestants while, allegedly, the RUC looked on.[69] But in *E v Chief Constable of the Royal Ulster Constabulary* the Lords held unanimously that the police in Northern Ireland had not breached the Human Rights Act 1998 in the manner in which they had sought to protect young children against inhuman and degrading treatment aimed at them by Loyalist demonstrators at Holy Cross Primary School in 2001.[70] And in a third case involving the police, *Ward v Police Service of Northern Ireland*, which concerned the investigation of the theft of £26.5 million from the Northern Bank in Belfast, the Lords approved the local judge's decision that, when the police wish to apply to extend the detention of a suspected terrorist for further questioning, they do not have to disclose the nature of the lines of inquiry they wish to pursue during that questioning.[71] In *Jordan v Lord Chancellor*, the House affirmed its earlier decision in *Re McKerr*,[72] to the effect that the duty under Article 2 of the European Convention to conduct thorough investigations of suspicious deaths does not apply to deaths occurring before the Human Rights Act came into force.[73] From a purely human rights

---

[65] ibid, 359–60.

[66] 'The House of Lords and the Northern Ireland Conflict—A Sequel' (2006) 69 MLR 383, 414.

[67] *Tweed v Parades Commission for Northern Ireland* [2007] 1 AC 650.

[68] [2008] NI 152.   [69] [2007] 1 WLR 2135.   [70] [2008] 3 WLR 1208.

[71] [2007] 1 WLR 3013. Mr Ward was later acquitted of all charges relating to the theft.

[72] [2004] 1 WLR 807.

[73] [2007] 2 AC 226. For a comment see M Requa and G Anthony, 'Coroners, Controversial Deaths, and Northern Ireland's Past Conflict' [2008] PL 443.

point of view that position is obviously regrettable, but their Lordships might have thought that the peace process in Northern Ireland was better served by not subjecting these 'old' cases to too much further forensic scrutiny. They did at least, in differing ways, make it easier for coroners' inquests to suggest that the death in question may have been the result of a crime.

In the other five recent appeals from Northern Ireland matters were raised which have a more general relevance to the United Kingdom as a whole, although two of them do not merit more than a mention here.[74] In *Miss Behavin'*, however, the Lords confirmed the rather unfortunate position they had adopted a year earlier in *Begum*,[75] namely, that they do not expect public authorities to be able to demonstrate that they took into account the human rights implications of their decisions, so long as the decisions themselves do not violate human rights in the eyes of the court.[76] On the other hand, a more progressive attitude was displayed in *Re G (Adoption: Unmarried Couple)*,[77] where the Lords said that they could interpret Convention rights in a way which went beyond how the European Court of Human Rights might have interpreted them in the case at hand, and that the United Kingdom's margin of appreciation in this regard could be developed not just by Parliament but also by the courts. In *Zalewska v Department for Social Development* the Lords confirmed the view of the Northern Ireland Court of Appeal that the UK's Accession (Immigration and Worker Registration) Regulations 2004 were compatible with EC law even though they made access to the labour market (and, indirectly, to income support) conditional upon the worker being registered with an authorised employer for a 12-month period: any breaks in that registration were fatal to eligibility.[78]

Conclusion

Northern Ireland may be a comparatively small part of the United Kingdom but it has contributed more than its fair share of judges and appeals to the House of Lords. Recent years would suggest that the flow of appeals is becoming more substantial and the Constitutional Reform Act guarantees that at least one of the

---

[74] *Re Maye* [2008] 1 WLR 315, on which categories of assets can be accessed in order to force compliance with a confiscation order; *Re D* [2008] 1 WLR 1499, on the standard of proof required before Life Sentence Review Commissioners decide not to release a prisoner recalled from release on licence.

[75] *R (SB) v Head Teacher and Governors of Denbigh High School* [2007] 1 AC 100.

[76] *Belfast CC v Miss Behavin' Ltd* [2007] 1 WLR 1420.

[77] [2009] 1 AC 173. See too ch 30 in this volume, p 555. On the Lords' earlier preference for 'the mirror principle', under which UK courts should not go any further than the European Court of Human Rights in protecting rights, see J Lewis, 'The European Ceiling on Human Rights' [2007] PL 720.

[78] [2008] 1 WLR 2602. Lady Hale dissented, finding the Regulations to be in breach of the Community law principle of proportionality.

United Kingdom's Supreme Court Justices will have experience of the practice of law in Northern Ireland. Future appeals may have less to do with the 'emergency' in Northern Ireland than with the rolling out of the peace process there, but otherwise there is no reason to suppose that the Supreme Court will be any less concerned with legal problems arising from that part of the country than the House of Lords has been to date.

18

The Interplay with the Judicial Committee of the Privy Council

*Kenneth Keith**

Introduction

Henry Brougham, in 1828 in his great law reform speech lasting six hours in the House of Commons, fortified by a hatful of oranges and informed by his practice before the Judicial Committee of the Privy Council, identified some of the challenges the Committee then faced. Because of the great variety of legal systems and the fact that many matters arising overseas were foreign to British experience, 'any judicial tribunal in this country must, of necessity, be an extremely inadequate court of review'. The difficulty, even incapacity, of the members of the Committee involved both ignorance of the law and unfitness to judge the facts. 'The judges should be men[1] of the largest legal and general information, accustomed to the study of other systems of law beyond our own, and associated with lawyers who have practised and presided in the colonial courts.' A specialist bar was needed, as were more sitting days: the Committee sat only nine days a year and many cases were 'compromised from hopelessness because of delays'. Not only were the Committee members not competent in many cases but they determined the most complex matters in a manner the most summary that can be conceived in this country. Improvements, he declared, were demanded to achieve justice for the 'countless millions...you desire to govern—all over the world'.[2]

At the time of that speech, the 'countless millions' were to be found in the Americas (the Caribbean, British Honduras, and British Guiana, as well as Canada), Gambia, Sierra Leone (including the Gold Coast), Cape Colony,

* Thanks to Rebecca Jenkin and Jonas Beaudry for help with the research for this paper and to John McGrath for comments. I have had to be very selective in preparing this paper and have made extensive use of the rich secondary literature.
[1] It was not until 2004 that a woman sat in the Judicial Committee—Dame Sian Elias, Chief Justice of New Zealand.
[2] For the reform period see PA Howell's valuable book *The Judicial Committee of the Privy Council 1833–1876* (Cambridge: CUP, 1979).

Mauritius, Ceylon, extensive regions of India (subject to the hegemony of the East India Company until the rebellion of 1857 which led to the British Government taking direct control), the Straits Settlements including Singapore, New South Wales, Heligoland, Gibraltar, Malta, and the Ionian Islands, as well as the Channel Islands and the Isle of Man, being parts of the British Isles which were not subject to the British court system. The population of India made up the great bulk of the millions to whom Brougham referred and their disputes were the source of much of the business of the Judicial Committee at that time and indeed throughout the nineteenth century and into the twentieth.

By the beginning of the twentieth century, the geographic reach of the Empire and of areas subject to British rule of one kind or another was much more extensive, covering about one quarter of the land mass of the world and about the same proportion of population. Britain had led the 'Scramble for Africa' (including Nigeria, the whole of South Africa, the protectorates there, the two Rhodesias and Nyasaland, Kenya and Uganda, Zanzibar, British Somaliland, and the condominium, with Egypt, of Sudan) and had also greatly extended its rule in Asia to include Burma, further parts of Malaya, North Borneo, Hong Kong, Papua, other parts of Australia, New Zealand, islands across the Pacific, and Cyprus and from 1922 the Irish Free State. That listing by itself highlights and magnifies Brougham's concerns. At that time, the cases before the Judicial Committee could raise, for instance, issues of French civil law (Québec and parts of the Caribbean—the custom of Paris; Mauritius and the Seychelles—the Napoleonic code), Roman-Dutch Law (Cape Colony and Ceylon), Roman law (Malta), Spanish law (Trinidad), customary law (West Africa), Turkish law (Cyprus), and especially Hindu law and Moslem law (India), as well as Norman-French law (Channel Islands).[3] Within the century after Brougham spoke the Judicial Committee's jurisdiction also included appeals from countries under League of Nations mandate such as Palestine and Tanganyika, those under various forms of protectorate, as in the Gulf area, and consular courts.

Over the past 70 years the jurisdiction of the Judicial Committee has been reduced to a shadow of its earlier self as many states within the Empire and later the Commonwealth became independent and either then or later decided to end appeals: the Irish Free State in 1933, Canada in 1933 and 1946, Palestine, Burma, India, Pakistan, and South Africa by 1950, almost all of the Commonwealth African States in the 1960s, Sri Lanka in 1971, Australia between the 1960s and 1980s, Guyana in 1970, Malaysia in 1978 and 1985, Singapore in 1989 and 1994, Hong Kong in 1997, New Zealand in 2003,[4] and Barbados in 2007 when it accepted the appellate jurisdiction of the Caribbean Court of Justice (CCJ).

---

[3] I exclude admiralty, prize, ecclesiastical and disciplinary appeals, the reference jurisdiction, and the recently created and soon to be abolished devolution jurisdiction.

[4] For a brief account of the New Zealand process see 'The Unity of the Common Law and the Ending of Appeals to the Privy Council' (2005) 54 ICLQ 197, 202–5; see BJ Cameron's valuable earlier account (1970) 2 Otago L Rev 172.

Jurisdiction remains in respect only of the other independent Caribbean countries, notably the Bahamas, Belize, Jamaica, and Trinidad and Tobago (now often the major source of appeals), Mauritius, Brunei in civil cases, the Channel Islands, the Isle of Man, and the remaining scattered British colonies. Forty-three of the 71 substantive decisions in 2007 were on appeal from the independent Commonwealth countries in the Caribbean.

Although the CCJ was established in 2005, only Barbados and Guyana have accepted its appellate jurisdiction. The Jamaican legislation to transfer the Judicial Committee's jurisdiction to the new Court was held in part unconstitutional by the Judicial Committee. While the Jamaican Parliament, it ruled, was able, by simple majority in each house of Parliament, to abolish appeals to the Committee, it was not able to substitute the CCJ for the Committee because the members of the new court did not have the necessary protection of tenure.[5] Experienced local observers have reported on the negative impact of the decision on the development of the court's appellate jurisdiction. Jamaican acceptance would have provided a powerful incentive for other smaller countries to follow suit and appeals from Jamaica would have enabled the court to increase its visibility and demonstrate its capacities. The reasoning of the Judicial Committee has also been strongly criticised, notably by Rt Hon Justice Michael de Bastide, the President of the new court and former Chief Justice of Trinidad and Tobago.[6]

Over the last century and most recently in the Caribbean, debates and decisions about ending or retaining appeals have concerned the quality and expertise of the local judges and those in London, the advantages and disadvantages of detachment and local knowledge and understanding, the value of the uniformity of the common law and the interpretation of legislation in force in Britain and other jurisdictions, costs and delays, and nationality and sovereignty. In the many cases where the appeal ended with independence, as with most African countries, the last appears to have been the principal or indeed the only reason.

This chapter considers aspects of the role of the Law Lords from the mid nineteenth century, when they move along Whitehall from the committee rooms in the Palace of Westminster and sit in the hearing rooms of the Judicial Committee of the Privy Council in Downing Street. What has their impact been on the law of countries and territories from which appeals came?

The answers given to that question varies greatly from place to place and time to time[7] and in respect of different areas of law. The material relevant to those questions is vast and this chapter must be selective. To begin, I recall some

---

[5] *Independent Jamaica Council for Human Rights v Marshall-Burnett* [2005] 2 AC 356. The court also has original jurisdiction to deal with disputes among the 13 members of CARICOM, a free trade organisation.

[6] 'Putting things right and the Caribbean Court of Justice' The Seventh William G Deman Memorial Lecture, 16 May 2006); see also Sir David Simmons, Chief of Justice of Barbados, 'The Caribbean Court of Justice: a Unique Institution of Caribbean Creativity' (2005) 31 Com Law Bull 71.

[7] For a valuable account from 70 years ago by a brilliant Australian scholar see RTE Latham, *The Law and the Commonwealth* (Oxford: OUP, 1937, republished 1949).

positive general answers. In 1900, with the Empire virtually at its full extent, Robert Haldane, already with many years' experience as counsel in the Privy Council and later to be Lord Chancellor and a prominent member of the Committee, spoke confidently of the Committee, 'that far reaching engine of imperial justice', as constituting 'a real and most important portion of the silken bounds which, with little friction, hold our great Empire together', and impartially examining the legality of the actions of the Queen's meanest subject and the Queen's Imperial Government.[8] In 1910 a leading Ontario judge who had appeared as counsel in the Judicial Committee went even further, emphasising 'the idea of fundamental union in all British communities—made manifest in one great Court of Appeal for all the lands beyond the seas . . . One name we bear, one flag covers us, to one throne we are loyal—and that court is a token of our unity.' He concluded that 'it is wholly beyond controversy that Canadians generally would deplore any attempt to interfere with their traditional right to apply for justice to the foot of the throne'.[9]

By 1921, following the carnage of the Great War, Haldane's tone is different; after outlining the work of 'the supreme tribunal of the Empire to which every subject of the King Emperor is entitled to go', the Lord Chancellor provided a cautious forecast: the British Empire, he thought, was a disappearing body, it would be a long time before it would disappear altogether, and accordingly he saw the real worth of the Judicial Committee as helping hold the Empire together.[10] In 1926 he declared, 'we sit as an Imperial Court which represents the Empire'.[11] Even in 1948, a former Attorney General of Palestine, who had earlier published a book on the Privy Council, assessed it as a model of an international court for human rights, referring to descriptions of it as the most august tribunal in the world and the golden link of the British Empire.[12]

A comment on time and context may be added. The Judicial Committee may be traced back to the fifteenth century, its jurisdiction in Britain was essentially abolished in 1641, it had jurisdiction until 1776 over all the American colonies, and, just within the last century, from a peak, its authority has drastically reduced, although more slowly than the executive and legislative powers of the British Crown and Parliament. In that century the 'Dominions' came to assert and be recognised as having independent status (with independent membership in the

---

[8] 'The Appellate Courts of the Empire' (1900) 12 Juridical Review 1.

[9] WR Riddell, 'The Judicial Committee of the Privy Council' (1910) 44 Am L Rev 161, 173, 174, 176; he does not mention that the Canadian Parliament, as long ago as 1888, had purported to abolish appeals in criminal matters, a measure held unconstitutional in *Nadan v The King* [1926] AC 482 only in 1926, shortly before the adoption of the Balfour declaration which was followed by 1933 legislation, in terms of the Statute of Westminster, repealing criminal appeals, upheld in *British Coal Corp v The King* [1935] AC 500 by the same committee and on the same day as the legislation abolishing the appeal for the Irish Free State was upheld (*Moore v AG for the Irish Free State* [1935] AC 484). Lord Sankey, the author of the Statute of Westminster, was by then Lord Chancellor and delivered both opinions.

[10] 'The Work for the Empire of the Judicial Committee of the Privy Council' (1923) 1 CLJ 143, 144.

[11] *Hull v M'Kenna* [1926] IR 402.   [12] Norman Bentwich (1948) 2 ILQ 392.

League of Nations, the Balfour declaration on Imperial relations in 1926, and the Statute of Westminster of 1931 being important constitutional markers), two major world wars and other armed conflicts were waged, international institutions and international law grew apace and in many respects have come to supplant and surpass the Imperial institutions and law as major underpinnings of globalisation, ideologies have come and gone, scientific and technological developments have occurred at a dizzying rate, new threats to humanity have appeared, Britain joined the European community, and nationalism took sharper forms with impacts on the law and court systems in different Commonwealth countries. The changing jurisdiction and work of the Judicial Committee must be seen against that wider background.

The judges

One of Henry Brougham's major reforms, to return to the mid-nineteenth century, was incorporated in the Privy Council Act 1833, an Act 'for the better administration of justice in Her Majesty's Privy Council'.[13] It limited those who could sit to certain categories of British judges who were members of the Privy Council, but included its President who was not necessarily a lawyer and who sat as late as the 1860s. Provision was also made for two additional members to be appointed, in practice judges and lawyers with extensive experience in India and Ceylon. From 1881 all members of the English Court of Appeal who were Privy Councillors could sit, as, from 1895, could the Chief Justices and Justices of the Australasian, Canadian, and South African superior courts, again if appointed to be Privy Councillors. That 1895 amendment was one response to pressure which continued into the first decade of the twentieth century for greater involvement of judges of the self-governing colonies in the Committee and more fundamentally for the creation of a single imperial tribunal, serving the United Kingdom as well as the empire.[14] In recent years some senior Caribbean judges have also been appointed. A 1915 amendment authorised the Committee to sit in more than one division, in effect allowing for one to deal, during the Great War, with Prize appeals and later with appeals from the subcontinent and the second with the remainder of the appeals. While the additional Indian members made up a regular and significant part of committees dealing with appeals from the subcontinent, the responsibilities of the judges from the self-governing colonies and dominions in their own jurisdictions meant that their contribution was limited. In the case of the New Zealand judges, who over the past century have made the largest contribution to the membership of the Judicial Committee, beyond of course the British and subcontinent members, only three sat before 1965. Over

---

[13] He also had a major hand in the passing of the Reform Act 1832 and the Anti-Slavery Act 1833.

[14] For a valuable summary of the developments around the turn of the century see R Stevens, *Law and Politics: The House of Lords as a Judicial Body 1800–1976* (London: Weidenfeld and Nicholson, 1978) 73–6; see also (2003) 1 New Zealand Journal of Public and International Law 3, 15–16.

the following 40 years, about 20 have sat, generally one or two each year for one to three months.[15] Given a major justification for the 1895 reform, it is striking that a New Zealand judge did not sit on a New Zealand appeal until 1971, and that, in the 1960s, as a matter of policy no Australian High Court judge sat on an appeal from any Australian Court. From the late nineteenth century it was the Law Lords who had the principal and almost the sole role in appeals from Canada, the Caribbean, Africa, Australia, and New Zealand.

Aspects of the composition and method of operation of the committee may conveniently be mentioned here. One is the potential significance, as will appear later, of the choice of a particular panel of members from a very large pool. On the one hand, the choice of a particular Law Lord in a series of cases may have a decisive continuing significance. On the other, variations in the composition and size of the panels may lead to conflicting decisions over a short period.

A second aspect is the role in the Judicial Committee for much of its history of the single advice, allowing no indication of dissent, as opposed to separate speeches in the House of Lords. Although the Privy Councillors' oath, set out in an order in council of 1627, was understood to require a single opinion, departures from that practice may be found in the nineteenth century. Following those departures, the old rule was re-imposed in 1878 and, notwithstanding an agreement at the Imperial Conference of 1911 to allow public dissent, that step was not taken until 1966, following pressure from Australian judges who were beginning to sit on a more regular basis. That change was first understood as allowing at most one judgment on each side, but practice recently has gone further, as with two concurrences by members of a unanimous committee dismissing an appeal from the Pitcairn Island Court of Appeal, and the members of the Committee in devolution appeals writing separately, as if they were sitting in the House of Lords.[16]

Speaking five years after the change, Lord Reid declared that this limit meant that from a long time back, from the point of view of developing the law, Privy Council judgments had been much inferior to those of the House of Lords. Thirty-five years later, the Senior Law Lord, Lord Bingham, expressed his agreement.[17] A related

[15] Lord Cooke of Thorndon, on his retirement from the Presidency of the New Zealand Court of Appeal in 1996, was appointed a Law Lord and until 2001 sat regularly in the Privy Council, as well as in the House of Lords; see eg Spiller (2003) 3 OUCLJ 29.

[16] On the single opinion debate, see DB Swinfen, *Imperial Appeal: The Debate on the Appeal to the Privy Council 1833–1986* (Manchester: MUP 1987) 221–46 and on the devolution practice R Munday (2002) 61 CLJ 612, 619–26. The Pitcairn appeal also saw a very early use in English courts of technology, unimaginable for almost all of the Committee's existence, with the lengthy trial record being on disk and immediately accessible, and a video link of the hearing to that remote island and its population of about 50 people, as had occurred at earlier stages when hearings were held in New Zealand.

[17] 'The Judge as law maker' (1972) 12 JSPTL 22, 28–9; 'The Rule of Law—Sixth Sir David Williams Lecture' (2007) 66 CLJ 67. Cases where the Law Lords take the opportunity of a Privy Council appeal to sort out English law may provide exceptions, as in *Agnew v Comr of Inland Revenue* [2001] 2 AC 710, overturning In re New Bullas Trading Ltd [1994] IBCLC 485, and the opinion (with two dissenting opinions) of a nine-member board in *AG for Jersey v Holley* [2005] AC 580, in effect overruling the decision of the House of Lords in *R v Smith* [2001] 1 AC 146.

matter, seemingly largely undocumented, is the procedure followed by the members of the Privy Council in settling the advice of the Committee. To what extent do they share their views with one another on the content and the expression of the reasons for that advice?[18]

A third aspect of the operation of the Committee, related to its Imperial role, concerns its place of sitting. According to Lord Radcliffe, speaking for the Privy Council in 1964 in an appeal from Ceylon, it is not a British institution; it is an integral part of the court structure of the countries from which appeals come.[19] It is simply as a matter of practice that it sits in the hearing room in the Privy Council offices in Downing Street. The question whether it should become peripatetic—with related issues about its composition and its possible consolidation with the House of Lords and the formation of a Commonwealth Court—was the subject of intermittent discussion in the Empire and Commonwealth at various times in the twentieth century, with the idea receiving its quietus as late as 1965 when it was raised both at the Commonwealth Heads of Government conference and the Commonwealth Law Conference in Sydney. Over the lengthy period, political, officials, and judges in London and elsewhere in the Commonwealth were concerned, in addressing those issues, with the composition of the Bench (Indian judges sitting on South African cases and vice versa, African judges sitting on Australian appeals...); judges from the Commonwealth sitting on English and Scottish appeals; the strain on members travelling long distances to places with difficult climates; delay; the quality of local counsel and of law libraries; the growing forces of nationalism which might be enhanced by the appearance of an itinerant court; the steady and increasingly rapid abolition of the appeal by many Commonwealth members; the growing understanding that the Committee was not well suited to deciding constitutional (especially federal) issues; and even the loss of mystery were the throne to come to the litigants ('the tradition, the ceremonial, the distance and the fact that the Court sits at the centre of the Empire would all be lost').[20]

It is remarkable in the light of that history, that, 40 years on, in 2007 and 2008, five Law Lords have sat in the Bahamas, which has consistently said that it will not replace appeals to the Committee with appeals to the Caribbean Court of Justice, and in Mauritius.

Indian appeals

The particular membership arrangements for Indian appeals meant that the Law Lords had a much more limited role than they did in other jurisdictions. Further,

---

[18] The recent experience of one New Zealand judge sitting in the Privy Council, shared by others, did not include 'the judges collegially sitting together, in meetings, settling the text of judgments delivered...' TM Gault (2002) 33 Victoria University of Wellington L Rev 631, 635.

[19] *Ibralebbe v R* [1964] AC 900, 921–2.

[20] R Stevens, *The Independence of the Judiciary: The View from the Lord Chancellor's Office* (Oxford: Clarendon Press, 1993) ch 8 provides a valuable account.

many of the cases had a particular local content and the jurisdiction ended well over 50 years ago. That extensive experience nevertheless highlights matters of more general application. One was about the structure and operation of the courts within India from which the appeals came, a matter which is often neglected when attention is focused on the final appeal court. Among the related debates and proposals were those leading to the establishment of a federal court for India along with the major reforms included in the Government of India Act of 1935. A second matter concerned the scope of the appeal: the distinctions between criminal and civil appeals; the choice between appeals of right or by leave and, in the latter case, the criteria for the grant of leave; and the weight to be given by the Privy Council to the concurrency of findings of fact in the courts in India.[21]

In general, across the Empire and Commonwealth, criminal appeals were only by special leave of the Judicial Committee, a leave which, until recently, as discussed later, was rarely given. In civil matters, appeals involving more than a fixed monetary limit (not always adjusted to take account of inflation) were often as of right, with the consequence that the Law Lords frequently had to deal with matters in the Judicial Committee which they would not have heard in the House of Lords; while administrative law appeals, for instance, by contrast, could be brought only with leave of the court from which the appeal came or the Committee.

A further matter of general application arising from Indian appeals are assessments over the years of the role of the Judicial Committee. In 1872 a London barrister, who had been a judge of the High Court of Madras, stated that the professional experience, as advocates or as judges, of home bred English judges, was defective in two respects: they were municipal lawyers rather than jurists (the legal education of English lawyers was neither scientific nor profound) and they had never been judges of fact. The defect of legal understanding was to be seen, he said, in judges struggling with a fundamental notion of Hindu or Roman Dutch law and misleading themselves by perpetually comparing it to apparently similar English legal notions. On the second defect, he recorded the recent abandonment by the Judicial Committee of the rule not to dissent from findings of fact except in very clear cases; that was one of the main reasons why judgments of the Judicial Committee were giving less satisfaction than earlier. The first defect led him to propose an admixture of retired colonial judges practically skilled in one or more of the alien systems of law which the court in London would have to administer, and the second to suggest changes in the scope of the appeal and the procedure and structures of the courts below. While he emphasised that his concern was only with Indian appeals which had made up more than three quarters of Judicial Committee appeals in the previous term, the

---

[21] For a recent discussion in the High Court of Australia, many years after the ending of appeals to London, of the Privy Council doctrine on this matter see Heydon J in *Roads and Traffic Authority of NSW v Dederer* [2007] HCA 42, paras 285–93.

defects he identified are essentially those identified by Henry Brougham nearly 50 years earlier and by many others since.[22]

Sharply contrasting views about the Judicial Committee were expressed by leading Indian politicians and lawyers in the debates there in 1925 about proposals for a Supreme Court of India. For the proponent, recent Privy Council decisions, particularly on Hindu and Muhammadan law, had not commanded universal and unqualified confidence. Pandit Nehru however saw the distance of six or seven thousand miles between the highest court of appeal and the Government of India as no bad thing; the time for a change would come when 'we are a self-governing people'. MA Jinnah strongly supported the proponent, arguing that 'the Privy Council have on several occasions absolutely murdered Hindu law, slaughtered Muhammadan law'. And, in the following year Mahatma Gandhi, expressing painful surprise at the opposition to the proposal, with the implication that we have lost all confidence in ourselves, expressed his firm belief that the Members of the Privy Council are not free from political bias and on highly intricate matters of custom, in spite of all their labours, they often make egregious errors.[23]

'The unity of the common law'

In the settled colonies (as opposed to those which were ceded or conquered or the subject of special treaty regimes), the law of England was considered to be applicable, subject, however, to the requirements of local circumstances. One early question concerned the attitude a colonial court was to take to the interpretation of an English statute applicable in the colony. Was the court bound by the interpretation given by the English Court of Appeal? In 1878 the Privy Council answered affirmatively:[24]

Their Lordships think the Court in the colony might well have taken this decision as an authoritative construction of the statute. It is the judgment of the Court of Appeal, by which all the Courts in *England* are bound, until a contrary determination has been arrived at by the House of Lords. Their Lordships think that in colonies where a like enactment has been passed by the Legislature, the Colonial Courts should also govern themselves by it ... It is of the utmost importance that in all parts of the empire where

---

[22] C Collett, 'The Judicial Committee of the Privy Council with Special Reference to India' (1872) I (4th ser) Law Magazine and Review 14. For an acute assessment of the arrangements for India from 1844 until the end of the late century see WC Petheram, 'English Judges and Hindu Law' (1900) 16 LQR 396, who saw potential value of the same English judge regularly sitting, assisted by assessors rather than by judges with Indian experience.

[23] All quoted in the valuable paper, GH Gadbois, 'Evolution of the Federal Court of India; An Historical Footnote' (1963) Journal of the Indian Law Institute 19, 24, 25, 26. For a devastating critique of a decision of February 1899 about Hindu law see WC Petheram, 'English Judges and Hindu Law' (1900) 16 LQR 77, expressing the fear that the persistent refusal by the Judicial Committee to recognise the right of a family in ancestral estates would not tend to strengthen the confidence of the people in the administration of justice.

[24] *Trimble v Hill* (1879) 5 App Cas 342, 344.

English law prevails, the interpretation of that law by the Courts should be as nearly as possible the same.

In 1927, a year after the adoption of the Balfour Declaration, the Privy Council stepped away from that position, asserting that it is not right to assume that an appellate Colonial (Dominion) Court is wrong if on a matter of English law it differs from an appellate court in England. But it was otherwise if the decision was one of the House of Lords for 'it is the supreme tribunal to settle English law, and that being settled, the Colonial Court, which is bound by English law, is bound to follow it'.[25] What was a court in a jurisdiction subject to Privy Council appeals to do if faced with conflicting decisions of the Privy Council and the House of Lords? By the end of the nineteenth century the House of Lords proceeded on the basis that it was bound by its earlier decisions while the Privy Council had for some time indicated that it was not.[26] Did that difference matter? Was the sequence of the decisions significant? Did it matter whether the later court pointed to an error in the earlier decision? Did the binding force of the Privy Council decision depend on its coming from the same jurisdiction? While these interesting questions did arise from time to time in Commonwealth Courts, legislation was increasingly supplanting the common law as Sir Robert Stout, Chief Justice of New Zealand, had pointed out as early as 1904.[27]

In the early 1930s, when Canada was actively looking at the ending of Privy Council appeals, the Alberta Court of Appeal, with hesitation, followed a ruling of the House of Lords in respect of negligence concerning negotiable instruments in preference to an earlier Privy Council decision not followed by the House of Lords. The Ontario Court of Appeal in a mental shock case went further, preferring to be guided by the views of English law expressed by the English Court of Appeal and an Irish court and not by a judgment of the Privy Council.[28]

One particular common law difference lasting into the 1960s, arising from decisions of the Privy Council and House of Lords, concerned Crown privilege. The Privy Council in an appeal from South Australia declared that it could assess the claim of the Minister to withhold state documents. In a later, wartime case the House of Lords said that the Minister's word was final and the courts had no role. What was a court in Australia or New Zealand to do? Was it bound by the (later) decision of the House of Lords, 'the supreme tribunal to settle English law', or by the decision of the Privy Council, the final court in the hierarchy and according to *Robins* equally able (with the House of Lords) to settle the law? In the 1950s and 1960s Canadian, Australian, and New Zealand courts decided that the Minister did not have the final say, at least as a general proposition, accordingly preferring

---

[25] *Robins v National Trust Co Ltd* [1927] AC 515, 519.
[26] *London Street Tramways v London CC* [1898] AC 375 and eg *Cushing v Dupuy* (1880) 5 App Cas 409, and *Tooth v Power* [1891] AC 284, 292.
[27] 'Appellate Tribunals for the Colonies' (1904) 2 Comm L Rev 3, 8.
[28] *Will v Bank of Montreal* [1931] 3 DLR 526 and *Negro v Pietro's Bread Co* [1933] 1 DLR 490.

the Privy Council position. That view of the law was also taken in the House of Lords in what appeared to be the first exercise by it of its recently rediscovered power to overrule its earlier decisions.[29] Much has been written about the reasons given by the various courts for taking the position they did. Two features of the reasoning may be recalled: on the whole, it was not a matter of the mechanical application of simple rules of precedent; rather the choice of result appears to be largely governed by the assessment by the judges of which approach was the better. That broader approach may be related to large changes in the perceptions of the judicial role from the 1960s, demonstrated, so far as British judges are concerned, particularly by Lord Reid on his becoming the senior Lord of Appeal and Lord Denning on his returning to the Court of Appeal as Master of the Rolls and, so far as judge made law is concerned, by the rapid development of the law of judicial review of administrative action, the latter in parallel with much legislative activity aimed at opening up public administration and subjecting it to greater control. For many Commonwealth jurisdictions the judicial development of that law, at that time, was through the House of Lords and the English Court of Appeal rather than the Privy Council where the two judges just mentioned rarely sat, in part because of the single opinion rule.

From the 1960s the uniformity of the common law was the subject of further challenges, not necessarily associated with differences between the Privy Council and the House of Lords. In 1963 the High Court of Australia, through its Chief Justice, Sir Owen Dixon, refused to follow as misconceived and wrong a much-criticised House of Lords decision, given by way of a single speech (a practice soon abandoned), in a murder case:

Hitherto I have thought that we ought to follow decisions of the House of Lords, at the expense of our own opinions and cases decided here, but having carefully studied *Smith*'s case I think that we cannot adhere to that view or policy. There are propositions laid down in the judgment...which I could never bring myself to accept...I think *Smith*'s case should not be used as authority in Australia at all.[30]

Soon after, in 1967, the Privy Council reinforced the existence of differences in the common law in a defamation appeal from Australia. The question was whether the award of punitive or exemplary damages in a libel case was limited to the categories stated recently by the House of Lords. The High Court of Australia, confirming its earlier position, had refused to follow that approach. The Privy Council asked whether in the face of the House of Lords' decision

the High Court of Australia were wrong in deciding not to change the law in Australia as it had been understood to be. There are doubtless advantages if within those parts of the Commonwealth (or indeed of the English-speaking world) where the law is built upon a common foundation development proceeds along similar lines. But development may

---

[29] eg P Hogg and P Monahan, *Liability of the Crown* (Toronto: Carswell, 3rd edn 2000) 88–100.
[30] *Parker v R* (1963) 111 CLR 610, 632. See also ch 32 in this volume.

gain its impetus from any one and not from one only of those parts. The law may be influenced from any one direction. The gain that uniformity of approach may yield is however far less marked in some branches of the law than in others. In trade between countries and nations the sphere where common acceptance of view is desirable may be wide.... But in matters which may considerably be of domestic or internal significance the need for uniformity is not compelling.

It concluded:

The issue that faced the High Court in the present case was whether the law as it had been settled in Australia should be changed. Had the law developed by processes of faulty reasoning or had it been founded upon misconceptions it would have been necessary to change it. Such was not the case. In the result in a sphere of the law where its policy calls for decision and where its policy in a particular country is fashioned so largely by judicial opinion it became a question for the High Court to decide whether the decision in *Rookes v Barnard* compelled a change in what was a well settled judicial approach in the law of libel in Australia. Their Lordships are not prepared to say that the High Court were wrong in being unconvinced that a changed approach in Australia was desirable.[31]

Within 10 years the High Court held that it was not bound by decisions of the Privy Council and did not regard itself as bound by decisions of the House of Lords.[32]

The recognition by the Privy Council of differences in the law within the Commonwealth and Empire is to be found not only in the 1930s and later, for instance in a number of New Zealand cases in the last three decades in which the Committee's deference to local assessment effectively denied the appellants in the Judicial Committee their right of appeal,[33] but also at the beginning of the century, in cases relating to indigenous or native rights or title. Those cases include valuable reminders of the danger of rendering native title to land in terms which had grown up under English law; a study of the history of the particular country and its usages was called for. According to Lord Haldane, 'Abstract principles fashioned a priori are of but little assistance, and are often as not misleading.'[34] In 1957, for example, the Judicial Committee stated the principle that the Crown intended that the rights of property of the inhabitants were to be fully respected, and, in the event of compulsory acquisition, they are to be entitled to compensation according to their interests even though the interests are of a kind unknown to English law.[35] That specific examination was however to be

---

[31] *Australian Consolidated Press v Uren* [1969] 1 AC 590, 641. For a valuable discussion of this and related decisions see WS Clarke, 'The Privy Council, Politics and Precedent in Asia Pacific Region' (1990) 39 ICLQ 741.

[32] *Viro v R* (1978) 141 CLR 88 and Sir Garfield Barwick (1977) 51 ALJ 480, 485. For comparable New Zealand developments see ch 19(a) in this volume.

[33] eg *Reid v Reid* [1982] 1 NZLR 147; *Invercargill CC v Hamlin* [1996] 1 NZLR 513; and *Lange v Atkinson* [2000] 3 NZLR 385.

[34] *Amodu Tijani v Secretary, Southern Rhodesia* [1921] 2 AC 399, 401–2, 404.

[35] *Oyekan v Adele* [1957] 1 WLR 876.

undertaken against the background of principles, based on established practice, which owed as much to the law of nations as it did the common law. Chief Justice John Marshall in 1823, for instance, had plainly distinguished between three things among others—the sovereignty of the colonising nations of Europe, the title which they might grant in exercise of their ultimate dominion, and the existing native rights to which that grant of title would be subject.[36]

Differences also arose in respect of the interpretation of legislation which was not of British origin and had a particular local character. This may be illustrated by the reaction of New Zealand judges to decisions given by the Privy Council early in the twentieth century. In the first decade of the century the Privy Council heard more appeals from New Zealand and allowed more of them than in any other decade until the 1990s.[37] In one case concerning Maori rights, the Privy Council's criticism not just of the Court of Appeal but also of the Solicitor General led to an extraordinary 'protest of bench and bar' at a special sitting, one Saturday morning, of the Court of Appeal.[38] The Chief Justice, Sir Robert Stout, saw the judgment as a direct attack on the probity of the Court of Appeal. Sir Joshua Strange Williams (later to be the first New Zealand judge to sit in the Privy Council), began his protest as follows:

For an inferior Court to criticize the judgment of a superior Court which reversed its decisions would be in general alike, unprofitable, and unseemly. But where the decision of the inferior Court has been not only reversed but has been reversed with contumely—where the inferior Court has been taunted with want of independence and subservience to the executive Government—it is right that the members of the Court who pronounced the decision in question should come forward and defend the honour of the Court they represent.

The stinging statements at the sitting manifested a strong view that the Law Lords were unaware of relevant provisions of New Zealand law and had made errors of law and fact. The special sitting was followed up by a protest from the Agent-General for New Zealand on the instructions of his Prime Minister:

the colony has been second to none in the respect entertained by it for the Privy Council, and in the value it has attached to maintaining the connection between its local judicial system and the great Imperial Tribunal. I can only express a sincere hope that the

---

[36] *Johnson v McIntosh* 5 US 503, 505 (1823), 521–2, a judgment well known in New Zealand in the early days of the colony; in 1901 the Privy Council cast doubt on the use of American authority in *Nireaha Tamaki v Baker* (1901) NZPCC 371, 384–5; compare *Attorney General v Ngati Apa* [2003] 3 NZLR 643 in which the judges of the Court of Appeal draw on US Supreme Court decisions and much else. JES Fawcett would probably see the above discussion as generous to the Judicial Committee. For him 'the impression left by the numerous decisions on acquisition of title to territory by the Crown . . . is one of a persistent ambiguity and a certain opportunism in the applications of international law and constitutional law': 'The Judicial Committee . . . and International Law' (1967) 42 BYIL 229, 252.

[37] Over the 150 years it exercised jurisdiction over New Zealand appeals, the Judicial Committee allowed about one third of the 320 appeals decided, a standard proportion.

[38] *Wallis v Solicitor General for New Zealand* [1903] AC 173; NZPCC 730.

unmerited words unfortunately used by Lord Macnaughten may not have the effect of weakening the feeling of reverence for the Privy Council which has always reflected itself in New Zealand's concept of a wise Imperial policy.[39]

The Chief Justice soon after contributed an article to the Law Quarterly Review asking what for him was a rhetorical question—'Is the Privy Council a Legislative body?'—in which he attacked a Privy Council interpretation of liquor legislation.[40] Campaigns for temperance and prohibition were waged very strongly through that period and again the sense was that their Lordships in London did not understand the context and particularly the purpose of giving popular control over the grant of liquor licences.

Federalism

The Judicial Committee faced differences within the Empire of another kind from the 1870s when cases about federalism began to appear. The first and principal source was the British North America Act 1867 and the issues it presented of the division of power within Canada between federal and provincial authorities. The judgments through to the 1930s underline the significance, apparently decisive, of the selection of the panel from the many available. Commentators have particularly stressed the roles of Lord Watson, who sat in all nine Canadian cases between 1894 and 1899 (the year he died) and gave the opinion five times, and Lord Haldane, who sat until 1928 and gave the opinion 19 times. They also refer to Lord Sankey, Lord Chancellor from 1929 to 1935, and Lord Atkin who sat with the same four colleagues[41] in six cases in 1937, in five of which federal legislation implementing the Canadian 'New Deal' was struck down. Atkin who was opposed to the Statute of Westminster gave five of those opinions.

Lord Watson, in the words of his great admirer, Lord Haldane, so covered with living flesh the bones of the Constitution of Canada that it took a new form; with his large political experience, he was able to be a statesman as well as a judge with

---

[39] Quoted in Swinfen (n 16) 166. Sir Frederick Pollock, editor of the Law Quarterly Review, tried to make a calming comment, recording 'an authoritative declaration that their Lordships had no intention of being personally offensive to the New Zealand Court' (1903) 19 LQR 249. Twenty-seven years later, JB Callan (later to become a judge) suggested that 'the very enormity of the offence the Judicial Committee committed... as a direct consequence of [its] failure, is our best assurance that it will not so fail again': 'The Appeal to the Privy Council' (1930) 6 NZLJ 94, 95.

[40] (1905) 21 LQR 9. At the end of the century comment might have been addressed to the Committee's interpretation of tax legislation with cases such as *Challenge Corporation v CIR* [1986] 2 NZLR 513 and *CIR v Auckland Harbour Board* [2003] 3 NZLR 289, para 11 (the statutory anti-avoidance provision being reduced to a 'long stop for the Revenue') being highlighted.

[41] One of the four was Sir Sidney Rowlatt, a retired tax judge who was said to have been persuaded to retire from the High Court in part by the offer of a Privy Councillorship, who sat in the Committee in his raincoat taking no notes, and who is thought to have provided the critical vote in some of the cases. See Lord Wright's tribute to Chief Justice Sir Lyman Duff (1955) 33 Can Bar Rev 1123 and MacKinnnon (1956) 34 Can Bar Rev 115, 117.

the task of immense importance and difficulty of silently developing and even altering the constitution of the country as it develops and alters.[42] In particular Watson, reversing the direction of early decisions of the Supreme Court of Canada, gave greater weight to 'provincial constitutional autonomy'. Haldane, on becoming Lord Chancellor, following the Watson line, treated the provinces as if they were, within their powers, 'sovereign states'. Lord Sankey had only a limited impact on that issue,[43] and is mainly remembered for decisions on other constitutional matters, notably for his rulings that the Canadian legislation abolishing criminal appeals to London was valid, and that women were 'persons' within the terms of the provisions of the 1867 Act regulating membership of the Canadian Senate. In the latter case he used a striking metaphor: the Act 'planted in Canada a living tree capable of growth and expansion within its natural limits'.[44] The object of the Act he declared to be 'to provide a constitution for Canada, a responsible and developing State'. The metaphor has been prominent over the past 25 years in cases in Canada on its Charter of Rights and Freedoms. Lord Atkin's 1937 decisions include an undisputed authoritative statement about the roles of the executive and the legislature in making and implementing treaties, and a metaphor, in sharp contrast to Sankey's, which recognises but gives no effect to the greatly different international role of Canada 60 years after the enactment of its constitution: 'While the ship of state now sails on larger ventures and into foreign waters she still retains the watertight compartments which are an essential part of her original structure.'[45]

A lasting consequence of the 1937 decisions is the 'great difficulty' they cause for implementing many treaties when their obligations call for changes in laws coming within the legislative competence of the provinces;[46] some have speculated about the outcome in those cases, had Lord Sankey been persuaded to sit, as was proposed.

More broadly, on the federal-provincial balance, Canada's leading constitutional lawyer of the present day, weighing as well the decisions of the Supreme Court of Canada over the six decades since the ending of Privy Council appeals, reaches three conclusions.[47] First, the Privy Council was biased in favour of the provinces in federal cases, going too far in restricting the powers of the central Parliament, but on the whole that served Canada well because a less centralised

---

[42] See the 1900 and 1923 articles, nn 8 and 10 above and (1899) 11 Juridical Review 281.

[43] But see the decisions of the Committee, with Sankey presiding, that air navigation and broadcasting were exclusively federal matters: *Re Regulation and Control of Aeronautics in Canada* [1932] AC 54 and *Re Regulation and Control of Radio Communications in Canada* [1932] AC 304.

[44] *Edwards v AG for Canada* [1930] AC 124.

[45] *AG for Canada v AG for Ontario* [1937] AC 326, 353.

[46] P Hogg, 'Canada: Privy Council to Supreme Court' in J Goldsworthy, *Interpreting Constitutions* (Oxford: OUP, 2006) 64.

[47] P Hogg and W Wright, 'Canadian Federalism, the Privy Council and the Supreme Court' (2005) 38 UBCL Rev 329, 352; see also P Hogg, *Constitutional and Law of Canada* (Toronto: Carswell, 5th edn 2007) ch 5.3(c), and ch 19(b) in this volume.

model is probably the right model for Canada. Second, the Supreme Court has expanded the scope of the federal heads of power, but not dramatically—a reasonable correction to the excesses of the Privy Council. And, third, in sum, 'Canada has not been badly served by either the Privy Council or Supreme Court.'

The early Privy Council cases on the Canadian constitution appear to have had another almost immediate and lasting, but this time liberating, effect, on the interpretation of the provisions of the Australian Constitution Act 1900. That measure was negotiated and drafted in Australia, approved by the colonial parliaments and endorsed by popular referendums. But the final necessary step was legislation at Westminster. The Government there had strong objections to a clause in the draft bill prohibiting appeals involving the interpretation of the federal or a state constitution, with however the qualification that the Privy Council would continue to have power to give special leave to appeal from the High Court in other cases but the Commonwealth Parliament would have the power to limit those cases. The draft said nothing about appeals direct from state supreme courts to the Privy Council. The Act as passed altered the provision relating to the interpretation of the Constitution—there were to be no appeals from the High Court to the Privy Council on the limits *inter se* of the constitutional powers of the Commonwealth and its states, or of the states *inter se*, unless the High Court certified that the question was one which ought to be decided by the Privy Council. Such leave was granted only once, in 1914 (when Lord Haldane took the opportunity to discuss the *Canadian* Constitution!).[48] There had earlier been a conflict between the High Court and the Privy Council, which, in a direct appeal from the Supreme Court of Victoria, had departed from a principle stated by the High Court. This litigation is notable for a number of things. Notwithstanding the decades of experience of limits on colonial legislative power and Canada's internal distribution of power, Lord Halsbury expressed difficulty in coming to grips with the notion of the legislative power of a state being limited by a federal structure: 'That is a novelty to me. I thought an Act of Parliament was an Act of Parliament and you cannot go beyond it. . . . I do not know what an unconstitutional Act means' and consistently with that position he refused to listen to the arguments based on American authorities. The High Court had an early opportunity to rule that that Privy Council decision was on an *inter se* issue and that it accordingly could ignore the decision. A second notable feature of the litigation is the explanation given in the second High Court decision for the compromise reached in London: there had been considerable dissatisfaction with the way the Privy Council had interpreted the Canadian Constitution and the framers of the Australian Constitution had greater familiarity with the constitutional work of the United States Supreme Court than had

---

[48] *AG for Australia v Colonial Sugar Refining Co* [1914] AC 237, 252–4.

the Law Lords—an opinion which Lord Halsbury's statement did nothing to dispel.[49]

The South Africa Act 1909 went even further than the Australian Constitution in the direction of restricting appeals: there was to be no appeal from the Supreme Court of South Africa but the King in Council continued to have the right to grant special leave to appeal. The intention, according to Lord Haldane speaking in 1921, was that the King's prerogative should be exercised in a very much restricted sense[50] and in fact leave was granted very rarely. But the grant of leave on the question of penalty and liquidated damages in contract, an extension of jurisdiction to matters of private law, and even more the decision in *Pearl Assurance Co Ltd v Union Government*[51] produced sharp criticism and a hardening of opinion against appeals. No 'great ground' of imperial or constitutional importance was involved. The Committee overruled the Appellate Division on a pure question of Roman-Dutch law in a judgment which was criticised as entirely incorrect:

To expound a system of law in which one was nurtured is anxious and exacting labour, a field of endeavour in which a life-time is all too short. It is no reflection on the members of the Judicial Committee, therefore, to say that neither in the past nor in the case under consideration have they been happy in the application of a system of law with which they were not even on a footing of nodding acquaintance. Not that they are to blame, but a ridiculous arrangement which charges them with an impossible task.[52]

Over the course of the last century or so, the Judicial Committee has faced a range of other constitutional issues in addition to many recent cases on bills of rights considered in the next section.[53] I mention a small selection. Some have concerned limits on the legislative power of colonial legislatures, especially in respect of legislation having 'extraterritorial effect'. An early controversial and poorly reasoned *obiter* statement on that matter which created difficulties for colonial legislature was perhaps overruled within 15 years, but it was only in 1931 that that limit was definitively removed by the Statute of Westminster.[54] Ninety years later, by contrast, any idea of the limits on the power of a Dominion legislature

---

[49] *Deakin v Webb* (1904) 1 CLR 585, *Webb v Outrim* [1907] AC 81, and *Baxter v Comr of Taxation* (1907) 4 CLR 1087, valuably discussed by Murray Gleeson, Chief Justice of Australia, in *The Influence of the Privy Council on Australia* (Anglo-Australian Lawyers Society, Sydney 31 May 2007); see also Pollock's pointed criticism, (1907) 23 LQR 119, 120.

[50] *Whittaker v Dunbar Corp* (1921) 90 LJPC 119, 120.   [51] [1934] AC 570.

[52] Aquilius, 'Immorality and Illegality in Contract' (1943) 60 SALJ 468, 476.

[53] Other constitutional cases include separation of powers matters, from Australia, Ceylon, and the Caribbean (eg recently in *Suratt v AG of Trinidad and Tobago* [2008] 1 AC 655, discussing Jamaican, Australian, and Sri Lankan cases), 'controlled' and 'uncontrolled' legislatures (eg *McCawley v R* [1920] AC 691 and *AG for New South Wales v Trethowan* [1932] AC 526), and emergencies and revolutions (*Re Marais* [1902] AC 51; *Tilonko v AG of Natal* [1907] AC 93; *Bhagat Singh v King Emperor* (1931) AIR PC 111; *King Emperor v Benoari Lal Sarma* [1945] AC 14; and *Madzimbamuto v Lardner-Burke* [1969] AC 645).

[54] *McLeod v AG of New South Wales* [1891] AC 455, criticised by Sir John Salmond in (1917) 33 LQR 117, and *AG for Canada v Cain* [1906] AC 542.

was completely forgotten by the Judicial Committee when they read New Zealand legislation enacted in 1928 as recognising all persons born in Western Samoa in the following 20 years as natural born British subjects in terms of New Zealand law.[55] That reading failed to have regard to the imperial and international context in which that legislation was enacted. It is perhaps significant that by 1981, the United Kingdom had been a member of the European Union for nearly a decade, almost all of the former Empire was independent, but the senior courts were not yet as inclined, as they are now, to read legislation in its international legal context.[56]

Notwithstanding the severe restrictions on Australian constitutional appeals, the Privy Council did hear a great number of appeals concerned with the 'free trade' guarantee incorporated in section 92 of the Constitution. That jurisprudence, along with many decisions of the High Court (140 in all), was essentially replaced in 1988 by a single unanimous judgment of the High Court aimed at removing 'a quite unacceptable state of affairs'; the court had been 'unable to give authoritative guidance or to express an authoritative view about the process of reasoning' needed.[57] One wise observer of the Australian scene stated in 1970 that 'in no case could it be said that the Board corrected palpable error in the High Court and it would have made remarkably little difference to the development of Australian law, public or private, if the appeal to London had been abolished in 1900'.[58]

Bills of Rights

From the 1960s, the Judicial Committee faced another new category of constitutional cases. They arose from bills of rights incorporated in the independence constitutions of new Commonwealth countries in Africa, South East Asia, and the Caribbean. The Bills owed their origin at least in part to the international human rights movement, especially as seen in the Universal Declaration of Human Rights 1948 and the European Convention on Human Rights and Fundamental Freedoms 1950 which had been extended to a number of the countries before they became independent. The legal tradition in which the Law Lords had been educated and practised was one which left the protection of human rights to the common law (or so it was said) and which was inclined, in

---

[55] *Lesa v AG* [1982] 1 NZLR 165.

[56] Compare for instance *R v Home Security, ex p Brind* [1991] AC 696 with *R v Immigration Officer at Prague Airport, ex p European Roma Rights Centre* [2005] 2 AC 1. For an earlier outstanding international law judgment, by Lord Sankey for the Committee, see *Re Piracy Iure Gentium* [1934] AC 572.

[57] *Cole v Whitfield* (1988) 165 CLR 360, para 7; see also para 20.

[58] G Sawer (1970) 2 Otago L Rev 138, 145. He had earlier observed that the Privy Council had never had a sufficient flow of Australian constitutional cases to develop a proper understanding of the Australian constitution but did have enough to do considerable damage.

Bentham's words, to condemn declarations of rights as 'nonsense on stilts'. An element of paradox may be seen in lawyers and politicians from that tradition being in part responsible for the preparation of many bills of rights and then having extensive experience as counsel and judges in their application and interpretation, valuable preparation, as it turned out, for the drafting, interpretation. and application of their own bill in the form of the Human Rights Act 1998.[59]

As the Law Lords and commentators alike have recognised, attitudes within the Judicial Committee to the understanding and interpretation of bills of rights are very different now from what they were in the earlier period. As early as 1964 Professor SA de Smith highlighted a basic choice for the judge arising from an introductory provision to some of the Bills setting out their general purport—the entitlement of every person to fundamental rights and freedoms—and used a phrase which Lord Wilberforce was to make famous in a Bermudan case in 1980 and which has often been repeated. Bills of rights, Lord Wilberforce declared, call for 'a generous interpretation avoiding what has been called "the austerity of tabulated legation" suitable to give the individuals the full measure of the fundamental rights and freedoms referred to'.[60]

Further, the interpretation of a constitutional instrument such as a bill of rights was to be according to suitable principles of interpretation, without necessarily accepting all the presumptions relevant to private law legislation. Australian and Canadian judges, addressing their constitutions had much earlier made the point that not all statutes were to be treated alike. By contrast, in 1887, the Judicial Committee, on appeal from Canada, had stated that it must treat the British North America Act of 1867 by the same methods of construction which it applied to other statutes.[61]

In earlier cases, a narrower legalistic approach may be seen. Given that many of the bills of rights cases arose from criminal prosecutions, that approach may be related to the reluctance at that time in respect of criminal matters (discussed in the next section of this paper). Three cases illustrate that approach. In a 1967 appeal from Southern Rhodesia the Board refused to consider whether the death penalty for the crime of complicity in arson of a residential building breached the prohibition in the Constitution of 'inhuman or degrading punishment'; the legislature, not the court, was to decide on the proportionate penalty.[62] In 2006, the Crown in an appeal from the Bahamas recognised that some might now call the decision 'barbaric' and offensive to a modern sense of justice. The Judicial Committee interpreted the relevant legislation as providing for a discretionary

---

[59] Lord Woolf, in one of the few references to the Judicial Committee in his recently published book of essays (C Campbell-Holt (ed)), *The Pursuit of Justice* (Oxford: OUP, 2008) 215–16, in explaining the 'smooth' implementation of the new Act, mentioned that the Privy Council experience of bills of rights was fortunate because it meant that the most senior judiciary were very familiar with the different techniques which a final court has to employ to give effect to human rights.

[60] SA de Smith, *The New Commonwealth and its Constitutions* (London: Stevens and Co, 1964) 194 and *Minister of Home Affairs v Fisher* [1980] AC 319, 328.

[61] *Lambe v North British Mercantile Fire & Life Insurance Co* (1887) 12 App Cas 575, 579.

[62] *Runyowa v R* [1967] 1 AC 26.

and not a mandatory death sentence, declaring that the Board in 1967 had effectively 'abdicated' its duty of constitutional adjudication.[63]

In 1975 a divided Privy Council held that the bar in the Jamaican Juveniles Law on the death sentence being pronounced on a person under 18 depended on the age at the date of sentencing and not at the date of offending, notwithstanding the prohibition in the Constitution on the imposition of 'a penalty which is severer in degree or description than the maximum penalty which might have been imposed for that offence at the time when it was committed'. That prohibition, said the Committee, was directed at invalidating laws passed after the offence was committed and the Juvenile Law was in force at that time.[64] Two judges of the New Zealand Supreme Court recently indicated why as a matter of principle they considered that that authority should not be followed, noting as well the change over the intervening 30 years in judicial attitudes to the protection of human rights.[65]

And in *Ong Ah Chuan v Public Prosecutor*, decided soon after Lord Wilberforce made his statement, but by a differently composed Committee, the Judicial Committee rejected a challenge, based on the guarantee of equality before the law, to Singapore's legislation which provided for a mandatory death sentence for conviction of trafficking in more than a specified weight of heroin; the argument was that the law offended against the principle of equality since it condemns to the highest penalty of death the addict who gratuitously supplied an addict friend with 15 kilograms from his store and a lesser penalty for a professional dealer caught selling for distribution to many addicts 14.99 kilograms. The Judicial Committee said that the principle of equality required that like be compared with like, by reference to similarity of circumstances, here in the offence: 'The questions whether this dissimilarity in circumstances justifies any differentiation in the punishment imposed upon individuals who fall within one class and those who fall within the other, and if so what are the appropriate punishments for each class, are questions of social policy.' Provided the dissimilarity in circumstances is not purely arbitrary and bears a reasonable relation to the social object of the law, there is no inconsistency with the Constitution, the Committee ruled. By 2004 the Judicial Committee declared that 'it is no longer possible to say', as it was at the time of *Ong Ah Chuan*, that there is nothing unusual in a mandatory death penalty. That penalty (as in the law of the United Kingdom until 1965) had predated any international arrangements for the protection of human rights. And the decision was made at a time when the international jurisprudence on human rights was rudimentary. The Judicial Committee then referred to 'the march of international jurisprudence' from the Universal Declaration of Human Rights, the regional human rights instruments, and the International Covenant on Civil and Political Rights.[66]

---

[63] *Bowe v R* 1 WLR 1623.   [64] *Baker v R* [1975] AC 774.
[65] *Mist v R* [2005] NZSC 77, paras 34–9.   [66] *Watson v R* [2004] UKPC 34, paras 29–30.

Bills of rights cases also raise other criminal law issues and matters such as freedom of expression and association, nationality, and property. Judgments on these matters demonstrate a growing familiarity with constitutional and human rights developments, with the related burgeoning sources with authorities from other Commonwealth countries, the United States, and Europe being drawn on, and different approaches to judging these matters being expressed and adopted. On the last matter references to a liberal and purposive interpretation and to the Wilberforce/de Smith *dictum* have become frequent, even routine, and the reality appears in significant measure to have matched the rhetoric.[67] As already mentioned, the legacy in this area is not simply across the Commonwealth but also in the United Kingdom itself.[68]

Criminal appeals

In 1932, in dismissing a petition for special leave to appeal against a conviction and sentence of death for a murder committed in India, Viscount Dunedin, for a committee which included two former Indian judges (Sir George Lowndes and Sir Dinshal Mulla), said that their Lordships had frequently repeated that they do not sit as a Court of Criminal Appeal. To interfere there must be something so irregular or so outrageous as to shake the very basis of justice. Such an instance had been found in *Re Dillet*,[69] 'the leading authority on those matters'. Alleged misinterpretation of the statutes and insufficiency of evidence did not qualify.[70] In *Dillet* their Lordships were 'of opinion that [the jury] directions were grievously unjust to the appellant and in many instances outraged the proprieties of judicial procedure. A conviction obtained by such unworthy means cannot be permitted to stand.'

In 1941 Lord Simon LC quoting from *Dillet* similarly declared that the Judicial Committee, broadly speaking, would interfere only when there had been an infringement of the essential principles of justice.[71] He instanced a refusal to hear the case of the accused, a trial in his absence, his not being allowed to call relevant witnesses, the tribunal being corrupt, not properly constituted, unable to understand the proceedings because of the language in which they were conducted, or not having jurisdiction.

---

[67] Note however that the varying composition of the Committees in recent death penalty appeals appears to be one reason for conflict between decisions: eg *Reckley v Minister of Public Safety and Immigration (No 2)* [1996] AC 527, *Lewis v AG of Jamaica* [2001] 2 AC 50, and *Boyce v R* and *Matthew v State* [2005] 1 AC 433 (discussed by Sir Fred Phillips in ch 20 in this volume; see also *Gibson v United States* [2007] UKPC 52 where by a majority of 4:3 the Committee overruled a decision given only three years earlier on a procedural issue already rectified by legislation.

[68] Of the very extensive writing, N Roberts, 'The Law Lords and Human Rights: The Experience of the Privy Council in Interpreting Bills of Rights' [2000] EHRLR 147, and J Gray, 'Evolving Constitutional Protection in the Caribbean Commonwealth and the Judicial Committee of the Privy Council' (2004) 4 OUCLJ 77 are valuable.

[69] (1887) 12 App Cas 459.   [70] *Mohinder Singh v King Emperor* (1932) 59 LR IA 233.

[71] *Muhammad Nawaz v R* (1941) 68 LR IA 126.

As recently as 1983 Lord Diplock speaking for the Judicial Committee, in a New Zealand appeal in which a jury direction was challenged, said that that issue fell within 'the category of questions to which (as the Board has had occasion to repeat at all too frequent intervals since the rule was stated . . . in *Ibrahim v The King*[72]) it is not the practice of the Board to substitute their own answer for the answer given by the local Commonwealth appellate Court—in the instant case a Court of Appeal composed of New Zealand judges familiar with the conduct of jury trials in New Zealand and the likely reaction of New Zealand juries'.[73]

The last decade demonstrates a major turnaround in practice. The Judicial Committee, although almost always hearing a second appeal, has increasingly demonstrated a willingness to act as a court of criminal appeal, often with bills of rights issues prominent. In many judgments (sometimes dissenting as well) its members now engage in a close assessment of the trial process and the evidence, examining, for instance, the failure by the prosecution to disclose possibly relevant evidence, the incompetence of trial counsel, the trial judges' decisions during the hearing, and their directions to the jury and apparent contradictions in the evidence.[74] The final test which they address is often put in terms of 'the safety of verdict'. Among the reasons for this major change may be the general availability over recent years of a right of appeal from criminal convictions, a right which did not exist when the Committee established its earlier firm practice, the increasing recognition by the legal profession and more widely of the rights of those charged with criminal offences, and the flow to the Judicial Committee of petitions for leave to appeal in criminal cases based on bills of rights. One consequence is that the Law Lords deal with many more criminal appeals in the Privy Council than they do in the House of Lords.

Conclusion

The impact of the Law Lords on the law of the countries and territories subject to the jurisdiction of the Judicial Committee may be assessed both in general and in particular terms. The particular impact appears clearly in Canadian constitutional

---

[72] [1914] AC 599.

[73] *R v McDonald* [1983] NZLR 252, 256. See the valuable account, as at 1966, by Sir Kenneth Roberts-Wray in his *Commonwealth and Colonial Law* (London: Stevens and Sons, 1966) 437–47. Even when leave was granted, appeals rarely succeeded: eg *Kurumar v R* [1958] AC 197, *Karamat v R* [1956] AC 256, *Aladesuru v R* [1956] AC 49.

[74] eg *Ramstead v R* [1999] 2 AC 92 (*Dillet* and *Ibrahim* cited in argument, not mentioned in judgment); *Arthurton v R* [2004] UKCPC 25; *Dial v State* [2005] UKPC4; *Teeluck v State* [2005] 1 WLR 2421; *Singh v State* [2006] 1 WLR 146; *Howse v R* [2005] UKPC 31; *Grant v State* [2007] 1 AC 1; *Bain v R* [2007] UKPC 33; *Dookran v State* [2007] UKPC 15, *Wizzard v Quin* [2007] UKPC 21, *Bernard v State* [2007] 2 Cr App R *Daniel v State* [2007] UKPC 39; *Charles v R* [2007] UKPC 47; *Persad v Trinidad and Tobago* [2007] 1 WLR 2379; and *Muirhead v R* [2008] UKPC 40 (see paras 30 and 39). For a notable New Zealand decision see *Taito v R* [2002] UKPC 15, leading to a number of rehearings and retrials and a legislative response.

law where, 60 years on, the federal-provincial division of power is little different from that struck by the Judicial Committee. In a negative sense that particular impact may be seen in Australia which, considering the Canadian experience to the end of the nineteenth century, avoided according any significant constitutional role in respect of the division of powers to the Committee.[75] By contrast, the Judicial Committee has undoubtedly made and continues to make a major contribution to the interpretation and understanding of bills of rights especially in the Caribbean. As noted, its attitude to that role, along with its role in criminal appeals, has changed markedly over the last 40 years and that experience has had a specific value for the United Kingdom itself as its judges and lawyers prepared for the introduction of its Human Rights Act. While it is sometimes difficult to disentangle the impact of the Law Lords sitting as Privy Councillors from their impact when sitting in the House of Lords in major areas—the law of negligence and many developments in equity and commercial law may be added to administrative law—this impact is manifestly from the House of Lords and not the Privy Council.

There remain the immensely important and immeasurable general influences of the Law Lords in the Judicial Committee, as one aspect of the inheritance throughout the Commonwealth of principles of constitutional government, including democracy, the rule of law, and the independence of the judiciary and of the profession.[76] It is something that must be nurtured and adapted within each society and culture. That nurturing and adapting takes many forms, one of which historically has appeared in the hearing room in Downing Street. One more specific influence arises from the marked changes in attitudes to the law-making role of the senior British judges over the last 40 or so years. The appeal provided a formal link to those matters, but the link is now much stronger and increasingly operational in many less formal ways, through the ready availability of law reports and other legal publications, the world wide web, meetings, conferences, and many personal contacts among lawyers and judges.[77]

And the future? Unrealised predictions, since at least the early 1920s, of the early ending of the Committee's role suggest caution. So too do some remarkable figures. Early in the twentieth century the Committee had jurisdiction over appeals from one quarter of the world population. A century on, the proportion is nearing one thousandth. The Committee nevertheless sits on about as many days—around 100 in recent years—as it did at that time and decides a

---

[75] In 2007 Hon Murray Gleeson, Chief Justice of Australia, declared that it is difficult to think of any Privy Council decisions about the Constitution that are now cited in argument to the High Court, n 49 above.

[76] See also the Declarations by Commonwealth Heads of Government beginning in Singapore in 1971, and declarations by Law Ministers and Chief Justices.

[77] On human rights matters see for instance the colloquia organised by the Commonwealth Secretariat, Interights and Lord Lester who gives an account in 'The Challenge of Bangalore: Making Human Rights a Practical Reality' [1999] EHRLR 273.

comparable number of cases (70–80).[78] That could not have been predicted. Nor could the major changes in the business, with many criminal law and bills of rights cases being decided. Other unpredictable elements are the potential role of the Caribbean Court of Justice and the attitudes of the members of the new Supreme Court towards this continuing, additional role.

---

[78] See the statistics included in R Stevens, *Law and Politics* (n 14) 72–3, a book which has been invaluable to me in preparing this chapter, as has been L Blom-Cooper and G Drewry, *Final Appeal: A Study of the House of Lords in its Judicial Capacity* (Oxford: Clarendon Press, 1972).

19

The Old Commonwealth

(a) Australia and New Zealand

Michael Kirby*

Two nations overwhelmingly populated by sheep

For a judicial body that is thousands of miles away, in a part of the world where the economic, social, cultural, and political circumstances are quite distinct from those prevailing in the southern hemisphere, the influence of the House of Lords on Australian and New Zealand courts has been extraordinary. Especially so because, from colonial times, the House has never been part of the formal judicial hierarchy. This chapter will focus on the influence of the House of Lords since the establishment of the Commonwealth of Australia in 1901 and the grant of Dominion status to New Zealand in 1907.

For a large part of the twentieth century a self-imposed tradition of largely unquestioning adherence to House of Lords decisions existed in both Australia and New Zealand. This practice was so strong that, in Australia, the Lords 'had sometimes been mistaken for a part of the Australian doctrine of precedent'.[1] Similarly, in New Zealand, English decisions were followed 'almost as a matter of course'.[2] Lionel Murphy, one time Australian Attorney General and High Court Justice, regarded the deference paid to English precedents as an attitude 'eminently suitable for a nation overwhelmingly populated by sheep'[3]—a comment specially apt for the two Southern outposts of the British Empire. Overall, this obedience was not altogether surprising. And, most of the time, it was substantially beneficial.

---

* Justice of the High Court of Australia. The author acknowledges the assistance of Ms Anna Gordon, Research Officer in the Library of the High Court of Australia, and members of the Faculty of Law, University of Otago in the preparation of this chapter.
[1] AR Blackshield, 'The High Court: Change and Decay' (1980) 5 Leg Serv Bull 107, 107.
[2] BJ Cameron, 'Law Reform in New Zealand' (1956) 32 NZLJ 72, 74.
[3] LK Murphy, 'The Responsibility of Judges', Opening Address for the First National Conference of Labor Lawyers, 29 June 1979, in G Evans (ed), *Law, Politics and the Labor Movement* (Melbourne: Legal Service Bulletin, 1980) 5.

The source of influence of the House of Lords

When Australia and New Zealand were colonised by Britain the colonists inherited so much of English case law and statute law as was applicable to 'their own situation and the condition of the infant colony'.[4] English law did not simply provide a foundation for Australian and New Zealand law, as 'the initial reception flowed without much distinction into the assumptions of precedent'.[5] In large part, English law was viewed as part of the precious birthright of the settlers.

The generally binding character of House of Lords decisions was affirmed by the Privy Council, which had undoubted jurisdiction as the final court for the antipodean colonies. In *Robins v National Trust Company*, Viscount Dunedin stated that the House of Lords 'is the supreme tribunal to settle English law, and that being settled, the Colonial Court, which is bound by English law, is bound to follow it'.[6]

A primary reason for treating House of Lords decisions as effectively binding was a recognition of the fact that the membership of the Privy Council substantially overlapped with participation in the judicial work of the House of Lords. This made it sensible and prudent for judges in Australia and New Zealand to write their judicial reasons with 'one eye to the prevailing English case law on the subject'.[7] So long as the right of appeal to the Privy Council remained, the policy of following House of Lords decisions was considered 'a practical necessity'.[8]

In the nineteenth century and throughout much of the twentieth century great weight was also placed on maintaining uniformity within the English common law or '*the* Common Law' as it was usually described. Indeed, as late as 1948, Sir Owen Dixon, later Chief Justice of Australia, considered that '[d]iversity in the development of the common law...seems to me to be an evil'.[9]

---

[4] There was statutory recognition of this principle in s 24 of the Australian Courts Act 1828 (Imp) (9 Geo IV c 83). In New Zealand, this principle was reflected in the English Laws Act 1858 (Imp), which likewise adopted the laws of England.

[5] PE von Nessen, 'The Use of American Precedents by the High Court of Australia, 1901–1987' (1992) 14 Adelaide L Rev 181, 182.

[6] [1927] AC 515, 519 (PC).

[7] WMC Gummow, 'The High Court of Australia and the House of Lords 1903–2003' in G Doeker Mach and KA Ziegert (eds), *Law, Legal Culture and Politics in the Twenty First Century* (Stuttgart: Franz Steiner Verlag, 2004) 44.

[8] P Brett, 'High Court—Conflict with Decisions of Court of Appeal' (1955) 29 ALJ 121, 122; see also Cameron (n 2) 74; *AG for Hong Kong v Reid* [1992] 2 NZLR 385, 392; *Kapi v MOT* (1991) 8 CRNZ 49, 55; A Mason, 'Future Directions in Australian Law' (1987) 13 Monash L Rev 149, 150.

[9] *Wright v Wright* (1948) 77 CLR 191, 210.

Australia

A wise general rule of practice

The binding effect of the decisions of the House of Lords upon Australian courts was emphatically stated in 1943 in *Piro v W Foster & Co Ltd*.[10] The High Court of Australia upheld the decision of a trial judge in South Australia to follow more recent House of Lords decisions regarding the general principles applicable to an action for damages,[11] instead of an earlier, contrary decision of the High Court.[12] Whilst acknowledging that House of Lords decisions were not 'technically' binding, Chief Justice Latham declared that:[13]

> ... it should now be formally decided that it will be a wise general rule of practice that in cases of clear conflict between a decision of the House of Lords and of the High Court, this court, and other courts in Australia, should follow a decision of the House of Lords upon matters of general legal principle.

Justice Williams was the strongest supporter of the authority of the House of Lords decisions, stating that '[i]t is the invariable practice for the Australian courts, including this court, to follow a decision of the House of Lords as of course, without attempting to examine its correctness, although the decision is not technically binding upon them ...'[14]

Professor Zelman Cowen, who was later to become Governor-General of Australia, commented that this decision 'formally [wrote] the House of Lords into the hierarchy of tribunals whose decisions bind Australian Courts'.[15]

The declaration of judicial independence

In 1963 the decision of the High Court of Australia in *Parker v R*[16] heralded a change of attitude towards English precedent in Australian courts. The High Court declined to follow the decision of the House of Lords in *DPP v Smith*,[17] which had established an objective test of intent for murder. On the issue of precedential respect, with the rest of the court concurring, Chief Justice Dixon stated:[18]

> Hitherto I have thought that we ought to follow decisions of the House of Lords, at the expense of our own opinions and cases decided here, but having carefully studied *Director*

---

[10] (1943) 68 CLR 313.

[11] *Caswell v Powell Duffryn Associated Collieries Ltd* [1940] AC 152 and *Lewis v Denye* [1940] AC 921.

[12] *Bourke v Butterfield and Lewis* (1926) 38 CLR 354.

[13] (1943) 68 CLR 313, 320. See also 325–6 (Rich J), 326–7 (Starke J), 336 (McTiernan J), and 341 (Williams J).

[14] ibid, 341.

[15] Z Cowen, 'The Binding Effect of English Decisions Upon Australian Courts' (1944) 60 LQR 378, 381.

[16] (1963) 111 CLR 610.   [17] [1961] AC 290.   [18] (1963) 111 CLR 610, 632–3.

of Public Prosecutions v Smith [1961] AC 290 I think that we cannot adhere to that view or policy. There are propositions laid down in the judgment which I believe to be misconceived and wrong. They are fundamental and they are propositions which I could never bring myself to accept... I wish there to be no misunderstanding on the subject. I shall not depart from the law on the matter as we have long since laid it down in this Court and I think that *Smith's Case* [1961] AC 290 should not be used in Australia as authority at all.

In time, the Privy Council would also follow the approach of the High Court, returning to more orthodox doctrine from which the Australian court would not be budged.[19]

Confirmation of the new approach

The general approach taken in *Parker v R* was confirmed in *Skelton v Collins*.[20] Again the High Court declined to follow the majority reasoning in a then recent House of Lords decision.[21] Instead, it applied an earlier House of Lords decision[22] concerning the assessment of compensation for the estate of an injured person who had later died. Justice Kitto stated:[23]

The Court is not, in a strict sense, bound by such decisions, but it has always recognised and must necessarily recognise their peculiarly high persuasive value. Moreover the reasoning of any judgment delivered in their Lordships' House, whether dissenting or concurring, commands and must always command our most respectful attention.

It was also decided that, where there is a clear conflict between a decision of the House of Lords and the High Court upon a matter of legal principle, other Australian courts ought to follow the High Court.[24] Justice Windeyer suggested that the High Court should be cautious in its treatment of authorities of the House of Lords which made 'reference only to English decisions... and seemingly to meet only economic and social conditions prevailing in England'.[25]

Following this decision, it was noted in Australia that '[a] new relationship of equality and mutual respect has emerged to replace the "colonial" attitude, clearly evident on both sides not so very long ago'.[26] Nevertheless, where there were no conflicting Privy Council or High Court decisions, decisions of the House of Lords continued to be treated as 'binding' by some Australian courts until as recently as the 1980s.[27]

---

[19] *Frankland v R* [1987] AC 576, 594.   [20] (1966) 115 CLR 94.
[21] *H West and Son Ltd v Shephard* [1964] AC 326.
[22] *Benham v Gambling* [1941] AC 157.   [23] (1966) 115 CLR 94, 104.
[24] ibid, 138–9 (Owen J (Windeyer J (at 133) and Taylor J (at 122) expressly concurred with these views)).
[25] ibid, 135.
[26] E St John, 'Lords Break from Precedent: An Australian View' (1967) 16 ICLQ 808, 816.
[27] See eg *Kelly v Sweeney* [1975] 2 NSWLR 720, 725 (Hutley JA); 738 (Mahoney JA). Cf Samuels JA; *Brisbane v Cross* [1978] VR 49; *Bagshaw v Taylor* (1978) 18 SASR 564, 578 (Bray CJ); *R v Darrington and McGauley* [1980] VR 353; *Life Savers (Australasia) Ltd v Frigmobile Pty Ltd*

Confirmation by the Privy Council

As an indication of the growing pragmatism affecting the relationship of courts in England and Australia, the Privy Council acknowledged, in *Australian Consolidated Press Ltd v Uren*,[28] the entitlement of the High Court to adhere to its own earlier decisions where they conflicted with an earlier House of Lords precedent.[29] The case concerned the question of when exemplary damages should be awarded in a successful action for defamation. Lord Morris of Borth-y-Gest, in delivering the advice of the Privy Council, stated in plain terms that '[t]heir Lordships are not prepared to say that the High Court were wrong in being unconvinced that a changed approach in Australia was desirable'.[30] These words 'sounded the death knell of mandatory uniformity of the common law'.[31]

Persuasiveness of the reasoning

Appeals to the Privy Council from Australian courts were finally abolished in 1986.[32] The leading case on the status of English decisions in Australian courts following the removal of the Privy Council from the Australian judicial hierarchy is *Cook v Cook*.[33] The High Court, while acknowledging that Australian courts would 'continue to obtain assistance and guidance from the learning and reasoning of United Kingdom courts', stated: 'Subject, perhaps, to the special position of decisions of the House of Lords given in the period in which appeals lay from this country to the Privy Council, the precedents of other legal systems are not binding and are useful only to the degree of the persuasiveness of their reasoning.'[34]

An emerging Australian common law

The statements made in the High Court in *Parker v R* and *Skelton v Collins*, and the abolition of appeals to the Privy Council, contributed significantly to the recognition in Australia of the existence of a distinctive 'Australian' common

---

[1983] 1 NSWLR 431, 433–4 (Hutley JA, with whom Glass JA agreed at 438); *Horne v Chester and Fein Property Developments* [1987] VR 913. Cf *X v Amalgamated Television Services (No 2)* (1987) 9 NSWLR 575, 584 (Kirby P).

[28] [1969] 1 AC 590. Later confirmed in *Geelong Harbour Trust Comrs v Gibbs Bright & Co* (1974) 129 CLR 576.

[29] *Rookes v Barnard* [1964] AC 1129.   [30] [1969] 1 AC 590, 644.

[31] WS Clarke, 'The Privy Council, Politics and Precedent in the Asia Pacific Region' (1990) 39 ICLQ 741, 743.

[32] Appeals to the Privy Council were abolished in stages: first in federal matters (Privy Council (Limitation of Appeals) Act 1968 (Cth)), secondly, appeals from the High Court (Privy Council (Appeals from the High Court) Act 1975 (Cth)), and finally, appeals from State Supreme Courts (Australia Act 1986 (Cth) and (UK)). In *Viro v R* (1978) 141 CLR 88 the High Court held that it was no longer bound to follow decisions of the Privy Council, with minor possible exceptions.

[33] (1986) 162 CLR 376.   [34] ibid, 390.

law.[35] Since these decisions, the High Court has deviated from the line taken by the House of Lords on a growing number of issues, for example in relation to damages for gratuitous services,[36] the availability of exemplary damages,[37] immunity for barristers' negligence,[38] the law of resulting trusts,[39] apprehended bias,[40] nervous shock,[41] the liability of local authorities,[42] and many other topics.

Consideration of House of Lords decisions in recent years

Today, at least in the High Court of Australia, it is never assumed that the judges will defer to House of Lords authority. Nevertheless, as Chief Justice Gleeson recently observed, '[t]he influence of English decisions, although no longer formal, remains strong.'[43] Just as in recent times the House of Lords has increased its use of authority from Commonwealth courts, the antipodean courts have repaid the compliment. There has actually been an increase in the citation of House of Lords decisions by the High Court in recent years.[44] The High Court sometimes applies House of Lords decisions where the House of Lords has considered a

---

[35] See eg J Toohey, 'Towards an Australian Common Law' (1990) 6 Aus Bar Rev 185; Mason (n 8); A Mason, 'The Common Law in Final Courts of Appeal Outside Britain' (2004) 78 ALJ 183; L Zines, 'The Common Law in Australia: Its Nature and Constitutional Significance' (2004) 32 Federal L Rev 337; J Chen, 'Use of Comparative Law by Australian Courts' in AE-S Tay and C Leung (eds), *Australian Law and Legal Thinking in the 1990s. A collection of 32 Australian reports to the XIVth International Congress of Comparative Law presented in Athens on 31 July–6 August 1994* (Sydney: Faculty of Law, University of Sydney, 1994) 64–5.

[36] *Hunt v Severs* [1994] 2 AC 350. Cf *Kars v Kars* (1996) 187 CLR 354.

[37] *Rookes v Barnard* [1964] AC 1129; *Broome v Cassell & Co Ltd* [1972] AC 1027. Cf *Uren v John Fairfax & Sons Pty Ltd* (1966) 117 CLR 118. Gummow J notes that 'in England, there are indications that the law may be turning, with the time being ripe for a reconsideration of *Rookes*' (Gummow (n 7) 52). See *Kuddus v Chief Constable of Leicestershire Constabulary* [2002] 2 AC 122.

[38] *Arthur JS Hall v Simons* [2002] 1 AC 615. Cf *D'Orta-Elenaike v Victoria Legal Aid* (2005) 223 CLR 1.

[39] *Tinsley v Milligan* [1994] 1 AC 340. Cf *Nelson v Nelson* (1995) 184 CLR 538.

[40] *Dimes v Proprietors of the Grand Junction Canal* (1852) 3 HLC 759, 10 ER 301; *R v Bow Street Magistrates, ex p Pinochet Ugarte (No 2)* [2000] 1 AC 119. Cf *Ebner v Official Trustee in Bankruptcy* (2000) 205 CLR 337.

[41] *Alcock v Chief Constable of South Yorkshire Police* [1992] 1 AC 310; *White v Chief Constable of South Yorkshire Police* [1999] 2 AC 455. Cf *Annetts v Australian Stations Pty Ltd* (2002) 211 CLR 317; *Gifford v Strang Patrick Stevedoring Pty Ltd* (2003) 214 CLR 269. See *W v Essex CC* [2001] 2 AC 592, where Lord Slynn considered that parents suffering from shock on learning of the sexual abuse of their children four weeks after the events might still come within a flexible concept of the immediate aftermath.

[42] *Anns v Merton LBC* [1978] AC 728. Cf *Sutherland Shire Council v Heyman* (1985) 157 CLR 424; *Jaensch v Coffey* (1984) 155 CLR 549. In *Murphy v Brentwood DC* [1991] 1 AC 398 however, the House of Lords overruled *Anns* and followed the High Court decision in *Sutherland*.

[43] AM Gleeson, 'The Influence of the Privy Council on Australia' (2007) 29 Aus Bar Rev 123, 133.

[44] See eg *Burge v Swarbrick* (2007) 232 CLR 336, in which case the High Court applied *George Hensher Ltd v Restawile Upholstery (Lancs) Ltd* [1976] AC 64; *A v State of New South Wales* (2007) 230 CLR 500, in which case the High Court followed *Glinski v McIver* [1962] AC 726; *Palmer Bruyn & Parker Pty Ltd v Parsons* (2001) 208 CLR 388, in which case the High Court approved *Smith New Court Securities Ltd v Scrimgeour Vickers (Asset Management) Ltd* [1997] AC 254; *Spies v R* (2000) 201 CLR 603, in which case the High Court approved *R v Scott* [1975] AC 819.

particular issue first, such as the cases concerning rape in marriage[45] and the statutory abrogation of legal professional privilege.[46] Justice William Gummow has reckoned that the extent of the interchange in decision-making by the High Court and House of Lords is possibly greater than before,[47] although this interchange 'does not necessarily yield to concurrence of outcome'.[48] The link is now one of rational persuasion in a context of substantially shared basic legal doctrine. It is no longer a relationship of obedience or subservience.

Australian influence on the House of Lords

It has been suggested that the decisions in *Parker v R* and *Skelton v Collins* contributed to the House of Lords decision in 1966[49] to abolish the rule that their own prior decisions on points of law were absolutely binding, so that their effect could only be altered by Parliament.[50] An experienced Australian advocate proposed that part of the reason for that change was 'undoubtedly the attempt to preserve the Australian link in particular and the uniformity of the common law in general' as the House of Lords would be able to 'make due allowance for the opinions of other common law judges, in Australia and elsewhere'.[51]

For most of the twentieth century, during the era of imperial authority, the House of Lords only very rarely drew upon decisions of Australian courts. In recent times, however, the House of Lords has often referred to High Court decisions on a broad range of issues. For example, in the *Deep Vein Thrombosis and Air Travel Group Litigation*, Lord Scott of Foscote said that the 'most important DVT authority is the recent decision of the High Court of Australia in *Povey v Qantas Airways Ltd* [2005] HCA 33'.[52] In *Gilles v Secretary of State for Work and Pensions*, a case concerning ostensible bias in a disability appeal tribunal, the House of Lords accepted my own reasoning in *Johnson v Johnson*[53] regarding the meaning of the fiction by which such questions are judged—the reasonable and well-informed observer.[54] In *R v Soneji (Kamlesh Kumar)*, Lord Steyn commented that the joint reasons by the High Court of Australia regarding the determination of the validity of an act done in breach of a statutory provision 'contains an improved analytical framework for examining such questions. In the evolution of this corner of the law in the common law

---

[45] *R v R* [1992] 1 AC 612; *R v L* (1993) 174 CLR 379. See Gummow (n 7) 54.

[46] *R (Morgan Grenfell & Co Ltd) v Special Comr of Income Tax* [2003] 1 AC 563; *Daniels Corp International Pty Ltd v Australian Competition and Consumer Commission* (2002) 213 CLR 543 at 582 [108], 593–4 [135]. The majority of the High Court limited the scope of the privilege in *Grant v Downs* (1976) 135 CLR 674. The House of Lords preferred the dissenting reasons of Barwick CJ in *Waugh v British Rlys Board* [1980] AC 521. The High Court subsequently qualified *Grant v Downs* in *Esso Australia Resources Ltd v Federal Comr of Taxation* (1999) 201 CLR 49.

[47] Gummow (n 7) 54.   [48] ibid.

[49] *Practice Statement (Judicial Precedent)* [1966] 1 WLR 1234.

[50] See St John (n 26) 810.   [51] ibid, 815.

[52] [2006] 1 AC 495, 505. See now *Povey v Qantas Airways Ltd* (2005) 223 CLR 189.

[53] (2000) 201 CLR 488.   [54] [2006] 1 WLR 781, 784, 787, 793.

world the decision in *Project Blue Sky*[55] is most valuable.'[56] There are many other instances.

House of Lords' influence on Australian law

It would exceed the ambit of this chapter to describe in detail the influence of House of Lords decisions on Australian law over the past two centuries. Virtually every area of the law has been affected by the reasoning in House of Lords cases. The fifth reported decision of the High Court of Australia in 1904 was *Chanter v Blackwood*,[57] an electoral case that involved the application of the principle stated by the Lords in *Julius v The Bishop of Oxford*.[58] Using such cases in their reasoning became second nature to all Australian judges and lawyers. The Appeal Cases and other reported series carried their Lordships' decisions to the other side of the world. The Australian Law Journal, the national legal journal of record, noted the main decisions and changes in the course of authority.[59] Members of the House of Lords were typically the principal guests at the recurrent Australian legal conventions. Sometimes such visiting English judges planted ideas that were to have a large impact on judicial administration (permanent intermediate appellate courts are an instance).[60]

Legal nationalism was a relatively quiescent force in the Australian judiciary and legal profession, even after the end of the Privy Council appeals which had reinforced the logic of using House of Lords authority. In part, this was the product of legal habits, legal education, and professional conservatism. In part, it was the result of having the authorised English reports on the shelves of judges and advocates—a large investment reinforced by daily usage. But mostly, it was a recognition of the practical utility and high intellectual distinction and persuasiveness of House of Lords reasoning. Every now and then, even today, judges in lower courts who have followed House of Lords authority unquestioningly, as if it were binding on them, need to be reminded of the new remit.[61]

However, for the most part, the borrowing from House of Lords authority has been advantageous for Australian law. It rescued Australian judges and lawyers in a huge but sparsely populated country from narrow legal parochialism. From

---

[55] *Project Blue Sky Inc v Australian Broadcasting Authority* (1998) 194 CLR 355, 390 [93] (McHugh, Gummow, Kirby, and Hayne JJ).

[56] *R v Soneji (Kamlesh Kumar)* [2006] 1 AC 340, 353.   [57] (1904) 1 CLR 39, 52, 66.

[58] (1880) 5 App Cas 214.

[59] MD Kirby, '*Australian Law Journal* at 80: Past, Present and Future' (2007) 81 ALJ 529, 534.

[60] R Evershed, 'The History of the Court of Appeal' (1950) 24 ALJ 346 stimulated the creation of the New South Wales Court of Appeal, later copied in most other courts. Apart from the decisions of the House of Lords, those of the English Court of Appeal were also normally followed in Australia in the absence of reliant High Court Authority: *Public Transport Commission v Murray-More* (1974) 132 CLR 336.

[61] See eg *Channel Seven Adelaide Pty Ltd v Manock* (2007) 82 ALJR 303, [138]–[141], a reference to the use of *Kemsley v Foot* [1952] AC 345. See also *Koompahtoo Local Aboriginal Land Council v Sanpine Pty Ltd* (2007) 82 ALJR 345, [104].

colonial times, it linked Australian law to one of the great legal systems of the world in the heyday of its imperial and economic influence.[62] If in recent decades it was noticed that there was a need to consider the imports more closely for their suitability for a somewhat different society, with different problems and values, this was merely another element in the evolution of the relationship of Britain and Australia—from one of dutiful obligation to one of friendship, shared interests, and mutual regard.

New Zealand

New Zealand courts were possibly even more obedient and unquestioning than Australian courts in their treatment of English precedent generally.[63] Prior to the establishment of a separate and permanent Court of Appeal in New Zealand, the primary policy concern of the New Zealand courts appeared to be to avoid any departures from the common law in England.[64] The New Zealand Court of Appeal was established in 1958. The influence of English precedent was particularly powerful in its early years.[65] Given the size and composition of the population, the resources of the legal profession and the continuation of Privy Council appeals, this was scarcely surprising.

Changing attitudes to English authority

The first murmurings of change in New Zealand occurred in *Corbett v Social Security Commission*,[66] when the New Zealand Court of Appeal followed a Privy Council decision[67] which conflicted with a House of Lords decision.[68] Later, in *Ross v McCarthy*[69] the New Zealand Court of Appeal expressly acknowledged that it was not bound to follow the House of Lords. The Court stated that decisions of the House of Lords were entitled 'to be treated with the very greatest of respect and only departed from on rare occasions where for some good reason or another the law in New Zealand has developed on other lines'.[70] Nonetheless, in *McCarthy*, the court applied the relevant House of Lords authority.

---

[62] FC Hutley, 'The Legal Traditions of Australia as Contrasted with those of the United States' (1981) 55 ALJ 63, 69.

[63] Decisions of coordinate courts in England were considered binding. See eg *Barker v Barker* [1924] NZLR 1078 where the court rejected a line of earlier New Zealand cases in order to follow a decision of an English divisional court, *Jackson v Jackson* [1924] P 19, despite the fact that at least two of the New Zealand judges considered the English decision unsatisfactory.

[64] BJ Cameron, 'Legal Change Over Fifty Years' (1987) 3 Canta L Rev 198, 209.

[65] ibid, 296.   [66] [1962] NZLR 878.

[67] *Robinson v State of South Australia (No 2)* [1931] AC 704.

[68] *Duncan v Cammell Laird and Co Ltd* [1942] AC 624.   [69] [1970] NZLR 449.

[70] ibid, 453–4 (North P, Turner J, and McCarthy J concurring).

The real break came in *Bognuda v Upton & Shearer Ltd*.[71] The Court of Appeal was faced there with established House of Lords authority that was at variance with perceptions of the requirements of modern New Zealand law and society. In the result, the New Zealand Court of Appeal declined to follow the House of Lords decision in *Dalton v Angus*.[72] Justice North, President, and Justice Woodhouse declared that, while House of Lords decisions were entitled to great respect, New Zealand courts were not bound by them as a matter of the law of precedent. The Court of Appeal clearly indicated a willingness to diverge from the House of Lords line of thinking where it was considered inappropriate to New Zealand's law and society. At the time, this decision was described as having 'created a landmark in the development of New Zealand legal identity'.[73]

After the decision of *Bognuda v Upton* the Court of Appeal demonstrated a 'much less inhibited approach to precedent and a greater readiness to use judicial reasoning to determine and develop the law'.[74] By 1982, it was observed that '[m]uch water has ... passed under the bridge and it cannot now be said that this Court is bound by the House of Lords.'[75] Unremarkable as a matter of legal logic—given that the institutional link of New Zealand courts was only to the Privy Council and not to their Lordships' House—the assertion of independence was still seen at the time as a striking and novel idea.

In 1996, the Privy Council recognised that the New Zealand Court of Appeal was entitled to depart consciously from English decisions on the basis that social conditions and the values of society in New Zealand were different from those of England.[76] The right to appeal to the Queen in Council was only abolished in New Zealand in 2003 with the establishment of the New Zealand Supreme Court as the nation's final appellate body.[77] The move was controversial in some circles in New Zealand, usually on the expressed basis of the small size of the population. However, once again, the evolution of independent institutions was a natural development, at once inevitable and appropriate.

An emerging New Zealand common law

As in Australia, a separate New Zealand common law began to emerge in the 1980s. By 1987, Sir Robin Cooke, then President of the New Zealand Court of Appeal and later himself a judicial member of the House of Lords, declared that 'New Zealand Law ... has now evolved into a truly distinctive body of principles

---

[71] [1972] NZLR 741; cf *Ross v McCarthy* [1970] NZLR 449.   [72] [1991] 6 AC 740.

[73] P Spiller, *New Zealand Court of Appeal 1958–1996: A History* (Wellington: Brookers Ltd, 2002) 391; J Smillie, 'Formalism, Fairness and Efficiency: Civil Adjudication in New Zealand' [1996] NZ L Rev 254.

[74] Cameron (n 64) 211.

[75] *North Island Wholesale Groceries Ltd v Hewin* [1982] 2 NZLR 176, 195 (Somers J).

[76] See *Invercargill CC v Hamlin* [1996] 1 NZLR 513 (PC). See also *Lange v Atkinson* [2000] 3 NZLR 385.

[77] Supreme Court Act 2003 (NZ).

and practices, reflecting a truly distinctive outlook'.[78] Thus, in *Lange v Atkinson*[79] the New Zealand Court of Appeal 'found the constitutional air of New Zealand too pure to be contaminated by uncertain English common law restrictions on political expression imposed by defamation law'.[80] The New Zealand Court of Appeal also deviated from the approach of the House of Lords in respect of recovery of economic loss,[81] intoxication as a defence to a criminal charge,[82] and recognition of invasion of privacy within tort law.[83] The House of Lords now considers decisions of New Zealand courts[84] as indeed the reasoning of other foreign courts when, as often happens, they touch upon common problems. The links of language and basic legal doctrine are a great legacy of our history. The transnational conversation between courts of high authority on issues of mutual interest is likely to expand still further with the creation of the Supreme Court of the United Kingdom.

Reasons for divergence and the future influence of the House of Lords

The reasons why divergences in legal principle occur from time to time vary. Divergences in the common law are often attributed to the differences in social conditions in various jurisdictions. However, as Justice Gummow suggests: '[A] greater part will be played by the strength of the submissions by the respective counsel, the degree of judicial research in judgment writing, and, in the end, by differing views of strong-minded and experienced judges upon issues of fundamental principle.'[85]

The growing influence of European law on the content of the law of the United Kingdom may limit the use of some English cases as precedents for the development of legal principles in Australia and New Zealand, at least in particular areas of the law. The fact that Australia does not have a constitutionally entrenched or statute-based national bill of rights is also significant.[86] Furthermore, the influence

---

[78] Sir R Cooke, 'The New Zealand National Legal Identity' (1987) 3 Canta L Rev 171, 182.

[79] [2000] 3 NZLR 385. See more recently *AG v Ngati Apa* [2003] 3 NZLR 643 and *Hosking v Runting* [2005] 1 NZLR 1.

[80] A Lester, 'The Magnetism of the Human Rights Act 1998' (2002) 33 Victoria University of Wellington L Rev 477, 477.

[81] *Invercargill CC v Hamlin* [1996] 1 NZLR 513. Upheld by the Privy Council in *Invercargill CC v Hamlin* [1996] 1 NZLR 513.

[82] *R v Kamipeli* [1975] 2 NZLR 610.

[83] See *Hosking v Runting* [2005] 1 NZLR 1.

[84] See eg *R (on the application of Hurst) v Comr of Police of the Metropolis* [2007] 2 AC 189; *JD v East Berkshire Community Health NHS Trust* [2005] 2 AC 373; *R v Smith* [2001] 1 AC 146; *Three Rivers DC v Governor and Company of The Bank of England* [2000] 2 WLR 1220; *Spring v Guardian Assurance plc* [1995] 2 AC 296.

[85] Gummow (n 7) 54. See also Mason (n 35) 190.

[86] See J Spigelman, 'Rule of Law—Human Rights Protection' (1999) Aus Bar Rev 29; Mason (n 35) 191. In recent years, however, statutory protection of basic rights has been introduced in the State of Victoria and the Australian Capital Territory.

of House of Lords decisions is also limited by encroachments into traditional areas of the common law by statute law. Nonetheless, the basic similarities of much legal doctrine remain. Habit, utility, a common language, and the traditionally practical way of looking at legal problems ensure that a sharing of learning and experience is bound to continue in the foreseeable future—probably more in Australia and New Zealand, in the long run, than in other Commonwealth countries outside the antipodes. Just the same, Australian and New Zealand courts now consult jurisprudence from many other jurisdictions, including civil law jurisdictions.[87] Almost certainly, this will also become a feature of the new Supreme Court of the United Kingdom as it is cut loose from its imperial past and traditional associations, stirring to mark out for itself a new and distinctive role in the world community of final, national courts.

Conclusion

For a substantial part of the twentieth century, the House of Lords of the United Kingdom, in its judicial role, exerted an immense influence on the courts of Australia and New Zealand. Only now, in the past decade or so, has the obedient, dependent attitude of courts in the former antipodean colonies begun to fade.[88] Australian and New Zealand courts are greatly indebted to the House of Lords for decisions on legal principle across the entire landscape of the common law. We continue to benefit from such decisions and now, the highest court in the United Kingdom is sometimes also assisted by decisions of Australian and New Zealand courts.

It is inevitable that the automatic application of the reasoning of the final court of the United Kingdom will decline, proportionately, in its influence on the elaboration of judicial opinions of the courts in Australia and New Zealand. Professional habits will change. New source materials will proliferate. Distinct linkages reflecting geography, the indigenous peoples, commerce, culture, and utility will be built. International law will grow in importance. Fresh contacts will be made, especially with other common law jurisdictions that represent the worldwide progeny of the courts that began by clustering around Westminster Hall.

Courts elsewhere now proclaim their own independence and integrity. Yet it is the greatest tribute that can be paid to the courts of England, including the House of Lords, that a strong element of imitation survives. The content of the law will change. But the integrity of courts, the judicial methodology, and the basic doctrines of the legal order constitute some of the most precious exports of the United Kingdom to the whole world. And the House of Lords has played a central role in this process during a time of imperial transition.

---

[87] See Gleeson (n 43) 133.
[88] MD Kirby, 'Reforming Thoughts from Across the Tasman' in G Palmer (ed), *Reflections on the New Zealand Law Commission: Papers from the Twentieth Anniversary Seminar* (Wellington: LexisNexis, 2007) 14.

(b) Canada

Robert J Sharpe

This paper traces the influence of the Judicial House of Lords in Canada from the pre-1949 era of obedience, when Canadian courts were required to follow its decisions, to the modern era of persuasion, when Canadian courts treat House of Lords decisions as authoritative but non-binding statements of common law principle.

The era of obedience: 1867–1949

English common law was received in colonial times in nine of Canada's 10 provinces where the common law continues to serve as the residual core body of law governing property and civil rights. Canada's codified criminal law was derived from English common law principles, as were significant aspects of our public and administrative law. Even in civilian Quebec, the common law and the decisions of the English courts have been influential. Until 1949, the Judicial Committee of the Privy Council was Canada's court of last resort in civil cases.

It is hardly surprising that Canadian courts followed the decisions of the House of Lords under this regime. The judicial members of the House of Lords were the dominant force on the Privy Council, and the Law Lords could be expected to speak with the same voice whether sitting at Westminster or in Downing Street. Indeed, obedience to English decisions was imposed on Canada by the Privy Council itself. The Privy Council considered itself bound by the decisions of the House of Lords[1] and, in *Trimble v Hill*, a case decided in 1879, the Privy Council proclaimed: 'It is of the utmost importance that in all parts of the empire where English law prevails, the interpretation of that law by the Courts should be as nearly as possible the same.'[2]

However, Canadian adherence to the decisions of the House of Lords cannot be explained solely as a matter of *stare decisis*. The imposition of the House of

[1] *Robins v National Trust* [1927] AC 515.
[2] Strictly speaking, the case only held that colonial courts were required to follow decisions of the English Court of Appeal when interpreting domestic statutes modelled on an English precedent.

Lords as the infallible oracle for the entire empire was readily accepted in Canada. As future Chief Justice Bora Laskin put it, English decisions 'were accepted and applied without any consciousness of obligation but because they reflected agreeable propositions of law'.[3]

Several factors contributed to this obedient attitude. First, Canadian judges revered and looked up to their English brethren, especially those who had reached the pinnacle of the House of Lords. This reverence was partially a product of colonialism, but it also flowed from a genuine admiration of the strength of the English Bench and Bar and a respect for the high quality of English decisions.

This reverence for the work of the English courts blended with the second factor, namely the Canadian profession's acceptance of Blackstone's theory of a universal and immutable body of common law, untouchable except by Parliament.[4] On this theory, the common law was conceived as an integral body of rules, there to be discovered by learned judges. The Canadian legal profession had no doubt that the most reliable and authoritative judges to ascertain and reveal the common law for the entire empire were the judicial members of the House of Lords.

A third factor was the remarkably strong Canadian adherence to legal formalism that lasted well into the 1960s and 1970s. The common law was seen as an internally coherent body of rules that could be objectively and mechanically deduced from prior decisions without reference to social, political, or economic context. As Paul Weiler put it in his stinging 1967 critique, the judges of the Supreme Court of Canada wrote 'their opinions as if there is already an established legal rule which binds them. The rule is applied because the law requires it, not because the judges believe it is a desirable rule.'[5] The formalist vision of the law and legal reasoning was inherently unreceptive to arguments that Canadian judges should shape the common law to reflect Canadian experience and conditions. The judicial role was limited to applying the common law as laid down by the highest authority. Order, predictability, uniformity, and stability of the law required an ultimate authoritative source for common law doctrine and that source was, without question, the House of Lords.

This powerful colonial-formalist legal tradition led Canadian judges to place the House of Lords on a pedestal. The Supreme Court of Canada saw the House of Lords—not the Privy Council—as 'la plus haute autorité judiciaire de l'empire'[6] and held that '[a] decision of the House of Lords should...be respected and followed though inconsistent with a previous judgment of this court.'[7] Justice

---

[3] B Laskin, *The British Tradition in Canadian Law* (London: Stevens & Sons, 1969) 61.

[4] I Bushnell, *The Captive Court: A Study of the Supreme Court of Canada* (Montreal: McGill-Queen's University Press, 1992) 292.

[5] P Weiler, *In the Last Resort: A Critical Study of the Supreme Court of Canada* (Toronto: Carswell/Methuen, 1974) 117.

[6] *Perrault v Gauthier* (1898) 28 SCR 241, 246. See also *Sweeney v Bank of Montreal* (1885) 12 SCR 661, 697.

[7] *Stuart v Bank of Montreal* (1909) 41 SCR 516, 548.

Frank Anglin wrote in 1923, a year before he was named Chief Justice of Canada, that the House of Lords 'carries authority almost equal to that of an Act of Parliament'.[8] Canadian courts readily acquiesced in the Privy Council's 1927 pronouncement that the House of Lords was 'the supreme tribunal to settle English law' and that a 'Colonial Court, which is bound by English law, is bound to follow' the pronouncements of the House of Lords.[9]

This admonition was obeyed even after the Statute of Westminster liberated the Supreme Court of Canada in 1931 from any formal obligation to behave as a 'Colonial Court'. From the time of its creation in 1875 until the early 1960s, the Supreme Court of Canada tended to await 'the last word from the English courts'[10] before daring to change the law, even in emerging areas. As the author of a leading study of the Supreme Court of Canada observes, the court's 'subservience to English cases was very much a Canadian creation'.[11] It was, wrote Bora Laskin in 1951, 'difficult to ascribe any body of doctrine to [the Court] which is distinctively its own, save, perhaps, in the field of criminal law'.[12] In 1959, another prominent Canadian scholar complained that Canadian judicial decisions read as if they were written by 'English judges applying English law in Canada, rather than those of Canadian judges developing Canadian law to meet Canadian needs with guidance of English precedent'.[13] It was not until the 1960s that the Supreme Court of Canada cited more Canadian than English cases.[14]

The first cracks in Canada's colonial-formalist legal foundation appeared in relation to constitutional law and the Privy Council's interpretation of the provisions of the British North America Act 1867 allocating legislative powers as between the federal and provincial governments. In a series of post-World War I decisions, the Privy Council restrictively interpreted two key federal powers, confirming the steady drift in its earlier decisions favouring provincial autonomy. The Privy Council refused to read the federal power in relation to 'trade and commerce' as conferring broad authority to regulate the national economy.[15] Similarly, the residual 'peace, order and good government' power, thought by many Canadian scholars to reflect the intention of the Fathers of Confederation to confer a general power to deal with matters of national concern, was reduced to little more than a power to respond to national emergencies.[16] These decisions were widely criticised as being 'the precise opposite of that which our fathers

---

[8] F Anglin, 'Some Differences between the Law of Quebec and the Law as Administered in the Other Provinces of Canada' (1923) 1 Canadian Bar Rev 33, 38.

[9] *Robins v National Trust* [1927] AC 515, 519.

[10] See eg *Village of Granby v Menard* (1900) 31 SCR 14, 22.   [11] Bushnell (n 4) 291.

[12] B Laskin, 'The Supreme Court of Canada: A Final Court of and for Canadians' (1951) Canadian Bar Rev 1038, 1075.

[13] HE Read, 'The Judicial Process in Common Law Canada' (1959) 37 Canadian Bar Rev 265, 268.

[14] P McCormick, 'The Supreme Court of Canada and American Citations 1945–1994: A Statistical Overview' (1997) 8 Sup Ct L Rev 527.

[15] *Re Board of Commerce Act 1919, and the Combines and Fair Prices Act 1919* [1922] 1 AC 191.

[16] *Toronto Electric Comrs v Snider* [1925] AC 396.

hoped and endeavoured to attain'[17] and seriously at odds with the needs of a modern federation.[18]

Particularly galling was the Privy Council's 1926 decision in *Nadan v The King*[19] striking down a section of Canada's Criminal Code that barred appeals to the Privy Council in criminal cases. Prominent constitutional litigator Newton Rowell described the Privy Council's decision as 'startling and reactionary'.[20] The suggestion that Canada could never have its own court of last resort provoked Chief Justice Frank Anglin, a judge who strongly supported the supremacy of the House of Lords on matters of common law, to take the unusual step of protesting to Prime Minister Mackenzie King: 'My Canadianism leads me to the opinion that we should finally settle our litigation in this country.'[21]

When the abolition of appeals was discussed at the 1926 Imperial Conference, the British Government readily agreed that rights of appeal to the Privy Council should be determined 'in accordance with the wishes of the part of the Empire primarily affected'.[22] Five years later, the Statute of Westminster 1931 cleared the way by formally liberating the Dominions from the last vestiges of colonial authority. But for almost 20 more years, the Canadian attachment to the ideal of a uniform body of common law enunciated by the courts of England remained more powerful than any concerns over the Privy Council's constitutional doctrines. The desire to keep Canadian 'jurisprudence in harmony with that of Great Britain and the Empire' and maintain the Privy Council's 'steadying influence on our jurisprudence', as well as the need to resist the strong pull of the United States, were cited as reasons to forego Canadian judicial autonomy.[23] It was not until 1949 that appeals to the Privy Council were finally abolished in civil cases.

The era of persuasion: 1949 to the present

The attraction of the colonial-formalist tradition was bound to fade once appeals to the Privy Council were abolished. The idea of a uniform body of common law that could apply throughout the empire was an impossible dream. The law must

---

[17] HA Smith, 'Residue of Power in Canada' (1926) 4 Canadian Bar Rev 432, 434.

[18] VC MacDonald, 'The Canadian Constitution Seventy Years After' (1937) 15 Canadian Bar Rev 401; WPM Kennedy, 'The British North America Act: Past and Future' (1937) 15 Canadian Bar Rev 393; FR Scott, 'The Consequences of the Privy Council's Decisions' (1937) 15 Canadian Bar Rev 485.

[19] [1926] AC 482.

[20] Rowell to King, 11 March 1926, quoted in M Prang, *NW Rowell: Ontario Nationalist* (Toronto: University of Toronto Press, 1975) 441.

[21] Quoted in JG Snell and F Vaughan, *The Supreme Court of Canada: History of the Institution* (Toronto: University of Toronto Press, 1985) 183.

[22] M Ollivier, *The Colonial and Imperial Conferences from 1887 to 1937, vol 3, Imperial Conferences Part II* (Ottawa: Queen's Printer, 1954) 150.

[23] Minutes of Convocation of the Law Society of Upper Canada, 1938 including the report of a special committee to review a bill to abolish appeals to the Privy Council.

adapt to distinctive local conditions, cultures, and mores. By the 1960s and 1970s, Canadian lawyers and judges began to recognise the House of Lords for what it was: an English court comprised of English judges deciding English cases in the light of English values. The House of Lords could certainly be relied upon as a source of English law. However, English judges could not be expected to understand, let alone consider, Canadian values when deciding English cases. There was bound to be a tension between our reverence for the English legal tradition and the authoritative pronouncements of England's highest court on the one hand and the inevitable failure of that court to understand or reflect our own experience when crafting its decisions on the other. This was not a criticism of the House of Lords—the problem rested in Canada where a rigid judicial adherence to legal positivism and formalism more or less immunised the authority of English decisions from being adapted to meet the exigencies of the Canadian experience.

Gradually, after 1949, Canadian courts began to develop what Chief Justice Brian Dickson described as 'a distinctively Canadian jurisprudence'.[24] Canadian courts continue to look to the House of Lords for authoritative statements of common law principle, but have adopted a more eclectic approach, often citing the decisions of other non-Canadian courts as well playing close attention to the pattern of Canadian case law.[25] English jurisprudence is no longer accorded automatic precedence, and its acceptance rests entirely upon its persuasiveness. The Judicial House of Lords continues to play an important role in the evolution of Canadian law, but this role is based upon persuasion rather than obedience. The Supreme Court of Canada recognises that 'the English legal background necessarily sets the stage for our own experience',[26] and when it is necessary to go to 'first principles'[27] the Court frequently looks to the House of Lords for non-binding but helpful guidance.

The nature of this relationship of persuasion rather than obedience may be illustrated by considering the impact of House of Lords decisions in the area of tort law. Here, as in other areas, early House of Lords decisions retain their foundational value. *Donoghue v Stevenson*[28] remains the core source and inspiration for the Canadian law of negligence, as do the landmark House of Lords decisions that followed in the 1960s and 1970s—*Hedley Byrne & Co Ltd v Heller & Partners Ltd*,[29] *Home Office v Dorset Yacht Co Ltd*,[30] and *Anns v Merton London Borough Council*.[31]

---

[24] R Sharpe and K Roach, *Brian Dickson: A Judge's Journey* (Toronto: University of Toronto Press, 2003) 317–20.

[25] Particularly when interpreting the Charter of Rights and Freedoms. See eg *Charkaoui v Canada (Citizenship and Immigration)* [2007] 1 SCR 350; *United States v Burns* [2001] 1 SCR 283; SK Harding, 'Comparative Reasoning and Judicial Review' (2003) 28 Yale J Intl L 409, 412–17.

[26] *Libman v R* [1985] 2 SCR 178, 184.

[27] *Geffen v Goodman Estate* [1991] 2 SCR 353, 374.   [28] [1932] AC 562.

[29] [1964] AC 465.   [30] [1970] AC 1004.   [31] [1978] AC 728.

The Supreme Court of Canada adopted the two-step *Anns* test to determine whether a duty of care exists in *Kamloops v Nielsen*.[32] The House of Lords subsequently overruled *Anns* in *Murphy v Brentwood District Council* on the grounds that 'it did not proceed on any basis of principle at all, but constituted a remarkable example of judicial legislation' and 'introduced a new species of liability governed by a principle indeterminate in character'.[33] At this point, Canadian and English tort law parted company. The Supreme Court of Canada continues to rely on the *Anns* test, insisting that *Anns*, not *Murphy*, harmonises better with the traditional law of negligence that flows from *Donoghue v Stevenson*. In *Canadian National Railway Co v Norsk Pacific Steamship Co*,[34] the Supreme Court of Canada 'refuse[d] to accept injustice merely for the sake of the doctrinal tidiness which is the motivating spirit of *Murphy*'. The Court saw the *Anns* approach as being in 'the best tradition of the law of negligence', and refused 'to be confined by arbitrary forms and rules where justice indicates otherwise'.[35] '[T]he incremental approach of *Kamloops*,' wrote McLachlin J, 'is to be preferred to the insistence on logical precision of *Murphy*' as it is 'more consistent with the incremental character of the common law. It permits relief to be granted in new situations where it is merited . . . [and] is sensitive to danger of unlimited liability.'[36] In *Cooper v Hobart*[37] the Supreme Court of Canada again reaffirmed the *Anns* test, but with a slight reformulation that explicitly imported policy considerations into the first step. This open acceptance of policy as an ingredient in decision-making and the willingness to pick and choose from various strands of authority on the basis of what best meets Canadian needs stands in stark contrast to the court's earlier colonial-formalist tradition.

In a similar vein, the Supreme Court of Canada rejected the restrictive *Rookes v Barnard*[38] approach to punitive damages as a widely criticised and unjustified divergence from the common law.[39] Similarly, the Supreme Court of Canada refused to follow the House of Lords' rejection of the tort of negligent investigation in *Hill v Chief Constable of West Yorkshire*.[40] Adopting the explicitly policy-oriented *Anns* test, McLachlin CJC concluded that '[v]iewed from the broader societal perspective, suspects may reasonably be expected to rely on the police to conduct their investigation in a competent, non-negligent manner.'[41]

On the other hand, the Supreme Court followed the House of Lords' decision in *Hussain v New Taplow Paper Mills Ltd*,[42] reaffirming the principle that

---

[32] *Kamloops (City of) v Nielsen* [1984] 2 SCR 2.   [33] [1991] 1 AC 398, 471.
[34] [1992] 1 SCR 1021.   [35] ibid, para 243.   [36] ibid, para 250.
[37] *Cooper v Hobart* [2001] 3 SCR 537.   [38] [1964] AC 1129.
[39] *Vorvis v Insurance Corp of British Columbia* [1989] 1 SCR 1085; *Whiten v Pilot Insurance Co* [2002] 1 SCR 595.
[40] [1989] AC 53.
[41] *Hill v Hamilton-Wentworth Regional Police Services Board* [2007] SCC 41.
[42] [1988] 1 All ER 541.

payments received for loss of wages from a private insurance policy should not be deducted from lost wage damages in a successful tort action,[43] a rule originally set down in *Bradburn v Great Western Rail Co.*[44] In doing so, the Supreme Court resisted opposing trends in the rest of the common law world.[45] Similarly, the Ontario Court of Appeal recently adopted the responsible journalism defence for media defendants in libel actions announced by the House of Lords in *Reynolds v Times Newspapers*[46] on the basis that it achieved an appropriate balance between protection of reputation and freedom of expression.[47]

A similar pattern of persuasion rather than obedience may be seen in criminal law and evidence. For example, in *R v Handy*[48] the Supreme Court of Canada acknowledged but declined to follow the view of the House of Lords in *R v H*,[49] which held that for the purposes of admissibility, similar fact evidence should be accepted as true in all but very exceptional cases and that the question of weight should be left wholly to the jury. Instead, Binnie J held that in considering whether to admit similar fact evidence, a trial judge must assess serious indicia of unreliability such as the possibility of collusion in the testimony of witnesses. On the other side of the ledger, in *R v Krieger*[50] the Supreme Court of Canada agreed with the decision of the House of Lords in *R v Wang*,[51] that a trial judge presiding over a criminal jury case cannot direct the jury to issue a verdict of guilty.

Decisions of the House of Lords are accorded significant weight in specialised areas where relatively little or no Canadian authority is available. *Sunrise Co v The Lake Winnipeg*[52] involved the question of the degree to which the owner of a ship that wrongfully causes another commercial ship to run aground is liable for the loss of profit resulting from the latter ship's repose in dry dock while undergoing repair. Unsurprisingly, the Supreme Court's decision relied heavily on a 1961 English treatise on the law of collisions at sea[53] and its discussion of two House of Lords decisions.[54]

In a less esoteric but still emerging area of law, namely intellectual property, the Supreme Court of Canada appears to cleave closely to the House of Lords' decisions. For example, in *Apotex Inc v Wellcome Foundation Ltd*[55] and *Whirlpool Corp v Camco Inc*,[56] the court applied two English patent law doctrines, the

[43] *Cunningham v Wheeler; Cooper v Miller; Shanks v McNee* [1994] 1 SCR 359.
[44] (1876) 10 Ex 1. [45] See *Cunningham*, 23 (McLachlin J dissenting).
[46] *Reynolds v Times Newspapers Ltd* [2001] 2 AC 127.
[47] *Cusson v Quan* 2007 ONCA 771. [48] [2002] 2 SCR 908, paras 104–14.
[49] [1995] 2 AC 596. [50] [2006] 2 SCR 501, paras 10–23. [51] [2005] 1 WLR 661.
[52] [1991] 1 SCR 3.
[53] KC McGuffie, *The Law of Collisions at Sea* (British Shipping Laws, vol 4) (London: Stevens & Sons, 1961).
[54] *The Haversham Grange* [1905] P 307; *Carslogie Steamship Co v Royal Norwegian Government* [1952] AC 292.
[55] [2002] 4 SCR 153. [56] [2000] 2 SCR 1067.

doctrine of sound prediction in assessing the usefulness of an invention,[57] and the doctrine of purposive construction in claim construal.[58] In the trademark context, the Supreme Court in *Ciba-Geigy Canada Ltd v Apotex Inc*[59] and *Kirkbi AG v Ritvik Holdings Inc*[60] endorsed the definition set down by the House of Lords in *Reckitt & Colman Products Ltd v Borden Inc*[61] of the elements of the action for 'passing-off' one's products as those of one's competitors. Canadian jurisprudence in this area may well remain harmonious with UK law, in line with the global trend toward the convergence of intellectual property regimes.

The Supreme Court of Canada has acknowledged the import of House of Lords decisions in another emerging area, namely the law's response to terrorism. In *Suresh v Canada (Minister of Citizenship and Immigration),*[62] holding that the protections of the Canadian Charter of Rights and Freedoms would generally prevent the Government from deporting a refugee claimant on national security grounds to a foreign state where he or she would face a substantial risk of torture, the court paid close attention to the House of Lords' decision on similarly fraught issues in *Secretary of State for the Home Department v Rehman.*[63] The court cited Lord Hoffmann's speech in *Rehman* both for its comments concerning the need to respect the executive's expertise and legitimacy on issues of national security, as well as the proposition that in light of the European Convention on Human Rights, torture is an illegitimate tool for combating terrorism.[64] Similarly, in *Charkaoui v Canada (Citizenship and Immigration),*[65] McLachlin CJC supported the Court's unanimous decision striking down the Immigration and Refugee Protection Act's security certificate detention system for non-citizens by citing *A v Secretary of State for the Home Department.*[66] In *A*, the House of Lords held that the United Kingdom's anti-terrorism provisions permitting indefinite detention of foreign nationals violated the European Convention on Human Rights. McLachlin CJC recognised that the weight to be accorded to the House of Lords' decision flowed not only from strict legal doctrine but also from shared experience with the problems posed by the threat of terrorism: 'Canada . . . is not alone in facing the problem of detention in the immigration context in situations where deportation is difficult or impossible.'[67]

---

[57] See *Apotex*, 57–66, citing *May & Baker Ltd v Boots Pure Drug Co* (1950) 67 RPC 23 (UKHL); *Mullard Radio Valve Co v Philco Radio and Television Corp* (1936) 53 RPC 323 (UKHL); *Olin Mathieson Chemical Corp v Biorex Laboratories Ltd* [1970] RPC 157 (Ch D).

[58] See *Whirlpool*, paras 39–50, citing, inter alia, *Catnic Components Ltd v Hill & Smith Ltd* [1982] RPC 183 (UKHL).

[59] [1992] 3 SCR 120, paras 32–33.   [60] [2005] 3 SCR 302, paras 65–66.

[61] [1990] 1 All ER 873.   [62] [2002] 1 SCR 3.   [63] [2003] 1 AC 153.

[64] See *Suresh*, paras 33, 74.   [65] [2007] 1 SCR 350, paras 124–8.

[66] [2005] 2 AC 68.   [67] *Charkaoui*, para 124.

Conclusion

The judicial House of Lords has always had significant influence over the evolution of Canadian law. House of Lords decisions, once binding on Canadian courts, are now regarded as authoritative, non-binding pronouncements, to be considered and weighed, together with Canadian decisions and those of other foreign courts, when resolving difficult legal issues.

(c) South Africa

Arthur Chaskalson

South Africa has had a troubled history. In itself this is not unusual, for it is true of most countries. However, to understand how the judicial House of Lords has been viewed from South Africa, it is necessary to refer to our legal history. I can give only a brief and superficial account of that history here. For detailed discussions of the relevant history, readers must look elsewhere.[1]

What is today the Republic of South Africa was not virgin territory when the first settlers from Europe arrived at the tip of the continent in the seventeenth century. It was the home of various African tribes, each with their own legal systems.[2] The Dutch were the first European settlers. In 1652 they established a refreshment station at the Cape, to supply their ships navigating the trade route to Batavia, and, as the settlement grew and became more permanent, courts were established to enforce local statutes and colonial legislation, and where they were silent, to apply Roman Dutch law, which was the law of the Netherlands at the time of the first settlement.[3] From 1795 to 1803 the British occupied the Cape, and then after a brief absence took the Cape again in 1806 and ruled it as the colonial power. Roman Dutch law remained in place as the common law of the European settlers, and became the common law of the Boer Republics and of the Natal Colony, as European settlement expanded over what is today South Africa.

The expansion of European settlement in Southern Africa is a story of imperial conquest, involving wars between the settlers and African tribes, wars between the British and the Boer Republics, various unsuccessful rebellions by settlers against colonial authorities, and by African communities against the colonial states. After the Boer Wars, which ended in 1902, there were four British colonies in Southern Africa, the Cape Colony, Natal, the Transvaal, and the Orange River Colony. In 1910, under the influence of the imperial

---

[1] M Channock, *The Making of South African Legal Culture 1902–1936: Fear, Favour and Prejudice* (Cambridge: CUP, 2001); R Zimmerman and D Visser (eds), *Southern Cross: Civil Law and Common Law in South Africa* (Oxford: Clarendon Press, 1996); C Forsyth, *In Danger for their Talents* (Cape Town: Juta, 1985); H Corder, *Judges at Work* (Cape Town: Juta, 1984); H Hahlo and E Kahn, *The South African Legal System and its Background* (Cape Town: Juta, 1968).

[2] TW Bennett, *A Source Book of African Customary Law for Southern Africa* (Cape Town: Juta, 1991).

[3] EA Walker, *A History of Southern Africa* (London: Longmans, Green & Co, 3rd edn 1957) 102.

Government, a union of the four colonies, the Union of South Africa, was established, as a British Dominion. Blacks were denied the franchise in the South Africa Act passed by the Imperial Parliament in 1909 and adopted by the new Union Parliament when it convened in 1910. Racial discrimination was legitimised by the legal order, and whites used their political and economic power to entrench and further their dominant social, economic, and political position. Racial discrimination was more deeply institutionalised from 1948 until 1994 by the system of apartheid. As a result of its apartheid policy, South Africa was forced to leave the Commonwealth, and in 1961 constituted itself as an independent Republic. The political leadership during this period was dominated by the Afrikaner majority within the white population, and this in turn had an impact on the attitude of South African courts to English law. I will return to this later.

After Union a uniform court structure was established with the Appellate Division as the highest court. Special courts were, however, constituted to deal with disputes between blacks. These courts were meant to apply African customary law, but in time they became instruments for the enforcement of apartheid laws.[4] The other courts, which were the dominant courts, dealt with cases that did not involve disputes between blacks. These courts, and legal practice and procedure, were strongly influenced by their colonial history. There was a divided bar with advocates (barristers) and attorneys (solicitors), in which only advocates had a right of audience in the higher courts.[5] The advocates' profession was modelled on the English Bar. There were senior and junior counsel,[6] a strict two-counsel rule in the bigger bars,[7] and by convention judges of the higher courts were appointed from the ranks of senior counsel.[8] Judges and counsel wore the same robes as their English counterparts, and procedure in the higher courts was similar to that of the English courts. Although the common law applied by these courts was Roman Dutch law, English law, and thus decisions of the House of Lords, had a strong influence on the early development of South African law, made stronger by the English doctrine of precedent which was adopted and applied by the courts. The influence of the English courts and ultimately of the House of Lords was also seen in the manner in which the higher courts functioned and judgments were written.

---

[4] For a description of these courts and how they came to be seen as providing an inferior system of justice, see Bennett (n 2) 139–41.

[5] This remained the position until 1995 when provision was made for attorneys to appear in the higher courts.

[6] King's Counsel and Queen's Counsel until South Africa left the Commonwealth in 1961, and Senior Counsel since then.

[7] This is no longer required, but in most important cases seniors will be briefed with juniors.

[8] There were exceptions, the most notable of which was probably the appointment of Mr Justice LC Steyn in 1951 from the position of Senior Law Advisor to the Government to the Bench of the Supreme Court in the Transvaal. Mr Justice Steyn was later elevated to the Appellate Division in 1955 and became the Chief Justice of South Africa in 1959.

In his Hamlyn Lectures on the contribution of English law to South African law,[9] Mr Justice Schreiner[10] observed that judgments of the House of Lords 'have often influenced South African decisions by the cogency of their reasoning and the clarity of their language'. That was certainly true of the period prior to his retirement from the Appellate Division in 1960, but the influence waned during the years of the apartheid republic. In 1959, shortly before Mr Justice Schreiner's retirement, Mr Justice LC Steyn[11] became Chief Justice. He held that position until 1971. Under his leadership the Appellate Division sought to develop a South African common law, based purely on Roman Dutch law,[12] free of the imperial influence of English law. This was already evident at the time of Schreiner's Hamlyn lectures in which he refers to judgments of the Appellate Division dealing with nuisance,[13] estoppel,[14] and defamation,[15] where the Appellate Division declined to follow long established principles that had entered our law through English law.

In *Regal v African Superslate (Pty) Ltd*,[16] the nuisance case, Steyn railed against a reliance on English authority which had been the practice in nuisance cases for over a century, saying that this had taken place without a comprehensive investigation of our common law. In *Trust Bank v Eksteen*,[17] the estoppel case, Steyn made his attitude, already well known to those who appeared in the court over which he presided, clear to all in the legal profession. The trial judge had said that the rules regarding estoppel 'are to be sought principally in the decisions of the English courts which have for long been the main guides to our courts'.[18] Steyn protested against this approach, saying that no court was entitled to substitute the law of any country for 'our law'.[19] Hoexter J who had been a member of the Appellate Division for many years before Steyn was appointed to that court, in a concurring judgment, began his analysis of the applicable legal principles, with this observation: 'I bear in mind that our Courts have pointed out over and over again that, in matters of estoppel, it is proper and safe to look for guidance to decisions of the English courts.'[20] But his was a lone voice in the court.

Edwin Cameron (now Mr Justice Cameron of the Constitutional Court of South Africa) trenchantly described Steyn's attitude to English law:[21]

[9] *The Contribution of English Law to South African Law; and the Rule of Law in South Africa* (London: Stevens & Sons, 1967), (Cape Town: Juta, 1967) 24.
[10] A member of the Appellate Division from 1945 to 1960, and generally regarded as one of the foremost South African judges of his time.
[11] See n 8 above.
[12] To be found largely in the writings of seventeenth and eighteenth century commentators as applied by the South African courts.
[13] *Regal v African Superslate (Pty) Ltd* 1963 (1) SA 102 (AD).
[14] *Trust Bank van Afrika Bpk v Eksteen* 1964 (3) SA 402.
[15] *Jordaan v van Biljon*, 1962 (1) SA 286 (AD); *Craig v Voortrekkerpers Bpk* 1963 (1) SA 149 (AD); *Nydoo v Vengtas* 1965 (1) SA 1 (AD).
[16] n 13.   [17] n 14.   [18] *Trust Bank v Eksteen* 1964 (1) SA 74 (N), 81.
[19] At 410–11.   [20] At 414.
[21] 'Legal Chauvinism, Executive Mindedness and Justice: LC Steyn's Impact on South African Law' (1982) 99 SALJ 38, 51. At the time Cameron was a young academic. Steyn had only recently retired from the Appellate Division, lauded by the apartheid legal establishment for his contribution

[He] wished to terminate the special bond [between English law and South African law]. This he proposed to do not only by firing broadsides but by embarking on a war of attrition which would eventually see the English elements in our legal system starved of their support by foreclosure of judicial amenability and congeniality to them.[22]

He did so by 'expressly [repudiating] what he considered to be unjustified reliance on English sources',[23] by '[ignoring] or all but [ignoring] English authority cited in argument by . . . counsel'[24] and by '[dismissing] English decisions which he felt constrained to mention as of no, or little, persuasive or informative value to the case before him or merely [expressing] a doubt as to their applicability in South African law'.[25] So hostile was Steyn to the citation of English authority that leading counsel at the Johannesburg Bar, briefed to appear in the Appellate Division, wryly considered whether there was an ethical duty to disclose to the court a decision of the House of Lords in their favour.[26] It would be fair to say that the view of the House of Lords from South Africa's highest court at this time was frosty.

This did not mean that English law, and the influence of the House of Lords, ceased to play a role in South African jurisprudence. The roots were too deep for that. The English law of evidence had been prescribed by statute to govern the admissibility of evidence in South African courts. When South Africa became a republic, the law of evidence at that date was declared by statute to be the law to be applied by the courts (in effect English law as at that date).[27] Criminal Procedure was prescribed by statute strongly influenced by English law;[28] so too the law of negotiable instruments.[29] The influence of English law and decisions of the House of Lords was also evident in fields of modern commercial law such as companies and insurance, and in the interpretation of statutes. The most important influence, however, was the strict adherence by the South African courts to the English doctrine of the supremacy of Parliament.

In dealing with the power of the legislature our courts consistently followed the principle of English constitutional law that Parliament is a sovereign body, and that no court can decline to enforce a statute on the grounds that it is unconstitutional, and therefore invalid.[30] Dismissing a challenge to the validity of the extension of the South African Terrorism Act to what was then the mandated Territory of

---

to South African law. Cameron's courageous criticism of Steyn's jurisprudence attracted considerable attention, and much hostility from the apartheid establishment.

[22] ibid, 50.   [23] ibid, 45.   [24] ibid, 49.   [25] ibid, 49–50.

[26] I first heard this from Rex Welsh QC, one of the leaders of the Johannesburg Bar at the time that Steyn presided in the Appellate Division. I have been told that the observation might have been made first by Mr Justice Schreiner after he retired, but I have not been able to verify its source.

[27] Generally in this regard, see WH Schmidt and H Rademeyer, *Law of Evidence* (looseleaf, Durban: LexisNexis Butterworths, 2003) paras 1311–13.

[28] DV Cowen, *The Law of Negotiable Instruments in South Africa* (Cape Town: Juta, 5th edn 1985) 146.

[29] WA Joubert et al, *The Law of South Africa* vol 19 (Durban: Butterworths, 1996) para 1.

[30] *R v McChlery* 1912 AD 199, 215, 218 and 224.

South West Africa, Steyn CJ had no difficulty in adhering to this principle.[31] Doing so he adopted, without comment, passages from an early Appellate Division decision in *R v McChlery*[32] which were said in that judgment to have been based on English law,[33] and went on to say: 'I cannot conceive of any British court declaring any Act of the British Parliament invalid on the grounds that it violates an obligation under a mandate. Under our Constitution our courts have no greater authority.'[34] The supremacy of Parliament, premised on the assumption that government is based on the will of the people to whom it is answerable for its legislative programme, had no legitimacy in the South African legal order, where Parliament was the preserve of the small white minority,[35] who used their power to entrench their position, and further their social, economic, and political interests.

The Appellate Division said: 'Parliament may make any encroachment it chooses upon the life, liberty, or property of any individual subject to its sway ... and it is the function of the courts of law to enforce its will.'[36] This was done as a matter of course under apartheid. Legislation could not be invalidated and where it was interpreted in a manner that did not meet the satisfaction of the Government, the 'loophole' could be closed by legislation. The doctrine of parliamentary supremacy thus protected apartheid legislation against any possible intrusion by the courts.

Most apartheid legislation was given effect through regulations made by the executive, and by administrators implementing government policy. Here too there was an English influence and initially greater scope for the courts. Soon after the adoption of apartheid as government policy, the Appellate Division, relying on *Kruse v Johnson*,[37] held that the policy of segregation on trains and waiting rooms, as implemented by the government-controlled rail services, was invalid because it was partial and unequal in its operation between different races.[38] The Government responded by enacting the Reservation of Separate Amenities Act[39] to sanction such discrimination, and this established a pattern of legislating for inequality that was subsequently followed. The courts did not interfere where this had been done, and went on to accept that substantial inequality could even be implicitly authorised by Parliament.[40]

In an attempt to immunise their decisions against judicial review, executive functionaries were vested with powers expressed in subjective terms. Wrenched from their context, *Kruse v Johnson*[41] and *Associated Provincial Picture Houses Ltd v Wednesbury Corporation*[42] provided grounds for the failure by the courts to

---

[31] *S v Tuhadeleni* 1969 (1) SA 153, 172–3.   [32] n 30.   [33] ibid.   [34] n 31, 177.
[35] At the time of apartheid whites made up approximately 15 per cent of the population.
[36] Stratford JA in *Sachs v Minister of Justice* 1934 AD 11, 37, referred to by C Hoexter, *Administrative Law in South Africa* (Cape Town: Juta, 2007) 12, and K O'Regan, 'Breaking Ground: Some Thoughts on the Seismic Shift in our Administrative Law' (2004) 121 SALJ 424.
[37] [1898] 2 QB 91.   [38] *R v Abdurahman* 1950 (3) SA 136 (A).   [39] Act 49 of 1953.
[40] *Minister of the Interior v Lockhat* 1961 (2) SA 587 (A). See in this regard, Hoexter (n 36) 296–8.
[41] n 37.   [42] [1948] (1) KB 223 (CA).

interfere with much of the injustice of apartheid. Where their decisions were questioned the *Wednesbury* rule was strictly applied.[43] *Cabinet of the Interim Government of South West Africa v Katofa*[44] is an illustration. Mr Katofa had been detained by the security forces on order of the Administrator-General pursuant to a power vested in him to detain any person if he was satisfied that such person had 'committed or attempted to commit or promote the commission of violence or intimidation of persons'. Responding to an application for habeas corpus the Administrator-General stated that he was so satisfied without giving any further details of what he was satisfied about or why. The High Court had adopted the approach of the House of Lords in *Secretary for State for Education and Science v Metropolitan Borough of Tameside*,[45] that 'if a judgment requires, before it is made, the existence of some facts, then although the evaluation of those facts is for the Secretary of State above, the court must enquire whether those facts exist and have been taken into account'.[46] Since no facts other than the 'satisfaction' of the Administrator had been given to justify the detention, the application for habeas corpus had been upheld. The Appellate Division reversed the decision of the High Court. Rejecting *Tameside* it held that the existence of the necessary facts to justify detention, as well as the evaluation of those facts, were matters for the Administrator and not the court. The Administrator had said that he was satisfied and his decision could therefore be set aside only if he had acted in bad faith or for an ulterior purpose. A hopeless task for the detainee who did not know and was not told what the Administrator's reasons were.

After Mr Justice Corbett was appointed as Chief Justice in 1989, the relationship between the Appellate Division and the House of Lords began to thaw. For instance,[47] staying with administrative law, the doctrine of legitimate expectation was 'imported' into our law,[48] and accepted by the Appellate Division as being a necessary development,[49] the views of the House in *Anisminic*[50] were taken into account in upholding a review in that case on the grounds of error of law,[51] and Lord Mustill's exposition of the requirements for procedural fairness[52] were cited with approval.[53]

---

[43] For instance, in *National Transport Commission v Chetty's Motor Transport (Pty) Ltd* 1972 (3) SA 726 (AD) the Appellate Division said that a claimant relying on unreasonableness as a ground for review of administrative action had to show that 'the decision was grossly unreasonable to so striking a degree as to warrant the inference of a failure to apply its mind (to the issues)—a formidable onus'.

[44] 1987 (1) SA 695 (A) (the judgment is in Afrikaans and I have translated into English the name of the case as it appears in the law reports).

[45] [1977] AC 1014 (HL).   [46] ibid, 1047.

[47] The examples are given as illustrations and are far from a complete list.

[48] Hoexter (n 36) 327.   [49] *Administrator, Transvaal v Traub* 1989 (4) SA 731 (A), 761.

[50] *Anisminic Ltd v Foreign Compensation Commission* [1969] 2 AC 147 (HL).

[51] *Hira v Booysen* 1992 (4) SA 69 (A).

[52] *R v Secretary for State for the Home Department, ex p Doody* [1993] 3All ER 92 (HL), 106.

[53] *Du Preez v Truth and Reconciliation Commission* 1997 (3) SA 204 (A), 231–3.

South Africa, again a member of the Commonwealth, is now a constitutional state with an extensive Bill of Rights entrenched as part of the supreme law. One of the entrenched rights is a right to just administrative action according to which 'everyone has the right to administrative action that is lawful, reasonable and procedurally fair',[54] and administrators can be required to give reasons for their decisions.[55] Legislation must be interpreted and the common law developed so as to promote the 'spirit, purport and objects of the bill of rights'[56] which include the values that underlie an open and democratic society.[57] The Constitutional Court,[58] now the highest court in such matters, has adopted the contextual approach to judicial review advocated by Lord Steyn in *R v Secretary for State for the Home Department, ex p Daly*,[59] and Lord Cooke's comments on the *Wednesbury* rule in *R v Chief Constable of Sussex, ex p International Traders Ferry Ltd*,[60] holding that reasonableness has a substantive component entitling a court to interfere with an administrative decision if it is one which 'a reasonable decision maker could not reach'.[61] Judgments of the House of Lords are frequently cited in argument to the highest courts of our country,[62] and once again carry the weight attributed to them by Mr Justice Schreiner in his Hamlyn Lectures.[63]

---

[54] Constitution of the Republic of South Africa, 1996, s 33(1).   [55] ibid, s 33(2).
[56] ibid, s 39(2).   [57] ibid, s 39(1).
[58] *First National Bank of SA Ltd t/a Wesbank v Minister of Finance* 2002 (4) SA 768 (CC), para 18.
[59] [2001] 3 All ER 433 (HL), 447.   [60] [1999] 1 All ER 129 (HL), 157.
[61] *Bato Star Fishing (Pty) Ltd v Minister of Environmental Affairs* 2004 (4) SA 490 (CC), paras 44–5.
[62] In the South African Law Reports for 2006, 144 decisions of the English courts are referred to.
[63] n 9.

(d) India

Adarsh Sein Anand[1]

This section traces, albeit briefly, the influence of the House of Lords on Indian law in general and on the Supreme Court of India since 1950 in particular. A brief reference is also made to the influence of the Supreme Court of India on the House of Lords. It is perforce restricted to selected areas.

Introduction

The Indian legal system is one of the oldest, dating back five thousand years to Vedic Times. It has changed and evolved over the centuries to imbibe influences from legal systems around the world. Various wise men first laid down the Laws of the Land which go by the name 'Smrithis' (commentaries on Vedas). These were administered by the judges, who functioned as supreme courts. During the Mughal period, there were various 'Adalats', which functioned as courts, and the Mughal Emperors functioned as supreme courts.

British colonial rule over India imposed a jurisprudence and legal system which have been retained by India in basic respects, even after independence. The growth of English common law in India since the eighteenth century is a fascinating tale of how a foreign system of law has found its roots in another country, thousand of miles from the home of its origin. Beginning with its application to the East India Company's factories in a few places in India, the common law of England with its statutory modifications and doctrines of equity deeply coloured and influenced the laws and judicial administration of the sub-continent, which even today bear the unmistakable stamp of their origin.

It was during British rule that a codified legal and judicial system was introduced in India, based on Anglo-Saxon jurisprudence, with the Judicial Committee of the Privy Council as the final court of appeal. The judicial members of the House of Lords dominated the Privy Council, which considered itself bound by the decisions of the House of Lords until at least 1935, when the British

---

[1] The author acknowledges the assistance of Shri Chetan Gupta, BCL (Oxon), Advocate, in the preparation of this piece.

Parliament enacted the Government of India Act 1935. The Federal Court of India was established under that Act and was inaugurated on 6 December 1937, though the Judicial Committee of the Privy Council continued to exercise its existing jurisdiction. By the Privy Council Abolition of Jurisdiction Act of 1949, appeals to the Privy Council were finally abolished and all pending appeals were transferred to the Federal Court, which also felt itself bound to an extent by the decisions of the House of Lords.

In the period leading up to its independence in 1947 and during the first several years of India's existence as an independent nation, a Constituent Assembly met to draft the nation's Constitution. The core of the Indian Constitution reflects the democratic ethos of eliminating inequalities and promoting social good. The Constituent Assembly decided to retain and adopt for the Republic the basics of the pre-independence judicial system.

The Constitution of India was adopted on 26 January 1950, when India became a Republic and the Supreme Court of India became its conscience keeper. Being reluctant to leave basic liberties undefined, unlike the English common law, the founding fathers enshrined them in Part III of the Constitution as Fundamental Rights for their better recognition and enforcement. This experiment has been followed in many other countries. In 1998, following the example of other Commonwealth countries and influenced by the European Convention on Human Rights, the United Kingdom enacted its own Human Rights Act.

The Supreme Court of India is the final court of appeal. It succeeded to the jurisdiction of the Federal Court and the Judicial Committee of the Privy Council. The Supreme Court of India was no longer 'bound' by the judgments of the Judicial Committee and no 'obedience' to those judgments was required— these only had some 'persuasive value'. Nonetheless, the judgments of the House of Lords continue to have a great influence and impact on Indian law. Considerations of respect and comity have played as large a part as those of convenience, as far as the use of decisions of the House of Lords by the Indian courts is concerned.

The judicial functions of the House of Lords originate from the ancient role of the Curia Regis as a body that addressed the petitions of the King's subjects. Prior to becoming the final appellate court for the United Kingdom, the House of Lords could even hear petitions presented directly to it. The evolution of the House into a final appellate body has, curiously enough, an Indian connection, for the practice of bringing cases directly to the Lords ended with the case of *Thomas Skinner v East India Co.*[2] Skinner had established a trading base in Asia while there were few restrictions on trade there. Later the base was seized by the British East India Company, which had been granted a monopoly, and a dispute broke out between the House of Lords and the House of Commons over whether the Lords ought to hear the case at first instance, with the Commons ordering the

---

[2] (1666) St Tr 710.

imprisonment of Thomas Skinner and the Lords retaliating by ordering the imprisonment of the company chairman. In 1670, King Charles II requested that both Houses abandon the case. When they refused, he ordered that all references to the case be expunged from the journals of both Houses and that neither body should continue with the dispute. The House of Lords then ceased to hear petitions in the first instance, considering them only after the lower courts had failed to remedy them. Today, the House of Lords continues to be the final appellate court for the United Kingdom, in all matters civil and criminal, although the High Court of Justiciary in Scotland is the final court of appeal in criminal matters for that jurisdiction.

Justice Krishna Iyer once commented that it is the waters of the Thames rather than those of the Potomac that fertilise the landscape of Indian legal thought.[3] Indeed, one of the principal tributaries to this cross-continental stream of legal thought has been the House of Lords rather than the Supreme Court of the United States. Amidst all the changes in the administration of justice both in India and in the United Kingdom, three pillars of Anglo-Saxon jurisprudence remain firmly rooted in our polity as they have been in the United Kingdom, namely, the sanctity of the liberties of the individual, the rule of law, and the independence of the judiciary. It is this fundamental similarity in judicial administration, born out of common historic traditions in the two countries, that has resulted in a close rapport between lawyers and judges of the two countries. The fact that most of the men who shaped India in the years immediately following independence happened to be lawyers who had been called to the Bar in England and were well versed in the common law, may also have something to do with the persistent influence of the English legal system. Mahatma Gandhi, father of the Nation, was called to the English Bar at the Inner Temple in 1891.[4] The conferences between lawyers and judges of the two countries through meetings of the Indo-British Legal Forum every second year have consolidated this relationship further.

The influence of the House of Lords on India's Supreme Court

It might be thought that the impact of the decisions of the House of Lords on Indian law is only natural, given that India inherited its legal system from the British and that because much legislation in force in India had parallels in the United Kingdom or crystallised the common law position at the time when they were enacted.[5]

---

[3] *Samsher Singh v State of Punjab* (1974) 2 SCC 831, 861, para 104.
[4] He was disbarred from practice in 1922 for his activities in connection with the Indian freedom movement and was only posthumously reinstated in 1988.
[5] An example of the former is the Indian Sale of Goods Act 1930, which was based on the Sale of Goods Act 1893 then in force in the United Kingdom. The Indian Contract Act 1872 is an example of the latter.

Indeed, this is to an extent true and in many of the cases discussed here, Indian courts looked to decisions of the House of Lords to see if the common law had evolved any further, or whether Indian legislation had made a conscious departure from the laws of the United Kingdom. This is very much in keeping with Oliver Wendell Holmes's characterisation of the English common law as 'not a brooding omnipresence in the sky but the articulate voice of some sovereign or quasi sovereign that can be identified'.

In the field of administrative law, the Supreme Court of India has generally followed the administrative law as expounded by British judges. The Indian jurisprudence on the application of principles of natural justice has certainly been influenced by decisions of the House of Lords. Prominent among these are the decisions in *Dimes v Grand Junction Canal*[6] and *Ridge v Baldwin*.[7] The former was relied on by the Indian Supreme Court even as recently as 2006 in *Rameshwar Prasad (VI) v Union of India*[8] when determining whether the Governor of a state had acted in a partisan manner and could be said to be biased.

Initially the Supreme Court felt itself hidebound by the approach taken in *Nakkuda Ali v Jayaratne*[9] and was therefore loath to interfere with administrative orders. *Nakkuda Ali* was a case from Ceylon involving the power of the Commissioner of Textiles to cancel any textile licence previously granted. The Privy Council held that the order cancelling the licence of a dealer was an entirely administrative order and not amenable to the writ jurisdiction of the court. But the Supreme Court of India freed itself from the shackles of *Nakkuda Ali* after Lord Reid delivered his judgment in *Ridge v Baldwin*.[10] In that case the House of Lords clearly held that where the action that was under challenge had affected a person's rights, the public body in question had to observe the principles of natural justice (or fairness) by informing the person of the charges against him and giving him a reasonable opportunity to be heard. If that was not done, the action taken would be held to be bad and unsustainable. *Ridge v Baldwin* has been hailed by Indian lawyers as the Magna Carta of writ jurisdiction. It has been cited in over 50 cases of the Indian Supreme Court, including *Maneka Gandhi v Union of India*[11] and *Olga Tellis v Bombay Municipal Corporation*,[12] which have gone on to become landmarks in their own right.

In the *Maneka Gandhi* case, the influence of the House of Lords was described in the following words by Justice Bhagwati (as he then was):

...in the epoch-making decision of the House of Lords in *Ridge v Baldwin* [citation omitted], which marks a turning point in the history of the development of the doctrine of natural justice, Lord Reid pointed out how the gloss of Lord Hewart, CJ, was based on a misunderstanding of the observations of Atkin LJ, and it went counter to the law laid down in the earlier decisions of the Court. Lord Reid observed: 'If Lord Hewart meant

---

[6] (1852) 3 HL Cas 759.   [7] [1964] AC 40.   [8] (2006) 2 SCC 1, 170, para 33.
[9] *Nakkuda Ali v Jayaratne* [1957] AC 66 (PC).   [10] n 7.   [11] (1978) 1 SCC 248.
[12] (1985) 3 SCC 545, 583, para 48.

that it is never enough that a body has a duty to determine what the rights of an individual should be, but that there must always be something more to impose on it a duty to act judicially, then that appears to me impossible to reconcile with the earlier authorities.' The learned Law Lord held that the duty to act judicially may arise from the very nature of the function intended to be performed and it need not be shown to be superadded. This decision broadened the area of application of the rules of natural justice and to borrow the words of Prof. Clar in his article on 'Natural Justice, Substance and Shadow' in Public Law Journal, 1975, restored light to an area 'benighted by the narrow conceptualism of the previous decade'. This development in the law had its parallel in India in *Associated Cement Companies Ltd v PN Sharma* (1965) 2 SCR 366, where this Court approvingly referred to the decision in *Ridge v Baldwin* . . .

In a catena of cases,[13] the Indian Supreme Court followed the lead of Sir Thomas Bingham MR (later Lord Bingham) in *R v Chief Constable of the Thames Valley Police Forces, ex p Cotton*[14] in rejecting the notion that a hearing can ever be a 'useless formality'.

A deep impact has also been made by the decision of the House of Lords in *Anisminic Ltd v Foreign Compensation Commission*[15] relating to errors of jurisdiction. A recent decision of the Indian Supreme Court, *Reliance Airport Developers (P) Ltd v Airport Authority of India*,[16] traces the impact of the *Anisminic* case and its progeny on Indian administrative law. Another case frequently relied upon by the Indian courts is *Padfield v Minister of Agriculture, Fisheries and Food*,[17] where it was held that if the Minister gave no reasons it meant that the Minister had no reasons to give, and his actions were, therefore, arbitrary. The principles that had fallen into disuse earlier were successfully rejuvenated in the *Padfield* case, which is now considered to be the last word on the subject. There are innumerable decisions of the Supreme Court of India following that decision.

Yet another case which has influenced the minds of Indian judges is *Council of Civil Service Unions v Minister for the Civil Service*,[18] where Lord Diplock said:

Judicial review had I think developed to a stage today when, without reiterating any analysis of the steps by which the development has come about, one can conveniently classify under three heads the grounds on which administrative action is subject to control by judicial review. The first ground I would call 'illegality', the second 'irrationality', and the third 'procedural impropriety'. That is not to say that further development on a case by case basis may not in course of time add further grounds.

The principle of reasonableness (or rationality) has become one of the most active and conspicuous among the doctrines to have vitalised administrative law in recent years.

---

[13] *State of Manipur v Y Token Singh* (2007) 5 SCC 65, 75, para 30; *Punjab National Bank v Manjit Singh* (2006) 8 SCC 647, 654, para 18; *Canara Bank v VK Awasthy* (2005) 6 SCC 321, 334, para 17; *MC Mehta v Union of India* (1999) 6 SCC 237, 246, para 22.
[14] [1990] IRLR 344.　　[15] [1969] AC 147.　　[16] (2006) 10 SCC 1, 59, paras 97–100.
[17] [1968] AC 997.　　[18] [1985] AC 374.

India has a written constitution with specific provisions for judicial review, unlike the United Kingdom, where the constitution as such is unwritten. Yet, in the realm of pure constitutional adjudication, the Supreme Court has relied on a judgment of the House of Lords to stress deference to the legislature. In *Gian Kaur v State of Punjab*,[19] a case concerning euthanasia and the right to die, the Indian Supreme Court referred to the decision of the House of Lords in *Airedale NHS Trust v Bland*[20] to hold that it would be reluctant to impinge on the field of legislative policy where complex matters such as the right to die were concerned.

The fact that the Indian Supreme Court often relies on decisions of the House of Lords, even when it has express statutory provisions on the basis of which to resolve the question presented, seems only to reinforce the thesis that such reliance is based as much on a feeling of fellowship and institutional comity as on necessity. Thus, in *CCE v Dunlop India Ltd*[21] the Indian court referred to the observations of Lord Diplock in *Cassell and Co Ltd v Broome*[22] on the importance of the lower courts observing the principle of *stare decisis* and following precedents, reinforcing Article 141 of the Indian Constitution which leaves no doubt that the decisions of the Indian Supreme Court are binding on all the courts in India.

Given the basic principles of the common law, it is hardly surprising that cases arising under commercial law have proved particularly receptive. The Indian Contract Act 1872 is a good example of a statute founded almost entirely on the common law. Decisions of the House of Lords such as *Derry v Peek*[23] formed the basis of the Indian analysis of the impact of fraud on a contract, with the Indian Supreme Court pointing to *Derry v Peek* as a 'leading English case' on the subject in decisions on contracts ranging from sales contracts[24] to lease agreements.[25] Similarly, *Dunlop Pneumatic Tyre v Selfridge and Co Ltd*[26] and *Bell v Lever Brothers Ltd*[27] are treated as the *loci classici* as far as privity of contract[28] and mistake[29] are concerned.

In company law, the landmark decision of the House of Lords in *Salomon v Salomon & Co*[30] is recognised by the Indian courts as a classic which establishes the basic proposition that a company has a distinct identity separate from its shareholders. The annals of the Indian Supreme Court are laden with references to the decision, variously describing it as 'well known'[31] and

---

[19] (1996) 2 SCC 648, 665, para 40.   [20] [1993] AC 789.
[21] (1985) 1 SCC 260, 268, para 6.   [22] [1972] AC 1027.   [23] (1889) 14 AC 337.
[24] *Ashok Leyland Ltd v State of Tamil Nadu* (2004) 3 SCC 1, 43, para 114.
[25] *Shrisht Dhawan (Smt) v Shaw Bros* (1992) 1 SCC 534, 553, para 20.
[26] [1915] AC 847.   [27] [1932] AC 161.
[28] See eg *MC Chacko v State Bank of Travancore* (1969) 2 SCC 343, 347, para 9.
[29] See eg *ITC Ltd v George Joseph Fernandes* (1989) 2 SCC 1, 23, paras 22–23, where *Bell v Lever Brothers Ltd* (n 27) was made the basis of the court's analysis, and the Indian court analysed the impact of that decision on the common law of England.
[30] [1897] AC 22.
[31] *CIT v National Finance Ltd* (1962) Supp (2) SCR 865, para 14; *State Trading Corp of India Ltd v CTO* (1964) 4 SCR 99, para 26.

'oft-quoted',[32] and refusing to deviate from it because it was a well-recognised principle of the common law.[33]

The impact of the House of Lords in the field of taxation is rather interesting. Its famous judgment in *Ramsay v IRC*,[34] which sets out the difference between tax avoidance and tax planning and sets to rest what was called the 'ghost' of *IRC v Duke Of Westminster*,[35] was relied upon heavily by the Indian Supreme Court in *McDowell & Co Ltd v CTO*,[36] which sought to draw the same distinction. The case is of particular interest because it demonstrates how closely the Indian Supreme Court tracked the development of this area of law by the House of Lords. In *McDowell* the Supreme Court referred to its previous decisions in *CIT v A Roman & Co*[37] and *CIT v BM Kharwar*,[38] which in turn had followed the *Westminster* case, and then went on to note subsequent developments in English law, including *IRC v Burmah Oil Co Ltd*,[39] and relied on the same to overrule impliedly the observations made in its previous decisions. Again, in *Mafatlal Industries Ltd v Union of India*,[40] a key case on unjust enrichment, it was noted that until 1992 the English position was that taxes paid under a mistake of law were not recoverable but that that position had been radically altered by the House of Lords in *Woolwich Building Society v IRC (No 2)*.[41]

This is not to say that the Indian Supreme Court has never departed from a decision of the House of Lords. Some of these departures can be attributed to the presence of a written constitution with an entrenched bill of rights, which expressly appoints the higher judiciary as its guardian,[42] and others to the peculiar socio-cultural conditions of India, which exert their own hydraulic pressures on the legal system. An example of the latter is the departure from the strict liability rule laid down by the House of Lords in *Rylands v Fletcher*[43] in favour of an absolute liability regime for hazardous industries. In *MC Mehta v Union of India*[44] the Supreme Court of India observed:

> ... We are certainly prepared to receive light from whatever source it comes, but we have to build our own jurisprudence and we cannot countenance an argument that, merely because the law in England does not recognize the rule of strict and absolute liability in cases of hazardous or inherently dangerous activities or the rule laid down in *Rylands v Fletcher* [citation omitted] as developed in England recognizes certain limitations and exceptions, we in India must hold back our hands and not venture to evolve a new

---

[32] *RL Arora v State of UP* (1964) 6 SCR 784, para 28; *Polestar Electronic (P) Ltd v Addl CST* (1978) 1 SCC 636, 654, para 11.

[33] *Tata Engineering and Locomotive Co Ltd v State of Bihar* (1964) 6 SCR 885, para 24.

[34] [1982] AC 300.   [35] [1936] AC 1, 19.

[36] (1985) 3 SCC 230, 236, paras 9–14.   [37] (1968) 1 SCR 10.

[38] (1969) 1 SCR 651.   [39] [1982] STC 30.

[40] (1997) 5 SCC 536, 597, paras 60–62.   [41] [1993] 1 AC 70.

[42] See for example *Kartar Singh v State of Punjab* (1994) 3 SCC 569, para 352, where the judiciary characterised itself as 'a sentinel on the qui vive' in respect of the Fundamental Rights enshrined in Part III of the Constitution.

[43] (1868) LR 3 HL 330.   [44] (1987) 1 SCC 395, 419, para 31.

principle of liability since English courts have not done so. We have to develop our own law and if we find that it is necessary to construct a new principle of liability to deal with an unusual situation which has arisen and which is likely to arise in future on account of hazardous or inherently dangerous industries which are concomitant to an industrial economy, there is no reason why we should hesitate to evolve such principle of liability merely because it has not been so done in England.

An example of the impact of entrenched judicial review is the Indian Court's acceptance of the doctrine of proportionality by reference to the House of Lords decision in *R v Secretary of State for the Home Department, ex p Daly*,[45] while the House of Lords itself remains cautious about accepting proportionality as a standard of review as a matter of English law (as opposed to the standard to be applied with respect to the European Convention on Human Rights).[46]

For years, in India as in the United Kingdom, the principle enunciated in *Associated Provincial Picture Houses v Wednesbury Corporation*[47] held the field. However, even as the House of Lords began to make cautious overtures towards the doctrine of proportionality in cases such as *Ex p Daly*, the Indian Supreme Court wholeheartedly adopted the doctrine. In cases such as *Commissioner of Police v Sayed Hussain*[48] (relating to the removal of a police officer from service), *State of MP v Hazarilal*[49] (on disproportionate criminal punishments), *Tri Oat Estate v UT Chandigarh*[50] (on the proportionality of forfeiture of the entire deposit for a minor infraction), *Moni Shankar v Union of India*,[51] and *Jitendra Kumar v State of Haryana*[52] (on the standard of review applicable with respect to the Government's appointment of officers), the Supreme Court has applied proportionality as a standard of review, albeit as an alternative standard of review, thereby advancing the doctrine further than the House of Lords itself is currently willing to do.

As an aside, it is a curious coincidence that in *R v Secretary of State for the Home Department, ex p Brind*,[53] the case in which the House of Lords refused to apply the doctrine of proportionality directly in domestic law, counsel for the appellants cited an Indian Supreme Court decision, *Ranjit Thakur v Union of India*,[54] in support of his argument that the proper standard of review was proportionality. *Thakur's* case in turn cited certain observations of Lord Diplock in *Council of Civil Service Unions v Minister for the Civil Service*[55] and then applied proportionality *stricto sensu*.

In a lecture delivered at the Victoria University, Wellington,[56] the Supreme Court of India was described by Lord Cooke of Thorndon, a former President of

---

[45] [2001] 2 AC 532.
[46] See eg *Brind v Secretary of State for the Home Department* [1991] 1 AC 696.
[47] [1948] 1 KB 223.
[48] (2003) 3 SCC 173, 176, paras 12–14.   [49] (2008) 3 SCC 273, 277, paras 11–15.
[50] (2002) 2 SCC 130, 146, paras 40–53.   [51] (2008) 3 SCC 484, 492, paras 17–18.
[52] (2002) 2 SCC 161, 183, paras 62–3.   [53] [1991] 1 AC 696.
[54] (1987) 4 SCC 611, paras 25–6.   [55] [1985] AC 374.
[56] 'Final Appeal Courts: Some Comparisons', December 2001.

the New Zealand Court of Appeal who after retirement sat not infrequently in both the Judicial Committee of the Privy Council and in the House of Lords, as 'probably the most constructive human rights court in the world'. He was appreciative of the manner in which the Supreme Court of India had become a vigilant defender of democracy, democratic values, and constitutionalism.

The influence of India's Supreme Court on the House of Lords

In India new content is being provided to criminal justice, resulting in prison reforms and the humanitarian treatment of prisoners and of people held on remand. The doctrine of equality has been employed to provide equal pay for equal work. Ecology, public health, and the environment are all now receiving attention from the courts. The rights of prisoners and of persons who have been arrested, and awards of compensation in cases of violation of fundamental rights, have been provided with a firmer jurisprudential base. Judicial activism has thus been used to search for the spirit of the law.[57] These developments have in turn had their impact on the House of Lords.

The House of Lords has in many cases referred to, and relied upon, judgments of the Supreme Court of India. For example, in *R (Amin) v Secretary of State for the Home Department*,[58] a case relating to a custodial death, Lord Bingham of Cornhill referred to *Nilabati Behera v State of Orissa*,[59] which placed a duty of care on police and prison authorities to protect the life of the inmate. Similarly, in *Reynolds v Times Newspapers Ltd*,[60] Lord Nicholls of Birkenhead found it useful to refer to the Indian decision in *Rajagopal (R) v State of Tamil Nadu*[61] in resolving the knotty issue of defamation with respect to public officials. On points of judicial practice and precedent the House of Lords has again had occasion to consider the rulings of the Indian Supreme Court. In *Re Spectrum Plus Ltd*[62] Lord Nicholls of Birkenhead discussed Indian precedents such as *Golak Nath v State of Punjab*,[63] *India Cement Ltd v State of Tamil Nadu*,[64] and *Orissa Cement Ltd v State of Orissa*[65] before coming to the conclusion that the House of Lords too had the power to overrule prospectively its previous decisions when exceptional circumstances so required.

After the judicial functions of the House of Lords have been transferred to the Supreme Court of the United Kingdom, pursuant to the Constitutional Reform Act 2005, the possibility of the Supreme Court of United Kingdom looking eastwards on issues concerning constitutional interpretation may become even more pronounced.

---

[57] See with advantage V Iyer, 'The Supreme Court of India' in B Dickson (ed), *Judicial Activism in Common Law Supreme Courts* (Oxford: OUP, 2007) 127ff.
[58] [2004] 1 AC 653, para 30.   [59] (1993) 2 SCC 746, 767.   [60] [2001] 2 AC 127, 199.
[61] (1994) 6 SCC 632, 650.   [62] [2005] 2 AC 680, 693–4, para 20.
[63] (1967) 2 SCR 762.   [64] (1990) 1 SCC 12.   [65] (1991) 2 SCR 105, 181.

20

Reflections from the New Commonwealth

Fred Phillips

Viewed from the New Commonwealth, the Appellate Committee of the House of Lords[1] was always considered a powerful, if amorphous, creation. The Judicial Committee of the Privy Council[2] was less so. Early in our legal life we learn that the judiciary should be 'a place apart' from the legislature and the executive. Our people have always found it inconceivable that the highest English tribunal, over which the Lord Chancellor presided, should physically have been located in the highest legislative chamber. That all the members of the House of Lords, including the presiding judge, could be permitted to take part in debates of the House was beyond comprehension. But that he should also be a senior member of the Cabinet, heading a Department of the Government, has boggled the mind. Little wonder that Lord Phillips of Worth Matravers, the then newly appointed Lord Chief Justice and Head of the Judiciary, who under the Constitutional Reform Act of 2005 assumed so many of the previous functions of the Lord Chancellor, must have been relieved to state on his formal assumption of duties in April 2006 that 'the reforms give transparent effect to the doctrine of the separation of powers'.

The two courts have sometimes been criticised by practitioners and academics—a matter to be endured by all such institutions, particularly courts of last resort. For instance, the Board's decision in *Ong Ah Chuan v Public Prosecutor*,[3] a Singapore drug case, was condemned by David Pannick, QC, a distinguished English practitioner.[4] Also, while the Privy Council was still Canada's final court, Professor Frank Scott, an erudite Canadian academic, found much fault with what he considered an erroneous tendency on the part of the Privy Council to give undue pre-eminence to the provinces over the federal government in issues relating to the distribution of powers under the British North

---

[1] The House of Lords Appellate Committee will in this chapter be variously referred to as 'the Lords', 'the House of Lords', 'the Judicial House', or 'the Judicial Council'.

[2] The Judicial Committee of the Privy Council will be referred to as 'the Privy Council', 'the Judicial Committee', or simply 'the Board'.

[3] [1981] AC 648.

[4] D Pannick, *Judicial Review of the Death Penalty* (London: Duckworth, 1982) 131.

America Act 1867.[5] Generally, he thought, the Privy Council misunderstood the nature of federation.

Despite the criticisms and imperfections, it cannot be disputed that the courts made an invaluable contribution to the common law jurisprudence in the New Commonwealth. Indeed, it has been observed that even after many of the countries have severed their judicial links with the Board, the judgments of the Privy Council (and *a fortiori* those of the Lords) have continued to be treated with respect and often quoted with approval. By coincidence, as this chapter was being drafted in June 2007, its author received from a judicial friend a judgment delivered in April 2007 by the Constitutional Court of Malawi[6] in which that court not only followed, but also extended, the recent decisions of the Privy Council in *R v Hughes* (a St Lucia case)[7] and *Reyes v R* (a Belize case)[8] in both of which the mandatory sentence of death was held to be invalid and unconstitutional to the extent of its mandatoriness, the relevant Malawi provision being couched in identical terms to the St Lucia and Belize provisions.

There can be no dispute that it is the common law that binds us together. A cursory assessment of the legal system under which the countries are governed shows that the one common denominator is the fact that it was the statutes that operated in England at specific times as well as the English common law and the doctrines of equity that the many jurisdictions took with them at the time of independence. In some territories the common law replaced the previous system of law by statute, as in the cases of British Guiana (now Guyana) and St Lucia—their previous systems being Roman-Dutch and French respectively. The laws of Mauritius, too, were inspired by English law and French law, and specifically by Acts of the Westminster Parliament. It is to be noted that independence came to all these countries over a 30-year period from the middle of the twentieth century and that between 1950 and 1980 the Privy Council adopted a conservative attitude in interpreting the provisions in the Constitutions—particularly the human rights provisions.

By 1980 the court had clearly taken notice of international bodies and instruments such as the European Court of Human Rights, the United Nations Covenant on Civil and Political Rights, and the Inter-American Commission on Human Rights, all of which were taking a liberal and generous approach to the interpretation of human rights. The Board in *Minister of Home Affairs v Fisher* had already signalled its intention to change course as far as constitutional interpretation was concerned, Lord Wilberforce stating that the rights were 'greatly influenced by the European Convention...which was signed and ratified by the United Kingdom...It was in turn influenced by the United Nations Declaration of Human Rights of 1948. These antecedents...call for a generous interpretation avoiding

---

[5] F Scott, *Essays on the Constitution* (Toronto: University of Toronto Press, 1977) 106.
[6] *Francis Kafantayene v AG*, Constitutional Court Case No 12 of 2005, decided 27 April 2007.
[7] [2002] 2 AC 259.   [8] [2002] 2 AC 235.

what has been called "the austerity of tabulated legalism" suitable to give to individuals the full measure of the fundamental rights and freedoms.'[9] It was in this context that the Privy Council discarded its conservative stance.

In the meantime, more and more countries were becoming independent and, often after a short period, severing their links with the Privy Council. Some of them created their own local final courts of appeal. Some joined final regional courts of appeal. The Caribbean, with a number of local appeal courts, continued to have the Privy Council as its final court, although the Guyana Court of Appeal was from 1980 that country's final court. It is a pity that the Privy Council idea of a peripatetic court now developing was not adopted in 1966 when Lord Chancellor Gardiner first suggested it in India.

One of the last jurisdictions eventually to establish a regional court was CARICOM, which in April 2005 launched the CCJ[10] (Caribbean Court of Justice). This forum was inaugurated as a multi-national tribunal with an original jurisdiction as an international entity, as well as an appellate jurisdiction as a superior Court of Record in a municipal situation when dealing with matters from the appeal courts of the region. The main mission of the court is stated to be 'to promote the development of a Caribbean jurisprudence, a goal which Caribbean courts are best equipped to pursue'. In the court's first public statement of its objectives, it promised that in promoting that jurisprudence it would 'naturally consider very carefully and respectfully the opinions of final courts of other Commonwealth countries and particularly the judgments of the Judicial Committee of the Privy Council which determine the law of those Caribbean States that accept the Judicial Committee as their final appellate court'.[11]

Such is the hope of the regional court in its proposed relationship with the Board. It is therefore relevant in this chapter particularly to address in some depth the stability of the judicial decisions emanating from the Board, bearing in mind that a court of last resort is not expected to reverse itself lightly. But there have been justifiable complaints on this score, both from the Privy Council itself[12] and from senior Caribbean judges.[13] The plea is for legal certainty and stability, without which credibility in the court of last resort is bound to be compromised. There must clearly be a balance between certainty and stability on the one hand and correctness on the other. That is why one understands that it was necessary for the House of Lords in 1966 to issue a Practice Statement under which it

---

[9] [1980] AC 319, 328G.

[10] See Duke Pollard's most instructive volume *The Caribbean Court of Justice: Closing the Circle of Independence* (Kingston, Jamaica: Caribbean Law Publishing Co, 2004). The writer of that book is currently a judge of the Caribbean Court of Justice.

[11] See para 18 of the Joint Judgment of the President of the CCJ and Saunders J in the *Joseph and Boyce* case—CCJ Appeal No CV 2 of 2005.

[12] One of the most comprehensive dissents, centred mainly on the doctrine of *stare decisis*, was that of Lord Hoffmann in *Lewis v AG of Jamaica* [2001] 2 AC 50, 87.

[13] See the comments of Saunders JA in *R v Hughes* (2001) 60 WIR 156 196. See also an admirable article by D O'Brien, 'The Privy Council overrules itself—again!' [2008] PL 28.

would no longer be bound by its own decisions.[14] Happily, since 1966 the House has only in the most exceptional circumstances re-opened its previous decisions— a policy the Board would do well to emulate.

The House will, however, depart from a previous decision where such a decision is based on the ground of public policy—the principle being that public policy is not immutable and is liable to change over time. The classic example of such a case was the policy of granting immunity from suit to advocates for negligence committed in the conduct of litigation. In a 1967[15] decision the Lords decided to maintain the immunity, but Lord Reid observed that public policy was not immutable and questioned the continued justification for such a concession. When a similar application reached the Lords in 1978[16] the court again upheld the immunity, which was then said to be an exception to the principle that a professional was under a special duty to exercise care and skill, and that no further concession was to be granted than was necessary for the due administration of justice. When the matter was referred to the Lords a third time, in the case of *Arthur JS Hall & Co v Simons*,[17] they held that the immunity should be abolished.

The reluctance to depart from previous decisions was underscored in *R v Kansal (No 2)*,[18] in which the House decided not to depart from a previous decision[19] even though three of the panel of five who had decided the previous case considered the judgment to be erroneous. In coming to that conclusion the court took to heart the dissent of Lord Hoffmann in the Privy Council case of *Lewis v Attorney General of Jamaica*[20]—a case in which the majority refused to follow their own decisions in three recent death penalty cases, which led Lord Hoffmann in his dissent to warn of the grave consequences that could arise if the power to overrule past decisions was exercised too liberally.

By the middle of the last century the Privy Council had imposed upon itself a degree of restraint. In a 1950 case before the Board from Swaziland,[21] Lord Porter remarked, on the question of respecting past decisions, that even though that body did not, like the House of Lords, have a formal code restraining reversal, the Board would re-open a decision on a given state of facts only with the greatest hesitation, and that an essential element to be considered was whether fresh material not previously communicated or fully presented to the original tribunal had been brought to light.

---

[14] Practice Statement (Judicial Precedent) [1966] 1 WLR 1234. See the clear dicta by Lord Wilberforce on precedent in the House of Lords in the case of *Fitzleet Estates Ltd v Cherry* [1977] 1 WLR 1345, 1349C–E. See too ch 9 in this volume.

[15] *Rondel v Worsley* [1969] 1 AC 191.   [16] *Saif Ali v Sydney Mitchell* [1980] AC 198.

[17] *Arthur JS Hall v Simons* [2002] 1 AC 615.

[18] [2002] 2 AC 69. See a very stimulating commentary on this case in BV Harris, 'Final Appellate Courts Overruling their Own "Wrong" Precedents: The Ongoing Search for Principle' (2002) 118 LQR 408.

[19] *R v Lambert* [2002] 2 AC 545.   [20] [2001] 2 AC 50.

[21] *Nkambule v R* [1950] AC 379, 397.

For the House of Lords, the statements made by Lord Lloyd of Berwick in the *Kansal* case[22] in support of his view that *Lambert* should not be overruled is very much in keeping with the reserve conveyed in Lord Porter's speech referred to in the preceding paragraph. Here is Lord Lloyd's magnanimous pronouncement as to the action to be taken:

> The reasoning in *Lambert* represents a possible view. Of that there can be no doubt. It has not been shown to be unworkable. In my view it should be followed. If we were to depart from *Lambert* today, who is to say that a differently constituted Appellate Committee, presented with fresh arguments, might not depart from our decision tomorrow?

For Lord Hope, *contra*, although he felt that the House should try to achieve consistency, 'looking at the wider picture' he was of the opinion that 'in the present context correction is more desirable than consistency'.[23]

Up to 1950 the Board endeavoured to achieve consensus in reaching its decisions. It did this no doubt on the basis that, while it was 'humbly advising' the Sovereign, the Sovereign was not to be faced with multiple opinions. By 1990, however, dissents seemed more frequent—a development that had the effect of making the law uncertain. Such uncertainty heightened when senior members of the Board issued discordant dicta. In *de Freitas v Benny*, Lord Diplock on the Board's behalf declared: 'Mercy is not the subject of legal rights. It begins where legal rights end.'[24] Later, in *Lewis*, Lord Slynn contradicted that dictum this way: 'Although on the merits there is no legal right to mercy, there is not the clear-cut distinction as to procedural matters between mercy and legal rights which Lord Diplock's aphorism...might indicate.'[25] In *Riley*[26] Lord Bridge averred that no delay, however protracted, could provide ground for holding an execution for murder unconstitutional as being a contravention of the constitutional provision against cruel and inhuman punishment or treatment. This view was subjected to a scathing dissent by Lords Scarman and Brightman which won the day by later being accepted by the Board in the now famous decision of *Pratt and Morgan v Attorney General of Jamaica*[27]—a case which reached the Privy Council on appeal from Jamaica requesting commutation of sentences of death to sentences of life imprisonment on grounds that the carrying out of death sentences after unconscionable delay constituted a contravention of the constitutional provision against inhuman or degrading punishment. Twenty-three men convicted of murder had been kept on death row for more than 10 years and 82 for between five and 10 years. The Board allowed the appeal and ruled that where execution was to take place more than five years after sentence there would be strong grounds for believing that the delay was such as to constitute inhuman or degrading punishment.

Recent dissents and reversals in appeals in death penalty cases from the Caribbean to the Privy Council have had an unsettling effect on this branch of

---

[22] [2002] AC 69, 93.   [23] ibid, 103.   [24] [1976] AC 239, 247G.
[25] *Lewis v AG of Jamaica* [2001] 2 AC 50, 70A.
[26] *Riley v AG of Jamaica* [1983] 1 AC 719.   [27] [1994] 2 AC 1.

the law—a situation that has caused unease even in the ranks of the membership of the Board. In this connection reference can be made to a lengthy dissent by Lord Hoffmann in the case of *Lewis v Attorney General of Jamaica*,[28] in the course of which the noble Lord referred with approval to the practice in the US Supreme Court in matters of *stare decisis*. It was pointed out that the Supreme Court had never considered itself bound by precedent and that accordingly it was prepared in *Brown v Board of Education*[29] to overrule its previous decision that racial segregation was lawful. However, in another case the Supreme Court examined the grounds upon which it would depart from precedent and decided *not* to overrule *Roe v Wade*.[30] In so doing the majority made use of the following statement: 'No judicial system could do society's work if it eyed each issue afresh in every case that raised it ... Indeed the very concept of the rule of law underlying our own Constitution requires such continuity over time that a respect for precedent is, by definition, indispensable.'[31] The grounds on which a court of last resort should normally depart from precedent, overruling its own previous decisions, are as valid in 2009 as they were when *Roe v Wade* was decided over 35 years ago.

Unfortunately the political twists of fortune in the United States Supreme Court in recent years brought into being a trend which is frightening in its implications. When President Bush appointed to the Supreme Court in quick succession two ultra-right-wing judges in the persons of Chief Justice John Roberts and Justice Samuel Alito, pundits predicted that there would be a revolution in the Court. That revolution was realised 'with breathtaking impatience'—according to Ronald Dworkin, who also described it as 'Jacobin in its disdain for tradition and precedent'.[32] It has been widely seen in the New Commonwealth as a move in the wrong direction, and one can only hope that such wanton tampering with precedent will not recur elsewhere. The two newly appointed judges were joining two existing equally right-wing justices—Antonin Scalia and Clarence Thomas. Those four have more often than not been supported by the swing vote of Justice Kennedy.

Dworkin describes the situation as 'an unbreakable phalanx bent on remaking constitutional law by overruling, most often by stealth, the central constitutional doctrines that generations of past justices, conservative as well as liberal, had constructed'. Justice Stephen Breyer was as a result to exclaim from the Bench: 'It is not often in the law that so few have so quickly changed so much.'

There have in the last two years been a number of cases in the Supreme Court with the same 5:4 majority and their decisions, sadly, have clearly been actuated not by a genuine desire to do right by the litigants, but rather by partisan and

---

[28] [2001] 2 AC 50, 87.   [29] 347 US 483 (1954).   [30] 410 US 113 (1973).
[31] *Per* O'Connor, Kennedy, and Souter JJ in *Planned Parenthood of Southeastern Pennsylvania v Casey* 505 US 833, 854 (1992).
[32] *New York Review of Books*, vol 54, no 14, 27 September 2007.

other motives. This point has been forcefully illustrated by Ronald Dworkin, who gives an admirable assessment of the cases as follows:

In their Senate confirmation hearings Roberts and Alito both declared their reverence for precedent; they might be reluctant openly to admit that they deceived the Senate and the people. It is therefore not absurd to suppose that this series of odd decisions covertly overruling important precedents is part of a strategy to create the right conditions for overruling them explicitly later. Roberts was careful to qualify his promise to senators not to overrule precedents by allowing that he might have to reconsider a precedent when its doctrinal bases . . . had been eroded by subsequent developments. He has not been a judge for long; his main training and experience is as a litigator, and the strategy I describe is familiar to that craft.[33]

Skilled corporate litigators think ahead like pool players: they argue for their clients on narrow grounds hoping for incremental victories that turn into much bigger ones later. Perhaps Roberts will keep his word and try in future years to build a new consensus that more faithfully reflects the Court's traditions. But I suspect that his Senate testimony was actually a coded script for the continuing subversion of the American constitution. The worst is yet to come.

One can only express the earnest hope that that 'worst' will not materialise; but such judicial behaviour must give cause for pause to other judiciaries around the world.

In the meantime the judges in the highest courts of the New Commonwealth must look to the day when they will, true to the solemn oaths they have taken, fulfil their mission of certainty, integrity, and impartiality according to law. They accept that they owe a special debt of gratitude to the Judicial Committee of the Privy Council and will in time wish to be remembered with the 'greats' of that Board.

Indeed, there are already clear indications that New Commonwealth judges are demonstrating that they are capable of rising to that occasion. This has been amply illustrated by the judges of the Caribbean Court of Justice (inaugurated in 2005) who at a very early stage have shown their mettle in judicial adjudication and law-making on a matter of great public importance.[34] The court has proven that it is a worthy successor to the Privy Council for those Caribbean states who see the wisdom in having their final appeals determined by a court sitting in the Caribbean, staffed by judges in the Caribbean. The new Supreme Court of the United Kingdom should be as ready to listen to this new voice as the Privy Council was to the appeal courts of the region before the new court came into being in the Caribbean. The rapid changes taking place throughout the world today demand common approaches by the modern judiciary in tackling similar problems and it behoves all courts of last resort to work together towards that end.

---

[33] ibid.

[34] See the judgment of the CCJ in the case of *Joseph and Boyce v AG of Barbados,* CCJ Appeal No 2 CV2 of 2006.

21

A Transatlantic Comparison

*Tom Zwart** *

Introduction

This contribution approaches the role of the Appellate Committee from a US perspective. Since the activities of the House of Lords and the US Supreme Court cover a vast area, the focus of this contribution will be on their operating systems, ie the conditions that directly determine the operation of both courts vis-à-vis the political branches in their jurisdiction.

To this end the case law of both institutions in the area of standing law will be described, followed by an analysis of the scope of review of acts of administrative agencies. After the difficulties that both courts face in handling the concept of non-justiciablity have been set out, the apparent contrast between the review of the constitutionality of legislation, which dominates the US constitutional scene, and the sovereignty of Parliament, which characterises the British system, will be discussed. Finally, some concluding observations will be made.

Standing

Under federal US law, a claimant needs to pass a three-pronged test in order to have standing.[1] First, he must have suffered an 'injury in fact', ie an invasion of a legally protected interest. This invasion must be concrete and particularised, and actual or imminent rather than conjectural or hypothetical. Second, there must be a causal connection between the injury and the conduct complained of. This means that the injury has to be fairly traceable to the challenged action of the defendant and should not be the result of the independent action of some third

* I am indebted to Gordon Anthony for his invaluable comments and insights on earlier drafts, Peter Morris for his very helpful suggestions, and David Wills, the Squire Law Librarian, and Peter Zawada, the Deputy Squire Librarian, Faculty of Law, University of Cambridge, for their trademark hospitality and effective assistance.
[1] Based on the majority opinion of Justice Scalia in *Lujan v Defenders of Wildlife* 504 US 555 (1992), 560–1.

party not before the court. Third, it must be likely, as opposed to merely speculative, that the injury will be redressed by a favourable decision by the court. US standing law is therefore close to the private interest model, which regards injury to body, property, or reputation as a prerequisite for standing. Overall, the Court has kept out those who could not claim to have a personal interest in the outcome.

Thus, in *Sierra Club v Morton*, the Sierra Club, an organisation with a special interest in the conservation of the national heritage of the US, had challenged the issuance of permits by federal officials for the development of a Walt Disney ski-resort in the Mineral King Valley of the Sequoia National Forest.[2] The Court acknowledged that environmental harm may constitute injury in fact. But it concluded that the Sierra Club lacked standing, because it had not claimed that any of its members had ever used Mineral King Valley. The Sierra Club had therefore failed to allege that it or its members would be affected in any of their activities by the proposed development and had not therefore suffered any injury. Justice White, who belonged to the majority rejecting the claim, is alleged to have said off the record:[3] 'Why didn't the Sierra Club have one goddamn member walk through the park and then there would have been standing to sue.' This decision seems very similar to that in *Rose Theatre Trust*,[4] which, of course, enjoyed a frosty reception in light of the judgment of the House of Lords in the *Fleet Street Casuals* case.[5]

The approach to standing in the US, where it is still very much a threshold issue,[6] contrasts sharply with the public interest approach that underlies English law. This approach is exemplified by the judgment handed down by the House of Lords in the *Fleet Street Casuals* case, which remains key to standing law in England & Wales.[7] In *Fleet Street Casuals* their Lordships emphasised that the subject matter of his application may provide an applicant with standing.[8] Standing should not, therefore, be regarded as a threshold issue isolated from the merits of the case. Their Lordships made clear that the applicant will have standing if he can make out a prima facie case that the respondent authority has committed an illegality,[9] or at least an illegality of sufficient gravity.[10]

---

[2] 405 US 727 (1972).

[3] R Woodward and S Armstrong, *The Brethren, Inside the Supreme Court* (New York: Avon, 1979) 164.

[4] *R v Secretary of State for the Environment, ex p Rose Theatre Trust Co* [1990] 1 QB 504.

[5] *R v Inland Revenue Comrs, ex p National Federation of Self-Employed and Small Businesses Ltd* [1982] AC 617.

[6] See the majority opinion of Justice Scalia in *Steel Co v Citizens for a Better Environment* 523 US 83 (1998), 88.

[7] Considering the broad approach adopted by the European Commission of Human Rights and the European Court of Human Rights regarding the 'victim' requirement, there would be no need for the English courts to resort to a more restrictive standing concept under the HRA. See T Zwart, *The Admissibility of Human Rights Petitions, The Case Law of the European Commission of Human Rights and the Human Rights Committee* (The Hague: Martinus Nijhofff, 1994) 50–87, and *R (Rusbridger) v AG* [2004] 1 AC 357, 367 *per* Lord Steyn.

[8] [1982] AC 617, 648 *per* Lord Scarman.

[9] ibid, 644 *per* Lord Diplock; 654–5 *per* Lord Scarman.

[10] ibid, 633 *per* Lord Wilberforce; 647 *per* Lord Fraser of Tullybelton; 662 *per* Lord Roskill.

Through their decision their Lordships reaffirmed the idea that injustices should be redressed regardless of who brings the action. It is this element to which Lord Diplock referred when he made the following remark:[11]

It would, in my view, be a grave lacuna in our system of public law if a pressure group, like the federation, or even a single public-spirited taxpayer, were prevented by outdated technical rules of locus standi from bringing the matter to the attention of the court to vindicate the rule of law and get the unlawful conduct stopped.

This judgment has clearly paved the way for citizen suits,[12] while standing is no longer an issue which courts need to address separately.[13]

The contrast between the American and English approaches to standing is perhaps surprising considering the fact that both are rooted in the early English case law regarding the prerogative writs, which had a distinctive public interest flavour. While applying for prerogative writs claimants who were motivated by the public interest have been remarkably successful, especially with regard to certiorari and prohibition. Thus, courts have held that while only 'persons aggrieved' may assume that the writ will be issued, it belongs to the discretion of the courts to also accept cases brought by persons who could not claim a particular grievance of their own.[14] Consequently, most cases brought by persons lacking a personal grievance have been deemed admissible.[15] In so doing, the courts have given the impression that that they attached much more value to being informed about an excess of jurisdiction than to the status of the person who raised the issue. This is exemplified by the judgment handed down by the Court of Common Pleas in *Worthington v Jeffries*,[16] which reads like a copy of the judgment in the *Fleet Street Casuals* case.

After the establishment of the Republic, American judges left the public interest path followed by English judges with regard to prerogative writs.[17] For example, in *Williams v Hagood* the plaintiff was denied standing because he had

---

[11] ibid, 644; see also Lord Woolf in 'Droit Public—English Style' [1995] PL 57, 62.

[12] P Cane, *Administrative Law* (Oxford: Clarendon Press, 4th edn 2004) 69.

[13] ibid, 67; thus, in *R (Campaign for Nuclear Disarmament) v Prime Minister* [2002] EWHC 2777 (QB), para 48, the court held that some suggested deficiency in CND's interest in the matter should not keep it from rendering judgment.

[14] *Forster v Forster and Berridge* (1863) 4 B&S 187, 199; *Chambers v Green* (1875) LR 20 Eq 552, 554–5; *R v Nicholson* [1899] 2 QB 455, 470–1; *R v Williams, ex p Phillips* [1914] 1 KB 608, 613; *R v Thames Magistrates' Court, ex p Greenbaum* (1955) 55 LGR 129, 135.

[15] *R v Grove* (1893) 57 JP 454, 456 *per* Lord Coleridge CJ; *R v Newborough* (1869) LR 4 QB 585, 589; *R v Stafford Justices, ex p Stafford Corporation* [1940] 2 KB 33, 43; *De Haber v Queen of Portugal* (1851) 17 QB 196, 214 *per* Lord Campbell CJ; *Mayor of London v Cox* (1867) LR 2 HL 239, 279; *Cooke v Gill* (1873) LR 8 CP 107, 114–15 *per* Bovill CJ; *Quartly v Timmins* (1874) LR 9 CP 416, 417 *per* Keating J; *Ellis v Fleming* (1875–76) LR 1 CPD 237, 514 *per* Brett J; *Farquharson v Morgan* [1894] 1 QB 552, 556 *per* Lord Halsbury; *R v Comptroller-General of Patents and Designs* [1953] 2 WLR 760, 764 *per* Lord Goddard CJ; *R v Greater London Council, ex p Blackburn* [1976] 1 WLR 550, 559 *per* Lord Denning MR.

[16] (1875) LR 10 CP 379.

[17] A Woolhandler and C Nelson, 'Does History Defeat Standing Doctrine?' (2003–4) 102 Mich L Rev 689, 709.

failed to claim that he had been or would be injured by the challenged action.[18] According to the court, the injury required was a wrong which directly resulted in the violation of a legal right. Consequently, underlying US standing law has traditionally been the need to show private injury as a prerequisite for litigation.[19] There are no indications that the Supreme Court will move closer towards the public interest model in the near future. On the contrary, during the past few decades the private law approach underlying US standing law has even been reinforced. Justice Scalia, who before being appointed to the Supreme Court bench warned that too low a standing barrier will be harmful to the separation of powers,[20] in particular has had a major impact on the Court's standing law, as exemplified by his majority opinion in *Lujan*.[21]

Scope of review

Both in American and English administrative law the scope of review used by the courts when reviewing administrative acts has emerged as a very important topic.

In the US, the decision in *Chevron v Natural Resources Defense Council* stands for the deference courts owe to administrative agencies.[22] Although the case deals with the scope of review of agencies' interpretations of Acts of Congress rather than administrative acts in individual cases, similar considerations apply. Not surprisingly, therefore, comparisons have been made between the *Chevron* decision and English case law on the deference owed to the decision-maker in individual cases.[23]

As is the case in Britain, courts in the US often have to deal with statutes the language of which is ambiguous. Until 1984 the courts used to determine on a statute-by-statute basis how to deal with these ambiguities. If the court felt that the ambiguity was accidental, in the sense that Congress had aimed at a particular result but had failed to express this, the court would consider itself best suited to clarify the issue. However, if the court came to the conclusion that the ambiguity was intentional, in the sense that Congress had avoided having to make a political choice by delegating to the agency, it would show deference towards the agency interpretation.

The Supreme Court changed course in *Chevron*. The case concerned rules issued by the Environmental Protection Agency (hereafter 'EPA') under the Clean Air Act. The Carter EPA had promulgated very strict regulations which were environmentally friendly, but did not go down very well with the business

---

[18] 98 US 72 (1878).   [19] Woolhandler and Nelson (n 17) 717–18.
[20] A Scalia, 'The Doctrine of Standing as an Essential Element of the Separation of Powers' (1983) 17 Suffolk UL Rev 881.
[21] *Lujan v Defenders of Wildlife* 504 US 555 (1992).   [22] 467 US 837 (1984).
[23] P Craig, 'Jurisdiction, Judicial Control, and Agency Autonomy' in I Loveland (ed), *A Special Relationship: American Influences on Public Law in the UK* (Oxford: OUP, 1995) 174; P Craig, *Administrative Law* (Oxford: OUP, 5th edn 2003) 513–16.

community. When the Reagan Administration came into office, the EPA replaced the existing rules by regulations which gave companies more leeway. Not surprisingly, these rules were then challenged by the National Resources Defense Council, an environmental organisation. Since these different sets of rules were rooted in an interpretation of the same statutory language, the question before the Supreme Court was how courts should treat agency interpretations of Acts of Congress. Should judges rely upon their own construction of the statute or should they respect the agency's interpretation?

The Supreme Court applied a two-step analysis which became known as the '*Chevron* two-step'. The first question is whether Congress has directly addressed the precise question. If the intent of Congress is clear, the agency and the court have to defer to the position of Congress, they cannot amend its views. If the court determines that Congress has not directly addressed the precise question, by being silent or ambiguous, the answer of the agency will be decisive. In such a case, a court may not substitute its own construction of a statutory provision for a reasonable interpretation made by the agency.

By holding in *Chevron* that courts should ordinarily yield to the agencies' interpretations of the statutes they administer, unless their construction was unreasonable, the court has replaced the statute-by-statute evaluation with an across-the-board presumption that, in the case of ambiguity, agency discretion is intended.[24] Courts must defer to the agencies out of respect for Congress's wish to entrust regulatory responsibility to agencies and to ensure that policy choices, which are a necessary element of interpreting statutes, are being made by persons answerable to the political branches rather than unelected judges. According to the Supreme Court in *Chevron*, it is the constitutional duty of the court to defer to agency interpretation of law, despite the fact that under that same Constitution it is the responsibility of the judicial branch to interpret the law.[25] Not surprisingly, *Chevron* has signalled a substantial increase in agency discretion to make policy through statutory interpretation.[26] However, although the *Chevron* position is still an important part of US administrative law, it appears to be losing some of its vigour. Two developments in particular have contributed to this watering-down.

First, courts do not always play by the *Chevron* book. Not surprisingly, judges have been unable to resist the temptation to try to establish the meaning of a provision in order to avoid having to go to step two. Thus, in *INS v Cardoza-Foncesca* Justice Stevens for the court's majority concluded that the agency's view could not pass *Chevron*'s first step, because Congress had directly spoken to the issue.[27] In reaching this conclusion Justice Stevens did not only rely on the

---

[24] A Scalia, 'Judicial Deference to Administrative Interpretations of Law' (1989) 39 Duke LJ 511, 516.

[25] *Marbury v Madison* 5 US (1 Cranch) 137 (1803), 177.

[26] CR Sunstein, '*Chevron* Step Zero' (2006) 92 Va L Rev 187, 190.

[27] 480 US 421 (1987), 446–8.

statutory language, but also on its legislative history.[28] This approach was criticised by Justice Scalia, who filed a concurring opinion. According to Justice Scalia, when a statute has a plain meaning courts should simply accept that meaning. When a statute does not have a plain meaning, courts should move to step two, rather than try to find a meaning by looking into the legislative history.[29]

Second, the enthusiasm for the *Chevron* approach is not shared by all. Some judges, like Justice Breyer, refuse to see *Chevron* as an absolute rule. Justice Breyer favours a case-by-case inquiry into whether a reasonable member of Congress, given the statutory aims and circumstances, would likely have wanted judicial deference.[30] Such deference would probably have been favoured by the reasonable Congressman if it concerns a minor question closely connected to the everyday administration of law, and would be less likely if it concerns a larger question concerning a central aspect of the statutory scheme.[31] Interestingly, the court seems to be moving his way.[32]

The deferential model chosen by the Supreme Court in *Chevron* contrasts with the growing dissatisfaction that exists regarding deference in English law. Objections have been raised not only to the use of the word,[33] but also to the concept as a whole.

Thus, Jowell has pointed out that, based upon the appropriate division of powers in a democracy, the legislature and the executive used to enjoy superior constitutional status to decide matters of public interest and policy, because they are responsible to the public through the democratic process.[34] He argues, however, that this constitutional position has changed as a result of the entry into force of the Human Rights Act 1998 (hereafter 'HRA'). In respect of qualified rights, it is now up to the courts to decide whether a breach of a right is justified in a democratic society because it promotes certain necessary public interests. It is for the public official or Parliament to justify that breach. The ultimate judgment whether the correct balance has been struck between the right in question, the public interest in overriding that right, and the essential requirements of a democratic society, is for the courts. Since under the HRA the courts are expected to guard democratic rights against unnecessary intrusion by the representatives of the popular will,[35] there is no need to defer to Parliament or its agents on the basis of their legitimacy as bodies which command 'majority approval'. However, the courts should be sensitive to the fact that their ability to determine the public

---

[28] ibid, 432–43.   [29] ibid, 452–5.

[30] S Breyer, *Active Liberty, Interpreting our Democratic Constitution* (New York: Knopf, 2005) 106.

[31] Sunstein (n 26) 199 and 231.   [32] ibid, 216–19.

[33] Lord Hoffmann in *R (Prolife Alliance) v BBC* [2004] 1 AC 185, 240.

[34] J Jowell, 'Judicial Deference: Servility, Civility or Institutional Capacity?' [2003] PL 592; J Jowell, 'Judicial Deference and Human Rights: A Question of Competence' in P Craig and R Rawlings (eds), *Law and Administration in Europe, Essays in Honour of Carol Harlow* (Oxford: OUP, 2003) 67.

[35] Jowell, 'Judicial Deference: Servility, Civility or Institutional Capacity?' ibid, 601.

interest is subject to limitations and shortcomings.[36] In Jowell's view, therefore, deference is not a constitutional imperative, but a concession made by a court that acknowledges that it is less well equipped to deal with a particular issue.

Hunt is critical of the way that deference has been conceptualised in the debate so far.[37] He rejects the use of 'spatial metaphors' that presuppose the existence of an area within which primary decision-makers are simply beyond the reach of judicial interference.[38] Hunt disagrees with this approach, because it treats certain areas of decision-making, or of a particular decision-maker's responsibilities, as being beyond the reach of legality, and within the realm of pure discretion.[39] In this way the progress that has been made in the area of public law by rolling back what were formerly considered to be zones of immunity from judicial review is threatened.[40]

The views of Jowell and Hunt seem to resonate with English judges. Thus, Lord Bingham in the *Belmarsh* case was unwilling to accept that the fact that judges are not elected and are not answerable to Parliament implies that they should yield to the other branches.[41] Judges are charged with interpreting and applying the law 'which is universally recognised as a cardinal feature of the modern democratic state, a cornerstone of the rule of law itself'. He therefore rejected the argument put forward by the Attorney General that the courts, being 'non-democratic' institutions, owe deference to the 'democratic' branches. In *Huang* their Lordships decided to ban deference from their vocabulary and perhaps even from their arsenal.[42] Their Lordships indicated that weighing up the competing considerations on each side and according appropriate weight to the judgement of a person with responsibility for a given subject matter and access to special sources of knowledge and advice, is part of the performance of the ordinary judicial task. In their view, giving weight to different factors is not, therefore, aptly described as deference.

The fact that deference is losing ground, especially in cases decided under the HRA, is not surprising. In those cases judges often face a dilemma. When an issue is raised in the area of national security or counter-terrorism, the court, on the basis of consistent case law, is to accord latitude to the decision-maker. However, when the decision taken affects the Convention rights of the claimant, the court is supposed to subject it to a more rigorous examination. This dilemma was described eloquently in Lord Walker's speech in the *Belmarsh* case.[43] His Lordship pointed out that since the case involved both national security and individual liberty, it called for the simultaneous application of two tests which contradict

---

[36] ibid, 595.
[37] M Hunt, 'Sovereignty's Blight: Why Contemporary Public Law Needs the Concept of "Due Deference"' in N Bamforth and P Leyland (eds), *Public Law in a Multi-Layered Constitution* (Oxford: Hart, 2003) 337.
[38] ibid, 338.   [39] ibid, 338–9.   [40] ibid, 347.
[41] *A v Home Secretary* [2005] 2 AC 68, 110.
[42] *Huang v Secretary of State for the Home Department* [2007] 2 AC 167, paras 16–17.
[43] [2005] 2 AC 68, 162.

each other. First, the court was expected to show a high degree of respect for the Secretary of State's appreciation, based upon secret intelligence sources, of the security risks. On the other hand, the court should subject to a very close scrutiny the practical effect which measures have upon individual human rights.

The crucial question, of course, is how to reconcile these two approaches in a satisfactory way. On the basis of *Kebilene* the courts should accord some degree of deference to the decision-maker, even if a fundamental or unqualified right is involved.[44] In *R (Farrakhan) v Home Secretary*, Lord Phillips MR used a test which did justice both to the need to defer to the authority and to rigorously examine the decision.[45] Lord Philips made the crucial observation that when a court applies a test of proportionality, the margin of appreciation or discretion it accords to the decision-maker is all-important. For it is only by recognising the margin of discretion that the court avoids substituting its own decision for that of the decision-maker. In the case at hand his Lordship found that the decision of the Secretary of State was proportionate, because he *provided a sufficient explanation for it*.[46] This demonstrates that his Lordship reviewed whether the decision of the Secretary of State was within a reasonable range of options, rather than assessing himself whether the right balance had been struck.

However, the test presented by Lord Philips has not been greeted with universal approval. Thus, Edwards has argued that this is a watered down version of the proportionality test that does not meet the level of scrutiny required by the HRA.[47] In his view the standard proposed by Lord Phillips amounts to 'judicial avoidance', and may even result in 'judicial abdication', of the courts' role under the HRA. His Lordship's following within the judiciary is also limited. In most cases where the challenged act belongs to the area of the discretionary judgment of the decision-maker, but at the same time affects a Convention right, the courts have subjected it to the rigorous examination associated with the HRA.[48] As a result, deference appears to be on its way out.

Justiciability

In both the US and England & Wales courts and commentators have acknowledged that there are so-called non-justiciable issues which are better left to resolution by the other branches. Complaints about these issues should be aired at the bar of public opinion and be resolved by the ballot box rather than by

---

[44] *R v Director of Public Prosecutions, ex p Kebilene* [2002] 2 AC 326, 381 *per* Lord Hope.
[45] [2002] QB 1391, 1417.   [46] ibid, 1419, emphasis added.
[47] R Edwards, 'Judicial Deference under the Human Rights Act' (2002) 65 MLR 859, 868 and 872.
[48] *R (Bloggs 61) v Home Secretary* [2003] 1 WLR 2724 and *R (Farrakhan) v Home Secretary* [2002] QB 1391 being the exceptions; see also S Sayeed, 'Beyond the Language of "Deference"' [2005] Juridical Review 111, 119–20.

invoking the aide of the courts.[49] In the US the concept of non-justiciability is usually referred to as the political question doctrine. Courts dealing with cases which include non-justiciable issues are faced with a dilemma which was eloquently described by Lord Justice Laws in *Marchiori*.[50] On the one hand, courts should not contemplate a merits review of decisions of government on grave matters of state. On the other hand, no matter how grave the policy issues involved, the courts should be alert so that no use of power exceeds its proper constitutional bounds.

Courts in both jurisdictions have found it difficult to develop a non-justiciability doctrine which would do justice to both principles. The authority to declare an issue non-justiciable is a discretionary power,[51] which the courts have at their disposal to preserve and protect the separation of powers. What is justiciable in one case may be non-justiciable in the next, because the circumstances are different. However, since by declaring an issue to be non-justiciable a court may allow an unlawful decision to stand,[52] some commentators have rejected the non-justiciability concept altogether.[53] They believe that there should be no place for such blind spots within the rule of law. Similar considerations may have led the US Supreme Court to rely on the concept less and less frequently.[54]

Other commentators accept the need for a non-justiciability concept, but find its discretionary nature unappealing. Thus, Barkow argues that nothing will keep the courts in check if they enjoy an unfettered discretion in this area.[55] Consequently, courts might use non-justiciability as a pretext to avoid cases they find less attractive or, on the other hand, may declare non-justiciable issues to be reviewable so as to be able to pronounce on them themselves, although they are committed to another branch. Harris is mainly concerned about potential inconsistencies. In his view the absence of clear and firm lines between justiciability and non-justiciability will create the risk of different judges drawing the lines in different places.[56] Consequently, both courts and commentators have tried to identify criteria and standards.

In the US the case of *Marbury v Madison* is usually considered the cradle of the non-justiciability doctrine.[57] In his opinion Chief Justice Marshall made a

---

[49] *R (Gentle) v Prime Minister* [2006] EWCA Civ 1689, para 43. For the view of the House of Lords see [2008] 2 WLR 879.

[50] *Marchiori v The Environment Agency* [2002] EWCA Civ 3.

[51] AM Bickel, *The Least Dangerous Branch, The Supreme Court at the Bar of Politics* (New Haven: Yale UP, 2nd edn 1986) 197; BV Harris, 'Judicial Review, Justiciability and the Prerogative of Mercy' (2003) 62 CLJ 631, 635.

[52] Harris, ibid, 633.

[53] TRS Allan, *Constitutional Justice* (Oxford: OUP, 2001) 173–4, 189–90; TRS Allan, *Law, Liberty and Justice* (Oxford: OUP, 1993) 212–18, 228–9. Chris Finn claims that the concept is redundant, 'The Justiciability of Administrative Decisions: A Redundant Concept?' (2002) 30 Fed L Rev 239.

[54] RE Barkow, 'More Supreme than Court? The Fall of the Political Question Doctrine and the Rise of Judicial Supremacy' (2002) 102 Colum L Rev 237.

[55] ibid, 263.   [56] Harris (n 51) 634–5.   [57] 5 US (1 Cranch) 137 (1803), 166.

distinction between decisions based on duties assigned by law and discretionary decisions. The former were suited to adjudication by the courts, while the latter ought to be decided by the political branches. In Justice Brennan's majority opinion in *Baker v Carr* the discretion/non-discretion distinction was replaced by a division into six categories.[58] According to Justice Brennan an issue is non-justiciable in case of a textually demonstrable constitutional commitment of the issue to a coordinate political department; a lack of judicially discoverable and manageable standards for resolving it; the impossibility of deciding the issue without an initial policy determination of a kind clearly not for judges to make; the fact that adjudication would result in a lack of respect for one of the coordinate branches; the need to adhere unquestioningly to a political decision already made; and the embarrassment that could be caused by more than one department pronouncing itself on the same question.

Prior to the judgment of their Lordships in the *CCSU* case,[59] decisions based on the use of prerogative powers were deemed to be non-justiciable. In *CCSU* their Lordships replaced this approach based on the source of the decision by one based on its subject matter. If the nature and subject matter of the prerogative are amenable to the judicial process, the decision will be reviewable.[60] Lord Roskill pointed out that under this 'subject matter test' there are some prerogatives which are excluded from judicial review altogether. He provided a list of these so-called 'excluded categories'.[61]

These and similar attempts to determine which issues are non-justiciable have not resulted in clear and practicable standards. The categorisation provided by Justice Brennan in particular has not proven to be very illuminating. Justice Scalia, who usually does not beat around the bush, observed in his plurality opinion in *Vieth v Jubelirer* that the tests are *probably* (emphasis added) listed in descending order of both importance and certainty.[62] When discussing Justice Brennan's framework, many commentators leave it to the readers to make sense of it by limiting themselves to quoting the relevant part of his judgment and stating that it is self-explanatory. However, it is anything but.

The solution may lie in abandoning the 'all or nothing' approach to which the courts have by and large resorted: they either operate on the patient, ignoring the risk of collateral damage, or they refuse to treat him, because they fear that surgery may do more harm than good. The micro-surgery introduced by the Court of Appeal in *Abbasi* appears to be a solution to this problem.[63]

In this case the mother of a British national, who was being held at Guantanamo Bay, challenged the decision of the Foreign Secretary not to commit

---

[58] 369 US 186 (1962), 217.
[59] *Council of Civil Service Unions v Minister for the Civil Service* [1985] AC 374.
[60] ibid, 418 *per* Lord Roskill.   [61] ibid.   [62] 541 US 267 (2004), 278.
[63] *R (Abbasi) v Secretary of State for Foreign and Commonwealth Affairs* [2003] UKHRR 76; in *Re Shuker's Application* [2004] NI 367 Kerr LCJ introduced the concept of reviewability which would allow the courts to proceed on a case-by-case basis.

himself to making the detailed representations she had requested. Lord Philips for the court admitted that the Foreign Office enjoys a wide discretion when deciding whether or not to intervene to protect British citizens. It is free to give full weight to foreign policy considerations. However, instead of applying the all or nothing approach that had characterised English law thus far, he came up with a more sophisticated solution. He did not so much ask himself if, but rather to what extent a decision taken by the executive in the field of foreign relations is justiciable. In other words, if the court can find a way to review the decision without entering the forbidden areas, it is allowed to do so.

In this case one of the questions was whether the Foreign Secretary had honoured a legitimate expectation, raised in a number of statements made by his Department, that he would make certain representations. Lord Philips felt perfectly capable of reviewing this aspect of the decision without impinging on any forbidden area.[64] By distinguishing the legal and policy components of the decision, while ensuring that a review of the legal component would not result in trespassing on the policy part, Lord Philips has developed a selective or partial non-justiciability concept which offers a very promising route out of the justiciability quagmire.

Review of the constitutionality of legislation

At first sight, as far as the judicial review of legislation is concerned, both courts could not be further apart. While under *Marbury v Madison* the US Supreme Court is allowed to review the constitutionality of legislation, English courts are barred from doing so as a result of the sovereignty of Parliament. But behind these constitutional facades important developments are taking place which may shed new light on constitutional orthodoxy.

First, in the US a stricter method to interpret the Constitution has been gaining ground. Traditionally, a large majority of the Justices have regarded the Constitution as a living document that has to be interpreted in the light of present-day conditions. Those who belong to this school of thought will try to interpret the document in such a way that it can assist the court in solving the problem at bar.[65] An important advantage of this approach is that the Constitution provides an answer to every question. Thus, the court in *Griswold* interpreted the Due Process Clause of the Fourteenth Amendment as including a right to privacy in order to be able to strike down a state law that banned the use of contraceptives by married couples.[66] This was despite the fact that the text of the Constitution does not contain such a right and it was not considered to be part of this clause when it was adopted.

---

[64] ibid, paras 83–107.
[65] S Breyer, 'Our Democratic Constitution' (2002) 77 NYU L Rev 254.
[66] *Griswold v Connecticut* 381 US 479 (1965).

A problem of this method is that reliable objective standards that support the construction are usually lacking. Consequently, there is a risk that the Justices' own beliefs will permeate their efforts to construe the Constitutional provisions, or that they will at least become vulnerable to claims of that nature. Thus, part of the criticism levelled at the ruling of the court in *Roe v Wade*,[67] which introduced a right to abortion in US law, is not aimed so much at its pro-choice outcome, but at the fact that the court's majority read this unenumerated right into the Due Process Clause of the Fourteenth Amendment.[68]

Alongside this 'living document approach' another method of construction has emerged which is called 'Originalism'.[69] The Justices who use this method subscribe to the view that when interpreting the Constitution judges should insulate themselves from their personal beliefs as much as possible. Originalists rely to a maximum extent on objective indicia in order to prevent subjective views from polluting their craftsmanship. Therefore, if they are unable to find the answer in the text of the Constitution itself, they will consult the original sources. Some, like Justice Thomas, will try to identify the intention of those who drafted the 1787 Constitution, called the Framers. Others, like Justice Scalia, will try to establish what the words meant to those living at the time the Constitution was drafted. He will use documents from that time period that reflect on this meaning, like the minutes of the ratification debates and the so-called Federalist Papers, which were written to explain the meaning of the Constitution to a sceptic New York audience. Interestingly, when the Framers have copied texts from other documents, like the Magna Carta or the Bill of Rights, Justice Scalia will try to establish what these texts meant at the time of their adoption.

A problem with this method of construction is that it does not provide an answer to every question raised before the court. If the Constitution is silent on an issue, Originalists will not be able to express an opinion thereon. Thus, in *Griswold* Justice Black expressed the view that the law that banned the use of contraceptives was ludicrous, but could not be struck down by the court, because it did not violate a provision in the Constitution.[70] Rather than adjusting the meaning of the Constitution to fit the case, the Originalists will leave it to the political process to amend the Constitution. Originalists like Scalia will be the first to admit that this method is not perfect. Sometimes the sources are unreliable, because they were used for partisan purposes, or they are lacking altogether.

A huge benefit of this method is that cases will be decided on the basis of objective standards. And these objective standards limit the Justices' room to manoeuvre. Although the 'living document approach' may still be dominant as

---

[67] 410 US 113 (1973).
[68] The criticism has not kept the right to abortion from becoming part of US law under *stare decisis*; see *Planned Parenthood of Southeastern Pennsylvania v Casey* 505 US 833 (1992), 845–6 *per* Justices O'Connor, Kennedy, and Souter.
[69] A Scalia, 'Originalism: The Lesser Evil' 57 U Cin L Rev 849.
[70] 381 US 479 (1965), 507–11.

far as the court is concerned, Originalism has had a huge impact.[71] Thus, the proponents of the living document approach have been encouraged to look for objective standards on which they can fall back when they interpret the Constitution. Justice Breyer has recently made a serious attempt to develop such objective standards.[72] More importantly, the Originalists at the court are succeeding in engaging their opponents on their favourite terrain. Thus, in *District of Columbia v Heller*, the case challenging the DC gun ban, the majority of the court, led by Justice Scalia, came to the conclusion that the Second Amendment to the Constitution protects an individual right to possess a firearm unconnected with service in a militia.[73] Not surprisingly, Justice Scalia reached this conclusion mainly by relying on founding era sources. However, one of the dissenting Justices, Stevens, defended the position that the Second Amendment protects the right to keep and bear arms for military purposes also by using these sources favoured by the Originalists. 'Originalism is in the game, even if it does not always prevail', as Justice Scalia has rightly pointed out recently.[74]

Second, in Britain the concept of Sovereignty of Parliament is becoming subject to important qualifications, like the United Kingdom's membership of the European Union and the adoption of the HRA. The scope, in particular, of section 3 of the HRA, which requires courts to read and give effect to legislation in a way that is compliant with Convention rights, may have important ramifications for the constitutional position of the courts. In *Ghaidan v Godin-Mendoza* their Lordships agreed that under section 3, a court may be required to read in words which change the meaning of the enacted legislation, so as to make it Convention-compliant.[75] Reassuringly, they added that the courts are not allowed to adopt a meaning that is inconsistent with a 'fundamental feature' of the legislation.[76] In his dissenting opinion Lord Millet expressed the cautious view that the obligation of the courts not to supply words which are inconsistent with a fundamental feature of the legislative scheme entails that they are not allowed to repeal, delete, or contradict the language of the offending statute.[77] While identifying the essential features of the legislative scheme, courts must rely in part at least on the words that Parliament has chosen to use.[78]

The majority of their Lordships, however, was willing to go much further. According to them the intention of Parliament in enacting section 3 was that a court can modify the meaning, and therefore the effect of primary and secondary legislation.[79] Thus, while Lord Millet would insist on preserving a relation, however tenuous, between the text of the provision and its interpretation by the court, the purposive approach adhered to by the majority would allow for a

---

[71] Which is by no means welcomed by all; see eg R Dworkin, 'The Supreme Court Phalanx' *New York Review of Books*, vol 54, no 14, 27 September 2007.
[72] Breyer (n 30).   [73] 554 US (decision of 26 June 2008).
[74] Justice A Scalia, 'Foreword' (2008) 31 Harvard JL & Pub Policy 871.
[75] [2004] 2 AC 557.   [76] ibid, 572 *per* Lord Nicholls.   [77] ibid, 586.
[78] ibid, 587–8.   [79] ibid, 571–2 *per* Lord Nicholls.

stand-alone interpretation of the statute. Such an interpretation, which would draw inspiration from the 'living document' approach adhered to by the Strasbourg Court, would be an amendment in everything but name. Not surprisingly, Lord Millet warned that the purposive method adopted by the majority may go beyond interpretation and may result in quasi-legislation, which could have a negative impact on the relationship between the legislature and the judiciary and ultimately the supremacy of Parliament.[80]

There is a striking contrast between the purposive interpretation of statutes, which is dominant in England & Wales, and the textualist approach, which is gaining ground in the US.[81] Textualists rely on the exact wording of a statute to determine its meaning. If the objective meaning of the statute cannot be ascertained from the text, textualists will try to discover it by resorting to canons of construction, dictionaries, rules of grammar, and other such tools. They will refrain from consulting other sources, like the purpose of the statute, the intent of the legislature, or legislative history. Textualism is a response to intentionalism, which interprets statutory language in the light of the intent of the legislature, which is reconstructed on the basis of the purpose and the history of the statute. Judges relying on intentionalism were often able to come up with a construction supporting their own preferences, by picking statements from the internally inconsistent legislative history or by emphasising only one of the many conflicting goals that Congress sought to further through the statute.[82]

Another important qualification was identified by Sir John Laws for the Administrative Court in the *Thoburn* case,[83] in which he introduced a rule of construction that put an end to the Midas touch of implied repeal. In his opinion Sir John indicates that he regards the Sovereignty of Parliament as a construct of the common law.[84] This means that the courts can extend, alter, or limit this concept at will: He that Giveth, also Taketh Away. According to Sir John this is already happening. In his opinion in *Roth* he has pointed out that the common law regarding the Sovereignty of Parliament is evolving.[85] In his view in its present state of evolution, the British system may be said to stand at an intermediate stage between parliamentary supremacy and constitutional supremacy.

Interestingly, this common law basis of the Sovereignty of Parliament has also been highlighted by Lord Steyn in *Jackson*.[86] Lord Steyn expressly relied on the

---

[80] ibid, 585.

[81] A Scalia, *A Matter of Interpretation, Federal Courts and the Law* (Princeton: Princeton UP, 1997) 3–47.

[82] RJ Pierce, Jr, 'The Supreme Court's New Hypertextualism: An Invitation to Cacophony and Incoherence in the Administrative State' (1995) 95 Colum L Rev 749, 751.

[83] *Thoburn v Sunderland CC* [2003] QB 151.

[84] ibid, paras 59–60; see M Elliott, 'Embracing "Constitutional" Legislation: Towards Fundamental Law?' (2003) 54 NILQ 25.

[85] *International Transport Roth GmbH v Home Secretary* [2003] QB 728, 759.

[86] *R (Jackson) v AG* [2006] 1 AC 262; B Dickson, 'Judicial Activism in the House of Lords 1995–2007' in B Dickson (ed), *Judicial Activism in Common Law Supreme Courts* (Oxford: OUP, 2007) 363, 371–2.

common law basis of the Sovereignty of Parliament. In his speech he indicated that the supremacy of Parliament was created by the judges and that they could be forced to qualify it when Parliament introduces oppressive or wholly undemocratic legislation.[87] Although none of the other Law Lords was prepared to go as far as Lord Steyn, several among them appeared to assume that Parliament's legislative power is constrained by certain common law fundamental rights.[88]

The idea that the common law may limit Parliament's legislative power has, of course, a long pedigree. Courts have traditionally relied on common law presumptions that Parliament intended to legislate in a particular way. These judge-made presumptions of legislative intent, in particular the hypothetical assertions about what Parliament could not or would not have intended, often do not coincide with Parliament's actual intentions. Willis has expressed the view that these common law presumptions of statutory interpretation, at least in part, compensate for the courts' lack of power to examine the constitutionality of Acts of Parliament.[89] In his view courts do not use common law presumptions of legislative intent as a means of discovering an unexpressed intent, but as a means of controlling an expressed intent of which they happen to disapprove: 'The presumption is now, in substance, a rule of constitutional law masquerading as a rule of construction.'[90]

Conclusion

This excursion was limited to a small area only and general conclusions should not, therefore, be drawn. However, an American observer would probably be struck by the fact that the English courts are gaining so much ground on the political branches. Although the US Supreme Court has the image of being an important constitutional player, the English judiciary, led by the House of Lords, is acquiring a similar status by stealth. In the area that has allowed the US Supreme Court to strengthen its hand, the judicial review of legislation, it is losing some of its room to manoeuvre, mainly as a result of the emergence of Originalism. The English judges, on the other hand, are making their mark through the use of section 3 of the HRA and their reliance on the common law when commenting on Acts of Parliament. This process is being reinforced by relaxing the standing rules considerably, making deference a redundant concept and by reducing the judicial no-go area through the introduction of partial or selective non-justiciability.

---

[87] [2006] 1 AC 262, 302–3.

[88] ibid, 303–4 *per* Lord Hope; 318 *per* Baroness Hale; 327 *per* Lord Brown.

[89] John Willis, 'Statutory Interpretation in a Nutshell' (1938) 16 Canadian Bar Rev 1; John Willis, 'Administrative Law and the British North America Act' (1939) 53 Harvard L Rev 251.

[90] Willis, 'Administrative Law and the British North America Act', ibid, 276.

22

A European Perspective

*Laurence Burgorgue-Larsen**

Introduction

For a lawyer brought up on the continent of Europe, an examination of the United Kingdom's legal system, particularly its highest court, the House of Lords, produces something of a shock. There is the initial shock that derives from seeing how two great legal cultures, embodying two distinct modes of thinking about the law, confront each other as they try to embed and extend their influence throughout the world. The sacrosanct dividing line between common law and Romano-Germanic law is a plain fact that cannot be denied and it strikes any casual observer forcibly. But a further shock flows from this first one. It relates to the place of the House of Lords at the heart of European constitutionalism. We all know that the highest British court is not itself a 'Constitutional Court', given that there is no written British constitution. But, notwithstanding the special nature of British constitutional law, the judicial arm of the House of Lords and the Judicial Committee of the Privy Council constitute two bodies, comprising mostly the same judges, which retain the power to interpret laws in the light of constitutional principles, in particular principles of common law, and also the power to control the division of competences between the constituent parts of the United Kingdom.[1] The House of Lords is therefore a kind of constitutional court, but its powers and ways of operating are clearly not within the mainstream which one French constitutional expert describes as 'the European constitutional justice model'.[2] The essential feature of this 'model' is judicial oversight of what is constitutional. But we should be careful not to delude ourselves. Continental constitutional

---

[*] Je tiens ici vivement à remercier Brice Dickson pour avoir assuré une excellente traduction de mon article et de m'avoir indiqué les derniers développements jurisprudentiels de la House of Lords.

[1] C Girard, 'Le réalisme du juge constitutionnel britannique. Un réalisme doucement réformé', *Les Cahiers du Conseil constitutionnel* (Paris, no 22, 2007) 256.

[2] See L Favoreu, *Les Cours constitutionnelles* (Paris: PUF, 1986). His students, sometimes referred to as representatives of the 'Aix' school, have taken up this vision: see L Favoreu, P Gaia, R Ghevontian, J-L Mestre, O Pfersmann, A Roux, G Scoffoni, *Droit constitutionnel* (Paris: Dalloz, 2008).

justice is heterogeneous in nature: its uniformity is deceptive.[3] The European constitutional justice model presents, on the surface, a certain uniformity, but when one looks more closely at European constitutional courts, the key characteristic which comes to the fore is diversity.

It is indisputable that the vast majority of states on the continent of Europe have, in effect, adopted the well-known Kelsen model of constitutional justice whereby responsibility for determining what is constitutional is allocated to an independent body outside the normal judiciary.[4] This approach demystifies the law, although sometimes history has demonstrated that this may not be a good thing. Parliamentary bodies find themselves subjected to oversight by the guardians of the constitution, with the result that the latter is magnified at the expense of the ordinary law. The House of Lords certainly does not conform to this pattern. The gap is a yawning one, first, because the highest British court is an integral part of the British judicial system—it does not in any way sit outside that system—and second, because parliamentary law, which is an expression of the wishes of the representatives of the people, cannot be challenged in Britain as it has an almost sacred status. The doctrine of Parliamentary sovereignty, developed by the unbending Professor Dicey, still reigns supreme and there is no way of challenging it, at any rate not directly. Today the House of Lords has practically no other function than to deal with appeals brought before it, whether in civil or criminal matters.[5] On the other hand, what seems normal in London— the establishment of the highest judicial body at the very heart of the parliamentary forum—appears on the continent of Europe to be a clear violation of the doctrine of separation of powers.[6]

If the gap between the House of Lords and continental constitutional courts is huge, we have to remember at the same time that the constitutional history of European states—indeed history itself—has been a powerful factor affecting the heterogeneity of the powers, the oversight mechanisms and, last but not least, the frames of reference for national constitutional courts on the continent. In short, the European 'model' of constitutional justice has left its mark on the mosaic. To

[3] C Grewe, 'A propos de la diversité de la justice constitutionnelle en Europe: l'enchevêtrement des contentieux et des procédures', *Les droits individuels et le juge en Europe, Mélanges en l'honneur de Michel Fromont* (Strasbourg: Presses universitaires de Strasbourg, 2001) 255–6.

[4] Although some states, like Denmark and Greece, have chosen to put in place a Supreme Court which has the ultimate say over constitutional issues, most countries have opted to create a constitutional court sitting outside the judicial system *stricto sensu*.

[5] N Lenoir, 'La Chambre des Lords à propos des projets actuels de réforme constitutionnelle', *Les Cahiers du Conseil constitutionnel* (1997, no 3) 59.

[6] The reform of the House of Lords introduced by the Constitutional Reform Act 2005 has definitely attenuated this critique and brings the British system closer to constitutional systems where separation of powers is better exemplified. See A Antoine, 'La réforme de la Chambre des Lords: chronique d'une révolution au long cours (1999–2007)' (2008) *Revue de droit public et de science politique en France et à l'étranger* 1331; and by the same author, 'Les enjeux de la création d'une cour suprême au Royaume-Uni et la Convention de sauvegarde des droits de l'homme et des libertés fondamentales' (2008) *Revue internationale de droit comparé* 283; Lord Hope of Craighead, 'The Reform of the House of Lords' (2008) *Revue internationale de droit comparé* 257.

examine the House of Lords today from the perspective of a continental lawyer is not easy, because the various courts which in general terms can be compared with the Law Lords do not themselves have a great deal in common. In fact, even if we confine ourselves to the extent of their powers, one might wonder what resemblance the French *Conseil constitutionnel* has to the Belgian *Cour d'arbitrage*, recently renamed the *Cour constitutionnelle*.[7] The former was created in 1958 with the specific aim of serving as a reliable mechanism for ensuring that Parliamentary activity was rational.[8] In a country which was essentially hostile to any oversight over constitutionality, the *Conseil* waited until 1971 before giving itself the freedom to be the ultimate arbiter of the legislator's output.[9] It is only very recently, on the occasion of the 24th amendment to France's Constitution of 4 October 1958, that France constructed an indirect mechanism for checking the constitutionality of laws.[10] The Belgian *Cour constitutionnelle*, for its part, was created in 1980 on the occasion of a revision of the Constitution designed to complete the federalisation of the country. Its powers were reduced to those it had first been given, namely overseeing the constitutionality of laws and decrees and supervising the division of responsibilities among the state, the communities, and the regions. In 1988 Parliament decided to enlarge its powers by giving individuals the right to lodge cases and by allowing it to deal with a significant number of constitutional disputes concerning the right to equality, freedom from discrimination, and education.

In the same way, one might ask, what are the links between the constitutional courts of Spain and Poland? On the one hand we have the Spanish Constitutional Court, where each year 98 or 99 per cent of the cases dealt with concern judicial review claims (*amparo*) by individuals arguing that one of their fundamental rights as laid down in the Constitution of 27 December 1978 has been violated.[11] In

---

[7] In May 2007 the Belgian *Cour d'arbitrage* joined the current mainstream European position whereby judges deciding constitutional issues are seen to be part of the constitutional judicial structure.

[8] See the special issue of the journal *Pouvoirs*, *Le Conseil constitutionnel* (Paris: PUF, 1991). On the numerous critical analyses of the way the *Conseil constitutionel* operates, see D Rousseau (ed), *Le Conseil constitutionnel en questions* (Paris: L'Harmattan, 2004).

[9] *Cons. Const.*, 16 July 1971, *Liberté d'association*, no 71-44 DC.

[10] Article 61 §1 of the French Constitution as amended on 23 July 2008: 'When, during the course of proceedings before them, it is maintained that a legislative provision is in breach of the rights and freedoms guaranteed by the Constitution, this question can be referred to the *Conseil constitutionnel* by the *Conseil d'Etat* or the *Cour de Cassation*, and the *Conseil* must pronounce on the question within a specified time. A constitutive law will set out the conditions subject to which this article will apply.'

[11] On the basis of Article 53§2 of the Spanish Constitution: 'Every citizen can invoke the protection of the freedoms and rights recognized by Article 14 and by section 1 of the second chapter before ordinary courts, in accordance with a procedure based on priority and urgency, and before the Constitutional Court through judicial review proceedings (*amparo*). This latter recourse is available when there is a conscientious objection recognized by Article 30.' See, for a summary of the powers of the highest Spanish court, P Bon, 'Le Tribunal Constitutionnel espagnol. Présentation', *Les Cahiers du Conseil constitutionnel* (1997, no 2) 38.

practice, along with the principle of equality (Article 14), it is the right to an effective judicial remedy (*tutela judicial efectiva* according to Article 24) which is the most frequently invoked, thereby transforming the *amparo* process into a mechanism for supervising the work of judges rather than of Parliament. To this must be added the means at the court's disposal for remedying the situation: it can, in effect, invalidate an act which has prevented the claimant from fully exercising his or her right, and can just as easily order the claimant to be returned to the position he or she was in before the right was interfered with. On the other hand, we have the Polish Constitutional Court, which began functioning in 1986 and to which has just been allocated, by virtue of the new Polish Constitution of 2 October 1997, the power to hear, in strictly limited circumstances, constitutional claims lodged by individuals. Such claims can be raised only in relation to the alleged unconstitutionality of the legislative provision underlying the decision which is under challenge. The decision itself cannot be challenged, on the grounds, for example, that the court has misinterpreted the legislation or has violated the claimant's procedural rights. One can see, therefore, that complaints have a much narrower reach than in Spain and that they tend to put in question the legislator rather than the judge, the exact opposite of the position prevailing in Spain.

These few examples serve to show that comparing jurisdictions is not simple. It can even be impossible, unless one chooses a rather specific perspective from which to analyse the situations being compared. Looking at the House of Lords from the point of view of continental European legal systems requires us to identify a link between the various European constitutional courts and the highest British court. Today this link can be found in the overriding duty to respect the rights accorded by the European Convention on Human Rights and Fundamental Freedoms. There is, then, something in common between the various courts: it takes the form of the need to adhere to Convention rights.[12] In this context it is useful to distinguish between the ways in which these rights are integrated into the different constitutional systems and the ways in which they are interpreted.

Ways of integrating human rights

If we have to systematise the ways in which the protection of European Convention rights has been integrated into continental legal systems by constitutional courts, we can differentiate between three effective methods. First, 'autonomous'

---

[12] Another link, just as important, is that created by Community law through the European Communities Act 1972. But despite the significance of this, not everything can be dealt with within this necessarily restricted framework. For fuller details on the influence in the UK of Community law, see the excellent thesis by J Cavallini, *Le juge national du provisoire face au droit communautaire. Les contentieux français et anglais* (Brussels: Bruylant, 1995).

integration; second, 'auxiliary' integration;[13] and third, what we might call 'surreptitious' integration. It will be interesting to see whether the way in which the House of Lords functions since the entry into force of the Human Rights Act 1998 on 2 October 2000 puts it into one of these three categories, or whether it falls into a separate category altogether.

Let us begin by looking at 'surreptitious' integration. This occurs whenever there is no reference made at all to the international norm and it does not feature in the reasoning of the constitutional court. This deliberate refusal to make such a reference and the focus instead on national constitutional norms, does not however prevent the court from drawing inspiration from the Convention and from the case law of the Court at Strasbourg. Everyone will recognise that this is the position adopted by the French *Conseil constitutionnel*, which has its own approach to making use of the European Convention, albeit in a very specific legal context. In effect the *Conseil* 'pays regard to' the jurisdictional issues, but only by means of a preliminary abstract assessment of the legislation in question.

'Autonomous' integration occurs whenever the rule which is being contested in front of the constitutional court, whether it is legislative in origin or not, is required to comply with the international norm, without the court having first to consider a national constitutional norm. Such a process always presupposes that international law has been integrated into national law (whether through incorporation or transposition) and that primacy has been accorded to the former over the latter. So in Bulgaria,[14] Hungary,[15] Slovakia,[16] and the Czech Republic,[17] to take just a few typical examples of new constitutions adopted by Eastern European countries after the fall of the Berlin Wall, constitutional courts are empowered, by the Constitution itself, directly to apply international treaties which the state has signed, especially human rights treaties, and above all the European Convention. The national constitution effectively confers on the

---

[13] This is a distinction made by M Verdussen (ed), *La justice constitutionnelle en Europe centrale* (Brussels: Bruylant, 1997). He uses the term autonomous and auxiliary 'application', but here I prefer the term 'integration'.

[14] As a result of the combined interpretation of Articles 5§4 et 149§1, para 4c of the Bulgarian Constitution of 13 July 1991, the Constitutional Court has the power to verify the compatibility of national laws with 'the norms of universally recognized international law' and with the treaties binding on Bulgaria.

[15] As a result of Article 1 of Law 32 of 1989 on the Constitutional Court, the Court can be asked to examine the question of whether a legal norm is or is not in harmony with an international treaty.

[16] Article 125 of the Slovak Constitution of 1 September 1992 empowers the Constitutional Court to adjudicate on the conformity of 'general legal rules in relation to international treaties promulgated in accordance with procedures established by legislation'.

[17] It is Article 87§1 of the Constitution of 16 December 1992 which authorises the Court to adjudicate on petitions seeking invalidation of laws, whether based on violation of the Constitition, on violation of a constitutional law, or on violation of an international treaty protecting human rights and fundamental freedoms, on condition that this treaty has been ratified and promulgated in accordance with the requirements of Article 10 of the Constitution. Violations of international law can also be invoked within the framework of 'constitutional complaints' lodged by individuals, when the petitioner can ask for the invalidation of the law in question.

constitutional court the responsibility for ensuring that the Convention is adhered to.

The final way in which the European Convention can operate in Romano-Germanic legal systems in Europe is through 'auxiliary integration'. This refers to situations where the reference to the international norm takes place through the intervention of a national constitutional norm, the latter restricting the former to a complementary role. In countries where the constitutional courts have not been given the power to ensure that national legislation complies with international treaties, the exercise of the standard function of each constitutional court—to apply the norms derived from the Constitution—can lead it to apply, through the medium of constitutional norms, norms derived from the international legal order. As a result, these latter norms are taken into account in the reasoning which underlies the decisions of the constitutional courts. In this way the interpretation clauses in national constitutions facilitate, or rather lead, the constitutional court to interpret the Constitution's provisions in the light of international treaties which have been signed and ratified by the state in question and where the European Convention has been given a privileged position. There are countries, such as Austria, Germany, and also Italy, however, where no constitutional provision triggers such an interpretative mechanism. In such cases the constitutional court, more or less easily, more or less readily, with more or less momentum and enthusiasm, manages nonetheless to interpret constitutional provisions in the light of the European Convention and Strasbourg case law. These are examples of 'spontaneous' interpretations.

The United Kingdom lies at the heart of this last way of applying the European Convention. At the risk of ignoring some important specificities, and of presenting a caricature of the present reality, one might say that before the entry into force of the Human Rights Act 1998[18] the way in which the Convention was applied was similar to the method used in Austria, Germany, and Italy, which, like the United Kingdom, are all dualist legal systems. In fact the House of Lords applied an interpretative approach favouring conformity with the European Convention in the *Brind* case,[19] but this was a case where a piece of national legislation was ambiguous. That meant that, in the presence of a clear legislative provision that was contrary to a relevant human rights treaty, the legislative provision had to take priority over the principles enshrined in the treaty.[20] Thus, while in the United Kingdom the dogma of the doctrine of parliamentary sovereignty prevented an interpretative approach being adopted which gave full effect to Convention rights,[21] in Germany

---

[18] M Hunt, *Using Human Rights Law in English Courts* (Oxford: Hart, 1997).

[19] *Brind v Secretary of State for the Home Department* [1991] 1 AC 696.

[20] See the remarkable thesis by Aurélie Duffy, which fills a wide gap in French doctrinal analysis of common law systems: *La protection des droits et libertés au Royaume-Uni* (Paris: LGDJ, La Fondation Varenne, 2007) 43.

[21] It should be noted that the obligation to interpret laws in conformity with Community law has revolutionised the British legal system even more drastically. For a recent illustration of this see *Dabas v High Court of Justice in Madrid, Spain* [2007] 2 AC 31, where on 28 February 2007 the House of Lords issued an important decision showing how committed British courts are to the development of

and Italy it is more the importance placed on the notion that a later law supersedes an earlier law which can present a barrier to such an interpretative approach. Be that as it may, all of these dualist systems have permitted courts, of their own motion, mindful of the importance of the obligations assumed by national governments, to try to give effect to Convention rights, without in so doing completely distorting the principles which govern their legal systems.

With the entry into force of the Human Rights Act in October 2000, the situation changed quite radically. This Act did not give to British courts, even the House of Lords, the power to declare pieces of primary legislation invalid (some continental lawyers would say 'still' did not give this power). This remains, and no doubt will remain for some time, a crucial difference between the British constitutional system, which is still based on the doctrine of Parliamentary sovereignty, and the continental constitutional systems. Nevertheless, the procedures introduced by this important piece of legislation, elevated to the level of 'constitutional legislation' in one important case,[22] come close in certain respects to the constitutional interpretative systems used in respect of Spanish, Portuguese, and even Romanian fundamental rights by putting in place a duty to interpret legislation in conformity with Convention rights and by giving a privileged status to Strasbourg case law.

Spain, Portugal, and Romania are the three countries in Western Europe which have integrated an interpretation provision into the heart of their constitutional texts. Article 10(2) of the Spanish Constitution of 27 December 1978[23] is

security, freedom, and justice. The House relied on express words used in the *Pupino* case (ECJ, C-105/03, [2006] QB 83), where the principle of interpreting national laws in accordance with EC law was imported into the framework of the EU's third pillar. The case is all the more remarkable in that the British court ignored a condition which Parliament had decided to add at the heart of the national law transposing the EC law and which effectively undermined the mechanism for handing over an alleged criminal. The Spanish claimant, suspected of having participated in the terrorist attacks in Madrid in 2004, contested being handed over to the Spanish authorities. The House of Lords pointed out the crucial objectives of the European Council Framework Decision and concluded that the fact that a Member State had decided, for reasons best known to itself, to subordinate the extradition procedure between states to the satisfaction of additional formalities would risk thwarting the objectives of the Framework Decision. The House went so far as to presume that Parliament could not have intended to produce a conflict between the British rules and the Framework Decision, nor to put in place a less cooperative extradition procedure than that which had existed before. As a result the House concluded that the arrest warrant was enough in itself to constitute the required evidence and that it was not necessary for the Member State issuing the warrant to supply a supplementary document. Lord Bingham's speech is a remarkable example of judicial adherence to the rule of law. He pointed out, at para 5, that Art 34(2)(b) of the EU Treaty makes Framework Decisions binding on Member States as to the result to be achieved but leaves to national authorities the choice of form and methods, but added that '[i]n its choice of form and methods a national authority may not seek to frustrate or impede achievement of the purpose of the decision, for that would impede the general duty of co-operation binding on Member States under Article 10 of the EC Treaty.'

[22] *Thoburn v Sunderland CC* [2003] QB 151 (Divisional Court). Sometimes referred to as 'the metric martyrs case'.

[23] This reads: 'The norms relating to fundamental rights and freedoms recognized by the Constitution must be interpreted in conformity with the Universal Declaration of Human Rights and with the international treaties and agreements having a bearing on the same issues that have been ratified by Spain.'

probably the best known of these provisions. It is a provision which, according to Eduardo Garcia de Enterria,[24] gives a direct constitutional value to the European Convention, which Spain ratified on 10 October 1979. This rule of interpretation has led the Spanish Constitutional Court to take into account not just the letter of the Convention but also the interpretation given to the Convention by the Court in Strasbourg when dealing with complaints lodged against Spain, even if it has to be remembered that non-compliance with the Convention cannot be directly invoked within the Spanish national legal framework because the Constitution is the only 'parameter of constitutionality'. For its part, Article 16(2) of the Portuguese Constitution of 2 April 1976 mentions both the duty to interpret laws in conformity with Convention rights and also the duty which flows from that, the duty to *apply* laws in conformity with Convention rights. However the Portuguese provision mentions only a soft law text, the Universal Declaration of Human Rights, which does not of itself have any binding force.[25] The Romanian Constitution must surely have been based on both the Spanish and Portuguese precedents because it amounts to a synthesis of each of them. Article 20(2) of the Constitution of 8 December 1991 effectively provides that the constitutional provisions relating to citizens' rights and liberties must be interpreted and applied in conformity with the Universal Declaration of Human Rights but also with the Covenants and other international treaties to which Romania is a State Party.[26]

The documents produced prior to the Human Rights Act show that the procedures currently in place in continental European constitutional systems were not at the centre of Tony Blair's thinking when his government introduced the reform. At that time fundamental rights were under severe attack in the United Kingdom.[27] It was, more logically, common law systems which influenced the thinking of Parliament, in particular the Canadian, New Zealand, and Hong Kong systems. It is clear, for example, that the ministerial 'statement of (in) compatibility' required by section 19 of the Human Rights Act 1998, takes its inspiration from section 7 of New Zealand's Bill of Rights Act 1990, which obliges the Attorney General 'to bring to the attention of the House of Representatives any provision in [a Bill] that appears to be inconsistent with any of

---

[24] E García de Enterría, 'Valeur de la jurisprudence de la Cour européenne des droits de l'homme en droit espagnol' in F Matscher and H Petzold (eds), *Protection des droits de l'homme: la dimension européenne. Mélanges en l'honneur de Gérard J Wiarda* (Cologne, Berlin, Bonn, Munich: Carl Heymanns, Verlag KG, 1990) 222.

[25] This reads: 'The constitutional and legislative norms relating to fundamental rights must be interpreted and applied in conformity with the Universal Declaration of Human Rights.'

[26] This reads: 'The constitutional provisions relating to the rights and liberties of citizens must be interpreted and applied in conformity with the Universal Declaration of Human Rights and with the covenants and other treaties to which Romania is a state party. If there is a conflict between the covenants and treaties relating to fundamental rights ... and the internal laws, the international rules take priority.'

[27] K Ewing and C Gearty, *Freedom under Thatcher: Civil Liberties in Modern Britain* (Oxford: Clarendon Press, 2nd edn 1990).

the rights and freedoms in this Bill of Rights'.[28] Similarly, the declaration of incompatibility which section 4 of the Human Rights Act allows for is analogous in certain respects to the provision in the Canadian Charter of Rights and Freedoms of 1982. It does not go so far as to allow the invalidation of a piece of primary legislation, but all of the declarations so far endorsed by the House of Lords have resulted in a change of law or practice. The most remarkable illustration of this is its 2004 decision in *A v Secretary of State for the Home Department*,[29] where a bench of nine Law Lords held, with only one dissenting voice, that indefinite detention without trial of non-British nationals was incompatible with the Convention right not to be deprived of liberty, and as a result Parliament allowed the offending legislative provision to lapse.[30] These various control mechanisms have no precise equivalents in continental legal systems. In fact the only relationship that can really be established is that between sections 2(1)[31] and 3[32] of the Human Rights Act and the provisions in Spanish, Portuguese, and Romanian law. There is an obligation on constitutional courts to interpret their constitutional provisions in the light of human rights law. Britain has requirements that Strasbourg jurisprudence be taken into account (section 2) and that legislation be interpreted so as to make it consistent with human rights (section 3)—though not with international human rights treaties in general, because the Act is focused on the European Convention and its Protocols, while other countries require compliance even with *soft* law. But the logic underlying the provisions is the same as in those other countries. The court has to do all that is possible to interpret the catalogue of constitutional rights in accordance with the catalogue of Convention rights as interpreted by the Court in Strasbourg. That is where the difficulties arise, because in spite of these interpretation clauses, the particularities of each legal system produce the variations in the way the content and reach of rights is interpreted nationally, as the next section of this chapter makes clear.

It should also be noted, however, that the House of Lords has given signs in recent times that, even in situations where the Human Rights Act does not apply, the courts are able to mine the resources of the common law in order to protect human rights. In *A v Secretary of State for the Home Department (No 2)* their Lordships held, reversing the Court of Appeal, that, when hearing an appeal under section 25 of the Anti-terrorism, Crime and Security Act 2001 by a person certified and detained under sections 21 and 23 of that Act, a court could not

---

[28] Duffy (n 20) 105.   [29] [2005] 2 AC 68.

[30] Replacing it with the Prevention of Terrorism Act 2005, ss 1–9, which allow 'control orders' to be issued against suspected terrorists. Some of these control orders have themselves been held by the House of Lords to be in breach of the right to liberty: see *Secretary of State for the Home Department v JJ* [2008] 1 AC 385.

[31] As a result of s 2(1), courts and tribunals determining a question which has arisen in connection with a Convention right must 'take into account' the judgments, decisions, declarations, and advisory opinions of the Court at Strasbourg.

[32] s 3(1) provides: 'So far as it is possible to do so, primary legislation and subordinate legislation must be read and given effect in a way which is compatible with the Convention rights.'

consider evidence which may have been procured by torture inflicted by officials of a foreign state.[33] In coming to this conclusion, the House found precedents not in the judgments of the European Court of Human Rights, nor in customary international law, but in the principles of English common law. Similarly, in *Jackson v Attorney General*, where the legality of the Hunting Act 2004 was under challenge because it had been passed without the agreement of the second chamber of Parliament, two Lords of Appeal said that they could conceive of situations (though this case was not one of them) where they would be entitled to strike down an Act of Parliament, or part of it, as unconstitutional.[34] Lord Steyn (who has since retired) could hardly have been more explicit: 'The classic account given by Dicey of the doctrine of the supremacy of Parliament, pure and absolute as it was, can now be seen to be out of place in the modern United Kingdom ... It is a construct of the common law. The judges created this principle. If that is so, it is not unthinkable that circumstances could arise where the courts may have to qualify a principle established on a different hypothesis of constitutionalism'.[35]

Ways of interpreting human rights

Whether we are considering continental constitutional courts, which have an interpretation clause at their disposal, or the Law Lords (since the entry into force of the Human Rights Act), the requirement to interpret legislation in a way that conforms with Convention rights and gives priority to the rights jurisprudence taken into account, this does not solve all the problems. There are not always systematically harmonious interpretations, despite the courts' efforts in that regard. Even if the reasons for divergences in the content and reach of human rights are to be found in the particularities of each constitutional system, it is nevertheless the case that these interpretative differences are a feature common to all legal systems, whether they are common law or civil law systems: interpretation of national constitutions does not always exactly coincide with interpretation of Convention rights.

The differences between different systems have many causes—the way judges are trained, the monist or dualist character of the constitution, the specificity of permitted constitutional review, the presence or absence of provisions requiring interpretation in compliance with rights, etc. These differences feed a constant dialogue with the European Court. In this regard one must keep in mind that a 'dialogue', a word with roots in the Latin term 'dialogus' which refers to a philosophical conversation in the manner of Plato's dialogues, is above all an exchange of views, a discussion, a conversation between two or more people.[36]

---

[33] [2006] 2 AC 221.
[34] [2006] 1 AC 262, *per* Lord Steyn (para 102) and Lord Hope (paras 107 and 120).
[35] ibid.
[36] See A Rey (ed), *Dictionnaire historique de la langue française* (Paris: Editions Le Robert, 2006) *sub verbo* 'Dialogue'.

Given this, and contrary to received wisdom, it can provoke just as much opposition, contradiction, and even discord as agreement. This is how today's relationship between the Strasbourg Court and constitutional courts can be characterised, including when the constitutional courts have to apply interpretation provisions. In order to appreciate this fact fully it is useful to look more closely at one of the three systems which, as we have seen, have constitutional courts which are particularly 'open' given that there is an interpretation provision in Article 10(2) of the Constitution—the Spanish system. The *Moreno Gomez* case,[37] which is about protection of the right to a healthy environment,[38] demonstrates the point perfectly.

Article 45(1) of the Spanish Constitution provides: 'Everyone has the right to enjoy an environment suitable for the development of the person, as well as the duty to preserve it.'[39] This is located in Part I of the Constitution, 'Fundamental Rights and Duties', in Chapter 3, which is headed 'Principles governing economic and social policy'. On account of this it benefits from only a small amount of protection, as provided by Article 53(3).[40] This means that it is impossible to resort to judicial review proceedings (*amparo*) in order to complain about a violation of the right to an appropriate environment. The Constitutional Court made this point in its decision of 3 December 1996,[41] where the claimant was complaining about how the criminal authorities, without having pursued them very strenuously, had classified the actions taken against the owners and exploiters of a petrol refinery in Galicia that was particularly pollutant.[42] The Constitutional Court recalled that, even though the right to an appropriate environment has taken on a special importance in contemporary society, it was only a 'principle' requiring public authorities to take care to ensure that all natural resources were rationally used so that the quality of life and of the environment could be protected and improved.[43] Notwithstanding this constitutional architecture, a

---

[37] *Moreno Gómez v Spain* (2005) 41 EHRR 40.

[38] For an analysis of comparative law which confirms that the environment is often linked by courts with the right to a private and family life, see L Burgorgue-Larsen, 'L'appréhension constitutionnelle de la vie privée. Analyse comparative des systèmes allemand, français et espagnol' in F Sudre (ed), *Le droit à la vie privée au sens de la Convention européenne des droits de l'homme* (Brussels: Bruylant, 2005) 69–115.

[39] Art 45 continues: '(2) The public authorities shall watch over a rational use of all natural resources with a view to protecting and improving the quality of life and preserving and restoring the environment, by relying on an indispensable collective solidarity. (3) For those who break the provisions contained in the foregoing paragraph, criminal or, where applicable, administrative sanctions shall be imposed, under the terms established by the law, and they shall be obliged to repair the damage caused.'

[40] This reads: 'Recognition, respect and protection of the principles recognized in Chapter 3 shall guide legislation, judicial practice and actions by the public authorities. They may only be invoked before the ordinary courts in accordance with the legal provisions implementing them.'

[41] Spanish Constitutional Court, 3 December 1996, no 199/1996.

[42] E Alberti, P Bon, and F Moderne, 'Chronique de jurisprudence constitutionnelle—Espagne' *Annuaire international de justice constitutionnelle* (1996) 611.

[43] For a similar decision see Spanish Constitutional Court, 26 June 1995, no 102/1995.

mechanism of indirect protection has been developed, European case law having been a powerful prompt in this regard. So there is justiciability, since judicial review proceedings can be taken, but it is an indirect form of justiciability. Proceedings can be taken only on the basis of the subjective rights in the Constitution (Articles 14 to 30), and not on the basis of the right to an appropriate environment. In this context, the decision of 24 May 2001 of the Constitutional Court is exemplary.[44]

In the *Moreno Gomez* case the claimant accused the municipality of Valencia of being responsible, due to its carelessness, for noise pollution generated by various establishments (bars and discotheques) situated in the immediate vicinity of his home. The claimant brought judicial review proceedings to the Constitutional Court complaining of a violation of both Article 15 (the right to physical and moral integrity) and Article 18 (right to personal and family privacy) of the Constitution. The decision in the case is quite remarkable for the broad scope it gives to the protection accorded by Articles 15 and 18 by extending them to cases of noise pollution, referring, as it does so, to the express words used in the Strasbourg cases of *López Ostra v Spain* and *Guerra v Italy*.[45] In this way the 'accidental protection' of rights has made an appearance in Spanish constitutional jurisprudence. The change of approach adopted by the guardian of the Constitution is totally exceptional in view of the initial conception of the right to an appropriate environment, which was as a simple 'directive principle' not capable of being protected through judicial review. The court actually said: 'One can conclude that prolonged exposure to clearly determined levels of noise which can be objectively classified as inevitable and unbearable, deserves the protection accorded to the fundamental right to personal and family privacy within the home, to the extent that the noise prevents or renders especially difficult the free development of the personality and this is the result of the acts of omissions of public bodies.'[46]

The Spanish Constitutional Court, therefore, thanks to the interpretative possibilities provided by Article 10(2) of the Constitution, considers the decisions of the Strasbourg Court as providing a criterion for interpreting the constitutional provisions protecting fundamental rights, being careful at the same time to emphasise the autonomy of the Spanish system. In fact this does not presuppose that the international norms have been transposed through being imitated, for the system of Convention rights pays no regard to the normative differences between the Spanish Constitution and the European Convention on Human Rights or to 'the need to restrict the scope of judicial review proceedings to its core functions'. These two points, which ensure the autonomy of the Spanish constitutional system as regards the interpretation of fundamental rights, help to explain the

---

[44] Spanish Constitutional Court, 24 May 2001, no 118/2001.
[45] *López Ostra v Spain* (1994) 20 EHRR 277; *Guerra v Italy* (1998) 26 EHRR 357.
[46] Spanish Constitutional Court, 24 May 2001, no 118/2001, at FJ no 6.

minimalist interpretation adopted in the end by the Constitutional Court in this case. Besides demanding 'serious and immediate' effects on health, the Court opted for a selective approach to protection against nuisances. One of the two dissenting judges did not want the Court's approach to be so narrow: he argued for a more innovative global approach to the range of exigencies in environmental matters.[47] And so, after a radical change of perspective in the indirect use of judicial review proceedings to protect the right to an appropriate environment, the Court dismissed the claimant's case and did not allow judicial review. Doubtless frightened by their own audacity in saying what they did about the relevant principles, the judges succumbed to the common temptation not to draw the practical consequences from their changed stance. In the end they chose a pusillanimous solution by rejecting the claimant's claim.

His claim having been dismissed by the Spanish Constitutional Court, the claimant naturally turned towards Strasbourg. What was that Court's decision? The scope of the Constitution's protection of the environment, through Article 18 of the Spanish Constitution, was not judged by the Strasbourg Court to be as restricted. The decision of 24 May 2001, which was for the Constitutional Court the means whereby it could align itself with the mechanism for indirectly protecting the environment developed by the European Court, was also the decision which suffered a buffeting from the European Court itself. That Court, in its decision in *Moreno Gómez v Spain*, pushed to one side the Spanish constitutional interpretation.[48] So, while the highest Spanish court rejected the claimant's request to be allowed to resort to judicial review proceedings, the Strasbourg Court declared her application admissible; and while the Spanish Constitutional Court adjudged that there had been no violation of Article 18 of the Spanish Constitution, the European Court held that there had been a violation of Article 8 of the European Convention.

The Strasbourg case law shows, time and time again, that a tradition of constitutional review is by no means the same thing as a tradition of human rights review, even when, paradoxically, the two courts refer to the same sources. Interpretative autonomy, and the internal constraints inherent in each legal system, inevitably introduce an element of chance.[49] Logically, the position can hardly be any different in the United Kingdom.

Analyses of the attitudes of British courts since the entry into force of the Human Rights Act have brought to light a rather exemplary consideration of

[47] E Alberti, P Bon, P Cambot, and J-L Requejo Pajes, 'Chronique de jurisprudence constitutionnelle—Espagne', *Annuaire international de justice constitutionnelle* (2001) 513–56, esp 542ff.

[48] *Moreno Gómez v Spain*, European Court of Human Rights, decision of 16 November 2004. For a commentary in English see Nico Krisch, 'The Open Architecture of European Human Rights Law' (2008) 71 MLR 183, 187–91.

[49] This was disclosed, very lucidly, by the former vice-president of the Spanish Constitutional Court: see F Rubio Llorente, 'La relation entre les juridictions espagnoles et les juridictions européennes', *Renouveau du droit constitutionnel. Mélanges en hommage à Louis Favoreu* (Paris: Dalloz, 2007) 1387, esp 1399.

Strasbourg case law by every level of jurisdiction in the United Kingdom, including the House of Lords. In fact, Strasbourg case law has in reality been directly applied,[50] rather than just being taken into account in compliance with the restrictive wording of section 2(1). This is all the more remarkable in that it has permitted the British courts to take into consideration the economic and social extensions to numerous rights, and to revisit areas where up to now there has been good protection, such as the area of freedom of expression (to the detriment of the right to privacy).[51] It is nonetheless the case that certain particularities of the British legal system still constitute barriers to a complete 'interpretative osmosis'. Aurélie Duffy has identified four such barriers which affect the level of protection of rights, whether they are civil and political or economic and social. The first relates to the fact that the Human Rights Act is not retroactive in effect, as was made clear in *R v Lambert*.[52] The second relates to the particular situation of certain holders of rights, such as detainees and foreigners; the third to the details of guaranteed rights in criminal matters; and the fourth to the need not to increase public expenditure.[53] Taken in the round, British case law is less protective of rights because in the midst of legal disputes it accords a certain 'deference' to the actions of public authorities. The result is that British courts—with the House of Lords at the top—give themselves a certain margin of appreciation when interpreting Convention rights, which guarantees the preservation of an autonomous approach. Certain authors have seen in that approach the mark of something specifically British—the court has been able to 'personalise' the list of rights.[54] But it is an odd way to personalise a list by opting for a reduction in the protection of rights. In this writer's opinion, more than the display of a mad desire to preserve a judicial space, these divergences in

---

[50] R Clayton and H Tomlinson, *The Law of Human Rights* (Oxford: OUP, 2nd edn 2008); Lord Lester and Lord Pannick (eds), *Human Rights Law and Practice* (London: LexisNexis, 3rd edn 2009).

[51] Analysis of recent case law shows, however, that there are still differences as regards the basis for protecting private life. The decision of the House of Lords in *Douglas v Hello! Ltd* [2008] 1 AC 1 obviously fits within this remodelling of the British judicial landscape, even if the highest court has still not yet recognised a right to one's image. The case concerned two stars of the big screen, the husband and wife couple Michael Douglas and Catherine Zeta-Jones. While preparing for their wedding they sold to the magazine *OK!* the exclusive right to photograph the festivities, warning all the guests that no other photography would be allowed. But some photographs of the wedding were then published in a rival magazine—*Hello!*. The House of Lords, affirming the Court of Appeal, ruled that *Hello!* was bound by a duty of confidentiality with regard to *OK!*. And it considered that this latter magazine, which had spent almost 1.5 million euros for the exclusive photography rights, had the right to protect itself and to seek redress from a court if a third party intentionally violated it. The reader can get some idea of the distance still remaining between the British and continental approaches from reading the speech of Lord Bingham (esp para 124), even if the particularities of the facts of the case serve to explain the position he took. It is not private life as such, and even less so the right to one's image, that was in the end protected, but only some information (the marriage of the two stars) which had to benefit, in conformity with the exclusive deal in question, from the law on confidentiality.

[52] *R v Lambert* [2002] 2 AC 545.   [53] Duffy (n 20) 260ff.

[54] F Klug, 'The Human Rights Act—A "Third Way" or "Third Wave" Bill of Rights' [2001] EHRLR 370.

interpretation derive, as they do in the remainder of European states, from the particularities of the British legal system—such as the attachment, indeed the (excessive?) deference, to the place of public authorities and the non-retro-spectivity of the Human Rights Act—which it is difficult for a court readily to brush aside with a wave of the hand.

Conclusion

The United Kingdom has not wholly joined the continental system for protecting rights. Although the House of Lords is a constitutional court (some of whose members have suggested a new hierarchy of norms with their pronouncements in *Jackson*), many differences remain. Its methods for choosing cases, the way it is composed, its mode of reasoning, its inability to invalidate primary legislation, etc, still make it distinct from continental constitutional courts. Nevertheless, despite the particularism of the British system, firmly and definitively anchored as it surely is in the common law, the influence of the Human Rights Act in the legal landscape across the Channel has also anchored it, to a degree, in a universe which is common to all European courts—that of the European Convention on Human Rights. Under the impact of House of Lords' decisions of recent years, the duties flowing from sections 2(1) and 3 of the Human Rights Act have brought the British system closer to the continental systems in that they impose, at the end of the day, the same constraint, namely, to respect and to apply the list of Convention rights. Despite the multitude of particularities peculiar to each constitutional system, the most important feature to note, without a doubt, is that they are all committed to a text which embodies 'common values'.

23

Views from Legal Practice

Although the House of Lords has confirmed that the right of access to justice is a fundamental feature of English common law, it has done relatively little to make that right into a meaningful reality. In particular it has not addressed the issues of the expense involved in taking an appeal to the Lords and the time required for the appeal process to run its course. The first section of this chapter gives one solicitor's perspective on the cost dimensions of the problem. The second section presents a barrister's view of the way the House has, rather idiosyncratically at times, gone about its business.

(a) Access to justice: a solicitor's view

Arthur Marriott

Introduction

By 1945 the English political and legal establishments were agreed that radical reform of the funding of civil litigation and an extension of the funding for criminal legal aid, which had been introduced by the Poor Persons Defence Act of 1930, were urgently required. Lord Rushcliffe's Committee, appointed in 1944, in the light of the extraordinary pressure on the provision of legal services during the war, particularly in matrimonial cases, had made a series of recommendations which the great reforming post-war Labour Government accepted in principle. These recommendations were designed to improve access to justice very substantially. The resulting legislation, the Legal Aid Act 1949, was to have far reaching effects on the development, growth, and financing of the English legal profession and the way in which English lawyers conducted contentious civil matters in the courts, before statutory tribunals, and in private arbitration. It was also to affect the conduct of criminal cases, expenditure on which rapidly absorbed the major part of state funding.

Introducing the bill in the House of Commons on 15 December 1948, the Attorney General, Sir Hartley Shawcross KC, said this:

I should be inclined to call this Bill a Charter. It is the charter of the little man to the British courts of justice. It is a Bill which will open the doors of the courts freely to all persons who may wish to avail themselves of British justice without regard to the question of their wealth or ability to pay...Magna Charta decreed that: 'to no one will we sell, deny or delay right or justice'...[I]t is an interesting historical reflection that our legal system, admirable though it is, has always been in many respects open to, and it has received, grave criticisms on account of the fact that its benefits were only fully available to those who had purses sufficiently long to pay for them.[1]

Magna Carta was a charter for the feudal aristocracy—what one commentator has described as 'one Baron, one vote'—hardly the poor, but Sir Hartley's intention was clear.

On the civil side, the Legal Aid Act made provision for state funding of civil legal advice and for the conduct of litigation. Arbitration and proceedings before statutory tribunals were excluded. Rushcliffe had recommended legal aid for representation before tribunals where solicitors and barristers had rights of audience. But the Government excluded that from the scope of the bill though, as Sir Hartley explained, there was no particular logic or justification for doing so. The bill addressed the vital question of liability to pay the other party's costs if the legally aided litigant was unsuccessful, by adopting Rushcliffe's recommendation that he should only be liable to pay such costs as the Tribunal thought reasonable and that his dwelling house should be exempt from execution.

In its rare excursion into the problem of the Legal Aid Act 1949 (and its successors) the judicial House of Lords warmly embraced this political exercise in social engineering. In *Hanlon v The Law Society*[2] Lord Edmund-Davies was unstinting in his praise for the system; he noted that an unsatisfactory state of affairs for some assisted litigants could not continue and would 'substantially erode our present pride in the legal aid system of the country'. And Lord Lowry went outside the strict judicial brief in suggesting the judicial reform, recommended by the Royal Commission on Legal Services,[3] that the matrimonial home should once again be freed from any charge. The Law Society, however, was statutorily entitled to exercise its discretion on whether the legally-aided wife could assert a charge on her asset, the matrimonial home.

As Sir Hartley had recognised in the debate on the second reading, the provisions still left the middle classes effectively denied access to the courts, a fact as true today as it was 60 years ago. However, for all its shortcomings and anomalies, the Legal Aid Act was to transform the practice of law in England. Solicitors and barristers developed flourishing and expanding legal aid practices across the country, both in civil and in criminal cases. Anyone who, like me, was in articles in the 1960s in a solicitors' firm in the London suburbs, is only too aware that legally-aided litigation, together with probate and conveyancing (the latter both

---

[1] HC Debs 1948-9, vol 459, col 1221.   [2] [1981] AC 124.
[3] Cmnd 7648, Vol I, 13, b4, p 149.

then governed by scale charges), constituted the pillars on which most suburban and provincial practices rested. It was High Street practices of that kind which made available to the citizen access to legal advice and the courts, supported also by a range of voluntary and quasi-voluntary organisations such as the Citizens Advice Bureaux.

The dominant problem of our legal system in the last 40 years has been the lack of access to justice. The two main characteristics of common law procedure are delay and expense. The civil justice system is today in a state of crisis for which the courts are only partly to blame, not having until the Woolf reforms of 1996 the power, or even the inclination, to manage the litigious process.

Right of access

The basic common law right of access to the courts is well entrenched. *Raymond v Honey*,[4] decided by the House of Lords in 1982, was an appeal and cross-appeal from the Divisional Court by the Governor of a prison who had been found to be in contempt because he stopped the respondent prisoner from lodging an application to the High Court to commit him for contempt. Lord Wilberforce said:

In considering whether any contempt has been committed by the appellant, there are two basic principles from which to start. First, any act done which is calculated to obstruct or interfere with the due course of justice, or the lawful process of the courts, is a contempt of court...Secondly, under English law, a convicted prisoner, in spite of his imprisonment, retains all civil rights which are not taken away expressly or by necessary implication...

Lord Bridge, in agreeing with Lord Wilberforce, added a third principle: 'Equally basic, that a citizen's right to unimpeded access to the courts can only be taken away by express enactment.' By contrast, the House of Lords, in denying prisoners the right to re-litigate their innocence in civil proceedings, was ungenerous as well as being arguably wrong in barring access to justice to the Birmingham Six.[5]

Funding

The critical issue for access to justice is the funding of civil and criminal litigation. *Airey v Ireland*[6] in the European Court of Human Rights established that 'Article 6(1) may sometimes compel the State to provide for the assistance of a lawyer when such assistance proves indispensable for an effective access to court...by reason of the complexity of the procedure or of the case.' It was, however, made

---

[4] [1983] 1 AC 1.   [5] *Hunter v Chief Constable of the West Midlands* [1982] AC 529.
[6] (1979) 2 EHRR 305.

clear that the decision cannot be considered as authority for a general principle that the state has a duty to fund impecunious litigants.

In the years 1988 to 1996/1997, expenditure on civil and criminal legal aid rose at a rate substantially in excess of inflation, with fewer cases being disposed of. Civil and criminal legal aid was the fastest rising item of Government expenditure overall. By 2004 the expenditure on civil and criminal legal aid had risen to over £2 billion. This expenditure produced some astonishing results. In the top 30 criminal cases during the year 2003/4 the average trial length was 67 working days, the average number of prosecution witnesses was 114, the average number of defendants was six, and the average legal cost was £2.6 million per case. In criminal legal aid, by 2004 over 50 per cent of Crown Court legal aid expenditure was consumed by 1 per cent of the cases.

The Lord Chief Justice, Lord Phillips, expressed 'horror' at the high cost of large civil litigation. Two notorious recent cases illustrate the extremes to which expenditure on cost can be driven. The *Equitable Life* case,[7] which was ultimately withdrawn, cost Equitable Life £30 million in its own costs. The *BCCI* case,[8] which also collapsed, is said to have incurred costs of £100 million. It led the Governor of the Bank of England to make severe and justified criticisms of the conduct of commercial litigation.

These litigious excrescences stemmed from two House of Lords decisions. In *Equitable Life Assurance Society v Hyman*[9] the Chancery judges in the lower courts—Sir Richard Scott at first instance and Sir Andrew Morritt (the Vice-Chancellor) dissenting in the Court of Appeal—had dismissed the policy-holder's claim against a scheme for restructuring pension provisions. A much disputed reversal of that equity view resulted in a fall-out of huge consequences—near-destruction of the Society, losses to policy-holders, and endless litigation in which even non-executive directors of Equitable Life were needlessly exposed to a protracted lawsuit that was abandoned. Furthermore, the decision has led to an astonishing number of departmental and other inquiries which eight years later are still not concluded, including the massive investigation by the Parliamentary Commissioner for Administration yet to be completed. There was an attempt by the defendants to halt the ensuing litigation before Mr Justice Langley, but that failed because of the restraint placed by the House of Lords on what constituted a reasonable cause of action. The *BCCI* litigation had been given the green light by the House of Lords in *Three Rivers District Council v Bank of England (No 6)*[10] simply because the threshold of the test for striking out a cause of action had been set at too low a level. It is all very well to uphold the right of access to the courts, but it is less than just to drag defendants into expensive court proceedings which are doomed to failure.

---

[7] *Equitable Life v Ernst & Young* [2003] EWCA Civ 1114.
[8] *Three Rivers DC v Bank of England* [2006] All ER (D) 17.
[9] [2002] 1 AC 408, and see ch 24 in this volume.   [10] [2005] 1 AC 610.

But it is not only the cost of massive litigation that is of concern. The cost of conducting even a claim of a few thousand pounds in value, arising from a breach of contract or act of negligence, is beyond the means of the overwhelming majority of citizens. Small and medium-sized companies are also effectively denied access to justice when the costs are not only high, but also disproportionate to what is at stake.

Contingency and conditional fee agreements

So far there has been no move to introduce contingency fee agreements such as fund a good part of US civil litigation. There are important differences between US litigation and English litigation, principally that in the civil jurisdiction in England there are no juries, limited class actions and, as a general rule, no punitive damages. Some believe that contingent fee agreements unlock the door to the courthouse. However, they do much more. The public policy issue is whether we wish to encourage litigation, for despite the abuse to which a contingent fee system is open, it increases access to the courts. Contingent fees help also to seek redress for wrongs by major corporations and government agencies, which would be well beyond the means of the majority of citizens to pursue. We may well see them introduced here.

The use of conditional fee arrangements was permitted by section 27 of the Access to Justice Act 1999 and we now have considerable experience in their use, often in conjunction with After the Event (ATE) insurance. The conditional fee agreements do not apply to criminal proceedings as a general rule, or to family proceedings. The Access to Justice Act 1999 also permits litigation funding agreements and certain conditions for such agreements are set out in a revised section 58B of the Courts and Legal Services Act 1990.

For generations litigation has also been funded by insurers, but a new feature is ATE insurance. By section 29 of the Access to Justice Act 1999:

Where in any proceeding a costs order is made in favour of any party who has taken out an insurance policy against the risk of incurring a liability in those proceedings, the costs payable to him may, subject in the case of court proceedings to rules of court, include costs in respect of the premium of the policy.

Callery v Gray[11] is a clear example of abuse of the arrangements for conditional fee agreements introduced by the Access to Justice Act 1999 and the attempt to recover, as part of a claimant's costs, the premium payable on ATE insurance. The Law Lords expressed concern at the potential for abuse of conditional fee agreements and ATE insurance, particularly in cases like *Callery v Gray*, which as Lord Hoffmann said 'was a typical straightforward personal injury claim'. In that case the claim was settled for £1,500 plus reasonable costs. Mr Callery's solicitors

---

[11] *(Nos 1 and 2)* [2002] 1 WLR 2000.

submitted a bill for £4,709.35. The House should have grasped the nettle of defining how such fee agreements should be implemented.

It is difficult to disagree with Professor Zander's conclusion that: '[t]he House of Lords in effect washed its hands of the whole business in *Callery v Gray*— saying the problem should be handled by the Court of Appeal'.[12] This is plainly a case in which, as Lord Hoffmann indicated, it is more rational to have levels of cost fixed by legislation which will not only be more likely to keep costs at a reasonable level, but also reduce disputes about costs.

There is also a long history of trade unions financing litigation on behalf of their members and a convention that in those circumstances the trade union pays the costs of the member, should a costs order be made against him.

Aiden Shipping

The concept of third party funding was at least extended by the House of Lords in *Aiden Shipping Company Limited v Interbulk Limited.*[13] Until 1986, it was thought that costs orders could be made only against a party to the litigation. But in the *Aiden Shipping* case the House of Lords decided that section 51(1) of the Supreme Court Act 1981 contained no implied limitation preventing costs orders against non-parties. Lord Goff, with whose speech all the other Law Lords agreed, said this:

I do not, for my part, foresee any injustice flowing from the abandonment of that implied limitation. Courts of first instance are, I believe, well capable of exercising their discretion under the statute in accordance with reason and justice. I cannot imagine any case arising in which some order for costs is made, in the exercise of the court's discretion, against some person who has no connection with the proceedings in question. If any problem arises, the Court of Appeal can lay down principles for the guidance of judges of first instance; or the Supreme Court Rule Committee can propose amendments to the Rules of the Supreme Court for the purpose of controlling the exercise of the statutory power vested in judges subject to rules of court.

In *Symphony Group plc v Hodgson*[14] Balcombe LJ summarised the various categories of case in which costs orders had been made against non-parties and emphasised:

An order for the payment of costs by a non-party will always be exceptional; see per Lord Goff in *Aiden Shipping* . . . the judge should treat any application for such an order with considerable caution.

In *Hamilton v Fayed*,[15] Simon Brown LJ took the view that:

The pure funding of litigation (whether of claims or defences) ought generally to be regarded as being in the public interest provided only and always that its essential

---

[12] M Zander, 'Where are we Heading with the Funding of Civil Litigation?' (2003) 22 CJQ 23.
[13] [1986] AC 965.   [14] [1993] 4 All ER 143.   [15] [2003] QB 1175.

motivation is to enable the party funded to litigate what the funders perceived to be a genuine case. This approach ought not to be confined merely to relatives moved by natural affection, but rather should extend to anyone—not least those responding to a fund raising campaign—whose contribution (whether described as charitable, philanthropic, altruistic, or merely sympathetic) is animated by a wish to ensure that a genuine dispute is not lost by default (or, as concerned Lord Portsmouth here) inadequately contested.

Simon Brown LJ was in favour of laying down a general rule that what he described as 'pure funders' are generally to be regarded as exempt from section 51 orders.

There have been a number of cases in the Court of Appeal which have addressed the issue of third-party funding in the light of Lord Goff's view in *Aiden Shipping*, that the Court of Appeal should have no difficulty in laying down guidelines of the exceptional circumstances in which third party costs orders may be appropriate.

Some of the authorities have suggested that there needed to be impropriety or unreasonableness as a factor in the exercise of the discretion, and referred to a decision of the Privy Council from New Zealand in *Dymocks Franchise Systems (SW) Pty Ltd v Todd*[16] that: '[t]he authorities established that, whilst any impropriety or the pursuit of speculative litigation may of itself support the making of an order against the non-party, its absence does not preclude the making of such an order.' The Privy Council in *Dymocks*—which notably contained four Law Lords and the Chief Justice of New Zealand, and whose judgment was given by Lord Brown (formerly Simon Brown LJ)—specifically considered the circumstances in which the third party in that case, a private company beneficially owned by one of the defendants' families, should pay the costs. The Privy Council set out a number of points by way of summary of what were described as the main principles:

1) Although costs orders against non-parties are to be regarded as 'exceptional', exceptional in this context means no more than outside the ordinary run of cases where parties pursue or defend claims for their own benefit and at their own expense. The ultimate question in any such 'exceptional' case is whether in all the circumstances it is just to make the order...

2) Generally speaking the discretion will not be exercised against 'pure funders', described in paragraph 40 of *Hamilton v Al Fayed* as 'those with no personal interest in the litigation, who do not stand to benefit from it, are not funding it as a matter of business, and in no way seek to control its course'...

3) Where, however, the non-party not merely funds the proceedings but substantially also controls or at any rate is to benefit from them, justice will ordinarily require that, if the proceedings fail, he will pay the successful party's costs... He himself is 'the real party' to the litigation...

[16] [2004] 1 WLR 2807.

4) Perhaps the most difficult cases are those in which non-parties fund receivers or liquidators (or, indeed, financially insecure companies generally) in litigation designed to advance the funder's own financial interests.[17]

The funding of our current civil justice system generally, raises extremely complex constitutional and public policy issues which will have to be resolved by Parliament, the courts, and the legal profession, as we continue to grapple with the seemingly intractable problem of the cost of access to justice. The reality is that much litigation will be and is being funded by third parties in various ways as a matter of course and not of exception. This is an inevitable consequence of the seemingly uncontrollable costs of civil litigation and the withdrawal of much public funding hitherto available.

The formulation of guidelines to give effect to reason and justice may be more complex in today's quite different and changing circumstances, than may have been contemplated in 1986 when the House of Lords was dealing in *Aiden's* case with the remedy of injustice caused by procedural constraints; and Lord Goff clearly anticipated that there would be no particular difficulty in the exercise of the discretion by a first instance judge. I believe that guidelines can be formulated to reflect the principle that third party funding is an essential part of our civil justice system as it now stands, but the funder is exposed to a cost order where either he is the real party in interest, or he has controlled or directed the conduct of the litigation, in a manner which has resulted in undue expense or hardship to the successful party.

The House of Lords has indicated that responsibility for procedural reform lies with the Court of Appeal. In *Callery v Gray*[18] Lord Bingham said:

The responsibility for monitoring and controlling the developing practice in a field such as this [conditional fees and after the event insurance] lies with the Court of Appeal and not the House, which should ordinarily be slow to intervene. The House cannot respond to changes in practice with the speed and sensitivity of the Court of Appeal before which a number of cases are likely over time to come. Although this is a final and not an interlocutory appeal, there is in my view some analogy between appeals and matters of practice and interlocutory appeals, of which Lord Diplock in *Birkett v James*... observed that only very exceptionally are appeals upon such matters allowed to come before the House.

A survey of the cases before the Appeal Committee would no doubt bear testimony to the Law Lords declining to accept in their judicial menu cases involving points of procedure.

Alternative dispute resolution

A particular aspect of civil procedure which is now part of the civil justice system is the use of Alternative dispute resolution (ADR), particularly mediation which

---

[17] ibid, para 25.   [18] *(Nos 1 and 2)* [2002] 1 WLR 2000.

has received government support. A series of decisions at first instance and the Court of Appeal appeared to be moving to a point where certainly in those courts, but not in the lower courts, the judges expected the parties to try to mediate the case and were prepared to make adjournment orders to that effect. Thus, for example, in *Hurst v Leeming*,[19] a professional negligence case, Mr Justice Lightman indicated that it would be a rare case of professional negligence (though *Hurst v Leeming* was one) that should not be mediated as a precondition of going to trial:

Practically all allegations of negligence against a professional man or body are serious, but that is no reason why an attempt should not be made at mediation. The reflection on the professional competence of a party may need to be reflected in the course of the negotiations and in any settlement, but cannot of itself take any ordinary case outside the purview of mediation.[20]

In *Cable and Wireless v IBM United Kingdom Ltd*, Coleman J in the Commercial Court upheld the validity of agreements to negotiate as part of a dispute resolution process. Unfortunately, in *Halsey*,[21] the Court of Appeal, whilst supporting the use of ADR, held that the mandatory referral or quasi mandatory referral approach such as the courts had been adopting, was contrary to public policy. The court also substituted the subjective view of the parties as to the desirability of mediation rather than the objective view of the judge. The court declared it to be contrary to Article 6 of the European Convention on Human Rights to require a mandatory reference to mediation. I fail to see how that can be the case. The argument is not that a litigant is being denied his day in court, but rather that a mediation is a prerequisite to a day in court. The EU has established a Directive on mediation and encourages it in both domestic and cross-border cases.

In my view, no serious procedural reform and improvement to access to justice is possible unless we adopt mandatory methods to promote settlement. That is the critical lesson which we have to draw from various attempts at procedural reform and the reform of funding. The experience we have so far had of court-attached non-mandatory ADR systems in the UK is that there is a 5 per cent take up, but within that 5 per cent we get the same percentage rates of settlement as we do for mandatory systems. Experience in the US shows us that we get the same rating of satisfaction of litigation whether parties are compelled to mediate or choose to do so.

All too often under our traditional system of litigation, settlements have been produced by the pressures of delay, cost, and uncertainty of litigation and the same has been true of arbitration. Properly mediated settlements are intrinsically fairer and more acceptable to the parties than those produced by the traditional pressures of expensive, lengthy, and unfair litigation. None of this has percolated through to the House of Lords. And no Law Lord has either endorsed or discouraged what has been said judicially in the lower courts.

---

[19] [2003] 1 Lloyd's Rep 379.   [20] ibid, 381.   [21] [2004] 1 WLR 3002.

Conclusion

To me, as an articled clerk in a suburban practice in Croydon, and subsequently as an assistant solicitor in a small City of London practice, the House of Lords in the 1960s was remote. To many of us learning our profession, the Lords seemed rooted in another time, certainly in another and much older generation. The reluctance of the House to review and depart from its own decisions[22] was disturbing at a time when traditional authority was under attack in this country, and elsewhere.

To this observer, it appeared that the Law Lords in the post-Reid/Wilberforce era—the last two decades of the twentieth century—with certain very obvious exceptions, withdrew into themselves. They failed to develop the common law and in particular to act decisively to protect the citizen against the power of the state. Decisions such as imposing the onus on a restricted mental patient to prove that, under section 73 of the Mental Health Act 1983, he did not need to be detained, took a long time to reverse.[23] The overruling, for example, of the *Anns* case[24] in *Murphy v Brentwood District Council*[25] was characterised by the intemperate criticism that Lord Wilberforce's reasoning in *Anns* was based on no principle at all, but amounted to a remarkable example of judicial legislation, to cite Lord Keith. Moreover, *Murphy's* case is remarkable for putting no coherent principled approach in the place of *Anns*.

The mood of the House of Lords in the past seemed narrow minded and very conservative, especially in matters relating to civil procedure, a topic that became professionally recognised and academically respectable only in recent times. Fortunately, that changed. By the mid-1990s the court was once again regarded as being of international significance, with Lords Goff and Browne-Wilkinson leading the way. There is little doubt that in the first decade of the twenty-first century, under the influence of Lords Bingham, Hope, Hoffmann, Nicholls, Steyn, and Lady Hale the House of Lords recovered the reputation that it had enjoyed under Lords Reid and Wilberforce, who were the judicial colossi of their times.

---

[22] The rule in *London Tramways Co v London CC* [1898] AC 375 (HL) was dominant, with the suggestion that the Lords might, extraordinarily, revisit a matter in *Practice Statement (Judicial Precedent)* [1966] 1 WLR 1234, very much a new development. See ch 9 in this volume.

[23] See *Reid v Secretary of State for Scotland* [1999] 2 AC 512; *R (H) v London North and East Region Mental Health Review Tribunal* [2002] QB 1.

[24] *Anns v Merton LBC* [1978] AC 728.   [25] [1991] 1 AC 398.

(b) Appellate advocacy: a view from the Bar

Mark Littman

In recent years counsel appearing in a case in the House of Lords would find themselves either in a committee room, or, very exceptionally, in the chamber of the House (before the Second World War, the Law Lords always sat in the chamber). If the hearing was in the main chamber the proceedings would occupy a tiny part of a vast, ornate chamber, quite empty save for a handful of the Law Lords hearing the case. Counsel would have to make their submissions from a modest space below the bar, hardly sufficient to accommodate themselves, their books, and their papers and evoking the sensation of being a horse in a stable. It was always a perilous exercise in constricted advocacy, tolerated only for its infrequency.

The Appellate Committee sat in the chamber only when Parliament was in recess in the month of October and possibly once a year at other times to assert its right to do so as the judicial arm of Parliament. At other times it sat in one of the committee rooms set aside for the hearing of appeals. Not infrequently, there were two committees sitting in adjoining rooms. In such a room the five or more Law Lords present would be seated in a semi-circle. In front of them would be the rostrum from which counsel made their submissions. There was ample room for the advocates, but less than adequate space for the public and the press. This arrangement was effective to create the maximum concentration of attention on the matter in hand to the exclusion of all irrelevances. It reminded one of the scene in the operating theatre of a hospital—St Thomas' Hospital across the Thames could be seen through the glass windows of Committee Room No 1—except that there was no visible patient but only the incorporeal body of the matter in issue.

So far as dress was concerned, the correct costume for counsel was the same as in the courts below—robes and wig—except that in the chamber of the House of Lords counsel were required to wear not the ordinary wig worn in court but a full-bottomed wig usually borrowed for the occasion and not particularly comfortable for advocacy. Their Lordships, however, whether in the chamber or in a committee room, wore ordinary civilian suits, something which to the uninformed member of the public did not adequately reflect the dull dignity of their office. To indicate that the decisions of the individual Law Lords were made in Parliament, the judgments were called 'speeches'.

More recently they have been described as 'opinions of the Lords of Appeal for judgment'.

Such dignity was, however, abundantly supplied by the quality of the intellect, learning, and character that their Lordships brought to bear on the matter in hand. Where the general standard was so high it might seem invidious to pick out particular names for special mention. A few, however, must be mentioned from those no longer with us. Names such as John Simon, James Scott Reid, Gavin Simonds, Cyril Radcliffe, Patrick Devlin, Tom Denning, Cyril Salmon, Kenneth Diplock, Jack Simon, and Richard Wilberforce will stand comparison with those of any judiciary in any country and at any time, including the previous period of the mid-twentieth century when Lords Wright, Atkin, and Macmillan graced the scene.

Nor was the range of their work in any way limited. For, being the final court of appeal from both the civil and criminal divisions of the Court of Appeal, their decisions as recorded in the official law reports cover the vast field of the common law, equity, admiralty, family, shipping, international, and statute law. But the contemporary observer of the Law Lords in action would note the predominance of cases in public law, rather than the familiar diet of private law that prevailed until the 1970s. The politics of judicial work is much more apparent nowadays.

As one would expect, the dominant consideration of such masters of the law was dedication to the rule of law. Yet one of the finest advocates of the period was Gilbert Paull, who always maintained that there was no tribunal more tender of the merits of the case, as contrasted with the strict application of the law, than the Appellate Committee of the House of Lords.

Nor was the House of Lords deterred in the pursuit of justice by the complication, obscurity, or novelty of the case. Thus, in *Fischler v Administrator of Roumanian Property* Lord Radcliffe said:[1]

My Lords, I regard this as a complicated case arising out of the special situation created by the Institution of the Anglo-Roumanian Clearing Office...and its subsequent dissolution. I do not think that it can be decided exclusively according to the ordinary conceptions of property, legal or equitable, that prevail in normal transactions.

The unusual circumstances of the case did not however prevent the House (Viscount Simonds, Lords Reid, Radcliffe, Cohen, and Denning) from unanimously reversing a unanimous decision of the Court of Appeal (Lord Evershed MR, Sellers and Pearce LJJ) and restoring the judgment of the trial judge.

The House of Lords, in hearing argument in one case, has always been astute to consider the possible effect a particular decision in that case might have on other cases. There was a solid devotion to the doctrine of precedent, even after the Practice Statement of 1966. The break with tradition was adumbrated in the early 1960s, as the case of *West v Shephard*[2] shows. This case also exemplifies another

---

[1] [1960] 1 WLR 917, 936.   [2] [1964] AC 326.

principle—how apparently modest cases can raise great issues. So it is perhaps worth spending a few minutes on its history. One day the present writer was in chambers at about 10.15am preparing for his morning coffee when Jack Jacob (later Sir Jack Jacob, Senior Master) came into his room and asked if he would mind taking over a case due to start at 10.30am before Mr Justice Paull (as he became). He said that the case was an ordinary 'running-down' case. His client, the woman plaintiff, while crossing the Euston Road, had been injured by a lorry which had shot the traffic lights. I protested on the grounds that, although I had appeared in many such cases, I did not really understand them and that consequently I had always been on the losing side. However, even at such short notice, I did eventually agree to do my best and rushed over to court to do so. In the event, Paull J, predictably, found for the plaintiff, and his decision was upheld in the Court of Appeal (Denning MR, Upjohn and Diplock LJJ) and by the House of Lords (Lords Tucker, Morris of Borth-y-Gest, and Pearce, Lords Reid and Devlin dissenting).

The speeches of the Law Lords in the House of Lords considered several very fundamental questions arising in the assessment of damages, especially those arising in cases such as the instant one, where the injured plaintiff suffered such damage by reason of the tortious act that she was totally (or almost totally) unaware of her injuries. This gave rise to questions as to the true basis of the law of damages in cases of serious personal injury. It definitively established that not too substantial damages should be awarded for loss of amenities in life to 'lame brain' accident victims, technically living but perpetually unconscious. Such parsimony was not replicated in the Australian and Canadian courts.[3]

It also gave rise to some more general questions such as the one put to me (appearing for the respondent—the injured party) by Lord Reid who invited me at 4.15 one afternoon to be prepared to address the Committee at the beginning of the next day on the question of whether the House was bound by its own previous decisions, a question which the House resolved three years later in the Practice Statement of 29 July 1966.[4] In the event, overruling a previous decision did not arise.

There is at least one respect in which House of Lords practice anticipated recent developments in the lower courts: namely, in the requirement that the parties reduce their principal submissions into writing before the hearing. The idea of skeleton arguments emerged in the Court of Appeal in the 1970s as a means of focusing attention on the essential areas of dispute. In the case of the House of Lords this took the form of rules providing for the submission of printed cases well in advance of the hearing. This gave the judges the opportunity of pre-hearing study. Such opportunity was not, however, always taken. Lord Reid, for example, normally preferred not to open his papers until he heard how

---

[3] *Skelton v Collins* (1966) 115 CLR 94; *Child v Stevenson* (1973) 6 WWR 140.
[4] See ch 9 in this volume.

the case was put by counsel orally. Other judges adopted the same attitude. Today, it is rare for the Law Lords to defer pre-hearing study. Time does not allow the deferment of knowledge about a forthcoming appeal.

However, the House of Lords has always attached importance to oral argument, much more so (for example) than is given to it in the Supreme Court of the United States (where speeches are limited to about 15–20 minutes) or in European courts. Nowadays, counsel are required in advance of the hearing to indicate the likely length of oral argument. It would be interesting to have a committee composed of representatives of the Bench and the Bar report on what would be the ideal balance between the written and oral elements in the resolution of the issues in the highest tribunals: to what extent should the distillation of the legal issues as displayed in the written submissions shorten the time given over reasonably to oral argument?

In recent years there has been a development of the practice of permitting the intervention of third parties—usually pressure groups like JUSTICE, Liberty, Amnesty International, and others—where there was thought to be an identifiable public interest that might not otherwise receive adequate consideration. This must be a necessary and valuable development, even if it lengthens the time taken in oral proceedings.

Less persuasive in the view of this writer is the introduction of the absolute age limit of 70. There should surely be some way of providing for exceptional cases, such as those of Lord Reid (who, because he was appointed before 1959, sat until he was 84) and Lord Wilberforce (who, because he missed obtaining the judicial freehold, being appointed as a judge only in 1961, had to retire in 1983). Both were fully capable of providing invaluable service well beyond that age. As Alan Paterson describes in his book *The Law Lords,*[5] the battle in an appellate court— in particular, the final appeal court—is not so much between the hired champions as between them and the Law Lords sequentially: the more appropriate analogy is to picture counsel as skilled anglers, with the Bench as the fish, the choice of fly depending on the conditions, the climate, and the weather prevailing at the relevant time. *Plus ça change.* The battle is always intellectually exacting and hugely pleasurable for the advocate.

[5] Basingstoke: Macmillan, 1982, 51.

24

A View from the City

Michael Blair

Introduction

How far, from 1875 onwards, did the Judicial House of Lords affect the City of London[1] and the financial services capital it has become? One answer to this question is, 'relatively little'. The City has always been more attuned to decisions taken or foreseeable elsewhere. While much of what is done there involves absorbing, influencing, and re-pricing in consequence of external factors, case law has only occasionally been such a factor. Compared to the Treasury, the Inland Revenue (including for this purpose the Special Commissioners), the Board of Trade,[2] and the European Commission, the House of Lords impinges only rarely on City thinking.

There are perhaps, however, four ways in which the impact of the House of Lords has been felt. Most of this chapter covers the fourth of these, and offers only a few thoughts on the other three; thus the reader should not look here for an exhaustive account of the relevant case law.

General commercial law

First, the City and the financial services industry are affected by developments in general civil and commercial law in the same way as other sectors of the economy. Many of the leading cases in contract, tort,[3] and indeed commercial

---

[1] By 'the City of London', a shorthand phrase, I include the other major financial centres of the United Kingdom, including Edinburgh, which strongly emphasises life assurance, fund management, and investment trusts. Also included are the allied sectors spread across the United Kingdom, including retail distribution systems through branch banking, retail arms, and independent financial advice.

[2] Later renamed the Department of Trade and Industry and then the Department for Business, Enterprise and Regulatory Reform (BERR).

[3] Such as the tort of misfeasance in public office, which was the subject of one of the most contentious decisions of the House of Lords in recent years: see *Three Rivers DC v Governor and Company of the Bank of England (No 3)* [2003] 2 AC 1. An account of this case is given later in this chapter.

practice and procedure have involved one or more financial institutions or individuals as parties. To a lesser extent, this is also true of some aspects of the criminal law, such as criminal intent, false pretences, and conspiracy to defraud.

Financial law

Secondly, the Judicial House of Lords has contributed to the part of commercial law relating specifically to financial matters. Examples are stock transfers, duties of disclosure in insurance law, and the relationship between banker and depositor.

Financial regulation

Thirdly, the House of Lords has had some limited involvement in the emerging topic of financial regulation, though perhaps less than might have been expected 20 years ago.

The glancing blow

Finally, and most importantly, the House of Lords is still remembered in the City because of at least three decisions which had nothing directly to do with finance, but which, in different ways, produced consequences of relevance to the nation's financial markets. Since the City is in the business of analysing, pricing, and packaging financial risk, any external event that impinges on financial risk or uncertainty is bound to touch on the City itself. For example, one of the three cases dealt with below was of close interest to the City even though, technically, it was about the *ultra vires* rule as it affected local authorities.

Analysis

Comments follow below on the first three areas described above. However, the fourth class (described as 'glancing blows') is the most important and must therefore come first. Here, three relatively recent cases in the House of Lords have fashioned the financial sector 'folk memory' about the judicial process. A question to the man on the Cheapside omnibus, 'For what in particular do you remember the judicial work of the House of Lords in your lifetime?' would almost certainly be met (after due thinking time) with one of three answers: 'Swaps', 'Equitable Life', or 'BCCI'.

There follows a brief description of each of the three cases followed by an assessment of their individual impact on City opinion and memory.

The 'glancing blow': three cases

The cases themselves

(a) The 'legal uncertainty' effect

The first case is *Hazell v Hammersmith and Fulham LBC.*[4] On the surface, this was a case on the inward topic of statutory powers of local authorities. However, it had massive commercial consequences for those City institutions that had entered into interest rate 'swaps' with the local authority. The banks and the Council had taken a different view as to the likely movement of interest rates over time, and entered into transactions that would have led to profit if they were right, and to loss if they were wrong. The central issue was whether the Council was legally empowered to enter into such transactions, and the House of Lords eventually decided that it was not. It could do things that were ancillary to the discharge of any of its functions, and those functions included borrowing. However, the House decided unanimously that entering into these swaps was not calculated to facilitate, or conducive or incidental to the discharge of, the borrowing power of the authority.

Once, therefore, the issue of the powers of the authority was raised by the auditor appointed by the Local Audit Commission, the banks had to meet an argument that, if right, meant that the Council could not be forced to pay on the swap transactions where it was the 'loser'. This argument succeeded at first instance, but was varied by the Court of Appeal, which accepted that the original transactions were tainted, but considered that later ones, designed to diminish the risk remaining in the earlier transactions, were validly made. Once, therefore, the Council had been made aware of the *vires* issue it could properly take action to mitigate its possible effects. In the House of Lords, the appeals by the auditor, and by the Council itself, against that part of the findings were allowed. Thus, though the case did not decide whether the old transactions could be reopened,[5] the banks could not recover under the still unsettled swap transactions where they were the 'winners'. Hence the case was widely seen as creating substantial 'legal uncertainty'.

(b) The 'financial disadvantage' effect

The second case is *Equitable Life Assurance Society v Hyman.*[6] This was a case in the financial arena, and might also belong to the second group, since it dealt with the powers of the board of a (mutual) life assurance society to take decisions on provision of benefits to policyholders. However, it is better classified as a 'glancing blow'; the analysis was corporate rather than financial, and its effects in financial

---

[4] [1993] 2 AC 1.   [5] This being treated as dependent on the facts of the individual case.
[6] [2001] 1 AC 408.

circles were political rather than legal. The Society had in the past contracted with some of its policyholders to provide a guaranteed level of benefit. Over time, the value of that guarantee began to be worthwhile, and by 1994 markedly so. Accordingly, the Society adopted a policy of declaring in relation to those policyholders a lower level of discretionary bonus, if they relied upon the guarantee, than if they elected to take another available option. So those claiming the benefit of the guarantee received lower bonus payments than two other classes of policyholder, that is, those who abandoned the right and those whose policy did not in any event fall into the class benefiting from the guarantee.

The validity of the Society's decision depended on a construction of one of its standard policies and on its own corporate constitution. At first instance, the judge, the then Vice-Chancellor, concluded that the Society was entitled to adopt that policy both under the contract and under its constitution. The effect was that the unexpected benefit of the guarantee was honoured, but the other policyholders were protected from the financial consequences of the payment of that benefit, since payment to all policyholders was adjusted so as, in a sense, to be fair to all.

This conclusion was reversed in the Court of Appeal, and the Society's appeal to the House of Lords was unsuccessful. It was held that the purpose of the guarantee was indeed that the policyholder who had the benefit of it was to be protected against market movement to a greater extent than if he had not got it, and it was not to be reasonably expected that the directors would exercise their, admittedly wide, discretion so as to nullify that advantage.

The effect on the City was one of 'financial disadvantage'. As a direct result of the decision, the Society gradually and inexorably became less able to maintain the previously impressive bonus record which had been one of its main selling points, and, over time, the amount paid out by way of discretionary bonus to all the policyholders, including those with the guarantee, began to shrink. Market value adjustments were required, and the expectations of prospective pensioners were dashed. In the end, one of the most venerable of City institutions had to close its doors to new business, and became a kind of 'run-off' fund. Many of those incensed at the loss of their prospective pension expectations were themselves in the City,[7] and it was often suggested in financial circles that, had the Lords of Appeal foreseen the long-term commercial effect of their decision, the decision might very well have gone another way.

(c) The 'cost of litigation' effect

The third case is *Three Rivers District Council v Governor and Company of the Bank of England (No 3)*.[8] It is often known as one of the 'BCCI' cases. The collapse of the Bank of Credit and Commerce International SA generated a

---

[7] Indeed, many of the disappointed policyholders were in the legal profession.
[8] [2003] 2 AC 1.

number of appeals to the Court of Appeal and the House of Lords. In that context, questions arose as to the underlying responsibility for the collapse. Some of the bank's depositors decided to test whether a claim for damages lay against the Bank of England as the (then) regulator of banks for the quality of its supervision of BCCI within the United Kingdom, even though BCCI's head-quarters were in Luxembourg. Possible bases of liability included the tort of misfeasance in public office, and obligations imposed on the systems of banking supervision in Europe under Community law. At first instance the claim relying on these two grounds was struck out, on the basis that there was no causal connection between the conduct of the Bank of England and the losses to the claimants, and because Community law had not created any right on the part of the claimants to damages resulting from the First EC Banking Co-ordination Directive of 1977.

The Court of Appeal upheld most of these two conclusions, except that it considered that the question of causation could not be determined until the facts were established. Despite that, the Court of Appeal struck out the statement of claim; even if further amended, there was in their view no realistic possibility of the claim becoming arguable. In the House of Lords, the appeal by the creditors succeeded by a 3:2 majority. The House was unanimous in its view of the scope of the tort of misfeasance in public office, and about Community law, but on the crucial question—whether the case should be allowed to continue to trial—the majority,[9] after the factual aspects of the appeal had been outlined to them, concluded that the claim could be amended and the case could proceed to trial. The minority[10] considered that the prospects of success at trial were so slight as not to justify the expense of proceeding.

In the result, therefore, the case proceeded to trial before Tomlinson J and occupied many court days[11] before eventually being abandoned in face of the ever-mounting costs of proceeding. The concern felt in the financial world about the case was therefore about the way in which litigation as a means of dispute resolution can have very substantial consequences in costs.

The consequences of each of the cases

Each of the three decisions left its mark on the life of the City in tangible ways.

(a) The uncertainty effect

The *Hammersmith and Fulham* case caused deep unease in the City. Those in financial circles had long been used to relying on the sanctity of contract, and on a stable and predictable legal environment within which to work. There had been little cause until then for concern about unpredictability and unclear legal

---

[9] Lords Steyn, Hope, and Hutton.   [10] Lords Hobhouse and Millett.

[11] The claimant's case was to be established on written evidence only, and through cross-examination. Accordingly, the claimant's opening speech was a very substantial one and is believed to be the longest one on record.

operating conditions. In late 1990/early 1991, however, when the case was decided, there were by coincidence two other new, unwelcome sources of uncertainty in the financial world, and the impact of the case was therefore correspondingly greater than it would have been at a time of less unease elsewhere. These two other areas of unease were the new statutory regulation of securities markets under the Financial Services Act 1986, commencing in 1988, and the decision in Europe to coordinate and harmonise the Community's financial markets as part of what later became the Financial Services Action Plan.

The general view in the City was that the *Hammersmith and Fulham* case was harsh on the banks. Why, it was asked, should a counterparty, and in particular a public counterparty, be able to rely on lack of its own capacity so as to escape from its (willingly entered into) obligations? Though the textbooks on contract contain numerous cases about the consequences of lack of capacity, in the context of minors and earlier of companies,[12] the notion that a counterparty was bound to inquire closely into the internal arrangements of the other side was seen as a real source of uncertainty and legal risk.

In the result, steps were taken to establish machinery to look for and to seek to eliminate other possible sources of legal uncertainty which could have an adverse impact on financial institutions of all kinds. The Financial Law Panel, funded initially by subscription, was set up under Lord Donaldson[13] and a number of changes were made to City practice, to regulation, and to other areas of law and contractual provisions. In due course, in 2002, this task was taken over by the public sector, in that the Bank of England established the Financial Markets Law Committee, initially under the Chairmanship of Lord Browne-Wilkinson and later under Lord Woolf.[14] The Committee was seen as relevant to the work of the Financial Stability wing of the Bank of England. It must be doubtful whether any of this would have happened without the stimulus of *Hammersmith and Fulham*, even with the advent of the large number of EC Directives that have occupied some of the time of the Financial Markets Law Committee over the last five years.[15]

(b) The financial effect

The *Equitable Life* case has also led to a number of political and public initiatives, many starting in and being driven by areas well removed from the City itself. The general purpose has been either to discover the underlying cause of the Equitable Life collapse, or to advance the claims of persons who claimed that they had lost

---

[12] The *ultra vires* rule for corporations was largely abolished in 1972 under the European Communities Act of that year.

[13] A former Master of the Rolls.

[14] See <http://www.fmlc.org>. A list of the current membership can be found at <http://www.flmc.org/members.html>.

[15] The FMLC website contains a full list of papers, letters, etc that form the final product of the work of the committee on over 100 items considered.

investment value in their life and pensions assets as a result of that collapse. The first initiative was an inquiry by Lord Penrose, who was asked by Treasury Ministers in August 2001 to inquire into the case to identify any lessons for the conduct, administration, and regulation of life assurance business.[16] Lord Penrose, a judge of the Court of Session, and thought by some to be one of the few UK judges qualified to carry out the inquiry and not conflicted out of doing so by virtue of his own private pension provision, delivered his report in December 2003.[17]

The Parliamentary Ombudsman (the Ombudsman) was invited in the meantime by a number of Members of Parliament to enquire into whether there had been a lapse in acceptable administrative standards in the supervision of the Equitable Life in the period leading up to the closure to new business in December 2000. Initially the Ombudsman of the day decided not to investigate the matter,[18] but his successor reviewed that decision on taking office in November 2002, and subsequently reported, in June 2003, that she did not find evidence to suggest regulatory failure, and that she could not go into the matter in greater depth as she was unable to investigate the circumstances surrounding the actions of the regulator including the advice and information provided to it.

Thereafter, there was a good deal of pressure on her to reconsider this initial verdict, and the matter once more came under the Ombudsman's scrutiny in late 2004.[19] The report was finally delivered, after some extensions of time, in the summer of 2008. In her report[20] the Ombudsman, Anne Abrahams, concluded that the Government Actuaries Department had been at fault in five specific ways[21] over the period 1991–8, and the Financial Services Authority, as agent for the Treasury, had been at fault in five further ways[22] over the period 1998–2000.

---

[16] The full terms of reference were 'To enquire into the circumstances leading to the current situation of the Equitable Life Assurance Society, taking account of the relevant life market background; to identify any lessons to be learnt for the conduct, administration and regulation of life assurance business; and to give a report thereon to Treasury Ministers'.

[17] See for instance the Treasury website, <http://www.hm-treasury.gov.uk>. The Penrose Report can be found at Press notice No 137/03 of 23 December 2003.

[18] The reasons for this were given in the (later) report of 30 June 2003: see <http://www.ombudsman.org.uk/improving_services/special_reports/pca/equitable03/p1overview.html/html>.

[19] The terms of reference for the inquiry, which commenced in November 2004, require the Ombudsman 'to determine whether individuals were caused an injustice through maladministration in the period prior to December 2001 on the part of public bodies responsible for the prudential regulation of the Equitable Life Assurance Society and/or the Government Actuary's Department; and to recommend appropriate redress for any injustice so caused'.

[20] 'Equitable Life, A Decade of Regulatory Failure' (published July 2008).

[21] Her first five 'findings of fact', involving judgments reached by her about the standard of conduct of the GAD, related to the initial appointment of a new Appointed Actuary in 1991, scrutiny of prudential returns for 1990–3, failure in 1994 by GAD to inform DTI about the introduction of the differential terminal bonus policy, further inadequate scrutiny of the returns for 1994–6, and in particular not questioning the basis for two particular valuations in those years.

[22] Her second set of five 'findings of fact', involving judgments reached by her about the standard of conduct of the FSA as the statutory agent of the Treasury, related to allowing a

At the time of going to press, the Treasury has published the Government's response[23] accepting the criticisms in part, and has invited the Right Honourable Sir John Chadwick to advise further as to compensation.

An inquiry by the European Parliament was mounted into *Equitable Life*, leading to a report by the Committee of Inquiry of June 2007.[24] This pressed the UK Government to accept responsibility for the losses, in view, among other things, of what they found to be a failure on the part of the UK Government to comply with the requirements of the Third EC Life Directive.[25] The Report was adopted by a plenary session of the European Parliament in June 2007.[26] At the time of writing, no response has been made by the UK Government to these recommendations, though it seems plain that the Government must have decided to await the outcome of the Ombudsman's lengthy inquiry before dealing with this additional issue.

There have been many other reviews, eg by the FSA itself, by the accountancy and actuarial professions into their relevant members, and, further, there have been several cases of satellite litigation. Some of these suits were brought by the Society against its former directors and auditors, and some brought against the Society by interested parties. Accordingly it is clear that the chapter on the Equitable Life matter is not yet closed, though the burden is now on the Government to decide whether the taxpayer should bear a substantial burden as a result of the recent history of the supervision of the Society. It is a matter for speculation whether any of this would have happened if there had not been a decision in the House of Lords in the opposite direction from the initial decision in the Chancery Division.

(c) The cost of litigation effect

The *Three Rivers* case also had some consequences, albeit perhaps to a lesser degree. It led the Governor of the Bank of England to make a trenchant set of comments on the fitness for purpose of the current adversarial system of litigation. In a speech in June 2006,[27] after the case was finally settled, he called it the 'most expensive fishing expedition in history' and asked for government consideration of the problem it had thrown into relief. This is the possible need to

---

financial reinsurance to count when it had not yet been concluded, failure to follow up on the Society's inadequate contingency analysis concerning the litigation, two errors surrounding the FSA's permitting the Society to remain open to new business after the *Hyman* case (not recording it, and not grounding it soundly in fact or law), and misleading communication to the public about the Society's solvency and compliance record in the aftermath of the closure to new business in December 2000.

[23] 15 January 2009 (Treasury Press notice 04/09).

[24] *Report on the Crisis of the Equitable Life Assurance Society*, European Parliament document A6-0203/2007 FINAL.

[25] See the Report at p 360.   [26] Voting by 602–13 with 64 abstentions.

[27] Mansion House speech to Bankers and Merchants, 21 June 2006.

overhaul the judge-made machinery for enabling cases that may turn out to be misconceived to be stopped at or near the outset.[28]

Since then, the Government has made no public announcement of any proposals to respond to this request.[29] However, the judiciary themselves have taken up the challenge. Following the criticisms arising from *Three Rivers*, and also from *Equitable Life*, a symposium was organised in October 2006 by the Commercial Court under the chairmanship of Mr Justice David Steel, the judge then in charge of that court. In the light of the views expressed before and at the symposium by client users and by those practising in or adjudicating in the court, a Working Party on Long Trials was set up under the chairmanship of Mr Justice Richard Aikens. The Commercial Court published the report of the Working Party in November 2007.

Key changes put forward were designed to secure earlier settlement, and more structured and shorter trials for those cases that did not settle, though there were also some recommendations designed to enable the court to be more proactive in preventing allegedly weak cases from proceeding. While no proposals were made directly on the legal tests to be applied in applications to strike out weak cases or to strike out a defence and enter summary judgment,[30] other proposals sought to stiffen the practice in applying the tests. In other fields, the main changes suggested included (a) limiting of the length of statements of case, and (b) the early creation of a judicially settled List of Issues, to take precedence for case management purposes over statements of case and to be used to set the parameters for disclosure of documents and the content of witness statements and expert reports. The List of Issues may also be useful in enabling the judge to offer a provisional view on the merits of the case even at the pre-trial stage, and thus encourage settlement out of court. As to costs, additional points explored relate to 'paperless litigation' (through the use of information technology) to reduce costs.

---

[28] He said, 'A legal framework for enforcing contracts and resolving disputes is not just an arcane process which allows professionals to earn vast fees, but an integral part of the structure of a successful market economy. It matters that there are simple, clear and timely ways of resolving disputes. What the BCCI case revealed was a legal system incapable of guaranteeing that. How can a case described by the trial judge himself as built "not even on sand but on air" take thirteen years and over £100 million in costs to come to a conclusion . . . A system that is powerless to prevent a case so hopelessly misconceived continuing for thirteen years requires examination. I very much hope that the Government will look carefully at this case, learn the lessons, and take steps to ensure that such an outcome can never occur again.'

[29] The Law Commission has had on foot, since at least October 2004, a project on Remedies against Public Bodies, and it held seminars on the subject in November 2004 and April 2007. However, the issue identified by the Governor does not appear to have been taken up then; indeed, this request for reform was not limited to the public sector but focused on any person facing what seemed, and eventually turned out to be, an unmeritorious set of proceedings.

[30] At part H of the Report (paras 84–104), the view was expressed that there could not be a different test for strike out or summary judgment in the Commercial Court from that prevailing elsewhere; nor could the avenues of appeal for such decisions be different; but, nonetheless, Commercial Court practice should lean somewhat more in favour of critical scrutiny (and thus potentially striking out the whole or parts of cases in that court), particularly when they are complex and heavy in documentation. For example, the judges are encouraged to raise proactively with the parties at the Case Management Conference whether a strike out or summary judgment application is appropriate.

The Report was adopted in the court for a trial period lasting until late 2008, and the experience under that experimental period is now being assessed.

Remaining analysis

I now turn, briefly, to the other three main areas of relevance to a view from the City of the House of Lords.

General commercial law

The first of the remaining three areas for analysis is the general law that is applied from day to day in the commercial life of this country. Plainly, the City depends on the predictability, fairness, and effectiveness of that area of law as much as any other sector of the economy. In general, while much of it is of critical importance to financial institutions,[31] I need say little about the field since it is covered fully in other chapters in this work, especially Chapter 36 of this volume on commercial law.

However, one point is worth stressing. The quality of our commercial law as a whole has been a help to the City in furthering its constant policy of securing a solid share of banking and other financial services in the world at large. While the strength of the financial institutions, and the quality of the workforce, have each been extremely important, it has also been of value that our legal arrangements for commercial business have had and retain healthy respect. The relative superiority in the world as a whole, and within Europe in particular, of the commercial legal apparatus in the United Kingdom has been a source of great strength to the City in recent decades and indeed in earlier times as well. English law has for many years been relatively popular in the international arena. It is a law which is frequently chosen by those with power to choose a law for the governing of their transactions. Further, London is also popular as a place of jurisdiction, where there is room for that choice to be exercised. London ranks with New York in terms of choice of law, and arguably even ahead of New York in terms of choice of court jurisdiction or choice of a place for arbitration. Various estimates have been offered over the years of the value in terms of invisible earnings of the great solicitors' firms in England and Wales, of the visiting law firms,[32] and indeed of

---

[31] For example, the leading case of *Hedley Byrne & Co Ltd v Heller and Partners Ltd* [1964] AC 465 involved a bank, and is known to every banker of any seniority. It established that a person may in certain circumstances owe a duty of care to a stranger, in tort, for negligent misstatement or advice. In that case the bank in question escaped liability only by virtue of its disclaimer. See also *Henderson v Merrett Syndicates Ltd* [1995] 2 AC 145.

[32] Increasingly, the major US law firms have bought or merged with existing firms or established branches themselves, and the same to a lesser extent is true of other law firms established in continental Europe and elsewhere.

the Bar; on any view the contribution made by these three sectors to the prosperity and reputation of the City has been very substantial.

Financial law

I turn to the second of the three remaining topics, which is the contribution made by the House of Lords to that part of commercial law that can best be described as financial law. It is surprising how little of this there is. For this there may be three principal reasons:

- First, there has been a strong Court of Appeal for as long as the House of Lords has been operating under the Appellate Jurisdiction Act 1876. Many of the leading decisions on financial law were settled at the level of the Court of Appeal[33] and have not needed to go any higher.
- Secondly, the bedrock of financial law has been in place for many years, and, indeed, some of the most fundamental decisions were arrived at before the commencement of the Appellate Jurisdiction Act 1876 itself.[34]
- Thirdly, arbitration, other forms of dispute resolution,[35] modern case handling in the Commercial Court, and indeed the tradition of robust commercial legal advice have all combined to keep a measure of control over the number of contested financial cases in this jurisdiction by comparison with the court lists and output elsewhere.

Financial regulation

The last of the three areas is financial regulation, as opposed to other areas of financial law.

For many years, until 1979, this subject did not really exist in its own right. Self-regulation under the old arrangements mainly run by the Stock Exchange, Lloyd's of London, and the Bank of England was the cement that held the City together. The subject began to appear in the banking field in 1979 but truly became identifiable as a result of the Financial Services Act 1986, which covered the securities field and part of the world of insurance.

---

[33] An outstanding example would be the classic decision of the Court of Appeal in 1904 in *Prudential Assurance Co v Comrs of Inland Revenue* [1904] 2 KB 658; this remains to this day the leading authority on the definition of a contract of insurance, a topic which as far as I know has never reached the House of Lords (the most recent exposition of the topic, in *Fuji Finance Ltd v Aetna Life Insurance Co Ltd* [1997] Ch 173, took place at the level of the Court of Appeal).

[34] See for instance *Foley v Hill* (1848) 2 HL Cas 28 on the basic proposition that the relationship between a banker and a depositor is that of a debtor and creditor; cf *Hopkinson v Forster* (1874) LR 19 Eq 283 on the absence of an equitable claim by an unpaid holder of a cheque against the banker. An even older example is *Carlos v Fancourt* (1794) 5 TR 482, 101 ER 272 establishing that there can be no contingency associated with a promise in a promissory note, and that a form of words that contains one will mean that the document is not such a note.

[35] Such as the City Disputes Panel.

That regime, based on a halfway house of practitioner-based regulation in a statutory framework, lasted a bare 13 years,[36] and was then replaced, in an early act of the incoming Labour Government in 1997, by a fully statutory system.

Apart from two appeals to the House of Lords, both in the field of investor compensation,[37] none of the litigation under the 1986 Act progressed beyond the Court of Appeal or the Inner House of the Court of Session. The record of the 2000 Act is even more remarkable, for a relatively contentious and ground-breaking piece of legislation, since there have to date been no appeals to the House of Lords arising out of it.

Conclusions

Generally speaking, the House of Lords has served the City well. It has never engaged heavily in City affairs, but what it has done has been helpful to the world of commerce rather than the reverse. However, there have been at least three cases in recent memory where there is still a strong strand of opinion that considers that the City and the financial services world would have been better served had the House of Lords upheld two of the decisions instead of reversing them,[38] and had it reversed the third decision instead of upholding it.[39] That said, City opinion would also have said much the same about the Court of Appeal, and would really have preferred the trial judge to have been upheld in all three cases, instead of in none.

---

[36] April 1988 to December 2001.

[37] Both were cases about the financial aspects of compensation following the default of an authorised firm, one brought by investors wanting to be paid more than the compensation company had decided upon, and the other concerning the true effect of the assignment which had to be executed by an investor as a condition of obtaining compensation: see *R v ICS, ex p Bowden* [1996] AC 261, and *ICS v West Bromwich* [1998] 1 WLR 896.

[38] ie, *Hammersmith and Fulham* and *BCCI (Three Rivers)*.   [39] ie, *Equitable Life*.

25

A Political Scientist's Perspective

Gavin Drewry

The location of the highest national appellate function in the second chamber of the legislature has long been recognised as one of the oddest features of the British Constitution. But, incongruous though this arrangement may seem, it is surely a feature of the British institutional landscape that might be expected to generate some shared interest, perhaps even collaboration, between academic lawyers and political scientists, particularly political scientists with a special interest in Parliament. Indeed, the very existence of such a glaring incongruity might have been expected to encourage this. And this is quite apart from the 'politics of the judiciary'—the role of the courts in any political system, and particularly the top courts in national judicial hierarchies, as arenas for holding governments to account, for reminding ministers and officials that the rule of law applies to them and not just to rank and file citizens, and for addressing disputatious issues that have high political impact. It was with these positive thoughts in his mind that this writer (a political scientist whose specialist interests include parliamentary and judicial mechanisms of public accountability) readily accepted his editorial colleagues' request to write about the judicial functions of the House of Lords from a political science perspective.

However, it soon became evident that the writing of this chapter would present at least two difficulties, the first, and lesser of the two being how to identify the precise location of the viewing point from which to offer a 'political scientist's view'. What is political science, as distinct from, for instance, constitutional history or organisational sociology? And is political theory really so very different from theoretical jurisprudence, given that they have so many founding fathers (Jeremy Bentham, Karl Marx, and John Rawls, to name but three) in common?

The second difficulty is much more significant and, indeed, goes to the heart of this chapter's subject matter. It arises from the inconvenient fact that very few political scientists in the UK (begging that identity question for the moment) have taken the slightest interest in the judicial functions of the House of Lords or indeed in most other aspects of law and legal institutions. The UK courts have, at least until quite recently, largely been treated as very marginal if not completely irrelevant to the academic study of UK politics. The middle part of this chapter will seek to demonstrate this.

So, if I had tried to interpret the title of this chapter literally—as promising an account of what political scientists have thought and written about the judicial functions of the House of Lords—the chapter would have been very short indeed. The author has sought to offset this inconvenience by taking a broader interpretation of his terms of reference by looking more generally at UK political scientists' interest in 'legal' aspects of their discipline—on the assumption that if any of them are interested in anything to do with law and the judicial process, then at least some of that interest must surely have focused (as is the case in the USA, where so much has been written about the political impact of the US Supreme Court) on the top court in the judicial hierarchy.

However, even with this wider and more elastically circumscribed agenda, relevant substantive material (other than insofar as a shortage of such material is itself 'relevant' as indicating a possible lack of interest) is in short supply. The latter part of this essay will be devoted to describing and explaining the latter phenomenon and reflecting on why, in the run-up to the transfer of the appellate jurisdiction to the new Supreme Court, we may just be beginning to detect some faint stirrings of interest in legal and judicial matters—perhaps even including the judicial functions of the House of Lords—in the British political science community.

What is 'political science'?

First, let me first address the 'what is political science?' issue. I will not make heavy weather of this because to do so would probably be seen as a self-indulgent digression in a volume of this kind—and many others have written on the matter in learned fashion and often at some length.[1] Suffice it to say that scholarly interest in politics (particularly in its normative, 'philosophical' aspects) can be traced back to Aristotle, c 350 BC, and perhaps beyond; but the modern study of politics as a branch of the social sciences began to take shape in the first half of the twentieth century and gained significant momentum after the Second World War, acquiring an important 'behavioural' dimension and attaching increasing weight to the use of quantitative methodologies. In recent years there has been growing interest in the use of economic models, particularly those associated with free-market 'public choice' accounts of social and political behaviour. The claims of the discipline to being a 'science' as opposed to a subject-area are quite modern (and are sometimes contested).

Political science has always been an eclectic discipline, drawing in particular upon (and contributing to) scholarly work in the areas of philosophy, economics, history, sociology—and law. So its boundaries are elastic and permeable. For the

---

[1] See, for instance, WJM Mackenzie, *Politics and Social Science* (Harmondsworth: Penguin, 1967); GA Almond, 'Political Science: The History of the Discipline' in RE Goodin and H-D Klingermann (eds), *A New Handbook of Political Science* (Oxford: OUP, 1996) 50–96.

purposes of this chapter the working definition of a 'political scientist' will, in recognition of this elasticity and permeability, be taken to mean an academic who is likely to belong to the relevant professional association (in post-war UK, the Political Studies Association) and/or all or most of whose published work appears in books and journals with a 'politics' Dewey Decimal library classification rather than the classmarks pertaining to 'economics' or 'law'. This very crude rule of thumb will probably not satisfy everyone, but it will suffice for our present purposes. There are inevitably some interesting hybrid cases—scholars who have crossed the bridge between politics and law, in one or the other direction—and some of these cases will be highlighted in the narrative that follows.

Law and political science—a natural affinity?[2]

That both the study and the practice of politics have, in the very nature of things, strong legal dimensions has long been recognised, not least in the United States, where the shadow of the US Supreme Court looms so large. In *Democracy in America*, Part I of which was published in 1835 (three decades after the path-breaking decision of the Supreme Court in *Marbury v Madison*), Alexis de Tocqueville observed that 'there is hardly a political question in the United States which does not sooner or later turn into a judicial one'. He opined that 'the power vested in the American courts of justice of pronouncing a statute to be unconstitutional forms one of the most important barriers which has ever been devised against the tyranny of political assemblies'.[3] The Founding Fathers—who were, of course, devising a republican constitution, embodying principles of limited government that would not allow a reversion to the oppression of the colonial past—laid the foundations for a constitution-based polity that was in sharp contrast to the uncodified constitutional arrangements in Britain. Herein lies the main explanation for the difference between the UK and the USA in respect of the 'legal' content of political science, to which we will return later.

In the United Kingdom, the metamorphosis of academic interest in political theory and institutions into a social science happened very slowly and somewhere along the way the legal ingredients seem to have gone missing. Consider the following passage from an important work by one of the leading figures of post-war political science, WJM Mackenzie:

In the generation before 1914 it would have been inconceivable that one should study political systems without also discussing legal systems. In England, Maine, Pollock, Maitland, Vinogradoff analysed policy and society in terms of the development of law. In Germany, theories of empire, state and nation were debated by Savigny and many others

---

[2] Parts of this section have been adapted from this writer's contribution to a *festschrift* to the late Geoffrey Marshall: G Drewry, 'Bridging the Chasm: Public Law and Political Science' in D Butler et al (eds), *The Law, Politics and the Constitution: Essays in Honour of Geoffrey Marshall* (Oxford: OUP, 1999) 203–21.
[3] A de Tocqueville, *Democracy in America*, abridged World Classics edition (Oxford: OUP, 1946) 83.

in terms of Roman law, canon law, and German law, of custom and codification. In France the debate about pluralism and the state was in one aspect a debate about the nature of law, involving legal scholars of the calibre of Duguit, Esmein and Carré de Malberg. In continental Europe the tradition survives in the Law Faculties; Anglo-Saxons rarely visit them except to enquire about the *Droit Administratif* or *Verwaltungsrecht*, concepts which make little sense when lifted out of the context of a general philosophy of law and the state.[4]

What is the basis of this natural affinity between the academic disciplines of law and political science? For one thing, the literature of political science is peppered with legal concepts and terminology, and some of it certainly addresses more or less directly and explicitly the relationships between law and politics and between legal and political actors and institutions. Constitutional issues, in particular, are frequently addressed from a hybrid legal and political science perspective, the balance of hybridity depending on whether the writer is primarily a lawyer or a political scientist. Public law is woven tightly into the fabric of public adminis-tration—albeit more tightly in some countries than in others.

The words of Mackenzie, just quoted, make clear the importance of law in the intellectual history of traditional political science. The serious study of politics has necessarily and inevitably involved the study of law, and vice versa. Some of the links are obvious. For one thing, constitutions and rules of public law, and the courts that interpret and apply them, set the formal ground rules of political practice and provide important mechanisms for governmental accountability and constraint. To take just one example, at the heart of the agenda of modern political science, any quantitative study of voting behaviour or legislative behaviour must be informed by a working knowledge of electoral or legislative rules if the research is to be done properly and the research findings made sense of.

International relations are underpinned by international law (and perhaps vice versa, given the importance of customary international law, based on state and inter-state practice). The decisions of international courts (in particular, so far as the UK is concerned, the European Court of Justice and the European Court of Human Rights) impinge heavily upon domestic law and domestic governance. Courts can be arenas for pressure group activity—via constitutional and legal challenges to government, public interest litigation, and test case strategies.[5] Judicial appointments to courts at all levels, and particularly to the constitutional and higher appellate courts in common law jurisdictions, is a matter of recurrent interest to politicians and political scientists as well as to lawyers who study or practise in such courts—the academic and media attention given to the ratifi-cation hearings by the US Senate of presidential nominations to the Supreme Court is a particularly high profile instance of this.

---

[4] Mackenzie (n 1) 278.
[5] C Harlow and R Rawlings, *Pressure through Law* (Oxford: Routledge, 1992).

Law and the enforcement of law underpin the very existence of the state, an entity characterised by Max Weber as possessing a monopoly of the legitimate use of force. Lawmaking is a clear manifestation of state authority. Laws are the medium through which policy is translated into action. Laws are an important resource for public policymaking.[6] Legislatures are not only, by definition, lawmaking bodies, they are also the arenas in which elected politicians operate—and in many countries a high proportion of legislators themselves have legal backgrounds: the convergence of legal and political and official careers has been a well recognised phenomenon—certainly since the time of de Tocqueville, who in 1835 opined, rather quaintly, that 'as the lawyers constitute the only enlightened class which the people does not mistrust they are naturally called upon to occupy most of the public stations'.[7] Such universal public faith in the trustworthiness of the legal fraternity might be less evident today, and full-time politics in an era of 'big government' leaves less time than was the case in de Tocqueville's day for a professional double life, but the criss-crossing of these career paths is still evident in many countries.

Like another Frenchman, Molière's M Jourdain in *Le Bourgeois Gentilhomme*, who was astonished to find that he had been talking prose all his life without realising it, even the most anti-legalistic political scientist may, when he or she starts to think about it, be surprised to find just how deeply legal ideas have penetrated the fabric and the day-to-day vocabulary of political theory and discourse. The social contracts discussed by Hobbes, Locke, and Rousseau have a strong legal resonance; so do ubiquitous concepts such as legitimacy, rights, and justice. Many of the 'great masters' of political thought—Machiavelli, Bentham, Marx, Hegel, et al—feature as prominently on the reading lists of university courses in theoretical jurisprudence as they do for courses on the history of political thought; moreover, they are often joined nowadays by more modern names like Rawls, Nozick, and Foucault. A quick glance at most current textbooks on legal theory or jurisprudence will serve to verify this.

So the close, almost symbiotic affinity between the practice of law and politics, and between academic law and political science, seems almost as predetermined as a law of nature. To what extent is this borne out by UK experience? And where, if anywhere, has the top appellate court fitted into the agenda of UK political science?

British political science in embryo—some ghosts from the LSE

The pre-history of modern political science in the UK really began in the decades straddling the Second World War—when most leading writers on politics and

---

[6] R Rose, 'Law as a Resource of Public Policy' (1986) 39 Parliamentary Affairs 297–314.
[7] de Tocqueville (n 3) 206–7.

political institutions had been educated in the older disciplines such as history and law. The ambiguous and ambivalent relationship between law and political science in this early phase can be illustrated by reference to three distinguished near-contemporaries who held chairs at the LSE during that period—and who collaborated on at least one major published work[8]—Harold Laski, William Robson, and Ivor Jennings. All three were interdisciplinary 'hybrids' of the kind mentioned earlier. It must be emphasised, however, that these three are chosen merely as illustrative of our present theme—were we writing a more comprehensive account of the early history of British political science, the names of several other important founding fathers would certainly have to be included.[9]

Even though the LSE—the London School of Economics *and Political Science*—was founded as long ago as 1895 (essentially as a Fabian project, led by Sidney and Beatrice Webb), political science was for a long time the poor relation of economics there.[10] The first LSE Professor of Political Science was appointed in 1920. He was the socialist Harold Laski, whose academic background was in the discipline of history, and who taught and wrote mainly about political concepts and the history of political philosophy.[11] Laski's academic career had begun at Harvard, and he retained strong links with the United States, including many friends in top American legal circles, including Brandeis, Holmes, and Frankfurter. He dedicated one of his many books, *Studies in Law and Politics*[12]—a work that includes an important early analysis of the party political affiliations of the higher judiciary, covering the period 1832 to 1906[13]—to Brandeis. So it is fair to say that 'law', broadly defined, was a significant weapon in the armoury of one early proponent of UK political science, but it was, so far as this writer has been able to ascertain, not the kind of law that engaged in any significant way with the judicial functions of the House of Lords.

It should be noted that the political science taught by Laski and his colleagues in those early days, and indeed as it subsequently developed at the LSE and elsewhere in the UK subsequently, lagged a long way behind its counterpart in the USA, where behavioural and economistic approaches were pioneered.[14] Bernard Crick has aptly referred to the discipline as 'the American science of politics'.[15] It could at least be said, however, that the LSE did much to encourage the treatment of law as one of the social sciences.

---

[8] HJ Laski, WI Jennings, and WA Robson (eds), *A Century of Municipal Progress* (London: Allen and Unwin, 1935).

[9] See D Kavanagh, 'British Political Science in the Inter-war Years: The Emergence of the Founding Fathers' (2003) 5(4) British J Politics and International Relations 594–613.

[10] R Dahrendorf, *A History of the London School of Economics and Political Science 1895–1995* (Oxford: OUP, 1995) 225–6.

[11] See I Kramnick and B Sheerman, *Harold Laski. A Life on the Left* (London: Hamish Hamilton, 1993).

[12] H Laski, *Studies in Law and Politics* (Princeton: Yale University Press, 1932).

[13] ibid, 164–80.   [14] See Dahrendorf (n 1) 226.

[15] B Crick, *The American Science of Politics* (Oxford: Routledge, 1959).

Sir Ivor Jennings (1903–65) is an interesting case in point. Called to the Bar in 1925, he took silk in 1949. He was another LSE man, holding posts first as lecturer then as Reader in English Law from 1929 to 1940. He ended his career as Vice-Chancellor of the University of Cambridge. Along the way he produced major, and in many ways pioneering, studies of constitutions and governmental institutions. As a member of the LSE law department, it is very doubtful that he would have relished, or even recognised, the label 'political scientist'—though he was probably as much of a member of that disciplinary fraternity as any of his academic contemporaries and is indeed recognised by David Apter, the distinguished Yale political scientist, as being (along with Ernest Barker and Harold Laski) one of the English founders of the study of comparative political institutions.[16] These (and other) 'institutionalists', Apter says, had in common 'not only an extraordinary empirical knowledge of how such institutions worked... but a common knowledge of classical medieval and social contract history and law'.[17]

One of Jennings' most celebrated works, *Parliament*, the first edition of which appeared in 1939, contains a two-page (in a book of 570 pages) outline of the history of the House of Lords as a court of record, with no mention of any recent cases, and summarily dismissing the judicial functions of the House as being 'of no political importance'[18]—a statement that carries strong resonance with the subject matter of this chapter.

The third member of the triumvirate, William Robson, was perhaps the most interesting 'hybrid' of them all. His career path at the LSE eloquently signalled his academic bipolarity: having been called to the Bar in 1922, he was lecturer in industrial and administrative law from 1926 until 1933; next Reader in Administrative Law, from 1933 to 1947; and he was then appointed as the first Professor of Public Administration in the University of London, a post that he held until his retirement in 1962. On the 'political science' side, he wrote extensively on a wide range of subjects in the fields of political economy and public administration. In 1930 he was one of the founders of *Political Quarterly* and served as one of the journal's co-editors until 1975. He was active in the Political Studies Association, the Fabian Society, and the Royal Institute of Public Administration; he was President of the International Political Science Association from 1950 until 1953.

But one of Professor Robson's most important contributions was to begin the long process of rescuing English administrative law from the shadow of misguided Diceyan dogma about the supposed threat that would be posed to the rule of law by introducing in Britain anything resembling the French *droit administratif*. The first edition of his pioneering work, *Justice and Administrative Law*, appeared in

---

[16] DE Apter, 'Comparative Politics, Old and New' in Goodin and Klingermann (n 1) 372–97, at 378.
[17] ibid.   [18] I Jennings, *Parliament* (Cambridge: CUP, 2nd edn 1957) 398.

1928, the second in 1947, and the third in 1951. Much of this work was concerned with the neglected (and at that time controversial) subject of tribunals and inquiries—Robson had given evidence to the Donoughmore Committee on Ministers' Powers (of which Laski was a member), whose report, published in 1932, is discussed at some length in the second and third editions of Robson's book. But it also includes some reference to case law—including some major House of Lords decisions: there is, for instance, a substantial commentary on the seminal decision of their Lordships in *Local Government Board v Arlidge*.[19] Robson also discusses such important topics as the nature and rationale of judicial independence. But—perhaps unsurprisingly, given the undeveloped nature of administrative law jurisprudence at that time—he makes no specific observations about the judicial role of the House of Lords in that context.

Post-WW2 developments

All three of these LSE luminaries survived the war—Laski died in 1950, but Jennings survived until 1965 and Robson until 1980. Their formidable contributions to scholarship grew cumulatively throughout their working lives, and are still respected to this day. But their writings moved inexorably down the reading lists of politics students as a new generation of political scientists and a new brand of political science emerged in the post-war era. Legal approaches to politics in Britain in the 1950s and 1960s came to be associated with the arid formalism of an earlier, 'pre-scientific' era and became casualties of the behavioural revolution imported from the United States. And, until the 1960s, despite the best efforts of William Robson and others, there was very little of the administrative law that might have tempted bold political scientists to wade (or perhaps one might say, Wade[20]) into the legal pond. Academic lawyers retreated to their end of the library, political scientists to theirs.

Two more names, a generation on from the three already discussed, merit special mention here: Professor JAG Griffith and Dr Geoffrey Marshall. The former was an academic lawyer, with political interests; the latter was a political scientist possessed, unusually for those professing that discipline, of formidable expertise in law.

Griffith was a student at the LSE from 1937 to 1940, the heyday of Laski, Robson, and Jennings (30 years later he edited the *festschrift* for Robson[21]).

---

[19] [1915] AC 120. See WA Robson, *Justice and Administrative Law* (London: Stevens, 3rd edn 1951) 473–83.

[20] The first edition of one important early textbook on the subject, by HWR Wade, *Administrative Law* (Oxford: Clarendon Press, 1961), was just 290 pages long, including indices. The 9th edition of Wade and Forsyth (2004) is 1035 pages long.

[21] JAG Griffith (ed), *From Policy to Administration: Essays in Honour of William A Robson* (London: Allen and Unwin, 1976).

He joined the staff of the Law Faculty in 1948, was appointed Professor of English Law in 1959, and then served as Professor of Public Law from 1970 until his retirement in 1984. In the meantime, in 1956, he became the first editor of the newly founded journal, *Public Law*—a post he occupied with distinction until 1981. This was and is probably the most 'political science-friendly' of all the UK law journals.

Griffith wrote several weighty monographs, but his first major claim to fame in political science circles was, or should have been, *The Politics of the Judiciary*,[22] his brilliantly subversive attack on the prevailing orthodoxy about the supposedly self-evident political neutrality of judges and the mechanistic nature of judicial decision-making. It was first published (in inexpensive paperback) in 1977, at about the time that the growing volume and political impact of judicial review were beginning to become more and more apparent—thereby underlining the importance of judicial independence and neutrality.

Griffith, a lifelong socialist, did not accuse English judges of conscious political bias; his claim—based on an impressively eclectic survey of judicial decisions in various areas of obvious political sensitivity (such as industrial relations, personal rights, censorship, and judicial review of official discretion)—was that a sub-conscious bias inevitably arises from the judges' professional experiences and social backgrounds. The book, which has gone through several subsequent editions, caused a great stir, and indeed some anger, in legal circles when first published. But it injected a much-needed sense of reality into discussions of judicial creativity and radically changed perceptions of the judicial role, to an extent that many of his general propositions are nowadays more or less regarded as commonplace orthodoxy. The book did attract some attention in political science circles—and probably raised some consciousness of the political relevance of the judicial process among at least some academics, but its main impact was on lawyers. Many of the cases critically discussed by Griffith were decided by the House of Lords, but this coverage is incidental to its main purpose.

A later book by Griffith—weightier in scholarship and of much greater potential relevance to the theme of this chapter—was his *Judicial Politics Since 1920*,[23] published in the Institute of Contemporary British History's series, 'Making Contemporary Britain'. The book contains well-documented accounts of the involvement of the courts—particularly the House of Lords and the Court of Appeal. It draws substantially on the research literature relating to the House of Lords; it includes thoughtful accounts of the contributions of individual Law Lords (including a particularly insightful pen portrait of Lord Reid); and commentaries on many leading House of Lords cases, particularly in the fields of public law and industrial relations law. It is probably a better book, at any rate by

---

[22] JAG Griffith, *The Politics of the Judiciary* (London: Fontana, 1977). Subsequent editions were published in 1981, 1985, 1991, and 1997.
[23] JAG Griffith, *Judicial Politics Since 1920: A Chronicle* (Oxford: Blackwell, 1993).

the usual academic criteria, than *The Politics of the Judiciary*—but it attracted much less attention than it deserved.

Griffith was a lawyer. Geoffrey Marshall is a rare example of a post-war British political scientist with a serious quantum of legal expertise (public lawyers with politics-related interests are much more commonplace). A critical admirer of some of Laski's constitutional writings, he was a fully paid-up member of the political science fraternity. The present writer recalls his own limited success in sustaining a specialist 'Law and Politics' group in the Political Studies Association throughout the 1980s. At most panel sessions of this group, meeting at PSA annual conferences, the audiences often failed to reach double figures. But Geoffrey Marshall was a loyal, and quite frequent, participant in these intimate events. His large output of authoritative publications—his interests ranged widely in the field of British and Commonwealth constitutional law and constitutional theory, with important forays into specific areas, including ombudsmen and police accountability—is recorded in the bibliography of his *festschrift*.[24] His knowledge of case law—including that of British appellate courts, was extensive, but, like most of the other luminaries cited here, he never engaged specifically with the appellate function as a discrete topic in its own right.

Political science and parliamentary studies

One place where we might expect to find political science engagement with the judicial functions of the House of Lords is in the sub-field of parliamentary studies. It is certainly the case that legislatures feature prominently in the political science literature around the world—unsurprisingly so, given their pivotal constitutional status as instruments for translating policy into law and as arenas for democratic debate and inter-party conflict. So far as the UK is concerned, the sub-field is relatively small—a fact that is probably attributable to the subordination of the House of Commons to the government of the day. Moreover, most of the parliamentary literature has focused on the Commons rather than on the Lords. So in our quest for a 'view from political science' we are faced with the dispiriting reality that not only have most UK political scientists been neglectful of the courts, they have also shown scant interest in the second chamber of Parliament in which the final court of appeal has been located. However, there are some honourable exceptions.

In 1964 Peter Bromhead (1919–2005) was appointed as the first Professor of Politics—'then a discipline in relative infancy', according to his Bristol colleague and obituarist, Donald Shell[25]—at the University of Bristol. Six years earlier, while at the University of Durham, he had published an important monograph

---

[24] Butler et al (n 2) 295–304.
[25] <http://www.bristol.ac.uk/politics/news/2005/021105%20Peter%20Bromhead>.

on the twentieth century House of Lords[26]—one of the few modern works devoted to exclusively to that institution, and still a minor classic in the literature of parliamentary studies. About five of the book's 283 pages are given over to an account of 'the Law Lords and other legal peers'.[27] This focuses mainly on the history of the conventions concerning political participation by Law Lords in the legislative business of the House, in particular the controversies surrounding Lord Carson's attacks in 1922—'with invective whose like had rarely been heard'[28]—on the coalition government over the Anglo-Irish Treaty. Bromhead notes subsequent episodes of judicial participation in debate—notably in the context of the death penalty and corporal punishment controversies of the 1940s and early 1950s—and comments that 'the experience which judges obtain in court, through the hearing of cases and the pronouncing of sentences, does not necessarily qualify them to be the interpreters of the will of society with regard to the deterrent and reformative effects of punishment'.[29]

The Bromhead-baton of House of Lords scholarship passed to another political scientist, Donald Shell, who has written extensively on the second chamber, his publications including a well-received textbook.[30] But the latter includes virtually nothing on the judicial function, apart from a brief reference to the role of Lord Chancellors, and a short account of some interventions by Law Lords in legislative debates on justice-related bills in the 1980s.[31] A subsequent collaboration between Shell and Nicholas Baldwin produced an interesting comparative study of second chambers, which includes a chapter by Meg Russell, of the Constitution Unit at UCL, entitled 'Responsibilities of Second Chambers: Constitutional and Human Rights Safeguards', which touches peripherally on the House of Lords' role in that context.[32]

Meg Russell has carried out substantial studies of House of Lords reform, from a cross-national comparative perspective. Her book on this subject, published in 2000,[33] drawing upon material from Australia, Canada, France, Germany, Ireland, Italy, and Spain, touched upon the role exercised by second chambers in some countries in appointing (sometimes in conjunction with the first chamber) members of the senior judiciary, and for oversight of judicial functions. She mentions the position of the Law Lords and suggests that the loss of legal expertise that would ensue from their removal from the House ('as many have proposed'—though at this stage the Constitutional Reform Act was not even a distant speck on the horizon) could be compensated by giving other senior lawyers *ex officio* membership of the House. Retired Law Lords might, in that event, be retained as members, to

---

[26] PA Bromhead, *The House of Lords and Contemporary Politics* (Oxford: Routledge and Kegan Paul, 1958).

[27] ibid, 67–72.   [28] ibid, 68.   [29] ibid, 72.

[30] D Shell, *The House of Lords* (London: Harvester Wheatsheaf, 2nd edn 1992).

[31] ibid, 159–60.

[32] N Baldwin and D Shell (eds), *Second Chambers* (Oxford: Routledge, 2001) 61–76.

[33] M Russell, *Reforming the House of Lords: Lessons from Overseas* (Oxford: OUP, 2000).

safeguard continuity. However, in conformity with the established pattern of UK political science, the judicial function is accorded marginal treatment.

Has the recent revival of interest in constitutional reform attracted the attention of political scientists? The answer is—some, but not much. When we look, for instance, at the work of Vernon Bogdanor, Professor of Government in the University of Oxford, and one of the most distinguished constitutional commentators among of the recent generation of political scientists, we find an immense output of top quality constitutional analysis, but only incidental and occasional engagement with the courts.[34] A recently published book by Anthony King (see below)[35] offers a little, but only a little, more encouragement in this context.

One rare collaborative venture between lawyers and political scientists was the workshop on the parliamentary and judicial roles of the House of Lords convened in Belfast in 1997 by one of my present co-editors, Brice Dickson, and Paul Carmichael, then Senior Lecturer (subsequently Professor of Public Policy/Government) at the University of Ulster. This exercise, and the co-edited book that resulted from it,[36] was genuinely cross-disciplinary and contains important discussion of the judicial functions of the Lords—notably, Dickson's own insightful analysis of the work of the Law Lords in the period 1967–96. But, even here, we have a volume that is in two separate parts—'The House as a Chamber of Parliament' and 'The House as a Supreme Court'—with the lawyers and the political scientists sticking, by and large, to their own respective disciplinary territories.

One important arena for parliamentary studies has been the Study of Parliament Group (SPG), founded in 1964 by a small group of academics and parliamentary clerks. It now has an elected membership of about 150—more or less equally divided between those two membership categories—and the academic membership has included an interesting mixture of lawyers and political scientists, including several people (Griffith, Marshall, Bromhead, Shell, Russell, Bogdanor, Norton) whose names feature in this chapter, as well as some contributors to this volume, and the present writer. The Group has produced a lot of cross-disciplinary discussions, collaborations, and publications,[37] but it has never directly tackled the judicial functions of the House of Lords. Its one substantial study of the House of Lords[38]—looking in depth at one parliamentary session—involved virtually no

---

[34] But see his interesting 2006 Sunningdale Lecture, 'Parliament and the Judiciary: The Problem of Accountability': <http://www.ukpac.org/bogdanor_speech.htm>.

[35] n 54.

[36] B Dickson and P Carmichael (eds), *The House of Lords. Its Parliamentary and Judicial Roles* (Oxford: Hart, 1999).

[37] The Group produced a collection of essays to mark the 40th anniversary of its foundation: P Giddings (ed), *The Future of Parliament: Issues for a New Century* (London: Palgrave Macmillan, 2005). This includes (at 270–5) a list of the Group's publications and of evidence given on its behalf to parliamentary select committees.

[38] D Shell and D Beamish, *The House of Lords at Work. A Study based on the 1988–1989 Session* (Oxford: Clarendon Press, 1993).

lawyer-members of the Group and did not look at all at the judicial work of the House. If these remarks imply any suggestion of guilt, then this writer is as guilty as anyone. A book on *The Law and Parliament*,[39] based on the work of an SPG study group and co-edited by Dawn Oliver and Gavin Drewry, contains hardly a mention of the judicial functions of the House of Lords (though it does contain an interesting chapter by Geoffrey Marshall on the significance of *Pepper v Hart*[40]).

Some rare exceptions

Moving outside the realm of 'parliamentary studies', an important exception to the depressing pattern of political science non-engagement with the judicial work of the House of Lords is the Oxford political sociologist, David Robertson, who has conducted an innovative analysis of House of Lords judgments.[41] Writing from a 'legal realist' perspective, his work includes an interesting statistical analysis of the Law Lords' judgments in the period 1986 to 1995, adapting the jurimetric methodologies that had been developed by American political scientists to throw light on the decision-making processes of the US courts. His concluding chapter, 'Legal Argument and Politics', includes an in-depth analysis of the judgments in *Airedale NHS Trust v Bland*,[42] a case that concerned the issue of whether the witholding of care from a person in a persistent vegetative state constitutes a criminal offence.

But has anyone else, in the world of UK political science, made any serious attempt to study the appellate functions of the House of Lords? Step forward, the present writer, who began his career as research assistant to Louis Blom-Cooper, working on the study that led to publication of *Final Appeal*—and whose co-editorship of the present volume signals his continuing interest in the subject, some 40 years later. Some readers may have suspected that the narrative up to this point might have been leading to this self-advertising *dénouement*—in which case, I am very much afraid that these unworthy suspicions will have been amply confirmed.

Neglect of the courts—some European straws in the wind?

A generation or so ago, it would have been quite possible—indeed quite usual— for undergraduates studying British politics and government in a UK university to emerge at the end of their course with not the slightest reference having been

---

[39] D Oliver and G Drewry, *The Law and Parliament* (London: Butterworths, 1998).
[40] 'Hansard and Interpretation of Statutes', ibid, ch IX.
[41] D Robertson, *Judicial Discretion in the House of Lords* (Oxford: Clarendon, 1998).
[42] [1993] AC 789.

made by their teachers to courts and judges and with their one lecture on 'The House of Lords' having made little or no mention of that institution's judicial function. The more perceptive among them might have paused briefly to ask themselves why their UK politics textbooks said nothing at all about the courts—even about the top appellate court—whereas the United States texts (including ones by UK political scientists)[43] would have contained repeated references to, and usually a chapter or more on, that country's Supreme Court; and texts dealing with the government of continental European countries would have talked a lot about administrative law and administrative courts and about constitutions and constitutional courts.

The explanation for this lay mainly, of course, in the absence of a codified British constitution and in the chronic underdevelopment of administrative law: for UK political scientists, a generation or more ago, the courts were not only formalistic and technically difficult to access by non-lawyers, they were also institutions whose activities impinged seldom and marginally on the political agenda. Judicial review was, in SA de Smith's famous phrase, 'sporadic and peripheral'. Such explanations were no doubt substantially valid, but the intellectual cost to political science of ignoring key legal dimensions of the discipline was considerable. This writer has spent much of his 40-year academic career trying to point this out, particularly to his fellow public administration specialists,[44] but, alas, to very little visible effect. The list of public law academics writing authoritatively and often in a highly theoretically-informed way about political and constitutional matters—descendents, perhaps, of some of the scholarly 'hybrids' discussed earlier—is long and ever-growing, but there has been all too little willingness on the part of political scientists to cross the disciplinary divide from the opposite direction.

Thus the 'view from political science' has been characterised by poor visibility and by a lack of curiosity on the part of political scientists about what they might find by peering through their legal telescopes—but there are some faint signs of interest in legal matters within the discipline. The growing volume and political impact of judicial review since the 1970s has made the courts very much harder to ignore. Even more important has been the impact of European law—both in its human rights aspects (particularly since the Human Rights Act 1998) and its EU manifestations. In the latter context, high profile cases like *Factortame*[45] and *EOC*[46] in the 1990s and the more recent *Thoburn*[47] (metric martyrs) case have

---

[43] There have been many UK political scientists who have specialised in the study of US politics and government and whose writings have included significant coverage of the Supreme Court. One who deserves special mention is Richard Hodder-Williams, author of a respected monograph on the subject, *The Politics of the US Supreme Court* (London: Allen and Unwin, 1980).

[44] See, for instance, G Drewry, 'Lawyers and Public Administrators: Prospects for an Alliance?' (1986) 64 Public Administration 173; G Drewry, 'Public Law' (1995) 73 Public Administration 41.

[45] *R v Secretary of State for Transport, ex p Factortame Ltd* [1991] 1 AC 603.

[46] *R v Secretary of State for Employment, ex p Equal Opportunities Commission* [1995] AC 1.

[47] *Thoburn v Sunderland CC* [2002] 4 All ER 156.

underlined the extent to which EU membership has juridified the British Constitution by requiring the courts—UK courts as well as the ECJ—to disapply legislation that is incompatible with EU Treaty obligations.[48] The factors that might once at least partially have excused political scientists' neglect of the courts no longer apply. In recent years, the House of Lords has become a court that specialises, substantially, in public law: and this, as this author and his colleagues have argued elsewhere, 'has interesting implications for the role and public perception of the final appeal court when it moves from the House of Lords and is rebadged with the evocative title of Supreme Court'.[49]

Let me end on a positive note. At last, undergraduate textbooks on UK politics are beginning to wake up to the importance of the courts. One good example is the widely used text by Bill Jones et al, *Politics UK*,[50] recent editions of which have included chapters on 'The Judiciary' by Professor Lord Norton—a political scientist who has published extensively on parliamentary and constitutional themes. Looking along my bookshelves and picking up a couple of recent volumes, more or less at random, I find a study of political institutions by the Strathclyde political scientist, David Judge, that includes some coverage of the role of the judiciary, alongside that of regulatory bodies;[51] and an elegant study of the British Constitution by the much respected British politics analyst, Anthony King, whose book includes interesting discussion of the legal implications of continuing developments in Europe, and of the growing importance of the judges in the political order.[52]

This is encouraging—but it is only a modest beginning. Apart from the European developments, mentioned earlier, constitutional reform—just one aspect of which is the Constitutional Reform Act, and the establishment of the new Supreme Court—has been near the top of the political agenda since the late 1990s. Whatever excuses there might once have been for UK political scientists to turn a blind eye to the political significance of the courts, and particularly the top court, no longer carry even the slightest conviction.

[48] G Drewry, 'The Jurisprudence of a British Euroscepticism: A Strange Banquet of Fish and Vegetables' (1997) 3(2) Utrecht L Rev 101. See also D Nicol, *EC Membership and the Judicialization of British Politics* (Oxford: OUP, 2001).

[49] G Drewry, L Blom-Cooper, and C Blake, *The Court of Appeal* (Oxford: Hart, 2007) 147.

[50] B Jones, D Kavanagh, M Moran, and P Norton, *Politics UK* (London: Pearson Longman, 6th edn 2007).

[51] D Judge, *Political Institutions in the United Kingdom* (Oxford: OUP, 2005) ch 6.

[52] Anthony King, *The British Constitution* (Oxford: OUP, 2007) chs 5 and 6.

PART E
SPECIFIC AREAS

26

International Law

Rosalyn Higgins

Introduction

Anyone attempting to trace attitudes towards international law from 1876 until the present time can readily see that the Law Lords have today become much more receptive to this field of law. It is clear to today's practitioner, and confirmed by a study of the cases in which matters of international law have been canvassed,[1] that this development has occurred not *in abstracto*, but in relation to certain great themes that run like threads across the years. These are: the relationship of international law to English law; the question of treaties in English law; state immunity; acts of state; the jurisdictional reach of English law; and international organisations and English law. Each of these themes will be addressed separately in this chapter. Together they show that the journey made by the House has been an impressive one.

International law and English law

Some eighteenth and nineteenth century cases are frequently invoked as authority for the proposition that international law was at that time perceived as part of 'the law of the land',[2] although on closer inspection that is not so certain.[3] In turn, a series of cases running from the beginning of the twentieth century suggested some preference for the so-called dualist view, whereby international law becomes part of English law only upon formal acceptance by the English authorities. In *The Cristina* Lord Macmillan spoke of the need for 'adoption in our municipal

---

[1] But not Prize law cases. Appeals from Prize Courts still lie with the Privy Council, not the House of Lords.

[2] eg *Barbuit's Case* (1737) 25 ER 777, *per* Lord Talbot; *Triquet v Bath* (1764) 97 ER 936, *per* Lord Mansfield; *De Wutz v Hendricks* (1820) 130 ER 326; *R v Keyn (The Franconia)* (1876) 2 Exch D 63, *per* Cockburn CJ.

[3] For a persuasive analysis, see J Collier, 'Is International Law Really Part of the Law of England?' (1989) 38 ICLQ 924.

law of a doctrine of public international law'[4] and a year later, in the Privy Council case of *Chung Chi Cheung v The King*, Lord Atkin said that: 'So far at any rate as the courts of this country are concerned, international law has no validity save insofar as the principles are accepted and adopted by our own domestic law',[5] but he then somewhat mystifyingly explained that our courts will ascertain what the relevant rule of international law is and 'having found it, they will treat it as incorporated into the domestic law, so far as it is not inconsistent with the rules enacted by statutes or finally declared by their tribunals'.[6] Thus matters remained, quietly but also uncertainly, for about 30 years.

In the 1970s English courts had to deal with the consequences of the expulsion from Uganda of large numbers of Asians said to be British protected persons. In the Court of Appeal Lord Denning, while (perhaps surprisingly) denying that international law required a state to accept into its territory its nationals thus expelled, added: 'rules of international law only become part of our law insofar as they are accepted and adopted by us'.[7] But he was to take an entirely different position a mere three years later, in *Trendtex Trading Corporation v Central Bank of Nigeria*.[8] In a very influential passage he there observed that international law is not subject to the English rule of *stare decisis*. It develops and sometimes changes, and an English court is free to give effect to those changes without any Act of Parliament, or any need to wait for a reversal by the House of Lords of one of its previous contrary judgments. This was because 'rules of international law, as existing from time to time, do form part of our English law'.[9] When the House of Lords came to address this same issue in 1980, in *I Congreso del Partido*,[10] the emphasis was on justice requiring the need to depart from previous case law. Theory about the place of general international law in English law was divided, save that Lord Wilberforce said in terms that he felt no need to wait for any changing enactment of Parliament.[11]

Today it is generally uncontroversial that customary international law is simply the law of the land. Its terms will need to be proved in a court of law by advocates who are there simply as counsel, not as experts in foreign law. The current vogue seems to be to add that it is received 'as common law'.[12] This has not, however, resolved all problems concerning the relationship between English law and customary international law. The application of the principle has proved difficult when international law has identified certain acts as international crimes. In *R v Jones*[13] one of the questions at issue was whether there was an international crime of aggression which was capable of being a 'crime' or 'offence' within the meaning of the Criminal Law Act 1967 and the Criminal Justice and Public Order Act

---

[4] *The Cristina* [1938] AC 485.   [5] [1939] AC 160, 167–8.   [6] ibid, 168.
[7] *Thakrar v Secretary of State for the Home Office* [1974] QB 684.   [8] [1977] QB 529.
[9] ibid, 554.   [10] [1981] 2 Lloyd's Rep 367.   [11] ibid, 371.
[12] An early trace of this is to be found in the reference by Lord Diplock in *Empson v Smith* to 'the common law of which the law of nations must be decreed a part': [1966] 1 QB 426, 431.
[13] [2007] 1 AC 136.

1994. The House of Lords unanimously answered this question in the negative. Some points in the reasoning were agreed by all five judges, but on other points their thinking diverged. They all accepted the proposition that international law is part of the law of England and Wales, although Lord Bingham thought it was probably too broadly stated.[14] They all also agreed that international law recognises aggression as a crime, rejecting the view of the Court of Appeal that it was too indeterminate a crime to be received into English law[15] and citing *Blackstone's Commentaries* to support the observation that in the past certain international law crimes had been automatically transposed into municipal law.[16] Lord Bingham offered the somewhat radical thought that it was 'at least arguable that war crimes, recognized as such in customary international law, would now be triable and punishable under the domestic criminal law of this country, irrespective of any domestic statute'.[17] At times the analysis in this case of what constitutes a crime in English law veers into analysis of the circumstances in which extraterritorial jurisdiction may be asserted.[18] International law declares aggression, war crimes, and genocide to be international crimes. As a result, each nation may exercise jurisdiction over these offences, no more no less. *This* is what is part of municipal law. States must cooperate to bring serious breaches of international obligations to an end, and not recognise or help maintain situations resulting from them.[19] However, there is no customary rule of international law (unlike in the Genocide Convention of 1948 and the Geneva Conventions of 1949) that requires, as a consequence, such permitted jurisdiction to be obligatorily exercised. As for aggression, it is widely agreed that this can be committed only by states.[20]

At the end of the day, the House of Lords thought that while *old* crimes in international law had been acknowledged as municipal law, new ones should not be so acknowledged without legislative intervention. In 1973, a unanimous House decided there no longer existed a power in the courts to create new criminal offences.[21] *R v Jones* entails reliance on alleged authority that is not authority at all and contains occasional worrying dicta.[22] And an international

---

[14] ibid, para 11.   [15] A view preferred by this writer.   [16] Book IV, ch 5, p 68.

[17] Para 22. The International Law Commission, when looking not at individual culpability but at the international responsibility of states, rejected the concept of 'international crimes' as applicable to states. Article 40 of its Articles of State Responsibility refers rather to 'serious breaches of obligations under peremptory norms of general international law' and the Commentary suggests that these include aggression, slavery, genocide, racial discrimination, apartheid, torture, and violations of the basic rules of international humanitarian law and of the right to self-determination: Draft Articles on Responsibility of States for Internationally Wrongful Acts, with commentaries (2001) 112.

[18] See Lord Bingham's agreement with the (rather different) observation of Buxton LJ in *Hutchinson v Newbury Magistrates' Court* (2000) 122 ILR 466, 506 (para 33).

[19] Article 41 of the ILC Articles on Responsibility of States (n 17).

[20] An exception is the International Military Tribunal at Nuremberg, which found 12 individuals guilty of crimes against peace, including planning and initiating a war of aggression.

[21] *Knuller Ltd v DPP* [1973] AC 435.

[22] eg 'It is, I think, true that customary international law is applicable in the English courts only where the constitution permits': *per* Lord Bingham, para 23, citing R O'Keefe, 'Customary International crimes in English Courts' (2001) LXXII BYBIL 293, 335.

lawyer cannot but be struck by the intermittent, but persistent, references to 'comity' by their Lordships. This term—unknown in international law—is used by national judges wishing to be sensitive to the reasonable position of courts in other forums. It is sometimes used as a synonym for 'international law', sometimes *in lieu* of 'international law', and sometimes in a way altogether mysterious to the international lawyer.[23] Its use persists, even alongside today's confident addressing of international law issues by the House of Lords. It could usefully disappear, suggesting as it does only an uncertainty about substantive international law rules.

Treaties

Unincorporated treaties

The treatment of unincorporated treaties has been a constant element in litigation and even now matters have not been fully settled by the House of Lords. Divergent views have also been expressed in the Court of Appeal and Privy Council. Thus, in 1967 the Court of Appeal in *Salomon v Customs and Excise Commissioners*[24] revealed divided opinions on the circumstances in which an unincorporated convention could be looked at. Lord Denning MR took a very robust approach, emphasising the need to make sure that the United Kingdom was in conformity with international law.[25] Lord Diplock, however, insisted that the sovereign power extends also to breaking treaties. In 1971, in *Woodend (KV Ceylon) Rubber and Tea Co Ltd v Commissioner of Inland Revenue*,[26] the Privy Council, referring also to the House of Lords' decision in *Inland Revenue Commissioners v Collco Dealings Ltd*,[27] insisted that no reliance could be based on the principle that legislation is presumed not to depart from an international obligation; the legislation alone should be considered.

The development in judicial attitudes to the question of what reference may be made to non-incorporated treaties over the last 25 years has occurred largely in relation to the European Convention on Human Rights. *Waddington v Miah*[28] is the first reported case in which the provisions of the European Convention were relied on in the interpretation of English law.[29] But developments in the

---

[23] See, eg, *Treacy v DPP* [1971] AC 537 (*per* Lord Diplock, 561–2) and *DPP v Stonehouse* [1974] AC 55 (*per* Lord Edmund-Davies, 83 and Lord Keith, 93).

[24] [1967] 2 QB 116.

[25] 'I am confirmed in my view by looking at the international convention which preceded the [Customs and Excise] Act of 1952 . . . I think we are entitled to look at it, because it is an instrument which is binding in international law: and we ought always to interpret our statutes so as to be in conformity with international law. Our statute does not in terms incorporate the convention, nor refer to it. But that does not matter. We can look at it.' ibid, 141E.

[26] [1971] AC 321.   [27] [1962] AC 1.

[28] [1974] 1 WLR 683. Lord Reid delivered the only judgment.

[29] See further *R v Secretary of State for the Home Department, ex p Bhajan Singh* [1976] QB 198; *R v Chief Immigration Officer, Heathrow Airport, ex p Salamat Bibi* [1976] 1 WLR 979. See R Higgins,

human rights context have undeniably had a knock-on effect in relation to other sorts of treaties. Within a couple of decades the battlelines were being drawn. In the final appeal in the *Spycatcher* case[30] the House held that there was no reason why the common law on limitations to freedom of expression should take a different approach from that enshrined in the Convention. Interestingly, Lord Goff made it clear that the principle of construction whereby a statute is to be interpreted if possible so as to be compatible with international obligations applies not only to statutory construction but more generally: 'I conceive it to be my duty, when I am free to do so, to interpret the law in accordance with the obligation of the cases under this treaty.'[31] However in the *Brind* case,[32] Lord Bridge, while declaring the attractiveness of the contention that it should be assumed that discretion conferred upon a Minister under a statute should be exercised within the limitations imposed by the European Convention, ultimately rejected that as 'introducing the Convention by the back door'.[33]

This issue of principle was one of several that lay at the heart of the important International Tin Council (ITC) litigation.[34] The ITC was an international organisation established by international treaty. Although the founding treaty—to which the United Kingdom was a party—had not been incorporated into English law, other treaty instruments relating to its headquarters and privileges and immunities were the subject of enabling Orders in Council, but these did not in terms accord the ITC legal personality in English law. It can only be described as regrettable that Lord Templeman, who gave the leading speech in the House of Lords, stated that a unincorporated treaty was ' . . . outside the purview of the Court not only because it is made in the conduct of foreign relations, which are a prerogative of the Crown, but also because, as a source of rights and obligations, it is irrelevant'. Lord Oliver was prepared to qualify this, allowing that a court could look at a treaty when it is incorporated into legislation, or where a statute enacted to give effect to it is ambiguous or obscure, or where domestic legislation 'either directly or by necessary implication' requires resort to a treaty for the purpose of construing its terms. This can be contrasted with the approach of Kerr LJ in the same case in the Court of Appeal. In a powerful analysis of the English case law he insisted that English courts, faced with unincorporated treaties, were not precluded from using them so long as the line was drawn to ensure that private rights claimed were not *dependent* upon the treaty. As the *ratio decidendi* for the House of Lords' decision did not turn on this matter, Lord Templeman's views do not constitute a formal overriding of those expressed by Kerr LJ, so they remain open for further argument.

'Dualism in the Face of a Changing Legal Culture' in M Andenas and D Fairgrieve (eds), *Judicial Review in International Perspective*, Liber Amicorum in Honour of Lord Slynn of Hadley, Vol II (The Hague: Kluwer Law International, 2000) 9, 12–13.

[30] *AG v Guardian Newspapers Ltd (No 2)* [1990] 1 AC 109.   [31] ibid, 283G.

[32] *R v Home Secretary, ex p Brind* [1991] 1 AC 696, 748.

[33] See also ch 30 in this volume.

[34] *JH Rayner (Mincing Lane) Ltd v Department of Trade and Industry* [1990] 2 AC 418.

In the event, this case seems to have been the high point of rigidity about non-incorporation.[35] In *McFarland v Secretary of State*[36] the House of Lords was fully prepared to assess whether a claim relating to section 133 of the Criminal Justice Act 1988 fell under Article 14(6) of the International Covenant on Civil and Political Rights. By the time we get to 2006 the House seems to have lost interest in dwelling upon whether treaties were incorporated into English Law. In *Kuwait Airways Corporation v Iraqi Airways Company*[37] it simply dealt with the substantive issues rather than dwelling upon whether particular Security Council Resolutions were part of English Law. All that mattered was that the United Kingdom was bound by these resolutions by virtue of Article 25 of the UN Charter.

The interpretation of treaties

Even while the European Convention on Human Rights remained unincorporated in the United Kingdom,[38] it was increasingly referred to not only for the principle that domestic legislation is presumed to be in conformity with treaty obligations but also to resolve perceived ambiguities. Thus, in *Attorney General v Associated Newspapers Ltd*[39] the House of Lords was not so much concerned with the then unincorporated status of the Convention but with whether section 8(1) of the Contempt of Court Act 1981 revealed an ambiguity which allowed the Convention to be referred to.[40]

The issue of possible language discrepancies in the authentic versions of an international convention came before the House in *James Buchanan and Co Ltd v Babco Forwarding and Shipping (UK) Ltd*.[41] The English text of the Convention was scheduled to the Carriage of Goods by Road Act 1965, and Article 23(4) of the Convention fell for interpretation. There was some possibility that reference to the French text (declared by the Convention itself to be equally authentic) might suggest a different interpretation of that paragraph from that suggested by the English text. Lord Wilberforce noted that in the particular context he found no 'assistance from methods said to be used in interpreting the Treaty of Rome by the Court of Justice of the European Communities', but he found the correct approach to be to interpret the English text in 'a manner appropriate for the interpretation of an international convention, unconstrained by technical rules of

---

[35] Together with the consequential contortions in *Arab Monetary Fund v Hashim (No 3)* [1991] 2 AC 114: see below.

[36] [2004] 1 WLR 1285.   [37] [2002] 2 AC 883.

[38] Technically the Convention has not been formally incorporated, but the long title to the Human Rights Act states that it is intended 'to give greater effect to rights and freedoms guaranteed under the European Convention on Human Rights'.

[39] [1994] 2 AC 238.

[40] ibid, 262, *per* Lord Lowry, who also referred to the Convention in *Spring v Guardian Assurance plc* [1995] 2 AC 296, 326G.

[41] [1978] AC 141. The Convention in question was the Convention on the Contract for the International Carriage of Goods by Road 1956.

English law'.[42] Having said that, he stated that the French text could also be looked at, not least because uniformity of interpretation of an international convention was desirable—and this could be done without any prior need for ambiguity on the face of the English text.[43] Lord Salmon agreed, while not in the event finding the study of the French text illuminating. Lord Edmund-Davies believed a prior ambiguity *was* needed in the English text before the French version could be looked at, and Viscount Dilhorne doubted the propriety of looking at the French text when Parliament had scheduled only the English text. While the approach of Lords Wilberforce and Salmon was more liberal, it is striking that their Lordships did not appear to feel that an international convention is best interpreted by the methods laid down in Articles 31–33 of the Vienna Convention on the Law of Treaties. Article 33 specifically addresses the interpretation of treaties authenticated in two or more languages and states that '[t]he terms of the treaty are presumed to have the same meaning in each authentic text.' Article 33 also provides that when a comparison of the authentic texts discloses a difference of meaning which neither a good faith interpretation of the ordinary meaning nor resort to the *travaux préparatoires* removes, 'the meaning which best reconciles the texts, having regard to the object and purpose of the treaty, shall be adopted'.[44]

By 1980 a strong majority in the House of Lords had affirmed the use of liberal, generally internationalist, methods of interpreting international conventions.[45] The use of *travaux préparatoires* to international treaties became admissible, even though background material relating to domestic statutes was still excluded.[46] Lord Diplock convincingly explained why this difference existed and Lord Scarman spoke of it being 'well settled' that English courts would respect the international currency of the Convention and also its international purpose. He stated that, in the specific task at hand, he would 'direct [him]self broadly along the lines indicated by Article 32 of the Vienna Convention on the Law of Treaties'.[47] And in an important dictum he stated that, howsoever the international convention had been brought into domestic law, '[o]nce it is a part of our law, its international character must be respected.'[48] While different outcomes were reached by their Lordships in this case, there was a striking consensus as to what could and could not be looked at when engaging in interpretation.[49] Lord Diplock stated that international courts and tribunals had recourse to *travaux préparatoires* and that 'this practice as respects national courts has now been confirmed by the Vienna Convention on the Law of Treaties'.[50] To the

---

[42] ibid, 152.   [43] ibid, 152–3.

[44] See also *Rothmans of Pall Mall (Overseas) Ltd v Saudi Arabian Airlines Corp* [1981] QB 368 (discrepancy between language texts: '*domicil*' and 'domicile').

[45] *Fothergill v Monarch Airlines Ltd* [1981] AC 251.

[46] See *Davis v Johnson* [1979] AC 264.   [47] [1981] AC 251, 293E.

[48] *Fothergill v Monarch Airlines Ltd* [1980] 3 WLR 209, at 233–4; ibid, 294B.

[49] Only Lord Fraser disagreed in principle with recourse to *travaux préparatoires*.

[50] [1981] AC 251, 282D.

international lawyer, both points in Lord Diplock's statement require qualification: it is only in restricted circumstances that international courts and tribunals may have recourse to *travaux préparatoires*, and it is less than clear that the reference in the Vienna Convention to when a court may look at *travaux préparatoires* was knowingly directed at *national* courts.[51] Lord Diplock seemed to go strikingly far in stating that for post-1969 treaties it would be a 'constitutional obligation...for an English court to look at their *travaux* when called upon to interpret them'.[52]

There has been a discernible trend to interpret provisions in international conventions in a way that is autonomous to the Convention and consistent with interpretations elsewhere. In *Sidhu v British Airways plc* Lord Hope stated in relation to the Carriage by Air Act 1961 that 'the code is intended to be uniform and to be exclusive also of any resort to the rules of domestic law'.[53] In *King v Bristow Helicopters Ltd*[54] the term 'bodily injury' fell for interpretation in a civil action brought for post-traumatic stress, a consequential peptic ulcer, and fear of flying. The Warsaw Convention, amended in 1955, is scheduled to the Carriage by Air Act 1961. It was agreed by all their Lordships that what 'bodily injury' means in any particular national system was irrelevant. Rather, it was the Convention meaning of that term that was to be sought—and this search was not to be controlled by technical rules of English law. That led Lords Hope, Steyn, and Mackay to the view that the meaning of the words would be that understood in 1929, which entailed recourse to the *travaux préparatoires*. Only Lord Hobhouse rejected the attempt to find a supposed state of affairs existing in 1929. He spoke forthrightly about the Warsaw Convention never being a 'historical document frozen in time'. Accordingly, the proper approach was to make use of the best current and scientific knowledge that is available.[55]

Sovereign immunity

Sovereign immunity and state trading

The late 1930s saw many cases in English courts arising out of the civil war in Spain. Many of these concerned claims to recover property, including requisitioned vessels, and the recognition of acts of *de facto* governments in that regard, and most were stayed pending the arrival in the House of Lords of the *Cristina* case,[56] which was destined to play in the following 35 years a central role in how issues of sovereign immunity were treated in the English courts. *The Cristina* was

---

[51] See [1966] *Yearbook of the International Law Commission*, Vol II, 218.
[52] [1981] AC 251, 283.   [53] [1997] AC 430, 453.   [54] [2002] AC 628.
[55] See the striking similarity to paras 80–2 in the *Arbitration Regarding the Iron Rhine Railway, between Belgium and Netherlands* (24 May 2005).
[56] (1938) 60 Lloyd's Rep 147.

a vessel registered in Bilbao, which had been captured on 19 June 1937 by the forces of General Franco. On 28 June the Spanish Government issued a decree requisitioning all Bilbao-registered ships. A later decree clarified that the earlier decree was intended to pass control over such ships wheresoever they were. *The Cristina* arrived in Cardiff on 8 July and on 22 July the owner issued a writ *in rem*. All five Law Lords held that the writ should be set aside because it impleaded a foreign sovereign. Lord Wright and Lord Atkin regarded international law as clearly stipulating that a foreign sovereign cannot be made party to legal proceedings against his will and that property owned and controlled by a foreign sovereign cannot be detained or seized by legal process. They further stated that this was part of English law. While agreeing with this reasoning, Lords Thankerton, Macmillan, and Maugham reserved the question of whether the property of a foreign sovereign which was not destined for public use, but was rather in commercial use, attracted such immunity. All previous cases relating to immunity had been decided by lower courts.[57] *The Cristina*—especially in the speech of Lord Atkin—provides the classic statement at the highest level of the doctrine of sovereign immunity from suit and execution. At the same time, it contained the seeds of the shift to a more restrictive immunity.

In 1952 the 'two principles' of immunity from suit and execution laid down by Lord Atkin in *The Cristina* were applied in the *United States of America and Republic of France v Dollfus Mieg et Cie SA and Bank of England*,[58] yet it was clear that several Law Lords were uncomfortable with the impact of the singularly English notions of possession and bailment. In the *Juan Ysmael* case[59] the Privy Council affirmed Lord Atkin's enunciation of the guiding principles, but the opportunity was taken to disagree with Lord Maugham's view that a mere claim of ownership by a sovereign was enough for immunity to apply. In *Rahimtoola v Nizam of Hyderabad*[60] the House was mainly concerned with whether the High Commissioner of Pakistan was an 'organ' or 'alter ego' of the state and it was agreed that, even if he was only an 'agent', he would be entitled to immunity. Lord Denning—now sitting in the Lords—argued that, as commercial transactions were involved, such immunity should not lie, and he urged the House to reconsider this part of the law. Sitting later as Master of the Rolls in the Court of Appeal, Lord Denning persevered in his advocacy of a restrictive doctrine of immunity in *Mellenger v New Brunswick Development Corporation*.[61]

---

[57] In particular *The Parlement Belge* (1880) 5 PD 197 and *The Porto Alexandre* [1919] 1 Lloyd's Rep 191. At the time of *The Cristina* the Brussels Convention of 1926 had been concluded, aimed at avoiding the negative consequences of immunity accorded to vessels engaged in State trading, but it was not in force for the United Kingdom.
[58] [1952] AC 582.   [59] *Juan Ysmael & Co Inc v Government of Indonesia* [1955] AC 72.
[60] [1958] AC 379.
[61] [1971] 1 WLR 604. See too *Thai-Europe Tapioca Service Ltd v Government of Pakistan, Directorate of Agricultural Supplies* [1975] 1 WLR 1485.

By 1976 the remarkable judgment of the Privy Council in *The Philippine Admiral* was finally to change matters, being clearly influenced by the changing international law perception of immunity for commercial acts. Even though counsel for the applicant had thought the absolute immunity rule was entrenched in English law, and could be changed only by Parliament, the Privy Council robustly decided that the earlier case of *The Porto Alexandre* should not be followed, notwithstanding the approval given to it by Lords Atkin and Wright in *The Cristina*. They contented themselves with the statement that 'the restrictive theory is more consonant with justice [and] they do not think that they should be deterred from applying it'.[62] As *The Philippine Admiral* was a trading vessel, albeit government owned, it would benefit from no immunity.

It was not until 1981 that the House of Lords had the opportunity to pronounce on the matter. In the meantime, in the *Trendtex* case,[63] Lord Denning MR had delivered himself of his celebrated dictum concerning the growing flood of cases applying a restrictive doctrine of immunity.[64] It fell to Lord Wilberforce (whose knowledge and interest in international law was to be of key importance to the Lords in this period) to state in *I Congreso del Partido* that 'the advance made' by *The Philippine Admiral* was not only right but extended also to actions *in personam*.[65] He expressly approved the Court of Appeal's decision in *Trendtex* and recognised a pattern of practice (in recent English case law, in judgments of respected foreign courts, and in writings of leading publicists) that evidenced 'a general seepage into international law of a doctrine of restrictive immunity.'[66] After this case the principle was settled, even if its application to the facts of some future cases led to judicial disagreements.

Sovereign immunity and human rights

The different, and very problematic issue that the House of Lords has had to wrestle with more recently is the relationship of the customary international law on immunity (and the 1978 Act) to a trend in international treaties to make immunity unavailable where grave violations of human rights are alleged.

In the first *Pinochet* case[67] a 3:2 majority found that to the extent that Senator Pinochet enjoyed immunity with regard to conduct within the 'functions' of a Head of State, the commission of international crimes was not within those functions and he had no immunity for those acts. However this ruling was set aside in the second *Pinochet* case due to the links between one of the Law Lords

---

[62] [1977] AC 373, 402.   [63] [1977] QB 529.
[64] 'Whenever a change is made, someone some time has to make the first move. One country alone may start the process. Others may follow. At first a trickle, then a stream, last a flood.' [1977] QB 529, 555.
[65] [1980] 2 Lloyd's Rep 367, 372.   [66] ibid.
[67] *R v Bow Street Metropolitan Stipendiary Magistrate, ex p Pinochet Ugarte* [2000] 1 AC 61.

and Amnesty International, an intervener in the case.[68] In the third *Pinochet* case[69] a 6:1 majority decided that Senator Pinochet could not benefit from immunity for the specific torture claims. The leading speech was given by Lord Browne-Wilkinson, who thought that after the affirmation of the Nuremberg Principles adopted by the General Assembly in 1946 there existed the concept of crimes in international law—originally linked to war, but then decoupled from that: 'I have no doubt that long before the Torture Convention of 1984 state torture was an international crime in the highest sense.'[70] In his view, the Torture Convention did not create a crime but established a system to fight it, one which required states to exercise jurisdiction or extradite. Still addressing the common law situation, he thought that immunity *ratione personae* was lost by a Head of State who was no longer in office, but his immunity in respect of official acts was preserved when he left office. However, the situation changed with the entry into force of the Torture Convention, which prohibited torture whether ordered by a Head of State or committed by an underling. If the former were to retain immunity *ratione materiae* after departure from office, the whole purpose of the Convention would be thwarted.

In the weighty speech of Lord Hope of Craighead the notion that it is not a function of state to commit acts which customary international law regards as crimes was held to be unsound in principle: '[T]he purpose for which [the acts] were performed protects these acts from any further analysis.'[71] He was of the view that there was no general agreement as to whether crimes contrary to *jus cogens* were removed from immunity under customary international law. There thus remained for Lord Hope the question of whether a former Head of State had immunity in the courts of a state which had jurisdiction to try the crime.[72] After an impressive analysis of international legal authority, he came to the conclusion that it could not be implied that the Torture Convention had removed immunity *ratione materiae* from former Heads of State for international crimes, but he then held that the immunity of Senator Pinochet could not survive Chile's agreement to the Torture Convention 'if the torture . . . was of such a kind or on such a scale as to amount to an international crime'.[73] Developments in international law were 'in place' by 1988 and 'the obligations which were recognized by customary international law in the case of such serious crimes by [the date of Chile's ratification of the Torture Convention] are so strong as to override any objection on the ground of immunity *ratione materiae* over crimes committed after that date'.[74]

---

[68] ibid, *(No 2)* [2000] 1 AC 119.   [69] ibid, *(No 3)* [2000] 1 AC 147.

[70] ibid, 198.

[71] ibid, 242. Today the 'purpose' of an act is not generally regarded as the criterion for differentiating between private and public acts: see *I Congreso del Partido* [1983] 1 AC 244.

[72] ibid, 243.

[73] ibid, 246. This suggests that certain types of torture, all of which is prohibited by the Convention, would not constitute a crime under international law, which must surely be questionable.

[74] ibid, 248.

Lord Saville of Newdigate agreed with Lord Nicholls in believing that immunity for parties to the Convention could not exist consistently with the terms of the Convention. To him there was no question of seeing if there had been an express or implied waiver:

Indeed it seems to me that it is those who would seek to remove such alleged official torturers from the machinery of the Convention who in truth have to assert that by some process of implication or otherwise the clear words of the Convention should be treated as inapplicable to a former head of state, notwithstanding he is properly described as a 'person who was acting in an official capacity'.[75]

Lord Millett stood alone on certain points of his reasoning. His view that no statutory authority was required for the courts to exercise jurisdiction over international crimes (of which torture was one even before the Torture Convention was agreed) stood in contrast to that of his colleagues, who believed that such authority was conferred for the first time by section 134 of the Criminal Justice Act 1988. He also agreed with Lords Nicholls, Hope, and Saville that the definition of torture in the Convention was entirely inconsistent with a plea of immunity *ratione materiae*: 'the official or governmental nature of the act, which forms the basis of the immunity, is an essential ingredient of the offence. No rational system of criminal justice can allow an immunity which is co-extensive with the offence.'[76] For Lord Millett, once a state was party to the Convention, there was no immunity to be waived. The implication would seem to be that that is so even so far as a current Head of State is concerned. By contrast, Lord Phillips of Worth Matravers thought the argument would only concern what immunity Senator Pinochet might have under the Torture Convention as a former Head of State. He thought it was still an open question whether international law recognised universal jurisdiction in respect of international crimes, but he held that 'no established rule of international law requires state immunity *ratione materiae* to be accorded in respect of prosecution for an international crime'.[77] He added: 'international crimes and extraterritorial jurisdiction are both new arrivals in the field of public international law ... I do not believe that state immunity *ratione materiae* can co-exist with them.'[78]

Lord Goff was the sole dissenter, sharing the views of Lords Slynn and Lloyd in the first appeal that no universal jurisdiction in respect of international crimes existed under customary international law. He found that, under section 20(1) of the State Immunity Act 1978, a former Head of State retained immunity for official acts and that the 1984 Convention had not altered that.

The various views of their Lordships have attracted both fierce support and trenchant criticism from human rights activists and international lawyers. But the relevant point for this chapter is that each and every one of the judgments is the product of an immersion in international law as it relates to customary law, treaty

---

[75] ibid, 267.   [76] ibid, 277.   [77] ibid, 289.   [78] ibid.

law, state immunity, and diplomatic immunity. That was true throughout the Divisional Court too. Each of the judges immersed himself in the international law on the subject, fully accepting the need to do so. Use was made of international and foreign case law, as well as of relevant conventions and legal writings.

In *Jones v Ministry of Interior, Saudi Arabia*[79] there was a further wide trawling of international law materials to assist in deciding whether Saudi Arabia could succeed in setting aside, under the State Immunity Act, service of civil proceedings brought by the claimant for, inter alia, torture by officers of the state. Lord Bingham accepted the findings in the second *Pinochet* case, but he distinguished the present case. He placed great emphasis on the fact that this case concerned a civil claim against a state as such. It was for him a point of great importance that the State Immunity Act was structured in terms of 'immunity save for specified exceptions', and that no exception for civil claims of torture outside of the United Kingdom was to be found.[80] And the European Court of Human Rights in *Al-Adsani v United Kingdom*[81] had recently found that, notwithstanding the *jus cogens* character of the prohibition on torture, international law does not currently provide that a state no longer enjoys immunity from civil suit in the courts of another state where acts of torture are alleged. The House's decision is indeed consistent with precedent, but the very narrow majority in *Al-Adsani*, the constant call in the UN for accountability for torture and their crimes, and the recent resolution of the Institut de Droit International stipulating an exception to the principles of immunity where international crimes are concerned,[82] all suggest that the legal principles are in transition. The distinctions highlighted by the Lords between civil and criminal actions, and between the Torture Convention and the State Immunity Act as it applies to torture, suggest a body of law that is straining to find internal coherence. This is a reflection not on those who are called upon to apply the law but on the corpus of law itself.

Acts of state

The act of state doctrine, concerning the judicial determination of the legal effect of an act of a foreign state or government, stands at the crossroads of private and public international law. In its practical application it is closely related to other legal rules, including those relating to recognition of a foreign state or government. Litigation concerning acts of state has regularly erupted at times of

---

[79] [2007] 1 AC 270.

[80] It is undeniably the case that the 2004 Convention on Jurisdictional Immunities of States and their Property (adopted by the UN General Assembly on 2 December 2004 (A/RES/59/38), but not yet in force) is also drafted in terms of 'immunity unless'. Extensive attempts were made to insert a human rights exception in the text, but they all failed.

[81] (2001) 34 EHRR 273.

[82] Draft resolution of the Third Commission of the Institut de Droit International, under consideration at its meeting in Santiago, Chile, in October 2007.

upheaval in foreign countries, where, for example, a private party before the court has claimed title to property by virtue of a foreign public act, or an entity claiming to be the government of a foreign state has sought the assistance of the English courts to retrieve property situated within the jurisdiction. The House of Lords has had a prominent role in such litigation and has contributed significantly to elaborating the circumstances in which the English courts will (or will not) give effect to the foreign act of state.

The Russian Revolution gave rise to many such cases in the English courts. It merits emphasis that, once it had been established that the act concerned was indeed that of a state or government recognised by the United Kingdom, the matter was not thereby to be treated as non-justiciable in the normal sense of that term. The content of the foreign act could be looked at to determine its meaning and scope, as the House of Lords showed in *Russian Commercial and Industrial Bank v Comptoir d'Escompte de Mulhouse*.[83] This had to be done, however, after hearing qualified experts in the foreign law.[84] But first it was necessary to know that the act concerned was indeed that of a foreign government—and it was in this regard that recognition by the United Kingdom played its part.[85]

The issue of recognition came to the House of Lords against the background of the establishment on 28 June 1945 of the communist provisional government in Warsaw. At that time the UK Government recognised the Polish Government in exile in London as the *de jure* Government but the later recognition of the Communist Government was treated as retroactive to this date.[86] This doctrine of retrospection was affirmed by the House in *Civil Air Transport Inc v Central Air Transport Corporation*.[87] A decade later the House was faced with some novel variations on foreign acts of state and recognition. In *Carl Zeiss Stiftung v Raynor and Keeler Ltd (No 2)*[88] their Lordships were concerned with whether a claim could be brought in the English courts by the Carl Zeiss company, a creation of the German Democratic Republic (GDR), which was not recognised as the Government of East Germany by UK authorities.[89] At the same time, there was much trade between GDR companies and UK companies. Their Lordships found help

---

[83] [1925] AC 112.

[84] See Lord Wright in *Lazard Bros v Midland Bank* [1933] AC 289.

[85] The Court of Appeal had held in *Luther v Sagor* [1921] 3 KB 532 that the recognition *de facto* of the Soviet government was a sufficient basis for the expropriating decree of the Soviet government to be given effect. The Court of Appeal further had held that the recognition, once given (a matter on which the Foreign Office certified by letter), had a retrospective effect to December 1917.

[86] *Gdynia Ameryka Linie Zeglugowe Spolka Akoyjna v Buguslawski* [1953] AC 11.

[87] [1953] AC 70. Several so called 'Russian bank cases' found their way to the House of Lords, dealing for the most part with private international law matters, eg *Comptoir d'Escompte de Mulhouse* (n 83); *Bank International de Commerce de Petrograd v Goukasson* [1925] AC 1950. The Italian invasion of Ethiopia in 1935 generated further comparable litigation, as did the Spanish Civil War. In *The Arantzazu Mendi* [1939] AC 256 the House of Lords was concerned with a somewhat different question, namely, whether a government recognised *de facto*, but not *de jure*, could insist on an entitlement to immunity from suit. It was held it could—a decision much criticised.

[88] [1967] 1 AC 853.

[89] eg H Lauterpacht, *Recognition in International Law* (Cambridge: CUP, 1947) 288H.

in the Foreign Office certificate as to recognition, which stated that the United Kingdom recognised the USSR as the *de jure* governing authority of East Germany. The House then held that the GDR was to be regarded as a subordinate entity of the USSR, and Carl Zeiss did therefore have standing to bring an action in the English courts. As in the much later case of *Arab Monetary Fund v Hashim*,[90] a conceptually troubling legal fiction was resorted to in order to accommodate the realities on the ground. A toe was put into the waters of reality by Lords Reid and Wilberforce, who perceived a trend in US courts to acknowledge such realities in the interests of justice and common sense.

In 1980 the Foreign and Commonwealth Office announced that it would cease formal recognition of foreign governments[91] (although the practice would continue for states). Recognition has thus faded as a preoccupying matter for courts, though certificates from the Foreign and Commonwealth Office continue to be sought on a variety of issues.[92] The focus has instead been on identifying the limits to the principle that English courts will give effect to the acts of foreign recognised states. In 1976, in *Oppenheimer v Cattermole*,[93] the House of Lords held that courts will *not* feel obliged under the act of state doctrine to give effect to the act of a foreign state in its own territory if the act was racially discriminatory and confiscatory and thus a grave infringement of human rights. That principle was affirmed by the House in *Williams and Humbert Ltd v W & H Trademarks (Jersey) Ltd*,[94] with a slightly wider formula being employed: 'English law will not recognise foreign confiscatory laws which, by reason of their being discriminatory on grounds of race, religion or the like, constitute so grave an infringement of human rights that they ought not to be recognised as laws at all.'[95]

The growing importance of international law in English courts, and the understanding that international human rights law is but a component part of international law, perhaps made it inevitable that the issue should be squarely faced of whether foreign acts of state entailing grave violations of international law should be given effect in English courts. It has been felt comfortable to clothe this in the garments of public policy. In *Kuwait Airways Corporation v Iraqi Airways Company*[96] one of the issues before their Lordships was whether UK courts should give effect to an Iraqi confiscatory decree promulgated in the wake of its

---

[90] [1991] 2 AC 114.

[91] *Hansard*, HL, vol 408, cols 1121–2 (28 April 1980). See RCA White, 'Recognition of States and Diplomatic Relations' (1988) 37 ICLQ 983–8; V Lowe and C Warbrick, 'Public International Law' (1992) 41 ICLQ 473–82.

[92] *Gur Corporation v Trust Bank of Africa Ltd* [1987] QB 599 (CA); *Arab Republic of Egypt v Gamal-Eldin* [1996] ICR 13 *Re B (A Child) (Care Proceedings: Diplomatic Immunity)* [2003] Fam 16; *Diepreye Solomon Peter Alamieyeseigha v Crown Prosecution Service* [2005] EWHC 2704 (Admin).

[93] [1976] AC 249.   [94] [1988] AC 368, 379.

[95] R Higgins, *Problems and Process: International Law and How We Use It* (Oxford: Clarendon, 1994) 218 (noting that it has been made clear that the English courts, as a matter of public policy, will not give effect here to foreign law that offends human rights).

[96] [2002] 2 AC 883.

invasion and purported annexation of Kuwait. Lord Nicholls of Birkenhead gave the leading opinion, and found as follows:

the courts of this country must have a residual power, to be exercised exceptionally and with the greatest circumspection, to disregard a provision in the foreign law when to do otherwise would affront basic principles of justice and fairness which the courts seek in the administration of justice in this country. Gross infringements of human rights are one instance, and an important instance, of such a provision. But the principle cannot be confined to one particular category of unacceptable laws. That would be neither sensible nor logical. Laws may be fundamentally unacceptable for reasons other than human rights violations.[97]

His Lordship referred to the Iraqi decree as a gross violation of rules of international law of fundamental importance. He added 'for good measure' that giving effect to this decree would be contrary to the UK's obligations under the UN Charter. He was joined in this analysis of the limits to the act of state doctrine by Lords Hoffmann and Steyn. Lord Steyn in particular thought the case 'a paradigm of the public policy exception' and elaborated in detail on the place of the Charter in international law and the binding Security Council resolutions on Iraq.[98] In establishing this constraint on the traditional giving of effect to an act of state, the House of Lords has emphasised with great clarity the importance of the international legal rules concerned.

It is also necessary to mention the singular 'English act of State' doctrine, formulated by Lord Wilberforce in *Buttes Gas and Oil Co v Hammer (No 3)*.[99] Lord Wilberforce said that 'there was a general principle ... of judicial abstention from adjudicating directly on the transactions of foreign sovereign states. The principle was not one of discretion but was inherent in the very nature of the judicial process.'[100] This pronouncement—which ironically came from the Law Lord of his generation with the deepest and strongest interest in international law—was to cast a long shadow, encouraging a somewhat undifferentiated recourse to non-justiciability. Indeed, such an approach was to be seen in their Lordships' judgments in the ITC litigation, where it was said that 'the transactions of independent states between each other are governed by other laws than those which municipal courts administer'.[101]

---

[97] ibid, para 18.

[98] It should be noted that Article 1(1) of the United Nations Act 1946 stipulates that if a resolution has been passed by the Security Council under Article 41 of the Charter (economic and diplomatic sanctions), the House of Lords may make the necessary Orders in Council to put this into effect. No such Order of Council was involved—but nor was this category of Security Council resolutions unknown to English law.

[99] [1982] AC 888.　　　[100] [2002] 2 AC 883, para 26.

[101] *JH Rayner (Mincing Lane) Ltd v Dept of Trade and Industry* [1990] 2 AC 418, 499G; see further below. In *Westland Helicopters Ltd v Arab Organization for Industrialization* [1995] 2 AC 387 Colman J, a judge greatly interested in matters of international law, who firmly insisted that the proper law of an international organisation was international law and not the law of the host state, did not then apply the relevant rules of international law, but rather concluded that matters relating to the AOI were non-justiciable.

The *Kuwait Airways* litigation gave an opportunity to the House of Lords to ensure that Lord Wilberforce's dictum was to be understood in a moderate way. Noting that Lord Wilberforce in *Buttes* had thought non-justiciability was the correct course when faced with issues of international law in which there are 'no judicial or manageable standards by which to judge [the] issues',[102] Lord Nicholls observed that Lord Wilberforce himself had accepted that in appropriate circumstances an English court *might* properly have regard to the content of international law. The non-justiciable principle did not mean, said Lord Nicholls, that the judiciary 'must shut their eyes to a breach of an established principle of international law committed by one state against another'.[103] In the present case the standard being applied was clear and manageable. Lord Steyn agreed. Lord Hope of Craighead was more circumspect, but was clearly willing to analyse the applicable international law in relation to the facts.

The jurisdictional reach of English law

The international law rules on jurisdiction serve the purpose of allocating jurisdictional competences among states. In *Treacy v DPP*[104] the House of Lords was concerned with the territorial reach of the Theft Act 1968, a person having made demands with menaces in a letter posted in England and received by the victim in West Germany. No geographical limitation on where the conduct took place or where its consequences were felt was to be found in the terms of the Act. Their Lordships were divided in their views as to where the offence was committed, the majority preferring the view that the offence was committed in England upon the posting of the letter. Only Lord Diplock (who was in the majority) addressed the issue as other than one concerning the interpretation of the terms of the Theft Act. Looking at the international aspects of the issue, he commented:

The Parliament of the United Kingdom has plenary power, if it chooses to exercise it, to empower any Court in the United Kingdom to punish persons in its territory for having done physical acts wherever the acts were done and wherever their consequence took place.[105]

He continued by observing that, while Parliament may move to legislate in so broad a fashion, the issue arises as to whether there will be resistance to such action by other states, invoking the rules of international law on jurisdiction. As to this, Lord Diplock offered a somewhat extraordinary reason for such long-arm jurisdiction:

... it would savour of chauvinism rather than comity to treat them [such acts in the field of criminal law] as excusable merely on the ground that the victim was not in the United Kingdom itself but in some other State.[106]

---

[102] [1982] AC 888, 938. [103] ibid, 1081A. [104] [1971] AC 537.
[105] ibid, 561E. [106] ibid, 562A.

A want of jurisdiction is not at all the same thing as classifying the act itself as 'excusable', as the International Court of Justice has been at pains to state on many occasions.[107]

International law has come, to a substantial degree, and depending on context, to recognise 'the effects doctrine', whereby jurisdictional competence may be asserted over acts committed overseas but which have their harmful and locally illegal effects within the jurisdiction of the forum. But the broader language of Lord Diplock—'wherever the acts were done and wherever their consequences took place'—envisages circumstances reserved for the very exceptional crimes that international law regards as entitling a state to exercise jurisdiction (such as war crimes or crimes against humanity). Lord Diplock's speech suggests that in the context of the *Treacy* case the rest of their Lordships may have been prudent to confine themselves to the interpretation of section 21 of the Theft Act 1968.

In *DPP v Doot*[108] Lord Salmon followed Lord Diplock in referring to 'the rules of international comity'. Lord Wilberforce addressed matters of international law more directly and confidently. He referred both to the objective territorial principle of jurisdiction and to the principle of universality. He then correctly added: 'the position as it is under international law is not, however, determinative of the question whether, under our municipal law, the acts committed amounted to a crime'.[109] As to that, he said, there was no mechanical answer.

Nor is there a mechanical answer to the converse question of whether there is a responsibility on the United Kingdom under international law for acts of its public servants committed abroad. The International Court of Justice has recently had occasion to confirm that acts of the military committed abroad, even if *ultra vires*, incur the international legal responsibility of the national state concerned. Thus, the fact that it was in the Democratic Republic of the Congo that the forces of Uganda violated international law did not avoid the legal responsibility of Uganda.[110] The UN's Human Rights Committee, interpreting the International Covenant on Civil and Political Rights, has also found that the duties of a state under that instrument are in play even when it is purporting to exercise jurisdiction outside its own territory. It stated that: 'a State party must respect and ensure the rights laid down in the Covenant to anyone within the power or effective control of that State Party, even if not situated within the

---

[107] See *Armed Activities on the Territory of the Congo (New Application: 2002) (Democratic Republic of the Congo v Rwanda)* [2006] ICJ Rep, para 127. See also: *Legality of Use of Force (Serbia and Montenegro v Belgium)*, Preliminary Objections, Judgment [2004] ICJ Rep, 279, 328; *Legality of Use of Force (Yugoslavia v Belgium)*, Provisional Measures, Order of 2 June 1999 [1999] ICJ Rep (I) 140, para 47; *Fisheries Jurisdiction (Spain v Canada)*, Jurisdiction of the Court, Judgment [1998] ICJ Rep 456, paras 55–6; *Aerial Incident of 10 August 1999 (Pakistan v India)*, Jurisdiction, Judgment [2000] ICJ Rep 33, para 51.

[108] [1973] AC 807.   [109] ibid, 817D.

[110] *Armed Activities on the Territory of the Congo (New Application: 2002) (Democratic Republic of the Congo v Rwanda)* Judgment [2006] ICJ Rep 168, 231, para 180.

territory of the State Party.'[111] The European Court of Human Rights, in *Banković v Belgium*,[112] has made clear that the reach of the European Convention is not in principle extraterritorial, unless certain exceptional circumstances exist such as occupation of a foreign territory. Such possibilities would 'require special justification in the particular circumstances of each case'.[113]

Jurisdiction over the actions of British forces in Iraq was under consideration in *Al-Skeini v Secretary of State for Defence*,[114] which concerned the deaths of six Iraqis caused by the actions of British soldiers in Basra. The first issue was whether the Human Rights Act 1998, which was silent as to its territorial reach, could apply to the actions of British forces overseas. Lord Bingham was alone in deciding this point in the negative. He noted that Article 1 of the European Convention did not find a place in the Human Rights Act, and that there was a specific procedure for the application of the Act to overseas territories. In his view a claim could not be made against the Secretary of State for acts or omissions of British forces serving overseas, but the forces could still be disciplined under the relevant procedures and could be tried for genocide, war crimes, and crimes against humanity. This approach would disallow governmental liability for purposes of the European Convention in circumstances in which such a responsibility under international law would undoubtedly lie.[115] Lord Rodger of Earlsferry thought that the purpose of the 1998 Act was to provide remedies in domestic law to those whose human rights are violated by a UK public authority. Jurisdiction was normally territorial so as not to violate the sovereignty of other states, but '[t]here is . . . nothing in the wider context of international law which points to the need to confine section 6 and 7 of the 1998 Act to the territory of the United Kingdom.'[116] Any other interpretation would leave victims without a remedy in the English courts. Baroness Hale was of the same view.

The second issue in *Al-Skeini* was the *extent* of any such jurisdiction outside of the United Kingdom. Here the majority was content to rely on the practice of the European Court of Human Rights. The Secretary of State conceded (even while challenging that any action could lie against him) that jurisdiction extended to a military prison in Iraq occupied and controlled by agents of the United Kingdom. Lord Carswell, referring to embassies and consulates abroad, as well as to such military prisons, thought that '[o]nce one goes past these categories, it would in my opinion require a high degree of control by the agents of the state of an area in

---

[111] HRC General Comment No 31, Nature of the General Legal Obligation Imposed on States Parties to the Covenant, CCPR/C/21/Rev1/Add 13, 26 May 2004. See also *Burgos/Delia Saldias de Lopez v Uruguay*, Communication No 52/1979 (29 July 1981), UN Doc CCPR/C/OP/1 at 88 (1984), a position endorsed by the ICJ in its *Advisory Opinion on Legal Consequences on the Construction of a Wall in the Occupied Palestinian Territory*, Advisory Opinion, ICJ Reports 2004, 136.
[112] App No 52207/99, decision of 12 December 2001.   [113] ibid, para 61.
[114] [2008] 1 AC 153.
[115] *Armed Activities on the Territory of the Congo (New Application: 2002)* (*Democratic Republic of the Congo v Rwanda*) Judgment, ICJ Reports 2006, 168, 231, para 180.
[116] [2008] 1 AC 153, para 97.

another state before it could be said that that area was within the jurisdiction of the former.'[117] The majority sought to see if the facts fell within the exceptions referred to in the *Banković* case by the European Court of Human Rights. Lord Rodger thought the Grand Chamber's findings in that case were inconsistent with the reasoning in the later case of *Issa v Turkey*[118] but, along with Baroness Hale, he found the former to be more persuasive. Lord Brown of Eaton-under-Heywood, in a highly detailed analysis of the European Convention case law, did not read *Issa* as in the event detracting from *Banković*.

The very nature of the issues under consideration in *Al-Skeini* will make the opinions there expressed controversial to some. The internationally minded way in which the complex issues were dealt with is undoubtedly impressive. The key issue has been clarified in a manner that is consistent with other rulings on international law.[119] In *Al-Jeddah*, in 2007, Lord Rodger was able simply to observe that the fact that an applicant was held in Iraq by UK forces was no bar as such to proceedings under the Human Rights Act 1998.[120]

International organisations

By the 1960s international organisations were beginning to make their presence felt in English courts.[121] In 1968, in *Nissan v Attorney General*,[122] the House of Lords needed to determine the status of national contingents within the UN Force in Cyprus. This force had been established by Security Council Resolution. At the heart of the litigation was the question whether British forces serving with the UN remained under the jurisdiction of the United Kingdom so far as criminal offences committed in Cyprus were concerned or whether they were then agents of the UN. In giving its judgment in favour of the former proposition, their Lordships examined UN resolutions, letters between the UN and Cyprus and between the UN and the United Kingdom, and myriad other UN documentation. Lord Pearce observed that '[t]he functions of the force as a whole are

---

[117] For findings on state responsibility in international law for the conduct of forces acting overseas, and notably in areas under occupation, see *Armed Activities on the Territory of the Congo (Democratic Republic of the Congo v Uganda)*, Judgment [2005] ICJ Rep 168, 231.

[118] (2004) 41 EHRR 27.

[119] See, eg, *Legal Consequences of the Construction of a Wall in the Occupied Palestinian Territory*, Advisory Opinion [2004] ICJ Rep 136, 179–80; *Coard v United States*, Case 10.951, Inter-Am CHR, Report No 109/99, P 39 (1999).

[120] [2008] 1 AC 332, para 48. See further below.

[121] In 1964 the Court of Appeal had to determine, in the context of deciding whether immunity lay from judicial process, whether the European Commission of Human Rights was an 'organ' of the Council of Europe. It also had to decide the temporal limit of any immunity attaching to the President of the European Commission. Only then could the statutory provisions of the International Organisations (Immunities and Privileges) Act 1950 be applied: *Zoernsch v Waldock* [1964] 1 WLR 675.

[122] [1970] AC 179.

international. But its individual component forces have their own national duty and discipline and remain in their own national service.'[123] Lord Morris firmly relied on UN documentation to find that:

it appears further that though national contingents were under the authority of the United Nations and subject to the instructions of the commander, the troops as members of the force remained in their national service. The British forces continued, therefore, to be soldiers of Her Majesty. Members of the United Nations Force were subject to the exclusive jurisdiction of their respective national states, in respect of criminal offences committed by them in Cyprus.[124]

These issues regarding criminal jurisdiction over, and responsibility for, British forces wearing the UN beret were fairly easily resolved, as were questions of the immunities of international officials. But before long there intruded more difficult problems. Some of these were perhaps self-inflicted. In 1978 the Foreign and Commonwealth Office advised that the Government would be willing officially to acknowledge that international legal entities enjoyed legal personality and capacity, allowing them to sue and be sued in this country, even in the absence of specific English legislation concerning them.[125] Notwithstanding this statement, courts embarked upon an inward-looking exercise in which the central focus became whether the international organisation was a legal person having its personality in English law. Realities became of little importance and a strictly dualist approach to international legal persons became the order of the day.

In the late 1980s a number of English courts were kept busy with issues arising out of the crash of the International Tin Council (ITC). This was an international organisation, operating at the relevant period under the Sixth International Tin Agreement (ITA), a treaty to which the EEC and some 23 states, including the United Kingdom, were parties. Under the ITA the ITC had legal personality, including the capacity to contract and to institute legal proceedings. Its headquarters were in London and a Headquarters Agreement was given effect in English law by International Tin Council (Immunities and Privileges) order in 1972, which said that it should have 'the legal capacities of a body corporate'. The ITA was not incorporated into English law (nor indeed was the Headquarters Agreement), but its provisions were reflected in the 1972 Order.

For various reasons the ITC became unable to meet debts owed to creditors, and some banks and brokers then brought actions against the member states of the ITC[126] and a receivership action was commenced.[127] This latter action had no success at any level. The House of Lords, led by Lords Templeman and Oliver, held that any rights that the members had against the ITC were rights under the ITA, and not enforceable in the English courts. An international organisation could thus not be wound up by reference to English Law. In the so-called 'direct

---

[123] ibid, 223E.   [124] ibid, 222E.   [125] See (1978) XLIX BYBIL 346–8.
[126] *JH Rayner (Mincing Lane) Ltd v Dept of Trade and Industry* [1989] Ch 72, 207.
[127] *Maclaine Watson & Co Ltd v International Tin Council* [1990] 2 AC 418.

actions' the House took a very formalist position, drawing a rigid distinction between English law and international law. The conclusion arrived at—that the actions against member states for the liabilities of the ITC could not succeed—is undoubtedly correct, but it is regrettable that it was not arrived at by examining the relevant treaties and related instruments.[128] This was an issue perfectly within the capabilities of their Lordships to address but the House preferred to avoid these issues of international law and insist that the whole matter was non-justiciable in English courts.

Disconcertingly, Lords Templeman and Oliver seemed to think that an English court could not only not deal with an unincorporated treaty (notwithstanding the 1972 Order in Council relating to it), but also not deal with rules of international law more generally. Private creditors, owed debts by an international organisation headquartered in London, entitled by its governing instrument to trade, given the capacities of a body corporate by the 1972 Order in Council, could apparently nonetheless only 'seek remedies in international law', such as in the International Court of Justice—which manifestly they could *not* do. Going much further than was needed for the disposal of the case, Lord Oliver even opined that the Order in Council 'created' an International Tin Council in the United Kingdom, and that it was *that* entity which entered into the contractual obligations that were not honoured. The ITC 'created' by the Order in Council was a 'separate *persona ficta* from the ITC created under the Treaty'. These regrettable findings not only took the United Kingdom along a path quite different from that taken by courts elsewhere dealing with comparable matters (in Canada, Malaysia, the Netherlands, and New York); it also departed from all reality into a world where there were parallel Tin Councils, one headquartered in London and with whom the United Kingdom had a Headquarters Agreement, the other 'created' by English law.

Ensuing problems were not long in coming. In *Arab Monetary Fund v Hashim (No 3)*[129] Hoffmann J was faced with an action brought by an international organisation established by treaty, well known in the City of London but in respect of which no Orders in Council existed. The United Kingdom was not a member. It was now apparently impossible to find that English law would recognise the legal personality of an entity which had been given its personality under a treaty. Hoffmann J—the House of Lords having started to hear these matters in the *ITC* case while *AMF* was under consideration—therefore decided that, as the treaty establishing the AMF had been incorporated into the law of Abu Dhabi, where it was headquartered, it could be recognised (by analogy with company law) as an entity with the capacity to sue in the English courts. The

---

[128] R Higgins, *Report on the Legal Consequences for Member States of the Non-fulfilment by International Organizations of their Obligations toward Third Parties* [1995] Ybk IIL Vol I, 252. The responsibility of international organisations is a topic under consideration by the International Law Commission: see Fifth Report of the Special Rapporteur, Mr Giorgio Gaja, 2007, UN Doc A/CN 4/583.

[129] [1991] 2 AC 114.

judge acknowledged that this reasoning was 'unappetising' and indeed it was. The reality of the existence of an international organisation was ignored and it was treated in English law (notwithstanding the Foreign and Commonwealth Office advice referred to above) as a creation of Abu Dhabi law. The House of Lords took a step back towards realism by finding that the common law recognises the personality in English law of an international organisation of which the United Kingdom is not a member, provided it has legal personality under the municipal law of at least one of its member states. But the House of Lords' decision in the *ITC* case left things in an anomalous position for no common law recognition was given to an international organisation with legal personality under one or more of its member states apparently because the United Kingdom was a member of the organisation. The organisation then needed to be 'created' in English law.

A few years later Colman J, in *Westland Helicopters Ltd v Arab Organization for Industrialization*,[130] decided that the finding of the House of Lords that the Arab Monetary Fund had been incorporated in 21 different states, and had its domicile and residence in the United Arab Emirates, did *not* mean that the organisation ceased to be an international body created by treaty: 'Questions as to the meaning, effect and operation of its constitution ... can only be determined by reference to the treaty and to the principles of public international law.'[131] To apply the law of any one state would ignore the terms of the treaty. The *Westland Helicopters* case was not appealed further, but it would be extremely surprising if the House of Lords were to read its findings in the *AMF* and *ITC* cases as having also determined that English law was the governing law of the organisation itself. (Commercial transactions between an organisation and third parties are, of course, a different matter.) The issue has not risen so sharply since, but the legal mood that has developed over recent years suggests that further legal issues concerning international organisations will now be dealt with in a more forthright and substantial way, with issues of status in English law no longer taking central stage.

In 2007, in *Al-Jeddah v Secretary of State for Defence*,[132] the House had occasion to revert to some of the issues addressed nearly 30 years earlier in the *Nissan* case. The appellant had been detained by British forces serving as part of the multinational force in Iraq but no charges were brought against him and he claimed that his rights under Article 5(1) of the European Convention had been violated. His internment was stated to be necessary for imperative security reasons. A first issue in the case[133] was whether the acts complained of were

---

[130] [1995] 2 AC 387.

[131] ibid, 303F. He found support for this view in Millett J's first instance decision in the *ITC* case [1987] Ch 419, 452D–E, and in Bingham LJ's dissenting judgment in the *AMF* case [1991] 2 AC 114, 140.

[132] [2008] 1 AC 332.

[133] Which arose only in the House of Lords, the Secretary of State relying for the first time on arguments derived from the recent decisions of the Grand Chamber of the European Court of Human Rights in *Behrami v France* and *Saramati v France, Germany and Norway*, App Nos 7141/01 and 78166/01, 2 May 2007, (2007) 45 EHRR SE10.

attributable at all to the United Kingdom, or to the United Nations and thus outside the scope of the European Convention. UN Security Council Resolutions authorised internment where it was necessary for imperative reasons of security. Lords Bingham, Carswell, and Brown and Baroness Hale all took the view that legal responsibility remained with the United Kingdom, with the European Convention thus becoming a relevant factor for further analysis. Their speeches all reveal a great ease in dealing not only with European Convention case law, as is now to be expected, but also with Security Council Resolutions, the UN Charter, the Fourth Geneva Convention, and the leading literature on various relevant matters of international law. Lord Bingham found that the key legal questions were: Were the UK forces placed at the disposal of the UN forces? Did the UN have effective command and control over the conduct of UK forces when they detained the appellant? Were the UK forces part of a UN peacekeeping force in Iraq? He answered all of these questions in the negative and said that any analogy with the situation in Kosovo[134] broke down, as the forces there had been established at the specific behest of the UN, and operated under its auspices, with UNMOVIC having the status of a subsidiary organ of the UN.

Lord Rodger of Earlsferry dissented on this first issue. He accepted that, in contrast to KFOR in Kosovo, the coalition forces had gone into Iraq some six months before the Security Council adopted Resolution 1511, authorising the adoption of the multinational force. But for him the key issue was that the resolution establishing that force (Resolution 1546) had been adopted before the British forces detained the appellant and regulated the legal position at the relevant time, and this situation he found entirely analogous with the Kosovo situation. He, too, traversed in an impressive manner the legal world of UN law and the attendant literature. His conclusion was that the Security Council, acting under Chapter VII of the UN Charter, had delegated functions to the multinational forces (just as it had earlier delegated functions to KFOR in Resolution 1244). That being so, he was convinced that the Strasbourg Court would hold that the acts of the United Kingdom, acting within the coalition forces, were attributable to the United Nations and not subject to scrutiny for compatibility with the Convention.

For the majority, it was necessary to move on to an issue which is becoming increasingly important,[135] namely, the interplay between UN Security Council

---

[134] The situation which had been under consideration in *Behrami* and *Saramati* (n 133).

[135] Recent cases at the European Court of Justice have also raised the question of the specific status of Security Council resolutions in the Community legal order, with parties alleging the illegality of Community acts purporting to implement Security Council decisions: Judgment of the Court of First Instance, *Ahmed Ali Yusuf and Al Barakaat International Foundation v Council of the European Union and Commission of the European Communities*, Case T-306/01 [2005] ECR II-3533; Judgment of the Court of First Instance, *Yassin Abdullah Kadi v Council of the European Union and Commission of the European Communities*, Case T-316/01 [2005] ECR II-3649; Judgment of the Court of First Instance, *Chafiq Ayadi v Council of the European Union*, Case T-253/02 [2006] ECR II-2139.

Resolutions (which are binding on all member states under Article 25 of the Charter and have priority over other obligations) and the European Convention. All agreed that the legal obligations of the United Kingdom under Security Council Resolution 1546 had to prevail. This finding by the House of Lords places it firmly within the mainstream of judicial decisions on the relationship between obligations under a *lex specialis* and obligations under Articles 25 and 103 of the UN Charter.

Concluding observations

The *International Tin Council* era, with its inward-looking preoccupation with matters of incorporation of treaties into national law, accompanied, one suspects, by an underlying desire to find the international law matters in contention to be non-justiciable, is long gone. Today the preoccupation with technical matters of English law is hardly to be discerned. There is strikingly little discussion on whether a treaty is or is not incorporated, or of whether a Security Council Resolution is or is not covered by Article 1 of the United Nations Act 1946. The House of Lords simply gets on with deciding the international law point in issue. The handling of international law issues is confident and positive in tone. There is an amplitude of judges serving on the Appellate Committee (and, indeed, in other courts also) who are thoroughly well versed in international law and prepared to treat it as any other field of law. Everything is treated as routine judicial work. The ready interest in international law may perhaps now require more rigour in differentiating what is put before their Lordships as 'showing' international law. Not all treaties, resolutions, drafts of the International Law Commission or findings of treaty bodies, qualify as sources of international law. Undifferentiated treatment of materials is particularly evident in, for example, *A v Secretary of State for the Home Department*.[136]

The pace of cases reaching the Lords relating to points of international law has undoubtedly greatly increased. In part, of course, this is due to the Human Rights Act 1998. But issues of international law increasingly play a component part in other matters that the House of Lords is called upon to determine. The House has had to concern itself with many of the great issues of international law of the day, including legal developments at the UN and the relationship between the law of the Charter and other legal obligations undertaken by this country.

Looking back over the years, many Law Lords have played their part in pronouncing upon the matters of international law that I have here described.[137]

---

[136] [2006] 2 AC 221.
[137] We may name Lord Thankerton (1928–48); Lord Russell (1929–46); Lord Cohen (1951–66); Lord Morris (1960–75); Lord Evershed (1962–5); Lord Upjohn (1963–71); Lord Edmund-Davies (1974–81); Lord Keith (1977–96); Lord Brandon (1981–91); Lord Brightman (1982–7); Lord Templeman (1982–94); Lord Griffiths (1985–93); Lord Mackay (1985–7); Lord Oliver (1986–91); Lord Nolan (1994–8); Lord Hope (1996–); Lord Saville (1997–); Lord Scott (2000–); Baroness Hale (2004–); Lord Brown (2004–).

Some among the Law Lords have played a very significant role in the matters here under discussion.[138] Lord Bingham, along with Lords Browne-Wilkinson and Goff before him, have ensured as presiding Law Lords that the House has become a leader in authoritative pronouncements by national courts on matters of international law. As we pass from the House of Lords to the new Supreme Court, this augurs well for the contribution to be made in the future.

[138] These include Lord Atkin (1928–44); Lord Denning (though more so in the Court of Appeal) (1957–62); Lord Devlin (1961–4); Lord Wilberforce (1964–83); Lord Diplock (1968–85); Lord Salmon (1972–80); Lord Scarman (1977–86); Lord Roskill (1980–6); Lord Bridge (1980–92); Lord Ackner (1986–92); Lord Mustill (1992–7); Lord Slynn (1992–2002); Lord Woolf (1992–2002); Lord Lloyd (1993–8); Lord Nicholls (1994–2007); Lord Steyn (1995–2005); Lord Hoffmann (1995–); Lord Hobhouse (1998–2003); Lord Millett (1998–2003); Lord Rodger (2001–); Lord Mance (2005–).

27

European Influences

Francis Jacobs and David Anderson

Introduction

The laws of other European states were from time to time the subject of valuable comparative analysis by the House of Lords.[1] The principal European influence on the work of the House of Lords came however not so much from these comparative excursions as from the law of the supranational organisations successively known as the European Economic Community, European Community, and European Union.[2] It is European law in that sense with which this chapter is concerned.

The growth of European law

For more than a third of a century, starting with UK accession in 1973 to what was then the European Economic Community,[3] the judicial House of Lords had jurisdiction to hear appeals founded in whole or in part on European law.

That period coincided with a huge expansion not only in the membership of the Community (from six Member States prior to UK accession to 27 in 2007), but also in the scope and influence of European law. In 1973, the Community could still be seen (notwithstanding the high ideals of its founders) as essentially a trade organisation, its main features being the customs union, common policies

---

[1] Two notable examples are the speech of Lord Goff in *White v Jones* [1995] 2 AC 207 and the speech of Lord Bingham in *Fairchild v Glenhaven Funeral Services Ltd* [2003] 1 AC 32. Such judicial journeys across the common law/civil law divide, though uncommon, appear to have been no more frequent in the other major European jurisdictions: see BS Markesinis, 'Foreign Law and Foreign Ideas in the English Courts' in *Always on the Same Path: Essays on Foreign Law and Comparative Methodology*, vol II (Oxford: Hart, 2001).

[2] The European Economic Community was renamed the European Community by the Maastricht Treaty of 1992 in recognition of the growing scope of its competence and activities. The European Union was created by the same Treaty in order to accommodate the European Community and two other 'pillars' (common foreign and security policy; justice and home affairs), whose structures were originally more intergovernmental in nature. The 2007 Lisbon Treaty was designed to render the European Community redundant and bring its activities within the scope of a single-pillared European Union.

[3] Together with its fellow organisations, the European Coal and Steel Community and Euratom, which have generated relatively little case law, none of it in the House of Lords.

for agriculture and external trade, and an embryonic competition policy. Successive Treaty amendments in 1986, 1992, 1997, and 2000[4] created the single market, the Euro, and the Schengen common travel area, whilst vastly extending the competence of the European Community and European Union in areas as diverse as social policy, consumer protection, public health, intellectual property, the environment, immigration, security, and judicial cooperation. European law had become the most developed system of international law operating anywhere in the world, and a significant influence on the legal landscape of every Member State.

The judicial development of European law was led throughout the period by the Court of Justice of the European Communities in Luxembourg (the European Court), assisted after 1989 by the Court of First Instance. Having proclaimed in one of its early judgments the primacy of European law over national law,[5] the European Court produced an extensive and coherent body of case law, distinguishing but rarely departing from its own precedents in a manner more familiar to common lawyers than to some of their civilian counterparts. It developed 'general principles of law',[6] many of them derived from national constitutional principles, which have become common currency across Europe and which may constitute grounds for invalidating Community and national rules alike. It breathed life into Treaty concepts of uncertain meaning, such as subsidiarity and European citizenship. It applied rights derived from European law in such a way as to produce effects even in areas of national competence where the Community legislator had not ventured: company taxation, civil procedure, and constitutional law.

National courts and European law

National courts also have a part to play in the application of European law. Indeed with limited exceptions,[7] they can and must do anything that the European Court can do. They are to give effect to rights contained in directly effective provisions of European law,[8] interpret national rules where possible in conformity with European law[9] and, where that is not possible, 'disapply' conflicting provisions of national law.[10] When in doubt as to the proper interpretation of European law, they are entitled, before giving judgment, to refer questions to the European Court for a definitive ruling. This preliminary ruling procedure, which finds its chief expression in Article 234 EC, has prompted the

---

[4] By, respectively, the Single European Act, Treaty of Maastricht, Treaty of Amsterdam, and Treaty of Nice. The 2007 Treaty of Lisbon would significantly expand the categories of justiciable acts, particularly in the field of justice and home affairs.

[5] Case 6/64 *Costa v ENEL* [1964] ECR 585.

[6] Including fundamental rights, equal treatment, proportionality, and legal certainty.

[7] In particular, the power to declare Community measures invalid, which is reserved to the European Court: Case 314/85 *Foto-Frost* v Hauptzollamt Lübeck-Ost [1987] ECR 4199.

[8] Case 26/62 *Van Gend en Loos* [1963] ECR 1.

[9] Joined Cases C-397/01 to C-403/01 *Pfeiffer* [2004] ECR I-8835, paras 110–19.

[10] Case 70/77 *Simmenthal* [1978] ECR 1453.

European Court to describe its relationship with national courts as cooperative rather than hierarchical,[11] based on mutual goodwill and respect.[12]

The ability of national courts to influence the shape of European law is however limited. It is true that the Member States remain 'the masters of the Treaties',[13] in the sense that the Community has only such powers as are attributed to it. But a Community dependent on the uniform application of European law looks to national courts for the loyal enforcement of that law rather than its creative development. Though many of the leading European law cases began in national courts, and returned there for judgment after being referred to Luxembourg, their significance derives not so much from the identification of the questions or the application of the preliminary ruling by the national court as from the preliminary rulings of the European Court itself, which are translated into all the Community languages and have binding force in all Member States. National courts below the final tier of appeal are entitled to interpret and apply European law without the assistance of a reference to the European Court, no matter how difficult or hotly contested the issue may be. Judgments of national courts given without the benefit of a preliminary ruling tend, however, to be infrequently cited as authority in other Member States. They are relied upon more rarely still in subsequent judgments of the European Court.

National courts of final appeal and European law

National courts from whose decisions there is no judicial remedy are—despite their seniority—the most restricted of all in their ability to influence the development of European law. By the third paragraph of Article 234 EC, they are not only entitled but also obliged to refer disputed questions of the interpretation of European law to the European Court for a preliminary ruling. That obligation is expressed in absolute terms. The Court has refined it, most notably in the so-called *CILFIT* guidelines, but only to the limited extent that a court of final appeal need not refer questions the answers to which are either covered by authority (*acte éclairé*) or otherwise completely obvious (*acte clair*).[14]

The purposes of the obligation to refer are to promote the consistency of application of European law across the Member States, and to prevent rights conferred on individuals by European law from being infringed.[15] The effect of the obligation has however been to remove from supreme courts, including the House of Lords, the power to decide any but the most straightforward questions of European law for themselves.

---

[11] Case 244/80 *Foglia v Novello (2)* [1981] ECR 3045, para 14.
[12] Case 13/61 *de Geus v Bosch* [1962] ECR 45, *per* Lagrange AG at 56.
[13] *Brunner v European Union Treaty* [1994] 1 CMLR 57.
[14] Case 283/81 *CILFIT* [1982] ECR 3415.
[15] See eg Case C-393/98 *Antonio Gomes Valente* [2001] ECR I-1327, para 17; Case C-224/01 *Köbler* [2003] ECR I-10239, para 35.

Whether this is the waste of a skilled judicial resource or a necessary price to pay for the uniform application of European law is a matter of opinion. The European Court has taken a strict view,[16] as underlined by recent judgments in which it has held that supreme courts which wrongly decide questions of European law without making a reference risk damages claims by the unsuccessful litigant[17] or—in the case of a persistently erroneous line of authority—infringement proceedings against their Member States at the suit of the European Commission.[18]

This has had the consequence that national courts of last instance, despite their pre-eminence within their own countries, tend to act as followers rather than leaders where European law is concerned. It is true that many such courts have from time to time been tempted to avoid the making of a time-consuming reference to the European Court by claiming the *acte clair* exemption even for cases that are not straightforward.[19] But any persuasive force that such judgments might otherwise have had, in the European Court or in other Member States, is inevitably diminished by the knowledge that, to the extent that they had anything novel or interesting to say about European law, they should not strictly speaking have been given at all.

The House of Lords as a court of European law

For the above reasons, it is not realistic to expect a national court, least of all a supreme court, to exert significant leadership in the substantive development of European law. The most that can be asked of it is an acceptance of the central principles of European law (notably, primacy and direct effect), a readiness to refer the difficult cases to the European Court, and an ability to decide the easy ones correctly. In its exercise of those functions, the judicial House of Lords proved itself largely beyond reproach.

Caseload of the House of Lords

The House of Lords gave almost 100 judgments with substantial European law content between 1981 and 2008.[20] The cases occurred at the rate of about one a year in the 1980s, four a year in the 1990s and five a year in the 2000s. Though

---

[16] Jacobs AG expressed the view in Case C-338/95 *Wiener* [1997] ECR I-6495, Opinion at para 64, that the *CILFIT* conditions should apply 'only in cases where a reference is truly appropriate to achieve the objectives of Article [234], namely where there is a general question and where there is a genuine need for uniform interpretation'. That view was pressed upon the European Court (without success) by the Danish Government in Case C-99/00 *Lyckeskog* [2002] ECR I-4839, [2003] 1 WLR 9.

[17] Case C-224/01 *Köbler* [2003] ECR I-10239; Case C-173/03 *Traghetti* [2006] ECR I-5177.

[18] Case C-129/00 *Commission v Italy* [2003] ECR I-14637.

[19] For examples from a number of Member States, see D Anderson and M Demetriou, *References to the European Court* (London: Sweet & Maxwell, 2nd edn 2002) 6-052–6-061.

[20] We are grateful to Sarah Love of Brick Court Chambers for her help in locating these cases.

these figures are not large, in the context of the 100 or so cases disposed of annually by the Appellate Committee of the House of Lords,[21] they do reflect the increasing importance of European law over the period.

Some subjects remained evergreen. The broad reach of the Treaty prohibition on measures having equivalent effect to quantitative restrictions on imports (Article 28, ex 30 EC), stated with notorious breadth by the European Court in *Dassonville*,[22] was asserted before the House of Lords over three decades by those seeking to avoid the application of domestic statute.[23] Private actions for breach of the competition rules were the subject of important decisions both at the beginning and the end of the period.[24]

Other areas had the attention of the House of Lords at different times. Intellectual property cases were clustered near the beginning of the period.[25] Employment cases, though a constant feature of all three decades, peaked with a series of references and other significant decisions in the 1990s.[26] The twenty-first century was dominated to a remarkable extent by tax cases, concerning both indirect taxation (nine cases concerning classification under the Sixth VAT Directive being decided or referred between 2001 and 2005)[27] and direct taxation (in which no fewer than six cases concerning the fallout from the ECJ decision in *Metalgesellschaft/Hoechst*[28] were decided between 2005 and 2007).[29] New developments brought new possibilities, such as the four cases on the European Arrest Warrant decided in recent years.[30]

---

[21] Judicial and Court Statistics, Ministry of Justice 2007: the annual number of appeals presented to the House of Lords ranged between 72 and 111 cases in the period 2000–7.

[22] Case 8/74 *Dassonville* [1974] ECR 837, para 5: 'All trading rules enacted by Member States which are capable of hindering, directly or indirectly, actually or potentially, intra-Community trade are to be considered as measures having equivalent effect to quantitative restrictions.'

[23] *R v Henn and Darby* [1981] AC 850 (pornography); *R v Goldstein* [1983] 1 All ER 434 (drugs); *Kirklees MBC v Wickes Building Supplies Ltd* [1993] AC 227 and *Stoke-on-Trent CC v B&Q plc* [1993] AC 900 (Sunday trading); *R (Derwin) v AG* [2008] 1 AC 719 (the hunting ban).

[24] *Garden Cottage Foods v Milk Marketing Board* [1984] 1 AC 130; *Crehan v Inntrepreneur Pub Co* [2007] 1 AC 333.

[25] *Wellcome Foundation Ltd. v S/S for Social Services* [1988] 1 WLR 635; *Allen and Hanburys v Generics (UK) Ltd* [1988] 3 All ER 1057; *Re Smith Kline & French Laboratories Ltd* [1990] 1 AC 64; *Asahi Kasei Kogyo KK's Application* [1991] RPC 485.

[26] See, in particular, *Foster v British Gas plc* [1991] 2 AC 306; *Webb v EMO Air Cargo (UK) Ltd* [1993] 1 WLR 49; *R v Secretary of State for Employment, ex p Equal Opportunities Commission* [1995] 1 AC 1; *Marshall v Southampton and South West Hampshire AHA (Teaching) (No 2)* [1994] 1 AC 530; *R v Secretary of State for Employment, ex p Seymour-Smith* [1997] 2 All ER 273; *Preston v Wolverhampton Healthcare NHS Trust* [1998] 1 All ER 528; *Barry v Midland Bank plc* [1999] 2 All ER 974.

[27] Including, most notably, the second reference in *Marks and Spencer plc v Customs and Excise Comrs* [2005] STC 1254.

[28] Joined Cases C-397/98 and C-410/98; [2001] Ch 620.

[29] Including, most notably, *Sempra Metals Ltd v IRC* [2008] 1 AC 561.

[30] *Office of the King's Prosecutor, Brussels v Cando Armas* [2006] 2 AC 1; *Dabas v High Court of Justice, Madrid* [2007] 2 AC 31; *Pilecki v Circuit Court of Legnica, Poland* [2008] 1 WLR 325; *Caldarelli v Court of Naples* [2008] 1 WLR 1724.

Acceptance of the central principles of European law

If any Law Lords shared the strong feelings on Europe that divided the political classes of the United Kingdom over much of the period, no trace of them is to be found in their judicial output. Politically, the period was characterised by a 1975 referendum over continued UK membership, bitter and sometimes tense parliamentary battles over the ratification of successive Community Treaties,[31] a short-lived policy of non-cooperation,[32] and the eventual opt-out of the UK from major parts of the European enterprise, including the Schengen common travel area and the Euro. In the courts, however, led by the judicial House of Lords, quiet acquiescence in the central requirements of European law was the order of the day. Constitutional conflicts did not arise or were diffused; the core principles of primacy and direct effect were accepted without demur; and all this was achieved, at least on the surface, without violence to traditional notions of parliamentary sovereignty.

An important reason for this lack of judicial controversy was the manner in which European law was incorporated by the European Communities Act 1972. The primacy of European law over 'any enactment passed or to be passed' was plainly provided for by sections 2(1) and 2(4). The question whether

anything short of an express positive statement in an Act of Parliament passed after January 1 1973, that a particular provision is intended to be made in breach of an obligation assumed by the United Kingdom under a Community treaty, would justify an English court in construing that provision in a manner inconsistent with a Community treaty obligation of the United Kingdom,

raised judicially by Lord Diplock in 1982,[33] has never had to be answered. Similarly, since section 3(1) requires questions of European law to be determined 'in accordance with the principles laid down by and any relevant decision of the European Court', the rulings of that court are treated as binding precedents and its authority in matters of European Law (even as regards the determination of the limits of Community power) has not so far been questioned.[34]

---

[31] Notably the Maastricht Treaty of 1992 and the Lisbon Treaty of 2007, when the battle spilled briefly into the courts: *R v Secretary of State for Foreign Affairs, ex p Rees-Mogg* [1994] QB 552; *R (Wheeler) v Office of the Prime Minister* [2008] EWHC 1409 (Admin).

[32] In May–June 1996, as a consequence of a Community ban on UK beef in the wake of the BSE crisis. The policy of non-cooperation (which prevented or delayed the adoption of some 100 Community measures) was described as 'the most serious breakdown in European Union functioning since President Charles de Gaulle of France adopted an "empty chair" policy in 1965': 'For the British beef war: a truce but no victory' *New York Times*, 24 June 1996.

[33] *Garland v British Rail Engineering Ltd* [1983] 2 AC 751, 771C.

[34] Contrast the insistence of the German Federal Constitutional Court, in its decision on the Maastricht Treaty, on its own competence to decide whether a Community act is *ultra vires* (a position at least theoretically contrary to the ruling of the ECJ in Case 314/85 *Foto-Frost v Hauptzollamt Lübeck-Ost* [1987] ECR 4199, under which this competence is reserved exclusively to the ECJ): *Brunner v European Union Treaty* [1994] 1 CMLR 57.

The obligation to interpret national law consistently with the directive which it implements was accepted by the House of Lords in some striking judgments,[35] though with an early and questionable reservation where the law in question was not intended to give effect to the directive.[36] The obligation was subsequently equated to the strong duty of interpretation under section 3 of the Human Rights Act[37] and extended to framework decisions.[38]

Asked for a case on the constitutional relationship between the United Kingdom and the Community, most students and teachers of law would name the Spanish fishermen's case, *Factortame*. There were important and engrossing issues in that case, which came three times before the House of Lords and three times before the European Court, about whether an Act of Parliament purporting to restrict the ownership of British fishing vessels to British citizens, resident and domiciled in the UK, was consistent with Community norms, including the right of establishment;[39] whether European law required an Act of Parliament to be suspended on an interim basis, notwithstanding the constitutional principle that injunctions were not awarded against the Crown;[40] and whether European law required damages to be paid to those injured by the application of statute.[41] Without doubt, *Factortame* was the case that brought home to the political and legal establishments in the United Kingdom the power of directly effective European law. The Spanish fishermen won on all points. Yet constitutionally, the case was on one view neither unorthodox nor surprising. European law was given primacy over a statute of 1988 because Parliament itself had said so. Furthermore, according to the House of Lords itself, this result was reached not on the heretical basis that Parliament had in 1972 succeeded in binding its successors, but because it had enacted an interpretation clause, section 2(4), which while it remains in force requires all statutes to be interpreted as if

---

[35] *Pickstone v Freemans plc* [1989] AC 66; *Litster v Forth Dry Dock and Engineering Co Ltd* [1990] 1 AC 546.

[36] *Duke v GEC Reliance Systems Ltd* [1988] AC 618, commenting upon the earlier decision in *Garland v British Rail Engineering Ltd* [1983] 2 AC 751.

[37] *Ghaidan v Godin-Mendoza* [2004] 2 AC 557, *per* Lord Steyn at para 45.

[38] In obedience to Case C-105/03 *Pupino* [2005] ECR I-5285 [2006] QB 83: see *Dabas v High Court of Madrid* [2007] 2 AC 31.

[39] This question was referred by the Divisional Court (*R v Secretary of State for Transport, ex p Factortame Ltd* [1989] 2 CMLR 353) and answered by the European Court (Case C-221/89, [1991] ECR I-3905).

[40] This question was referred by the House of Lords (*R v Secretary of State for Transport, ex p Factortame Ltd* [1990] 2 AC 85). The accelerated ruling of the European Court (Case C-213/89, [1990] ECR I-2433) was then applied by the House of Lords in another reasoned judgment ([1991] 1 AC 603). As the court of last instance, the House of Lords was technically correct to refer, even though the consequent delay caused considerable loss which later had to be compensated. A bolder approach had been taken by the Divisional Court ([1989] 2 CMLR 353), which without a reference decided the issue in the fishermen's favour—a result subsequently reached by the European Court.

[41] The House of Lords affirmed the rulings of the Divisional Court (after a reference) and the Court of Appeal to the effect that damages were payable: [2000] 1 AC 524.

they contain a section stating that its provisions are without prejudice to directly enforceable Community rights.[42]

Exercise of the jurisdiction to refer

By the end of 2008, 38 references had been made by the House of Lords to the European Court. This was less than 10 per cent of the modest UK total of 448 a small proportion but one which may simply reflect the relatively light caseload of the House of Lords compared to final-instance courts in some other Member States.

There was none of the initial reluctance to refer that was associated with some other national supreme courts. Indeed, in the first European law case to come before the House, a question that was considered to be 'free from any doubt' was nonetheless referred for the sole reason that the Court of Appeal had taken a different view:[43]

Later years saw a reduction in the willingness of the House of Lords to make references. This can be explained in part by a wish to avoid the delay consequent upon a reference to the European Court (which could add up to two years to the progress of an appeal), and in part by a greater confidence on the part of the Law Lords in their own ability to find the right answer. The House of Lords attracted criticism from commentators in the 1980s and 1990s for what they perceived as an excessive willingness to decide debatable points of European law for itself[44] (though interestingly, no such criticisms tended to be made of 'pro-European' decisions).[45]

In the new century, the tendency of the House of Lords to go it alone increased further. In the *BCCI* case, the House found it possible to conclude without a reference that the First Banking Directive did not require the Bank of England to be liable to depositors, although both the High Court and Court of Appeal had explicitly found that the question was not *acte clair*, and despite a powerful dissenting judgment on the substance of the question by Auld LJ in the Court of

---

[42] *R v Secretary of State for Transport, ex p Factortame Ltd* [1990] 2 AC 85, *per* Lord Bridge at 140 B–D, an analysis confirmed in *ICI v Colmer* (Inspector of Taxes) [2000] 1 All ER 129. Some commentators have however taken the view that the House of Lords 'elected to allow the Parliament of 1972 to fetter the Parliament of 1988': HWR Wade, 'Sovereignty—Revolution or Evolution' (1996) 112 LQR 568, and cf P Craig, 'Sovereignty of the United Kingdom Parliament after *Factortame*' (1991) 11 YBEL 221.

[43] *R v Henn and Darby* [1981] AC 850, *per* Lord Diplock at 906A.

[44] See, eg, Arnull [1988] PL 313, 319–20 and (1989) 52 MLR 622–39; Szyszczak (1990) 15 EL Rev 480, 485–9 and (1994) 19 EL Rev 214, 220; Weatherill (1992) 17 EL Rev 299–322, referring variously to *Re Sandhu* (*The Times*, 10 May 1985); *Duke v GEC Reliance* [1988] AC 618; *Finnegan v Clowney* [1990] 2 AC 407; *Freight Transport Association Ltd v London Boroughs Transport Committee* [1991] 1 WLR 828; and *Kirklees MBC v Wickes Building Supplies Ltd* [1993] AC 227.

[45] eg *R v Secretary of State for Employment, ex p EOC* [1995] AC 1, in which the House of Lords declared, contrary to the opinion of both the Divisional Court and the Court of Appeal, that certain provisions of the Employment Protection (Consolidation) Act 1978 were indirectly discriminatory against women, contrary to Article 119 of the EEC Treaty.

Appeal.[46] Whilst a second reference was made in *Marks and Spencer plc v Customs and Excise Commissioners*, Lord Hoffmann stated that he would have considered the remaining issue to be *acte clair* in the Commissioners' favour, were it not for the fact that the Advocate General (echoing the Commission) had previously expressed the view that it was 'manifestly clear' in the other direction.[47] In a number of other cases, no reference was made despite the House of Lords itself being divided as to the correct interpretation of European law.[48] It is difficult to square these decisions with the *CILFIT* guidelines.[49]

Cases not referred

As will be evident by now, the House of Lords gave a number of judgments on European law issues which, on a strict application of the *CILFIT* guidelines, should probably have been referred.[50] It does not appear to have been deterred from doing so, in recent years, by the prospect of actions for infringement or for damages in respect of its judgments (the latter at least a largely theoretical prospect, given the need to show a manifest disregard for Community obligations).[51]

It is not easy to point to any substantive judgment of the House of Lords that is 'wrong', in the sense that the European Court would plainly have come to a different conclusion on a reference. Some of them might, however, be described as questionable.

Influence of the House of Lords on European law?

Despite its late entry to the Community, the United Kingdom influence on European law and legal process is undoubted.[52] On the whole, however, that

---

[46] *Three Rivers DC v Governor of the Bank of England (No 3)* [2003] 2 AC 1.

[47] [2005] STC 1254, *per* Lord Hoffmann at para 12.

[48] See eg *Customs and Excise Comrs v Plantifor Ltd* [2002] 1 WLR 2287 (VAT); *CR Smith Glaziers (Dunfermline) Ltd v Customs and Excise Comrs* [2003] 1 WLR 656 (VAT); *R (Junttan Oy) v Bristol Magistrates' Court* [2004] 2 All ER 555 (health and safety at work). In *R v Secretary of State for Health, ex p Imperial Tobacco* [2001] 1 WLR 127, Lords Hoffmann and Millett found an issue to be *acte clair* notwithstanding the contrary opinion of their three colleagues (one of whom, Lord Slynn, was a former judge of the European Court) that a reference of the issue—which had by then become moot—would have been necessary.

[49] Contrast, however, *OB v Aventis-Pasteur SA* [2008] 4 All ER 881, in which the House of Lords made a second reference despite the fact that four of the five Law Lords found the meaning of the earlier preliminary ruling to be clear. The reference was made because Lord Rodger considered the contrary view to be not beyond reasonable argument.

[50] See eg, in addition to those judgments referred to at n 44 above, *Three Rivers* [2003] 2 AC 1; *Rutherford v Secretary of State for Trade and Industry* [2006] ICR 785; *Crehan v Inntrepreneur* [2007] 1 AC 333; *Sempra Metals Ltd* [2008] 1 AC 561.

[51] Case C-129/00 *Commission v Italy* [2003] ECR I-14637 (infringement action); Case C-224/01 *Köbler* [2003] ECR I-10239; and Case C-173/03 *Traghetti* [2006] ECR I-5177 (damages).

[52] Sir David Edward, Judge of the European Court, identified the principal such contributions as the British tradition of advocacy, the habit of detailed citation of precedent, the approach to the teaching of European law, the quality of writing about European law, and the reports of the House of

influence did not take the form of judicial contributions to the development of substantive law. The student will look in vain for the equivalent in European law of the *Pinochet* case in public international law:[53] a case in which the ruling of the House was eagerly awaited, studied, and imitated across the world. Nor did the 'dialogue' between the House of Lords and Luxembourg prove as influential on the latter court as the equivalent dialogue, over a much shorter period, with the European Court of Human Rights in Strasbourg—a dialogue in which the UK courts have made 'a major and distinctive contribution' to the Strasbourg case law, including by 'urging caution when the Court has gone too far'.[54]

Evidence for the influence of national courts on the European Court might be expected to be found in the Opinions of its Advocates General which, as the work of a single hand, tend to be more discursive and fully reasoned than its collective judgments.[55] Yet a database search of those Opinions for references to judgments of the House of Lords produces meagre returns. Having discounted references which merely help to explain the procedural context of the case, or the content of the national law applicable to the dispute,[56] and having noted the occasional borrowing of a phrase which encapsulates or illuminates the issue in dispute,[57] one is left with only a handful of cases in which a judgment of the House of Lords is cited by the Advocate General to support a proposition of European law. Even in those cases, the impression is given that the House of Lords is looked to for confirmation of a course that the Advocate General was already minded to advise, rather than for guidance or inspiration.

Lords Select Committee on the European Communities (as it was then known): 'The Development of Law and Legal Process in the EU' in BS Markesinis (ed), *The British Contribution to the Europe of the Twenty-First Century* (Oxford: Hart, 2002).

[53] *R v Bow Street Magistrate, ex p Pinochet (No 1)* [2000] 1 AC 61; *R v Bow Street Magistrate, ex p Pinochet (No 3)* [2000] 1 AC 147.

[54] Sir Nicolas Bratza, the serving UK judge on the European Court of Human Rights, in 'Winds of Change in the Strasbourg Court', 17 May 2007, online at <http://www.slynn-foundation.org>. Examples of House of Lords judgments which can be said with confidence to have materially influenced the approach of the European Court of Human Rights are *Barrett v Enfield LBC* [2001] 2 AC 550 (immunities in tort), *R v Spear* [2003] 1 AC 734 (court martials), and *R (Alconbury Developments Ltd) v Secretary of State for the Environment, Transport and the Regions* [2003] 2 AC 295 (administrative decision-making). In *McCann v United Kingdom* (13 May 2008), the reasoning of the Strasbourg Court was grounded on the dissenting speeches in *Qazi v London Borough of Harrow* [2004] 1 AC 983 and *Kay v Lambeth BC* [2006] 2 AC 465.

[55] The Advocates General, currently eight in number, are members of the European Court who in most cases prepare, after the conclusion of argument, an individual Opinion for the guidance of the Court.

[56] For example, the citation in Case C-498/03 *Kingscrest Associates Ltd v Comrs of Customs and Excise* [2005] ECR I-4423 of the definition of 'charitable' by the House of Lords in *Income Tax Comrs v Pemsel* [1891] AC 531; and the citation in Case C-196/04 *Cadbury Schweppes plc v Comrs of Inland Revenue* [2007] Ch 30 of *Ramsay v IRC* [1982] AC 300 for its supposed relevance to the thinking of the Special Commissioners who had referred the case to the European Court.

[57] See eg the citation in the first paragraph of the Opinion in Case C-423/04 *Richards v Secretary of State for Work and Pensions* [2006] ECR I-3585 of Lord Nicholls' description of transsexual persons in *Bellinger v Bellinger* [2003] 2 AC 467.

The principal substantive citations by Advocates General of judgments of the House of Lords are as follows:

a. In two Opinions concerning the circumstances in which Member States should be liable for damages when they breach European law,[58] an Advocate General referred to the fact that the House of Lords had been prepared to accept (though in both cases *obiter*) that damages for breach of European law might be awarded in ordinary civil actions, and that the decision of a majority of the Court of Appeal that no such liability existed (in the absence of misfeasance) in actions against the Government was open to question.
b. Judgments of the House of Lords have occasionally been cited to confirm the Advocate General's proposed interpretation of a directive.[59]
c. The 1966 Practice Statement was once cited in a discussion of the circumstances in which the European Court should be prepared to depart from its own rulings.[60]

These sparse references should not be a cause for surprise. There are two principal ways in which national courts of last instance have (for better or worse) been able to exert influence on the content of European law. The House of Lords, in common with many other national courts, made little use of the first and none of the second.

The first possible avenue of influence is to use the reference procedure not simply to ask questions but to suggest to the European Court the answer that it should give and the legal route by which that answer should be reached. This is the usual practice of the German courts, which may be credited with introducing the European Court, by that means, to such general principles of law as fundamental rights and proportionality.

Until recently, such expressions of opinion by the House of Lords were rare. In common with other United Kingdom courts, the Law Lords may have felt that it would be pointless for them to opine on a question which it was for the European Court to answer, or been reluctant to put the parties to the expense of the longer hearing that a fuller exploration of the questions might have required. Three recent examples point to a more active approach, however. In *'The Front*

---

[58] Opinions of Léger AG in Joined Cases C-46/93 and C-48/93 *Brasserie du Pêcheur SA v Germany* and *R v Secretary of State for Transport, ex p Factortame Ltd* [1996] 2 WLR 506; Case C-5/94 *R v MAFF, ex p Hedley Lomas (Ireland) Ltd* [1996] ECR I-2553, paras 87 and 204. The cases he referred to (see fnn 16–18 of his Opinion in Joined Cases C-46/93 and C-48/93) were *Garden Cottage Foods v Milk Marketing Board* [1983] 1 AC 140 and *Kirklees MBC v Wickes Building Supplies* [1993] AC 227, the latter doubting the correctness of *Bourgoin v Minister of Agriculture Fisheries and Food* [1986] 1 QB 716.

[59] Case C-262/88 *Barber v Guardian Royal Exchange Assurance Group* [1991] QB 344, Opinion of van Gerven AG at fn 31 (citing *Hayward v Cammell Laird* [1988] ICR 464); Case C-201/02 *R, ex p Wells v Secretary of State for Transport, Local Government and the Regions* [2004] ECR I-723, Opinion of Léger AG at fn 29 (citing *R v North Yorkshire CC, ex p Brown* [2000] 1 AC 397).

[60] Joined Cases C-267/95 and C-268/95 *Merck & Co Inc v Primecrown Ltd* [1996] ECR I-6285, Opinion of Fennelly AG at para 139.

Comor,[61] a unanimous House's reference was accompanied by a forthright explanation of why it opposed the suggestion that antisuit injunctions in support of arbitration clauses were prohibited by the Brussels Regulation.[62] In *R (M) v HM Treasury*,[63] a Report of the Judicial Committee indicated in 17 crisp paragraphs why it preferred one of the competing interpretations of a sanctions regulation to the other. In *OB v Aventis-Pasteur SA*,[64] Lord Hoffmann indicated how he believed that a previous ruling of the European Court was to be interpreted. In the latter case, the Law Lords may in effect have been inviting the European Court to dispose of their reference by reasoned order under the accelerated procedure provided for by Article 104(3) of its Rules of Procedure.[65]

The second avenue of influence, less welcome from a Community perspective, is to invoke national constitutional law in order to resist the application of European law,[66] or to accept it only on conditions.[67] Such statements of position by national courts (less common in recent years) have occasionally drawn a response from the European Court. Thus, the initial impetus for the development of the European Court's fundamental rights jurisprudence,[68] and its increased caution in relation to the use by the Community institutions of Article 308 (ex 235) EC as a legal basis for legislation,[69] have each been attributed to qualifications placed by national courts (principally, but not only, the Federal Constitutional Court of Germany) on their willingness to accept the primacy of European law.

The House of Lords, under the clear direction of the European Communities Act 1972, never sought to use this second avenue of influence. It did not question

---

[61] *West Tankers Inc v Riunione Adriatica di Sicurta SpA* [2007] 1 Lloyd's Rep 391.

[62] Lord Hoffmann, having pointed out that such injunctions are issued by competing arbitration centres such as New York, Bermuda, and Singapore, concluded: 'There seems to be no doctrinal necessity or practical advantage which requires the European Community to handicap itself by denying its courts the right to exercise the same jurisdiction.' The Advocate General addressed in her Opinion the views expressed by the House of Lords (Case C-185/07 *Allianz SpA v West Tankers Inc*, Opinion of 4 September 2008 at paras 38 and 63–5), though (like the Court) she did not share them.

[63] [2008] 2 All ER 1097.   [64] [2008] 4 All ER 881.

[65] An anonymous Law Lord (speaking under Chatham House rules) was reported to this effect by A Le Sueur in 'A Report on Six Seminars about the UK Supreme Court at the School of Law, Queen Mary, University of London', November 2008, p 51.

[66] Historical examples of this tendency from the case law of eg France and Italy are given in A-M Slaughter, AS Sweet, and JHH Weiler (eds), *The European Courts and National Courts— Doctrine and Jurisprudence* (Oxford: Hart, 1997).

[67] See, classically, the two *Solange* judgments and the Maastricht judgment of the German Federal Constitutional Court: *Solange I* [1974] 2 CMLR 540; *Solange II* [1987] 3 CMLR 225; *Brunner v European Union Treaty* [1994] 1 CMLR 57.

[68] The development by the European Court of the general principle of fundamental rights was caused by 'an incipient rebellion against supremacy, led by national courts': AS Sweet, 'Constitutional Dialogues' in Slaughter, Sweet, and Weiler (n 66) 317–19.

[69] The Federal Constitutional Court of Germany warned in its Maastricht judgment (*Brunner v European Union Treaty* [1994] 1 CMLR 57) that an interpretation by the Community institutions of Article 308 EC in a sense that equated to an extension of the Treaty would 'not have any binding effect on Germany', a concern which was addressed by the European Court in Opinion 2/94 [1996] ECR I-1788, para 30, but which was subsequently echoed by the Danish Supreme Court in its own Maastricht judgment: *Carlsen v Rasmussen* [1999] 3 CMLR 854.

fundamental doctrines such as primacy and direct effect. It did not depart from the European Court's case law by claiming the power to decide for itself the limits of Community competence (*Kompetenz-Kompetenz*) within the United Kingdom.[70] Nor did it seek to use the threat of non-recognition in order to influence the substantive content of European law. As Lord Bingham once said, extra-judicially: 'The supremacy of Community law has been accepted by the English courts with a readiness and applied with a loyalty which, if equalled in one or two other member States, has been exceeded in none.'[71]

The contrast between the political equivocation towards 'Europe' and the wholehearted acceptance of its law by United Kingdom courts is certainly a striking one. The House of Lords might, in the manner of other senior national courts, have sought to use its leverage to influence in specific respects the development of European law. In the event, its influence was of a different nature. By its loyal compliance with the requirements of European law, the House of Lords used its considerable authority within Europe to support the legitimacy of a legal order which has always depended for its acceptance on the courts of the Member States.

European law as an influence on English law

Principles of interpretation

In 1980, Lord Diplock could say:

> The European court, *in contrast to the English courts*, applies teleological rather than historical methods to the interpretation of the Treaties and other Community legislation. It seeks to give effect to what it conceives to be the spirit rather than the letter of the Treaties; sometimes, indeed, to an English judge, it may seem to the exclusion of the letter.[72]

The case before him, in which the Court of Appeal had held that an absolute prohibition on the importation of certain goods was not a quantitative restriction or measure having equivalent effect within the meaning of the EEC Treaty, provided a striking illustration of the point he was making.

Judges (following Lord Denning's exhortation to 'divine the spirit of the Treaty and gain inspiration from it'[73]) soon learned to interpret European law in

---

[70] The closest that the courts of the United Kingdom have come to a warning shot across the bows of the Community institutions is the following dictum from the judgment of the Court of Appeal in *Thoburn v Sunderland CC* ('*Metric Martyrs*') [2003] 1 QB 151, *per* Laws LJ at para 69: 'In the event, which no doubt would never happen in the real world, that a European measure was seen to be repugnant to a fundamental or constitutional right guaranteed by the law of England, a question would arise whether the general words of the 1972 Act were sufficient to incorporate the measure and give it overriding effect in domestic law. But that is very far from this case.'

[71] '"There is a World Elsewhere": The Changing Perspectives of English Law' (1992) 41 ICLQ 513, reprinted in *The Business of Judging* (Oxford: OUP, 2000) 87.

[72] *R v Henn and Darby* [1981] AC 850, 905B, emphasis added.

[73] *HP Bulmer v J Bollinger SA* [1974] Ch 401, 426C–E.

the approved Community manner. Of course, 'the blinkered gaze traditionally attributed to English judges'[74] must not be exaggerated. It seems likely however that 'European' principles of interpretation had some influence, however indirect, on the more purposive approach to the interpretation of domestic law by which the period was characterised, even if the extent of that influence is difficult to quantify.

Substantive law

It should not be surprising that judges who had acquired a working knowledge of European law should have thought from time to time to apply its principles to domestic law, even in the absence of any legal obligation to do so. It is still less surprising that they should have done so in circumstances where domestic litigants had been left disadvantaged by comparison with their counterparts from other Member States.

That was the case in relation to the long-standing rule prohibiting the grant of injunctive relief against the Crown. In its second *Factortame* judgment,[75] the House of Lords disapplied the rule in favour of Community nationals. It then relied specifically on this fact when deciding subsequently that the rule did not apply even in situations where no European law rights were at stake.[76]

More often, European law was referred to as background support for a development of the case law that was thought desirable for other reasons. Thus:

a. Lord Goff drew upon European precedent (though only as the sixth of six reasons favouring his conclusion) when holding in *Woolwich Equitable Building Society v Inland Revenue Commissioners* that money paid to a public authority pursuant to an *ultra vires* demand is prima facie recoverable as of right.[77]

b. The practice of the European Court was one of the factors that induced the House of Lords to acknowledge in *Re Spectrum Plus*[78] that a previous judgment might in principle be overruled with prospective effect only.

c. In a case concerning the recoverability of compound interest, Lord Hope after a brief review of European legal materials thought it 'reassuring, although hardly surprising, to find that the compound interest method is the Commission's method of choice in the field of Community law in not dissimilar circumstances'.[79] Lord Walker went further, describing the judgment of the

---

[74] *AB Bofors UVA v AB Skandia Transport* [1982] 1 Lloyd's Rep 410, *per* Bingham J at 412.

[75] *R v Secretary of State for Transport, ex p Factortame Ltd* [1991] 1 AC 603.

[76] *M v Home Office* [1994] 1 AC 377 at 422G. That authority was not however followed in Scotland: *McDonald v Secretary of State for Scotland (No 1)* 1994 SLT 692.

[77] [1993] AC 70. Lord Goff commented: 'at a time when Community law is becoming increasingly important, it would be strange if the right of the citizen to recover overpaid charges were to be more restricted under domestic law than it is under European law.'

[78] [2005] AC 680.

[79] *Sempra Metals Ltd v Inland Revenue* [2008] 1 AC 561, *per* Lord Hope at para 40.

European Court in Joined Cases C-397 and 410/98 *Hoechst* as 'a powerful encouragement for this House to reconsider the basis on which a monetary award reversing unjust enrichment can and should take account of the time value of money'.[80]

Is it possible to discern a more general influence from Luxembourg, notably in the growth of public law that characterised the late twentieth and early twenty-first centuries?

European law was certainly an important part of the background. It provided an early vehicle for the consideration by the UK courts of fundamental rights which were subsequently given effect in the Human Rights Act 1998.[81] While the phrase 'legitimate expectation' was introduced to English administrative law prior to EEC accession,[82] the jurisprudence of the European Court has been influential in the development of that elusive concept in England.[83] Less tangibly, European Law formed part of the personal experience not only of many advocates before the House of Lords (including successive Treasury Devils, each of whom graduated to the Bench) but also of some of its judicial members. As well as Lord Slynn, who had served as Advocate General and Judge of the European Court before his appointment to the House of Lords, one would wish to mention those others who combined their judicial work with the chairmanship of Sub-Committee E (Law and Institutions) of the European Union Committee of the House of Lords, to the undoubted benefit of both.[84] It may well be that a degree of familiarity with the workings of the Community increased the receptiveness of the House of Lords to European influences.

The willingness of the House of Lords to give effect to European law when it was required to do so was however not always mirrored by an equivalent readiness to adapt the principles of domestic public law to the European template. Indeed

---

[80] ibid, para 183.

[81] See eg *Hodgson v Comrs of Customs and Excise* [1997] ELR 117, in which Article 6 ECHR was analysed and applied because of the need to interpret the governing Directive in conformity with it.

[82] *Schmidt v Secretary of State for Home Affairs* [1969] 2 Ch 149, *per* Lord Denning MR at 170.

[83] A practical example of this osmosis is *R v Ministry of Agriculture, Fisheries and Food, ex p Hamble (Offshore) Fisheries Ltd* [1995] 2 All ER 714, in which Sedley J prefaced his legal analysis by recording (at 724) that '[n]either counsel submits that there is any material difference between [the jurisprudence of the European Court on legitimate expectations] and the domestic law of England and Wales.' The House of Lords appears to have adopted the doctrine of substantive legitimate expectation, as expounded by the Court of Appeal in *R v North Devon Health Authority, ex p Coughlan*, even though as was recently remarked it has not considered it in depth: *R (Bancoult) v Secretary of State for Foreign Affairs* [2008] 3 WLR 995, *per* Lord Carswell at para 135.

[84] The European Union Committee (formerly the Select Committee on the European Communities) is unrivalled among national parliaments for the quantity and quality of its reports into EU affairs. The loss to the highest court of the expertise in topical areas of EU law that has for many years been provided to it by the judicial chairmanship of Sub-Committee E might be considered one of the less happy consequences of the strict separation of powers that resulted in the displacement of the Law Lords from the Palace of Westminster.

the borrowing of principles from European public law was marked by a high degree of caution. Thus:

a. The adoption of proportionality as a ground for review in English administrative law, first mooted by Lord Diplock in 1985[85] and advocated many times since,[86] has still not occurred.[87]

b. There remains no general duty on administrative decision-makers to give reasons for their decisions, equivalent to that contained in Article 253 of the EC Treaty.[88]

c. The House of Lords declined to assimilate the mental element required for the domestic tort of misfeasance in a public office to the standard applicable to the liability of a public authority for breach of European law, whilst affirming that where European law was in issue, that standard would be loyally applied.[89]

Some of the progressive developments in English public law, for example in relation to standing[90] and defendants' duty of disclosure,[91] were in areas where European law has remained conservative by comparison. The rapid development of public law principles in Commonwealth jurisdictions whose judges and lawyers have had little exposure to European law is also a warning against attributing exclusively to Europe an influence that may have been felt just as strongly outside it.

Procedure

The European Commission is in 2002 believed to have shown interest in the practice of the House of Lords not to give reasons for refusing leave to appeal in cases which raised an arguable point of European law. Infringement proceedings were averted on the basis that in future brief reasons for refusal would be given, as

---

[85] *CCSU v Minister for the Civil Service* [1985] AC 374; see also Lord Bridge and Lord Roskill in *R v Secretary of State for the Home Office, ex p Brind* [1991] 1 AC 696.

[86] By Lord Slynn in *R (Alconbury Ltd) v Secretary of State for the Environment, Transport and the Regions* [2003] 2 AC 295, 320–1, by Lord Steyn in *R (Daly) v Secretary of State for the Home Department* [2001] 2 AC 332, para 32 and by the Court of Appeal in *R (Association of British Civilians: Far Eastern Region) v Secretary of State for Defence* [2003] QB 1397, para 34 (which, however, stated in relation to the *Wednesbury* test of unreasonableness that it was 'not for this court to perform its burial rites').

[87] The House of Lords refused leave to appeal in the latter case. Lord Hope remarked in *Somerville v Scottish Ministers* [2007] 1 WLR 2734 that it was 'not the occasion to embark on an examination of this issue, which is plainly one of considerable importance and difficulty'.

[88] *Stefan v General Medical Council* [1999] 1 WLR 1293; *R v Secretary of State for the Home Department, ex p Doody* [1994] 1 AC 531.

[89] *Three Rivers DC v Bank of England (No 3)* [2003] 2 AC 1, *per* Lord Steyn at 196. See now Law Commission Consultation Paper No 187, *Administrative Redress: Public Bodies and the Citizen* (3 July 2008), which drew heavily on EU principles in its proposals for new rules governing the liability of public bodies.

[90] *R v IRC, ex p National Federation of Self-Employed and Small Businesses Ltd* [1982] AC 617; contrast Case C-50/00P *UPA* [2002] ECR I-6677.

[91] *Tweed v Parades Commission for Northern Ireland* [2007] 1 AC 650.

has since been done, although the reasons given are summary in nature. Because it seemed unsatisfactory that there should be a difference of practice between EC and domestic cases, the same practice is now followed generally. This may be counted a positive development, the impetus for which came from Brussels.

Some European law practitioners displayed an early tendency to model their written Case for the House of Lords on the full written observations that it was usual to submit before the European Court, rather than on the more exiguous document suggested by the House of Lords in *Yorke Motors v Edwards*.[92] Whether or not as a consequence, that tendency is now widespread.

The recent custom of the House of Lords of holding advocates to an informal timetable was not derived directly from the strict time limits applied by the European Court to advocates at its own, very much shorter, oral hearings. The European Court model, of which many advocates before the House of Lords had personal experience, may however have contributed to the general acceptance of the timetabling of submissions.

Conclusion

European law was conscientiously interpreted and applied by the House of Lords in approaching 100 cases over the period of UK membership, not always with obvious enthusiasm but with courtesy and generally without fuss. Some issues the House of Lords resolved for itself; others it referred to the European Court for a ruling to which it then faithfully gave effect. Some of its references for preliminary rulings raised interesting points which resulted in the development of European law by the European Court.[93]

From time to time, and increasingly in recent years, the House of Lords decided cases which it should strictly have referred. But few if any of its judgments have proved especially controversial, or were demonstrably wrong. In addition, Law Lords felt sufficiently confident in their understanding of European law to use its principles from time to time, without any legal obligation to do so, as models for the development of domestic law.

As a court of European law, the House of Lords must therefore (by the modest standards applicable to national courts) be counted a success. One might wish that it had arrived earlier at the practice of conveying its own opinions to the European Court along with its references for preliminary rulings: its authority would have guaranteed an attentive audience for its views. But a major role for the

---

[92] [1982] 1 WLR 444. In both *Factortame* appeals, counsel for the fishermen thought it politic to apologise at the start of their written cases for taking this course.

[93] Sir David Edward, a judge of the European Court between 1992 and 2004, singled out the references by the House of Lords in Case C-213/89 *Factortame* and Case C-453/99 *Courage v Crehan* [2002] QB 507 as of particular interest: 'The Development of Law and Legal Process in the EU' in Markesinis (n 52).

House of Lords in the substantive development of European law was largely precluded by the Treaties and by the terms of the European Communities Act 1972. Its most significant contribution may prove to have been the loyal and constructive way in which it applied European law as declared in Luxembourg. By its own practice and by force of example, the House of Lords contributed to a Europe-wide task which had, at the time of UK accession, been by no means assured of success: the grafting of a new legal order on to the established national institutions which it needed for its legitimacy and effectiveness.

28

Constitutional Law

Brigid Hadfield

Introduction

A constitutional law case may be defined as one that is concerned with the judges' determination of the borders of their regulation of public power, primarily but not exclusively governmental power, and with the judicial formulation of the principles on which such power should be exercised. As such, of course, these cases reflect, directly or indirectly, the judicial perceptions of the judicial role within the United Kingdom constitutional order. That is, although clearly the House of Lords can only address those issues which parties deem appropriate for litigation (and which the Law Lords are prepared to take on appeal), the approach of these judges should also reflect their views on who or what institutions are the (ultimate) formulators and custodians of the state's constitutional values, a role of no minor importance in the absence of a codified, *a fortiori*, entrenched constitution.

For the first 60 to 70 years of the twentieth century there appear to have been precious few such cases.[1] That is, the constitutional law role of the House of Lords was exceedingly limited (and largely confined to wartime or other emergency cases) and constitutional 'law' was primarily focused on and through political and not judicial channels. From the 1970s onwards, however, the growing number of constitutional law cases, as defined, could just as easily be included under other, burgeoning, branches of public law.

In brief, during the first six to seven decades of the twentieth century, judicial control of the exercise of parliamentary power was effectively blocked by such a widespread adherence to the doctrine of parliamentary sovereignty proclaiming the absence of legal limits upon an Act of Parliament that no case reached the House of Lords on the question (after 1842) prior to the United Kingdom's accession to the European Community from January 1973, although the first

---

[1] Although the book covers the 133 years from 1876, given that the key constitutional law cases within this period begin at the end of the First World War, reference will be made in this chapter to 'the last hundred years' or to 'the twentieth century' as a shorthand for the longer period.

challenge after that date, to a private Act of Parliament, was not connected with the European Community. Membership of the European Community also exposed constitutional (and other branches of the) law to the principles articulated by the judges of the European Court of Justice and binding upon all organs of the state. So far as review of governmental power was concerned, administrative law was in the doldrums until well into the 1960s and its revivification led to its separation from constitutional law, if only for pedagogic purposes. In terms specifically of the relationship between public power and the individual, the case law on civil liberties from the earlier decades of the last century was largely confined to a limited number of cases on public order and police powers. Few of these (criminal law?) cases reached the House of Lords anyway. Then, from the early 1970s, the evolving and increasingly influential jurisprudence of the European Commission and Court of Human Rights, the albeit incomplete development of the common law as a home for human rights values, and finally the enactment of the Human Rights Act 1998 transformed civil liberties into human rights law, and its consequent expansion created a new category of public law. Not surprisingly, therefore, there are separate chapters in this book on Administrative Law, on Human Rights, and on European influences on the House of Lords. The challenge for a separate chapter on constitutional law and the House of Lords turns on the key question of the identity of constitutional law cases. Are they solely those cases left over from the major selections made by administrative, human rights, and European public lawyers, or, fractionally better, those cases that illustrate the major principles underpinning these areas of the law? Alternatively, is there a discernible 'corpus' of constitutional law cases in their own right?

Key constitutional law cases: selection and overview

The following may be suitable candidates for the key constitutional law cases of the last hundred years, of which there are not many and not all of which will be considered more fully below. They are grouped partly chronologically and partly by substance. There are, broadly defined, three non-discrete categories of case: the role of the judiciary in time of emergency; the courts and the royal prerogative; and the courts and Acts of Parliament. Collectively, these cases present a rather uneven picture of the constitutional sense of the judges.

The first group of cases in particular provides an insight into the constitutional possibilities of the rules of statutory interpretation. They address most acutely the principles governing the triangular set of relationships: Parliament and the Government; the Government and the courts; and the courts and Parliament.[2]

---

[2] At this stage at least this geometry is more fruitful than the depiction of sovereignty in the bi-polar terms of the Queen in Parliament and the Queen in her courts.

The Zamora,[3] which set the scene for the dominant judicial attitude to executive power in time of emergency for the whole of the twentieth century,[4] would otherwise lead the list, but as a decision of the Judicial Committee of the Privy Council on appeal from the Prize Court, it is outside the remit of this chapter. Pride of place, therefore, is given to *R v Halliday, ex p Zadig*[5] which concerned the validity of a Defence of the Realm regulation of the First World War and contained a noble dissent from Lord Shaw of Dunfermline, constitutionally at least the equal of the more famous dissent of Lord Atkin in *Liversidge v Anderson*[6] on similar but not identical questions which arose during the Second World War.[7] These two dissents, as will be argued below, are, probably uncontroversially, the most significant of all the constitutional speeches from the House of Lords over the last hundred years: significant in substance, that is, but not in (immediately) engendering a change in judicial stance.

This line of cases on the judicial perception of the judicial role *vis-à-vis* statutory emergency powers vested in the Government, but in far less acutely dangerous times, continues in the 1960s[8] with *McEldowney v Forde*,[9] a case which, like the *Burmah Oil* case,[10] is also notable for its consequences. Finally, from the most recent era, *Secretary of State for the Home Department v Rehman*[11] and *A v Secretary of State for the Home Department*,[12] decided by a nine-judge House of Lords,[13] relate to the question as to what changes, if any, the effluxion

---

[3] [1916] 2 AC 77 *per* Lord Parker of Waddington, who delivered the opinion of the Privy Council, at 106–7: '[T]heir Lordships are of opinion that the judge ought, as a rule, to treat the statement on oath of a proper officer of the Crown to the effect that the vessel or goods which it is desired to requisition are urgently required for use in connection with the defence of the realm, the prosecution of war, or other matters involving national security, as conclusive of the fact...Those who are responsible for the national security must be the sole judge of what the national security requires.'

[4] In *Council of Civil Service Unions v Minister for the Civil Service* [1985] AC 374 (the GCHQ case) the House of Lords established the justiciability of an exercise of the royal prerogative but in reliance on *The Zamora* refused to exercise it.

[5] [1917] AC 260.   [6] [1942] AC 206.

[7] *Greene v Secretary of State for Home Affairs* [1942] AC 284 was decided by the House of Lords on the same day as *Liversidge* but decided differently on the facts.

[8] See too *Chandler v DPP* [1964] AC 763.   [9] [1971] AC 632.   [10] [1965] AC 75.

[11] [2003] 1 AC 153; decided by the House of Lords in 2001.   [12] [2005] 2 AC 68.

[13] The other cases involving nine judges are *R v Ball* [1911] AC 47, *AG's Reference (No 2 of 2001)* [2004] 2 AC 72, *A v Secretary of State for the Home Department* [2005] 2 AC 68, *Jackson v AG* [2006] 1 AC 262, and *R (Gentle) v The Prime Minister* [2008] 1 AC 1356. A nine-judge House was convened in February 2008 in the discontinued case between the President of the State of Equatorial Guinea and *inter alios* Simon Mann. All bar the case of *Ball* may be regarded as being of constitutional concern and the recent 'proliferation' of such cases may show the House of Lords moving into Supreme Court mode on constitutional issues. *R (Bancoult) v Secretary of State for Foreign and Commonwealth Affairs* [2007] 3 WLR 955 however, was heard by only five judges, surprisingly and, given the 3:2 outcome, perhaps significantly. See, in a different context but nonetheless as a point of wider application, Lord Hoffmann (in the majority in *Bancoult*) in *White v Chief Constable of South Yorkshire* [1999] AC 455 at 502, who described *McLoughlin v O'Brian* [1983] 1 AC 410 as 'one of those cases in which one feels that a slight change in the composition of the Appellate Committee would have set the law on a different course'.

of time and the Human Rights Act 1998 have had on the judges. This is a question to be answered primarily by the Human Rights chapter of this volume and is only adverted to here.

The second category of constitutional case involves the exercise of the royal prerogative powers and involves the common law powers of the courts. Here the *GCHQ* case[14] is the leading case. It reversed 300 years of law with, on this point, brevity of words perhaps unparalleled in legal history for a matter of comparable significance. Prior to this decision, it was clear and long established law that the courts would review whether a claimed prerogative power existed and its extent but they would not review the exercise of a recognised prerogative power. As it happens, no case on the prerogative came before the House of Lords after the seventeenth century Revolution Settlement until the immediate aftermath of the First World War.

Attorney General v De Keyser's Royal Hotel,[15] a case arising out of the taking of property under statutory powers for use in time of war, involved the relationship between an extant statute and the royal prerogative. The later cases of *Burmah Oil Co Ltd v The Lord Advocate,*[16] reversed by a retrospective Act of the sovereign Parliament, namely the War Damages Act 1965, (very peripherally) *Attorney General v Nissan,*[17] and *R v Secretary of State for the Home Department, ex p Fire Brigades Union*[18] complete the list.[19] Again, these cases, like the first category, involve a spread of dates across the last century.

The third and final group of cases, those concerned with the sovereignty of Parliament, a cornerstone constitutional principle which did not surface in the House of Lords after 1842[20] until the 1970s, include *Pickin v British Railways Board*[21] on the challenge to the validity of a private Act of Parliament, and *Jackson v Attorney General*[22] concerning the validity of the Parliament Act 1949. The cases of *R v Secretary of State for Transport, ex p Factortame Ltd (No 2)*[23] on the impact of EC law on this doctrine, in which an Act of Parliament was 'disapplied', and *R v Secretary of State for Employment, ex p Equal Opportunities Commission,*[24] in which the House of Lords granted a declaration that the provisions of an Act of Parliament were contrary to European Community law,

---

[14] *Council of Civil Service Unions v Minister for the Civil Service* [1985] AC 374.

[15] [1920] AC 508. The only other (non-House of Lords) case on the extent of the royal prerogative after the seventeenth century was the Court of Appeal decision in *Re a Petition of Right* [1915] 3 KB 649.

[16] [1965] AC 75.   [17] [1970] AC 179.

[18] [1995] 2 AC 513. This case is also noteworthy because of the difficulty of convening a court of five judges who had not debated the relevant Criminal Justice Bill when it was before the legislative House of Lords.

[19] The decision in *Bancoult* [2008] UKHL 61 came too late to be fully integrated into the text but brief mention of it will be made below. Lord Bingham's (dissenting) speech in that case is a cameo gem both on the royal prerogative and on constitutionalism, a worthy valedictory to his time as Senior Law Lord.

[20] *Edinburgh & Dalkeith Rly v Wauchope* (1842) 8 ER 279 (a three-judge House of Lords).

[21] [1974] AC 765.   [22] [2006] 1 AC 262.   [23] [1991] 1 AC 603.

[24] [1995] 1 AC 1.

either add fine (linguistic) nuances to the doctrine of Parliamentary sovereignty or provide its *coup de grâce*.[25] To be read alongside these cases, although not itself a sovereignty decision, is *Anisminic v Foreign Compensation Commission*,[26] in which the reasoning of a majority of their Lordships on the validity of an absolute ouster clause may justifiably be considered as one of the greatest constitutional law decisions of the twentieth century. In this case, a profound exposition on constitutionalism, almost completely dressed by their Lordships in necessarily narrow legal terms, serves as a key marker of the potential judicial contribution to constitutional values within the context of the doctrine of the sovereignty of Parliament.

Judges and the executive in times of emergency: two classic dissents

Such cases accentuate constitutional issues most acutely and are also the most likely group of constitutional cases on their facts to give rise to litigation. The problems for the courts are clear. Who should determine the nature and extent of the emergency, evaluate the available evidence, some of which of its nature will be highly secret, and determine and secure the appropriate response to the emergency? To what extent can an Act of Parliament be expected to deal with an emergency in anything but the most general of terms, necessarily leaving the Government to supply the often vitally important 'detail' through non-sovereign delegated legislation and/or administrative action? Is the doctrine of ministerial responsibility any guarantee against an abuse of delegated powers, regarding either their extent or their application? To what extent should the protection in this context of fundamental individual rights (such as liberty and a procedurally fair and open hearing) be left vulnerable to only (very) limited judicial protection?

In *Zadig*,[27] the familiar salient element in emergency cases is present, namely legislation passed with minimal and largely uncritical (or, if critical, unavailing) scrutiny from Parliament. If Parliament, the third element in the triangular set of relationships, fails adequately to discharge its scrutiny powers over the executive, should the courts step in to fill the breach and, if so, on what principles? The Defence of the Realm Consolidation Act 1914 by section 1(1) conferred upon the King in Council the power during the continuance of the War to issue regulations for 'securing the public safety and the defence of the realm'. Regulation 14B, made in 1915, empowered the Secretary of State to provide for the internment without trial of persons of hostile origins or associations where it appeared to him expedient to do so for the fulfilment of the stated statutory aims. It will be noted that the Act did not expressly confer the power to intern.

---

[25] An absence of challenges to the doctrine in the courts may, of course, be regarded as a sign of its strength.

[26] [1969] 2 AC 147.

[27] [1917] AC 260; D Foxton, '*R v Halliday ex parte Zadig* in retrospect' (2003) 119 LQR 455.

An advisory committee which, as required, included in its membership two High Court judges, Sankey and Younger JJ, was appointed under the Regulation to advise the Secretary of State on the exercise of his powers. The internee could make representations to the committee. At the time Zadig, a naturalised British subject, was interned, the committee, regulating its own procedure and sitting in private, provided the internee with no reason for the detention, the evidence given against him was not released to him, and representation by solicitor not counsel was permitted, only occasionally and for the sole purpose of the giving of evidence and not for advocacy.[28] Zadig did not directly challenge the decision to detain him under the Regulation but challenged the validity of the Regulation itself. His counsel, relying on the constitutional essence of the principles of statutory interpretation,[29] argued, inter alia, that 'some limitation must be put upon the general words of the statute',[30] that 'general words in a statute cannot take away the vested rights of the subject or alter the fundamental laws of the Kingdom', and that 'where one of two possible constructions is repugnant to the traditions and Constitution of this country, that construction ought to be rejected in favour of the more reasonable construction'.

The House of Lords (composed of one Englishman, three Scotsmen, and an Irishman[31] and, even more interestingly, four former Government law officers[32]) by a majority of four to one, almost summarily dismissed Zadig's arguments: the statute was passed at a time of extreme national danger; Parliament had sought to address the possibility of abuse by providing safeguards which effectually guarded against 'all injustice or abuse in the administration of the regulation' (*per* Lord Atkinson[33]); in the event of an egregious abuse (as in illustrations given by Lord Dunedin[34]) Parliament would repeal the parent Act; and 'however precious the personal liberty of the subject may be there is something for which it may well be sacrificed by legal enactment, namely national success in war'.[35]

---

[28] Lord Finlay at 269: 'It seems obvious that no tribunal for investigating the question whether circumstances of suspicion exist warranting some restraint can be imagined less appropriate than a Court of Law.'

[29] The constitutional value of these rules, which also include the presumption that a criminal law statute should be construed strictly, that is in favour of the accused and against the prosecution, is often overlooked. Cf, on this specific presumption, Lord Atkinson at 274 of *Zadig*. For a consideration of the non-use of side notes and more generally the appropriate approach to the interpretation of the Official Secrets Act 1911, see *Chandler v DPP* [1964] AC 763.

[30] Zadig's counsel's suggestion that a judicial interpretation of the Regulation as conferring unlimited powers upon the executive could sanction the imposition of the death penalty without trial was 'answered' thus by Lord Finlay LC at 268–9: '. . . it may be necessary in time of great public danger to entrust great powers to His Majesty in Council, and that Parliament may do so feeling certain that such powers will be reasonably exercised'. Lord Dunedin at 270–1 said: '. . . the fault, if fault there be, lies in the fact that the British Constitution has entrusted to the two Houses of Parliament, subject to the assent of the King, an absolute power untrammelled by any written instrument obedience to which may be compelled by some judicial body. The danger of abuse is theoretically present; practically, as things exist, it is in my opinion absent.'

[31] Lord Wrenbury, Lords Finlay LC, Dunedin, and Shaw, and Lord Atkinson respectively.

[32] Lord Wrenbury was the exception. Foxton (n 27) 480–1.   [33] [1917] AC 260, 276.

[34] ibid, 271. Cf Lord Finlay (n 30).   [35] ibid, Lord Atkinson, 271.

Lord Shaw's dissent, the sole dissent of the 13 judges[36] who heard Zadig's case, is a classic rehearsal, in advance of its time, of both historic and contemporary constitutional values. The other judgments, he stated, 'constitute a suspension and a breach of those fundamental rights which are protective of British liberty'. In his opinion, 'Parliament never sanctioned either in intention or by reason of the statutory words employed...such a violent exercise of arbitrary power'. Parliament in the 1914 Act had indeed employed the words 'public safety and defence of the realm' but it had not included any phrase about 'hostile origins or associations' and so had given 'no express sanction' for Regulation 14B which 'fundamentally affected the rights' of the subjects. Consequently, he continued, the argument to which he was unable to accede was that Parliament, 'not expressly dealing with a matter pre-eminently demanding careful delimitation, must be held to have accomplished by implication this far-reaching subversion of our civil liberties'.[37]

Emphasising the constitutional need for the judiciary to approach such *vires* questions in a spirit of independent scrutiny rather than compliance with the Government,[38] Lord Shaw, addressing the Attorney General's argument that the principle of perfect generality[39] applied to the interpretation of the Regulation, used words of considerable constitutional resonance. Saying that this would mean that for the duration of the War 'the Government has been allowed at its own hand to do anything it likes',[40] including the repeal of 'laws as deep as the foundations of the Constitution' and the subversion of 'ordinary fundamental and constitutional rights' by for example permitting the imposition of the death penalty without trial, he added: 'Under this the Government becomes a Committee of Public Safety. But its powers as such are far more arbitrary than those of the most famous Committee of Public Safety known to history.'[41] As Lord Atkin would later say (but in English): *'inter arma leges non silent'*,[42] but a dissent, though not silent, is a dissent just the same and the majority view in *Zadig* prevailed.

---

[36] Five judges sat in the Divisional Court and three in the Court of Appeal.

[37] [1917] AC 260, 276–8.   [38] ibid, 287.

[39] That is an interpretation subject only to two limitations, that of time (the duration of the War) and that of identified purpose, namely, public safety and the defence of the realm. As Lord Shaw said, at 288, the latter limitation was 'illusory': 'As to what acts of State are promotive or regardful of that purpose, can a Court of law arrest the hand of a responsible Executive?...[No] [c]ourt of law could dare to set up its judgment on the merits of an issue—a public and political issue—of safety or defence...judges are not fitted to interpose on these.'

[40] At that point, Lord Shaw added, the law is effectively 'over-mastered' and the only law left is that which 'the Bench must accept from the mouth of the Government'. He then quoted from Juvenal's *Satires*: '*Hoc volo, sic jubeo; sit pro ratione voluntas*', that is, 'I will it, I order it; let (my) will stand for a reason.' Ibid, 288.

[41] ibid, 289–91. The 'Committee' to which he refers was during the French Revolution's reign of terror; in French *'la grande terreur'*.

[42] *Liversidge v Anderson* [1942] AC 206, 244: 'In this country, amid the clash of arms, the laws are not silent. They may be changed but they speak the same language in war as in peace.' Cicero's *'Silent enim, leges inter arma'* from *Pro Milone* was quoted by Lord Shaw in *Zadig* at 289.

Lord Shaw's dissent echoed loudly in the Second World War detention case of *Liversidge v Anderson*,[43] where Lord Atkin's[44] own dissent then carried forward these values into a conflict of far greater magnitude in terms of both the internal dangers already faced in the blitz of Britain from the summer of 1940 and the 'external' situation then facing the United Kingdom.[45] That factor, alongside the unprecedented hostile response of the other judges to Lord Atkin,[46] expressed in both public and private, render Lord Atkin's speech certainly the better known (and the more courageous, if not original) dissent.

The main issue in *Liversidge* was not legally the same as in *Zadig* in that section 1(2) of the Emergency Powers (Defence) Act 1939 expressly conferred the power upon the King in Council to make provision for the detention of persons whose detention appeared to the Secretary of State to be expedient in the interests of public safety or the defence of the realm. The appellant was detained, by order of the Home Secretary, under Regulation 18B of the Defence (General) Regulations 1939, which provided that if the Secretary of State had 'reasonable cause to believe any person to be of hostile origins or associations' and that by reason thereof 'it is necessary to exercise control over him', he may make a detention order. There was no argument over the *vires* of the Regulation under which Liversidge had been detained. His sole argument concerned the construction of its words: that is, whether or not the phrase 'reasonable cause' imported an objective or subjective requirement.[47] If the former test were correct then the Home Secretary would be required to lead evidence as to the reasonableness of his belief, that is, the grounds on which he exercised his discretion. If the latter test were correct, then a simple affidavit stating his belief that he had reasonable cause would suffice. This argument had only recently become necessary. In the Court of Appeal in another Regulation 18B case, *R v Secretary of State for Home Affairs, ex p Greene*[48] (the appeal being heard in the House of Lords[49] immediately

---

[43] *Liversidge v Anderson* [1942] AC 206.

[44] Lord Atkin, as Atkin J, had agreed with the lawfulness of Zadig's detention: *R v Halliday* [1916] 1 KB 738, 743: 'I think that the regulation is well within the power given by section 1 of the Act and I can see no reason for invoking any limitations upon it.' In *Liversidge* [1942] AC 206 at 239, Lord Atkin simply stated that *Zadig* had nothing to do with the issue in *Liversidge*. The contrast in his dicta in the two cases may nonetheless be dryly commented upon; it can equally be said that Lord Atkin matured in his thinking as a judge or that even at the time of Lord Shaw's dissent, Atkin J listened.

[45] G Lewis, *Lord Atkin* (London: Butterworths, 1983) 132, points out that the time during the argument and judgment in *Liversidge*, September to November 1941, was the 'low point in the War. The Balkans and Crete had been overrun; the invasion of Russia had carried the Germans close to Leningrad and Moscow; the British summer offensive in the Western Desert had failed; the Japanese menaced the Malayan Peninsula and Singapore; Pearl Harbour was to follow in the next month and the United States were not yet in the War.'

[46] ibid, 138ff. See also JAG Griffith, *Judicial Politics since 1920* (Oxford: Blackwell, 1993) 36–48.

[47] There was an additional question of on whom the burden fell: the Home Secretary to establish reasonable cause or the detainee to establish lack of it? Once the courts held that the test was a subjective one the burden on the Home Secretary became that of merely stating by affidavit that he indeed had reasonable grounds for his belief.

[48] [1942] 1 KB 87.   [49] *Greene v Secretary of State for Home Affairs* [1942] AC 284.

following *Liversidge*), the Government had for the first time argued that the Home Secretary had to establish only that he believed that he had reasonable cause. Prior to that case the Government had accepted the requirement and the burden of showing reasonable cause.[50]

The majority of the House of Lords in *Liversidge* had little difficulty in disposing of the need for an objective test. Viscount Maugham[51] rejected the appellant's argument that the construction of the Regulation should if possible be in favour of the liberty of the subject. If there were any reasonable doubt about the meaning of the Regulation, he said, 'we should prefer a construction which will carry into effect the plain intention of those responsible for the Order in Council rather than one which will defeat that intention'. The words 'reasonable cause' were, he argued, capable of bearing both the meaning of 'if there is in fact reasonable cause' and also (especially where a person is conferred with an exclusive discretion or the matter is within his exclusive knowledge) 'what a person thinks is reasonable cause'. His reasons for preferring the latter meaning were as follows. First, the Home Secretary must have reasonable cause to believe that a person is of hostile origin and that it is by reason of that fact necessary to exercise control over him. As the latter decision was so 'clearly a matter for executive discretion' not subject to the discussion, criticism, and control of a judge, it 'necessarily follows' [*sic*] that the same is true of all the facts which he is required to have reasonable cause to believe. Secondly, since the Home Secretary was not acting judicially under Regulation 18B, that is, he could act on hearsay, without legal evidence, and without the constraint of the *audi alteram partem* rule, then it would be 'strange if his decision could be questioned in a court of law'. Thirdly, as the Home Secretary would often be acting on confidential information, which could not, without risk to the defence of the realm, be communicated to the detainee or to a court, even sitting *in camera*, it would be 'impossible for the court to come to a conclusion adverse to the opinion of the Secretary of State in such a matter'. Fourthly, the person entrusted with the powers under the Regulation was a Secretary of State, a position not comparable with, for example, that of a police constable. The Home Secretary was a principal 'member of the Government answerable to Parliament for the proper discharge of his duties' and not to the courts; he was assisted by an advisory committee; and he was required to report to Parliament once a month on the exercise of his powers.[52] *Ça suffit*.

The sole dissentient judge, Lord Atkin, emphasised that the decision to detain the individual concerned not only the defence of the realm but also the liberty of

[50] *R v Secretary of State for the Home Affairs, ex p Lees* [1941] 1 KB 72 at 78 *per* Humphreys J for the Divisional Court and at 84 *per* MacKinnon LJ in the Court of Appeal; *R v Home Secretary, ex p Budd* [1941] 2 All ER 749.

[51] Elder brother of the author Somerset Maugham, former Lord Chancellor and author of a letter to *The Times* on 6 November 1941 criticising Lord Atkin.

[52] [1942] AC 206, 219–22.

the individual and was, further, one taken by an executive minister and not a judicial officer. He also, by extensive consideration of the legislative use of the word 'reasonable' and judicial response thereto, sought to establish that the words in the Regulation 'have only one plain and natural meaning', a matter capable of being resolved by the judges. It is the following phrases of his speech, however, which have made Lord Atkin's dissent most memorable:

I view with apprehension the attitude of judges who on a mere question of construction when face to face with claims involving the liberty of the subject show themselves more executive minded than the executive... In this country amid the clash of arms the laws are not silent. They may be changed but they speak the same language in war as in peace. It has always been one of the pillars of freedom... that the judges are no respecters of persons and stand between the subject and any attempted encroachments on his liberty by the executive, alert to see that any encroachment is justified in law. In this case I have listened to arguments which might have been addressed acceptably to the Court of King's Bench in the time of Charles I... I know of only one authority which might justify the (majority's) suggested method of construction... Humpty Dumpty[53]

... who used words to mean solely what he chose them to mean.

Ewing and Gearty have argued that Lord Shaw's speech in *Zadig* is 'certainly unequalled eclipsing by far the better known contribution of Lord Atkin twenty-five years later'[54] but for the reasons given above, the latter's speech too remains one of the greatest constitutional law judgments ever delivered.

A paean of praise to two dissentient judgments[55] over a quarter of a century apart, however, with no other cases cited hardly constitutes a thrilling tribute to the constitutional awareness of the House of Lords judges. The paucity of case law and the constitutionally limited jurisprudence of the majority judgments in both cases should not be hidden by the dramatic nature of two dissents. Yet, the essence of constitutionalism and of the spirit of much constitutional law history is well served by Lords Shaw and Atkin, and a chapter such as this should delight in such judgments, however atypical they may be. Ahead of their time and well before debates on civil liberties transmuted into human rights (and before the birth of the sound-bite), these judges demonstrated that within constitutional law proper human rights values have a place. The rules of statutory interpretation when used expansively and liberally may serve every bit as well as references to the rule of law and human rights.[56]

---

[53] ibid, 244–5.

[54] KD Ewing and C Gearty, *The Struggle for Civil Liberties* (Oxford: OUP, 2000) 86–7.

[55] In *IRC v Rossminster Ltd* [1980] AC 952, Lord Diplock, from the massively safer position of a peacetime interpretation of a tax statute, said at 1011: 'For my part I think the time has come to acknowledge openly that the majority of this House in *Liversidge v Anderson* were expediently and at that time, perhaps, excusably, wrong and the dissenting speech of Lord Atkin was right.'

[56] Cf I Jennings, *The Law and the Constitution* (London: University of London Press, 5th edn 1959) in his then necessarily short chapter on The Courts and the Constitution, 254: 'The courts are free to act, however, only within a sphere of small diameter, for the possibility of interpretation is limited by the legislation passed.'

National security and the judges: a later evaluation[57]

The judges in *Rehman*[58] and *A*,[59] on issues arising from either side of the coming into force of the Human Rights Act 1998 and decided well over 80 years after *Zadig*, scarcely match the constitutional language of the dissents of Lords Shaw and Atkin. What may have changed is the willingness of a greater number of judges to espouse such language but even then rarely in situations involving national security. It is important, however, that the lure of high constitutional language does not mask the fact that, as Lord Hoffmann said in *Rehman*, the cost of failure in issues at the heart of the defence of the realm or national security is high. Whilst the protective role of the judges of human rights against executive (and now parliamentary) encroachment is constitutionally vital so too is the role of a Government in protecting the state. Constitutional law needs both sorts of protection, and needs and receives judicial recognition of this. This has been confirmed in both *Rehman* and *A*. The constitutional protection of human rights requires a continuous dialogue between the different institutions of the state based fully on an articulation of their respective competences and mutual respect for them. The doctrine of the separation of powers by no means automatically justifies expansionist judicial power.[60]

Rehman concerned the decision of the Home Secretary, under section 3(5)(b) of the Immigration Act 1971, to deport a Pakistani national on the grounds that it would be conducive to the public good in the interests of national security. Rehman sought to challenge the decision on the ground that as a number of the Home Secretary's claims against him could not be factually substantiated, the Minister could not be said to have satisfied the statutory requirement. The House of Lords heard the case in May 2001 and the judgments were published exactly a month after '9/11'. They held that the section 3 decision was prima facie a matter for the executive discretion of the Home Secretary: although matters of national security did not fall beyond the scrutiny of the courts, it was 'self evidently right that national courts must give great weight to the views of the executive on matters of national security';[61] Lord Hoffmann placed his reliance for such a conclusion on the separation of powers. In a postscript to his speech written after 9/11, he emphasised the 'need for the judicial arm of the government to respect such decisions of Ministers of the Crown' both because of government access to special information and expertise and also because

such decisions, with serious potential results for the community, require a legitimacy which can be conferred only by entrusting them to persons responsible to the community

---

[57] See Feldman, ch 30 in this volume.   [58] [2003] 1 AC 153.   [59] [2005] 2 AC 68.
[60] See *Duport Steels v Sirs* [1980] 1 WLR 142, esp Lord Diplock at 157.
[61] [2003] 1 AC 153, 187.

through the democratic process. If the people are to accept the consequences of such decisions, they must be made by persons whom the people have elected and whom they can remove.[62]

The powers conferred upon the judiciary by sections 3 and 4 of the Human Rights Act gave an enhanced democratic legitimacy to the more penetrative exercise of judicial powers, but have largely left unaltered the respect of the judiciary for the Government's national security powers, as can be seen in *A*, the Belmarsh detainees case.

Constitutional cases and their consequences

The restrictive hand of the rules of statutory interpretation may be seen in the case of *McEldowney v Forde*,[63] which came towards the end of the largely quiescent time for the judges, at a time when they were fully controlled by the Kilmuir rules[64] and their public profile, in so far as they had one, was in chairing political hot potato Government Committees and Commissions. In *McEldowney*, a case involving freedom of political expression in Northern Ireland,[65] the *facts* occurred during the first half of 1968 and it is thus not a case during the Northern Ireland 'Troubles' which are usually dated as beginning at any time from October 1968 (when a key civil rights march was affected by violence) to the summer of 1969 when the first deaths took place and the army was deployed. The Northern Ireland Parliament, however, had enacted the law concerned amidst earlier civil conflict during the era immediately after the partition of Ireland. The Civil Authorities (Special Powers) Act (Northern Ireland) 1922 by

[62] At 195. Cf Lord Hoffmann (dissenting) at 132 in *A*: 'The real threat to the life of the nation, in the sense of a people living in accordance with its traditional laws and political values, comes not from terrorism but from laws such as these. It is the true measure of what terrorism may achieve. It is for Parliament to decide whether to give the terrorists such a victory.'

[63] [1971] AC 632, judgment delivered June 1969. Note, in the context of the infrequent number of twentieth century constitutional cases, that Lord Guest, at 648–9, pointed out that he had been unable to find any case since *Zadig* in which a statutory instrument had ever been challenged and that consequently 'it must be plain that the task of a subject who endeavours to challenge the validity of such a regulation is a heavy one'. But cf *Chester v Bateson* [1920] 1 KB 829; *R v Sheer Metalcraft Ltd* [1954] 1 QB 586; *Comrs of Customs and Excise v Cure & Deeley Ltd* [1962] 1 QB 340.

[64] Named after the then Lord Chancellor who issued them in December 1955. The rules sought to keep the judiciary 'insulated from the controversies of the day' and effectively prevented the judges from contributing to both radio and television broadcasts. When Lord Mackay became Lord Chancellor in 1987 he rescinded the rules, regarding them as an infringement of the independence of the judiciary. For one consequence of a higher judicial profile affecting a Law Lord, see Lord Steyn, 'Laying the Foundations of Human Rights Law in the United Kingdom' [2005] EHRLR 349, n 4 and related text: 'Due to a challenge to my neutrality as a Law Lord made by the Government... I did not sit in *A*.'

[65] S Livingstone, 'The House of Lords and the Northern Ireland Conflict' (1994) 57 MLR 333, 346–8. Although the present book contains separate contributions on both Scotland and Northern Ireland it nonetheless seems important to include at least one major case from these jurisdictions in this chapter.

section 1(3) conferred the power upon the Northern Ireland Minister of Home Affairs to make regulations for the preservation of peace and the maintenance of order. Regulation 24 of the Special Powers Regulations made in 1922 made it an offence to become or remain a member of an unlawful organisation. Five republican organisations were expressly deemed by the Regulation to be unlawful organisations. In 1967 this list was amended to include 'republican clubs or any like organisation howsoever described'.

McEldowney was acquitted by the magistrates of an offence under this amendment, no evidence at all being led against him or his club of any activities that constituted a threat to peace, law, and order. The Northern Ireland Court of Appeal by a majority (Lord McDermott CJ dissenting) overturned this decision. It held that the Regulation was *intra vires* the parent Act and that the listing of the various organisations had been intended to prevent the Government from needing to establish in every case the threat to peace and order posed by them. A key question became whether the courts had a role in deciding if the Regulation did in fact further peace and order. McEldowney's appeal to the House of Lords challenged the *vires* of the amended Regulation on the grounds 'that it was not necessary for and did not make provision for the preservation of peace and maintenance of order'. He also argued that its terms 'were so wide that it was unreasonable, bad for uncertainty and duplicity, ambiguous and unenforceable in law'.[66] The House of Lords ruled by three votes (Lords Hodson, Guest, and Pearson) to two (Lords Pearce and Diplock dissenting) that the amended Regulation was not *ultra vires* the 1922 Act and (in the absence of bad faith) it was for the Minister to determine whether or not an organisation should be listed as unlawful as a threat to peace and order. Lord Pearson said:

The Northern Ireland Parliament must have intended that somebody should decide whether or not the making of some proposed regulation would be conducive to the 'preservation of peace and the maintenance of order'. Obviously it must have been intended that the Minister of Home Affairs should decide that question. Who else could ? . . . The courts cannot have been intended to decide such a question, because they do not have the necessary information, and the decision is in the sphere of politics which is not their sphere.[67]

Calvert heralded the decision thus: ' . . . the House of Lords has abolished the doctrine of the separation of powers. Its scope in the common law was always limited.'[68]

More tellingly than Calvert in terms of consequences, given Lord Pearson's exclusion of the political from the judicial domain, Boyle, Hadden, and Hillyard, in a chapter published in 1975 and entitled 'Civil Rights: The Failure of Law and Lawyers', wrote: ' . . . there can be no doubt of [the decision's] symbolic importance in showing the futility of pursuing the civil rights campaign through

---

[66] This argument failed too.
[67] [1971] AC 632, 655. Note that this is not phrased in terms of national security etc but in terms of politics.
[68] H Calvert, 'The "Republican Clubs" Case' (1970) 21 NILQ 191.

the courts. It is significant that the forces of law and order in Derry and Belfast broke down within weeks of the final rejection of the claim in the House of Lords.'[69] Although, as with virtually everything about Northern Ireland politics and the constitution, one could add 'Discuss' and then receive a multiplicity of opinions on the matter, the point is an important one and a salutary reminder of the deep waters within which constitutional law cases may operate.[70]

The royal prerogative and the judges

The first two twentieth century cases to reach the House of Lords on the royal prerogative powers of the Crown, *de facto* the Government, both concerned a traditional issue for the courts, namely the existence or the lawful extent of a claimed prerogative power: as it were, the legality question of the heads of judicial review. It probably is important that these cases too involved the taking of property, for certainly in the interpretation of statutes there is a presumption against the taking of property without compensation.

In *De Keyser*[71] the facts were as follows. In May 1916 the 'Crown' took (compulsory) possession of the De Keyser's Royal Hotel in London to serve as the headquarters of the Royal Flying Corps. It acted either under the Defence of the Realm Regulations made under the Defence of the Realm Consolidation Act 1914 (as stated in the War Office's requisitioning letter) or, as later argued before the courts, under the royal prerogative. The Defence Act 1842 provided for compensation for the taking of possession of lands or buildings by the Crown for the defence of the realm whether acquired voluntarily or compulsorily; the 1914 Regulations were silent on the matter of compensation.[72] The main question before the House of Lords was whether the Crown was bound to pay

---

[69] K Boyle, T Hadden, and P Hillyard, *Law and State: The Case of Northern Ireland* (London: Martin Robertson, 1975) 15.

[70] For views on their Lordships' decision in *Robinson v Secretary of State for Northern Ireland* [2002] NI 390 see B Hadfield, 'Does the Devolved Northern Ireland need an Independent Judicial Arbiter?' in N Bamforth and P Leyland (eds), *Public Law in a Multi-Layered Constitution* (Oxford: Hart, 2003); and B Dickson, 'The House of Lords and the Northern Ireland Conflict—A Sequel' (2006) 69 MLR 383. Note too the political composition of the Northern Ireland Executive formed after Assembly Elections in March 2007.

[71] [1920] AC 508.

[72] The Regulations' Parent Act of 1914 under s 1(1) empowered the King in Council to make Regulations during the continuance of the war for securing the public safety and the defence of the realm and under s 1(2) enabled such Regulations to suspend any restrictions on the acquisition or user of land or the exercise of any power under inter alia the Defence Act 1842 which remained the source for the power to take the land etc. It was not clear under which subsection of the 1914 Act the key Regulation had been made. The 1842 Act provided for certain conditions to be satisfied where there was no agreement to the land etc being taken. The 1914 Regulations were held to have removed those restrictions but not the provisions on compensation which were classified not as a restriction on but as a consequence of the taking of property. Lord Atkinson said at 542: 'Neither public safety nor defence of the realm requires that the Crown be relieved of a legal liability to pay for the property it takes from one of its subjects.'

compensation *ex lege* for the use and occupation of the hotel or whether an offer to pay compensation *ex gratia* was sufficient, the answer requiring a consideration of whether the hotel had been taken under statutory or prerogative powers.

The House of Lords found that the Crown had taken under legislation and that being the case there could be no resort to the royal prerogative. The legislation, superseding the prerogative, put it into abeyance during the life of the legislation. The Crown could only act under the legislation and in accordance with its requirements. As Lord Atkinson said, it would be 'useless and meaningless' for the legislature to impose restrictions on the Crown by legislation if the Crown could disregard them through resort to the royal prerogative: 'One cannot in the construction of a statute attribute to the Legislature (in the absence of compelling words) an intention so absurd.'[73]

Because the case was resolved under the legislative provisions, it left open the question of whether or not compensation would have been due under the prerogative power for the taking of property during time of war. The war prerogative was notoriously vague and eventually fell for consideration in *Burmah Oil*, a Scottish appeal, heard by their Lordships in 1964, but the facts of which stem from a part of the Government's military policy in the Second World War. Following the Government's scorched earth policy, in 1942 the retreating British army destroyed Burmah Oil's installations near Rangoon in Burma[74] to prevent the advancing Japanese troops availing themselves of these resources. The destruction was carried out the day before the Japanese forces occupied Rangoon. Other installations to the north were destroyed over the following weeks. By the time the case came before the Lords, it was accepted by both parties that the destruction of the property was carried out under the royal prerogative; the question for the House of Lords to decide was whether that exercise of the prerogative gave rise to an entitlement to compensation to the persons who had suffered loss as a consequence. The House of Lords (by 3 to 2) held that it did,[75] although the basis on which the claim would be based was left vague.[76] Although demolitions falling under the head of battle damage, that is, arising directly out of military operations, would not give rise to a claim for compensation (it was

---

[73] At 539.

[74] Then a Crown Colony and not covered by legislation; the position for compensation for action taken by the Government in the exercise of emergency powers in the UK was regulated (and limited) by the Compensation (Defence) Act 1939. The key policy issues, as in *de Keyser*, are balancing public/community needs in the pursuit of the war and the burden of damage suffered and inflicted in its duration and whether, and to what extent, the individual or the public purse should bear the loss.

[75] Viscount Radcliffe and Lord Hodson dissented on the ground that that they preferred to classify the action taken as acts of war taken in the face of the enemy (and so justified by a doctrine of necessity) and not part of a war prerogative the limits of which were exceedingly hard to define. There was thus no right to compensation: pp 133 and 134, and 141. See too on the uncertain nature of the prerogative and foreign territory, *AG v Nissan* [1970] AC 179.

[76] AL Goodhart, 'The Burmah Oil Case and the War Damage Act 1965' (1966) 82 MLR 97 points out at 98 that their Lordships' decision would have granted the appellants more generous compensation rights than those conferred upon British residents by the 1939 Act.

unanimously held), here the action was taken at the approach of the enemy forces and not during engagement with them.

The longer term constitutional significance of the case lies more in its consequences than in its substance, namely the enactment of the retrospective War Damages Act 1965 which removed the right to the compensation granted by the House of Lords. The fact as well as the substance of this enactment could be regarded as casting doubt on the rule of law and the independent role of the judges who actually decided the case well aware that retrospective legislation would be forthcoming in the event of a decision in favour of Burmah Oil.[77] The enactment of the 1965 Act (and even more so the timing of the indication of its likely enactment) clearly marks the judges as subordinate to the will of Parliament, a statement of constitutional import made by both main political parties. The Conservative Government instigated the principle of the bill and when it lost office at the October 1964 general election, it was then enacted at the behest of the new Labour Government.

Both the above cases are concerned with the extent of the prerogative and its relationship to statute. The *GCHQ* case,[78] in 1984, raised the question of the reviewability of the exercise of a recognised prerogative power, a power previously disavowed by the courts. Although national security resolved the specific outcome of the case, its more important outcome established principles which would operate to control the exercise by the Government of prerogative powers well beyond the national security situation itself. Their Lordships in a profoundly under-stated way extended the perimeters of the judicial role. It may have helped that the exercise of this particular prerogative power, the regulation of the terms and conditions of employment in the civil service, was exercised under a prerogative Order in Council (that is, was delegated rather than direct), thus making the facts more akin to the exercise of a statutory power. Lord Scarman spoke in terms of the centuries' old limitation on the courts' review of the exercise of a prerogative power as having been 'overwhelmed by the developing modern law of judicial review'.[79] Lord Diplock stated that he saw no reason 'why simply because a decision-making power is derived from the common law and not a statutory source, it should for *that reason only* be immune from judicial review'.[80] Lord Roskill, in similar vein, referred to the development of our administrative law 'building upon but unhampered by our legal history'.[81] Full stop in terms of reasons given for the

---

[77] G Wilson, *Cases and Materials on Constitutional and Administrative Law* (Cambridge: CUP, 2nd edn 1976) 254 provides the letter written while the case was pending in the lower court by the Deputy Treasury Solicitor to the company. Pointing out the Government's opinion that the case was unfounded in law and anyway that the claim should not be met by the British taxpayer, he added that the Government had accordingly decided that 'in the unlikely event of your company succeeding, legislation would be introduced to indemnify the Crown . . . against your company's claim'. The legislative House of Lords for a time sought to remove the retrospective clause from the Bill.

[78] *Council of Civil Service Unions v Minister for the Civil Service* [1985] AC 374. See Craig, ch 29 in this volume.

[79] At 407. [80] At 410. Emphasis in original. [81] At 417.

change in judicial attitude, but this is the start not the end of the story. It is a powerful illustration of judicially wrought light-touch constitutional reform.

The final case in this category—not, for once, involving national security—is *Fire Brigades Union*,[82] which perhaps for one of the first times since *Liversidge* provided a sustained analysis of its issues in the language of constitutionalism. The facts briefly were that a scheme of criminal injuries compensation introduced via a Government White Paper under the prerogative powers (if such they were) was replaced by a more generous statutory scheme under the Criminal Justice Act 1988, which was not then brought into force (a distinguishing factor from *de Keyser*). As is often the case, the Secretary of State was empowered to bring the relevant provisions of the 1988 Act into force on a day to be appointed by him. Subsequently, the Government, deciding not to bring the Act into force, sought to introduce a new scheme under the White Paper procedure. The House of Lords held that there was no duty on the Secretary of State to bring the Act into force but (by a majority, Lords Keith and Mustill dissenting) that he was under a continuing duty to consider doing so and that he could not lawfully bind himself not to do so, at the same time as introducing a scheme inconsistent with the 1988 Act. Lord Browne-Wilkinson's speech resonates with the principles of a constitutional order that stress the need to avoid allowing the *Government* to be in a position to subvert the expressed legislative wishes of *Parliament*. As Lord Browne-Wilkinson said, whilst it is undesirable that the courts should 'intervene in the legislative process' by requiring that an Act be brought into effect, equally the Secretary of State himself was not free to 'decide at will' whether or not to bring the legislation into force: 'It is for Parliament, not the executive, to repeal legislation.'[83] The dissentient view regarded this approach as an infringement of the separation of powers and an intrusion of the judiciary into the political domain. Lord Mustill said that it was not for the court to comment upon the relationship between the executive and Parliament and if the attitude of the Secretary of State were 'out of tune with the proper respect due to parliamentary processes that is a matter to which Parliament must attend'. In a concluding section on the separation of powers, he included the key phrase: '[I]t is the task of Parliament and the executive in tandem, not of the courts, to govern the country.'[84] Lord Keith, also dissenting, stated that to find for the appellants 'would represent an unwarrantable intrusion by the court into the political field and a usurpation of the function of Parliament'.[85] In many

---

[82] [1995] 2 AC 513.   [83] ibid, 550, 551, and 552 respectively.

[84] ibid, 560 and 567 respectively.

[85] ibid, 546. His use of the word 'usurpation' gives the opportunity to refer to what is perhaps the most quotable, although fortunately not prevailing, dictum from the House of Lords of the twentieth century: *per* Viscount Simonds in *Magor & St Mellons RDC v Newport Corporation* [1952] AC 189 at 191, arguing against the desirability of filling judicially discerned gaps in legislation: it would be 'a naked usurpation of the legislative function under the thin disguise of interpretation'. See also *Pepper v Hart* [1993] AC 593 which provides scope for the Government to influence the meaning and impact of legislation through a way extraneous to the words of the legislation itself (admissibility under certain conditions of Government statements from *Hansard*).

ways, however, to use the language of the later case of *A*,[86] the emphasis on 'relative institutional competence', a phrase that has more creative possibilities in this context than the 'separation of powers', should be based on an articulated awareness of the contribution each institution can make to constitutional checks and balances. To close one's judicial eyes to the frequent impotence of Parliament to Government excess is not an adequate judicial response. Judicial self-restraint is dependent for its constitutional effectiveness on the existence of effective restraints within Parliament. In their absence the judges must seek a deeper constitutional logic for a more intrusive role.

It was that logic that drove the majority of the House of Lords in *Anisminic v Foreign Compensation Commission*[87] to close the door on absolute ouster clauses. Faced with a statutory provision protecting the determinations of the Commission from being called in question in any court of law, the House of Lords held that the word 'determination' protected only a valid and not a purported (or void) determination, the latter but not the former, of course, needing the protection of the ouster clause. Again the House, well aware of (from one constitutional perspective) the justifiably 'evasive' nature of its decision, resorted to and effectively used the rules of statutory interpretation. Lord Reid indicated that it is a 'well established principle that a provision ousting the ordinary jurisdiction of the court must be construed strictly',[88] that is, construed in a way that preserves the jurisdiction of the court. In reaching this conclusion, by pushing back the boundaries of jurisdictional error, the courts were carrying out the intention of the legislature. It would thus be a 'misdescription to state it in terms of a struggle between the courts and the executive'.[89] Although *Anisminic* is usually claimed as an Administrative Law case, its very essence is at the heart of constitutionalism: an independent judiciary, interpreting legislation (as it alone should), keeping the courts open,[90] and

---

[86] Cf Lord Bingham both in *A v Secretary of State for the Home Department* [2005] 2 AC 68, 102 (the phrase is from Liberty's written submission in that case) and in *Jackson v AG* [2006] 1 AC 262, 287 and quoted below.

[87] [1969] 2 AC 147. Lords Reid, Pearce, and Wilberforce in the majority, Lords Morris (error within jurisdiction) and Lord Pearson (no error) dissenting. Wade, in *Constitutional Fundamentals* (London: Stevens, revised edn 1989) 81, states that the case may be seen as 'the ultimate in judicial enterprise', adding (at 82): 'The net result was that (the judges) had disobeyed the Act, although nominally they were merely construing it in a peculiar but traditional way.' Labelling this as 'judicial policy on the constitutional level', he continued: 'The judges appreciate, much more than does Parliament, that to exempt any public authority from judicial control is to give it dictatorial power, and that this is so fundamentally objectionable that Parliament cannot really intend it.' Cf JAG Griffith, *Politics of the Judiciary* (London: Fontana, 5th edn 1997) 108, who in this context writes of this 'extreme case of judicial interference with the powers of public authorities'.

[88] [1969] 2 AC 147, 170.

[89] ibid, *per* Lord Wilberforce at 208. See the Foreign Compensation Act 1969, s 3 for the Government's mixed response to the case.

[90] See the later dicta, on the (probable) impregnability, even against a sovereign Parliament, of access to the courts, of Lord Steyn and Lady Hale in *Jackson v AG* [2006] 1 AC 262, 302–3, and 318 respectively.

thereby avoiding the creation of autocratic power vested in the Commission or for that matter in a Government Minister.

Sovereignty and the courts

The constitutional principle of the sovereignty of Parliament, the long-standing, and possibly crumbling, keystone of the constitution, which insists that there are no legal limits on the powers of Parliament as expressed in an Act of Parliament, has been tested in two non-EC contexts. In *Pickin v British Railways Board*[91] a challenge to a Private Act of Parliament on the ground that the Act had been fraudulently procured was easily dismissed, although at least the issue was sufficiently triable with regard to a Private Act as to reach the House of Lords. The decision of the House, however, stands foursquare on the traditional doctrine. Lord Reid said in classic style: 'The function of the court is to construe and apply the enactments of Parliament... for a century or more both Parliament and the courts have been careful not to act so as to cause a conflict between them.' Lord Morris referred to the 'firm rule that the courts must accept and give full binding effectiveness to an Act of Parliament' and to sovereignty principles which are both 'desirable and reasonable'. Lord Simon of Glaisdale, emphasising the privileges of Parliament, not least under Article 9 of the Bill of Rights 1689, spoke of the corollary of parliamentary democracy in the United Kingdom being the lack of power in the courts to declare enacted law invalid; he referred to the need for both the courts and Parliament to play their own particular role in the constitution and to the dangers that collision between the two institutions would cause to the protection of constitutional rights.[92]

In *Jackson*[93] by contrast, the House of Lords was asked to entertain a challenge to the Hunting Act 2004 and hence to the Parliament Act 1949, under the terms of which the 2004 Act had been passed. Both are Public Acts of Parliament. The 1949 Act, passed without the consent of the House of Lords under the Parliament Act 1911 procedure, reduced the delaying power over bills of the legislative House of Lords. There was little expectation that the judges would strike down the 1949 Act as an *ultra vires* 'law' of a subordinate (or derivative) legislature seeking to enlarge its own powers. What is significant is that the House of Lords heard the case at all, that a bench of nine judges heard the case, and that five of the seven judges who expressed an opinion said (albeit *obiter*) that Parliament could not repeal the sole remaining veto power of the House of Lords under the Parliament Act procedure and then proceed to defer the holding of a general election with only the consent of the House of Commons

---

[91] [1974] AC 765.   [92] At 787–8, 793, and 798–9 respectively.
[93] *Jackson v AG* [2006] 1 AC 262.

and the Royal Assent. What is significant too is the language used by (some of) the judges in their *obiter dicta*.[94]

Lord Bingham, after a masterly exposition of the history of the Parliament Act 1911, referred to the possible dangers of an unbalanced constitution caused by the diminished powers of the House of Lords under the Parliament Acts, but regarded it as 'quite inappropriate for the House in its judicial capacity to express or appear to express an opinion upon them'.[95] The constitutionally most sparkling judgment, however, is Lord Steyn's valedictory (closely followed by that of Lord Hope). Referring to the United Kingdom's membership of the European Union, to the Human Rights Act, and to devolution, Lord Steyn proclaimed that we do not 'have an uncontrolled constitution . . .' and continued:

The classic account given by Dicey of the doctrine of the supremacy of Parliament, pure and absolute as it was, can now be seen to be out of place in the modern United Kingdom . . . [It remains] the *general* principle of our constitution. It is a construct of the common law. The judges created this principle. If that is so, it is not unthinkable that circumstances could arise where the courts may have to qualify a principle established on a different hypothesis of constitutionalism. In exceptional circumstances (for example the abolition of judicial review) . . . the new Supreme Court may have to consider whether this is a constitutional fundamental which even a sovereign Parliament acting at the behest of a complaisant House of Commons cannot abolish.[96]

Key constitutional judgments: the best and the representative?

By way of conclusion, five House of Lords judgments are offered as the most outstanding constitutional judgments of the last 100 years. Coincidentally (almost) they occurred approximately once every 20 years or so. The criteria for selection into this category are: a judicial respect for the doctrine of Sovereignty of Parliament combined with an awareness of the limitations both of that doctrine and of ministerial responsibility (and of the consequences of those limitations); an emphasis upon the need for a balanced constitution; the desire to limit (the potential for) autocratic power; and a (consequent) refusal to accept any ouster of the jurisdiction of the courts. A key element, thus, is an allegiance shown to the enacted and judicially interpreted will of Parliament that is not equated with the will of the executive. These are the cases that finely balance judicial adherence to the doctrine of parliamentary sovereignty with the judicial formulation of

---

[94] For a 'criticism' of the views of some of his colleagues in *Jackson* (views quoted with approval in this chapter), see Lord Bingham in his lecture: 'The Rule of Law and the Sovereignty of Parliament', King's College London Commemoration Oration, 31 October 2007. See too, for criticism more forcefully expressed, R Ekins, 'Acts of Parliament and the Parliament Acts' (2007) 123 LQR 91, esp 103.

[95] *Jackson v AG* [2006] 1 AC 262, 287.

[96] ibid, 302–3. See too Lord Hope at 304: 'The rule of Law enforced by the courts is the ultimate controlling factor on which our constitution is based.'

constitutional principles which serve to constrain executive power which itself is not sovereign.[97] It is fully appreciated that this role may be seen as being or as becoming too intrusive into the political domain, too subversive of the allegiance owed to the Sovereign enacted wishes of Parliament, too restrictive of the mandate and capabilities of those who have been elected, including the Government. In a constitution in which Parliament has the last word, at least as against the domestic judges, however, such concerns may be misplaced.

The five selected best judgments, according to these criteria, are those by Lord Shaw of Dunfermline in *Zadig*, Lord Atkin in *Liversidge*, Lord Reid in *Anisminic*, Lord Roskill in *GCHQ*, and Lord Steyn's valedictory (especially the final two paragraphs) in *Jackson*. Perhaps the third and fourth judgments deserve a brief explanation. It is true that Lord Reid's speech is not necessarily more outstanding than the two other majority speeches in *Anisminic* but it would be unfortunate in many regards to omit such an outstanding judge altogether from this list. The other issue, whether or not *GCHQ* should be represented at all, rather than, say, the *Fire Brigades Union* case, arises because it is an essentially under-stated case in its presentation of constitutional issues but the principle of the reviewability of the royal prerogative was of profound importance and the case cannot easily be omitted.

These judgments are not the most representative of their generations or overall across the century. Those delivered by Lord Shaw and Lord Atkin were ahead of their time constitutionally, Lord Steyn's is probably ahead of its time on sovereignty, but all five judgments are constitutional classics. It may be argued that such judgments, even if they are not typical, are necessary: as a goad to majority judicial opinion, to keep the judicial formulation of constitutional principles constantly galvanised and evolving and to foster an essential inter-institutional debate on key constitutional principles. Constitutional growth and change feed on the creative tension between those judgments here labelled the classic and those labelled the representative. Both, it is suggested, are necessary.

A list of the five House of Lords constitutional judgments more representative of the last hundred years, that is more cautiously focused on parliamentary sovereignty widely understood and on the value of Ministerial accountability combined with a sense of a narrower judicial role, would, it is suggested, be composed as follows: Viscount Maugham in *Liversidge*, Lord Pearson in *McEldowney*, Lord Simon in *Pickin*, Lord Mustill (dissenting) in *Fire Brigades Union,* a case that nonetheless can be regarded as heralding a more overt articulation of constitutional values by the House of Lords largely eschewed by the majority until then, and Lord Bingham in *Jackson*.

---

[97] In those cases not involving Parliament, of which *R (Bancoult) v Secretary of State for Foreign and Commonwealth Affairs* is a prime example, the key principles include an 'equality of arms' between judicial and executive power and the judicial desire not to facilitate an executive autocracy.

Bancoult:[98] postscript and prelude

Possibly the last, and certainly one of the last, constitutional law decisions to be delivered by the Appellate Committee of the House of Lords is *R (Bancoult) v Secretary of State for Foreign and Commonwealth Affairs* in which the Government appealed against the decision of the Court of Appeal that section 9 of the British Indian Ocean Territory (Constitution) Order 2004, a (legislative) prerogative Order in Council, was invalid. Section 9 precluded the Chagossians, who had been removed from their island home between 1968 and 1971 'with callous disregard for their interests',[99] in pursuance of a defence agreement between the United Kingdom and the United States of America, from returning home. This was contrary to a promise made in November 2000 by the then Foreign Secretary, Mr Robin Cook, in response to earlier litigation (a promise held by the majority in *Bancoult* not to give rise to a legitimate expectation).

Their Lordships' decision, upholding the appeal by a majority of three to two, Lord Bingham and Lord Mance dissenting, is a sad concluding note to the House of Lords' constitutional jurisprudence. Lord Hoffmann, stating that the right of abode, a creature of the law and 'not in its nature so fundamental that the legislative powers of the Crown simply cannot touch it', had to be weighed in the balance with the state's defence, diplomatic, and indeed economic[100] interests. Consequently a legislative body was rationally entitled to take such practical consequences into account when deciding to legislate to remove the right of abode, which, on the facts here, Lord Hoffmann regarded as purely symbolic and its assertion as akin to a right to protest in a particular way.[101]

Lord Bingham's dissenting speech, by contrast, which merits a place in the 'best category' above, incisively states the key principles of constitutionalism: the reviewability of the prerogative,[102] of its existence, its extent and its exercise; the absence of any (previous exercise of the) prerogative power to 'exile an indigenous population from its homeland', a point significantly reinforced by the equating of the claimed rights of 'those whose homes are in former colonial territories' with the rights of citizens of the United Kingdom. The absence of any legal power to make section 9 rendered it void.

---

[98] [2008] UKHL 61, judgment delivered 22 October 2008.

[99] *Per* the Secretary of State and referred to by Lord Hoffmann at para 10. See also para 53: 'the deed has been done, the wrong confessed, compensation agreed and paid'. Compensation had been paid by the Government in 1982.

[100] At paras 54–5: 'Funding is the sub-text of what this case is about.'

[101] At paras 45 and 53.

[102] At para 69 he describes the prerogative power to legislate by Order in Council as 'an anachronistic survival'. The fact that the equivalent end could have been reached by way of an Act of Parliament was addressed (at para 70) by the constitutionally important riposte, 'it could, but not without public debate in Parliament and democratic decision'.

If, however, there were a prerogative power to make section 9, Lord Bingham continued, then it was anyway irrational 'in the sense that there was, quite simply, no good reason for making it', and also (thus retaining substantial value in the concept of legitimate expectation) it was in breach of the Government undertaking given in 2000.

This case involves many key aspects of constitutional law and the role of the judges: Government resort to the use of the legislative royal prerogative, the Order in Council being placed before the Queen for her approval, without any prior public or parliamentary debate, five days before its existence was made public;[103] human rights; and the judicial (non) evaluation of the defence, economic, and diplomatic interests of the United Kingdom. It encapsulates much of the essence of the previous 133 years of constitutional jurisprudence, engendering a varied judicial response, and as such is a fitting case with which to conclude this chapter.

---

[103] *Bancoult* in the Court of Appeal [2007] 3 WLR 768, paras 95–6 *per* Waller LJ.

29

Administrative Law

Paul Craig

Introduction

The object of this chapter is to chart the contribution of the House of Lords to some of the main developments in administrative law, with particular attention being given to the second half of the twentieth century. The chapter does not address the impact of the Human Rights Act 1998, since this topic is dealt with by Professor Feldman in chapter 30 of the present work.

Administrative law in the UK did not of course begin in the twentieth century. Judicial review on both procedural and substantive grounds has existed in developed form from at least the seventeenth century. It would, however, be impossible within the confines of this chapter to chart the House of Lords' contribution to the evolution of administrative law over this period. It is for this reason that the primary focus is the twentieth century and the revival or reinvigoration of judicial review in the second half thereof.

The limits of review in the early decades of the 20th century

It is common to tell a story about administrative law in the twentieth century in the following terms. In the early decades the courts were crabbed and confined in their exercise of judicial review. This was by way of contrast to the more expansive role arrogated by the courts in the seventeenth and eighteenth centuries. The self-imposed shackles were progressively shed as a result of seminal decisions in the 1960s and 1970s. There is, as we shall see, truth in this. There are, however, dangers in depicting complex bodies of jurisprudence in overly black and white terms. It is nonetheless fitting to begin with the evidence that substantiates this reading of doctrinal development.

The 'gateways' to administrative law were more narrowly confined at that time. This was true in relation to standing, remedies, and natural justice. Standing determines who will be able to complain to the courts about suspect administrative action. The relevant case law is complex, but there was certainly a body of jurisprudence that limited such challenges to those who possessed private rights, narrowly defined. It was only when an individual was settling a private dispute which he or she had with the administration that judicial review was available.[1] There were doubts about the application of the remedies, in particular the prerogative orders.[2]

Similar limitations were apparent in the context of natural justice. The courts deployed a range of doctrinal devices which cumulatively served to limit the applicability of process rights.[3] The dichotomy between rights and privileges, and that between administrative and judicial decisions, had the effect of limiting the scope of natural justice. So too did the idea that there had to be a super-added duty to act judicially before process rights were held to be applicable. Substantive judicial review was also limited. Challenges for jurisdictional error were subject to the vagaries of the collateral fact doctrine, the application of which had little in the way of *ex ante* certainty or *ex post facto* rationality.[4] The courts were reticent about challenges to the exercise of administrative discretion, and the doctrine of Crown privilege meant that it could be difficult to discover the information necessary to sustain an action.[5] The courts' approach was mirrored by the Diceyan distrust of administrative tribunals, and the denial that we possessed any separate administrative law.[6]

The picture of doctrinal development sketched above should nonetheless be kept within perspective. In terms of the primary case law there were tensions between the idea that administrative agencies were 'odd' creations, to be controlled at all costs, and the actual doctrines applied by the courts. Thus, for example, the private rights theme, apparent in the law of standing and natural justice, served to limit those bodies that would be amenable to judicial review. In terms of the secondary literature, this period saw the flowering of writing about public law which did not conform to the Diceyan paradigm. The benefits of administrative agencies, as the institutions chosen to deliver welfare state reforms, were recognised. While it was acknowledged that some control was desirable, the whole approach to these institutions was more positive and functional. The emphasis was on how law could be used to ensure the effective delivery of valuable services.[7]

The expansion of judicial review from the 1960s

It would be a mistake to think that the revival or reinvigoration of administrative law doctrine occurred at a particular point in time. There were nonetheless

---

[1] P Craig, *Administrative Law* (London: Sweet & Maxwell, 6th edn 2008) ch 24.
[2] ibid, 828–41.   [3] ibid, 373–5.   [4] ibid, 439–41, 464–5.   [5] ibid, 931–3.
[6] See, eg, Lord Hewart, *The New Despotism* (London: Ernest Benn, 1929).
[7] See C Harlow and R Rawlings, *Law and Administration* (London: Butterworths, 2nd edn 1997) ch 3.

doctrinal decisions that were individually of importance, and which taken together revitalised the courts' power of judicial review. The House of Lords was at the forefront of these developments from the 1960s onwards.

Procedural review

We have already noted the ways in which the courts placed limitations on the applicability of procedural protection in the middle years of the twentieth century. The decision of the House of Lords in *Ridge v Baldwin*[8] was a turning point in this area of the law. Their Lordships held that a chief constable who could be dismissed only for cause was entitled to notice of the charge and an opportunity to be heard before being dismissed. The importance of the case lies in the general discussion of natural justice, especially that given by Lord Reid.

His Lordship reviewed the nineteenth century case law which evidenced the broad application of natural justice and then proceeded to consider why, given these authorities, the law had become confused. Lord Reid gave three reasons for this. The first was that natural justice could have only a limited application in the context of the wider duties or discretion imposed upon a minister. The courts had however applied those limited notions of natural justice to other areas where the constraints were unnecessary.[9] The second reason was that the principle had received only limited application during the war. Again, Lord Reid felt that special considerations which might be pertinent during wartime should not affect the ambit of natural justice now. The third was the confusion between rights and remedies evident in the alleged requirement of a super-added duty to act judicially as a requirement of certiorari, and the way in which this had stilted the development of natural justice.[10] The judicial element should be inferred from the nature of the power and its effect on the individual.

Their Lordships therefore revived the principles of natural justice in two connected ways. They rediscovered the nineteenth century jurisprudence that had applied the principle to a broad spectrum of interests and a wide variety of decision-makers. They disapproved of impediments which had been created in the twentieth century: the requirements of a *lis inter partes* and a super-added duty to act judicially were said to be false constraints. However, little positive guidance is to be found in the case as to when natural justice should apply. The closest it comes to any general formulation is in the idea that the applicability of natural justice will be dependent on the nature of the power exercised and its effect upon the individual concerned.

The years following *Ridge* were therefore marked by a host of cases concerned with the criterion for the applicability of natural justice. The dominant judicial approach has been to render the applicability of natural justice dependent upon

---

[8] [1964] AC 40.   [9] ibid, 71–2.   [10] ibid, 72–8.

the courts' determination of whether a duty to act fairly is warranted on all the facts of the case.

There have also been significant developments in relation to the content of procedural protection that should apply in any particular case. In general terms the courts will balance three different types of factor in this respect: the individual interest at issue; the benefits to be derived from added procedural safeguards; and the costs to the administration, both direct and indirect, of complying with these procedural safeguards.

The House of Lords has, for example, recently reaffirmed in strident tones the importance of the right to notice. Thus in *Anufrijeva*[11] the claimant was an asylum seeker, whose income support was terminated after the Home Secretary rejected her asylum application. This determination was not however communicated to the claimant. Lord Steyn held that notice of a decision was essential in order to enable the person affected to challenge it. It was an 'application of the right of access to justice', which was a 'fundamental and constitutional principle of our legal system'.[12] The rule of law required that a constitutional state should accord to individuals the right to know of a decision before their rights could be affected. The 'antithesis of such a state was described by Kafka: a state where the rights of individuals are overridden by hole in the corner decisions or knocks on doors in the early hours'.[13] Lord Steyn acknowledged that there could be exceptional cases where notice was not possible, such as with arrests and search warrants, but held that the present case fell within the ambit of the general rule requiring notice. The right to notice was a fundamental right and could therefore only be excluded by Parliament expressly or by necessary implication. He concluded that Parliament had not done so in the relevant legislation.

The House of Lords has also recognised more generally the background principles that are pertinent to this area. Procedural rights perform an instrumental role, in the sense of helping to arrive at an accurate decision on the substance of the case.[14] Procedural rights are also seen as having a non-instrumental role in protecting human dignity, by ensuring that individuals are told why they are being treated unfavourably, and by enabling them to take part in that decision.[15] These twin rationales for the existence of procedural rights were recognised in *Doody*,[16] which was concerned with whether prisoners given a life sentence for murder should be told the reasons behind the length of their imprisonment. Lord Mustill stated that a prisoner would wish to know why the particular term was selected, 'partly from an obvious human desire to be told the reason for a

---

[11] *R (on the application of Anufrijeva) v Secretary of State for the Home Department* [2004] 1 AC 604.
[12] ibid, para 26.   [13] ibid, para 28.
[14] eg J Resnick, 'Due Process and Procedural Justice' in J Pennock and J Chapman (eds), *Due Process* (New York: New York University Press, 1977) 217.
[15] eg F Michelman, 'Formal and Associational Aims in Procedural Due Process' in *Due Process*, ibid, ch 4.
[16] *R v Secretary of State for the Home Department, ex p Doody* [1994] AC 531, 551.

decision so gravely affecting his future, and partly because he hopes that once the information is obtained he may be able to point out errors of fact or reasoning and thereby persuade the Secretary of State to change his mind, or if he fails in this to challenge the decision in the courts'. The non-instrumental and instrumental justifications for procedural protection are readily apparent in this quotation.

Jurisdictional review

The expanded application of natural justice heralded by *Ridge* was matched but a few years later by the broadening of jurisdictional review in *Anisminic*. The problem of jurisdictional review is endemic to all legal systems. A tribunal is given authority to decide upon a particular issue. If a furnished tenancy exists the tribunal may adjudicate on the rent. If a person is unfairly dismissed she may be awarded compensation. All such grants of authority may be expressed in the following manner: if X exists, the tribunal may or shall do Y. X may consist of a number of different elements, factual, legal, and discretionary. An individual then wishes to complain of the tribunal's findings.

Prior to the decision in *Anisminic* the dominant approach was the collateral or jurisdictional fact doctrine. This encapsulated the idea that certain elements within the 'if X' inquiry would be regarded as jurisdictional, with the consequence that the courts would substitute their judgment for that of the initial decision-maker. Other matters that formed part of this inquiry would be left to the initial decision-maker, unless there was an error of law on the face of the record. It was however very difficult to determine *ex ante* which way the court would characterise a particular issue. This uncertainty was compounded by the difficulty of making any sense of the case law *ex post facto*.[17]

The House of Lords' decision in *Anisminic Ltd v Foreign Compensation Commission*[18] expanded the courts' competence over these inquiries and laid the seeds for a test based on error of law. Lord Reid stated that jurisdiction in a narrow sense meant only that the tribunal was entitled to enter upon the inquiry. There were, however, a number of ways in which, having correctly begun the inquiry, the tribunal could do something which rendered its decision a nullity. Misconstruction of the enabling statute so that the tribunal failed to deal with the question remitted to it, failure to take account of relevant considerations, and asking the wrong question were, said Lord Reid, examples of this.[19]

Lord Reid's judgment significantly broadened the potential scope of review. A court, if it wished to interfere, could always characterise an alleged error as having resulted from asking the wrong question, or having taken account of irrelevant considerations. However, the courts could choose whether to utilise this armoury. If the court did not wish to intervene, it could achieve this result by stating that

---

[17] Craig (n 1) ch 14. [18] [1969] 2 AC 147. [19] [1969] 2 AC 147, 171.

there was no error at all, by characterising the error as one within jurisdiction, or by defining jurisdiction itself more narrowly than in *Anisminic*. In fact the courts continued to equivocate as to whether the traditional approach should be maintained. Put more accurately, individual judges may have been clear as to their preferences, but those preferences did not always coincide.[20]

It was to take over 20 years before the seeds sown in *Anisminic* were fully reaped in *R v Hull University Visitor, ex p Page*.[21] Lord Browne-Wilkinson, who gave the leading judgment, held that *Anisminic* had rendered obsolete the distinction between errors of law on the face of the record and other errors of law, and had done so by extending the *ultra vires* doctrine. Thenceforward, it was to be taken 'that Parliament had only conferred the decision-making power on the basis that it was to be exercised on the correct legal basis: a misdirection in law in making the decision therefore rendered the decision *ultra vires*'.[22] In general, therefore, 'any error of law made by an administrative tribunal or inferior court in reaching its decision can be quashed for error of law'.[23]

Review of discretion

The framework for judicial review of discretion was laid down not by the House of Lords, but by Lord Greene MR in the *Wednesbury* case,[24] but it has nonetheless been markedly affected by House of Lords' decisions.

Lord Greene MR used the word 'unreasonableness' in two different senses. On the one hand it connoted the various grounds of challenge that went to the legality of the public body's actions, propriety of purpose, and relevancy. He also gave unreasonableness a substantive meaning, which became the '*Wednesbury* test': if an exercise of discretion successfully negotiated the hurdles of propriety of purpose and relevancy it could still be invalidated if it was so unreasonable that no reasonable body could have reached such a decision. If the challenged decision really was so unreasonable that no reasonable body could have made it, then the court was justified in quashing it. The very fact that something extreme would have to be proven to come within this criterion provided both the legitimation for the judicial oversight, and served to defend the courts from any allegation that they were thereby overstepping their remit and intervening too greatly on the merits.

The last 30 years have seen the courts expand their control over the substance of discretionary decisions. They relaxed or loosened the test and applied it to discretionary decisions which could not, whether right or wrong, be classified as so unreasonable that no agency could have made them, and this judicial approach was applied even in cases that were not concerned with rights. This received

---

[20] See, eg, the differing judgments in *Re Racal Communications Ltd* [1981] AC 374.
[21] [1993] AC 682.   [22] ibid, 701.   [23] ibid, 702.
[24] *Associated Picture Houses Ltd v Wednesbury Corp* [1948] 1 KB 223.

explicit support from Lord Cooke in the *ITF* case,[25] who regarded the formulation used by Lord Greene as tautologous and exaggerated. It was not, said Lord Cooke, necessary to have such an extreme formulation in order to ensure that the courts remained within their proper bounds as required by the separation of powers. He advocated a simpler and less extreme test: was the decision one which a reasonable authority could reach?

The courts, following the lead of the House of Lords, also explicitly varied the intensity of the *Wednesbury* test, and applied it with more searching scrutiny in cases concerned with rights, even prior to the Human Rights Act 1998.[26] In such cases, Lord Bridge in *Brind*[27] said that the court must inquire whether a reasonable Secretary of State could reasonably have made the primary decision being challenged, and that it began its inquiry from the premise that only a compelling public interest would justify the invasion of the right. Sir Thomas Bingham MR's formulation was very similar.[28] The court was to consider whether the decision was beyond the range of responses open to a reasonable decision-maker, and the greater the interference with human rights the more the court would require by way of justification.

The House of Lords moreover took the important step of aligning the position at common law with that under the European Convention on Human Rights. Following dicta in the *Spycatcher* case,[29] the House of Lords in the *Derbyshire* case[30] expressed the view that there was no difference in principle between the common law protection of rights and that secured by the Convention. The 'green light' given by the House of Lords was not lost on lower courts. It became normal for there to be more searching scrutiny in rights-based cases.[31]

A related, albeit distinct, development was the House of Lords' creation of a priority rule, to the effect that legislation will not be held to allow an interference with a common law constitutional right unless this was sanctioned by Parliament. This is apparent in *Simms*.[32] Legislation was to be read subject to a principle of legality, which meant that fundamental rights could not be overridden by general or ambiguous words. This was, said Lord Hoffmann, because there was too great

---

[25] *R v Chief Constable of Sussex, ex p International Trader's Ferry Ltd.* [1999] 1 All ER 129.

[26] Sir John Laws, 'Wednesbury' in C Forsyth and I Hare (eds), *The Golden Metwand and the Crooked Cord: Essays in Honour of Sir William Wade* (Oxford: OUP, 1998) 185–202.

[27] *R v Secretary of State for the Home Department, ex p Brind* [1991] 1 AC 696, 748–9.

[28] *R v Ministry of Defence, ex p Smith* [1996] QB 517.

[29] *AG v Guardian Newspapers (No 2)* [1990] 1 AC 109, 283–4.

[30] *Derbyshire CC v Times Newspapers Ltd* [1993] AC 534.

[31] See eg *R v Secretary of State for the Home Department, ex p Leech* [1994] QB 198; *R v Ministry of Defence, ex p Smith* [1996] QB 517; *R v Secretary of State for the Home Department, ex p McQuillan* [1995] 4 All ER 400; *R v Secretary of State for the Home Department, ex p Moon* [1996] Imm AR 477; *R v Lord Chancellor, ex p Witham* [1998] QB 575, 585–6; *R v Secretary of State for Social Security, ex p Joint Council for the Welfare of Immigrants* [1997] 1 WLR 275.

[32] *R v Secretary of State for the Home Department, ex p Simms & O'Brien* [2000] 2 AC 115; *R (on the application of Morgan Grenfell & Co Ltd) v Special Comr of Income Tax* [2003] 1 AC 563; *R (on the application of Anufrijeva) v Secretary of State for the Home Department* [2004] 1 AC 604.

a risk that the full implications of their unqualified meaning might have passed unnoticed in the democratic process. In the absence of express language or necessary implication to the contrary, the courts would therefore presume that even the most general words were intended to be subject to the basic rights of the individual. Parliament had, therefore, to squarely confront what it was doing and accept the political cost. Lord Hoffmann left open the possibility that a fundamental right could be overridden by necessary implication, as well as by express words. It seems clear that he would only accept that this was so in extreme cases, and this is the import of the phrase 'necessary implication'.[33]

Review of discretion and prerogative power

The discussion in the preceding section was concerned with the way in which review of discretion pursuant to the *Wednesbury* test has changed in more recent years, and the contribution of the House of Lords to that development. The House of Lords was also responsible for expanding review of discretionary power by making it clear that the manner of exercise of prerogative power was subject to judicial control. Traditional orthodoxy had hitherto maintained that the courts would only control the existence and extent of prerogative power, and would not inquire into the manner of exercise of an admitted prerogative. Some judges, notably Lord Denning MR in the *Laker Airways*[34] case, asserted a broader power of judicial review, but it was clear that change in this respect required a decision of the House of Lords.

This was forthcoming in the *GCHQ*[35] case, which broke down the barriers by holding that the courts could, subject to certain limitations, control the manner of exercise of an admitted prerogative. The House of Lords held that, as a matter of principle, the exercise of prerogative power was reviewable. Their Lordships recognised that in the past review had been confined to determining whether a prerogative existed and the limits thereof. They held, however, that matters had moved on and that the manner of exercise of an admitted prerogative power should also be open to scrutiny. Thus Lord Scarman stated that that 'if the subject matter in respect of which prerogative power is exercised is justiciable, that is to say if it is a matter upon which the courts can adjudicate, the exercise of the power is subject to review in accordance with the principles developed in respect of the review of the exercise of statutory power', and that the 'controlling factor in determining whether the exercise of prerogative power is subject to judicial review is not its source but its subject matter'.[36] Lord Diplock was of like mind, holding that the mere fact that a power was derived from a common law and not a

---

[33] See also *R v Lord Chancellor, ex p Witham* [1998] QB 575, 585–6.
[34] *Laker Airways Ltd v Department of Trade* [1977] QB 643. See also, *Chandler v Director of Public Prosecutions* [1964] AC 763; *R v Criminal Injuries Compensation Board, ex p Lain* [1967] 2 QB 864.
[35] *Council of Civil Service Unions v Minister for the Civil Service* [1985] AC 374.
[36] ibid, 407.

statutory source should not for that reason alone render it immune from judicial review.[37] These sentiments were echoed by Lord Roskill, who put the matter succinctly. If the executive was to act lawfully it must have some power to do the act in question. This power would, in the modern day, normally come from Parliament as a statute, and when it did so it would be subject to the normal principles of judicial review. Occasionally the executive would act pursuant to the prerogative. His Lordship could see no 'logical reason why the fact that the source of the power is the prerogative and not statute should today deprive the citizen of that right of challenge to the manner of its exercise which he would possess were the source of the power statutory'.[38]

Their Lordships placed qualifications upon judicial review of the exercise of prerogative power, which were primarily based on subject matter. Thus Lord Roskill felt that prerogative powers relating to the making of treaties, the defence of the realm, the prerogative of mercy, the grant of honours, the dissolution of Parliament, and the appointment of ministers were not suitable for judicial review because of their subject matter.[39] Lord Diplock more generally doubted whether prerogative powers could successfully be challenged on grounds of irrationality.[40]

The House of Lords, moreover, found against the applicants on the facts of the case. It decided that while they would normally have had a good case to argue that there had been a breach of procedural propriety, based upon the failure to consult, these requirements of fairness were outweighed by considerations of national security. It was, said their Lordships, for the executive, rather than the courts to decide on the balance between fairness and national security.

Notwithstanding these qualifications, the *GCHQ* case significantly extended the courts' control by affirming that they would consider the manner of exercise of prerogative power. The central message was that where the executive exercised prerogative power it should be subject to the same types of control as for statutory powers. The executive was not, therefore, to have any advantage when it acted pursuant to prerogative power. In this sense the central message of the case was one of 'equivalence': the executive, when acting pursuant to the most legitimate discretionary power, that given by statute, was subject to controls relating to its manner of exercise; given that this was so, the controls that operated on the exercise of prerogative discretionary power should not be markedly different. The jurisprudence since the *GCHQ* decision has shown that the courts are willing to assess the manner of exercise of prerogative powers. They have viewed with scepticism claims that such powers are wholly non-justiciable.[41]

---

[37] ibid, 410.   [38] ibid, 417.   [39] ibid, 418.   [40] ibid, 411.
[41] *R v Secretary of State for Foreign and Commonwealth Affairs, ex p Everett* [1989] 1 All ER 655; *R v Secretary of State for the Home Department, ex p Bentley* [1993] 4 All ER 442; *R v Ministry of Defence, ex p Smith* [1996] QB 517; *R v Secretary of State for the Home Department, ex p Fire Brigades Union* [1995] 2 AC 513; *R (on the application of Bancourt) v Secretary of State for Foreign and Commonwealth Affairs* [2008] UKHL 61.

Discovery, Crown privilege, and public interest immunity

The developments in relation to procedural and substantive review must be viewed in conjunction with the important conceptual shift from Crown privilege to public interest immunity.

Until 1968 the Crown possessed Crown privilege.[42] It could refuse to reveal certain documents because to do so would be contrary to the public interest. This principle was widely drawn.[43] Documents could be withheld either if the disclosure of the contents of a particular document would injure the public interest, or where the document was one of a class of documents which must be withheld in order to ensure the proper functioning of the public service. Moreover, a statement by a minister in the proper form that a document fell into one of these two categories would it seems not be challenged by the courts. Dissatisfaction with this state of affairs led the Lord Chancellor in 1956 to announce that the Government would henceforth not claim privilege in certain areas.[44] While this self-denying ordinance was to be welcomed, it proved to be a double-edged sword. The areas where privilege would not be claimed had little if any analytic coherence.

The House of Lords took the opportunity to revise the law in *Conway v Rimmer*.[45] The plaintiff was a former probationary police constable who began an action for malicious prosecution against his former superintendent. The Secretary of State objected to the production of five documents, certifying that they fell within classes of documents disclosure of which would be injurious to the public interest. The House of Lords expressly asserted the power of the courts to hold a balance between the public interest as expressed by the minister who wished to withhold certain documents, and the public interest in ensuring the proper administration of justice. While their Lordships were unanimous in this respect, the formulations as to how the balancing was to operate differed somewhat. These ambiguities should not, however, be allowed to cloud the importance of the main principle that was unequivocally asserted by the House of Lords: the courts would balance the competing public interests to determine whether disclosure should be ordered. If the court was in doubt as to the outcome of this balancing it could inspect the documents before ordering production. This was in fact done and the court concluded that the documents should be produced. Class claims and contents claims for public interest immunity persisted after *Conway*, but the House of Lords' judgment made clear that all such claims would be subject to the balancing test.

Given the nature of the balancing operation that the *Conway* case requires, the name 'Crown privilege' was obviously inappropriate. The Crown cannot simply

---

[42] J Jacob, 'From Privileged Crown to Interested Public' [1993] PL 121.
[43] *Duncan v Cammell, Laird & Co Ltd* [1942] AC 624.
[44] *Hansard*, HL, vol 197, col 741 (6 June 1956).   [45] [1968] AC 910.

decide whether to withdraw a category of documents from the court. That the title was indeed misleading was recognised in *Rogers v Secretary of State for Home Department*.[46] Lord Reid[47] stated that the term 'privilege' was misleading, and that the real issue was whether the public interest in not disclosing the document outweighed the interest of the litigant in having all the evidence before the court.

The nature of the discretion possessed by ministers and the like who might claim public interest immunity was clarified by the House of Lords in *Wiley*.[48] Lord Woolf, speaking for the House, accepted that public interest immunity could not be waived *after* the court had determined that the public interest against disclosure outweighed that of disclosure. Matters were, however, different in relation to the situation *before* that final determination had been made. His Lordship held that ministers possessed discretion as to whether to claim public interest immunity. Thus it was open to the Secretary of State acting on behalf of his department, or the Attorney General, to decide that the public interest in documents being withheld from production was outweighed by the public interest in disclosure. While the court was the ultimate arbiter on this balance, his Lordship made it clear that it would be extremely rare for the court to reach a different conclusion where the minister was of the view that the documents could be disclosed. This was equally true of class claims and contents claims.[49]

Standing

There was considerable diversity in the older case law on standing, both within each remedy and as between them. Even when the same words, such as 'private right', 'special damage', 'person aggrieved', or 'sufficient interest' were used, it could not be assumed that they had the same meaning. The principal cause for this confusion was the failure to adopt a clear view as to what the remedies were seeking to achieve, and truth to tell the House of Lords did little to clarify the confusion during this period. There were indeed House of Lords decisions that reinforced existing narrow conceptions of standing for reasons that were contestable.

This can be exemplified by *Gouriet*.[50] The Post Office Act 1953, sections 58 and 68, made it an offence to interfere with the mail. The Union of Post Office Workers (UPW) had called on their members not to handle letters being sent to South Africa. Gouriet sought the consent of the Attorney General to a relator action, but this was not forthcoming. When the case went to the House of Lords

---

[46] [1973] AC 388.   [47] ibid, 400. See also 406, 408, 412.
[48] *R v Chief Constable of the West Midlands Police, ex p Wiley* [1995] 1 AC 274.
[49] The position is however rather different where parties other than government departments are in possession of documents in respect of which immunity could be claimed on a class basis.
[50] *Gouriet v Union of Post Office Workers* [1978] AC 435.

the plaintiff no longer asserted that this refusal of consent could be reviewed, rather that the failure to secure the approval was not fatal to the claim. Their Lordships rejected this argument. They were clearly concerned because the case was about a relator action 'in support' of the criminal law.

It is however the more general reasoning that is of relevance. The House of Lords' reasoning is permeated by a conception of the role of the citizen in public law. Put shortly, the citizen has no such role. In the absence of the Attorney General a citizen could enforce his or her private rights, but public rights could be enforced only through the Attorney General as representative of the public interest. It therefore followed that consent to a relator action was not something fictitious or nominal, to be circumvented at will: it was the substantive manifestation of the principle that public rights were to be represented by the Attorney General.[51]

The decision illustrates a conception of standing based on the vindication of private rights. There were numerous difficulties with this approach, one of which was that an applicant who sought a prerogative order was not tied to the enforcement of private law rights. The person was in effect vindicating the public interest to some degree. The premise underpinning *Gouriet*, to the effect that individuals enforce private rights and the Attorney General enforces public rights, could not therefore be unqualifiedly accepted as an accurate description of what the courts had been doing.

The House of Lords has however interpreted the sufficient interest test in section 31(3) of the Supreme Court Act 1981 more liberally, as is evident from the *IRC* case.[52] Casual labour was common on Fleet Street newspapers, the workers often adopting fictitious names and paying no taxes. The Inland Revenue ('IRC') made a deal with the relevant unions, workers, and employers whereby if the casuals would fill in tax returns for the previous two years then the period prior to that would be forgotten. The National Federation argued that this bargain was *ultra vires* the IRC, and sought a declaration plus mandamus to compel the IRC to collect the back taxes. The IRC argued that the National Federation had no standing. Their Lordships found for the IRC.

The *Gouriet*[53] decision was distinguished in the *IRC* case. It was treated as referring only to *locus standi* for declaration and injunction in their private law roles, and as having nothing to say about the standing for those remedies in public law. To regard *Gouriet* as concerned only with standing in private law is to allow form to blind one to substance. The parties in *Gouriet* might appear 'private': a trade union and a private citizen. The real argument in that case was, however, as to whether a private citizen should be able to vindicate the public interest without

---

[51] [1978] AC 435, 477–80, 483, 495, 498–9, 508. Cf the view in the Court of Appeal [1977] 1 QB 729, 768–72, 773–9.

[52] *R v Inland Revenue Comrs, ex p National Federation of Self-Employed and Small Businesses Ltd* [1982] AC 617; P Cane, 'Standing, Legality and the Limits of Public Law' [1981] PL 322.

[53] [1978] AC 435.

joining the Attorney General. This was how the case was argued, and this was how their Lordships responded to the argument.[54]

Gouriet and the *IRC* case in fact reflect different philosophies. The former conceived the private citizen as having no role in enforcing the public interest, and thus preserved the dichotomy in the standing criteria for the prerogative orders and declaration and injunction. This ignored the fact that the private citizen was to some extent vindicating the public interest when seeking pre-rogative relief. The *IRC* case eschewed the historical distinction between the remedies, and took as its touchstone the more liberal rules for prerogative relief, to which standing for declaration and injunction were then assimilated.

The more liberal approach in the *IRC* case is also evident in the judicial assumption that standing should be developed to meet new problems, and that there should not be an endless discussion of previous authority. This furthered the tendency towards a unified conception of standing based upon sufficiency of interest, notwithstanding the ambiguities in some of the judgments. It is therefore not surprising that arguments that the test for standing should differ depending upon the particular remedy being sought have been generally absent from sub-sequent case law. It should, however, be recognised that even when the courts adopt a uniform test this does not mean that individual judges share the same view as to what should count as a sufficient interest. This is evident from the *IRC* case itself.[55]

The House of Lords has in the post-*IRC* era been willing to countenance some public interest challenges. Thus in the *Equal Opportunities Commission* case,[56] the EOC sought *locus standi* to argue that certain rules concerning entitlement to redundancy pay and protection from unfair dismissal were discriminatory and in breach of EC law. The duties of the EOC included working towards the elim-ination of discrimination, and promoting equality of opportunity between men and women.[57] The House of Lords held that the EOC had standing. Lord Keith, giving the majority judgment, reasoned that if the contested provisions were discriminatory then steps taken by the EOC to change them could reasonably be regarded as working towards the elimination of discrimination. It would, said his Lordship,[58] be a retrograde step to hold that the EOC did not have standing to 'agitate in judicial review proceedings questions related to sex discrimination which are of public importance and affect a large section of the population'.

---

[54] Insofar as this was the real question at stake in *Gouriet*, it clearly was 'about' public law, and this is nonetheless true even though the issue of whether a citizen should be able to vindicate the public interest can arise in a non-public law case. This view is reinforced by the fact that both older and more recent authority, in what were indubitably public law cases, have expressed the test for standing in terms of private rights and special damage, where a declaration is being sought outside of s 31. See eg *Stoke-on-Trent CC v B & Q (Retail) Ltd* [1984] AC 754.
[55] Compare eg [1982] AC 617, 644 (Lord Diplock), 661 (Lord Roskill).
[56] *R v Secretary of State for Employment, ex p Equal Opportunities Commission* [1995] 1 AC 1.
[57] Sex Discrimination Act 1975, s 53(1).   [58] [1995] 1 AC 1, 26.

Remedial reform

The judicial interpretation accorded to the reforms in the law of remedies has proven contentious. The Report of the Law Commission led to revision of Order 53,[59] which was the principal procedural mechanism for seeking a prerogative order. The basis of the reform was the concept of application for judicial review. The prerogative orders and declaration and injunction were subject to this mechanism, and declarations and injunctions could be granted pursuant to an application for judicial review if the court considered, having regard to the nature of the matters and the nature of the persons and bodies against whom a remedy may be granted by the prerogative orders, and all the circumstances of the case, that it would be just and convenient for the declaration to be made or for the injunction to be granted.

The application for judicial review was, however, significantly affected by the decision in *O'Reilly v Mackman*.[60] This case limited the circumstances in which a declaration or an injunction in a public law case could be sought outside Order 53. Lord Diplock gave judgment for the House of Lords, and reasoned as follows. The prerogative orders had, prior to the reforms, been subject to a number of limitations. There was no right to discovery, damages could not be claimed in conjunction with one of the orders, and cross-examination upon affidavits occurred very rarely, if at all. These limitations justified the use of the declaration under Order 15, rule 16. However, the reformed Order 53 had removed the above defects by providing for discovery, allowing damages to be claimed, and making provision for cross-examination. The reformed procedure also provided important safeguards for the public body, including the requirement of leave to bring the case and a time limit short enough so that the public body would not be kept unduly in suspense as to whether or not its actions were valid. In the light of these changes it would normally be an abuse of process to seek a declaration outside of Order 53. Two exceptions were mentioned: certain types of collateral attack and cases where none of the parties objected to a remedy being sought outside Order 53.

The decision in *O'Reilly* gave rise to a large number of cases where applicants sought to bring their cases outside Order 53, principally in order to escape the narrow time limit applying thereunder. The courts were forced to grapple with the ambit of the private rights exception laid down in *O'Reilly* itself, and a number of such cases reached the House of Lords.[61] The cases decided in the immediate aftermath of *O'Reilly* revealed the difficulty of deciding whether a particular interest should be characterised as a private right. The precise effect of this characterisation was also unclear. Did the presence of a private right mean

---

[59] SI 1977/1955.   [60] [1983] 2 AC 237.

[61] *Cocks v Thanet DC* [1983] 2 AC 286; *Davy v Spelthorne BC* [1984] AC 262; *Wandsworth LBC v Winder* [1985] AC 461.

that the principle in *O'Reilly* should be deemed no longer applicable at all? Or was the existence of such a right merely an important factor that could lead the court to make a discretionary exception to the *O'Reilly* principle?

This ambiguity was brought to the fore in the important House of Lords decision, *Roy v Kensington and Chelsea and Westminster Family Practitioner Committee*.[62] It is clear that Lord Lowry preferred the former view, and this has generally been the approach adopted by the courts in later cases.[63] This approach was reinforced by dicta of Lord Steyn in *Boddington v British Transport Police*.[64] His Lordship held that case law[65] had made it clear that procedural exclusivity would only be insisted upon where the sole object of the action was to challenge a public law act or decision. It did not apply in a civil case when an individual sought to establish private law rights which could not be determined without an examination of the validity of the public law decision. Nor did it apply where a defendant in a civil case sought to defend himself by questioning the validity of the public law decision. Nor, equally, did it apply in a criminal case where the liberty of the subject was at stake.[66]

It may indeed be the case that that the exceptions to *O'Reilly* go beyond these. This seems to be so from a reading of the House of Lords' decision in *Mercury*.[67] In 1986 two companies, Mercury ('M') and British Telecommunications ('BT'), made an agreement for the provision of services pursuant to condition 13 of BT's licence. The agreement provided for a reference to the Director General of Telecommunications ('DGT') where there was a dispute between M and BT. The parties referred a matter to the DGT concerning pricing for the conveyance of calls. The DGT made his determination and M challenged this, arguing that the DGT had misinterpreted the costs to be taken into account when resolving the pricing issue. M's challenge was by way of originating summons for a declaration. The DGT and BT argued that the case should have been brought by way of Order 53. Lord Slynn gave the judgment for a unanimous House of Lords in favour of M.

His Lordship acknowledged the rationale for the presumptive exclusivity of this procedure given in *O'Reilly*, but noted also that this exclusivity was only ever presumptive rather than conclusive in nature. The criterion that should be used to decide whether a case could be brought outside Order 53 was whether 'the proceedings constitute an abuse of the process of the court'.[68]

---

[62] [1992] 1 AC 624.

[63] *Lonrho plc v Tebbit* [1992] 4 All ER 280; *Trustees of the Dennis Rye Pension Fund v Sheffield CC* [1998] 1 WLR 840; *British Steel plc v Customs and Excise Comrs* [1997] 2 All ER 366.

[64] [1999] 2 AC 143.

[65] Lord Steyn referred to *Roy* [1992] 1 AC 624, *Winder* [1985] AC 461, *Chief Adjudication Officer v Foster* [1993] AC 754, and *Mercury Communications Ltd v Director General of Telecommunications* [1996] 1 WLR 48.

[66] [1998] 2 WLR 639, 663.

[67] *Mercury Ltd v Director General of Telecommunications* [1996] 1 WLR 48.   [68] ibid, 57.

The abuse of process test does not on its face require the existence of any private right as a condition precedent for an applicant to be able to proceed outside Order 53. That this is so is further confirmed by the way in which this test was applied in *Mercury* itself. In allowing M to bring its case by way of originating summons Lord Slynn did not mention the rights-based criterion derived from *Roy*. Nor did he frame his judgment that M should be allowed to bring its case by way of originating summons on the ground that its private rights were at stake. It would have been difficult to find private rights that M had as against the DGT. Lord Slynn held that there was no abuse of process, in part because the essence of the action was a contractual dispute between M and BT, and in part because the relevant issues could be better determined by the Commercial Court, rather than via Order 53.

It would seem that if an applicant has private rights then the case will be allowed to proceed outside Order 53, even if it does involve a public law matter, and this will be deemed *ipso facto* not to be an abuse of process. However, even where there are no such rights it will be open to an applicant to convince the court that recourse to an ordinary action does not constitute an abuse of process.

The impact of this reasoning on the decision in *O'Reilly* is significant. In *O'Reilly* the assumption was that it would be an abuse of process for an applicant to proceed outside Order 53, precisely because this would deprive the public body of the protections enshrined in the Order 53 procedure. This starting assumption was qualified, but not undermined, by the exceptions concerning consent and private rights. In *Mercury* the same concept, abuse of process, has a very different meaning. Here the assumption is that an applicant should be allowed to bring a case outside Order 53, unless this constitutes an abuse of process. The fact that the public body will be deprived of the protections contained in Order 53 does not, however, appear to constitute, in itself, such an abuse. Provided that the applicant can convince the court that there are good reasons for allowing the claim to be brought by way of ordinary action, no such abuse will be found.

It is perhaps not going too far to conclude that the House of Lords created the doctrine of presumptive exclusivity, and has been steadily backing away from it ever since.[69] The Law Commission's approach to procedural exclusivity was very close to that of the courts: the exclusivity principle should be preserved for pure public law cases with generous exceptions for cases involving private rights and complex factual disputes.[70]

---

[69] For academic comment, see, S Fredman and G Morris, 'Public or Private: State Employees and Judicial Review' (1991) 107 LQR 298, and 'A Snake or a Ladder: *O'Reilly v Mackman* Reconsidered' (1992) 108 LQR 353.

[70] Law Commission Consultation Paper No 126, *Administrative Law and Statutory Appeals* (1993), 18–19, para 3.23; Law Commission, *Administrative Law: Judicial Review and Statutory Appeals* (Report No 226, HC 669, 1994), para 3.15.

Conclusion

Judicial review has, as is apparent from the preceding discussion, undoubtedly been reinvigorated from the 1960s onwards. The incidence and nature of such review continues to evolve. The most important influences have been the Human Rights Act 1998 and membership of the EU. The Human Rights Act has in many ways transformed judicial review. A great many cases will now feature some rights-based claim, either instead of, or in addition to, common law grounds of judicial review. The judiciary has necessarily been forced to make difficult judgments concerning the limits of human rights. Membership of the EU has moreover had a marked impact on administrative law, since the courts will not only have to apply EU principles of judicial review in cases that have a Community law dimension, but they will also have to decide whether to apply such principles in cases that do not have a Community law dimension, as exemplified by the continuing debate concerning the status of proportionality in UK law.

30

Human Rights

David Feldman

Examining the contribution of a single tribunal to an area of law is an odd exercise, especially when it is a top appellate tribunal. The House of Lords does not act in a vacuum. Access to it is strictly controlled by a requirement for leave to appeal, so most new developments take place in lower courts.[1] The Law Lords react to those developments, to counsel's submissions, and to each other; they rarely strike out in a wholly unexpected direction, and when they do the result is sometimes less than ideal.[2] This chapter focuses on the important contributions that the House has made to protecting human rights in the UK, but it should be remembered throughout that its jurisprudence is only the tip of a mass of judicial activity which has often stimulated the House to move in a particular direction.

Fundamental rights independent of the Human Rights Act 1998

Our judges have long regarded certain common law rights as fundamentally important, especially rights to property, freedom of contract, and freedom from unjustified detention. However, the judicial work of the House of Lords in respect of rights guaranteed under international treaties or customary international law took off only in the last quarter of the twentieth century. Human rights treaties were rare before 1950, and the UK's broadly dualist approach to them restricted their impact on domestic law.[3] It is therefore unsurprising to find no explicit mention of them in Law Lords' speeches before the 1970s,[4] even when counsel cited them.[5]

---

[1] B Dickson, 'Comparing Supreme Courts' in B Dickson (ed), *Judicial Activism in Common Law Supreme Courts* (Oxford: Oxford University Press, 2007) ch 1, at 7.

[2] See Sir Richard Buxton, 'How the common law gets made: *Hedley Byrne* and other cautionary tales' (2009) 128 LQR 60.

[3] M Hunt, *Using Human Rights Law in English Courts* (Oxford: Hart Publishing, 1997) chs 1, 4, 5, and 6.

[4] A search of Lexis on 5 February 2008 for (human right! and (COURT-NAME) House of Lords and (JUDGMENT-DATE) before 1946) yielded a nil return.

[5] See eg *J v C* [1970] AC 668, 676 (Robert Alexander); *Royal Government of Greece v Governor of Brixton Prison* [1971] AC 250, 273 (Louis Blom-Cooper).

In 1974 Lord Reid referred to the Universal Declaration of Human Rights and the European Convention on Human Rights (ECHR) as reinforcing the strong common law presumption that criminal legislation is not retrospective.[6] The first substantive judicial discussion of human rights by the House occurred in *Oppenheimer v Cattermole*[7] in 1975. Significantly, it concerned rights in customary international law, which has never been subject to the dualist principle. The majority opined (*obiter*) that English courts would, on public policy grounds, refuse to recognise a German law of 1941 depriving German Jews who were ordinarily resident outside Germany of their German nationality, because it violated fundamental human rights of refugees from Nazi persecution. However, the impact of human rights as public policy considerations was limited. That same year, in *Blathwayt v Baron Cawley*,[8] the House rejected an argument that freedom of religion under the ECHR could operate as an aspect of public policy to override freedom of testamentary disposition in relation to a will which had taken effect in 1936 depriving a legatee of his life interest if he were to become a Roman Catholic.

The year 1979 illustrated the limited weight given to treaty rights. In *R v Lemon* an argument that the House should not allow continued operation of the obsolescent crime of blasphemous libel unless it complied with the ECHR was turned on its head when Lord Scarman said that the right to freedom of religion and belief impliedly imposed an obligation on individuals not to offend the religious sensibilities of others.[9] In *Science Research Council v Nassé*[10] Lord Wilberforce considered that, as the rules of public interest immunity were developed to secure a fair hearing in difficult circumstances, it was unnecessary to refer to Article 6 of the ECHR to establish the scope of the immunity. In *R v IRC, ex p Rossminster Ltd* Lord Wilberforce accepted that the integrity of a man's home and place of business was 'an important human right', but did not regard that as sufficient reason to interpret legislation as requiring a search warrant to specify the offence being investigated.[11]

During the 1980s human rights formed a point of reference in Law Lords' opinions in 12 cases. As a general principle, the House accepted that courts could use the ECHR as a guide to the construction of legislation which was ambiguous or otherwise difficult to construe. However, their Lordships only rarely addressed the substantive applicability of Convention rights.[12] In some cases they

---

[6] *Waddington v Miah (otherwise Ullah)* [1974] 1 WLR 683, 693–4.   [7] [1976] AC 249.
[8] [1976] AC 397.
[9] [1979] AC 517, 622 (Louis Blom-Cooper QC), 465 (Lord Scarman). In *Gleaves v Deakin* [1980] AC 477, the House also rejected an argument that a person should not be committed for trial on a charge of criminal libel unless it could be shown to be justified under ECHR Art 10.
[10] [1980] AC 1028, 1068.   [11] [1980] AC 952, 997. Lord Salmon dissented.
[12] *Champion v Chief Constable of Gwent* [1990] 1 WLR 1, 14, *per* Lord Ackner (ECHR Art 8 not engaged by refusal of Chief Constable to allow officer, a school governor, to sit on the governors' appointment sub-committee).

mentioned rights merely to announce that they were irrelevant.[13] In others there was a passing reference to the ECHR or the European Court of Human Rights, perhaps to explain the background to a piece of legislation or another international treaty.[14] Law Lords who treated human rights as relevant considerations were usually dissenting.[15]

Nevertheless, there were some signs of growing receptiveness. In *Attorney General v BBC* Lord Fraser of Tullybelton accepted that judges should have regard to the ECHR in cases in which the law was not firmly settled, and Lord Scarman referred to a rebuttable presumption that English law is intended to be consistent with the UK's international obligations, including those under human rights treaties.[16] The ECHR was becoming part of the legal background against which municipal law would be developed, a process encouraged by the use of the ECHR in the European Court of Justice when applying the Treaty of Rome and general principles of Community Law.[17] In the second *Spycatcher* case, Lord Goff said of the ECHR, '. . . I conceive it to be my duty, when I am free to do so, to interpret the law in accordance with the obligations of the Crown under this treaty.'[18] It was used in this way in *Lord Advocate v Scotsman Publications*, when Lord Templeman took Article 10 of the ECHR as a basis for analysing the balance to be struck when deciding whether to restrain a breach of confidence in a national security case.[19] In *R v Secretary of State for the Home Department, ex p Bugdaycay* Lord Bridge suggested that administrative decisions affecting fundamental rights might attract an enhanced standard of review when he said that removing asylum seekers to a country where their right to life was threatened called for 'most anxious scrutiny',[20] although such anxiety does not seem to have affected outcomes.

The 1990s began unpromisingly when the House refused to use freedom of expression under the ECHR to justify any review more rigorous than *Wednesbury* unreasonableness of a decision not to allow the voices of IRA sympathisers to be broadcast, lest it result in the back-door incorporation of the ECHR in municipal

---

[13] *Williams and Humbert Ltd v W & H Trade Marks (Jersey) Ltd* [1986] AC 368; *Harman v Secretary of State for the Home Department* [1983] 1 AC 280, 299 *per* Lord Diplock.

[14] *AG v English* [1983] 1 AC 116, 143 *per* Lord Diplock; *Re Lonrho plc* [1990] 2 AC 154, 208.

[15] *Harman v Secretary of State for the Home Department* [1983] 1 AC 280, 316–17 *per* Lord Scarman and Lord Simon of Glaisdale; *Secretary of State for Defence v Guardian Newspapers* [1985] AC 339, 361 *per* Lord Scarman; *AG v Guardian Newspapers* [1987] 1 WLR 1248, 1286 *per* Lord Bridge.

[16] [1981] AC 303 at 353 *per* Lord Fraser and 354 *per* Lord Scarman.

[17] See eg *R v Henn* [1981] AC 850, ECJ (on a reference from the House of Lords), 870–1 where Advocate General Warner referred extensively to the case law of the European Court of Human Rights, and *Gold Star Publications v DPP* [1981] 1 WLR 732, 735 (Lord Wilberforce), 742 (Lord Simon, dissenting).

[18] *AG v Observer Ltd* [1990] 1 AC 109, at 283 *per* Lord Goff of Chieveley. In the event his Lordship was not surprised to be able to hold that English law was consistent with the right to freedom of expression under Art 10.

[19] [1990] 1 AC 812, 822 (Lord Keith), 823 and 826 (Lord Templeman).

[20] [1987] AC 514 at 531.

law.[21] Yet there were other signs that Law Lords were conscious of human rights, and that rule of law and human rights standards were generating more stringent review as the 1990s wore on.[22] They mentioned the ECHR and its case law in several cases,[23] providing a context for discussion of municipal law.[24] Occasionally this generated a discussion as to the applicability of Convention rights on the facts of the case.[25] In *Abnett v British Airways plc* analysis of the relationship between human rights treaties and other treaties given effect in municipal law led the House to hold that Scottish courts should not use the ECHR to interpret the obligations of airlines under the Warsaw Convention of 1955, given effect by the Carriage by Air Act 1961, because it was desirable for all states to implement a convention in the same way, and not all parties to the Warsaw Convention were parties to the ECHR.[26] At the same time there was a further mention that legal professional privilege was a fundamental right under the ECHR and as a matter of

---

[21] *R v Secretary of State for the Home Department, ex p Brind* [1991] 1 AC 696.

[22] See Stephen Livingstone, 'The House of Lords and the Northern Ireland conflict' (1994) 57 MLR 333; B Dickson, 'The House of Lords and the Northern Ireland conflict: a sequel' (2006) 69 MLR 383.

[23] *Re L (A Minor) (Police Investigation: Privilege)* [1997] AC 16 (mentioning ECHR Arts 6 and 8); *R v Brown (Winston)* [1998] AC 367, 381 (Lord Hope, making a passing reference to ECHR Article 6(3)).

[24] *Pickering v Liverpool Daily Post and Echo Newspapers plc* [1991] 2 AC 370, 413 *per* Lord Bridge, noting that an amendment to the Mental Health Review Tribunal Rules 1983 had been made in response to a decision of the Strasbourg court holding that the earlier version had violated the Convention; *R v Preston* [1994] 2 AC 130, 142 *per* Lord Jauncey, noting that the Interception of Communications Act 1985 had been passed to overcome the shortcoming in English law that had led the Strasbourg court to hold that telephone tapping had violated Article 8 of the ECHR in *Malone v United Kingdom* (1984) 7 EHRR 14; *Re D (Minors) (Adoption Reports: Confidentiality)* [1996] AC 593, 613–14 *per* Lord Mustill, noting that disclosure of reports to parties in family litigation generally helps to protect the rights to respect for family life and a fair hearing, and ordering disclosure; *R v Khan (Sultan)* [1997] AC 558, holding that it was not necessary to exclude evidence obtained from an unauthorised listening device attached to the wall of a home because using the evidence would not make the defendant's trial unfair, even though there had been violations of ECHR Arts 8 and 13: *Khan v United Kingdom*, Eur Ct HR, Judgment of 12 May 2000 (2001) 31 EHRR 45; *R v Secretary of State for the Home Department, ex p Simms* [2000] 2 AC 115, 129–30 *per* Lord Steyn, referring to *Silver v United Kingdom* (1983) 5 EHRR 347 on prisoners' correspondence as part of context for deciding that a prisoner was entitled to talk to a journalist to seek help in getting his case referred back to the Court of Appeal.

[25] See *X Ltd v Morgan-Grampian (Publishers) Ltd* [1991] 1 AC 1, 49 *per* Lord Templeman, suggesting (wrongly, as it turned out when the case went to Strasbourg) that it had been 'necessary' to order Mr Goodwin, a journalist, to reveal his sources from the points of view of both s 10 of the Contempt of Court Act 1981 and Art 10(2) of the ECHR; *R v Secretary of State for the Home Department, ex p Francois* [1999] 1 AC 43, 51 (Lord Slynn), accepting that in interpreting ambiguous legislation one could take account of international human rights obligations, but holding that changing the rules on early release of prisoners so that some stayed in prison longer than expected did not violate ECHR Art 7; *Dawson v Wearmouth* [1999] 2 AC 308, 321 (Lord Mackay), 329 (Lord Hobhouse): father could not assert a right under ECHR Art 8 in respect of his child's name; *Lord Mayhew of Twysden's Motion* [2002] 1 AC 109 (Committee of Privileges), 118–19 (Lord Slynn), holding that Convention rights did not prevent legislation from withdrawing the right to sit in the House of Lords from most hereditary peers.

[26] [1997] AC 430, 443–4 (Lord Hope).

common law,[27] and the 'anxious scrutiny' idea from *Bugdaycay* was invoked, though without obvious effect.[28]

This does not mean that the House was unconcerned with the values that underpin human rights. Both before and after the Human Rights Act 1998 (hereafter HRA, or 1998 Act) it decided important cases on anti-discrimination legislation, applying the legislation to fields such as immigration in which discrimination (at least on the ground of nationality) is inherent.[29] In asylum cases the House has given a relatively generous interpretation to the Convention on the Status of Refugees.[30] It has interpreted the term 'persecuted for reasons of... membership of a particular social group' as including women in Pakistan (or women who were accused of adultery there) who were liable to mistreatment, people persecuted by reason of being part of a particular family, and women in Sierra Leone subject to the threat of female genital mutilation and of persecution for opposing it.[31]

But this did not produce a consistent human rights ethos. The Law Lords differ in their approaches to interpreting international humanitarian treaties, sometimes applying a broad, evolutionary approach in the light of commentators' views and those of the UNHCR, sometimes using a literal interpretation, and sometimes seeking the drafters' original intention through the *travaux préparatoires*.[32] Individual judges themselves are not always consistent. There is a major division between those Law Lords who see human rights as essentially legal concepts to be interpreted and applied in a more or less formal way with a view to maximising certainty, and those who interpret them in an evolutionary way in the light of developing social and moral values. For a long time, the former approach dominated. There were signs of a possible thaw in the general resistance of UK municipal law to international human rights law, but no more. Human rights had emerged from darkness, but struggled to make an impression on judicial decision-making. Only when the HRA and the devolution legislation had been passed, and the process of implementing them was under way, did all Law Lords have to take human rights seriously in their decisions. The approach then changed significantly at several levels.[33]

[27] *R v Derby Magistrates' Court, ex p B* [1996] AC 487, 507 *per* Lord Taylor.

[28] *R v Secretary of State for the Home Department, ex p Abdi* [1996] 1 WLR 298, 305 *per* Lord Slynn (dissenting).

[29] See eg *Mandla v Dowell Lee* [1983] 2 AC 548, *R (European Roma Rights Centre) v Immigration Officer at Prague Airport* [2005] 2 AC 1.

[30] *R v Secretary of State for the Home Department, ex p Adan* [2001] 2 AC 477; *Januzi v Secretary of State for the Home Department* [2006] 2 AC 426.

[31] See eg *R v Immigration Appeal Tribunal, ex p Shah* [1999] 2 AC 629; *K v Secretary of State for the Home Department; Fornah v Secretary of State for the Home Department* [2007] 1 AC 412.

[32] See eg *R v Asfaw* [2008] 1 AC 1061 on Art 31(1) of the Refugee Convention. Lords Bingham, Hope, and Carswell applied an evolutionary approach, Lord Rodger used a literalist approach, and Lord Mance (with Lord Rodger concurring) was an originalist, looking to the *travaux préparatoires*.

[33] See B Dickson, 'Safe in their hands? Britain's Law Lords and human rights' (2006) 26 LS 329–46.

The impact of the HRA

The most obvious effect of the 1998 Act was a huge growth in the human rights case load, which between 2002 and 2008 averaged 37.5 per cent of the House's total case load.[34]

Secondly, the House has extended previously rare practices to help it to grapple with unfamiliar challenges. It has allowed a far larger number of organisations to intervene in cases than ever before,[35] usually in written submissions but sometimes orally. In *E v Chief Constable of the Royal Ulster Constabulary* Lord Hoffmann said, 'the expectation is that their fund of knowledge or particular point of view will enable them to provide the House with a more rounded picture than it would otherwise obtain', but he stressed that interveners must do more than reiterate points already made adequately by one of the parties.[36]

Some Law Lords have also started to consider a range of material, going beyond the Strasbourg case law of which section 2 of the Act requires account to be taken. Like the Strasbourg court, the Law Lords have interpreted Convention rights in the light of the UK's obligations under other human rights treaties to which the UK is party, which form part of the matrix of standards and rules in which the ECHR operates. Law Lords also regularly refer to academic writing, and permit citation of 'soft law' such as the preparatory works for treaties, and reports and opinions of international institutions like the UN Human Rights Committee and national bodies such as the Parliamentary Joint Select Committee on Human Rights. For example, Lord Carswell, with the agreement of the other members of the House, has said of the UN Convention on the Rights of the Child (1989) that, although not directly enforceable in municipal law in the UK, its requirements are 'a relevant consideration which should be taken into account by the state and its emanations in determining upon their actions'.[37] It has to be said, however, that judges vary widely in their propensity to make explicit use of such material as part of the reasoning in their

---

[34] I treated as a human rights case any decision concerning the interpretation or operation of the HRA and any decision in which at least one Law Lord's opinion gave serious consideration to a question of substantive international or domestic human rights law.

[35] They have included the responsible government minister in a case where a declaration of incompatibility has been or might be made under s 4 of the HRA (see Report of the Appeals Committee of 7 March 2001, [2001] All ER (D) 215 (Mar)), Amnesty International, Campaign to End Rape, Child and Woman Abuse Studies Unit, Children's Law Centre, the Commonwealth Lawyers Association, the Equality and Human Rights Commission, INQUEST, Joint Council for the Welfare of Immigrants, JUSTICE, Justice for Women, Northern Ireland Commissioner for Children and Young People, Rape Crisis Federation of England and Wales, The Redress Trust, and the Speaker of the House of Commons.

[36] [2008] 3 WLR 1208, paras 2–3.

[37] *E v Chief Constable of the Royal Ulster Constabulary* [2008] 3 WLR 1208, para 60 *per* Lord Carswell. See also *Dyer v Watson, K v HM Advocate* [2004] 1 AC 379, a devolution case on the effect of delay on minors under ECHR Art 6.

speeches: Lord Bingham and Baroness Hale have referred to it liberally,[38] but others have done so less often.

Thirdly, these quantitative and methodological changes are matched by a qualitative development. The Law Lords engage in rigorous analysis of the case law of the Strasbourg court, and the care and ingenuity with which they mould it when seeking solutions to novel and intractable issues command the respect of the Strasbourg court. In part this is a response to legislative requirements. Apart from the 1998 Act, a growing body of legislation and case law requires (or has been interpreted as requiring) decision-makers to ensure that they do not infringe the human rights (or certain rights) of applicants in, for example, immigration, asylum, and extradition processes.[39] A request for extradition is to be refused (save in relation to European Arrest Warrants) where there is a risk that the accused would be likely to be denied a fair hearing or suffer violation of the right to be free of inhuman treatment or punishment in the requesting jurisdiction;[40] and it has been held that refugees cannot show a well founded fear of persecution for the purpose of claiming asylum unless they face discrimination in relation to a recognised human right.[41] But it is also, in part, a result of a changing judicial ethos.

Using Strasbourg jurisprudence

The House not only takes account of the case law of the Strasbourg court, as section 2 of the HRA requires. Their Lordships analyse it as carefully as they would the judgments of domestic courts, and it often determines the case. The House takes the view that the purpose of the Act is to allow people in the UK to obtain protection for Convention rights from municipal courts equivalent to that which the Strasbourg court would offer them. Before the Act came into force, some commentators expected that courts would be able to develop distinctively UK interpretations of Convention rights, sometimes offering greater protection than would have been provided by the Strasbourg court.[42] Others argued that they must be subject to the same limits as in international law (except so far as the restrictions had been relaxed by Act of Parliament).[43] It gradually became clear that the House generally regards the content and reach of Convention rights in

---

[38] See eg *A v Secretary of State for the Home Department* [2005] 2 AC 68, paras 22–4, 34, 42–3, 57–65, 69 *per* Lord Bingham; *R (European Roma Rights Centre) v Immigration Officer at Prague Airport* [2005] 2 AC 1; *A v Secretary of State for the Home Department (No 2)* [2006] 2 AC 221, paras 35–44 *per* Lord Bingham.

[39] See eg *Re Al-Fawwaz* [2002] 1 AC 556; *Sepet v Secretary of State for the Home Department* [2003] 3 All ER 304; *R (Wellington) v Secretary of State for the Home Department* [2009] 2 WLR 48.

[40] *Re Al-Fawwaz* [2002] 1 AC 556; *R (Wellington) v Secretary of State for the Home Department* [2009] 1 AC 335.

[41] *Sepet v Secretary of State for the Home Department* [2003] 3 All ER 304.

[42] See eg D Feldman, *Civil Liberties and Human Rights in England and Wales* (Oxford: Oxford University Press, 2nd edn 2002) 83.

[43] Sir Richard Buxton, 'The HRA and private law' (2000) 116 LQR 48.

municipal law as being the same as in international law,[44] although the mechanics of their application in municipal law are a matter for municipal law.[45]

The House decided quite early that, 'in the absence of some special circumstances', it should follow the 'clear and consistent jurisprudence of the Strasbourg court'.[46] As Lord Bingham explained in *Ullah*, this was because 'the Convention is an international instrument, the correct interpretation of which can be authoritatively expounded only by the Strasbourg court ... The duty of national courts is to keep pace with the Strasbourg jurisprudence as it evolves over time: no more, but certainly no less.'[47] This remains the orthodox view,[48] especially in the field of economic and social policy,[49] although (as we shall see) it is coming under pressure at the margins. It has compelled the House to develop the art of reading Strasbourg judgments respectfully and creatively, if not uncritically. For example, in *R (Pretty) v Director of Public Prosecutions*[50] the issue was whether the right to life (among others) included a right to be helped to die when life became intolerable, without any threat of criminal proceedings against the helper. Their Lordships considered a wide range of Strasbourg authorities and concluded that it did not. The Law Lords' argumentation was adopted almost entirely by the European Court of Human Rights (save in respect of the applicability of Article 8) when the case made its way to Strasbourg.[51]

Their Lordships engaged equally sensitively and creatively with the Strasbourg case law in *R (Baiai) v Secretary of State for the Home Department (Nos 1 and 2)*, concluding that the Home Secretary had violated the right to marry under Article 12 of the Convention by requiring immigrants awaiting a decision on their immigration status to obtain a rarely granted certificate from the Home Secretary before they would be allowed to marry in the UK.[52]

The House has developed a context-sensitive analysis of discrimination cases when considering what kinds of personal characteristic amount to a protected 'status': it has carefully distinguished between involuntary characteristics—such as homelessness or being a young, single adult—which amount to a

[44] *R (Al-Skeini) v Secretary of State for Defence* [2008] 1 AC 153; *R (Al-Jedda) v Secretary of State for Defence* [2008] 1 AC 332.
[45] *R (Ullah) v Special Adjudicator* [2004] 2 AC 323, para 20 *per* Lord Bingham of Cornhill; *Re McKerr* [2004] 1 WLR 807.
[46] *R (Alconbury Developments Ltd) v Secretary of State for the Environment, Transport and the Regions* [2003] 2 AC 295, para 26 *per* Lord Slynn of Hadley.
[47] *R (Ullah) v Special Adjudicator* [2004] 2 AC 323, para 20 *per* Lord Bingham of Cornhill.
[48] See *R (Animal Defenders International) v Secretary of State for Culture, Media and Sport* [2008] 1 AC 1312, paras 37, 53, 55, 56 *per* Lord Bingham, Baroness Hale, Lord Carswell, and Lord Neuberger of Abbotsbury respectively.
[49] *R (Ullah) v Special Adjudicator* [2004] 2 AC 323; *Bellinger v Bellinger* [2003] 2 AC 467.
[50] [2002] 2 AC 800.
[51] *Pretty v United Kingdom* (2002) 35 EHRR 1.
[52] [2008] 3 WLR 549. The House has also followed the Strasbourg court in holding that a right to a non-contributory disability benefit is a possession protected by Art 1 of Protocol 1 to the ECHR: *R (RJM) v Secretary of State for Work and Pensions* [2009] 1 AC 311, following *Stec v United Kingdom* (2006) 43 EHRR 1017 (though interference was held to be justified on the facts).

status,[53] and freely chosen membership of groups or activities—such as partici-pating in hunting with dogs—which do not.[54] Unmarried heterosexual couples might be thought to have freely chosen not to marry, but in *Re P* the House decided that, as the Strasbourg court had treated marriage as a status, unmarried relationships also involve a status.[55] The House has also distinguished between a core protected status, such as sex or race, where courts should strictly scrutinise the reasons for any difference of treatment, and more peripheral grounds for discrimination, such as age and country of residence, where judges would only require some rational justification.[56]

Positive obligations under the European Convention provide another example of the acuity of the Law Lords in using the Strasbourg jurisprudence. The obligation of states under Article 1 of the Convention to secure the Convention rights to all within their jurisdiction gives rise to obligations on the state not merely to avoid violating rights, but also sometimes to take positive steps to protect people against violation of their rights by third parties, whether other states, private persons, or even force of circumstances. The House has shown itself adept at giving effect to these obligations while ensuring that the burdens imposed on the state are not impracticably heavy. Positive obligations apply both to institutional structures and policies and to operational activities, ensuring that the structures protect vulnerable people effectively: there is a special responsibility towards people who are detained and denied the ability to make autonomous decisions.[57] Their Lordships have stressed that it will not be easy to satisfy courts that the operational duty has been breached,[58] but that does not mean that a case must be exceptional in order to justify a finding of a breach of a positive obligation.[59]

Thus in *Limbuela* their Lordships accepted that Article 3 of the Convention imposed a duty on the state to provide a safety-net through the social security system for those at risk of degradation and destitution, including asylum seekers and illegal immigrants awaiting removal from the country.[60] Yet at the same time they have stressed that positive obligations implied into the ECHR, even in relation to the absolute and non-derogable rights, apply only where the claimant has an arguable claim that the public authority concerned has breached the core,

---

[53] *R (RJM) v Secretary of State for Work and Pensions* [2008] 3 WLR 1023; *AL (Serbia) v Secretary of State for the Home Department* [2008] 1 WLR 1734 (though differential treatment was held to be justified on the facts of those cases).

[54] *R (Countryside Alliance) v AG* [2008] 1 AC 719.   [55] *Re S* [2008] 3 WLR 76.

[56] See eg *R (Carson) v Secretary of State for Work and Pensions, R (Reynolds) v Secretary of State for Work and Pensions* [2006] 1 AC 173.

[57] *R (Amin) v Secretary of State for the Home Department* [2004] 1 AC 653; *R (L) v Secretary of State for Justice* [2008] 3 WLR 1325; *Savage v South Essex Partnership NHS Foundation Trust* [2009] 2 WLR 115.

[58] *Re Officer L* [2007] 1 WLR 2135; *Van Colle v Chief Constable of the Hertfordshire Police* [2009] 1 AC 225; *E v Chief Constable of the Royal Ulster Constabulary* [2008] 3 WLR 1208.

[59] *Savage v South Essex Partnership NHS Foundation Trust* (n 57 above).

[60] *R (Limbuela) v Secretary of State for the Home Department* [2006] 1 AC 396.

negative obligation,[61] and extend only to taking such steps as are reasonable in the circumstances, without imposing impossible or disproportionate burdens on the state, to protect people against a real and immediate risk, of which the state is or should be aware, of violation of a Convention right.[62] In a series of cases the Law Lords have been prepared to impose obligations under a range of Convention rights on immigration decision-makers, while insisting that removing an alien from the country would violate one of the non-absolute Convention rights, such as respect for family life, only if the person concerned would be likely to suffer a flagrant breach of the right such as to deny entirely, or nullify the core of, the right.[63]

This balanced approach prevents the ECHR from imposing judicially enforceable obligations on the UK to guarantee social and economic rights to anyone who arrives in the country, with the financial and administrative burden that that would entail. Where the positive obligation arises in relation to an unqualified right such as freedom from inhuman treatment, it is an absolute obligation, but is still only an obligation to take such steps as are reasonable in the circumstances to prevent a real and immediate risk of harm: a proportionality assessment enters into the calculation of the scope of the duty.[64] Nevertheless, it is not always easy to establish the limits of the obligation. In *N v Secretary of State for the Home Department* the House followed the later of two Strasbourg decisions in order to limit the positive obligation under Article 3 to ensure that failed asylum seekers could receive medical treatment for serious illness by allowing them to stay in the UK indefinitely for treatment. The House interpreted the Strasbourg jurisprudence as applying only to people in exceptional need.[65]

Generally, the House has done well in elucidating the scope of rights, even where it has not been easy, as when trying to decide whether administering corporal punishment to children in obedience to biblical texts was a 'manifestation of religion' given qualified protection by ECHR Article 9.[66] The main problem area has been fair hearing rights, especially in criminal cases. The House has given a narrow interpretation to the term 'determination of a criminal charge' in Article 6(1), excluding the making of an anti-social behaviour order and a finding that a person who is unfit to plead to a criminal charge did the act forming the actus reus of the offence, despite the fact that the consequences of

---

[61] *R (Gentle) v Prime Minister* [2008] 1 AC 1356.

[62] *Osman v United Kingdom* (1998) 29 EHRR 245, para 116.

[63] *R (Ullah) v Special Adjudicator* [2004] 2 AC 323; *R (Razgar) v Secretary of State for the Home Department* [2004] 2 AC 368; *Beoku-Betts v Secretary of State for the Home Department* [2008] 3 WLR 166; *Chikwamba v Secretary of State for the Home Department* [2008] 1 WLR 1420; *EM (Lebanon) v Secretary of State for the Home Department* [2008] 3 WLR 931.

[64] *Van Colle v Chief Constable of the Hertfordshire Police* [2008] 3 WLR 593; *E v Chief Constable of the Royal Ulster Constabulary* [2008] 3 WLR 1208, esp at para 10 *per* Baroness Hale of Richmond.

[65] [2005] 2 AC 296. The House followed comments of the Strasbourg court in *Bensaid v United Kingdom* (2001) 33 EHRR 205, para 40 in preference to the decision in *D v United Kingdom* (1997) 24 EHRR 423.

[66] See *R (Williamson) v Secretary of State for Education and Employment* [2005] 2 AC 246.

such decisions are based on criteria and have characteristics that are similar to criminal convictions.[67] There has also been a tendency to read the right to a hearing within a reasonable time and the right to be presumed innocent until proved guilty as if they were merely subordinate elements of a fair hearing, instead of giving them their proper weight as special requirements without which no hearing can meet the requirements of Article 6.[68] In the early days of the HRA this was understandable: there was a pragmatic concern not to allow opponents of the Act to paint it as undermining law and order, and sometimes the Strasbourg court has followed the House rather than vice versa. When the Privy Council in *Brown v Stott*[69] gave less weight to the privilege against self-incrimination as an aspect of the right to a fair hearing under Article 6(1) than might have been expected in the light of the Strasbourg case law, the Strasbourg court qualified its own approach, moving to one giving more weight to the public interest in regulating the use of dangerous vehicles based on a balancing exercise taking account of the 'nature and degree of compulsion used to obtain the evidence, the existence of any relevant safeguards in the procedure, and the use to which any material so obtained was put'.[70]

But where principles arguably derivable from the Strasbourg jurisprudence are consistent with a well established principle of the common law, the House will sometimes treat the Strasbourg principle as of general application, not limited to the factual circumstances in which it was developed. For instance, in *R v Davis*[71] the accused had been convicted on the strength of evidence from witnesses whose names and addresses were not disclosed to the defence, and who were shielded from the defendant (though not his counsel). The House held that there was a fundamental right both at common law and under the ECHR to know who one's accusers were. A trial would be unfair if a conviction was based solely or decisively on evidence which the defendant did not have the chance to challenge effectively. The Crown argued that the Strasbourg court had not used the 'sole or decisive evidence' test in relation to witnesses who give evidence in person in court (albeit anonymously), but the House decided that the test was of general application even though it had never before been applied to a case such as *Davis*.[72]

The Law Lords have regularly taken a light-touch approach to assessing the justifications for an interference with a right, and the Strasbourg court may demand a more rigorous evaluation. In *R (S) v Chief Constable of South Yorkshire Police*[73] the police had taken and retained fingerprints and DNA samples from

---

[67] *R (McCann) v Manchester Crown Court* [2003] 1 AC 787; *R v H (Fitness to Plead)* [2003] 1 WLR 411.

[68] See eg *AG's Reference (No 2 of 2001)* [2004] 2 AC 72.   [69] [2003] 1 AC 681, PC.

[70] *O'Halloran and Francis v United Kingdom* App Nos 15809/02, 25624/02, judgment of 29 June 2007, para 55.

[71] [2008] 1 AC 1128.

[72] The practical effect of the decision was almost immediately reversed by Act of Parliament, which will no doubt eventually fall to be assessed for compatibility with Art 6.

[73] [2004] 1 WLR 2196.

people arrested on suspicion of offences and either acquitted or not prosecuted. The claimants said that this violated their right to respect for private life under ECHR Article 8. The House decided that the interference with their right was relatively minor, and that the retention in pursuance of a general policy without consideration of the circumstances of individual cases was justified as a proportionate response to a pressing social need to prevent and detect crime. When the case reached Strasbourg, the Grand Chamber of the European Court of Human Rights unanimously took a far more rigorous approach to analysing the supposed justification, and decided that a blanket policy to retain information about fingerprints and DNA of people who have not been convicted of any offence without review of individual cases could not be justified.[74] In relation to prevention of crime the House has sometimes adopted narrow readings of rights and broad readings of exceptions.[75]

Doubts, difficulties, and philosophical differences

It has sometimes been necessary to find a way forward where the Strasbourg case law is developing in a way that is only questionably predictable, or has created principles that are not easy to articulate or apply, or provides lines of authority that seem to conflict. In these cases the House has often struggled to find a way forward, and has tended to give the smallest possible scope to rights. This is regularly done where the Strasbourg case law appears to be contradictory,[76] although sometimes it has been possible to reconcile the two lines of authority, deny any divergence, and give effect to a reasonably wide scope for the right.[77]

Where there is no clear guidance from Strasbourg on the scope of a right, philosophical differences between Law Lords have free rein. This is apparent in control order cases such as *JJ v Secretary of State for the Home Department*. The Strasbourg case law on the meaning of deprivation of liberty for the purpose of Article 5 of the ECHR rejects any bright-line rule, offering instead a collection of factors without any formula for deciding what weight to give each of them. One

---

[74] *S and Marper v United Kingdom*, App Nos 30562/04 and 30566/04, judgment of 4 December 2008.

[75] See also *R (Gillan) v Comr of the Metropolitan Police* [2006] 2 AC 307, holding that authorising searches without reasonable suspicion under the Terrorism Act 2000 did not violate Convention rights and would in any case be justifiable (subject to concern about discriminatory use): *Austin v Comr of Police of the Metropolis* [2009] 2 WLR 372.

[76] eg regarding the extra-territorial application of Convention rights in *R (Al-Skeini) v Secretary of State for Defence* [2008] 1 AC 153, preferring the strict control approach found in *Banković v Belgium* (2001) 44 EHRR SE5 to that based on responsibility in *Ilaşcu v Moldova and Russia* (2004) 40 EHRR 46.

[77] See eg *Savage v South Essex Partnership NHS Foundation Trust* [2009] 2 WLR 115, reconciling the approaches to the operational responsibilities of state bodies under ECHR Art 2 for people detained and vulnerable to the risk of suicide in *Keenan v United Kingdom* (2001) 73 EHRR 38 and *Powell v United Kingdom* (2000) 30 EHRR CD 362.

can sympathise with the desire of Lord Brown of Eaton-under-Heywood to enhance certainty by treating the period of detention as determinative, even though that is inconsistent with the Strasbourg approach.[78]

Cases like these can give rise to a question as to the circumstances in which it is proper for the House to depart from Strasbourg case law. Lord Hoffmann has said that he 'would have considerable doubt' as to whether decisions of the Strasbourg court should be followed if they 'compelled a conclusion fundamentally at odds with the distribution of powers under the British constitution'.[79] Law Lords have sometimes been very reluctant to hold legislation encapsulating parliamentary balance struck between the rights of individuals and the interests of other people, or society generally, or the integrity and efficiency of the political or legal system, to be incompatible with Convention rights.[80] Where the Strasbourg case law relates particularly to the United Kingdom, the House has asked whether the Strasbourg court correctly understood the position in domestic law. If the Strasbourg court understood it correctly, the House follows the Strasbourg decision.[81] But if the House thinks that the Strasbourg court has misunderstood the domestic position the House has declined to follow it.[82] Sometimes the Strasbourg court has responded by adjusting its jurisprudence in the direction favoured by the House.[83]

Many Strasbourg decisions rely on the scope of a state's margin of appreciation in assessing justifications advanced for interfering with rights. As the margin is inapplicable to municipal law, UK judges have more freedom to go their own way on questions of justification than in relation to the scope of rights. In *R (Animal Defenders International) v Secretary of State for Culture,*

---

[78] [2008] 1 AC 385. See also *Secretary of State for the Home Department v MB* [2008] 1 AC 440; *Secretary of State for the Home Department v E* [2008] 1 AC 499.

[79] *R (Alconbury Developments Ltd) v Secretary of State for the Environment, Transport and the Regions* [2003] 2 AC 295, para 76.

[80] *R (Animal Defenders International) v Secretary of State for Culture, Media and Sport* [2008] 1 AC 1312, paras 44–45 *per* Lord Scott of Foscote; *Harrow LBC v Qazi* [2004] 1 AC 983; *Kay v Lambeth LBC* [2006] 2 AC 465; *Doherty v Birmingham CC* [2008] 3 WLR 636, para 80 *per* Lord Scott of Foscote.

[81] *R (Anderson) v Secretary of State for the Home Department* [2003] 1 AC 837, paras 18 *per* Lord Bingham of Cornhill, 54 *per* Lord Steyn, and 73–8 *per* Lord Hutton.

[82] See eg *Barrett v Enfield LBC* [2001] 2 AC 550, criticising the decision of the Strasbourg court in *Osman v United Kingdom* (1999) 29 EHRR 245 relating to ECHR Art 6(1) as failing to appreciate the distinction between absence of a duty of care and a special procedural immunity for particular defendants. The European Court of Human Rights subsequently departed from its decision in *Osman* on this point, taking account of criticisms in *Barrett*. See also *R v Spear* [2003] 1 AC 734, paras 12 *per* Lord Bingham of Cornhill and 65–97 *per* Lord Rodger of Earlsferry (courts martial), and *Doherty v Birmingham CC* [2008] 3 WLR 636, paras 80, 83–8 *per* Lord Scott of Foscote.

[83] In *Z v United Kingdom*, App No 29392/99, judgment of 10 May 2001, para 100 the Strasbourg court accepted that it had misunderstood the law of negligence when deciding the Art 6 point in *Osman*, and changed its approach accordingly. In *Cooper v United Kingdom*, (2004) 39 EHRR 8, the Grand Chamber departed from a decision of a Chamber in *Morris v United Kingdom* (2002) 34 EHRR 1253 that potential pressure on junior members of a court martial from senior officers undermined their independence, in the light of criticism of *Morris* by Lord Bingham and Lord Rodger in *R v Spear*, n 82 above.

Media and Sport,[84] the claimant argued that the ban on political advertising on radio and television in section 321(2) of the Communications Act 2003 violated its right to freedom of expression under Article 10 of the ECHR. The Strasbourg court had held that a similar prohibition in Switzerland was an unjustifiable restriction on freedom of expression, although a prohibition on religious advertising could be justified.[85] The House decided that several of the considerations that had led the Strasbourg court to uphold the ban on broadcast religious advertising (particularly the administrative discretion that any lesser restriction would entail) applied just as powerfully to political advertising, although Lord Bingham and Lord Scott accepted that there might be a violation on different facts.[86] Had the arguments been deployed as powerfully in the political advertising case as in that concerning religious advertising, the Strasbourg court might have allowed more scope for states to decide what restrictions were necessary to protect democracy.[87]

Where Strasbourg jurisprudence is inconsistent or unsettled, the House has generally taken the latest Strasbourg judgment, especially if from the Grand Chamber, as offering the best indication of the direction in which the jurisprudence is going.[88] The House normally follows new leads,[89] although an occasional voice may ask whether the new departure in Strasbourg is sufficiently settled to justify following it, bearing in mind that no doctrine of *stare decisis* applies.[90]

On occasions the House consciously limits the application of Strasbourg case law because of reluctance to apply rights in ways that would not have been supported by the representatives of the High Contracting Parties to the ECHR in 1950. For instance, in *R (Gentle) v Prime Minister* their Lordships read Article 2 in the light of general principles of conceptions of the duties of states when the Convention was negotiated: states could not have imagined that the right to life could restrict the freedom of a sovereign state to make war abroad and to deploy troops for that purpose.[91] Another way to restrict the impact of Strasbourg decisions is to stress their fact-sensitive nature. There is also a desire to protect domestic legal and constitutional arrangements, particularly if they would upset established procedures in the UK (as in *Kay v Lambeth LBC*)[92], or impose a major burden on the state (as in *N v Secretary of State for the Home Department*[93]). This

---

[84] [2008] 1 AC 1312.
[85] *VgT Verein gegen Tierfabriken v Switzerland* (2001) 34 EHRR 159 (political advertising), distinguished in *Murphy v Ireland* (2003) 38 EHRR 212 (religious advertising).
[86] *Animal Defenders International*, n 84 above paras [34], [41]–[42].
[87] *Animal Defenders International* especially at paras 28–35 *per* Lord Bingham of Cornhill, 48–49 and 52 *per* Baroness Hale of Richmond.
[88] See eg *N v Secretary of State for the Home Department* [2005] 2 AC 296.
[89] See eg *R (Anderson) v Secretary of State for the Home Department* [2003] 1 AC 837; *Bellinger v Bellinger* [2003] 2 AC 467.
[90] See *Re G (Adoption: Unmarried Couple)* [2008] 3 WLR 76.   [91] [2008] 1 AC 1356.
[92] *Kay v Lambeth LBC* [2006] 2 AC 465.   [93] [2005] 2 AC 296.

can produce some uncertainty, but it also allows dialogue with the Strasbourg court which can lead to a realignment of the jurisprudence in each jurisdiction to re-establish consistency.

Gaps in the Strasbourg case law can also cause uncertainty. Where the Strasbourg court has not decided an issue directly but has made decisions in an analogous field which suggest what answer it would give, or has decided that the matter lies within states' margin of appreciation, the House has begun to go beyond the minimum scope of rights for which clear Strasbourg authority can be shown. In *Re G*,[94] the claimants, an unmarried heterosexual couple, lived in Northern Ireland, where a statutory instrument prevented courts making an adoption order in favour of an unmarried couple. They argued that this violated their right to be free of discrimination taken together with their right to respect for family life under Articles 14 and 8 of the ECHR. The Strasbourg court had not decided whether denying an unmarried, heterosexual couple the opportunity to adopt violated Article 14, but the Grand Chamber had recently held that preventing adoption by a lesbian, whose same-sex partner was unwilling to shoulder any parental responsibility, was outside the state's margin of appreciation.[95] A majority of the House felt that they could detect that the Strasbourg jurisprudence was moving towards a position where it was likely that a ban on unmarried adopters would be considered to violate Articles 14 and 8. But where a matter was treated as being within the state's margin of appreciation, national authorities, including courts,[96] had to make their own decisions as to the justifiability of an interference with rights. The 'no less but no more protection' principle could not apply to matters within the state's margin of appreciation. The *Ullah* approach is more appropriate when delineating the boundaries of a right than when considering whether an interference with it is justified; in the latter context, local conditions and cultural traditions are likely to be relevant when assessing pressing social need and proportionality, and outcomes may properly vary from place to place even within a single state.[97]

Constitutional propriety, parliamentary sovereignty, and deference

Whilst it is generally agreed that municipal constitutional proprieties may act as a brake on the domestic operation of Convention rights derived from international

---

[94] *Re G (Adoption: Unmarried Couple)* [2009] 1 AC 173.

[95] *EB v France*, Application No 43546/02, (2008) 47 EHRR 21, GC, departing from *Fretté v France* (2002) 38 EHRR 438. See Andrew Bainham [2008] CLJ 479.

[96] [2008] 3 WLR 76, esp at paras 47–8 *per* Lord Hope. Lord Walker dissented on this point and Baroness Hale had some doubts: paras 82 and 119.

[97] ibid, paras 41 *per* Lord Hope, 80 *per* Lord Walker (dissenting). Baroness Hale suggested that this may cut two ways: there may be a duty to protect people's rights against particularly restrictive cultural traditions in one jurisdiction that would justify overriding a legislature's assessment of the best general rule on a sensitive social issue: paras 121–2.

law, there are different views as to what the constitution requires. A case like *Re S* shows the complexity of the division between constitutional functions of courts and legislatures, particularly in the fields of economic and social policy. The case was concerned with subordinate legislation, not an Act of Parliament, which may explain the willingness of the majority to impose a judicial view of Convention rights in preference to the legislative provisions. Yet even in relation to Acts of Parliament municipal courts have not surrendered their responsibility to determine the limits of Convention rights. Convention rights protect the politically weak and socially vulnerable against politically and socially dominant groups. Making human rights part of municipal law entails recognition that political might does not equate to moral right. The weight to be given to a parliamentary assessment of the appropriate balance between individuals' rights and the needs of society varies, as Lord Bingham has said, with circumstances and subject matter. Where the two Houses have clearly given careful consideration to the human rights implications of legislation relating to the integrity of the democratic process of which Parliament has particular understanding, and have laid down a general rule to reflect that understanding, their assessment is entitled to special respect from judges.[98] Where those factors are absent, the judgment of Parliament carries less weight, especially when there have been legal or social developments between enactment and litigation.[99] An initially compatible legislative provision may become incompatible if, for instance, the case law on the scope of the relevant Convention right develops, or social standards change.[100]

For all these reasons, when deciding whether a statutory interference with a right is justified, the House has been vigilant to assert judicial responsibility as the ultimate arbiter of such issues as legitimacy of aim and proportionality, even in national security cases, subject to the limits inherent in the judicial role. To that end, it has held that disclosure of documents may properly be ordered somewhat more readily than is usual in judicial review proceedings.[101]

The House has had to grapple with the separation of legislative and judicial functions in several contexts under the HRA. First, the obligation in section 3 of the Act to read and give effect to legislation in a manner compatible with Convention rights applies only so far as it is possible to do so.[102] Decisions must be based on a reading of the text of the legislation, but it must be a reading, not a

---

[98] *R (Animal Defenders International) v Secretary of State for Culture, Media and Sport* [2008] 1 AC 1312, para 33.

[99] *Wilson v First County Trust Ltd (No 2)* [2004] 1 AC 816, para 62 *per* Lord Nicholls of Birkenhead.

[100] See Lord Walker of Gestingthorpe (dissenting) in *Re S* [2008] 3 WLR 76, para 83.

[101] See eg *R (Daly) v Secretary of State for the Home Department* [2001] 2 AC 532, paras 27–8 *per* Lord Steyn; *A v Secretary of State for the Home Department* [2005] 2 AC 68, especially *per* Lord Bingham of Cornhill at paras 37–42; *Huang v Secretary of State for the Home Department* [2007] 2 AC 167, para 13; *Tweed v Parades Commission for Northern Ireland* [2007] 1 AC 650 (disclosure of documents in judicial review proceedings).

[102] HRA, s 3(1).

wholesale re-writing; the latter would be legislation, not interpretative adjudication. However, the labels 'interpretation' and 'legislation' do not tell us where the line between them should be drawn; they only describe a conclusion about the constitutional acceptability of the action taken. When deciding on the constitutional appropriateness of judicial action under section 3 to support a right, the House takes account of the significance and nature of the right itself and of Parliament's 'emphatic adjuration' to give effect to it.[103]

On this basis the House has read legislation preventing a defendant charged with a sexual offence from raising the complainant's previous sexual activity as subject to an implied proviso allowing evidence and questions which are truly probative in relation to a matter on which the defendant's fair opportunity to put his case depends, to permit a fair hearing under ECHR Article 6.[104] Legislation requiring a defendant to show some fact has been read as imposing only an evidential burden (requiring the accused to produce some credible evidence that puts the fact in issue, after which the probative burden is borne by the prosecution) rather than a legal, or persuasive, burden (requiring proof on the balance of probabilities), if a legal burden would place a disproportionate burden on the accused and unreasonably interfere with the presumption of innocence under Article 6(2) of the ECHR.[105] Again, where the House had held before the 1998 Act came into force that the Rent Act 1977, allowing a person living with a secure tenant as his or her husband or wife to succeed to the tenancy on the tenant's death, applied to unmarried heterosexual couples but not to same-sex couples, the House by a majority treated section 3 of the 1998 Act as permitting and extended reading of 'person who was living with the original tenant as his or her wife or husband' as including the survivor of a same-sex couple, in order to make the legislation compatible with the right to be free of discrimination taken together with the right to respect for private life and the home.[106] In these cases it was said that nothing alien to the drafter's meaning was being introduced to the legislation, and the readings were consistent with the structure of the legislation.

This seems to be true of most of the cases, but it is not self-evident, particularly in the 'rape shield' case. In this area, drawing the line between interpretation and legislation calls for delicate judgement. Judges' views can be expected to have particular authority when determining what is essential to a fair trial. For example, in *R (Hammond) v Secretary of State for the Home Department* legislation provided that the minimum term of imprisonment to be served by certain life-sentence prisoners should be set or reviewed by a High Court judge, but the prisoner was not to be entitled to an oral hearing. The House held that this

---

[103] *R v A (No 2)* [2002] 1 AC 45, para 44 *per* Lord Steyn.   [104] ibid.

[105] *R v Lambert* [2002] 2 AC 545; *AG's Reference (No 4 of 2002)* [2005] 1 AC 264, paras 50–2 *per* Lord Bingham of Cornhill in relation to s 11 of the Terrorism Act 2000, with whom the other Law Lords agreed. Compare *Sheldrake v Director of Public Prosecutions*, ibid at para 41, holding the reverse onus rule in s 5(2) of the Road Traffic Act 1988 to be justified and not to violate Art 6.

[106] *Ghaidan v Godin-Mendoza* [2004] 2 AC 557, on Rent Act 1977, Sch 1, para 2(2).

violated the prisoner's right to a fair hearing and accepted the Home Secretary's concession that section 3(1) of the HRA should be applied so as to subject the legislation in question to an implied discretion on the part of the High Court judge to order an oral hearing when that is necessary to secure the prisoner's right to a fair hearing.[107]

Of course, it sometimes seems clear to the House that making legislation compatible with rights would require more interference with it than the judiciary could justify. Judges could not properly read into legislation a scheme for maintaining oversight of a local authority's making and implementing of decisions on child care when one of the main planks of the legislation was the removal of courts from that process (save by way of judicial review), even if the authority was failing to protect the children's Convention rights.[108] Nor could they read out of legislation express provisions requiring the Home Secretary to act as the final arbiter of the period of imprisonment to be served by a life-sentence prisoner before being considered for release on licence.[109] It was regarded as improper to change the consistent approach of lower courts in interpreting the statutory requirement for the parties to a valid marriage to be respectively male and female as leaving gender reassignment therapy out of account, mainly because reading in a special proviso for people who had undergone gender reassignment therapy would have required the court to specify the stage of treatment at which the law should recognise the change of gender, and would have had far-reaching implications for other areas of law such as social security, pensions, and discrimination.[110]

These interpretative questions thus fall to be settled within a rich mix of constitutional principles and structures and Convention rights. One factor is the availability of a declaration of incompatibility under section 4 of the 1998 Act, to be used if it proves impossible to read a piece of primary legislation compatibly with Convention rights. Partly because the Government and the Queen in Parliament have so far legislated to address, more or less convincingly, final declarations of incompatibility under section 4, even in sensitive, terrorism-related cases, the Law Lords feel able to limit their intrusion on legislative functions under section 3. They are all the more ready to use section 4 as it leaves the incompatible legislation in force until it is amended or repealed, so judges need not take the apparently controversial step of striking down legislation or work out transitional measures.[111] The House has successfully established clear

---

[107] [2006] 1 AC 603, though only Lord Brown, para 46, unequivocally accepted that the concession was correct.

[108] *Re S (Minors) (Care Order: Implementation of Care Plan)* [2002] 2 AC 291.

[109] *R (Anderson) v Secretary of State for the Home Department* [2003] 1 AC 837.

[110] *Bellinger v Bellinger (Lord Chancellor intervening)* [2003] 2 AC 467, especially at paras 36–49 *per* Lord Nicholls of Birkenhead, 68–9 *per* Lord Hope of Craighead, 76 *per* Lord Hobhouse of Woodborough, and 83 *per* Lord Rodger of Earlsferry.

[111] See A Kavanagh, 'Choosing between sections 3 and 4 of the HRA: judicial reasoning after *Ghaidan v Mendoza*' in H Fenwick, G Phillipson, and R Masterman (eds), *Judicial Reasoning under the UK HRA* (Cambridge: Cambridge University Press, 2007) ch 5.

principles in relation to the novel device of section 4. First, a declaration of incompatibility is only available after the legislation has been assessed by reference to section 3 and found incompatible.[112] Secondly, it cannot be used where the Act is inapplicable, whether *ratione temporis* or *ratione personae*.[113] Thirdly, declarations of incompatibility alert the Government and legislature to a problem with legislation, so there is no point in making one where the legislation has already been amended,[114] although it is proper to make one where amending legislation has been drafted but not yet passed, in order to provide vindication (though not a proper remedy) for the victim's violated right.[115] These principles respect constitutional proprieties while giving proper effect to section 4.

Another problem arising from parliamentary sovereignty has been the meaning of section 6(2) of the HRA, which provides that it is not unlawful for a public authority to act incompatibly with a Convention right if—

(a) as the result of one or more provisions of primary legislation, the authority could not have acted differently; or (b) in the case of one or more provisions of, or made under, primary legislation which cannot be read and given effect in a way which is compatible with the Convention rights, the authority was acting so as to give effect to or enforce those provisions.

Each of these paragraphs has two possible readings, one giving a wide exemption to public authorities, the other a narrower one. Lord Hope has been the leading exponent of reading both paragraphs as broadly as possible, giving the maximum protection to public authorities implementing statutory schemes. In *R v Kansal (No 2)*, evidence of a self-incriminatory statement obtained from the defendant under statutory compulsion had been used as evidence against him, incompatibly with ECHR Article 6. Lord Hope alone suggested that the prosecutor who acted incompatibly with Article 6 could not have been acting unlawfully under section 6(1) of the HRA, because he had been giving effect to the statutory scheme.[116] However, the legislation had merely obliged the defendant to answer questions without benefit of privilege against self-incrimination or exclusion of the replies from evidence at trial. It had not compelled the prosecutor to use the evidence so obtained.

Choosing between wide and narrow interpretations of section 6(2) has become important in at least three cases before the House. In *R (Hooper) v Secretary of State for Work and Pensions*[117] the claimants were widowers who challenged a decision of the Secretary of State to give effect to legislation entitling a widow, but

---

[112] *Wilson v First County Trust Ltd (No 2)* [2004] 1 AC 816.
[113] ibid; *R (Rusbridger) v AG* [2004] 1 AC 357.
[114] *Doherty v Birmingham CC* [2008] 3 WLR 636.
[115] *Bellinger v Bellinger* [2003] 2 AC 467.
[116] [2002] 2 AC 69, paras 85–8. The legislation amended following the decision of the Strasbourg court in *Saunders v United Kingdom* (1997) 27 EHRR 313.
[117] [2005] 1 WLR 1681.

not a widower, to certain payments on the death of her husband, and not to make equivalent payments to widowers *ex gratia*. The House accepted that the statutory scheme was discriminatory, violating ECHR Article 14 taken together with Article 1 of Protocol 1. However it concluded that the Secretary of State was saved from unlawfulness by section 6(2)(b), because he had merely been giving effect to the statutory scheme. The HRA could not turn a discretion to make *ex gratia* payments into an obligation.[118]

In *R (Wilkinson) v Inland Revenue Commissioners*, on the other hand, the Inland Revenue Commissioners were held to have no power to make an extra-statutory concession allowing widowers to claim a statutory bereavement allowance, restricted in a discriminatory way to widows only, in order to pursue equality between men and women, rather than deal pragmatically with hardship or transitory anomalies or make policy in the interstices of tax legislation. It followed that their refusal to make such a concession was protected by section 6(2)(a).[119]

In cases concerning social security payments and tax policy, there are good reasons for protecting the authorities which administer the system against liability if they are simply doing what primary legislation requires. The alternative approach would both cross a line carefully drawn by Act of Parliament and impose an additional burden on the exchequer and tax-payers. However, it is less clear that this is equally appropriate where legislation confers a discretion or power, rather than a duty, on a public authority. This issue arose squarely in *Doherty v Birmingham City Council*.[120] Birmingham City Council, exercising its statutory power to manage a council-occupied caravan site, served notice on gipsies to leave the site where they had been living for about 17 years, then brought County Court proceedings for possession. Section 5(1) of the Mobile Homes Act 1983 provided that normal protection against eviction did not apply to 'land occupied by a local authority as a caravan site providing accommodation for gipsies...' The gipsies wanted to argue that the possession proceedings violated both substantive and procedural rights to respect for their home under ECHR Article 8.[121] However, they were precluded from doing so by majority decisions of the House of Lords holding that the legislation had established by a bright-line rule that it would never be justifiable to restrict a landowner's proprietary or contractual rights in order to protect an occupier's right to respect for

---

[118] ibid, *per* Lords Nicholls, Hoffmann, and Hope at paras 6, 48–52, and 72–5 and 82 respectively. Lord Brown of Eaton-under-Heywood at paras 105–26 (with whom Lord Scott of Foscote at para 90 agreed) thought that it would have been an unlawful abuse of power for the Secretary of State to make *ex gratia* payments to widowers under the prerogative when that was inconsistent with the statutory scheme, so the case fell under paragraph (a) rather than (b).

[119] [2005] 1 WLR 1718, paras 20–3 *per* Lord Hoffmann, with whom Lords Nicholls, Hope, Scott and, in relation to s 6(1)(a) but not various *obiter dicta*, Lord Brown, agreed.

[120] [2008] 3 WLR 636.

[121] See *Connors v United Kingdom* (2005) 40 EHRR 189; *McCann v United Kingdom* [2008] LGR 474.

the home. Any challenge was therefore limited to an application for a declaration of incompatibility, which would leave the legislation effective, or reliance on ordinary judicial review principles, particularly *Wednesbury* unreasonableness, in rare cases where such a claim could credibly be asserted.[122] When the issue appeared again before the Lords in *Doherty*, the council relied heavily on section 6(2)(b) of the HRA. Lord Hope agreed that section 6(2) protected a public authority which 'is doing what it has been authorised to do by the primary legislation' even if it did so partly in reliance on a non-statutory power.[123] Lord Walker, likewise, deprecated any 'distortion' of the principle of parliamentary sovereignty.[124]

Lord Mance took a narrower view of section 6(2), pointing out that nothing in the 1983 Act made it improper for the council to take account of Convention rights.[125] This view gives proper weight to the rights and the fact that the HRA is itself an Act of Parliament, requiring judges to give more significance to Convention rights than merely treating them as relevant considerations. It also takes seriously the distinction between making a statutory provision otiose and controlling the manner of its implementation; between a public authority having a statutory duty to act in a particular way and having a discretion; and between doing something that will always be incompatible with a right and doing something that might be compatible in a manner that makes it incompatible. Both points of view represent political choices, but Lord Mance's, giving more weight to Convention rights, is, it is respectfully submitted, to be preferred. It avoids the risk of emasculating the rights whenever a public authority is acting within a statutory framework, a danger which the House confronted, not entirely convincingly, in *Huang v Secretary of State for the Home Department*[126] when trying to explain why the approach adopted by the majority in *Kay v Lambeth London Borough Council* in relation to housing was not equally applicable to the review of immigration decisions, as counsel for the Home Secretary had argued.

In these tangled constitutional thickets judges have sought to simplify their paths by seeking principles for dealing with inter-institutional relationships. Two such principles, much trumpeted, are the discretionary area of judgment and deference. Even before the 1998 Act came fully into force, Lord Hope had said that where individual rights and social needs compete, necessitating an assessment of proportionality, '[i]n some circumstances it will be appropriate for the courts to recognise that there is an area of judgment within which the judiciary will defer, on democratic grounds, to the considered opinion of the elected body or person whose act or decision is said to be incompatible with the Convention.' His

---

[122] *Harrow LBC v Qazi* [2004] 1 AC 983 (Lord Bingham of Cornhill and Lord Steyn dissenting), as explained by the majority of a seven-judge Committee in *Kay v Lambeth LBC, Leeds CC v Price* [2006] 2 AC 465, especially at para 110 *per* Lord Hope of Craighead (Lord Bingham of Cornhill, Lord Nicholls of Birkenhead, and Lord Walker of Gestingthorpe dissenting on this point).

[123] ibid, para 21.

[124] ibid, paras 97–104. Lord Rodger agreed with Lord Hope and Lord Walker: para 89.

[125] ibid, paras 141–53. The quotation comes from para 153.

[126] [2007] 2 WLR 581, para 17 *per* Baroness Hale.

Lordship suggested that the area of judgment would more readily be recognised in relation to qualified rights, social or economic policy, and terrorism than in respect of rights which are not expressly qualified in the Convention or are of high constitutional importance or 'of a kind where the courts are especially well placed to assess the need for protection'.[127] Furthermore, the proportionality of an interference with a right is ultimately always a question of law of which judges are the final arbiters; it is not open to judges to abrogate this responsibility by way of deference.[128] This is a matter of constitutional propriety: judges must decide on the allocation of power between branches of government on the basis of legal principles.[129] Another basis for deference may be an assessment of expertise: which body is most competent to make the decision? Where a general rule is needed, a legislature will normally be the more competent body. Where the challenge is to the Convention compatibility of a decision about an individual case, the court may be as well placed to make a decision as anyone else, unless the subject matter is highly specialised, in which case the view of a specialist decision-maker may carry considerable weight.[130]

To some extent, this over-simplifies the matter, since threats to rights often stem from a mixture of rules and individualised decisions relating to them, or of social policy and fundamental rights.[131] Enumerating potentially relevant factors does not resolve tensions between them, although the list may remind courts to stay within their review function and not to step into the shoes of the primary decision-maker.[132] The problem is the weight to be accorded to the views of

---

[127] *R v Director of Public Prosecutions, ex p Kebilene* [2000] 2 AC 326, 381, citing Lord Lester of Herne Hill QC and D Pannick, *Human Rights Law and Practice* (London: Butterworths, 1st edn 1999), para 3.21 on the 'discretionary area of judgment'.

[128] *A v Secretary of State for the Home Department* [2005] 2 AC 68. This may require a narrow interpretation of common law powers of public authorities: see eg *R (Laporte) v Chief Constable of Gloucestershire Constabulary* [2007] 2 AC 105 (preventing breach of the peace).

[129] *R (ProLife Alliance) v British Broadcasting Corporation* [2004] 1 AC 185, paras 75–6 *per* Lord Hoffmann.

[130] For examples of the latter, see the deference shown by the majority of the House to the Special Immigration Appeal Commission's assessment of the existence of a public emergency threatening the life of the nation in *A v Secretary of State for the Home Department* (n 126); the Foreign Secretary's assessment (rather than that of the Commission) of the effect on the UK's national security of allowing a person to engage in terrorism abroad from UK soil in *Secretary of State for the Home Department v Rehman* [2003] 1 AC 153; and the assessment of the Director of the Serious Fraud Office, having been consulted by the Attorney General who, in turn, had been consulted by the Ministry of Defence, the Cabinet Secretary, and the Prime Minister, that the Director had to accept the view of the Government that continuing to investigate alleged bribery in relation to an arms contract between the UK Government and Saudi Arabia would damage the UK's national security: *R (Corner House Research) v Director of the Serious Fraud Office* [2008] 3 WLR 568. See also *International Transport Roth GmbH v Secretary of State for the Home Department* [2003] QB 782, paras 83–7 *per* Laws LJ (dissenting).

[131] See *Re S* [2008] 3 WLR 76, para 48 *per* Lord Hope, stepping back slightly from his earlier dicta in *R v Director of Public Prosecutions, ex p Kebilene* [2000] 2 AC 326.

[132] See *R (ProLife Alliance) v British Broadcasting Corporation* [2004] 1 AC 185, paras 137 and 139 *per* Lord Walker of Gestingthorpe. For examples, see *A v Secretary of State for the Home Department* (n 128), and *Re S* [2008] 3 WLR 76.

different decision-makers. Where no reasons have been given, as is typically the case where legislation has established a bright-line rule that encapsulates its choice of balance between competing interests, that choice will be given considerable weight (though not to the extent of preventing the courts from deciding whether the rule interferes unjustifiably with a Convention right, as the court must be the ultimate authority on the question whether the right has been violated).[133] Where the legislature has merely created a discretion, for example by establishing a licensing or regulatory regime, the balance will be struck (either generally or in individual cases) by a subordinate, usually executive, body with its own level of democratic legitimacy and specialist competence which will be taken into account in deciding how much weight to give to the reasoning (if any) of that body on the issue of justification. Where the decision-maker gives reasons for striking the balance in a particular way a reviewing court should give considerable weight to them, taking account of the constitutional position and expertise of the body concerned. The more evidence there is that the decision-maker gave careful consideration to the balance to be struck in the light of human rights consider-ations, the more weight its assessment will be given.[134] But if that body gives no reasons, it does not mean that the rule or decision will be treated as violating the right, because judges have to decide whether there has been a violation, not whether the decision-maker or rule-maker has given adequate reasons.[135] It simply means that the court must make its own assessment of the balance without that assistance, behaving as if it were the primary decision-maker to that extent.[136]

It seems, therefore, that the idea of deference or discretionary area of judgment is merely shorthand for complex notions of constitutional propriety and insti-tutional competence which affect not justiciability but the weight which courts will give to an assessment by another decision-maker of the justification for an interference with a Convention right (or, to put it another way, the intensity of review).[137] Their Lordships have rightly not generally treated the notion as a practical aid to concrete decision-making.

Law Lords have had difficulty in working out the implications of constitutional principles where the HRA overlaps the devolution legislation, another consti-tutional innovation. Under the devolution legislation, Convention rights operate as limits on the legal competence of devolved legislative and executive bodies.

---

[133] *R (Williamson) v Secretary of State for Education and Employment* [2005] 2 AC 246; *Kay v Lambeth LBC* [2006] 2 AC 465.

[134] This applies even where the decision-maker is the Queen in Parliament enacting an Act of Parliament: *R (Animal Defenders International) v Secretary of State for Culture, Media and Sport* [2008] 1 AC 1312, para 33 *per* Lord Bingham of Cornhill.

[135] *R (SB) v Governors of Denbigh High School* [2007] 1 AC 100; *Belfast CC v Miss Behavin' Ltd* [2007] 1 WLR 1420.

[136] *Huang v Secretary of State for the Home Department* [2007] 2 AC 167; *Belfast CC v Miss Behavin' Ltd.* [2007] 1 WLR 1420, para 37 *per* Baroness Hale of Richmond.

[137] *R (ProLife Alliance) v British Broadcasting Corporation* [2004] 1 AC 185 at paras 132–9 *per* Lord Walker of Gestingthorpe, discussing Lord Steyn's exposition of the principle of proportionality in *R (Daly) v Secretary of State for the Home Department* [2001] 2 AC 532, paras 27–8.

Under the HRA, by contrast, the rights impose obligations on all public authorities, and individuals may obtain both public and private law remedies to vindicate victims' rights. The rights thus apply to different bodies (though there is some overlap) and serve different purposes. The possibility of divergent meanings in different constitutional and legal contexts has divided the House, largely on national lines. The Scottish Law Lords have supported autonomous interpretation of rights for the constitutional context of devolution, but most English Law Lords have reacted strongly in favour of uniform interpretation. In *HM Advocate v R*[138] the Privy Council sat with three Scottish judges and two judges whose experience had been within the English system. The issue was whether undue delay by the Scottish Executive in bringing a prosecution violated the right to a hearing within a reasonable time under ECHR Article 6(1), so that HM Advocate, as a Scottish minister bound by the Scotland Act 1998, would act beyond competence in continuing the prosecution. The majority, consisting of the Scottish judges, decided that the right to a hearing within a reasonable time acted as a bar to prosecution in the context of the devolution system.

Yet in a non-devolution case from England the House of Lords took a different view. An Appellate Committee of nine Law Lords sat in *Attorney General's Reference (No 2 of 2001)*.[139] Of these, seven could be described as 'English' judges and only two were Scots. The House held that it would not be appropriate to stay criminal proceedings on the ground of delay unless the delay made a fair hearing impossible. The majority went out of their way to say that their decision was irreconcilable with *HM Advocate v R*, in effect disapproving the Privy Council decision. The two Scottish Law Lords dissented. With respect, the majority were wrong on two grounds. First, they disregarded the constitutional differences between England and Scotland under the Scotland Act 1998. The English approach focused on how a defendant could be compensated for delay, and confused that with the question whether the right to a hearing within a reasonable time had been violated. This cannot apply where, as in Scotland, delay deprives the prosecuting authority of competence to continue the prosecution. In view of the constitutional differences between England and Scotland, there was no good reason why Scotland and England should not have gone their own ways, as long as each of them gave at least as much protection to the right to a hearing within a reasonable time as is required by Article 6 of the ECHR. Secondly, the majority gave too little weight to the separation in ECHR Article 6(1) between the different but complementary rights to a fair hearing and to a hearing within a reasonable time. The English majority, in their pursuit of uniformity of interpretation of Convention rights across the UK, failed to recognise the significance of changes made by the devolution settlement to the constitutional structure of the UK, which may require different responses to threatened violations of Convention rights in devolved and non-devolved matters.

---

[138] [2004] 1 AC 462.   [139] [2004] 2 AC 72.

Territoriality and Convention rights

Two difficult issues have arisen in relation to the territorial scope of Convention rights. The first is whether the rights have a different content in purely domestic cases as compared with those with an international element, such as removal of immigrants and extradition. As noted earlier,[140] the House was able to hold that public authorities may sometimes act unlawfully under the 1998 Act if they remove a person from the UK to another country where he or she would be at significant risk of suffering violation of Convention rights. But their Lordships have identified an ambiguity in the Strasbourg case law as to the *content* of obligations under the ECHR in cases with an international element. Absolute rights, such as that under Article 3, remain absolute in all circumstances, but the resulting positive obligation on the state to protect people against threats from third parties, while absolute, is only to take such steps as are reasonable in the circumstances to counter a real and immediate threat.[141] It is hard to categorise obligations towards people from whom the state contemplates withdrawing active assistance, or whom it plans to send to another state, as positive or negative. If the right to be free of inhuman treatment or punishment under Article 3 has the same content in international as in purely domestic cases, people would be entitled to protection from UK authorities against any treatment in another state's institutions that would be treated as violating Article 3 in the UK. That might make it impossible for the UK to remove or extradite people to many states which are not party to the ECHR, including at least some states of the USA. In *Soering v United Kingdom*[142] the Strasbourg court seemed to contemplate a degree of relativism in relation to the meaning of inhuman or degrading treatment in extradition cases to take account of the importance of international cooperation in the prosecution of offences, allowing the extraditing state to ask whether the treatment would be disproportionate to the alleged crime. However, in *Kafkaris v Cyprus* the court observed, *obiter*, that an irreducible sentence of life imprisonment without realistic possibility of parole 'may raise an issue' under Article 3,[143] while in *Saadi v Italy*[144] the court reasserted the absolute nature of Article 3 and denied any possibility of watering it down with a proportionality assessment.

In *R (Wellington) v Secretary of State for the Home Department*,[145] the House had to grapple with this difficulty. The applicant was the subject of a request for extradition to the state of Missouri charged with first degree murder. If convicted

---

[140] See the text at n 63 above.
[141] *Saadi v Italy* Application No 37201/96, judgment of 28 February 2008; *E v Chief Constable of the Royal Ulster Constabulary* [2008] 3 WLR 1208, para 10 *per* Baroness Hale of Richmond.
[142] (1989) 11 EHRR 439.
[143] Application No 21906/04, judgment of 12 February 2008, GC, para 97. The sentence in that case was held on the facts not to be irreducible.
[144] See n 141 above.   [145] [2009] 1 AC 335.

there he faced life imprisonment without the possibility of parole. The majority of the House decided that, in relation to the risk of inhuman or degrading treatment or punishment (though not torture), treatment had to inflict greater suffering to violate Article 3 in extradition cases than in purely domestic cases. This relativism, authorised by *Soering*, was said not to have been qualified by *Saadi*, and to be consistent with the Strasbourg court's judgment in *Kafkaris v Cyprus*, which had not suggested that a full-life term would always violate Article 3 in extradition cases. The minority took a different view. As they correctly observed, the text of Article 3 did not justify distinguishing between torture and inhuman or degrading treatment. Nor, they considered, did the case law of the Strasbourg court (including *Saadi*, which they considered to mark a departure from the relativism of *Soering*) justify giving a narrower meaning to any part of Article 3 in extradition cases merely on account of the public interest in prosecuting suspected offenders.[146] Their Lordships ultimately refused to interfere with the extradition because life imprisonment would become inhuman or degrading only at the point where a convict had been imprisoned for so long that the punishment became disproportionate to the original offence,[147] but the criticisms levelled by Lords Brown and Scott at the reasoning of the majority are, with respect, compelling. The majority's fears about the practical difficulties facing the international extradition regime should be addressed by maintaining a high threshold to be overstepped by anyone claiming to have suffered inhuman or degrading treatment, not by introducing relativism to an absolute right.

The second international issue is the extent to which obligations under the HRA bind UK public authorities when exercising functions in or in respect of territories outside the UK. Article 1 of the ECHR requires the High Contracting Parties to secure Convention rights to everyone within their 'jurisdiction'. Unnecessarily, UK courts have treated the interpretation of ECHR Article 1 in international law as determining the reach of Convention rights in municipal law under the HRA. The judges have taken the view that international law must govern because of the 'no more and no less protection' principle articulated in *Ullah*. They have therefore had to resolve difficult and controversial questions of international law, whereas the issue should have been viewed through the lens of domestic constitutional law.

One group to have suffered as a result are people in some of the UK's colonies and dependent territories. Where the UK Government had not previously declared under Article 56 of the ECHR that the ECHR extended to South Georgia and the Sandwich Islands, in *R (Quark Fisheries Ltd) v Secretary of State for Foreign and Commonwealth Affairs* the House held that the Crown acting in right of that territory when licensing fishing operations was not subject to the requirements of the Convention.[148] In *R (Bancoult) v Secretary of State for Foreign*

---

[146] ibid, paras 85–7 *per* Lord Brown of Eaton-under-Heywood.   [147] ibid, paras 88–9.
[148] [2006] 1 AC 529.

and Commonwealth Affairs (No 2) they held that the ECHR had no application to the Chagos Islands because the UK had made no declaration extending it to them.[149]

The House has faced even greater difficulty in relation to the duties owed by or to British forces abroad, particularly when operating as part of the UN-sanctioned multinational forces in Iraq and Afghanistan. The House has found three grounds for limiting these duties. First, it has held that any obligation to service personnel in committing them to military action is very limited, if it exists at all. There is presumably an obligation under Article 2 of the ECHR not to kill them, but the decision to go to war does not engage their right to life under Article 2, and the positive obligations under Article 2 (such as the duty to hold an effective, independent investigation into the cause of violent death) apply only where the death itself might have amounted to a violation of the obligation not to kill.[150]

Secondly, the House has limited the obligation to foreign nationals caught up in military action abroad by reference to the nature of the rights in international law. While recognising that the Strasbourg jurisprudence was not altogether consistent,[151] it has decided that duties could only extend to geographical areas where UK forces and administrators exercised sufficient control to make it practical to expect them to secure Convention rights effectively to the population. Local people caught up in an exchange of fire in Southern Iraq therefore did not suffer a violation of their Convention right to life.[152] However, where death or detention occurred in an area that was clearly within the control of UK forces, for example at a military camp or prison run by them, Article 2 or 5 applied unless there was a special reason for excluding it.[153]

Thirdly, the House has held (following Strasbourg) that obligations may be restricted by other rules of international law. One of these applies where UK personnel are acting as part of an operation supported or required by a UN Security Council resolution to uphold international peace and security under Chapter VII of the Charter. In *R (Al-Jedda) v Secretary of State for Defence*,[154] concerning detention by British forces of a suspected insurgent in Iraq, the House of Lords struggled to protect the integrity of UK constitutional law against assertions that its human rights standards had been excluded by the Strasbourg court, which in *Behrami v France*[155] had attributed responsibility for implementation of such resolutions by a military force, KFOR, in former Yugoslavia to the UN rather than to the states that contributed to that force. The House (by a majority) partially got round the problem of attribution of responsibility by distinguishing *Behrami* on the ground that it had been concerned with a different

---

[149] [2008] 3 WLR 955.   [150] *R (Gentle) v Prime Minister* [2008] 1 AC 1356.
[151] Compare the decision in *Banković v Belgium* (2001) 44 EHRR SE5 with that in *Ilaşcu v Moldova and Russia* (2004) 41 EHRR 46.
[152] *R (Al-Skeini) v Secretary of State for Defence* [2008] 1 AC 153.
[153] *Al-Skeini*, ibid; *R (Al-Jedda) v Secretary of State for Defence* [2008] 1 AC 332.
[154] [2008] 1 AC 332.   [155] *Behrami v France* (2007) 45 EHRR SE10, GC.

mission, that to Kosovo which had full UN Security Council authority, rather than that to Iraq, in relation to which the Security Council had merely passed a resolution to manage the occupation of Iraq after the invasion had occurred. However, the House broadly accepted the view of the Strasbourg court that, as a matter of public international law, UN Security Council resolutions under Chapter VII of the UN Charter overrode rights under the ECHR by virtue of Article 103 of the Charter. This is a questionable view,[156] as demonstrated by the European Court of Justice later when it protected rights in EU law against the effect of Chapter VII Resolutions.[157] It is understandable that a national court would tread carefully where the European Court of Human Rights refuses to step at all, but the issue can probably not be ducked indefinitely.

The temporal application of Convention rights

In relation to the temporal application of Convention rights, the House entangled itself in complications. The presumption that legislation does not apply retrospectively applies to the HRA.[158] After a period in which it was assumed that the Act could apply in appeals against decisions made before 2 October 2000 (the date on which the Act came fully into force),[159] the House backtracked, holding by a majority that it applied only to cases arising on or after that date.[160] In *R v Kansal (No 2)*[161] a pre-Act conviction based on compelled self-incrimination was referred back by the Criminal Cases Review Commission on the ground that the use of the evidence was incompatible with the right to a fair hearing under ECHR Article 6. A majority of the House thought that the House's earlier decision in *R v Lambert*[162] had been wrongly decided, but four Law Lords (Lord Hope dissenting) thought that it would have been inappropriate to depart from *Lambert*, so the wrong decisions stood to be applied in later cases.[163] As a result, it has proved impossible to provide a domestic remedy for people whose convictions violated Convention rights before 2 October 2000.[164] Fortunately this embarrassing confusion related only to a transitional problem, albeit one of great importance.

---

[156] See D Feldman, 'The role of constitutional principles in protecting international peace and security through international, supranational and national legal institutions' in C Geiringer and DR Knight (eds), *Seeing the World Whole: Essays in Honour of Sir Kenneth Keith* (Wellington, New Zealand: Victoria University Press, 2008) 17–47.

[157] Joined Cases C-402/05 P *Kadi v Council and Commission* and C-415/05 P *Al Barakaat International Foundation v Council and Commission*, Grand Chamber, 3 September 2008, as yet unreported.

[158] *Wilson v First County Trust Ltd (No 2)* [2004] 1 AC 816.

[159] *R v Director of Public Prosecutions, ex p Kebilene* [2000] 2 AC 326.

[160] *R v Lambert* [2002] 2 AC 545 (Lord Slynn of Hadley, Lord Hope of Craighead, Lord Clyde, and Lord Hutton; Lord Steyn dissented).

[161] [2002] 2 AC 69.   [162] [2002] 2 AC 545.

[163] *R v Rezvi; R v Benjafield* [2003] 1 AC 1099.   [164] See eg *R v Lyons* [2003] 1 AC 976.

The meaning of 'public authority' and the effect of Convention rights on private law

Significant problems have divided the House in identifying 'hybrid' public authorities under section 6(3)(b) of the HRA, which provides that a private person or body is a public authority, and so is generally required by section 6(1) to act compatibly with Convention rights, when it is exercising 'functions of a public nature'. It has proved difficult to find satisfactory criteria for deciding when a private party is exercising a function of a public nature. In *Aston Cantlow and Wilmcote with Billesley Parochial Church Council v Wallbank*[165] the House appeared to prefer the functional test, holding that a parochial church council enforcing a right to have the church's chancel roof repaired at the expense of a lay rector was a private (religious) body enforcing a private property right. This seemed to establish that religious institutions are not all-purpose public authorities (even the Church of England, despite its special constitutional status), and that one has to look in detail at exactly what a private body is doing (in that case, enforcing a private-law right rather than exercising a public-law power) when deciding whether it is exercising a public function so as to be a 'hybrid' public authority.

But what is the position where an all-purpose public authority such as the NHS contracts with a private provider to deliver services which are ultimately the responsibility of the public authority? In *YL v Birmingham City Council* the House divided on the issue. The majority refused to treat private providers as public authorities.[166] The effect is to protect private providers but to deprive a large number of vulnerable people of the protection of Convention rights, significantly limiting the potential reach of the HRA. Like the cases on possession proceedings discussed above, this may reflect the common lawyer's traditional resistance to letting human rights dilute the absolute character of property and contractual rights. Other cases in which a private party seeks to rely on Convention rights in support of a statutory or common law claim against another private party have elicited similarly divided reactions. Uncertainty about this is built into the structure of the Act. While the scheme of the Act makes it clear that the main impact of Convention rights will be vertical—ie operating against public authorities rather than public bodies—the Act requires horizontal effect where the result of the case depends on the reading or effect given to a statute,[167] and where a court is considering making an order affecting the right to freedom of expression, especially in cases concerning journalistic, literary, or artistic material or the right of a religious organisation to exercise its freedom of thought, conscience, and religion.[168] Views of commentators have

---

[165] [2004] 1 AC 546.   [166] [2008] 1 AC 95.   [167] HRA s 3.
[168] HRA ss 12 and 13.

differed,[169] but in the event the House has edged towards a degree of horizontal effect, though slowly and with some reluctance. In *Wainwright v Home Office*[170] the House rejected the claim that there was at common law a tort of invasion of privacy, or that the common law had to develop such a tort in order to give effect to Article 8 of the ECHR. So far as there had been a gap in protection required by Article 8 it related to interference with privacy by public authorities. That gap had been filled by the HRA, which might also produce some protection against invasion of privacy by private persons by way of horizontal effect. If it did not, any such extension would need detailed legislation. Lord Walker subsequently spoke of the 'spectre' of having to develop the common law to make it fully compatible with Convention rights having been firmly rejected.[171]

A similarly discouraging message came from the majority of the House in *Smith v Chief Constable of Sussex Police*, where the claimant had suffered serious injuries at the hands of his former partner having informed the police about many specific death-threats that the partner had made against him. The claimant sued the police in negligence. His claim was struck out on the ground that the police were immune from suit, and he appealed. Lord Bingham would have used ECHR Articles 2 and 3 to restrict the public interest immunity of the police from negligence liability in respect of the investigation and prevention of crime. His Lordship wanted to develop negligence liability in harmony with the obligations of the state under Article 2 of the ECHR and with liability of the police under the HRA.[172] The other Law Lords rejected the suggestion that the common law should be developed to reflect liability under the ECHR and the 1998 Act. If common law liability reflected the HRA, there would be no need for it, and the desirability for harmony with the HRA could not justify going further than required by Article 2. The majority also considered that the purpose of a claim under the 1998 Act was different from one in tort. The Convention, unlike tort, did not generally aim to compensate people for losses, but rather to vindicate fundamental rights and establish violations by states.[173]

This clearly reflects a mindset which remains slightly uncomfortable about using human rights to determine private relationships. In *R (Greenfield) v Secretary of State for the Home Department*[174] the claimant had been denied an independent tribunal and legal assistance in prison disciplinary proceedings, violating ECHR Article 6. The question was whether he should receive damages. The House held that the finding of a violation constituted just satisfaction in

---

[169] Sir William Wade, 'Human rights and the judiciary' [1998] EHRLR 520, esp at 524ff; M Hunt, 'The horizontal effect of the Human Rights Act' [1998] PL 423; N Bamforth, 'The true "horizontal effect" of the Human Rights Act' (2001) 117 LQR 34; Sir Richard Buxton, 'The HRA and private law' (2000) 116 LQR 48.

[170] [2004] 2 AC 406. This case arose before the HRA took effect, so comments about the effect of the Act are, technically, *obiter*.

[171] *Doherty v Birmingham CC* [2008] 3 WLR 636, para 99.   [172] ibid, 58.

[173] See particularly Lord Hope at 82, Lord Phillips at 98–9, and Lord Brown at 137–8.

[174] [2005] 1 WLR 673.

itself. Apart from the factors violating Article 6, the claimant had received an otherwise fair hearing. The House held that courts should not try to apply a tortious measure of damages to claims under the HRA, but should normally award damages only where there was pecuniary loss and causation was established, or where damages were needed, exceptionally, to provide just satisfaction for non-pecuniary loss.

On this view of human rights, they operate in public law against the state; they should not be used acquisitively, and they have different purposes from private law. This allowed the House by a majority to accept that it might in exceptional cases declare at the instance of an unaffected third party in public interest litigation that a statute should be interpreted in a specific, Convention-compatible way if it would serve a useful purpose.[175] Yet Law Lords have also suggested that human rights should not be invoked for symbolic or public interest purposes, or as part of a political campaign, but only to safeguard the real interests of a victim of an alleged violation.[176] If the latter view is right, human rights are there essentially to protect private interests, like tort, and there is no reason not to use a tortious measure of damages. If the former view is correct, there is nothing wrong with using human rights to improve the quality of public administration by using them to complement a wider, political or public interest campaign, as long as the claimant claims to be a victim of the violation. But neither is exclusively correct. The Law Lords' response to the function of the rights and their role in private law and public interest litigation has not been consistent.

In one area—breach of confidence—the HRA has stimulated a development in common law liability, though it is easier to say what the position now is than to identify the principles justifying the move to that position. The main authority is *Campbell v MGN Ltd*,[177] where a newspaper published a photograph of a well-known model leaving premises of Narcotics Anonymous, with stories referring to her alleged addiction to narcotics. The model sued for breach of confidence, the newspaper relied by way of defence on the right to freedom of expression, and the claimant referred in turn to the right to respect for private life. The House decided that, in the light of the developing case law of the European Court of Human Rights and the Court of Appeal, the English law of breach of confidence could and should be regarded as providing a tort of misuse of private information, giving a remedy against publication of information, including photographs, concerning a person's activity in public space if that obviously affects a matter within the scope of his or her private life or the person has a legitimate expectation of privacy in relation to that matter.[178] The decision that the woman's rights had been infringed on the facts was reached by a three-two majority, but what is

---

[175] *R (Rusbridger) v AG* [2004] 1 AC 357.

[176] *R (Bancoult) v Secretary of State for Foreign and Commonwealth Affairs (No 2)* [2008] 3 WLR 955, para 53 *per* Lord Hoffmann, 116 *per* Lord Rodger, and 120 *per* Lord Carswell. Lord Mance disagreed with the suggestion that any right was symbolic only: para 138.

[177] [2004] 2 AC 457.   [178] ibid. See especially Lord Nicholls of Birkenhead at para 14.

interesting for our purposes is that none of the Law Lords gave a clear explanation of the legal justification for using the Convention right to respect for private life in private law proceedings in this way. The most convincing justification has come from Sedley LJ in the Court of Appeal.[179] As a result, Buxton LJ has referred to the difficulty that has been experienced in explaining how the state's obligation in international law under a human rights treaty could be 'articulated and enforced in actions between private individuals'. He continued:

> However, judges of the highest authority have concluded that that follows from s 6(1) and (3) of the HRA, placing on the courts the obligations appropriate to a public authority... The effect of this guidance is, therefore, that in order to find the rules of the English law of breach of confidence we now have to look in the jurisprudence of arts 8 and 10. Those articles are now not merely of persuasive or parallel effect but... are the very content of the domestic tort that the English court has to enforce.[180]

This illustrates how in this field the House has been content to leave lower courts to develop the theoretical foundations for development, and has not so far produced a consistent view of the effect of Convention rights on the common law. The present position is unsatisfactory for two reasons. First, the requirements of the ECHR change with the Strasbourg court's case law, and more recent decisions, notably *Von Hannover v Germany*,[181] show that the state may have obligations to change law (including constitutional law) to protect people's rights against private, commercial undertakings. Secondly, whilst the ECHR itself does not compel the change to be effected by a particular institution or legal technique within the state, there is no obvious reason why the courts should be unable to respond incrementally through common law development on a case-by-case basis if the law allows Convention rights to be applied horizontally. The question is whether and when the law allows that.

Conclusion

In the last 20 years, and particularly since 2000, human rights have become central to the work and thinking of the Law Lords. This reorientation of values has significantly changed public law and may come to affect private law as well: it can no longer be said, generally, that the Law Lords 'display a political and professional elitism which discourages interference with discretionary decisions of government and professional administrators'.[182] Principled consistency is becoming more important than substantive rationality and pragmatism in most cases, although the search for consistent principles is proving difficult and the

---

[179] In *Douglas and Zeta-Jones v Hello! Ltd* [2001] QB 967, paras 133–6.
[180] *McKennitt v Ash* [2008] QB 73, CA, at paras 10–11 *per* Buxton LJ (citations omitted).
[181] Eur Ct HR, App No 59320/00, judgment of 24 June 2004.
[182] D Feldman, 'Public law values in the House of Lords' (1990) 106 LQR 246–76, 275.

essential requirements that judicial decisions should be workable and ultimately acceptable still operate. There have been a few embarrassing episodes, especially the confusion over the temporal application of the Act, and the over-wide interpretation of section 6(2) of the HRA which threatens to emasculate Convention rights as part of a losing struggle to protect County Courts against having to consider Convention rights in possession proceedings brought by local authorities. But those are isolated embarrassments, and they arise from pragmatic concerns as much as errors of principle.

These are contentious issues, and the Law Lords have varied attitudes. There have been notable divisions over the separation of powers between judiciary and legislature and over the impact of parliamentary sovereignty on the HRA, and deep uneasiness over the extra-territorial application of rights and the relationship between national and international law. The changing structure of the UK's constitutional settlement continues to stretch understanding and cause problems. In respect of the purpose of the HRA and of Convention rights, which affects many aspects of adjudication, their Lordships have not found any one model—public or private law, respecting international law or developing municipal law—consistently satisfying for all purposes. Nor is it yet clear how far (if at all) the House will qualify the common law's traditional commitment to absolute proprietary and contractual rights. But arguments about fundamental principles are never finally settled. Nobody can fail to be impressed by the seriousness and rigour with which the Law Lords, led by Lords Bingham, Nicholls, and Steyn, and despite their differences, have tackled the novel task of making human rights fully part of our law.

31

Non-discrimination and Equality

*Brenda Hale**

Equality before the law is one aspect of the Diceyan concept of the rule of law in which most of the Law Lords were brought up: no man is above the law and all are subject to its constraints and disciplines.[1] Formal equality, in the sense of a right to be treated equally by the law, by public officials, and by private suppliers of worthwhile goods, is a much more recent concept.[2] Universal suffrage arrived only in 1929;[3] anti-discrimination laws began only very tentatively in 1965 but have since developed in scope if not so much in concept;[4] the equal right to the enjoyment of fundamental human rights and freedoms arrived only with the Human Rights Act 1998;[5] and the United Kingdom has still not signed or ratified the 12th Protocol to the European Convention on Human Rights, with its open-ended guarantee of the equal protection of the laws.[6] Substantive

---

* I am deeply indebted to my legal assistant, Corinna Ferguson, for her help in researching the case law and discussing the issues. Errors and opinions are, of course, all my own.

[1] AV Dicey, *An Introduction to the Study of the Law of the Constitution* (London: Macmillan, 10th edn 1959) 193.

[2] It did not feature at all in the preceding study, L Blom-Cooper and G Drewry, *Final Appeal: A Study of the House of Lords in its Judicial Capacity* (Oxford: Clarendon Press, 1972).

[3] The Representation of the People Act 1928 gave women the right to vote on the same terms as men.

[4] Race Relations Act (RRA) 1965, replaced by RRA 1968, and then by RRA 1976, still (with amendments) the governing statute. In other fields the principal legislation is the Equal Pay Act (EPA) 1970 (as amended) and Sex Discrimination Act (SDA) 1975 (as amended); the Disability Discrimination Act (DDA) 1995 (as amended in particular by the DDA 2005); the Employment Equality (Sexual Orientation) Regulations 2003, SI 2003/1661 (as amended), the Employment Equality (Religion or Belief) Regulations 2003, SI 2003/1660 (as amended), the Employment Equality (Age) Regulations 2006, SI 2006/1031 (as amended); the Equality Act 2006; and the Equality Act (Sexual Orientation) Regulations 2007, SI 2007/1263. Additionally the following enactments apply in Northern Ireland: the Equal Pay Act (Northern Ireland) 1970 (as amended), the Sex Discrimination (Northern Ireland) Order 1976 (as amended), the Race Relations (Northern Ireland) Order 1997 (as amended), and the Fair Employment and Treatment (Northern Ireland) Order 1998 (as amended).

[5] Providing remedies in UK law for violations of the rights protected by the European Convention on Human Rights and the Protocols to which the UK is party, including Article 14 (see p 589 below).

[6] The UK has ratified the International Covenant on Civil and Political Rights 1966, art 26 of which is in very similar terms to the 12th Protocol, but this has not become part of UK domestic law.

equality, the recognition that difference between individuals is a strength to be treasured in any democracy, and may from time to time require that reasonable accommodation be made to cater for those differences, is an even more recent concept.

The Law Lords themselves, though diverse in their characters, attitudes, politics, and legal practices, and coming from all parts of Great Britain and Ireland, have been remarkably similar in their backgrounds and education.[7] Not until very recently would it have occurred to anyone to be embarrassed that half the population was not reflected in their ranks, any more than were the visible minorities who have been an increasing proportion of the population over the past 50 years. The first Jewish Law Lord was appointed in 1951[8] but there have been several since then; the first, and so far the only, woman was not appointed until 2004. It would be tempting to look for some correlation between the (slowly) growing diversity among their Lordships and a growing appreciation of the scope and complexity of equality issues. But this would be mere speculation. It is fairer to comment that the House has become comfortable with formal equality but is somewhat less comfortable with the accommodation of difference.

The early twentieth century House of Lords cases showed how inadequate the conventional concepts of the common law, including the canons of statutory interpretation, were to redress traditional and deep-seated sex or race discrimination, whether in statute, by administrative or professional bodies, or in the market place. In *Nairn v University of St Andrews*,[9] the House refused to interpret the word 'person' in the Representation of the People (Scotland) Act 1868 to include women graduates who otherwise fulfilled the qualifications for voting in the election of the Member of Parliament for the Universities of Edinburgh and St Andrews. In *Weinberger v Inglis*,[10] the House refused to interfere with the blatantly discriminatory decision of the committee of the London Stock Exchange to refuse to re-elect a blameless member of 22 years' standing, simply because he had been born in Bavaria; yet he had long been naturalised as a British subject, there were no doubts about his loyalty and allegiance, and members of his family had made significant contributions to the war effort. In *Viscountess Rhondda's Claim*,[11] the majority of the Committee for Privileges held that the Sex Disqualification (Removal) Act 1919 had not removed the inability of a woman who was a peeress in her own right to sit and vote in the House of Lords. According to the Lord Chancellor and the majority, this was not a disqualification comparable to age or bankruptcy but a life-long incapacity.[12] And in *Roberts v*

---

[7] In this respect, not much has changed since Blom-Cooper and Drewry, *Final Appeal* (n 2); see ch VIII, 159–67, esp Table 13 at 160–3, and B Dickson, 'The Lords of Appeal and their Work 1967–1996' in P Carmichael and B Dickson (eds), *The House of Lords, Its Parliamentary and Judicial Roles* (Oxford: Hart, 1999) 131–6, esp Table 7.2 at 133–5. See, now, Appendix 4.

[8] Lionel Cohen served as a Lord of Appeal in Ordinary from 1951 to 1960.

[9] [1909] AC 147.   [10] [1919] AC 606.   [11] [1922] 2 AC 339.

[12] Viscount Birkenhead LC, at 362.

Hopwood,[13] the House ruled it unlawful for a local authority to decide, as a matter of principle, to pay their women workers as much as men, without regard to the actual jobs done or how much it would have cost them to secure the women's labour in the market place.

These last two cases, in particular, may suggest that their Lordships were slow to adapt to the growing egalitarianism of the times. Yet there are tantalising hints that even then they might have done better. According to a vociferous minority in *Viscountess Rhondda's Claim*, it made no difference whether the word incapacity or disqualification was used: a woman peer could not sit and vote because of the age old disability of all women to perform the public functions which they would otherwise have been entitled to perform—a disability which was expressly removed by the 1919 Act.[14] The reluctance of the majority to hold that the legislature had 'departed from the usage of centuries' was not shared by the Privy Council in *Edwards v Attorney General for Canada*.[15] Only 20 years after *Nairn*, the Board felt able to construe the word 'persons' in the British North America Act of 1867 to include women, so that women could be appointed members of the Canadian Senate. Although the Board could not say so, the fact that women had since been granted the right to vote for and sit in the Lower House may have affected their thinking.

In *Weinberger*, the majority thought that the House could only intervene if the committee had not acted in good faith; Lord Atkinson broadened this to 'arbitrarily or capriciously'; but this could not be inferred, because 50 of the candidates of German or Austrian origin had been elected and 57 had not; the committee had no obligation to give its reasons. However, the concept of reasonableness in rule-making bodies had already been established and the Divisional Court had recognised that even local authority by-laws might be struck down if they were 'partial or unequal in their operation'.[16] Nearly 50 years later, but a decade before the Sex Discrimination Act, the Court of Appeal was able to hold it unlawful for the Jockey Club to deny a woman a trainer's licence simply because she was a woman.[17] And Lord Buckmaster in *Roberts* would not have interfered had it been shown that the council had decided to pay women the same rate for the same job; it was the decision to pay all their lowest grade workers the same minimum wage irrespective of their job content to which he objected. Eventually, the common law did develop the notion that 'treating like cases alike and unlike cases differently is a general axiom of rational behaviour',[18] so that failure to do so might be a ground for judicial review of administrative action: but even this was haphazard and controversial.[19]

---

[13] [1925] AC 578.   [14] n 11 above, Viscount Haldane, at 386; Lord Wrenbury, at 394.
[15] [1930] AC 124.   [16] *Kruse v Johnson* [1898] 2 QB 91, at 99.
[17] *Nagle v Feilden* [1966] 2 QB 633.   [18] *Matadeen v Pointu* [1999] 1 AC 98, at 109.
[19] See J Jowell, 'Is Equality a Constitutional Principle?' (1994) 47 CLP 1, 14, where equality is described as a 'well-disguised rabbit to be hauled occasionally out of the Wednesbury hat'.

Otherwise, the duty not to discriminate against certain kinds of people in certain kinds of ways is the creature of relatively recent statute and treaty.[20] The House of Lords' jurisprudence does not cover the whole spectrum of issues arising even under those instruments. The random way in which cases reach the appellate committee has meant that some of the key areas that have troubled the lower courts have not been considered by their Lordships at all. Even so, there have been over 70 judgments concerning equality or discrimination since the first Race Relations Act in 1965. Well over half of these have been in the last ten years. This may suggest a greater appreciation of the importance of the issues by those giving leave to appeal.[21] It may also reflect the role of the statutory Commissions which have either supported[22] or intervened[23] in many of the appeals. This trend may develop further with the new Equality and Human Rights Commission which has a brief, not only to enforce domestic anti-discrimination law, but also to promote human rights, including equality.[24]

We are also beginning to see some recurring themes. In brief, we can see how the formal notion that like cases should be treated alike has been developed by statute to require that certain differences should be disregarded however material some might think them to be. But the problem remains of identifying which cases are alike in other respects and should therefore be treated alike—and which cases are different and should therefore be treated differently. The problem is intensified by the legislative refusal to accept that direct discrimination on the prohibited grounds can ever be justified.[25] This leads to an understandable reluctance in the courts to hold that what seem to be rational and sensible distinctions amount to discrimination at all. One person's obvious common sense can be perceived by its victims as obvious discrimination. In theory, this problem should not arise under the Human Rights Act; Article 14 of the European Convention on Human Rights prohibits only those differences in treatment that cannot be justified, although differences of treatment on grounds such as race or sex are much harder to justify than differences of treatment on other grounds. But even here there has been a reluctance to find that the cases are otherwise alike, and should be treated alike unless the difference in treatment can be explained and justified.

---

[20] See n 4 above and n 51 below.

[21] In *Archibald v Fife Council* [2004] ICR 954, p 588 below, counsel for the respondent council suggested in argument that, had it been an English case, it would not have been given leave to appeal. Their Lordships, however, considered it an important case, as do the disability rights groups.

[22] eg, the Disability Rights Commission supported the appellant in *Archibald v Fife Council* [2004] ICR 954, p 588 below.

[23] eg, the Racial Equality, Equal Opportunities, and Disability Rights Commissions intervened jointly in the victimisation case of *Derbyshire v St Helen's MBC* [2007] 3 All ER 81, p 585 below.

[24] See Equality Act 2006, s 30.

[25] The difficulties of distinguishing between direct and indirect discrimination are well illustrated by the Court of Appeal case of *R (Elias) v Secretary of State for Defence* [2006] 1 WLR 3213.

Value judgments are required in this as in many other areas of the law. In *Ghaidan v Godin-Mendoza*,[26] the House found that discrimination between same-sex and opposite-sex couples in the succession provisions of the Rent Act 1977 could not be justified. Yet in *M v Secretary of State for Work and Pensions*,[27] the majority found that discrimination between same-sex and opposite-sex couples in the child support scheme was justified because of historical disapproval of same-sex relationships, although it was not suggested that this disapproval could be justified:

Ms M's complaint of discrimination is in my view anachronistic. By that I mean that she is applying the standards of today to criticise a regime which when it was established represented the accepted values of our society, which has now been brought to an end because it no longer does so but which could not, with the support of the public, have been brought to an end very much earlier.[28]

It was not explained why this case differed from *Ghaidan* in which the self-same argument had been rejected. At a deeper level, it is difficult to accept that past exclusion can justify the continued inequality of the excluded group.[29] The place of past exclusion in modern equality law is to justify continued attempts to redress it in order that the historically disadvantaged can arrive at substantive equality with the historically more advantaged.[30]

Interpreting the modern anti-discrimination legislation

In the early days of the Race Relations and Sex Discrimination Acts, people trying to establish their rights had mixed fortunes in the House of Lords. In *Ealing London Borough Council v Race Relations Board*,[31] the House drew a distinction between 'national origins' and 'nationality', thus permitting discrimination against foreigners in the supply of housing.[32] In *Charter v Race Relations Board*[33] and again in *Dockers' Labour Club and Institute v Race Relations Board*,[34] the House held that a Conservative club and a working men's club were not providing facilities and services to a 'section of the public', thus permitting them to

---

[26] [2004] 2 AC 557.   [27] [2006] 2 AC 91.   [28] *Per* Lord Bingham, para 6.
[29] *Per* Baroness Hale, para 115.
[30] See eg *R (Hooper) v Secretary of State for Work and Pensions* [2005] 1 WLR 1681, p 592 below.
[31] [1972] AC 342.
[32] Lord Simon's lively comments, at 364, on the national characteristics of the Scots, the English, and the Welsh, despite their common nationality, are an interesting example of stereotyping which might raise eyebrows today: the Scots are a nation, inter alia, 'because of frugal living and respect for learning', the English 'because of the common law and of gifts for poetry and parliamentary government', the Welsh 'because of musical gifts and religious dissent'.
[33] [1973] AC 868.
[34] [1976] AC 285. Children in the care of a local authority, on the other hand, are a 'section of the public' to whom foster parents provide facilities and services: *Applin v Race Relations Board* [1975] AC 259.

operate a colour bar. And in *Amin v Entry Clearance Officer Bombay*[35] the House held, by a majority, that the anti-discrimination legislation did not apply to the performance of public duties such as entry clearance—this was not a service or facility for the public or the section of the public seeking entry to this country but the operation of the public duty of immigration control. Each of these distinctions has since been disregarded or removed by legislation.[36]

More recently, however, the House has been inclined towards wider rather than narrower protection for people claiming to be victims of discrimination. Three developments in particular stand out. First, in *Science Research Council v Nasse*,[37] the House recognised how difficult it could be to obtain evidence of discrimination in employment without disclosure of confidential records kept on other employees or candidates and gave guidance on how the competing requirements of doing justice to the applicants and maintaining the duty of confidence to third parties might be reconciled. In similar vein, in *Glasgow City Council v Zafar*,[38] the House recognised that discrimination claims 'present special problems of proof for complainants since those who discriminate on the grounds of race or sex do not in general advertise their prejudices: indeed they may not even be aware of them'. Inferences might therefore have to be drawn from the lack of any explanation for less favourable treatment.[39]

Second, in *Mandla v Dowell Lee*,[40] the House recognised Sikhs as a racial group defined by reference to their ethnic origins, although they are not biologically distinguishable from other people from the Punjab. Interestingly, there is no mention of the view taken in earlier cases that the Jews are also a distinct racial group.[41] Protecting Sikhs and Jews when other religions were not protected was later to reinforce the case for granting protection from discrimination on grounds of religion or belief on the same terms as race discrimination.[42]

---

[35] [1983] 2 AC 818.

[36] The Judicial Committee of the Privy Council declined to follow the *Ealing* case in *Thompson v Bermuda Dental Board* (2008) 24 BHRC 756. Nor did the House distinguish between national origins and nationality when applying ECHR, Art 14 to the indefinite detention of foreign suspected terrorists in *A v Secretary of State for the Home Department* [2005] 2 AC 68. The other two were corrected by Parliament in what are now RRA 1976, ss 25 and 19B respectively.

[37] [1980] AC 1028.

[38] [1998] ICR 120, *per* Lord Browne-Wilkinson at 125; approving guidance given by Neill LJ in *King v Great Britain China Centre* [1992] ICR 516, at 528–9.

[39] See also the Sex Discrimination (Indirect Discrimination and Burden of Proof Regulations) 2001, SI 2001/2660, amending the SDA to implement Council Directive 97/80/EC on the burden of proof in claims of sex discrimination in employment and vocational training.

[40] [1983] 2 AC 548.

[41] See *Clayton v Ramsden* [1943] AC 320 for numerous references to the Jewish race and Jewish blood; also in the Court of Appeal in *Keren Kayemeth le Jisroel v Comr for Inland Revenue* [1931] 2 KB 465, affirmed by the House of Lords at [1932] AC 650.

[42] In the Equality Act 2006, Part 2, adding to the provisions of the Employment Equality (Religion or Belief) Regulations 2003, SI 2003/1660.

But most important of all was the line of cases beginning with *Birmingham City Council v Equal Opportunities Commission*,[43] where the House held it unlawful for the council to provide fewer grammar school places for girls than for boys. The council did not want to discriminate against the girls; but for historical reasons, there were only three girls' grammar schools while there were five for boys. As these were mostly voluntary aided schools, it would have been difficult to redress the balance without abandoning selection altogether. But the Act did not require there to be any intention or motive to discriminate if the result was that the girls were less favourably treated than the boys because of their sex. This important principle was reaffirmed in *James v Eastleigh Borough Council*,[44] where the majority held it direct discrimination to charge men for entry to the council's swimming baths until they reached the age of 65, while women were allowed free entry from the age of 60. It made no difference that the council had simply linked their charges to the state pension age. The subjective reason for the differential treatment was quite irrelevant. The council had had the best of motives—to benefit those whose resources were likely to have been reduced by retirement. However, as Lord Goff reiterated, the question was simply: would the husband have received the same treatment as his wife, but for his sex?[45] The same approach was later applied to victimisation claims by the majority in *Nagarajan v London Regional Transport*.[46]

Once, therefore, it is established that the reason for the less favourable treatment is a prohibited ground, the motivation or purpose or explanation for the difference is irrelevant. It is difficult to put this point clearly, because it involves two different sorts of 'why' question: despite Lord Goff's insistence on a simple 'but for' test in *James v Eastleigh Borough Council*,[47] Lord Nicholls has since emphasised that even the first, 'on grounds of' or 'by reason of', question is not an objective question of causation as that term is usually understood by lawyers, but a subjective test: why did he do as he did?[48] Nevertheless, it is convenient to label them the 'causation' and the 'motivation' questions, because without clearly distinguishing between the two, much obvious discrimination might go without a remedy. Their Lordships have recognised that to require conscious bias or active hostility would deprive the legislation of much of its force.

Apart from these three important developments, there have also been expansive decisions on narrower points. In *Hampson v Department of Education and Science*,[49] the protection given to acts of discrimination 'in pursuance of any instrument made under any enactment by a Minister of the Crown'[50] was

---

[43] [1989] AC 1155; Lord Goff gave the only opinion, with which all the others agreed.
[44] [1990] 2 AC 751.   [45] [1990] 2 AC 751, at 774.   [46] [2000] 1 AC 501.
[47] [1990] 2 AC 751, at 774.
[48] *Khan v Chief Constable of the West Yorkshire Police* [2001] ICR 1065, para 29; see also the discussion in *Nagarajan v London Regional Transport* [2000] 1 AC 501, *per* Lord Browne-Wilkinson at 507–9, Lord Nicholls at 511–13, Lord Steyn at 519–20.
[49] [1991] 1 AC 171.   [50] RRA 1976, s 41(1)(b).

confined to acts done in the necessary performance of an express obligation in such an instrument and did not extend to acts done in the exercise of a power or discretion which it conferred. In *Barclay's Bank v Kapur*,[51] a generous interpretation was given to when time begins to run for limitation purposes. In *Relaxation Group v Rhys-Harper*,[52] the legislation was held to apply to discrimination taking place after the employment relationship had ended, as long as it arose from that relationship. And in *Percy v Board of National Mission of the Church of Scotland*,[53] the House held that the Sex Discrimination Act applied to an associate minister in the Church of Scotland, who was employed under 'a contract personally to execute any work or labour',[54] the anti-discrimination legislation giving wider protection than the unfair dismissal and redundancy legislation, which is confined to people employed under a contract of service.

The House was able to reach that conclusion without recourse to European Community law. Nevertheless, Community law was the original inspiration for the equal pay and sex discrimination legislation (and has more recently extended to discrimination in the fields of occupation and employment on other grounds).[55] The House has adopted a cautious approach when in doubt as to the reach of Community protection and made many references to the European Court of Justice.[56] Some of these have arisen from the exclusion of 'provision in relation to death and retirement' from the domestic but not from Community law. In *Garland v British Rail*[57] the House was told by the European Court of Justice that it was against community law to continue travel concessions for the families of retired male employees but not for the families of retired female employees; accordingly the House concluded that this was not 'provision in

---

[51] [1991] 2 AC 355.   [52] [2003] ICR 867.   [53] [2006] 2 AC 28.

[54] SDA 1975, s 82(1).

[55] Principally, EC Treaty Art 119, now Art 141; Council Directive 75/117/EEC on the approximation of the laws of Member States relating to the application of the principle of equal pay for men and women (the Equal Pay Directive); Council Directive 76/207/EEC on the implementation of the principle of equal treatment for men and women as regards access to employment, vocational training and promotion, and working conditions (the Equal Treatment Directive), amended by Directive 2002/73/EC (the Amended Equal Treatment Directive); Council Directive 79/7/EEC on the progressive implementation of the principle of equal treatment for men and women in matters of social security, followed up in Directives 86/378/EEC and 96/97/EC; Council Directive 86/613/EEC on the application of the principle of equal treatment between men and women engaged in an activity, including agriculture, in a self-employed capacity, and on the protection of self-employed women during pregnancy and motherhood; Council Directive 97/80/EC on the burden of proof in cases of discrimination based on sex, extended to UK by CD 98/52/EC; all of the above Directives were consolidated and updated by Directive 2006/54/EC (the Recast Equal Treatment Directive), and will be repealed from 15 August 2009; Council Directive 2000/43/EC implementing the principle of equal treatment between persons irrespective of racial or ethnic origin (the Race Directive); and Council Directive 2000/78/EC establishing a general framework for equal treatment in employment and occupation (the 'Framework Directive'). See also Council Directive 97/81/EC concerning the Framework Agreement on part-time work concluded by UNICE, CEEP, and the ETUC, extended to UK by CD 98/23/EC.

[56] For *Webb v EMO Air Cargo* [1993] 1 WLR 49, *Webb v EMO Air Cargo (No 2)* [1995] ICR 1021, see p 586 below.

[57] [1983] 2 AC 751.

relation to retirement'. In *Foster v British Gas*,[58] the House was told that the Equal Treatment Directive was directly effective against British Gas, so that female employees could not be required to retire earlier than male. And the long-running saga of *Preston v Wolverhampton Healthcare NHS Trust*[59] concerned the battle of part-time workers to gain retrospective access to the employers' occupational pension schemes.

Most troubling has been the identification and justification of indirect discrimination. The concept is easy enough to state: the employer may apply a rule or a practice which is sex-neutral on its face but puts one sex at a disadvantage compared with the other because fewer of the former can comply with it. In *R v Secretary of State for Employment, ex parte Seymour-Smith (No 2)*[60] the House had sought guidance from the ECJ on the principles to be applied in assessing whether there was such a disparate impact. The complaint was that fewer women than men would be able to satisfy the two-year qualifying period for claims for unfair dismissal. The ECJ endorsed a statistical approach, comparing the proportions of men who could and those who could not satisfy the requirement with the proportions of women who could and could not do so. Over the relevant years, very roughly three quarters of men and two thirds of women could qualify. Three of their lordships thought this significant; two did not. However all of them thought that the requirement was justified in order to encourage recruitment by employers.

The statistical approach has been used on other occasions, most recently in *Secretary of State for Trade and Industry v Rutherford (No 2)*.[61] But it can obscure a difficult conceptual question. Male workers complained that their rights to claim compensation for unfair dismissal and redundancy ceased at the age of 65. They argued that this was sex discrimination because it affected more men than women, as more men than women chose to remain in work until 65. But of course it affected all those who did so choose equally. The House held, therefore, that it was not indirect sex discrimination. It was not treating men less favourably than women because of their different working patterns in the same way that arbitrary age qualifications or excluding part-time workers from pensions and other benefits is. Women who wanted what the men wanted would have been treated in the same way.

Kicking against the pricks?

It will have been noted that, while all their Lordships agreed with the opinion of Lord Goff in *Birmingham City Council v Equal Opportunities Commission*,[62] the follow-up decisions in *James v Eastleigh Borough Council*[63] and *Nagarajan v*

---

[58] [1991] 2 AC 306.
[59] [1998] 1 All ER 528, *Preston v Wolverhampton Healthcare NHS Trust (No 2)* [2001] 1 ICR 217; see also *Preston v Wolverhampton Healthcare NHS Trust (No 3)* [2006] ICR 606.
[60] [2000] ICR 244.   [61] [2006] ICR 785; see also *Barry v Midland Bank* [1999] ICR 859.
[62] [1989] AC 1155.   [63] [1990] 2 AC 751.

London Regional Transport[64] were reached by a majority. This is not surprising. Their Lordships have a keen eye to what they see as the merits of the particular case, perhaps because there was a good reason for doing what was done or because there was no conscious intention to discriminate.

Once direct discrimination or victimisation is shown, there is no defence of justification (and indeed indirect discrimination through imposing requirements which bear more heavily against one race or sex than against others could in the original formulation only be excused if the requirement could be justified independently of its discriminatory effect). Difficult though it might have been to resolve the historical imbalance in educational provision for boys and girls in Birmingham, no one could suggest that there was any longer (if there ever had been) an objective justification for providing girls with fewer educational opportunities than boys. But it might well be thought that there was an objective justification for the swimming pool charges. The state pension age has been different for men and women since 1940.[65] Employers have organised their own pension schemes on the basis that women would retire at 60 and men at 65. Both the Equal Pay and Sex Discrimination Acts[66] excluded 'provision in relation to death and retirement'; and the House had at first held, in *Duke v GEC Reliance Ltd*,[67] that this allowed employers to insist that women retired at 60. So this was all part of the sensible and laudable object of making various benefits, including those of healthy and enjoyable exercise, available to those who were less likely to be able to afford them, albeit on a broad-brush basis. In the victimisation case of *Nagarajan*, the tribunal had held that the employers had been influenced, consciously or subconsciously, by their knowledge of a previous discrimination claim brought by the complainant. Lord Browne-Wilkinson, in the minority, was reluctant to accept a strict 'but for' test and could not agree that unconscious discrimination was unlawful.[68]

Generally speaking, however, their Lordships have been prepared to accept the rigours of the law, including the lack of any justification defence, but they have sometimes tried to avoid its uncomfortable rigidity. The two techniques used have been 'causation' and comparison. Thus in *James v Eastleigh Borough Council* itself, the minority held that the council had not discriminated on the ground of sex but on the ground that the wife was a pensioner whereas the husband was not.[69] More recently, in *R (Gillan) v Commissioner of Police of the Metropolis*,[70] the same technique has been used, albeit *obiter*, by two of their Lordships to distinguish that case from the uncomfortable but unanimous decision in *R (European*

---

[64] [2000] 1 AC 501.   [65] Old Age and Widows' Pension Act 1940.

[66] EPA 1970, s 6(1A)(b); SDA 1975, s 6(4).

[67] [1988] ICR 339; but cf *Foster v British Gas* [1991] 2 AC 463, where Community law trumps domestic law.

[68] [2000] 1 AC 501, at 510.   [69] [1990] 2 AC 751, *per* Lord Griffiths and Lord Lowry.

[70] [2006] 2 AC 307.

Roma Rights Centre) v Immigration Officer, Prague Airport.[71] It is worth considering these two cases in more detail.

Roma Rights concerned an operation by British immigration officials at Prague airport designed to prevent potential asylum seekers from travelling to the United Kingdom. Once arrived at a UK airport, a person who claims asylum cannot be sent back and will be granted temporary admission until his asylum claim is determined, sometimes years later. The Roma Rights Centre claimed that the immigration officers screening would-be travellers at Prague airport were routinely treating ethnic Roma less favourably than ethnic Czechs: subjecting them to longer and more intrusive questioning, requiring proof of matters taken on trust from the Czechs, and refusing would-be visitors whose bona fides there was no more reason to doubt. The immigration authorities denied that they were doing this, but the evidence amassed in support of the claim was pretty clear. The reasons for doing it were entirely understandable. The vast majority of asylum seekers coming from the Czech Republic are Roma; hardly any are ethnic Czechs. It is much more likely that an ethnic Roma will claim asylum on arrival in the UK than that an ethnic Czech will do so. These facts certainly made it rational for the immigration officers to treat the Roma with more suspicion than the Czechs. Indeed, the majority in the Court of Appeal found it quite inevitable that they would do so. Had there been a justification defence the facts might, perhaps, have afforded a justification. But that avenue was not available. So the majority of the Court of Appeal found that the officials had not discriminated on grounds of race: if they had discriminated at all, it was on the ground of rational suspicions about the would-be travellers' intentions.

The House of Lords unanimously allowed the appeal. The fact that the officials might have had a good reason for treating the Roma less favourably was neither here nor there. They had singled out the Roma for such treatment simply because they were Roma (and indeed visibly different from the ethnic Czechs). This was just the sort of stereotyping that the anti-discrimination legislation is designed to prevent: it is the same as treating an individual woman less favourably than a man simply because, statistically, women are more likely to take time off work for pregnancy and other caring responsibilities than are men. As Lord Hoffmann was later to put it in *R (Carson) v Secretary of State for Work and Pensions,*[72] 'that offends the notion that everyone is entitled to be treated as an individual and not a statistical unit'.

Roma Rights was entirely consistent with the earlier line of authority in *Birmingham City Council v Equal Opportunities Commission,*[73] *James v Eastleigh Borough Council,*[74] and *Nagarajan v London Regional Transport.*[75] The conduct of the immigration officials met the 'but for' test as adumbrated by Lord Goff. But it was probably the first time that that approach had been applied to the public

---

[71] [2005] 2 AC 1.   [72] [2006] 1 AC 173, para 16; see further p 591 below.
[73] [1989] AC 1155.   [74] [1990] 2 AC 751.   [75] [2000] 1 AC 501.

functions newly brought within the race relations legislation following the Macpherson Report into the Stephen Lawrence case.[76] In the wake of the atrocities of 11 September 2001 and 7 July 2005, the same issue was bound to arise in the context of anti-terrorist activities by the police.

R (Gillan) v Commissioner of Police for the Metropolis[77] concerned the legality of the Commissioner's authorisation of random stop and search powers under the Terrorism Act 2000. The House held that the authorisation was lawful and that its exercise in this case was not incompatible with Convention rights. The complainants did not belong to the ethnic groups most likely to be targeted by the police. But, *obiter*, Lord Brown of Eaton-under-Heywood questioned whether targeting people of Asian origin would be discriminatory in the light of the *Roma Rights* case. He had great difficulty in distinguishing the two, yet clearly thought it only common sense that the police should be able to concentrate their attentions upon people of the same ethnicity as those who had been involved in previous terrorist activities. He concluded that, in *Roma Rights*, the House had held that the Roma had been targeted *solely* because of their ethnicity rather than because of other matters which had aroused suspicion.[78] Lord Hope emphasised that there must always be some other reason in addition to ethnicity for exercising the stop and search power.[79] Essentially, therefore, each was relying on 'causation' as a way out of the dilemma. Nevertheless, each was contemplating that it might be acceptable to begin by concentrating on people of a particular ethnic appearance,[80] though it has long been accepted that the prohibited ground need not be the only reason for the less favourable treatment.[81]

A similar problem has arisen in victimisation cases, where once again there is no justification defence. In *Khan v Chief Constable of the West Yorkshire Police*[82] the Chief Constable had refused to give a reference for an officer who was pursuing a complaint of race discrimination against him. The House held that the Chief Constable was simply applying his normal policy to protect his position when there were proceedings of any kind brought against him by an officer and was not therefore acting 'by reason of' the fact that the claimant had complained of race discrimination.[83] There was no reference to European Community law, which had not yet been extended to race discrimination.[84] In *Derbyshire v St Helen's Metropolitan Borough Council*,[85] women members of the school catering

---

[76] *The Stephen Lawrence Inquiry, Report of an Inquiry by Sir William Macpherson of Cluny*, Cm 4262 (London, HMSO, 1999) ch 47, recommendation 11.

[77] [2006] 2 AC 307.   [78] Paras 83–92.   [79] Paras 40–7.

[80] Lord Scott, para 68, found a preferable solution in the possibility of statutory exception; and see the critique by Karon Monaghan, *Equality Law* (Oxford: OUP, 2006) para 1.05, note 22, and para 6.90.

[81] *Nagarajan v London Regional Transport* [2000] 1 AC 501, *per* Lord Nicholls at 512.

[82] [2001] ICR 1065.   [83] RRA 1976, s 2(1).

[84] Race Directive, 2000/43/EC, implemented in the Race Relations Act 1976 (Amendment) Regulations 2003.

[85] [2007] 3 All ER 81.

staff (dinner ladies) complained that the employers had written, not only to them but also to their colleagues, warning them of serious consequences for the school meals service, the children who used it, and the catering staff who worked in it, if they continued to pursue the claims for equal pay which others had settled. The Employment Tribunal, the Employment Appeal Tribunal, and the House rejected the employers' argument that they were merely trying to settle the case. European law requires that people who bring discrimination claims are given effective protection against dismissal or other adverse treatment as a reaction to their complaints.[86] The letters had gone beyond the ordinary conduct of litigation and inflicted a detriment upon the women because they were pursuing their claims. The same approach should now apply to race and other grounds of discrimination to which Community law has been extended.[87] Even so, it has been suggested that the majority, by approving the actual result in *Khan*, did not sufficiently distance themselves from its approach.[88]

The other way of denying that discrimination has taken place is to find that the claimant's case is not truly comparable with that of a real or hypothetical person who has been or would be treated more favourably than the claimant. Their cases are not alike and therefore they do not have to be treated alike. The difficulty here lies in deciding in what ways the two cases have to be alike. An obvious and acute example is pregnancy and maternity leave. There is no exact male equivalent. It was tempting, therefore, to look for the nearest comparable case, that of a man who is absent from work because of sickness. In *Webb v EMO Air Cargo*,[89] however, the House referred the question to the European Court of Justice and received the unequivocal answer that there could be no question of comparing a woman who was unable to work because of pregnancy with a man who was unable to do so because of illness. In *Webb v EMO Air Cargo (No 2)*,[90] therefore, the House was obliged to hold that to dismiss a worker because she was pregnant was sex discrimination. In that case, the woman had been specifically recruited to fill a vacancy caused by another woman's maternity leave, but this made no difference as she had been recruited for an indefinite period. The House was sufficiently concerned about adverse reactions from employers to point out that a woman who had been recruited for a specific period to cover for another's absence might have been treated differently.[91] Pregnancy provision is therefore an example of the principle of reasonable accommodation to inescapable differences

---

[86] Equal Pay Directive, 75/117/EEC, art 5; Equal Treatment Directive, 76/207/EEC, art 7, as amended by Directive 2002/73 following *Coote v Granada Hospitality Ltd* (Case C-185/97) [1999] ICR 100.

[87] n 55.

[88] M Connolly, 'Discrimination Law and Victimisation: Reinterpreting *Khan*—Easy Case Makes Bad Law' (2007) 36 Industrial Law Journal 364; Baroness Hale appears to be exonerated at 368.

[89] [1993] 1 WLR 49.   [90] [1995] ICR 1021.

[91] *Per* Lord Keith at 1027. For a very 'black-letter' approach to construing the SDA in the context of pregnancy-related illness see *Halfpenny v IGE Medical Systems* [2001] 1 ICR 73.

in order to 'level the playing field'.[92] The principle is well known in the context of disability but not in the context of sex or race, where positive discrimination, even to redress historic disadvantage, is usually not permitted.

But usually the attempts to identify the proper comparison of like with like are more subtle.[93] The problems are well illustrated by *Shamoon v Chief Constable of the Royal Ulster Constabulary*.[94] A chief inspector with the urban traffic branch complained that she had been removed from the role of 'counselling officer' in the appraisal of constables while two male chief inspectors had not. The House held that this was not the true comparison, because there had been complaints from constables and from the Police Federation about the way she conducted the appraisals. It had not been shown that, had similar complaints been made against male chief inspectors, they would have been treated any differently. How then could it be proved that such hypothetical men would have been treated differently if the question had never arisen? In *Watt (formerly Carter) v Ahsan*[95] Lord Hoffmann suggested that it might be uncommon to find a real person who qualified as a statutory comparator, because their circumstances would so often be different. However, it might be possible to infer the way in which a hypothetical comparator would have been treated from the way in which a real, though different, person had been treated. In *Ahsan*, it could be inferred that the complainant had been rejected as a candidate because of his ethnicity from the fact that a white candidate who was on the face of it less well qualified to represent the ward than he was had been selected.

That inference was not drawn in *Shamoon*, however, and one is left with the disturbing possibility that the model of appraisal and command with which the constables felt comfortable was intrinsically male and that they had difficulties in coming to terms with a woman in charge. How is one to know whether the complaints themselves were justified or the effect of systemic sexism in the constabulary? It might have been more satisfactory if the difference in treatment could have been recognised and a proper inquiry held into whether it had been justified by the complaints which had been made. But this the legislation does not permit and the *Ahsan* case illustrates some of the pitfalls. Several Labour Party ward branches had been suspended following press allegations of Pakistani councillors helping people to jump the queue of housing grants and recruiting suspect party

---

[92] The law on pregnancy discrimination in employment has since been clarified and developed by the Employment Equality (Sex Discrimination) Regulations 2005, SI 2005/2467, regs 4 and 36, amending the EPA and SDA in the light of Directive 2002/73/EC, amending CD 76/207/EEC on the implementation of the principle of equal treatment for men and women as regards access to employment, vocational training and promotion, and working conditions.

[93] In *Rainey v Greater Glasgow Health Board* [1987] AC 224, it was held that the fact that a man had previously been employed in the private sector meant that for equal pay purposes he was not comparable with a woman who had not. Had it been a sex discrimination claim, rather than an equal pay claim, it might have been held that the discrimination was on the ground of previous employment rather than sex.

[94] [2003] 2 All ER 26.   [95] [2008] 1 AC 696.

members. These had proved unfounded but the party seemed still to think that there was a problem associated with the Pakistani community. Lord Hoffmann[96] rejected the suggestion that, had there indeed been such a problem, rejecting a Pakistani candidate might have been legitimate:

It is no more than the old plea that you have nothing against employing a black person but the customers would not like it. In essence it is a defence of justification based on political expediency. It may salvage the purity of the personal motives of the selection panel but it does not in my opinion satisfy the terms of the 1976 Act, which does not allow any justification for direct discrimination.

Accommodating difference

As we have seen, the race and sex discrimination legislation adopted a principle of formal equality. The differences of race and sex were to be ignored but in all other respects like cases were to be treated alike. There was a glimmering of a principle of substantive equality, of reasonable accommodation of difference, in the community law approach to pregnancy and maternity leave. When disability discrimination legislation came along in 1995, it had perforce to require employers (and providers of goods, facilities and services, but not initially of premises) to make reasonable adjustments to cater for disabled people,[97] defined as those whose disabilities made ordinary day-to-day activities substantially more difficult for them.[98] The House had a rare opportunity to consider the scope of that duty in *Archibald v Fife Council*.[99] Mrs Archibald had been employed as a road sweeper but a complication of surgery had left her unable to walk and sweep. She retrained successfully for office work but the council required her to compete with others for office vacancies; she was eventually dismissed for incapacity after failing to obtain any of them. The House decided that there was a duty to make reasonable adjustments, even though she was now incapable of doing the job for which she had initially been employed. And it could be reasonable to require them to appoint her to a different job, even at a slightly higher grade, provided that she was qualified for it, without subjecting her to open competition with others.

The 1995 Act defined two different kinds of discrimination: treating someone less favourably than he would treat another 'for a reason which relates to the disabled person's disability'[100] and failing to comply with the duty to make reasonable adjustments.[101] But what does treating someone less favourably for a

---

[96] Para 47.   [97] Disability Discrimination Act 1995, ss 6 (now s 4A) and 21.
[98] DDA 1995, s 1(1).   [99] [2004] ICR 954.
[100] DDA 1995, ss 5(1) (now s 3A(1), 20(1) and 24(1)).
[101] DDA 1995, ss 5(2) (now s 3A(1) and (2)) and 20(2); there is a reasonable adjustment duty upon providers of goods, facilities, and services, in s 21, but there was none upon providers of premises until introduced by DDA 2005.

reason related to his disability mean? That a disabled person is treated less favourably than someone to whom the reason for the treatment does not apply where the reason has something to do with the disability? Or that a disabled person is treated less favourably than someone to whom the same reason applies but has nothing to do with a disability? In *Clark v Novacold*,[102] the Court of Appeal held that it meant the former: employers had to be kinder to people whose absences were caused by disability than to people who were not absent at all.

Unfortunately, the issue came before the House in a case concerning premises, at a time when there was no reasonable adjustment duty and the possible justifications for less favourable treatment were narrowly defined. In *Lewisham London Borough Council v Malcolm*,[103] the House of Lords held, by a majority, that *Clark v Novacold* was wrongly decided. The treatment of the disabled person had to be less favourable than the treatment of a non-disabled person who had supplied the same reason for the landlord's treatment: thus evicting a mentally ill tenant who had sublet his flat was not discrimination because a non-disabled person who had sublet his flat would have been treated in exactly the same way. This limits the concept to simple direct discrimination and is probably not what was originally intended. Parliament undoubtedly intended to cover indirect discrimination and employment law will probably have to be amended to comply with the European Directive 2000/78/EC. But the actual result was not surprising: otherwise a social landlord might have been obliged to tolerate conduct by their disabled tenants that they would never have tolerated in a non-disabled person. Somehow, there has to be a principle which requires the provider of employment, goods and services, or premises to make reasonable adjustments to cater for the disability but provides a justification defence in which the competing interests can be properly balanced in accordance with proportionality principles.

Human rights

Article 14 of the European Convention on Human Rights reads as follows:

The enjoyment of the rights and freedoms set forth in this Convention shall be secured without discrimination on any ground such as sex, race, colour, language, religion, political or other opinion, national or social origin, association with a national minority, property, birth or other status.

Several aspects of this have come before the House since the Human Rights Act 1998 came into force in October 2000. First there is the vexed question of what is meant by 'the enjoyment of the rights and freedoms set forth in this Convention'. Article 14 is not a freestanding guarantee of equal treatment. On the other hand, it would add nothing if it only applied where there had been a violation of one of the substantive rights. It is aimed, therefore, at discrimination in the ways in

---

[102] [1999] 2 All ER 977.   [103] [2008] 1 AC 1399; Baroness Hale dissenting on this point.

which a state gives effect to, protects, or respects another Convention right: as the Strasbourg court puts it, it must fall 'within the ambit' or 'affect the modalities' of another Convention right. In *Ghaidan v Godin-Mendoza*[104] the violation consisted of unjustified discrimination between opposite and same-sex couples in the rules relating to respect for a person's home, a core value protected by Article 8. In *M v Secretary of State for Work and Pensions*,[105] on the other hand, the majority held that discrimination between opposite-sex and same-sex relationships in the calculation of child support did not 'fall within the ambit' or 'affect the modalities' of the paying parents' right to respect for either their family or their private life because the impact upon each was so remote. 'The further a situation is removed from one infringing those core values [which the article is intended to protect], the weaker the connection becomes, until a point is reached when there is no meaningful connection at all.'[106] In the minority view, the state was discriminating in one of the ways it chose to respect family life, in particular the family lives which these parents had with their children.

The second question is whether the ground of distinction complained of falls within the enumerated grounds or the open-ended 'other status'. Article 14 cannot be aimed at all kinds of classification, because otherwise there would have been no need of the list, save perhaps to remind the reader of some of the more obviously objectionable classifications. The list itself generally concentrates on personal characteristics which the individual did not choose and cannot or should not be expected to change.[107] But it is hard to put one's finger on the type of classification intended by the words 'other status'. The point is not always taken in the European Court of Human Rights, but the expression 'personal characteristic' is sometimes used.[108] In *R (S) v Chief Constable of the South Yorkshire Police*,[109] the House held that the historical fact of having been arrested and detained in a police station was not a 'status' for this purpose; retaining the DNA samples and fingerprints even of those who were not subsequently charged or convicted, while those of other innocent people could only be retained with their consent, did not call for justification under Article 14. This was followed in *R (Clift) v Secretary of State for the Home Department*.[110] Differences between the parole regimes for prisoners sentenced to more than 15 years' imprisonment and for prisoners serving life sentences did not fall within Article 14. Differences between the regimes of prisoners liable for deportation and others did fall within Article 14, because they were on the ground of 'national origins'. Nationality and

---

[104] [2004] 2 AC 557.   [105] [2006] 2 AC 91.

[106] *Per* Lord Bingham at para 4; for a critique of these decisions see B Hale, 'Same Sex Relationships in the House of Lords' [2007] Juridical Review 247.

[107] *AL (Serbia) v Secretary of State for the Home Department* [2008] 1 WLR 1434, para 26.

[108] Citing *Kjeldsen, Busk, Madsen and Pederson v Denmark* (1976) 1 EHRR 711, para 56.

[109] [2004] 1 WLR 2196: the case went on to the European Court of Human Rights, where it was held that ECHR Art 8 had been violated and that it was therefore unnecessary to consider the complaint under Art 14.

[110] [2007] 1 AC 484.

immigration status seem to have been regarded in the same way as 'national origins' since *A v Secretary of State for the Home Department*,[111] where a nine-judge committee held that a provision allowing for the indefinite detention without trial of foreign suspected terrorists, but not the home grown, could not be justified. In *R (Carson) v Secretary of State for Work and Pensions*,[112] it was observed that Strasbourg had taken an expansive view of 'other status', so that the country of habitual residence was included. In *R (RJM) v Secretary of State for Work and Pensions*,[113] street homelessness was treated as a personal characteristic. Lord Walker likened personal characteristics to a series of concentric circles: at the core are the most personal, innate and largely immutable characteristics such as sex, colour, sexual orientation and disability; then there are nationality, language, religion and politics, which may be almost innate; and further out are other acquired characteristics, such as military status or domicile.[114]

However, the most important issues in Article 14 are, first, are the cases sufficiently alike that treating them differently requires justification; and secondly, if so, is the difference in treatment justifiable? In the domestic law of race and sex discrimination, as we have seen, the intrinsic differences between men and women, white and black, are ignored in deciding whether the two cases are alike. In *Ghaidan v Godin-Mendoza*,[115] the House rejected the argument that opposite-sex and same-sex couples were intrinsically different (because the latter could not have children together) and that it was not discrimination to treat them differently. Once again the prohibited ground was disregarded. But in *Carson*, the majority held that the intrinsic differences between residence in the United Kingdom and residence in South Africa, the prohibited ground of discrimination, were so relevant to the system of entitlement to contributory state benefits that it was not discrimination for the scheme to treat them differently.[116] Lord Carswell, in the minority, held that the state was called upon to justify the discrimination (and that this had not been done). In the linked case of *R (Reynolds) v Secretary of State for Work and Pensions*,[117] all took the view that differences in living costs between different age groups (the prohibited ground of discrimination) were so relevant to the income support scheme that the cases did not have to be treated alike. In each case, the classifications were not particularly objectionable and the subject matter was essentially one of social and economic policy which Parliament is usually better fitted than the courts to assess. Some might have thought it preferable to acknowledge the difference in treatment but also the justifications for it.

If discrimination does have to be justified, it must 'pursue a legitimate aim' and 'there must be a reasonable relationship of proportionality between the means

---

[111] [2005] 2 AC 68.   [112] [2006] 1 AC 173.   [113] [2009] 1 AC 311.
[114] Para 5.   [115] [2004] 2 AC 557.
[116] For a critique, see A McColgan, 'Cracking the Comparator Problem' [2006] EHRLR 650. The appellant also lost in Strasbourg, but the Chamber's decision has now been referred to the Grand Chamber.
[117] [2006] 1 AC 173.

employed and the aim sought to be realised'.[118] While the protection of the traditional marital family is in principle capable of being an important legitimate aim,[119] discrimination between unmarried opposite-sex and same-sex couples is not rationally related to that aim. In *Ghaidan*, it could not be explained how the traditional family was protected by treating people who were unable or strongly unwilling to marry even less favourably than those who could do if they chose. In *In re G (Adoption Unmarried Couple)*,[120] a blanket ban on joint adoptions by unmarried couples (whether of the same or opposite sexes) could not be justified: it was irrational to turn a reasonable generalisation, that it was usually in the best interests of a child to be adopted by a married couple, into an irrebuttable presumption, that it could never be in the best interests of a child to be adopted by an unmarried couple.

It is harder to justify discrimination on some grounds than on others. In *AL (Serbia) v Secretary of State for the Home Department*[121] the House rejected a rigid approach to 'suspect' grounds derived from the US jurisprudence. But as Lord Walker said in *R (RJM) v Secretary of State for Work and Pensions*, 'the more peripheral or debateable any suggested personal characteristic is, the less likely it is to come within the most sensitive area where discrimination is particularly difficult to justify'.[122] Race and sex discrimination are undoubtedly in that area. But much discrimination between the sexes is the result of the historical division of labour within the home and the related disadvantage of women in the market place. As Strasbourg pointed out long ago, 'certain legal inequalities tend only to correct factual inequalities'.[123] In *R (Hooper) v Secretary of State for Work and Pensions*,[124] the House was concerned with three state benefits available for widows but not for widowers—a one-off widow's payment, a widowed mother's allowance for those left with dependent children to bring up, and a widow's pension for those widowed or reaching the end of their widowed mother's allowance over a certain age. The UK had accepted that the discrimination should be phased out, but the question was how and when? Should the position be levelled up or levelled down? In fact the solution chosen was to make all three available to both widows and widowers but to limit the duration of the widowed person's pension. The House held that the earlier discrimination was justified by the historical disadvantage of women in the labour market. It was very much a matter for political judgment when that had been so sufficiently overcome that benefits targeted at widows alone could no longer be justified.[125] It seems, therefore, that Article 14 is a more flexible tool than domestic anti-discrimination

---

[118] Oft repeated, eg in *Stec v United Kingdom* (2006) 43 EHRR 1017, para 51.
[119] *Karner v Austria* (2003) 38 EHRR 528.   [120] [2008] 3 WLR 76.
[121] [2008] 1 WLR 1434.   [122] [2008] UKHL 63, para 5.
[123] *Belgian Linguistics Case (No 2)* (1968) 1 EHRR 252, para 10.
[124] [2005] 1 WLR 1681.
[125] In *R (Wilkinson) v Inland Revenue Comrs* [2005] 1 WLR 1718, the Government did not dispute that the legislation which granted a bereavement tax allowance to widows but not to widowers violated Art 14; so the real dispute was whether the Revenue could have acted differently for the purpose of HRA 1998, s 6(2).

law, in that it can permit distinctions to be drawn with a view to achieving substantive rather than purely formal equality. It seems less likely, however, that it could have been taken further and positively required the state to continue to discriminate in favour of widows until the 'gender pay gap' had been all but eliminated.

Conclusion

If nothing else, this swift survey of the House of Lords' jurisprudence on discrimination and equality illustrates how complicated and controversial the issues can be. At a particular time in the battle for equality it may be necessary to fight for the right to be treated in the same way as the dominant group. At another stage it may be necessary to fight for the recognition of difference so that true substantive equality can be achieved. As the prohibited grounds of discrimination in domestic law are broadened to include age, sexual orientation, and religion or belief, the issues are likely to become even more complicated and controversial as these may well be inconsistent with one another.[126] There is still much work to be done, by the courts as well as in Parliament.[127]

---

[126] As exemplified by the debate over the application of the Equality Act (Sexual Orientation) Regulations 2007, SI 2007/1263, to adoption and fostering agencies run by the Roman Catholic and other Churches.

[127] See eg *Fairness and Freedom: The Final Report of the Equalities Review* (London: Cabinet Office, 2007).

32

Criminal Law

JR Spencer

In this chapter I shall try to evaluate the contribution of the House of Lords to the development of English criminal law. By this, I mean substantive law: for reasons of space, and to avoid overlap with other chapters, the broader aspects of criminal justice will not be touched upon. The chapter begins with an introduction, with some dates and figures, and other background matters. It continues with a central section in which the work of the House of Lords is examined. For reasons of space again, the number of topics covered there is severely limited—and apologies are offered in advance to those who wish that other topics had been chosen. In the final section, I try to *faire le bilan*: to weigh up the strengths and weaknesses of the Law Lords' contribution to this area of law, and express a personal view as to which way the final balance tips.

Introduction—figures, facts, and dates

In criminal justice, the body of reported case law[1] from the House of Lords from 1876 to 2007 consists of just under 400 decisions, of which about 175 are concerned (more or less) with substantive criminal law. Of these, the over-whelming majority were decided during the last 40 years, reflecting the fact that, before 1960, access to the House of Lords in criminal cases was severely limited.

From 1876 until 1908 there was virtually no way a criminal case could reach the House of Lords, and during that period I believe there were only two that made the journey, neither of which raised an issue of substantive criminal law.[2] The Criminal Appeal Act 1907, which created the Court of Criminal Appeal, established a route to the House of Lords, provided the Attorney General gave a certificate that the case raised 'a point of law of exceptional public importance',

---

[1] I confess that I have not searched the court records themselves.

[2] *Castro, orse Orton, orse Tichborne v R* [1180–1] 6 App Cas, which was the final legal round of the famous *Tichborne* case; and *Mews and Oastler v R* [1883] AC 339, a case deciding which pocket of the public purse was responsible for paying the costs of keeping a 'criminal lunatic' in a mental asylum.

and that it was 'in the public interest that a further appeal should be brought'.[3] Although this Act came into force in January 1908, it was not until three years later that the first case under the new procedure—a prosecution appeal that eventually succeeded—reached the House of Lords.[4] It caused muddle and confusion, because the Criminal Appeal Act had not specified what the effect of a successful prosecution appeal should be, and while the courts were puzzling over this the defendant, who was at liberty, vanished.[5] The first case to reach the House of Lords that raised a point of substantive criminal law (as against a point of criminal procedure or evidence) seems to be *Beard*, decided ten years later in 1920.[6] And during the next 40 years, the reported cases in which the House of Lords addressed a point of substantive criminal law numbered only 12.[7]

In 1960 the Attorney General's fiat was abolished in favour of the present system whereby appeal lies from the Criminal Division of the Court of Appeal (as it now is) if that court certifies that 'a point of general public importance' is involved, and either that court, or the House of Lords, gives leave on the ground that 'the point is one which ought to be considered by that House'. And at the same time, a right of appeal in criminal cases was created, on similar terms, from decisions of the Divisional Court.[8] (But there has never been any appeal from Scotland in its criminal jurisdiction, although the Law Lords sitting in the Privy Council heard cases raising points of criminal law arising out of devolution.)

The rising number of criminal cases that began to find their way to the House of Lords as a result of these new arrangements was unwelcome, and provoked the spat between Lord Dilhorne and the Court of Appeal that Gavin Drewry and Louis Blom-Cooper describe in chapter 4, the outcome of which was that the Court of Appeal, feeling bruised, adopted a policy of certifying points of public importance readily but refusing leave, so letting the House of Lords itself decide which points should be examined further.

This policy of restraint did not reduce the number of appeals in criminal cases to pre-1960 levels; indeed, over the next decades it continued to rise steadily. But it meant (and still means) that the House of Lords exercises considerable influence over the development of the criminal law not only by the way it decides cases, but also by its choice of cases to decide; and in retrospect, its choice of areas of criminal law to review, or not review, has sometimes seemed a little odd. Thus

---

[3] Criminal Appeal Act 1907, s 1(6).

[4] *R v Ball and Ball* [1911] AC 305. This was a prosecution under the Punishment of Incest Act 1908, and the issue was the admissibility of certain evidence.

[5] (1910–11) 6 Cr App R 49, 54.   [6] [1920] AC 479.

[7] *Woolmington v DPP* [1935] AC 462; *Andrews v DPP* [1937] AC 576; *Milne v Metropolitan Police Comr* (1939) 27 Cr App R 90; *Mancini v DPP* [1942] AC 1; *Holmes v DPP* [1946] AC 588; *Joyce v DPP* [1946] AC 347; *Wicks v DPP* [1947] AC 362; *Bedder v DPP* [1954] 1 WLR 1119; *Board of Trade v Owen* [1957] AC 602; *DPP v Head* [1959] AC 83; *DPP v Smith* [1961] AC 290; *Welham v DPP* [1961] AC 103. Between 1920 and 1960 it also decided another six cases that turned on points of criminal procedure and evidence—making, with *Beard*, a total of 19 criminal cases in 40 years.

[8] Administration of Justice Act 1960, s 1.

in 2005, in *Dica*,[9] it refused leave to appeal a case where the Court of Appeal had (to the surprise of some commentators[10]) ruled that criminal liability exists for recklessly infecting another person with HIV: an issue which seems no less important than the finer details of the law relating to drinking and driving, which have occupied the earnest attention of the House of Lords on at least 21 occasions[11]—many of them in cases where the House itself gave leave.

In the next section of this chapter I propose to examine the contribution of the House of Lords to the development of English criminal law in three areas of central importance. They are: the authority to create new criminal offences; the interpretation of criminal statutes, and (by analogy) the outer limits of common law offences; and the mental element in crime.

The House of Lords and English criminal law: its work in three areas

The authority to create new criminal offences

The most fundamental issue in criminal law is: who makes it? Which person, or group of persons, has the power to extend its range by the creation of new criminal offences? In modern times it has been generally accepted that, in democratic states, this is a function of the legislature; and in those with written constitutions, this will commonly provide that nothing is criminally punishable unless it is made so by a statute that was in force at the time the relevant act or omission took place.[12] In Western Europe, this rule was incorporated into the European Convention on Human Rights as Article 7 in 1950. In the light of this, there was surprise (to put it mildly) when in 1961 the House of Lords, by a majority, declared that in England and Wales new common law offences can be created *ex post facto* by the courts themselves.

---

[9] [2004] QB 157; for the refusal of leave, see the Minutes of the House of Lords, 14 December 2005.

[10] Though not this one, whose arguments in an article in the *New Law Journal* the Court of Appeal adopted; but *Dica*, and *Konzani* [2005] 2 Cr App R 14 (198), which applies and extends it, have generated a large amount of comment, some of which is very hostile.

[11] *Pinner v Everett* [1969] 1 WLR 1266; *DPP v Carey* [1970] AC 1072; *Sakhuja v Allen* [1973] AC 152; *Rowlands v Hamilton* [1971] 1 WLR 647; *Bourlet v Porter* [1973] 1 WLR 866; *Baker v Foulkes* [1975] 1 WLR 1551; *Metropolitan Police Comr v Curran* (1975) 62 Cr App R 131; *Spicer v Holt* [1977] AC 987; *Walker v Lovell* [1975] 1 WLR 1141; *Morris v Beardmore* [1981] AC 446; *Pascoe v Nicholson* [1981] 1 WLR 1061; *Clowser v Chaplin* [1981] 1 WLR 837; *Fox v Chief Constable of Gwent* [1986] AC 281; *Cracknell v Willis* [1988] AC 450; *Gumbley v Cunningham* [1989] AC 281; *DPP v Warren* [1993] AC 319; *DPP v Butterworth* [1995] 1 AC 381; *DPP v McKeown* [1997] 1 WLR 295; *DPP v Jackson* [1999] 1 AC 406; *Russell v Devine* [2003] 1 WLR 1187; *Sheldrake v DPP* [2005] 1 AC 264.

[12] For example, Article 16 of the Dutch Constitution: 'Nothing is punishable except by virtue of a pre-existing statutory rule of criminal law.'

As older readers will remember, this pronouncement was made in *Shaw v DPP*,[13] the celebrated 'Ladies' Directory' case, in which a man who had published a directory of London prostitutes found himself prosecuted, inter alia, for the common law offence of conspiracy to corrupt public morals. His defence was that no such crime existed. After an examination of various slender and antique precedents, four members of the House of Lords held that it did; and for good measure added (in effect) that if it did not exist before, it did so now, because they had the power to create it. The view of the majority was put, with great force, by Viscount Simonds. With an approving backward reference to the Court of Star Chamber, he said that the higher courts still have 'a residual power, where no statute has yet intervened to supersede the common law, to superintend those offences which are prejudicial to the public welfare'; and with a glance ahead to a future in which Parliament might decriminalise homosexual acts between consenting males, he said the courts could then be expected to use their crime-creating power to punish anyone who might presume, 'even without obscenity', to advocate or encourage homosexual practices. The fifth member of the court, Lord Reid, delivered a long and strongly worded dissent.

This decision drew a barrage of academic criticism of unequalled ferocity,[14] and a few years later the House reversed its position on the power of the courts to create new offences. In *R v Bhagwan* in 1970 a group of Law Lords, including two from the majority in *Shaw,* declined to apply it, holding that where some immigrants smuggled themselves into the United Kingdom without actually breaking any of the ill-drafted provisions of the existing immigration laws they could not be prosecuted for common law conspiracy to evade the policy of the statute.[15] In *R v Knuller*, two years later, all the Law Lords (including one member of the majority in *Shaw*) went out of their way to retract the remarks in *Shaw* about the existence of a judicial power to create new offences.[16] And a final rejection of any overt judicial power to extend the criminal law took place in *DPP v Withers*, where it was held that there is no such offence as a conspiracy to commit a public mischief.[17]

Much more recently, the House of Lords revisited this area again in *R v Jones*.[18] In this case a group of defendants who were prosecuted for various criminal acts arising out of protests against the Iraq war claimed in their defence that their acts were legal, being done to prevent the commission of a crime—namely the crime of 'aggression' as recognised by public international law during the course of the twentieth century. This offence had not been incorporated into UK internal law by statute, and, said a unanimous House of Lords, it could not become a criminal offence under internal law by the judges ruling it to be so. As Lord Bingham said:

[13] [1962] AC 220.

[14] JC Smith [1961] Crim L Rev 468; C Turpin [1961] CLJ 144; Seaborne Davies, 'The House of Lords and the Criminal Law' (1961) VI JSPTL (NS) 104.

[15] [1972] AC 60.   [16] [1973] AC 435.   [17] [1975] AC 842.

[18] [2007] 1 AC 136; and see too *Norris v Government of the USA* [2008] 1 AC 920.

'...there now exists no power in the courts to create new criminal offences as decided by a unanimous House in *Knuller*. While old common law offences survive until abolished or superseded by statute, new ones are not created.'[19]

Looking back on this piece of legal history nearly 50 years later, what are we to make of it? In defence of the House of Lords as an institution, it can be said that it got there in the end. In defence of the majority in *Shaw*, it could also be said that English judges undoubtedly had power to create new common law offences in the distant past, and that in the more recent past they had vigorously defended it, even to the point, in the middle of the nineteenth century, of using its existence as a reason to oppose the creation of a criminal code.[20] But even if the majority judges in *Shaw v DPP* were not entirely alone in the position they took,[21] by the 1960s their views were completely out of step with mainstream educated legal thought. The decision was, in fact, a most bizarre performance; and all the more so when we recall that Viscount Simonds, who took the lead, was in matters of civil law an extreme opponent of judicial activism, who ten years earlier had famously castigated Lord Denning's liberal approach to the interpretation of statutes as 'a naked usurpation of the legislative function under the thin disguise of interpretation'.[22]

The interpretation of existing criminal offences

Something almost as important as the source of the power (if any) of the courts to create new criminal offences are the principles that the courts follow when construing old ones. With this in mind, some countries that have criminal codes have furnished them with preliminary articles that set out the basic rules. Article 111-4 of the French *Code pénal*, for example, provides that '*La loi pénale est d'interprétation stricte*'. In England and Wales there is no criminal code; and in its absence, the final court of appeal might be expected to formulate some principles in this area. And looking at criminal law through twenty-first century spectacles, I think we might expect these principles to include at least the following. First, since the power of the courts to create new offences has been rejected, one rule should be that existing common law offences should not be extensively construed—because to extend a vague common law offence to penalise new forms of conduct is open to the same principled objections as declaring the existence of new common law offences. Secondly, we would expect to find some clear guidelines on the construction of statutory offences. These, one would have thought, would start with a basic rule that the courts begin by giving the words of a criminal statute, like any other type of statute, their natural meaning.

---

[19] ibid, [28]; cf Lord Hoffmann at [61], and Lord Mance at [102].
[20] G Williams, *Criminal Law: The General Part* (London: Sweet & Maxwell, 2nd edn 1961) 595.
[21] In 1968 (or thereabouts), I heard Sir Norman Skelhorne, the Director of Public Prosecutions, vigorously defend it when addressing Cambridge University Law Society.
[22] *Magor and St Mellons RDC v Newport Corp* [1952] AC 189, 191.

They would continue with a rule that, where there are several natural meanings, the court looks for clues as to the intention of Parliament in the legislative background and history, and the broader legal context; and where these sources provide no intelligible clues, the courts would apply a rule of 'strict construction' and resolve the ambiguity in favour of the defendant, unless the result of doing so was obviously absurd.[23] But on these matters the case law of the House of Lords, taken as a whole, presents a picture that is anything but clear. Whilst cases can be found that support all of these propositions, others can be found that ignore them, or—in some cases—state the opposite.

In a series of cases during the 1960s and 1970s the House of Lords showed great willingness to expand the reach of common law offences: both by confirming the existence of some which were in doubt and by expanding the outer limits of others whose existence, if nothing else, was certain. So in *Sykes v DPP*[24] the House of Lords affirmed the existence, hitherto disputed, of an offence of 'misprision of felony'—the failure by a person who was aware of the commission of a felony to denounce it to the authorities. The defendant, whose conviction was upheld, had played a peripheral role in the theft of firearms from the United States Air Force and their subsequent delivery to the IRA; but the offence of which he was convicted, assuming it existed, was equally applicable to the failure of a father who failed to inform upon his son (or vice versa), or a householder who failed to report a boy to the police for stealing apples—objections which Lord Goddard dismissed by saying, 'the law is nowadays administered with dignity and common sense'.[25] In *Button and Swain*[26] the House breathed new life into the common law offence of affray by holding, contrary to some authorities, that it could be committed in a private place as well as in a public one, and further life in *Taylor*[27] where, discarding yet more authorities, it held that the offence could be committed by one person acting on his own, as well as by a group. In *Shaw* the offence of conspiracy, as we saw in the last section, was held to cover conspiracy to corrupt public morals, and in *Kamara*[28] to cover agreements to commit at least some torts as well. In *DPP v Doot*[29] the House of Lords decided that conspiracy, though committed the moment A and B agree, is a 'continuing offence' which goes on being committed afterwards—so enabling those who conspire abroad to be prosecuted in England once they get here. In *Scott v Metropolitan Police Commissioner*[30] the House of Lords, by a majority of three to two, adopted an extensive definition of conspiracy to defraud. In *Whitehouse v Lemon*[31] the House of Lords gave a broad interpretation to the common law offence of blasphemy, holding that the offence consisted of the publication of any matter seriously offensive to the feelings of Christians, irrespective of the intentions of the

---

[23] See AP Simester and GR Sullivan, *Criminal law, Theory and Doctrine* (Oxford: Hart, 3rd edn 2007) 45ff.
[24] [1962] AC 528. [25] ibid, 569. [26] [1965] AC 591. [27] [1973] AC 964.
[28] [1974] AC 104. [29] [1973] AC 807. [30] [1975] AC 819. [31] [1979] AC 617.

publisher. And in *Verrier v DPP*[32] the House ruled that the long-standing assumption that the maximum penalty for a common law misdemeanour was two years' imprisonment was incorrect: and so, in principle, any offence at common law is potentially punishable by imprisonment for life.

In some of the cases—like *Scott v MPC*—the extension of the law was well received, whereas in others—like *Sykes* and *Whitehouse v Lemon*—it was highly controversial. But in none of them was much awareness shown, except in dissenting speeches, of any need for caution when extending common law offences. And during this period there were hardly any cases where, confronted with the chance to construe a common law offence widely, the Law Lords declined to take it.[33]

In 2004, a much different House of Lords adopted a completely different approach to common law offences. In the combined appeals in *Rimmington and Goldstein*[34] the issue was the scope of the common law offence of public nuisance. Having examined this singularly vague offence in the light of Article 7 of the European Convention, the House adopted a definition of the offence that contained it, holding that it is restricted to behaviour that affects the public generally: and hence that it does not apply to the repeated commission of a criminal offence against a large number of individuals, for example, by sending obscene or threatening letters to a lot of people. It also held that it would usually be improper (and hence, presumably, a potential abuse of process) to prosecute a person for public nuisance where his behaviour was covered by some statutory offence. In the course of delivering the leading speech, Lord Bingham said that there was an arguable case for abolishing the crime of public nuisance, but added that, just as the courts today have no power to create new offences, so they are unable to abolish those that currently exist.[35] And four years later, in *Norris v US*,[36] the House of Lords took a similarly restrictive approach to the crime of conspiracy to defraud, holding—contrary to the views of the Court of Appeal—that it did not cover an agreement between suppliers to fix prices.

The record of the House of Lords in construing statutory offences is also rather patchy.

As one would expect, there are many cases in which the House of Lords has approached the construction of criminal statutes in the way suggested earlier in this chapter. Thus in *Bentham*,[37] for example, it stressed that the first thing to

---

[32] [1967] 2 AC 195.

[33] The only examples of which I am aware are *Withers* (n 17) and, from just before this period, *Board of Trade v Owen* [1957] AC 602.

[34] [2006] 1 AC 459.

[35] Although not able to abolish an overbroad offence, the courts may be able to neutralise its ill effects by halting a prosecution under it as an 'abuse of process'. As already mentioned, this possibility was hinted at in *Rimmington and Goldstein*. And this was the result achieved in *Asfaw* [2008] 1 AC 1061, where the House of Lords thought that for the defendant to be convicted in the circumstances of the case would put the United Kingdom in breach of its international obligations under the 1951 Refugee Convention.

[36] [2008] 1 AC 920.   [37] [2005] 1 WLR 1057.

consider, when construing a criminal statute, is the literal meaning of the words: if this is plain and unambiguous, there is no room for arguments of policy as to whether they should be extended or reduced. So where a statute made it an offence for a person to have 'in his possession a firearm or imitation firearm', this phrase could not be read to cover falsely pretending to possess a firearm—as by putting his hand in his pocket with his fingers extended and saying 'Stick 'em up!'[38] As Lord Wright had put it in a much earlier case, 'The Act must be construed according to the natural meaning of the language used, all the more so since it is an Act creating a criminal offence.'[39]

Similarly, where (as usual) the words are capable of different meanings the Law Lords' next port of call is usually the legislative background—including any White Paper[40] that preceded the legislation, and any official Report[41] on which it was known to be based. A classic example of this approach is *Attorney General's Reference (No 1 of 1988)*,[42] where the point at issue was whether a person 'obtained' information for the purpose of the statutory offence of insider dealing only when he actively sought it, or whether he also 'obtained' it where it was volunteered to him; and the House adopted the wider meaning after examining other sections of the relevant statute, and the White Paper on which it had been based. In recent years the Government, when introducing legislation, has adopted the practice of publishing Explanatory Notes; and in several recent cases the House has made it plain that it will also consider these as an aid to the construction of criminal statutes.[43] On many occasions, too, the House has reaffirmed that where the legislative background gives no clear answer to the conundrum, the narrower interpretation should be adopted:[44] accepting, as Lord Diplock neatly put it in one case, that 'A man should not be gaoled upon an ambiguity.'[45]

On the other hand, every criminal lawyer is painfully aware of a list of famous decisions where the House of Lords has departed from these principles of statutory interpretation to go off on what tort lawyers would call 'a frolic of its

---

[38] An added reason was that, if the defendant's fingers were an 'imitation firearm', the police would be entitled to confiscate them!

[39] *Milne v MPC; Boundford v MPC* (1939) 27 Cr App R 90, 126; a case in which the defence team, whose arguments prevailed, consisted of the future Lord Denning and HC Leon, better known by his pseudonym, Henry Cecil.

[40] eg *AG's Reference (No 1 of 1988)* [1989] AC 971.

[41] See eg *R v Bloxham* [1983] 1 AC 109 (reference to the 10th Report of the Criminal Law Revision Committee on Theft and Related Offences when construing the offence of handling stolen goods contrary to s 22 of the Theft Act 1968); *R v Allen* [1985] AC 27 (reference to the 13th Report of the Criminal Law Revision Committee when construing the offence of making off without payment contrary to s 3 of the Theft Act 1978). In *R v Z (AG for Northern Ireland's Reference)* [2005] AC 645 it considered at length and in detail the history of anti-terrorist legislation.

[42] [1989] AC 971; mentioned with approval by Simester and Sullivan (n 23).

[43] *Montila* [2004] 1 WLR 3141, *per* Lord Hope at [35]; *AG's Reference (No 5 of 2002)* [2005] 1 AC 167, *per* Lord Bingham at [21].

[44] See, eg, *Bloxham* (n 41) 114E, and *Allen* (n 41) 1034E–F.

[45] *DPP v Goodchild* [1978] 1 WLR 578.

own'. So in *Anderton v Ryan*[46] a majority consisting of Lords Fraser, Bridge, Keith, and Roskill declined to look at the Report of the Law Commission on which the Criminal Attempts Act 1981 was based, and so contrived to interpret the new law as perpetuating the difficulties about 'impossible attempts' that it was designed to solve. No lasting harm was done here, because after a spanking administered by Professor Glanville Williams[47] the House reversed this decision the following year, with the only Law Lord who had sat in the earlier case admitting with the best of grace that he and his brethren had got it wrong.[48] The same, alas, cannot be said of the equally controversial decision in *R v Caldwell*,[49] in which a majority led by Lord Diplock set at nought the legislative history of the Criminal Damage Act 1971, which made it clear 'beyond the possibility of honest doubt'[50] that the word 'recklessness' had been used to mean acting with actual foresight of the risk of causing harm, in order to impose upon the law a new definition of his own devising according to which the term caught those who were merely negligent as well. The confusion created by this decision, which was equally disliked by academics and the judges in the courts below, lasted for 22 years, until—long after Lord Diplock's death—it was finally overruled in *R v G* in 2003.[51]

In practical terms, the effect of Lord Diplock's speech in *Caldwell* was to extend the scope of criminal liability for a range of serious offences: and to reach this destination it not only disregarded the legislative history of statute that was the subject of the appeal, but also made no mention of the 'strict construction' principle—the principle that, in cases of genuine doubt, the court adopts the interpretation that is most beneficial to the defendant. And no mention of this principle is to be found in another group of well-known cases, the effect of which was to extend, by a very wide margin, the reach of the offence of theft.

The issue in these cases was the meaning of the word 'appropriation', which is the central ingredient of the basic offence under section 1 of the Theft Act 1968, and which is rather loosely defined by section 3(1), according to which 'any assumption by a person of the rights of an owner amounts to an appropriation'. This definition leaves a number of obvious questions open. Does 'appropriation' potentially include acts done to the property to which the owner consents? If yes, is this so generally, or only where the consent is tainted by force, fraud, or mistake? And if the consent of the owner is generally irrelevant, does 'appropriation' even extend to cover acts the legal effect of which is to transfer all proprietary rights in the subject matter of the alleged theft to the defendant, in circumstances where the civil law would not intervene to make him give it back? The outcome of a series of four well-known House of Lords cases is that the answer to all these three questions is a resounding 'yes'—with the result, in effect,

---

[46] [1985] AC 560.
[47] 'The Lords and Impossible Attempts, or *quis custodiet ipsos custodes?*' [1986] CLJ 33–83.
[48] *R v Shivpuri* [1987] AC 1; the Law Lord who admitted the mistake was Lord Bridge.
[49] [1982] AC 341.   [50] G Williams, 'Recklessness Redefined' [1981] CLJ 252–83, 263.
[51] [2004] 1 AC 1034.

that any conduct in relation to another person's property is theft if there was intention permanently to deprive, and the tribunal of fact regards such conduct as 'dishonest'.

As to whether the resulting law is unduly harsh, and can operate without undesirable collisions with the civil law, opinions are divided. But whatever the answer to those two questions is, there was no need for the House of Lords to give this extraordinarily wide definition to the offence of theft in order to catch villains, because those who dishonestly cheat others into giving them their property are also guilty of a range of other serious criminal offences.[52] And even if the only people who get caught in the broad net of theft are rogues and villains there is still an issue of 'fair labelling', because some of them will have done things that are far removed from any popular conception of the crime of theft. This extensive approach is in stark contrast to the narrow and technical approach that the House adopted to a range of fraud offences in *Preddy*,[53] which produced a law of fraud so unworkably narrow that it had to be amended by Parliament as a matter of urgency.[54] How did it manage to go so far to the opposite extreme with the crime of theft?

In retrospect, it seems that the huge extension of the scope of theft came about more or less by accident. In the first case, *Lawrence v Metropolitan Police Commissioner*,[55] the issue was whether a dishonest taxi driver who had demanded and received an excessive fare from a foreigner had thereby committed the offence of theft—given that the passenger had apparently consented, and that the taxi driver was undoubtedly guilty of the separate offence of obtaining property by deception. In an extremely brief speech in which his brethren concurred, Lord Dilhorne said (in effect) 'of course'—missing the point as he did so. The key issue was hardly discussed, nothing was said about the legislative background to the Theft Act, no mention was made of the principle of 'strict construction', and a significant part of Lord Dilhorne's speech was spent complaining that he and his brethren had had to waste their time on a problem of such triviality.[56] In the second case, *Morris*,[57] the issue was whether a dishonest shopper in a supermarket who swapped labels in the hope of paying a reduced price at the checkout was guilty of a theft. In a brief speech in which his brethren concurred, and from which his impatience with the subject matter was also clear, Lord Roskill said that he was. Appropriation, Lord Roskill said, obviously required 'an act by way of adverse interference with or usurpation' of the owner's rights: but this was present here, because the shopkeeper had not consented to the labels being swapped. These remarks were of course inconsistent with the *ratio* of *Lawrence*, insofar as it had one; but Lord Roskill did not tell us whether that case was distinguishable,

---

[52] Until 15 January 2007, obtaining property by deception contrary to s 15 of the Theft Act 1968, and thereafter, fraud under the Fraud Act 2006.
[53] [1996] AC 815. [54] Theft (Amendment) Act 1996 (now repealed by the Fraud Act 2006).
[55] [1972] AC 626. [56] See further ch 4 in this volume.
[57] *Anderton v Burnside; R v Morris* [1984] AC 320; comment [1984] CLJ 7.

right for the wrong reasons, or impliedly overruled. As in *Lawrence* the House made no reference to the legislative background to the Theft Act, or to the principle of 'strict construction'. The very different House of Lords which returned to the issue nine years later in *Gomez*[58] cannot, unlike its predecessors, be criticised for want of effort; but most of this was expended in discussing the two earlier cases, and trying to make sense of them. Because there now existed case law on the subject, the majority said that it was now too late to look at the legislative background;[59] and neither the majority, nor Lord Lowry, who dissented (and who did look at the legislative background), made any mention of the principle of strict construction. The group of Law Lords who considered the issue for the fourth and final time in *Hinks*[60] also took the issue seriously, and Lord Steyn, in whose speech the rest of the majority concurred, also confronted the issues of policy. But once again, much of their combined effort was focused on discussing the earlier cases—and nobody, not even the dissenting minority, mentioned the principle of strict construction.

From this brief survey of the work of the House of Lords as an interpreter of criminal offences I believe that two conclusions can be drawn. First, its performance has improved with time, and secondly, it (or its successor) could in future do still better. In particular, when construing statutory offences our highest court should adopt the principled approach suggested earlier in this chapter, and not be deflected into a minute examination of the earlier cases, especially those which are devoid of an intelligible *ratio decidendi*. In the world of computers, there is a well-known proverb, brief and rather coarse, which means that time spent processing inherently defective data is time wasted. It applies to legal analysis as well.

No discussion of the House of Lords as an interpreter of criminal offences would be complete without a mention of *R v R*,[61] where it extended the reach of the crime of rape by abolishing the common law rule that a husband cannot be prosecuted for raping his wife—supposedly preserved by the phrase '*unlawful* sexual intercourse' in the statutory definition of the offence of rape.[62] Much has been written about this case, and here there is little room to add to it. But in answer to those who have criticised the Law Lords for extending the criminal law when this ought to be left to Parliament, two points in my view can be made. The first is that the 'marital exemption' in rape was a rule which, at the end of the twentieth century, nobody defended on the merits. And the second is that the 'marital exemption' was an anomalous rule which conflicted with a broader and more important principle: that to be valid, a person's consent to acts done to his or her body must subsist at the time the act takes place, and if given in advance, can be withdrawn.

---

[58] [1993] AC 442. [59] ibid, Lord Keith at 464C–D. [60] [2001] 2 AC 241.
[61] [1992] 1 AC 599. [62] Sexual Offences (Amendment) Act 1976, s 1(1).

The mental element in crime

One of the basic principles of criminal law upon which most theorists agree is the notion that criminal liability should be based on fault. And for most academic lawyers, this means (i) that strict liability, if admitted at all, should be limited to the minor offences; (ii) 'fault' means fault in relation to the elements of the offence—a notion that is sometimes called the 'correspondence principle'; (iii) fault may consist, in descending order of gravity, of intention, recklessness, or negligence; and (iv) the more serious the offence, the higher the level of fault the law requires. The principles are usually reflected in the criminal codes of countries which have them—and in this country, which does not, they are to be seen in the Draft Code drawn up 20 years ago by the Law Commission. In the light of this, one might have expected to see them reflected in the decisions by which the House of Lords has shaped English criminal law over the last hundred years. How far is this the case?

As regards strict liability, I believe most academic lawyers would say that it has done rather well. It got off to a spectacularly bad start in *Warner v MPC*,[63] in which it held, by a majority, that the offence of possessing dangerous drugs—for which the defendant in that case had been sentenced to two years' imprisonment—carries strict liability; and hence, even if Warner had been telling the truth when he said that he was unaware of what the contents of the package was, he was still guilty. This decision was ill received, and Parliament later reversed it, creating for this particular crime a 'no negligence' defence.[64] But when the issue of strict liability came before the House again, this time in the context of the related offence of being 'concerned in the management' of premises used for drug-taking, a different line was taken. Lord Reid, who had vocally dissented in *Warner*, delivered the leading speech, which contained a pronouncement that has been much quoted since. Having pointed out that many criminal statutes are silent as to whether mens rea is required or not, he said that in such cases

there has for centuries been a presumption that Parliament did not intend to make criminals of those who were in no way blameworthy in what they did. That means that whenever a section is silent as to mens rea there is a presumption that, in order to give effect to the will of Parliament, we must read in words appropriate to require mens rea.

In later cases the House has said that this presumption can be rebutted in the case of a 'regulatory offence', conviction for which carries little moral obloquy; but where the offence carries a heavy maximum penalty, or where a conviction for it would leave a dark stain on the defendant's character, it cannot.[65] In recent years

---

[63] [1969] 2 AC 256.

[64] Misuse of Drugs Act 1971, s 28; a provision which the Home Office then dragged its heels about implementing: see JC Smith and B Hogan, *Criminal Law* (London: Butterworths, 3rd edn 1973) 73.

[65] Compare *Westminster CC v Croyalgrange* [1986] 1 WLR 674 and *Pharmaceutical Society of Great Britain v Storkwain* [1986] 1 WLR 903.

it twice took this line, spectacularly, in the context of sexual offences involving minors, holding that defendants were guilty of these offences only where they knew or suspected that the victim was under age.[66] In the first of these, *R v B (A Minor)*, Lord Steyn said that the fact that Parliament had recently quintupled the maximum penalty for the offence to make it carry ten years' imprisonment instead of two was a factor that should make the courts particularly wary about holding that liability for this offence was strict.[67]

A related issue is what is usually called the 'correspondence principle': the notion that the fault element of a crime should extend to all the elements of the actus reus. Here the House of Lords has done less well, because it has delivered a series of decisions which reaffirm, without questioning the principle, the existence of a series of constructive crimes. It has done so, first and foremost, in the context of the crime of murder. In *R v Beard*,[68] the first case in which the reconstructed House of Lords considered a point of substantive criminal law—it resoundingly reaffirmed 'constructive murder': the rule that a death caused in the course of committing a felony is automatically a murder, whether or not the accused foresaw death or bodily harm as the result. Then, after the felony-murder rule had been abolished by section 1 of the Homicide Act 1957, in a trilogy of well-known cases it contrived to hold that it is still murder to cause the death of another by an act intended to cause grievous bodily harm, whether or not the actor foresaw the possibility of death.[69]

In *DPP v Newbury and Jones*[70] the House reaffirmed the existence of constructive manslaughter, a crime of which a defendant is guilty if he causes death by an act that is 'unlawful and dangerous'—for example, dropping a large stone over a bridge in the path of a train—irrespective of whether he himself foresaw any bodily harm to anyone. And in *R v Savage and Parmenter*[71] the House held that the statutory offence of assault occasioning actual bodily harm[72] is a constructive crime, of which the defendant who intends to commit an assault or battery is guilty irrespective of whether he intended or foresaw bodily harm as a result; and in similar vein, the statutory offence of maliciously wounding or inflicting grievous bodily harm[73] is a constructive crime, in that a person is guilty

---

[66] *B (A Minor) v DPP* [2000] 2 AC 428; *R v K* [2002] 1 AC 462.

[67] A very different spirit, alas, animates the speeches of the majority in the recent case of *G* [2008] 1 WLR 1379, the first case where the new law on sexual offences created by the Sexual Offences Act 2003 came before the House of Lords. The majority had no difficulty in accepting that Parliament had really meant the offence of sexual intercourse with a person under 13 to carry strict liability as to the victim's age; or that this rule should equally apply to a defendant who was only 15 himself; or that the resulting offence should carry the stigmatic label 'rape', and the possibility of life imprisonment, even where the girl concerned had not only consented, but also deceived the defendant by lying about her age; and one member of the majority, Baroness Hale, endorsed this outcome with evident enthusiasm.

[68] [1920] AC 479.   [69] *DPP v Smith* [1961] AC 290, *Hyam v DPP* [1975] AC 55.
[70] [1977] AC 500.   [71] [1992] 1 AC 699.
[72] Offences Against the Person Act 1861, s 47.   [73] ibid, s 20.

if he foresaw any bodily harm resulting from his act, even if it was not a 'wound' or 'grievous bodily harm'. For those who support the correspondence principle, this group of cases are an obvious disappointment.

In defence of the House of Lords, it might be said that the bulk of the existing case law pointed in the direction that they took, and the Law Lords could hardly have done other than they did. But as against this, it could be said that in *Hyam*, which held that mens rea for murder includes intention to cause grievous bodily harm, the House split 3 to 2, with Lords Diplock and Kilbrandon powerfully dissenting. Had they persuaded one of their brethren to join them, murder would no longer be, in any sense, a constructive crime. It was, as the Duke of Wellington said about the Battle of Waterloo, 'a damned nice thing'.

On identifying the different types of fault, and the distinctions between them, the House of Lords has a rather chequered record; but it is one which can (I think) be fairly described as successful in the end.

The efforts of the House of Lords to define intention have taken place in the context of the crime of murder, and of what is meant by 'an intent' to cause death or grievous bodily harm. The story begins with *DPP v Smith*[74] where, as everyone presumably remembers, Smith had driven his car off at speed with a policeman clinging to the side, zig-zagging in an apparent attempt to throw him off, so killing the policeman when he fell into the path of an oncoming vehicle. The Court of Criminal Appeal quashed Smith's conviction for murder, and substituted a conviction for manslaughter with a sentence of ten years' imprisonment, because the trial judge had failed to make it explicitly clear to the jury that the key question was what Smith himself actually foresaw or intended. Concurring in a speech delivered by Viscount Kilmuir LC,[75] the House restored the murder conviction and laid down a definition of intention that was wholly objective. Once a person is 'unlawfully and voluntarily doing something to someone', it said, he is deemed to intend any consequences of his conduct that a reasonable man would have foreseen, irrespective of what he intended or foresaw himself.

At a practical level this 'objective' definition of intention was extraordinarily severe—and at a theoretical level it was objectionable because it extended the boundaries of intention so widely as to swallow up recklessness and even trespass into the territory previously thought to belong to negligence.[76] The decision was much criticised, and in 1967 Parliament reversed it by a statute which made it clear that, where intention or foresight are required, what counts is what was actually foreseen or intended by the defendant.[77]

---

[74] [1961] AC 290.

[75] The other Law Lords being Lord Tucker, Lord Denning, Lord Parker CJ, and Lord Goddard, his 83-year-old predecessor. The author of the speech is said to have been Lord Parker: see TP Morris and L Blom-Cooper, *A Calendar of Murder* (London: Michael Joseph, 1964) 163.

[76] Although, as Viscount Kilmuir pointed out, it had the support of OW Holmes in *The Common Law* (1881).

[77] Criminal Justice Act 1967, s 8.

Its next attempt to lay down a workable definition of intention in murder was scarcely any better. In *Hyam v DPP*[78] the House said that intention includes both desire for the outcome and, in certain cases, conscious risk-taking: but between them, the Law Lords used a wide range of phrases to describe the degree of risk which, if foreseen, meant that the defendant's mental state counted as intention.[79] So just as the test in *DPP v Smith* was unsatisfactory because it blurred the distinction between intention and negligence, so the test in *Hyam v DPP* was unsatisfactory because it blurred the line between intention and recklessness. Eventually, after two further efforts to redraw the line more appropriately,[80] in *Woolin*[81] the House of Lords eventually decided that conscious risk-taking may amount to intention if, but only if, the risk-taker foresaw the consequence as 'a virtual certainty'. Although this test does not please everybody,[82] it seems to be workable in practice—and it does draw a clear line between intention and subjective recklessness.

In *Caldwell*, as we saw earlier, the House of Lords also made a false start in its efforts to define recklessness. In that case it rejected a well-established view which limited the concept to conscious risk-taking, and redefined it to also include unconscious risk-taking by someone who 'has not given any thought to the possibility of there being any such risk'. This decision blurred the line between recklessness and negligence, just as *DPP v Smith* had earlier blurred the line between negligence and intention; and there was general relief when in 2003 a House of Lords under the leadership of Lords Bingham and Steyn overruled it and restored the narrower definition of recklessness, in which one of the ingredients is actual foresight of the risk in question.[83]

So far, the House of Lords has not been required to discuss the meaning of simple negligence for the purpose of criminal proceedings. But in the context of manslaughter it has been faced with the task of giving a meaning to the concept of 'gross negligence'. And once again, the story is one of a series of confusions, with a relatively successful outcome in the end. In *Andrews v DPP*[84] the House of Lords gave its qualified approval to the remarks of Lord Hewart CJ in *Bateman*,[85] where he had said that for manslaughter the negligence of the accused must go 'beyond a mere matter of compensation between subjects' and show 'such disregard for the life and safety of others as to amount to a crime against the State and conduct deserving punishment'; but having done so, it muddied the waters by saying that '...of all the epithets that can be applied "reckless" most nearly

---

[78] [1975] AC 55.   [79] See Glanville Williams's note, [1974] CLJ 200.
[80] *Moloney* [1985] AC 905 and *Hancock and Shankland* [1986] AC 455.
[81] [1999] 1 AC 82.
[82] One criticism of the test is its uncertainty, because the test it lays down is exclusive, but not conclusive: the tribunal of fact 'may' find intention where the defendant believed that the consequence was virtually certain, but is not obliged to do so; see D Ormerod (ed), Smith and Hogan, *Criminal Law* (Oxford: OUP, 12th edn 2008) 99–100. Another is that it is in some respects too narrow: Antje Pedain, 'Intention and the Terrorist Example' [2003] Crim L Rev 579.
[83] *R v G* [2004] 1 AC 1034.   [84] [1937] AC 576.   [85] (1925) 19 Cr App R 8.

covers the case'. Then nearly 50 years later, in *Seymour*,[86] it muddied them further by saying that the appropriate test for criminal liability for manslaughter in this type of case was the new 'objective' test of recklessness, recently created in *Caldwell*. And then at last in *Adomako* a new generation of Law Lords cleared up the confusion between gross negligence and recklessness with a decision which anathematised *Seymour*, reinstated the test in *Bateman*, and made it plain that negligence is, in principle, a failure to behave as a reasonable person in the defendant's position would, and 'gross' negligence is (in effect) missing that standard by a particularly wide margin. Although this test of gross negligence has been criticised as circular,[87] the law that emerges from *Adomako* is certainly much clearer than it was before. And when taken together with the decisions in *Woolin* and *R v G*, the result is that in English law the lines between intention, recklessness, and negligence are now relatively clear.

The fourth aspect of the fault principle is the idea that the more serious the offence, the higher the level of fault the law requires. In general, the decisions of the House of Lords apply this notion. In *Morgan*[88] it held that on principle the mental element in rape must be intention or recklessness, and not mere negligence; and to incur criminal liability a man must in principle be aware of at least the possibility that the victim did not consent. And more recently in *Saik*[89] it held that, to be guilty of the crime of conspiracy, a defendant must actually know the facts that make the conduct he has agreed to perform amount to a criminal offence; with the result that where a defendant is prosecuted for conspiracy to launder money, the prosecution must show that he was aware that the money he agreed to handle had criminal origins: even recklessness is not enough—and nor, *a fortiori*, is mere negligence.

Conclusion

The dominant view among those who have commented on the contribution of the House of Lords to the development of English criminal law is that, to put it crudely, it has made a mess of it. Thus many years ago, Meredith Jackson wrote, 'It cannot be said that the House of Lords have made adequate contributions to criminal law';[90] more recently David Robertson wrote: 'By common consent, including at least some of the Law Lords themselves and many of their juniors in

---

[86] [1983] 2 AC 493; In my note on the case at [1983] CLJ 187 I concluded that 'it must count as one of the most unsatisfactory pronouncements on criminal law which has fallen from the House of Lords over the last twenty years', and in retrospect I do not think this comment was too severe.

[87] See Smith and Hogan (n 82) 531.

[88] [1976] AC 182.   [89] [2007] 1 AC 18.

[90] *The Machinery of Justice in England* (Cambridge: CUP, 5th edn 1972) 152; his comments became progressively stronger in later editions.

the Court of Appeal, the Law Lords have not shone in their task of controlling and developing the criminal law.'[91]

This view was broadly justified, I believe, by the performance of the House of Lords in criminal cases up to the end of the 1980s. A good decision from the final appeal court on a point of criminal law should (i) see the point, (ii) address it with intellectual honesty, (iii) answer it in a way which is both consistent with general legal principles and not shocking to the moral sense of civilised people, and (iv) state the answer with sufficient clarity to enable the lower courts to decide future cases without generating more appeals. And in systems that make use of juries, as we do, there is a further quality much to be desired: (v) to present the law in a form which makes it possible for judges to give directions to juries that are intelligible to lay people. Some of the decisions of the reformed House of Lords in criminal cases during its first 110 years met these criteria, but—alas—a significant number did not.

Why was this so?

One reason that has sometimes been put forward as an explanation is the virtual absence from among their Lordships of anyone who had much of a background in the criminal law. During the crucial 25 years following the abolition of the Attorney General's fiat in 1960, when the House of Lords first had a real chance to make its mark on the criminal law, there were only three Law Lords who, before their appointment, had made any kind of name for themselves as experts in the criminal law: Lords Devlin, Lane, and Edmund-Davies; and of these three, only Edmund-Davies stayed there long enough to make his mark. Of the overwhelming majority who, both during that period and later, reached the House of Lords with little or no previous experience of the criminal law, some, like Lord Goff, developed a keen interest in it when they got there.[92] But some others, like Lord Roskill in *Morris*, let their impatience with the subject show; others again, like Lord Diplock in *Caldwell*, thought that it was an area in which they could make up new rules as they went along; and at least one admitted that it was beyond him. In his speech in *Hyam*, Lord Cross confessed that he had failed to grasp one of the main points in the case until the end, adding, 'My failure to appreciate this may well have been partly due to the fact that I have never before had to grapple with this obscure and highly technical branch of the law . . .'[93]

---

[91] D Robertson, *Judicial Discretion and the House of Lords* (Oxford: OUP, 1998); AH Manchester, *A Modern Legal History of England and Wales 1750–1950* (London: Butterworths, 1980) 175, 200.

[92] In 1988 he published a learned article in the LQR entitled 'The Mental Element in the Crime of Murder' 104 LQR 30, which provoked a response from Glanville Williams ('The Mens Rea for Murder: Leave it Alone' (1989) 105 LQR 387).

[93] *Hyam* [1975] AC 55, 97. Though a Chancery practitioner by origin, Cross did in fact have some criminal experience, having been Deputy Chairman of Suffolk Quarter Sessions, and sitting in the Criminal Division of the Court of Appeal after he became a Lord Justice of Appeal; so this self-deprecating comment may have been intended to blunt his rebuke to the appellant's counsel for failing to raise the point with sufficient clarity at the outset.

As a barrister Lord Edmund-Davies had practised in the criminal courts, as a judge he had extensive experience of criminal work both at first instance and on appeal, and for many years he was a member of the Criminal Law Revision Committee, where he worked closely with his friend and compatriot Glanville Williams. When he reached the House of Lords, his speeches in criminal cases, as might have been expected, showed a strong grasp of principle and a good sense of its practical application; qualities that make us suspect that, if the other two credible criminal lawyers, Devlin and Lane, had stayed longer, the performance of the House of Lords in criminal cases during this key period would have been a good deal better than it was. But Devlin, as is widely known, retired after three years because he found the House of Lords 'boring', and Lane, who also found the work there little to his taste,[94] left after less than a year to become Lord Chief Justice. In that capacity he regularly presided in the Criminal Division in the Court of Appeal, where his judgments certainly helped to develop a coherent set of principles in the criminal law. As the author of his obituary in *The Times* said, 'Given more time in the House of Lords he would have been able to craft and refine his judgments in a way that pressure of business does not permit in the criminal division of the Court of Appeal.'[95] And if the record of the House of Lords in criminal cases suffered from the departure of Devlin and Lane before their time, it probably also suffered from the failure of at least one other judge with a distinguished record in criminal cases to get there. Although Sir Frederick Lawton had his critics, particularly on the liberal left, his technical grasp of the criminal law was excellent, as is clear from his judgments in the court below.

From the 1990s onwards, the standard of judgments in criminal cases in the House of Lords has been consistently much better. Most of its decisions in criminal cases in recent years have been characterised by seriousness of purpose, thoughtfulness, and clarity of expression. This is so, I believe, not only in the areas that were examined in this chapter, but also in others which were left aside for reasons of space: among them, general defences,[96] and the burden of proof.[97]

To this improved state of affairs I believe a number of factors have contributed. One is the growing quantity and quality of academic writing in this area, and the willingness of the courts to refer to it. Another is the quality of the Law Lords who have been appointed, and their general willingness—unlike that of some of their predecessors—to treat criminal law as worthy of their attention. And a third is their reducing age, brought about by the gradual effect of section 26 of the Judicial Pensions and Retirement Act 1993, a provision for which (in my view) the name of the Lord Chancellor of the day, James Mackay, should be for ever

---

[94] To me, and a group of other visitors from Cambridge, he said that during his short time in the House of Lords he had 'used up a whole bottle of smelling-salts just to keep awake'!

[95] *The Times*, 24 August 2005.

[96] In particular, *R v Kingston* [1994] 2 AC 355; *R v Z* [2005] 2 AC 467.

[97] *Lambert* [2002] 2 AC 545; *Johnstone* [2003] 1 WLR 1736; *Sheldrake v DPP and AG's Reference (No 4 of 2002)* [2005] 1 AC 264.

blessed. As old professors sometimes lose their faculties, so old judges—alas—sometimes lose their judgement;[98] but whereas a bad book or article damages only the reputation of the author, a bad judgment also does injustice to the parties and, where it is final court of appeal that delivers it, it can also injure the very fabric of the law.

But if recent years have seen a new spirit in the judicial House of Lords towards criminal law, they have also seen a new and different spirit in the legislature. Parliament, in the grip of politicians who are in turn in the grip of public opinion as mediated by the editors of the tabloid newspapers, has busied itself in creating new criminal offences almost every aspect of which offends against the concept of a civilised system of criminal law as preached for many years by academic lawyers, and as practised in recent years by the judicial House of Lords. In the new criminal offences that have been created in huge numbers by both primary and secondary legislation in recent years,[99] the fault element (if any) is usually no more than negligence.[100] The Sexual Offences Act 2003—a piece of legislation of which the then Home Secretary, David Blunkett, has said he was particularly proud[101]—has reversed a whole series of House of Lords decisions, ratcheting the fault element in sexual offences downwards so that some very serious offences that previously required intention or recklessness are now offences of negligence, or even strict liability. The Road Safety Act 2006 has created a new range of constructive crimes: causing death by careless driving, and causing death by driving when disqualified, unlicensed, or uninsured—all punishable, of course, with imprisonment. To some offences of strict liability, Parliament has even decreed that a mandatory prison sentence shall apply.[102] The academic lawyer who looks at all this gets the feeling that the barbarians are at the gates—and prays, though perhaps with little hope, that the new Supreme Court will be strong enough to keep them at bay.

---

[98] The average age of the Appellate Committee that decided *Shaw v DPP* was 71 and Viscount Simonds, who delivered the leading speech, was 80; Lord Goddard, when he delivered the speech in *Sykes v DPP* (n 24), was 84.

[99] In 2006, Nick Clegg MP, then the Liberal Democrat's spokesman for home affairs, stated that no fewer than 3,000 new criminal offences had been created in the ten years since Tony Blair came to power: a claim which Channel Four News investigated, concluding that 'Clegg seems to be on pretty solid ground'. On 25 November 2005, Baroness Scotland, in answer to a parliamentary question from Lord Tebbit, admitted to 404 new offences emanating from the Home Office alone. She could not speak for other Departments: 'More detailed information is not held and could be identified and listed only at disproportionate cost.'

[100] See for example the offence of failing to protect a vulnerable member of the family contrary to s 5 of the Domestic Violence, Crimes and Victims Act 2004 (an offence of negligence, punishable with 14 years); Human Tissue Act, s 5(3) (an offence of negligence, punishable with three years' imprisonment, where a person carries out various procedures in relation to human body parts without the necessary authorisation).

[101] S Pollard, *David Blunkett* (London: Hodder and Stoughton, 2005) 307.

[102] Criminal Justice Act 2003, s 287, imposing mandatory prison sentences for a range of offences relating to possession of firearms.

33

Fair Trial: 'One Golden Thread'

Anthony Hooper[1]

Reginald Woolmington

The case against Reginald Woolmington was strong. At the age of 21, Reginald, a dairy man, killed his newly wedded wife, Violet, aged 17 and a half. Three months after the marriage took place, Violet had left Reginald and went to live with her mother. Reginald wanted her back. Violet refused. Less than a month later, on 10 December 1934, Violet's aunt, Mrs Daisy Brine, who lived next door, heard Reginald saying: 'Are you coming back or not?' and, 'Where's your mother?' Then Mrs Brine heard a gunshot. She saw the appellant mount his bicycle and ride away. She went next door and there found her niece lying on the mat. Violet had been shot through the heart.

In the House of Lords Viscount Sankey, Lord Chancellor, set out the appellant's account:[2]

According to Reginald Woolmington's own story, having brooded over and deliberated upon the position all through the night of December 9, he went on the morning of the 10th in the usual way to the milking at his employer's farm, and while milking conceived this idea that he would take the old gun which was in the barn and he would take it up that morning to his wife's mother's house where she was living, and that he would show her that gun and tell her that he was going to commit suicide if she did not come back. He would take the gun up for the purpose of frightening her into coming back to him by causing her to think that he was going to commit suicide. He finished his milking, went back to his father's house, had breakfast and then left, taking with him a hack saw. He returned to the farm, went into the barn, got the gun, which had been used for rook shooting, sawed off the barrels of it, then took the only two cartridges which were there and put them into the gun. He took the two pieces of the barrel which he had sawn off and the hack saw, crossed a field about 60 yards wide and dropped them into the brook. Having done that, he returned on his bicycle, with the gun in his overcoat pocket, to his father's house and changed his clothes. Then he got a piece of wire flex which he attached

[1] I am very grateful to Professor David Ormerod and to my wife Fiona Baigrie Hooper for the help they have given me in writing this chapter.

[2] *Woolmington v DPP* [1935] AC 462.

to the gun so that he could suspend it from his shoulder underneath his coat, and so went off to the house where his wife was living. He knocked at the door, went into the kitchen and asked her: 'Are you coming back?' She made no answer. She came into the parlour, and on his asking her whether she would come back she replied she was going into service. He then, so he says, threatened he would shoot himself, and went on to show her the gun and brought it across his waist, when it somehow went off and his wife fell down and he went out of the house. He told the jury that it was an accident, that it was a pure accident; that whilst he was getting the gun from under his shoulder and was drawing it across his breast it accidentally went off and he was doing nothing unlawful, nothing wrong, and this was a pure accident . . . [W]hen he was arrested at 7.30 on the evening of the 10th and charged with having committed murder he said: 'I want to say nothing, except I done it, and they can do what they like with me. It was jealousy I suppose. Her mother enticed her away from me. I done all I could to get her back. That's all.'[3]

He left a note which, so he claimed, he had written after the shooting:[4]

Good bye all.

It is agonies to carry on any longer. I have kept true hoping she would return this is the only way out. They ruined me and I'll have my revenge. May God forgive me for doing this but it is the Best thing. Ask Jess to call for the money paid on motor bike (Wed.). Her mother is no good on this earth but have no more cartridges only 2 one for her and one for me. I am of a sound mind now. Forgive me for all trouble caused

Good bye

ALL

I love Violet with all my heart

Reg.

At the conclusion of his first trial, which lasted one day, the jury could not agree. At his second trial, the trial judge, Swift J, directed the jury on the issue of burden of proof in the following way:

If you come to the conclusion that she died in consequence of injuries from the gun which he was carrying, you are put by the law of this country into this position: The killing of a human being is homicide, however he may be killed, and all homicide is presumed to be malicious and murder, unless the contrary appears from circumstances of alleviation, excuse, or justification. 'In every charge of murder, the fact of the killing being first proved, all the circumstances of accident, necessity or infirmity are to be satisfactorily proved by the prisoner, unless they arise out of the evidence produced against him: for the law will presume that the attack would be founded in malice unless the contrary appeareth' [Foster, *Crown Law* (1762), page 255]. That has been the law of this country for all time since we had law. Once it is shown to a jury that somebody has died through the act of another, that is presumed to be murder, unless the person who has been guilty of the act which causes the death can satisfy a jury that what happened was something less, something which might be alleviated, something which might be reduced to a charge of manslaughter, or was something which was accidental, or was something which could be justified.[5]

---

[3] ibid, 471–2.　　　[4] ibid, 464.　　　[5] ibid, 473.

After a retirement of just over an hour, the jury convicted the appellant and he was sentenced to death.[6] A month later the Court of Criminal Appeal dismissed the appeal, saying that there was ample authority for the proposition of law relied upon by the judge. The Attorney General then gave his fiat certifying that the appeal involved a point of law of exceptional public importance and that, in his opinion, it was desirable in the public interest that a further appeal should be brought. The House of Lords allowed the appeal and quashed the conviction, holding that the trial judge had misdirected the jury on the issue of the burden and standard of proof. Viscount Sankey LC gave the only speech, with which Lord Atkin, amongst others, concurred. (It was Lord Atkin who, a few years later, in *Liversidge v Anderson*[7] delivered probably the most well-known dissent in any case in the House of Lords. Lord Atkin took to task those judges who, 'when face to face with claims involving the liberty of the subject, show themselves more executive-minded than the executive.')[8]

It was in *Woolmington* that Viscount Sankey famously said:

Throughout the web of the English Criminal Law one golden thread is always to be seen, that it is the duty of the prosecution to prove the prisoner's guilt subject to what I have already said as to the defence of insanity and subject also to any statutory exception... No matter what the charge or where the trial, the principle that the prosecution must prove the guilt of the prisoner is part of the common law of England and no attempt to whittle it down can be entertained.[9]

One significant obstacle to the search for the 'golden thread' was the passage in Foster's *Crown Law* relied upon by the trial judge. Viscount Sankey said that Sir Michael Foster, although a distinguished judge, was, for the purpose of deciding whether the proposition of law was correct, to be regarded 'as a text book writer'. 'He did not lay down the doctrine in any case before him, but in an article which is described as the "Introduction to the Discourse of Homicide" published in 1762.'[10]

Viscount Sankey pointed out that the first part of this passage appears in 'nearly every text-book or abridgement which has since been written', including *Stephen's Digest of the Criminal Law* and *Archbold, Criminal Pleading, Evidence*

---

[6] A valuable full account of the trials can be found in BB Block and J Hostettler, *Famous Cases: Nine Cases That Changed the Law* (Hook: Waterside Press, 2002) ch 3. The authors reveal that Reginald and Violet had a son and that after his release, Reginald disappeared into obscurity.

[7] [1942] AC 206.

[8] ibid, 244. He also said, in what must be one of the most well-known passages in any House of Lords decision (245): 'I know of only one authority which might justify the suggested method of construction: "When I use a word," Humpty Dumpty said in rather a scornful tone, "it means just what I choose it to mean, neither more nor less." "The question is," said Alice, "whether you can make words mean so many different things." "The question is," said Humpty Dumpty, "which is to be master—that's all."' (*Lewis Carroll, Through the Looking Glass*, c vi.)

[9] n 2, 481.   [10] ibid, 474.

and Practice, and that it appears almost textually in *Russell on Crimes* and *Halsbury's Laws of England*. Viscount Sankey asked whether it was correct to say, 'and did Foster mean to lay down, that there may arise in the course of a criminal trial a situation at which it is incumbent on the accused to prove his innocence?' There was, Viscount Sankey said, no authority before Foster for such a proposition, contradicting the trial judge who had said that it had 'been the law of this country for all time since we had law'.

Having examined a number of treatises and cases, Viscount Sankey examined *R v Greenacre*[11] in which the passage from Foster was incorporated by the 'very distinguished judge' Tindal CJ.[12]

Viscount Sankey went on to say:

If at any period of a trial it was permissible for the judge to rule that the prosecution had established its case and that the onus was shifted on the prisoner to prove that he was not guilty and that unless he discharged that onus the prosecution was entitled to succeed, it would be enabling the judge in such a case to say that the jury must in law find the prisoner guilty and so make the judge decide the case and not the jury, which is not the common law.

The last word rests with the jury

Many years later, in *R v Wang*,[13] the House of Lords relied, in part, on this passage. When called upon to answer the following question of law: 'In what circumstances, if any, is a judge entitled to direct a jury to return a verdict of guilty?' the House of Lords said that there are no circumstances in which a judge is entitled to direct a jury to return a verdict of guilty. In *Wang*, the appellant had been in possession of a bag containing a curved martial arts sword, in its sheath, and a small Ghurkha-style knife. The appellant had subsequently been indicted on two counts of having an article with a blade or point in a public place, contrary to section 139(1) of the Criminal Justice Act 1988; one count relating to the sword, the other to the knife.

The appellant had testified that he was a Buddhist and that he practised Shaolin, a traditional martial art. Those who practised Shaolin were Buddhists and were called Shaolin followers. To learn Shaolin, one was instructed how to behave and keep the spirit. It was necessary to have a good personality. Shaolin followers learned to help society and protect people, to which end they relied

---

[11] (1837) 8 C & P 35, 173 ER 388.

[12] In addition to successfully defending Queen Caroline at her trial for adultery, Tindal CJ made an important contribution to the development of the modern law of provocation in *R v Hayward* (1833) 6 C & P 157 and presided over the panel of judges who advised the House of Lords in *M'Naughten's Case* (1843) 10 Cl & F 200, 8 ER 718.

[13] [2005] 1 WLR 661.

on Buddhist teaching, especially love without denominations or limitations. The sword was one of 18 weapons in which a Shaolin follower must become expert, and the knife was a 'willow leaf knife', the use of which required much skill. One who excelled would become the teacher of all followers in the future. To practise Shaolin was not to worship Buddha but to keep the spirit of the people.

On the day in question, the appellant, so he claimed, had been on his way to see his solicitor. He had taken the sword and knife with him because he did not like to leave them in the place where he was staying in Clacton, and he liked to stop at remote and uninhabited places to practise Shaolin.

Possession not being in issue, the judge told counsel that he could see no defence to these two counts. Counsel for the appellant made plain his reliance on section 139(4) and (5)(b) of the 1988 Act, which provide:

(4) It shall be a defence for a person charged with an offence under this section to prove that he had good reason ... for having the article with him in a public place. (5) Without prejudice to the generality of subsection (4) above, it shall be a defence for a person charged with an offence under this section to prove that he had the article with him – (b) for religious reasons; ...

The judge ruled that he did not have a defence because as a matter of law he had no good reason for having the article with him in a public place, and directed the jury to convict.

Lord Bingham, giving the considered opinion of the Committee, held that the judge should have left the matter to the jury. There being no circumstances where the judge can direct the jury to convict, it will follow, as Lord Bingham accepted, 'that there will be acquittals of such high profile defendants as *Ponting*, *Randle* and *Pottle*'. Of these acquittals, he said that they

have been quite as much welcomed as resented by the public, which over many centuries has adhered tenaciously to its historic choice that decisions on the guilt of defendants charged with serious crime should rest with a jury of lay people, randomly selected, and not with professional judges.[14]

Lord Bingham continued:

That the last word should rest with the jury remains, as Sir Patrick Devlin, writing in 1956, said (Hamlyn Lectures, pp 160, 162),

'an insurance that the criminal law will conform to the ordinary man's idea of what is fair and just. If it does not, the jury will not be a party to its enforcement ... The executive knows that in dealing with the liberty of the subject it must not do anything which would seriously disturb the conscience of the average member of Parliament or of the average juryman. I know of no other real checks that exist today upon the power of the executive.'

[14] ibid, para 16.

Foster put to rest

I return to Viscount Sankey's speech in *Woolmington*. Viscount Sankey gave what may be described as a generous interpretation of the passage in Foster and the decision in *Greenacre*:

All that is meant is that if it is proved that the conscious act of the prisoner killed a man and nothing else appears in the case, there is evidence upon which the jury may, not must, find him guilty of murder. It is difficult to conceive so bare and meagre a case, but that does not mean that the onus is not still on the prosecution.[15]

And a little later Viscount Sankey said:

Just as there is evidence on behalf of the prosecution so there may be evidence on behalf of the prisoner which may cause a doubt as to his guilt. In either case, he is entitled to the benefit of the doubt. But while the prosecution must prove the guilt of the prisoner, there is no such burden laid on the prisoner to prove his innocence and it is sufficient for him to raise a doubt as to his guilt; he is not bound to satisfy the jury of his innocence.[16]

Viscount Sankey continued by saying that if, however, the passage in Foster and the decision in *Greenacre* were to be interpreted as the trial judge had done in Reginald Woolmington's trial, then they are wrong.[17] In murder cases, he went on,

[w]hen evidence of death and malice has been given (this is a question for the jury) the accused is entitled to show by evidence or by examination of the circumstances adduced by the Crown that the act on his part which caused death was either unintentional or provoked. If the jury are either satisfied with his explanation or, upon a review of all the evidence, are left in reasonable doubt whether, even if his explanation be not accepted, the act was unintentional or provoked, the prisoner is entitled to be acquitted.[18]

The modernisation of the reasonable doubt test

Although the popular view is that the prosecution must prove the case beyond a reasonable doubt, difficulties with the meaning of 'reasonable doubt' (or perceived difficulties in explaining to a jury what is or is not a reasonable doubt)

---

[15] [1935] AC 462, 480.   [16] ibid, 481.   [17] ibid, 482.

[18] ibid, 482. In *Bratty v AG for Northern Ireland* [1963] 1 AC 386, the House of Lords held that the burden of disproving automatism was on the prosecution unless the only suggested cause for the automatism was a defect of reason caused by a disease of the mind, ie insanity within the M'Naughten Rules, in which case the burden is on the defendant, the standard being the balance of probabilities. Section 2 of the Homicide Act 1957, which created the statutory defence of diminished responsibility, places the legal burden on the defendant.

have led to the abandonment, in practice, of the reasonable doubt test. Juries are now told, in the words of the current Judicial Studies Board Specimen Directions:[19]

How does the prosecution succeed in proving the defendant's guilt? The answer is—by making you sure of it. Nothing less than that will do. If after considering all the evidence you are sure that the defendant is guilty, you must return a verdict of 'Guilty'. If you are not sure, your verdict must be 'Not Guilty'.

According to the Specimen Directions:

Normally, when directing a jury on the standard of proof, it is not necessary to use the phrase 'beyond reasonable doubt'. But where it has been used in the trial, e.g. by counsel in their speeches, it is desirable to give the following direction: 'The prosecution must make you sure of guilt, which is the same as proving the case beyond reasonable doubt'...

I do not believe that Viscount Sankey would object to the change, although I am unaware of any decision in the House of Lords that has considered the change and approved it.

Reginald Woolmington goes free

The House of Lords refused to apply the 'proviso'. In the words again of Viscount Sankey:

We were then asked to follow the Court of Criminal Appeal and to apply the proviso of Section 4 of the Criminal Appeal Act, 1907, which says: 'the Court may, notwithstanding that they are of opinion that the point raised in the appeal might be decided in favour of the Appellant, dismiss the appeal if they consider no substantial miscarriage of justice has actually occurred'. There is no doubt that there is ample jurisdiction to apply that proviso in a case of murder. The Act makes no distinction between a capital case and any other case, but we think it impossible to apply it in the present case. *We cannot say that if the jury had been properly directed they would have inevitably come to the same conclusion.*[20]

Thus Reginald Woolmington was saved from hanging and was released some four months after Violet's death. Today a new trial would be ordered, but long gone are the days when the House of Lords was able to consider a conviction appeal within four months of the alleged crime: it is likely to take more than four months just to bring the defendant to his first trial, let alone his second.

---

[19] Judicial Studies Board, *Crown Court Benchbook*, Specimen Directions available from the JSB website: <http://www.jsboard.co.uk>.
[20] [1935] AC 462, 482–3, emphasis added.

Would the jury inevitably have come to the same conclusion, absent the error?

The italicised sentence in the just cited quotation is of the greatest importance. The test there laid down is now applied by the Court of Appeal (Criminal Division) whenever there has been an error in the trial process, whether, for example, by reason of a misdirection or the admission of inadmissible evidence or prosecution non-disclosure of material which the defence would have relied on at trial. After a 'wobble' in *Stafford v Director of Public Prosecutions,*[21] the House of Lords in *R v Pendleton*[22] confirmed that the same test applied in fresh evidence cases:

First ... the Court of Appeal ... is not and should never become the primary decision-maker. Secondly, ... the Court of Appeal ... has an imperfect and incomplete understanding of the full processes which led the jury to convict. The Court of Appeal can make its assessment of the fresh evidence it has heard, but save in a clear case it is at a disadvantage in seeking to relate that evidence to the rest of the evidence which the jury heard. For these reasons it will usually be wise for the Court of Appeal, in a case of any difficulty, to test their own provisional view by asking whether the evidence, if given at the trial, might reasonably have affected the decision of the trial jury to convict. If it might, the conviction must be thought to be unsafe.[23]

The golden thread

The golden thread is so deeply woven into the fabric of our society that it is perhaps difficult for us to understand the importance at the time of *Woolmington*, not only in this country but in the numerous Dominions and Colonies which then formed part of the British Empire. The requirement of proof beyond a reasonable doubt in criminal cases was embedded in the laws of all those countries which then formed part of that Empire. Sadly, as I shall show shortly, Parliament is less attached.

Proof beyond reasonable doubt is likewise embedded into the law of the United States. In 1970 in *Re Winship*[24] Justice Brennan, delivering the opinion of the majority in the Supreme Court, said:

The requirement that guilt of a criminal charge be established by proof beyond a reasonable doubt dates at least from our early years as a Nation. The 'demand for a higher degree of persuasion in criminal cases was recurrently expressed from ancient times, [though] its crystallization into the formula 'beyond a reasonable doubt' seems to have occurred as late as 1798. It is now accepted in common law jurisdictions as the measure

---

[21] [1974] AC 878.   [22] [2002] 1 WLR 72.
[23] At para 19. Cf *Dial v The State (Trinidad and Tobago)* [2005] 1 WLR 1660 (PC).
[24] 397 US 358 (1970).

of persuasion by which the prosecution must convince the trier of all the essential elements of guilt.' [C McCormick, *Evidence* § 321, pp 681–2 (1954); see also J Wigmore, *Evidence* § 2497 (3rd edn, 1940).] Although virtually unanimous adherence to the reasonable doubt standard in common law jurisdictions may not conclusively establish it as a requirement of due process, such adherence does 'reflect a profound judgment about the way in which law should be enforced and justice administered.' [*Duncan v. Louisiana*, 391 US 145, 391 US 155 (1968)].[25]

Quoting the 1895 decision of the Supreme Court in *Coffin v United States*,[26] Justice Brennan said that the reasonable doubt standard plays a vital role in the American scheme of criminal procedure:

It is a prime instrument for reducing the risk of convictions resting on factual error. The standard provides concrete substance for the presumption of innocence—that bedrock 'axiomatic and elementary' principle whose 'enforcement lies at the foundation of the administration of our criminal law' ... [27]

Re Winship is itself of considerable importance because, by a majority, the Supreme Court applied the requirement of proof beyond a reasonable doubt test to the trial of juveniles, relying in part on the landmark 1967 decision of the Court in *Re Gault*.[28] In that case the Court, having referred to Dean Roscoe Pound who wrote in 1937 that 'the powers of the Star Chamber were a trifle in comparison with those of our juvenile courts ...', went on to ensure that juvenile defendants were entitled to the due process safeguards enjoyed by adult defendants. It was in *Re Gault* that the Court said:

Then, as now, goodwill and compassion were admirably prevalent [in juvenile courts]. But recent studies have, with surprising unanimity, entered sharp dissent as to the validity of this gentle conception. They suggest that the appearance as well as the actuality of fairness, impartiality and orderliness—in short, the essentials of due process—may be a more impressive and more therapeutic attitude so far as the juvenile is concerned.[29]

Although, as far as I am aware, the European Court of Human Rights has not expressly said that proof of guilt beyond a reasonable doubt is required under the Convention, it has said:

The Court considers that, in addition to being specifically mentioned in Article 6 § 2, a person's right in a criminal case to be presumed innocent and to require the prosecution to bear the onus of proving the allegations against him or her forms part of the general notion of a fair hearing under Article 6 § 1.[30]

Given the significant role of British lawyers in the drafting of the 1950 European Convention for the Protection of Human Rights and Fundamental Freedoms, it

---

[25] ibid, 361–2.   [26] 156 US 432, 453 (1895).   [27] n 24, 363.
[28] 387 US 1 (1967).   [29] ibid, 26.
[30] *Phillips v UK* (2001) (App No 41087/98), decision of 5 July 2001, para 40.

seems likely that the decision in *Woolmington* has had a profound effect on the domestic law of many countries which have not inherited a common law system.

I have also noticed that 'proof beyond a reasonable doubt' is sometimes translated in the French text as *l'intime conviction*, [31] the expression used in civil law jurisdictions to describe the necessary level of satisfaction before a criminal charge may be found proved.

The statutory exceptions, judicial intervention

Viscount Sankey accepted, as he had to, that the presumption of innocence was subject to any statutory exceptions. With the advent of the Human Rights Act 1998, the House of Lords in 2001 in *R v Lambert*[32] was able to do what the House of Lords in *Woolmington* could not do, that is, critically examine the statutory exceptions and reduce their number.[33] In *Lambert* the appellant had been found in possession of a duffle bag containing two kilos of cocaine. His defence was that he did not believe or suspect or have reason to suspect that the bag he was carrying contained cocaine, or any other controlled drug. The trial judge had directed the jury, in accordance with the law at the time, that on a charge of possession of cocaine with intent to supply, contrary to section 5 of the Misuse of Drugs Act 1971, the prosecution had to prove that the defendant had a bag in his possession and that the bag contained cocaine. It was for the defendant to prove on the balance of probabilities that he did not know that the bag contained a controlled drug. In lawyer's language, the burden on the defendant was not merely evidential but legal. The appeal was dismissed on the grounds that the Human Rights Act 1998 did not have retrospective effect, but their Lordships took the opportunity to give opinions on what are often called reverse onus of proof clauses.

Lord Steyn started the material part of his speech (at para 32) with a reference to *Woolmington* and the golden thread, and followed it with some statistics:

The *Woolmington* principle was, however, subject to Parliament legislating to the contrary. It is a fact that the legislature has frequently and in an arbitrary and indiscriminate manner made inroads on the basic presumption of innocence. Ashworth and Blake *(The Presumption of Innocence in English Criminal Law,* 1996 Crim LR 306, at 309) found 219 examples, among 540 offences triable in the Crown Court, of legal burdens or presumptions operating against the defendant. They observed that no fewer than 40% of the offences triable in the Crown Court appear to violate the presumption. In 1972 a most distinguished Criminal Law Revision Committee had observed that 'we are strongly of the

---

[31] See *John Murray v UK* (1996) 22 EHRR 29.   [32] [2002] 2 AC 545.
[33] Lord Bingham CJ had earlier in the Divisional Court expressed strong views about the compatibility of reverse onus clauses in terrorism legislation with Article 6(2): see *R v DPP, ex p Kebilene* [2000] 2 AC 326.

opinion that, both on principle and for the sake of clarity and convenience in practice, burdens on the defence should be evidential only': *Eleventh Report, Evidence (General)* Cmnd 4991 of 1972, para 140. Nevertheless, the process of enacting legal reverse burden of proof provisions continued apace.

More recent legislation, concerned with terrorism and money laundering, has been replete with reverse onus clauses. The Sexual Offences Act in section 75 creates a number of evidential presumptions[34] and section 76 creates, in inelegant language, a conclusive presumption to be applied when a person is being tried for the more serious sexual offences.[35]

Lord Steyn then turned (at para 33) to the impact of human rights conventions and the Human Rights Act:

In the meantime the human rights movement came into existence. The foundation of it was the Universal Declaration of Human Rights (1948), which has been the starting point of subsequent human rights texts. In article 11(1) it provided: 'Everyone charged with a penal offence has the right to be presumed innocent until proved guilty according to law...' Borrowing this language almost verbatim, article 6.2 of the European Convention for the Protection of Human Rights and Fundamental Freedoms (1950) provided: 'Everyone charged with a criminal offence shall be presumed innocent until proved guilty according to law'. Article 14.2 of the International Covenant on Civil and Political Rights (1966) which was signed by the United Kingdom in 1966 is to the same effect. Nevertheless, and despite the right of petition to the European Court of Human Rights created for the United Kingdom in 1961, there was no constraint in our domestic law to legislative incursions on the presumption of innocence. But by the 1998 Act Parliament has provided that, subject to the ultimate constitutional principle of the sovereignty of Parliament, inroads on the presumption of innocence must be compatible with article 6.2 as properly construed. If incompatibility arises, the subtle mechanisms of the 1998 Act come into play.

---

[34] Section 75(1) provides that 'the complainant is to be taken not to have consented to the relevant act unless sufficient evidence is adduced to raise an issue as to whether he consented, and the defendant is to be taken not to have reasonably believed that the complainant consented unless sufficient evidence is adduced to raise an issue as to whether he reasonably believed it'.

[35] Section 76 provides:

Conclusive presumptions about consent

(1) If in proceedings for an offence to which this section applies it is proved that the defendant did the relevant act [defined in section 77, eg penetration] and that any of the circumstances specified in subsection (2) existed, it is to be conclusively presumed—

   (a) that the complainant did not consent to the relevant act, and

   (b) that the defendant did not believe that the complainant consented to the relevant act.

(2) The circumstances are that—

   (a) the defendant intentionally deceived the complainant as to the nature or purpose of the relevant act;

   (b) the defendant intentionally induced the complainant to consent to the relevant act by impersonating a person known personally to the complainant.

On the vital importance of the presumption of innocence, Lord Steyn (at para 34) cited Sachs J in the South African Constitutional Court:

In *HM Advocate v McIntosh, PC* [2001] 3 WLR 107 Lord Bingham of Cornhill recently referred to the judgment of Sachs J of the South African Constitutional Court in *State v Coetzee* [1997] 2 LRC 593. It is worth setting out the eloquent explanation by Sachs J of the significance of the presumption of innocence in full, pp 677–678, para 220:

'There is a paradox at the heart of all criminal procedure in that the more serious the crime and the greater the public interest in securing convictions of the guilty, the more important do constitutional protections of the accused become. The starting point of any balancing enquiry where constitutional rights are concerned must be that the public interest in ensuring that innocent people are not convicted and subjected to ignominy and heavy sentences massively outweighs the public interest in ensuring that a particular criminal is brought to book... Hence the presumption of innocence, which serves not only to protect a particular individual on trial, but to maintain public confidence in the enduring integrity and security of the legal system. Reference to the prevalence and severity of a certain crime therefore does not add anything new or special to the balancing exercise. The perniciousness of the offence is one of the givens, against which the presumption of innocence is pitted from the beginning, not a new element to be put into the scales as part of a justificatory balancing exercise. If this were not so, the ubiquity and ugliness argument could be used in relation to murder, rape, car-jacking, housebreaking, drug-smuggling, corruption... the list is unfortunately almost endless, and nothing would be left of the presumption of innocence, save, perhaps, for its relic status as a doughty defender of rights in the most trivial of cases'.

The logic of this reasoning is inescapable.

Lord Steyn then rejected the argument that there was a valid distinction to be drawn between constituent elements of an offence and excuses. He agreed (at para 35) with the reasoning of the Supreme Court of Canada in *R v Whyte*:[36]

The exact characterization of a factor as an essential element, a collateral factor, an excuse, or a defence should not affect the analysis of the presumption of innocence. It is the final effect of a provision on the verdict that is decisive. If an accused is required to prove some fact on the balance of probabilities to avoid conviction, the provision violates the presumption of innocence because it permits a conviction in spite of a reasonable doubt in the mind of the trier of fact as to the guilt of the accused.[37]

Lord Steyn accepted that not all reverse onus of proof clauses would be incompatible with Article 6(2). He asked whether the reverse onus clause at issue was justified and proportionate. While finding that there was justification for imposing the legal burden of proof upon the defendant, he concluded that to do so was disproportionate. Having reached that conclusion, he held that the

---

[36] (1988) 51 DLR (4th) 481, 493.

[37] In *McIntosh v Lord Advocate* [2003] 1 AC 108 the Privy Council, on an appeal from the Appeal Court of the High Court of Justiciary of Scotland, held that the presumption of innocence did not apply to the post-conviction regime of confiscation orders. The House of Lords applied *McIntosh* in *R v Benjafield* [2003] 1 AC 1099.

legislation could be read down so as to impose only an evidential burden. Three other members of the Appellate Committee reached the same conclusion, namely Lord Slynn, Lord Hope, and Lord Clyde.

In *Sheldrake v Director of Public Prosecutions and Attorney General's Reference (No 4 of 2002)*,[38] the House of Lords upheld one reverse onus clause in the Road Traffic Act and, by a majority, held that a reverse onus clause in section 11 of the Terrorism Act 2000, concerned with proscribed organisations, should be read down to impose only an evidential burden. Lord Bingham, having described the principle in *Woolmington* as 'supremely important', went on to examine the European Court of Human Rights authorities in detail, concluding (at para 21):

From this body of authority certain principles may be derived. The overriding concern is that a trial should be fair, and the presumption of innocence is a fundamental right directed to that end. The Convention does not outlaw presumptions of fact or law but requires that these should be kept within reasonable limits and should not be arbitrary. It is open to states to define the constituent elements of a criminal offence, excluding the requirement of *mens rea*. But the substance and effect of any presumption adverse to a defendant must be examined, and must be reasonable. Relevant to any judgment on reasonableness or proportionality will be the opportunity given to the defendant to rebut the presumption, maintenance of the rights of the defence, flexibility in application of the presumption, retention by the court of a power to assess the evidence, the importance of what is at stake and the difficulty which a prosecutor may face in the absence of a presumption. Security concerns do not absolve member states from their duty to observe basic standards of fairness. The justifiability of any infringement of the presumption of innocence cannot be resolved by any rule of thumb, but on examination of all the facts and circumstances of the particular provision as applied in the particular case.

Lord Bingham then considered *Lambert* and another case in the House of Lords, *R v Johnstone*,[39] reminding lower courts (and, in particular, the Court of Appeal Criminal Division) that nothing said in *Johnstone* suggests an intention to depart from *Lambert*.

The presumption of innocence and offences which do not require proof of blameworthiness

Whereas legislative attempts to undermine the presumption of innocence by reversing the burden of proof are, following *Lambert*, subject to judicial scrutiny, the numerous legislative provisions expressly creating offences which do not require proof of blameworthiness, known as offences of total or partial strict liability/responsibility, are essentially immune from that same judicial scrutiny, as the House of Lords has recently confirmed in *R v G*.[40] If the definition of an

---

[38] [2005] 1 AC 264.   [39] [2003] 1 WLR 1736.
[40] [2009] 1 AC 93. See too p 608 above.

offence is such that it may be committed in the absence of any blameworthiness *vis-à-vis* some or all of the ingredients of the offence, the presumption of innocence cannot be prayed in aid to require proof of blameworthiness. Thus if, after *Lambert*, the legislature had made it an offence to be in possession of a controlled drug with intent to supply even though the defendant did not know or believe or have reason to believe that the item he intended to supply was a controlled drug, the courts, so the House of Lords has held, would be powerless to intervene.

In the absence of a clear legislative intention to punish conduct in the absence of blameworthiness *vis-à-vis* an ingredient of the crime, there is, so the House of Lords has held, a presumption that a subjective mental element is required. In the words of Lord Nicholls in *B v Director of Public Prosecutions*:[41]

In these circumstances the starting point for a court is the established common law presumption that a mental element, traditionally labelled *mens rea*, is an essential ingredient unless Parliament has indicated a contrary intention either expressly or by necessary implication. The common law presumes that, unless Parliament indicated otherwise, the appropriate mental element is an unexpressed ingredient of every statutory offence. On this I need do no more than refer to Lord Reid's magisterial statement in the leading case of *Sweet v. Parsley* [1970] AC 132, 148-149:

'. . . there has for centuries been a presumption that Parliament did not intend to make criminals of persons who were in no way blameworthy in what they did. That means that whenever a section is silent as to *mens rea* there is a presumption that, in order to give effect to the will of Parliament, we must read in words appropriate to require *mens rea* . . . it is firmly established by a host of authorities that *mens rea* is an essential ingredient of every offence unless some reason can be found for holding that that is not necessary.'[42]

In *B* the House held that a defendant is entitled to be acquitted of the offence of inciting a child under 14 to commit an act of gross indecency, contrary to section 1(1) of the Indecency with Children Act 1960, if he holds or may hold an honest belief that the child was aged 14 years or over. Parliament had not expressly or by necessary implication provided to the contrary.

I return to the decision in *G*. In that case, the appellant, aged 15 at the time of the alleged offence, had pleaded guilty to the offence of rape of a child under the age of 13, contrary to section 5 of the Sexual Offences Act 2003:

(1) A person commits an offence if—

    (a) he intentionally penetrates the vagina, anus or mouth of another person with his penis; and

    (b) the other person is under 13.

---

[41] [2000] 2 AC 428, 460.

[42] See also *R v Hunt* [1987] AC 352, a decision that was not referred to in *B* but which made it easier to find that the burden of proof was on the defendant.

(2) A person guilty of an offence under this section is liable, on conviction on indictment, to imprisonment for life.

The prosecution ultimately accepted the appellant's version of the facts, namely, that the complainant, aged 12 at the time, had consented to intercourse and that he believed and reasonably believed that she was 15. Indeed the complainant had, it was agreed, told him that she was 15. One of the appellant's grounds of appeal was that the conviction violated his right to a fair trial and the presumption of innocence under Article 6 of the Convention, because it was an offence of strict liability. In the words of Lord Hoffmann (at para 3),

> The mental element of the offence under section 5, as the language and structure of the section makes clear, is that penetration must be intentional but there is no requirement that the accused must have known that the other person was under 13. The policy of the legislation is to protect children. If you have sex with someone who is on any view a child or young person, you take your chance on exactly how old they are. To that extent the offence is one of strict liability and it is no defence that the accused believed the other person to be 13 or over.

It is worthy of note that a requirement that the defendant knew or reasonably believed that the consenting other party was over the age of 13 would still have left the defendant guilty of an offence against section 13,[43] punishable with five years' custody.

The House of Lords in *G* held that the content and interpretation of domestic substantive law is not engaged by Article 6(2) and by the presumption of innocence. In the words of Lord Hope (at para 27):

> So when article 6(2) uses the words 'innocent' and 'guilty' it is dealing with the burden of proof regarding the elements of the offence and any defences to it. It is not dealing with what those elements are or what defences to the offence ought to be available.

Although, according to Lord Hope,[44] an absolute offence may subject a defendant to conviction in circumstances where he has done nothing blameworthy, Article 6(2) and the presumption of innocence cannot assist him or her. I say 'him or her' because Baroness Hale, who agreed that Article 6(2) did not avail the defendant, seems to have seen the issue in terms only of males offending. She said:

> Thus there is not strict liability in relation to the conduct involved. The perpetrator has to intend to penetrate. Every male has a choice about where he puts his penis. It may be difficult for him to restrain himself when aroused but he has a choice. There is nothing unjust or irrational about a law which says that if he chooses to put his penis inside a child who turns out to be under 13 he has committed an offence (although the state of his

---

[43] By virtue of the oddly worded s 13, a person under 18 commits an offence if he does anything that would be an offence under any of ss 9 to 12 if he were aged 18.

[44] At para 30.

mind may again be relevant to sentence.) He also commits an offence if he behaves in the same way towards a child of 13 but under 16, albeit only if he does not reasonably believe that the child is 16 or over. So in principle sex with a child under 16 is not allowed. When the child is under 13, three years younger than that, he takes the risk that she may be younger than he thinks she is. The object is to make him take responsibility for what he chooses to do with what is capable of being, not only an instrument of great pleasure, but also a weapon of great danger.

Whilst many might agree with the proposition in the last sentence, it should be remembered that a female child over the age of nine commits an offence against section 7 of the Sexual Offences Act (an offence punishable with a maximum of 14 years' custody) if she intentionally touches a boy under the age of 13 with his consent, if the touching is sexual and even though she believes and reasonably believes he is 13.

Conclusion: the golden thread

It is a great tribute to the House of Lords that in 1935 it confirmed in the common law the presence of the golden thread and that it has, since then, done much to conserve and burnish it.

34

Torts

Robert Stevens

Introduction

The modern law of torts is dominated by decisions of the House of Lords. In other areas of private law this is not so. Within contract law, for example, the leading cases are frequently those of the Court of Appeal[1] or even first instance judges.[2] Another feature of the law of torts is how many of the leading cases are relatively recent. Again, this hyperactivity in modern times is not the case in other areas, notably the law of contract where many of the leading cases are relatively old.[3] Although the foundations of the law of torts are ancient, the building we currently live in is of very recent construction. It is perhaps unsurprising therefore that the large number of cases over a relatively short period of time has caused the law of torts to be perceived as a 'mess'.[4]

The large volume of cases which the House of Lords has decided in this area makes it impossible to provide anything more than a selection of topics, and an overview of those chosen. That is what is attempted in this chapter.

Comparisons

In most, if not all, respects the law of torts as administered by the House of Lords is the law of the United Kingdom. This is so even if the body of law is given a different label (delict) north of the border. English and Scottish law have converged as a result of the House of Lords tying the two systems together in this

---

[1] eg *Carlill v Carbolic Smoke Ball Co* [1893] 1 QB 256; *Hong Kong Fir Shipping Co v Kawasaki Kisen Kaisha* [1962] 2 QB 26.

[2] *Central London Property Trust Ltd v High Trees House Ltd* [1947] 1 KB 130 (Denning J).

[3] eg *Stilk v Myrick* (1809) 2 Camp 317 170 ER 1168; *Adams v Lindsell* (1818) 1 B and Ald 681, 106 ER 250.

[4] D Ibbetson, 'How the Romans Did for Us: Ancient Roots of the Tort of Negligence' (2003) 26 UNSWLJ 475.

area. Many of our leading torts cases come from Scotland,[5] including, of course, the most well known of all.

It is noticeable how many of our leading decisions from the House of Lords were pre-figured by those from the United States, particularly those of the New York Court of Appeals from that court's golden era.[6] In this context at least, an English, or indeed British, lawyer finds that when they talk about the law of torts with a counterpart from the United States, there is still a common law between them. More importantly, these matching pairs of cases reflect the core of rational principle at the heart of the common law, so that the law's structure is, at least arguably, not simply a matter of policy choice for individual judges.

Given this Anglo-American proximity, the more recent divergence in the outcome of torts cases heard before the highest court of the United Kingdom and the equivalent courts in Australia, Canada, and New Zealand is all the more striking, and disturbing.[7] Although in legal terms these countries have only recently been freed from the Privy Council's yoke, their ultimate appellate courts have frequently chosen a different path from the House of Lords. In some ways this is arguably healthy. Different ultimate appellate courts each independently determining what the best version of the common law is, without deferring to an ultimate superior, keeps all of them on their toes. However, the most obvious point to make about this divergence within the Commonwealth is that the clear

---

[5] eg *Donoghue v Stevenson* [1932] AC 532; *McGhee v National Coal Board* [1973] 1 WLR 1; *Junior Books Ltd v Veitchi Ltd* [1983] 1 AC 520; *Macfarlane v Tayside Health Board* [2000] 2 AC 59.

[6] We may pair *MacPherson v Buick Motor Co* 217 NY 382, 111 NE 1050 (1916) (Cardozo J) with *Donoghue v Stevenson* [1932] AC 562; *Palsgraf v The Long Island Railroad Co* 248 NY 339, 162 NE 99 (1928) (Cardozo CJ) with *Bourhill v Young* [1942] AC 92; *Glanzer v Shepard* 233 NY 236, 23 ALR 1425 (1922) (Cardozo CJ) with *Hedley Byrne & Co v Heller & Partners* [1964] AC 465; *Robins Dry Dock v Flint* 275 US 302 (1927) (Holmes J) with *Leigh and Sillavan Ltd v Aliakmon Shipping Co Ltd, The Aliakmon* [1986] 1 AC 785; *Ultramares Corp v Touche* 174 NE 441 (1931) (Cardozo CJ) with *Caparo Industries plc v Dickman* [1990] 2 AC 605; *Biakanja v Irving* 49 Cal 2d 647, 320 P 2d 16 (1958) with *White v Jones* [1995] 2 AC 207; *Dillon v Legg* 68 Cal 2d 728, 441 P 2d 912 (1969) with *McLoughlin v O'Brian* [1983] 1 AC 410; *East River Steamship Co v Transamerica Delaval Inc* 476 US 858 (1986) with *D & F Estates v Church Comrs for England* [1989] AC 177; *Thing v La Chusa* 48 Cal 3d 644, 771 P 2d 814 (1989) with *Alcock v Chief Constable of South Yorkshire Police* [1992] 1 AC 310; *Summers v Tice* 33 Cal 2d 80, 199 P 2d 1 (1948) with *Fairchild v Glenhaven Funeral Services Ltd* [2003] 1 AC 32. The different approaches to the intentional infliction of economic harm (compare *Allen v Flood* [1898] 1 AC 1 with *Tuttle v Buck* 119 NW 946 (1909)) is probably the most significant divergence.

[7] Compare, for example, *Rookes v Barnard* [1964] AC 1129 with *Uren v John Fairfax and Sons Ltd* (1966) 117 CLR 118 (High Ct of Australia); *British Rlys Board v Herrington* [1972] AC 877, with *Hackshaw v Shaw* (1984) 155 CLR 614 (High Ct of Australia); *D & F Estates v Church Comrs for England* [1989] AC 177 with *Winnipeg Condominium Corp v Bird Construction Co* [1995] 1 SCR 85 (Sup Ct of Canada); *Leigh and Sillavan Ltd v Aliakmon Shipping Co Ltd, The Aliakmon* [1986] 1 AC 785 with *Canadian National Rly Co v Norsk Pacific Steamship Co* [1992] 1 SCR 1021; *Alcock v Chief Constable of South Yorkshire Police* [1992] 2 AC 310 with *Annetts v Australian Stations Pty Ltd* (2003) 211 CLR 317 (High Ct of Australia); *Gorringe v Calderdale MBC* [2004] 1 WLR 1057 with *Brodie v Singleton Shire Council* (2001) 206 CLR 512; *Murphy v Brentwood DC* [1991] 1 AC 398 with *Invercargill CC v Hamlin* [1994] 3 NZLR 513 (NZ Ct of Appeal).

pattern in the law of torts is for the House of Lords to adopt a more conservative (or, less pejoratively, pro-defendant) approach than its counterpart Commonwealth courts. It has resisted the expansion of liability. In some respects, the English law of torts now more closely resembles the law found in the United States than that now prevailing in some other parts of the Commonwealth. Some academic commentators disapprove of this relative conservatism,[8] whilst others do not.[9]

Beginnings

One possible starting point would be to go back to *Ashby v White*[10] where the House of Lords adopted the dissenting judgment of Holt CJ in holding that the prevention of the claimant from voting by a constable on the pretext that he was not a settled inhabitant was actionable in damages. This was so even though the claimant's preferred candidate was elected and so he had no loss of any kind consequential upon the infringement of his right to vote. However this was a decision of lay peers and arguably tells us more about the politics of the times than anything very much about the future judicial role of the House.[11]

Of course, for many, the *alpha* and *omega* of the law of torts is the House's most famous decision within private law: *Donoghue v Stevenson*.[12] The most important development in the twentieth century was the 'staggering march'[13] of the 'tort' of negligence, and this was an important staging post on the ramble. However, what from today's perspective is most surprising about the case is that the doctrinal error that *Donoghue* corrected—that someone who in performing a contract negligently injures a third party could not be sued, because it was thought that this would offend the doctrine of privity of contract[14]—survived as long as it did, not that it was removed. The decision in *Donoghue* was not a revolution, and had been anticipated over a decade earlier by the decision of the great Cardozo J in the New York Court of Appeals in *MacPhearson v Buick Motor Co*.[15] In any event, just as sexual intercourse did not really begin in 1963,[16] the law of torts did not commence in 1932.

---

[8] eg B Markesinis and G Fetke, 'Damages for the Negligence of Statutory Bodies. The Empirical and Comparative Dimension to an Unending Debate' [2007] PL 299.

[9] eg R Stevens, *Torts and Rights* (Oxford: OUP, 2007) 348.

[10] (1703) 2 Ld Raym 938, 92 ER 126.

[11] For discussion see *Watkins v Secretary of State for the Home Department* [2006] 2 AC 395, [24]–[25] *per* Lord Bingham.

[12] [1932] AC 562.

[13] T Weir, 'The Staggering March of Negligence' in P Cane and J Stapleton (eds), *The Law of Obligations: Essays in honour of John Fleming* (Oxford: OUP, 1997) 97.

[14] *Winterbottom v Wright* (1842) 10 M & W 109, 152 ER 402.

[15] 217 NE 382, 111 NE 1050 (1916).

[16] 'Sexual intercourse began / In nineteen sixty-three (Which was rather late for me) / Between the end of the Chatterley ban / And the Beatles' first LP.' Philip Larkin, 'Annus Mirabilis'.

The attitudes of an earlier era are reflected in the fact that *Donoghue* was decided by a bare majority. That the pursuer in *Donoghue* had a free standing right, against all others who could reasonably foresee that their conduct could injure her, that they take care with respect to her, which was wholly independent of the contract of sale to which she was not a party, seems obvious today. That the generality of this right was not obvious at the time is reflected in *Robert Addie & Sons (Colliers) Ltd v Dumbreck*[17] which the House decided three years earlier. A four-year-old boy was crushed to death by the wheel of a haulage machine operated on the defendant's land. The boy was a trespasser, playing in a field which the defendant knew was being used as a playground. The machine was unguarded and easily accessible. The machine was started by an employee of the defendant who did not check whether any children were playing on it. The House of Lords held that the defendant was not liable, there being no duty of care to a trespasser, but merely a duty not to intentionally or recklessly injure.

How was the child's right not to be negligently injured, a right good against everyone who could foresee such injury, lost with respect to the landowner by the innocent trespass committed? A cynic, or realist, would suggest that *Dumbreck* reflected not a slip in legal analysis but an excessive deference to the interests of landowners. The Court of Appeal limited its impact by imputing fictitious licences to enter; Lord Denning MR, to his credit, would have gone further and removed the bar on trespasser recovery.[18] That the conservatism of the House of Lords can be sometimes unfortunate is reflected in the fact that in 1972 in *British Railways Board v Herrington*[19] this step was not taken. Whilst *Dumbreck* was overturned, the duty of an occupier to a trespasser was characterised as being of a lower level than that owed to persons generally, one of 'common humanity'.[20] It was only with the statutory intervention of the Occupiers' Liability Act 1984 that the error of *Dumbreck* from more than 50 years earlier was finally corrected.

The earlier forays of the House pre-*Donoghue* into liability for negligence in the nineteenth century were in an era when the judge had the responsibility to remove the case from the jury when there was insufficient evidence of the defendant's carelessness.[21] However, for the modern law these decisions are of little relevance. German machine guns brought to an end the use of jury trials in England in most actions for torts after the First World War. There were not enough jurors left. That questions of fact are now for the judge may have been one reason behind the willingness to move towards more generalised rules in the twentieth century. This is exemplified by *Donoghue* and the growth of such open

---

[17] [1929] AC 358.

[18] *Videan v British Transport Commission* [1963] 2 QB 650, CA, 665–7. A step the High Court of Australia took in *Hackshaw v Shaw* (1984) 155 CLR 614.

[19] *British Rlys Board v Herrington* [1972] AC 877.

[20] ibid, 909 *per* Lord Morris, 922–3 *per* Lord Pearson.

[21] *Bridges v North London Rly Co* (1874) LR 7 HL 213; *Metropolitan Rly Co v Jackson* (1877) 3 App Cas 193.

textured rules as reasonable foreseeability as a touchstone of liability. The end of the use of the impenetrable black box which is the jury arguably allowed a twentieth century liberalisation in torts law. However, the case for this link between the end of the civil jury and the liberalisation of the law is not clear cut. First, precisely the same developments took place earlier in the United States, where the use of juries in civil actions is still widespread. Second, there is no indication in the judgments in, say, *Donoghue*, that the House itself thought that change was appropriate because of the change in the identity of the trier of fact.

A nineteenth century decision which is still of some importance, and almost as famous as *Donoghue*, is that in *Rylands v Fletcher*.[22] However, there are at least three reasons why this 'spectacular example of judicial constructivism'[23] cannot be our starting point. First, it came before the House of Lords judicial committee as a fully professional appellate body was established by the Appellate Jurisdiction Act 1876. Second, the important judgment is really that of Blackburn J in the Exchequer Chamber, rather than that of any member of the House. Third, in England at least, the 'rule in *Rylands v Fletcher*' has been emasculated. Here, the House of Lords has subsequently confined the rule to isolated[24] escapes[25] from land. Only such damage which is reasonably foreseeable as a consequence of such an escape is now recoverable.[26] Today it is an anomalous aspect of the general law of nuisance. Only one reported claim based upon it has succeeded since the Second World War.[27] The Australian High Court, showing either a healthy lack of respect for icons of the past or an unacceptable degree of judicial activism[28] (according to taste), has taken the step of abolishing it.[29] It is only in the United States where *Rylands v Fletcher* has truly matured into a freestanding rule of defensible scope. There it is a general rule of strict liability in relation to abnormally dangerous activities.

Injuria **and** *damnum*

Our modern law really begins neither with Mrs Donoghue nor with the escaping reservoir in *Rylands*, but with a trio of decisions of the House of Lords in the 1890s. In each case the claims brought failed. These decisions embedded into

---

[22] (1868) LR 3 HL 330.

[23] D Ibbetson, *A Historical Introduction to the Law of Obligations* (Oxford: OUP, 1999) 183.

[24] *Cambridge Water Co v Eastern Counties Leather* [1994] 2 AC 264.

[25] *Read v Lyons* [1947] AC 156.

[26] *Cambridge Water Co v Eastern Counties Leather* [1994] 2 AC 264; *Transco v Stockport MBC* [2004] 2 AC 1.

[27] *Mason v Levy Auto Parts of England* [1967] 2 QB 530 (McKenna J).

[28] *Transco v Stockport MBC* [2004] 2 AC 1, [43] 'inconsistent with the judicial function' (Lord Hoffmann).

[29] *Burnie Port Authority v General Jones Pty* (1994) 179 CLR 520. However liability was still imposed by the sleight of hand of conjuring up a non-delegable duty.

our law the division between *injuria* and *damnum*. In English we express this distinction as being that between injury and harm, a civil wrong and its consequences, rights and loss. It is central to understanding the law of torts.

In the first case in the series, *Mogul Steamship Co v McGregor Gow & Co*,[30] a group of shipowners, in order to secure control of the tea trade with China, offered freight rebates to all shippers prepared to deal with them exclusively. The rebate was withdrawn from shippers who traded with carriers outside of the association. The claimants were rival shipowners who suffered economic loss, as they could no longer carry tea profitably. As the defendant shipowners had not infringed any right of the claimant the loss was not actionable, it was *damnum sine injuria*.[31]

In *Bradford v Pickles*[32] the claimants acquired land in order to sink a borehole to obtain a water supply for local residents. The defendant acquired land further up the slope from the claimants' works and sunk a bore of his own in order to prevent water percolating through to the claimants' land. This was done with the intention of extracting from the claimants a high price for the land purchased. The defendant had no other commercial object by his actions. It was held that the claimants had no (property) right to the percolating water. Without a right exigible against the rest of the world to the percolating water, no tort was committed when the supply was cut.

Finally, in the 'great case'[33] of *Allen v Flood*[34] the claimants were shipwrights, engaged each day to work on their employer's ship. The defendant was the secretary of a union who informed his employer that if the claimants continued to be re-engaged the union members would not work. The employer consequently refused to re-engage the claimants, who claimed their consequent economic loss from the defendant. The claim failed. The intentional infliction of economic harm is not actionable. Without a right, there is no wrong.

Although *Allen v Flood* is sometimes criticised,[35] it was recently reaffirmed by the House of Lords.[36] The importance of this trio of cases and the fact that they form the foundation of the law of torts has perhaps been lost sight of because of the apparent rag-bag of exceptions which seem to be found within the 'economic' torts. However, that we have a right not to be told lies we believe,[37] or that the actions of one conspirator in carrying out an agreement can be attributed to all of

---

[30] [1892] AC 25.

[31] See also *Victoria Park Racing and Recreation Grounds Co Ltd v Taylor* (1937) 58 CLR 479 (High Ct of Australia).

[32] [1895] AC 587.

[33] WN Hohfeld, 'Some Fundamental Legal Conceptions as Applied in Judicial Reasoning' (1913) 23 Yale LJ 16, 40. See also Tony Weir, *Economic Torts* (Oxford: OUP, 1997) 21.

[34] [1898] AC 1.

[35] eg P Devlin, *Samples of Lawmaking* (Oxford: OUP, 1962); J Finnis, 'Intention in Tort Law' in D Owen (ed), *Philosophical Foundations of Tort Law* (Oxford: OUP, 1995) 229.

[36] *OBG Ltd v Allan* [2008] 1 AC 1.   [37] *Derry v Peek* (1889) 14 App Cas 337.

them so that a tort by one is a tort by all,[38] or the accessory right against non-parties that they do not procure the breach of an agreement[39] are not truly exceptions. These so-called 'economic' torts do not have anything very much doctrinally in common one with another. True, anomalies existed such as liability for 'lawful means conspiracy', which was openly acknowledged as illogical upon its introduction by the House in *Quinn v Leathem*,[40] and it is easy to view this decision cynically as a means of by-passing the logic of *Allen v Flood* in order to hold a trade union liable for industrial action. However, although not formally overruled, the House subsequently distinguished *Quinn* out of existence.[41]

The modern House was shown at its best in the recent decision of *OBG Ltd v Allan*[42] which did much to sort out the mess the Court of Appeal had managed to create in this area. Unfortunately some of this good work was almost immediately undone by their subsequent decision in *Total Network SL v Her Majesty's Revenue and Customs*.[43] The latter concerned what 'unlawful' means in the context of unlawful means conspiracy. The case is notable for heavy citation of, and quotation from, authorities which were not binding on the House, with little substantive analysis of why unlawful means conspiracy is, in principle, actionable, when the intentional infliction of loss is not.[44] Because at ultimate appellate level the court is, technically at least, not bound to follow any prior decision, the principled answer to legal questions must take central stage in the analysis. At a lower level in the hierarchy, the mechanical citation of authorities will in many cases be sufficient to dictate the result. At the highest level it never is. As we shall see, this pattern of removal and addition of mistakes over time almost always provides a more satisfactory explanation for the condition of our current law, than does any shift in outlook of the members of our highest court.

The rise and fall of the 'tort' of negligence

One story that is sometimes told goes like this.

Once upon a time courts were reluctant to adopt any general rule of liability for harm caused by fault. Then a general principle of liability for negligently injuring persons and property was established in *Donoghue v Stevenson*.[45] As we have seen, this is sometimes attributed to the disappearance of juries. The

---

[38] *Brooke v Bool* [1928] 2 KB 578.   [39] *Lumley v Gye* (1853) 2 E & B 216, 118 ER 749.

[40] [1901] AC 495, 506: 'every lawyer must acknowledge that the law is not always logical' *per* Lord Halsbury.

[41] *Crofter Hand Woven Harris Tweed Co Ltd v Vietch* [1942] AC 435.

[42] [2008] 1 AC 1. For earlier ground clearing see *Lonrho v Shell* [1982] 1 AC 173; *Lonrho v Fayed* [1990] 1 AC 448.

[43] [2008] 1 AC 1174.

[44] For understated but powerful analysis of *OBG* and *Total Network SL* see H Carty, 'The Economic Torts in the Twenty-First Century' (2008) 124 LQR 641.

[45] [1932] AC 562.

form of harm which was actionable was expanded by the House of Lords in *Hedley Byrne v Heller*[46] to allow recovery for pure economic loss, at least where the loss was caused by a negligent misrepresentation. This was then generalised still further by the House of Lords in *Anns v Merton London Borough Council*[47] into a general principle of recovery for all loss negligently caused, save where reasons of policy dictated otherwise. The highpoint of this approach was the Scottish appeal to the House of Lords in *Junior Books v Veitchi*.[48]

Then, so it is said, more timid or conservative[49] members of the House of Lords, such as Lord Keith of Kinkel, took control in the 1980s and 90s and set about reversing the progress that had been made. General principle was abandoned and the law was once again returned to unprincipled compartments of recovery through the adoption of an incrementalist approach.[50] In particular, recovery for 'pure' economic loss was re-confined to cases of negligent misrepresentation, and the liability of public bodies for negligence was cut back because of misconceived policy concerns. Recovery has been confined to 'pockets' of liability,[51] resembling the law as it stood before *Donoghue*.

Almost everything about the above story is incorrect. It conflates or ignores the distinction between *injuria* and *damnum*. Its starting point is scepticism about the reality of the specified duties, with correlative rights, owed to others to take care not to injure them. An early exponent of this scepticism was Oliver Wendell Holmes:[52]

Take the law of tort or civil liability for damages apart from contract and the like. Is there any general theory of such liability, or are the cases in which it exists simply to be enumerated, and to be explained each on its special ground, as is easy to believe from the fact that the right of action for certain well known classes of wrongs like trespass or slander has its special history for each class? I think that there is a general theory to be discovered, although resting in tendency rather than established and accepted. I think that the law regards the infliction of temporal damage by a responsible person as actionable, if under the circumstances known to him the danger of his act is manifest according to common experience, or according to his own experience if it is more than common, except in cases where upon special grounds of policy the law refuses to protect the plaintiff or grants a privilege to the defendant. I think that commonly malice, intent, and negligence mean only that the danger was manifest to a greater or less degree, under the circumstances known to the actor, although in some cases of privilege malice may mean an actual malevolent motive, and such a motive may take away a permission knowingly to inflict harm, which otherwise would be granted on this or that ground of dominant public good. But when I stated my view to a very eminent English judge the

---

[46] [1964] AC 465.   [47] [1978] AC 728.   [48] [1983] 1 AC 520.

[49] See the *ad hominem* attack on Lord Hoffmann by B Markesinis and G Fetke, 'Damages for the Negligence of Statutory Bodies. The Empirical and Comparative Dimension to an Unending Debate' [2007] PL 299.

[50] eg *Caparo Industries plc v Dickman* [1990] 2 AC 605.

[51] See J Stapleton, 'Duty of Care and Economic Loss: A Wider Agenda' (1991) 107 LQR 249.

[52] OW Holmes, 'The Path of Law' (1897) 10 HL Rev 457, 471–2.

other day, he said: 'You are discussing what the law ought to be; as the law is, you must show a right. A man is not liable for negligence unless he is subject to a duty.' If our difference was more than a difference in words, or with regard to the proportion between the exceptions and the rule, then, in his opinion, liability for an act cannot be referred to the manifest tendency of the act to cause temporal damage in general as a sufficient explanation, but must be referred to the special nature of the damage, or must be derived from some special circumstances outside of the tendency of the act, for which no generalized explanation exists. I think that such a view is wrong, but it is familiar, and I dare say generally is accepted in England.

That the very eminent English judge was right[53] and Holmes wrong is reflected in the contemporaneous decisions of the House in *Mogul Steamship Co v McGregor Gow & Co*, *Bradford v Pickles*, and *Allen v Flood* discussed above. The infliction of damage, or loss, without the violation of a right is not actionable. Actionable loss, or harm, is always suffered subsequent to, and as a consequence of, a wrong that has been suffered. A wrong, or injury, occurs immediately and is not ongoing. It is meaningless to talk of a duty not to be caused loss; as loss is always suffered as a result of a breach of a duty, it cannot go to the definition of the duty itself. Although some torts are not actionable per se, such as the general rule in slander, so that *damnum* is required in addition to *injuria,* it is the latter which is the essential requirement. That sight can be lost of the fundamental difference between *injuria* and *damnum* is perhaps because in English 'injury' and 'harm' are commonly treated as synonyms. The modern day tendency to refer to the law of torts as protecting 'interests' similarly elides the distinction between the right and consequential loss.[54] It is within liability for negligence that the greatest confusion has arisen. One or more cock-ups in analysis, and the steps to correct them, more easily explains the apparent shifts in the House's approach than any alleged move from a 'liberal' court with Lord Wilberforce as Senior Law Lord, to a differently composed court with the senior position taken by such 'arch-conservatives' as Lord Goff or Lord Bingham.

The *Anns v Merton London Borough Council* disaster

Anns v Merton London Borough Council[55] concerned the liability of a local authority for negligently failing to inspect the foundations of building work. The claimants were lessees who subsequently acquired their interest in the premises. Cracks began to appear in the plaster on their walls, and the claimants successfully argued that the local authority owed them a duty of care, and were consequently potentially liable for expenditure necessary to restore the dwelling to a condition

---

[53] The 'learned judge' was probably Lord Davey, who had spoken to Holmes about the near contemporaneous case of *Allen v Flood*: M DeWolfe Howe (ed), *Pollock-Holmes: Letters vol 1* (Cambridge: CUP, 1942), 77: Holmes to Pollock, 9 August 1897.
[54] eg P Cane, *Tort Law and Economic Interests* (Oxford: OUP, 1996).   [55] [1978] AC 728.

in which it was no longer a danger to health and safety. It is now clear that *Anns* was wrong, and set running a number of unfortunate hares into the common law which it has subsequently taken the House of Lords decades to chase down. There were six such hares.

The 'two-stage' test for a 'duty of care'

The most significant error in *Anns* was the conflation of injury and harm. This is apparent from the two-stage test for a 'duty of care' in negligence set out in the speech of Lord Wilberforce.[56] The first limb of this test is that the defendant could have reasonably foreseen that his negligence would cause the claimant loss. The second limb enables any considerations which ought to negative the duty to be taken into account. For example, it is sometimes said that imposing a duty upon a public body in carrying out its functions may lead to 'over-deterrence',[57] or the imposition of liability upon an accountant for carelessly prepared accounts to all those investors who suffered loss as a result would lead to liability of indeterminate scope and amount.[58]

Whilst this two-stage approach purports to be a definition of a *duty* of care, the label no longer describes its contents. The first limb defines the 'duty' in terms of loss, *damnum*. *Injuria*, the right, has disappeared from the picture altogether. The duty is not a *real* duty, with a correlative right held by specific others. Rather it has become, under its second limb, a 'control device'[59] or 'incidence rule'[60] for defining when loss caused by negligence must be paid for.

Although this test remains, at least in theory, that which is applied in Canada,[61] the House of Lords soon retreated from it. A three-stage test was suggested, which Lord Keith of Kinkel took the lead in formulating.[62] First, was the claimant's loss as a result of the defendant's negligence reasonably foreseeable? Second, was there a relationship of proximity? Third, would imposing liability be fair, just, and reasonable? However the approach adopted in *Anns* persisted as the 'duty' is still not defined in relation to a correlative right of the claimant, but rather in terms of the loss suffered. *Injuria* is still missing, replaced by a vacuous search for reasons

---

[56] Arguably pre-figured by *Home Office v Dorset Yacht Co* [1970] AC 1004, 1027 *per* Lord Reid.
[57] eg *X v Bedfordshire CC* [1995] 2 AC 633.
[58] *Caparo Industries plc v Dickman* [1990] 2 AC 605.
[59] J Fleming, 'Remoteness and Duty: The Control Devices in Liability for Negligence' (1953) 31 Canadian Bar Rev 471; *Dorset Yacht Co Ltd v Home Office* [1969] 2 QB 412, 426 *per* Lord Denning MR; *D v East Berkshire Community NHS Trust* [2005] 2 AC 373, [94] *per* Lord Nicholls.
[60] J Stapleton, 'Evaluating Goldberg and Zipursky's Civil Recourse Theory' (2006) 75 Fordham L Rev 1529, 1532–5.
[61] *Kamloops (City) v Nielsen* [1984] 2 SCR 2; *Cooper v Hobart* [2001] 3 SCR 537.
[62] *Peabody Donation Fund v Sir Lindsay Parkinson & Co Ltd* [1985] AC 210, 239–41 *per* Lord Keith; *Yuen Kun-Yeu v AG of Hong Kong* [1988] AC 175 (PC), 190–4 *per* Lord Keith; *Rowling v Takaro Properties Ltd* [1988] AC 473 (PC), 501 *per* Lord Keith; *Hill v Chief Constable of West Yorkshire* [1989] AC 53, 60 *per* Lord Keith; *Caparo Industries plc v Dickman* [1990] 2 AC 605, 617–18 *per* Lord Bridge, 633 *per* Lord Oliver, 658 *per* Lord Jauncey.

of proximity and fairness. One does not have to be temperamentally cynical to take the view that the change from one test to another was obfuscatory. Today although lip service is paid to the three-stage test,[63] it plays hardly any substantive role in the analysis of the courts.

Property damage

Perhaps the easiest error in *Anns* to spot was the position adopted that the claim concerned damage to property,[64] so that it was thought that the claim was analogous to someone negligently damaging someone else's car. If this had been correct there would potentially have been injury, the infringement of the property right to the house. However, if I buy a car from a supplier which does not work because of the negligence of the manufacturer, the manufacturer has not committed a tort because no (property) right of mine has been violated. The car to which my property right relates is defective from the moment of its acquisition. The position of the House of Lords in *Anns* seems to have been that the claimants' right to the plaster on their walls was separate from their right to the foundations of their house. When cracks in the plaster appeared, because the foundations were defective, this was seen as a new injury to the separate right to the plaster. If it had also been shown that the claimants would have had a competent survey carried out on their own behalf had the local authority not intervened thereby making them worse off, assuming the divisibility of rights, the result would have been entirely orthodox. Unfortunately, it is incorrect. The claimants had leased a single asset, a house, which was defective from the moment it was acquired. The lessee has one indivisible right to the building. The foundations and the plaster accede to the greater whole. The error in relation to the divisibility of our rights to things was subsequently corrected, first by the House of Lords in *D & F Estates Ltd v Church Commissioners* by overruling a decision of the Court of Appeal where the defendant had been the property's builder,[65] and then by formally taking the step of overruling *Anns* itself in *Murphy v Brentwood DC*.[66] The result in *Murphy* followed *a fortiori* from *D & F Estates*. These later decisions to deny the claim based upon a tort are sometimes unfairly criticised for being empty of substantive reasoning;[67] certainly there is no extensive discussion of whether it does or does not make good sense in policy terms to give the purchasers of houses a claim in damages against local authorities for negligent surveys. There was no doctrinal basis for a claim based upon a tort as no right was infringed. *Anns* was wrong, and little more needed to be, or could be, said.

---

[63] eg *Comrs of Customs and Excise v Barclays Bank plc* [2007] 1 AC 181.

[64] *Anns v Merton LBC* [1978] AC 728, 759 *per* Lord Wilberforce. See also *Dutton v Bognor Regis UDC* [1972] 1 QB 373, 396 *per* Lord Denning MR.

[65] *Dutton v Bognor Regis UDC* [1972] 1 QB 373 overruled by *D & F Estates Ltd v Church Comrs* [1989] AC 177.

[66] [1991] AC 398.   [67] eg R Cooke, 'An Impossible Distinction' (1991) 107 LQR 46.

This was not a counter-putsch by forces of reaction, but the correction of a mistake of law.

Failure to confer a benefit

The third error made in *Anns* has proven to be the most pernicious. There is no general duty to confer benefits upon other people, which includes the absence of any general duty to protect others from harm. This was recently and forcefully re-stated by the House in *Sutradhar v National Environment Research Council*.[68] The absence of any such general duty is true both of individuals and of public bodies alike. I have a right that you do not punch me on the nose, or that you do not negligently tear my clothes, or that you do not call me an axe murderer in print. I do not have a right that you cure my illness, mend my car, or speak well of me. Of course, if I assume a duty towards someone else, as for example a bailee does towards a bailor when he accepts possession of goods, this assumed duty requires me to take positive steps to offer protection. Similarly, legislation may impose positive duties both on individuals and state bodies, such as the duty on Highway Authorities to take positive steps to maintain the highway created by the Highways Act 1980.

If, therefore, in exercising a statutory power or carrying out a statutory duty a public body fails to confer a benefit upon someone, it cannot without more be liable. It does not matter that the failure of the public body was grossly below the standard of conduct which could have been expected. That this is the law was established by the House of Lords in *East Suffolk Rivers Catchment Board v Kent*.[69] The claimant's land flooded as a result of a breach in a sea wall. The defendant public body in the exercise of their statutory powers took on the job of repairing the wall. Because of the inefficient way in which the work was carried out, the repair work took much longer than was necessary. The claimant, a farmer, sought compensation for the loss consequent upon the land being flooded for longer than it would have been if all reasonable care had been taken. The majority of the House of Lords dismissed the claim. It was not shown that the claimant, or anyone else, would have repaired the wall if the authority had not intervened. No right to the claimant's land was therefore infringed. There was no implicit assumption of responsibility as the efforts of the defendant did not exclude anyone else from effecting repairs. The legislation under which the public body had the power to act did not create a right good against it for the careful completion of the work.

Lord Atkin dissented in *East Suffolk*, and much like his dissent in *Liversidge v Anderson*[70] this undermined the weight subsequently attached to the majority's decision. The dissent in *East Suffolk* was given particular weight, coming as it did from the founding father of the neighbour principle in *Donoghue*. Unfortunately,

---

[68] [2006] 4 All ER 490.   [69] [1941] AC 74.   [70] [1942] AC 206.

whilst in *Liversidge v Anderson* Lord Atkin was arguably right, in *East Suffolk* he was plainly wrong. In *Anns* the House of Lords followed the approach of Lord Atkin, whilst not formally overruling *East Suffolk* itself. Although purchasers or lessees of property do not have a right against persons generally that they provide them with the benefit of a careful house inspection, and the legislation under which the local authority acted did not on its true construction confer such a right, the House in *Anns* conferred upon the lessee a claim for damages where the local authority had failed to confer upon them this benefit anyway.

Although *Anns* itself was overturned in *Murphy*, this was not on the basis that the court could not take the step of imposing a positive duty to confer a benefit where this was not discoverable in the wording of the legislation under which the public body acted. Where the injury which the public body had reasonably foreseeably failed to prevent was property damage or personal injury, it remained arguable even after *Murphy* that liability should be imposed. The attempt to retreat from this misstep has led to a continuing stream of cases coming before the House of Lords and Privy Council on the liability of public bodies for failure to confer benefits,[71] such as against the police for failing to catch criminals.

Eventually, orthodoxy was re-established first in respect of the exercise of statutory powers by a bare majority of the House of Lords in *Stovin v Wise*[72] and subsequently more decisively in respect of the carrying out of statutory duties by a unanimous decision in *Gorringe v Calderdale Metropolitan Borough Council*.[73] So, the negligent failure of a public body to paint a 'STOP' sign on the highway was not actionable by someone injured as a result, any more than the failure by anyone else to confer such a benefit would be actionable absent a statutory duty conferring a right upon the claimant. However, 26 years of confusion cannot be eradicated overnight, and the law is still not generally understood, at least not apparently by the Court of Appeal[74] or the Law Commission.[75] If one starts from the position that we are each of us entitled to be placed in the position we would be in if a public body is careful, the error is easy to make. For example the High Court of Australia initially correctly refused to follow *Anns*[76] on this point but

---

[71] eg *Yuen Kun-Yeu v AG of Hong Kong* [1988] AC 175 (PC); *Rowling v Takaro Properties Ltd* [1988] AC 473 (PC); *Hill v Chief Constable of West Yorkshire* [1989] AC 53; *Murphy v Brentwood DC* [1991] 1 AC 398; *X v Bedfordshire CC* [1995] 2 AC 633; *Stovin v Wise* [1996] AC 923; *Barrett v Enfield LBC* [2001] 2 AC 550; *Phelps v Hillingdon LBC* [2001] 2 AC 619; *Gorringe v Calderdale MBC* [2004] 1 WLR 1057; *D v East Berksihire Community NHS Trust* [2005] 2 AC 373; *Brooks v Comr of Police for the Metropolis* [2005] 1 WLR 1495.

[72] [1996] AC 923 Lord Goff, Lord Jauncey of Tullichettle, and Lord Hoffmann; Lord Nicholls and Lord Slynn dissenting.

[73] [2004] 1 WLR 1057.

[74] *Smith v Chief Constable of Sussex* [2009] 1 AC 225 overturned by *Chief Constable of the Hertfordshire Police v Van Collel* [2008] 3 WLR 593.

[75] Law Commission for England and Wales, *Administrative Redress Public Bodies and the Citizen* (2008) LCCP no 187, 45–46.

[76] *Sutherland Shire Council v Heyman* (1985) 157 CLR 424.

subsequently and almost inadvertently reversed its position,[77] so that Australian and British law have criss-crossed one another.

The policy-operational divide

In order to keep the *Anns* principle within some sort of limit, Lord Wilberforce adopted from the law of the United States a division between operational and policy matters,[78] policy matters being non-justiciable and therefore incapable of attracting liability. If the liability of public bodies for torts were a branch of public law, concerned with the regulation of government decision-making, this division would make sense. However, if the law of torts is actually concerned with the (private) rights we have against everyone else, it is obviously unacceptable to allow a public body to avoid liability for a prima facie wrong, such as knocking down a house or creating a nuisance, on the basis that this decision is a policy matter. Conversely, the mere fact that an activity is operational, as in *Anns*, cannot alone give the claimant a cause of action for its negligently being carried out. The House of Lords has more recently rejected this division.[79]

Recovery for 'pure' economic loss

As we have seen, their Lordships in *Anns* thought that they were dealing with a case of damage to property. However, that this was not so, and that Lord Wilberforce's two-stage test was defined in terms of loss, gave support to the view that 'pure' economic loss was actionable, ie that it was unnecessary to establish the violation of a right before recovery was allowed.[80] In support of this many commentators adopted, and still adopt, the position that their Lordships had given the green light to recovery for 'pure' economic loss, *damnum sine injuria*, in their earlier decision of *Hedley Byrne v Heller*.[81] *Anns* was seen as another breach in the dike.

In fact, *Hedley Byrne v Heller* was not the novelty which it is sometimes portrayed as being. Whenever one party assumes responsibility towards another, a duty of care arises. The most well-known example of this is bailment, which need not be contractual. When loss is suffered as a consequence of such an assumption of responsibility it is recoverable. What *Hedley Byrne* achieved was to bring back into the light a line of authority, exemplified by *Wilkinson v Coverdale*,[82] which textbook writers had failed to give prominence to. Where, as in *Hedley Byrne*

---

[77] *Brodie v Singleton Shire Council* (2001) 206 CLR 512.

[78] [1978] AC 728, 754 taken from *Indian Towing Co Inc v United States* (1955) 350 US 61. The US Supreme Court subsequently repudiated this distinction in *Berkovitz v United States* (1988) 486 US 531; *United States v Gaubert* (1991) 499 US 315.

[79] *Stovin v Wise* [1996] AC 92, 951 *per* Lord Hoffmann; see also *Rowling v Takaro Properties Ltd* [1988] AC 473, 501 *per* Lord Keith.

[80] eg Cooke (n 67).   [81] eg Stapleton (n 51).   [82] (1793) 1 Esp 75, 170 ER 284.

itself, the defendant made it clear that no assumption of responsibility was made, by disclaiming liability, no claim on this basis was possible. The right relied upon in *Hedley Byrne* was quite different from that relied upon by Mrs Donoghue.

Unfortunately, another issue which arose in *Hedley Byrne* was whether there were any special limitations upon recovery where the defendant's negligence took the form of words rather than actions. The House of Lords concluded, correctly, that there were not. Unfortunately, in the minds of some the two issues were not kept separate and so it was thought that economic loss was recoverable whenever it was the consequence of a negligent misrepresentation. This error found its way into the House's decision in *Smith v Eric S Bush*,[83] a case which is almost indistinguishable from *D & F Estates* save for the fact that the latter does not concern a misrepresentation. It was only in the mid-1990s that orthodoxy re-asserted itself, with the basis of *Hedley Byrne* again being stated to be the defendant's assumption of responsibility, and not any distinction between words and action.[84]

Academic scepticism[85] as to the reality of the courts finding such an assumption of responsibility through conduct seemed to be confirmed by the decision of the House of Lords in the case of the disappointed legatees: *White v Jones*.[86] Lord Goff was prepared to 'deem' there to be an assumption of responsibility by the solicitor instructed to draw up a will in favour of the intended beneficiaries, so as to support a claim for loss they suffered as a result of his failure to amend the testator's will in their favour. This unfortunate descent into a fiction disguises whatever justification there is for *White v Jones*.[87] This has led some commentators to throw the assumption of responsibility baby out with the fictional bathwater.

Policy

The open invocation of policy concerns, that is, those reasons unrelated to what is just as between claimant and defendant, which *Anns* helped to usher in has not, for good or ill, disappeared along with the two-stage test. So, in one of its most difficult decisions to support in recent years, the House refused claims by parents and children for harm suffered as a result of the *intentional* taking away of children from their parents by the agents of public bodies, even though the legislation under which they acted conferred no privilege to act in this manner.[88] Concerns such as over-deterrence or the diversion of public funds into defending

---

[83] [1991] 1 AC 831.

[84] *Henderson v Merrett Syndicates (No 1)* [1995] 2 AC 145; *Spring v Guardian Assurance plc* [1995] 2 AC 296; *Williams v Natural Life Health Foods* [1998] 1 WLR 830.

[85] eg K Barker, 'Wielding Occam's Razor: Pruning Strategies for Economic Loss' (2006) 26 OJLS 289.

[86] [1995] 2 AC 207.

[87] For this writer's attempt to justify the result see Stevens (n 9) 176–82.

[88] *X v Bedfordshire CC* [1995] 2 AC 633.

potentially ill-conceived claims were relied upon. That the rights of children not to be seized by strangers, and of parents that others do not remove their offspring without any statutory authority, may be overridden by one or more of a basket of contentious policy concerns is somewhat surprising. The error of analysis, although now corrected,[89] was caused by a too ready willingness to try to answer the question posed by reference to extra-legal concerns. From time to time, members of the House of Lords in torts actions have disavowed the usage of policy concerns.[90] Unfortunately, once the policy genie was out of the bottle it has proved extremely difficult to put back.

Nervous shock

For those who would argue that the law of torts was liberalised in the 1970s, only to be cut back by judicial reactionaries in the 1980s and 90s, the law in relation to psychiatric injury is a central example. The mistaken generalisation made in *Anns* caused judicial doubts to arise in relation to all generalisations of principle in the law of torts. Indeed, at one stage, it was thought that there was a 'risk that the law of negligence will disintegrate into a series of isolated decisions without any coherent principles at all, and the retreat from *Anns* will turn into a rout'.[91]

The subject of 'nervous shock' covers a number of different issues. One is the issue of whether a physical injury, such as a haemorrhage[92] is actionable where it is inflicted through the mechanism of shock. The House of Lords in *Bourhill v Young*[93]—a decision which deserves a more prominent place in the Pantheon of great cases than it currently enjoys—concluded that it was necessary for the claimant to show that the defendant's negligence was in relation to her. Negligence in thin air, or in the abstract, does not suffice. As this relational negligence could not be shown, the claim failed.

More difficult is where the claimant suffers psychiatric injury, without physical injury. Such injury may not necessarily be suffered through a shock, and it is certainly inappropriate to nowadays refer to such illness as a 'nervous disorder' with its connotations of Elizabeth Barrett Browning. In *McLoughlin v O'Brian*,[94] the House of Lords came within 'a hair's breadth'[95] of treating our right to psychiatric health as being a species of our general right to bodily safety when it allowed a mother a claim for her psychiatric injury consequent upon the death of her daughter and the physical injury of other family members. Although there

---

[89] *D v East Berkshire Community Health NHS Trust* [2004] QB 558 (CA).

[90] eg *McLoughlin v O'Brian* [1983] 1 AC 410, 430 *per* Lord Scarman; *McFarlane v Tayside Health Board* [2000] 2 AC 59, 76 *per* Lord Slynn, 83 *per* Lord Steyn, 97 *per* Lord Hope of Craighead, 105 *per* Lord Clyde, 108 *per* Lord Millett.

[91] *Marc Rich & Co AG v Bishop Rock Marine Co Ltd* [1996] 1 AC 211, 230 *per* Lord Lloyd of Berwick.

[92] *Hambrook v Stokes Brothers* [1925] 1 KB 141.   [93] [1943] AC 92.   [94] [1983] AC 410.

[95] *White v Chief Constable of South Yorkshire* [1999] 2 AC 455, 502 *per* Lord Hoffmann.

were decisions of the Court of Appeal which had moved in this direction,[96] the change was not brought about following a careful consideration of why the common law had historically set its face against the recognition of such a right, nor was there any analysis of whether this approximation was now appropriate. The 'why not?' approach of *Anns*, which was still dominant at the time, was taken as sufficient.

The retreat from *McLoughlin* was rather more shambolic than the retreat from *Anns* itself. So, in *Alcock v Chief Constable of South Yorkshire Police*[97] where the claims were brought by spectators suffering psychiatric injury because of a disaster at a football stadium as a result of police negligence, 'more or less arbitrary'[98] restrictions on recovery were imposed, under the rubric of 'proximity'. Once this step had been taken, the House considered that distributive equity required that the same restrictions should be placed upon claims by police officers for this form of harm arising from the same incident, despite the presence of a relationship of employment between the claimant officer and the defendant chief constable.[99] The movement was not all one way, however, so a surprisingly expansive approach was taken in categorising psychiatric injury as of the same 'type' as physical injury for the purposes of remoteness,[100] although the House has begun to retreat from this.[101] Nobody could pretend that the current condition of the law is satisfactory.

Causation

Outside of the context of the duty of care, the most intractable and recurrent problem in the recent history of the common law of torts is that of evidentiary gaps. What happens if the claimant has suffered a loss, such as that caused by a disease, which may have been the result of a wrong committed by the defendant, but which the claimant cannot show on the balance of probability was so caused? Can the claimant recover the lost chance of avoiding the loss, or, even more radically, 'jump'[102] the evidentiary gap altogether and recover in full?

The orthodox answer is that unless a loss is shown to have been caused by the defendant's wrong it cannot be recovered.[103] However, in *McGhee v National Coal Board*[104] the House did permit the pursuer to jump the gap, and allowed recovery for dermatitis resulting from the exposure to brickdust. Their Lordships relied upon their own earlier decision of *Bonnington Castings v Wardlaw*[105] as

---

[96] *Boardman v Sanderson* [1964] 1 WLR 1317 (CA); *Chadwick v British Rlys Board* [1967] 1 WLR 912.

[97] [1992] 1 AC 310.

[98] *White v Chief Constable of South Yorkshire* [1999] 2 AC 455, 502 *per* Lord Hoffmann.

[99] ibid.

[100] *Page v Smith* [1996] 1 AC 155.   [101] *Grieves v FT Everard & Sons Ltd* [2008] 1 AC 281.

[102] Jane Stapleton, 'Lords a'Leaping: Evidentiary Gaps' (2002) 10 Torts LJ 276.

[103] eg *Jobling v Associated Dairies* [1982] AC 794,   [104] [1973] 1 WLR 1.

[105] [1956] AC 613.

providing authority for this, but it is now generally recognised that a proper reading of that case lends no support for the result in *McGhee*.[106]

The potential revolution which *McGhee* heralded was such that the House's initial response was to deny that anything new had been done at all.[107] However this was never a tenable interpretation of the change wrought by *McGhee*, leading one of their Lordships, writing extra-judicially, to ask 'James McGhee: A Second Mrs Donoghue?'[108] It is now quite clear that the answer is 'no'.

The question needed to be answered because of a large number of claims by employees who had developed mesothelioma, a fatal cancer, developed as a result of exposure to asbestos dust whilst at work. The claimants had worked for a series of employers who had each exposed them to this dust. Mesothelioma is not made cumulatively worse according to the length of exposure to asbestos, but is rather triggered by it, possibly by a single strand. It was impossible to show on the balance of probabilities as against any individual employer that the disease was triggered by the period of working for them. The House of Lords in *Fairchild v Glenhaven Services Ltd*[109] followed *McGhee* and allowed the gap to be leaped, and the claims to proceed against each employer.

However, an orthodox approach was re-established shortly afterwards by the majority decision in *Barker v Corus (UK) Ltd*[110] where the House of Lords confined the employees' recovery to the lost chance of avoiding the disease: a loss they could show that they had suffered on the balance of probabilities as a result of the wrong. The case which had seemed to stand in the way of this result was the earlier decision in *Hotson v East Berkshire Area Health Authority*[111] where, at least on one reading of the case, the House had refused to allow recovery for a lost chance of avoiding an injury which the claimant might have avoided if his medical treatment had been careful. The cases were unsatisfactorily reconciled on the basis that there was a special rule where the injury was caused by a 'single agent': in *Barker* asbestos dust. This is a rule with no normative attraction which has been adopted simply as a means reconciling cases which are, in reality, irreconcilable. It is a rule that is the result of the order in which the cases have been decided and the need to square one with another, rather than one which anyone would *ex ante* have adopted. No other legal system adopts it, and it may be doubted whether it will survive.

Worse still, litigants were emboldened by *Fairchild* to attempt to obtain recovery in situations where the issue was unrelated to that of there being an evidentiary gap. So, in *Gregg v Scott*[112] the claimant sought to recover for the

---

[106] *Fairchild v Glenhaven Services Ltd* [2003] 1 AC 32, [21]–[22] *per* Lord Bingham, [44]–[45] *per* Lord Nicholls, [65] and [70] *per* Lord Hoffmann, [142]–[144] *per* Lord Rodger of Earlsferry.
[107] *Wilsher v Essex Area Health Authority* [1988] 1 AC 1074.
[108] Lord Hope (2003) 62 CLJ 587.   [109] [2003] 1 AC 32.
[110] [2006] 2 AC 572. The result in *Barker* itself in relation to claims for mesothelioma was reversed by the Compensation Act 2006, s 3.
[111] [1987] AC 750   [112] [2005] 2 AC 176.

increased risk of avoiding a harm he had not yet suffered, a claim rejected by a majority.[113] Subsequently in *Grieves v FT Everard & Sons Ltd*[114] a claim was brought for symptomless pleural plaques, coupled with the anxiety and the increased risk that a disease may develop in the future, a claim rejected unanimously. More surprisingly, a majority of the House in *Chester v Afshar*[115] allowed a claim for injuries by a patient who claimed that a surgeon had negligently failed to warn her of the risks associated with an operation, although she would have gone ahead with the same procedure, albeit at a later time, even if warned. That harm which is coincidental to a wrong (ie the risk of this harm was not increased by the wrong) is irrecoverable had been established 50 years earlier, but this authority was not properly examined.[116]

Some of the most recent decisions on causation are marred by their length. Admittedly, *Allen v Flood* occupies 181 pages of the law reports, but this reflects its foundational importance within the law of torts, its political sensitivity, and the decision to summon eight judges of the High Court to give opinions, alongside seven members of the House of Lords. There can be less excuse for the modern phenomenon of the lengthy multiple speeches in, say, *Fairchild* or *Gregg v Scott*. Excessive quotation from, as opposed to citation of, other judgments is a particular problem. No academic submitting an article to a journal would expect to get away with such length and flabbiness. It cannot be appropriate to require someone who needs to know the law on causation to read and reconcile hundreds of pages of different judgments from many cases. The common law approach itself is compromised unless restraint is shown. The change in style of judgment is probably attributable to the use of computers, and the production by counsel of lengthy skeletons. A similar problem arose in the Supreme Court of Canada, which that court has now corrected.[117]

Fault

A much more glowing term report for the past century can be given in relation to the House's clarification of what constitutes fault within the law of negligence. In a series of cases in the 1950s,[118] of which the most important is that in *Bolton v Stone*, the factors to be taken into account in determining whether a duty of care had been breached were settled, and have proven almost[119] uncontroversial since

---

[113] Lord Hoffmann, Lord Phillips, and Baroness Hale. Lord Nicholls and Lord Hope dissenting.
[114] eg *Grieves v FT Everard & Sons Ltd* [2008] 1 AC 281.   [115] [2005] 1 AC 134.
[116] *Carslogie SS Co Ltd v Royal Norwegian Government* [1952] AC 292.
[117] Compare the length of *Canadian National Rly Co v Norsk Pacific Steamship Co* [1992] 1 SCR 1021 with *Mustapha v Culligan of Canada Ltd* 2008 SCC 27 (Sup Ct of Canada).
[118] *Paris v Stepney* [1951] AC 367; *Bolton v Stone* [1951] AC 850; *Latimer v AEC* [1953] AC 643; *Morris v West Hartlepool Steam Navigation Co* [1956] AC 552.
[119] Cf *Jolley v Sutton LBC* [2000] 1 WLR 1082.

that time. Occasionally the Court of Appeal falls asleep and needs correcting, as happened in *Tomlinson v Congleton Borough Council,* where Lord Hobhouse felt compelled to remind the courts below:[120]

Does the law require that all trees be cut down because some youths may climb them and fall? Does the law require the coast line and other beauty spots to be lined with warning notices? Does the law require that attractive water side picnic spots be destroyed because of a few foolhardy individuals who choose to ignore warning notices and indulge in activities dangerous only to themselves? The answer to all these questions is, of course, no.

In general, however, the principles are satisfactory and well settled.

Similarly, the House has maintained the position that no fault is required in torts such as trespass and conversion,[121] something the Court of Appeal has forgotten from time to time.[122] So, in *Governor of Brockhill Prison, ex p Evans (No 2)*[123] false imprisonment was held to be made out even though the prison governor responsible for detaining prisoners for a period longer than authorised by legislation was wholly blameless in doing so.

Nuisance

Compared with the travails of negligence, the law of nuisance has been progressed relatively serenely.

It may be argued that the approach in the early decision of the House in *St Helens Smelting Co v Tipping*[124] of making the nature of the locality of the activity relevant to whether it constituted a nuisance, entrenched the division between the leafy suburbs and sink estates, but planning law has long since played a much greater role in regulating what is built and where it is done than the the law of nuisance, the impact of which is relatively minor.

The requirement that positive steps must be taken by a landowner to alleviate a nuisance of which he is aware, even if not responsible for its creation, does not reveal a libertarian attitude to property rights.[125] The House has however consistently interpreted the statutory authorisation of public bodies to create a nuisance very restrictively, reluctant to accept the cutting back of our common law rights.[126]

The attempt in *Hunter v Canary Wharf*[127] to expand private nuisance, a tort protecting the right to the quiet enjoyment of land, to protect other interests, such as privacy, was decisively rejected. That someone with no right to use the

---

[120] [2004] 1 AC 46, at [81].   [121] *Hollins v Fowler* (1875) LR 7 HL 757.
[122] eg *Wilson v Pringle* [1987] 1 QB 237.   [123] [2001] 2 AC 19.
[124] (1865) 11 HLC 642.   [125] *Sedleigh-Denfield v O'Callaghan* [1940] AC 880.
[126] *Geddis v Proprietors of the Bann Reservoir* (1878) 3 App Cas 430; *Metropolitan Asylum DC v Hill* (1881) LR 6 App Cas 193; *Manchester Corp v Farnsworth* [1930] AC 171; *Tate & Lyle Industries Ltd v GLC* [1983] 2 AC 509; *Allen v Gulf Oil Ltd* [1981] AC 1001.
[127] [1997] AC 655.

land has no standing to sue for interference with its use is, one would have thought, axiomatic. Again, *damnum sine injuria* is irrecoverable. Lord Goff pointedly stated in relation to the academic commentary asserting the contrary that 'a crumb of analysis is worth a loaf of opinion'.[128]

Vicarious liability

Until relatively recently the House's pronouncements on vicarious liability have caused few ripples. Admittedly, in *Lloyd v Grace Smith & Co*[129] a solicitor's firm was held liable for the fraud of one of its clerks, even though he was acting for his own benefit and not that of the firm, something which had been thought to exclude vicarious liability. The general pattern, however, was a conservative one. For example, in *Morgans v Launchbury*[130] the Court of Appeal's attempts to expand vicarious liability where the owner of a car gave permission to someone else to use it for purposes other than the owner's were rejected, with the court refusing to take into account the underlying insurance position. Similarly, in *Lister v Romford Ice and Cold Storage Co*[131] an employee was required to indemnify an employer for the latter's liability because of the employee's injuring a third party. The court ignored, quite correctly, the fact that the substantive claimant was the employer's insurance company, seeking to pass on the loss which it had been paid a premium to absorb.[132] In *The Ocean Frost*[133] the House concluded that an employer could not be vicariously liable for fraudulent statements made by an employee acting without actual or ostensible authority. Finally, in *Dubai Aluminium Co Ltd v Salaam*,[134] where the party held vicariously liable sought to bring a contribution claim against another wrongdoer he was treated as the person who had committed the wrong, and not as an innocent party held liable for the wrong of someone else.

This pattern of relative conservatism was broken by *Lister v Hesley Hall Ltd*[135] where the House, following the Supreme Court of Canada,[136] abandoned the traditional Salmond test for determining when an employee's actions are within the course of his employment. Could an employer be held vicariously liable for the abuse of a child by a teacher whilst the child was at school? As the abuse was neither authorised nor an unauthorised mode of an authorised act, the orthodox answer would have been 'no'. The rule was changed so that it sufficed that the wrong was sufficiently closely related to what the employee had been employed to do, which was so whenever the enterprise created or materially enhanced the risk of the wrong.

---

[128] [1997] AC 655, 694.   [129] [1912] AC 716.   [130] [1973] AC 127.
[131] [1957] AC 555.
[132] For a similar deliberate ignoring of the insurance position see *Hunt v Severs* [1994] 2 AC 350.
[133] [1986] AC 717; cf *Credit Lyonnais Bank Nederland NV v Export Credit Guarantee Department* [2000] 1 AC 486.
[134] [2003] 2 AC 366.   [135] [2002] 1 AC 215.   [136] *Bazley v Curry* [1999] 2 SCR 534.

Again, the cock-up theory probably explains this change best. It does not seem to have been argued by counsel that the school owed a non-delegable duty to the children on the basis of a voluntary assumption of responsibility for their well-being whilst at school. Although one cannot bail boys, the duty assumed was the same sort of duty that a bailee assumes towards a bailor. The result in *Lister* is correct but this did not require the radical step taken.

The decision in *Lister* also saw the House seek to justify vicarious liability in policy terms, in particular in terms of internalising to an enterprise the losses its activity caused. This policy-based approach was also reflected in *Majrowski v Guy's & St Thomas's NHS Trust*[137] where the House, albeit *obiter*, adopted the 'servant's tort' theory of vicarious liability (ie the theory that the employer is not committing a tort but is actually held liable for someone else's). Although not everyone approves of these developments,[138] they reflect both current academic orthodoxy and the influence it has upon the thinking of the modern court.

Conclusion

Both the strengths and weaknesses of judge made law are reflected in the recent history of the law of torts before our ultimate appellate court.

Law which is made on a case-by-case basis tends to lack any systematic ordering. The judge does not have the luxury of time and space, which a textbook writer or academic possesses. To give the law a rational overall structure it is necessary to stand back, something a judge faced with the pressing question of the justice here and now between the parties before her does not always have the luxury of being able to do. The simplification of the law concerning the negligent damage to person and property which took place in *Donoghue* subsequently led to the creation of an over-arching 'tort' of negligence, encompassing much of the old law of trespass,[139] the action on the case,[140] and many voluntarily assumed obligations previously seen as within *assumpsit*.[141] This over-simplification has been at significant cost, with the different characteristics of the different claims hidden behind the swollen 'tort' of negligence. Some of our other torts fare little better, being, as presented in the standard textbooks, little more than a random collection of formulas for relief, with little underlying order. However, the blame for this does not lie with the courts in general or the House of Lords in particular, but with those whose task it is to give an overall account of an area of law. It is the academic community that has failed. Given this failure, the law itself is in remarkably good shape, if somewhat untidy.

---

[137] [2007] 1 AC 224.
[138] R Stevens, 'Vicarious Liability or Vicarious Action' (2007) 123 LQR 30.
[139] eg *Letang v Cooper* [1965] 1 QB 632.   [140] eg *Donoghue v Stevenson*.
[141] eg *Hedley Byrne v Heller*.

For a brief period it seemed as if the fundamental difference between a wrong and it consequences, *injuria* and *damnum*, was to be abandoned for a general rule that all loss caused by negligence was prima facie actionable. The conservatism of our highest court, which is entirely appropriate given that it is not fulfilling a legislative function, happily corrected this error.

The number of cases concerning the law of torts annually decided by the House of Lords is very large. The prevalence of arbitration, which has cut back the number of commercial contract cases which are now heard by appellate courts, has not affected claims based upon torts. The law of torts is now largely embodied in decisions of the House of Lords, something which was not true 50 or 60 years ago. There is no sign that the recent flood is abating. It should not be thought that this is some indication of a 'compensation culture' running rampant. In relation to all claims, the number of claims heard by the House of Lords is small, providing little evidence of what is happening lower down.

At one time the most able members of the judiciary were not found at the ultimate appellate level. Certainly this was so during the late nineteenth and early twentieth centuries. The Court of Appeal of Scrutton, Bankes, and Atkin LJJ was more than a match for any five drawn from the House at that time. Today the same could not be said. Over the last quarter century, the House of Lords has been the intellectual driving force in developing a defensible law of torts. We have recently had, and have, an ultimate appellate court which is more than a match for any found elsewhere in the common law world. It is to be hoped that we do not look back with nostalgia to our present and most recent past as a golden era which was lost.

In Australia it is generally accepted that the judicial outlook of the court under Chief Justice Mason was rather different from that under the current Chief Justice. One advantage of our not having had a Chief Justice was that the court was not associated with the attitudes of any one individual. In England although individual judges may be perceived as more conservative than others, the House of Lords as a corporate judicial body has not been perceived as having a markedly different character under one Senior Law Lord or another. The change of direction in the approach to claims in torts since the 1970s is not best explained as the court becoming more conservative over time. If it were, it would be expected that this shift would be reflected in other areas of law, which it is not. The better view is that errors in legal analysis were corrected, rather than different policy choices being made. Cock-ups and their correction are less interesting than left-right battles, but here at least it is the more plausible story.

In the United States, the Supreme Court has essentially become, especially after the Judiciary Act of 1925, a constitutional court. Something is lost if an appellate court does not deal with private law issues, and the damage is not confined to private law itself. A court that is forced on a daily basis to deal with questions which raise no issue of a politically sensitive nature will be one where technical competence in the law is the criterion by which judges will be assessed by their peers and others. At appellate level a judge should be judged by the ability to correctly analyse complex tax law matters or the technical aspects of the conflict of laws. A court comprised of such judges will not become partisan in its operation, so that even such apparently banal issues as the standing of an assignee of a contractual right to sue does not split along a predictable conservative/liberal divide.[142] The United Kingdom's ultimate appellate court has not given us a *Dred Scott v Sandford*[143] or a *Bush v Gore*.[144] Perhaps paradoxically, a court which is forced to deal daily with issues which, to the layman, may appear unimportant, such as snails in bottles of ginger beer, will more competently, impartially, and uncontroversially deal with the questions of great constitutional weight which it is also required to answer. It is important for the law to be as boring as possible. The law itself is compromised if a cynical or 'realist' view is allowed to take hold.

---

[142] Cf *Sprint Communications Co v APCC Services Inc* (US Sup Ct) decision no 07-552 decided 23 June 2008. Breyer, Stevens, Kennedy, Souter, and Ginsburg, JJ; Roberts, CJ, Scalia, Thomas, and Alito, JJ, dissenting.
[143] (1857) 60 US (19 How) 393.   [144] (2000) 531 US 98.

35

Libel, Privacy, and Freedom of Expression

*Eric Barendt**

Introduction

At the beginning of his speech in *Reynolds v Times Newspapers*, in which the House of Lords significantly extended the scope of the qualified privilege defence to libel, Lord Nicholls said the appeal concerned the relationship of two fundamental rights: freedom of expression and the right to reputation.[1] This observation does not appear particularly striking, now that we have become accustomed to the incorporation of the European Convention (ECHR) right to freedom of expression into United Kingdom law by the Human Rights Act 1998. But it would probably have astonished most of the Law Lords who considered libel appeals in the course of the preceding century. They developed the principles of defamation law, without generally paying much attention to the implications of their decisions for freedom of speech and of the press.

One explanation for the apparent neglect of these freedoms is that the common law did not give them any positive recognition; freedom of speech could only be exercised when the law did not interfere.[2] It is only during the last 20 years under the influence, and then the incorporation, of the ECHR that the House of Lords has treated freedom of expression as a right of comparable weight to the reputation right; indeed, interestingly, it has been in libel cases that members of the House have referred to a constitutional right to freedom of speech.[3] There is therefore a marked contrast between the approach taken by the House to libel law in most of the decisions considered in the next section of this

---

* I am grateful to Richard Rampton, QC for his comments on a draft of this chapter.

[1] [2001] 2 AC 127, 190 (Lord Nicholls); for discussion of this case, see p 657 below.

[2] See Lord Bingham in *R (Laporte) v Chief Constable of Gloucestershire Constabulary* [2007] 2 AC 105, para 34. However, the Court of Appeal took account of the common law right of free speech to justify its decision in *Bonnard v Perryman* [1891] 2 Ch 269 that interim injunctions should not be granted to stop further publication of a libel where the defendant has put forward a defence of truth or fair comment.

[3] *Cassell and Co Ltd v Broome* [1972] AC 1027, 1133 (Lord Kilbrandon), and *Reynolds v Times Newspapers* (n 1) at 207 (Lord Steyn).

chapter, and that taken in more recent cases where freedom of expression arguments have been given full consideration.

In comparison with its rich libel jurisprudence, the House has given relatively few rulings on the protection of personal privacy. Only five years ago it refused to recognise a common law privacy tort, holding in *Wainwright v Home Office*[4] that it would be inappropriate for the courts to formulate a broad right of uncertain scope. But the law of confidentiality has been developed to protect personal (and official) information against disclosure by the media; this topic is discussed in the section begining on p 661. The section following that is concerned with contempt of court and the open justice principle, where the House of Lords has been inconsistent in the weight it attaches to freedom of speech and of the press.

Libel law

General principles of identification and meaning

In the last 20 years of the nineteenth century the House of Lords considered a few libel cases involving issues of meaning.[5] But its first seminal decision in the modern period was that in *E Hulton and Co v Jones* in which it established the rule that the intention and knowledge of the publisher are irrelevant in determining whether the words referred to the claimant or are defamatory of him.[6] The newspaper in that case could not argue that it had not heard of the claimant, let alone intended to defame him. The material question was how the article would be understood by reasonable readers; if, in the view of the jury, they would think it defamatory of the claimant, the defendant would be liable in the absence of any defence. What was unusual, perhaps unprecedented, was that the House of Lords, over which Lord Loreburn, LC, presided, gave extempore speeches on such an important point after only a day's argument;[7] the issues had divided the Court of Appeal, with Fletcher Moulton LJ dissenting in a long judgment. The decision remains good law, though recent developments have somewhat reduced its significance.[8]

Knupffer v London Express Newspaper[9] is another significant ruling: if a defamatory allegation is made of a class of people, an individual member can only

---

[4] [2004] 2 AC 406.
[5] In particular, see *Capital and Counties Bank Ltd v George Henty and Sons* (1882) 8 App Cas 741 and *Lord William Nevill v Fine Art and General Insurance Co Ltd* [1897] AC 68.
[6] [1910] AC 20.
[7] RFV Heuston, *Lives of the Lord Chancellors 1885–1940* (Oxford: OUP, 1964) comments on Lord Loreburn's tendency during his early years as Lord Chancellor to dispose of cases quickly.
[8] See the offer of amends defence provided by the Defamation Act 1996, ss 2–3, and *O'Shea v MGN* [2001] EMLR 943, in which it was held that to apply *Hulton v Jones* to a look-alike situation would be an unjustifiable interference with freedom of expression.
[9] [1944] AC 116.

bring a libel action if it is understood as referring to him; there are no special rules precluding actions by members of a class. In some circumstances, all members of a large group might be able to bring libel proceedings, though generally it would be difficult for them to show that they were individually referred to. One can have no quarrel with the general approach of the House, but its decision that the article—an attack on the Young Russia fascist movement—was not capable of referring to the claimant is questionable; the British branch of the movement had only 24 members, and four witnesses had given evidence that they considered the article referred to him.

The House of Lords indicated the correct approach to questions of meaning in one of its most important post-war libel decisions, *Lewis v Daily Telegraph*.[10] Among the principles is the 'reasonable reader' test, under which the meaning of an allegation is determined by asking what an ordinary person, 'not avid for scandal', would read into the words complained of...'.[11] So a report that officers of a fraud squad are inquiring into the affairs of a company should not be understood to imply guilt. Judges should direct juries to exclude from the range of possible meanings those which would not be given to the text by ordinary readers. This approach has been followed in a number of cases,[12] including another decision of the House of Lords, where it held that ordinary readers would usually not only look at the headlines of an article and an accompanying photo from which a defamatory meaning might be inferred, but that they would also read the caption to the photo and the full text, which made it plain that the claimants had not been defamed.[13]

One of the more extraordinary decisions of the House on these points was that of a 3:2 majority in *Morgan v Odhams Press Ltd*.[14] It held that the claimant was entitled to bring libel proceedings in respect of a tabloid article stating that a girl involved in a dog doping scandal had been kidnapped. Although the article did not name or point to the claimant, he could sue because it could be understood by some readers as implicating him in the kidnapping; they knew that the girl had stayed voluntarily with the claimant before the article was published. It was, moreover, immaterial whether readers believed the allegations against the claimant. Lord Guest, dissenting, thought the decision had worrying implications for freedom of speech.[15]

Public authorities not entitled to bring libel proceedings

In *Derbyshire County Council v Times Newspapers*, one of its most remarkable decisions in libel law, the House held that public authorities may not bring

---

[10] [1964] AC 234.   [11] ibid, 260 (Lord Reid).
[12] See eg *Jones v Skelton* [1963] 1 WLR 1362 (PC); *Slim v Daily Telegraph Ltd* [1968] 2 QB 157 (CA); *Mapp v News Group Newspapers Ltd* [1997] EMLR 397 (CA).
[13] *Charleston v News Group Newspapers Ltd* [1995] 2 AC 65.   [14] [1971] 1 WLR 1239.
[15] ibid, 1261.

defamation proceedings, because such actions 'must inevitably have an inhibiting effect on freedom of speech'.[16] It is important that democratically elected bodies are open to public criticism, so they should not be able to sue to protect their reputation. The House considered authorities from South Africa and the United States, including the famous decision of the US Supreme Court in *New York Times v Sullivan*.[17] It reached its conclusion on common law principles, while the Court of Appeal had come to the same decision on the basis of the ECHR, not yet incorporated into English law.[18] Later cases have extended the *Derbyshire* principle to preclude libel actions by public corporations and political parties;[19] individual politicians remain free to bring them, though defendants now find it much easier to argue that defamatory allegations about such claimants are covered by a defence of qualified privilege.[20]

Defences of truth and fair comment

Several rulings of the House have developed this area of libel law, though it would be difficult to describe any of them as seminal. *Sutherland v Stopes* concerned a vitriolic attack on the integrity of Marie Stopes, the birth control pioneer.[21] By 4:1, the House reversed the Court of Appeal, which had allowed her appeal from the judgment of Lord Hewart, LCJ.[22] The jury had found that the allegations were true, but not fair comment; the House held there was no evidence to support the latter finding, so the judge had correctly entered a verdict for the defendant.[23] In the earlier of two cases in the 1950s,[24] it held that complaints by film producers that a film critic was 'out of touch with the tastes and requirements of the picture-going millions' were comment; the fact that there were economic motives for the complaints did not provide evidence of malice. *Kemsley v Foot*[25] established the important point that a comment need not set out the facts on which it is based; it is enough that it refers to subject matter well known to the public, for example, a play or film on which a reviewer is commenting. *Kemsley* was itself distinguished by the House of Lords in its controversial ruling in *Telnikoff v Matusevitch*.[26] By a 4:1 majority it held that the question whether statements in a letter to a newspaper, in reply to an article in that paper, amounted to fact or comment should be determined by reference to the letter alone, not in conjunction with the terms of the article. In a strong dissent, Lord

---

[16] [1993] AC 534, 547 (Lord Keith).   [17] 376 US 254 (1964).   [18] [1992] QB 770.
[19] *British Coal Corp v NUM* 28 June 1996, unreported, French J; *Goldsmith v Bhoyrul* [1997] 4 All ER 268, Buckley J.
[20] See pp 657–8 below.   [21] [1925] AC 47.
[22] See R Hall, *Marie Stopes* (London: André Deutsch, 1977) ch 13 for an account of this very controversial case. It is surely worthy of note that the House was composed of five Law Lords whose ages ranged from 68 (Viscount Cave, LC) to 82 (Viscount Finlay).
[23] The decision also contains important dicta that the defendant is required to prove the sting, not the detail, of defamatory imputations: [1925] AC 47, 78–9 (Lord Shaw).
[24] *Turner v MGM* [1950] 1 All ER 449.   [25] [1952] AC 345.   [26] [1992] AC 343.

Ackner argued that the decision meant that the fair comment defence could not be used where readers were unaware of the material commented on; further, it was odd to allow the jury to look at the article to determine the fairness of a letter or review, but not to determine whether it was comment. On the other hand, all the Law Lords were agreed that the defendant does not have to show that the comment reflected his own opinion; it is enough that it is a comment which could be made honestly by someone.[27]

Qualified privilege

It is here that the House of Lords has recently made its most important contributions to the development of libel law in England and Wales. For the first half of the twentieth century, qualified privilege was an issue in only a handful of cases.[28] The most important, *Adam v Ward*,[29] established that it is for the judge to determine whether there was a privileged occasion and whether the privilege had been exceeded. The jury's role is to find the facts relevant to determining whether the occasion was privileged. Reciprocity of duty and interest between the publisher and recipient of the communication is essential.[30]

English common law did not recognise that qualified privilege could cover the publication of defamatory allegations by the media to the general public until the decision of the House in *Reynolds v Times Newspapers Ltd*,[31] where the *Sunday Times* published an article alleging that Albert Reynolds, who had just resigned as Prime Minister of Ireland, had lied to the Dáil and misled his Cabinet colleagues about the circumstances concerning his resignation. The House declined to extend qualified privilege to include the publication of any 'political information' irrespective of the circumstances, because that step would mean that the reputation of political figures could never be protected, and further it would be wrong to distinguish political discussion from the treatment of other issues of general importance. But it did recognise that the media could claim a qualified privilege for the communication of defamatory allegations to the public; whether the claims should succeed would depend on the circumstances. Lord Nicholls, in the leading speech, indicated factors which trial judges might consider in deciding whether the media could claim the defence: for example, whether it had reliable sources, the steps taken to verify the story, and whether it had approached the claimant for comment. The common law did not set 'a higher standard than that of responsible journalism . . . '.[32] In this case the publication was not protected, for it had presented serious allegations as statements of fact, without mentioning

---

[27] The House rejected the contrary view of the Supreme Court of Canada in *Cherneskey v Armadale Publishers* (1979) 1 SCR 1067.

[28] *London Association for Protection of Trade v Greenlands Ltd* [1916] 2 AC 15; *Minter v Priest* [1930] AC 558.

[29] [1917] AC 309.   [30] ibid, 334 (Lord Atkinson).   [31] [2001] 2 AC 127.

[32] ibid, 202 (Lord Nicholls).

Mr Reynolds' own explanation of events; it could not, therefore, be said that the public had a right to know them.

Reynolds is a landmark decision. It offered the media greater freedom to investigate and report stories of public interest, provided it behaved responsibly in the ways indicated by Lord Nicholls; it was no longer decisive that it could not establish the truth of defamatory allegations of fact. The speeches in the House are remarkable for their copious reference to leading authorities in other common law jurisdictions and for their full discussion of the libel jurisprudence of the European Court of Human Rights. Indeed, one explanation for the House's innovative approach to qualified privilege is that it was anticipating the consequences of the incorporation of the ECHR by the Human Rights Act 1998; from October 2000 the courts have been required to protect the Convention right to freedom of expression and to take account of decisions in Strasbourg.

Although *Reynolds* has had a significant impact on media practice,[33] the expanded qualified privilege defence has rarely succeeded in the courts. The main reason is that judges tended to treat the 'check-list' of factors indicated by Lord Nicholls as a set of hurdles, all of which must be surmounted by the press before it can claim the privilege. The House of Lords put matters right in its recent decision in *Jameel v Wall Street Journal Europe SPRL*.[34] Indeed, it has probably expanded the scope of what has become known as 'Reynolds privilege', jurisprudentially distinct from the traditional form of qualified privilege.[35] It applies whenever the subject matter of the publication, taken as a whole, is a matter of public interest. In the view of some members of the House, it was no longer necessary to ask whether the media had a duty to publish a story and whether the public had an interest in receiving it. On the question whether it was right for the defendant to include the particular defamatory allegations, some discretion should be left to the editor to determine whether it was necessary to do this to make the story more presentable or to add to its credibility; the defence would fail if they were included gratuitously. Finally, it should be asked whether the defendant had satisfied the requirements of responsible journalism; it was wrong in that context to insist that all the tests suggested by Lord Nicholls must necessarily be satisfied. In *Jameel* itself, there was no need for the newspaper to obtain the comments of the claimant on its story that his company's bank accounts were being monitored by the Saudi authorities, because he would have nothing useful to say about it.

The most significant aspect of this ruling is the emphasis placed on the story as a whole in determining whether the publication is covered by qualified privilege; it is no longer necessary to ask, as common law courts have traditionally done, whether the recipients had an interest in, or right to know, the *particular*

---

[33] A Kenyon, *Defamation: Comparative Law and Practice* (London: UCL Press, 2006) 223–31, 236–7.

[34] [2007] 1 AC 359.

[35] See Lord Phillips MR in *Loutchansky v Times Newspapers Ltd (Nos 2, 3, and 5)* [2002] QB 783, para 35.

defamatory allegations published by the defendant. In conjunction with the deference accorded the judgment of editors in deciding to include the allegations, this principle significantly widens the freedom of the media to report stories with defamatory implications. As Lady Hale put it, 'our defamation law should encourage, rather than discourage' serious journalism of the kind found in the Wall Street Journal.[36] Lord Hoffmann said that until recently defamation law had been weighted against defendants.[37] These are not remarks which would have been made in the House of Lords before *Reynolds*; they show, as Ward LJ said in a recent Court of Appeal libel judgment, very clearly 'which way the wind from the House of Lords is blowing'.[38]

At much the same time as these developments, the House has interpreted the legislation conferring a privilege for the fair and accurate reports of public meetings liberally to the benefit of the press.[39] The judge and Court of Appeal in Northern Ireland had held that a meeting—a press conference convened to support the release of a soldier convicted of serious criminal offences—could not be regarded as 'public' because there was a nexus between its organisers and those attending it. The House of Lords held that this was too narrow an approach to the legislation, which had been enacted to enable the media to report any meeting open to everyone, where the media had been invited to ensure its coverage for the benefit of the general public. Lord Steyn in particular stressed that the qualified privilege of newspapers existed to protect and promote freedom of expression, a right of constitutional significance and weight.

Lastly, the decision in *Horrocks v Lowe* should be mentioned.[40] Lord Diplock for the House clarified the meaning of 'malice' for the purpose of rebutting a defence of qualified privilege, in that case the common law qualified privilege claimed by a local authority councillor speaking in a debate. There is express malice if it is shown that the publisher knew that the communication was untrue, or was reckless or indifferent whether it was true or false. Alternatively, malice may defeat a plea of qualified privilege (but not fair comment) if it is proved that an allegation was made predominantly for reasons of spite or for personal advantage, even if the speaker believed in its truth. This ruling is perhaps now less significant than it used to be. One reason is that malice has a narrower meaning in the context of fair comment,[41] while it is also doubtful whether there is any room for malice in the context of

---

[36] ibid, para 150.   [37] ibid, para 38.

[38] In *Charman v Orion Publishing Group Ltd* [2008] 1 All ER 750, para 66(7); the Court of Appeal applied the principles in *Reynolds* and *Jameel* to hold protected by qualified privilege allegations made about a police officer in a book, *Bent Coppers*.

[39] *McCartan Turkington Breen (a firm) v Times Newspapers Ltd* [2001] 2 AC 277. On another, subsidiary, issue the House held that the contents of a press release constitute part of 'the proceedings' of the meeting, for the purpose of the reporting defence, even though the release has not been read out at the meeting.

[40] [1975] AC 135.

[41] See the judgment of the Hong Kong Court of Appeal, given by Lord Nicholls in *Paul v Cheng* [2001] EMLR 777.

'Reynolds privilege'. That type of privilege can be claimed only if the defendant has met the standards of responsible journalism; if that is so, it follows that she has not acted with express malice.

Damages for libel

The House has considered the assessment of damages in a few cases.[42] In *Plato Films v Speidel*[43] it declined to reconsider the rule under which evidence of specific acts of misconduct on the part of a claimant (as distinct from evidence of his general bad character) cannot be introduced to reduce the amount of damages to which he is entitled. Viscount Simonds characteristically rejected the argument that it would be proper for the House acting judicially to revise this well-established, but much criticised, rule.[44]

Much the most important of its decisions in this area is that in *Cassell and Co Ltd v Broome*,[45] although the case should not really have reached the House. The Court of Appeal had dismissed an appeal from the award to the claimant of punitive damages in addition to a modest sum of compensatory damages. Had the Court of Appeal merely confirmed the award, leave to appeal to the House would probably not have been granted, but it had ruled that it was not bound by the principles for the award of punitive damages formulated by Lord Devlin in *Rookes v Barnard*.[46] Consequently, an Appellate Committee of seven Law Lords heard argument over 13 days, much of it on the question whether the Court of Appeal had been right to treat *Rookes* as decided per incuriam for ignoring earlier relevant House of Lords decisions. The House was clearly keen to correct the Court of Appeal, and in particular Lord Denning, MR, on this point of precedent. But it also took the opportunity to confirm some fundamental principles of damage awards in defamation cases. Lord Hailsham, LC, highlighted the constitutional role of the jury in libel actions, including its power to determine the appropriate award. The purpose of damages is not only to compensate the claimant for his losses and provide solace for injured feelings, but also to vindicate his reputation in the eyes of the public; that is why libel damages could not be compared with the awards in personal injuries cases. The House approved the restrictions imposed by Lord Devlin on the award of punitive (or 'exemplary') damages: they could not be awarded in libel, unless it was shown that the defendant had calculated that he would make a profit from publishing the defamatory allegations.[47]

---

[42] In addition to the decisions mentioned in the text, see *Ley v Hamilton* (1935) LT 384.
[43] [1961] AC 1090.
[44] ibid, 1123–4, declining to reconsider the rule in *Scott v Sampson* (1882) 4 QBD 491, Cave J.
[45] [1972] AC 1027.
[46] [1964] AC 1129. The case concerned the tort of intimidation, not libel.
[47] These principles have been refined by the Court of Appeal, notably in *Elton John v MGN* [1997] QB 586.

Miscellaneous cases

A few other House of Lords decisions on libel law should be mentioned. Lord Atkin in *Sim v Stretch* provided one of the many alternative tests for what constitutes a *defamatory* allegation: would the words tend to lower the claimant in the eyes of right-thinking members of society generally?[48] In 1980 the House considered a prosecution for criminal libel,[49] now an extremely rare proceeding. A libel must be 'serious' to justify a criminal prosecution; Lord Diplock doubted whether the offence is compatible with the European Convention, because under the criminal law the defendant must show not only that the allegations are true, but also that publication is in the public benefit. In *Berezovsky v Forbes, Inc*,[50] by a 3:2 majority, the House held that the claimant, a Russian businessman, resident for some of the year in England, could bring libel proceedings here in respect of allegations in a magazine which had a circulation of only about 2,000 subscribers in England out of a total circulation of 788,000; claimants such as Berezovsky often prefer to bring proceedings in England, rather than in the United States, where the law offers the media wider defences. That is why London is considered the libel capital of the world.

Finally, in *Grobbelaar v News Group Newspapers Ltd*,[51] one of the least satisfactory libel cases in the last few years, the House allowed an appeal by the claimant against a Court of Appeal ruling that the jury decision in his favour was perverse and should be set aside. The House held that appellate courts should interpret the jury's decision on liability, if possible, to avoid the conclusion that it was perverse; but it was evident that its award of £85,000 could not be supported, as it must have found on the evidence that the claimant, a famous premiership goalkeeper, had entered into corrupt agreements to fix matches. The House used its inherent power to exercise a statutory authority granted the Court of Appeal; the latter now has authority to substitute for a jury award the sum which it considers appropriate, rather than order a new trial,[52] so the House could reduce the award to nominal damages of £1. The decision perhaps shows an unnecessary attachment to the sanctity of jury decisions on liability; jury trial of libel actions is now becoming relatively uncommon, so it is unlikely that the points in *Grobbelaar* will come before the House again.

Confidentiality and privacy

The House declines to recognise a privacy tort

English common law does not recognise a discrete tort of privacy either generally or in the particular context of media infringement. The House of Lords rejected

---

[48] [1936] 2 All ER 1237, 1240.   [49] *Gleaves v Deakin* [1980] AC 477.
[50] [2000] 1 WLR 1004.   [51] [2002] 1 WLR 3024.
[52] Courts and Legal Services Act 1990, s 8(2).

an invitation to recognise the tort as recently as 2003, although the case presented favourable circumstances for its recognition. *Wainwright v Home Office*[53] did not involve the media or freedom of expression. The claimants argued that their privacy had been infringed when they had been required to submit to strip-searches on visiting a relative in prison; the searches had been conducted without statutory authority. The House held the claimant could not sue for invasion of privacy. Lord Hoffmann in the leading speech said, '[t]here was a great difference between identifying privacy as a value which underlies the existence of a rule of law . . . and privacy as a principle of law in itself'.[54] The courts should not formulate a general right in an area where Parliament had declined to intervene; if there was a serious gap in the law it should be filled by detailed legislation, rather than the common law.[55] The difficulty with this argument, in the context of media intrusion, is that governments and Parliament are reluctant to introduce privacy laws which would make them unpopular with the press. It would be much easier for the Law Lords (or the Supreme Court) than for Parliament to establish a privacy right; legislation would then be necessary to clarify the scope of the right and provide the media with appropriate defences. The decision in *Wainwright* should be seen as a missed opportunity, indicating a failure on the part of the House to appreciate how an innovative decision would encourage the legislature to act.[56]

In the context of press and media infringement of personal privacy, other well-established causes of action may provide adequate protection. One possibility is a libel action to compensate a claimant whose real complaint is that his image has been exploited, without consent, to present him in an offensive or false light.[57] But the main surrogate for the privacy tort in this context has been the long-established equitable jurisdiction in cases of breach of confidence.

Breach of confidence before the HRA

The most important contributions of the House of Lords in this area were made in the notorious *Spycatcher* cases,[58] where the Government attempted to

---

[53] [2004] 2 AC 406.   [54] ibid, para 31.

[55] ibid, para 33. The HRA did not apply, as the incident occurred before it came into force. The House rejected the argument that incorporation of the ECHR, including the right to respect for private life, guaranteed by Article 8, strengthened the case for recognition of privacy rights. The Strasbourg court has now held that the UK infringed this Convention right: *Wainwright v UK* (2007) 44 EHRR 40.

[56] Lord Bingham, a member of the Committee that decided *Wainwright*, has argued extra-judicially that the courts might formulate common law privacy rights, if Parliament failed to act: 'Should there be a Law to Protect Rights of Personal Privacy?' [1996] EHRLR 450.

[57] See the decision of the House in *Tolley v Fry* [1931] AC 333 (caricature of amateur golfer, with carton of chocolate protruding from his pocket, carried defamatory innuendo that he had consented to use of his image for advertising, so damaging his reputation as an amateur). Percy Winfeld considered that the defendant should have been liable for offensive invasion of privacy: 'Privacy' (1931) 47 LQR 23, 39.

[58] *AG v Guardian Newspapers Ltd* [1987] 1 WLR 1248; *AG v Guardian Newspapers Ltd (No 2)* [1990] 1 AC 109.

prevent the reporting of allegations made by Peter Wright, a former member of the Security Service, of serious irregularities on its part during the period he had been working for it. There was a bitter division of opinion between the Law Lords whether to continue the interim injunction granted the Crown until full trial of the breach of confidence action. The majority (Lords Templeman, Brandon, and Ackner) held that it should be continued, primarily to preserve morale among members of the Security Service. The dissents of Lords Bridge and Oliver considered it futile to continue the injunction, when it was easy for the public to buy the *Spycatcher* book abroad or to read the allegations in newspapers in the United States, Canada, and Europe. Lord Bridge correctly predicted that the order would not survive a challenge in the European Court of Human Rights.[59] The majority decision naturally attracted much criticism in the press; certainly it now appears to have been an aberration.

The House, however, refused to uphold the Crown's claim for a permanent injunction when the case came back a year later. Applying a principle stated in the *Crossman Diaries* case[60] and by the High Court of Australia,[61] the House held the Crown had not shown that it was in the public interest to maintain the injunction, since the contents of *Spycatcher* were no longer secret as a result of its worldwide publication.[62] The principles of breach of confidence were restated with great clarity, particularly by Lord Goff in a passage frequently cited in later cases:[63]

...a duty of confidence arises when confidential information comes to the knowledge of a person (the confidant) in circumstances where he has notice, or is held to have agreed, that the information is confidential, with the effect that it would be just in the circumstances that he should be precluded from disclosing the information.

Lord Goff explained that the duty did not arise only when information had been confided in the course of a contract or other relationship; a third party such as a journalist could be liable if he disclosed the contents of an 'obviously confidential document, such as a private diary'. But an action for breach of confidence could not be brought if the information was too trivial to be regarded as confidential, if it had entered the public domain, or if the public interest in confidentiality was outweighed by the public interest favouring disclosure.

---

[59] [1987] 1 WLR 1248, 1280. For the Strasbourg decision holding the UK in breach of Art 10 of the ECHR, see *Observer and Guardian v UK* (1992) 14 EHRR 153.

[60] *AG v Jonathan Cape Ltd* [1976] 1 QB 752, Widgery LCJ.

[61] *Commonwealth of Australia v John Fairfax and Sons Ltd* (1980) 147 CLR 39.

[62] The same principle was applied by the House of Lords in *Lord Advocate v The Scotsman Publications Ltd* [1990] 1 AC 812.

[63] [1990] 1 AC 109, 281.

The protection of privacy and confidentiality after the HRA

The House of Lords has considered privacy and confidentiality in three major cases after the Human Rights Act came into force.[64] In *Campbell v MGN Ltd*,[65] by a 3:2 majority, it held that Naomi Campbell could recover damages for breach of confidence when the *Daily Mirror* disclosed that she had been having treatment for her drug addiction at Narcotics Anonymous and published a photograph of her leaving one of its meetings. The Law Lords all recognised that personal information could be protected against media disclosure through a breach of confidence action; moreover, the law had to be developed in conformity with the ECHR rights to respect for private life and to freedom of expression. Neither right was automatically entitled to priority, but should be balanced on the basis of the particular facts. Even the dissenting speeches of Lords Nicholls and Hoffmann agreed that breach of confidence should now be seen in these circumstances as protecting privacy or human autonomy and dignity, rather than relationships of trust and confidence; Lord Nicholls indeed thought that the tort is now more appropriately termed 'misuse of personal information'.[66] The House acknowledged the importance of the Convention rights and the Strasbourg Court's jurisprudence on how they should be balanced. But it stopped short of recognising a discrete privacy tort, even in the limited context of media disclosure of sensitive personal information. In contrast, the House unanimously refused to grant an injunction to prevent disclosure of the identity of a woman charged with the murder of her older son and publication of their photographs, even though publication by the media would infringe the privacy of the woman's younger son, then aged eight.[67] The freedom of the press fully to report legal proceedings trumped his privacy.

In the third case, the House of Lords has adapted breach of confidence to protect the commercial interests of celebrities. An issue in *Douglas v Hello! Ltd (No 3)*[68] was whether Michael Douglas and Catherine Zeta-Jones, who had granted *OK!* magazine the right to publish approved pictures of their wedding, had confidentiality rights to secure compensation for the publication by *Hello!* of unauthorised pictures. The Court of Appeal upheld the actions by the Douglases for breach of confidence; that issue was not taken to the House. But the Court of Appeal rejected the claim by *OK!* to invoke against *Hello!* an exclusive right to publish any photographs of this occasion. By a 3:2 majority, the House allowed *OK!*'s appeal.[69] For Lord Hoffmann, it was unrealistic not to recognise that *OK!* had paid £1 million for the benefit of the obligation of confidence imposed on all

---

[64] The House has formulated the principles under which interim injunctions and other temporary orders to preserve confidentiality or personal privacy may be granted under the HRA 1998, s 12(3): *Cream Holdings Ltd v Banerjee* [2005] 1 AC 253.

[65] [2004] 2 AC 457.   [66] ibid, paras 11–17 (Lord Nicholls) and 49–51 (Lord Hoffmann).
[67] *Re S (A Child)* [2005] 1 AC 593.   [68] [2006] QB 125.
[69] *OBG Ltd v Allan* [2008] 1 AC 1.

those attending the wedding not to publish *any* photographs. The obligation could be imposed to allow a media outlet to be the only source of information.[70] In strong dissents, Lords Nicholls and Walker pointed out that the unauthorised photographs contained no non-trivial confidential information, not revealed by publication of the approved photographs. The decision clearly stretches the law of breach of confidence beyond the terms set out by Lord Goff in *Spycatcher*, and enables celebrities to market their image for commercial purposes by entering into exclusive publishing agreements. Potentially, it is a significant decision.

Contempt of court and open justice

The strict liability rule

It seems astonishing that the House of Lords hardly considered contempt of court before its decision in *Attorney General v Times Newspapers Ltd* in 1973.[71] It held there that prejudgment by the media of the issues which would come before the court in pending litigation amounted to a contempt even if, as in this case, the trial would be conducted by a judge without a jury, so there would be no likelihood that the publicity would influence the decision. Trial by newspaper was inherently objectionable, because it could lead to disrespect for the law; treating the discussion as a contempt would not unduly fetter freedom of speech. The *Sunday Times* disagreed, and so did a majority of the European Court of Human Rights in one of its first rulings on Article 10 of the ECHR.[72]

That decision led to the enactment of the Contempt of Court Act 1981, limiting the scope of the 'strict liability rule'. It also provides that a publication which is part of a good faith discussion of public affairs is not a contempt, if the risk of prejudice is merely incidental to that discussion.[73] In *Attorney General v English*[74] the House of Lords allowed a newspaper's appeal from the Divisional Court, holding that it was immaterial whether the passages creating the risk of prejudice were necessary to the statement of the theme of the article.

Common law contempt

As a result of two decisions of the House of Lords, it is a contempt of court, say, for a newspaper intentionally to prejudice the administration of justice by publishing material, the disclosure of which has been stopped by an injunction taken against another paper. The rule was formulated by the House in one of the *Spycatcher* cases, when the *Sunday Times* and other newspapers published the

---

[70] ibid, paras 117–24.
[71] [1974] AC 273: see Sir David Eady and ATH Smith (eds), *Arlidge, Eady and Smith on Contempt* (London: Sweet & Maxwell, 3rd edn 2005) para 1.87.
[72] *Sunday Times v UK* (1979) 2 EHRR 245.   [73] s 5.   [74] [1983] 1 AC 116.

allegations covered by the interim injunctions which had been taken out against the *Guardian* and the *Observer*.[75] Although not, of course, parties to the injunction, their publication amounted to a contempt of court. The House later clarified the law concerning this type of contempt in *Attorney General v Punch*,[76] where the editor of the magazine published an article by a former officer of the Security Service, containing information which the officer had been prevented by an injunction from disclosing until full trial of the Crown's action against him. The editor could not argue as a defence to contempt proceedings that the terms of the injunction were too wide, nor that he himself had not intended to prejudice national security; he was liable for contempt as he had deliberately published material covered by the order against the officer.

The open justice principle

These contempt decisions are important. But they pale in comparison with the seminal ruling of the House of Lords in *Scott v Scott*.[77] In that case it decided that it was wrong to hear nullity proceedings in private in order to spare one of the parties embarrassment. But much more significant than the actual decision are the principles declared by the Law Lords. Viscount Haldane LC said:[78]

While the broad principle is that the Courts of this country must, as between parties, administer justice in public, this principle is subject to apparent exceptions...As the paramount object must always be to do justice, the general rule as to publicity, after all only the means to an end, must accordingly yield. But the burden lies on those seeking to displace its application in the particular case to make out that the ordinary rule must...be superseded by this paramount consideration.

The House instanced some particular types of case where the open justice principle need not be observed in the interests of justice—wardship disputes or litigation concerning trade secrets—but these were exceptions and did not include cases where the only argument was that the evidence would be particularly sensitive. Lord Shaw considered the open justice principle a constitutional right, and referred to Jeremy Bentham's argument for publicity as 'the very soul of justice'.[79]

Scott v Scott is almost invariably cited when the media assert their rights to attend or report legal proceedings. Its principles were extensively discussed by the House in the *Leveller* case, when it held that it was not a contempt to disclose the name of a witness who had been permitted to give evidence in an official secrets prosecution without disclosing his identity; even assuming that the court had authority to order the media not to identify him, it had failed to do this with a clear direction.[80] This case is now the leading authority on the circumstances in

---

[75] *AG v Times Newspapers Ltd* [1992] 1 AC 191.   [76] [2003] 1 AC 1046.
[77] [1913] AC 417.   [78] ibid, 437–8.   [79] ibid, 477.
[80] *AG v Leveller Magazine Ltd* [1979] AC 440.

which a party or witness may be allowed anonymity, a lesser intrusion on media freedom than holding the hearing, or part of it, in private. On the other hand, in *Home Office v Harman*[81] a majority of the House ruled that a solicitor was in contempt of court when she allowed a journalist to see documents disclosed to her on discovery, which had been read out by counsel during the proceedings. The journalist then used them as a basis for an article on conditions in a special prison unit. Lord Diplock denied that the case involved freedom of speech or the press, or the open justice principle. Lord Scarman dissented vigorously, arguing that it was wrong to uphold contempt proceedings for the disclosure of information to which the public had access under the open justice rule. Subsequently, the European Human Rights Commission held admissible an application that the House of Lords decision infringed the right to freedom of expression.[82]

The privilege not to disclose sources of information

The House of Lords has often considered the scope of the 'journalists' privilege' not to reveal their sources of information. Generally, they have taken a cautious approach to the privilege, in contrast to the more generous stance of the European Court of Human Rights. In *British Steel Corporation v Granada Television Ltd*[83] it declined to recognise a common law privilege as an integral aspect of freedom of the press. Its other decisions have concerned the scope of the qualified statutory privilege conferred by the Contempt of Court Act 1981:[84] there is a privilege unless the applicant shows that disclosure is necessary for one of the prescribed ends. The first involved the circumstances in which an order may be made to disclose a source 'in the interests of national security'.[85] A majority of the House ordered disclosure to identify the leaker (of a document indicating how the Government would deal with controversy following the arrival of cruise missiles in Britain) in order to avert the risks of any further, more damaging, leaks. It decided that an order is 'necessary... for the prevention of... crime' when it is 'really needed' to stop crime in general; disclosure of a source is not limited to the prevention of an identified offence.[86] In *X Ltd v Morgan Grampian Ltd*[87] the House ruled that disclosure of the source is necessary 'in the interests of justice' whenever the applicant, in this case a company anxious to keep its financial affairs confidential, argues that it needs to know who leaked the information in order to exercise its legal rights, for instance, to dismiss a disloyal employee. The House rejected the alternative interpretation of the provision which would have allowed disclosure only to enable justice to be done in specific legal proceedings.

---

[81] [1983] AC 280.   [82] 10038/82, *Harman v UK* 38 D & R 53.
[83] [1981] AC 1096.   [84] s 10.
[85] *Secretary of State for Defence v Guardian Newspapers* [1985] AC 339.
[86] *Re An Inquiry under the Company Securities (Insider Dealing) Act 1985* [1988] AC 660.
[87] [1991] 1 AC 1.

The European Court of Human Rights held that the United Kingdom by this decision had infringed freedom of expression; it was not necessary to order disclosure of the source of the leak to protect the company's commercial confidentiality, since it had been granted an injunction to stop the journalist and his paper from revealing its financial problems.[88] The Government left it to the courts to interpret the provision in conformity with the Strasbourg ruling. In its most recent pronouncement in this area,[89] the House has accepted that the privilege constitutes an integral aspect of press freedom, but it granted a mental hospital an order to disclose the identity of the person, presumed to be an employee, who had disclosed the medical records of a patient, via an intermediary, to a newspaper. It was essential to discover his identity to stop any further leaks of confidential patient records and to remove suspicion from other employees.[90]

Conclusions

It is, of course, silly to criticise past judicial decisions for not reflecting modern values. Inevitably, they were shaped by contemporary culture as well as by legal doctrine, itself influenced by the ideas of previous generations. Victorian and early twentieth century society prized reputation more than we do.[91] Equally, we probably attach greater importance to freedom of expression, and we are certainly more aware of the impact of libel and privacy laws on its exercise. But even allowing for these considerations, the jurisprudence of the House of Lords in libel and the other areas of law considered here is curiously uneven. Some decisions have established canonical principles, notably the open justice principle in *Scott*[92] and, I predict, the expanded qualified privilege formulated in *Reynolds*[93] and *Jameel*.[94] Others, including some which have long been authoritative, may now be vulnerable to legislative or judicial qualification.[95] It would also be difficult to claim much for the literary quality of the individual judgments in cases considered in this chapter. One might perhaps expect judges to take particular care over their judgments in libel law, where the precise meaning of words is often of fundamental importance, but this has not always been apparent. Some judgments are, however, a pleasure to read; among them are the speeches of Lords Haldane

---

[88] *Goodwin v UK* (1996) 22 EHRR 123.
[89] *Ashworth Hospital Authority v MGN Ltd* [2002] 1 WLR 2003.
[90] Subsequently, a court refused to order the intermediary, Ackroyd, to disclose his source, because in the absence of further leaks it was not 'necessary...in the interests of justice' to order disclosure: *Mersey NHS Trust v Ackroyd* [2006] EMLR 12, Tugendhat J.
[91] On the changing values of reputation, see R Post, 'The Social Foundations of Defamation Law: Reputation and the Constitution' (1986) 74 California L Rev 691.
[92] [1913] AC 417.   [93] [2001] 2 AC 127.   [94] [2007] 1 AC 359.
[95] See *Hulton and Co v Jones* [1910] AC 20 (text at n 6) and perhaps *Telnikoff v Matusevitch* [1992] AC 343 (text at n 26).

and Loreburn in *Scott,* of Lord Nicholls in *Reynolds,* and of Lady Hale in both *Campbell* and *Jameel.*

One further point in conclusion should be made. The European Human Rights Court has on four occasions held that the United Kingdom infringed the ECHR through decisions of the House of Lords on points discussed in this chapter;[96] it is also likely it would have upheld the application in the *Harman* case, if that had been referred to it after the Commission had ruled it admissible.[97] This is a matter of some concern, especially as the European Court is hardly radical, affording national courts a margin of appreciation when they apply Convention rights. None of these cases involved libel law. Perhaps surprisingly, it is in the areas of privacy and contempt that recent House of Lords decisions have been vulnerable to scrutiny on human rights grounds.

[96] See the decisions in *Wainwright v UK* (2007) 44 EHRR 40; *Observer and Guardian v UK* (1992) 14 EHRR 153; *Sunday Times v UK* (1979) 2 EHRR 245; and *Goodwin v UK* (1996) 22 EHRR 123.

[97] See nn 81–2 above.

36

Family Law

Stephen Cretney

Introduction: changing judicial and family values

Between 1877 (when the Appellate Jurisdiction Act 1876 came into force) and 2005 (when the Constitutional Reform Act established the machinery whereby the Supreme Court will replace the House of Lords as the court of final appeal) there were enormous changes in the English law governing family relationships. These changes are vividly illustrated by a comparison of two outstanding pieces of judicial oratory.

In 1923 Lord Chancellor Birkenhead, concurring in the dismissal of a wife's appeal against the court's refusal to grant her the divorce she sought, said:[1]

It is an unfortunate circumstance that [the wife] should . . . be tied for life to a dangerous, violent and homicidal lunatic, after having for many years suffered, both in body and in spirit, from his unfaithfulness and his cruelty. He is forty-one years of age and she is forty. We need take little account of his feelings. As regards her, we are bound to note that during many more years, unless death remove him or release her, she must look forward to a loneliness from which she can escape only by a violation of the moral law. To some this may appear a harsh, and even an inhumane result; but such, my Lords, such is the law of England. Your Lordships cannot, because of the sympathy which you must all feel for this unhappy victim of our marriage law, impeach the chastity of a woman, equally innocent, who also is entitled to the sympathy and shelter of the law. The true remedy lies outside any Court of law; it lies beyond the scope of your Lordships' faculties, sitting as the Supreme Appellate Tribunal. It rests with Parliament (if and when it thinks proper) to end a state of things which in a civilized community, and in the name of morality, imposes such an intolerable hardship upon innocent men and women.

In 2004 Baroness Hale of Richmond, concurring in a decision that the survivor of a same-sex relationship was entitled under the housing legislation to succeed to a tenancy in the same way as would the survivor of a different-sex relationship,[2] said this:

[1] *Rutherford v Richardson* [1923] AC 1, 12. The ground for the decision was that there was insufficient evidence of adultery against the woman named in the wife's petition.

[2] The Rent Act 1977 gave a person who had been living with a tenant 'as his or her wife or husband' the right to succeed on the tenant's death. Baroness Hale's remarks are directed to

Homosexual relationships can have exactly the same qualities of intimacy, stability and inter-dependence that heterosexual relationships do . . . [M]arried and unmarried couples, both homosexual and heterosexual, may bring up children together . . . Homosexual couples can have exactly the same sort of inter-dependent couple relationship as heterosexuals can . . . Some people, whether heterosexual or homosexual, may be satisfied with casual or transient relationships. But most human beings eventually want more than that. They want love. And with love they often want not only the warmth but also the sense of belonging to one another which is the essence of being a couple. And many couples also come to want the stability and permanence which go with sharing a home and a life together . . . In this, people of homosexual orientation are no different from people of heterosexual orientation.

The comparison certainly illustrates how, in the course of 80 or so years, the scope and nature of the 'family law' with which the Appellate Committee has been concerned have broadened. In the 1920s, there were appeals in divorce and other 'matrimonial causes', there was the occasional case about contractual or property matters with a 'family' flavour,[3] there were cases about parentage, and, occasionally, cases about parental rights,[4] but little else. In contrast, in the twenty-first century the Appellate Committee has already had to deal with issues arising from the sophisticated and complex structure created to meet the state's concern for safeguarding the welfare of children, and the interpretation of international conventions dealing with improper removal of children across frontiers, not to mention the housing legislation which so often has an important impact on family life.

The kinds of issues that today routinely come before the courts include some of a kind which could scarcely have been imagined in Lord Birkenhead's time. In 1926, statute law first recognised—and that very tentatively—the creation of an 'artificial' family unit through the institution of legal adoption.[5] Eighty years on, techniques of human assisted reproduction, enabling genetic and social parentage to be separated, are widely used and are regulated within an elaborate legislative framework; and there are difficult issues for the courts to resolve, not least in the context of dealing with disputes about the upbringing of the children of same-sex couples.[6] It is certainly difficult to believe that Lord Birkenhead and his colleagues could have envisaged that their successors on the Appellate Committee would have to assess the adequacy of the legislative response to the

---

establishing that the nature of a committed same-sex relationship is indistinguishable from a committed different-sex relationship, and that accordingly to deny a tenant's homosexual partner the statutory succession right given to a tenant's heterosexual partner infringed the homosexual partner's rights under the Human Rights Act: *Glaidon v Godin-Mendoza [2004]* 2 AC 557, [142].

[3] eg *Debenhams v Mellon* (1880) 6 App Cas 24; *Edwards v Porter* [1925] AC 1.

[4] Notably *Ward v Laverty* [1925] AC 102; and see also *Barnado v McHugh* [1891] AC 388 and *Barnado v Ford* [1892] AC 326.

[5] Adoption of Children Act 1926: see SM Cretney, *Law, Law Reform and the Family* (Oxford: OUP, 1998) ch 8.

[6] See *Re G (Children)* [2006] 1 WLR 2305.

situation of transsexual people who had successfully received gender reassignment therapy.[7]

In the 1920s the law which the House administered was not only highly technical but also left little scope for judicial discretion. Even when the words of a statute—for example the Married Women's Property Act 1882[8]—might be interpreted as giving a court some discretion, the judicial climate long continued to favour a restrictive approach to its exercise.[9] In contrast, at the beginning of the twenty-first century English family law has shifted emphatically towards accepting the exercise of a wide judicial discretion as appropriate for regulating such matters as the financial and other consequences of relationship breakdown.

Finally, it is striking how the style of Lord Birkenhead's speech reflects his background as a combative politician and an outstandingly successful courtroom advocate—a background which he shared with most of those who held the Great Seal from 1876 until the end of the twentieth century. Baroness Hale's appointment in 2004 as a Lord (*sic*) of Appeal in Ordinary marked an important break with tradition, not only in respect of gender but also in terms of her professional experience—markedly different from that of all her predecessors. The contrast is also clearly reflected in the two extracts.

Many of these changes can be seen as part of a process of gradual and natural evolution, but the enactment of the Human Rights Act 1998 is in a different category, adding a new dimension to decision-making even in cases in which the law might have appeared to be settled by the clear words of statute or by case law.[10] To quote Baroness Hale once more: 'Parliament has entrusted us with the task of deciding whether its legislation is compatible with the Convention rights. If it is not, it is our duty to say so. The fact that the issue raises moral questions on which views may legitimately differ does not let us off the hook.'[11]

In 1926 Lord Birkenhead's views on the divorce law were controversial;[12] and another decade was to pass before there was any statutory response to the plea for the reforms of which he was a committed advocate. In 2004 the extent to which the law should equate same-sex and different-sex relationships was also a matter

---

[7] *Bellinger v Bellinger (Lord Chancellor Intervening)* [2003] 2 AC 467.

[8] s 17: judge dealing with a question of title to or possession of property had power to 'make such order . . . as he thinks fit'.

[9] 'No Parliament of that era could possibly have intended to put a husband's property at the hazard of the unfettered discretion of a judge (including a county court judge)': *Pettitt v Pettitt* [1970] AC 777, 793 (Lord Reid).

[10] See eg *Ghaidan v Godin-Mendoza* [2004] 2 AC 557. A striking illustration of the impact of the Act is provided by *Re G (Adoption: Unmarried Couple)* [2008] 3 WLR 76 where the House held (Lord Walker of Gestingthorpe dissenting) that a provision in Article 14 of the Adoption (Northern Ireland) Order 1987 preventing unmarried couples from applying to adopt a child was incompatible with Convention Rights. It appeared that 95 per cent of respondents in a government consultation were opposed to removal of that bar, but the Appellate Committee considered that this majority view lacked any rational basis.

[11] *R (Countryside Alliance) v AG* [2008] 1 AC 719.

[12] See SM Cretney, *Family Law in the Twentieth Century, A History* (Oxford: OUP, 2005) 208–49.

on which opinions differed;[13] but whereas in Lord Birkenhead's time all that the Appellate Committee could do was demonstrate the hardship and injustice caused by the existing law, today it has the much greater opportunities afforded by the Human Rights Act itself to reform the law (or at least use a declaration of incompatibility as a strong lever for legislative action). The recognition that the Appellate Committee can properly be described as a 'branch of government' may indeed raise issues about the accountability of the judiciary which are more explicitly recognised in some other jurisdictions where the separation of the legislative, judicial, and executive branches of government has been a fundamental principle.

Family law in the judicial House of Lords 1857–2007

Marriage and divorce

The Matrimonial Causes Act 1857 introduced a statutory code governing the grant of decrees for restitution of conjugal rights, judicial separation, and divorce. This reflected the policy of the law that marriage was a relationship to which legal rights and duties were attached and it was the function of the courts to enforce these in much the same way as it enforced the performance of contracts. For example, husband and wife were under a legal duty to cohabit, and although 'cruelty' was a ground for separation the courts were bound to apply the principles laid down before 1857 by the ecclesiastical court[14] in interpreting what this meant. Thus, in 1897 the Committee had no doubt that a wife's conduct in publicly and repeatedly alleging that the husband was a homosexual could properly be described in ordinary language as 'cruel', but held that for legal purposes only an 'absolute impossibility' of discharging 'the duties of married life' could suffice: there had to be 'danger to life, limb or health or a reasonable apprehension of such injury'.[15]

There was no formal judicial discretion in such cases; but inevitably what the courts (ultimately the House of Lords) had to decide was what was within (and what was beyond) the scope of acceptable behaviour between man and wife. For more than half a century the House resolutely upheld a view of marital relationships which today seems antediluvian. For example, the Matrimonial Causes Act 1937 added desertion to the grounds for divorce and introduced 'wilful refusal' to consummate as a ground upon which a marriage could be annulled.

---

[13] The Civil Partnership Act 2005 has now established a marriage-like legal regime into which same-sex couples can opt.

[14] Matrimonial Causes Act 1857, ss 16, 22.

[15] *Russell v Russell* [1897] AC 395. The petitioner (the second Earl Russell) subsequently obtained a decree of divorce in the United States, was convicted by his peers of bigamy and sentenced to imprisonment, and was subsequently prominent in the campaign for reform of the divorce laws.

But this did little for many men and women who experienced serious and apparently irremediable sexual difficulties: in 1947 the House refused to terminate the marriage of a couple who had succeeded in having intercourse only three times (and that in the first year of a six-year marriage). They were still under the same roof, and factual separation was a prerequisite for divorce.[16] The following year, the House held[17] that a wife who consistently refused to allow intercourse unless her husband used a condom had not refused to consummate the marriage: the marriage had been consummated on the one occasion when the husband had unwillingly used a condom. True, 'the procreation of children' had traditionally been regarded as one of the main purposes of marriage, and it was argued that to deny a spouse the possibility of becoming a parent necessarily involved a repudiation of the obligations of marriage. But Lord Chancellor Jowitt denounced the suggestion that the law of the land should be co-extensive with the moral law as 'dangerous and fallacious' and insisted that the answer to questions coming before the courts depended 'not on a consideration of the Christian doctrine of marriage . . . but on the true construction of the relevant Acts of Parliament'.[18]

It was not only in cases concerning the grant of 'matrimonial relief' that the difficulties inevitably caused by the fact that marriage is not only a legal construct but also a human relationship became apparent. *Fender v St John-Mildmay*[19] was an action for breach of promise of marriage. The (not self-evidently meritorious) defence was that it would be contrary to public policy to award damages since the defendant was at the relevant time a married man. In fact the promise had been made after the court had pronounced a decree nisi of divorce: the marriage was thus legally (albeit not factually) in existence. The Committee divided three to two,[20] the majority preferring to consider the reality of the situation to the legal theory. But the view of Lord Atkin (a progressively minded lawyer) demonstrates the tenacity of conservative views about the respective roles of judge and legislator down to the beginning of the Second World War:

It is the province of the statesman, and not the lawyer, to discuss, and of the Legislature to determine, what is best for the public good, and to provide for it by proper enactments. It is the province of the judge to expound the law only; the written from the statutes: the unwritten or common law from the decisions of our predecessors and of our existing Courts, from text writers of acknowledged authority, and upon the principles to be clearly deduced from them by sound reason and just inference; not to speculate upon what is best, in his opinion, for the benefit of the community.[21]

Against such a background it is surprising to find that decisions of the House eventually proved to be influential in preparing the ground for the reforms of the

---

[16] *Weatherley v Weatherley* [1947] AC 628.   [17] *Baxter v Baxter* [1948] AC 274.
[18] *Weatherley v Weatherley* [1947] AC 628, 633.   [19] [1938] AC 1.
[20] Lords Atkin, Thankerton, and Wright in the majority; Lords Russell of Killowen and Roche dissented.
[21] [1938] AC 1, 11.

divorce law effected by the Divorce Reform Act 1969. The first (and historically perhaps most significant) move came in 1943 with the decision in *Blunt v Blunt*:[22] husband and wife both sought a divorce, but the Court of Appeal held that since neither was 'innocent' there should be no divorce. The House disagreed: in deciding whether to exercise the statutory discretion to grant a decree to a 'guilty' party courts should strike a balance between 'respect for the binding sanctity of marriage and the social considerations which make it contrary to public policy to insist on the maintenance of a union which has utterly broken down'. Both the policy which Lord Chancellor Simon[23] and his colleagues laid down and the language in which it was expressed marked a significant change of approach evidently influential in the development of the law. It is true that in 1956 the Royal Commission on Marriage and Divorce (chaired by Lord Morton of Henryton, a Lord of Appeal in Ordinary) rejected, on grounds which some considered 'legalistic', proposals to allow a marriage which had broken down to be dissolved irrespective of the parties' moral culpability; but eight years later two appellate decisions of the House—*Williams v Williams*[24] and *Gollins v Gollins*[25]—reinforced the view that the underlying question in deciding whether the statutory grounds for divorce had been established was whether the respondent's conduct was such that the petitioner ought to have a remedy. Thenceforth, the notion that the matrimonial offences should be regarded in the same way as criminal offences was discredited, and the force of the arguments for the legislation to be founded solely on the issue of breakdown correspondingly stronger.

Financial and property matters

The two world wars saw many changes in social and economic circumstances, of which two were especially relevant to the development of family law. First, there was a huge increase in the demand for divorce which, in spite of the restrictive statutory provisions, the legal system was increasingly able to meet; secondly, property ownership (and especially ownership of the family home) became much more widespread than it had been at the beginning of the century. Yet the divorce courts' powers to make orders dealing with capital were restricted and so if the marriage broke down the question whether the wife had, as a matter of law, any beneficial interest in the home—legal title to which was often vested in the husband—became one of great importance.

---

[22] [1943] AC 517.
[23] Simon's failure as Foreign Secretary (and especially his association with the policy of appeasement in the 1930s) may have led to a failure to recognise his achievements as a liberal Home Secretary and Lord Chancellor: see SM Cretney, 'Simon: A Lawyer in Politics', All Souls College, Chichele Lectures, 2002, *All Souls and the Tradition of Public Service in the Twentieth Century*.
[24] [1964] AC 598. In both this case and in *Gollins* (below) the Appellate Committee was divided 3:2.
[25] [1964] AC 644.

Ownership of family property: the 'cold legal question'[26]

In the years following the Second World War judgments in the Court of Appeal sought to find a solution by invoking concepts of 'trust' and 'equity' (notably the so-called 'deserted wife's equity') in a way surprising to orthodox property lawyers. In 1965 the House of Lords in *National Provincial Bank Ltd v Ainsworth*[27] took a principled stand for orthodoxy: a wife might indeed have personal rights enforceable against her husband to be provided with housing, but that was a right *in personam*, of its nature incapable of binding third parties such as a bona fide purchaser (or mortgagee) of the property. Both argument and judgment are examples of traditional legal discourse at a very high level; and it would be difficult to find a clearer example of the House's role in demonstrating the need for statutory reform. In 1967 the Matrimonial Homes Act gave a spouse who lacked a proprietary interest in the home 'rights of occupation' capable of binding third parties.

Although the 1967 Act provided a basis for reform it did not solve all problems. The Act was hastily drafted (and a serious flaw in it was revealed by the House six years later[28]). More significantly, the Act was tailored to deal primarily with the case where one spouse owned the house, and it did not seek to deal with the situation in which a wife claimed that, although the legal estate was unquestionably vested in her husband, the contributions which she had made were such as to give her a claim, recognisable in equity, to a beneficial interest by way of implied, resulting, or constructive trust. On this issue, the House spoke with a less clear voice. True, in *Pettitt v Pettitt*[29] it unanimously held that such claims had to be dealt with in accordance with the traditional rules of equity, and that the Married Women's Property Act 1882 did not allow the courts to vary established proprietary rights merely on the ground that it would be just to do so. But unhappily the House has not succeeded in defining with precision what conditions have to be satisfied for a 'trust' interest to be successfully claimed.[30] By the beginning of the twenty-first century other means have been found of recognising marriage[31] as an economic as well as an emotional partnership.

---

[26] *Gissing v Gissing* [1969] 2 Ch 85, 93 (Lord Denning MR).　　[27] [1965] AC 1175.
[28] *Tarr v Tarr* [1973] AC 254.　　[29] [1970] AC 777.
[30] In *Gissing v Gissing* [1971] AC 886 the House did (unanimously) reject the notion that so-called 'family assets' were a discrete category to which special rules applied; whilst some of the opinions in *Lloyds Bank v Rosset* [1991] 1 AC 107 suggested an apparently almost contemptuous approach to the value of the contributions made by the traditional 'homemaker'. However, *Stack v Dowden* [2007] 2 AC 432 may represent some shift towards greater recognition.
[31] In *Barclays Bank plc v O'Brien* [1994] 1 AC 180, 198 Lord Browne-Wilkinson emphasised that it was recognised that unmarried cohabitation had become 'widespread'; and note *Stack v Dowden* [2007] UKHL 17. It may be that the Supreme Court will have to resolve the question of how far the traditional distinction with marriage—and now civil partnership—in terms of legal consequences can be justified.

The discretionary power to make financial orders on divorce

In 1970 the legislature responded to fears that the introduction of 'no fault' or 'breakdown' divorce would cause hardship and be unfair, especially to economically vulnerable wives, by giving the divorce court wide powers to make orders dealing with virtually all the available economically valuable resources. The exercise of those powers was to be wholly at the court's discretion: 'all the circumstances' were to be considered, and the court should seek to exercise its powers so 'as to place the parties, so far as it is practicable and, having regard to their conduct, just to do so, in the financial position in which they would have been if the marriage had not broken down and each had properly discharged his or her financial obligations and responsibilities towards the other'.[32] But in 1984, prompted in part by agitation on the part of divorced men who claimed that they and their new families were unfairly treated, Parliament made a number of changes, including the removal of the direction to seek to reproduce what might be called the *status quo ante*. The breadth of the courts' discretion over money and property correspondingly broadened.[33]

For some years, the lower courts creatively developed conventions on a pragmatic case-by-case basis about how different kinds of situation should be dealt with, and this approach seemed to attract the Appellate Committee's approval in the only case[34] on the assessment of the amount of financial relief to have reached the House in the twentieth century. But three later cases in which leave was given have demonstrated the inherent weakness of a legislative scheme which confers a wide discretion but does not lay down any single principle governing its exercise. The first, *White v White*,[35] involved a couple married for more than 30 years and both working in the family farming business: the Court of Appeal awarded the wife 40 per cent of the assets, and that award was upheld by the House. What was novel about the case was the outspoken proclamation of an underlying principle: this was the need to avoid 'discrimination' between husband and wife and 'bias' in favour of the money earner and against the home maker, with the consequence that, even in cases of the very wealthy, there would often be an equal division of assets. Two years later[36] the Appellate Committee reiterated this as the underlying policy objective. The different members of the Committee discussed, often in rather general terms, a variety of factors—compensation, financial need, sharing, contributions—which might be relevant

---

[32] Matrimonial Proceedings and Property Act 1970, s 5 (subsequently consolidated as Matrimonial Causes Act 1973, s 25(1)).

[33] The Matrimonial and Family Proceedings Act 1984 emphasised the desirability of bringing about a 'clean break' to encourage (as Lord Scarman had put it in *Minton v Minton* [1979] AC 593, 608) the parties 'to avoid bitterness after family breakdown' by settling their money and property problems once and for all, and thereby 'to put the past behind them and to begin a new life...not overshadowed by the relationship which has broken down'.

[34] *Piglowska v Piglowski* [1999] 1 WLR 1360.   [35] [2001] 1 AC 596

[36] *Miller v Miller, McFarlane v McFarlane* [2006] 2 AC 618.

in different factual situations. A surprising feature of the cases is that in none of them did the House alter the disposition of capital assets ordered by the court below.

Time will tell whether the various opinions provide adequate guidance to the courts and profession; but it seems not unlikely that one outcome will be that the wealthy will increasingly make nuptial contracts seeking to regulate the outcome on any future separation. English law has traditionally been reluctant to allow a private contract to operate in this way: in 1929 in *Hyman v Hyman*[37] the House asserted that the court's power to make maintenance provisions had been conferred 'not merely in the interests of the wife, but of the public';[38] and, although various techniques are available to minimise the impact of this principle on 'private ordering', it may be that—at least in the absence of any fresh statutory provision—the House will be called upon to review this area of the law in the light of the economic and social changes that have occurred since *Hyman* was decided nearly 80 years ago. The evidence[39] suggests that the House is likely to be much more responsive to those changes than could have been predicted in Lord Birkenhead's (or even Lord Atkin's) time.

Children

In the twentieth century the legal system increasingly played an important part in decisions about the status and upbringing of children. There has been a mass of legislation, and judicial decisions which at first sight seem to depend on narrow and technical points of statutory construction often turn out to involve important and difficult questions of social and juristic policy.[40] The Appellate Committee has played a full and important part in resolving such cases, but although many of the issues have now been resolved by legislation (especially the Children Act 1989) it seems that the Human Rights Act 1998 may facilitate a more 'rights-based' approach to cases involving children.

Legal parentage and its attributes

It is not surprising that in an environment dominated by hereditary peers the resolution of disputes about parentage should have been regarded as of first importance; but until the second half of the twentieth century there were no reliable scientific means of determining the truth. There was no alternative to

---

[37] [1929] AC 601.

[38] *Hyman v Hyman* [1929] AC 601, 614 (Lord Hailsham). Statutory provisions seem also to reflect this policy: see Matrimonial Causes Act 1973, s 34. The House adopted a practical approach to problems which arose when circumstances had changed after the court had made a so-called clean break order: *Barder v Barder* [1988] AC 20, and see *Livesey (formerly Jenkins) v Livesey* [1985] AC 424.

[39] Notably *MacLeod v MacLeod* [2008] UKPC 64.

[40] See eg *Lewisham LBC v Lewisham Juvenile Court* [1980] AC 273, where the narrow point was whether a child was still 'in care' until actually removed from the Local Authority.

relying on presumptions, and the Appellate Committee adopted a conservative approach to the admission of evidence seeking to rebut the presumption of legitimacy. In *Russell v Russell*[41] the question for decision was whether the wife had committed adultery. The husband's case was based on the allegation that she had given birth to a child of whom he could not be the father. By a 3:2 majority, the Appellate Committee held that evidence that there had been no intercourse should not have been admitted, and accordingly the decree which he had obtained should be rescinded. The majority refused to accept the argument that the principle of not admitting evidence of non-access (long accepted in legitimacy proceedings) should not apply equally in divorce cases. In Lord Birkenhead's words:[42]

> We have not to ask whether we should ourselves have laid [the rule] down; still less to consider whether changed social conditions have undermined its authority. We find the rule living and authoritative... [The policy which it reflected] was a deeply seated domestic and social policy rendering it unbecoming and indecorous that evidence should be received from such a source; upon such an issue; and with such a possible result.

It was left to Lord Sumner in a dissenting opinion to point out that notions of the sanctity of married relationships had passed into the 'limbo of lost causes and impossible loyalties' with the coming of judicial divorce (which, at least in legal theory, involved an investigation of the whole of a couple's married life). But this was not an approach that appealed to the majority. Happily, in the second half of the twentieth century reliable scientific evidence of parentage became routinely available and the Appellate Committee[43] ruled not only that it was in the interests both of the child and of justice that such evidence should be obtained and admitted, but that in general the interests of a child were best served by ascertaining the truth.

Parental rights and children's welfare

What did it mean to be legally a child's parent? In the 1870s the conventional judicial view was that the father was the head of his house, with control of the family, and that no court should interfere with his right to decide questions of where and how his children should be educated and in what religion they should be raised.[44] In the first quarter of the century the women's movement successfully saw off opposition from those who were convinced that to allow any erosion of that principle would 'allow the state to steal your children'; and in *Ward v Laverty*[45] the Appellate Committee was prepared to recognise that greater stress

---

[41] [1924] AC 687.   [42] [1924] AC 687, 699.

[43] *S v McC (orse S) and M* [1972] AC 24. Statute was to provide detailed procedural rules: Family Law Reform Act 1969.

[44] See eg *Re Agar-Ellis* (1878) 10 Ch D 49.

[45] [1925] AC 101 (NI) (Viscount Cave). However, the wishes of the father were only to be displaced if a sufficient case could be made out for doing so, and the facts do not make easy reading.

should be laid on the welfare and happiness of children than had been done in the past. But it had taken much campaigning to get the principle that the 'child's welfare should be the first and paramount consideration' embodied in statute;[46] and nearly half a century later, it was the Appellate Committee that completed the move from the 'father-centred' attitudes of Queen Victoria's time to the more 'child-centred' approach of the 1960s and 1970s.

The decision in *J v C*[47] meant that the court's assessment of the child's welfare would almost invariably be what determined the outcome, and it appeared that this criterion applied not only where the dispute was between the two parents[48] but equally to those in which the dispute was with a third party. The result was that a ten-year-old Spanish Roman Catholic child was to remain in England in the care of English Protestant foster parents notwithstanding the wishes of his 'unimpeachable' parents that he return to them in Spain. Such an outcome may not have been what Parliament would have contemplated in 1925[49] and it is certainly true that two decades later the Children Act 1989 was to take a much more subtle approach to cases where there was a conflict between Social Services departments and the birth family. But the decision in *J v C* seems to have reinforced the view that parental rights had to yield to children's interests even if the time was not yet ripe for ready acceptance of the view that children have rights of their own—as the United Nations Convention on the Rights of the Child and the Human Rights Act were to emphasise in 1989 and 1998 respectively.[50]

In *J v C* the Appellate Committee had insisted that there remained a fundamental distinction between the *legal adoption* of a child (which involved a complete legal transfer of parentage from birth parents to adopters) and decisions relating only to custody and upbringing; and it had certainly been the case for many years that a refusal of parental consent to adoption would often be conclusive: the courts would rarely hold that refusal was 'unreasonable' (the statutory precondition for dispensing with it). But a year after *J v C* the Appellate Committee shifted the balance towards giving greater weight to the claims of the child's welfare in deciding whether to overrule a parental refusal to agree. The child's welfare was (said Lord Hailsham LC[51]) always relevant and would be decisive 'in those cases in which a reasonable parent would so regard it'. In effect the question became whether, given the evidence of professionals about the benefits of adoption to the child, any reasonable parent could refuse to consent.

---

[46] Guardianship of Infants Act 1925, s 5.   [47] [1970] AC 668.

[48] It is no doubt true that 'in the ordinary way' it will be for the benefit of the child to be cared for by the biological parents: see *Re G (Children)* [2006] 1 WLR 2305.

[49] See SM Cretney, *Law, Law Reform and the Family* (Oxford: OUP, 1998) 175–9. The question of the return of children wrongfully removed is now the subject of international convention, but difficult cases can still arise, especially where those conventions do not apply: see eg *Re J (A Child)* [2006] 1 AC 80.

[50] The waning of 'parental rights' was also exemplified by *R v D* [1984] AC 778 (father could be guilty of kidnapping his own child).

[51] [1971] AC 682, 699–700.

Subsequently statute[52] was further to erode the distinction between legal adoption and other procedures for securing the welfare of children.

The child's rights

Gillick v West Norfolk and Wisbech Area Health Authority[53] was on the face of it a straightforward application for a declaration about the accuracy of the wording of a government circular setting out policy on the provision of contraception to the young. But in reality the case raised difficult issues about children's rights to confidential health care and the rights and duties of parents, health care professionals, and others affected. The opinions in the case demonstrate that this was still an area in which there were sharply differing attitudes amongst the Law Lords. On the one hand there was Lord Templeman:

I doubt whether a girl under the age of 16 is capable of a balanced judgment to embark on frequent regular or casual sexual intercourse fortified by the illusion that medical science can protect her in mind and body and ignoring the danger of leaping from childhood to adulthood without the difficult formative transitional experience of adolescence. There are many things which a girl under 16 needs to practise but sex is not one of them.

For Lord Templeman (and Lord Brandon, the other judge in the minority) the fact that statute criminalises sexual activity between people under 16 was a powerful indicator of the policy to be adopted: Parliament (said Lord Templeman) had the power to declare his view to be out of date[54] but until it did so a girl under 16 had no right to contraception merely in order to minimise the risks attached to an illegal activity. The majority (albeit with different emphases) rejected this: Lord Scarman, believing that the law ought to be 'sensitive to human development and social change' and that it was unrealistic to impose fixed rules to determine when a person should be treated as 'grown-up', had no doubt that parental rights had to yield to the rights of those children who did have sufficient understanding and intelligence to be capable of making up their own minds.[55]

Controlling the exercise of the state's powers and duties in relation to children

In the years after the end of the Second World War, public concern for the neglected and deprived child ceased to be primarily the concern of individuals

---

[52] Most recently, the Adoption and Children Act 2002.   [53] [1986] AC 112.

[54] The provisions of the Sexual Offences Act 2003 (which broaden the range of sexual activity involving young people now criminalised) perhaps indicate rather that Parliament wished to reassert traditional values in this regard.

[55] *Re B (A Minor) (Wardship: Sterilisation)* [1987] AC 199 is another important case, in which the Appellate Committee ruled that a 17-year-old mentally handicapped girl could be sterilised, that being in the circumstances in her best interests.

and voluntary organisations (notably the National Society for the Prevention of Cruelty to Children[56]) and increasingly came to be expressed through the medium of a professionalised bureaucracy, usually based in Local Authority Social Services departments There were important cases attempting to define the boundary between the courts and the legal system on the one hand and local authorities and administrative action on the other, especially in taking decisions about children 'at risk' or in need. These cases[57] demonstrated some of the failings of the statutory provisions, and played a significant part in creating a climate of opinion favourable to the comprehensive legislative restructuring effected by the Children Act 1989.

But no legislation could eliminate the need for the House to determine cases involving difficult policy issues, even when at one time the issue might have been seen as no more than a simple exercise in statutory construction. In *Re M (A Minor) (Care Order: Threshold Conditions)*[58] the Court of Appeal overturned a care order made in respect of a baby who was present when the father brutally murdered the mother: the legislation stipulated that intervention required that the child be suffering significant harm or likely to suffer such harm, and *at the date of the hearing* the child was being well cared for. Nor could it be said that the child was likely to suffer such harm if no order were made: a relative was able and willing to provide good quality care. The Local Authority successfully appealed, the Appellate Committee accepting that the Court of Appeal's restrictive inter-pretation of the statute would make it impossible for local authorities properly to discharge their child protection role. But the child was to stay under the sensitive nurture of the mother's cousin, in whose care he had developed into a 'boisterous, healthy and happy' little boy. This was not what the social workers had predicted: they had convinced the trial judge that the cousin lacked the ability to provide the special quality of care he needed; and it is a reminder of the inevitable fallibility of decision-taking in this area that it was only because the Court of Appeal ruled (in law, wrongly) that the trial judge had had no jurisdiction to make the order that experience demonstrated that keeping the child in his birth family was more in the child's interests than the 'adoption outside the family' solution which the social workers had favoured.

Other cases have demonstrated the difficulties of fact finding in cases where 'abuse' is alleged: the Appellate Committee has steered skilfully between the view that where a child's welfare is at risk suspicion is a sufficient basis for action[59] and

---

[56] The NSPCC remained active in its traditional child protection role for many years; and in 1977 the Appellate Committee's ruling that the Society should not be obliged to disclose the identity of an informant recognised the Society's special position as a body authorised by law to discharge a vital public function: *D v National Society for the Prevention of Cruelty to Children* [1978] AC 171.

[57] Notably *Lewisham LBC v Lewisham Juvenile Court Justices* [1980] AC 273; *Liverpool CC v A* [1982] AC 363; and *Re W (A Minor) (Wardship: Jurisdiction)* [1985] AC 791.

[58] [1994] 2 AC 424.

[59] *Re H (Minors) (Sexual Abuse: Standard of Proof)* [1996] AC 563; *Re O and anor (Minors) (Care: Preliminary Hearing)* [2004] 1 AC 523.

the kind of certainty sought in criminal prosecutions where the evidence must point beyond reasonable doubt to an identified individual. For example, in *Lancashire County Council v B*[60] the evidence demonstrated that a seven-month-old baby had suffered violent shaking, causing brain damage. But there was no evidence identifying which of three adults involved was the perpetrator. The Appellate Committee rejected the view that the statutory provisions required the person responsible to be identified; but equally it emphasised that the fact that the 'threshold condition' laid down in the Children Act 1989 has been satisfied does no more than open the way to the *possibility* that a care or other order will be made if the court concludes that this is what needs to be done to safeguard the child's welfare.[61]

Conclusion

This, of necessity highly selective, study of the role of the judicial House of Lords in relation to family law does demonstrate the value of a judicial body which has increasingly refused to be confined to a formalistic and mechanistic view of the judicial role. It also provides illustrations of the self-evident truth that judicial attitudes change, as do attitudes in society generally, and that attitudes amongst the individual judges active at any particular time will also differ. The application of the law governing family relationships may sometimes be particularly susceptible of being influenced by individual judges' personalities, beliefs, and attitudes. In this context it is pertinent to observe that, whereas the Lords of Appeal have been appointed on the advice of Prime Ministers (no doubt usually accepting the recommendation of the Lord Chancellor), Justices of the Supreme Court must first be selected 'on merit' by a selection commission. The impact of the complex process laid down in the Constitutional Reform Act 2005 on appointments remains to be seen. As evidenced by the opinions delivered by the Lords of Appeal in the *Gillick* case—all highly competent lawyers—the concept of appointment 'on merit' may (especially where judgments of social and public policy have to be made) not be as self-evident as is often assumed.

---

[60] [2000] 2 AC 147.

[61] Other tribunals continued to find difficulty in the application of the law. In *Re B (Children)* [2009] 1 AC 11 the Appellate Committee categorically rejected the notion that a 'heightened' or 'enhanced' civil standard of proof applied in care proceedings: the time had come 'to say, once and for all, that there is only one civil standard of proof and that is proof that the fact in issue more probably occurred than not' (Lord Hoffmann, at para 13). This is the appropriate standard both in finding the facts necessary to establish the threshold condition set out in s 31(2) of the Children Act 1989 and in assessing the welfare considerations in accordance with s 1 of the Act (Baroness Hale of Richmond, para 70).

37

Land Law

Derek Wood[*]

Introduction

Land law has a direct impact on the personal, business, and public lives of the nation. Flats are let. Homes are bought and sold. The construction and occupation of commercial property is underpinned by leasing. Much of the surface of the United Kingdom is covered by farmland. The letting and use of agricultural property are both regulated and encouraged by law. Development is strictly controlled by local authorities and central government.

Until the nineteenth century land law was the province of the common law, moderated in its earliest history by medieval statute and in later centuries by the development in the Courts of Chancery of the rules and doctrines of equity. Since the Victorian age land law has attracted increasing attention from Parliament. The beginnings were modest: the compulsory acquisition of land for canals and railways, driving the industrial revolution; some protection for Scottish and English farmers; a start on the tidying-up of conveyancing. The First World War brought in the Rent Acts. The many facets of Lord Birkenhead's 1925 property legislation created new platforms for practice, and continuing reform. The Landlord and Tenant Acts of 1927 and 1954 gave important rights to business tenants. From 1947 to 1995 statutory codes were introduced to regulate the letting of farms. The Town and Country Planning Act 1947 and its successors have revolutionised the way in which we are able to use or develop land. Entirely new professional specialisms have grown up in the wake of planning and compulsory purchase legislation. Leases and tenancies of public and private housing are still in the grip of complex statutory codes.

The House of Lords in its judicial capacity has not been frequently sighted in these big landscapes. There are, without question, landmark decisions. But they are few. The Digests of the Official Law Reports, beginning in 1865 with the HL

[*] I am grateful to Sir John Lindsay and to my colleagues Jonathan Gaunt QC, Anthony Radevsky, Barry Denyer-Green, and Charles Harpum for their comments on a draft of this chapter.

and App Cas series of reports, some 12 years before the Appellate Committee was established, provide a good snapshot of the volume of activity in this field in our highest appeal court. The table below lists the main topic headings of interest to property lawyers. With some re-titling and re-classification, and a small amount of double-counting, the numbers of real property cases heard in the House of Lords and officially reported are shown against each category.

(The table does not include cases of land transactions which exemplify more general principles of law, such as fraud, duress, or undue influence. Nor does it include Scottish appeals, some of which are discussed below.)

Table of digested cases

	1865–1950	1950–2008
Agricultural holdings	1	5
Compulsory purchase	20	17
Easements	12	1
Land charges/registration	0	8
Landlord and tenant	41	62
Licence/tenancy	0	5
Limitation (including adverse possession)	9	2
Mines and minerals	26	0
Mortgages (land only)	15	2
Planning	1	40
Proprietary estoppel	1	1
Restrictive covenants	0	2
Specific performance (land only)	1	1
Vendor and purchaser	13	5

Conveyancing and mortgages

Sale of land

Conveyancing probably accounts for more legal business, at least in terms of quantity of transactions, than any other type of work. Inevitably some disputes reach the courts. During the period of this review they have overwhelmingly been disposed of at first instance by the judges of the Chancery Division. Relatively few have progressed to the Court of Appeal, far fewer to the House of Lords.

One probable explanation is that the sale and purchase of land, and any disputes, must be settled quickly. Chancery procedures have on the whole helped parties in a hurry. The appeal processes do not. In addition the Chancery judges have an expertise in land law which makes them a particularly reliable specialist tribunal; and it is said that the House of Lords is traditionally reluctant to entertain challenges to settled conveyancing practice.

MEPC v Christian-Edwards,[1] described in his speech by Lord Russell as 'a curious case', is a rare example of a dispute in which it was worth the parties' while to pursue over more than two years, no doubt in a falling market, the question whether an anxious vendor could require a reluctant purchaser to accept a title which the purchaser (wrongly) said was defective.[2] Otherwise the leading cases in the field have been concerned with questions of damages for breach of contract, after the issue of completion or non-completion has faded away.

The long-lived but finally ill-fated rule in *Bain v Fothergill,*[3] which excluded purchasers whose vendors could not show a good title from claiming damages for breach of contract, restricting them to recovery of their deposit and legal expenses, was described by Balcombe LJ in the Court of Appeal[4] as 'impossible to justify,' serving 'no useful purpose anywhere in England or Wales'. It was finally abolished in 1989.[5]

Of much greater stature and importance are the decisions in *Johnson v Agnew*[6] and *Rainieri v Miles,*[7] which in their different ways placed contracts for the sale of land firmly into the main stream of general contract law. In *Johnson* Lord Wilberforce addressed a confusion in law which was

due partly to the mystification which has been allowed to characterise contracts for the sale of land, as contrasted with other contracts, partly to an accumulated debris of decisions and text book pronouncements which has brought semantic confusion and misunderstanding into an area capable of being governed by principle.

It was held that where a vendor obtains an order for specific performance which is not complied with, the contract remains alive and the vendor has not lost the right to return to the court for an award of damages. Whether awarded at common law or under Lord Cairns' Act the measure of damages would be the same.

The speeches of Lords Edmund Davies and Fraser in *Rainieri* were powerful enough to persuade Lord Russell to abandon his own draft.[8] They follow the decision in *Stickney v Keeble*[9] and are a—the—text-book analysis of the effect at common law and in equity of a contract to complete a sale and purchase on a stated date, time not being of the essence. If one of the parties fails to complete on the date stated in the contract, damages are recoverable at common law even though either party—'even the contract-breaker'—can specifically enforce the contract at a later date; and the entitlement to common law damages is not affected by a notice to complete making time of the essence of a later completion date.

---

[1] [1981] AC 205.

[2] The objection was an uncompleted contract for sale made in 1912 which had sunk without trace in the 1930s. 'Beyond reasonable doubt' the vendor was held to have a marketable title, and it was not open to the Land Registry to register the contract as an incumbrance.

[3] (1874) LR 7 HL 158.   [4] *Sharneyford Ltd v Barrington Block & Co* [1987] 1 Ch 305, 318.

[5] Law of Property (Miscellaneous Provisions) Act 1989, s 3.

[6] [1980] AC 367.   [7] [1981] AC 1050.   [8] ibid, 1095.   [9] [1915] AC 386.

Mortgages

Six cases of major importance on mortgages span the period from 1892 to 1914.[10] Collectively these decisions set limits to the ability of mortgagees of land or other assets to exploit their superior bargaining position by keeping the borrower in debt for commercial purposes which go beyond protection of the security—'clogging the equity of redemption'. A variant of this topic was explored in *Esso Petroleum Co Ltd v Harper's Garage (Stourport) Ltd.*[11] The Appellate Committee did not look at mortgages again until it heard the case of a statute-barred debt in 2005.[12]

Easements and restrictive covenants

Until the recent decisions in *Bakewell Management Co v Brandwood*[13] and the Scottish case of *Moncrieff v Jamieson*[14] the House of Lords had not considered any case on easements for many years. The seminal decision on the acquisition of easements in *Dalton v Angus,*[15] under the *ancien régime*, was essentially the product of the advice of the judges. *Home and Colonial Stores v Colls*[16] set the standard for actionable interference with rights of light. The remaining private law cases were concerned with the question of what rights could be implied as ancillary or reasonably necessary to an express grant. In *Pwllbach Colliery Co Ltd v Woodman*[17] the Appellate Committee rejected a claim by a colliery that it had acquired under its sub-lease an implied easement to commit a nuisance by spreading coal dust to a neighbouring tenant, who took his lease subject to all existing rights and easements. In the absence of proof that the business could not be carried on otherwise, a right to commit this nuisance could not be regarded as reasonably necessary for the enjoyment of rights granted by the head lessor. The discussion in *Moncrieff* returned to this question. It was held that the grant of a servitude of access by vehicles carried with it, in the unusual circumstances of the case, an ancillary right to park, which was necessary for the comfortable use and enjoyment of the right granted. Lord Rodger considered it necessary for the effective use of the servitude.

---

[10] *Salt v Marquis of Littlehampton* [1892] AC 1; *Noakes & Co v Rice* [1902] AC 24; *Reeve v Lisle* [1902] AC 461; *Bradley v Carritt* [1903] AC 253; *Samuel v Jarrah Timber & Wood Paving* [1904] AC 323; and *Kreglinger v New Patagonian Meat & Cold Storage Co* [1914] AC 25.

[11] [1968] AC 269: covenant in a mortgage to purchase only the mortgagee's petrol for 21 years held to be an unreasonable restraint of trade and void as contrary to public policy.

[12] *West Bromwich BS v Wilkinson* [2005] 1 WLR 3203.

[13] [2004] 2 AC 519: committing a criminal offence (driving across a common) does not prevent the acquisition of a right of way under the lost modern grant rule.

[14] [2007] 1 WLR 2620.   [15] (1881) 6 App Cas 740.   [16] [1904] AC 179.

[17] [1915] AC 634.

The rules for the acquisition of easements and similar rights arising out of private law transactions do not apply in the case of compulsory purchase. In *Sovmots v Secretary of State for the Environment*[18] it was held that a local authority which wished to acquire compulsorily empty maisonettes in the upper floor of an office building could not take advantage of the rule in *Wheeldon v Burrows*[19] or section 62 of the Law of Property Act 1925 and acquire by implication easements which were necessary for the enjoyment of the flats.

There is no corresponding decision anywhere on restrictive covenants, which is all the more surprising because (section 84 of the Law of Property Act 1925 apart)[20] they comprise a substantial body of law which is entirely judge-made, founded on principles of equity developed as recently as the mid-nineteenth century.[21] These covenants affect much of the development which was carried out in the first half of the twentieth century. The state of the law as it had been developed by the lower courts was however accepted by Lord Templeman in his speech in *Rhone v Stephens,*[22] in which he held that, in contrast with restrictive covenants, the burden of positive covenants does not generally run with land. Lord Wilberforce, whose interests as a racegoer were well known, would not have taken pleasure in forming part of the minority in the Aintree racecourse case[23] in which it was held that a covenant 'not to cause or permit' land to be used otherwise than for the purpose of horse racing and agricultural purposes would not be broken by an owner selling the land to a third party for housing development, even though the purchaser's intentions were fully publicised.[24] Happily the development never took place.

Land charges and land registration

One of the intended outcomes of the 1925 reforms was that matters affecting title to land should be registered and accessible to purchasers, mortgagees, and other interested third parties. In the case of unregistered land, an incumbrance capable of being registered as a land charge under the Land Charges Act 1925 would not bind a third party if it had not been registered, even if that party had actual knowledge of it. Incumbrances on registered land, to be binding, had to be entered on the register of title. But to this there were exceptions. The rights of persons in actual occupation at the date of the transaction were also preserved, even if unregistered.[25]

---

[18] [1979] AC 144.   [19] (1879) 12 Ch D 31.
[20] Jurisdiction of the Lands Tribunal to modify or discharge restrictive covenants.
[21] *Tulk v Moxhay* (1848) 2 Ph 774 41 ER 1143.   [22] [1994] 2 AC 310.
[23] *Sefton v Tophams Ltd* [1967] AC 50.
[24] The overall judicial head-count was against the final decision by 5 to 4, Stamp J and two of the judges in the Court of Appeal supporting Lords Reid and Wilberforce, the 2:3 minority in the House.
[25] Land Registration Act 1925, s 70(1)(g), now replaced with modifications by the Land Registration Act 2002, Sch 3 para 2.

These rules have been put to the test in six cases in the House of Lords. In the case of unregistered land the law according to Lord Wilberforce in *Midland Bank Trust Co Ltd v Green*[26] is plain. A father granted his son an option to purchase a farm of which the son was tenant. The son's solicitor failed to register the option as a charge. Later the father sold the farm, now worth about £40,000, to his wife for £500. She knew of the option; but the sale was for valuable consideration and it overrode the son's interest. The mother was not acting fraudulently in taking advantage of a mandatory system of registration which left the son vulnerable.

Where title to land was registered the rights of persons in actual occupation had to be addressed. In *National Provincial Bank v Ainsworth*[27] it was held that the rights asserted must be proprietary, not merely personal. Rejecting suggestions in the lower courts that there might be 'a deserted wife's equity' it was held that a wife's right to occupy the matrimonial home is personal, arising from her status, and will not bind a mortgagee.[28]

In contrast, contributing to the purchase price (or, as it has been held in later cases, helping with mortgage payments or paying for improvements) will advance the status of the wife or other occupier to the position of beneficial tenant in common with the legal estate owner: *Williams and Glyn's Bank Ltd v Boland, Same v Brown*.[29] This was held to give rise to a right covered by section 70(1)(g). The decision in *Boland* had a profound effect on conveyancing practice, resulting in (among other things) far more careful inquiries by mortgagees lending to individuals. More comfort for lenders was derived from the decision in *City of London Building Society v Flegg*.[30] Where the legal estate was held on trust for sale by two or more trustees, the rights of beneficial owners would be overreached under section 27 of the Law of Property Act 1925, and converted from a proprietary right into an interest in the proceeds of sale.

In two further cases—*Abbey National Building Society v Cann*[31] and *Lloyds Bank plc v Rosset*[32]—the Appellate Committee has examined more closely what is required to establish actual occupation. It must exist at the date of completion of the disposition (purchase or mortgage). If it is delayed until the date of registration of the interest it is too late. In *Cann* it was also held that acts preparatory to taking up occupation, such as carpet-laying and moving in furniture, were not 'occupation' within the meaning of section 70(1)(g). In *Rosset* it was emphasised that contributions in kind, such as carrying out home decorating or making improvements, as opposed to pecuniary contributions, were not enough to create the type of beneficial interest discussed in *Boland*.

Improvements in conveyancing practice and these later decisions may have rendered *Boland* less alarming to lending institutions than first appeared. But

[26] [1981] AC 513. [27] [1965] AC 1175.
[28] The Matrimonial Homes Act 1967, now Family Law Act 1996, ss 30–32 and Sch 4 have ameliorated the problem. See also the discussion by Stephen Cretney in ch 36 of this volume.
[29] [1981] AC 487. [30] [1988] AC 54. [31] [1991] 1 AC 56.
[32] [1991] 1 AC 107.

Lord Wilberforce stated in *Boland* that the principle was not limited to wives, and in *Barclays Bank plc v O'Brien* Lord Browne-Wilkinson pointed out that 'unmarried cohabitation, whether heterosexual or homosexual, is widespread in our society' and that 'the law should recognise this'.[33] The reasoning in *Stack v Dowden*[34] (equities arising from ownership of a home held in joint names by unmarried partners) also highlights the continuing importance of *Boland*.

Landlord and tenant

Common law

The common law of landlord and tenant was given its shape by Sir Edward Coke in his great *Commentary upon Littleton* (Co Litt) which was published in 1628. The early editions of the nineteenth century textbooks—Woodfall and Foa—faithfully follow the form and much of the content of Co Litt. The Appellate Committee has continued to cast light on some persistent common law questions.

Rye v Rye[35] addressed the question whether a person can be landlord and tenant of the same property: not as beneficial owner. Lord Denning in *St Marylebone Property Co Ltd v Fairweather*[36] and Lord Millett in *Barrett v Morgan*[37] both invoked Coke to explain the doctrine of surrender of leases, Lord Millett distinguishing it from a tenant's notice to quit. In *Prudential Assurance Co v London Residuary Body*[38] Coke provided the basis for the decision that a tenancy for a term of uncertain duration is void.

In *National Carriers Ltd v Panalpina (Northern) Ltd*[39] the Committee revisited its earlier hesitations in *Cricklewood Property and Investment Trust Ltd v Leighton Investment Trust Ltd*[40] and held by a majority that the doctrine of frustration applies to leases, preferring 'hardly ever' to 'never'. The question whether a lease can be repudiated was the subject of a lively public debate between Neuberger J (as he then was) and Lord Millett in 2000[41] but has not yet reached the highest court.

Into a dark area of law in which important rights and obligations may critically depend on the service of procedural notices some daylight has penetrated. Lord Diplock's controversial analysis of the fusion of law and equity in *United Scientific Holdings Ltd v Burnley Borough Council*[42] produced a decision that time is not of the essence for serving a notice triggering a rent review at a stated date, unless the parties say so, or the lease contains express indications to the contrary. In *Mannai*

---

[33] [1994] 1 AC 180, 198.   [34] [2007] 2 AC 432.
[35] [1962] AC 469.   [36] [1963] AC 510, 548.   [37] [2000] AC 264.
[38] [1992] 2 AC 386.   [39] [1981] AC 675.   [40] [1945] AC 221.
[41] Blundell Lecture cited by Lloyd LJ in *Reichman v Beveridge* [2007] 1 EGLR 37, para 27.
[42] [1978] AC 904.

Investment Co Ltd v Eagle Star Life Assurance Co Ltd[43] it was held that a right, exercisable by formal notice, to break the term of a lease on a stated date could be validly exercised by a notice which gave the wrong date if 'the reasonable recipient' of the notice, as Lord Steyn put it, would know what was intended.[44]

Statute

The bulk of the digested cases are the product of statutory interference with the common law, which Parliament over a long period has thought to be over-protective of the interests of landlords. The reach of statutory intervention has been comprehensive: homes, business premises (very widely defined), and farmland. The law has changed again and again, and many of the reported decisions are concerned with the meaning of provisions long since repealed. But some big and lasting themes can be picked out.

First, the House of Lords has been unwilling to accept the argument that property statutes passed to protect tenants, or serve some other social purpose, should be construed restrictively to minimise their impact on vested property rights. The consistent aim has been to understand and carry into effect the policy underlying the statute.[45]

Secondly, and closely connected with that, the House of Lords does not like attempts at avoidance. The sentiment against avoidance goes back a long way. In the Scottish case of *Cathcart v Chalmers*[46] it was held that a clause in an agricultural lease depriving the tenant of statutory compensation was void. In *Elmdene Estates Ltd v White*[47] an attempt by a landlord to avoid the prohibition on charging a premium on the grant of a rent-controlled tenancy by requiring the tenants to sell their present house at an under-value to a third party, as a condition of the grant, received scathing criticism. But the speeches in these cases do not match the eloquence of Lords Salmon and Hailsham, invoking memories of national food shortages in the Second World War, in *Johnson v Moreton*,[48] in which a clause in an English agricultural lease aimed at depriving the farmer of security of tenure was held to be contrary to public policy.

The task of unravelling the meaning and purpose of an Act, especially in the ever-changing field of housing law, has produced important statements on the very exercise of statutory interpretation. Lord Simon's speeches in *Maunsell v Olins*[49] and *Farrell v Alexander*[50] are mature reflections on the process of

---

[43] [1997] AC 749.

[44] His claim that he was bringing a breath of commercial fresh air into the technical area of land law, however, does less than justice to earlier groundbreaking decisions in the lower courts: see this author's ch 1 in S Bright (ed), *Landlord and Tenant Law: Past, Present and Future* (Oxford: Hart, 2006) 3–4.

[45] A good example is the speech of Lord Griffiths in *R v Burke* [1991] 1 AC 135 at 146–7 (prosecution for harassment under the Protection from Eviction Act 1977).

[46] [1911] AC 46.   [47] [1960] AC 528.   [48] [1980] AC 37.   [49] [1975] AC 373.

[50] [1977] AC 59.

statutory drafting by an outstanding lawyer who served as MP and Law Officer as well as judge. The highest court of appeal is now occupied exclusively by judges who have not had hands-on experience in Parliament. The influence of other parliamentarians on the interpretation of statutes passed in their time in government[51] deserves further study.

Street v Mountford

The decision in *Street v Mountford*[52] can also be looked at through the lens of anti-avoidance. Since the Rent Acts and their replacements, and Part II of the Landlord and Tenant Act 1954, have only protected tenants strictly so-called,[53] landlords have been tempted to induce tenants to sign documents declaring them to be no more than licensees. The type of agreement offered has been a far cry from the Appellate Committee's first and definitive discussion of licences in *Winter Garden Theatre (London) Ltd v Millennium Productions Ltd.*[54] The device was finally scotched by Lord Templeman in *Street v Mountford.* He held that the grant of exclusive possession for a term at a rent creates a tenancy. The decision has generated a substantial literature. It was distinguished in *AG Securities v Vaughan,*[55] followed in *Antoniades v Villiers,*[56] and more controversially followed in *Bruton v London and Quadrant Trust.*[57] The Trust was held to be 'landlord' even though it had no legal title to the property, but was a licensee only. For its clear and simple explanation of the nature of tenancy the decision in *Street v Mountford* probably stands as the most important leading case in this branch of the law.

Landlord and Tenant Act 1954, Part II

In the more technical field of statute law the legislation which has received the most enduring attention from the House of Lords is Part II of the 1954 Act, conferring a statutory right on business tenants to claim a new tenancy at the end of the current tenancy, subject to certain limited grounds of refusal. Between 1956 and 1996, 13 decisions were handed down on different provisions of this far-reaching Act. They include its application to tenancies at will;[58] the concept of 'occupancy' for business purposes;[59] the terms on which any new tenancy should be granted;[60] the nature and timing of the 'intention' to redevelop or occupy the tenant's premises which a landlord must prove to defeat a claim for a new

---

[51] eg Lord Hailsham LC in *O'May v CLRP* [1983] 2 AC 276 (see below).
[52] [1985] 1 AC 809.
[53] The same mistake was not made under the Agricultural Holdings Acts.
[54] [1948] AC 173.   [55] [1990] 1 AC 417 (no exclusive possession).
[56] ibid (two purported agreements to be read together).   [57] [2000] 1 AC 406.
[58] *Wheeler v Mercer* [1957] AC 416.
[59] *Graysim Holdings Ltd v P&O Property Holdings Ltd* [1996] AC 399.
[60] *O'May v CLRP* [1983] AC 276.

tenancy;[61] and the ability of parties to waive or otherwise overcome some of the procedural rigidities built into the Act.[62] The decision in *Re 'Wonderland' Cleethorpes*[63] exposed shortcomings in the formula for calculating compensation on quitting which resulted in amendments to the Act.

Leasehold enfranchisement

Intriguingly the enfranchisement of long leases, beginning with the Leasehold Reform Act 1967 in relation to houses, and now extended by the Leasehold Reform, Housing and Urban Development Act 1993 to flats, has claimed an almost equal amount of attention. (London flats seem to be a particular focus of interest.) The meaning of the word 'house' itself has been considered more than once.[64] In *Majorstake Ltd v Curtis*[65] stringent tests were imposed on landlords seeking to defeat tenants' claims on the ground of an intention to develop premises in which the flat in question is contained. In each of these cases the Committee has recognised and given effect to an underlying legislative policy that long leaseholders should own their own home. Even more significantly, the Appellate Committee has unequivocally endorsed the abolition of the requirement that enfranchising tenants should satisfy a residence test, extending rights generally to non-resident investors.[66]

Rent Acts, Housing Acts, and other legislation

Despite a steady flow of appeals in residential cases, an evaluation of the Appellate Committee's impact on other branches of statute law is more difficult to carry out because of the continuing flux of the law itself.[67] Courage and imagination were shown in *Ghaidan v Godin-Mendoza*[68] in a field in which these qualities are rarely called for, the work of applying statute to fact being mostly a hard grind.

Adverse possession

The Appellate Committee's only incursions into the contentious area of adverse possession have resulted in two leading cases. In some of their past decisions the

---

[61] *Betty's Cafés Ltd v Phillips Furniture Stores Ltd* [1959] AC 20. See also *Heath v Drown* [1973] AC 498: landlord not entitled to oppose a new tenancy for redevelopment where there is a contractual right under the existing tenancy to enter to carry out the intended works.

[62] *Kammins Ballrooms Ltd v Zenith Investments Ltd* [1971] AC 850. [63] [1965] AC 58.

[64] *Parsons v Henry Smith's Charity* [1974] 1 WLR 435; *Tandon v Trustees of Spurgeon's Homes* [1972] AC 755; *Malekshad v Howard de Walden Estates* [2003] 1 AC 1013; and *Boss Holdings Ltd v Grosvenor West End Properties* [2008] 1 WLR 289.

[65] [2008] 1 AC 787. [66] *Howard de Walden Estates v Aggio* [2009] 1 AC 39.

[67] Who now consults *Palser v Grinling* [1948] AC 291 (definition of a furnished tenancy) except for the discussion of the meaning of 'substantial'?

[68] [2004] 2 AC 557: defendant living in a stable and permanent homosexual relationship with a protected tenant held to be residing with him 'as his or her wife or husband' for the purposes of the Rent Act 1977, also discussed in chs 31 and 36 of this work.

lower courts, faced with hard cases, had made confusing and bad law. The Appellate Committee's decisions, in particular the second, have now substantially put this subject to rest.

St Marylebone Property Co Ltd v Fairweather[69] concerned a shed in Hampstead which straddled two back gardens. It was held that the right of one of the freeholders to recover its part of the shed was not impaired by the fact that its lessee's right of recovery had been barred by very long adverse possession by the neighbour on the other side during the term of the lease. When the dispossessed lessee surrendered his lease the freeholder acquired an immediate right to advance its own claim.

In *Pye v Graham*[70] the owner of registered land with development potential licensed a farmer in 1983 to graze the land for 11 months. When the agreement ended the owner asked the farmer to leave but took no further action until 1998. At first instance Neuberger J held on those facts that the owner's title was barred, regretting the state of the law that required him to do so.[71] The Court of Appeal[72] found a way to reverse him, but he was unanimously upheld in the House of Lords. Lord Browne-Wilkinson, giving the leading speech, pointed out that 'the apparently straightforward statutory provisions' had given rise to considerable difficulties in earlier cases in the Court of Appeal.[73] Paying generous tribute to the way in which Slade J in a case at first instance had previously reconciled these authorities[74] he delivered a speech which is a masterpiece of clear exposition. Simple factual possession—a sufficient degree of occupation and control—is enough to entitle a squatter to claim ownership, irrespective of the parties' relationship, or their private understanding or intentions.

The case has two sequels. An argument advanced by the claimant that the law as described by Lord Browne-Wilkinson would violate owners' human rights was dismissed, but was taken up by the owners against the United Kingdom in the European Court of Human Rights. A Chamber of the Fourth Section of the Court by a majority of four votes to three held that Article 1 of Protocol 1 had been violated. By a majority of 12 to five the majority of the Grand Chamber disagreed.[75] It considered that the balance struck between individual property rights and the rules barring stale claims was not disproportionate.

To the diminishing amount of land which remains unregistered the decision therefore still applies with full force. In the case of registered land its practical effect has been mitigated by the Land Registration Act 2002. The concept of adverse possession remains unaltered, but the Act has abrogated the 12-year limitation period. It entitles occupiers who have been in adverse possession for

---

[69] [1963] AC 510.   [70] [2003] 1 AC 419.   [71] [2000] Ch 676, 709–10.
[72] [2001] Ch 804.   [73] [2003] 1 AC 419, para 31.   [74] ibid.
[75] *JA Pye (Oxford) and JA Pye (Oxford) Land Ltd v United Kingdom* (2008) 46 EHRR 45.

ten or more years to apply for a registered title, but they must give the owner of the paper title a fair opportunity to challenge their claim and reassert ownership, irrespective of the amount of time that has elapsed.[76]

Ramsden v Dyson revisited

In *Ramsden v Dyson*[77] Lord Kingsdown[78] had said that where a person enters into a verbal agreement for 'a certain interest in land', or is encouraged by the owner to expect to receive such an interest, and takes possession and expends money on the land, a court of equity will compel the owner to give effect to the promise or expectation. In the same case Lord Cranworth LC had said[79] that where a promise is known to be made which is binding in honour only, the jurisdiction of courts of equity as well as law is excluded.

After 142 years of extensive travel throughout the common law world the doctrine of proprietary estoppel found its way back to the House of Lords in *Yeoman's Row Management Ltd v Cobbe*.[80] Lords Scott and Walker reviewed the doctrine, and the allied concept of constructive trust, in depth. Equity is not to be overstretched. The expression 'certain interest' was intended to be restrictive. The object of the estoppel must be capable of close definition. The court cannot satisfy an expectation of a contract when its terms have not been sufficiently worked out. Moreover, an undertaking which is known to be binding in honour only cannot be converted into a beneficial interest in property. Equitable estoppel is not, Lord Walker said, 'a sort of joker or wild card to be used when the court disapproves of the conduct of a litigant who seems to have the law on his side'.[81] The doctrine can be safely sent back into orbit.[81a]

Planning and compensation

Compulsory purchase

The compulsory acquisition of privately-owned land for the great projects of the nineteenth century—canals, railways, tramways—can still be viewed as a shock to a system of land tenure based on contract and inheritance. Indeed in the earlier phases the beneficiaries of compulsory purchase were themselves private business ventures, proceeding by private Act of Parliament. Public authorities, which now dominate the field, did not begin to have these overwhelming powers to any great extent until the time of the First World War. It is then no surprise that the period

[76] See Land Registration Act 2002, s 97 and sch 6.   [77] (1866) LR 1 HL 129.
[78] ibid, 170.   [79] ibid, 145–6.   [80] [2008] 1 WLR 1752.   [81] ibid, para 46.
[81a] But while this book was being proofed the House resurrected the doctrine of proprietary estoppel in *Thorner v Major* [2009] 1 WLR 776.

between 1865 and 1907 contains the greatest number of appeals: 25 digested cases, including Scottish Appeals.[82]

The scheme of compulsory purchase, consolidated in various Lands or Railways Clauses Consolidation Acts and others, and routinely incorporated into each private Act, was designed to exclude judicial intervention. The Acts defined the powers of acquisition and laid down the procedure for their exercise. Compensation was fixed by arbitrators. But compensation was payable not simply for the land taken. Its acquisition might adversely affect other land retained by the owner or in the ownership of a third party ('severance' or 'injurious affection'). The early decisions on these two heads of compensation have retained their authority.

With little legal material to guide it the House turned to the law of tort. Compensation for severance or injurious affection could only be recovered in respect of a head of loss claimable at common law. The temporary obstruction of a street causing loss of trade[83] and the emission of smoke, noise and vibration from a railway[84] would not count. The Duke of Buccleuch had better luck against the Metropolitan Board of Works building the Thames Embankment.[85] It was held in the Duke's favour that compensation for injurious affection was recoverable not just for the taking of the land but also the permanent use to which it would then be put.

The common law of damages received payment in return in the decision in *Bwllfa & Merthyr Dare Steam Collieries v Pontypridd Waterworks Co.*[86] The colliery company was entitled to be paid for the loss of unworked coal seams, fixed by the arbitrator some two and a half years after the seams had been surrendered. Should they be valued at the date of surrender or at the date of arbitration, when values had increased? Lord MacNaghten's rhetorical questions[87] continue to resonate through the law of damages. 'Why should he listen to conjecture on a matter which has become an accomplished fact? Why should he guess when he can calculate? With the light before him, why should he grope in the dark?'

In 1947 the Judicial Committee of the Privy Council handed down its decision in *Pointe Gourde Quarrying and Transport Co Ltd v Sub-Intendent of Crown Lands.*[88] This case may rank as the most important decision in this field. It was held that the value of land taken by compulsory purchase cannot include any

---

[82] A very similar story emerges from the pattern of digested cases on mines and minerals, which assumed great importance in both private conveyancing and compulsory purchase in the nineteenth and early part of the twentieth centuries: 25 English and Scottish appeals down to 1913, and only one after that, in 1945, shortly before these resources were nationalised.

[83] *Ricket v Metropolitan Rly Co* (1867) 2 HL 175.

[84] *Hammersmith and City Rly Co v Brand* (1869) 4 HL 171, followed in *London, Brighton and South Coast Rly v Truman* (1885) 11 App Cas 45 and by the Appellate Committee in *Argyle Motors (Birkenhead) Ltd v Birkenhead Corp* [1975] AC 99 and *Wildtree Hotels Ltd v Harrow L BC* [2001] 2 AC 1.

[85] *Duke of Buccleuth v Metropolitan Board of Works* (1872) 5 HL 418 followed in *Cowper Essex v Acton Local Board* (1889) 14 App Cas 153.

[86] [1903] AC 426.   [87] ibid, 426.   [88] [1947] AC 465.

increase in value which is entirely due to the scheme for which the land has been taken. The decision has been debated by the Appellate Committee on a number of occasions.[89] Most importantly it was fully analysed and its scope more rigorously defined by Lord Nicholls in his speech in *Walters v Welsh Development Agency*[90] where the value of the land taken depended critically upon the definition of the 'scheme' for which it was being acquired.

Other cases before the Appellate Committee have demonstrated the interchange between concepts of private and public law in the field of compulsory purchase. In *Smith v East Elloe RDC*[91] it was held that a compulsory purchase order could not be challenged on the ground that it had been made and confirmed in bad faith, but the aggrieved owner would have a remedy in private law. The wide scope of powers inherent in a compulsory purchase order was emphasised in *Simpson's Motor Sales (London) Ltd v Hendon Corporation*,[92] in which it was held that land acquired specifically for the construction of flats could be held for a larger redevelopment scheme to take place at a future indefinite date, there being no excess of powers or unconscionable conduct in holding onto it.

Town and country planning

If the law of compulsory purchase engages both private and public law concepts, the jurisprudence of planning law moves land law into the public sphere and merges in the much wider field of judicial review, outside the scope of this chapter. Some of the history of the Appellate Committee's treatment of this branch of the law can nevertheless be traced here.

Planning law effectively begins in the period of reconstruction after the Second World War. The spirit of the age is caught in the first of the Appellate Committee's post-war decisions—*Franklin v Minister of Town and Country Planning*[93]—implementing the New Towns Act 1946. The speed of decision-making puts the modern planning system to shame. In January 1946 the Reith Committee recommended Stevenage as the site of a new town. In April 1946 the New Towns Bill was published and in May the Minister himself (Mr Lewis Silkin) spoke at a public meeting in Stevenage Town Hall. The meeting was turbulent. He was barracked. He said, 'It is no good your jeering: it is going to be done.' There were cries of 'Dictator!'. He promised to consult as far as possible all the local authorities but said, '[I]f people are fractious and unreasonable, I shall have to carry out my duty'. Someone shouted 'Gestapo!'. The Act was passed, the appropriate Order laid in August 1946, and a two-day public inquiry held in

---

[89] See *Davy v Leeds Corp* [1965] 1 WLR 445; *Margate Corp v Devotwill Investments* [1970] 3 All ER 864; and *Rugby Joint Water Board v Foottit, Same v Shaw-Fox* [1973] AC 262.
[90] [2004] 1 WLR 1304: wetlands forming part of the Cardiff Bay barrage project.
[91] [1956] AC 736.   [92] [1964] AC 1088.   [93] [1948] AC 87.

October. The inspector reported later that month and Stevenage was designated in November.

An application to the High Court to have the decision quashed on the ground of procedural irregularity and bias, made in December 1946, was dismissed by the Appellate Committee on 24 July 1947 after argument in June.[94] The House dryly observed that the Minister was acting in a purely administrative and not a quasi-judicial capacity. Modern commentators are divided on the merits of the decision.[95] On whichever side of the line it might fall, it remains a boundary-marker for judicial interference in politics.

In other planning cases the Appellate Committee has exercised a more orthodox function. In *Slough Estates Ltd v Slough BC*[96] it was held that external documents (in that case the submitted plans) were to be taken into account in construing a planning permission. Almost as important as the grant of planning permission are the conditions which are attached to it. Lord Denning's statement of the law in the Court of Appeal in *Pyx Granite Co Ltd v Minister of Housing and Local Government*,[97] that conditions must fairly and reasonably relate to the permitted development and cannot be used to achieve an ulterior object has been followed and applied in a number of cases in the House of Lords. In *Fawcett Properties Ltd v Buckingham CC*,[98] within those constraints, a liberal and pragmatic approach to the interpretation of conditions was advocated. *Mixman's Properties Ltd v Chertsey UDC*[99] emphasised that conditions must be related to the use of the land and cannot be used in effect to dictate the terms upon which the landowner can let plots on his site. It was held in *Kingsway Investments Ltd v Kent CC*[100] that a time condition—permission ceasing to have effect after three years—could validly be annexed to an outline planning permission. In *Newbury DC v Secretary of State for the Environment*[101] a condition, attached to permission to use unsightly aircraft hangars for the storage of materials, that the structures should be demolished after ten years was quashed on *Pyx Granite* grounds. *Grampian Regional Council v City of Aberdeen DC*[102] paved the way for the requirement that development should be carried out in an orderly fashion, the prior completion of essential infra-structure being a lawful condition to implementing the principal scheme.

The durability of pre-existing lawful uses was explored in *Young v Secretary of State for the Environment*[103] and *Pioneer Aggregates v Secretary of State*.[104] The notion that planning policies, while they cannot (normally) be aimed at

---

[94] The Attorney General Sir Hartley Shawcross (leading Mr Hubert Parker) submitted that it was 'idle to talk of natural justice in a case of this kind or of any necessity for an appearance of justice'.
[95] Contrast *De Smith's Judicial Review* (London: Sweet & Maxwell, 6th edn 2007) para 6-039 with ch 14 of this work (Louis Blom-Cooper and Gavin Drewry).
[96] [1971] AC 958.   [97] [1958] 1 QB 554, 572.   [98] [1961] AC 635.
[99] [1965] AC 735, a decision under the Caravan Sites etc Act 1960.   [100] [1971] AC 72.
[101] [1981] AC 578.
[102] (1983) 47 P & CR 633, remarkably not reported in the Appeal Cases series.
[103] [1983] 2 AC 662.   [104] [1985] AC 132.

individuals, can legitimately protect specific classes or groups of occupiers was upheld in *Westminster City Council v Great Portland Estates plc.*[105]

The Appellate Committee has recently concentrated upon the current pressing concern for environmental protection, reflected in *Berkeley v Secretary of State*[106] and *R (Barker) v Bromley LBC.*[107] In *Berkeley* a decision by the Secretary of State to grant planning permission was quashed on the ground that no adequate environmental impact assessment had been carried out as required by both European and domestic law. In *Barker* it was held, after a referral to the European Court of Justice, that where outline permission had been granted without such an assessment, but it became apparent later, when reserved matters fell to be considered, that the project would be likely to have significant effect on the environment, permission granted without an assessment would be invalid notwithstanding the apparent effect of Regulations made under UK legislation.

Conclusion

Property lawyers, echoing the question raised by the Judaean Liberation Front in *Life of Brian*, might ask: What did the House of Lords ever do for us? It has always responded energetically and purposefully to new legislation. Analysing the policy underlying an Act of Parliament, carrying it into effect, and setting appropriate boundaries have been its main areas of activity. The large areas of law and practice which lie outside social or economic policy have benefited at most from sporadic raids. The answers to many practical problems in those areas still lie in the decisions of the lower courts, and the textbooks.

[105] [1985] AC 661, a victory for the tailors of Savile Row, among others.
[106] [2001] 2 AC 603.   [107] [2007] 1 AC 470.

38

Commercial Law

*Francis Reynolds**

The area potentially covered by the term 'commercial law' is not defined, but is on any view extensive. In this chapter the subjects addressed are basic contract law, shipping law in general including marine insurance, sale of goods, bills of exchange and banking, company law, and some parts of the conflict of laws. More could be added, but they would strain the writer's competence (as indeed do some of those included) and perhaps not add much to any overall impression that can be drawn from what is discussed.

An important point to note at the start is that from the point of view of the steady development of commercial law through judicial decisions, the picture presented by the House of Lords' decisions is incomplete. A large number of commercial decisions have also emanated from the Privy Council: during the first 30 years of the twentieth century significant cases, especially in banking and insurance, came from Canada, Australia, and New Zealand; in the mid to late twentieth century from Australia and New Zealand; and until quite recently still from New Zealand. These are outside the scope of the chapter but their existence should not be forgotten. Whatever their true precedential status, all can be used in argument, and some of them are regularly cited as marking key developments in English commercial law.[1]

As is pointed out in chapter 24 of this volume, 'A View from the City', a satisfactory system of commercial law, valid for the solution of international disputes, is based on the existence of good general principles, and this usually means good general principles of contract. In English law there is no code to fall back on, so there is a need for a constantly evolving body of case law, well adapted

---

* I have been much helped in the preparation of this chapter by the Rt Hon Lord Justice Longmore, Professor Adrian Briggs, Profesor EP Ellinger, Professor DD Prentice, and Professor FD Rose, to all of whom I am most grateful.

[1] A slightly dramatic example is provided by the four cases dealing with different ways of extending the benefit of a main contract (of carriage in these cases) to subcontractors: *The Eurymedon* [1975] AC 154; *The New York Star* [1981] 1 WLR 138 (stevedores: 'Himalaya' clause); *The Pioneer Container* [1994] 2 AC 324; *The Mahkutai* [1996] AC 650 ('actual carriers': bailment on terms). They were finally considered by the House of Lords in another actual carrier case, *The Starsin* [2004] 1 AC 715.

to its subject matter, the basic principles of which can be reliably stated at any one time (even if problems continue to present themselves in unfamiliar or unexpected ways). A surprising number of House of Lords cases, many of them (as is appropriate) fairly recent, though arising in completely disparate contexts, do actually provide, or reinforce, this. To see this, it is convenient to go through the topics within the law of contract as they are customarily set out in present day textbooks.

There are at least 12 House of Lords cases, in multifarious contexts, on formation of contract. (Perhaps just as well), the (to students) well-known and rather stultifying cases on letters of acceptance were not decided in the House of Lords, which enabled a flexible view to be enunciated in more recent times—as it happens, in a case on telex transactions and the conflict of laws;[2] on the other hand the House took a (perhaps inappropriately) strict view against the notion of a contract to negotiate quite recently.[3] The unique common law concept of consideration was worked out before 1875, but trouble has been caused for more than a century by the decision of Lord Selborne (but doubted by Lord Blackburn) in the rather homely context of a landlady and her lodger, *Foakes v Beer*,[4] that consideration is required for the modification of a contract. This is perhaps the oldest case still relevant to basic contractual principle. Rather contrived and unreliable invocations of equity have more recently been displaced (though not completely) by seeking a solution through manipulating the idea of consideration, or through a doctrine of waiver,[5] but the underlying difficulty, surprisingly, remains, and the awkwardness of the attempts to solve it show up a 125-year-old problem which, had the guidance of Lord Blackburn been followed, probably should not exist. Almost the only case directly concerning intention to create legal relations is a House of Lords decision on an agency contract for the sale of carbon paper containing an 'honourable pledge' clause.[6] As regards terms of the contract, statements of the principles of incorporation and interpretation of exemption clauses have been made in more than one case and context, and the saga of 'fundamental breach', developed by Lord Denning after the Second World War and originally prominent in the context of oppressive terms in hire purchase contracts, required three House of Lords cases (in different contexts) to bring it to an end at a time when the matter had come to be perceived as better regulated by statute.[7] The very limited student topic of mistake in contract is not dead: it generated leading cases in 1932[8] and 2004,[9] the latter in connection with the old

---

[2] *Brinkibon v Stahag Stahl, etc, GmbH* [1983] 2 AC 34.
[3] *Walford v Miles* [1992] 2 AC 128, criticised on this account by Sir Patrick Neill QC in (1992) 108 LQR 405.
[4] (1884) 9 App Cas 605.   [5] See *The Kanchenjunga* [1990] 1 Lloyd's Rep 391.
[6] *Rose & Frank Co v JR Crompton & Bros Ltd* [1925] AC 445.
[7] The *Suisse Atlantique* case [1967] 1 AC 361; *Photo Production Ltd v Securicor Transport Ltd* [1980] AC 827; and *George Mitchell Ltd v Finney Lock Seeds Ltd* [1983] AC 803.
[8] *Bell v Lever Bros Ltd* [1932] AC 161.
[9] *Shogun Finance Ltd v Hudson* [2004] 1 AC 919, a hire purchase case.

problem of two innocent parties defrauded by a third. Misrepresentation cases date back to the days of company flotation in Victorian times: the unexpected decision in *Derry v Peek*[10] provided a block, albeit cured immediately by a specialised statute; but a more general route to circumvention by means of contract law was rejected in 1913.[11] Though the original block was removed in 1964 in the banking case of *Hedley Byrne & Co Ltd v Heller & Partners Ltd*[12] the problem had already been perceived as requiring a statute, and such was soon after passed.[13] Banking cases likewise have recently provided guidance on undue influence,[14] and industrial action cases on duress.[15] The policy against allowing contracts unduly to restrict trade was first articulated in the *Nordenfeld* case (arising in connection with the manufacture of Maxim guns) in 1894[16] and has been developed since, to a considerable extent in connection with the petrol industry.[17]

The question of third party rights in contract has eventually been solved by statute,[18] but the problem had not been a serious one as it was not difficult for a lawyer specifically wishing to draft so as to create such rights to do so by means of the trust. On the other hand the related privity point of the effect of contract clauses in favour of subcontractors sued in tort did require solution and was, as is stated above,[19] solved in the maritime context, and by the Privy Council. After some unsatisfactory experimentation with the sale of goods technique of conditions and warranties and reasoning used in sale of land cases, the proper formulation of the rules for discharge of contract by breach was the subject (as he at least once described it) of many years' work by Lord Diplock, who connected it with the doctrine of frustration.[20] Lord Wilberforce[21] and Lord Roskill[22] also intervened, with the result of preserving the notion of the contract term requiring strict compliance (the condition)—something that may or may not have been welcome to Lord Diplock.

The application of the doctrine of frustration has been, probably because of the amount of money likely to be involved, the subject of at least 15 House of Lords cases, mostly in the context of hostilities and (though not all) ships; but Lord Reid's formulation of it in a construction case in 1956 still stands as the leading guide.[23] The law relating to contract damages, too easily dismissed as procedural, and often assumed to be based on some rather imprecise statements (known

---

[10] (1889) 14 App Cas 337.
[11] *Heilbut Symons & Co v Buckleton* [1913] AC 30 (leading speech by Lord Haldane).
[12] [1964] AC 465.   [13] The Misrepresentation Act 1967.
[14] Most recently the *Etridge* case [2002] 2 AC 777.   [15] *The Evia Luck* [1992] 2 AC 152.
[16] [1894] AC 535.   [17] *Esso Petroleum Ltd v Harpers Garage (Stourport) Ltd* [1968] AC 269.
[18] Contract (Rights of Third Parties) Act 1999.   [19] See n 1.
[20] See his speech in *Photo Production Ltd v Securicor Transport Ltd* [1980] AC 827, modifying remarks of his own in the Court of Appeal in *Hong Kong Fir Shipping Co Ltd v Kawasaki Kisen Kaisha Ltd* [1962] 2 QB 26.
[21] *The Diana Prosperity* [1976] 1 WLR 989.
[22] *Bunge Corp v Tradax Export SA* [1981] 1 WLR 711.
[23] *Davis Contractors Ltd v Fareham UDC* [1956] AC 696.

throughout the common law world) in the carrier case of *Hadley v Baxendale* in 1854[24] was the subject of careful consideration and discussion of terminology, again by Lord Reid, in a case of 1969 concerning late arrival under a charterparty and the sale of bulk sugar.[25] Several cases have subsequently developed this, some of them a specialised group related to negligent professional advice and an unanticipated drop in property values, but others concerned to relax strict rules as to the type of loss recoverable. The distinction between damages and penalties has also required attention over a period. (The House has, however, given two recent decisions on contract damages which by commercial criteria are not as happy as some.)[26] Finally, Lord Reid once more took the lead in an important affirmation of the significance of the action in debt for a fixed sum in contrast to damages.[27]

To this account should be added an important decision of the House in recent years which, accompanied by other cases, laid down more relaxed principles of interpretation of documents than those previously believed to operate: in particular in permitting reference to matters outside the document, including those arising in negotiation.[28] It is at least partly for the commercial community to make known whether these are realistic, and the contexts, if any, in which they are not; and this question has already been the subject of discussion.

Maritime law has always been a conspicuous force in English decisions, and the reasoning in maritime contract cases has been extremely influential in formulations of general law. There are too many overlaps of classification for exact numbers to be given, but there are at least 200 such cases in App Cas and AC between 1875 and 2007, and this does not include cases only in Lloyd's Reports, the true number of which is difficult to ascertain.[29]

Here the great variation of sub-topics means that the material is best considered in historical order. The first case heard by the newly constituted House of Lords and reported in vol 1 of App Cas concerned compulsory pilotage, but a noticeable feature of the cases that follow is how many concern ship collisions. About 28 such cases had reached the House of Lords by 1912, not all heard by Lords with experience in the area. Such disputes of course continue: in 1967 there was a decision concerning a collision involving the Harwich-Hook of Holland ferry near Harwich harbour,[30] by which time there had been about 48 cases.

In this area of law there is a steady stream of perfectly competent maritime cases, most of which would however not be cited today (though some are: a bill of lading case was won in the Court of Appeal in 1970 by junior counsel Mr John Hobhouse discovering an obscure decision of the House, not mentioned in the

---

[24] (1854) 9 Exch 341.   [25] *The Heron II* [1969] 1 AC 350.
[26] See below, nn 94–6 and text.
[27] *White & Carter (Councils) Ltd v McGregor* [1962] AC 413.
[28] *Investors Compensation Scheme Ltd v West Bromwich BS* [1998] 1 WLR 896.
[29] Also there were at the time of writing 618 House of Lords cases, not of course all maritime, in the Weekly Law Reports since their establishment in 1953; and there are some cases sometimes only in other series.
[30] *The Koningin Juliana* [1975] 2 Lloyd's Rep 111.

books, of an appeal from Scotland in 1916).[31] Two leading decisions of the 1880s considered the notion of 'perils of the sea'[32] (in one rather bathetically constituted by rats eating into a salt-water pipe): the meaning of a 'deviation' was illustrated in 1893,[33] part of its significance was considered in 1912,[34] and the true nature of this strange doctrine investigated, but not conclusively determined, in a famous case of 1936 which did not qualify for an appearance in the official Law Reports.[35] In 1924 came the long-notorious *Elder Dempster* case[36] concerning an actual carrier claiming protection of the bill of lading, the reasoning of which was regularly declared (even by Lord Diplock) incomprehensible, but which would now be regarded as a fairly normal, if obscurely reasoned, case on bailment. After the adoption of the Hague Rules, Scrutton LJ (who strongly believed in freedom of contract) ceased to edit his book *Scrutton on Charterparties*. There were soon two House of Lords cases on the Rules, in 1928 and 1935,[37] and others followed later[38] (some in the Privy Council).

Some time after the Second World War, shipping litigation became more frequent. A rather unusual and perhaps contorted view on the application of the Hague Rules to loading and unloading devised by Devlin J in 1954 was accepted in a different context by the House of Lords in 1955[39] and then in 2006 treated by the House as too well established to alter.[40] Perhaps surprisingly Lord Simonds, a Chancery lawyer often regarded as somewhat unbending, presided in 1957 over a landmark case permitting the incorporation of the Hague Rules into charterparties in a very flexible way,[41] and shortly afterwards (1961) held the seaworthiness obligation under the Hague Rules to create a non-delegable duty on the shipowner—a bold step.[42] However, in 1962 he took a strongly conservative line on privity of contract (in the application of the Rules to stevedores) which has taken much ingenuity over the years to sidestep.[43]

In the late 1970s and beyond, perhaps because of the economics of the shipping industry at the time, there seems to have been a cult of fighting charterparty cases, sometimes to the highest level. (The same was true in the commodity trades.) The tip of the iceberg showed in the House of Lords. A series of cases on the operation of laytime and hence demurrage in respect of delayed ships

---

[31] *Love & Stewart Ltd v Rowtor SS Co Ltd* [1916] 2 AC 527, cited in *The Dunelmia* [1970] 1 QB 289.

[32] *The Xantho* (1887) 12 App Cas 503; *Hamilton Fraser & Co v Pandorf & Co* (1887) 12 App Cas 518.

[33] *Glynn v Margetson & Co* [1893] AC 351.   [34] *Kish v Taylor, Sons & Co* [1912] AC 604.

[35] *Hain SS Co Ltd v Tate & Lyle Ltd* (1936) 41 Com Cas 350.

[36] [1924] AC 522 (leading speech by Lord Sumner).

[37] *Gosse Millerd Ltd v Canadian Government Merchant Marine* [1929] AC 223; *Stag Line Ltd v Foscolo Mango & Co Ltd* [1932] AC 328.

[38] See below, n 49.   [39] *Renton & Co Ltd v Palmyra Trading Corp* [1957] AC 149.

[40] *The Jordan II* [2005] 1 WLR 1363.

[41] *Adamastos Shipping Co v Anglo-Saxon Petroleum Co* [1959] AC 133.

[42] *The Muncaster Castle* [1961] AC 807 (where the report of the argument occupies 28 pages).

[43] *Midland Silicones Ltd v Scruttons Ltd* [1962] AC 446; for the devices used see above, n 1.

was fought in the early 1970s,[44] and in the late part of the decade came three well-known cases on withdrawal of a ship for (slightly) late payment of time charter hire.[45] (Linked to the problem came a later case denying the landlord-and-tenant remedy of relief against forfeiture in such situations.)[46] The emphasis returned to the allocation of delay risk in a case concerning the duty to nominate a safe port—did it have to remain safe?—the decision of which was, however, said to have gone contrary to expectations in the industry.[47] In several of these cases, when Lord Diplock was presiding, the practice was followed of having one opinion only from one of the 'commercial' lords—Lord Diplock himself, Lord Brandon of Oakbrook, Lord Roskill—with which all the others concurred. The purpose was presumably to promote certainty; but not all agreed with the certainties created.

Parties who for some reason could not establish title to sue in contract experimented with attempts to establish the right of others to sue for their loss,[48] and with title to sue in tort (which tended to fail if the loss claimed was purely economic).[49] A slight lull in the litigation was followed quite recently by a group of cases on bills of lading and the operation of the Hague Rules,[50] and on the statute that had been passed to deal with accrued problems of right to sue, the Carriage of Goods by Sea Act 1992.[51] The cumulative effect of all these cases by the early 1980s was to give great prominence to the law of carriage by sea (which Lord Goff of Chieveley once described in a lecture as the typical English contract); but this, and the volume of litigation involved (which was mostly international), has more recently tended to diminish, partly because of a new statute facilitating arbitration. Prominent in many or most of these decisions, and also in those on marine insurance mentioned below, have been the 'commercial' Law Lords. To mention names is from one viewpoint invidious, but listing a few is appropriate to indicate the power exercised in the common law by particular personalities. Though several others could be in any comprehensive list, we may mention Lord Wilberforce (like others, far from solely 'commercial'), Lord Diplock, Lord Brandon of Oakbrook, Lord Roskill, Lord Goff, Lord Lloyd of Berwick, and Lord Mustill; more recently Lord Steyn and Lord Hobhouse of Woodborough; and others could be added. And no one writing on the House

---

[44] *The Darrah* [1977] AC 157; *The Laura Prima* [1982] AC 1; *The Johanna Oldendorff* [1974] AC 479 (establishing what came to be called the 'Reid test'); *The Maratha Envoy* [1978] AC 1; and at an earlier time *The Aello* [1961] AC 135.

[45] *The Laconia* [1977] AC 850; *The Chikuma* [1981] 1 WLR 314; *The Afovos* [1983] 1 WLR 195 (Lord Diplock's (slightly puzzling) last word on discharge of contract by breach).

[46] *The Scaptrade* [1983] 2 AC 694.   [47] *The Evia* [1983] 1 AC 736.

[48] *The Albazero* [1977] AC 774; the possibility was subsequently further developed by the House in construction cases.

[49] See *The Aliakmon* [1986] AC 785; *The Mineral Transporter* [1986] AC 1.

[50] *The Giannis NK* [1998] AC 605 (dangerous goods); *The Starsin* [2004] 1 AC 715; *The Jordan II* [2005] 1 WLR 1363 (loading and unloading operations); and *The Rafaela S* [2005] 2 AC 423 ('straight' bills of lading).

[51] *The Berge Sisar* [2002] 2 AC 205.

of Lords in the latter part of the twentieth century can fail to recognise the influence of Lord Reid in all areas.

The topic of marine insurance is of course closely related to that of carriage by sea, for example in interpretation of the excepted perils. The common law was codified in 1906 by a statutory restatement of not only the rules of specifically marine insurance but also of many of the relevant general principles of insurance law, in an Act[52] which, though it probably requires updating and proposals are indeed up in the air, still seems adequate for purpose. The majority of cases relevant to the present day concern interpretation of the statute, or of particular clauses such as 'perils of the sea'[53] and 'warlike operations'[54] (some of which cases have been significant precedents). A leading case of 1925 considered the notion of insurable interest,[55] but this topic has now lost much of its significance. Four recent cases have been prominent. The first is *The Popi M*,[56] concerning the cause of an unexplained ship loss, where the judge of first instance selected the least improbable cause, but the House of Lords reverted to the general principle that a claimant must prove his case, which can also be invoked elsewhere in this part of the law. The second, *The Good Luck*,[57] concerns the controversial marine insurance notion of warranty, finding that breach of it operates automatically to displace the insurance: this, while it seems correct in principle, causes difficulties in connection with the applicability of waiver, and also raises concerns as to the requirement of strict compliance at present imposed in this part of the law. In the third, *Pan Atlantic Insurance Co Ltd v Pine Top Insurance Co Ltd*[58] (a non-marine case interpreting, as often, the 1906 Act) the House delivered an eagerly awaited interpretation of the statutory formulation of the duty of disclosure (which had already been determined to give rise to a right to rescind only). The difficulty was as to how far the requirement that the information would affect the judgment of a prudent insurer meant that it also had to be material to the risk and to inducement of the insurer in question. The House laid down the necessity for reliance but was less clear about that of materiality. The last case, *The Star Sea*,[59] concerned alleged non-disclosure of the unseaworthy state of a vessel which later became a constructive total loss, and decided that any obligations of disclosure during litigation was governed by the Civil Procedure Rules only. Though the last three decisions are probably by and large steps forward, they have caused considerable disappointment among those who would like to see more clarification in, and perhaps reform of, the rules as to warranties, *uberrima fides*, the pre-contractual duty of disclosure, and whether, when, and why there is a post-contractual duty of disclosure.

The topic of sale of goods goes with carriage by sea, since many of the big sales are international in some way. The law was of course codified by the Sale of

---

[52] The Marine Insurance Act 1906.
[53] See the cases cited above, n 32, which are equally valid for marine insurance.
[54] eg *The Coxwold* [1942] AC 691.   [55] *Macaura v Northern Assurance Co* [1925] AC 619.
[56] [1985] 1 WLR 948 (the 'yellow submarine' case).   [57] [1992] 1 AC 233.
[58] [1995] 1 AC 501.   [59] [2003] 1 AC 469.

Goods Act 1893.[60] Since then the House has decided several cases on the meaning of the quality term, including two lengthy ones against an international background[61] (the term was subsequently modified by statute, partly in response to difficulties demonstrated by those cases). On the international front, it was also decided as early as 1877 that the time of shipment could be part of the description of the goods;[62] and the requirement of strict compliance with description, which has been a strong feature of English law, was affirmed with supporting reasoning in a case of 1933 relating to the import of Russian timber.[63] A number of cases, in fact from the first half of the twentieth century, assisted in determining the nature of and the rules applicable to the cif contract.[64] In the second half, helped by the technique of requiring an arbitral tribunal to state a case, disputes were more involved and technical: the most recent concerned theoretical complications connected with the two rights to reject documents and goods.[65] On a more domestic front, the House in 1895 decided the case that affirmed the efficacy of hire purchase as a method of sales financing[66] and has contributed to the law applicable to that contract subsequently.[67]

If one asks whether the House has dealt with pure financial law, one finds a number of earlier cases determining points on bills of exchange and cheques, the law on which had been codified in 1882. A famous judgment of Lord Herschell considers the extent to which, in interpreting a codification, reference may be made to the law as it stood previously;[68] and there were important decisions that an original payee cannot be a holder in due course,[69] on the duty to draw cheques in a way that does not facilitate fraud,[70] and on estoppel against setting up a defence of forgery.[71] As regards the wider area of banking law, the nature of the relationship of banker and customer was determined by Lord Cottenham in the House of Lords long before 1875,[72] but development of practice has led in the second part of the twentieth century to sophisticated discussion of rights to combine accounts and set-off,[73] the pleading of fraud under letters of

[60] Replaced, with amendments, by the Sale of Goods Act 1979 and further amended subsequently.

[61] The *Hardwick Game Farm* case [1969] 2 AC 31 (cattle and poultry feed); *Christopher Hill Ltd v Ashington Piggeries Ltd* [1972] AC 441 (Norwegian herring meal).

[62] *Bowes v Shand* (1877) 2 App Cas 455.

[63] *Arcos Ltd v EA Ronaasen & Son* [1933] AC 470. There were other cases on such disputes decided at lower levels.

[64] Conspicuous examples are *Horst v Biddell Bros* [1912] AC 18 and *Ross T Smyth & Co Ltd v TD Bailey Sons & Co* [1940] 3 All ER 60 (Lord Wright).

[65] *Gill & Duffus SA v Berger & Co Inc* [1984] AC 382.

[66] *Helby v Matthews* [1895] AC 471.

[67] eg *Bridge v Campbell Discount Co* [1962] AC 600 (penalty); *Branwhite v Worcester Works Finance Ltd* [1969] 1 AC 552 (finance company's liability in respect of fraud by dealer).

[68] *Bank of England v Vagliano Bros* [1891] AC 107.

[69] *Jones Ltd v Waring & Gillow Ltd* [1926] AC 670.

[70] *London Joint Stock Bank v Simmons* [1892] AC 201 (Lord Halsbury).

[71] *Greenwood v Martins Bank Ltd* [1933] AC 51.   [72] *Foley v Hill* (1848) 2 HL Cas 28.

[73] eg *Halesowen Presswork and Assemblies Ltd v National Westminster Bank Ltd* [1972] AC 785.

credit,[74] and of the nature of a bank's possible security rights over customers' accounts.[75] Beyond that, developments in recent banking law draw on and also influence the general law—the law of tort in respect of bankers' references;[76] the application of equitable principles concerning fiduciary duties and accessory liability for breach of trust or for knowing receipt of trust property,[77] which certainly impinge on bankers; *Quistclose* trusts;[78] and large parts of what is nowadays (under the guidance of Lord Goff) recognised as and termed the law of restitution take effect in a banking context.[79]

Company law was much regulated by statute before 1875 and has continued to be so. It is, however, firmly rooted in common law principles of contract and fiduciary obligations in equity. The House of Lords' greatest contribution was undoubtedly the decision in *Salomon v Salomon & Co Ltd*,[80] where the House drew from the not-at-all-clearly drafted legislation an intention that the company was an entity separate from its members: thus the corporators, including Mr Salomon, were not liable for the debts of the company. This judgment of a strong Committee[81] proved to be seminal. But the House of Lords had already in 1875, but before its establishment in its present form, formulated a doctrine that a contract outside a company's objectives was ultra vires and not enforceable, the purpose of which was to protect shareholders from having corporate money used for purposes in which they had not invested.[82] It did not work entirely satisfactorily, and there has subsequently been difficulty in disentangling it from the common law principles of agency. There was also from 1855 what came to be called an 'indoor management rule', which was directed towards protecting third parties dealing with the company in good faith, which likewise became entangled with agency principles and ideas of notice.[83] Already before the *Salomon* case the House had sought to protect the company's capital by preventing it from purchasing its own shares.[84] All these developments had their difficulties, and have

---

[74] *The American Accord* [1983] 1 AC 168. The basic requirements of conformity under such credits were laid down by the House in *Equitable Trust Co of New York v Dawson Partners Ltd* (1927) 27 Ll L Rep 49.

[75] *Re Bank of Credit and Commerce International SA* [1998] AC 214.

[76] *Hedley Byrne & Co Ltd v Heller & Partners Ltd* [1964] AC 465.

[77] See *Twinsectra Ltd v Yardley* [2002] 2 AC 164, developing an earlier Privy Council judgment and itself subsequently 'explained' in another Privy Council case.

[78] Deriving from the speech of Lord Wilberforce in *Barclays Bank Ltd v Quistclose Investments Ltd* [1970] AC 567.

[79] Especially the 'swaps' cases: eg *Westdeutsche Landesbank Girozentrale v Islington BC* [1996] AC 669.

[80] [1897] AC 22. See Lord Cooke of Thorndon, *Turning Points in the Common Law* (Hamlyn Lectures 1996) (1997) ch 1.

[81] Lord Halsbury LC, Lord Watson, Lord Herschell, Lord Macnaghten, Lord Davey, and Lord Morris (the last of whom, however, confined himself to concurring in the 'judgment which has been announced'). See the hesitating acceptance by Pollock in (1897) 13 LQR 6.

[82] *Ashbury Carriage Co v Riche* (1875) LR 7 HL 653.

[83] These were largely dealt with in lower courts. A House of Lords decision is *Houghton & Co v Nothard Lowe & Wills* [1928] AC 1.

[84] *Trevor v Whitworth* (1887) 12 App Cas 409; and after the *Salomon* case *Ooregum Gold Mining Co v Roper* [1892] AC 125 (sale of shares at a discount).

been or are being dismantled in stages and superseded by statute, a tendency given impetus by EU attempts to harmonise company law in Europe. The underlay nevertheless is one of the common law; and in parallel the general principles of equity that impose fiduciary obligations in various circumstances, for instance on an agent, solicitor, partner, or bank, can largely be traced to early cases on company promoters and directors.[85] Sometimes general principle may be evolved from legislation: a significant recent judgment on a statutory provision has elaborated the principles on which relief may be given where the company is being conducted in a way that may be 'unfairly prejudicial' to the interests of a member or members[86]—a matter on which the common law had failed to provide an effective remedy.

Finally, the House has undoubtedly risen to the challenge raised by the expanding and increasingly sophisticated international commerce of the second half of the twentieth century in ways normally discussed under the heading of the conflict of laws. Most (not all) of these developments occurred in or after the 1970s, at more or less the same time as the rise in shipping litigation and commercial litigation generally—a large number of the cases brought involving only one, or no, UK party. A number of judgments on choice of law in contract established the right of parties to choose a governing law, at least in an international context[87] (which was not at all clear from the jurisprudence of the 1930s), and for its ascertainment where there was no clear choice.[88] A group of cases introduced an entirely new feature of allowing damages to be claimed and calculated in foreign currencies.[89] Finally, over a series of cases the House developed a doctrine, not previously extant except in Scotland, of *forum non conveniens*, enabling a court to determine whether and when it should hear a case with international features.[90] Unfortunately decisions of the European Court of Justice, with several of which it is difficult to agree, have seriously diminished the scope of such reasoning, but it remains for purely international litigation. An associated development is that of the anti-suit injunction to prevent parties seeking to litigate or arbitrate in places other than those on which they have agreed,[91] though this has likewise encountered difficulties with EU law. Nevertheless, it is by reason of these and similar courageous developments that the

---

[85] eg *Gluckstein v Barnes* [1900] AC 240; *Regal (Hastings) Ltd v Gulliver* (1942) [1967] 2 AC 134n.

[86] *O'Neill v Phillips* [1999] 1 WLR 1092 (Lord Hoffmann).

[87] See *R v International Trustee* [1937] AC 500, where Lord Atkin said that a choice of law would be 'conclusive'; this was subsequently reinforced by Lord Wright in the Privy Council.

[88] *Cie Tunisienne de Navigation SA v Cie d'Armement Maritime SA* [1971] AC 572; *Amin Rasheed v Kuwait Insurance Co Ltd* [1984] AC 50; though the law in this area is now much modified by an international convention (the 'Rome Convention').

[89] *Miliangos v George Frank (Textiles) Ltd* [1976] AC 443; *The Despina R* [1979] AC 685.

[90] Starting with *The Atlantic Star* [1974] AC 436; a leading recent case is *Lubbe v Cape plc* [2000] 1 WLR 1545. The doctrine is primarily associated with Lord Goff.

[91] The jurisdiction was first examined and restated in the Privy Council, but the House considered it in *Airbus Industrie GIE v Patel* [1999] 1 AC 119.

English courts can claim expertise in the resolution of international litigation in accordance with the principles of freedom of contract.

In quite different times and in a quite different context, a *Morning Chronicle* article in 1838 stated, 'The commercial part of the community have little reason to thank God...that there is a House of Lords.'[92] Though there have been hiccups, surprises, and unpopular decisions, by and large the development of the law since the third-tier appeal was preserved in 1876, and especially in the second half of the twentieth century,[93] has meant that the commercial part of the community should since that time have had cause to think differently. It seems clear, however, that despite the heavy load of the Court of Appeal, which points to the value of a third tier in the court system, the number of commercial cases heard by the Lords has declined of late. Whether this is due to a policy regarding the granting of leave to appeal, or to increased use of arbitration, or to any other cause—or whether it is simply accidental—is not clear.

Paradoxically, in its penultimate year, the House decided two appeals on the law of damages, as applied in the context of charterparty disputes; in both of them it so happened that charterers prevailed over owners, not necessarily justly. The cases were decided by two different (with one exception) panels of the House; only one commercial lawyer was involved in either of them, and he dissented. The first, *The Golden Victory*,[94] has been described by a former Commercial Court judge as 'the worst decision on any aspect of English commercial law, and certainly shipping law, that has come out of the House of Lords in my entire career in the legal profession'.[95] The second, *The Achilleas*,[96] is less obviously unacceptable. But it is difficult to say more than that; and both put one in mind of the views expressed in 1838. Nevertheless, despite reservations induced by these two decisions, especially the first, it is to be hoped that the new Supreme Court will not be reluctant to take the opportunity of continuing the line of significant rulings which has hitherto, and especially in the last 50 years, been so important to the regulation (and hence development) of national and international commerce.

---

[92] 15 August 1838 (in connection with the prosecution of Cobbett), quoted in *Gower's Modern Company Law* (London: Sweet & Maxwell, 6th edn 1997) 36 n 3.

[93] Lord Cooke (n 80), at 4, suggested (though largely by reference to tort cases) that the 1990s 'may prove to be vintage years'.

[94] [2008] 2 AC 353.

[95] The Hon Sir Anthony Colman, in an address to the London Maritime Arbitrators Association, reproduced in its Newsletter for Autumn 2008. See also Lord Mustill, '*The Golden Victory*: Some Reflections' (2008) 124 LQR 571; F Reynolds, '*The Golden Victory*: A Misguided Decision' (2008) 38 HKLJ 333.

[96] [2009] 1 AC 61.

39

Intellectual Property

Robin Jacob

Final Appeal, by Louis Blom-Cooper and Gavin Drewry, was published in early 1972. I had a small hand in it: the Acknowledgements include the statement 'Mr Robin Jacob initiated us into the mysteries of patent, trade mark and copyright law'. *Final Appeal* did not use the term 'intellectual property' (hereafter IP). It was hardly ever used then, and in so far as it was, it meant only copyright and like rights (matters of the 'intellect' rather than vulgar trade). The term 'industrial property' was used for patents and industrial designs. IP, nationally and internationally, was something of a commercial and legal backwater. We did not know then that it was about to grow into the giant it has now become—occupying a key position worldwide. Decisions of important national courts in the field of IP are now studied all over the world the moment they appear. A House of Lords decision (or even the fact that leave to appeal has been given) will be the subject of almost immediate comment and discussion across the internet well before anything appears in any legal journal concerned with IP (there are many of these now, virtually none then). So it is that the international importance of the judicial House of Lords in IP has grown since *Final Appeal*. Most importantly of all this has been in the field of patents, as I shall discuss more fully later.

My main task for *Final Appeal* was to produce a potted summary[1] of each of the IP cases for Part B, entitled 'the House of Lords in Action 1952–68'. The summaries were used by whoever wrote the actual text. Perhaps it was Louis, but he feigns not to remember. This time I get to write the text.

What I intend to do is review what I see as the key features and cases following those considered in *Final Appeal*—those from 1969 to 2007. But I must start by going back in time to consider the place of the House of Lords in IP up until the pre-*Final Appeal* period, until 1952. By and large it performed a valuable and cohesive function. Thus patent law was developed for the capitalist economy during the nineteenth century into a workable body of rules even before the

---

[1] This was an invaluable exercise for a young barrister, providing a sure foundation for practice. For the present task I have been similarly (but more ably) assisted by James Whyte, a barrister of 8 New Square, Lincoln's Inn. I am very grateful.

partial codification in 1932[2] of the grounds of invalidity and their complete codification in 1949.[3] Prior to that time the substantive governing law was essentially still the Statute of Monopolies 1620. And the rules for determining the scope of a patent, what amounted to infringement, remained uncodified until the new, European system, took over in 1977.[4] So it fell to the judges—ultimately the House of Lords—to work out the rules. Key figures in this process were the two IP giants of the early twentieth century, Lords Parker and Fletcher Moulton. They each had a special interest in IP.[5] (It seems to be a feature of the House of Lords that from time to time a member of the court takes a shine to the subject, particularly patents.)[6] Lord Parker created the modern law of passing off in *Spalding v Gamage*.[7] He, along with Fletcher-Moulton LJ in the Court of Appeal, also created the cautious British approach to the registrability of trade marks.[8] The 20s to 50s were fairly quiescent for IP. The 30s saw some hostility, particularly to patents.[9] The 40s and 50s, particularly under Lords Russell and Simonds, continued a restrictive approach to the scope of patents—one which we would now regard as unsatisfactory: in particular an approach consisting of regarding the claims as so distinct from the context of the specification and the drawings that the latter should only be considered as an aid to construction where there is ambiguity of claim[10] has long gone. Much the same has, of course, applied generally to questions of construction of all sorts of documents—'strict' has given way to 'purposive'.

I turn to the period under review. First, some statistics. In the 16 years reviewed in Final Appeal there were 24 IP cases in the House of Lords; in the subsequent 38½ years (1969–mid-2008) 55 if one counts a few cases which might be called borderline IP.[11] Of these 26 were on patents, 12 on copyright, nine on registered trade marks, two on passing off, two on registered designs and four on breach of confidence. Numbers have not been significantly on the increase, notwithstanding the increased importance of the subject. But the actual numbers do not tell the full story, particularly for patents. The cases heard have,

---

[2] By the Patents Amendment Act 1932.   [3] By the Patents Act 1949.

[4] The year of implementation of the European Patent Convention.

[5] Fletcher Moulton piloted the Trade Marks Act 1905 through the House of Commons and is said to have drafted much of it himself. Parker chaired a wartime committee to look into the alleged deficiencies in UK patent law. There was a perception that pre-War Germany had used the patent system so as to advantage its (particularly chemical) industry as against British industry by suppressing UK manufacture. I am not convinced of that, but it was wartime.

[6] Lords Reid, Diplock, and Hoffmann are more recent examples of this.

[7] (1915) 32 RPC 273, building on nineteenth century HL cases, *Reddaway v Banham* [1896] AC 199, *Powell v Birmingham Vinegar* [1897] AC 710 and *Montgomery v Thompson* [1891] AC 217. Lord Parker's key contribution was to identify that the action protected not property in a name or trade mark but in the goodwill attached to a name or trade mark.

[8] *W&G du Cros' Appn* [1913] AC 83 and *per* Fletcher Moulton LJ in *Crosfield's Application* (1909) 26 RPC 837.

[9] For instance the patent for the pentode was struck down as being too wide, *Mullard v Philco* (1936) 53 RPC 323, a decision which is generally regarded as wrong or, at best, unsatisfactory.

[10] An approach endorsed by the House of Lords in *EMI v Lisson* [1939] AC 83.

[11] In particular four cases concerned with breach of confidence.

in the main, had more legal significance than many of the cases in the earlier period.[12] Then it was not difficult to get leave to appeal, often from the Court of Appeal. Being under the naïve impression that only questions of important legal principle came before the House, as a pupil in 1967 I asked my master, Anthony Walton, what principle was involved in *Ransburg v Aerostyle*,[13] where the Court of Appeal had given leave. His answer summed up the ease with which leave could then be obtained: '£100,000 worth of principle'. By contrast, in the period under review I cannot think of a single case where the mere amount of money involved has been enough to get leave. Big money cases did not get leave unless there was an element of public interest, for instance an important question of law. So although the rate of cases has been fairly constant, their importance has been more significant.

A change during the review period has been the length of hearings. At the beginning of the review period, IP appeals, and particularly patent appeals, were apt to take a long time. Hearings were often five days or more. In 1963 Lord Reid had protested about the length (19 days) of *Van der Lely v Bamfords*[14] but nothing really changed for a long time. Even in 1980, *Catnic v Hill & Smith*,[15] concerning a simple mechanical invention, took ten days. By the 1990s and 2000s hearing times were somewhat down, even though the technical subject matter was much more complex. Most notably, the key case of *Kirin-Amgen v Transkaryotic Therapies (No 2)*[16] had only nine hearing days. The subject matter, recombinant technology, was vastly more complicated than that in *van der Lely* (a hay rake) and the law was also much more complex (European and American authorities were considered in detail).

Another feature of IP cases in the review period has been the low level of dissenting opinions, particularly in relation to cases involving substantive IP law.[17] There have been no dissents in such cases since 1974.

The figures include three appeals from Scotland.[18] There is no leave requirement for these. It is doubtful whether two of the cases would have got leave if they had been English or Northern Irish. The third, *Johnstone*, raised an important point of trade mark law[19] (though in a criminal context, the point is of wider significance) but these days, with the last word on trade marks now lying with the European Court of Justice, the decision cannot be ultimately determinative.

---

[12] Many of the cases—particularly patent cases—though reported, were seldom, if ever, cited, deciding, as they did, no important question of law.

[13] [1968] RPC 217.   [14] [1963] RPC 61.   [15] [1982] RPC 183.

[16] [2005] RPC 9.

[17] Lord Diplock dissented in *American Cyanamid v Upjohn* [1971] RPC 425 and Lords Reid and Morris in *Bristol Myers (Johnson's Application)* [1974] AC 646.

[18] *Buchanan v Alba Diagnostics* [2004] SC(HL) 9; *Redrow Homes v Bett Bros* [1999] AC 197 and *R v Johnstone* [2003] FSR 42.

[19] Does the defendant's use have to indicate trade origin to infringe? The ECJ is still working its way through this topic: see eg *Arsenal TM* Case C-206/01 [2002] ECR I-10273, *Hölterhoff v Freiesleben* Case C-2/00 [2002] ECR I-4187 and most recently *O2 v Hutchison* Case C-533/06 [2008] WLR (D) 193—see also [20] of the Attorney General's opinion to the effect that the case law on this topic is all at sea.

Next, a bit about the leading personalities. The review period commenced with what can fairly be called Lord Reid's court. He presided in nearly all IP cases until his retirement on 10 January 1975. You cannot get a better picture of Lord Reid in action than to read the vivid report of argument in *GE TM*.[20] I well remember his way of asking a seemingly innocuous question to which counsel gave the self-evident answer. That would be followed by a similar question, with the same result. Then the old man, looking surprisingly small for a man of his height, would lean forward with his hands clasped together just below his chin, his eyes bright behind those round spectacles: 'Very well then, so does it follow that . . . ?' A pit opened up.

Lord Diplock was the next dominant Law Lord in IP. He gave the leading (often the only) speech time and time again. His interest in IP probably stemmed not only from the fact that he had a degree in chemistry but also from the fact that his father had been a patent agent. He even, whilst a Law Lord, sat as a judge of first instance in a patent trial.[21] Even his last 'speech' was in a patent case, being delivered posthumously by Lord Fraser in *Allen & Hanbury v Generics*.[22] After Diplock it fell to Lord Oliver, with less evident enthusiasm for the subject, and Lord Templeman, with enthusiasm to cut back IP rights,[23] to take the lead roles. When Lord Hoffmann arrived in the House of Lords in 1995 he immediately took over and has given the leading speech in nearly every IP case since.[24] We may expect Lords Walker and Neuberger each to take a similar interest in IP and take over as the leading IP judges of the new Supreme Court when Lord Hoffmann retires, as he will in April 2009.[25]

I turn now to consideration of the cases. They are of two sorts, those about the core rules of IP law and those which, although having an IP right in the background, were really about some more general question.

The general cases

Norwich Pharmacal

I begin with perhaps the most important case of all, *Norwich Pharmacal v Customs & Excise*.[26] I will tell the whole story: it is one worth telling and if I not do it here

---

[20] [1973] RPC 297. The argument was reported by Peter Prescott who, working from the transcript, captured all the key interchanges, generally with the exact words. It reads like a play.

[21] *Standard Fabrics v Reeves* [1972] RPC 47.

[22] [1988] 3 All ER 1057.

[23] He realised that, particularly in the field of 'soft IP' (a patent lawyer's term for rights in non-technical subject matter such as copyright and trade marks), the new enthusiasm for IP was getting out of hand, with a resulting risk of overprotection and the stultification of proper competition.

[24] They include all nine patent cases and the only copyright case of importance, *Designers' Guild v Russell Williams* [2001] FSR 11.

[25] Both sat on a number of IP cases, including patent cases, both at first instance and in the Court of Appeal.

[26] [1974] AC 133.

it may never be told. It is difficult, if not impossible, to remember or even picture procedural law before the era of the *Norwich*, *Anton Piller*, and *Mareva* orders. They all emerged in the early 70s. The first and seminal case was *Norwich*, changing as it did the whole ethos of what remedies a court could grant.

It started in 1967 when I was Anthony Walton's pupil. The drug company Smith Kline & French had an exclusive licence under Norwich Pharmacal's patent for a chicken food additive called furazolidone. SK&F noticed that statistics of imported products published in the 'special chemical register' by the Customs included furazolidone. Clearly it infringed the patent.[27] The amounts and dates of import but not the names of the importers were published. SK&F asked Customs for the names. Customs said it could not and would not supply them. It could not because the names were confidential to the supplier of the information and moreover by implication statute[28] precluded disclosure. It would not because if it did supply the names that would imperil the integrity of the special chemical register in that dishonest people would lie about what they were importing. SK&F went to Antony Walton. He suggested that the thing to do was to sue Customs claiming it was infringing because the infringing product passed through its control. This was seen as a long shot but the idea was to bring some pressure on Customs, possibly to get the names on discovery of documents and somehow make use of them, or even to lose but make some political capital out of that with a view to getting legislation to deal with this manifest injustice. The idea of an action for discovery as such was so alien that it never crossed the mind of anyone.

An action for infringement was started in 1969. It was not pursued with great enthusiasm, given its prospects. But one day, looking through four Chancery Division reports for something wholly unconnected with this case, Walton's eye accidentally, and serendipitously, fell upon p 97, the 1876 case of *Orr v Diaper*. There it was, or seemed to be, an order for discovery of the name of a trade mark infringer. The order was against a shipper of goods bearing a spurious trade mark to find out who the exporter was. The Norwich writ was amended to include a claim for discovery. Customs listed documents which would disclose the names, but claimed Crown privilege.[29] So a summons for inspection was issued. It came before Graham J. He, the practical business-minded judge that he was, held that discovery should be given, against the arguments of Mr Templeman QC and Mr Jean-Pierre Warner for the Crown. The Court of Appeal reversed Graham J with a resounding thump—there was no such thing as an action for discovery against anyone who was not himself a wrongdoer and in any event the information both could not as a matter of law and should not on the grounds of Crown privilege be disclosed. Lord Denning MR's judgment was particularly conservative—even

---

[27] Save on the improbable hypothesis that it was an SK&F product bought in the UK, exported, and re-imported.
[28] In the shape of s 3 of the Finance Act 1967.
[29] As public interest immunity was called in those days.

accepting the argument that the Crown should protect wrongdoers in the interests of keeping the statistics accurate.[30] Leave to appeal was refused.

So it was on an application for leave that the case first reached the House of Lords. As I recall it the oral argument lasted for most of the day. It was in the Moses room rather than one of the two usual Committee rooms. Oddly, what interested the three Lords[31] who heard it most was the point about whether statute precluded disclosure. Leave was given.

Thus the stage was set for a right royal battle. By then Mr Templeman had gone to the Bench and Mr Warner to be the UK's first Advocate-General in the ECJ. The new Crown team were Peter Oliver QC leading, as first junior, Mr Peter Gibson. By then the amount of legal research which had been done was truly massive. We had trawled the English Reports, early American and Commonwealth authorities, and the leading textbooks of the nineteenth century. All the authorities had been photocopied and put in five large, bound volumes.[32]

Walton decided to start with the statutory prohibition/Crown privilege points —these were seen as the soft target because the idea of the Crown protecting wrongdoers was obviously unattractive. The plan failed at the first moment. Before he had got further than 'May it please your Lordships I appear with...' Lord Reid interrupted: 'Mr Walton, there are two points in this case. Their Lordships would like you to start with the question of whether there is an action for discovery.' Clearly there was some scepticism about this. Walton embarked on the exercise taking them through the detailed stuff we had found. There was much intervention. Some progress seemed to be made but not, it seemed, enough when Peter Oliver got up on, I think, the third day. At some point thereafter, either the Thursday or the following Monday, Lord Kilbrandon did not appear— he was sick. Lord Reid said the court would press on with four. So Peter Oliver finished his response on the discovery appeal and Walton had about a day and a bit to reply. By now they were really interested. At about midday on the Wednesday of the second week the argument on this point was complete. We were turned out of Committee room number 1 while the four debated what to do. Lunch came and went. We all walked up and down that corridor, seemingly for ever. At about quarter to four the door was flung open and the usher called 'Counsel'. In we went. Reid said: 'Mr Walton and Mr Oliver. Their Lordships are evenly divided. Lord Kilbrandon will be better by Monday. We would like you to re-argue the question. The rest of us will endeavour not to interrupt.'

---

[30] The dishonest infringing importers might lie if they knew that their identity might be exposed.

[31] Lord Cross was one; I cannot remember the other two.

[32] Not just ring binders. Photocopying a few, unreported cases had been done once or twice before but this was an exercise on a different scale. The exercise was repeated in *Zamir v Secretary of State for Home Affairs* [1980] AC 930 to the distaste of Lord Wilberforce, who deprecated the cost of photocopying at public expense through the legal aid scheme. *Norwich* was, I believe, the first time reported authorities had ever been photocopied. Before that the House and counsel all worked with actual volumes of reports.

After that it was all downhill. After the action for discovery the other point was easy. In the result it was a 5:0 decision.

I, and all others in the case, long wondered which two changed their minds. None of us ever found out. A possible mind-changer was Lord Cross. For a few days after the argument was over counsel got a letter from him.[33] He had discovered a case of 1887 in the Supreme Judicial Court of Massachusetts, *Post v Toledo*,[34] which he thought supported the existence of the action. If I were asked to speculate now as to the other mind-changer I would say Lord Morris. He had played a lesser part in the debate, and I think, by nature, was rather more conservative than the others.

Norwich set in train a whole series of cases about the limits of the rule itself (journalists' sources, malicious informers, and so on); it changed the very notion of using litigation to obtain information.[35] It changed lawyers' attitudes to creative procedural litigation. If this unthinkable thing could be done, why not others? So came *Anton Piller*,[36] *Mareva*,[37] orders against third party banks for production of documents,[38] passport seizure orders where an alleged debtor was likely to abscond,[39] and others. I do not think any of these things would have happened as quickly or even at all but for the sea-change brought about by *Norwich*.

---

[33] I do not know how many times such a post-hearing letter had happened before.

[34] (1887) North Eastern Reporter 540. The Judgment was by Associate Justice Holmes, the future Justice Holmes of the US Supreme Court. Actually Peter Prescott's (he was second junior) researches had already found this case but we did not cite it because we thought it distinguishable on the grounds that the defendant was in effect a wrongdoer. We were not so purist as to say that it did not help after Lord Cross had found it and thought it was in our favour!

[35] A quick early example was *D v NSPCC* [1978] AC 171, where a mother, wrongly accused of child abuse, sought an order that the identity of the informer be disclosed by the NSPCC. The HL refused the order on the ground of public interest—the doctors, teachers, relatives, and neighbours who are the regular informants to the NSPCC of cases of suspected child abuse would all dry up if their names could come out. Curiously a recent author, Ruth Costigan, has asserted that 'there is no appellate authority on whether a public interest defence can defeat a *Norwich Pharmacal* claim': 'Protecting Journalists' Sources' [2007] PL 464, 475. She cites a Court of Appeal case where the point was assumed, *Mersey NHS Trust v Ackroyd* [2003] EMLR 36. Is *D* so old that everyone has forgotten it? And is *Norwich* itself no longer read? For in *Norwich* the question of public interest was a live defence, only failing on the merits.

[36] [1976] Ch 55. I am quite sure this would never have happened but for *Norwich*. Following *Norwich*, record companies who were facing the new phenomenon of piracy quickly sought disclosure orders against retailers as to their sources. It usually turned out that by the time action against these was taken they said they had nothing left and had only sold a few. The need to 'get in there' provoked legal research by Hugh Laddie into the nineteenth century cases for a justification for such an order. About eight were granted in favour of record companies until the Chancery judges decided that the order needed the sanction of the Court of Appeal. The ninth case, where it was refused, *Anton Piller*, happened not to be a record piracy case. It was one of breach of confidence. When taken to appeal, Lord Denning MR was much in favour of the order (the contrast with his attitude to *Norwich* is marked). And so it was that the name of this obscure German company entered the language of the law.

[37] [1975] Lloyd's Rep 509.   [38] *Bankers Trust v Shapira* [1980] 1 WLR 1274.

[39] *Bayer v Winter (No 1)* [1986] 1 WLR 497, CA.

American Cyanamid v Ethicon[40]

This was Lord Diplock at his most prescriptive, indeed virtually legislative. Until the 1960s interlocutory injunctions in patent cases were seldom granted. The general practice was, unless the patent was old and well established, to refuse an injunction where counsel asserted that validity was to be challenged. That changed essentially when the business-minded Graham J went on the Bench. The rule became, broadly, that if the plaintiff could establish a 'strong prima facie case'—ie show that he was likely to win—he would get an injunction.

Now that was all very well for simple patent cases. The court could realistically form such a view.[41] But when you tried to work out who was really likely to win in a high-tech case of some complexity with conflicting expert evidence on affidavit, the job of assessing who was likely to win became impossible. *American Cyanamid* was such a case. The parties put piles of affidavits before the court and, over many days, argued about whether or not there was a 'strong prima facie' case. Graham J held there was. The Court of Appeal held there was not, following an eight-day hearing. The case came before the House (the House having given leave) with an estimate of 12 hearing days. It took three. The House, through Lord Diplock, took both sides by surprise by refusing to go much into the question of how strong the plaintiff's case was. Instead he decided to lay down completely general rules about the grant of interlocutory injunctions. He set aside the 'strong prima facie' case rule and set out the well-known formula, which I summarise here:

(1) Has the plaintiff 'any real prospect of success'?[42] If no, no injunction; if yes:
(2) Would damages be an adequate remedy and could the defendant pay? If both yes, no injunction; if either no:
(3) Would the defendant, if ultimately successful, be adequately compensated under the plaintiff's undertaking as to damages and could the plaintiff pay? If yes to both, injunction, if either no:
(4) How tips the 'balance of convenience?' Injunction or not depends on how the balance tips, a multifactorial assessment.
(5) If the factors are 'evenly balanced' preserve the status quo by granting an injunction.

There are two other important points. First, Lord Diplock went out of his way to say that, if damages were an adequate remedy and the defendant could pay, there should be no injunction, 'however strong the plaintiff's claim appeared to be'. Secondly, he allowed that the court could consider who would be the likely winner only as an item in step 4 (balance of convenience), where 'it is apparent

---

[40] [1975] AC 396.
[41] See eg *Carroll v Tomado* [1971] RPC 401, about a simple and short patent for a domestic plastic-coated wire frame 'airer/drier'.
[42] Which means 'Is there a serious question to be tried?'

upon the facts as disclosed by evidence as to which there is no credible dispute that the strength of one party's case is disproportionate to that of the other party'.

Following *Cyanamid* (another word to have entered the language of the law) there have been I do not know how many decisions trying to work out the implications. Often you see courts struggling to get out of the *Cyanamid* straightjacket, trying to grant or withhold an injunction depending on the merits of the case. I have long thought that this decision was wrong and harmful. The apparent logic is itself deeply flawed. Here are some of my objections:

(1) It makes no sense to withhold an injunction 'however strong the plaintiff's claim appears to be'.

(2) The whole exercise gives neither side much of a basis to settle the case since the court is going out of its way not to give a clue as to who it thinks has the better case.

(3) The questions of whether damages would be an adequate remedy or whether the undertaking as to damages would be adequate are themselves difficult to assess. The court is led into considering a whole lot of 'what if' scenarios.

(4) Likewise investigations about whether a party has enough money to pay involves both speculation as to how much would be involved and as to the financial standing of the party concerned. There can be and often is a mini-trial about this.

(5) The test is apt to tilt things in favour of plaintiffs, particularly rich ones—to get past the first hurdle is relatively easy and then you are mainly into questions of money rather than legal merits.

(6) You can tilt things back in favour of defendants by taking a wide view of what is meant by damages being an 'adequate remedy'. Some judges have taken that to mean 'capable of assessment' in the sense that the court could come up with a figure. But in reality assessment of damages is apt to be a complicated and to some extent broad-brush exercise.[43] Trying to put someone back in the financial position they would have been but for an infringement, or but for the fact they were 'wrongly' injuncted, is a task to be avoided if one can.

So far as I know, no other jurisdiction in the world considers the prospects of ultimate success at trial as such a minor factor at the interlocutory stage. *Cyanamid* has not taken root in any common law country. And I am not surprised. I think it a pity that the Civil Procedure Rules did not do away with *Cyanamid*.[44] And it would be a good thing if the House of Lords in its dying days or the new Supreme Court in its early days re-considered it. Of course there will be cases where one cannot realistically express a view on the merits, cases where there is an acute conflict of evidence, or cases where the whole thing is too

---

[43] See eg the assessment of damages for patent infringement in *Gerber v Lectra* [1995] RPC 383, [1997] RPC 443 (CA).

[44] But then the CPR in the main just re-state the old rules in language which is more prolix although supposed to be more 'user friendly'.

complicated,[45] but it makes no sense in other cases to demote the ultimate merits. You are more likely to get an unjust result if you do.

LB Plastics v Swish[46] and *British Leyland v Armstrong*[47]

The House does not come well out of this pair of cases. Following the Design Copyright Act 1968, a general realisation grew that copyright law could be used to prevent the copying of most industrial artefacts. The basic reasoning was simple:[48] most things are first designed by drawings. Copyright will subsist in these, in those days for 50 years from the year of death of the author for things with no eye appeal and 15 years from first marketing of articles which had eye appeal. It is an infringement of the copyright in a drawing to copy it. That includes copying it indirectly and in three dimensions by copying the designer's article, itself made from the drawing.

Such had been the position established by the cases in the lower courts when *LB Plastics* reached the House. It was about a 'knock-down drawer system'. The defendants had based their rival system on that of the plaintiffs. Their drawers would fit those of the plaintiffs. They had denied copying. If one looks at the actual pictures of the two sides' articles set out in Reports of Patent Cases one can see why—the individual parts are very different in appearance. The main point argued was that the only feature actually copied was an unusual feature called 'a reverse countersink'. The House treated the case as mainly being about burden of proof—once you have proof of some copying and some visual identity, the burden of proof shifts to the defendant to prove that he did not copy. The trial judge held that the defendants were liars and the House had little sympathy for them.

This 'main' argument meant that the most important point did not get the attention it deserved and should have had. Was this bizarre rule of copyright, creating effectively perpetual protection against copying of most mechanical items, right? It was argued that, if and to the extent the defendants had copied, all they had taken was the 'idea'. The argument was brushed aside. It was advanced briefly by junior counsel for the respondents. It was not considered significant enough even to be summarised in the report of argument.

It seems fairly clear that the House[49] did not appreciate what was really at stake: should copyright confer the extraordinary degree of protection which the lower courts had established in the 70s? It treated the case as mainly one about fact and onus of proof. To be fair, that may well be because of the way it was argued.

---

[45] Patent cases can often be of this sort—*Cyanamid* was.   [46] [1979] RPC 551.
[47] [1986] AC 577.
[48] This is not the place to go into the detailed provisions or the cases.
[49] Which consisted of Lords Wilberforce, Hailsham, Salmon, Fraser, and Keith. None of these had much experience of IP.

When the rule started to become established, manufacturers realised they could use it to maintain monopolies in spare parts.[50] So they did, either reserving the market in spares to themselves or licensing others to make spares on payment of substantial royalties. In the motor car business one of those manufacturers[51] was British Leyland. Armstrong, who made spare exhaust systems for BL cars, refused to take a licence saying they did not need to do so for a variety of reasons. Those reasons included technical arguments under copyright law, an alleged implied licence to repair, custom and usage under the law merchant, and that enforcement of the copyright would be contrary to the competition rules of the EEC.

All these reasons had failed up to the Court of Appeal decision. Most were re-run before the House. In addition it was invited to reverse *Swish*, using the 1966 Practice Statement, even though it had been decided only a few years before. By a majority of four to one it refused to do so. Lord Griffiths alone was prepared to hold that *Swish* had missed the point: 'I am equally satisfied that it was not the intention of Parliament to bestow upon a manufacturer through the draughtsman in his drawing office protection for a purely functional object that could not be obtained through either patent or design copyright legislation.' What the majority did (Lords Templeman and Bridge, Lords Scarman and Edmund-Davies effectively concurring) was truly remarkable. All the appellants' arguments were rejected, but the House found a new one of its own.[52] And it did so without hearing argument on the point or giving the respondents an opportunity of commenting on the argument or the authorities used to justify it. If a lower court had done that it would have been rightly castigated. I doubt that the present House of Lords would do anything similar—Article 6 is now in everyone's minds. The contrast with Lord Cross's letter in the *Norwich* case stands out.

The explanation for this extraordinary case undoubtedly lies in the Lords' hostility, particularly that of Lords Templeman and Bridge, to over powerful monopoly rights. Actually the pricing and availability (short and long term) of spares is a very complicated economic matter,[53] much more suitable for investigation and control by industry self-regulation[54] or competition

---

[50] *British Northrop v Texteam Blackburn* [1974] RPC 57.

[51] Ford and Volvo were others and had their own litigation against spare part makers.

[52] The point was based on a supposed inherent 'right to repair' coupled with a borrowing from land law rules and cases under which a grantor of a right may not derogate from his grant. It has not received much acceptance since. Parliament changed the law of copyright in 1988 so as to remove the most over-protective aspects of copyright law. The Privy Council in *Canonkabushiki kaisha Co (Hong Kong) Ltd v Green Cartridge* [1997] AC 728, 737F (via Lord Hoffmann, who else?) cut the doctrine back and made it fairly clear that it thought *Leyland* an aberration: 'It is of course a strong thing (not to say constitutionally questionable) for a judicially-declared head of public policy to be treated as overriding or qualifying an express statutory right.'

[53] For instance the supplier of spare parts will only be interested in those that are profitable, but an original equipment manufacturer as a practical matter will probably have to maintain supplies of all parts, most of which would be unprofitable in a stand-alone market.

[54] eg a code under which spares for a particular model will be made available for a fixed period after the model becomes obsolete.

authorities[55] than the blunt instrument of an IP court concerned, as it must be, with black or white rules of law. Most would say now that the House should have left the problem to the legislature, as indeed it was invited but refused to do.

Polaroid (Land's) Patent[56]

I put this in mainly for fun, but also to ask rhetorically, why is this not done more often, not only by the House of Lords but by other appellate tribunals? Leave had been given by the Court of Appeal. These are the speeches in full:

Lord Diplock: My Lords, the reasons given by Buckley, LJ, for the Court of Appeal, from which this appeal to your Lordships' House is brought, are, in my opinion, obviously right and expressed in terms so clear and convincing that I do not think I can improve upon them. I would dismiss this appeal.
    Lord Russell of Killowen: I concur.
    Lord Lowry: I also concur.
    Lord Emslie: I too concur for the same reasons.
    Lord Bridge of Harwich: My Lords, I concur.

I love the little elaborations in the concurring speeches too.

Patent law

The House of Lords has served patent law well over the review period. I start with what is generally the most important question in a patent case, the scope of the monopoly covered by the patent. The 1960s, which ended the period covered by *Final Appeal*, left some unfinished business about this. There had been two 3:2 decisions, *Van der Lely*[57] and *Rodi*.[58] The majority view in each case was that the monopoly was confined to that which was covered by the claims properly construed. Moreover claim construction required a strict approach. The minority view was that patent law should prevent what Lord Reid called 'sharp practice',[59] namely taking the idea of the claim without falling within its strict meaning as a matter of language.[60] In the jargon of the time this was called the 'doctrine of pith and marrow'. The majority view did not formally say that the doctrine was dead, but it was, given the strict constructionalist approach, as a practical matter impossible to imagine a case where it would apply.

---

[55] And was a live subject at the time with a Competition Act investigation into Ford's pricing and spare parts policies.
[56] [1981] FSR 578.   [57] *Van der Lely v Bamfords* [1963] RPC 61.
[58] *Rodi & Weinenberger v Henry Showell* [1969] RPC 367.   [59] *Van der Lely* (n 57) 77.
[60] In the case in point, the claim was directed at a hay rake device constructed so that the 'hindmost' wheels could be taken off the frame and attached to the front. The alleged infringement worked in exactly the same way, save that the foremost wheels were taken off and attached to the rear.

Lord Diplock, in *Catnic v Hill & Smith* [61] resolved this old problem, created a more liberal approach to claim construction, but went on to create a new puzzle which came to be known as the 'Catnic questions'. He resolved the old problem by declaring, with a Stalinesque re-writing of legal history, that there never had been a doctrine of pith and marrow, that the differing opinions given in the two great cases of the 60s were simply about construction of the patent claims. They obviously were not. No one could have or had ever read them that way,[62] including the lower courts in *Catnic* itself. That resolved the matter for the time being—all was just a question of claim construction.

The advance Lord Diplock made in claim construction was to require a much more intelligent approach. The emphasis was to be on how 'those likely to have a practical interest in the subject matter of [the] invention' would read the claim in context. 'A patent specification should be given a purposive construction rather than a purely literal one derived from applying to it the kind of meticulous verbal analysis in which lawyers by their training are too often tempted to indulge.' Lord Diplock went on to elaborate this with a series of questions about what was to be done if there was 'a variant' from a particular descriptive word used in a claim. This was the least successful part of his speech. The questions were not easy as they stood. Hoffmann J tried to restate them in *Improver v Remington*.[63] The order was a bit more logical, but nonetheless the approach was too complicated—it involved considering first the acontextual meaning of the word.

When he reached the House of Lords, Lord Hoffmann took the opportunity of not so much rejecting the *Catnic* questions as elegantly making them irrelevant. This was in *Kirin-Amgen*. *Catnic* had been the last case concerned with scope of patent monopoly under the common law. In 1978 the European Patent Convention (EPC) came into effect, implanted in UK law by the Patents Act 1977. This was a messy attempt to reconcile the perceived English and German approaches to the problem. The perceived English approach was strict constructionism of the kind which had been the approach in the 30s until, at the latest, the early 70s—read the claim as a freestanding piece of language, resorting to context (specification and drawings) only in the case of ambiguity. The perceived, indeed actual, German approach was to use the claims only as a guideline. The compromise was provided by Article 69 of the EPC and a Protocol upon it. Article 69 says: 'The extent of the protection conferred by a European patent...shall be determined by the terms of the claims. Nonetheless, the description and drawings shall be used to interpret the claims.' The Protocol, in summary, rejects both approaches to construction. The approach of Article 69 is to be one which 'combines a fair protection for a patentee with a degree of certainty for third parties'.

---

[61] [1982] RPC 183.
[62] How could you with passages such as 'I am not suggesting that the doctrine of pith and marrow is dead' (*per* Lord Morris in *Rodi* at 384).
[63] [1990] FSR 181.

Lord Hoffmann provided a masterful analysis of the whole subject of determination of scope of patent. He covered not only the European rules but contrasted (and criticised) the US rules, which clearly include a 'doctrine of equivalents'.[64] His intended audience was not just the UK. He was seeking to persuade other European judges to eschew woolly rules—a doctrine of equivalents which meant that some things just outside the claim were also within the monopoly. He was warning of the consequences of such an approach. One can confidently expect *Amgen* to form part of the future debate about scope of patents for many years to come. The battle is not yet over. Many Continental judges think there is a 'doctrine of equivalents' though there is nowhere near a consensus as to what it is. For the present, the UK rule is: 'The determination of the extent of protection conferred by a European patent is an examination in which there is only one compulsory question, namely that set by Art 69 and its Protocol: what would a person skilled in the art have understood the language of the claim to mean?' Lord Hoffmann has also now tackled all the other major areas of patent law, namely the most important questions concerning validity. The requirements of novelty[65] and sufficiency[66] have been clarified. His last contribution to patent law was his consideration of obviousness in *Conor v Angiotech*.[67] Two experienced patent judges (Nicholas Pumfrey at first instance) and a Court of Appeal including me were reversed, Lord Hoffmann preferring the opinion of the Dutch Court which had held the patent valid. It is perhaps too early to say how important this decision is: on one view he has endorsed the patentability of what in essence is a research programme to find out if the idea works—if indeed there is an invention.

Finally on the subject of validity, Lord Oliver's contribution in *Asahi*[68] is worthy of mention. For the House clearly and finally decided that under the EPC, the old common law muddled thinking about prior disclosure or commercialisation (the problem was which really mattered?)[69] had been superseded by a new rule: only a prior disclosure (whether by use or in a document) which *enabled* a skilled person to perform an invention counted.

One other contribution of Lord Hoffmann needs mentioning—the judicial teach-in. In *Kirin-Amgen* he arranged for the panel, in advance of the hearing, to have technical seminars about recombinant technology from Professor Yudkin of

---

[64] Under this there can be infringement by something which is *outside* the language of the claim properly construed. Some equivalents will do, but others not: which? The problem is, what are the limits of the doctrine? It is still not settled in the US and may never be. Lord Hoffmann thought probably not: '[O]nce the doctrine is allowed to go beyond the claims, a life of its own is exactly what it is bound to have.' And 'American litigants pay dearly for results which are no more just or predictable than could be achieved by simply reading the claims.'

[65] *Merrell Dow v Norton* [1996] RPC 76; *Synthon v SmithKline (No 2)* [2006] RPC 10.

[66] *Biogen v Medeva* [1997] RPC 1.   [67] [2008] 4 All ER 621.

[68] *Asahi Kasei Kogyo's Application* [1991] RPC 485.

[69] The split decision and varied reasoning in *Bristol Myers (Johnson's Application)* [1974] RPC 646 show the problem of trying to reconcile distinct grounds of attack, prior disclosure, and prior secret commercialisation.

Oxford University. The parties consented to this so there could be no objection. But the technique is clearly of general application to high technology cases and may come into more general use even if they object.[70] Some purists might question the court being taught in private in this sort of way, but I think that is unrealistic—provided any genuine point of difficulty pointed out by the 'teacher' is raised with the parties, that should satisfy any fair-minded observer as to the openness and fairness of the trial.[71]

The result of all this vigorous activity in relation to core patent law is twofold: first, the House of Lords in its last years has established clear, practical, and sensible rules which are likely to serve UK law for some years ahead. Secondly, in the event that a truly European (either EU or freestanding) patent court is established, these decisions will form valuable contributions to what will be a new, European, jurisprudence in patent law. If such a court comes,[72] then, as has already happened with trade marks and will happen with registered designs, the position of 'top' court for IP will be passed on. The recent decisions and a few more would be the last of a UK-only final court of appeal.

As regards non-core patent subjects, the House has also been active in the review period. The ragbag of subjects covered, important though they are, does not warrant detailed coverage here, particularly since in most cases they are about now-repealed or obsolete provisions of the Act.

Registered trade marks

In the review period the House considered nine trade mark cases. Seven of these were concerned with the provisions of the 1938 Act, repealed in 1994 and replaced by new, EU-based legislation. In the early part of the period Lord Diplock took a commanding position. His speech in *GE TM*[73] is a genuine masterpiece, outlining the early nineteenth century law of trade marks in the common law and at equity. It is about the need for accommodation of marks independently developed in small markets but which come into conflict later. Much of what he says is of value for today in the wider context of the European Union, where conflicting trade marks can and do emerge perfectly lawfully in different member states. His speech is still considered by European trade mark jurists today.

---

[70] The Court of Appeal recently sat with a scientific advisor who provided similar pre-hearing instruction in a case concerning computer modelling of rock drill bits: *Halliburton v Smith* [2006] EWCA Civ 1715.

[71] If a court cannot use a live teacher, is it precluded from reading books or searching the internet? All these things must surely be open to a court, provided that any point emerging is put to the parties.

[72] It is possible in the next ten years or so, but given that the project is already 50 or so years in the making, one should not hold one's breath.

[73] [1973] RPC 297.

Also of interest is Lord Diplock's speech in *SK&F's TM*.[74] An application to register as trade marks the appearance of a number of pharmaceutical capsules succeeded. The appearance was fancy, the system of colouring being to have one end of a particular colour, the other transparent through which you could see small spheres, some white, some coloured (like hundreds and thousands). Again his speech is a masterpiece. Clearly the panel that, ten years later, vehemently rejected the registration of the shape of a Coca-Cola bottle,[75] thought *SK&F* wrongly decided. But by then, as has already been observed, an anti-monopoly mood had set in. Actually the requirements of industry do extend, in appropriate cases, to registration of shapes and containers. The European Trade Marks Directive explicitly allows this.[76] The consequence, thus far, of allowing registration of shapes as famous as that of the Coca-Cola bottle, has not been the disaster for proper competition which Lord Templeman thought it would be.

Conservatism was also displayed in *York Trailer Holdings' Appn*.[77] Most people who have driven behind large lorries will have seen the trade mark York. Yet registration of the mark was refused. Lord Wilberforce gave the leading speech. It followed the official line that registration might be a restriction upon competition—a trailer maker or trader in York might be put in difficulty. Personally I thought this a bit of nonsense, though I had argued the official line for the Register of Trade Marks. Again the new European law has swept this on one side.

Passing off

The review period contains just two passing off cases. The first, *Erven Warninck v Townend*[78] decided that where a number of traders use a common term for their product (in the case concerned, 'advocaat', in the case approved, 'champagne') they can each sue a third party who deceptively uses the name for the non-genuine thing (egg-flip or 'Spanish champagne'). Lord Diplock laid down a fivefold test which, in retrospect, was not particularly successful. So the later decision, *Reckitt & Colman v Borden*,[79] went back to the 'classical trinity', reputation, misrepresentation, and damage. The only remarkable thing about the case was that the plaintiffs had been able to prove all three in relation to a lemon-shaped container of lemon juice.[80]

---

[74] [1976] RPC 511.   [75] *Coca-Cola's TM Appn* [1986] 1 WLR 695.
[76] EC 89/104 but only where the 'sign' is distinctive: see Arts 2, 3.1(b).
[77] [1984] RPC 231.   [78] [1979] AC 731.   [79] [1990] 1 All ER 873.
[80] I also got some personal satisfaction persuading my other former pupil master, Lord Bridge. He did not like it—'If I could find a way of avoiding this result, I would. And '[W]ith undisguised reluctance I agree with my noble and learned friends that this appeal should be dismissed.'

Copyright

The review period covers 11 cases involving copyright. The first [81] was something of a disaster jurisprudentially. The issue was whether the prototype for a mass-produced sofa was a 'work of artistic craftsmanship'. All five members of the court agreed it was not. But their reasons were, to put it bluntly, all over the shop. No one, here or abroad,[82] has been able to reconcile the speeches. The most interesting is that of Lord Simon of Glaisdale, who traced the phrase back to the arts and crafts movement of the late nineteenth century.

CBS v Amstrad [83] was about the provision of means (double-headed tape recorders) for copying. Could phonographic copyright owners sue the sellers of such machines because it was near certain that the machines would be used to copy recordings still in copyright? Not surprisingly the answer was no, but the problem has not gone and will not go away. Increasingly those who provide the means for copyright infringement, particularly on the internet, are likely to be made or held liable, either by courts determining existing law or by legislation. If the only way to stop piracy is to shoot the messenger, the messenger is likely to be shot.

The only other copyright case I wish to mention is *Designers Guild v Russell Williams*.[84] It was about a fabric design. The trial judge, disbelieving the defendants' claim of independent derivation, held that they had infringed. The Court of Appeal reversed on the grounds that none of the detail had been taken. The House, led by Lord Hoffmann, restored the trial judge's decision. It laid down that this sort of decision is not to be interfered with unless the judge was plainly wrong. Some members of the IP world, including the late Pumfrey LJ, were and are still surprised by the result. Some indeed say that, like *LB Plastics*,[85] the case is really authority for the proposition that liars lose.

Designs

Early in the review period the House decided *Amp v Utilux*.[86] Purely functional articles (connecting parts to go inside a washing machine), having no 'eye appeal', could not be registered as designs. The reasoning is elegant, particularly that of Lord Reid, but the result was wholly unintended. For if an article could not be registered as a design, ordinary copyright protection would run for the life of the author plus 50 years. This is what upset the House so much in *Leyland*. Whether,

---

[81] *Hensher v Restawile* [1976] AC 64.
[82] Particularly Australia, where the same phrase appears in their Copyright Act.
[83] [1988] AC 1013.   [84] [2001] FSR 11.   [85] [1979] RPC 551.
[86] [1972] RPC 103.

if the House had realised the consequence, it would have so held, remains a matter of conjecture.

Conclusion

The House has generally served IP well, and has particularly served patents very well. IP law is a lot better off for the second tier of appeal.

40

Tax Law

John Tiley and Stephen Oliver

In this chapter we look at the House of Lords and its contribution to tax law. We shall consider how a number of issues raised by Louis Blom-Cooper and Gavin Drewry in their magisterial work[1] have fared since 1970. We shall then look at the most overwhelming change, which is that tax statutes are no longer treated as distinct from other statutes;[2] as we shall see, the cases show the courts moving on from the attitudes of the *Duke of Westminster* case[3] with its strict construction and unimaginative approach to the facts. Further change may be imminent. As the final section on indirect tax shows all too well, civil law notions of fraud on the law have infiltrated the UK system through VAT. It is not correct to say that civil law notions are relevant to VAT but not to direct tax, since similar notions of 'abuse' are to be found in the European Court of Justice's decisions in direct tax matters, such as cases on relief for cross-border losses, thin capitalisation, and controlled foreign companies. One may note that while the terms 'abuse' and 'abusive transactions' have become part of the language of the European Court of Justice, there is much work still to be done in that jurisdiction to determine the nature, substance, and extent of this approach. Such cases may well in due course come before the UK's final court of appeal and it may be a matter of regret—though not surprise—that no mention was made of this dimension in *Barclays Mercantile Business Finance Ltd v Mawson*.[4] A future book reviewing the work of the new Supreme Court in this area should have much of interest and excitement to consider in relation to how these two approaches fit together.

---

[1] L Blom-Cooper and G Drewry, *Final Appeal: A Study of the House of Lords in its Judicial Capacity* (Oxford: Clarendon Press, 1972).
[2] Obvious exemplars are Lord Steyn in *IRC v McGuckian* [1997] 1 WLR 991, and Lord Nicholls speaking for the House of Lords in *Barclays Mercantile Business Finance Ltd v Mawson* [2005] 1 AC 684.
[3] *IRC v Duke of Westminster* [1936] AC 1.
[4] See *Barclays Mercantile Business Finance Ltd v Mawson* [2005] 1 AC 684.

Old issues

Numbers

In Chapter 15 of *Final Appeal*, on Revenue and Rating Appeals, Blom-Cooper and Drewry consider 133 Revenue Appeals and 23 Rating Appeals for the years 1952–70. That chapter raises a number of issues which we can address and update. The first is the number of appeals. Taking the period 1971–2008 and using the cases reported in the Tax Cases reports supplemented by some recent decisions,[5] we have had 128 direct tax appeals to the House of Lords. Cases staying at the tier below numbered 201, so just over one third of tax appeals (128/329) went on from the Court of Appeal or equivalent to the House. This is a major change from 1952–70,[6] when two out of every three cases went from the lower court.

Reversal rate

In the 128 appeals, the House reversed the court from which the appeal had come in 58 cases. However the rate of reversal is higher in recent years. Of the 26 cases heard between 1990 and 1999, the House reversed in 13; during this period 67 cases did not get beyond the Court of Appeal or equivalent. For the period since 1999 the House has reversed in 14 appeals out of 27. For 1980–9 the House reversed in 16 cases out of 45 appeals with 70 cases left at the lower level; for 1970–9 the House reversed in 13 out of 37 appeals with 46 left at the level below.

Dissents

In 128 appeals, no fewer than 103 were unanimous. Of the other 25, 15 were 3:2 splits (including *Pearson*) and ten were 4:1. Like flu, the dissenting habit was catching—in the sequence of 128 cases, five cases of dissent occurred between 25 and 31 and six between 91 and 100. The VAT cases are considered below. One VAT case was a leapfrog from the Divisional Court (the House agreed with the Divisional Court).

Reasons for decline

Explanations for the decline in the number of revenue cases reaching the Lords— in so far as one can detect it—include the virtual disappearance in 1998 of the Court of Appeal giving leave to appeal. It is clear from the conversations recorded

---

[5] And the House of Lords' decision in *Pearson v IRC* [1981] AC 753, which inexplicably did not appear in the Tax Cases reports.
[6] Blom-Cooper and Drewry (n 1) 321 n 2.

in the Tax Cases reports that before 1998 the Court of Appeal was quite willing to grant leave of its own initiative.[7] Another possible reason for the decline is that fewer appeals are now taken to the Special or General Commissioners anyway; however, this is not relevant to the proportion of appeals reaching the Lords or the rate of reversal.

Leapfrog appeals

Blom-Cooper and Drewry commented on the recent innovation of the leapfrog appeal—direct from the High Court to the House of Lords. These are started by a certificate from the High Court judge.[8] Just when one thought the leapfrog procedure moribund, one finds the combined appeals *Revenue and Customs Commissioners v William Grant & Sons Distillers Ltd* and *Small (Inspector of Taxes) v Mars UK Ltd*.[9] The *Grant* case came on appeal from the Court of Session.[10] The *Mars* case concerned exactly the same issue and had been heard by Lightman J.[11] The case as reported in the House of Lords states that leave was given under s 12 of the Administration of Justice Act 1969, though this is not mentioned in the reports of Lightman J's judgment.

Overruling cases: the 1966 Practice Statement

The first case in which the House was invited to use the Practice Statement to overrule one of its own decisions was *Fitzleet Estates Ltd v Cherry*,[12] where it was invited to overrule its (to most people very unsatisfactory) decision in *Chancery Lane Safe Deposit and Office v IRC*.[13] The judges went out of their way to say that *Chancery Lane* was correctly decided and that, even if that were not so, to overrule would impair certainty in the law which the Statement declared to be an indispensable foundation. Lord Edmund Davies put the case for overruling the earlier case in the following deliberately unconvincing form: 'The most that could be

---

[7] Leave was granted by the CA in *Colmer* [1993] STC 710 at 719, and in *Nuclear Electric plc v Bradley* [1995] STC 1125. It was refused by the Court of Appeal in *IRC v Willoughby* [1995] STC 143, *McKnight v Sheppard* [1997] STC 852, *Walker v Centaur* [1999] STC 19, [1999] STC 19, 28, and *MacNiven v Westmoreland Investments Ltd* [2001] 1 AC 311.

[8] Administration of Justice Act 1969, s 12, followed by application to the House of Lords Committee under s 13. Megarry J refused an application under s 12 in *IRC v Church Comrs* [1975] 1 WLR 251. The procedure was used in *Fitzleet v Cherry* (1977) 51 TC 708 (below); since the only point was whether the House should overrule one of its own earlier decisions this seems sensible. Leapfrog appeals were authorised in five other cases between 1978 and 1984 (by Brightman J in *Ben Odeco v Powlson* [1978] STC 360; by Walton J in *Vestey v IRC* [1977] STC 414; by Nourse J in *IRC v Metrolands Property Finance Ltd* [1981] STC 193 (a development land tax case); by Nourse J in *Pilkington Bros Ltd v IRC* [1981] STC 219; and by Vinelott J in *Payne v Barratt Developments Ltd* [1984] STC 65 (where the issue was whether *IRC v Clydebridge Properties Ltd* 1980 STC 68 should be overruled).

[9] [2007] 1 WLR 1448.   [10] [2006] STC 69.

[11] [2005] STC 958 (see All ER Rev 2005, 27.35-27.38).   [12] (1977) 51 TC 708.

[13] [1966] AC 85. See also ch 9 in this work.

properly urged on their behalf was that the 3:2 division of opinion in their Lordships house in the earlier case showed that it was a "near thing", that the decision might well have gone the other way and that the time has now come when it should.'[14] The case in which the House used the Statement to overrule its own previous decision was *Vestey v IRC (Nos 1 and 2)*.[15] Lord Wilberforce overruled *Congreve v IRC*,[16] preferring to overrule it rather than confining it to its own particular facts.[17] One may note that when the House came to overrule *IRC v Plummer*[18] in *IRC v Moodie*[19] it did so on the basis that *Plummer* was inconsistent with *Ramsay v IRC*.[20]

Three tiers or two?

Can one tell a story as to the usefulness of the tiers of appeal? Under the Taxes Management Act 1970 the normal appeal process, in England and Wales, goes from the Commissioners (Special or General) to the High Court (Chancery Division); later appeals take effect under the normal statutes regulating appeals, viz: the Administration of Justice Acts 1934 and 1969 and the Appellate Jurisdiction Act 1876 to the Court of Appeal and from there to the House of Lords. In Scotland, as shown by *IRC v Brander and Cruickshank*[21] at the start of our period and *R and C Commissioners v William Grant*[22] at the end, the appeal goes from the Commissioners (Special or General) to the Inner House of the Court of Session sitting as the Court of Exchequer in Scotland and then to the House of Lords. There is no statistical or other basis on which one can say that the House of Lords is more fallible in English cases than in Scottish ones.[23]

Has the House played a useful role?

As we have seen, the House has often overruled the lower court—and even more so recently. However, this does not show that the Court of Appeal's function is superfluous. Its members are constrained by the doctrine of precedent, and *Ramsay* represented new law because the House responded to a new argument. What would be of interest is to know what the members of the Court of Appeal, possibly sitting as a court of five, would have done if they had been the final court of appeal and the new argument had been put to them. In *Ramsay* the Court of Appeal held in favour of the Revenue on the ground that this was a debt on a

---

[14] n 12 at 721F. [15] [1980] AC 1148. [16] [1948] 1 All ER 948.
[17] [1980] STC 10, 23. [18] [1979] STC 793. [19] [1993] STC 188.
[20] Lord Templeman [1981] STC at 194e: 'If it were necessary to invoke the Practice Statement I have no doubt that this would be an appropriate course to take but in my opinion it is sufficient to state that the decision in *Plummer* would have been different if the appeal had been heard after the enunciation by this House of the *Ramsay* principle. Note the view of Sir Louis Blom-Cooper in ch 7 that *Plummer* may not have been a proper candidate for application of the Practice Statement.
[21] (1970) 46 TC. [22] [2007] STC 680.
[23] The great reforms about to be implemented make Scotland and Northern Ireland move to the English model of three tiers.

security.[24] In *Furniss v Dawson*[25] they held in the taxpayers' favour and were roundly criticised for their trouble; however, as *Craven v White* was to show, they may have been closer to the truth after all.

The Appellate Committee of the House and its membership

All members of the House have contributed to the development of our subject. Usually at least one Scottish Law Lord has sat—because of the application of tax law throughout the United Kingdom. Significantly there were two Scottish Law Lords in *Craven v White*;[26] they agreed with Lord Oliver while the other two English Law Lords, Lord Templeman and Goff, were for the Revenue.

If one looks as the actual membership of the Appellate Committee, one finds few judges with extensive tax experience. The most obvious example is Lord Nolan, who sadly found himself called to other areas of public service. However, of those currently in office in the 2000s, Lord Walker had quite wide tax experience at the Bar, while Lord Hoffmann had broad commercial experience, as did the Scottish Law Lords. Looking at earlier generations one finds many famous names having little hesitation in getting their minds round the tax legislation, so we may infer that tax expertise is not essential to an individual judge—although it may be helpful to the panel to have someone with such expertise. However there does seem to have been some resistance to appointing tax judges earlier; why else, for example, would Vinelott J have been left in the Chancery Division? What this may also reflect is the fact that tax law as an area of practice was relatively small in the 1950s. It takes time for the effects of change to seep through to the composition of the Committee, whether in relation to women, ethnic minorities, or practice minorities such as tax specialists.[27]

With the exception of *Pepper v Hart*,[28] the panel has been five; only four gave speeches in one case but only because one Lord had died after the hearing but before the speeches were delivered. In *Pepper v Hart* the first hearing was before five, but, having heard the submissions on the interpretation of the provisions, the House invited the parties to make submission on what became the rule in *Pepper v Hart*.[29] Lord Emslie, the only Scottish Law Lord on the first panel, did

---

[24] Templeman, Scarman, and Ormerod, [1979] STC 583.   [25] [1984] AC 474.

[26] [1989] AC 398.

[27] Lord Bingham was appointed Senior Law Lord in 2000; from 2002 to 2008 the Second Senior Law Lord was Lord Nicholls. Much more work will have to be done to determine the influence of these two very important individuals. Casual conversation suggests that they were seen to have been working hard to reach agreed positions and to try extremely hard to avoid very damaging 3:2 splits.

[28] [1993] AC 593.

[29] The members have contributed to the literature of the subject, notably Lord Walker (2004) 120 LQR 412, Lord Hoffmann [2005] British Tax Rev 197, and of course Lord Templeman, who in (2001) 117 LQR 575 gave the dissenting speech he would have given in *MacNiven v Westmoreland Investments* [2001] 1 AC 311 if he had not retired. The topic of tax avoidance was also touched on in Lord Oliver's address to the Annual General Meeting of the Statute Law Society, published in [1992] Statute L Rev 3.

not take part in the second hearing but this was more than made up for by the addition of Lord Mackay and Lord Keith of Kinkel—along with Lord Ackner: a heavyweight team to resolve a heavyweight issue.

In our area the bulk of issues arising has, inevitably, been on the interpretation of the tax legislation. However, the House has also made important contributions in other areas such as the use of *Hansard* in *Pepper v Hart,* and of course restitution, where *Woolwich*[30] and *Deutsche Morgan Grenfell*[31] stand out. Other issues include the question of when one can rely on statements made by a Revenue/state official[32] and the scope of legal privilege.[33] Other constitutional law issues include the standing of extra-statutory concessions under which HMRC agree not to impose tax in various situations—*IRC v Vestey*[34] and *R v IRC, ex p National Federation of the Self Employed.*[35] On trusts we have *Carver v Duncan*[36] and *Pearson v IRC.*[37]

Interpretation and application

The predominant concern of the House has been to modernise its approach to questions of interpretation—and application—and to explore the limits of its powers to control avoidance. In 1972 Blom-Cooper and Drewry wrote that their text highlighted the attitudes of the court towards matters of construction which, while usually speaking in favour of strict construction, did not always do so. Some judges protested that tax statutes should be treated similarly to other statutes. Beginning probably in 1981 with *IRC v Ramsay*[38] but with hints of exasperation in earlier cases, the House has been on something of a journey. The journey proper began with *Ramsay,* because that was when the composite transaction approach was first put to the House of Lords itself. A series of transactions began with a share purchase and two loans. By the alchemy of a series of transactions this was converted, it was hoped, into an allowable loss on the shares and a non-chargeable gain on the loans because they were debts as opposed to debts on a security. The transactions were not only interconnected but also self-cancelling, like particles in a gas chamber; they were also completely freestanding, having no connection with any business or other transaction; in that sense—and probably in many others—the transactions were artificial. For the tax system to have allowed such a scheme to succeed would have been disastrous.

---

[30] *Woolwich Equitable Building Society v IRC* [1993] AC 70. [31] [2007] 1 AC 558.
[32] *Matrix Securities v IRC* [1994] 1 WLR 769.
[33] *R v Special Comr, ex p Morgan Grenfell* [2002] STC 786.
[34] [1980] AC 1148.   [35] [1981] All ER 93.
[36] [1985] AC 1082 (Lord Diplock dissenting)
[37] [1981] AC 753. Here the majority in favour of the Revenue consisted of Lords Dilhorne, Keith, and Lane; Lords Salmon and Russell dissented. As the Court of Appeal (unanimously) and Fox J had also been for the taxpayer, six judges were for the taxpayer and just three were for the Revenue.
[38] [1982] AC 300.

The story culminates in *Barclays Mercantile Business Finance Ltd v Mawson*.[39] *Barclays* is a culmination, in that it settled the nature of the doctrine, almost to the point of saying it was not a doctrine at all but simply an approach to questions of interpretation of law and the analysis of facts.[40]

One explanation sometimes offered for the tradition of strict construction was that the judges were not familiar with the interstices. That is no longer necessarily so. The final examination for both the Bar Council and the Law Society came to require an understanding of Revenue Law for those wanting to practise in this country, even though the Bar later relaxed this requirement. Whether or not they were familiar with the tax legislation, no one could accuse judges of our era of being reticent on such matters.[41]

In *Ramsay*, Lord Wilberforce went to great lengths to show that the decision of the House was consistent with the *Duke of Westminster* case.[42] It did not undermine what he called 'the cardinal principle' of *Inland Revenue Commissioners v Duke of Westminster* that where a document or transaction is genuine, the court cannot go behind it to some supposed underlying substance.[43]

The cardinal principle was noted by Lord Diplock in *IRC v Burmah*, though he added[44] that it did not tell one very much about which methods of ordering one's affairs would be effective after *Ramsay*. Further doubts were raised by the decision in *Furniss v Dawson*,[45] where the House extended the approach to a transaction which had not gone full circle and so was still linear. Further, it applied it to a transaction of corporate reorganisation which was miles away from the scheme in *Ramsay*.[46] In *Furniss v Dawson* the issue was whether a transfer made by A to B and then by B to C should be treated as two distinct transfers, in which case a deferral of tax arose under the reorganisation rules, or whether it was treated as one transfer (from A to C) so that there was no deferral.

In *Furniss v Dawson* Lord Brightman famously said:[47]

... [T]he rationale of the new approach is this. In a pre-planned tax saving scheme, no distinction is to be drawn for fiscal purposes, because none exists in reality, between (i) a series of steps which are followed through by virtue of an arrangement which falls short of

---

[39] [2005] 1 AC 684.

[40] *Barclays* is also a culmination in the sense that a series of later House of Lords decisions have been determined in favour of the Revenue, which might not have been so decided earlier. Such victories include *Macdonald v Dextra Accessories Ltd* [2005] 4 All ER 107 and the Captial Gains tax case of *West v Trennery* [2005] 1 All ER 827; they may also have been surprised by their success in the *Scottish Provident* case [2004] 1 WLR 3172.

[41] For the dominating early influence of Lord Wilberforce (*Ramsay*) and Lord Diplock (*IRC v Burmah*) see D Robertson, *Judicial Discretion in the House of Lords* (Oxford: OUP, 1998).

[42] *IRC v Duke of Westminster* [1936] AC 1.

[43] Interestingly, the *Westminster* case was not even cited in *Barclays Mercantile Business Finance Ltd v Mawson* [2005] 1 AC 684.

[44] [1982] STC 30, 320.   [45] [1984] AC 474, [1984] STC 153.

[46] A corporate reorganisation had also been in issue in *Burmah Oil* but there the transaction had gone full circle.

[47] [1984] AC 474, 527, [1984] STC 153, 166g.

a binding contract, and (ii) a like series of steps which are followed through because the participants are contractually bound to take each step seriatim . . . *Ramsay* says that the fiscal result is to be no different if the several steps are preordained rather than pre-contracted.

So *Ramsay* is an approach to schemes whose steps are 'preordained' rather than contractually binding. Then we have 'the rule', taken from Lord Diplock in *Burmah,* who had expressed what Lord Brightman called the limitations of the *Ramsay* principle:[48]

First, there must be a preordained series of transactions; or, if one likes, one single composite transaction. This composite transaction may or may not include the achievement of a legitimate commercial (ie business) end. The composite transaction does, in the instant case; it achieved a sale of the shares in [the companies] by [A] to [C]. It did not in *Ramsay.* Secondly, there must be steps inserted which have no commercial (business) *purpose* apart from the avoidance of a liability to tax—not 'no business *effect*'. If those two ingredients exist, the inserted steps are to be disregarded for fiscal purposes. The court must then look at the end result. Precisely how the end result will be taxed will depend on the terms of the taxing statute sought to be applied.

The problem *Furniss v Dawson* left was the nature and scope of the new rule (or principle or approach) and judges went out of their way to stress the early nature of the development. Towards the end of the journey, in the *MacNiven* case, Lord Nicholls said:[49]

My Lords, I readily accept that the factual situation described by Lord Brightman is one where, typically, the *Ramsay* approach will be a valuable aid. In such a situation, when ascertaining the legal nature of the transaction and then relating this to the statute, application of the *Ramsay* approach may well have the effect stated by Lord Brightman. *But, as I am sure Lord Brightman would be the first to acknowledge,* the *Ramsay* approach is no more than a useful aid. This is not an area for absolutes. The paramount question always is one of interpretation of the particular statutory provision and its application to the facts of the case.

Notwithstanding Lord Nicholls' eminence and valuable contributions in this area, the historian may doubt whether Lord Brightman would have made that acknowledgement. Most likely he would not have rejected it either and it was far more likely that he would have said that it was too early to say.

The deliberate intellectual vacuum resulting from *Furniss v Dawson* was not appreciated by judges in some jurisdictions in which the *Westminster* approach was accepted doctrine. In Canada, Estey J said that the UK case law was to be rejected if it introduced a general business purpose test; the best he could do was to assist the Revenue authorities by introducing a purposive approach to interpretation.[50] This is of course where the UK courts have ended up after *Barclays.*

48 [1982] STC 30, 320; emphasis in the original.
49 *MacNiven v Westmoreland Investments* [2001] 1 AC 311, at [8]; emphasis added.
50 *Stubart Investment Ltd v R* [1984] CTC 294.

The Canadian court also said that the presence of Canada's statutory General Anti-Avoidance Rule (or GAAR, as tax lawyers like to refer to such things) was a reason not to adopt the general business purpose test. From Ireland we have *McGrath v McDermott*,[51] where the Supreme Court also rejected the doctrine of 'fiscal nullity' as set out in *Furniss v Dawson*. The Irish Tax Appeal Commissioners had decided that the new approach in the leading UK cases qualified the *Duke of Westminster's Case*; the higher judges held that they did not. The Irish court cited the *absence* of a GAAR in their system as a reason for not following *Ramsay*. The Australian High Court also rejected the 'fiscal nullity' version of the new approach—in *John v Commissioner of Taxation*.[52] Like the other two cases, this decision was just too early to take account of the decision of the House of Lords in *Craven v White*.[53] The court also said that the presence of Australia's statutory GAAR 'made it impossible to place upon other provisions of the Act a qualification which they do not express for the purpose of inhibiting tax avoidance'.[54]

Uncertainty as to the nature of the new approach was inherent in the journey the judges had chosen to take. The Inland Revenue, taking a literal rather than contextual approach to what the judges had said, regarded it as a rule to be applied in many situations. If it was a rule, was it a rule like the pre-1964 rule against perpetuities, which was one of almost mathematical precision, or was it a principle like *Donoghue v Stevenson*?

Clarification first came in three joined appeals in 1988. In *Craven v White* the House decided that the doctrine applied to join up the various steps and make the transfer one from A to C only where it was 'practically certain' at the time of the first transfer (from A to B) that the B–C transfer would follow—and did. This narrowing was designed to make the rule workable and to reconcile the words of the judges and the words of the statute. Further clarification came in *MacNiven*,[55] where the Revenue presented the House with a circular transaction. The House held that the very question whether the doctrine applied was a question of construction. So the mere fact that the transaction could be made to fit within Lord Brightman's words did not mean that the words had to be applied; the prior question of construction had to be addressed. It was an approach, not a rule.

That should have been the end of things, but Lord Hoffmann offered an explanation of the case law rule in terms of a distinction between concepts that were commercial (where the approach applied) and those that were legal (where it did not). This proved unhelpful and even unworkable, and caused much (increasingly despairing) argument over the next few years. Such straitjackets were quietly jettisoned in the *Barclays* case.[56]

It is tempting to be judgmental about the performance of the judges in this area and criticise them for their deliberate lack of clarity. The detail—and an

[51] [1988] IR 258.   [52] (1988) 166 CLR 417.   [53] [1989] AC 398.
[54] Citing Gibbs J in *Federal Comr of Taxation v Patcorp Investments Ltd* (1976) 140 CLR at 292.
[55] *MacNiven v Westmoreland Investments* [2001] 1 AC 311.
[56] *Barclays Mercantile Business Finance Ltd v Mawson* [2005] 1 AC 684, para 32.

account of the intervening case law—are best left to the professional journals and books. One may, however, argue that the judges were right to be hesitant and that they needed to see more areas of avoidance so as to get the scale of the problem before committing themselves too firmly. One may note, though, that part of the problem with the case law was the Inland Revenue's analysis of what the judges had done. The persistence with which they argued for some sort of rule rather than an approach to questions of construction led to their downfall in *MacNiven* and *Barclays*. As Lord Hoffmann said of the proposition put forward in *MacNiven*:[57]

I am bound to say that this does not look to me like a principle of construction at all . . . [Counsel/Mr McCall's] formulation looks like an overriding legal principle, superimposed upon the whole of revenue law without regard to the language or purpose of any particular provision, save for the possibility of rebuttal by language which can be brought within [his final parenthesis].

The Revenue would have been much better advised to have taken the 'practical certainty' approach in *Craven v White* and argue that while, as a matter of construction, this very severe test might be right for corporate reorganisations, it was not the only test and that some less demanding test might be relevant in other areas. Whether they also need a statutory General Anti Avoidance Rule is a matter for them and for Parliament—it is not for the judges to give them one. Meanwhile, and for connected reasons, the state of the tax statute book gets worse and worse—with long, detailed, and highly prescriptive provisions which, Lord Hoffmann has pointed out, do not give the judges much leeway in reaching 'purposive' interpretations.

The House of Lords' contribution to indirect taxes

The contribution of the House of Lords to VAT law has been sparing. This reflects the position of VAT law, which falls substantially within the framework of the EC Sixth Council Directive of 1977 (the Sixth Directive). The decision of the European Court of Justice in *Becker v Finanzamt Munster-Innenstadt*[58] established that the Sixth Directive had direct effect, always so long as the Community law provision relied upon was 'clear and precise' and 'unconditional'. This signalled the primacy of the ECJ in indirect tax disputes. The issues of principle have been determined by the ECJ and the House of Lords has been left to interpret and apply the ECJ's rulings.

The figures are significant. In the 35 years since VAT was introduced, there have been 16 appeals to the House of Lords; four of those resulted in references to

---

[57] *MacNiven v Westmoreland Investments* [2001] 1 AC 311, para 29.
[58] Case 8/81 [1982] ECR 53.

the ECJ. In 2006, when no VAT appeals were heard by the House of Lords, the ECJ dealt with 30 references in VAT matters; one third of those came from the UK under the Article 234 reference procedure and half of those were made by the tribunal of first instance (the VAT and Duties Tribunals). The practitioners in this field of the law have come to realise that a reference to the ECJ by the tribunal is a cheaper and quicker way of resolving the dispute than taking the potentially long climb through the High Court and the Court of Appeal to the House of Lords and then possibly finding the matter referred on to the ECJ.

Until the impact of *Becker* was felt, the more important VAT rulings of the House of Lords had focused on the scope of the tax and on the jurisdiction of the VAT Tribunal. In *Customs and Excise Commissioners v Thorn Electrical Industries Ltd*[59] the *vires* of regulations issued under the Finance Act 1972 that treated as a supply the discharge of obligations under a hiring agreement entered into before VAT had been introduced was in issue; the House of Lords ruled that the regulations were effective. In *Customs and Excise Commissioners v JH Corbitt (Numismatists) Ltd*[60] the jurisdiction of the tribunal was in issue. Was there a right of appeal against the exercise of the discretion given to Customs and Excise refusing permission for the use of the second-hand 'margin scheme'? The House of Lords ruled that the VAT Tribunal had only a conventional appellate jurisdiction; in the result that domestic law was modified to bring such appeals into the VAT Tribunals' jurisdiction.

Since *Becker* the Lords have been concerned with no further issues relating to the structure and management of VAT. *Customs and Excise Commissioners v Fine Art Developments*[61] was the last of the appeals on VAT relating purely to domestic law. There the Lords had the opportunity to develop restitutionary principles in the field of tax and thereby recognised the right of a taxpayer who had overpaid output tax in past accounting periods to deduct the amounts overpaid from the tax due under its current return.

In *Fleming v R and CCC*[62] the House held that a time limit introduced by the UK Parliament broke a general principle of EC law. The UK had introduced a three-year time limit without warning and without transitional provisions. This deprived many businesses of the right to reclaim tax overpaid in earlier years or to claim relief for those years. The House ruled that this violated the EC principle of effectiveness and referred the matter back to the UK authorities to devise an appropriate transitional period.

The focus of the issues before the Lords in the last 20 years has been on the application of words and phrases of the Sixth Directive. What was the Community law meaning to be given to the term 'consideration'? The traditional English law sense was too narrow; instead the Lords adopted the concept of 'direct link'. Those were the issues in *Customs and Excise Commissioners v Apple*

---

[59] [1975] 1 WLR 1661.   [60] [1981] AC 22.   [61] [1989] AC 914.
[62] [2008] 1 WLR 195.

and *Pear Development Council*[63] and in *Customs and Excise Commissioners v Professional Footballers' Association (Enterprises) Ltd.*[64] Can one package of supplies with taxable and exempt ingredients be split into two separate supplies, or must it rank as a single composite supply and take its taxable character from the dominant element? The House of Lords in *Card Protection Plan v Customs and Excise Commissioners*[65] referred the matter to the European Court of Justice and later interpreted this ruling in a manner that has provided a solid route map that has clarified what had been a divergent set of principles. That led on to the conclusion in *HMRC v College of Estate Management*[66] that a supply of printed materials (normally zero-rated) was part of a wider exempt supply of education.

What was the extent of the expression 'economic activities' in the Sixth Directive? *Institute of Chartered Accountants in England and Wales v Customs and Excise Commissioners*[67] established that the statutorily governed regular activities of the Institute were outside their scope, notwithstanding that they were provided to members for a consideration. Then came *Redrow Group plc v Customs and Excise Commissioners*,[68] an important decision on the direction of supply. Did the house builder who paid for the supplies of estate agents' services to potential purchasers of new houses receive the supplies, or were they received by the direct beneficiaries, the prospective purchasers?

So far we have looked at those few opportunities presented to the House of Lords where they have enlightened the VAT code. But what contribution has the House of Lords made in the field of VAT avoidance?

In contrast to the proactive approach of the House of Lords to the avoidance of direct taxes, its approach to VAT avoidance has been deferential. The court took a lead from Lord Hoffmann in *Robert Gordon College v Customs and Excise Commissioners*[69] and later in *Customs and Excise Commissioners v Thorn Materials Supply*.[70] Lord Hoffmann declined to admit any approach that involved taking a 'global' view of a series of transactions that were accepted to have been genuine contracts carried out to achieve a tax avoidance objective. The *Ramsay* principle had no application to VAT avoidance. That message signalled the start of eight years of energetic VAT avoidance of unimaginable ingenuity.

But the attention of the House of Lords and the tax planners had not been caught by the distant drums of the emerging principle of 'abuse of rights' developing case by case in the European Court of Justice throughout the 1990s. As it happened, *Mawson*[71] was presented to the House of Lords without any mention of the fact that, at the same time, the full Chamber of the ECJ was considering the reference from England in *Halifax*, a VAT avoidance case.[72] There are in consequence two anti-avoidance judge-made doctrines, the product

---

[63] [1986] STC 192.   [64] [1993] 1 WLR 153.   [65] [2002] 1 AC 202.
[66] [2005] STC 1579.   [67] [1999] STC 398.   [68] [1999] STC 161.
[69] [1996] 1 WLR 201.   [70] [1998] STC 725.
[71] *Barclays Mercantile Business Finance Ltd v Mawson* [2005] 1 AC 684.
[72] Case C255/02 [2006] STC 919.

of the two courts; and there is a now joined-up revenue authority with an interest in a reconciliation between the two approaches. A start might have been made—but was not advanced—in *R and CCC v Principal and Fellows of Newnham College*.[73] With the parties' agreement they approached the matter on 'traditional' lines. The College, described by Lord Hoffmann as 'famously poor', sought relief for the input tax incurred on the costs of a new library building.

No relief would have been available if the college had been in occupation of the premises; so the College leased the library and seconded the library staff to a company controlled by it, and sold the library assets to the company and hired them back for the use of its members. Taking the traditional approach rather than re-analysing the transaction on *Halifax* lines, the (bare) majority of the House decided in favour of the College. The College had not been in occupation of the library premises and so was entitled to reclaim the input tax.

As we noted at the beginning of this chapter, the Supreme Court will no doubt have further work in this area.

[73] [2008] 1 WLR 888.

Lords of Appeal in Ordinary from 1876

	Name and title/ Lifespan	Period served [y = years m = months]	Appointed by [Prime Minister and (party)/ Lord Chancellor]	Age when first appointed
1	Blackburn of Killearn (Colin) 1813–96	1876–87 10y 3m	Disraeli (Conservative)/ Cairns	63
2	Gordon of Drumearn (Edward) 1814–79	1876–9 2y 10m	Disraeli (Conservative)/ Cairns	62
3	Watson (William) 1827–99	1880–99 9y 5m	Gladstone (Liberal)/ Selborne	53
4	FitzGerald of Kilmarnock (John) 1816–89	1882–9 7y 4m	Gladstone (Liberal)/ Selborne	66
5	Macnaghten (Edward) 1830–1913	1887–1913 26y 1m	Salisbury (Conservative)/ Halsbury	57
6	Morris (Michael) 1827–1901	1889–1900 10 y 5m	Salisbury (Conservative)/ Halsbury	62
7	Hannen (James) 1821–94	1891–3 2y 7m	Salisbury (Conservative)/ Halsbury	70
8	Bowen of Colwood (Charles) 1835–94	1893–4 7m	Gladstone (Liberal)/ Herschell	58
9	Russell of Killowen (Charles) 1832–1900	1894 1m	Gladstone (Liberal)/ Herschell	62
10	Davey (Horace) 1833–1907	1894–1907 12y 6m	Gladstone (Liberal)/ Herschell	61
11	Lindley (Nathaniel) 1828–1921	1899–1905 6y 7m	Salisbury (Conservative)/ Halsbury	62
12	Robertson (James) 1845–1909	1899–1909 9y 3m	Salisbury (Conservative)/ Halsbury	54
13	Atkinson (John) 1844–1932	1905–28 22y 1m	Campbell-Bannerman (Liberal)/ Loreburn	61
14	Collins (Richard) 1842–1911	1907–10 3y 5m	Campbell-Bannerman (Liberal)/ Loreburn	65
15	Shaw of Dunfermline (Thomas) 1850–1937	1909–29 20y 3m	Asquith (Liberal)/Loreburn	59
16	Robson (William) 1852–1918	1910–12 2y	Asquith (Liberal)/Loreburn	58
17	Moulton (John Fletcher) 1844–1921	1912–21 8y 5m	Asquith (Liberal)/Loreburn	68

(cont.)

[1] Sources: *Oxford Dictionary of National Biography* (2004); Maxwell Barrett, *The Law Lords* (2001); www.the peerage.com (last visited 2 January 2009).

	Name and title/ Lifespan	Period served [y = years m = months]	Appointed by [Prime Minister and (party)/ Lord Chancellor]	Age when first appointed
18	Parker of Waddington (Robert) 1857–1918	1913–18 5y 4m	Asquith (Liberal)/Haldane	56
19	Dunedin (Andrew [Murray]) Viscount from 1926 1849–1942	1913–32 18y 6m	Asquith (Liberal)/Haldane	64
20	Sumner (John [Hamilton]), Viscount from 1927 1859–1943	1913–30 16y 3m	Asquith (Liberal)/Haldane	54
21	Cave (George) Viscount from 1918 1856–1928	1918–22 3y 11m	Lloyd George (Liberal)/ Finlay	62
22	Carson (Edward) 1854–1935	1921–9 8y 6m	Lloyd George (Liberal)/ Birkenhead	67
23	Blanesburgh (Robert [Younger]) 1861–1946	1923–37 13y 6m	Bonar Law (Conservative)/ Cave	62
24	Atkin (Richard – Dick) 1867–1944	1928–44 16y 5m	Baldwin (Conservative)/ Cave	61
25	Tomlin (Thomas) 1867–1935	1929–35 6y 6m	Baldwin (Conservative)/ Hailsham	62
26	Thankerton (William [Watson]) 1873–1948	1929–48 19y 1m	Baldwin (Conservative)/ Hailsham	56
27	Russell of Killowen (Frank) 1867–1946	1929–46 17y 1m	MacDonald (Labour)/ Sankey	62
28	Macmillan (Hugh) 1873–1952	1930–9 and 1941–7 15y 5m	MacDonald (Labour)/ Sankey	57
29	Wright (Robert) 1869–1964	1932–5 and 1937–47 13y 5m	MacDonald (Labour)/ Sankey	63
30	Maugham (Frederic) Viscount from 1939 1866–1958	1935–8 and 1939–41 4y 2m	Baldwin (Conservative)/ Hailsham; Chamberlain (Conservative)/ Caldecote	69
31	Roche (Alexander) 1871–1956	1935–8 2y 3m	Baldwin (Conservative)/ Hailsham; Chamberlain (Conservative)/ Maugham	64
32	Romer (Mark) 1866–1944	1938–44 6y 7m		72
33	Porter (Samuel) 1877–1956	1938–54 16 y 7m	Chamberlain (Conservative)/ Maugham	61
34	Simonds (Gavin) Viscount from 1954 1881–1971	1944–51 and 1954–62 14y 11m	Churchill (Conservative)/ Simon; Churchill (Conservative)/Kilmuir	63
35	Goddard (Rayner) 1877–1971	1944–6 1y 6m	Churchill (Conservative)/ Simon	67
36	Uthwatt (Augustus) 1879–1949	1946–9 3y 3m	Attlee (Labour)/Jowitt	67
37	Du Parcq (Herbert) 1880–1949	1946–9 3y 3m	Attlee (Labour)/Jowitt	66
38	Normand (Wilfrid) 1884–1962	1947–53 6y 9m	Attlee (Labour)/Jowitt	63

(cont.)

	Name and title/ Lifespan	Period served [y = years m = months]	Appointed by [Prime Minister and (party)/ Lord Chancellor]	Age when first appointed
39	Oaksey (Geoffrey Lawrence) 1880–1971	1947–57 10y	Attlee (Labour)/Jowitt	67
40	Morton of Henryton (Fergus) 1887–1973	1947–59 12y	Attlee (Labour)/Jowitt	60
41	MacDermott (John) 1896–1979	1947–51 3y 11m	Attlee (Labour)/Jowitt	51
42	Reid (John Cumberland Scott) 1890–1975	1948–75 26y 4m	Attlee (Labour)/Jowitt	58
43	Greene (Wilfrid) 1883–1952	1949–50 11m	Attlee (Labour)/Jowitt	66
44	Radcliffe (Cyril) Viscount from 1962 1899–1977	1949–64 5y 4m	Attlee (Labour)/Jowitt	50
45	Tucker (Frederick) 1888–1975	1950–61 11y	Attlee (Labour)/Jowitt	62
46	Asquith of Bishopstone (Cyril) 1890–1954	1951–4 3y 4m	Attlee (Labour)/Jowitt	61
47	Cohen (Lionel) 1888–1973	1951–60 8y 11m	Churchill (Conservative)/ Simonds	63
48	Keith of Avonholm (James) 1886–1964	1953–61 7y 2m	Churchill (Conservative)/ Simonds	67
49	Somervell of Harrow (Donald) 1889–1960	1954–60 5y 3m	Churchill (Conservative)/ Simonds	65
50	Denning (Thomas) 1899–1999	1957–62 5y	Macmillan (Conservative)/ Kilmuir	58
51	Jenkins (David) 1899–1969	1959–63 4y 8m	Macmillan (Conservative)/ Kilmuir	60
52	Morris of Borth-y-Gest (John William) 1896–1979	1960–75 15y	Macmillan (Conservative)/ Kilmuir	64
53	Hodson (Charles) 1895–1984	1960–71 10y 6m	Macmillan (Conservative)/ Kilmuir	65
54	Guest (Christopher) 1901–84	1961–71 10y 7m	Macmillan (Conservative)/ Kilmuir	60
55	Devlin (Patrick) 1905–92	1961–4 2y 3m	Macmillan (Conservative)/ Kilmuir	56
56	Evershed (Raymond) 1899–1966	1962–5 2y 9m	Macmillan (Conservative)/ Kilmuir	63
57	Pearce (Edward Holroyd) 1901–90	1962–9 7y 1m	Macmillan (Conservative)/ Kilmuir	61
58	Upjohn (Gerald) 1903–71	1963–71 7y 2m	Douglas-Home (Conservative)/ Dilhorne	60
59	Donovan (Terence) 1898–1971	1964–71 7y 11m	Douglas-Home (Conservative)/ Dilhorne	65

	Name and title/ Lifespan	Period served [y = years m = months]	Appointed by [Prime Minister and (party)/ Lord Chancellor]	Age when first appointed
60	Wilberforce (Richard) 1907–2003	1964–83 17y 5m	Douglas-Home (Conservative)/ Dilhorne	57
61	Pearson (Colin) 1899–1980	1965–74 9y 7m	Wilson (Labour)/Gardiner	66
62	Diplock (Kenneth) 1907–85	1968–85 17y 1m	Wilson (Labour)/Gardiner	61
63	Dilhorne (Reginald [Manningham-Buller]), Viscount from 1964 1905–80	1969–80 11y 2m	Wilson (Labour)/Gardiner	64
64	Cross of Chelsea (Geoffrey) 1904–89	1971–5 4y 7m	Heath (Conservative)/ Hailsham	66
65	Simon of Glaisdale (Jocelyn [Jack]) 1911–2006	1971–7 6y 5m	Heath (Conservative)/ Hailsham	60
66	Kilbrandon (Jim) 1906–89	1971–6 5y 3m	Heath (Conservative)/ Hailsham	65
67	Salmon (Cyril) 1903–91	1972–80 8y 9m	Heath (Conservative)/ Hailsham	68
68	Edmund-Davies (Herbert) 1906–92	1974–81 7y	Wilson (Labour)/ Elwyn-Jones	68
69	Fraser of Tullybelton (Ian) 1911–89	1975–85 10y 10m	Wilson (Labour)/ Elwyn-Jones	63
70	Russell of Killowen (Charles) 1908–86	1975–82 6y 10m	Wilson (Labour)/ Elwyn-Jones	67
71	Keith of Kinkel (Harry) 1922–2002	1977–96 19y 10m	Callaghan (Labour)/ Elwyn-Jones	54
72	Scarman (Leslie) 1911–2004	1977–86 9y	Callaghan (Labour)/Elwyn- Jones	66
73	Lane (Geoffrey) 1918–2005	1979–80 8m	Thatcher (Conservative)/ Hailsham	61
74	Roskill (Eustace) 1911–96	1980–6 5y 9m	Thatcher (Conservative)/ Hailsham	69
75	Bridge of Harwich (Nigel) 1917–2007	1980–92 11y 5m	Thatcher (Conservative)/ Hailsham	63
76	Brandon of Oakbrook (Henry) 1920–99	1981–91 10y	Thatcher (Conservative)/ Hailsham	61
77	Brightman (John) 1911–2006	1982–7 5y 3m	Thatcher (Conservative)/ Hailsham	71
78	Templeman (Sydney) 1920–	1982–94 12y	Thatcher (Conservative)/ Hailsham	62
79	Griffiths (Hugh) 1923–	1985–93 8y 4m	Thatcher (Conservative)/ Hailsham	61
80	Mackay of Clashfern (James) 1927–	1985–7 2y 1m	Thatcher (Conservative)/ Hailsham	58

(cont.)

	Name and title/ Lifespan	Period served [y = years m = months]	Appointed by [Prime Minister and (party)/ Lord Chancellor]	Age when first appointed
81	Ackner (Desmond) 1920–2006	1986–92 6y 8m	Thatcher (Conservative)/ Hailsham	66
82	Oliver of Aylmerton (Peter) 1921–2007	1986–91 5y 11m	Thatcher (Conservative)/ Hailsham	64
83	Goff of Chieveley (Robert) 1926–	1986–98 11y 2m	Thatcher (Conservative)/ Hailsham	59
84	Jauncey of Tullichettle (Charles) 1925–2007	1988–96 8y 8m	Thatcher (Conservative)/ Mackay	62
85	Lowry (Robert) 1919–99	1988–94 5y 5m	Thatcher (Conservative)/ Mackay	69
86	Browne-Wilkinson (Nicholas) 1930–	1991–2000 8y 9m	Major (Conservative)/ Mackay	61
87	Mustill (Michael) 1931–	1992–7 5y 3m	Major (Conservative)/ Mackay	60
88	Slynn of Hadley (Gordon) 1930–2009	1992–2002 10y 7m	Major (Conservative)/ Mackay	62
89	Woolf (Harry) 1933–	1992–6 3y 8m	Major (Conservative)/ Mackay	59
90	Lloyd of Berwick (Anthony) 1929–	1993–8 5y 3m	Major (Conservative)/ Mackay	64
91	Nolan (Michael) 1928–2007	1994–8 4y 9m	Major (Conservative)/ Mackay	65
92	Nicholls of Birkenhead (Donald) 1933–	1994–2007 12y 3m	Major (Conservative)/ Mackay	61
93	Steyn (Johan) 1932–	1995–2005 10y 9m	Major (Conservative)/ Mackay	62
94	Hoffmann (Leonard) 1934–2009	1995–2009 14y 2m	Major (Conservative)/ Mackay	60
95	Clyde (James) 1932–	1996–2001 5y	Major (Conservative)/ Mackay	64
96	Hope of Craighead (David) 1938–	1996–	Major (Conservative)/ Mackay	58
97	Hutton (Brian) 1931–	1997–2003 7y	Major (Conservative)/ Mackay	65
98	Saville of Newdigate (Mark) 1936–	1997–	Blair (Labour)/Irvine	61
99	Hobhouse of Woodborough (John) 1932–2003	1998–2003 5y 3m	Blair (Labour)/Irvine	66
100	Millett (Peter) 1932–	1998–2003 5y 3m	Blair (Labour)/Irvine	66
101	Phillips of Worth Matravers (Nicholas) 1938–	1999–2000 1y 5m 2008–	Blair (Labour)/Irvine; Brown (Labour)/Straw	60
102	Bingham of Cornhill (Thomas) 1933–	2000–8 8y 4m	Blair (Labour)/Irvine	66

Name and title/ Lifespan	Period served [y = years m = months]	Appointed by [Prime Minister and (party)/ Lord Chancellor]	Age when first appointed
103 Scott of Foscote[2] (Richard) 1934–	2000–9 9y 2m	Blair (Labour)/Irvine	65
104 Rodger of Earlsferry (Alan) 1944–	2001–	Blair (Labour)/Irvine	57
105 Walker of Gestingthorpe (Robert) 1938–	2002–	Blair (Labour)/Irvine	64
106 Hale of Richmond (Brenda) 1945–	2004	Blair (Labour)/Falconer	58
107 Carswell (Robert) 1934–	2004–9 5y 6m	Blair (Labour)/Falconer	69
108 Brown of Eaton-under-Heywood (Simon) 1937–	2004–	Blair (Labour)/Falconer	66
109 Mance (Jonathan) 1943–	2005–	Blair (Labour)/Falconer	62
110 Neuberger of Abbotsbury (David) 1948–	2007–	Blair (Labour)/Falconer	58
111 Collins of Mapesbury (Lawrence) 1941–	2009–	Brown (Labour)/Straw	67
112 Kerr (Brian) 1948–	2009–	Brown (Labour)/Straw	61

[2] Lord Scott is due to retire on 30 September 2009, to be replaced on 1 October 2009 in the Supreme Court of the United Kingdom by Lord Clarke who, as Sir Anthony Clarke, has served as Master of the Rolls since 2005.

Who Succeeded Whom?

The Appellate Jurisdiction Act 1876 allowed for two Lords of Appeal to be appointed immediately, and for up to two more to be appointed when vacancies arose among the salaried judicial posts in the Privy Council. The first such vacancy occurred in 1882 and the second in 1891.

The maximum permitted number of Lords of Appeal was then raised to six by the Appellate Jurisdiction Act 1913, to seven by the Appellate Jurisdiction Act 1929, to nine by the Appellate Jurisdiction Act 1947, to 11 by the Appellate Jurisdiction Act 1968, and to 12 by the Maximum Number of Judges Order 1994 (SI 1994/3217).

The number of Lords of Appeal appointed kept pace with the maximum number permitted until September 1968, when only one additional judge (Lord Diplock), not two as permitted, was appointed under the Appellate Jurisdiction Act 1968, making the number in office ten, rather than the permitted 11. This remained the position until January 1975, when Lords Reid and Morris both retired. But rather than replace both of those Lords of Appeal, or appoint three, to bring the number up to the permitted maximum, only one was appointed (Lord Fraser). This left the number of Lords of Appeal in post at nine.

The number in post did not rise to ten until the appointment of Lord Lane in September 1979, but it was reduced again to nine in 1980 with the retirement of Viscount Dilhorne. It was a full five years before a tenth Lord of Appeal was again appointed (Lord Griffiths). The number fell again to nine in June 1987 (when Lord Brightman retired) and to eight in October 1987 (when Lord Mackay took over as Lord Chancellor), but it rose again to nine in February 1988 (with Lord Jauncey's appointment) and to ten in August 1988 (Lord Lowry).

Lord Slynn's appointment in March 1992 brought the complement to 11 for the first time, 24 years after the authorisation to do so. The twelfth position in the Lords was made available in 1994 and was taken almost immediately by Lord Hoffmann. Since then there have been 12 Lords of Appeal in post at any one time (except between June 1996, when Lord Woolf became master of the Rolls, and January 1997, when Lord Hutton took the vacancy), although other commitments (such as Lord Saville's chairing of the Bloody Sunday Tribunal of Inquiry, and Lord Hutton's chairing of the Inquiry into the death of Dr David Kelly) have from time to time meant that the number of Lords of Appeal actually available to deal with appeals has been less than the maximum.

In the Table that follows, the names of five judges appear twice. Lord Macmillan was first appointed in 1930 but in 1939 he took up a Ministerial post for two years. He was reappointed as a Lord of Appeal in 1941. Lord Wright was first appointed in 1932 but was then made Master of the Rolls in 1935. He was reappointed as a Lord of Appeal in 1937. Lord Maugham was first appointed in 1935 but from 1938 he served for a brief period as Lord Chancellor. Shortly after relinquishing that position he was reappointed as a Lord of Appeal in 1939. Lord Simonds had the same experience as Lord Maugham: he was first appointed in 1944 but then served as Lord Chancellor from 1951 to 1954 before being reappointed in the latter year as a Lord of Appeal. Finally, Lord Phillips served first from 1999 to 2000 but was then Master of the Rolls from 2000 to 2005 and Lord Chief Justice from 2005 to 2008, when he was again appointed as a Lord of Appeal.

Four Lords of Appeal were sons of previous Lords of Appeal. Lord Thankerton (1929–48) was the son of Lord Watson (1880–99). Lord Russell (1929–46) was the son of Lord Russell of Killowen (1894), and a third Lord Russell (1975–82) was in turn the son of Lord Russell (1929–46). Lord Keith of Kinkel (1977–96) was the son of Lord Keith of Avonholm (1953–61). Lord Romer (1938–44) was related through marriage to both Lord Maugham (1935–8 and 1939–41) and Lord Russell of Killowen (1929–46). Neither Lord Morris (1960–75) nor Lord Kilbrandon (James Shaw) (1971–6) was related to their earlier serving namesakes.

The youngest person to be appointed a Lord of Appeal is Lord Radcliffe, who was 50 at the time. The oldest is Lord Romer, who was 72. The longest serving Lord of Appeal is Lord Reid (26 years and 4 months); the shortest serving is the first Lord Russell of Killowen, who was appointed Lord Chief Justice of England after just a month in office as a Lord of Appeal. The first woman to be appointed was Lady Hale of Richmond in 2004.

Of the 112 Lords of Appeal appointed, five served at some time in their career as Lord Chancellor (Lords Cave, Maugham, Simonds, Dilhorne, and Mackay). Six served at some time as Lord Chief Justice (the first Lord Russell and Lords Goddard, Lane, Woolf, Phillips, and Bingham). Lord Chief Justice Parker of Waddington (1958–71) was the son of the Lord Parker who served as a Lord of Appeal from 1913 to 1918, but he himself was never appointed as a Lord of Appeal. On the other hand, Lord Oaksey, a Lord of Appeal from 1947 to 1957, was the son of Lord Trevethin, who was Lord Chief Justice from 1921 to 1922. Nine Lords of Appeal also served as Master of the Rolls (Lords Lindley, Collins, Wright, Greene, Evershed, Denning, Woolf, Phillips, and Bingham). Lords Woolf, Phillips, and Bingham all served as both Master of the Rolls and Lord Chief Justice.

The Scots Law Lords who also served as Lord President of the Court of Session (the senior civil position) and as Lord Justice General (the senior criminal position)—the two offices have always been combined in modern times—are Lords Dunedin, Normand, Hope of Craighead, and Rodger of Earlsferry. The Law Lords from Northern Ireland who also first served as Lord Chief Justice of Northern Ireland (the top civil and criminal post) are Lords Lowry, Hutton, Carswell, and Kerr.

1 (1876–)	2 (1876–)	3 (1882–)	4 (1891–)	5 (1913–)	6 (1913–)	7 (1929–)	8 (1947–)	9 (1947–)	10 (1968–)	11 (1968–)	12 (1994–)
Blackburn 1876–87	Gordon 1876–80	FitzGerald 1882–9	Hannen 1891–3	Dunedin 1913–32	Sumner 1913–30	Tomlin 1929–35	Morton 1947–59	MacDermott 1947–51	Diplock 1968–85	Slynn 1992–2002	Hoffmann 1995–
Macnaghten 1887–1913	Watson 1880–99	Morris 1889–99	Bowen 1893–4	Wright 1932–5	Macmillan 1930–9	Maugham 1935–8	Jenkins 1959–63	Asquith 1951–4	Ackner 1986–92	Walker 2002–	Collins 2009–
Parker 1913–18	Robertson 1899–1909	Lindley 1899–1905	Russell 1894	Roche 1935–8	Maugham 1939–41	Porter 1938–54	Upjohn 1963–71	Somervell 1954–60	Woolf 1992–6		
Cave 1918–22	Shaw 1909–29	Atkinson 1905–28	Davey 1894–1907	Romer 1938–44	Macmillan 1941–7	Simonds 1954–62	Cross 1971–5	Morris 1960–75	Hutton 1997–2003		
Blanesburgh 1923–37	Thankerton 1929–48	Atkin 1928–44	Collins 1907–10	Simonds 1944–51	Normand 1947–53	Evershed 1962–5	Russell 1975–82	Lane 1979–80	Carswell 2004–9		
Wright 1937–47	Reid 1948–75	Goddard 1944–6	Robson 1910–12	Cohen 1951–60	Keith 1953–61	Pearson 1965–74	Templeman 1982–94	Roskill 1980–6	Kerr 2009–		
Oaksey 1947–57	Fraser 1975–85	Du Parcq 1946–9	Moulton 1912–21	Hodson 1960–71	Guest 1961–70	Edmund-Davies 1974–81	Nicholls 1994–2007	Goff 1986–98			
Denning 1957–62	Mackay 1985–7	Radcliffe 1949–64	Carson 1921–9	Simon 1971–7	Kilbrandon 1971–6	Brandon 1981–91	Neuberger 2007–	Hobhouse 1998–2003			
Pearce 1962–9	Jauncey 1988–96	Wilberforce 1964–82	Russell 1929–46	Scarman 1977–86	Keith 1977–96	Browne-Wilkinson 1991–2000		Hale 2004–			
Dilhorne 1969–80	Hope 1996–	Brightman 1982–7	Uthwatt 1946–9	Oliver 1986–91	Clyde 1996–2001	Bingham 2000–8					
Griffiths 1985–93		Lowry 1988–94	Greene 1949–50	Mustill 1992–7	Rodger 2001–	Phillips 2008–					
Lloyd 1993–8		Nolan 1994–8	Tucker 1950–61	Saville 1997–							

1 (1876–)	2 (1876–)	3 (1882–)	4 (1891–)	5 (1913–)	6 (1913–)	7 (1929–)	8 (1947–)	9 (1947–)	10 (1968–)	11 (1968–)	12 (1994–)
Phillips 1999–2000		Millett 1998–2003	Devlin 1961–4								
Scott 2000–		Brown 2004–	Donovan 1964–71								
			Salmon 1972–80								
			Bridge 1980–92								
			Steyn 1995–2005								
			Mance 2005–								

Lord Chancellors From 1876

Name	Period served	Appointed by (Prime Minister)	Prime Minister's political party
Earl Cairns	1874–80	Benjamin Disraeli	Conservative
Earl of Selborne	1880–5	William Gladstone	Liberal
Lord Halsbury	1885–6	Marquess of Salisbury	Conservative
Lord Herschell	1886	William Gladstone	Liberal
Lord Halsbury	1886–92	Marquess of Salisbury	Conservative
Lord Herschell	1892–5	William Gladstone	Liberal
Earl of Halsbury	1895–1905	Marquess of Salisbury	Conservative
Earl of Loreburn	1905–12	Henry Campbell— Bannerman	Liberal
Viscount Haldane	1912–15	Herbert Asquith	Liberal
Lord Buckmaster	1915–16	Herbert Asquith	Liberal
Lord Finlay	1916–19	David Lloyd George	Liberal
Earl of Birkenhead	1919–22	David Lloyd George	Liberal
Viscount Cave	1922–4	Andrew Bonar Law	Conservative
Viscount Haldane	1924	Ramsay MacDonald	Labour
Viscount Cave	1924–8	Stanley Baldwin	Conservative
Lord Hailsham	1928–9	Stanley Baldwin	Conservative
Viscount Sankey	1929–35	Ramsay MacDonald	Labour
Viscount Hailsham	1935–8	Stanley Baldwin	Conservative
Lord Maugham	1938–9	Neville Chamberlain	Conservative
Viscount Caldecote	1939–40	Neville Chamberlain	Conservative
Viscount Simon	1940–5	Winston Churchill	Conservative
Viscount Jowitt	1945–51	Clement Attlee	Labour
Lord Simonds	1951–4	Winston Churchill	Conservative
Viscount Kilmuir	1954–62	Winston Churchill	Conservative
Lord Dilhorne	1962–4	Harold Macmillan	Conservative
Lord Gardiner	1964–70	Harold Wilson	Labour
Lord Hailsham of St Marylebone	1970–4	Edward Heath	Conservative
Lord Elwyn–Jones	1974–9	Harold Wilson	Labour
Lord Hailsham of St Marylebone	1979–87	Margaret Thatcher	Conservative
Lord Havers	1987	Margaret Thatcher	Conservative
Lord Mackay	1987–97	Margaret Thatcher	Conservative
Lord Irvine	1997–2003	Tony Blair	Labour
Lord Falconer	2003–7	Tony Blair	Labour
Jack Straw MP	2007–	Gordon Brown	Labour

Pen Portraits of the Lords of Appeal

Ackner (Desmond)

Attended Highgate School and Cambridge University. Served in the Army during World War II. Called to the English Bar at age 25. Acted for the families of victims at the public inquiry into the Aberfan disaster in 1967 and for victims of thalidomide in the late 1960s. Spent nine years as a High Court Judge, six years on the Court of Appeal, and six years as a Lord of Appeal (1986–92).

Asquith of Bishopstone (Cyril)

Attended Winchester College and Oxford University. The fourth son of the Liberal Prime Minister Herbert Henry Asquith. Served in the Army during World War I. Called to the English Bar at age 30. Spent eight years as a High Court Judge, five years on the Court of Appeal, and three years as a Lord of Appeal (1951–4). Died in office.

Atkin (Richard—'Dick')

Attended Christ College, Brecon and Oxford University. Early days in Brisbane, Australia, where his father was a member of the Queensland Assembly. Raised in Wales by his mother after his father died. Called to the English Bar at age 24. Spent six years on the High Court, nine years on the Court of Appeal, and 16 years as a Lord of Appeal (1928–44). Delivered leading judgment in *Donoghue v Stevenson* (1932) and a famous dissent in *Liversidge v Anderson* (1941). Died in office.

Atkinson (John)

Attended Belfast Academy and Queen's College Galway. Called to the Irish Bar at age 21. Appointed as Solicitor General for Ireland in 1889 and became Attorney General for Ireland in 1892. Elected as Conservative MP for North Londonderry in 1895. The first Irish barrister to be appointed a Law Lord directly from his practice at the Bar. Spent 23 years as a Lord of Appeal (1905–28).

Bingham of Cornhill (Thomas)

Attended Sedbergh School and Oxford University, where he read History. Called to the English Bar at age 25. Became Queen's Counsel aged 38 and High Court Judge at age 46. Appointed as Master of the Rolls in 1992 and as Lord Chief Justice of England and Wales in 1996. In 2000, became the first appointed Senior Law Lord, a position formerly assumed by the longest serving Lord of Appeal. Served in this capacity until retiring in 2008.

Blackburn (Colin)

Attended Eton College and Cambridge University. Called to the English Bar at age 25. Became better known as a law reporter than as an advocate but as a judge he acquired a reputation for great lucidity. Spent 17 years as a High Court Judge. Became one of the first two Lords of Appeal in Ordinary, with Lord Gordon, and spent over ten years in that capacity (1876–87).

Blanesburgh (Robert [Younger])

Attended Eton College, Edinburgh University, and Oxford University. Called to the English Bar at age 23. Spent four years as a High Court Judge in the Chancery Division, four years on the Court of Appeal, and 13 years six months as a Lord of Appeal (1923–37). Fellow of the Royal College of Music and received honorary doctorates from Edinburgh, Oxford, and St Andrews Universities.

Bowen (Charles)

Went to school in Lille, France, before attending Rugby School and Oxford University. Won many classical scholarships and became a Fellow of Balliol College, Oxford, in 1858. Called to the English Bar at age 26. Wrote verse translations of classical works. Spent three years as a High Court Judge, 11 years on the Court of Appeal, but just one year as a Lord of Appeal (1893–4). Died in office.

Brandon of Oakbrook (Henry)

Attended Winchester College and Cambridge University. Served in the Army during World War II, attaining the rank of Major in the Royal Artillery. Awarded the Military Cross in 1942 while serving in Madagascar. Called to the English Bar at age 26. Spent 12 years as a High Court Judge, three years on the Court of Appeal, and ten years as a Lord of Appeal (1981–91).

Bridge of Harwich (Nigel)

Attended Marlborough College. Served in the Army during World War II, attaining the rank of Captain. Called to the English Bar at age 30. Spent seven years as a High Court Judge, five years on the Court of Appeal, and over 11 years as a Lord of Appeal (1980–92). One of the very few Lords of Appeal without a university degree, but studied mathematics in his retirement and graduated from the Open University at the age of 86.

Brightman (John)

Attended Marlborough College and Cambridge University. Served in the Navy during World War II, attaining the rank of Lieutenant Commander. Called to the English Bar at age 30. Appointed Attorney General of the Duchy of Lancaster in 1969, but relinquished this in 1970 when promoted to the Bench. Spent seven years as a High Court Judge, five years on the Court of Appeal, and five years as a Lord of Appeal (1982–7).

Brown of Eaton-under-Heywood (Simon)

Attended Stowe School and Oxford University. Served in the Royal Artillery from 1955 until 1957, attaining the rank of Second Lieutenant. Called to the English Bar at age 24. Recorder and First Junior Treasury Counsel from 1979 until 1984. Spent eight years as a High Court Judge and 12 years on the Court of Appeal before becoming a Lord of Appeal in 2004. Was the Intelligence Services Commissioner from 2000 to 2006.

Browne-Wilkinson (Nicolas)

Attended Lancing College and Oxford University. Called to the English Bar at age 23. Spent six years as a High Court Judge, eight years on the Court of Appeal, and almost nine years as a Lord of Appeal (1991–2000). Senior Law Lord from 1998 until 2000, at the time of the *Pinochet* affair.

Carson (Edward)

Attended Portarlington School, Wesley College, Dublin, and Trinity College Dublin. Called to the Irish Bar at age 23. Elected as MP for Trinity College Dublin and served as Solicitor General for Ireland. Called to the English Bar at age 39 and served as Solicitor General for England. Represented Marquess of Queensbury when he was sued by Oscar Wilde. Became leader of the Unionist cause in Ulster at age 56. Spent eight years as a Lord of Appeal (1921–9). Received a state funeral in Belfast.

Carswell (Robert)

Attended Royal Belfast Academical Institution, Oxford University, and Chicago University. Called to the Bar of Northern Ireland at age 23, becoming a Queen's Counsell at 37. Counsel to the Attorney General for Northern Ireland 1970–1, and Senior Crown Counsel in Northern Ireland 1979–84. Spent nine years as a High Court Judge and four years as a Lord Justice of Appeal in Northern Ireland. Served as Lord Chief Justice of Northern Ireland from 1997 until 2004 and as a Lord of Appeal from 2004 to 2009.

Cave (George)

Attended Merchant Taylors' School, London and Oxford University. Called to the English Bar at age 24. Elected as Unionist MP for the Kingston Division of Surrey. Served as Solicitor General and as Home Secretary. Spent almost four years as a Lord of Appeal (1918–22). Became a viscount in 1918. Served as Lord Chancellor from 1922 until 1924 and from 1925 until 1928. Became Chancellor of Oxford University in 1925.

Clyde (James)

Attended Edinburgh Academy, Oxford University, and Edinburgh University. Son and grandson of men who were each Lord President of the Court of Session and Lord Justice General. Served in the Intelligence Corps from 1954 until 1956. Called to the Scottish Bar at age 27. Became Chancellor to the Bishop of Argyll in 1972. Senator of the College of Justice in Scotland from 1985 to 1996. Served on the Courts of Appeal of Jersey and Guernsey for six years and spent five years as a Lord of Appeal (1996–2001). Was Justice Oversight Commissioner in Northern Ireland from 2003 to 2006.

Cohen (Lionel)

Attended Eton College and Oxford University. Called to the English Bar at age 30. Spent three years as a High Court Judge in the Chancery Division, five years on the Court of Appeal, and almost nine years (1951–60) as a Lord of Appeal. Chaired several Royal Commissions, including one on Awards to Inventors, which acknowledged scientists who made technological advances during World War II. The first Jew to be appointed as a Lord of Appeal.

Collins of Mapesbury (Lawrence)

Educated at the City of London School and Downing College, Cambridge. Admitted as a solicitor in 1968 and a partner in Herbert Smith Solicitors from 1971 to 2000. Became a

Queen's Counsel in 1997. Served as a High Court Judge (Chancery Division) from 2000 to 2007 and on the Court of Appeal from 2007 to 2009. Replaced Lord Hoffmann as a Lord of Appeal in April 2009, the first solicitor to be appointed.

Collins (Richard)

Attended Dungannon School, Trinity College Dublin, and Cambridge University. Called to the English Bar at age 25. Spent six years as a High Court Judge, ten years on the Court of Appeal, and three years as a Lord of Appeal (1907–10). Served as Master of the Rolls from 1901 until 1907. Represented the United Kingdom on the Venezuela Boundary Commission, which was established in 1899.

Cross of Chelsea (Geoffrey)

Attended Westminster School and Cambridge University and became a Fellow of Trinity College, Cambridge. Called to the English Bar at age 26. Spent six years as a High Court Judge in the Chancery Division, ten years on the Court of Appeal, and four years as a Lord of Appeal (1971–5). Chancellor of Durham University from 1959 until 1960.

Davey (Horace)

Attended Rugby School and Oxford University. Called to the English Bar at age 28. Elected as Liberal MP for Christchurch in 1880, but lost his seat in 1885. Appointed as Solicitor General in 1886. Elected as MP for Stockton-on-Tees in 1888, but lost this seat in 1892. Spent one year on the Court of Appeal and 12 years and six months as a Lord of Appeal (1894–1907). Died in office.

Denning (Alfred Thompson—Tom)

Attended Andover School and Oxford University. Called to the English Bar at age 24. Spent four years as a High Court Judge, nine years on the Court of Appeal, and five years as a Lord of Appeal (1957–62). Returned to the Court of Appeal as Master of the Rolls, an office which he held for the next 20 years. A frequently controversial judge who was not afraid to reconsider established precedent. Published several books after retiring. Died aged 100.

Devlin (Patrick)

Attended Stonyhurst College and Cambridge University. Called to the English Bar at age 24. Spent 12 years as a High Court Judge, one year on the Court of Appeal, and just over two years as a Lord of Appeal (1961–4). First independent chairman of the Press Council from 1964 until 1969 and High Steward of Cambridge University from 1966 until 1991.

Renowned for his debates about morality and the law with Professor Herbert Hart in the 1960s.

Dilhorne (Reginald [Manningham-Buller])

Attended Eton College and Oxford University. Called to the English Bar at age 22. Elected as Conservative MP for Daventry in 1943. Junior minister in Winston Churchill's government. Elected as MP for Northamptonshire South in 1950. Served as Solicitor General, Attorney General and, from 1962–4, Lord Chancellor. Became a viscount in 1964. Appointed a Lord of Appeal in 1969. Died in office in 1980. The last Lord of Appeal to have previously served as a Member of Parliament.

Diplock (Kenneth)

Attended Whitgift School and Oxford University, where he read Chemistry. Called to the English Bar at age 25. Spent five years as a High Court Judge, seven years on the Court of Appeal, and 17 years as a Lord of Appeal (1968–85). Chaired a Commission set up in 1972 to consider legal measures against terrorism in Northern Ireland, leading to the establishment of 'Diplock' courts in which judges decided criminal cases without the assistance of juries.

Donovan (Terence)

Attended Brockley School. Served in the Army and the Royal Air Force during World War I. Called to the English Bar at age 26. Elected as Labour MP for Leicester East in 1945, and for Leicester North East in 1950. Spent ten years as a High Court Judge, three years on the Court of Appeal, and seven years as a Lord of Appeal (1964–71). Died in office.

Du Parcq (Herbert)

Born in Jersey. Attended Victoria College, Jersey, and Oxford University. Called to both the English Bar and the Jersey Bar at age 26. Specialised in commercial litigation. Spent six years as a High Court Judge, eight years on the Court of Appeal, and three years as a Lord of Appeal (1946–9). A member of the Permanent Court of Arbitration at The Hague. Died in office.

Dunedin (Andrew [Murray])

Attended Harrow School, Cambridge University, and Oxford University. Called to the Scottish Bar at age 25. Elected as Conservative MP for Bute and Caithness in 1891. Served as Solicitor General for Scotland, Lord Advocate, and Secretary of State for Scotland. After leaving Parliament, spent eight years as Lord President of the Court of Session and Lord

Justice General, and 18 years and six months as a Lord of Appeal (1913–32). Created a viscount in 1926.

Edmund-Davies (Herbert)

Attended Mountain Ash Grammar School, London University, and Oxford University. Won the Vinerian Scholarship. Called to the English Bar at age 23. Lectured at the London School of Economics from 1930 until 1931. Served in the Army Officers' Emergency Reserve and in the Royal Welch Fusiliers during World War II. Spent eight years as a High Court Judge, eight years on the Court of Appeal, and seven years as a Lord of Appeal (1974–81). Noted for his chairmanship of the Aberfan tribunal in 1966.

Evershed (Raymond)

Attended Clifton College and Oxford University. Served in the Army during World War I, attaining the rank of Second Lieutenant. Called to the English Bar at age 24. Spent two years as a High Court Judge in the Chancery Division and 15 years on the Court of Appeal. Master of the Rolls from 1949 until 1962. Spent almost three years as a Lord of Appeal (1962–5).

FitzGerald of Kilmarnock (John)

Attended Trinity College Dublin. Called to the Irish Bar at age 22. Became Queen's Counsel at the early age of 31. Elected as Liberal MP for Ennis in 1852. Served as Solicitor General for Ireland and Attorney General for Ireland. Spent 22 years as a High Court Judge (in Ireland)and was then appointed directly into the House of Lords. Served seven years as a Lord of Appeal (1882–9). Died in office.

Fraser of Tullybelton (Ian)

Attended Repton School, Oxford and Glasgow Universities. Lectured at Glasgow University and Cambridge University. Served in the Army during World War II. Called to the Scottish Bar at age 25. Attempted to become a MP, standing unsuccessfully as the Conservative candidate for East Edinburgh. Spent ten years as a Senator of the Court of Justice in Scotland and ten years as a Lord of Appeal (1975–85).

Goddard (Rayner)

Attended Marlborough College and Oxford University. Called to the English Bar at age 22. Stood for Parliament as an Independent Conservative candidate in 1929, but was unsuccessful. Spent six years as a High Court Judge, six years on the Court of Appeal, and 18 months as a Lord of Appeal (1944–6). Then served as Lord Chief Justice of England for 12 years, the first Lord Chief Justice to hold a law degree.

Goff of Chieveley (Robert)

Attended Eton College and Oxford University. Served in the Army from 1945 until 1948. Fellow and Tutor at Lincoln College, Oxford. Called to the English Bar at age 25. Spent seven years as a High Court Judge and four years on the Court of Appeal. Served as a Lord of Appeal for over 11 years (1986–98), being the Senior Law Lord for his last two years. Called back from retirement to sit on the second *Pinochet* appeal.

Greene (Wilfrid)

Attended Westminster School and Oxford University. Called to the English Bar at age 25. Became King's Counsel at age 39 and went directly into the Court of Appeal at age 52. Spent 14 years on the Court of Appeal, including 12 as Master of the Rolls. Served as a Lord of Appeal for only 11 months (1949–50) before being forced to retire due to bad health. Remembered for his Court of Appeal judgment in *Associated Provincial Picture Houses Ltd v Wednesbury Corporation* (1948).

Gordon (Edward)

Attended Royal Academy, Inverness, and Edinburgh and Glasgow Universities. Called to the Scottish Bar at age 21. Elected as Conservative MP for Thetford and later for Glasgow and Aberdeen Universities. Served as Solicitor General for Scotland and as Lord Advocate and was one of the first two Lords of Appeal appointed under the Appellate Jurisdiction Act 1876 (with Lord Blackburn). Died in office in 1879.

Griffiths (Hugh)

Attended Charterhouse School, and Cambridge University. Served in the Welsh Guards during World War II, receiving the Military Cross in 1944. Called to the English Bar at age 26. Spent nine years as a High Court Judge, five years on the Court of Appeal, and eight years as a Lord of Appeal (1985–93). A keen sportsman, he became captain of St Andrews Golf Club the year after he retired and was later President of the MCC.

Guest (Christopher)

Attended Merchiston Castle School, and Cambridge and Edinburgh Universities. Called to the Scottish Bar at age 24. Stood for Parliament as a Unionist candidate for the

Kirkcaldy Burghs in 1945, but was unsuccessful. Served as a senator of the College of Justice in Scotland from 1957 to 1960. Appointed a Lord of Appeal during the Macmillan administration. Served for ten years in this capacity (1961–71).

Hale of Richmond (Brenda)

Attended Richmond High School for Girls and Cambridge University. Called to the English Bar in 1969. Worked primarily in academia for 18 years and became Professor of Law at Manchester University and a member of the Law Commission for England and Wales. Spent five years as a High Court Judge and five years on the Court of Appeal. Was only the second woman to be appointed to the Court of Appeal. Became the first female Lord of Appeal in 2004.

Hannen (James)

Attended St Paul's School and Heidelberg University. Called to the English Bar at age 27 and was made Queen's Counsel at age 47. Became a High Court Judge in 1868 and was appointed directly into the House of Lords as a Lord of Appeal in 1891. Served for two years seven months in this capacity (1891–3). Acted as a government investigator in the Charles Stewart Parnell case.

Hobhouse of Woodborough (John)

Attended Eton College and Oxford University. Worked abroad in Australia and New Zealand. Called to the English Bar at age 23 and became Queen's Counsel at age 41. Specialised in commercial law. Spent 11 years as a High Court Judge, five years on the Court of Appeal, and five years as a Lord of Appeal (1998–2003).

Hodson (Charles)

Attended Cheltenham College and Oxford University. Served in the Army during World War I, receiving the Military Cross. Called to the English Bar at age 26 and specialised in divorce law. Spent 14 years as a High Court Judge in the Probate, Divorce and Admiralty Division, nine years on the Court of Appeal, and more than ten years as a Lord of Appeal (1960–71). A member of the International Court of Arbitration at The Hague from 1949 until 1971.

Hoffmann (Leonard)

Born in South Africa. Attended South African College School, and Cape Town and Oxford Universities (the latter as a Rhodes Scholar). Won the Vinerian Scholarship. Called to the South African Bar at age 24. Stowell Council Law fellow at University

College, Oxford from 1961 to 1973. Called to the English Bar at age 30 and took silk in 1977. Spent seven years as a High Court Judge in the Chancery Division and three years in the Court of Appeal. Appointed as a Lord of Appeal in 1995, serving as Second Senior Law Lord from January 2007 until his retirement in April 2009.

Hope of Craighead (David)

Attended Edinburgh Academy, Rugby School, and Cambridge and Edinburgh Universities. Called to the Scottish Bar at age 27. Dean of the Faculty of Advocates from 1986 until 1989. Was appointed direct from the Bar in 1989 to be Lord President of the Court of Session and Lord Justice General, which offices he held for seven years. Became a Lord of Appeal in 1996, assuming the mantle of Second Senior Law Lord in April 2009. Chancellor of the University of Strathclyde since 1998.

Hutton (Brian)

Attended Shrewsbury School, Oxford University, and Queen's University Belfast. Called to the Northern Ireland Bar at age 23, becoming a Queen's Counsel at age 39. Senior Crown Counsel in Northern Ireland from 1973 to 1979. Spent nine years as a High Court Judge before being appointed as the Lord Chief Justice of Northern Ireland in succession to Lord Lowry in 1988. Served in this capacity for nine years. Spent seven years as a Lord of Appeal (1997–2004). Chaired the inquiry into the death of Dr David Kelly (2003–4).

Jauncey of Tullichettle (Charles)

Attended Radley College, and Oxford and Glasgow Universities. Served in the Royal Naval Volunteer Reserve during World War II. Called to the Scottish Bar at age 24. Spent nine years as a senator of the Court of Justice in Scotland and eight years as a Lord of Appeal (1988–96). A member of the Royal Company of Archers.

Jenkins (David)

Attended Charterhouse School and Oxford University. Served in the Army during both World Wars. Called to the English Bar at age 24 and became King's Counsel at age 38. Held the office of Attorney General of the Duchy of Lancaster. Spent two years as a High Court Judge, ten years on the Court of Appeal, and four years as a Lord of Appeal (1959–63).

Keith of Avonholm (James)

Attended Hamilton School and Glasgow University. Served in the Army with the Seaforth Highlanders during World War I. Called to the Scottish Bar at age 25. Spent 16 years as a senator of the Court of Justice in Scotland and over seven years as a Lord of Appeal

(1953–61). One of his three children became a Lord of Appeal in 1977, taking the title Lord Keith of Kinkel (see below).

Keith of Kinkel (Harry)

Attended Edinburgh Academy, and Oxford and Edinburgh Universities. Son of a previous Lord of Appeal, Lord Keith of Avonholm. Served in the Scots Guards during World War II. Called to the Scottish Bar at age 28. Spent six years as a member of the Scottish judiciary and 19 years as a Lord of Appeal (1977–96). Was the most senior Law Lord for the last ten of these years.

Kerr (Brian)

Attended St Colman's College, Newry, and Queen's University Belfast, being called to the Northern Ireland Bar in 1970. Became a Queen's Counsel in 1983 and served as Senior Crown Counsel from 1988 to 1993. Appointed to the High Court of Northern Ireland in 1993, becoming Lord Chief Justice of Northern Ireland in 2004. The 112th (and last) person to be appointed as a Lord of Appeal, in 2009.

Kilbrandon (Jim [Shaw])

Attended Charterhouse School, and Oxford and Edinburgh Universities. Called to the Scottish Bar at age 26. Spent 12 years as a senator of the Court of Justice in Scotland and five years as a Lord of Appeal (1971–6). Served as Chairman of the Scottish Law Commission from its inauguration in 1965 until 1970. Chaired the Royal Commission on the Constitution from 1970 until 1973.

Lane (Geoffrey)

Attended Shrewsbury School and Cambridge University. Served in the Royal Air Force during World War II. Called to the English Bar at age 28. Spent eight years as a High Court Judge, five years on the Court of Appeal, but only eight months as a Lord of Appeal (1979–80) as he was then appointed Lord Chief Justice of England and Wales, serving in that capacity for 12 years.

Lindley (Nathaniel)

Attended University College School and London University. Called to the English Bar at age 22. Practised in the Chancery courts. Spent six years as a High Court Judge and

19 years on the Court of Appeal. Appointed Master of the Rolls in 1897 and served in this capacity for three years. Spent six years as a Lord of Appeal (1899–1905).

Lloyd of Berwick (Anthony)

Attended Eton College, and Cambridge and Harvard Universities. Became a Fellow of Peterhouse College, Cambridge. Called to the English Bar at age 26. Spent six years as a High Court Judge, nine years on the Court of Appeal, and five years as a Lord of Appeal (1993–8). Chaired an inquiry into anti-terrorism legislation in 1996. Active in the House of Lords after retiring as a Lord of Appeal.

Lowry (Robert)

Attended Royal Belfast Academical Institution and Cambridge University. Son of a Unionist MP who later became a High Court Judge. Served in the Army during World War II, attaining the rank of Major. Called to the Northern Ireland Bar at age 28. Spent seven years as a High Court Judge and from 1971 to 1988 as Lord Chief Justice of Northern Ireland, in succession to Lord MacDermott. Chaired the Constitutional Convention in Northern Ireland, 1975–6. Spent over five years as a Lord of Appeal (1988–94).

MacDermott (John)

Attended Campbell College, Belfast and Queen's University Belfast. Called to the Irish Bar at age 25. Elected as Unionist MP for Queen's University Belfast in 1938. Served in the Army during World War II, attaining the rank of Lieutenant. Spent three years as a High Court Judge and almost four years as a Lord of Appeal (1947–51). Was then appointed Lord Chief Justice of Northern Ireland, a post he held until 1971. Often sat in the House of Lords even after returning to work in Northern Ireland in 1951.

Mackay of Clashfern (James)

Attended George Heriot's School, and Edinburgh and Cambridge Universities. Called to the Scottish Bar at age 28. Appointed as Dean of the Faculty of Advocates in 1976. Served as Lord Advocate of Scotland for five years . Spent one year as a Senator of the College of Justice in Scotland and two years as a Lord of Appeal (1985–7) before being appointed as Lord Chancellor, the first Scottish advocate to serve in that capacity. Retired as Lord Chancellor in 1997. Editor in Chief of *Halsburg's Laws of England* since 1998.

Macmillan (Hugh)

Attended Collegiate School, Greenock, and Edinburgh and Glasgow Universities. Called to the Scottish Bar at age 24. Served as Solicitor General. Appointed directly to the House of Lords from the Bar. Served as a Lord of Appeal from 1930 until 1939 and then spent a period as Minister for Information during World War II. Served again as a Lord of Appeal from 1941 until 1947.

Macnaghten (Edward)

Attended Dr Cowan's School, Sunderland, Trinity College Dublin, and Cambridge University. Became a Fellow of Trinity College, Cambridge. Called to the English Bar at age 27. Elected as Conservative MP for County Antrim in 1880, exchanging this seat five years later for that of North Antrim. Appointed directly to the House of Lords from the Bar. Spent 26 years as a Lord of Appeal (1887–1913), second only to Lord Reid in length of service.

Mance (Jonathan)

Attended Charterhouse School and Oxford University. Called to the English Bar at age 22 and took silk at age 39. Spent six years as a commercial judge in the High Court and six years on the Court of Appeal. Became a Lord of Appeal in 2005. Served as Chairman of the Banking Appeals Tribunal from 1992 until 1993, Chairman of the Consultative Council of European Judges from 2000 to 2003, and President of the British Insurance Law Association from 2000 until 2002. Husband of Lady Justice Arden.

Maugham (Frederic)

Attended Dover College and Cambridge University. Called to the English Bar at age 24. Spent six years as a High Court Judge and four years on the Court of Appeal. Served as a Lord of Appeal for three years (1935–8) and then spent one year as Lord Chancellor. Served two further years as a Lord of Appeal (1939–41). Presided in *Liversidge v Anderson* (1941). Created a viscount in 1939.

Millett (Peter)

Attended Harrow School and Cambridge University. Served in the Royal Air Force as a Flying Officer from 1955 until 1957. Called to the English Bar at age 23 and took silk age 41. Practised at the Chancery Bar. Spent eight years as a High Court Judge, four years on the Court of Appeal, and five years as a Lord of Appeal (1998–2004). Retired early to take up the Treasurership of Lincoln's Inn. A non-permanent judge of the Court of Final Appeal, Hong Kong, since 2000. Editor in Chief of the *Encyclopaedia of Forms and Precedents* since 1998.

Morris (Michael)

Attended Galway College and Trinity College Dublin. Called to the Irish Bar at age 23. Elected as a Liberal MP for Galway in 1865. Became a Conservative and took office in Lord Derby's administration as Irish Solicitor General. Later appointed as Irish Attorney General. Spent 20 years as a High Court Judge, two years on the Court of Appeal, and ten years as a Lord of Appeal (1889–99).

Morris of Borth-y-Gest (John William)

Attended Liverpool Institute and Cambridge and Harvard Universities. Served in the Royal Welch Fusiliers during World War I. Called to the English Bar at age 25. Stood for Parliament twice as a Liberal candidate for the seat of Ilford, but was unsuccessful on both occasions. Spent six years as a High Court Judge, nine years on the Court of Appeal. and 15 years as a Lord of Appeal (1960–75).

Morton of Henryton (Fergus)

Attended Kelvinside Academy and Cambridge University. Called to the English Bar at age 25. Served in the Highland Light Infantry during World War I, winning the Military Cross. Spent six years as a High Court Judge, three years on the Court of Appeal, and 12 years as a Lord of Appeal (1947–59). An Honorary Fellow of St John's College, Cambridge and later a Deputy High Steward of Cambridge University.

Moulton (John Fletcher)

Attended Kingswood School and Cambridge University. Called to the English Bar at age 30. Elected as Liberal MP for Clapham, South Hackney, and a Cornwall constituency. Appointed directly to the Court of Appeal, where he spent six years. Served as Director General of the Explosives Department during World War I. Spent eight years and five months as a Lord of Appeal (1912–21). Died in office.

Mustill (Michael)

Attended Oundle School and Cambridge University. Served in the Royal Artillery from 1949 until 1951. Called to the English Bar at age 24 and took silk at age 40. Chairman of the Civil Service Appeal Tribunal from 1971 until 1978. Spent seven years as a High Court Judge, seven years on the Court of Appeal, and five years as a Lord of Appeal (1992–7), retiring prematurely. Served as Chairman of the Judicial Studies Board from 1985 until 1989, and as President of the British Maritime Law Association from 1995 to 2003.

Neuberger of Abbotsbury (David)

Attended Westminster School and Oxford University. Employed by Rothschilds, the merchant bank, for three years. Called to the English Bar at age 26. Served as a High Court Judge for eight years, the last three of which as Supervisory Chancery Judge of Midlands, Wales and Chester, and Western Circuits. Spent three years on the Court of Appeal before being appointed a Lord of Appeal in 2007.

Nicholls of Birkenhead (Donald)

Attended Birkenhead School and Liverpool and Cambridge Universities. Called to the English Bar at age 25 and took silk at age 41 . Spent three years as a High Court Judge and five years on the Court of Appeal. Served as Vice Chancellor of the Supreme Court from 1991 until 1994. Spent over 12 years as a Lord of Appeal (1994–2007), the last five as Second Senior Law Lord. Served on the Hong Kong Court of Final Appeal from 1998 to 2004.

Nolan (Michael)

Attended Ampleforth College and Oxford University. Served in the Royal Artillery from 1947 until 1949. Called to the English Bar at age 25 and to the Northern Ireland Bar at age 46. Spent nine years as a High Court Judge, two years on the Court of Appeal, and four years as a Lord of Appeal (1994–8). Chaired the Committee on Standards in Public Life from 1994 until 1997, giving his name to the Nolan Principles. Chancellor of Essex University from 1997 until 2002.

Normand (Wilfrid)

Attended Fettes College, Edinburgh and Oxford, Paris, and Edinburgh Universities. Served in the Royal Engineers during World War I. Called to the Scottish Bar at age 26. Elected as Unionist MP for West Edinburgh in 1931. Served as Solicitor General for Scotland and then as Lord Advocate. Spent 12 years as Lord President of the Court of Session and Lord Justice General, and six years as a Lord of Appeal (1947–53).

Oaksey (Geoffrey [Lawrence])

Attended Haileybury School and Oxford University. Son of a Lord Chief Justice of England. Served in the Royal Artillery during World War I and was mentioned twice in despatches. Called to the English Bar at age 26. Spent 12 years as a High Court Judge, three years on the Court of Appeal, and ten years as a Lord of Appeal (1947–57). Served as the British President of the Nuremburg War Crimes Tribunal in 1945–6.

Oliver of Aylmerton (Peter)

Attended the Leys School, Cambridge and Cambridge University. Later became an Honorary Fellow of Trinity Hall, Cambridge and also University Commissary. Served in the 12th Battalion Royal Tank Regiment during World War II and was mentioned in despatches. Called to the English Bar at age 27. Spent six years as a High Court Judge in the Chancery Division, six years on the Court of Appeal, and five years as a Lord of Appeal (1986–91).

Parker of Waddington (Robert)

Attended Westminster School and Eton College, and then Cambridge University. Called to the English Bar at age 27. Served as junior counsel to the Treasury from 1903 until 1906. Spent seven years as a High Court Judge and was then appointed directly to the House of Lords as a Lord of Appeal. Served for five years in this capacity (1913–18). Died in office. His son served as Lord Chief Justice of England from 1958 to 1971.

Pearce (Edward Holroyd)

Attended Charterhouse School and Oxford University. Called to the English Bar at age 24. Spent nine years as a High Court Judge, five years on the Court of Appeal, and seven years as a Lord of Appeal (1962–9). After retiring as a Law Lord, became Chairman of the Press Council, serving in this capacity until 1974. An accomplished landscape artist.

Pearson (Colin)

A Canadian who came to England at age 7. Attended St. Paul's School and Oxford University. Called to the English Bar at age 26. Worked at the Treasury Solicitor's office during World War II. Spent ten years as a High Court Judge, four years on the Court of Appeal, and nine years as a Lord of Appeal (1965–74). Served as Chairman of the Law Reform Committee and of the Royal Commission on Civil Liability and Personal Injury.

Phillips of Worth Matravers (Nicholas)

Attended Bryanston School and Cambridge University. Undertook national service with the Royal Navy. Called to the English Bar at age 24 and took silk at age 40. Spent eight years as a High Court Judge, three years on the Court of Appeal, and one year as a Lord of Appeal (1999–2000). Appointed as Master of the Rolls in 2000 and served in this capacity until 2005, when he became Lord Chief Justice of England and Wales. Succeeded Lord

Woolf on both occasions and succeeded Lord Bingham as Senior Law Lord in October 2008. Is President-elect of the UK Supreme Court. Chaired the inquiry into Bovine Spongiform Encephalopathy (BSE) from 1998 to 2000.

Porter (Samuel)

Attended Perse School and Cambridge University. Called to the English Bar at age 28. Spent four years as a High Court Judge and was then appointed directly to the House of Lords where he served for 16 years as a Lord of Appeal (1938–54). Dissented in the treason trial of William Joyce ('Lord Haw-Haw'), concluding that the Crown had not satisfied the burden of proof.

Radcliffe (Cyril)

Attended Haileybury School and Oxford University. Became a Fellow of All Souls College, Oxford. Called to the English Bar at age 25. Served as Director General of the Ministry of Information during World War II. Chairman of the Boundary Commission which resulted in the division of Pakistan and India. Appointed directly to the House of Lords, the youngest ever Lord of Appeal at age 50, and served for 15 years (1949–64). Created a viscount in 1962, the last Lord of Appeal to be granted an hereditary peerage.

Reid (James Cumbernauld Scott)

Attended Edinburgh Academy, and Cambridge and Edinburgh Universities. Served in the 8th Royal Scots during World War I. Called to the Scottish Bar at age 24. Elected as Unionist MP for Stirling and Falkirk from 1931 to 1935 and for Glasgow Hillhead from 1937 to 1948. Served as Solicitor General for Scotland and as Lord Advocate. Appointed directly to the House of Lords in 1948 and served longer than anyone else as a Lord of Appeal – 26 years (1948–75).

Robertson (James)

Attended Royal High School, Edinburgh, and Edinburgh University. Called to the Scottish Bar at age 22. Elected as Conservative MP for Buteshire from 1885 to 1891. Served as Solicitor General for Scotland and as Lord Advocate. Appointed as Lord President of the Court of Session and Lord Justice General in 1891. Rector of Edinburgh University from 1893 until 1896. Served as a Lord of Appeal for over nine years (1899–1909). Died suddenly in France while still in office.

Robson (William)

Educated privately and at Dr Brace's School in Newcastle before attending Cambridge University. Called to the English Bar at age 28. Elected as Liberal MP for Bow and Bromley from 1885–6 and for South Shields from 1895 to 1910. Served as Solicitor General for England and Wales from 1905 until 1908 and as Attorney General for England and Wales from 1908 until 1910. Appointed directly to the House of Lords and served for two years as a Lord of Appeal (1910–12).

Roche (Alexander)

Attended Ipswich School and Oxford University. Called to the English Bar at age 25 and became King's Counsel at age 41. Spent 17 years as a High Court Judge, one year on the Court of Appeal and over two years as a Lord of Appeal (1935–8).

Rodger of Earlsferry (Alan)

Attended Kelvinside Academy, and Glasgow and Oxford Universities, completing a doctorate at the latter. Became a Junior Research Fellow at Balliol College, Oxford and then a Fellow of New College, Oxford. Called to the Scottish Bar at age 30 and took silk at age 41. Became Solicitor General for Scotland and then Lord Advocate, serving in each post for three years. Served as Lord President of the Court of Session and Lord Justice General from 1996 to 2001, succeeding Lord Hope. Appointed a Lord of Appeal in 2001.

Romer (Mark)

Attended Rugby School and Cambridge University. Called to the Bar at age 24 and became Queen's Counsel at age 40. Spent seven years as a High Court Judge in the Chancery Division, nine years on the Court of Appeal, and six years as a Lord of Appeal (1938–44). Died in office. Related to two other Lords of Appeal – his sister married Lord Maugham and his wife's sister married Lord Russell of Killowen.

Roskill (Eustace)

Attended Winchester School and Oxford University. Called to the English Bar at age 22. Spent nine years as a High Court Judge, nine years on the Court of Appeal, and almost six years as a Lord of Appeal (1980–6). Served as Chairman of the Fraud Trials Committee, which reported in 1986 and was the impetus for the setting up of the Serious Fraud Office.

Russell of Killowen (Charles Arthur)

Attended St. Malachy's College, Belfast, Castleknock College, and Trinity College Dublin. Called to the English Bar at age 27. Elected as a Liberal MP for Dundalk from 1880 to 1885 and for South Hackney from 1885 to 1894. Served as Attorney General and was appointed as a Lord of Appeal in 1894, but served in this capacity for less than a month before becoming Lord Chief Justice. His son and grandson also became Lords of Appeal.

Russell of Killowen (Charles Ritchie)

Attended Beaumont College and Oxford University. Called to the English Bar at age 23. Served in the Army during World War II. Won the French *Croix de Guerre* and was mentioned in despatches. Spent seven years as a High Court Judge in the Chancery Division, 13 years on the Court of Appeal, and almost seven years as a Lord of Appeal (1975–82). His father and grandfather were also Lords of Appeal.

Russell of Killowen (Frank)

Attended Beaumont College and Oxford University. Called to the English Bar at age 26. When appointed to the High Court, chose to refuse the customary knighthood. Spent nine years on the High Court, one year on the Court of Appeal, and 17 years as a Lord of Appeal (1929–46). His father was a Lord of Appeal and his son also served in this capacity. Died in office.

Salmon (Cyril)

Attended Mill Hill School and Cambridge University. Called to the English Bar at age 22 and became King's Counsel at age 42. Served in the Army during World War II. Spent seven years as a High Court Judge, eight years on the Court of Appeal, and eight years as a Lord of Appeal (1972–80). Chairman of the Royal Commission on Tribunals of Inquiry in 1966.

Saville of Newdigate (Mark)

Attended Rye Grammar School and Oxford University, where he won the Vinerian Scholarship. Called to the English Bar at age 26 and took silk at age 39. Spent eight years as a High Court Judge and three years on the Court of Appeal. Became a Lord of Appeal in 1997. Appointed in 1998 to chair the second Bloody Sunday Inquiry into the events of 30 January 1972 in Londonderry, Northern Ireland, so has rarely sat on House of Lords appeals.

Scarman (Leslie)

Attended Radley College and Oxford University. Called to the English Bar at age 25. Served in the Royal Air Force during World War II. Spent 12 years as a High Court Judge, four years on the Court of Appeal, and nine years as a Lord of Appeal (1977–86). Highly respected first Chairman of the Law Commission of England and Wales (1965–72). Chaired public inquiries into disturbances in Northern Ireland and race riots in Brixton. Early advocate of incorporating the European Convention on Human Rights into English law.

Scott of Foscote (Richard)

Born in India. Attended Michaelhouse College in Natal, South Africa, and then Cape Town and Cambridge Universities. Won a blue in rugby at Cambridge. A fellow at the University of Chicago for one year. Called to the English Bar at age 25, talking silk at age 40. Spent eight years as a High Court Judge in the Chancery Division. Appointed a Lord Justice of Appeal in 1991 and Vice Chancellor of the Supreme Court in 1994. Chaired the 'Arms to Iraq' Inquiry from 1992 to 1996. Appointed a Lord of Appeal in 2000, due to retire at the end of September 2009. A Judge of the Hong Kong Court of Final Appeal since 2003.

Shaw (Thomas)

Attended Dunfermline High School and Edinburgh University. Admitted to the Scottish Bar at age 25. Hamilton Fellow in Mental Philosophy at Edinburgh University. Elected as Liberal MP for Hawick Burghs from 1892 to 1909. Served as Solicitor General for Scotland from 1884 until 1885 and as Lord Advocate from 1905 until 1909. Spent 20 years as a Lord of Appeal (1909–29).

Simon of Glaisdale (Jocelyn—'Jack')

Attended Gresham's School, Holt, and Cambridge University. Called to the English Bar at age 23. Served in the Royal Tank Regiment during World War II. Elected as Conservative MP for Middlesbrough West. Served as Solicitor General. Spent nine years as President of the Probate, Divorce and Admiralty Division of the High Court and was then appointed directly to the House of Lords as a Lord of Appeal, serving for six years in that capacity (1971–7). The last person to be elevated directly from the High Court to the House of Lords. No relation to Viscount Simon, the Lord Chancellor from 1940 to 1945.

Simonds (Gavin)

Attended Winchester College and Oxford University. Called to the English Bar at age 25. Spent seven years as a High Court Judge and was then appointed directly to the House of Lords as a Lord of Appeal. Served in this capacity from 1944 until 1951 and from 1954 until 1962. Lord Chancellor from 1951 until 1954. Created a viscount in 1954.

Slynn of Hadley (Gordon)

Attended Sandbach School, and London and Cambridge Universities. Called to the Bar at age 26 and took silk at age 44. Lectured at the London School of Economics. Appointed a High Court Judge at 46, serving for five years before becoming President of the Employment Appeal Tribunal for three years. Became Advocate General at the European Court of Justice in 1981 and a Judge of the European Court of Justice in 1988. Served for ten years as a Lord of Appeal (1992–2002), being Second Senior Law Lord from 1998. President of the Court of Appeal of the Solomon Islands from 2001 until 2006.

Somervell of Harrow (Donald)

Attended Harrow school and Oxford University. Became a Fellow of All Souls College, Oxford. Served in the Army during World War I. Called to the English Bar at age 27. Elected as Conservative MP for Crewe from 1931 to 1945. Served as Solicitor General, Attorney General, and Home Secretary. Appointed directly to the Court of Appeal, where he spent eight years. Served for over five years as a Lord of Appeal (1954–60).

Steyn (Johan)

Born in Cape Town. Attended Jan van Riebeeck school, and Stellenbosch and Oxford Universities (the latter as a Rhodes Scholar). Called to the South African Bar at age 26, becoming Senior Counsel in South Africa at age 37. Moved to England in 1973 and joined the English Bar, specialising in commercial law. Spent six years as a High Court Judge, three years on the Court of Appeal, and ten years as a Lord of Appeal (1995–2005). Went public while still a Lord of Appeal with his opposition to the detention system at Guantánamo Bay.

Sumner (John [Hamilton])

Attended Manchester Grammar School and Oxford University. Called to the English Bar at age 24. Spent three years on the High Court, one year on the Court of Appeal, and over 16 years as a Lord of Appeal (1913–30). Worked on the Treaty of

Versailles 1918 and chaired the London Reparation Committee. Created a viscount in 1927.

Templeman (Sydney)

Attended Southall Grammar school, and Cambridge University. Called to the English Bar at age 27. Served in the Army throughout World War II and was mentioned in despatches with the Rifles Gurkha. Took silk at age 44. Spent six years on the High Court in the Chancery Division, four years on the Court of Appeal, and 12 years as a Lord of Appeal (1982–94). Served on The Royal Commission on Legal Services 1976–9.

Thankerton (William [Watson])

Attended Winchester College and Cambridge University. Called to the Scottish Bar at age 26. Elected as Unionist MP for Lanark South in 1913 and for Carlisle in 1924. Served as Solicitor General for Scotland and as Lord Advocate. Appointed directly to the House of Lords as a Lord of Appeal, serving for 19 years in that capacity (1929–48). Died in office. Son of a previous Lord of Appeal, Lord Watson.

Tomlin (Thomas)

Attended Harrow School and Oxford University. Called to the English Bar at age 24 and became King's Counsel at age 46. Spent six years as a High Court Judge in the Chancery Division and was then appointed directly to the House of Lords as a Lord of Appeal, serving for six years (1929–35). Died in office.

Tucker (Frederick)

Attended Winchester College and Oxford University. Son of a member of the South African Parliament. Called to the English Bar at age 26 and became King's Counsel at age 45. Served in the Army during World War I. Spent eight years as a High Court Judge and five years on the Court of Appeal. Served for 11 years as a Lord of Appeal (1950–61).

Upjohn (Gerald)

Attended Eton College and Cambridge University. Called to the English Bar at age 26 and became King's Counsel at age 40. Served in the Welsh Guards during World War II, attaining the rank of Brigadier. Sat on the Lynskey tribunal on corruption in government in 1948. Spent nine years on the High Court in the Chancery Division, three years on the Court of Appeal, and over seven years as a Lord of Appeal (1963–71). Died in office.

Uthwatt (Augustus)

Born in Australia. Attended Ballarat College, and Melbourne and Oxford Universities. Called to the English Bar at age 25. Spent five years as a High Court Judge and was then appointed directly to the House of Lords as a Lord of Appeal, serving for three years (1946–9). Died in office.

Walker of Gestingthorpe (Robert)

Attended Downside School and Cambridge University. Called to the English Bar at age 22 and became Queen's Counsel at age 44, practising at the Chancery Bar. Spent three years as a High Court Judge in the Chancery Division and five years on the Court of Appeal. Appointed to the House of Lords as a Lord of Appeal in 2002.

Watson (William)

Attended Glasgow and Edinburgh Universities. Called to the Scottish Bar at age 24. Appointed Solicitor General for Scotland and later as Lord Advocate. Elected as MP for Glasgow and Aberdeen Universities from 1876 to 1880. Appointed directly into the House of Lords as a Lord of Appeal, serving for 19 years (1880–99). Died in office. His son became a Lord of Appeal in 1929 as Lord Thankerton.

Wilberforce (Richard)

Attended Winchester College and Oxford University. Lived in India as a child and was the son of a judge of the Lahore High Court, and great-great-grandson of William Wilberforce. Became a Fellow of All Souls College, Oxford. Called to the English Bar at age 25. Served in the Army during World War II. Spent three years as a High Court Judge in the Chancery Division and was then appointed directly to the House of Lords as a Lord of Appeal, serving for over 17 years (1964–82). Died in 2003, aged 95.

Woolf (Harry)

Attended Fettes College in Scotland and University College London. Called to the English Bar at age 21. Spent seven years on the High Court, six years on the Court of Appeal, and almost four years as a Lord of Appeal (1992–6). Returned to the Court of

Appeal as Master of the Rolls, remaining in that office until 2000, when he was appointed Lord Chief Justice of England, serving until 2005. In each post he succeeded Lord Bingham. Chaired an inquiry into disturbances at Strangeways Prison in 1990 and helped to prompt radical reform of civil procedure through his *Access to Justice* report in 1996. Helped to established a 'Concordat' between the judges and government in 2004. A Judge of the Hong Kong Final Court of Appeal since 2003.

Wright (Robert)

Educated privately and at Trinity College, Cambridge University. Called to the English Bar at age 31. Spent seven years as a High Court Judge and was then appointed directly to the House of Lords as a Lord of Appeal. Served in this capacity from 1932 until 1935, when he became Master of the Rolls, a post he held until 1937. Then served as a Lord of Appeal for a further ten years (1937–47). The first Chairman of the United Nations War Crimes Commission.

Index